Pratt's

Guide to Venture Capital Sources

Tenth Edition

Pratt's

Guide to Venture Capital Sources

Tenth Edition

Edited by:

Stanley E. Pratt
Jane K. Morris

Tenth Edition

To the memory of our friend and colleague,
Brian Haslett

In appreciation for his many years of
dedication to entrepreneurship and to the
development of the venture capital profession.

Preface

The United States was founded and has thrived on the principles of entrepreneurship and individual and collective risk-taking. In many ways, the nation owes its development to the willingness of entrepreneurs and investors to assume the major risks inherent in new business development. The imagination, boldness and energy of entrepreneurs and small business owners, combined with the involvement and persistence of experienced venture capital investors, has often led to the creation of new industries and new technologies, which in turn have increased the productivity of the nation's economic process and of its workers. If the nation is to perpetuate its history of growing economic affluence, it must continue to nurture the traditions of individual capitalism.

In the spirit of revitalizing these traditions, this book is dedicated to those men and women who are willing to make the personal sacrifices required to build significant businesses, and to those venture capitalists with the skills, fortitude and foresight to participate in new business development.

The relationship between the entrepreneur and the venture capitalist is often the key element in a successful venture and understanding this unique relationship is a necessary first step for the prospective entrepreneur. The entrepreneur brings fresh ideas, management skills and personal commitment to this relationship, while the venture capitalist brings financial backing and extremely valuable new business development experience. Although the entrepreneur and the operating management team are normally the most critical elements in the relationship (since the venture capitalist cannot perform his role without an entrepreneur), the partnership of entrepreneurial management and venture investors usually enables a developing business to achieve objectives faster and more efficiently. In today's dynamic and competitive marketplace such an investor/management partnership is often critical to the survival and ultimate success of new business development.

The industry has expanded dramatically in the past seven years from a total industry size of $2.5 billion in 1977 to over $18 billion at end of 1985. Yet the industry is grievously small when compared with commercial banks with over $1 trillion in assets, pension fund assets of $920 billion and insurance companies with over $500 billion. Because it is so small, the effective matching of entrepreneurs with venture capitalists is a very important process.

Venture capitalists invested over $6 billion in new and growing businesses in the past two years. The companies which attracted these dollars will require continued financial support to fuel their growth. These follow-on investments as well as commitments to new quality investment opportunities will more than absorb the capital currently available in the industry. As supply continues to produce demand, the competition for those dollars intensifies. This book is designed to increase the entrepreneur's chances for success in finding venture capital by assisting the entrepreneur identify, approach and work with the right venture capitalists for his or her business development.

As editors of the *Tenth Edition* of *PRATT'S GUIDE TO VENTURE CAPITAL SOURCES,* we wish to express thanks and appreciation to the contributing authors and to our staff members who worked so diligently to achieve its publication.

Stanley E. Pratt
Jane K. Morris
Editors

Contents

Introduction

This *Tenth Edition* of *PRATT'S GUIDE TO VENTURE CAPITAL SOURCES* has been updated and expanded to incorporate current information on the venture capital investment process, a directory of active venture capital investment firms and advice to entrepreneurs and smaller business managers who seek capital for business development. *PRATT'S GUIDE* is designed as a tool to assist entrepreneurs and managers understand how the process of raising capital works and to help them locate compatible venture capital investors.

Background information on the venture capital industry and guidelines to be followed by companies seeking financing are provided in the articles written by professional venture investors. In these unique expositions, venture capitalists discuss their views on the key aspects of venture financing and clearly describe the requisite criteria for their investments. The directory section provides detailed information on venture capital companies in the United States and Canada. In addition, there is a directory of U.S. underwriters specializing in small companies. To further aid the reader, indexes of U.S. venture capital companies and their key personnel follow the directory sections.

The text of *PRATT'S GUIDE* is divided into five sections relevant to the new business development process: 1) *Background on Venture Capital;* 2) *How to Raise Venture Capital;* 3) *Sources of Business Development Financing;* 4) *Perspectives;* and 5) *When and How to Go Public.*

Prospective entrepreneurs should find the background section helpful in penetrating the mystique that still surrounds the venture investment process. Not only is the nature of a venture capitalist's involvement described, but the characteristics of successful entrepreneurial management teams are also delineated.

Raising venture capital can be a traumatic experience for the uninitiated, yet if one is aware of the expectations of the venture capitalists, much frustration and wasted energy can be avoided. The articles in the section *How to Raise Venture Capital* are written by professional venture capitalists who seek to do just that — save their own time and energy, as well as that of the entrepreneur — by clearly laying out realistic expectations and normal procedures for approaching a venture capitalist.

Sources of business development financing are found in both the private and public sectors. Among the private venture capital sources discussed in this book are: private partnerships and corporations, publicly held venture firms, venture capital funds formed by banks and bank holding companies, divisions of major corporations, affiliates of investment banking firms, and direct venture investment activity by insurance companies, pension funds or investment advisory firms. Several sources of government assisted funding are reviewed including Small Business Investment Companies (SBICs) and Minority Enterprise

Small Business Investment Companies (MESBICs) which are privately capitalized venture capital firms, licensed and regulated by the Small Business Administration. They are eligible to receive federal loans to leverage and augment the private funds invested in them. Both SBICs and MESBICs are privately managed and are operated in much the same manner as other venture firms. MESBICs are chartered to make equity investments in businesses owned by minority groups such as Black Americans, Hispanic Americans, American Indians and Vietnam veterans. Also discussed are R&D limited partnerships which provide a unique source of early financing.

Understanding the different viewpoints involved in the venture development process increases the chances of establishing a productive, working relationship with a venture capitalist. Such relationships have, many times, proven to be the critical element that determines a venture's success or failure. The information in the *Perspectives* section provides an insight into the personal characteristics that venture capitalists look for in their clients, as well as a view of the venture process from an entrepreneur's perspective.

While the primary thrust of this book is to obtain financing from private venture capital firms, we have included a section on *When and How to Go Public,* as well as a directory of U.S. small company underwriters. Not all businesses are able to attract private financing. In those years that the public market has a strong appetite for new issues of small companies, it is a viable alternative that has nurtured many successful developments.

The differences between private and public financing of venture developments are significant. Private venture capitalists may be defined as "participating investors seeking to add value through ongoing longer-term involvement." As such, they are concerned investors and, in contrast to passive investors, will accept responsibility for better or for worse. Public investors, however, are passive investors; when problems develop — as they always do — the liquidity of a public market investment enables investors to walk away from one situation in search of another. Doing business in the goldfish bowl of the public market, operating managements have additional, unsophisticated pressures for performance, and each misstep is clearly exposed. A normal progression of business development financing would entail private investment until such time as a business' success was clearly evident, and its profitability had provided a margin for error to overcome subsequent problems. At this time, subsequent financing from the public marketplace can provide funds for significant expansion as well as establishing liquidity for management and early investors.

The underwriters included in the directory section are only those that make firm commitments in which they agree to purchase the entire issue, thereby staking their firm's capital and reputation upon successful placement of the issue.

Venture capital financing was primarily regarded as the early-stage financing of relatively small, rapidly growing companies. Since the recession of 1974, however, venture capitalists have taken on an expanded role in business development financing. Today, their investment activity covers a broad spectrum of investment interests encompassing virtually all phases of business development. In addition to early-stage development funding, venture capitalists provide expansion financing for companies that have overcome initial hurdles and require additional capital for growth but do not yet have access to public or credit-oriented institutional funding. In addition, venture capitalists, together with entrepreneurs and business managements, finance leveraged buyouts, i.e. purchase of ailing corporate divisions or absentee-owned private businesses with the objective of revitalizing them.

Definitions for the stages of business development funding referred to in this book are given below:

Early-Stage Financing

- *Seed Financing* — a relatively small amount of capital provided to an inventor or entrepreneur to prove a concept and qualify for startup capital. This would generally involve product development and market research. And also, if outcomes are positive, the building of a management team and the development of a business plan.

- *Research and Development Financing* — a tax advantaged partnership set up to finance product development for startup as well as more mature companies. Investors secure tax writeoffs for their investments as well as a later share of the profits if the product development is successful.

- *Startup* — financing provided to companies for use in completing product development and initial marketing. Companies may be in the process of being organized or they may have been in business a short time (one year or less), but have not sold their product commercially. Usually, such firms will have made market studies, assembled the key management, developed a business plan and generally be ready to do business.

- *First-Stage Financing* — financing provided to companies that have expended their initial capital (often in developing and market testing a prototype), and require funds to initiate full scale manufacturing and sales.

Expansion Financing

- *Second-Stage Financing* — working capital for the initial expansion of a company which is producing and shipping, and has growing accounts receivable and inventories. Although the company has clearly made progress, it may not yet be showing a profit.

- *Third-Stage or Mezzanine Financing* — funds provided for major expansion of a company whose sales volume is increasing, and that is breaking even or profitable. These funds are utilized for further plant expansion, marketing, working capital, or development of an improved product.

- *Bridge Financing* — financing for a company expecting to go public within six months to a year. Often bridge financing is structured so that it can be repaid from the proceeds of a public underwriting. It can also involve restructuring of major stockholder positions through secondary transactions. Restructuring would be undertaken if there were early investors who wanted to reduce or liquidate their positions, or if management had changed and the stockholdings of the former management, their relatives and associates, were to be bought out to relieve a potential oversupply of stock when public.

Acquisition/Buyout Financing

- *Acquisition Financing* — funds provided to a firm to finance its acquisition of another company.

- *Management/Leveraged Buyout* — funds provided to enable an operating management group to acquire a product line or business (which may be at any stage of development), from either a public or private company; often these companies are closely held or family owned. Management/leveraged buyouts usually involve revitalizing an operation, with entrepreneurial management acquiring a significant equity interest.

Deciding which method or what venture capital firm or type of firm is best suited to handle a specific situation is an issue that must be resolved by the company seeking financing and by its advisors. Each venture capital firm has its own preferences, methods of investigating and selecting investments, and its own type of legal investment agreements. Since no two venture firms operate in exactly the same way, it is essential that entrepreneurs and business managers analyze their own needs and attempt to match those requirements with the skills and interests of an appropriate venture capital firm.

While the venture capital firms included in *PRATT'S GUIDE* have been selected because they are devoted primarily to venture financing, there is no assurance that, at any given time, a specific group will be receptive to an approach or have funds immediately available. At the present time, however, most venture capitalists are actively seeking new investment opportunities. Even with the current availability of investment capital, we should point out that the majority of new investment proposals are not financed. Convincing venture capitalists that a potential development represents a unique opportunity is truly the first major sale by a new company. Further, a good working partner relationship must be established and maintained for the optimum benefits of venture capital investment.

Each firm listed has different capacities for servicing client companies and it is critical for the entrepreneur or business management to understand those capabilities. Some firms can provide a wide range of financial and managerial services, while others may have specialized talents that would be valuable to some new business developments but relatively unimportant to other specific situations. The active involvement of venture capitalists does vary in both nature and extent. Generally the most successful venturers are actively involved in the companies they finance. While the directories in *PRATT'S GUIDE* attempt to delineate preferences, as well as levels of activity and involvement, it is incumbent upon the entrepreneur and management team to develop a means of evaluating the ongoing role of the venture investor.

Preparing a listing of venture capital firms is a difficult task—some firms maintain a low profile and are unknown to all but a few professionals. A number of the active firms listed in this directory supplied the requested data only because of this book's comprehensive nature. Most venture capital firms are not interested in reviewing situations that are clearly not going to meet their stated preferences. Consequently, a careful review of both the articles and the information presented in the directories should help capital seekers to start and develop a productive investment relationship with the firms listed.

The unique character of the venture capital industry demands special qualifications to develop a truly useful guide for dealing with the industry. Venture Economics, Inc. also publishes *VENTURE CAPITAL JOURNAL* — the principal source of current information on venture investing for 25 years. In addition, Venture Economics provides information services, research and consulting to corporations, institutions and government agencies regarding the venture capital investment process. Seminars for investors, entrepreneurs and major corporations are often sponsored by *VENTURE CAPITAL JOURNAL*. The *First Edition* of *GUIDE TO VENTURE CAPITAL SOURCES* was published in 1970, and updated versions in 1972, 1974, 1977, 1981, 1982, 1983, 1984 and 1985 have added new and useful information. This specialized experience and Venture Economics' continuing active role as a recognized authority on the venture capital industry make this *Tenth Edition* the most authoritative edition to date. The information presented in the directory section is organized on a computer database to facilitate continuous updating. In addition, entrepreneurs will find the industry preferences index following the listings of venture capital firms particularly helpful in identifying venture capital investors.

While we possess extensive knowledge of the venture capital business, we have had to rely on the representations of the private firms and could not personally verify all of the information received. There have also been numerous companies organized in the venture capital industry in the past few years and there are many still in the formative stages. Given these caveats, however, we are confident that the *Tenth Edition* of *PRATT'S GUIDE TO VENTURE CAPITAL SOURCES* is the most comprehensive and authoritative source of information on the venture capital industry and new issue underwriters at this time. We also feel assured that *PRATT'S GUIDE* will be of great assistance to entrepreneurs, managers of smaller businesses, and potential participants in the venturing process. We wish all of you much success with your endeavors.

Background on Venture Capital

Venture capital has traditionally been a low profile, private industry. In the past few years the national media has directed increased attention to the venture capital process and yet misconceptions about the industry continue to proliferate. It is the objective of this book to provide a realistic view of what the entrepreneur can expect from venture capital financing and a long-term relationship with professional venture capital investors. The first article in this section, "Overview and Introduction to the Venture Capital Industry," examines those factors that characterize the venture capital business — the long-term nature of the investments and the "value-added" to a new business by ongoing involvement of professional venture capitalists — and it reviews the industry's development and evolution from its original orientation towards early-stage investments to the present range of activities which encompass all stages of business development.

The unique qualities of entrepreneurs are examined in "Characteristics of an Entrepreneurial Management Team" which outlines the characteristics most necessary to create and grow a new venture. Also included are criteria that can be used to judge a new venture's viability, its potential and its major risks.

Understanding the operations of the venture capital industry and the process of new business development, as well as the individual roles involved, is of critical importance to the potential entrepreneur. The two following articles begin to build that understanding.

Overview and Introduction to the Venture Capital Industry

Stanley E. Pratt

Stanley E. Pratt *is chairman of Venture Economics, Inc. and publisher of its monthly publication, VENTURE CAPITAL JOURNAL, which has been reporting and analyzing business development investing since 1961. Venture Economics specializes in research/ information services and publications related to venture capital. An active venture capitalist prior to assuming his present responsibilities in 1977, Mr. Pratt has become recognized as a leading authority on the venture capital business.*

What is Venture Capital?

Venture capital is often thought of as "the early-stage financing of new and young companies seeking to grow rapidly." Although this has been, and remains, the main focus of most professional venture investors, the venture capital industry today covers a broader spectrum. In addition to providing seed, startup and first stage financing, venture capitalists also fund the expansion of companies that have already demonstrated the viability of their businesses but do not yet have access to the public securities market or to credit-oriented institutional funding sources such as banks or insurance companies. They also provide management/leveraged buyout financing to assist operating managements purchase and revitalize a division of a major corporation or an absentee-owned private company. Venture capitalists also sometimes employ their skills and experience in public stock market securities, where patient, supportive investment can assist ongoing business development.

While the long-term involvement between the venture capitalists and the entrepreneurial teams that manage the companies in their portfolio differentiates venture capitalists from the world of passive investors, two additional characteristics of venture capital must be stressed:

- the actual or potential equity participation of the venture capitalist either via a direct purchase of stock, or through warrants, options or convertible securities

- a long-term investment discipline that requires the venture capitalist to wait usually five to ten years for investments to provide a significant return.

History of the Venture Capital Industry

While venture capital was instrumental in the discovery of America — remember Queen Isabella's backing of Columbus?— and in its development — from the trading and trapping companies to Pierre DuPont's investment in General Motors — its institutionalization did not begin until after World War II. Prior to that time, most venture investments were made by wealthy individuals, syndicates organized by investment bankers, or by a few family organizations employing professional managers. Several of these pioneering venture investment firms such as Bessemer Securities, Venrock Associates (formerly Rockefeller Family & Associates) and J. H. Whitney & Co. continue to be active today.

The formation of American Research and Development Corporation (ARD) in Boston in 1946 was one of the first steps towards the institutionalization of the venture investment process. The next major milestone was the passage in 1958 of the Small Business Investment Company Act which provided for the creation of Small Business Investment Companies (SBICs) as vehicles for small business financing. With tax advantages and potential Government lending for leverage, SBICs were the first vestige of a true venture capital industry.

Although initial acceptance was slow, the SBIC program soon took off. From 1960 through 1962 585 SBIC licenses were approved. The industry was off on a fast track, but pulled up lame almost immediately. The infant industry was almost destroyed by unreasonable expectations, inadequate private capitalization, a short-term investment orientation, excessive government regulation, poor economic and market conditions, a lack of management experience, and widespread misunderstanding of venture investment disciplines.

SBICs were, nonetheless, a major factor in building a venture capital industry. Today the survivors of those early years, along with many new SBICs, form an important core of the venture capital investment community. Largely because of the early failure of SBICs to take full advantage of an attractive segment of the venture investment market, a number of new private venture capital firms were formed in the late 1960s and early 1970s.

These new firms were structured to avoid many of the problems that had become evident in the SBIC program, such as constricting governmental regulations and inadequate private capitalization. While most new firms were formed as limited partnerships, a number of the largest firms were structured as corporations. Funding came principally from institutional investors (such as insurance companies, pension funds, endowments and bank trust departments) and wealthy individuals and families. These investors sought exceptional aggregate rewards from a portfolio of "high risk" venture investments. By this time, the success of ARD and its investment in Digital Equipment had become visible. New capital could be and was attracted by the evident potential benefits of venture investing under disciplined management. Raising some $450 million between 1969 and 1973, new groups became active venture investors, and soon experienced some of the difficulties inherent in long-term private investment.

The early to mid-1970s was a traumatic but educational period for the young venture capital business. Many of the new venture groups initially made classic early-stage venture investments. As a result, they experienced a myriad of difficulties before some of the early stage companies in their portfolio emerged as viable businesses. With losses becoming evident early and the ultimately successful businesses experiencing nerve wrenching growing pains, the feasibility of venture capital as a reasonable investment strategy was questioned by many of the institutional investors. Even sophisticated and supposedly long-term investors found it difficult to believe that the sun would eventually shine on the apparent chaos of the venture investment portfolios. In addition, portfolio companies starting to achieve success were stung by the recession of 1974 and 1975. However, by the late 1970s, as the venture capital partnerships began to mature, it became apparent that investment returns from business development portfolios would exceed those of alternative investment vehicles by 10% or more.

Of even greater significance than these initial investment returns were the many lessons learned and the disciplines adopted by both venture capitalists and their investors as the industry evolved during difficult economic times.

Perhaps the most important skill developed by venture capitalists during this formative period was the capability to work with operating managements over an extended period of time. The illiquidity of investment positions forced the venture investors to become involved on a continuing basis and thereby demonstrated the powerful value-added effect of personal involvement in long-term investments.

In addition, adverse economic pressures resulted in the emergence of two new strategies — wider investment interests and greater industry cooperation — which strengthened the industry and filled a widening gap in financing the nation's new, high

growth potential businesses. Although venture capitalists initially concentrated on early-stage investments, the declining public market for new issues forced venture capitalists to become more involved in expansion financings to support the development of existing portfolio companies (small company underwritings decreased from almost $1.4 billion in 1969, to only $16 million in 1975).

With the increased demand from capital-starved, newer businesses, venture capitalists began to operate across a far broader spectrum of investment interests. Later-stage expansion financings for companies that would have formerly received growth capital from public market underwritings provided adequate investment returns at a far lower risk exposure than early-stage developments. Startup activity was focused on principally the most qualified managements with achievable expectations. Developing these exceptional opportunities gave venture investors an insight into the requisite parameters for successfully developing new businesses. Well-structured, management/leveraged buyouts provided excellent returns with less need for continuing involvement. In 1974, venture capitalists perceived opportunities in the depressed stock market and many found — with their longer-term outlook, concerned involvement, and understanding of emerging growth company development — the public marketplace provided another area of opportunity.

This diversity of opportunities enabled venture capitalists to balance their activities in terms of time involvement, risk acceptance and reward potential, while providing ongoing assistance to developing businesses. Some firms tailored their operations to those specific segments of the venture investment process where their particular skills would be most effective, while others developed the capability to operate across the entire spectrum of investment opportunities.

The Venture Capital Industry Today

As 1986 begins, the organized venture capital community and the entrepreneurs, through which new business development is accomplished, are operating in a favorable environment. The increased amounts of capital available for investment and the role model effect of prior successful developments has attracted entrepreneurs to bring about a myriad of venture investment opportunities. The dramatic expansion of the venture capital industry which began in 1978 under the impetus of the 1978 capital gains tax reduction continues today. With over $18 billion in committed capital, the industry has more than four times the resources it did only five years ago.

The past few years have also seen expansion of venture capital management resources. A blend of classic startup and early-stage investors, generalists providing early-stage and expansion financing, and specialists for specific industries as well as for management/leveraged buyouts, now provides attractive sources of financing for more entrepreneurs and managers than ever before. In 1983 and 1984 venture capitalists disbursed an estimated $2.8 billion and $3 billion, respectively, across the entire spectrum of their investment interests. Disbursements are expected to exceed $2.5 billion in 1985 as well.

As a classic example of greater supply producing greater demand, the entire business development process has become healthy and vibrant. Individual investors in venture developments have also reemerged, including many successful entrepreneurs who are investing their profits in new businesses. The public marketplace is once again financing smaller businesses; there was a dramatic increase in underwritings of companies with a net worth of $5 million or less in 1982 and 1983. And, though the pace of such underwritings slowed significantly in 1984, by the end of 1985 the pace had picked up.

Perhaps the most remarkable social development of the late 1970s and early 1980s, however, is the reemergence of entrepreneurship in the nation. Colleges today are bursting with young entrepreneurs. Experienced business managers, driven by the apparent availability of funds, are creating more business development investment opportunities than ever before and each successful funding stimulates other attempts. While it should be noted that venture capitalists are, and must remain, highly selective in allocating capital investment to business developments with a perceived high likelihood of success; more entrepreneurs than ever are receiving the financing necessary to prove their capabilities. Even after this screening process, many developments will not be successful, but those that are will provide exceptional benefits to entrepreneurs, their investors and the nation's economy.

Governmental attitudes towards venture capital are now far more favorable than in the past due to the increased visibility of the innovation and productivity benefits of venture capital investment.

A study conducted by the U.S. General Accounting Office (GAO) concluded that "the venture capital process can greatly contribute to the nation's economy and can significantly improve productivity in the 1980s." The study, "Government-Industry Cooperation Can Enhance The Venture Capital Process," targeted 72 companies which received a total of $209 million from venture capital investors during the 1970s. By 1979, these companies had combined sales of $6 billion, which in the last five years of the decade grew at a 33% annual sales growth rate. These venture-backed developments had created 130,000 jobs, over $100 million in corporate tax revenues, $350 million in employee tax revenues, and $900 million in export sales. Moreover, data compiled for the GAO by Venture Economics, Inc. showed that of $1.4 billion invested by professional venture capitalists in 1,332 companies from 1970 to 1979, $886 million or 61%, was invested in 725 companies, or 54%, that were involved in productivity related products, systems and services. In 1983 77% of all companies financed by venture capitalists provided products or services which improved productivity.

Beyond the increased reliance of the Reagan Administration upon private sector initiatives, state and regional economic development activity is placing more emphasis on new business development. Rather than focusing on "smoke-stack chasing" for large employers to relocate, economic developers are seeking a more diversified economic base through public and private sector cooperation to stimulate new growing businesses. These attitudes are conducive to new opportunities for both entrepreneurs and venture investment managers while providing greater economic productivity.

The venture capital industry should maintain and build upon its present momentum in the rest of the 1980s because of the exciting synergy produced by the cooperation and coordination of capital sources, venture development investors and entrepreneurial managers. This nation's future growth and productivity can be dramatically enhanced by a more effective utilization of these available resources.

Characteristics of a Successful Entrepreneurial Management Team

Alexander L. M. Dingee, Jr., Brian Haslett
and Leonard E. Smollen

Alexander L. M. Dingee, Jr., *is a cofounder and president of Venture Founders Corporation, Waltham, Massachusetts and directs the investment activities of several early-stage venture capital funds dedicated to creating and investing in seed, startup and first-stage situations. Previously he had successfully started two companies, both of which were sold for capital gain.*

Brian Haslett *was a co-founder of Venture Founders Corporation and played a lead role in establishing its U.K. subsidiary and in helping many American and British entrepreneurs create and finance their new enterprises. He subsequently was a contributor to VENTURE CAPITAL JOURNAL. Mr. Haslett died during 1985.*

Leonard E. Smollen, *is executive vice president and a cofounder of Venture Founders Corporation and involved with Dingee in the startup and seed venture investment activities of BDG '81. He previously held executive positions at EG&G, Inc.*

What are the personal characteristics required to be a successful entrepreneur? Before making the great personal sacrifices required to start and build a major enterprise, would-be entrepreneurs should engage in serious soul-searching to be sure that they have enough of the capabilities needed to thrive in the toughest jungle in the business world.

To assist in such self-judgments, the following guidelines were prepared by principals of Venture Founders Corporation (VFC). Founded in 1970 to design and apply new approaches to venture development and financing, VFC presently serves investor clients both in the United States and in the United Kingdom. These clients have committed capital to funds that finance new and young ventures being built by entrepreneurs that are found, evaluated and assisted by VFC.

Venture capitalists say that they prefer a grade A entrepreneur with a grade B business idea to a grade B entrepreneur with a grade A idea. And it is generally a strong management team not a lone entrepreneur that they back.

So, the first two questions that the would-be entrepreneur must ask himself or herself are: Do I have adequate *commitment, motivation,* and *skills* to start and build a major business — to be a successful entrepreneur? Does my management team have the necessary complementary skills to enable us to succeed in building a particular venture.

If these two questions can be answered affirmatively, then a third question must be answered before it is wise to take the time needed to develop a comprehensive business plan and mount a search for venture capital: Do I have a viable venture idea?

This article will consider these three vital questions with most emphasis placed on the first, and most important, one.

Am I an Entrepreneur?

A good way to answer this question is to compare yourself to a successful entrepreneur in a thorough and objective manner. Begin this comparison by studying the following key characteristics that successful entrepreneurs, venture capitalists, and behavioral scientists say are important for entrepreneurial success:

Drive and energy level: Success as an entrepreneur demands the ability to work long hours for sustained periods with less than the normal amount of sleep.

Self-confidence: You need self-confidence — a belief in yourself and your ability to achieve your goals and a sense that events in your life are self-determined.

Setting challenging but realistic goals: You need the ability to set clear goals and objectives that are challenging, yet realistic and attainable.

Long-term involvement: You have to be able to commit yourself to projects that will see completion in five to seven years and to work towards goals that are that far away. This means having the ability to immerse yourself totally in your business and to concentrate on attaining these distant goals.

Using money as a performance measure: Money, in the form of salary, profits, or capital gains, should be viewed more as a measure of how you are doing than an end in itself.

Persistent problem solving: You must have an intense and determined desire to solve problems so you can complete tasks.

Taking moderate risks: Entrepreneurial success generally results from taking moderate, calculated risks, where the chances of winning were not so small as to make the effort a gamble, nor so large as to make it a sure thing, but which provided a reasonable and challenging chance of success.

Learning from failure: You have to be able to use your failures as learning experiences. You need to understand your role in causing failures so that you can avoid similar problems in the future. You should be disappointed but not discouraged by failure.

Using criticism: You need to demonstrate a capacity to seek and use criticism of the style and substance of your performance.

Taking initiative and seeking personal responsibility: You need to possess the desire to seize opportunities and put yourself in situations where you are personally responsible for success or failure. You should be able to take the initiative to solve problems or fill leadership vacuums. You should enjoy being involved in situations where your impact on a problem can be measured.

Making good use of resources: Can you identify and use expertise and assistance that is relevant to the accomplishment of your goals? You should not be so involved in the achievement of your goals and in independent accomplishment that you will not let anyone help you.

Competing against self-imposed standards: Do you tend to establish your own standard of performance, which is high yet realistic, and then compete with yourself?

No one individual can be adequately strong in all 12 of these attributes. Weak spots can often be covered by other members of your management team. Do remember, though, *you* are the *most* critical risk. Rate yourself on each of these key characteristics "strong," "average," or "weak" compared with others you know and respect. Be as honest and accurate as you can. If you think you are average or low on most of them, then do yourself, your family, and your would-be backers, partners, and employees a favor — do not start a business.

If you rate yourself high on most traits, we urge you to review these possibly unrealistic ratings of yourself with people who know you well. Wives, teachers, peers, and professional advisors are all likely to have a somewhat different view of you, both in terms of your past accomplishments and your potential. Take enough time with each reviewer to explain *why* you rate yourself as you do. Be prepared to alter your ratings in the light of

their opinions. If people you know tell you that you are likely to fail as an entrepreneur, they may be right. But both you and they should be aware that making such an evaluation realistically is no quick-and-easy task.

Once you believe that you have made an adequate assessment of yourself, be on the lookout for personal experiences that call for entrepreneurial strengths. Reflect on these experiences and see if you behaved in a manner consistent with your rating. Self-deception is a dangerous enemy in this process of self-evaluation.

If, after a while, you can convince yourself and others whom you consult that you have enough entrepreneurial traits to start and build a major business, you still have to evaluate your management skills. If you lack some of the skills needed in your venture, they can be provided by others on your management team — but only if you perceive the need for such skills and are aware of your personal shortcomings. To this end, you should systematically audit your managerial experience and accomplishments in the functions of marketing and sales; operations; research, development, and engineering; finance and accounting; general management and administration; personnel; and the legal and tax aspects of business. To rate yourself, we suggest the following standards.

Strong = Know thoroughly and have proven ability
Average = Have limited knowledge and accomplishments and will need backup perhaps part-time
Weak = Unfamiliar and need someone else probably full-time

Individuals are rarely equally strong in all elements of any of these seven functions. It is unwise to generalize about anyone's ability to perform an entire function from his other strength in one or two of its elements. The different nature of each element makes this unlikely. For example, a powerful direct salesman probably will not show equal strength in market research and evaluation.

Before giving yourself an overall rating on each of these functions, we suggest that you break each function into its principal elements and rate yourself on each element. Note that the elements of any function that are critical may vary somewhat with each venture: the marketing and sales function includes market research and evaluation and marketing planning as well as sales management and merchandising, direct selling, service, and distribution. The latter will not be critical if you market through distributors.

A listing and brief description of representative elements of all seven functions is presented at the end of this article.

We suggest that you review your self-evaluation of your management skills with people who are most exposed to them on a day-to-day basis, i.e. those with whom you work or have worked. Bear in mind that bosses, peers, and subordinates may all see a different side of you. When, with the help of friends and colleagues, you have made a thorough evaluation of your entrepreneurial traits and your management skills, you should be better able to evaluate the personal risks you will run if you try to create a business.

If your dream is to build a multi-million dollar business, it might also be wise to check your evaluation with one or more of the professionals who are active and respected in the fields of career counseling and entrepreneurial behavior. A man with a weak heart may only ask his wife about taking a gentle stroll up a small grassy hill, but he would be wise to consult a doctor before trying to climb a rocky mountain.*

Does My Team Have the Necessary Complementary Skills?

Research into successful ventures shows that teams perform better than one individual. Knowing this, venture capitalists always look for a balanced team. So your next task is to analyze the business you contemplate and determine what abilities and skills are critical to its success in the first two or three years. Then you should set about building a management team that includes people who are strong where you are weak.

In a new company, you may not want (or may not be able to afford) to have all functions performed by full-timers. You should, however, be just as careful in choosing part-timers since you may want some of them to come on board later. Avoid the trap of teaming up with a school friend whom you only know in social and classroom situations or a colleague in the lab or office whose skills match your own. It is tempting to do this because you think you know these friends well. Such choices rarely work out well. Successful venture capitalists are rapidly turned off by a team that is all one of a kind — be they all engineers, salesmen, or relatives.**

Do I Have a Viable Idea?

Imagine that you are sitting in a venture capitalist's chair and you have just analyzed what you did with the few hundred business proposals you examined last year. Your analysis shows that you handled the various proposals in these ways.

* For a discussion and appraisal of such evaluations, see "Business Leadership Training: A Six-Month Evaluation," a paper by Jeffry A. Timmons, D.B.A., and John L. Hayes.

** For further discussion, see "The Entrepreneurial Team: Formation and Development" by Jeffry A. Timmons, D.B.A., a competitive paper presented at the annual Academy of Management meeting in 1973.

1. Rejected 60% of them after a 20-to-30 minute scanning.
2. Reviewed another quarter for a few hours and then discarded them.
3. Investigated about 15%, in depth, and then turned two-thirds of them down because of one or more serious flaws in the management team or the business plan — flaws that could not be remedied or at least not remedied in less than one year.
4. Decided to invest in 5% of them but could only negotiate acceptable terms with the entrepreneur(s) and other existing stockholders with 3%.

The 15% that you investigated in some depth were presented by strong, well-balanced management teams who had been able to show you relevant accomplishments in marketing, finance, and operations and had developed (perhaps with some prodding by you) a comprehensive business plan.

Now, return to your real role — that of an entrepreneur. Think what that venture capitalist's analysis means to you: you have a three-in-a-hundred chance of securing capital from any one source on terms acceptable to you and the venture capitalist; you have only a 15% chance of even being considered seriously for investment by the venture capitalist and you need a comprehensive business plan to qualify for such consideration.

You should approach several venture capitalists to identify those most likely to be interested. But, their *standards* will not differ widely. So, if you are really serious about going into business for yourself, you should start to develop a comprehensive business plan. Remember, though, if the plan is done properly and completely, it will probably take you 150 to 300 hours of hard work. Even when it is done, there is no guarantee that you will raise enough investment capital.

Is there any way to avoid going to all this effort only to have your plan rejected after a mere 20-minute scanning? Try looking at your business startup idea in the same way that the venture capitalist will — in a cold, critical, unemotional manner.

Before developing your business plan, ask yourself those simple but vital questions that the venture capitalist has in his mind when he is scanning a plan to determine if it is worth studying and calling a meeting to discuss. The first vital question: *What exactly will be sold to whom?* Other key market questions are:

- Why will the customer buy *your* product?

- Who are its ultimate users and what major influences on their purchasing habits are beyond your control?

- Who will be your competitors? Are they profitable now? Why do you think you can successfully compete with them?

- Is your market large and growing? Does it offer a multi-million-dollar potential for your company?

- Are you or will you be in a recognized growth industry?

You should then ask and answer several questions about the other major aspects of the business you contemplate, questions about your team, your financial needs and the risks you are running. Such questions may include:

- What is the *maximum* amount of dollars and length of time that will be needed before your product is ready for market?

- What is the depth of your team's knowledge and extent of their reputations in the types of markets, technologies, and operations in which you will be active?

- What are your team's management skills in the three *key* areas of marketing, finance, and operations?

- How many unproven marketing, technical and manufacturing approaches do you contemplate?

- What are the strengths, weaknesses, and major risks of your venture?

Careful thought about the key areas listed should enable users of this guide to take a reasonable first look at their own venture ideas and to evaluate their potential and their major risks. If you are comfortable with your own answers in all of the areas discussed, you can probably justify developing a business plan. See the article in this guide, "Preparing A Business Plan," for an outline for doing this in a fashion most likely to attract and convince a professional venture capital investor. If you are uneasy in any area, is this because you lack data? Or does your venture have a basic flaw?

In Summary

The risks in entrepreneurship are you, your team, and any fundamental flaws in your venture idea. You must make a reasonable first evaluation of these risks. You should then be able to put together a business plan and avoid many of the early errors (for example, team inadequacies; underpricing; weak cash management) that so often cripple new ventures. You should also be able to improve your chances of securing financing and launching a successful venture.

Representative Elements of Seven Management Functions

1. Marketing and sales
   a. *Market research and evaluation:* Ability to design and conduct market research studies and to analyze and interpret study results; familiarity with questionnaire design and sampling techniques.
   b. *Strategic sales:* Experience in developing marketing strategies and establishing forces and then planning appropriate sales, advertising, and promotion programs and setting up an effective network distributor or sales representative organization.
   c. *Sales management and merchandising:* Ability to organize, supervise, motivate, and provide merchandising support to a direct sales force; ability to analyze territory and account sales potential and to manage a sales force to obtain target share of market.
   d. *Direct selling:* Experience in identifying, meeting, and developing new customers; demonstrated success in closing sales.
   e. *Service:* Ability to perceive service needs of particular products; experience in determining service and spare parts requirements, handling customer complaints, and managing a service organization.
   f. *Distribution management:* Ability to organize and manage the flow of the product from manufacturing through distribution channels to the ultimate customer, including familiarity with shipping costs, scheduling techniques, carriers, etc.
   g. *Overall marketing skills:* Give yourself a combined rating reflecting your skill level across all of the above marketing areas.

2. Operations
   a. *Manufacturing management:* Knowledge of the production processes, machines, manpower, and space requirements to produce the product; experience in managing production to produce products within time, cost, and quality constraints.
   b. *Inventory control:* Familiarity with techniques of controlling inprocess and finished goods inventories of materials.
   c. *Quality control:* Ability to set up inspection systems and standards for effective control of quality in incoming, inprocess and finished materials.
   d. *Purchasing:* Ability to identify appropriate sources of supply, material into inventory; familiarity with economical order quantities and discount advantage.
   e. *Overall operations skills:* Give yourself a combined rating reflecting your skill level across all of the above operations areas.

3. Research, development, and engineering
   a. *Direction and management of applied research:* Ability to distinguish and keep a prudent balance between long-

range projects at the frontiers of your technology, which attract the most creative individuals, and shorter range research in support of current product development activity.

b. *Management of development:* Ability to plan and direct work of development engineers and to use time and cost budgets so that perfectionists do not ruin you and yet product performance, appearance, and production engineering needs can be met; ability to distinguish between bread-board, field and pre-production prototype programs.

c. *Management of engineering:* Ability to plan and direct engineers in the final design of a new product for manufacture and in the engineering and testing of the production process to manufacture that new product.

d. *Technical know-how:* Ability to contribute personally to research, development, and/or engineering because of up-to-date in-depth knowledge of the technologies in which your company is involved.

e. *Overall research, development, and engineering skills:* Give yourself a combined rating reflecting your skill level across the above areas.

4. Financial management

   a. *Raising capital:* Ability to decide how best to acquire funds for startup and growth; ability to forecast the need for funds and to prepare budgets; familiarity with sources and vehicles of short- and long-term financing.

   b. *Money management:* Ability to design, install, maintain, and use financial controls; familiarity with accounting and control systems needed to manage; ability to set up a project cost control system, analyze overhead/contribution/absorption, prepare profit and loss and balance sheets, and manage a bookkeeper.

   c. *Specific skills:* Cash flow analysis; break-even analysis; contribution analysis; budgeting and profit-planning techniques; profit and loss, balance sheet, and present value analysis of return on investment and payback.

   d. *Overall financial skills:* Give yourself a combined rating reflecting your skill level across all of the above financial areas.

5. General management and administration

   a. *Problem solving:* Ability to anticipate potential problems and plan to avoid them; ability to gather facts about problems, analyze them for real causes, and plan effective action to solve problems; thoroughness in dealing with the details of particular problems and in follow-through.

   b. *Communications:* Ability to communicate effectively and clearly, both in speech and in writing, to the media, the public, customers, peers, and subordinates.

   c. *Planning:* Ability to set realistic and attainable goals, identify obstacles to achieving the goals and develop detailed action plans to achieve those goals; ability to schedule own time very systematically.

   d. *Decision making:* Ability to make decisions on your best analysis of incomplete data.

   e. *Project management:* Skill in organizing project teams, setting project goals, defining project tasks, and monitoring task completion in the face of problems and cost/quality constraints.

   f. *Negotiating:* Ability to work effectively in a negotiating situation; ability to quickly balance value given and value received.

   g. *Personnel administration:* Ability to set up payroll, hiring, compensation, and training functions.

   h. *Overall administrative skills:* Give yourself a combined rating reflecting your skill level across all of the above administrative areas.

6. Personnel management

   a. *Leadership:* Ability to understand the relationships between tasks, the leader, and the followers; ability to lead in situations where it is appropriate; willingness to manage actively, supervise, and control activities of others through directions, suggestions, inspiration, and other techniques.

   b. *Listening:* Ability to listen to and understand without interrupting or mentally preparing your own rebuttal at the expense of hearing the message.

   c. *Helping:* Ability to ask for and provide help and to determine situations where assistance is warranted.

   d. *Criticism:* Ability to provide performance and interpersonal criticism to others that they find useful; ability to receive feedback from others without becoming defensive or argumentative.

   e. *Conflict resolution:* Ability to confront differences openly and to deal with them until resolution is obtained.

   f. *Teamwork:* Ability to work well with others in pursuing common goals.

   g. *Selecting and developing subordinates:* Ability to select and delegate responsibility to subordinates and to coach them in the development of their managerial capabilities.

h. *Climate building:* Ability to create, by the way you manage, a climate and spirit conducive to high performance; ability to press for higher performance while rewarding work well done.

i. *Overall interpersonal skills:* Give yourself a combined rating reflecting your skill level across all of the above personnel management areas.

7. Legal and tax aspects

a. *Corporate law:* Familiarity with legal issues relating to stock issues, incorporation, distribution agreements, leases, etc.

b. *Contract law:* Familiarity with contract procedures and requirements (government and commercial), including default, warranty, and incentive provisions; fee structures; overhead, general and administrative expenses allowable, and so forth.

c. *Patent law:* Experience with preparation and revision of patent applications; ability to recognize a strong patent; familiarity with claim requirements.

d. *Tax law:* Familiarity with general state and federal reporting requirements for businesses and with special provisions concerning Subchapter S corporations, tax shelters, fringe benefits, etc.

e. *Overall legal and tax skills:* Give yourself a combined rating reflecting your skill level across all of the above legal and tax areas.

How to Raise Venture Capital

This section provides a step by step guide to obtaining venture capital financing. Written by experienced venture capitalists, each article explores one of the practical considerations in dealing with the venture capital process. Beginning with guidelines for contacting and working with venture capitalists, the articles continue with an outline of the type of detailed business plan that will facilitate a venture capitalist's investment decision, and the discussions offer entrepreneurs guidance in: approaching the venture capitalist and presenting the business plan; anticipating the pricing and structure of the financing; and understanding the legal requirements. The articles also point out what the venture capitalist is looking for, what he seeks to avoid, what will be required of the entrepreneur, and how the investment decision is made. Examining the venture capitalist's objectives and decision-making processes, together with the structured business plan, should help the entrepreneur to locate and build a productive investment relationship.

Guidelines for Dealing with Venture Capitalists

Stanley E. Pratt

See previous background description.

The relationship between entrepreneur and venture capital investor is unique and it can be a very significant factor in determining the success of a business development. Often referred to as a marriage, the venture capitalist/entrepreneur association, as any union, can achieve common purposes if the partners complement and support each other's capabilities, respect and understand different perspectives, and develop sensitivity to each other's actions and reactions. Successful rapport contributes to the "value-added" that differentiates business development from passive investment and helps achieve the substantial rewards envisioned from venture capital investment.

Experienced venture capitalists should be viewed as a resource that goes beyond the provision of investment capital. The extent to which the benefits of professional venture capitalist involvement are realized depends upon the quality and chemistry of the relationship between a business' operating management team and the venture capitalist.

Initial Contact

It is important to begin the relationship with the venture capitalist on the right foot. For the entrepreneur there are several important "do's" and "don'ts" to keep in mind.

It is important to give serious consideration to which venture capitalist should be approached for funding a particular type of venture. The information presented in the listings in this book's directory section provides useful criteria for selecting among venture capital firms. The directory should not be used as a mass-mailing list to send unsolicited proposals, but rather as a guide to determine the potential fit and interest of several venture capital firms. Devoting insufficient time and thought to selecting prospective venture capital investors wastes the time and money of both the entrepreneur and the venture capitalist. More importantly, venture capitalists can be apprehensive if they feel a deal has been too aggressively "shopped around" and rejected by several of their peers. The article by Jackson Tankersley in *PRATT'S GUIDE* provides detailed information on choosing and approaching a venture capitalist to achieve the right "fit."

Presentation

The heart of the presentation is a written business plan through which the venture capitalist evaluates the potential development of a business and the capabilities of a proposed management team. Venture capitalists are constantly exposed to innovative and exciting new products, but products do not make a business — successful businesses create and develop successful products. The management team must demonstrate an understanding of the market and an ability to thoroughly think through and evaluate the actions in its business plan to attract the attention of venture capitalists.

The business plan, together with management's discussion of it, enables potential investors to focus upon management's planning skills and experience. It must be a product of the principal managers, rather than a polished exposition by outside consultants, since it documents management knowledge and expertise in the disciplines necessary for independent business development. It should combine a historical factual review with careful research and understanding to produce a realistic future plan. It is not a selling document, but shows the anticipated developments and the structures necessary to enable financing the proposal. Finally, it provides a mechanism for measuring potential and actual progress. Most business plans presented are far too optimistic, but those that are too conservative will not attract an investor's attention. It is thus important to present reasonable expectations that both the management and the venture capitalist can accept as achievable.

Perhaps the most important part of the business plan and its presentation is the clear identification of the existing and future market needs as well as the niche that will allow a new or smaller growing business to exist and successfully expand. Too often, entrepreneurs are enthusiastic about a marvelous product and they expect the potential investor to recognize the product's need without documentation as to why or how the customer will purchase the product.

If presentations are made with adequate homework, facts are presented to avoid unpleasant surprises, and a natural and realistic exposition is made; the proper chemistry may be developed with venture capitalists to bring about a remarkable amount of assistance even prior to any final decision.

Investigation

Perhaps the most frustrating aspect of dealing with venture capitalists is the time required during the period from original introduction to the closing of an investment. Realistic planning should allow for at least three to six months for contact, courtship and investigation. When a business needs funds yesterday, the process is even more problematic than usual and only the most intuitive venture capitalists will respond. Adequate investigation and familiarization takes time, and venture capitalists are just as busy and jealous of time as operating managements. Time frames should be discussed initially and reasonable schedules should be set up and maintained. One of the best ways to judge a venture capitalist's interest is in the time allocated for substantive investigation.

After an initial meeting, the responsible venture capital firm will indicate within a week or two whether it is interested in seriously considering a proposal. If so, the investigation begins in earnest with extensive checking of the management, an analysis of product, technical and marketing considerations and a financial analysis. While these studies require a great deal of time and effort on the part of both parties, they are necessary to establish the understanding required for long-term involvement; and an entrepreneur generally benefits from such a review.

At the same time, the entrepreneur should be conducting an investigation and analysis of the venture capital firm. Some investors can offer a great deal more than others, especially in specific industries or in particular stages of business development. The experience and expertise of the investor should be carefully reviewed. Perhaps the best way to check on venture capitalists is to contact the managements of other companies in which the venture capitalist has invested. This should include successful businesses, as well as disappointing experiences and outright failures, to determine how a potential investor will react to both good and bad developments. The nature and frequency of communications between the venture capitalist and the managements of portfolio companies should be noted. In general, the entrepreneur should seek strong rather than relatively passive investors, much the same as venture investors desire to back strong management teams. It is critical to determine each side's capacities to establish mutual trust and working relationships.

Negotiations

Once the investigations have been completed the final details of the investment are subject to the give and take of direct negoti-

ation. Usually the negotiations are handled by the chief executive officer of the operating management team and the venture capitalist. Advisors such as attorneys and accountants can be helpful, but decisions cannot be delegated since management must live with final determinations during the difficult times of building a business. Generally, compromise is necessary for both parties and it is important that both sides feel that a fair deal has been reached. Each side must leave a little bit at the table and not burden the relationship with unrealistic projections or expectations. If unrealistic expectations are created initially, the entrepreneur will be suffering from a credibility gap right from the start. An open and honest relationship will reduce the number of surprises later.

Too often, entrepreneurs confuse ownership with control. Management controls a business and the venture capitalist's role is generally supportive — enabling greater growth than might have been accomplished without such involvement. If a business fails to develop in accordance with planned expectations, venture capitalists as owners may push for changes through the board of directors. Directors may seek changes in the controlling management of the business, but ownership positions in developing businesses are seldom responsible for such restructuring. Most often, venture capitalists operate through persuasion in the expectation that their original decision to back a particular management team was correct.

The structure of a financing determined in these negotiations must be clearly understood by all parties. The amount of capital investment is usually determined with the expectation that additional funds will be made available in a series of steps that are dependent on the development of the business. The use of debt and equity will be structured in accordance with the requirements and capabilities of the business as well as the objectives and needs of the investor.

Depending upon the stage of development of the business being financed, the venture capitalist seeks a potential return of five to 10 times his investment and a means of assuring future liquidity. Factors relating to these liquidity requirements are a part of the venture capitalist's negotiating objectives.

The most important point to remember about the negotiations is that, while there may be disagreements, the overall tenor of the negotiations will often set the tone for ongoing relationships.

The Continuing Relationship

The entrepreneur should strive to delineate his own objectives and understand those of the venture capitalist. This facilitates discussions around those objectives, particularly in the early stages. Objectives change with time and different conditions, and it is necessary to air and discuss these changes to determine how the relationship might be affected. The most important point is to "stay close" and to "keep on top of each other's thinking." Continuing communication is critical to maintain an ongoing productive relationship.

The entrepreneur should learn as much as possible about the venture capitalist's capabilities and should attempt to exploit specific talents to create opportunities and solve problems. This is the essence of how the venture capitalist adds value to investments.

The common trait differentiating professional venture capitalists from other investors is long-term, ongoing involvement — they are not normally passive investors. Enhanced returns are expected through the value added by specialized, experienced assistance. Independent business development re-

quires unique skills that may not have been necessary in the larger corporation where the entrepreneur acquired management training. Venture capitalists provide assistance in: policy determination for small, growing businesses; long-range planning; financial assessments and arrangements; management evaluation and recruitment; relations with outside technical consultants and vendor/suppliers; relations with shareholders; and provisions for the eventual liquidity of ownership positions. With this valuable assistance available to, and focused on, the entrepreneur, it is incumbent upon operating managements to maintain working relationships to take advantage of that experience and expertise. There may be times when one side or the other is difficult to convince, but a frank, ongoing relationship produces the value added to investments that creates extremely rewarding business partnerships.

Preparing a Business Plan*

Brian Haslett and Leonard E. Smollen

See previous background descriptions

Before you begin in earnest to develop the comprehensive business plan that you will need to raise venture capital, you should try to convince yourself that:

- You are indeed an entrepreneur with *some* demonstrated management ability.

- You have a viable idea for the startup or expansion of a business that is selling in a market that you (or a partner) have preferably worked in or at least have studied thoroughly.

- You can secure the commitment of one or two other people, whose skills and experience complement your own, to work with you to build your business. (To help you think these issues through, you should review "The Characteristics of a Successful Entrepreneur" in this *GUIDE*.)

Developing a business plan that will attract the professional venture investors' interest and, more important, their financial commitment, is a major challenge because it is likely that you are preparing such a plan for the first time. Even if you have an MBA, you could well not have learned how to put together a comprehensive business plan.

To ease the entrepreneur's task, Brian Haslett and Leonard Smollen, two of the founders of Venture Founders Corporation, Waltham, Massachusetts, prepared the detailed guidelines that follow. They interviewed many successful venture capitalists about their experiences and used their own experience in analyzing numerous venture proposals in writing this article. Their aim is to help the entrepreneur comprehend the scope of what is required and appreciate how much detail is needed to establish the fundamentals on which a good startup or expansion are based. VFC's staff has been working with entrepreneurs in the various parts of North America and Northern Europe since 1972,* helping to develop their management teams and business plans.

Though entrepreneurs often find this process of building their teams and preparing their plans harder and more lengthy than

they anticipated, those who "completed the course" are generally able to raise the capital they need and proceed to moving their businesses ahead successfully.

Businesses that have been developed with the assistance of VFC principals range from manufacturers of tents in Kentucky and of rock drilling equipment in Florida, to a manufacturer of automated cash processing systems in England, and a re-manufacturer of mining tools in Canada. All of these businesses were planned with guidelines similar to those set out below. Several are now profitable, multi-million dollar corporations.

Using These Guidelines

When raising equity capital, your business plan is a vital sales tool. Before risking their funds for what is likely to be a period of five years or longer, most venture capital investors will want to satisfy themselves that you have thought through your plan carefully and that you and your partners have enough skill and experience in your chosen business area to manage effectively, seize opportunities, solve problems, *and* make profits. These prospective backers will — or should — insist on reviewing your proposal *before* considering any investment seriously. Some will not even meet with an entrepreneur without first seeing his or her business plan. For this reason, your plan must be well-prepared and very persuasive in conveying the potential of your company. It should cover all major issues and yet not be so detailed that the investor-reader is "turned off." Fifty pages should suffice for most businesses.

Use common sense in applying to your particular business the guidelines described here because they are meant to cover a wide variety of manufacturing and service businesses. It is not possible or desirable to follow them slavishly. (For example, a plan for a service business clearly does not require any discussion of manufacturing or product design.)

When starting up or expanding a business in your particular industry or market, there are certain currently critical issues of which you ought to be aware and with which you must deal in

* Originally published and copyrighted (1972) by the Institute for New Enterprise Development (INED). Revised for this book by the authors.

your plan. In the chemical industry, issues of significance can, for example, include the following:

- Reduced availability of raw materials and resultant bartering and allocation

- Increasingly strict regulations at all government levels, covering the use of chemical products and the operation of chemical processes

- Diminishing viability of the high capital cost, special-purpose chemical processing plant serving narrow markets

Make whatever investigations are needed to develop a list of special issues that are significant to your particular businesss.

These guidelines, because they contain a list of potentially *relevant* issues, will help you develop your list. But it is up to you to determine, at the time you are preparing your plan, which issues are *significant* to the future development of your business.

Professional venture capitalists are not the only people who find business plans invaluable. For the entrepreneur, the careful preparation of a plan is an important opportunity to think carefully through all of the facets of a business expansion or startup, to examine the consequences of different marketing, operations, and financing strategies, and to determine what human, physical and financial resources are required. Much of this *can* be done effectively on paper without the often crippling expense of trial-and-error operation.

In one venture that we helped develop, the discipline of writing his business plan caused the entrepreneur to realize that the major market for his biomedical product was in nursing homes, not in hospital emergency rooms as he had previously supposed. He changed the focus of his marketing effort accordingly.

Another successful entrepreneur with whom we worked has told us that, besides using his plan to help raise $650,000 startup capital, it helped him monitor his company's performance during its first 18 months. Then, when he needed to increase his company's credit lines, and to secure long-term financing for building and equipment, he was able to update his plan in two or three days. Had he not had a plan, he would have needed two to three weeks which would have been almost impossible to find.

Summary of the Plan

Many investors like to read a one- to three-page summary of a business plan that highlights its important features and opportunities so that they can quickly decide if it is worth their while reviewing the whole plan carefully. Do not write your summary until you have written your plan. As you draft each section of the plan, circle a few sentences that you think are important enough to be included in a summary.

Allow plenty of time to write an appealing and convincing summary. Remember that this summary is probably the first thing about you and your business that the would-be investor is going to read. Unless it is appealing and convincing, it may also be the last!

We suggest that your summary should contain *very brief* statements about

1. your company's origins, activities, management and performance,
2. any distinguishing features of your product or service,
3. the attractiveness of your market,
4. a summary of your financial projections,
5. the amount of money you now seek, in what form (equity or debt or both), and for what purpose.

We suggest that you persuade several people to review your summary while it is still in draft form. They should be people whose business realism you respect, but who are not involved in your venture. Then evaluate their reactions realistically. Did they quickly grasp what you are proposing to do? Were they "turned on" by what they read? Did they ask you how much stock you were willing to sell them? They should provide you with some useful indications of how the professional venture capital investor is likely to react.

Description of Your Business and Its Industry

In this section, you should provide the reader with some background for what you are going to present in subsequent sections about your product/service, your market opportunity, and the people and plans that you have for going after that opportunity. You should *briefly* describe what product or service you are offering, to whom, and sketch the nature and current condition of your industry to show where and how you fit in it.

Your Company

Describe the business you are in or intend to enter. Describe your product/services, possible customers, and regions of operation.

Trace the history of your business: when it was formed; how its products/services were chosen and developed; and what roles each of the principals played in bringing the business to where it is today.

If your company is already trading and is now seeking further development or expansion financing, review its market penetration and its financial performance (sales, profits, return on equity).

If, as is to be expected, your company has had early setbacks and incurred losses, describe these and say what you are doing to avoid recurrences. Omission of any reference to past problems can make your proposal appear too good to be true.

Your Industry

Present your view of the nature, current status and prospects for the industry in which your business does, or will, operate. Describe the principal participants and how they are performing; growth in sales and profits and also any published forecasts for the current year; companies that have recently entered or left these markets and why; and what major economic, social, technological, or regulatory trends are affecting your business.

In this section you should not go into too much detail. That is done later. Each topic should be covered summarily in two or three sentences.

Features and Advantages of Products or Services

The potential investor wants to know *exactly* what you are going to sell, what kind of special know-how and protection you have, and what its advantages and drawbacks are.

- *Description.* Describe, in more detail than previously, the products or services that you sell or intend to sell and what needs they satisfy. Use diagrams, sketches, and pictures if illustration will improve understanding and heighten interest. Emphasize any distinctive features of your product or service by highlighting the differences between what competitors currently have on the market and what you have or will offer. State candidly each feature's advantage or disadvantage.

- *Proprietary Position.* Describe any patents, trade secrets, or other proprietary features. Discuss any head start that you have or could have that would enable you to achieve a favored or entrenched position in your industry.

- *Potential.* Discuss any opportunities for the logical extension of your existing line or the development of related products or services. Investors like to know what you can do for an encore.

Market Research and Analysis

In this section of your plan, you should present enough facts to convince the investor that the market for your product or service is such that you can achieve your sales target in the face of the competition. The discussion and the guidelines below should help you do this.

This is probably the most difficult section for entrepreneurs to do well. And, because choice of marketing strategies, size of operating work force and facilities, and requirements for inventory and receivables financing are all to be derived from sales forecasts, it is also the most crucial. Because of this, we advise you to prepare this section of your business plan *before you do any other and to take enough time to do it really well.*

Customers

Define your markets clearly. Explain who the major purchasers for your product or service are, where they are, and why they buy. Discuss and indicate by rank order the significance of price, quality, service, personal contacts, and political pressures. When do they buy? Discuss the significance of seasonality — when the buying is done, and how it affects your offering.

List some actual or potential customers who have purchased, or expressed an interest in, your product or service and indicate why. List any actual or potential customers who have dropped, or shown no interest in, your product or service, and explain why this was so. Explain what you are doing to overcome negative customer reaction. The absence of some frank discussion about the negatives of your offering leads readers to wonder if you are telling your whole story.

Market Size and Trends

What is the size of the current total market for the product you have or service you do or will offer? This market should be determined from discussions with potential distributors, dealers, sales representatives, and customers, as well as a review of whatever published data are available. Do not rely solely on published data. It is often inadequate and known to be so by industry insiders. Give the size of the total market in both units and dollars. Be careful to include *only* the market you are in fact going after. If you intend to sell regionally, show the regional market size.

Describe the potential annual growth of the total market for your product or service. Market projections should be made for at least three future years. Discuss in more detail than previously how the major factors, such as industry trends, new technical developments, new or changing customer needs, are affecting market growth and review previous trends of the market. Any differences between past and projected future growth rates should be explained. If you are assuming that past trends will continue, say why. Entrepreneurs tend to overestimate the size of their market. If potential investors become dubious about your market size and growth estimates, they may lose interest in the rest of your proposal.

Competition
Make a realistic assessment of the strengths and weaknesses of competitive products and services and name the companies that supply them. State the data sources used to determine which products are competitive and the strengths of the competition.

You should compare your products or services with your competitors' on the basis of price, performance, service, warranties, and other pertinent features. A table can be an effective way of presenting these data.

Then review the managerial and financial strengths and weaknesses of your competitors. Give your assessment of each competitor's capability in marketing, operations, and finance, and their recent trends in sales, market share, and profitability. If they are not doing well, explain why you expect to succeed.

Conclude this section by explaining why customers buy from your three or four key competitors. Then, from what you have presented above about their operations, explain why you think that you can capture a share of their business — *if* that is how you plan to grow.

Entrepreneurs often know less about their competition than they should. Professional investors are very wary of proposals in which competition is treated lightly.

Estimated Market Share and Sales
Identify any major customers who have made or are willing to make purchase commitments. Indicate the extent of these commitments.

Sales and market share data									
		1st year				*2nd year*			
		Q1	*Q2*	*Q3*	*Q4*	*Q1*	*Q2*	*Q3*	*Q4*
Estimated total market	Units								
	Dollars								
Your estimated sales	Units								
	Dollars								
Your estimated market share	Units								
	Dollars								

Estimate the share of the market and the sales in units and dollars that you think that you can achieve. Base this estimate on your assessment of your customers and their acceptance of your product or service, your market size and trends, and the competition, their offerings and their share of sales in prior year. The growth of your sales and your estimated market share should be related to the growth of your industry and customers and the strengths and weaknesses of your competitors. The data should be presented in tabular form, as shown above. If yours is an existing business, also indicate the total market, your market share, and sales for two prior years.

Marketing Plan
Your marketing plan should describe *how* you will achieve your sales target. The marketing plan should include a description of your sales and service policies and pricing, distribution and advertising strategies that you will use to achieve your goal. The marketing plan should make clear *what is to be done, how it will be done,* and *who will do it.*

Marketing Strategy
A description of your marketing strategy should include a discussion of the kinds of customers who will be targeted for initial heavy selling effort, customers who will be sought for later selling efforts, method of identifying specific potential customers and of contacting them, and the features of the product or service (quality, price, delivery, warranty) that will be emphasized to generate sales.

If the sales of your product or service are seasonal, discuss this and indicate any ideas you have for obtaining out-of-season sales.

Pricing

Many entrepreneurs, after convincing the investors that they have a superior product, then say they intend to sell it for less than their competitors. This makes a bad impression for two reasons. First, if their product is as good as they say it is, the entrepreneurs can be judged as poor sales people if they have to offer their product at a lower price than the competition. Second, costs do tend to be underestimated. If you start out with low prices, there is little room to maneuver if costs run over budget. Price hikes are tougher to make stick than price cuts.

Your pricing policy is one of the more important decisions you make. Your "price must be right" to penetrate your market, maintain your market position, and produce the profits you project. Devote enough time to considering a number of pricing strategies and convincingly present the one you select.

Discuss the prices to be charged for your product and service and compare your pricing policy with those of your major competitors. Explain how the price you set will enable you to:

- secure/increase acceptance of your offering,

- maintain and desirably increase your market share in the face of competition, and

- produce profits.

Justify any price increases over competitive items on the basis of newness, quality, warranty, and service. If your product is to be priced lower than your competitors' products, explain how you will do this and maintain profitability.

Sales Tactics

Describe how you will sell and distribute your product or service. Do you or will you use your own sales force, sales representatives, and distributors? Are there ready-made manufacturers' sales organizations already selling related products that you already use or can use? If distributors or sales representatives are used, describe how they have been or will be selected, and the areas they will cover. Discuss the margins to be given to retailers, wholesalers, and your commissions to sales representatives, and compare them to those given your competition. Describe any special policies regarding such items as discounts and exclusive distribution rights.

If a direct sales force is being introduced, indicate how it will be organized and at what rate it will be built up. Show the sales expected per salesman per year and what commission incentive and/or salary they will receive. Explain how these figures compare to those of your competition.

Service and Warranty Policies

If your company will offer a product that will require service and warranties, indicate the importance of these to the customer's purchasing decision and discuss your method of handling service problems.

Advertising, Public Relations, and Promotion

Describe the program you will use to bring your product to the attention of prospective customers. Indicate your plans for public relations, trade show participation, trade magazine advertisements, direct mailings, and the preparation of product sheets and promotional literature. If advertising will be a significant part of company expenses, details of how and when these costs will be incurred should be presented.

Design and Development Plans

If any of your products or services require design and development before they are ready to be placed on the market, the nature and extent of this work should be fully discussed. The costs and time required to achieve a marketable product or service should be indicated.

Such design and development might be the engineering work necessary to convert a laboratory prototype to a finished product, the design of special tooling, the work of an industrial designer to make a product more attractive and salable, or the identification and organization of manpower, equipment, and special techniques or to implement a service business, for example, the equipment, new computer software, and skills required for computerized credit checking.

Development Status and Tasks

Describe the current status of the product or service and explain what remains to be done to make it marketable. Describe briefly the competence or expertise that your company has or will acquire to complete this development. Indicate the type and extent of technical assistance that will be required, and state who will supervise this activity within your organization, and give his or her experience in related development work.

Difficulties and Risks
Identify any major anticipated design and development problems and approaches to their solution. Discuss their possible impact on the timing of the market introduction of your product or service and the cost of design and development.

Costs
Present and discuss a design and development budget. The costs should include labor, materials, consulting fees, etc. Design and development costs are often underestimated. This can seriously impact cash flow projections. Accordingly, consider and perhaps show a 10% to 20% cost contingency. These cost data will become an integral part of the financial plan.

Operations Plan
The operations plan should describe the kind of facilities, space requirements, capital equipment, and labor force (part and full time) that are required to deliver the forecast quantities of the company's product or service. For a manufacturing business, discuss your policies regarding purchasing, "make or buy decisions" (which parts of the product will be purchased and which operations will be performed by your work force), inventory control, and production control. A service business should describe the appropriateness of location, and lease of required equipment, and competitive productivity from a skilled or trained labor force.

The discussion guidelines given below are general enough to cover both product and service businesses. Only those that are relevant to your venture — be it product or service — should be used in preparing the business plan.

Geographic Location
Describe the location of the business and discuss any advantages or disadvantages of the site in terms of wage rates, labor unions, labor availability, closeness to customers or suppliers, access to transportation, state and local taxes, state and local laws, utilities, and zoning. For a service business, proximity to customers is generally a "must."

Facilities and Improvements
If yours is an existing business, describe the facilities currently used to conduct the company's business. This should include plant and office space, storage and land areas, machinery, special tooling, and other capital equipment.

If your venture is a startup, describe how and when the necessary facilities to *start* production will be acquired. Discuss whether equipment and space will be leased or acquired (new or used), and indicate the costs and timing of such actions. Indicate how much of the proposed financings will be devoted to plant and equipment. These cost data will become part of the plan.

Discuss how and when plant space and equipment will be expanded to the capacities required for future sales projections. Discuss any plans to improve or add to existing plant space or to move the facility. Explain future equipment needs and indicate the timing and cost of any acquisitions. A three-year planning period should be used for these projections.

Strategy and Plans
Describe the manufacturing processes involved in your product's production and any decisions with respect to subcontracting component parts rather than manufacturing them in house. The "make or buy" strategy adopted should consider inventory financing, available labor skills and other nontechnical questions as well as purely production, cost, and capability issues. Justify your proposed "make or buy" policy. Discuss any surveys you have completed of potential subcontractors and suppliers and who these are.

Present a production plan that shows cost-volume information at various sales levels of operation with breakdowns of applicable material, labor, purchased components, and factory overhead. Discuss the inventory required at various sales levels. These data will be incorporated into cash flow projections. Explain how any seasonal production loads will be handled without severe dislocation, for example, by building to inventory, using part-time help, or subcontracting the work.

Briefly, describe your approach to quality control, production control, and inventory control. Explain what quality control and inspection procedures the company will use to minimize service problems and associated customer dissatisfaction.

Discuss how you will organize and operate your purchasing function to insure that adequate materials are on hand for production, that the best price and payment terms have been obtained, and that raw materials and in-process inventory, and, hence, working capital have been minimized.

Labor Force
Explain, exclusive of management functions (discussed later), to what extent local labor force has the necessary skills in sufficient quantity and quality (lack of absenteeism, productivity)

to manufacture the product or supply the services of your company to whatever quality, time and cost standards you have established. If the skills of the labor force are inadequate for the needs of your company, describe the kinds of training that you will use to upgrade their skills. Discuss how your business can provide and pay for such training and still offer a competitive product both in the short term (first year) and long term (two to five years).

Management Team

The management team is the key to a successful business. Investors look for a committed management team with a balance in marketing operations and financial skills and experience in doing what is proposed.

Accordingly, this section of the business plan will be of primary interest to potential investors and will significantly influence their investment decisions. It should include a description of the key members of the management team and their primary duties, the organizational structure, and the board of directors.

Organization

In a table, present the key management roles in the company and name the person for each position.

Discuss any current or past situations in which the key management people have worked together that indicate how their skills and personalities complement each other and result in an effective management team. If any key individuals will not be on hand at the start of the venture, indicate when they will join the company or what you are doing to locate and secure commitments from such individuals.

In a new business, it may not be possible to fill each executive role with a full-time person without excessively burdening the overhead of the venture. One solution is to use part-time specialists or consultants to perform some functions. If this is your plan, discuss it and indicate who will be used and when they will be replaced by a full-time staff member.

If the company is established and of sufficient size, an organization chart can be appended as an exhibit.

Key Management Personnel

Describe the exact duties and responsibilities of each of the key members of the management team. Include a brief (three or four sentence) statement of the career highlights of each individual to focus on accomplishments that demonstrate ability to perform the assigned role.

Complete resumes for each key management member should be included here or as an exhibit to the business plan. These resumes should stress education, training, experience, and accomplishments of each person in performing functions similar to that person's role in the venture. Accomplishments should be discussed in such concrete terms as profit and sales improvement, labor productivity gains, reduced operating costs, improved product performance, and ability to meet budgets and schedules. When possible, it should be noted who can attest to accomplishments and recognition or rewards received, such as pay increases and promotions.

Management Compensation and Ownership

The likelihood of obtaining financing for a startup is small when the founding management team is not prepared to accept modest initial salaries. If the founders demand substantial salaries in excess of what they received at their prior employment, the potential investor will conclude that their psychological commitment to the venture is a good deal less than it should be.

State the salary that is to be paid to each key person and compare it with the salary received at his last independent job. Set forth the stock ownership planned for the key management team members, the amount of their equity investment (if any), and any performance-dependent stock option or bonus plans that are contemplated. Mention any loans made to the company by management, indicating on what terms they were made and under what circumstances they can be converted to equity.

Board of Directors

Identify board members and include a one or two sentence statement of the member's background to show how he or she can benefit the company and what investment (if any) has been made.

Management Assistance and Training Needs

Describe candidly the strengths and weaknesses of your management team and board of directors. Discuss the kind, extent, and timing of any management training that will be required to overcome any weaknesses.

Supporting Professional Services

State the legal (including patent-counsel), accounting, public relations, advertising, banking, and other service organizations that you have selected for your venture. Supporting service organizations that are reputable *and* capable (remember reputations often live on after capability diminishes) not only provide professional assistance, but can also add significantly to the credibility of your business. In addition, properly selected professional organizations can help you establish good contacts in the business community, identify potential investors, and help you secure financing.

Overall Schedule

A schedule that shows the timing and interrelationship of the major events necessary to launch the venture and realize its objectives is an essential part of a business plan. In addition to being a planning aid and showing deadlines critical to a venture's success, a well-prepared schedule can be an extremely effective sales tool in raising money from potential investors. A well-prepared and realistic schedule demonstrates the ability of the management team to plan for venture growth in a way that recognizes obstacles and minimizes risk.

Prepare, as a part of this section, a month-by-month schedule that shows the timing of activities such as product development, market planning, sales programs, and operations. Sufficient detail should be included to show the timing of the primary tasks required to accomplish each major goal.

Show on the schedule the deadlines or milestones critical to the venture's success. This should include events as follows:

- Incorporation of the venture (for a new business)
- Completion of prototypes. This is a key date. Its achievement is a tangible measure of the company's ability to perform
- When sales representatives are obtained
- Dates of displays at trade shows
- When distributors and dealers are signed up
- Order of materials in sufficient quantities for full-time operation
- Start of operation. This is another key date because it is related to the production of income
- Receipt of first orders
- First sales and deliveries. This is a date of maximum interest because it relates directly to the company's credibility and need for capital
- Payment of first accounts receivable (cash in)

The schedule should also show the following and their relation to the development of the business.

- Number of management personnel
- Number of operations personnel
- Additions to plant or equipment

Discuss in a general way the activities most likely to cause a schedule slippage and what steps you would take to correct such slippages. Discuss the impact of schedule slippages on the venture's operation, especially on its potential viability and capital needs. Keep in mind that the time to do things tends to be underestimated — even more than financing requirements. So be realistic about your schedule.

Critical Risks and Problems

The development of a business has risks and problems, and the business plan invariably contains some implicit assumptions about them. The discovery of any unstated negative factors by potential investors can seriously undermine the credibility of the entrepreneur and his venture and endanger its financing.

On the other hand, identifying and discussing the risks in your venture demonstrates your skill as a manager and increases your credibility with a venture capital investor. Taking the initiative to identify and discuss risks helps you demonstrate to the investor that you have thought about them and can handle them. Risks then tend not to loom as large black clouds in the investor's thinking about your venture.

Accordingly, identify and discuss the major problems and risks that you think you will have to deal with to develop your venture. This should include a description of the risks relating to your industry, your company and its personnel, your product's market appeal, and the timing and financing of your startup. Among the risks that might require discussion are the following.

- Price cutting by competitors
- Any potentially unfavorable industry-wide trends
- Design or operating costs significantly in excess of estimates
- Development schedule not met
- Sales projections not achieved by target date
- Difficulties or long lead times encountered in the procurement of parts or raw materials
- Difficulties encountered in obtaining needed bank credit line because of tight money
- Larger than expected innovation and development costs to stay competitive
- Lack of availability of trained labor

This list is *not meant to be in any way comprehensive* but only indicative of the kinds of risks and assumptions involved.

Indicate which business plan assumptions or potential problems are most critical to the success of the venture. Describe your plans for minimizing the impact of unfavorable developments in each risk area on the success of your venture.

The Financial Plan

The financial plan is basic to any investor's evaluation of your business and should represent your best estimates of future operations. Its purpose is to indicate the financial potential of your venture and its capital needs. The financial plan should also serve as an operating plan for financial management of your business.

In developing your financial plan, three basic exhibits must be prepared.

- Profit and loss forecasts for three years

- Cash flow projections for three years

- Pro forma balance sheets at startup, semi-annually in the first year, and at the end of each of the first three years of operation.

In the case of an existing business seeking expansion capital, balance sheets and income statements for the current and two prior years should be presented in addition to these financial projections.

After you have completed the preparation of the financial exhibits, briefly highlight in writing the important conclusions that can be drawn. This might include such items as the maximum cash requirement, the amount to be supplied by equity and debt, the level of profits as a percent of sales, and how fast any debts are repaid.

Profit and Loss Forecast

The preparation of your business' projected income statements is the planning-for-profit part of your financial plan. Crucial to the earnings forecasts, as well as other projections, is the sales forecast. The methods for developing sales forecasts have already been described in these guidelines, and the sales forecasts made there should be used here.

The following list is a group of headings that can be used in drawing up your profit and loss (P&L) forecast for prospective investors. Italics indicate items that should be included in the figures for that heading but not listed separately in the statement.

Sales
   Less: Discounts
   Less: Bad debt provision
   Less: Materials used
      Direct labor
      Manufacturing overhead
        includes rent, utilities, fringe benefits, telephone
      Other manufacturing expense
        leased equipment, etc.
      Depreciation
  Total cost of goods sold
Gross profit (or loss)
   Less: Sales expense
      Engineering expense
      General and administrative expense
        office supplies, accounting and legal services, management, etc.

Operating profit (or loss)
   Less: Other expense
      (*e.g., interest*)
Profit (or loss) before taxes
Income tax provision
Profit (or loss) after taxes

Figures should be projected for three years. The first year should show a breakdown by month for each item. The second and third years should project quarterly figures. Figures for all three years should appear on a single sheet of ruled paper — make sure the paper you use is large enough. Tape two pages together, if necessary.

Once the sales forecasts are in hand, production costs, or operations costs for a service business, should be budgeted. The level of production or operation that is required to meet the sales forecasts and also to fulfill inventory requirements must be determined. The material, labor, service, and manufacturing overhead requirements must be developed and translated into cost data.

Sales expense should include the costs of selling and distribution, storage, discounts, and advertising and promotion. General and administrative expense should include management salaries, secretarial costs, and legal and accounting expenses. Manufacturing or operations overhead includes such items as rent, utilities, fringe benefits, and telephone.

If these earning projections are to be useful, they must represent your realistic and best estimate of probable operating results.

Discussion of Assumptions
Because of the importance of profit and loss projections, you should explain any assumptions that you made in their preparation. Such assumptions could include the amount allowed for bad debts and discounts and sales expenses or general and administrative costs as a fixed percentage of costs or sales.

Cash Flow Forecast
For a new business, the cash flow forecast can be more important than the forecasts of profits because it details the amount and timing of expected cash inflows and outflows. Usually the level of profits, particularly during the startup years of a venture, will not be sufficient to finance operating cash needs. Moreover, cash inflows do not match the outflows on a short-term basis. The cash flow forecast will indicate these conditions.

The following headings can be used in preparing the pro forma cash flow analysis. Like the income statement, the cash flow analysis should cover three years, with the first year broken down into 12 monthly figures and the second and third year projected by quarters. Again, this analysis should be made on a single large sheet of ruled paper.

Cash balance: Opening
Add: Cash receipts
    Collection of accounts receivable
    Miscellaneous receipts
    Bank loan proceeds
    Sale of stock
        Total receipts

Less: Disbursements
    Trade payables
    Direct labor
    Manufacturing overhead
    Leased equipment
    Sales expense
    Warranty expense
    General and administrative expense
    Fixed asset additions
    Income tax
    Loan interest @ _____ %
    Loan repayments
    Other payments
        Total disbursements

Cash increase (or decrease)
Cash balance: Closing

Given a level of projected sales and capital expenditures over a specific period, the cash flow forecast will highlight the need for and timing of additional financing and show you your peak requirements of working capital. You must decide how this additional financing is to be obtained, on what terms, and how it is to be repaid. Part of the needed financing will be supplied by the professional venture capitalists, part by bank loans for one of five years, and the balance by short-term lines of credit from banks. This information becomes part of the final cash flow forecasts.

If the venture is in a seasonal or cyclical industry, in an industry in which suppliers require a new firm to pay cash, or if an inventory buildup occurs before the product can be sold and produce revenues, the cash flow forecast is crucial to the continuing operation of your business. A detailed cash flow forecast that you understand can enable you to direct your attention to operating problems without the distractions caused by periodic cash crises that you should have anticipated.

Discussion of Assumptions
This should include assumptions made on the timing of collection of receivables, trade discounts given, terms of payments to your suppliers, planned salary and wage increases, anticipated increases in any operating expenses, seasonality characteristics of the business as they affect inventory requirements, and capital equipment purchases. Thinking about such assumptions when planning the operation of your business is useful for identifying issues that may later require attention if they are not to become significant problems.

Balance Sheet Forecasts
The balance sheets are used to show the assets required in the operation of your business and, through liabilities, how these assets are to be financed. Investors and bankers look to the projected balance sheets for such information as debt to equity ratios, working capital, current ratios, and inventory turnover. The investor will relate them to the acceptable limits required to justify future financings that are projected for the venture.

The following headings may be used to prepare the balance sheet forecasts.

ASSESTS

Current assests
  Cash
  Marketable securities
  Accounts receivable
  Inventories
    Raw materials and supplies
    Work in progress
    Finished goods
      Total inventory
Prepaid items
  Total current assets

Plant and equipment
      Less: Accumulated depreciation
Net plant and equipment

Deferred charges
Other assests (identify)
      Total assets

LIABILITIES AND STOCKHOLDER'S EQUITY

Current liabilities
  Notes payable to banks
  Accounts payable
  Accruals
  Federal and state taxes accrued
  Other
        Total current liabilities

  Long-term notes
  Other liabilities

  Common stock
  Capital surplus
  Retained earnings

      Total liabilities and stockholder's equity

Forecasted balance sheets should be prepared at startup, semi-annually for the first year, and at the end of each of the first three years of operation.

Cost and Cash Flow Control

Your ability to meet your income and cash flow projections will depend critically on your ability to secure timely reports on, and effectively control, your operating costs. For this reason, investors will want to know what kind of cost and cash control systems you have or will use in your business. The financial plan should include a brief description of how you will design, install, and maintain systems for controlling costs and cash flows appropriate to the nature and size of your business, who will be responsible for getting cost data, how often cost data will be obtained, and how you will take actions to reduce costs that are running higher than you expected.

Proposed Company Offering

The purpose of this section of the plan is to indicate the amount of capital that is being sought and to briefly describe the uses that will be made of the funds raised. The discussion and guidelines given below should help you do this.

Desired Financing

Summarize from your cash flow projections how much money you will need over the next three years to carry out the development and expansion of your business that have been described. Indicate how much of this money you expect to obtain now from the sale of stock and how much you think you can borrow from a bank. Describe the kind (common stock, convertible debenture, etc.), unit price, and total amount of securities to be sold in this offering. Also show the percentage of the company that the investors of this offering will hold after the offering is completed or after any exercise of stock conversion or purchase rights.

Capitalization

Show in a table the names of your current shareholders and the number of shares each holds. Also indicate how many shares of your company's common stock will remain authorized but unissued after the offering.

Use of Funds

Investors like to know how their money is going to be spent. Provide a brief description of how the capital raised will be used. Summarize as specifically as possible what amount will be used for such things as product development, capital equipment, marketing, and general working capital needs.

Market Information Sources for the Entrepreneur

James R. Fries

James R. Fries *is the business administration and engineering librarian at Feldberg Library, Dartmouth College, Hanover, New Hampshire. Feldberg serves the Amos Tuck School of Business Administration and the Thayer School of Engineering. Mr. Fries has 11 years of professional experience in academic and industrial research libraries.*

Introduction

Market research is among the most important tasks an entrepreneur must complete before presenting a business plan to potential venture capital investors. The entrepreneur's analysis and understanding of the market, and what differentiates the company's product or service from others in the industry, are crucial in helping a venture capitalist decide if the new company is a good investment.

To complete the market research section of the business plan, an entrepreneur needs current information on all aspects of the commercial environment. Two key aspects, the industry and competitors, should be carefully assessed. This is especially important in technology-based industries where industry and competitive developments occur daily.

One way to monitor the business environment is to scan information sources that regularly report on companies, industries, technologies and market news. Since emerging companies lack the resources for a large market research function, inexpensive and readily-available information sources must be exploited whenever possible to supplement management's awareness and knowledge of the market.

Purpose/Scope

The purpose of this article is to highlight and describe major sources of market and industry information. This is not an exhaustive list, but a guide to key resources. Its goal is to save the entrepreneur time when collecting data for market research and suggest ways of finding answers that might not otherwise have been considered. The chapter focuses on sources covering markets, industries, competitors, technologies, economic trends and other factors in the business environment. Since these sources are widely available and often inexpensive, they should be consulted in an early phase of the market research task.

General Sources of Market and Industry Information

Virtually any question confronting the entrepreneur during the market research phase of business planning can be at least partially answered using secondary sources found outside the company. The problem is that so much published data exists it is difficult to know where to begin to look.

The general sources mentioned below should be consulted early in the data-gathering part of market research because they are widely available, easy to contact and cost very little to use. By using any one of these general sources, the entrepreneur has access to hundreds of publications, data sources and resource people and is able to draw on expert knowledge to locate the key sources that should be used for market research.

Business Libraries

Public, college and university libraries often have a business reference collection. This should be the first source used when collecting market data for several reasons. First, the reference librarians can probably save hours or even days of the researcher's time. Second, an experienced and knowledgeable business librarian can suggest relevant sources that the researcher did not know even existed. Third, business libraries found in large cities or associated with business schools have excellent collections of U.S. government documents, patents, trade magazines, directories and other resources. Most libraries today use electronic networks to locate and order magazine articles and books not available locally. Thus the entrepreneur can draw on the resources of major research libraries without having to travel a great distance.

Federal Government Sources

The U.S. Government is the largest publisher in the world. Data collected by the U.S. Government is used by market research firms, economic forecasting services, business publishers and other organizations. Entrepreneurs should be aware of and use Federal agencies and their publications because they are inexpensive and contain considerable amounts of useful economic data. For example, the Commerce Department issues hundreds of publications and special reports containing economic, demographic and industry data. Patents issued by the U.S. Patent and Trademark Office and technical reports from the National

Technical Information Service are excellent sources for tracking product development or technical consulting work done by U.S. companies. The directories listed below — found in most libraries — list and describe the publications and reports issued by the Federal Government.

1. *Federal/State Executive Telephone Directory*
   Directory of names, addresses and telephone numbers for officials in Federal and State Government. Updated only annually, so some agencies' or individuals' numbers may change and not be noted in the directory. One use of the directory would be to locate (and then direct-dial) market and industry analysts at the U.S. Department of Commerce.

2. *American Statistics Index (ASI)*
   Monthly abstract/index source describing all Federal statistical publications. It is an invaluable source of economic, demographic and social data, both primary and secondary.

3. *Statistical Abstract of the United States*
   Convenient annual reference for U.S. economic, political, demographic and social data. Also a handy guide to hundreds of U.S. statistical publications and sources. While ASI has descriptive details about each publication, the Statistical Abstract is useful because it summarizes so much data and so many publications.

4. *Congressional Information Service (CIS)*
   Monthly abstract/index service published by the same firm that issues ASI. CIS has index/abstract coverage of all publications from the U.S. Congress, including their research reports, hearings and other documents.

Other Federal Sources to Consult

5. *Official Gazette of the United States Patent and Trademark Office*
   (issued in two parts, one covering patents, one covering trademarks) Weekly source to all new patents and trademarks issued by the U.S. PTO. Each issue of the gazette has an index by patentee, either the individual or company name.

6. *Government Reports Announcements and Index*
   Published every two weeks by the National Technical Information Service, this is a central source for information about all U.S. Government-sponsored research, development and engineering reports. GRA&I is a major source for tracking advanced technology work performed under government sponsorship.

7. *Commerce Business Daily*
   A daily list of business opportunities with the U.S. Government, it lists contract awards, procurement invitations, subcontracting leads and other commercial activities of the Federal Government.

8. *Census of Manufacturers*
   Published every five years, this is a principal source of data and facts about the structure and condition of U.S. manufacturing industries. The reports cover production, inventories, employment, number of establishments, capital expenditures, value added, cost of material and other factors.

9. *Current Business Reports and Current Industrial Reports*
   Issued monthly, these reports are important indicators of retail and wholesale trade and industrial activity.

Federal sources generally do not track economic and business activity below the county level. State organizations (government or private) are more familiar with local and regional issues and can be helpful.

1. *The National Directory of State Agencies*
   Annual guide with names, addresses and telephone numbers for state officials and agencies in all 50 states. Excellent source for locating state officials and agencies concerned with economic and commercial development.

2. *Johnson's Worldwide Chamber of Commerce Directory*
   A small guide, but packed with useful contacts. It includes a list of chambers of commerce — with addresses and telephone numbers — in all 50 states as well as internationally. In addition, the directory has U.S. chambers of commerce abroad, American embassies, consulates and key U.S. officials throughout the world. Finally, foreign embassies and foreign consular offices in the U.S. are included.

Industry and Trade Associations
Trade associations follow trends on developments in particular industries. They are an excellent source of industry data. Associations that represent a large number of manufacturers, suppliers or other industry segments can be a valuable information source.

1. *Encyclopedia of Associations*
   Annual guide to over 18,000 associations. This is the most widely quoted and used directory of associations. Each listing has a full association description, address and telephone number. One useful feature is a list of any association publications available.

2. *National Trade and Professional Associations of the United States*
Annual directory for over 6,000 U.S. trade and professional associations and labor unions. Each listing includes association name, address, telephone number and (like the Encyclopedia of Associations), a list of publications. The association's annual budget, an indicator of its size and importance, is also given. Excellent directory of associations that would probably be of interest to entrepreneurs. The introduction explains the role of trade associations and their activities.

Sources of Company and Industry Information
The general sources described above will lead to the company and industry information sources noted here. Using these publications, the entrepreneur can get a good overview of industry trends and activities of both public and private companies.

1. *Standard and Poor's Industry Surveys*
S&P is a leading publisher of business information. *Industry Surveys* tracks 22 key industries and about 1,300 companies and has two parts — Basic and Current Analysis. Basic Analysis examines industry trends and problems. Extensive text for each industry is accompanied by statistical tables and charts allowing one to compare performance among the industry's leading firms. *Current Analysis* includes recent developments along with industry, market and company statistics.

2. *U.S. Industrial Outlook*
This annual publication is subtitled "Prospects for Over 350 Manufacturing and Service Industries." Specialists at the Department of Commerce prepare each chapter of the book. Excellent source for learning about historical trends, the current situation and outlook for each industry analyzed.

3. *Predicasts F&S Index*
Excellent source for tracking industry, company and technology-related issues and developments. Published weekly, *F&S Index* includes references to company, product and industry information from over 750 business publications, newspapers, trade magazines and market reports. The publication has two parts, one covering industries and products and the other covering companies.

4. *Predicasts Basebook and Forecasts*
Companion publications to the *F&S Index,* the *Basebook and Forecasts* give historical trends and future prospects by industry. These two sources extract only the data from tables, charts, graphs, etc. found in the approximately 750 publications indexed by the *F&S Index*. The *Basebook and Forecasts* are extremely useful for getting a general picture of how different factors such as sales, employment and production have changed and are expected to change over time.

5. *Predicasts Review of Markets and Technology*
Monthly service that scans more than 1,000 trade magazines, market studies and other sources reporting on technology-based industries. PROMT has strong coverage of companies' research, new products, general market and industry trends. Abstracts, or short summaries, are included for each article.

6. *Ward's Directory* (2 volumes)
Unusual and very useful directory. Volume 1 includes data for 51,000 firms — over 8,000 public and 43,000 private companies ranked by industry, and within industry by sales and employee size. There are many special features — for example, 51,000 companies are ranked geographically by state and zip code. Volume 2 includes 49,000 private companies, also ranked within industry by sales and employee size. It includes the same features found in Volume 1. None of the companies listed in Volume 1 duplicate those in Volume 2.

7. *Moody's Manuals*
Moody's is another leading publisher of business information. The *Moody's Manuals* cover sectors such as banking, industrial, transportation and utilities. The weekly reports (and the annual books) are a valuable guide to (publicly traded) companies news. Events reported include new product announcements, personnel changes and financial statement releases.

8. *Standard and Poor's Corporation Records and Stock Reports*
These two publications contain information similar to that found in Moody's listed above. *Corporation Records* is issued daily, while the *Stock Reports* appear quarterly. Together, the two give a good picture of the condition of publicly traded companies.

9. *Million Dollar Directory* (Dun and Bradstreet)
This directory reports on about 160,000 U.S. companies whose net worth is over $500,000. Company name, address, telephone number, officers, sales and employee size are given for the companies listed. Along with Moody's and Standard and Poor's, Dun and Bradstreet is a third leading publisher of business information.

10. *Standard Directory of Advertisers*

    This directory is a guide to the advertising expenditures and advertising media used for over 17,000 companies. It has two parts — one organized by industry and the other by state. Besides advertising budget, each company listing includes address, telephone number, sales, number of employees, officers and advertising agency.

11. *Corporate Technology Directory*

    This new directory covers technology-based companies. The 3 volume set has data on more than 12,000 companies. Special features include industry and geographic indexes. Data provided includes indicators of sales and employee size ranges.

Computer Databases for Collecting Market Information

Microcomputer hardware and software technology are powerful tools for collecting market information. Using a microcomputer and a modem connected to telecommunications links, the entrepreneur can search on-line databases of market, company and industry information. If one does not own a microcomputer or prefers not to search on-line databases, this service is often available at university and public libraries for a nominal fee. Several commercial firms provide access to the databases. Listed below are the major services and what they offer.

Dow Jones News Retrieval Service

Dow Jones and Company, Inc.
P.O. Box 300
Princeton, NJ 08540
(800) 257-5114

Rates depend on the type of service the subscriber wants. Hourly fees range from $6 to $72. There are over 20 databases on DJNRS. Among them are the full text of the *Wall Street Journal,* financial statements for companies listed on the New York, American and OTC Exchanges, daily stock price data and other databases. A new service, Track, allows one to automatically monitor news and information about a pre-defined set of companies.

Nexis

Mead Data Central
9393 Springboro Pike
P.O. Box 933
Dayton, OH 45401
(513) 865-6800

Nexis is a major player among vendors of on-line databases. It offers a wide variety of subject groups (business, finance, government, general news, trade/technology) and contains the complete text of articles in its databases. Over 150 newspapers, magazines, newswire services and other sources are included in Nexis. (Contact Nexis for price information.)

BRS After/Dark

BRS Information Technologies, Inc.
Latham, NY 12110
(800) 345-4277

After/Dark costs include a sign-up fee of $75. Per-hour costs for searching the databases on After/Dark are about $12. The business information databases on BRS have summaries and references to magazine articles, not the full text of articles. After/Dark is available after 6:00 p.m. (and on weekends) and is a menu-driven system designed for those who have never used on-line databases. The business databases are updated monthly and generally begin with the mid-1970s.

Knowledge Index

Dialog Information Services
3460 Hillview Avenue
Palo Alto, CA 94304
(800) 227-1927

Knowledge Index is similar to BRS After/Dark. The sign-up fee is $35, but per-hour search costs are slightly higher than for After/Dark. Knowledge Index is available only in the evening after 6:00 p.m. As with After/Dark, the business information databases do not have the full text of magazine articles, but references to and summaries for each article are included. The business databases begin their coverage in the mid-1970s.

Compuserve

Compuserve, Inc.
5000 Arlington Centre Blvd.
P.O. Box 20212
Columbus, OH 43220
(800) 848-8199

Compuserve specializes in computer-based information services for business professionals. Among the databases offered is "Supersite," which provides demographic and sales potential information. The data in "Supersite" is organized by state, county and zip code. Other databases cover stock market activity, newswire services and other business-related sources. (Contact Compuserve for price information.)

NewsNet
Bryn Mawr, PA 19010
(215) 527-8030
NewsNet specializes in business newsletters. Its coverage is very broad and includes stock market activity, research and development issues and advanced technology trends, company news and other subjects.

Conclusion

This article has outlined major sources of market and industry data for entrepreneurs. It is meant as a guide to key sources of information about markets, competitors and technologies. Using readily-available information sources will save valuable time and provide data useful in making business decisions regarding products, markets and competitors. The entrepreneur must fully understand all aspects of the commercial environment before introducing a product or service, and published business information can provide valuable insights about the marketplace.

Investments of Interest to Venture Capitalists

Elwood D. Howse, Jr.

Elwood D. Howse, Jr., *is president of Cable, Howse & Cozadd, Inc., a private venture capital fund management company which he co-founded in 1977. In 1982, he co-founded Cable, Howse & Ragen, an institutionally focused investment banking firm specializing in high technology and Pacific Northwest companies. Mr. Howse was also formerly with Data Science Ventures, a venture capital firm in Princeton, New Jersey; and was the chief financial officer of Seattle Stevedore Company. He has a B.S. degree in engineering and an M.B.A. from Stanford University.*

In this 1986 edition of *PRATT'S GUIDE TO VENTURE CAPITAL SOURCES* there are over 700 venture capital firms listed. With this number, there is no sure way of divining whether a particular business would be of interest to one or more of them. The aim of this article is to explain the characteristics that venture capitalists typically look for and how preferences may vary from firm to firm. Three fundamental characteristics are:

1. *Potential of the business* to achieve a significant scale in a few years.

2. *Quality of the management group* aiming to make this happen.

3. Probability that the business could, assuming it reaches the planned scale, be merged, acquired or sold to the public to provide *ultimate liquidity* for the venture capital firm.

Business Potential

Until an entrepreneur has focused on a specific opportunity, he or she cannot put together the most appropriate management group. So, although most venture capitalists put "management excellence" as their top priority, the potential for scale is really the first consideration. The attributes of a business that has the potential for scale include:

- A product or service with sustainable proprietary features.
- An "unfair" advantage in terms of technical know-how or lead time.
- A market niche or segment in which these features/advantages show a clear economic benefit; higher quality, lower cost or improved productivity.
- A market whose size is potentially large enough and growing fast enough so that a believable share represents a substantial sales revenue in a few years.
- Access to that market through existing channels of distribution to identifiable customers.

- High gross margins to allow for errors that inevitably occur in rapidly growing companies and (if technology-based) to provide for substantial R&D expenditures.

No one business opportunity is necessarily going to have all these attributes; opinions will differ on what represents a substantial revenue ($30 million, $50 million or $100 million) and in how few years the revenue rate should be reached (5, 7 or 10 years). This will depend on the venture capitalist, perception of the risk, rate of return objectives and the stage of development of the business being considered. In what industries and companies are these characteristics to be found? If venture capitalists' past actions are a relevant indicator, the following table showing venture capital investment activity in 1983 and 1984 should provide the answer.

	Percent of Number of Companies Financed	
	1984	1983
Computer Hardware and Systems	23%	24%
Software and Services	15	13
Telephone and Data Communications	11	9
Other Electronics	12	10
Total Electronics Related	61	56
Medical/Health Care Related	11	10
Commercial Communications	3	3
Genetic Engineering	3	3
Energy Related	2	4
Industrial Automation	4	4
Industrial Products and Machinery	4	4
Consumer Related	6	8
Other Products and Services	6	8
Total	100%	100%

	Percent of Dollar Amount Invested	
	1984	1983
Computer Hardware and Systems	32%	33%
Software and Services	11	9
Telephone and Data Communications	12	10
Other Electronics	13	10
Total Electronics Related	68	62
Medical/Health Care Related	8	8
Commercial Communications	4	3
Genetic Engineering	2	3
Energy Related	2	3
Industrial Automation	2	3
Industrial Products and Machinery	3	3
Consumer Related	6	9
Other Products and Services	5	6
Total	100%	100%

The reason for the popularity of the electronic and medical/ health care segments is that the technologies used in these industries are changing more rapidly than in others. Therefore more opportunities exist to develop proprietary products. Remember, though, that venture capitalists are fundamentally in the business of developing successful new businesses. If your business is not on the above table but has the attributes cited, you should pursue venture capital. Each venture capitalist is looking for that rare opportunity where the herd has not trampled.

Not withstanding the distribution of interest indicated in the above lists, popularity of certain areas will increase or decrease as markets change. For instance, investments in early-stage consumer software companies are less desirable than they were. It appears that the attributes needed to build a successful software company relate more to the quality of distribution and the ability to market a broad line of quality products. The products no longer need to be on the leading edge of technology, rather they need to fill the customer's needs, be easy to use and reliable. Proctor and Gamble or Pepsi Cola marketing and sales skills are the current key to success. Another investment area that is now of less interest is genetic engineering. High development expense, long time to reasonable revenue stream and a multiplicity of existing companies attacking similar markets with products difficult to differentiate discourage potential investors.

A strategy that some venture capitalists follow is to look for a component supplier in a field they judge has become over

populated. An example of this is in the computer disk memory market. Certainly large and rapidly growing, this market has been populated by more than 50 companies, many of which have lusted to be the industry leader. It is increasingly difficult to differentiate the participants. As a supplier to most all of those firms, the primary independent volume producer of thin film read/write recording heads, Cybernex, illustrates a unique opportunity. Since its technology provides greater storage density with a reliable, lower cost, consistent product, investors in Cybernex can participate in this industry without having to judge which of the disk manufacturers will be successful.

Sometimes a venture capitalist will not wait for an entrepreneur to find a business opportunity but will discern one themselves and act on it. This may be done by their seeking out an interesting company with relevant attributes or taking the initiative and starting a company themselves. The best known example of this approach is the oft-cited formation of Tandem Computers in 1974. Started by an associate at Kleiner & Perkins, a San Francisco venture capital firm, the Tandem product concept was tested prior to major investment by examining, with the help of consultants, the primary risk areas of hardware and software development with the help of consultants. After the basic concept proved valid, the company obtained major investment to finance equipment development and other business building phases. An increasing number of venture capitalists specializing in providing seed capital are willing to test initial concepts and help coalesce the management and financial resources if testing results are positive. Do not be discouraged if all you have is a concept. You may still be of interest.

Excellence of Management

Regardless of what caused the formation of a company, excellence of management is a priority consideration. In determining whether an investment is of interest, venture capitalists do not necessarily require a management team to be complete or contain all the functions. However, the nucleus present must have the qualities to attract the full team needed to build a successful company. These qualities include such things as experience, knowledge, perseverance, leadership, creativity and stamina. In assessing the team there is no direct way that these qualities are determined. The challenge in presenting a business to a venture capitalist is to show these qualities by displaying a thorough understanding of the business and an ability to articulate in verbal and written form its nuances and the key decisions that led to selecting the business strategy.

Management should, in seeking to attract interest, try to develop a rapport with potential investors. Investors are reluctant to commit even to the most exciting company if they cannot get along with management. Maintaining a positive attitude and developing such rapport is difficult when management is confronted with intense questioning and skepticism by experienced investors. Tolerance, good listening, reasoned responses and good humor are needed to build the desired relationship. Realize that the venture capitalist is most interested in finding a strong team that, while having conviction, can quickly adapt to the rapid unexpected changes affecting most businesses.

While entrepreneurs should be prepared to modify their stance, they should not be too flexible. Venture capitalists' skeptical probing is intended to gauge the judgment and depth of thought of management. Indignation will not result in the trusting relationship that must develop to result in investment by the venture capitalist. While in the courtship phase there seems to be a "we-they" mentality at times, after the investment is made a partnership attitude is the most beneficial.

Liquidity

Assuming the management team is sound and the business is attractive, the issue the venture capitalist then addresses is ultimate liquidity, i.e. is the business capable of being merged, acquired or sold to the public. The entrepreneur who is determined to remain independent as a private company can assume there will be no interest from venture capitalists. Assuming the entrepreneur can contemplate one of the exit routes and will seek private or public partners, the projected profits five years out multiplied by the appropriate price/earnings ratio must result in a valuation that could give the venture capitalist the gain sought on the capital to be employed.

Conclusion

To have an investment of interest, management must prove its excellence through the presentation of a business opportunity that can achieve profitability, scale and, ultimately, liquidity.

How to Choose and Approach a Venture Capitalist

G. Jackson Tankersley, Jr.

G. Jackson Tankersley, Jr. is a founder and managing general partner of The Centennial Fund, Centennial Fund II and Centennial Business Development Fund, which represents the largest pool of venture capital headquartered in the Rocky Mountain Region. Prior to co-founding Centennial, he was a vice president of Continental Illinois Venture Corporation and Continental Illinois Equity Corporation. He is a graduate of Denison University and received his M.B.A. from Dartmouth's Amos Tuck School of Business Administration.

Introduction

Why is only one out of every 50 to 100 investment opportunities reviewed by any given venture capitalist actually financed? More importantly, how does an entrepreneur improve on these odds? Many proposals are rejected because the management clearly lacks the entrepreneurial skills necessary to build a business, or because the venture capitalist does not believe in the market opportunity or the product feasibility. In too many cases, however, turndowns stem from entrepreneurs' lack of familiarity with a particular venture capitalist's tastes, requirements or specializations. In the article on page 38, there is a review (by Elwood D. Howse) of the characteristics of businesses venture capitalists generally find attractive. This article focuses on choosing the right firm and how to approach it.

Choosing the Right Venture Capital Firm

Identifying the most appropriate pool of venture capitalists to approach is a critical decision. It is surprising how little research many entrepreneurs conduct before they begin the time-consuming task of raising capital. There are two dangers in approaching too many venture capitalists unprepared. First, once an investment opportunity is rejected, it is very difficult to get it reconsidered, even with a proper introduction. Second, if an investment opportunity is rejected by a number of firms, it may get an "overshopped" reputation. Venture capitalists freely trade information and a turndown by one firm may influence others.

Increased media coverage makes it easier to collect useful snapshots of venture capital. But once you start to focus your search, you need the sort of data on specific venture capital firms that is in the directory section of this guide. These data include geographic location, amount of capital managed, amount of capital invested in the first six months of the previous year, industries of interest and stage of development at which investments are preferred.

This information is important as it provides five ways of choosing venture capital firms that are most likely to respond to your approach.

The first way is *geographically.* This may be the single greatest factor today. If you cannot attract a "local lead" investor you will have a significantly more difficult time raising capital. Although there are many firms investing nationwide, the closer the venture capitalist is to the investment, the easier it is to "add value" and to "monitor" the investment, especially in early-stage companies. In fact, the industry has witnessed an increase in regional investment focus for this reason.

Secondly, many venture capitalists have a *stage of development* bias. There are some who prefer the seed capital arena while others are only interested in later stage investing. Make certain that the stage of development of your company meets with the preferred stage of development of the venture firm which you are approaching. One word of caution: many in the venture capital industry invest in "startups" but definitions vary between firms. A startup for one firm can actually be a later stage investment for another. So beware of inconsistent uses of stage of development terms. Generally accepted definitions can be found in the directory introduction of this book.

The third basis is *amount of capital* needed. There are many firms which state a preference regarding an upper and lower limit to the size of an investment. If your project falls much outside a firm's range, it is better not to approach them. Also, it is unwise to inflate the amount of capital you need to meet their "minimum." Some venture capitalists, on the other hand, shy away from very large dollar syndications and do prefer to invest a few hundred thousand dollars to give them a meaningful position in a company. These firms may be more appropriate for your initial requirements.

The venture capital industry is witnessing greater *industry specialization* than ever before. There are venture capital firms and individual venture capitalists which specialize in medical

41

technology, communications, consumer products, distribution and many other industries. Clearly, if a venture capital firm has a stated investment preference in your industry, not only is it more likely to understand your opportunity but it will also be in a position to add value to your company. This industry expertise is often acknowledged and respected by other venture capitalists who may provide additional funding. In addition, a number of venture capital firms have excluded certain investment categories such as real estate, oil and gas, or even computer software investment opportunities.

Finally, in every successful venture capital financing, there is a need for *venture capital leadership*. There are a number of funds who are active investors and are willing to lead a financing while others serve as passive investors. In order to complete a syndication, you will need venture capital leadership. It is unwise to approach passive investors until after a lead investor is identified. Therefore, try to identify venture capitalists which have historically taken early leadership roles in syndications similar to your opportunity.

Using these five criteria as a basis, prepare a target pool of venture capitalists to approach. Make certain that this target pool is of a reasonable size. No one likes to receive a business plan which is numbered 128, knowing it has been sent to a mass audience.

A simple matrix may assist this effort. For example, subjectively rate a venture firm's investment orientation compared to your company's criteria on a scale of 1 to 10. The venture capitalists with the highest ratings should be the initial targets.

	VC #1	VC #2	VC #3
Geography	8	8	5
Stage of Development	9	9	9
Capital Required	6	3	8
Industry	7	1	8
Leadership	2	6	8
Total	32	27	38

Obvious trade-offs occur. Which is more important, industry focus or geography? However, in the above example, VC #3 is probably the most likely firm to approach, VC #1 should be approached after the lead investor has been identified and there is no obvious reason to contact VC #2.

Before you approach a venture capitalist that you have targeted, you should research the selected venture firms. Most have a brochure, which has been prepared to provide information to entrepreneurs as well as various "deal sources." A simple phone call to the receptionist of most firms can get you a copy of the brochure. Most brochures have been thoughtfully prepared to generate investment opportunities which fit the firm's interests while discouraging opportunities which obviously do not.

Using the brochure or other resources, try to identify what investments the individual venture capitalist has made. Venture capitalists are known by past successes, which can be keys to their areas of personal interest and expertise.

Now that the target pool has been identified and background information has been obtained, it is now time to approach the venture capitalist.

How to Approach

The *best* way to approach a venture capitalist is through an *introduction*. Venture capitalists are more likely to turn down an unsolicited, non-introduced business plan without giving it much attention. An introduction, in order to be successful, should be a quality introduction. It can be a banker, a lawyer, an accountant, another entrepreneur or even another venture capitalist. If your banker, lawyer or accountant appears unwilling to provide an introduction, they are probably telling you something. Their unwillingness may indicate they do not think you and/or your product is financeable and, therefore, do not want their name associated with it. If your contact does not know venture capitalists, you may have the wrong banker, lawyer or accountant. If you are close to, and are held in high regard by a successful entrepreneur who has received funding from a specific venture capitalist, this is often the best introduction as venture capitalists pay particular attention to such contacts. Be careful with venture capital references. If one venture capitalist you ask for an introduction has turned you down, others will want to know why. If the venture capitalist which you ask is a passive investor and he introduces you to an active investor with the comment "if you invest, we want to do it with you," that could be positive. The same holds true if a firm has become fully invested and is not making new commitments.

The Purpose of the Initial Contact

The initial contact following the introduction should be by telephone. The purpose of the telephone call should be to get the venture capitalist to request your business plan and to get that business plan read upon receipt. There have been many articles and books prepared on what a business plan should contain. One is in *PRATT'S GUIDE.* A number of service organizations (including accounting firms, consultants and investment bankers) are now making this a specialty. It should be clearly understood by the entrepreneur that initially *the sole purpose of the business plan sent to a venture capitalist is to get a meeting.* Let the significance of a meeting be clear. If one out of 100 investment opportunities ultimately gets funded by a specific venture capitalist, probably no more more than 30 have a meeting. Therefore, if you are invited to a meeting with the venture capitalist, you have just increased your odds by a factor of three.

The plan should be concise, well written and include a summary that covers at least four points.

1. What is this business? Many people say their business is building this product or marketing this concept when in fact the fundamental business is something all together different. Understand your business and articulate it.

2. Who are the people and why/how are they qualified to succeed in this endeavor? Venture capitalists consistently state that they invest in people not products or markets. Therefore, the people who are responsible for making it happen must be highlighted.

3. How well has the business done? Any business, even a seed capital entity has a history. What is its history? What has been done with the time and resources devoted to date?

4. How well do you expect it to do? Most businesses that do not meet a venture capitalist's expectations fail due to the size or the scope of the potential businesses. As a rule of thumb, a company should have the potential to be worth at least $30 million within three to five years to be of interest.

It is unfortunate, but often true, that in the initial review venture capitalists generally look for reasons to turn down an investment rather than search for reasons to invite you for a meeting. Typographical errors, incomplete or erroneous market information, ill conceived organizations are all potential negatives.

Meeting the Venture Capitalist

Assuming that you have carefully selected a pool of venture capitalists, have received quality information from them, established introductions, made telephone contacts, had your business plan read and scheduled a meeting, then be prepared at the meeting to make a formal presentation. However, be prepared and able to deviate from your agenda if necessary. The venture capitalist is using the meeting to learn about the product and market but is primarily focusing on sizing up the entrepreneur and the team. Remember, you may have limited time to make a positive impression and to leave the venture capitalist excited about your company.

The entrepreneur should likewise use the meeting to size up the venture capitalist. Do not hesitate to ask a venture capitalist for references, especially portfolio entrepreneurs. Call them, find out how well they have worked together from the entrepreneurs' perspectives.

Summary

In the past three years, over $12 billion was raised by venture funds. Funds are now available in the venture capital industry to finance companies in virtually any geographic area, in many industries at any stage of development, and with almost any capital requirements. It is the task of the entrepreneur to select and approach the venture capitalist. If you do so wisely, going through the steps outlined above and checking out the venture capitalists as they do you, you will improve those odds. Your ideal backer is one who contributes more than capital to your business through understanding your industry thoroughly and by building a close working relationship with you.

Meeting with the Venture Capitalist

Wayne B. Kingsley

Wayne B. Kingsley is chairman of InterVen Partners, Inc., a venture capital firm affiliated with First Interstate Bank with offices in Los Angeles and Portland. He has 14 years of venture capital experience. Prior to joining InterVen in 1983, Mr. Kingsley was a vice president of Norwest Venture Capital Management, Inc., a Minneapolis-based Small Business Investment Company. From 1972 to 1976, he was chief operating officer of Cascade Capital Corporation, which was acquired by Norwest in 1976. Mr. Kingsley is a graduate of Miami University of Ohio and holds an M.B.A. degree from the Darden School at the University of Virginia.

Obtaining financing for your firm is no different than any other selling task. Every step is important. One of the more critical steps is the first meeting with your customer, the venture capitalist. The impressions formed during this meeting will be the basis for his or her subsequent regard for you and your proposal. Your initial objective is to convince him that your proposal merits spending time and money to investigate. Other chapters in this book have dealt with the preparation of a written business plan. Your task in this meeting is to present the essence of your plan in a clear, concise manner.

One would hope the venture capitalist had studied your plan before meeting with you, but the chances are he has just skimmed it. Even worse, his only knowledge of the proposal may be from your telephone conversation with him or the two page summary you sent. So assume he remembers very little about your business and also that present in the meeting may be other partners or junior associates totally unfamiliar with your proposal who are there to render advice or do subsequent investigation work. This meeting will probably last about an hour to an hour and a half.

In preparation, you should plan and rehearse a one-half hour explanation of your proposal which sets forth the company's business, the market and external environment in which it operates, the strengths of the management team and similarities to other successful ventures. The presentation should emphasize the strengths in your proposal. Obvious weak points should be addressed, to illustrate that you recognize them. Then discuss your planned corrections. You should also state why this will be a profitable investment for the venture capitalist. To do this you have to state your objectives for the company and how you will attain them. Be reasonable. Even if you firmly believe you will achieve $200 million in sales your first year, revise your projections to something more conservative and consistent with the average, successful venture-backed company.

What image should you convey? First, you should be natural. If you and the venture capitalist want to continue discussions, this will be the first of many meetings. You are going to see each other in the best and worst moments. So a good starting point is the "real you." Beyond this, be confident. You are offering the investor an opportunity to invest in a very promising company, one in which you have decided to risk a part of your life and assets. The venture capitalist, if he invests, will become your partner. So you want to demonstrate that you are a good potential partner. Just let your natural abilities as a leader and a builder show through. Let the venture capitalist see that you are a smart, reasonable, classy, knowledgeable, tough, chief executive officer. Always use reason rather than argument.

If the venture capitalist expresses interest, tell him you would really like to work with him but that you are also talking with others.

When you have concluded your presentation, you want your listeners to have a clear and concise understanding of your business, what is unique about it and how you will achieve your projections. Something they could easily explain to others. It is most important they understand what is unique about the proposal, if it is not the product then the management team or the location or something else. Very few venture capitalists will invest in something which is a "me-too" product going against established competition.

The use of visual aids to make your presentation is strictly a matter of preference. This author's preference is for limited or no use of fancy aids. Part of the reason for the meeting is to establish rapport. Overhead projections, slides and video tapes cut down on eye contact and may minimize the give and take of a head-on presentation. However, many venture capitalists' offices, including the author's, have the necessary equipment to accommodate visual presentations, so do what you think is necessary to present yourself in a natural, easy going manner.

Handling Questions

During and after your presentation, you should be prepared for questions. You may assume the venture capitalist knows something about your business and will ask some of the obvious questions. He may also ask some penetrating questions and may also challenge your assumptions. He may ask some blunt questions or expose some preconceptions with which you disagree. He may also ask some dumb questions or not question you at all in areas you expected questions. In other words, the response may be off-the-wall.

How do you handle this? If you have done your homework and know your business you should be able to answer most questions in a brief and concise manner. If you do not know the answer or have to prepare an answer, this is an ideal opportunity to arrange another meeting to deliver the necessary information. If you disagree with a statement the venture capitalist makes, say why and then offer to provide additional information on the subject. Do not get sidetracked from your objective by arguing a small point. In the case of an obvious objection which was not raised, you may want to raise it and answer it yourself so that it does not become a problem when the venture capitalist thinks of it after you have gone.

Even if the person you are talking to is a technological whiz kid in your field, try to keep the meeting focused on the big picture and not get off on details of a technology which he may not be able to fully comprehend in a brief first meeting. Instead talk about the quality of the technology capability in your company and the accomplishments of the technologists. To assess technology, most venture capitalists will hire consultants and check the reputations of the technical people in your company, rather than rely on their own technological capability. They will probably be more concerned in this first meeting with your ability to demonstrate your overall business acumen and understanding of the business.

Maintaining Momentum

If the venture capitalist indicates interest, find out what the next step in the process will be. Even the best intentioned people can get sidetracked onto a new proposal or dealing with the many flash fires which occur in any portfolio. What you want to do is get a tentative schedule set up with dates and milestones which, if things go well, will lead to an investment. Once set up, you want to keep your due dates religiously and gently prod the venture capitalist into keeping his. If he starts to fall seri-

ously behind schedule or becomes too distant, his interest in your proposal has probably waned or he is just waiting to see what other people will do. If this happens, you will probably have to find another, more active investor to replace him. Do not be surprised, however, if later a deal starts to go together, and he then becomes very interested and active again.

Entrepreneurs are always trying to develop a magic money raising strategy. If investors cannot be convinced of the merits of the investment, no amount of intrigue or cosmetics will improve your chances for funding. However, how you present and market your proposal can influence the value investors place on it, as well as their degree of comfort with you and the other members of the management team.

Camp Followers

One common strategy question is whether or not to involve "camp followers" in the project. Camp followers may be of two types. The first is a series of smaller investors who "seed" the deal to establish price and credibility and the second type is the well-known person who becomes an advisor or a director, primarily to establish credibility. This type may also make a small investment to further indicate faith in the project.

Do not add camp followers to your project if there is no *operational benefit* from doing so. Small, unsophisticated investors can complicate a larger venture financing by making compliance with securities laws more difficult, by balking at the seemingly onerous terms of the professional financing, by "helping" negotiate the terms and by presenting an unstated but always present risk of suit in the future. New and growing companies often go from crisis to crisis before achieving success. These crises are usually better met by the professionals who deal with them daily. On the other hand, a number of companies are started and grow successfully with only the help of smaller investors. If small investors are essential to your company, by all means embrace them. If, later, you plan an institutional venture financing, prepare them for this event.

A number of successful companies have included well-known business people on their board of directors. Sometimes these people are sought out as advisors or merely passive investors. Far too often the inclusion of these people is for strictly cosmetic purposes, not unlike an athlete endorsing a particular brand of shaving cream. Rarely do such endorsements actually hurt a company, except perhaps to bring into question management's confidence in its own abilities. But far too often the inclusion of these people adds nothing to the company. Occasionally it can be detrimental, if they try to become too involved and do not really understand small businesses. On the other hand, a talented person, with proven ability who has worked, and intends to continue working with a business can be an invaluable asset. The key to this decision is whether or not the person will actually take time to work with the company and has the specific talents required to add value.

A few additional helpful hints:

Requiring signed secrecy agreements can be an impediment to obtaining financing. Before you decide to ask for these, make sure what you are asking to be kept secret is really worth all the effort and involves an easily definable thing — like the formula for Coke.

When dealing with investors, they will generally want some rights and information which do not at first appear reasonable. It is perfectly proper to argue but not about everything. Pick your battles and fight only those things which seem most important to you. If the investor does the same thing, the chances are neither of you will be left with many substantive areas of disagreement.

Do not get discouraged. Every venture capitalist is different. Sometimes a number of them like the same proposal. Often one will like and fund a proposal which others do not like. Diversity makes a horse race. Keep looking until you find the person who likes your company.

The investor will usually negotiate price and terms after he has investigated your proposal. In the beginning, you should talk about price only to ensure his expectations are in a reasonable range. At the end of the process, you and the investor will have considerable time and money invested in each other and will have incentive to strike a deal you each can accept. If you try to negotiate price in the begining of the relationship, it is much easier to walk away from each other.

For the venture capital relationship to be successful, it has to be built on trust and mutual respect. When negotiating price it is adversarial, when working through problems and facing a competitive world, it must be supportive. If either party suspects such a relationship cannot be perfected, it should be abandoned. Be open and honest with your current and prospective investors and demand the same from them.

Venture Capital: More Than Money?

Dr. Jeffry A. Timmons

Dr. Jeffry A. Timmons *was the Paul T. Babson Professor of Entrepreneurial Studies at Babson College, Wellesley, Massachusetts from 1982 to 1984. He joined Babson permanently as Professor of Entrepreneurial Studies and Management in July 1984. At Northeastern University, Boston, during 1973, he launched the new ventures and entrepreneurship major, the first in the U.S.A. He has authored and co-edited eight books including NEW VENTURE CREATION (2nd edition, Irwin, 1985), co-authored THE ENCYCLOPEDIA OF BUSINESS RESOURCES (Harper & Row, 1984), and has authored nearly 100 articles and papers on venture creation, venture capital and entrepreneurship, including five articles for HARVARD BUSINESS REVIEW. He has served as a consultant to venture capital firms operating in the U.S.A., United Kingdom, Australia, Canada and Sweden, and to numerous startup and rapid growth ventures.*

You've survived the startup — thanks to your own sweat equity, help from some friends, your wits, guts and a lot of dedication. Your aspirations and the responses from your marketplace are agreeing more and more: your business can become a substantial one. Your ambitious expansion plans indicate a voracious appetite for cash and today venture capital is a prime source. If it is the first time that you have sought venture capital, you wonder if it is worth it. You know it can take weeks, months, sometimes a year or more to secure finance, all the while diverting scarce management resources away from building and running your fledgling firm. And besides, you wonder if you really want outsiders involved in *your* company? You ponder a vital question: even if you have raised venture capital before: what real value will the venture capitalist infuse in your venture, beyond the money?

To gain some insights into this, I talked with members of the management team, and some of the original venture capital investors at NBI, Inc. of Boulder, Colorado. NBI is one of the most successful and rapidly growing new firms in the wordprocessing and office automation industry. Launched in 1973, the firm attained sales of $167,000 in the first year NBI's president, Tom Kavanagh, and two partners joined the venture to propel its growth. By 1982, three rounds of venture capital and subsequent public offerings later, NBI sales had exceeded $100 million and its rapid growth is continuing.

For entrepreneurs contemplating raising venture capital, or having the good fortune to be narrowing the choices, the NBI experience provides a good illustration of ways a lead venture capital investor can become immersed in helping to grow a business in ways that are highly constructive. Tom Kavanagh has found significant "value-added" in his venture capital partners, enough so that he succinctly expressed what I shall call "Kavanagh's Law": "It is far more important whose money you get than how much you get or how much you pay for it."

The following narrative demonstrates a number of ways in which a lead venture investor made contributions deemed by the NBI management team to be of great value. As you will see throughout, this is a case where excellent personal chemistry developed between the venture capitalist and the management team. This is illustrative of a relationship that enables the value-adding process to work: the importance of this cannot be overemphasized.

Early Stages: Vital Contributions in Recruiting Key Management

Judging by the experience of Kavanagh and his top three vice presidents, having the right venture capital partner during the startup and fragile early stages of a venture can make a tremendous difference in the odds favoring survival and success. In their minds, there is no doubt about it: recruiting the key management team members was "probably the most indispensable value-added" by their venture capital partners. Even though, compared to most small fledgling firms, NBI's ambitions and plans were impressive, it was very difficult to entice the kind of high-performing executive from a top-notch large company to join in the launching and building of an embryonic firm. For Kavanagh, the lead investor that played an invaluable role in recruiting two of three top people was Burton J. McMurtry, then a general partner of Institutional Venture Associates and now of Technology Venture Investors, Menlo

Park, California. These two key management additions, Mark Stevenson as Vice President of Marketing, and David Klein as Vice President of New Business Development, have been central contributors to NBI's explosive growth.

McMurtry was always available to assist in searching for candidates and to do the research to find top people. In addition, he extensively examined the backgrounds, track records and experience of possible additions to the team. In many cases, venture capital investors have developed this fine art with an elaborate network of thousands of contacts, leads and reliable sources of intelligence and verification that is unique. But you can have all that and still wind up with unfilled management gaps. The real trick, according to Tom Kavanagh, is to convince a really top-notch person to give up all they have built, for instance, at a Xerox or an IBM, and take the plunge with you. How does a venture capital partner make a critical difference in this process?

Perhaps you are in a situation similar to Tom Kavanagh's in 1975. Your business plan is being well received. You know this because more than one venture capitalist has taken the time to get to know you and to review your plan carefully. Further, they have expressed more than casual interest in your venture. But there is one real hitch: without an outstanding marketing person — someone who really knows your business inside and out — with a top track record, the investors simply decline to act. You have been pursuing your number one candidate for over two months, and you hope to celebrate Thanksgiving with his acceptance of your offer. The call comes. His message is clear, "I like you, your prospective backers, your company, your product and your philosophy. But we've moved eight or nine times. I am very happy in what I am doing, and believe I can achieve my income, position, and personal financial goals while becoming a driving force in the industry right where I am." Now what? You cannot bootstrap it forever. Once your prospective backers find out, and word gets around the industry that your top prospect said "no," well . . .

With a professional venture capital partner, however, the odds are that stomach-bending setbacks such as this can be overcome. It is not uncommon to discover a flow of ingenuity and utter determination that turns the fragile balance back to your favor. How can investors make a difference in crises like these? Professional venture capitalists cannot be "armchair deal-creators." McMurtry found Mark Stevenson, then a national sales manager for Xerox, through his contacts with exceptional performers and entrepreneurially-inclined managers. And when the crisis hit at this embryonic stage for NBI, his reaction was to roll up his sleeves and attack the problem, rather than dump it back to Tom Kavanagh. What is more, at this point in time, McMurtry's

Institutional Venture Associates had yet to actually invest any capital in NBI. The final decision was contingent on securing a key marketing person.

Working together, Kavanagh and McMurtry combined analytical insight and creativity — just the kind of "chemistry" that can make the difference between success and failure. After talking through the reasons Stevenson had given for his rejection, McMurtry was convinced that Stevenson had "not really thought it through completely, particularly the financial consequences," and had thus declined for the wrong reasons. The next day the two of them were on a plane from San Francisco to Dallas to meet with Stevenson. The eye-ball to eye-ball meeting extended well beyond dinner. The next day Stevenson quit his job at Xerox and joined NBI as Vice President of Marketing. What had happened?

According to Stevenson, "there is no question that without Burt I would not have done it. His very professional, straightforward way convinced me. He said that he and Tom wanted to sit down with me and my wife, and my two children to talk over the reasons why we should reconsider. He had the sensitivity to know that, if my wife also understood the reasons why we might want to change our minds, it would make all the difference. The offer really was not any different in terms of salary and stock. What he was able to do was enable me to see the decision in a different context: what it could mean to be in control of my own destiny, while also achieving those other personal aims." Several months later, David Klein, a close colleague from Stevenson's prior job also decided to join NBI even though Klein had originally been the one to talk Stevenson out of it in the first considerations. He found Kavanagh and McMurtry a persuasive team. As Klein put it "I would not have joined if it were not for Burt. His understanding of what had to happen to make it a good deal for both of us was the key. He was able to convey in a very professional and credible way that he could not get rich unless we did." The advantages of having venture capitalist recruiting assistance are not only with exceptional top managers. At NBI "100 times or more" McMurtry played a key role in closing with numerous prospective suppliers, dealers and customers.

Beyond Recruiting: Unique Industry Savvy

Knowledge of the industry is a must in order to develop a credible business plan. For the aspiring entrepreneur, it is critical to have an in-depth understanding of the markets to be served. Yet, if it is your first startup, and the industry is only beginning to emerge, then the market data is grayer, the boundaries fuzzier, and the customers more elusive than in the more mature business that you left. This is an area where the venture capitalist, because of the richness of his first hand experience and depth of knowledge in several industries usually can be of significant help to test the reality of your business plan, goals, objectives and assumptions. For instance, a lot of the operating characteristics in an industry, particularly an emerging one, simply are not written down anywhere. Reliable assumptions, such as aging of receiveables and payables, certain costs and margins, and other ratios, especially for new customers and new products, are not readily available. But more often than not, if you are working with the right venture capitalists for your business, a great deal of that knowledge will be available from his prior experience. Being able to test your own notions against such a rich knowledge base can be invaluable. As Tom Kavanagh put it, "The know-how an experienced venture capitalist can provide is not available any place else. There just is not any other source on a lot of these things."

In-depth knowledge of an industry involves frequent contact with other CEOs, customers, and suppliers in the same business. One of the most difficult linkages for early-stage entrepreneurs in an emerging industry to acquire is with other CEOs. Aside from possible legal prohibitions, it is very delicate to obtain access to possible competitors or near-competitors. The linkages and integrity of a professional venture capitalist enables a sharing of a perspective on the business to which most entrepreneurs simply never have access.

A Sounding Board

According to Kavanagh, the Devil's Advocate Role is a third contribution which the venture capitalist can make in ways that are very difficult to obtain elsewhere. Having someone to discuss your plans and ideas, before your are firmly committed, can help to avoid costly sidetracks. The need for a savvy outsider is ironically rooted in one of the strengths of the management team. In developing an effective relationship, they come to work together so closely and intimately that they begin to think alike. New product ideas, strategies and directions start to look as if they came out of one mind, according to Kavanagh. The risks of this tendency are obvious, and the outside investor, because of a reasonably objective view, can react better to the rationale of plans, ideas, and initiatives.

One of the things that happens in a small company, according to David Klein, NBI Vice President of New Business Development, is that it is tough to get "tests of reasonableness." In contrast, he found that at an IBM or Xerox you are forced to do so. The "implementors" challenge your innovative decisions. But at NBI, as in most smaller ventures in the early

going particularly, each of the top management team has their area of accountability, and you are pretty much on your own, according to Klein. In this case, Burt McMurtry deliberately made it a point to talk with each member of the top management team, often several times a week. It was extremely valuable, this group reports, to have someone there vitally concerned, and asking numerous constructive questions. One of McMurtry's favorite questions was, "What decisions did you make last week that you were most uncomfortable with?"

Fostering an Entrepreneurial Climate

Another area that had a lot to do with NBI's success was what I would call a high sense of clarity about what it takes to create and perpetuate an "entrepreneurial climate and commitment." Kavanagh credits McMurtry's extensive experience with similar startup and early-stage ventures in assisting him to create just such a climate. The heart of it appears to be an incentive system that spawned a great deal of teamwork, instead of rewards for just individual success. As one NBI vice president put it, "Getting promoted simply did not matter since we did not pay ourselves much anyway. All the payoffs were based on what was good for NBI." The key executives were convinced that they could all achieve their financial goals if they could drive NBI to accomplish its business objectives. This spirit continues to permeate the company today.

The Long Haul

Financing for the Long Haul is a fourth consideration in sizing up what a venture capitalist has to offer besides money. For the company with potential and aspirations compelling enough to attract venture capital investors in the first place, it is almost a given that subsequent rounds of financing will be necessary as the venture succeeds. Unlike many other sources of finance, professional venture capitalists must possess both the patience and bravery for the longer haul. If you have found the right one for your company, then you can expect him to be 100% behind you to arrange for subsequent rounds of financing. In doing so, such an investor will look out for the best interests of the company, rather than simply what is most advantageous for the venture capital firm.

In NBI's case, McMurtry was the vital link in attracting two other highly regarded venture capitalists to participate in the later rounds, William Hambrecht of Hambrecht & Quist and David Dullum of Frontenac Venture Capital. According to Kavanagh, Dullum has served the company very effectively as a director and member of the audit committee. As an investor and member of the board of NBI, Hambrecht served a critical role when it came to determining the most suitable structure and timing of subsequent public offerings. Their contributions complemented McMurtry's and are considered invaluable by the management team. And as one of them put it, they were smart enough and professional enough to get involved when and where they could make the biggest contribution.

Extent of Involvement

Entrepreneurs often express concern over the extent to which a venture capitalist is involved in the company. The key consideration, of course, is the bottom line effect of such involvement, whether the additional effort and support, in fact, achieves recognized value. On the other hand, is the involvement considered to be investor meddling, that must be accepted as a courtesy. At NBI, the management team feels the relationship was positive.

Especially in the early going, most ventures cannot afford the relatively high priced resources available from top-notch consulting or accounting firms. The venture capitalist can be a resource center of names, contacts and credibility. Since the venture investors are seeking capital gains, their interests are driven by doing as much as they can to nurture the venture along. But the perception of involvement often depends upon whether you talk to the founders or the investors. An MIT study recently asked both "how much involvement the investor had in the company?" The answers were revealing: the investors typically said, we are heavily involved in aiding the company to grow: the entrepreneurs responded just the opposite — not much at all, we only see them one or two days a month!

For NBI, the involvement was described as "complete immersion, but never any meddling." Particularly in the early stages the serious venture partner, usually as a member of the board, may be involved one or two days a month in person, and as much as several hours a week on the phone. What kind of activities? At NBI these are some good illustrations of the nature of his immersion. The investors became immersed in the operating details of the business in order to know the markets, products, people and customers thoroughly to become familiar with every aspect of the business viewed as critical to success. But they did not meddle in the operating decisions. Management was assisted and advised, supplemented but not supplanted.

An area where immense help can be contributed is in securing key customers and accounts. Again, in the fragile startup period and early-stages every customer can be crucial. Venture capitalists can often articulate the company's cause in a more objective manner than the founders. What they can add is a sufficient comfort level to enable big company buyers to cast their fate as customers of a new or small firm. Venture investors can outline by phone why they invested in the venture and the reasons for their confidence. A sense of professional objectivity can shift doubt to confidence. According to the NBI team, McMurtry spent untold hours doing just these kinds of things. He also prepared a carefully documented letter explaining the rationale for investing in NBI which was a source of considerable comfort to buyers and vendors alike.

Still another example of the kind of immersion NBI experienced centered on the need for longer range planning, initiating some strategic thinking, even though the immediate pressures of the startup or expansion seem to be overwhelming. Tom Kavanagh stresses that it was McMurtry who "gets lots of credit for getting us to do it first. He got the process on track and going a good two years earlier than we would have without his prodding, and you never do it soon enough."

When the Cannons Go Off . . .

Roaring cannons are inevitable for most fledgling firms that grow as rapidly as NBI. There are crises, periods of doubt, even some desperation; it never seems to be simple. The fragile process of launching and building such an enterprise requires more of an investor than an uncanny degree of ingenuity, the shirt-sleeves perseverance, and other virtues just noted. Beyond their objectivity and insight another vital contribution emerged — support with patience and fortitude.

When things start to go badly— some missed deadlines, a lost key account, an unexpected resignation, and the inevitable cash and confidence crisis, there is nothing more disturbing than to have a backer with a weak heart, and a weaker pocketbook. If you are promising enough to attract an experienced professional venture investor, you are more likely to discover what the NBI team did when "the cannons went off." No matter how bad things got, there was a calmness in Burt. "Never once," according to Mark Stevenson, "did he step on your hands when you were lying flat on your back." In short, that kind of professional behavior meant there were no "I told you so's" or threats to withhold future financial backing, or a panicky haste to start changing management, strategies or product. In the case of NBI, the message was one of concern but accompanied by a continuing full level of confidence in the team and how they were going about it.

In Summary

The successful development of a business can be critically impacted by the interaction of the management team and the involved venture capitalists. If a peer relationship can be established, the value-added synergy can be a powerful stimulant for success.

It is not fair to conclude that all venture capitalists are exactly like those NBI was able to attract, nor that every founder-investor partnership will evolve as this one has. Yet, many aspiring founders may overlook some of the very high "value-added" contributions that professional venture capital investors are accustomed to making and erroneously opt for a "better deal," or a debt backer. If you have progressed far enough to gain the serious interest of professional venture investors, they will welcome as thorough an examination of their credentials and track record as they will conduct on you, your team and venture. By taking the time to talk to entrepreneurs they have backed, you are more likely going to discover many of the exceptional qualities among them that NBI found in their backers. Money cannot buy such outside resources, but the potential for substantial capital gains by growing a high potential company can. Having just such resources on your team can be the subtle difference in making such visions become reality for investors and intrepreneurs alike.

Structuring the Financing

Stanley C. Golder

Stanley C. Golder *is a general partner of Golder, Thoma & Cressey, Chicago, Illinois, which was founded in 1980 and currently manages $160 million in two venture capital funds. For the prior nine years, he was president of the Equity Group of First Chicago Corp., one of the largest and most successful bank holding company business development investment affiliates. He is a past president of both the National Association of Small Business Investment Companies and the National Venture Capital Association. In addition, Mr. Golder teaches a course on venture capital at Northwestern University's J.L. Kellogg Graduate School of Management, Evanston, Illinois. Golder, Thoma & Cressey is an active investor with a diversified investment philosophy.*

Introduction

The structuring of venture capital investments follows no set formula nor is there any perfect structure: the objective is to reconcile the differing needs and concerns of the venture capitalist and the entrepreneur in a way that is satisfactory to both parties. Since each situation is different, structures vary widely.

There are three issues which relate to the process of formalizing a venture investment: (1) the financial structure, i.e. the form of securities instruments used, (2) the pricing and (3) the terms of the agreement. The last two are discussed in two other articles in *PRATT'S GUIDE,* so I will concentrate on the securities instruments, their advantages and disadvantages and how they can be used to provide a fair and equitable structure.

Needs and Concerns

The needs of the venture firm and the company will vary based on the stage of development of the company, the risk, and the ultimate potential as well as the requirements and the philosophy of the individual venture firm. However, there are a number of factors that venture capitalists and entrepreneurs typically consider when creating any investment.

Primary considerations for the venture capitalist include:

- Reasonable reward given the level of risk.
- Sufficient influence on the development of the company, usually through board representation.
- Management's relative contribution to capital. (This assures that managers have more at stake than just their egos.)
- Minimization of taxes resulting from the various types of cashflows to investors (dividends versus interest, versus capital gains).
- Future liquidity in the event that the company is successful or stagnates.

- Voting control, which is particularly desirable if performance is substantially below expectations and the management team must be replaced.
- Protection from having any remaining investor dollars split with the entrepreneur in the event that the company is unsuccessful and dissolves.
- Current yield in the case of a Small Business Investment Company (SBIC), which has debt to service.

Primary considerations for the typical entrepreneur include:

- Ability to lead the creation of the business that they have conceptualized (operating and strategic control).
- Financial rewards for creating the business.
- Adequate resources needed to achieve their goal.
- Minimization of tax exposure for buying cheap stock.
- Value of substantive contribution from board members.

Common considerations for both sides include:

- Flexibility of structure:
  - room to enable additional investments later,
  - incentives for future management, and
  - retention of stock if management leaves.
- Balance sheet attractiveness to suppliers and debt financiers.
- Retention of key employees through adequate equity participation.

Many of these factors are discussed in the pricing and investment agreement chapters. In this chapter we focus on sharing of future rewards, the means whereby liquidity is achieved and investor capital protected and on where control rests.

The structuring process will include laying out the needs and concerns of both parties; evaluating all the alternatives; and choosing and negotiating a structure which will be consistent with the company's financial needs and capabilities and which will provide liquidity and, in extenuating circumstances, control for the investors.

Securities Instruments Commonly Used

The structure of a venture capital financing can involve the use of a range of securities instruments from straight debt to debt with equity features (convertible debt to debt with warrants) to common stock. Following is a summary of the securities which are often used in combination with one another:

- *Senior Debt* — Generally used for long-term financing for low risk companies or for mezzanine (later stage) financings.

- *Subordinated Debenture* — This is a type of debt that is subordinated to financing from other financial institutions such as banks and may be unsecured. It is usually convertible to common stock or accompanied by warrants to purchase common shares. Senior lenders accept this as equity and therefore allow increased debt from other sources.

- *Preferred Stock* — Generally convertible to common stock. Preferred stock gives the venture capitalists "preference" over common shareholders and some rights while from the entrepreneur's perspective it improves the company's debt-to-equity ratio. A disadvantage is that if dividends are attached, they are not tax deductible.

- *Common Stock* — Generally the most expensive in terms of ownership given to the venture capitalist because it has the most risk. But from the venture capitalist's view it is also the least flexible. It affords no protection, allows the least amount of control over management and since there is generally no dividend, provides no return until the stock is sold.

Choosing the "Right" Instruments

The advantage to debt instruments from the venture capitalist's perspective is that they can be designed to provide (1) preference in case of liquidation, (2) some current income and (3) remedies in case of default. A Small Business Investment Company (SBIC) which has used its leverage and thus has debt to service will prefer an income bearing security. However, for the company, excessive debt can strain the company's credit standing and make future long-term financing difficult and, in case of default, places the venture capitalist in a position of control. On the other hand, common stock or (as it is often termed) straight equity provides no protection for the venture capitalist and as a result will ultimately be very costly for the entrepreneur in terms of equity give-up.

You, the venture capitalists and your respective attorneys can be creative in modifying traditional securities to meet the needs of a particular situation. Most venture capital financing structures are a combination of debt and equity which satisfies both parties. The often used preferred stock structure is a compromise between common stock and note structures for several reasons. First, preferred stock has more protection than common stock, but less than subordinated notes. Second, preferred stock usually carries a dividend, but it can only be paid if the company is profitable. Also, preferred stock is a separate class of stock, and accordingly, has certain rights established in the articles of incorporation which are stronger than the rights of common shareholders, but usually not as strong as noteholders. Finally, preferred stock may be redeemable, which would allow investors to obtain a return of principal, assuming that sufficient capital is available for redemption.

Other combinations and unique hybrid structures can often provide preference in sale, liquidation or merger; and current income plus capital gain for the venture capitalist without weighing the balance sheet with too much debt.

A no-load convertible preferred, for example, has no dividend attached; has liquidation preference; converts to common at the option of the holder and automatically at a public offering; votes as if common stock; is considered equity; and requires a board seat, monthly reports, registration rights and a right of first refusal for future financings. This is typically used for startup and early stage financings and is atractive to the entrepreneur because there is no dividend obligation.

Common stock may be used in a larger successful company while senior debt with warrants may be more appropriate in a turnaround situation.

Flexibility of Structure

The structure adopted initially affects the ability to take actions subsequently and therefore should be as flexible as possible. Firstly, the rights of initial investors to participate in subsequent financing rounds should be established so as to provide as little obstacle as possible to their being completed. Secondly, there needs to be provision made for providing stock that can motivate key management brought in subsequent to the financing. Thirdly, if management members leave, some or all of their stock should be retained by the company. These last two issues can be dealt with by having a class of stock for management differing from that issued to investors. Reserves can be escrowed. Care needs to be paid to the tax implications so that members of management are not faced with unexpected liabilities in connection with their holding this stock.

Another point on structure of transactions, which seems obvious, but is often ignored, is that an investor in an early stage company who puts in considerably more dollars than the entrepreneur should generally not lose money on their investment, while an entrepreneur makes money. This, again, mitigates toward using a senior instrument so as to protect the investor's position.

Obviously, it is in the best interest of both the investor and the entrepreneur that the instruments used be considered equity and be leverageable as the company grows. Preferred stocks should cause no problems as they are clearly equity, even though they may have redemption requirements. These are easily handled by senior lenders if and when the company is capable of acquiring debt. Subordinated debt can be accommodated to this need, but has a few more problems vis-a-vis senior lenders as the company grows. In either case, however, these instruments should be equity as far as any senior creditors are concerned, so that appropriate leverage can be obtained when necessary.

Many venture capitalists prefer not to make outright purchases of common stock except in cases where the majority ownership is in the hands of an investor group. Even then, there are many arguments for preferred stocks. Before taking a common equity position, there can be a waiting period to determine if the company performs as expected and to see if management's objectives are similar to those of the investors and will protect the investors' interest.

The question of ultimate liquidity is also very significant. While there are differences in various parts of the country, we still prefer an ultimate maturity on our investments, which either provides liquidity or the ability to negotiate toward liquidity when the company has not reached its objectives, but is viable.

In most cases, we think only of success or failure in our investments, but it is a distinct possibility that a company will move relatively sidewards (sometimes called the living dead) or plateau in its growth and therefore be unable to achieve a public market. Even if companies go public, the market will not usually accept a large amount of stock from inside investors, unless the company makes major progress. The only way for the venture capitalist is a sale or merger of the company. At this point, the goals of the entrepreneurs or managers of the company may differ from the investor's objectives. Consequently, contractual arrangements to achieve liquidity become most important and can be best achieved at the inception of the investment.

Control
Another problem which is handled by appropriate structuring is the very serious aspect of control. Every businessman approaches the venture capitalist with the idea that he should control his own business, but history has shown that many entrepreneurs do not have the desire, may not have the ability and certainly do not have the experience to run a business as it grows. Most venture capitalists do not want to run companies but do feel that it is their basic responsibility to see that the companies in which they invest are well run and, if management changes are appropriate, they can be achieved. Various types of senior instruments can give the investor the opportunity to have his interests protected as these types of problems develop. This is not a means to financially disadvantage the equity interest of the entrepreneur. In fact, it is designed to help that interest and to enable a board of directors to make changes in management if they deem appropriate.

There are major differences between investors and not all of the companies in the industry have the same philosophies. Having been involved with many successful companies and hearing many successful entrepreneurs speak who have been backed by venture capitalists, you will find that control is a bogey man with inexperienced investors and entrepreneurs but not with those who have been successful. De facto day-to-day control needs to be distinguished from voting control.

Conclusion
It has been the author's experience that the appropriate structuring of a transaction cannot make a bad investment good; it can, however, influence the results of investments that are not meeting the initial expectations.

In making every investment, the parties presume a high level of success. The record proves, over the years, that only a small percentage are truly successful. Therefore, achieving liquidity and/or return of capital and the possible remedies available by using instruments other than common stock can be helpful to the investment process and beneficial to both the entrepreneur and venture capitalists.

Avoid inflexible structures. More often than not, an inflexible structure will exaggerate a strategic problem rather than provide a simple solution. For example, there have been situations where an inflexible deal structure enabled one very small player to obstruct an entire round of badly needed financing. Therefore, the best advice for entrepreneur and venture capitalist alike is to keep the structure simple and flexible and to be sure to understand the terms so that the relationship between the two will be a good, constructive one.

The Pricing of a Venture Capital Investment

Jane Koloski Morris

Jane Koloski Morris *is vice president of Venture Economics, Inc., Wellesley Hills, Massachusetts, and editor of its monthly publication, VENTURE CAPITAL JOURNAL, which has been reporting and analyzing business development investing since 1961. In addition, she is editor of PRATT'S GUIDE TO VENTURE CAPITAL SOURCES and moderator of the firm's national seminar series on "How to Raise Venture Capital." Prior to joining Venture Economics in 1977, Ms. Morris was director of public relations and marketing at the Boston Stock Exchange.*

The following article summarizes comments made by venture capital investors and entrepreneurs at over 40 "How to Raise Venture Capital" seminars co-sponsored by VENTURE CAPITAL JOURNAL. It also incorporates a large portion of an article written by Stanley C. Golder of Golder, Thoma & Cressey which appeared in prior editions of the GUIDE.

The pricing of a venture capital investment is perhaps the most subjective and most controversial topic in the negotiation process. It is actually far less negotiable than the structure although differences in opinion on what the price should be can often be mitigated by changes in the structure.

Pricing refers to the valuation of the company before and after the financing determined after an analysis by the venture capitalist of the risk versus the potential reward. The entrepreneur, the optimist, wishes to secure the highest price possible for his company. The venture capitalist, the skeptic, recognizing that things never proceed according to plan, wants a lower valuation. The ultimate pricing will generally fall somewhere between with both parties leaving something on the table so that the tone is set for a harmonious working relationship.

This article will discuss the return objectives of the venture capitalists as well as summarize the key factors which play an important role in determining the valuation of an investment opportunity.

Profit Targets Set by Venture Capitalists

The return on investment (ROI) expected by the venture capitalist will vary based on the risk perceived and the differing expectations of specific venture investors. To illustrate the internal rates of return the following table was prepared by Stanley Golder of Golder, Thoma & Cressey:

Profit Targets of Venture Capitalist	Compounded Annual Rates of Return (pre-tax)
Triple their money in three years	44%
Triple their money in five years	25%
Four times their money in four years	41%
Five times their money in three years	71%
Five times their money in five years	38%
Seven times their money in three years	91%
Seven times their money in five years	48%
Ten times their money in three years	115%
Ten times their money in five years	58%

As a general rule, if venture capitalists are financing seed or startup companies, they are looking for returns on the high end of the scale — 50% compounded or more. For second stage financings, venture capitalists tend to look for 30% to 40% while later stage investors may only expect returns in the range of 25% to 30% compounded per annum.

Factors Affecting Pricing

Pricing is an art not a science. As Woody Howse of CH Partners often comments, "It's very difficult to forecast, especially if you are talking about the future." Therefore, in determining price, the venture capitalist must assess the various risks involved in the investment: the product risk, i.e. the concept or idea;

the market risk; and the management risk. If the potential reward compensates for the risk, the venture capitalist will make the investment. The greater the risk perceived by the venture capitalist, the higher will be the expected return and therefore the more equity the venture capitalist will need to have in your company. The venture capitalist uses some analytical tools in assessing the risk and future potential of your company but in dealing with the unknown the final determination of valuation will be judgmental based on the knowledge, experience and intuition of the individual investor.

The quantitative analysis performed by the venture capital investor refers primarily to:

- The *potential of the company*. What is the potential upside (how big is it and how long will it take to get there) versus the potential downside (how bad it might be). If all goes according to plan, or close to plan, what will be the revenues of this company at some point in the future? To determine this, venture capitalists will look at other companies in the same industry. This would include industry leaders, medium sized companies and small firms. Key operating statistics for each company will be compared to your company's projections, in the case of a startup, as well as historic performance in the case of a later stage company. These include sales, operating costs, gross profits and margins, overhead and administrative expenses, and net profit and its ratio to sales. Net worth and return on equity will also be calculated, together with long term debt and current ratios. Price earnings ratios in the current market will be compared: if stocks of the leading firms are selling at 25 times, medium companies at 15 times and small companies at eight times, there will be a hesitancy to consider a price earnings ratio of more than 10 to 12 in estimating what the venture equity could be worth at the time of the sale.

- The venture capitalist will be looking at your business plan closely to determine the *accuracy of your financial projections*. These projections, if too conservative, could result in underpricing of the company but if too optimistic, they could impair your credibility and cause the investor to be more cautious than necessary.

- The *future dilution* based on anticipated additional rounds of financing.

- *Exit*. How attractive will this company be as a publicly traded firm, or as an acquisition candidate if the business cannot survive as a viable independent entity?

- *Elapsed time until profitability*. The profit target is based on the best estimate of when liquidity on investment is probable and the return threshold expectations of the venture firm.

- *Performance to date*. If the investment is a follow on funding, has the company met its projections to date? Very often benchmarks are set up at the initial investment against which performance is measured to determine the price of subsequent rounds. It is to the advantage of the entrepreneur to set realistic goals which can be met or exceeded. Unrealistic goals, if accepted by the venture investor, may increase the valuation in the initial round of financing. However, failure to achieve them — even if the company has done very well — is likely to result in a reduced valuation in a subsequent round. Your objective should be to increase the value of your company at each successive round.

- *Capital gains versus current income*. Will the structure of the investment provide some current income in the form of interest or dividends or is the return based solely on an eventual capital gain?

If it is determined that the product and market are viable, can this management team build the product and exploit the market? This requires a far different type of analysis. The factors affecting the risk will be the strength of the team and the stage of development of the company.

The venture capitalist's assessment of management will be judgmental and intuitive. This is by far the most critical element in determining whether or not the venture capitalist will make the investment and in terms of the affect management strength has on the potential and risk perceived, it is also of utmost importance in the pricing.

As a general rule, the more relevant accomplishments and experience of the management team, the higher the valuation of the company will be. The qualifications, the track record and the credibility of the management will be subjected to very close scrutiny.

The venture capitalist will also determine the commitment of the management team. How much of their net worth are they willing to commit? Entrepreneurs will be more constrained from walking away when things are not going well if they are financially committed to the company's success.

Also of importance in the determination of risk will be the personal chemistry between the management and the venture investors. Good chemistry can go a long way toward increasing the comfort level of the venture capitalist.

Fund Raising Environment
In addition to all the internal factors which are examined to determine the ultimate pricing, the environment in which you are raising capital for your company can dramatically impact valuation. The environment includes the general state of the economony particularly the public stock market as well as the state of the venture capital industry and the entrepreneurial climate.

The Stock Market
There is a direct relationship between venture pricing and the overall condition of the securities market. When the stock market is high and speculative, pricing will be on the high side. Pricing will be vastly different during a down period.

In 1982 to 1983, the stock market was receptive to the issues of new companies and it was willing to pay a high price for them. The confidence level of investors was increased by this buoyant market and entrepreneurs were able to obtain very favorable valuations.

Later-stage companies in particular were able to achieve premium valuations from investors (institutional as well as venture capitalist) who anticipated quick returns from a public offering. The pendulum swung to the opposite extreme in 1984 and 1985 when the public market for new issues declined.

Companies which had raised capital in 1983 at very high valuations often saw their valuations drop dramatically in 1984 when they raised additional dollars.

Venture Industry and Entrepreneurial Climate
A venture capitalist once commented that the venture capital industry changes every 90 days. Although this may be an exaggeration, it emphasizes the variable character of this small segment of the investment community.

Pricing will be affected by the supply of venture capital and the appetite of the venture capital investors. From 1979 to 1983 as more capital was being raised by venture firms, they were eagerly seeking investment opportunities. Startup activity was at an all-time high in 1981 and the competition for the "best" deals tended to increase valuations. In fact, it was often said that there were too many dollars chasing too few deals. Raising capital in 1984 was far more difficult for the entrepreneur as the demands on capital increased and venture firms began to concentrate on retaining additional funds for companies already in their own portfolios. The supply of capital for new investment opportunities declined and even existing portfolio companies were subject to greater scrutiny. Consequently, valuations of expansion financings declined dramatically from the abnormally high levels of 1982 to 1983.

It should be noted that while expansion financing valuations can vary significantly in different cycles, startup pricing has far less variation due to the domination of business risk in early stages over the financial and pricing risk.

Determining Value
Before you have your initial meeting with a potential venture capital investor, you should have calculated a value for your company. Although you will not be negotiating price in early meetings, the venture capitalist may want to know how much equity you will be willing to sell for the capital which you require to see if your expectations are in line with his.

To do this you should:

1. Consider the business risk associated with the financing to determine the rate of return which will be expected by the venture capitalist. The business risk is generally high in a startup company while the pricing risk is low. In a later stage business much of the business risk may have been eliminated but the pricing risk is high since the investor may only be looking for a three to five times return on his investment versus a 10 times return on a startup.

2. Estimate the price/earnings ratio based on comparable publicly held companies. The market value of the company can then be projected by multiplying forecasted annual earnings by the P/E ratio for comparable companies.

3. Divide the estimate of the total dollar return the venture capitalist wants by the projected market value of the company. This will yield the percentage of ownership the venture capitalist will need, as of the future date, to realize the desired return. Dilution from any additional equity financings required during the interim period must be considered in making these calculations.

When you have arrived at a valuation for your company, confirm your analysis with experienced professionals — lawyers, accountants, bankers. The following two examples were prepared by Peat, Marwick, Mitchell & Co. to illustrate the calculations involved in determining valuations.

Example One — XYZ Company, Inc., a startup, needs $500,000. The company's product appears to have excellent potential. However, because the product is new and unproven, an investment in the company would be extremely risky. Accordingly, it is reasonable to estimate that a venture capitalist would want a potential return of at least 10 times his total investment in five years. Management estimates that the company should be able to "go public" at 20 times earnings in five years. Projected after-tax earnings for the fifth year is $1,250,000. Additional long-term financing of $500,000 will be needed at the beginning of the third year.

In the calculations below it is assumed that the venture capitalist who provides the initial financing ($500,000) also provides the subsequent financing ($500,000), and that he wants a return equal to 10 times both. However, it should be noted that if the company made satisfactory progress during the first two years, it would be reasonable to assume that the venture capitalist will be satisfied with a lower return on the subsequent financing since it would involve less risk.

Estimate of Total Dollar Return Required

Total Investment	$ 1,000,000
Estimate of Return Required	x 10
	$10,000,000

Projected Market Value in Fifth Year

Projected Earnings	$ 1,250,000
Estimate of P/E Ratio	x 20
	$25,000,000

Percentage Ownership Needed in Fifth Year

Estimate of Total Dollar Return Required	$10,000,000
Projected Market Value of Company in Fifth Year	25,000,000
	40%

Example Two — In this set of calculations it is assumed that a second investor provides the subsequent financing ($500,000). The calculations show that the venture capitalist who provides the initial financing ($500,00) would need 20% ownership as of the fifth year to realize the return he wants. However, since the ownership to be given up for the subsequent financing will reduce his ownership position, he will want more than 20% ownership initially. For example, if it is assumed that 15% ownership will have to be given up for the subsequent financing, the venture capitalist who provides the initial financing would need 23% ownership initially to end up with 20% ownership in the fifth year.

Estimate of Total Dollar Return Required

Total Investment	$ 500,000
Estimate of Return Required	x 10
	$ 5,000,000

Projected Market Value in Fifth Year

Projected Earnings	$ 1,250,000
Estimate of P/E Ratio	x 20
	$25,000,000

Percentage Ownership Needed in Fifth Year

Estimate of Total Dollar Return Required	$ 5,000,000
Projected Market Value of Company in Fifth Year	25,000,000
	20%

Thus, it appears that the investment ($500,000) may be attractive to an interested venture capitalist if the principals of XYZ Company, Inc. are willing to give up approximately 23% ownership.

The following models used by Stanley Golder when he was at First Chicago Corporation illustrate the underlying rationale behind pricing decisions.

First Chicago Pricing Model

There are three basic directions a venture situation can take.

1. Successful: profitable to the point of being a solid public company

2. Sideways: marginally profitable with limited growth — not a viable public company but able to service debt over a period of years

3. Failure: bankruptcy or reorganization

Cash Flow for the Successful Investment

The cash flow to the investor if the company is quite successful might look like this (assume capital gains are realized in Year 4; figures are in thousands).

Year	1	2	3	4	5	6	7
Principal	0	0	0	0	0	0	0
Interest	21	21	21	18	0	0	0
Capital gain	0	0	0	X	0	0	0

Cash Flow for the Sideways Investment
The cash flow to the investor would be different, however, if the company became a limited growth situation (figures are in thousands).

Year	1	2	3	4	5	6	7
Principal	0	0	0	75	75	75	75
Interest	21	21	21	18	13	8	3
Capital gain	0	0	0	0	0	0	0

Cash Flow for the Failure Investment
If, unfortunately, the investment turned out to be a disaster, the cash flow might follow this pattern (assume a 10% recovery in Year 2; figures are in thousands).

Year	1	2	3	4	5	6	7
Principal	0	30	0	0	0	0	0
Interest	21	0	0	0	0	0	0
Capital gain	0	0	0	0	0	0	0

Compared Cash Flows
Comparing the cash flows for each of the three directions a venture investent might take produces the following (figures are in thousands).

Year		1	2	3	4	5	6	7
Successful	↑	21	21	21	18+X	0	0	0
Sideways	→	21	21	21	93	88	83	78
Failure	↓	21	30	0	0	0	0	0

Probability Selection
The next step in this method involves assigning probabilities (P) to each of the three possible directions. The sum of these probabilities must, of course, equal 1.0. For the purposes of this example, we have chosen the following probabilities, but each type of project might well receive different weighting for probabilities of success and failure.

P ↑ = .3 (3 chances in 10)
P → = .5 (5 chances in 10)
P ↓ = .2 (2 chances in 10)
1.0

Total Pricing Layout
After having selected an appropriate discount factor (for the entire portfolio), the overall layout is as follows (we have assumed an annual 20% compounded target portfolio return; figures are in thousands).

Discounted value of dollar		.83	.69	.58	.48	.40	.33	.28
Year		1	2	3	4	5	6	7
P ↑	.3	21	21	21	18+X	0	0	0
P →	.5	21	21	21	93	88	83	78
P ↓	.2	21	30	0	0	0	0	0

Reduction to Present Value Equivalents
The next step is to reduce these numbers to their present value equivalents by multiplying them by the discount factor at the head of the column.

Year		1	2	3	4	5	6	7
P ↑	.3	17	15	12	9+.48X	0	0	0
P →	.5	17	15	12	45	35	27	22
P ↓	.2	17	21	0	0	0	0	0

Pricing Equation
We now total each row and then construct the basic equation that will provide the desired output.

Probability Row Total

P ↑ .3   53+.48X
P → .5   173
P ↓ .2   38

$$300 = P(\uparrow)(53 + .48X) + P(\rightarrow)\,173 + P(\downarrow)38$$

Using the probabilities shown above,

$$300 = (.3)(53 + .48X) = (.5)(173) + (.2)(38)$$

Decision Matrix

P1	P2	P3	X	Percentage of firm needed at		
				P/E10	P/E15	P/E30
0.8	0.0	0.2	648.0	6.8	4.5	2.3
0.7	0.1	0.2	704.7	7.4	4.9	2.5
0.6	0.2	0.2	780.3	8.2	5.5	2.7
0.5	0.3	0.2	886.1	9.3	6.2	3.1
0.4	0.4	0.2	1,004.9	11.0	7.3	3.7
→**0.3**	**0.5**	**0.2**←	**1,309.5**	**13.8**	**9.2**	**4.6**
0.2	0.6	0.2	1,838.7	19.4	12.9	6.5
0.1	0.7	0.2	3,426.2	36.1	24.0	12.0

The row set in bold type shows the present value of $300,000 if a 20% compounded growth rate is to be achieved, based on different probability assumptions shown on each line. The line marked ← → shows the assumptions given in this problem about success, failure, or sideways movement of the investment.

Thus, if a price-earnings multiple of 15 is to be used to calculate the value of the company, a 9.2% equity will be required to achieve the compound growth rate of 20%, given the probability requirements in the example. The columns headed P/E 10 and P/E 30 show the percentage of equity needed under those price-earnings multiples.

Comparison of Three Pricing Methods
The percentage of equity required under the three pricing methods is as follows: traditional, 12.9%; fundamental, 5.3%; First Chicago, 9.2%.

Effect of Varying the Interest Rate
What happens if the interest rate on the debenture is doubled, from 7% to 14%, for example?

P1	P2	P3	X	Percentage of firm needed at		
				P/E10	P/E15	P/E30
0.8	0.0	0.2	529.0	5.6	3.7	1.9
0.7	0.1	0.2	566.3	6.0	4.0	2.0
0.6	0.2	0.2	615.9	6.5	4.3	2.2
0.5	0.3	0.2	685.2	7.2	4.8	2.4
0.4	0.4	0.2	789.2	8.3	5.5	2.8
0.3	**0.5**	**0.2**	**982.5**	**10.1**	**6.8**	**3.4**
0.2	0.6	0.2	1,369.1	13.8	9.2	4.6
0.1	0.7	0.2	2,348.9	24.7	16.5	8.2

This table shows that the equity percentage required on the investment will drop from 9.2% to 6.8% and still produce the same return to First Chicago if the interest rate on the debenture doubles, from 7% to 14%.

Effect of Varying the Time Horizon
What is the effect of pushing out the realization of capital gains to Year 7?

P1	P2	P3	X	Percentage of firm needed at		
				P/E10	P/E15	P/E30
0.8	0.0	0.2	1,119.7	11.8	7.9	3.9
0.7	0.1	0.2	1,217.7	12.8	8.5	4.3
0.6	0.2	0.2	1,348.4	14.2	9.5	4.7
0.5	0.3	0.2	1,531.2	16.1	10.7	5.4
0.4	0.4	0.2	1,805.6	19.0	12.7	6.3
0.3	**0.5**	**0.2**	**2,262.8**	**23.8**	**15.9**	**7.9**
0.2	0.6	0.2	3,177.2	33.4	22.3	11.1
0.1	0.7	0.2	5,920.5	62.3	41.5	20.8

This table shows the effects of moving the realization of capital gains from the fourth to the seventh year, keeping all other assumptions the same. The investment now will require a 15.9% equity interest rather than 9.2%.

Conclusion
The valuation of your company will be determined through both quantitative analysis and the personal judgment and bias of the venture capital investor.

It is based on the perceived value by the investors of the future growth of the company and the talents and skills of the management team to exploit the opportunity. In addition, the current money raising environment will also be an important consideration. As an entrepreneur, you must be realistic in evaluating these factors and opportunistic in exploiting them. The final consideration you must make is whether you want the highest valuation or the best investors. Professional venture capital may be an expensive route for the entrepreneur but if the value added provided by these investors will accelerate the growth and ultimately result in a larger more successful company, it may be well worth the cost. In the last analysis it is the size of the pie and not the width of the slice which is significant.

Preliminary Legal Considerations in Forming a New Enterprise

Michael P. Ridley, Esq.

Michael P. Ridley *is a principal in the Los Angeles law firm of Riordan, Caps, Carbone & McKinzie, specializing in venture capital and corporate finance. He and his firm represent numerous venture capital funds and small business investment companies and a large number of companies that have been financed by venture capital sources. Mr. Ridley is a graduate of Stanford University and Yale Law School.*

The following article is a summary of the key legal concerns of the entrepreneur in the planning stages and startup of a business.

Relations with Prior Employers

Venture capitalists typically invest in enterprises headed by superior managers with prior track records. It is therefore likely that founders and key employees in a new business will have recently left or are considering leaving their present employment. As such, it will be important during the formation process to ensure that the founders and key employees do not misappropriate the trade secrets of prior employers or otherwise engage in unfair competition with the prior employer.

Trade Secrets

Although employees are free to leave employment and start a competing enterprise, they are not free to utilize their employer's trade secrets or compete while still employed. Most litigation involving the improper use by a departing employee of an employer's trade secrets will center on whether the information used by a departing employee is in fact a trade secret. Definitions of what constitutes a trade secret will vary from state to state. As a general rule a trade secret means "information, including a formula, pattern, computation, program, device, method, technique or process that (1) derives independent economic value, actual or potential, from not being generally known to the public or to other persons who can obtain economic value from its disclosure or use; and (2) is the subject of efforts that are reasonable under the circumstances to maintain its secrecy." Uniform Trade Secret Act.

It will be important for the new enterprise to avoid situations in which it is involved in the misappropriation of trade secrets of prior employers for several reasons: (a) certain jurisdictions make it a criminal offense to misappropriate trade secrets, e.g., California Penal Code Section 499(c) makes it a misdemeanor punishable by up to one year in prison and up to $5,000 in fines to steal, copy or use without authorization trade secrets; (b) the prior employer has legal recourse to enjoin the new enterprise's use of the employer's trade secrets and to seek damages, including royalties and, where appropriate, punitive damages, which recourse could very well mean the termination of the startup's activities and, at a minimum, the incurrence in a very short period of time of substantial legal fees and management time diverted from the enterprise; and, last, but not least, (c) venture capitalists, depending upon their respective involvement in formulating the startup and whether they knew or should have known that the startup they were financing had misappropriated trade secrets, may themselves be liable for damages to the prior employer.

Although one can never obtain 100 percent assurance that a departing employee will not be sued by a prior employer, the departing employees should follow certain steps:

1. Review all non-disclosure and assignment of invention agreements executed by founders and new employees, particularly those sections relating to prior discoveries. Certain jurisdictions provide that inventions developed on an employee's own time not relating to the employer's business constitute the property of the employee. Any work on technology to be utilized by a startup should be done on the employee's time with the employee's own resources. Employment agreements should be reviewed to determine the existence of and enforceability of covenants not to compete.

2. Prepare the business plan on the employee's individual time.

3. Do not use the prior employer's premises or equipment in preparing the business plan or doing preparatory work in setting up the new venture. Calls to future suppliers, employees and funding sources should be done at home or during the employee's free time.

4. Turn in all customer lists, product specifications, marketing plans, etc. Do not bring copies of proprietary information to the startup.

5. A problem area will exist where the founder is not an employee but rather an officer or director of the former

employer. The fiduciary relationship to the former employer may be breached by failing to offer the opportunity to the employer. Corporate opportunity problems may be solved by having the prior employer decline to pursue the opportunity or invention which the startup is formed to pursue.

6. The safest course of action is for the employee to depart from the employer prior to competing with the employer and to disclose preparations to compete if such failure to disclose preparation would be harmful to the employer. Departing employees should inform the prior employer of plans rather than have the prior employer learn of plans from reference checks of venture capitalists or in a newspaper.

Solicitation of Fellow Employees

The general rule is that, absent unfair or deceptive means, the public interest of the mobility of employees enables the startup to hire employees, after departure, of former employer. A problem arises if the solicitation occurs while the founders are still employed by the former employer or if the employees are hired not for their skills but rather to obtain the prior employer's trade secrets.

Solicitation of Business of Former Employer

The general rule is that, absent a valid noncompete agreement, employees may solicit customers of former employers after departing unless proprietary customer lists or confidential information, such as pricing, is used. A problem area is often in the area of defining what constitutes customer lists. To the extent that the identity of customers, purchasing agents, required terms a vendor must meet, etc., are known to the public, the more likely a customer list will not be found.

Ownership and Protection of Technology

If technology will be important to the success of the startup, steps should be implemented on formation to protect the technology. There are several alternatives to follow in protecting technology — trade secrets, patents and copyrights. The best method to be used is dependent on the type of technology involved.

Trade Secrets

The general rule is that a trade secret is lost if it is disclosed to the general public or competitors or if the person seeking to protect a trade secret does not take reasonable steps under the circumstances to ensure its confidentiality. A startup should require that all employees and founders, prior to and as a condi-tion of employment, execute non-disclosure and assignment of invention agreements that (a) set forth recognition of employee of the nature of the importance of trade secrets to the company and agreement to keep all such information in confidence; (b) set forth the prior inventions that are being brought by the employee to the company; (c) represent that no trade secrets of prior employers are being brought to the new enterprise and require that the employee will not disclose to the company trade secrets which may have been obtained as a result of prior employment; and (d) assign all inventions to be used by the company or which are developed during the course of employment, except those inventions which are developed entirely on an employee's own time and do not relate either to the business of the employer or to the employer's actual or anticipated research or development or do not result from any work performed by the employee for the employer.

The company should seek a proper balance between the cost to implement certain procedures designed to restrict the flow of information to protect the confidentiality of trade secrets and the necessity for information to flow within the enterprise. At minimum, the company should consider the following:

1. Sensitive areas should be under lock and key with only specified employees having access and that access should be logged. Access to computer files should similarly be controlled. Visitors to the facility should not be shown sensitive areas containing trade secret information, such as a manufacturing process or computer programs. Visitors and consultants or possible purchasers or suppliers should sign non-disclosure and confidentiality agreements. Confidential documents should not be left in open view or unattended in areas in which employees or other persons not authorized to have access to the information would have access. Courts are often impressed with a lock box for blue prints or source and object codes.

2. Proprietary documents and information should be legended as such with restrictions on copying or disseminating the same.

3. Departing employees should be interviewed to ensure no trade secrets are being withdrawn or in the possession of the departing employee and to reiterate the company's claim of trade secrets.

4. Employees must be made aware of the fact that they are dealing with trade secrets, that such trade secrets are the property of the employer and are of vital importance to that employer, and that the company will prevent the improper use of the company's trade secrets.

Patent

A 17-year monopoly created by statute for "new and useful process, machine, manufacture or composition of matter, or any new and useful improvement thereof." The invention must be "new" to be patentable. 35 U.S.C. 102(b) prevents issuance of patent if the invention has been in public use for over a year or if the invention has been described in a publication that has been published for over a year prior to the application. It is important for the company to see patent counsel early to determine patentability, particularly on the issue of when public use has occurred, whether a patent would be the most appropriate method of protection and the scope of the license to be granted by the inventor. Patent protection extends only to jurisdictions in which it is filed. Major disadvantages relate to the fact that the invention must be disclosed, patent litigation is expensive, and, until recently, most inventors were not successful in patent claims.

Copyright

A limited monopoly is granted for the term of the author's life plus 50 years for an original work of authorship, including computer software, but not ideas, principles, concepts or discoveries. To perfect, an author must deposit a copy of the work with the Library of Congress and the Copyright Office. An author may deposit the first and last 25 pages of a computer program which may prevent disclosure of integral workings of the program. Material must be marked to indicate copyright protection.

Trademark

The company should, at a very early stage after determining its name and the names of its proposed products, conduct a trademark availability search. It makes no sense to incur significant advertising, printing and marketing costs only to find that a desired name has been registered by a third party as a trademark. Federal registration of a trademark can occur after a mark eligible for registration has been used in an interstate sale and is good for 20 years. Federal registration gives right of holder of trademark to seek damages, including treble damages, for infringement of trademark.

Securities Issues

Shares Issues for Compensation

Founders, hopefully, should receive shares in the startup at a fraction of what the venture capitalists are paying. As such, the company should be organized and shares issued as soon as possible during the formation process. The founders should avoid situations in which the founders are incorporating the enterprise on day one at a low valuation, and on the same or the next day with no other event having occurred, the venture capitalists are being issued shares at a much higher valuation.

If shares are issued for services and will be subject to a risk of forfeiture, regardless of whether the founder is paying fair market value, employees and founders should file 83(b) elections with the Internal Revenue Service within 30 days of issuance of such shares to elect to have the value of the securities in excess of the cost to the employee (which should be zero) treated as income in year of issuance. Failure to file will mean that when the risk of forfeiture lapses, the employee will be taxed at ordinary income rates on the difference between what was paid for the shares and their value at the date the restrictions lapse. If the company is successful, the effect will be disastrous to the founders and employees, since the shares may not then be marketable but may have great value.

An emerging area of the law is wrongful termination of employment. All stock purchase or option agreements should provide that no employment agreement is intended and that the company has the right to terminate employment.

Shareholder Agreements

The founders should execute rights of first refusal giving the company and the other founders rights of first refusal in the event of any transfer to a third partner. Restrictions may also be imposed upon transfer by any of the founders during the first years of the enterprise. Venture capitalists will typically insist upon such restrictions; it is far better to obtain them while the only value of the company is as perceived in the business plan, or in an untested prototype as opposed to after the financing is in place and value is more apparent.

The founders should also consider the propriety of the vesting of shares based on length of service to the company and the granting to the company a right to repurchase unvested shares at cost. Although the founding team, at the onset, may appear quite compatible, as the enterprise grows it is entirely possible that certain elements of that team will not be up to the task and, as such, a portion of those shares should be made available to bring in new people. Venture capitalists will usually insist upon some vesting requirements. It is far easier to obtain the same while there is little proven value in the business enterprise.

If the initial funding is from friends and families and includes notes, such persons should be made aware of venture capitalists' typical demands that such notes either should be contributed to capital at closing or subject to deferred pay-out. As such, the founders should ensure that amendments to such notes be made by other than unanimous consent of the note holders.

Regulatory Compliance

Securities issued to the founders and pre-venture capital sources of funds should be issued in compliance with applicable state blue sky laws and the Securities Act of 1933. Failure to do so gives rights of rescission and will delay and/or hinder a subsequent public offering. The general rule for state purposes is that no securities may be issued without a permit unless an exemption is otherwise available. Exemptions will vary from state to state but will be predicated on the type of security, the qualification of the purchaser and/or the amount of financing or number of purchasers. Even if an exemption is available for the issuance of securities to sophisticated individuals, the company may wish to issue shares to all employees, regardless of their sophistication. Very early in the formation process the company should implement a restricted stock purchase plan or incentive stock option plan and obtain permit for the same. A problem area relates to promises made to new employees for shares in absence of permit or exemption.

Under the Securities Act of 1933, securities may not be issued unless registered or unless an exemption from registration is available. The typical exemption would be Regulation D adopted by the SEC on April 15, 1982 which sets forth a means wherein an issuer may issue securities without the need for registering the same.

Rule 504: $500,000 limit in 12 months preceding issue, no requirement of disclosure (caveat: fraud rules still applicable), no advertising, restrictions on resale.

Rule 505: $5,000,000 limit in 12 months preceding issue, no more than 35 unaccredited purchasers, no requirement of disclosure to "accredited investors" but disclosure of information on Part 1 of form S-18 if "nonaccredited," no advertising, restrictions on resale.

Rule 506: No limit as to dollar size, no more than 35 nonaccredited investors, no requirement of disclosure to "accredited investors" but disclosure of information on Part 1 of form S-18 if "nonaccredited," no advertising, restrictions on resale.

The issuer must complete and file Form D with SEC with 15 days of first sale.

Conclusion

These are just a few of the potential problem areas to consider prior to forming a new business. It is wise to consult with an attorney experienced in new company formations very early in the planning process to avoid future difficulties.

The Legal Process of Venture Capital Investment

Richard J. Testa, Esq.

Richard J. Testa is a partner in the Boston law firm of Testa, Hurwitz & Thibeault. He and his firm have served as counsel for several national and international venture capital firms as well as for a large number of high technology and other businesses that have been financed by venture capitalists.

Section I. General Considerations Relating to Legal Documentation

A key element in the attainment of a successful relationship between a young business enterprise and its venture capital investors is the careful crafting of the legal structure of the investment transaction. Venture capital investing is a long-term commitment of support to a company. As such, the parties involved in structuring and implementing the investment transaction must bring to the process a sensitivity to the changing and different objectives and requirements (financial, legal, personal, etc.) of the business and its principal participants. The legal documents must foresee the evolution of the enterprise from a development stage startup to a publicly held company or viable acquisition candidate. Not only do the investment documents represent a charter of the legal rights of the parties spanning the growth cycle of the business but they also set the tone of the relationships between the management/entrepreneurs and the financial backers of the enterprise, serving as a model for resolution of their often differing interests.

Despite increasing standardization of the venture capital process, it remains, fundamentally, highly idiosyncratic, with each transaction reflecting the particular chemistry between entrepreneur and investor. Accordingly, there exists no such thing as the "perfect model" of legal documentation for the investment transaction. Each set of documents should be tailored to reflect the unique combination of styles and interests involved. Generally, however, each transaction will encompass the following common set of documents:

1. the *term sheet*, summarizing in broad strokes the principal financial and other terms of the investment

2. the *investment agreement*, detailing the terms of purchase and provisions of the securities (equity or debt) being acquired

3. the *stockholders agreement*, containing restrictions upon the transfer and voting of securities by management and (occasionally) investors

4. *employee stock purchase or stock option agreements*, governing the current and future allocation of equity in the business to key employees

5. *employee confidentiality and proprietary rights agreements*, assuring the retention by the business of its valuable trade secrets and business rights

6. *legal opinion* of company counsel

Section II. The Term Sheet

The handshake "agreement" between investor and entrepreneur is often set forth in a written term sheet or letter of intent. Although the term sheet may take a variety of forms, from a cursory and informal letter to a more detailed and formal memorandum, it is intended to accomplish the following purposes:

1. to reflect the agreed upon valuation of the business and to quantify the proposed allocation of that value between the entrepreneurs and investors;

2. to summarize key financial and legal terms of the transaction which will serve as the basis for preparing definitive legal documents; and

3. on occasion, to impose enforceable legal obligations upon the parties, such as requiring payment of expenses in the event the investment does not close or prohibiting negotiations with other parties pending the completion of the transaction.

Above all, the term sheet should be used by the venture capitalist to elicit those concerns of the entrepreneurs which, if unaddressed and unresolved, might later develop into "deal killers." For example, if the venture capitalist intends to require that the entrepreneurs submit their stock ownership in the enterprise to buy-back or forfeiture restrictions in the event they sever employment, such a condition should be covered in the term sheet since it encroaches in an area in which the entrepreneur will be especially sensitive. Similarly sensitive topics are the composition of the board of directors and matters relating to the terms of employment of the entrepreneurs.

A term sheet is particularly valuable for the entrepreneur who has never seen venture terms before. The new chief executive officer is being introduced to a large number of new concepts. By contrast, the venture capitalist is usually experienced and familiar with numerous levels of permutations on possible terms. The term sheet is particularly useful in bridging these differences in background knowledge and experience.

Section III. The Investment Agreement

A. *Principal Purposes and Legal Consequences*

The long form investment agreement has four principal business objectives:

1. Most importantly, it sets forth the detailed substantive terms of the investment.
2. It serves as the basic disclosure document in which the relevant historical, business, financial and legal data relating to the enterprise is set forth or referenced.
3. It presents, through the use of conditions precedent to closing, a "stop-action" photograph or image of the issuer that must exist at the time of closing. The level of detail of this photograph will vary depending upon the round of financing involved in the transaction and the simplicity or complexity of the company's operations.
4. It defines the several business parameters within which the enterprise must operate in the future. The several commandments to management range from relatively simple "thou shall not's" to complex "thou shalt's."

The legal effect of the investment agreement is similar to that of many commercial contracts. The most common consequence of a breach of agreement in the capital investment context is the ability of the investor to refuse to close the transaction because of the company's failure to satisfy a condition precedent or the existence of a significant misrepresentation by the company. Once the closing has occurred, remedies in the nature of rescission are rare. Moreover, while claims for damages do arise, they are uncommon in the high risk venture area. Common remedies available for breach of covenant are specific performance and injunctive relief. As a practical matter, however, remedies that are self-executing, such as ratchet-down provisions in an anti-dilution formula or extraordinary voting rights granted to a class of preferred stock, are more formidable than those remedies which frequently amount to waving a stick in the air, such as accelerated repayment of debt securities.

B. *Description of the Transaction*

The investment agreement memorializes the terms of the transaction. Consequently, the agreement should include a description of the securities being purchased, the purchase price and a requirement that the securities be properly authorized.

If the investor acquires a note (whether or not convertible) or a stock purchase warrant, the form of the security should be attached as an exhibit to the investment agreement. If the investor acquires a class of stock other than conventional common stock, the terms of the class of stock as set forth in the corporate charter should be attached to the investment agreement as an exhibit.

If more than one investor participates in the financing, they may be listed or referenced in an exhibit to the agreement. In some cases, the company will execute separate but identical investment agreements with the other investors. A condition of each investor's obligation to purchase may be that identical investment agreements have been executed simultaneously with each investor, such agreements have not been amended and are in full force on the closing date and a specified minimum number of dollars has been raised by the company.

In some transactions, the entire investment proceeds will not be made available to the company at a single closing. The purchase may be made in two or more installments over fixed periods of time, in which event the major condition precedent to closing each successive installment is the absence of any material adverse changes affecting the company since the initial closing. In a "staged" investment, the purchase of additional securities at subsequent closings is conditioned upon the accomplishment of certain financial or operational goals, such as the attainment of specified revenue levels or completion of development work on a new product, as well as the absence of adverse changes. A staged investment serves as an incentive to management to proceed diligently with the development of its product as outlined in its business plan and enables the venture capitalist to target his investment with a maximum impact on the development of the business.

C. *Representations and Warranties of the Company*

It is a rare issuer company that is totally "clean," that is, a company which has no stated exceptions to the several business, financial and legal topics addressed by the representation and warranty section of the investment agreement. Only a new startup company with neither employees nor sales is likely to fall into this category. Since the venture capitalist has already conducted a thorough factual review of the company's business prior to issuing his term sheet or letter of intent, the representations and warranties are not intended to "screen" the company for suitability as an investment (although the disclosure of significant adverse information not previously known to the investor may scuttle the investment) but rather to provide full disclosure of the fine details of the company's operations which may be relevant in advising management with regard to the future conduct of the business.

The following list of specific representations and warranties are common in most venture capital investment agreements. Each category is prefaced by an affirmative declaration or affirmation of compliance, subject to stated exceptions which are normally appended as an exhibit.

1. *Organization and authority:* The company is properly organized, in good standing and has legal authority to conduct its business.

2. *Corporate action:* All necessary actions under state corporate law, and the company's corporate charter and bylaws have been taken to authorize the transaction and to issue the securities.

3. *Governmental approvals:* All consents and approvals of governmental agencies necessary to complete the transaction have been obtained. In particular, this covers compliance with state securities laws and environmental regulations.

4. *Absence of litigation:* No litigation or other proceedings exist, or are threatened, which would adversely affect the company's business or the financing transaction.

5. *Employment of key personnel:* No restrictions exist relating to employment of key personnel or use of business information, particularly as a result of prior employment of such personnel by another enterprise.

6. *Compliance with other agreements:* No violations of the company's corporate charter, bylaws or other valid agreements exist, or will exist as a result of the financing.

7. *Ownership of properties and assets:* The company possesses sufficient ownership rights in its business assets, particularly its patent, copyright, trademark and other intellectual property rights, to conduct its business.

8. *Financial information:* Audited and internal unaudited financial statements have been prepared in accordance with generally accepted accounting principles and fairly present the financial position and operating results of the company. Statements as to specific categories of items, such as in-

ventory valuation and status of accounts receivable, may be included. No adverse changes have occurred since date of the most recent financial statements furnished.

9. *Transactions with insiders:* Disclosure is made of any direct or indirect transactions between the company and its directors, officers and stockholders.

10. *Third-party guaranties or investments:* Absence of continuing financial involvements with third parties.

11. *Compliance with federal securities laws:* Certification that the transaction complies with federal and state securities laws, including the possibility that the transaction may be integrated with other securities sales.

12. *Registration rights:* Absence of rights to cause the company to file any registration statement under the federal securities laws or any right to participate in any such registration statement.

13. *Disclosure:* The business plan used to seek financing is accurate and complete and all material disclosures have been made to investors either in the business plan or in legal documents relating to the transaction.

14. *Brokerage:* Disclosure of any finder's or broker's fees or commissions payable in connection with the transaction.

15. *Capitalization:* Description of the company's authorized capitalization and status of outstanding securities, including warrants, options and convertible securities. Any transfer restrictions, repurchase rights or preemptive rights are also described.

D. *Covenants and Undertakings of the Company*

The covenants section of the investment agreement contains several affirmative and negative undertakings of the company relating to the future conduct of its affairs. Affirmative covenants are actions, positions or results that the company promises to achieve or undertake. Negative covenants are actions, positions or results that the company promises to avoid.

If, under the terms of the investment agreement, the board of directors is to be controlled by inside management, the covenants are frequently extensive. In an equity-oriented venture capital investment, however, where the investors will frequently control the board of directors, the covenants are often kept to a minimum. In such a situation, the affirmative covenants might merely provide that the investor will receive periodic financial information and will be represented on the board. The negative covenants might limit only the company's ability to amend its corporate charter or merge or sell its assets without the investor's consent. A venture capital firm with board control will generally rely upon this control to influence the development of a company and will not, as a rule, find it necessary to impose extensive contractual restrictions on the conduct of the business by insisting on strict affirmative and negative covenants.

Both affirmative and negative covenants may remain in effect as long as the investors hold any of the investment securities or, alternatively, may terminate upon the occurrence of certain events, such as the completion of an initial public offering, conversion of debt-oriented convertible securities into equity or mere passage of time.

Among the customary *affirmative* covenants which are found in venture capital investment agreements are the following:

1. *Payment of taxes and claims:* The company will pay all lawful taxes, assessments, and levies upon it or its income or property before they become in default. This covenant sometimes provides that all trade debt and principal and interest on debt securities acquired by the investor will be paid when due.

2. *Property and liability insurance:* The company will maintain insurance against hazards and risks and liability to persons and property to the extent customary for companies engaged in the same or similar businesses.

3. *Maintenance of corporate existence:* The company will maintain its corporate existence and all rights, licenses, patents, copyrights, trademarks, etc. useful in its business, and will engage only the type of business described in the business plan.

4. *Legal compliance:* The company will comply with all applicable laws and regulations in the conduct of its business.

5. *Access to premises:* The investor or his representatives will generally be permitted to inspect the company's facilities, books and records. To the extent that confidentiality of corporate business information may be compromised by such rights of access, investors generally agree to confidentiality restrictions or to limiting access to lead or other major investors.

6. *Accounts and reports:* The company may be asked by the investor to agree to maintain a standard system of accounting in accordance with generally accepted accounting principles consistently applied, and to keep full and complete financial records.

7. *Repair and maintenance:* The company will keep all necessary equipment and property in good repair and condition, as required to permit the business to be properly conducted.

8. *Approval of budgets:* The investor will frequently require management to produce comprehensive annual operating and capital budgets for approval by the investor or by the board of directors. Revisions of such budgets during the year may also require advance approval.

9. *Protection of proprietary rights:* The company will agree to take all necessary steps to protect proprietary developments made in the future, including causing all key employees to sign confidentiality and proprietary rights agreements.

10. *Compliance with key agreements:* The company will enforce its rights under key agreements, such as the stockholders agreement, and will cause future stockholders to join the agreement.

11. *Life insurance:* The investor will often require the company to maintain insurance on the lives of key officers and employees. The face amount in some cases may be as much as the purchase price of the securities, and the insurance proceeds are often payable directly to the investor, particularly if the investor holds debt securities.

12. *Board of directors:* Venture capital firms will generally seek assurances that they will be represented on the company's board of directors. The right to be represented on the board may be backed up by voting agreements with the principal stockholders. If the investor is not to be represented on the board, the company may be required to notify the investor of the time and place of board meetings, to permit the investor or his representative to attend such meetings and to receive written materials disseminated to directors. Frequency of board meetings and financial arrangements may also be covered.

13. *Financial and operating statements:* The company will invariably agree to provide the investor with detailed financial and operating information. The information to be provided may include annual, quarterly, and sometimes monthly reports of sales, production, shipments, profits, cash balances, receivables, payables, and backlog; all statements filed with the Securities and Exchange Commission or other agencies; notification of significant lawsuits or other legal proceedings; and any other information that the investor may need for his own voluntary or involuntary filing requirements. Particularly where an investor is acquiring debt securities or preferred stock containing extensive financial and other covenants, financial statements are

required to be accompanied by a certificate from the company's chief executive or financial officer and, in the case of audited financial statements, its auditors, to the effect that the company is in compliance with all provisions of the investment agreement. The right to receive financial information is often terminated when the company goes public in order to avoid dissemination of "inside" information. Although companies generally concede the legitimate interests of investors to receive business information, negotiation over the scope and form of this information may be considerable in view of the operational burden and potential liabilities it can impose upon management.

14. *Current ratio, working capital, or net worth:* These covenants normally are included only in debt financings and are agreements to maintain the current ratio, working capital or net worth, either at a minimum amount or as specified for various time periods. They may be keyed to projections made by the company; accordingly, care should be taken by the company in preparing the business plan to project financial results and conditions which management is comfortable in undertaking to attain on a contractual basis.

15. *Use of proceeds:* Often the company will agree to apply the proceeds received from the financing to a specified use. The investor will sometimes require that the proceeds be applied within a narrow area of the business in connection with a specific financing plan or may simply require that the funds be used for working capital.

In contrast to affirmative covenants, which generally exhort the company to undertake actions which it would ordinarily choose to take in the normal course, the negative covenants contained in the investment agreement have more teeth and serve to limit the company from actions it otherwise might be inclined to take, unless the investors have consented in advance. Typically these negative covenants relate to matters which would affect the fundamental nature of the business in which the investment has been made (e.g., mergers and acquisitions) or would alter the balance of control between the investors and entrepreneurs reached in the investment agreement (e.g., controls of dilution). Since the negative covenants limit the scope of managerial flexibility, they are often the subject of sharp negotiation. This is all the more so because the investor's remedy upon material breach by the company may result in the immediate acceleration of indebtedness in the case of debt securities and may sometimes trigger rescission rights in the case of equity securities. As suggested above, there is a trade-off between the degree of investor control of the voting power and board of direc-

tors and the strictness of the negative covenants imposed on the company. Many typical *negative* covenants are described below:

1. *Mergers, consolidations, and sale or purchase of assets:* Mergers, consolidations, acquisitions, and the like are generally prohibited without the investor's advance approval. Liquidation and dissolution of the company and the sale, lease, pledge or other disposition of substantial assets without consent may also be barred. Restrictions may also be placed on the company's purchase of capital assets.

2. *Dealings with related parties:* The company will covenant that no transactions between the company and any officers, directors or stockholders of the company shall be effected unless on an arm's length basis and on terms no less favorable to the company than could be obtained from nonrelated persons. Approval of all transactions with affiliates by either the board or the investors may be required.

3. *Change in business:* The company will not change the nature of its business as described in its business plan.

4. *Charter amendments:* The investor may prohibit the company from amending its corporate charter or bylaws without the consent of the investor. More narrowly drawn covenants might prohibit only certain specified actions (such as a change in the capital structure) without the investor's consent.

5. *Distributions and redemptions:* The company typically agrees not to make any dividend distributions to stockholders. Dividends may be prohibited until a given date or until the completion of a public offering of the company's stock, or may be limited to a fixed percentage of profits above a set amount. In addition, the company may covenant not to repurchase or redeem any of its securities except in accordance with the terms of the securities purchased by the investor (e.g., redeemable preferred stock), employee plans (e.g., forfeiture of stock upon termination of employment) or agreements with stockholders (e.g., right of first refusal).

6. *Issuance of stock or convertible securities:* The investor may prohibit the company from issuing any securities that would result in dilution of the investor's position. This includes restrictions on the issuance of securities of the type purchased by the investor and any securities convertible into such securities at a price less than that paid by the investor. Alternatively, an "anti-dilution" formula may be employed so that such an issuance will automatically trigger an improved conversion rate for the securities purchased by the investor. Frequently these covenants are included in the terms of the securities themselves.

7. *Liens and encumbrances:* The investment agreement (generally for debt-oriented securities, including redeemable preferred stock) may provide for restrictions on liens, pledges, and other encumbrances, with exceptions for such liabilities as real estate mortgages. Separate restrictions can be placed on leases of real property or equipment.

8. *Indebtedness:* The company may agree to restrictions on future indebtedness, with exceptions for institutional senior borrowings, indebtedness on personal property purchase money obligations and trade indebtedness, up to certain limits in the ordinary course of business. Again, this provision is most typical of investments in debt-oriented securities.

9. *Investments:* Restrictions against investing in other companies may be imposed by the investor. Exceptions are made for investments in wholly owned subsidiaries.

10. *Employee compensation:* The company may agree to limit employment and other personal service contracts of management or key personnel to a maximum term and a maximum amount of annual compensation. In addition, the investment agreement may prohibit the acceleration or termination of vesting schedules applicable to transfers of stock held by officers, directors and employees.

11. *Financial covenants:* Negative financial covenants are frequently imposed upon a company in a debt-oriented investment, such as prohibiting key ratios or financial conditions from exceeding certain limits or limiting the company from incurring losses in excess of a certain amount. Semantics often determine whether a financial covenant is affirmative or negative in nature. Clear definition of financial and accounting terms is critical. Short of resulting in a default on securities, failure to comply with financial covenants may trigger adjustments in conversion ratios of securities or give rise to preferential voting or other rights for the investor.

In addition to the numerous affirmative and negative covenants described above, the venture capital investment agreement will customarily contain a number of more complex undertakings by the company, which are generally set apart in the agreement. Two of the more typical of these covenants pertain to registration rights and rights to participate in future financings. Another such provision, indemnification of the investors for breach of the investment agreement, is also discussed briefly below:

1. *Registration rights:* The right to register securities for public sale under the Securities Act of 1933 and state securities laws represents the most advantageous vehicle for a venture capital investor to achieve liquidity and realize a return on his investment. The potential of an enterprise to achieve a size conducive to a public offering is an imperative of most venture capital investments; accordingly, the right of the investor to participate in the public market for the company's securities is an area in which the venture capitalist will concede few limitations on his flexibility of action. Registration rights are intricately bound up in the complexities of federal and state securities regulation and must be thoroughly understood by the investor and his counsel. The key elements of a registration rights provision in a venture capital investment agreement generally include the following:

a. *Securities available for registration:* Registrable securities will invariably be limited to common stock, including shares issuable on conversion of other securities. After-acquired common stock held by the investor may also be included. If the investor is participating in a second or third round financing, he must consider to what extent his registration rights will be coordinated or "pooled" with registration rights granted to investors in previous financings.

b. *"Piggy-back" registration rights:* Investors will have the right to include shares in any registration which the company undertakes either for its own benefit or for the account of other holders of securities. Exceptions are generally made for registrations involving employee stock plans or acquisitions. "Piggy-back" registrations will frequently be unlimited in number on the theory that no significant burden is imposed on the company by requiring it to include additional shares in a registration which it is otherwise undertaking. Except for the company's initial public offering, investors may be guaranteed a minimum participation in "piggy-back" registrations.

c. *Demand registration rights:* Investors frequently obtain the right to require an issuer to register their shares upon demand and without regard to the registration of shares for the account of any other person. Demand rights assure the investor access to the public market. Theoretically, unrestricted demand registration rights enable an investor to force a company to go public; as a practical matter, demand rights are rarely, if ever, used to this end, although their presence may influence the decision of a company to go public. Because of the expense involved, demand rights may be limited in number, unless registration is available on a short-form registration statement such as Form S-3. In addition, investors may agree to limit the exercise of demand rights to the holders of a minimum specified percentage of registrable securities to avoid unduly small registrations.

d . *Marketing rights:* "Piggy-back" registration rights generally contain provisions enabling the underwriters managing the public offering to cut back the number of shares to be registered by selling securityholders on a pro rata basis if, in the underwriters' opinion, such a cutback is necessary or desirable to market the public offering effectively. If securityholders other than the venture capital investors also hold registration rights, the relative marketing priorities of the various groups, including management, in the event of a cutback must be addressed.

e . *Indemnification:* Each party will agree to indemnify the other against liabilities for which it is responsible arising out of a registration. Although the extensive indemnification provisions of an underwriting agreement will frequently supersede the terms of the investment agreement, they are nevertheless important because underwriters will typically look to the company and any major selling shareholders for indemnification on a joint and several basis and will leave those parties to their own devices to allocate any liabilities among themselves.

f . *Procedural covenants:* Many registration right provisions contain undertakings to comply with certain procedural matters involved in a registration, such as participation in the preparation of a registration statement, qualification under state securities laws and entitlement to legal opinions and accountants' comfort letters.

g . *Availability of Rule 144:* The company will agree that once it has gone public, it will file all reports and take all other action necessary to enable the investors to sell shares (which they did not include in the registration statement persuant to registration rights) in the public market under the exemption from registration contained in Rule 144 under the Securities Act of 1933.

h . *Expenses of registration:* Because of the cost involved in a registration of securities, investors will typically require the company to agree at the time of the initial investment to bear the expenses of registration, exclusive of underwriters discounts or commissions applicable to the investors' included shares.

2 . *Rights to future financings:* Venture capitalists often insist upon a right to participate in future financings by the company. On the upside, this offers the investor an opportunity to maintain or increase its interest in the success of the enterprise; on the downside, the investor receives some protection against dilution or loss of his initial investment in the event financing must be sought under distress situations. The right to participate may include:

a . *rights of first refusal* to assume the entire financing (each investor on a pro rata basis with other members of the investor group).

b . *preemptive rights* to participate in the financing to the extent that the investor's ownership percentage of the company's securities will be the same after the financing as before.

c . *rights of prior negotiation* to discuss and negotiate financing opportunities with the company prior to the company making offers to others.

First refusal and preemptive rights typically contain oversubscription rights to permit an investor to absorb any portion of the securities not subscribed for by another investor or securityholder.

3 . *Indemnification for breach of agreement:* Particularly in the case of startups, venture capital investors may require founders and/or top management to share personal responsibility for the representations and warranties made by the company in the investment agreement and to indemnify the investors for any breaches thereof. From the investors' point of view, imposing the spectre of personal liability on the insiders can be an effective means of assuring complete and accurate disclosure of all material business information. Indemnification by insiders also circumvents the anomaly of investors seeking indemnification from the company out of the capital which they have invested in the business. On the other hand, personal liability for disclosure matters which may be outside the reasonable knowledge of the entrepreneur may be an unfair burden to place on him. For this reason, in cases where personal responsibility for representations and warranties is desired, care should be taken to focus that responsibility in areas of special knowledge of the entrepreneur (e.g., ownership of proprietary rights, compliance with prior employment arrangements, etc.) and to distinguish between the risks assumed by the company and those assumed by the individual (e.g., unqualified representations versus "best knowledge" representations). Termination of indemnifica-

tion obligations often occur after a stated period of time, usually not exceeding two years, or after the issuance of audited financial statements covering a one- or two-year period.

D. *Conditions to Closing*

The use of "conditions precedent to closing" in the investment agreement, or more appropriately the satisfaction of conditions at or prior to the closing, is a device used for two principal purposes. The most obvious is to guarantee that certain fundamentals relating to the securities and the particular transaction are in place, with receipt of favorable legal opinions being a classic example. In addition, conditions are used as negotiating tools to change or affect the affairs of the company. For example, a common closing condition may involve the contemporaneous execution of a bank loan agreement satisfactory to the investor or the consummation of a significant commercial transaction with a customer.

Many venture financings contemplate a simultaneous signing of the investment agreement and closing. Consequently, there is no technical need for a set of conditions designed to cover the time period between execution of the agreement and a subsequent closing. Notwithstanding a simultaneous signing and closing, the use of express conditions serves to expedite the negotiations and to assist the closing process by serving as a checklist of actions to be taken in connection with the implementation of the transaction.

Closing conditions that are commonly seen in the capital formation process include: opinion of counsel for the company; opinion of counsel for the investor; execution of the several ancillary agreements, including employment, noncompetition and stock restriction agreements; elections and resignations of directors; and compliance certificates by senior management. Descriptions of certain of these ancillary agreements and documents are included in Section IV below.

Section IV. Terms of Investment Securities

A. *General Considerations and Descriptions*

Selection of the appropriate investment security for a specific transaction will depend upon the relative importance to the venture capitalist and the issuer of a number of factors, including the level of risk of the venture, investment objectives of the investors, capital requirements of the company, the relative interests and contributions of other securityholders, the degree to which management control by the investors is desirable, liquidity of the securities, and so on. Among the securities which are commonly used in a venture capital financing are:

- common stock
- convertible preferred stock
- convertible debt
- non-convertible preferred stock or debt coupled with common stock or common stock purchase warrants

Generally the venture capitalist will prefer to invest in a senior security which is convertible into, or carries rights to purchase, common equity. A convertible senior security affords the investor downside protection, in terms of the opportunity to recover the investment on a priority basis through redemption, repayment or liquidation preferences, with the upside potential of a liquid equity security traded at significantly appreciated values in the public market. Discussion of the relative merits and disadvantages of the various types of investment securities is beyond the scope of this article. Described in the following sections, however, are certain of the principal provisions of typical preferred stock and debt securities.

B. *Principal Terms of Preferred Stock*

Preferred stock is the investment security most frequently involved in venture capital financings because of the flexibility it offers the company and the investor in tailoring the critical issues of the investment — principally management control and recovery/return on investment. Typically the preferred stock utilized in a venture transaction is convertible into common stock and contains redemption provisions designed to enable the investor to recoup his investment if the enterprise fails to achieve its anticipated success. Convertible preferred stock provisions should address the following major issues:

1. *Dividends:* "Plain vanilla" convertible preferred stock does not generally carry mandatory dividend rights. Preferred will, however, participate with common to the extent dividends are declared. If dividends are desired, they may be on a cumulative or non-cumulative basis. Cash flow considerations will affect the ability of a startup to pay dividends.

2. *Liquidation:* Holders of preferred stock will have a priority claim over the common stockholders to the assets of the corporation in a liquidation. The liquidation preference will typically equal the original purchase price of the security plus accrued dividends. Participating preferred may also share pari passu with common stock after the liquidation preference has been distributed. Convertible preferred stock provisions usually permit the investors to elect liquidation treatment in the event of a merger or acquisition in which the company is not the surviving entity.

3. *Voting rights:* Convertible preferred stock issued in venture capital transactions often votes with the common stock on all matters and is entitled to one vote for each share of common into which the preferred may be converted. In addition, the holders of convertible preferred stock, voting separately as a class, may have the right to veto certain corporate transactions affecting the convertible preferred stock (such as the issuance of senior securities, mergers, acquisitions and amendment of stock terms or charter provisions). Other preferential voting rights may include:

a. class vote for election of directors.

b. extraordinary voting rights to elect a majority of the board of directors upon a breach of the terms of the convertible preferred stock, such as a failure to pay dividends or make mandatory redemptions or default in the performance of financial or other covenants which may be contained in the convertible preferred stock provisions or underlying investment agreement.

4. *Conversion:* Holders of convertible preferred stock may convert their shares into common stock at their discretion (except as limited by automatic conversion obligations). Conversion provisions should address the following matters:

a. automatic conversion upon the occurrence of certain events, principally the completion of a public offering or the attainment of specified financial goals.

b. mechanics of conversion.

c. conversion ratio, usually expressed by a formula based upon original purchase price, which initially yields a one-for-one conversion factor.

d. adjustment of conversion ratio to take into account (i) stock splits, stock dividends, consolidations, etc. and (ii) "dilutive" common stock issuances, that is, sales of common stock at prices lower than those paid by the investors.

e. Certification of adjusted conversion ratios by independent accountants.

The nature of the anti-dilution adjustments can have a dramatic effect on the number of common shares issuable upon conversion of the preferred stock. "Rachet-down" anti-dilution provisions apply the lowest sale price for any shares of common stock (or equivalents) sold by the company after the issuance of the preferred stock as the adjusted conversion value.

"Formula" or "weighted average" anti-dilution provisions adjust the conversion value by application of a weighted average formula based upon both sale price and number of common shares sold. Anti-dilution provisions generally carve out a predetermined pool of shares which may be issued to employees without triggering an adjustment of the conversion ratio.

5. *Redemption:* Redemption offers the investor a means of recovering his initial investment and the issuer an opportunity to eliminate the preferential rights held by the holders of the senior security. Topics to be addressed include:

a. optional or mandatory redemption.

b. stepped-up redemption price or redemption premium designed to provide investors a certain appreciated return on the investment (NB: "unreasonable redemption premium" issue under IRC Section 305).

c. desirability of a sinking fund.

d. redemption call by the company.

It should be noted that the prospect of mandatory redemption or redemption upon call by the issuer may force the holder of convertible preferred stock to exercise his conversion privilege lest he lose the upside potential of his investment.

C. *Principal Terms of Debt Securities*

The purchase of debt securities will enable the venture capitalist to receive a current return on his investment through receipt of interest payments. In the case of a convertible debt instrument, the interest rate will be below market rates because of the equity feature coupled with it. Although the terms of convertible debt may be structured to resemble preferred stock in many aspects, significant differences between the two securities do exist. First, debt securities do not carry the right to vote for the election of directors or on other stockholder matters. Accordingly, the investor's ability to influence management of the company directly is diminished and he must resort to voting agreements and proxies in order to participate in the election of directors or, alternatively, rely on indirect means of influence such as the affirmative and negative covenants contained in the investment agreement. It should further be noted that the investor's status as a creditor of the company in any bankruptcy proceedings may be affected by principles of "equitable subordination" to the extent that equity-like control is exercised, with the result that the investor's debt security is subordinated in right of payment to the claims of other third party creditors of the company who do not exercise control. Second, the investor's right to receive interest under a debt instrument is more secure than the right to receive dividends on a preferred stock, inasmuch as payment of dividends may be restricted by state corporate laws relating to legally available funds and by the requirement that dividends must be declared by the board of directors. Finally, although a debt security may rank prior to preferred stock in terms of a claim on corporate assets in liquidation, this advantage is at the cost of creating a weaker balance sheet, which may have adverse effects in terms of trade and commercial bank credit, even where subordination provisions are present.

The following principal issues are generally addressed in the structuring of a venture capital investment in debt securities:

1. *Interest rate:* Interest will be at a fixed rate, below market if debt is convertible or coupled with common stock or stock purchase warrants. Because of cash flow considerations of the issuer, interest payments may be deferred for a period of time.

2. *Repayment:* Repayment of principal is often scheduled in quarterly, semi-annual or annual installments commencing four to six years into the term, or in a single "balloon" payment at maturity.

3. *Optional prepayment:* The company may elect to prepay the debt, often at a premium. Since prepayment will have the effect of extinguishing any conversion rights, the right to prepay will be deferred generally to such times as initial principal installments fall due. Issuance of stock purchase warrants in lieu of a conversion feature in the debt instrument will avoid this problem.

4. *Conversion:* The debt instrument may be converted into common stock at a fixed price at any time. Conversion terms, including anti-dilution provisions, will be similar to convertible preferred stock.

5. *Subordination:* Debt is generally subordinated to bank and other institutional borrowings and may be thus viewed as equity by lenders. Complex subordination provisions are often required to regulate the relationships between senior lenders and subordinated noteholders in the event of defaults, insolvency, etc.

6. *Affirmative and negative covenants:* Debt instruments are tied into extensive affirmative and negative undertakings by the company, which are usually contained in the purchase agreement. In addition to standard covenants used in a venture capital financing, these may include lengthy financial covenants of the variety typical in a commercial lending transaction.

7. *Defaults:* Defaults include material breaches of representations and warranties; breach of covenants which are not remedied within a cure period; non-payment of principal and interest on debt instruments; acceleration (cross-default) of senior debt; insolvency and bankruptcy.

8. *Security:* Generally a debt instrument will be issued to a venture capitalist on an unsecured basis, although collateral is sometimes given in asset-based transactions such as leveraged buyouts.

Another common exception to the general rule is an SBIC financing, in which adequate collateral and personal guaranties are often required.

Section V.   Ancillary Agreements and Documents

A.   *Stockholders Agreement*

The stockholders agreement is designed to control the transfer and voting of the equity securities of the company by key stockholders so that stable ownership and management of the enterprise may be maintained for the term of the investment. This is accomplished through restrictions on the sale of stock by insiders, which have the effect of limiting the stockholder group to persons who are known quantities to the investors, and through voting agreements, which assure that the balanced composition of the board of directors will be perpetuated. The principal provisions contained in a typical stockholders agreement to achieve these results are:

1. *Right of first refusal:* Key management stockholders will grant the company and/or the investors the right to purchase their shares on the same terms as those contained in a bona fide offer from a third party. Investors participate in the right of first refusal on a pro rata basis and have oversubscription rights to acquire any offered shares which are not picked up by another investor. Rights of first refusal are generally not extended to the company or insiders by the investors since the existence of such terms would tend to chill any sale of an entire block of shares by the investors to a third party. Transfers of shares by way of gift to members of an insider's family or as collateral in a bona fide loan transaction are permitted, provided the transferee or pledgee also agrees in writing to be bound by the agreement.

2. *Buyout provisions:* Some stockholder agreements provide that the company and/or the investors will have an option to purchase the shares of any insider at fair market value upon the occurrence of certain contingencies, such as death, personal bankruptcy or attachment of shares by legal process as in the divorce context. Detailed procedures, usually involving one or more appraisals by disinterested persons, are provided to assure a fair valuation of the stock.

3. *Right to participate in insider sales:* Although philosophically at odds with a right of first refusal, a stockholder agreement may provide that the investors have a right to

participate alongside management insiders in any sale to third parties. Although rarely exercised, this "co-sale" right limits the ability of management to bail out of the company leaving the investors at risk to recover their investment. Often this right of co-sale is triggered only by a sale which would have the effect of transferring actual or effective voting control to a third party.

4. *Voting requirements:* All parties will generally agree to vote all shares for the election of directors in favor of specified nominees of the respective groups.

Restrictions under applicable state law need to be examined to determine the legality of stockholder agreements in any given jurisdiction, as well as to verify compliance with state procedural and substantive requirements. Unless otherwise limited by state law (ten years in Massachusetts), stockholder agreements will generally terminate upon the earlier of a public offering by the company or the expiration of a stated period of time.

B. *Employee Stock Purchase Agreements*

Venture capital investors typically insist that appropriate equity incentives be implemented to attract, retain and motivate key employees. Both the entrepreneurs and investors are willing to suffer dilution of their respective equity interests (anywhere in a range from 5% to 15% of fully diluted equity) to achieve this end. The investment agreement will specify a pool of shares to be set aside for employee purchases and exempt the issuance of those shares from the various negative covenants, anti-dilution provisions and pre-emptive rights contained in the investment agreement and the terms of the investment securities. Establishment of appropriate employee stock plans is frequently a condition of closing of the investment. Incentive objectives and tax considerations play a significant role in determining the shape of an employee equity program. Among the typical employee equity incentives are the following:

1. *stock purchase plans,* providing for an outright sale to key employees, often at a bargain price, with the company retaining an option to repurchase the shares on a lapsing basis (generally over four or five years) if the employee terminates employment for any reason.

2. *incentive stock options,* enabling the employee to purchase shares with advantageous tax consequences at the fair market value on the date the option was granted.

3. *non-qualified stock options,* which may be granted in amounts which exceed the aggregate dollar limitations for incentive stock options under the Internal Revenue Code

and which may have exercise prices less than fair market value at date of issuance and other terms not available under incentive stock options.

4. *"junior" common stock,* which is an equity security bearing only a percentage of the voting, dividend, liquidation and other rights of a straight common stock and which is automatically converted into common stock upon the attainment of certain specified objectives, such as revenue and profit goals. Although "junior" common stock was a popular incentive vehicle through the end of 1983, its continued use and attractiveness as a method of compensating management have been called into question by recent actions taken by the Securities and Exchange Commission and proposed to be taken by the Financial Accounting Standards Board (FASB).

In all circumstances (other than incentive stock options) consideration must be given to the application of Section 83 of the Internal Revenue Code to issuances of stock to employees. Section 83 provides that an employee is required to recognize income in respect of property (including corporate securities) transferred to him in connection with the performance of services in an amount equal to the difference between the fair value of the property and the amount paid therefor. In the case of property subject to restrictions which lapse over time (such as forfeiture restrictions or repurchase options) the income is recognized at the time the restrictions lapse. Thus, an employee who acquires stock at a low purchase price in the early years of an enterprise and whose rights to those shares "vest" as forfeiture restrictions lapse over a period of years will recognize income based on the appreciated value of those shares as each installment lapses. Section 83(b) of the Code ameliorates the harsh effect of this provision by permitting a taxpayer to elect to include the value of the transferred property in income in the year of receipt by filing a special election.

In *Alves et al. v. Commissioner,* 79 TC 864, CCH Tax Court Reports Dec. 39, 501 (1982), the Tax Court applied Section 83 to a founding stockholder of a new company who acquired shares subject to a repurchase option granted to the company and exercisable upon his termination of employment prior to the end of a specified period. As a result of this decision, founding stockholders should consider taking the precaution of filing Section 83(b) elections when shares are initially acquired in order to prevent assessment of significant tax liabilities when those shares vest at appreciated values in later years.

C. *Employee Confidentiality and Proprietary Agreements*

Protection and preservation of the "intellectual capital" of an enterprise is of paramount importance to the venture capital investor, especially where the portfolio company is engaged in product development activities on the leading edge of technologies. to secure the company's claim to its valuable proprietary and business rights, investors are increasingly requiring that founders and other key employees enter into confidential non-disclosure and invention agreements with the company. These agreements typically provide that the employee (i) will not disclose company trade secrets or rights to third parties or use such rights for any purpose, in each case other than in connection with the company's business; and (ii) will disclose and convey to the company all inventions developed by the employee during the course of employment. Such agreements often obtain the commitment of the employee to cooperate with the company, even after his employment is terminated, to the extent necessary to perfect the company's record ownership of the inventions.

In addition, such agreements often contain acknowledgment that the individual is not bound by any obligations to a former employer which would prevent or restrict his employment with the company and that his performance of services for the company does not involve the violation of the proprietary rights of any former employer. Founding stockholders may also agree to non-competition covenants.

D. *Legal Opinion*

The favorable legal opinion of company counsel generally covers the legality of the securities, compliance with state and federal securities laws and related matters. If the company is involved in litigation, company counsel may be requested to express a position. Likewise, if patents are critical to the company's business, a favorable opinion of patent counsel may also be required. A common error is to confuse the opinion of legal counsel with due diligence. Counsel is not a surety for business or legal uncertainties; the opinion is not a substitute for factual investigation.

Venture Capital in Practice: A Case History

Timothy M. Pennington

Timothy M. Pennington *is a general partner of Brentwood Associates, Los Angeles, a venture capital firm active in a wide range of investments, from startups to established companies, as well as special situations. Mr. Pennington, originally an engineer, has been involved with venture capital and corporate finance since 1966. In 1972, he left the investment banking firm of Blyth & Co. as a vice president to join Brentwood Associates at its formation.*

How does the venture capitalist actually make an investment decision? How does he put into practice the principles described in the other articles in this book?

The following is a case history of how an investment opportunity was pursued by our firm. Some information has been changed to conceal the identity of the specific situation. An important thought to keep in mind is that each investment opportunity is unique and has its own distinctive characteristics, therefore, details covered in this case history may not apply to other projects. Furthermore, situations will vary because venture capitalists have their own ideas of the relative importance of the various aspects of a business venture. Different venture groups, therefore, attach varying degrees of importance to the elements of a given investment opportunity. Also, the key elements often vary between differing situations.

This is a case history of a startup project. The description does not include all of the investigation and analysis that was done, but highlights the most important aspects. The project involved four men in their mid-30s with an idea. Working out of their homes, these four men had written a business plan and had developed a working prototype of the product they intended to exploit.

The Business Plan and the Management

Our firm started with a thorough reading of the business plan. The plan was extremely well formulated and written. This was an important positive factor because there were not many historical facts and figures to analyze in this startup venture. The product involved was a labor- and cost-saving electromechanical device. It didn't do anything in a revolutionary way, but it was an evolutionary improvement over existing products in terms of cost/performance. It was a "medium technology" device — meaning it utilized existing state-of-the-art knowledge and materials — and was not pushing any new frontiers of esoteric technology.

The company wanted to raise $500,000, which their projections showed would last until positive cash flow from operations was reached. This was one of the items that would need careful scrutiny because the amount of capital required is a pivotal element in all deals.

After becoming interested in the opportunity from reading the business plan, we had an initial meeting with the four men and discussed all aspects of the venture as a general overview. We asked for an extensive list of references for the men because the requirement of good management, very important in all deals, is even more critical in a startup. We spent a considerable amount of time telephoning these references. In addition to the references provided by the men, we developed our own additional references wherever possible. As one might expect, it is infrequent that critical references are volunteered. The additional references might come from any number of sources, including the superiors, peers, and subordinates from prior business relationships of the men. What we learned was that the CEO was considered bright, hard working, honest, experienced, and excellent in the marketing area, a good leader, strongly motivated to succeed, a little headstrong with a large ego, decisive and able to make tough decisions, weak in manufacturing and engineering, and, overall, very highly regarded. His weaknesses included a tendency to be overly optimistic and excessively loyal to his people, which he manifested by being too slow to make necessary personnel changes. The number-two man was also highly regarded and was somewhat similar in strengths. The technical members of the team seemed to be quite competent, but, due to the nature of their employment history references, we were not able to obtain answers to questions we had about them. We decided to investigate further in this area.

During the reference-checking effort, we continued to make our own personal appraisal of the people through additional face-to-face business meetings, as well as through a few social dinner visits.

We think it is very important to get to know people through several meetings and in different kinds of circumstances. A much better working relationship, both before and after a financing, can be developed if good communication, understanding, and rapport can be established. The determination of the degree to which people "wear well" is important to both parties.

Our overall impression of the management people at this point was very positive. The one element that was bothersome was evidence of a tendency toward stubbornness, coupled with procrastination in the personnel area. We considered this a potential major negative because, as the deal had been presented to us, management would own slightly over 50% of the company and, therefore, would be able to ignore counsel if they chose.

Product Development

The incomplete development of the product was, of course, a concern to us, particularly because one functional element had not yet been proven. Management claimed this function was not very important and, in any case, easy to complete. Our marketing analysis convinced us that the function was important.

That raised two questions for us: (1) Was management not well informed about its own market, or were they not leveling with us? (2) What were the technical risks that would be assumed by going ahead with the financing before development was completed?

To answer the first question, we decided to do further market research by talking to additional people in the field, including potential users of the product and industry experts. We also recontacted some of the previous references, with more concentration on this particular question. What we found was a bigger area of gray. To some potential users the feature in question was not critical; to others it was so important that they wouldn't purchase without it. And, of course, there were attitudes between these two extremes. This indicated that, if the technical problems could not be overcome, the company wouldn't necessarily be out of business, but the total market size would be substantially reduced. The implication was that the valuation of the company (the price) would have to be lower to compensate for the possibility of a much smaller upside investment potential.

Additional discussions with management concerning the importance of the product feature convinced us that the difference in views we held from those we thought they held was honest and explainable and not the result of misrepresentations, which would have killed the deal immediately from our standpoint. There was, however, still a meaningful difference of opinion as to the impact on the company if this functional element could not be incorporated into the product.

To help us answer the question about the technical risk, and to evaluate the competence of the two technical people, we hired a consultant. We used a man who was employed in another company in which we had an investment. Because of our past experience with him, we had a high degree of confidence in his abilities and judgment and felt that his competence was high in the areas we were asking him to appraise. His report indicated that he believed the feature could be developed, but he was concerned about the amount of development time and dollars required. There was, of course, no assurance of success.

Market Analysis

Our analysis of the market included talking to industry experts, reading industry surveys and literature of the competing companies, and detailed questioning of the management. In obtaining an industry expert, you would like to find the universally best informed person who has had direct experience with the particular subject and is, in fact, an expert. Often, such a person does not exist or is a competitor. However, usually a number of persons can be identified who have sufficient experience to be of meaningful help. In this case, we were partially lucky. We could not find anyone who was broadly enough based to cover all aspects of the market that was being addressed by the company because its product cut across several market segments. Therefore, we tried to separate the problem. The company suggested one person, and we found a second one by following leads through several levels of subsequent references. With the two men, we were able to develop most of the information we felt was appropriate in making a decision.

From all of the above, we became convinced that the product was a very real advance and that the market was large and ready to accept the product, providing the company used a reasonable marketing effort.

The size of the market is usually a very important factor. We felt that, in five years, the annual shipments of products to the market in which this company would be competing could reach $200 million. Assuming that the technical feature in question was made part of the company's product offering, we believed that the company could attain about a 20% share of the market, or $40 million. Without the technical feature, however, the market size might be cut in half. This judgment ("guess" is probably a more accurate word) suggested that the risk of the functional technical feature's not working changed the potential of the operation from a high profit margin $40 million revenue business to a medium profit margin $20 million business, with an even greater impact on potential value. Instead of earning an expected $3.2 million (8% net after tax on $40 million in sales) and being worth, say, $57.6 million (a price/earnings ratio of

18) the company might earn $1.0 million (5% on $20 million) and be worth $10 million (a price/earning ratio of 10). This was more than a fivefold reduction in potential value. Obviously, there are other factors involved in a return on investment evaluation, such as the amount of additional capital and, therefore, dilution that must be obtained as growth continues. The figures given only illustrate the effects of potential market size and market share on company value.

In appraising the market share that might be achieved, competition needed to be considered. There was no existing competitor who would be offering a comparable product. However, it was expected that, as a sizable market developed, competition would appear. Existing manufacturers of the products for this market could be expected to react with new features, new products, price reductions, or all of these. In addition, once the new product becomes visible and begins to make a market impact, new competitors will become interested in the market. These will include other startup companies and product introductions by companies in an associated field who recognize the market potential. In this case, the market appeared to be big enough to accommodate active, forceful competition.

The recognizable potential competitors were studied, their relative strengths appraised, and estimates made as to possible new company efforts. This, coupled with our market analysis, led to our guess that this company could reasonably capture 10% of the market.

Capital Adequacy

After sizing up the market and the company's potential, the question of capital adequacy was considered. Doing this is of major importance, because, if not enough money is raised, the investor is faced with several negative situations. First, more money will have to be raised, which will dilute the investor's ownership and lower the rate of return on which the investment decision was based. Second, if the company cannot raise the money, the investor is faced with the prospect of having to put up more money, if he is legally or financially able to do so, or lose a significant part of the original investment even though the company may be making good progress. Times change, and even though the company is progressing, outside money may not be available. Third, the company management will have to devote a substantial amount of time to the money-raising effort and, therefore, will be forced to reduce its attention to the problem of running the business. This is a high and very real cost to a young company, and sometimes it can be near fatal.

All of the above elements need to be balanced against trying to raise too much money. The greater the amount of money, the greater the number of partners needed in the deal, the more time

it will take, and the greater the dilution to management and to the investor. The answer to "what is the right amount of money" depends on a number of factors. These include the investors' cash resources and willingness to provide future financing, the length of operating time that seems reasonable under the circumstances before reentering the "money-raising mode," and the probability that the indicated time will have enabled the company to make sufficient progress so that it can obtain additional funds at a higher price to reduce dilution.

In the case in question, management's projections seemed unrealistic in several ways: sales growth rate and profit margins both seemed too high, and the debt position also seemed too large, relative to equity. A slower sales buildup would decrease the expected need for cash due to a lower requirement for working capital, but, in this case, lower profits would more than offset this benefit. The net result was a belief that at least another $1 million would be needed in 12 to 18 months, and probably a third financing would be required in the third or fourth year.

We then did an analysis of the company's prospective viability. We put emphasis on the salability of its products and the cost and capital structure of the business. In the product area, we took a user's point of view in looking at the benefits and costs of buying the company's product. We applied both the payback and present value methods of analysis. We looked at the various elements of user savings: reduced labor, high productivity, reduced material costs, less downtime, and some intangibles such as safety and easier governmental compliance. We then compared the savings that would be made over a period of time with the initial costs plus extra marginal operating costs. It appeared to us that in a typical user environment, the product would achieve payback within two years and an internal rate of return of approximately 40% per year, which, in this industry, was considered highly attractive. Based on this analysis and on our discussions with prospective customers, we concluded that customers would be willing to pay the proposed or even a higher sales price.

We then concentrated on the company's cost and capital structure. The cost of goods sold, operating expense levels, planned personnel levels, development expense levels, and the like, were carefully evaluated for reasonableness. We concluded that, while the company's projections were too optimistic, there was sufficient margin in the product to sustain a profitable business. The overall business plan was well formulated in most areas, including manpower loading, new product development, marketing strategy, and overall business strategy.

We summed up our view of the proposal's pluses and minuses, made our own forecasts of the company's sales, earnings, and capital requirements, and did an analysis of the expected return on our investment at the proposed financing terms. We concluded that the return was not high enough for the risks we perceived. We weren't willing, therefore, to invest on the basis suggested by management, although we were sufficiently interested to want the investment on modified terms.

Making the Deal
After much discussion with the company on the terms of the deal, which, in addition to price, included type of security, seniority, and income, we, and the company, were able to narrow the gap substantially. The only major problem was the more optimistic view of the future held by management, as is generally the case. We were only able to break the deadlock by reluctantly agreeing to a "performance deal." This was accomplished by investing at a price that was acceptable to management but considered by us as too high with a stipulation that the price would be subject to downward adjustment if the company did not meet its projections.

Successive levels of profit achievement, or lack thereof, were stipulated at which the price of our investment would be reduced, thereby increasing our ownership of the company. If management performed anywhere near its projected levels, they would receive their asking price, and we would be quite happy with that kind of performance. If they didn't perform, the price we paid would be reduced and the percent of the company we owned would be increased, thereby bringing the valuation more in line with the "real value" as perceived by us. This also reduced our concern about the shortcomings of management, since our influence increased as results became less positive.

We dislike this kind of arrangement, however, and use it very infrequently because it can create a conflict or differences in motivations on certain issues and can get in the way of the most objective business decisions. For example, increasing research expenditures might be a wise, long-run decision, but it decreases near-term earnings, thereby reducing the investment price and, therefore, diluting management's equity.

In this case, we had high regard for the people involved, felt their objectives and ours were quite compatible, and were able to agree on how potential conflict situations would be handled in the future. We made the investment on that basis.

As mentioned, each investment is different and subject to varying degrees of objectivity, ranging from precise statistical analysis, to almost total, seat-of-the-pants guessing. However, in the last several years, investment decisions within the venture community have increasingly involved very careful objective analysis and less reliance on instinctive reactions and guesswork.

The Key to Successful Leveraged Buyouts: Analysis of Management

Gregory P. Barber

Gregory P. Barber *joined Narragansett Capital Corporation, Providence, Rhode Island, one of the nation's largest publicly held venture capital companies, as a vice president in October 1978. He is responsible for new investments. Prior to joining Narragansett, Mr. Barber was a vice president in the National Accounts Division at Industrial National Bank of Rhode Island. He holds a Bachelor of Arts degree from Boston College.*

There are many quantitative and qualitative aspects to the analysis undertaken by an outside equity investor considering a leveraged buyout proposal. It is difficult to segregate any of these aspects and place it uppermost on the list of ingredients that make a leveraged buyout successful. Clearly, the financial profile of the investment must be right. The product or service must have market acceptance, the financing must be appropriate, and the people must be capable of managing the company. Far too often the outside equity investor becomes enamored with quantitative items, such as profit margins, market share, historical growth rates, and so on, and becomes strictly qualitative about the people who will be responsible for producing the results necessary for a successful venture. We have tried to augment our own judgment (often called "gut feeling") with a quantitative review of the management we propose to support in an investment. We have also learned that risk increases proportionately with the learning curve that management must overcome. We have divided the risk spectrum into three sections which are described below.

1. We have found that the safest leveraged buyout is one that contemplates no management changes whatsoever. A good example of this is a corporate divestiture to the management group that has (and has had for some time) the operating responsibility for the business being divested. Not only is there a zero learning curve, but also the management will have full knowledge of potential problems that are not readily apparent to outsiders seeking to purchase the business.

   We always undertake a thorough investigation to uncover hidden liabilities, but nonetheless, we get great comfort from knowing that the individuals who have been running the business are willing to invest their own hard-earned money in the same venture.

   This type of situation is less traumatic for customers and vendors of the company, as they will continue to deal with the same people. Our investment in Company # 1, which is described later in this article, exemplifies this type of management risk.

2. If an attractive opportunity presents itself and it does not include existing management, the risk is enhanced. This is obvious, as there is no longer an "insider" for the outside equity investor to participate with in the acquisition evaluation, and hidden liabilities could later surface. To hedge against this risk, the new investor can ask for more representations and warranties in the purchase agreement. These are valuable only if the seller is financially capable of satisfying future claims or a sufficient escrow is arranged. Nonetheless, an operating risk has been created, for the new management must take control and overcome a learning process.

   When this type of opportunity arises, we feel most comfortable if the new management has a successful track record in precisely the same business. This normally means that the new management has been with a direct competitor of the company being acquired. This competitive experience proves helpful in assessing acquisition risks in addition to shortening the learning curve.

   On the plus side, new management might very well bring a new perspective and vitality to the company. This type of situation represents greater risk and greater reward than the "status quo" example described earlier. Our investment in Company # 2 typifies this kind of situation.

3. When an outside equity investor ventures beyond the management parameters described in Examples 1 and 2, the risk factor will increase dramatically. At Narragansett Capital Corporation (NCC) we are fully aware that the leveraged financial approach we employ creates sufficient risk without being compounded by the uncertainty of whether management can be successful in the business under consideration. To underscore this concern, I have described our investment in Company #3. We did much

soul-searching as to management's ability to make a transition from an industrial products to a consumer products business before agreeing to provide the necessary financing. This investment is off to a healthy start, and it is used to exemplify the outer limit of the management risk spectrum that we will entertain.

Company #1

The financial profile of this investment created immediate interest on our part. As part of an overall corporate strategy to concentrate on branded consumer products, the parent company decided to divest this division, which operates as a converter of fabric for the home furnishings and home decorative industries. The price was set at a slight premium over book value and was fair as a multiple of historic and projected earnings. This financial profile suggested that our highly leveraged approach could be utilized, and the following financing package was arranged:

Senior Bank Revolving Credit	$4,250,000
INCC 10-year Subordinated Loan	2,450,000
Equity	500,000
Total	$7,200,000

The earnings and cash flow of the business showed that the acquisition debt could be serviced properly, and our investigation revealed that the industry outlook was satisfactory. As for management, our investigation revealed the following:

The president and CEO: had full profit and loss responsibility for this business for over 10 years. Furthermore, he had been a stockholder of the company when it was originally sold to the parent company in the early 1970s and had spent over 30 years with the company. The record showed that he was a consistent and proven money-maker in this industry, and his knowledge of the company was unquestionable. Clearly, he was a "10" on a scale of 10.

As for the second-tier operating managers, all of whom became our shareholder partners, their depth of experience was equally impressive. Among three individuals, there were nearly 90 years of experience in the industry of which 60 had been spent at this particular company. This combined in-depth knowledge of the industry and the company proved to be very helpful in negotiating a satisfactory agreement with the seller.

We expect the business to be run exactly as it had been in the past. The continuation of their fine record will result in an excellent return on investment for all shareholders. These management characteristics, coupled with a sound financial profile, make for a very sound and safe investment from an outside equity investor's point of view.

Company #2

This company operates 24 discount health and beauty aid stores in the greater Pittsburgh area. The two owner/managers decided to sell, and we were approached by an outside group seeking to purchase the company. This did not look like an attractive opportunity on the surface because of a relatively flat sales and earnings performance in recent years. Our interest in the investment changed dramatically after meeting the proposed new management team. The key operating manager had excellent credentials in the health and beauty aid business. His 17 years of experience began at the level of assistant store manager and progressed through his present position as a district manager with profit and loss responsibility for 60 stores. His two proposed partners augmented this "hands-on" operating experience with strong administrative and control skills developed in running their own successful wholesale drug business.

During the initial meetings, it became obvious that our proposed partners had identified the strengths and weaknesses of the business. This, in itself, was not particularly significant, but their detailed plan to exploit strengths and correct weaknesses led us to believe that they had an excellent chance of improving the present performance. The new CEO proposed to revamp all key areas, including purchasing, merchandising, staffing, and so on, while the other partners would concentrate on the implementation of new inventory controls and management information systems. The demonstrated track record of all the individuals in the areas in which they would contribute convinced us to make this investment.

It should be noted that the financial profile of this investment was fairly conservative. In other words, the price was a relatively low multiple of earnings, and the new company would be able to meet its debt obligations even if earnings decreased. The debt service coverage ratio was initially over two-to-one, and it would increase to three or four-to-one once projections were met. It would be ill-advised to introduce new management into an investment that financially offers little or no margin for error. We consider this type of investment to have more opportunities for a higher return on investment than Example #1 because new management will implement new ideas and bring needed vitality to a rather stagnant company. Nonetheless, we will only attempt this if our downside position is limited by a conservative financial structure.

Company #3

This 100-year-old company became available in mid-1979 when the major shareholder chose to devote more time to personal activities. It was brought to our attention by an individual who had been seeking to purchase a company for the past several months. The business itself had an excellent record as a manufacturer of hair care products, and the proposed price was fair relative to earnings and assets being acquired. Our leveraged formula appeared to be appropriate, and the following financing was arranged:

Senior Bank Term Loan	$ 900,000
NCC 10-year Subordinated Loan	900,000
Equity	200,000
Total	$2,000,000

The proposal looked acceptable financially, and the business had a stable earnings record. The management analysis was considerably more difficult. First, there were to be no members of existing management included as stockholders. In addition, the present top management planned to leave the company almost immediately after the sale. There would be no employment or consulting contracts with these individuals. Second, the new team (our partners) were coming from outside of the industry. The company operated as a consumer products business selling to the major chains and mass merchandisers. Our partners had backgrounds in the plastics industry, but of a commercial rather than consumer nature. Nonetheless, after considerable deliberation, we decided to proceed.

What factors induced us to take this risk?

1. It was a very conservative capitalization in which historical earnings would enable the new company to pay interest and principal on its debt and have a substantial surplus. This conservative capitalization would enable the business to withstand a few errors in judgment made by the new management.

2. The capabilities of the new management were verified by a number of good references who emphasized the strong integrity of the individuals. The latter is important in any evaluation of management, but especially so in this case. We felt that it was absolutely necessary for management to communicate freely and honestly with us as they underwent the learning process in their new business. They have, in fact, encountered problems that were not fully exposed prior to closing. We have been kept fully informed, however, and many of these problems are now behind us. The investment seems to be headed in the right direction. We feel strongly at NCC that good news can wait, but bad news cannot.

Management analysis can be a very difficult process. We feel that while "gut feeling" and the "right chemistry" are important factors, the outside equity investor should have hard data to support convictions about management. Our business is one of selecting winners, and we must always use all available resources to make decisions.

Sources of Business Development Financing

Most entrepreneurs are unaware of the myriad of financing sources available to developing businesses. This section of *PRATT'S GUIDE* describes a variety of capital and other resources available for potential entrepreneurs.

The organized venture capital industry has widespread interests, presently has more capital available for investment than at any other time in its history and its professional managers are actively seeking new investment opportunities in all stages of business development. Informal investors such as family, friends and business associates are reemerging and they are a primary source of pre-startup financing. In addition, there have been a number of funds formed in the past few years specifically to provide seed capital and to work with the entrepreneur in the early stages of the development of the business. Research and development partnership or equity partnership financing offers excellent tax advantages for investors and, in many cases, can work successfully in conjunction with later venture capital financing. The Small Business Administration (SBA) programs including both Small Business Investment Companies (SBICs) and SBA-guaranteed loans can be an excellent source for those companies meeting the SBA's criteria. More than $3 billion has been invested by SBICs in the last 25 years. Minority Enterprise Small Business Investment Companies (MESBICs), an arm of the SBIC program, assist minority and socially disadvantaged entrepreneurs in financing their businesses. In addition, venture capital subsidiaries of major corporations are becoming significant providers of independent business development financing.

This section highlights the unique characteristics of each source and presents analyses of the investment objectives as well as of the preferred type of investments and structures of these sources. This information should assist the entrepreneur in identifying those sources most apt to finance his venture.

The Organized Venture Capital Community

Stanley E. Pratt

See previous background description.

Peter Drucker, in his 1976 book, "The Unseen Revolution: How Pension Fund Socialism Came to America," discusses the profound changes in U.S. capital markets brought about through the growing domination of investment capital by pension funds. "We are organizing a capital market totally unequipped to supply entrepreneurial capital needs," he said, and further pointed out that "the problems of the small but growing business are dissimilar from those of the established big or fair-sized businesses. They require a different investment policy, different relationships to management, and a different understanding of business economics, management, and dynamics." As a solution, he proffered that, "What is needed, therefore, are new capital market institutions specifically provided to give these new, young, growing businesses the capital (and the management guidance) they need; and which, at the same time, can act as investment vehicles suited for the fiduciary, the asset manager trustee."

The organized venture capital community has been evolving since the 1960s to perform this role, and now serves as an effective vehicle to distribute capital for business development investment. While the total capital committed to professional venture investment management is still a small segment of the nation's vast financial marketplace, a recognized, disproportionately large benefit is accruing from its investment in the most productive segment of the American economy.

As a result of the productivity of these investments, and the current emphasis on investment versus consumption, the capital committed to professional venture capital firms is increasing. Total capital committed to this pool was approximately $2.5 billion to $3 billion in 1969 and remained at about that level through 1977 (additions roughly equaled withdrawals during that period). In 1978, however, with the capital gains tax reduction, a dramatic expansion commenced such that by the end of 1985 the pool totaled over $18 billion. Annual venture capital disbursements from this pool averaged approximately $365 million per annum from 1970 through 1977, grew to $550 million in 1978, almost doubled to about $1 billion per annum in 1979 and 1980, and increased dramatically to $2.8 billion in 1983 and $3 billion in 1984. During the past decade, there have been approximately 400 to 600 firms involved in making business development investments, with today's active participants better capitalized and more experienced than ever before. The major components of the venture industry are: independent private venture capital firms, Small Business Investment Companies (SBICs) and venture capital subsidiaries of large financial institutions and industrial corporations.

Independent Private Venture Capital Firms

The principal institutional source of venture capital is independent private venture capital firms. These include the family groups involved with venture capital investment such as the Rockefeller, Phipps and Whitney organizations that were the predecessors for the industry today. However, greater significance is now allotted to the professional partnerships and corporations funded by pension funds, major corporations, individuals and families, endowments and foundations, insurance companies and foreign investors. There are presently over 300 independent firms in the U.S. — approximately 200 of which were formed in the last seven years — which invest principally in equity in the full range of situations from seed and startups to relatively mature companies and management/leveraged buyouts. These funds range in capital size from $10 million to $60 million, although some are smaller or larger. Investment activity is normally at a rate of 10 to 15 new commitments per year with each commitment receiving from $250,000 to more than $1 million.

As the major source of classic venture development funding, independent firms adopt substantially different investment orientations. Some groups specialize in early-stage business developments such as startups and even seed financings, while others prefer expansion financings or management/leveraged buyout transactions. Management/leveraged buyouts enable the operating management of a division of a larger corporation, or of a privately owned business, to purchase the existing business. Also, a number of groups operate balanced funds which invest across the entire spectrum of business development investment interests. Most of these groups invest the major portion of their funds in technology-related businesses, although a growing number are seeking other manufacturing, distribution and even consumer-oriented investments. The most critical considerations for these investors are a credible management team, an identified market niche for a product with high growth potential, and the resulting possibility of developing a major new business.

Independent venture firms are generally active investors that work in conjunction with the operating managements to develop a significant business within a five to seven year time frame. They are seldom passive investors, and they will provide assistance in such areas as planning, personnel development, marketing, supplier relationships and future financing requirements. Seasoned venture capitalists can bring their experience in prior new business development to support new entrepreneurs. Independent venture firms also carefully monitor ongoing operations, serve as a sounding board for problem resolution and are active participants in business development decisions.

Small Business Investment Companies (SBICs)
Of the approximately 375 regular SBICs licensed by the Federal government, some 200 are primarily oriented towards venture capital investments. The balance are principally engaged in making loans to small businesses or in making investments in specific businesses such as grocery markets or movies. Lending SBICs represent the only institutional source of long-term capital for those small businesses that may be successful but clearly lack the potential to become major businesses. SBICs usually have a minimum private equity capital of $500,000 and this may range as high as $10 million. In addition, they have access to Government loans to achieve three-to-one (for lenders) or four-to-one (for venture capital investors) leveraging of the private equity capital, thereby providing a total investment potential of four or five times the private capital. Lending SBICs often make numerous small investments, but the venture investment oriented firms normally make five to 10 new commitments per year ranging from $100,000 to over $1 million for each portfolio company. Because SBICs generally borrow a portion of their investment capital and this requires servicing the interest, they usually avoid straight equity investments in early-stage companies in preference to income producing preferred stock or debt instrument investment structures.

The larger venture capital-oriented SBICs, with at least $1 million to $2 million in private capital, operate very similarly to the independent private venture capital firms. Larger SBICs operate across the broad spectrum of venture investment interests, including startups, expansion financings and management/leveraged buyouts. There is far more diversity among SBICs than among independent firms in the type of investments they will consider. SBIC emphasis on technology-related investments is not as great as in independent firms, and SBICs represent an excellent source of financing for businesses with more moderate growth prospects and lower potential risk.

In addition to the regular SBICs, there are now approximately 150 Minority Enterprise Small Business Investment Companies (MESBICs) that are privately owned and managed firms. These firms are licensed to provide financing to small businesses that are at least 51% owned by socially or economically disadvantaged persons, such as members of minority groups and U.S. military Vietnam veterans. Private capital in MESBICs ranges from $300,000 to more than $4 million, and those with private capital of $500,000 or more are eligible to receive Government leverage of four-to-one. Most MESBICs operate in a manner very similar to SBICs and pursue the common objective of adequate investment returns, but they also possess the added expectation that social benefits will result from successful investments.

Venture Capital Subsidiaries
A number of financial corporations, most notably commercial bank holding companies, have established separate subsidiaries (often in addition to SBICs), to invest in business development situations that do not meet the parent's usual investment or loan criteria, or that would not qualify under SBIC regulations. While these groups do not generally announce specific capital commitments, they are limited to 5% of the parent's capital and they range from $5 million to more than $200 million. Investments by these groups are most often in later-stage business developments and management/leveraged buyouts. These subsidiaries are usually managed by the group's venture investment management team and commitments to individual portfolio companies generally range from $1 million to $5 million.

Venture capital investment divisions have been formed by 30 to 40 large industrial corporations including General Electric, Lubrizol, Texaco and Xerox, and they represent a substantial venture capital investment source. These groups typically invest in situations where the product, market, or technology is related to the parent company's operations or where the business is of interest as a diversification opportunity. Some of them, however, operate more autonomously from the parent and have a wide range of investment interests.

The corporate subsidiary segment of the venture capital community has shown notable growth since 1977 with more than a 100% increase in the total dollars committed, and it is becoming a significant factor.

In the late 1960s and early 1970s, a large number of major corporations, as well as a few insurance companies, began investing directly in venture capital situations. Both groups contributed substantial funds to those operations, yet in most cases the efforts were misguided and the results were not fruitful. Corporations stressed the "window on technology" concept to the exclusion of developing a profitable, independent new business, and insurance investors attempted to employ their credit-oriented investment analysis techniques without recognition of the specialized skills and efforts needed for equity investment requiring ongoing involvement.

The resurgence of corporate venture investment activity, however, appears to be taking place with better planning and with recognition that such groups must be independent of normal corporate activities. Corporate groups are now employing proven venture investment disciplines, such as independent profitability and a five to seven year investment time frame, in the attempt to create successful venture investment divisions. In many cases the corporations are investing in, and participating with, completely independent venture capital firms. If corporations are able to maintain these disciplines, the corporate subsidiary segment of the venture capital community could become a very productive component since it already represents a very significant source of capital.

Geographic Considerations

Historically, the bulk of the nation's professionally managed venture capital has been concentrated in the Northeast and the San Francisco Bay Area with secondary centers in Chicago and Minneapolis. Today, venture capital funds are being formed in new areas at a rapid rate.

The following charts provide leading state and regional breakdowns of the dollars raised by independent private venture capital firms in 1983 and 1984:

Distribution of Capital Commitments
(Independent Private Firms Only)
Annual New Capital Commitments
(millions)

	1984	1983
California—Southern	$ 47.0	$ 208.9
— Northern	1,134.4	745.1
New York	639.1	957.5
Massachusetts	481.0	459.5
Connecticut	196.7	320.0
Illinois	144.9	35.1
Maryland	103.2	133.7
Colorado	102.6	27.0
Texas	78.0	126.4
Pennsylvania	66.1	32.0
Minnesota	58.7	123.0
New Jersey	37.8	24.0
Other States	169.4	290.9
Total	$3,258.9	$3,483.1

Regional Breakdown
(millions)

	1984	1983
Northeast (CT, MA, NJ, NY, PA, RI)	$1,420.7	$1,823.4
Southeast (FL, GA, MD, VA)	163.4	195.4
Midwest (IA, IL, MI, MN, WI)	276.1	239.9
Northwest (WA)	7.0	109.3
Southwest (CO, NM, TX)	210.3	161.1
West Coast (CA)	1,181.4	954.0
Total	$3,258.9	$3,483.1

Although New York, California, Massachusetts and Connecticut venture firms have continued to secure the largest percentages of new capital commitments, the tremendous increase in total capital raised has resulted in a windfall for many new areas. Venture firms outside these states raised $792 million in 1983 (up from $191 million in 1982) and $761 million in 1984 highlighting the recent regional shifts to new geographic locations.

In addition, venture funds located in the traditional areas are agressively seeking investment opportunities in these new regions as increased amounts of capital become available.

Although most venture capital firms still prefer to invest in companies located close to their offices, increasing cooperation among venture capital firms has led to a sharing of responsibility for local monitoring and ongoing involvement. When considering an attractive venture investment opportunity in a distant area, venture capitalists today often try to involve another group located within a 200 mile radius of the business opportunity. Thus, by sharing potential responsibilities and rewards, many venture capital firms now operate virtually coast-to-coast. A major stimulus to this cooperation has been the development of two major trade associations, the National Association of Small Business Investment Companies (NASBIC) and the National Venture Capital Association (NVCA).

A Healthy and Expanding Industry

While the organized venture capital industry certainly does not represent the nation's entire venture capital investment activity, its vibrancy and prosperity set the tone for overall activity. With remarkable accomplishments evident in the past several years, the venture capital industry currently enjoys excellent health from a record amount of available investment capital, the experience of two decades of development and an entrepreneurial climate favorable for venture development investment.

Informal Investors — When and Where to Look

William E. Wetzel, Jr.

William E. Wetzel, Jr. is Professor of Finance at the Whittemore School of Business and Economics at the University of New Hampshire in Durham. With sponsorship from the Office of Advocacy of the U.S. Small Business Administration he directed a study of the cost and availability of informal risk capital in New England. The emphasis of the study was on firms without access to traditional venture capital sources or the public equity markets. Results of the study led to the formation of Venture Capital Network, Inc. — an experimental service designed to link entrepreneurs with individual investors (business angels). Professor Wetzel, a former commercial loan officer, serves on the boards of directors of a multi-bank holding company, and several other corporations, including a successful high technology startup. He is a Director of Venture Capital Network, Inc.; the Small Business High Technology Council of New Hampshire; and the Smaller Business Association of New England. He has written extensively on the subjects of venture capital, entrepreneurship, and economic development.

Entrepreneurs seeking venture capital should be aware that the venture capital markets are both diverse and dispersed. Sources of venture financing range from the public new issues market, through professional venture capital funds and wealthy individuals, to local investors with a few dollars to back an acquaintance or relative. Investment objectives are equally broad. For example, investors vary dramatically in their taste for risk, ranging from investors willing to back inventors with unproven ideas to those preferring second or third round financing for established firms. Investors differ as well in the size of the investment they will consider, their exit horizons or level of patience for cash flow, the extent of their professional involvement with a venture, their geographic and industrial preferences, their rate of return requirements and in the significance of non-financial factors in their investment decisions.

For many entrepreneurs seeking venture capital, informal investors (business angels) represent the most appropriate source of funds, if not the only source. Informal investors tend to be financially sophisticated individuals of means, often with previous investment or management experience in new or rapidly growing ventures. There is evidence to suggest that informal investors represent the largest pool of risk capital in the country and that they finance 20,000 or more ventures per year.

If a venture proposal is economically sound in terms of market potential, competitive advantages, production and distribution capability and a competent management team is either in place or can be built, then there are definable circumstances under which a search for risk capital from informal investors would be appropriate.

Financing Technology-Based Inventors

Informal investors, in particular individuals with past experience in the formation of ventures in related fields of technology, are often the most likely source of capital for technology-based inventors prior to the startup of a business enterprise. Venture capital firms typically have little interest in inventors. The odds of picking a winner are slim, downside risks are substantial, relatively small amounts of money are typically involved, the costs of investment supervision and guidance are high, and the length of time between investment and cash recapture generally exceeds the limits of venture capital firms. Informal investors may accept the risks, costs and limited liquidity of inventor financing in view of perceived non-financial benefits such as the satisfaction of business creation or the stimulation of involvement with innovative technology, but professional venture capitalists consider the financial risk/reward relationship to be paramount.

The successful commercialization of new technology often depends more upon "demand-pull" than upon "technology push." An individual investor with technical and managerial experience in the commercialization of related technology can bring a "sense of the market" to the work of a technology-based inventor. Personal satisfaction derived from a fresh involvement with emerging technology may also convert what would be a cost to a professional investor into a significant non-financial benefit for the right individual investor. Technology-based inventors should be aware, however, that despite the potential attractiveness of participation in new technology, the financial risks are high, and therefore the cost of financial backing will be high. Capital gains potential on the order of 50 to 100 times or more within five to 10 years is not unreasonable and may require sale of a major share of equity to attract funds. By reducing the risk and the waiting period for investors, the longer an inventor/entrepreneur can survive on personal funds and "sweat equity," the lower will be the cost of external capital.

Increasingly, technology-based inventors and small firms can turn to public and quasi-public organizations for venture financing. These relatively recent programs have been created in recognition of the contribution of young, technology-based firms to the generation of new jobs and to the pace of technological innovation, and in recognition of the difficulty these ventures encounter in raising small amounts of very high risk seed financing. For example, the Federal Small Business Innovation Research Program (SBIR) was initiated in 1982 to fund high quality research proposals on scientific or technical opportunities that could have significant public benefit if the research is successful. A second goal of the SBIR program is the conversion of funded research into advanced commercial applications by private firms. The SBIR program is designed to increase the incentive and opportunity for small firms to undertake high risk research that has a high potential payoff and can effectively lower the risk for follow-on investors. Several states have created their own programs to stimulate economic growth by providing venture financing for firms with promising ideas and innovations.

Financing Business Startups

The 1978 and 1981 reductions in capital gains tax rates, a revival of the new issues market for smaller companies and changes in ERISA regulations governing pension fund investments have swelled venture funds under professional management to over $17 billion, six or seven times pre-1978 levels. However, according to *VENTURE CAPITAL JOURNAL,* less than a third of the industry's annual rate of new investment goes into startup situations, and then only for firms with the prospect of a public share offering or merger with a larger, established firm within five to 10 years. These ventures typically anticipate revenues from $20 million to $50 million within five years and ultimately sales in excess of $100 million. At best, professional venture investors back less than 1,000 startups annually. For ventures that are likely to generate revenues up to $20 million in five years and that are likely to remain privately held, individual investors and groups of individuals are the most likely sources of startup financing.

Providing seed capital or startup financing to an inexperienced management team can be enormously time consuming. Many of the management decisions involved in creating a new venture are unique to the startup process and will set the course of the venture through its perilous early years. Investors experienced with seed capital and startup situations can provide invaluable guidance to first-time entrepreneurs. Ideally, investors in new enterprises would also be experienced in related fields of business or technology. In other words, finding the "right" investors should be an important objective in the search for funds. The right investors will also be individuals who are fully aware of the risks involved and who are emotionally, as well as financially, able to bear those risks; who recognize the inevitability of unforeseen delays and other problems; who are prepared to invest additional funds if the venture succeeds and/or are realistic about the cost of additional outside equity capital; whose exit expectations are consistent with those of the founder and with the cash flow requirements of the venture; and, finally, whose role in the management of the venture is compatible with the needs of the venture and the founder.

Financially sophisticated individuals and groups of individuals are an appropriate source of startup funds under some or all of the following conditions:

a) *When the total financing required is over $50,000 but under $500,000.* The lower boundary represents the minimum equity capital required to start anything but a "Mom & Pop" operation. The upper boundary represents the minimum investment typically required to interest a professional venture capital firm or equity-oriented SBIC, though they will occasionally entertain proposals involving less than $250,000.

A 1981 survey of 51 of the largest and most active professional venture capital firms disclosed that the range of individual investments was from $300,000 to $4 million. The size of a typical individual investment was over $800,000. The figures were similar for equity-oriented SBICs, but substantially higher for corporate venture affiliates. (See D.E. Gumpert and J.A. Timmons, "Disregard Many Old Myths About Getting Venture Capital," *Harvard Business Review,* January-February 1982). The available data indicate that venture financing in the $50,000 to $500,000 range is the domain of angels.

b) *When the sales potential of the venture is between $2 million and $20 million per year within five to 10 years.* Techniques for liquidating a venture investment are limited to public offerings, acquisitions by larger firms, or buy-back arrangements with the venture or its founders. Companies with potential revenues in excess of $20 million and growth rates of 30% per year or more are generally necessary to provide the prospect of cash recovery through a public share offering or merger with a larger firm within the typical five to seven year investment cycle of a professional venture fund. Many informal investors are more patient and can accommodate ventures with slower growth rates. Young, privately held companies with sales under $20 million are an important source of new job opportunities and are a major source of technological innovation. At the startup stage these companies are often financed by informal investors. Entrepreneurs seeking startup financing from informal investors should identify the cash recapture expectations of these investors early in their negotiations and be prepared to offer appropriate buy-back arrangements or other liquidation options as an alternative to traditional exit mechanisms.

c) *When the proposed new venture is expected to generate "psychic income" for an investor in addition to adequate financial rewards.* More than impersonal financial incentives usually influence the investment decisions of informal investors. For example, a sense of civic or social responsibility often motivates individuals of means. A wealthy citizen in a community suffering from chronic unemployment may have more than a pecuniary interest in backing a venture expected to create 50 to 100 new jobs over a period of five to 10 years. Other individuals may derive "psychic income" from financing an inventor/entrepreneur involved in the commercial development of a new technology with significant social benefit, e.g. medical technology or energy-related technology. Other informal investors, in particular previously successful entrepreneurs, are often interested in investing both their funds and their experience in assisting promising new ventures get started. The rewards are partly financial and partly the satisfaction and stimulation of playing a role in the entrepreneurial process. The influence of psychic income, or so-called "hot buttons," is a characteristic that distinguishes informal investors from professional venture capitalists. Entrepreneurs sensitive to the match between the characteristics of their ventures and the personal tastes of investors should be able to raise funds on terms that are attractive to both parties.

Financing Growing Established Businesses

When sales grow, assets must grow. For manufacturing ventures every additional sales dollar typically requires between 50 cents and one dollar of additional assets and, therefore, additional financing in the same amount.

Retained earnings provide the principal source of new equity capital required to finance the growth of established corporations whether public or privately held. General Electric's retained earnings are five times its paid-in capital, Kodak's seven times and General Motors' 10 times. For privately held corpo-

rations retained earnings are generally the only source of new equity capital. For example, there are over two million incorporated businesses in the United States, but only about 12,000 (approximately one-half of one percent) enjoy sufficiently wide ownership to be considered publicly owned. The shares of about 4,000 firms are traded on organized national or regional stock exchanges. In other words, the public equity markets are not a source of capital for most corporations.

For practical purposes, the public equity markets represent a source of growth capital only for medium-sized and large corporations, those with after-tax earnings of $1 million or more. After-tax profits of $1 million to $2 million imply sales of $20 million or more, given typical after-tax margins of 5% to 10%. Only the exceptional expanding firm with sales between $2 million and $20 million can expect to raise funds in the public equity markets. In addition, professional venture capital firms concentrate on businesses with prospective growth rates high enough to propel a venture into public offering status within five to 10 years, or to attract a major corporate acquisition.

In the absence of alternative external equity sources, growth rates for small firms are constrained by the growth in internally generated equity. A firm earning a 20% return on equity and paying no dividends can grow no faster than 20% per year without distorting the debt/equity proportions of its balance sheet. Typically growth rates in excess of 40% per year are necessary to attract the interest of institutional venture investors. The troublesome firm to finance is the established firm growing faster than retained earnings and internal cash flow can support but not fast enough to attract venture capital. These troublesome but attractive growth rates tend to fall between 20% and 40% per year. Passage of the Small Business Investment Incentive Act of 1980 and the SEC's new Regulation D simplifying the raising of relatively small amounts of long-term capital indicate an awareness of the financing problems of smaller established firms.

For privately held firms growing at a rate too slow to attract venture capital, individual investors are the most likely financing source. A great deal of time can be wasted talking with institutional venture capital sources about deals which they are very unlikely to do. In some cases, national and regional investment banking firms can be helpful in placing financing privately with individual investors.

Profile of Informal Investors

Any attempt to describe a "typical" informal investor or business angel is bound to result in a profile with as many exceptions as examples. In the first place, these individuals exhibit a natural tendency toward anonymity when it comes to their

93

investment activity. In the second place, the personal backgrounds and investment objectives of informal investors are so diverse that generalizations about these characteristics are, at best, only suggestive.

The importance of informal investors to the vitality of entrepreneurial ventures prompted the Whittemore School of Business and Economics at the University of New Hampshire to undertake an examination of the volume and characteristics of informal risk capital financing in New England. The research was sponsored by the Office of Advocacy of the U.S. Small Business Administration, and focused on the role of informal investors as a source of funds for three types of investment situations:

1. financing technology-based inventors;
2. startup and early stage financing for emerging firms; and
3. equity financing for small established firms growing faster than internal cash flows can support.

A comprehensive investment history and interest questionnaire was employed in the research. Responses were received from 133 informal investors, a sample large enough to at least draw tentative conclusions about the characteristics of individual venture investors.

Research results confirmed generally held impressions that informal investors are a significant source of risk capital for technology-based inventors, and for both emerging and established firms without access to traditional venture capital sources or the public equity markets. Useful generalizations about the characteristics of informal investors can be drawn from the sample data. Of equal significance, however, is the degree of variation in characteristics represented by individual investors. They are a characteristically diverse as well as a geographically dispersed group and therefore difficult to profile.

Respondents reported risk capital investments totaling over $16 million in 320 ventures during the five years from 1976 through 1980, an average of one deal every two years for each investor. Classified by number of investments, 44% went to startup ventures, 18% to firms under one year old, 18% to firms between one and five years old, and the balance to established firms. The average size of their investments was in the neighborhood of $50,000, while the median investment size was about $20,000. In over 60% of their investments, those investors participated with other individuals to finance larger transactions.

The data suggest that venture capital financing by informal investors is at least equal in dollar volume to the equity-type funds provided by professional venture investors and that, by investing in smaller amounts, informal investors finance perhaps 20 times as many ventures. Data contained in a 1981 study by

the SEC of Rule 146 private placements support these conclusions. The SEC's study of financing under Regulation D during its initial year (April 1982 to April 1983) provides additional insight to the informal risk capital market.

The research data indicate that informal investors are an appropriate source of small amounts of very early, very high risk financing. One-third of the sample expressed a "strong interest" in financing technology-based inventors and 78% expressed a "strong interest" in startup and early stage financing for emerging firms. Investors interested in inventors and startups tend to limit their interest to fields with which they are familiar. In both cases investors tend to have post-graduate college training, prior startup management experience and expect to maintain an active relationship with ventures in which they invest, typically a consulting role or service on a working board of directors. As a result of this active relationship, informal investors tend to invest close to home — typically within a day's drive, more often within 50 miles.

Approximately one respondent in five expressed a "strong interest" in growth financing for established small firms. Investors interested in established firms typically consider investments in the neighborhood of $75,000 in any one firm. The incidence of advanced technical training and startup management experience was lower among investors interested in established firms than among investors interested in either technology-based inventors or in early stage financing for emerging firms.

The investment size and venture age preferences of informal investors combined with a high frequency of post graduate college training (51%), frequently technical, and prior startup management experience (75%) fill a need for risk capital financing typically not met by professional venture capital firms or the public equity markets. In addition, the tendency of informal investors to participate with other financially sophisticated individuals adds flexibility to the total financing available for any given venture and permits venture financing approaching the typical $250,000 to $500,000 interest thresholds of venture capital firms and equity-oriented SBICs.

Informal investors generally learn of investment opportunities through friends and business associates. During the course of the research it was not uncommon to discover that finding one informal investor led to contacts with several others. A network of friends and associates appears to link these individuals. However, the majority of respondents were less than satisfied with the effectiveness of existing channels of communication between bonafide entrepreneurs seeking risk capital and investors like themselves. Over 80% expressed an interest in a referral service that would permit them to examine a broader range of investment opportunities. These widely held opinions suggest that an appropriately designed network linking investors with opportunities could materially improve the efficiency of the informal risk capital market. Confidentiality and timeliness appear to be two essential characteristics of such a network. (See the description of Venture Capital Network, Inc.)

Generalizations about a group as diverse as the informal investor population are hazardous. Nevertheless, the data reveal a number of interesting characteristics. Despite the pitfalls, and as a starting point for discussion and further research, the following profile of the mythical, "typical" angel is offered:

INFORMAL INVESTOR PROFILE

1. Age 47.
2. Education: Post-graduate degree, often technical.
3. Previous management experience with startup ventures.
4. Typically invests from $20,000 to $50,000 in any one venture.
5. Invests at a rate of approximately once every two years.
6. Typically participates with other financially sophisticated individuals.
7. Prefers to invest in startup and early stage situations.
8. Willing to finance technology-based inventors when technology and markets are familiar.
9. Limited interest in financing established, moderate growth, small firms.
10. Strong preference for manufacturing ventures, high technology in particular.
11. Invests close to home — within 300 miles and usually within 50 miles.
12. Maintains an active professional relationship with portfolio ventures, typically a consulting role or service on a board of directors.
13. Diversification and tax sheltered income are not important objectives.
14. Expects to liquidate investment in five to 10 years.
15. Looks for compound annual rates of return on individual investments ranging from 50 + % from inventors to 20% to 25% from established firms.
16. Looks for minimum portfolio returns of about 20%.
17. Often will accept limitations on financial returns or accept higher risks in exchange for non-financial rewards.
18. Learns of investment opportunities primarily from friends and business associates.
19. Would like to look at more investment opportunities than present informal system permits.

Having enumerated the above characteristics, it must be said that exceptions to all of the above abound. There appear to be few bonafide opportunities for which an appropriate individual investor cannot be found. Copies of the complete research report, *Informal Risk Capital in New England,* can be obtained from the National Technical Information Service (NTIS), U.S. Department of Commerce, 5285 Port Royal Road, Springfield, Virginia 22161. Cite NTIS accession number PB81-196149. See also "Angels and Informal Risk Capital," *Sloan Management Review,* Summer, 1983.

Informal investors, essentially individuals of means and successful entrepreneurs, are a diverse and dispersed group with a preference for anonymity. Creative techniques are required to identify and reach them. Currently, inventors and entrepreneurs must find their own way through the maze of channels leading to informal venture capital. Private market makers are unable, by and large, to reap the substantially public benefits of improving the efficiency of the informal capital market. Therefore, entrepreneurs can expect to find little guidance in preparing sound investment proposals and in identifying potential individual investors, and investors themselves will continue to rely largely on random events to bring investment opportunities to their attention.

Venture Capital Network, Inc.

In an attempt to overcome the problems that entrepreneurs and individual investors encounter in trying to locate each other, the Business and Industry Association of New Hampshire (BIA) and the Office of Small Business Programs of the University of New Hampshire created Venture Capital Network, Inc. (VCN). VCN is a private sector experiment in capital formation. A not-for-profit corporation, VCN: (1) solicits, compiles and profiles information describing opportunities for risk capital investment in new or emerging ventures; (2) identifies active, informal investors and profiles their distinguishing investment objectives; and (3) provides a timely, confidential and objective referral system serving both entrepreneurs and investors. VCN assumes no fiduciary, advisory or evaluative role in such referrals.

VCN focuses its efforts on the six-state New England Region. However, VCN places no geographic restrictions on its services. During its experimental first year, VCN enrolled over 300 investors from 32 states and 133 entrepreneurs from 26 states. Seven hundred and sixty-five investor/entrepreneur introductions were initiated, an average of between five and six per entrepreneur. While VCN's contact with investors and entrepreneurs ceases with an introduction, at least five ventures are known to have been funded by VCN investors.

With the support of a group of professional sponsors, including the Shawmut Bank of Boston; Deloitte, Haskins & Sells; and Peat, Marwick, Mitchell & Co., VCN is significantly expanding its services to entrepreneurs and investors. VCN is also assisting in the formation of VCN counterparts in other regions of the United States and several foreign countries. Entrepreneurs and investors interested in VCN can obtain further information by writing to Venture Capital Network, Inc., Box 882, Durham, New Hampshire 03824.

Summary
Wealthy individuals, successful entrepreneurs in particular, are a significant source of venture capital for certain types of situations. These informal investors are a diverse and dispersed group about which very little is known. Situations suggesting a search for venture capital from an appropriate individual, or group of individuals, include the following:

1. Financing technology-based inventors prior to commercialization of an invention or innovation.

2. Financing business startups, especially for firms with five to 10 year sales potential between $2 million and $20 million and requiring from $50,000 to $500,000 of venture capital.

3. Financing business startups with the prospect of providing psychic income in addition to adequate financial rewards.

Examples of non-financial incentives for informal investors include the creation of jobs in a community experiencing chronic unemployment, participating in the commercialization of a socially useful new technology or innovation, and the satisfaction of playing an active role in the entrepreneurial process.

4. Financing privately held, established businesses growing too fast to finance from internal cash flows but not fast enough to attract institutional venture investors. Attractive but troublesome growth rates tend to fall between 20% and 40% per year.

Under the best of circumstances, the search for informal venture capital can be frustrating. Entrepreneurs with sound ideas, strong management skills and well-documented proposals may find the search productive. Venture Capital Network, Inc. is designed to help. Financially sophisticated individuals will often undertake investments that are smaller, riskier and less liquid than those that interest professional venture investors. Appropriate incentives are necessary to offset the costs, risks, and limited liquidity of these investments and entrepreneurs seeking informal venture capital will find it essential to carefully match their objectives with those of their financial partners.

How to Organize and Finance the Startup
The Role of the Seed Capital Fund

John B. Mumford and Frederick J. Dotzler

John B. Mumford and Frederick J. Dotzler *are general partners of Crosspoint Venture Partners, a seed venture capital fund with offices in Mountain View and Newport Beach, California. Crosspoint's perspective is that of both entrepreneurs and venture capitalists since the fund's managers had previously founded and managed over a dozen successful new businesses.*

Seed capital is the money used to finance the very early stages of a business, before a management team has been assembled and even before a strategy has been formulated. It is used to finance initial research and development, build a prototype, do market research, organize the business and write a business plan.

Historically, this seed capital has been raised almost exclusively from personal savings of the founders, friends, relatives, or personally-guaranteed bank loans. In recent years this capital has also become available from specialized seed funds such as Crosspoint that invest exclusively in early-stage ventures and from other venture funds that occasionally make seed investments. The business risks are so great and venture capital management involvement is so intense at this seed/startup stage that successful operating experience in early stage ventures is necessary for seed capital investors. Their approach differs from later stage investors.

At Crosspoint we invest in seed, startup and very early stage businesses structured as equity partnerships as well as corporations. We actually like to get involved at the product concept stage with an inventor or technical team and participate in developing the business strategy, the financing strategy and hiring the remaining key management team. We often participate like a founder by bringing early-stage business and management know-how to the situations.

At this seed stage, we are usually the only investor. Once the product is developed, the management team is complete and the company has confirmed the market for the product by obtaining customer orders, we then bring in strong institutional venture capital groups to finance follow-on rounds.

Different Types of Startups

There are three typical types of startups from a venture capitalist's perspective:

1. *A qualified and experienced management team presents a well-defined business plan.* A number of early-stage venture capital firms are interested in these types of startups. Typically, the venture investor evaluates the following: viability of the business concept, technical risk, potential market size and projected growth, competition and management team qualifications. This process largely involves checking and verifying what is written in the business plan. If all of these factors are positive, the parties begin to negotiate the investment structure and pricing.

    Example—Personal CAD Systems, Los Gatos, California, was formed by a team of experienced engineers and managers from the semiconductor, computer and CAD industries to develop electronic design automation software for the IBM personal computer family. Early in 1983 this team approached Crosspoint to explore a "seed round" to finance the company. Previously, Personal CAD received an offer from two large institutional funds who were willing to invest a minimum of $1.5 million for 65% of the equity. Crosspoint's staged financing approach was to determine exactly what capital was required to develop the products, complete the team and obtain initial user feedback.

    The entrepreneurs decided to have Crosspoint invest the $500,000 required to complete these initial milestones. In return, the founders gave up 30% of the initial equity.

    The company achieved its milestones successfully and was profitable on sales of approximately $9 million in 1984. Personal CAD Systems has raised two additional rounds of venture capital totaling $6.5 million at significantly increased valuations. Even with these additional financings, the entrepreneurs and management still own 37 % more of the company than they would have if they had accepted the initial $1.5 million financing proposal.

2. *Product innovator or technical team presents an undeveloped product concept for financing.* This is a startup which needs a seed venture capital investor. Typically the founder does not have a complete business plan or strategy, so the process involves a more in-depth evaluation of the commercial potential of the business and/or technology. It requires initiating market research to determine if there is a significant market for the business concept. The investing firm must decide if the inventor or technical team has entrepreneurial qualities and determine what other members of the team must be attracted to the business. An initial business plan is then drafted. This plan outlines the product development program, initial sales and marketing programs, personnel and management hiring requirements, and detailed funding requirements that are based upon achievement of certain technical milestones.

Example — Laserpath Corporation, Sunnyvale, California, developed proprietary technology that allows them to manufacture prototype and production volumes of highly complex, large semi-custom VLSI logic circuits approximately 10 times faster than current practice allows. In 1983 the inventor, Morgan Johnson, approached Crosspoint to evaluate the concept. At that point he had developed a number of mathematical interconnect patterns and researched the patentability of the concept.

Crosspoint helped the inventor to develop a business strategy and product research and development plan with milestones to be achieved with a $1 million seed funding. During the 18 month development period Crosspoint provided much of the general management, technical review, marketing and accounting support to this new venture. Laserpath was initially set-up in our "incubator" R&D facility.

By early 1985, the company had demonstrated technical feasibility on a prototype gate array chip, had assembled a top technical and management team and had raised a $5 million follow-on venture capital round to complete the product development and begin marketing first generation products.

3. *Initiation of a business concept by the venture capital firm.* A few venture capitalists, including Crosspoint, will on

occasions start companies if they have been unable to find someone to back to take advantage of a market opportunity that capitalizes on a unique technology. The venture firm conducts the necessary market research and technical evaluation and then launches the new company. At Crosspoint, we typically have one of our partners act as president during the initial startup phase with responsibility to hire the key technical team and a permanent president to run the business.

Example — CXC Corporation, Irvine, California, was founded by Jim Willenborg and John Mumford, partners of Crosspoint, to develop a fully distributed voice/data switch. In 1981, the founders believed that bringing state of the art VLSI, computer, networking and software technologies to the office communications market could result in a significant business opportunity. CXC was formed with a $150,000 seed financing to allow the founders, including Joe Leonardi, the CXC president who was a proven computer industry executive, to develop the system architecture and develop a comprehensive business plan.

CXC has now raised $50 million of venture capital to complete this major product development effort, develop manufacturing capability, build a sales and marketing organization and successfully introduce the CXC Rose system.

Issues to Consider when Starting a Company
What are the entrepreneur's first considerations about starting a company, and what is the venture capitalist looking for from the entrepreneur in making a startup investment? It is assumed that a valid and attractive business concept has been identified and that the entrepreneur has a strong conviction that this is an outstanding opportunity. This conviction is important because much effort is required to take a business from concept to fruition, and many setbacks must be overcome. Although venture capitalists may temporarily help fill in a few of the gaps, they will usually look to the entrepreneur and his team to be the experts and have the answers. The entrepreneur must have thoroughly researched the business and thought out how to organize and manage it before trying to interest others.

Investors will usually not finance just a product or product idea. They want to see a complete business. They look for a well-structured marketing plan in which potential customers have been identified, the method of distribution has been analyzed, the competition thoroughly investigated and follow-on products conceptualized.

It is important for the entrepreneur or a designee to contact potential customers and the distribution channels to help assess demand for the product as early as possible. (A well prepared questionnaire or interview guide will help ensure that all topics of interest are covered during these market research sessions.) Interviews with prospective customers can be summarized in the business plan to help potential investors gauge the market's interest in the product. Letters of intent to purchase the product, if they can be obtained, will certainly help sell the business proposal.

These interviews can also be used to test product strategy. If a majority of potential customers want a feature not included in the original design or balk at the proposed pricing, the entrepreneur may have to adjust the plan.

In addition to the original founder or founders, it is usually necessary to supplement the team with the right mix of talents and expertise that together can convince the investor that they can build a substantial business. The most important player is the chief executive officer, usually the president, the team leader and the final word on all decisions. A chief executive must be able to inspire confidence in all employees, to motivate them and also be able to hire the very best in his industry. If that individual is not on-board, we require that a plan for hiring the key manager be agreed upon prior to our investing and that funds be budgeted in the financing for an executive search to find the president.

The founders should decide how to divide and share equity among themselves and any planned key additions soon after deciding to build a company. A complete management team (research and development, marketing, manufacturing, accounting and finance, etc.) must be assembled. The founder or founders should be willing to share equity with these key players to induce them to join the team and to motivate them. The amount of equity allocated to each should be commensurate with expected contribution to the long-term performance of the company. A stock vesting program is ideal for insuring that the equity payoff is directly related to each team member's continued employment.

A business plan or statement that presents a thorough and concise description of the business and a plan of action for the company must be developed. It should set forth the financial requirements and expected financial rewards. The business plan is a statement of corporate strategy; it sets the focus and direction of the company. It also becomes a contract of sorts between investors and management. A good business plan is a reflection of the entrepreneur and his ability and is the guide against which he will be measured in the future.

An entrepreneur should come to grips with the "financial partner" issue before seeking seed equity capital. Any serious amount of financing, and consequently any thought of obtaining rapid growth, requires financial partners in the enterprise. Whenever founders are reluctant to give up equity in return for needed growth capital, the probability of a major success is lessened.

There is no standard way to get started. A couple of people working weekends and nights may formulate a business plan and, without benefit of even a prototype to demonstate, try to raise money with nothing more than the plan and their own backgrounds and reputations. On the other hand, the product development may be nearly completed, a prototype may have been built on the entrepreneur's own money, or perhaps a company may have been formed to sell a few products to customers. The founder may have raised several thousand dollars of "seed" money from personal savings, relatives or friends.

The Role of the Venture Capitalist in Assisting the Startup Process

A seed startup venture capitalist should have extensive startup operating experience and be a proven manager. Emerging companies often encounter problems that can be solved quickly with input from someone who has managed a new company.

Crosspoint uses a "matrix management" approach to helping manage seed startups. Although one partner manages the investment, three partners who are functional specialists are available to assist the company with technology review and management of product development; sales, marketing and business strategy; and accounting systems and operating organization.

We also provide an incubator facility to start and support companies during the conceptual and development stages. This facility provides administrative office and shop space during the development of an engineering prototype and the preparation of the business plan.

One of the most valuable contributions made by the seed venture capitalist is to provide feedback and assistance in developing the product strategy, marketing strategy and overall business strategy for the company. In addition, the venture capitalist will help to identify individuals for the management team — determine the type of individual required and help sell them on the business opportunity.

The venture capitalist will also identify professionals, including lawyers and accountants, skilled in helping startup businesses. In addition to providing the seed capital, a professional venture capitalist will help in organizing later rounds of financing.

Conclusion

The venture capital industry has expanded both in terms of dollars available and the number of firms. Some firms have specialized by investing in companies at specific stages in their evolution. Others have decided to focus on certain industries.

Each entrepreneur starting a company has a unique set of requirements and needs for support beyond seed capital. It is by providing this support that the seed venture capitalist with early-stage business and management know-how can make a useful contribution. As the company grows, institutional venture investors that specialize by industry or by later stage financings can play an increasingly useful role and provide expansion capital as needed.

Seed capital fund managers are specialists who must build a very close working relationship with entrepreneurial management teams. The personal chemistry and mutual respect between entrepreneurs and seed venture capitalists is a very critical factor in this type of business development.

SBA Programs for Financing a Small Business

David J. Gladstone

David J. Gladstone is president of Allied Capital Corporation, Washington, D.C., a publicly traded venture capital and lending company with three major wholly owned subsidiaries. Allied also manages one venture capital partnership, Allied Venture Partnership. Assets being managed total $100 million. Allied Investment Corporation is one of the nation's oldest Small Business Investment Companies (SBIC) which makes equity-type venture capital investments in small growth-oriented companies. Allied Financial Corporation is a Minority Enterprise Small Business Investment Company (MESBIC) making investments in companies owned by "disadvantaged" individuals and specializing in companies owned by Viet Nam era veterans. Allied Lending Corporation is a participating lender with the U.S. Small Business Administration and makes guaranteed loans to small business concerns. Allied Venture Partnership was established to co-invest with Allied Capital's subsidiary and to invest in some equity venture capital investments. Mr. Gladstone has been with Allied for 12 years. He received his BA in Government and Economics from University of Virginia, his MA in Computer Science from American University and his MBA from Harvard Business School.

There are two basic U.S. Small Business Administration (SBA) programs that have been used most frequently to finance small business. The first program provides funds through Small Business Investment Companies (SBICs and MESBICs) licensed by the SBA and the second program provides financing through banks and financial companies whereby the SBA guarantees up to 90% of the loan being made.

SBIC FINANCING

During the last two and one-half decades, the SBIC-MESBIC industry has developed into a unique source of funds for small business in the United States. During these past 25 years, SBICs have invested billions in small businesses, with small losses to the SBA. SBICs have contributed to the creation of millions of jobs by their investments in small business. By any test, the SBIC program has been a success. It has been an ideal marriage between public policy and private enterprise.

Each SBIC or MESBIC is a private company owned by investors and has equity capital contributed by the stockholders. During the last 26 years, the number of licensed SBICs has changed. At first, there was a rapid growth in the number of SBICs, then a period of no growth, and finally a decline. In the last five years, the number of SBICs has been increasing dramatically. Currently, there are approximately 500 active SBICs in the United States. Each must invest its funds only in U.S.-based small businesses. To receive a list of the most active SBICs, see the directory section of this book or write to the National Association of Small Business Investment Companies, 1156 15th Street N.W., Suite 101, Washington, D.C. 20005.

The most noticeable changes in the SBIC industry in recent years has been the increase in the number of professional managers. Most managers have advanced business degrees and experience in the field of lending or equity financing. They are able to act in a knowledgeable and professional manner. Another change that a small business should be aware of is the trend of the SBIC community into a narrow spectrum of structuring SBIC investments. SBICs borrow most of their funds from the SBA — up to $4.00 in loans from the SBA for each $1.00 of private capital — and this limits the type of capital they can offer to a small business. Since SBICs borrow most of their funds, they must lend their money to small businesses rather than purchase equity from them.

As with most things in this world, the cost of SBIC borrowing has increased during the last 10 years. Recently, SBICs were paying the SBA 12% interest for their funds. Therefore, the problem in structuring an investment to a small business is based on the situation that the SBIC has borrowed most of its money and, therefore, needs to charge interest on the money it disburses to the small business so it may pay the SBA for the interest on its own capital. Usually, SBICs lend their money at 13% to 15%

interest. Most of the interest paid by the small business to the SBIC is, in turn, paid to the SBA. Any difference is used to cover operating overhead in the SBIC.

As one can see, most of the interest income from small businesses does not generate a great profit for the stockholders of the SBIC. Rather, the SBICs make their profit by having an option to own equity in the small business to which they have loaned money. It is important to note that the entrepreneur will have to give up less equity in his company if he obtains money from an SBIC because the SBIC will get some of its return as interest. The typical types of financings made by SBICs in order of their frequency is outlined as follows:

Convertible Debenture

A convertible debenture for eight years, five years interest only, then three years of amortization; 12% to 14% interest, unsecured with conversion privileges to purchase 25% to 40% of the stock of the borrower at a reasonable price. This is usually a second round financing for the small business.

Loan with Options to Buy Stock

A loan for seven years, three years interest only, then four-year amortization; 13% to 15% interest; usually subordinated to institutional lenders, with stock options to purchase 10% to 20% of the company's stock at a low exercise price. This is usually a third round financing.

Straight Loan

A loan at 17% to 18% interest with a straight amortization over five to seven years, secured by specific assets. This is usually financing for a mature company secured by specific collateral of the small business.

Preferred Stock

Preferred stock redeemable after 8 years, with an 8% to 12% dividend, with an option to convert to common stock of approximately 40% to 80% of the company. This is usually first round financing.

Notice that these investments, except for the last one, are loans and not equity. Few SBICs make common stock equity investments because of their SBA interest obligations discussed above. Most analysts of the SBIC program now recognize that if the program is to be equity-oriented, the SBA must change its program and purchase preferred stock from SBICs. In return, the SBICs will be required to purchase equity in the small business.

Many small businessmen don't understand why SBICs don't want to purchase stock in their small business. On the other hand, most small businessmen will not borrow money from their bank to purchase stock in a friend's company. Obviously, SBICs have the same problem, due to the funds borrowed from the SBA. So, the best advice to a small business seeking financing from an SBIC is to structure the proposed investment as a loan with equity options, or in a format as set out above. To structure the proposed financing any other way will risk a premature turndown by the SBIC.

Another analysis of SBICs is by the types of investments the SBICs make. This can be segmented by the stage of development of the business. A compendium is set forth below.

Startups or First Round Financings

These are the most difficult situations to finance through an SBIC because a new company usually needs equity and not debt. The new company needs to retain its cash flow in the initial years to use internally, rather than pay interest on SBIC debt. However, some SBICs will invest a portion of their funds in early-stage financings and approximately 33% of the funds invested by SBICs today are in new companies.

Second Round Financing

In this situation, the company has created a product or service and is marketing it with some degree of success. The company needs funds to finance the business' growth and its negative cash flow. In this case, a convertible debenture is normally the structure. Most SBICs invest a large portion of their funds in second round financings.

Third Round Financing

Third round financing is needed when a company is running well and has generally established profitability, but needs growth capital. A loan with warrants will typically be the structure from an SBIC. Many SBICs invest funds in this area also.

Public Offering

Sometimes, an SBIC will purchase preferred stock or a convertible debenture that is part of a public offering or a semi-public offering. In this instance, the company is usually well along in its development cycle and investment risk can be more clearly analyzed. This is an infrequent area for SBICs to invest.

Leveraged Buyout

In many cases, a company may be purchased by new owners with most of the capital as debt. Often, the current operating management participates in the purchase. Those businesses usually have demonstrated cash flow to service such debt. SBICs often provide subordinated debt in the form of loans with warrants. The SBIC debt in fact, supports senior debt since it may be unsecured or so far down the ladder from security that a senior lender really thinks of it as equity. Most SBICs are eager to invest in leveraged buyouts because the cash flow is more easily predictable.

Debt Without Equity

There are a number of SBICs that make collaterized loans for a simple high interest rate and no ownership in the small business. This may occur when the SBIC has excess funds; however, there are many SBICs and MESBICs that concentrate in this type of financing usually in a specific industry.

Turnaround

Some SBICs finance turnaround situations — companies in trouble (even bankruptcy) which need money and management assistance. Usually, a turnaround deal is structured as debt with equity options. Where possible, the SBIC will seek security for its investment. Not many SBICs are investing in turnaround opportunities.

In summary, a small business is more likely to receive financing from an SBIC if it is seeking a second or third round financing or is trying to finance a leveraged buyout.

A potential borrower from an SBIC must know the type of SBIC that may be interested in financing their concern. There are various types of SBICs with different investment objectives.

Public Companies

Some of the largest SBICs are owned by public stockholders and their stock trades on the stock exchanges. Because of the problems of operating a venture capital company and meeting the requirements of the Investment Company Act of 1940 (and the 1980 Act), there are not many public SBICs. Before their demise, many of the public companies tended to be the greatest risk takers. With a few exceptions, however, most of the remaining public SBICs are now making second and third round financings and leveraged buyouts. Not long ago, the two largest public companies announced they would discontinue being public companies and cited SEC regulations as the reason. This reduces the amount of public money available to small businesses. During the bull market for new issues, several new small public venture capital companies were created.

Private Companies or Partnerships

Most of the SBICs today are privately owned which gives them great flexibility to meet the needs of the small business. Since the management of the SBIC answers only to a few private stockholders, needs of the entrepreneur can be met more easily and more quickly. Often, the management of the SBIC is also the owner. Much of the funds available to small business is from private SBICs.

Bank-Related

Many SBICs are owned by banks. Too often, these are merely extensions of the bank loan department. In larger banks, however, the SBIC is generally a profit center with its own management team which can accommodate the small business on a variety of terms and conditions. Infrequently, the bank loan department teams up with the SBIC where the bank makes a working capital loan on inventory and receivables and the SBIC makes an equity-type, long-term loan. In the larger banks, the two work independently. In major money center banks, the SBIC is a true high risk/high reward venture capital company. This is a substantial area of funds for small business.

Venture Capital-Related

Some SBICs are wholly owned subsidiaries of a pool of capital used for venture investment. Here, the SBIC may invest with long-term debt, while the venture arm may invest in common stock, which is a nice combination. However, most venture funds do not have SBICs.

Specialty SBICs

There are some SBICs set up specifically to make investments in one industry. These industries include: real estate development, broadcasting, fast-food franchises, movie production, grocery stores and drug stores, just to name a few.

Unfortunately, most SBICs are small. The normal loan amount available may be only $100,000 to $300,000 per small business. Because many SBICs are small, the larger investment opportunities are often syndicated, which means several SBICs may invest together in the company. Usually, one SBIC plays a "lead investor" role and the borrowing small business meets principally with the lead investor. A group of SBICs can put up $3 million without too much trouble. Over $5 million may be difficult to arrange from the SBIC community.

It pays for a potential borrower to do his homework on specific SBICs to recognize specialties and areas of particular interest.

Some like the retail trade while others will invest only in manufacturing. To find the SBIC which will understand the needs of a specific small business, it's wise for the small businessperson to obtain background information on the SBIC he (she) intends to approach. With information on SBICs, let's turn to the second principal form of financing through the SBA — SBA guaranteed loans.

SBA GUARANTEED LOANS

Probably 2,500 banks in the United States make SBA 90% guaranteed loans and there are a few non-bank companies which handle such financings. Even with this large number, only several hundred lending institutions are actively making SBA guaranteed loans. In the past few years, the SBA selected approximately 500 of the most active lenders with the best loan records to be designated as "Certified Lenders."

As a Certified Lender, the SBA attempts to give three-day turnaround service. The paperwork necessary for a loan has been reduced substantially, thereby reducing the processing time dramatically. (In Allied's case, it reduced the processing time from eight to twelve weeks to one to two weeks.) Thus, in these cases, an SBA guaranteed loan processed through a certified lender takes no longer to process than a regular loan from a commercial bank. The small businessperson who wants to utilize a guaranteed loan is advised to contact their local SBA office for a list of Certified Lenders. This listing may also be obtained by writing to the Deputy Director of Finance, Small Business Administration, 1441 L Street N.W., Washington, D.C. 20416. SBA has a pilot program for "Preferred Lenders," where the lender makes the loan, then tells SBA what has been guaranteed. SBA is still experimenting but the outlook is promising.

The chief benefits from an SBA guaranteed loan are (a) obtaining better terms and (b) securing enough money to adequately capitalize the small business.

Better Terms

Most lending institutions will not lend long-term, but with SBA guaranteed loans, much of the risk of a long-term loan is shifted to the SBA. SBA gives lenders an incentive to go longer-term by giving the lender permission to charge a higher interest rate on loans over seven years. The maximum terms are seven years for working capital, 10 years for machinery and equipment, and 25 years for real estate including leasehold improvements.

Interest rate maximums are on two scales: (1) a variable rate loan has a maximum of 2-3/4% over prime and the rate is adjusted monthly; or (2) a fixed rate loan has the fixed rate set at 2-3/4% over prime at the time the loan is submitted and stays at that rate for the life of the loan. Thus, when the loan is submitted to the SBA lender, the fixed rate maximum that the lender can propose to the SBA is 2-3/4% over the current prime rate. Because long-term rates are higher than short-term rates, it is difficult for lenders to make a long-term loan that has its maximum rate held down by short-term prime rates. Currently, SBA is running a pilot program in several regions where there are no maximums. Remember these are the maximum; the lender can always charge less.

Enough Money

Because of the SBA guarantee, the lender can provide more money than conventional credit terms. It is common for a small business to receive 100% financing on land and buildings where the small business lacks the standard downpayment funds. The same is true on machinery and equipment. However, this can only occur where there is sufficient equity in the business.

To some extent, working capital loans guaranteed by the SBA have been abused and now working capital loans are more difficult to obtain. The SBA guarantee program is not set up for revolving lines of credit, but rather it is oriented to long-term loans. Some banks have tried to make term loans secured by accounts receivable and inventory, but have found it difficult to monitor and manage when the inventory and receivables rise and fall. The best use of SBA guaranteed loans is for long-term asset financing such as real estate, machinery and equipment and other fixed assets.

The maximum loan amount that can be made under the guaranteed loan program is $550,000. While this is usually sufficient for a small business it is not adequate for a growing business. Currently, SBA has limited guarantee authority for loans and the outlook for guarantee loans is not promising. It seems likely that Congress will limit the guarantee authority last year to about $1.8 billion, down from $2.2 billion last year. Even with this credit squeeze, SBA guaranteed loans are a major source of funds for small business.

In summary, both SBA programs can benefit a small business. SBA loans can provide long-term debt financing for specific assets, while SBIC financing can provide growth capital. Any good small business should be able to obtain funds through either program.

The MESBIC Connection: Venture Capital for the Forgotten Entrepreneur

Walter M. McMurtry, Jr.

Walter M. McMurtry, Jr. is a founder and president of the Inner-City Business Improvement Forum (ICBIF), Detroit, one of the largest minority business development corporations in the U.S. He has also served as President of the MESBICs, Independence Capital Formation, Inc. and Inner-City Capital Access Center, Inc. As of May 1983 the above MESBICs have merged, with the new entity, Inner-City Capital Access Center, Inc., surviving. Mr. McMurtry is a director and past president of the American Association of MESBICs and participates in the Economic Development Administration's Financial Round-table as well as numerous other federal, state and city commissions.

That minority enterprise small business investment companies (MESBICs) have grown steadily in size, number, and wisdom is testimony to their strength.

MESBICs started when Robert Dehlendorf, then president and CEO of the Arcata National Corporation of Palo Alto, California proposed, and his board accepted, a plan to inject 2% of Arcata's net profits into an investment company. The year was 1968, the 2% of net profits amounted to about $150,000, and the investment company he proposed would operate on a simple investment philosophy.

"What we will try to do," Dehlendorf said, "is to back the right man with the right idea in the right marketplace." This time, however, the right man was to be a minority entrepreneur. Arcata National also planned to invest an additional $150,000 each year for the next five years. If this plan had been followed, Arcata Investment Company (AIC) would have had a private capital base of $900,000 by 1972. Today, the largest MESBIC has $4.7 million.

AIC, of course, had not yet become a MESBIC. It was happy to join the SBIC program, which the Small Business Administration had operated since 1958. In August 1968, Arcata Investment became a chartered SBIC, the only SBIC — out of more than 500 — to specialize in venture capital for the minority business community. The SBA had barely handed AIC its small business investment company license before the White House heard about it.

On November 6, 1969, President Richard M. Nixon announced "Project Enterprise," a key ingredient of which was something called a MESBIC. Very quickly — too quickly it now seems — everyone in the government became active. The President issued his Executive Order. The SBA was charged with licensing, regulating, and leveraging this new industry. A special Office of Minority Business Enterprise within the Department of Commerce was asked to stimulate interest in MESBICs as it went about implementing the President's general directive.

Even Secretary of Commerce Maurice Stans promoted MESBICs, and especially AIC, as he spoke to corporate and business audiences around the country about minority economic development. Stans envisioned the creation of 100 MESBICs by June 1970 and another 400 within the next several years. If this goal could be met, he argued, over a billion dollars would be available for minority business investment by the mid-1970s.

At year-end 1982, however, 128 MESBICS have raised only approximately $121.4 million in private capital, a pool that the SBA has increased by another $164.8 million by purchasing debentures and non-voting preferred stocks.

MESBICs did not sprout like mushrooms under that plan. They did not even enjoy the boom regular SBICs experienced from 1958 to 1964. The reasons are obvious and represent a stage of growth the industry is glad to have behind it. Business and banking investors responded with too much financial caution and too little real commitment in terms of time and "hands on" assistance to the MESBICs and their portfolio companies. Philanthropic groups were committed, but imprudent. No one won: you cannot invest just a little money on a "social" problem — nor are noble objectives a substitute for a good accounting system and hard cash.

AIC, which started as the first MESBIC, soon illustrated what could go wrong. It restricted its minority small business operations to "mom and pop" operations. Loans ranged in size from $10,000 to $25,000, and either the loans were not adequately monitored or the management and marketing assistance did not arrive in time. Many of these businesses were lost, and AIC soon found itself depleted of operating capital. It stopped making loans in 1971.

The SBA now requires a minimum of $1 million in private capital commitment for all SBICs and MESBICs, but our own experience suggests $1 million to $2 million is needed to establish a viable venture capital company, and it takes considerably more to make them truly effective. SBICs have learned this the hard way. After 20 years, SBICs have finally turned profitable as an industry, but they lost approximately two-thirds of their original members doing it.

MESBICs are still part of the SBIC industry, but they have their own special investment charter and focus. MESBICs are privately owned venture capital companies licensed to provide debt and equity financing to small business firms that are at least 51% owned by socially or economically disadvantaged persons, such as members of minority groups.

MESBIC investments to an entrepreneur can take several forms. Some of the most common are:

- **Loans with warrants** — In return for a loan, the borrower issues warrants to the MESBIC to purchase common stock in the business at a specified price during a fixed period of time.

- **Convertible debentures** — The MESBIC receives a debenture in exchange for a loan. The debenture can be repaid with interest or converted to an equivalent amount of common stock in the business.

- **Common stock** — The MESBIC purchases common stock equity in the business.

- **Preferred stock** — The MESBIC purchases preferred stock in the business. This stock can be repaid through redemption or converted to common stock equity.

- **Straight loans** — Although the MESBIC usually will want the opportunity to share in the growth and potential profits of the small companies they finance, they will in some cases make loans involving no equity features. Interest rates, terms of repayment, and collateral requirements are determined by negotiations subject to state laws and SBA regulations. Loans can be for a minimum of four years, but five years is the usual minimum.

In almost all cases, a MESBIC also provides management assistance to its clients. This is an extremely important supplement and may prove as valuable to the small business owner as the financing itself. Second and third round financings are possible with a number of MESBICS, especially when the investor has had ongoing involvement.

MESBIC deals range across the entire business landscape. Independence Capital Formation, a former MESBIC superseded by its sister MESBIC, Inner-City Capital Access Center, of which I am president, has invested in such diverse industries as banks and fast food operations; a rubber manufacturer; a toy manufacturer; a railroad; and automobile dealerships. Other MESBICS have been involved in the communications, service, and transportation industries; and in wholesale distribution. When financing larger deals, such as the acquisition of a CBS-affiliated television station in Rochester, New York, several MESBICs joined in a syndicate, with one of them taking the lead. In these larger deals, MESBICs act as a catalyst for attracting traditional lenders. Their equity then becomes subordinated debt to a senior lender (in this case, the Chase Manhattan Bank). In 1982, MESBICs made 764 financings for a total of $47 million. Forty-three percent of those deals were startup situations but the current economic climate argues that MESBICS, like other venture capital firms, move more toward expansion financing and acquisition of existing businesses.

Individual MESBICs set their own investment patterns. They also determine their maximum loan size and concentrate in certain business areas while taking no interest in others. Qualified entrepreneurs should put their packages together well, then check with several MESBICS before concluding that MESBICs "don't know a good deal when they see one." The industry has outgrown its old reputation as the "banker of last resort" for the minority community.

By law, MESBICS are prohibited from participating in most real estate transactions, cannot invest in nonprofit organizations or in individual projects (as opposed to ongoing businesses), and, of course, MESBICs cannot do business with a firm that is part of the MESBIC itself.

MESBICs can now be limited partnerships, but most are private for-profit corporations subject to state usury law ceilings. MESBICs have not offered their own stock for public sale as Narragansett Capital and other regular SBICs have done, but some MESBICs are discussing this option. The businesses MESBICs invest in can, of course, offer public stock, and that is a financing option that should be discussed with the MESBIC and any other investors.

What can minority businesses do to ensure a sympathetic hearing from MESBICs? Here are some suggestions:

- Have a strong knowledge of the industry in which you will be doing business

- Have a strong knowledge of the market area you will be servicing

- Have a sound management team

- Have a sound operational plan for success, which is the most important factor

The American Association of MESBICs, located at 915 Fifteenth Street, NW, Washington, D.C. 20005, publishes a monthly newsletter and bi-monthly bulletin on the MESBIC industry that will keep the entrepreneur abreast of developments in the industry. Successful businesses are not created quickly, but MESBICs are committed to a more equitable opportunity for all enterprising Americans.

Dealing with the Corporate Venture Capitalist

Kenneth W. Rind

Kenneth W. Rind *is a general partner of Oxford Partners, Stamford, Connecticut, which manages venture capital funds provided by both corporate (strategic) and financially oriented investors. Prior to that, he was a principal of Xerox Development Corporation, the corporate development and venture capital subsidiary of Xerox Corporation.*

Introduction

Corporate venture capital generally differs from conventional venture investing in that motivations beyond strictly financial reward are present. Typically, a corporation will be seeking to gain exposure to new markets/technologies, generate new products, identify/assess acquisition candidates, assure a source of supply, and/or assist a customer. Corporations also may utilize venture capital concepts to initiate new ventures internally, or to spin off businesses which are not appropriately kept inside. Though corporate venturers represent only a small part of the venture capital community, their importance is growing and their involvement in technology businesses, in particular, has been out of proportion to their size. This article will describe the unique benefits as well as the problems an entrepreneur will have in dealing with a corporate venture capital source which has strategic motivations.

History of Corporate Venture Capital

Probably the first corporate venturer was DuPont. When one of its important new customers ran out of funds in 1919, it purchased a 38% equity interest and brought in a new president, Alfred Sloan. General Motors has grown substantially since that investment.

After World War I, American Telephone, General Electric and Westinghouse bought out the British interests in American Marconi. They subsequently changed the name of their venture to Radio Corporation of America, now RCA.

Right after the Second World War, a small company, Haloid Corporation, funded the commercialization of a new technology developed by Chester Carlson and the Battelle Memorial Institute. Haloid later changed its name to Xerox Corporation.

Another corporate venturer probably became interested in the concept because its largest stockholder was a man whose father had previously been the venture capitalist behind the formation of IBM. Fairchild Camera and Instrument financed a group of eight technologists leaving Shockley Transistor in 1957. They later acquired this venture, Fairchild Semiconductor, the grandfather of many of the companies now populating Silicon Valley.

Many corporations became active venture capitalists in the 1960s seeking a "window on technology." However, the lack of profit orientation and the decline of the market in 1970 brought about the exit of most of those established corporate venture capitalists, including such major names as: DuPont, Ford, Alcoa, Union Carbide, Northrop, Scott Paper and Singer, as well as some newer venturers such as Memorex, California Computer, Dataproducts, Electronic Memories, Mohawk Data and Applied Magnetics.

Public interest in the stock market recovered in 1971 and 1972, before almost collapsing entirely in 1974 and 1975, driving many other corporate venturers from the business.

Corporations Become More Active

In the last few years there has been a renewal of interest in direct corporate venture capital investments, fueled mainly by a desire to keep pace with technology developments coupled with an awareness of the "success" of a few corporate venture groups. For example, 36 of the 50 largest United States electronics companies have made direct venture investments since 1980. In addition, the entry of foreign corporations into the field has become a major new factor.

It is estimated that today there are more than 60 industrial corporations which directly invest over $500 million annually in ventures. This figure includes funds only under direct corporate control. There has also been a growing tendency for corporations to invest in venture pools managed by others, both as a supplement to their direct investments, and as a first step into the area.

A particular focus has been investments in semiconductor manufacturers by domestic and foreign corporations in order to assure a viable supplier. The success of such attempts remain to be proven, but the trend has not yet abated. Recent examples include: Intel, International Microelectronic Products, LSI

Logic, Siliconix, VLSI Technology, Xicor, and Zymos. Some noteworthy companies that presently have or have had participation by corporate venture capitalists include:

- *Computers* — Amdahl, Altos, Apple, Convergent, Cray, Fortune Systems, Modular Computer, Stratus, Tandem, Trilogy, Wang
- *Medical Electronics* — ADAC, Coherent, Cordis, Kolff Medical, Orion Research
- *Telecommunications* — Comdial, Intecom, Lynch Communications, MCI, Network Systems, Paradyne, Quotron, Rolm, Ungermann-Bass, VMX
- *Biotechnology* — Advanced Genetic Sciences, Amgen, Biogen, Cetus, Collaborative Research, Genentech, Genex
- *Terminals* — Datapoint, Lee Data, Ramtek, Syntrex, Telxon
- *Peripherals* — Centronics, Computer Memories, Decision Data, Evans & Sutherland, Seagate, Zitel
- *Instruments* — Analog Devices, Nicolet, Waters Associates
- *Robotics* — Adept Technology, Advanced Robotics, Applied Intelligence Systems, Automatix, Diffracto, Robotic Vision Systems, Synthetic Vision Systems, View Engineering
- *Miscellaneous* — Businessland, Data Card, Data I/O, Federal Express, Key Pharmaceutical, Siltec, Scope, Xidex

Problems of the Corporate Venturer

Although financial rewards are usually a secondary concern, corporate venture capital funds that have been run by professionals, even if not strictly for maximum return, have performed as well as any fund with reported compounded annual returns of 20% to 100%.

On the other hand, many corporations have failed as venturers. A 1978 survey of corporate venture capital organizations made by Tektronix stated that only 7% of corporate venture capital organizations regarded themselves as being very successful, with over half not even rating themselves as marginal successes. The difficulties experienced by a corporation seeking to become a venture capitalist usually arise from one of these sources:

- *Lack of appropriately skilled people*
  A venture capitalist must be entrepreneurially motivated, patient, realistically optimistic, good at negotiation, persuasive and able to evaluate people as well as businesses. Also he must be more than superficially familiar with accounting principles, tax regulations, corporate finance structures, securities analysis, and securities law. Good internal people

are generally unwilling to leave a company's main-stream activities even if they possess the appropriate skills. Experienced people from the outside are difficult to attract and retain without special compensation packages which are almost impossible to structure.

- *Contradictory rationales*
  A corporate venture capital program may find it difficult to act in the best interests of both the investee company and the parent. For example: if the goal of the venture group is to acquire, then equity financing by others is undesirable; if the rationale is an exclusive marketing arrangement or a preferred supplier role, then the investee's operations may be unduly limited. A desire to have continuous profit increases by the parent is also incompatible with the normal results of a venture operation. The entire problem can be exacerbated by an improper reporting structure. For example, having the venture group report to the Vice President of Finance is likely to shift focus to profitability; to the Vice President of R&D to technology; to the Vice President of Corporate Planning to market information, etc.

- *Legal problems*
  A corporate venturer must be extremely careful to organize its activities so that it will not run afoul of conflict of interest problems, including "fiduciary responsibility" and "corporate opportunity" doctrines. Several corporations have left the field, incorrectly believing that legal constraints would necessarily totally inhibit the strategic benefits they wanted out of a venture program.

- *Inadequate time horizon*
  A venture activity usually shows its losses and problems early, with the successes taking more time to develop than anticipated. Unless a corporation's commitment to venture capital is made for at least seven to 10 years, its venture fund generally will be terminated in its early stages.

Selecting a Corporate Partner

In order to assure the viability of a long-term relationship and avert common problems that arise in co-investing with a corporation, the following points should be considered:

- *Compatibility of goals*
  As previously noted, corporations make venture capital investments for diverse reasons including: assisting potential suppliers or customers, gaining exposure to new technologies/markets, growing possible acquisitions, and

obtaining a financial return. The business interests of both parties may either reinforce the possibility of success or lead to future conflicts.

- *Longevity*
Many corporate venture groups have been shut down due to a lack of early success, an inability to set clear objectives or even just shifts in corporate strategy. A failure of continuing support will probably arise at a poor time in the economy for raising funds from others. Make sure there is a true long-term commitment to the concept.

- *People*
If the corporate group is not managed by experienced venture capitalists, unnecessary conflicts may develop. There may also be a desire for the staff to return to a career path inside the corporation, thereby requiring continual efforts at educating new people. Finally, the corporation may not provide adequate financial resources to build an independent operation.

- *Flexibility*
The route necessary for decision-making may be short or tortuous. It is essential for the investee corporation that the venture group has appropriate autonomy to ensure that crises can be met quickly. Major corporations often measure performance against a set plan, whereas entrepreneurs must have the flexibility to react and restructure a plan to overcome a myriad of unexpected problems.

- *Interference*
Unless the relationship is well-structured, the corporation may attempt to require its conventional reporting and staff policies which are inappropriate for a venture situation. Curiosity visits may also become an annoyance.

- *Time horizon*
Not all corporate venture capitalists realize the length of time that may be necessary to bring a new business to profitability. If the corporation does not react rationally to unforeseen slippage, then substantial difficulties will be created.

- *Style*
Corporate venture groups, like non-corporate ones, differ in attitudes, approaches and interests. A feeling of sympatico,

which should have developed before the investment, is generally extremely helpful to a successful relationship and must be fostered in the aftermath.

Corporate Investors Bring Advantages
Corporate venture capitalists believe they should be preferred investors. In addition to the usual financial and strategic assistance given by conventional venture capitalists, corporations also may offer:

- Assistance in almost all facets of corporate endeavor, e.g. setting up financial systems, qualifying suppliers, meeting government regulations;

- Credibility with customers, banks and other investors both from a technical and financial standpoint;

- Relief, if desired, from the full range of corporate activities, e.g. the corporate investor may take on marketing responsibilities or may license the product;

- Immediate income from an R&D or consulting contract if appropriate;

- Customer interface with an interested party;

- An investor with an infinite lifetime, though his time horizon for profitability will be shorter;

- Additional capital where warranted;

- A merger partner, if and when appropriate;

- A more flexible financing package since return on investment may not be the only criterion.

Conclusion
Corporate venture capitalists can be good partners. However, it is important to note that there have been many abrupt terminations of such activities by the parent corporations; several of them despite excellent returns. In fact, no strategically oriented corporate venture capital group has succeeded in keeping its key personnel for more than seven years. For this and other previously described reasons, it is incumbent upon the entrepreneurial team to exercise the same thoroughness in choosing a potential corporate investor as a venture group does in choosing its investments.

Tax Advantaged Financing Sources Through Limited Partnerships

Jane Koloski Morris

See previous background description.

Tax advantaged limited partnerships are often used as investment vehicles to provide development capital for seed, startup or very early stage company financings, as well as for research and product development in established businesses. Alternatively called a "wondrous low risk financing tool," a "way to minimize equity giveup" or a "potential disaster," it is difficult to judge whether the tax incentive orientation will be an important new financing vehicle, or whether the inherent complexity of a structure to serve two masters will, in fact, hinder business development investment.

A well-structured limited partnership offers tax shelter advantages and potential rewards to investors as well as apparently lower cost financing for entrepreneurs. In theory, the tax advantaged limited partnership is a boon for investors and entrepreneurs. In practice, however, it is a complicated financing structure which requires careful consideration and the knowledge of professionals experienced in these structures to avoid significant legal, tax and business development problems.

Based on a 1954 enactment created to stimulate research and development, and clarified by a 1974 Supreme Court decision which approved the tax deductibility of expenses by investors in a partnership performing research and development, it is only in the last few years that these vehicles have gained acceptance and increasing popularity as legitimate financing tools. Initially, and still predominantly, R&D partnerships have been set up to finance product development for businesses which could not afford such significant expense within the company's financing structure. The concept is to reduce the risk and exposure of the sponsoring company, which is primarily oriented to manufacture and market products, and at the same time to enable investors to finance such development with pretax dollars.

The controversy surrounding this type of financing is based on the inherent problems of any vehicle that seeks to do all things for all people. Popularity among investors seeking an immediate reduction of tax liabilities has subjected tax oriented partnerships to abuses by scam artists. Since these investors often seek conservation of capital — retention of funds that may be paid in taxes — rather than the long-term potential rewards from such investments, the indications of future potential are often not well-scrutinized. The "sizzle" in many R&D investments offerings is often just that, and the chances of tasting the elusive steak may be remote. In addition, the complex tax questions can, paradoxically, inject a substantial amount of risk into the investment consideration.

Neither the Internal Revenue Service nor the accounting community is comfortable with tax structures employed to accomplish the desired objectives of these partnerships and, as result, each partnership must be examined carefully for both questionable tax deductions and the ultimate tax treatment of investment returns. There is as yet no standard format for the structure to assume and no guarantee that the tax advantages proclaimed in an offering are viable. Although the entrepreneur might be initially satisfied with the receipt of capital whether or not the IRS disclaims investor tax write-offs, such problems can destroy a developing business. Major future tax liabilities in a growing business can cause disaster and no entrepreneur needs or wants angry investors. Investors facing surprise tax payments will take recourse far beyond the syndicator — the future viability of the business may not be their central issue. The benefits and risks of tax shelter financing require unique structuring and careful analysis to avoid serious problems for both investors and business managements.

Classic R&D Partnerships

There are numerous forms tax sheltered development partnerships may assume, although two have become the most popular. The first is the classic R&D partnership which is the dominant vehicle for product development. These have been used for both startup and established businesses to fund research and applications development of specific products. Investors, generally individuals, invest their capital as limited partners in a partnership managed by a general partner. The partnership then contracts with the corporation to perform research on behalf of the partnership. Ownership rights — which must be clearly defined — to the technology and products developed as a results of this research are held by the partnership and the limited parer investors are generally entitled to tax writeoffs in the first year totalling 80% to 90% of their invested capital. If the research and development produces a product, the corporation has the option of purchasing the technology from the partnership and would then pay the partnership a prenegotiated royalty on the sale of the products. This may typically be 7% to 10%

of sales and may or may not have a "cap" — a maximum amount — on the dollars to which the partnership is entitled. Gains received by the partnership from the corporation payments hopefully receive long-term capital gains treatment.

Equity Partnerships

The second type of tax advantaged financing source and the one most often used in conjunction with venture capital type new business development is the equity/operating partnership. While these vehicles are initially structured similarly to the R&D partnership discussed above, there are important differences to reflect the anticipated long-term involvement of the investors. While the limited partner investors will receive their pro rata allocations of development expenses as a tax writeoff, the primary appeal of these vehicles is to provide an equity interest in the planned business from the fruits of the research and development — with particular emphasis on the development. In these instances the investors are primarily concerned with long-term growth of asset values through market capitalization of income earned by the business and tax considerations are generally considered merely a way of reducing exposure. In equity partnerships a corporate vehicle is normally structured from the onset to serve as the corporate general partner of the partnership and provide a means of converting successful developments into the permanence of corporations for continuing businesses. Through this means, the investors will become shareholders of an ongoing corporation which succeeds the partnership.

Advantages of Tax Advantaged Financing Sources
For the Entrepreneur

1. A means of financing research and product development outside of the financial constraints of a growing business. Since funding for development purposes is normally extremely restricted in smaller and rapidly expanding businesses, the ability to have outside investors finance development on a project basis can be very attractive. If the project is unsuccessful, the other aspects of the business would be less seriously impacted, but if successful, the project can be moved into the main stream of company operations.

2. A source of seed capital, or very early stage development funds from independent investors. Historically, most seed capital for product development has been in short supply and was often provided by family and friends. This, of course, is a very high risk investment and generally requires

an element of faith in the entrepreneur's capabilities that cannot be supported with meaningful objective evaluation. Potential tax savings can stimulate this earlier investment.

3. Product development and conceptual seed financing can often be accomplished at a lower equity and financial cost to the entrepreneurial management team. Since investors in a tax advantaged partnership are receiving the initial benefits of tax writeoffs, they may be satisfied with less of a continuing interest to achieve their specific objectives.

4. Since research and development can thus be funded on an independent basis, the management team retains greater control over business operations of the company.

For the Investor

1. The ability to invest with pretax and not after tax dollars, which means that in a 50% tax bracket, the investor is receiving 80% to 90% leverage on the net exposed investment. A front end tax benefit reduces investment exposure immediately.

2. An opportunity to participate in a venture development at a very early stage when the potential return is often the greatest. The high risk of such investment is partially offset by tax benefits.

3. Potential participation in a royalty income stream from classic R&D partnerships, or ownership interests in a business from equity partnerships. If the partnership vehicle is properly structured, the financial benefits are expected to be received on a capital gains, rather than an ordinary income, tax basis.

Disadvantages of Tax Advantaged Financing Sources
For the Entrepreneur

1. The complexity of tax oriented investment vehicles injects serious potential consequences beyond the control of the management team. The entrepreneur and the business are exposed to structuring errors inherent in new and untried vehicles that will be scrutinized by tax and regulatory authorities which often have divergent objectives from those of building a business. If perceived tax benefits are disallowed, the company and the investors can receive significant impact and can often be pushed into working at cross purposes.

2. The payment of royalties on sales — an off the top financial obligation — severely hampers the company's ability both to generate internal cash and external financing for growth just when it needs it the most.

3. The potential corporate benefit of tax loss carryforwards has been removed by passing these tax losses through to investors. Here again, the company may be forced to expensive financing just when it has demonstrated the viability of the product. It should be noted that in the case of an equity partnership with a corporate general partner, tax loss carryforwards may be recouped if the deductibility of partnership expenses is disallowed by the IRS.

4. Tax advantaged partnership financing must normally be viewed as a temporary solution to financing problems. Project financing, which is often the basis for tax advantaged partnerships, is not always integrated with ongoing business development financing requirements.

5. Short-term tax considerations will often attract short-term oriented investors and even if they perceive potential growth in asset values, their ongoing support may be unduly influenced by short-term performance. The company's best source of support is generally involved investors. Equity partnerships are normally structured with early and continued involvement on behalf of the investor group.

For the Investor:

1. If the partnership is not structured properly, all tax benefits may be disallowed by the IRS.

2. The project financing aspect of tax advantaged partnerships often limits the potential investment return to a specific product development.

3. As with the entrepreneur, the investor must be concerned with potential barriers to future financing requirements of a continuing business.

4. The complex structure of a tax advantaged partnership can lead to difficulties in having profits categorized as long-term capital gains. The high income investor that normally participates in such partnerships could receive a dramatic reduction in net investment returns if cash benefits received are declared to be ordinary income.

An Example of an Equity Partnership

Since classic research and development financing through tax advantaged royalty partnerships can be researched through available documentation on such transactions as De Lorean Motors, Storage Technology and Trilogy, the following example should be useful to outline the successful use of an equity partnership.

XYZ Technology, L.P. was formed as a limited partnership with the principal founders serving as the general partner. There were two classes of limited partners: the investors as Class A partners and the management employees as Class B partners. Capital of $2 million was provided by a group of individual investors in increments to be invested over the next year based upon the achievement of technical milestones, although the full amount had been committed at the time the partnership was organized. For this commitment the investors received approximately 60% of the partnership interests with management holding 40%. The development of the product was completed in approximately 14 months with shipments commencing at that time. The partnership's original capital was supplemented with $3.2 million of which $1 million was provided by individuals and investment partnerships who invested as limited partners and the balance was provided by institutional venture capitalists in the form of loans to the partnership to be converted into convertible preferred stock upon the incorporation of the business. Over the first two calendar years of this development, the limited partners received an allocation of losses equal to approximately 89% of their contributed capital. The second round $3.2 million financing involved an equity dilution of approximately 25%. Several months later the company was incorporated and the partners received common stock for their partnership interests. Twenty-seven months after the company was originally formed as a partnership the new corporation completed an institutional financing of $6.5 million, with an equity dilution of less than 10%, which valued the business at more than $75 million. At this point, investors who had provided some $11.7 million were holding some 75% of the equity with an imputed valuation of $56 million and the management team held 25% of the equity earned through sweat equity and nominal cash, with an imputed value of $19 million. The company is now a successful and growing business.

Summary and Conclusion

Tax advantaged financing sources should be considered as an alternative vehicle. As in any newly utilized vehicle, there are many unknown factors that must be considered and the complexity of any tax related program requires specialized expertise. The best advice for entrepreneurs considering this source of financing is to contact a professional firm who has successfully structured prior tax advantaged partnerships.

Perspectives

Venture-backed companies have achieved notable success as industry leaders and innovators. Companies such as Intel Corp., Apple Computer, Tandem Computers and Federal Express were pioneers creating new industry sectors. The role of the venture capitalist in the success of new business development and the unique character of venture-backed companies and their founders are discussed in this section of *PRATT'S GUIDE*.

The relationship between the entrepreneur and the venture capitalist is often a critical factor in the success or failure of a new business. To develop a productive, honest working relationship, it is helpful to recognize the biases, prejudices and pressure points that have emerged from the experiences of both venture capitalists and entrepreneurs.

Before investing in any management team, venture capitalists look for the right skills and disciplines, but they also look for a chemistry or "gut feeling" that gives them the personal go-ahead signal regarding management. This section also examines the techniques employed by several professional venture capitalists in evaluating management teams and offers some valuable advice for the entrepreneur on early relationships with the venture capitalist.

Presented are the views of two entrepreneurs who have worked with, and established the respect of, a number of venture capitalists. Their insights are valuable as a guide, and they place the entrepreneur/venture capitalist relationship and the money raising process in a unique perspective.

The Art of Venturing

Frederick R. Adler

Frederick R. Adler is a senior partner of the law firm of Reavis & McGrath, New York City, and is the managing general partner of Adler & Company, a venture capital firm also located in New York City. In the late 1960s Adler became intrigued with venture capital and began investing in early-stage ventures that were primarily technological. Since then, Adler has invested in about 80 enterprises, perhaps the most successful being Data General Corp., now the nation's second largest independent minicomputer manufacturer. Adler is considered an entrepreneur in the venture capital field.

Choosing and continually evaluating a first rate management team lies at the very heart of a successful venture capital investment. The problem is that a significant part of identifying and then continually auditing such talent is a very esoteric exercise to which there is no scientific approach. Once the initial management has been selected, the auditing process is frequently skimmed over until the new enterprise is in deep trouble. Resumes and even past history are not an insurance policy against failure. Unfortunately, I don't know any solution other than initial and continued inquiry.

Once past a qualification and detailed screening process, using our own people and outside "search" firms, we "psych out" the prospective management team. We try to get to know them in the best possible manner — not in a conference room, but on the floor of the plant, or the lab or what have you. How do they function in periods of extreme pressure, the condition under which most small companies grow? How well are they going to survive under the need to meet next week's payroll? Small comments often can provide a clue to management's thinking and capability, not as they relate merely to running a small company, but also to the creation and management of a large, successful company.

The need is to constantly monitor the quality of management's judgment. When in doubt, make probes that are designed partly to aggravate or irritate an insecure manager to see how he will react. Investigate potential flaws and weaknesses in the management structure. Usually weak managers will try to cover up or blame others for flaws in their own operation rather than develop and execute a balanced business plan for their area of responsibility. If there are too many uncured weaknesses, or if the weaknesses are too great, management stability is not going to equal management ambition, and the whole project will either not make sense to begin with or, if we are so unfortunate as to have invested, will go nowhere.

Warning Signals

There are some things said or positions taken by entrepreneurs in meetings that serve as major warning signals or at least indicate weakness in judgment.

"There is nothing like this product on the market today." Most, but not all of the time, this statement indicates that a man has not done his homework or that he may have designed a perfect product for a market that does not exist.

One of the major dangers with startups is that they often involve products for which the market is exceedingly difficult to assess. Venture capitalists rarely back totally new products. They usually back improvements on existing products, such as cases where a new manufacturing technique will reduce manufacturing costs. The Data General financing was only a startup from a technical viewpoint. The management team had designed computers and built software for Digital Equipment Corporation. They had designed and developed 12-bit, general purpose small computers. Obviously there was no question that they could design and build a general purpose computer for the new company. The question was, how good are these men going to be at managing their own business? Thus, the key risks were not product risks, although some new design techniques were employed; instead, they primarily related to marketing and management. The central question almost always comes down to whether the product can be sold, not whether it is the only such product on the market. Even the right decisions change with time, and management had better be flexible enough to adapt.

"There isn't really a great widget available on the market today that will interchange with a particularly successful existing piece of equipment." Often the product and development costs for a special piece of equipment that is fully interchangeable with other manufacturers' units are so excessive that the business will never be able to recoup the costs. Striving for perfection in a new product so that it is fully interchangeable with

everything usually poses major problems, and it is far better to develop a very good product, for which a real demand exists, that can be put into production at a reasonable cost.

Another major warning signal is an inordinate concern with salary, company cars, and other fringe benefits at the time of the original negotiation for financing. Venture capitalists hate to see money wasted, and particularly in a new enterprise, every dollar must be marshaled very carefully if the business is to be assured of survival. An entrepreneur's focus on such things as a car, the size of the office, travel expenses, and so forth, usually indicates a mental approach and lack of dedication that would divert attention away from developing a major business success.

The entrepreneur who is concerned about having full use of a secretary, a large car, and a 15′ x 16′ office, tends to be thinking more like an employee than a partner. He or she is not likely to be as concerned about how much money is spent to develop a product or to be concerned that his or her share of the equity is being dissipated by such high capital expenditures. The results are usually very negative from the investor's point of view.

The Tortoise or Hare Approach
There are two ways of viewing a new project or startup venture. One is that it is of utmost importance to get into the market quickly with a new product to beat competitors. To accomplish this target, substantial additional monies often must be invested. The other alternative is to bring the best product with excellent price/performance characteristics to the market slowly and carefully before the original product obsolesces. Although the danger of competition due to lost time is increasing, I lean toward the slow side and tend to avoid early investment projects that are trying to beat the clock and short cut needed early investment and the difficult process of building primary demand.

Management as a Popularity Contest
Another negative feature is exhibited by the manager who is running a contest for the affection of the co-workers. The successful entrepreneur must step up and bite the bullet when critical decisions are required. When demand slacks, production must be cut and this means layoffs. Middle management must be used to the fullest possible extent to avoid overhead expenses under these conditions. Trying to keep all employees while hoping for the business to pick up can often be a disastrous strategy. The company may not be around by the time demand increases.

The Market Plunger
One petty irritation is the stock market approach — that is, the approach of a manager who spends a lot of time being concerned with the price of relative equities of similar kinds of business. Moreover, managers who make presentations based on this type of analysis usually overprice their projects. One of the obvious tenets of profitable venturing is to attempt to gain entry into a new project at the fairest possible valuations, subject to the caveat that it pays to pay more for the really first rate high potential deal than a little for a second rate deal. However, the team that demands too much of the pie seldom receives financing.

Shotgun Product Development
A rather common problem is the failure of management to focus on the major objectives of the business. All venture capitalists have been exposed to managers who keep starting new product development programs and are unable to focus on the specific product that will make the company highly successful. The manager who proposes to work on 10 products, even though they may be good ones, seldom develops the one excellent product from which the company can make a major success.

The Genuis
Perhaps someday I will meet "The Genius," but I doubt it. My definition is someone I have heard about. No one has the experience or time to be first-rate in everything. The smartest people are those who make use of the smartest people they know in order to get the job done. They use management personnel, bankers, venture capitalists, and anyone who can give them information or an advantage.

The Ideal Entrepreneur
In a sense, every venture capitalist is looking for the entrepreneur with excellent management experience and past profit and loss responsibility who is greedy, hungry, and yet honest and sincere. He or she must have the intellectual integrity to admit mistakes and to recognize and reward other people's talents. This founder must be technically qualified to do the job, but must not be so immersed in the technology to lose sight of the need to build a profitable business rather than a bunch of fancy products. The leader must have a strong ego. Without a large ego, he or she is not going to view the obstacles with sufficient confidence. Yet if too egocentric and one-sided, he or she will make some serious, dumb decisions by refusing to take input from others.

The manager must be tough enough to make very hard decisions if the venture is to survive, and that means firing one's best friend if necessary. Yet the entrepreneur must be smart and mature enough so that this toughness is tempered and so that the key people will not leave because of attitudes which irritate them.

The venture capital business is one of persistence. Every venture capital deal has experienced unexpected problems. They happen daily, weekly, or monthly, and there are enough big ones to scare every manager and venture capitalist. Good managements overcome these problems. The weaker ones fall by the wayside.

To be successful in developing a new project, management must be aggressive, but at the same time cannot let ambition outstrip its pocketbook. A major problem in the venture business is that almost every early-stage project has a limited source of funds, unless it achieves instant success (a great rarity). Ambitions must be measured and desires reined in to the very tight limits of the pocketbook.

Characteristics of Successful Projects

In our most successful investments, management has had a very close working relationship, both financially and operationally, with our venture capital group. Senior management has tended to operate in a very open-minded, flexible, questioning way in order to obtain everyone's views. Exploring alternatives and brainstorming important decisions with all of the high-caliber people involved has been a key aspect in making sound management decisions.

Perhaps this is a contradiction of the theory of the great leader, but it may be that there is no such person. Generally speaking, it is interaction that produces good management decisions.

At most of the companies in which I am heavily involved, the top management personnel are extremely capable and mature, and they run the company in every sense. Yet, in spite of my "non-involvement" with actual operations, we still find time to get together at regular intervals varying with need. In most cases, we talk by phone at least two or three times a week. When there is nothing specific to discuss, we try to keep each other informed of everything that is or eventually could be a major problem. Again, I emphasize that our discussions usually do not cover day-to-day operations, which should be in the hands of competent management. But they do cover the broader policy and planning aspects of managing the business, particularly in finance, strategic planning, acquisitions, senior personnel and other critical decisions. I try to teach them to be their own management consultants, their own venture capitalists. The more they talk to us because they like to bounce ideas rather than need our decisional abilities, the better off they, their companies and ultimately the venture capitalists, will be.

People who are good managers take advantage of each other by interacting as much as possible. They "truth seek" rather than advocate. Building a company from a small base entails a world of possible mistakes, and the trick is to avoid those that are fatal. By talking to enough bright people, particularly those with direct experience in building a business, management should be able to avoid such mistakes. However, there are no supermen, and it is only by great effort and conscientious attention to detail that businesses can be effectively managed and sustain a competitive edge during their early growth periods. In business, paranoia isn't a psychosis, it is reality, it is survival, it is success.

The Entrepreneur's Perspective

Donald J. Kramer

Donald J. Kramer *is a partner of TA Associates, a Boston-based venture capital firm with over $400 million under management. Before joining TA in 1984, he was president and chief executive officer of Hendrix Electronics, Inc., Manchester, New Hampshire, a venture capital financed manufacturer of text management systems, video display terminals and optical character recognition scanners. Since 1970, he was with Modicon Corporation, a company backed by a number of venture capitalists which manufactured and sold programmable controllers. He became president of Modicon in 1973 and joined Gould, Inc. as a vice president when that company acquired Modicon in 1977.*

After a technical type high school education, I started college in engineering, which I soon found I hated and consequently only lasted six months. Joining the Navy for four years gave me a different type of education, learning about people, and I came out with an incredible passion to succeed. Back in college, I graduated number one in my class majoring in accounting at Northeastern University, and was accepted at graduate school. With family responsibilities, however, eating became the most important habit to satisfy, so I went to work, although I did ultimately get my MBA from a combination of study at Syracuse University and Boston University.

My career path has been a progression from big companies to small, and I soon became a small business addict. Smaller business management is my narcotic. I am hooked and would find it difficult to go back to larger companies' bureaucratic structures. My first exposure to the world of venture capital came when I helped form a new facsimile company in the late 1960s with a corporate sponsor for funding and technology. This was a noteworthy failure for me and for my meager savings which I had invested, although I learned more from that failure than from a lot of subsequent successes. After a typically euphoric two years, we were asked to sell the business when the parent had some problems. We successfully sold it five times and every time the parent's assessment of the value went up until the parent decided it was so good they would keep it. I decided to move on, but I learned that one of the most important keys to business success is to understand the objectives and motivations of the business' investors.

About Venture Capitalists

The primary importance of venture capitalists to an entrepreneur is MONEY, and they all have money, but investors do differ in objectives, motivations, and capabilities. The relationship between operating management and the business' outside investors can help or harm a business' development. Understanding objectives is the first way to help that relationship. During the negotiation process the objectives should be uncovered.

Corporate venture capitalists may have entirely different objectives from the financial orientation of most venture investors. Corporations may only be interested in research and development off the balance sheet or off the P & L statements. I am generally uncomfortable with corporate investors because their objectives and mine are likely to be quite different.

The majority of individual venture capitalists are personally compensated on the basis of the success of their portfolios and most pools, if not all, have a finite life. As venture partnerships end, they are primarily seeking return as opposed to new investments. It is important to understand where the potential investor is in that life cycle, and whether they intend to put together another fund with similar objectives. One has to recognize that these objectives can change due to money market changes, liquidity needs or what-have-you. Perhaps the initial objective can be laid out, but the ultimate comfort that they are never going to change cannot be made.

In initial dealings with venture capitalists, they will check on your background and references and it is just as important for you to do the same to them. It is perfectly reasonable to ask for references from those who may invest in you. Next, there is the personal chemistry — a very important factor. This must be seen and felt early since future events and problems will strain most relationships. Find out whether or not they have the necessary skills to assist you in *your* particular venture. Lastly, remind yourself that they are the stockholders, they do, in fact, own the company.

Venture capitalists are all different and each fund is different. Some are very good at startups, but there are probably fewer of those than any other kind. In my opinion, this requires operating skills in order to help a new management over some rough spots. Usually a company cannot afford to hire all the talent it needs, it has to get advice and there are times when a venture capitalist can provide this. Many differences depend on where they get their money and whether they are looking for an incremental percentage return, whether they hope to shoot the moon, whether they are in for five years or forever.

People have different skills and venture capitalists are no different. Some are good technically, although they are rare. There are not too many good marketers — even though most all venture capitalists think they are because marketing is relatively easy to understand. I find whenever I get into a box with a venture capitalist, I start talking "bits and bytes," even though I don't know them, because it usually backs them off. They don't understand it either. A few venture capitalists are aware of technical aspects, most feel they understand the marketing but the only thing they really understand is venture capital. They know what kind of a deal will sell and to whom it will sell.

Venture firms tend to hire very bright guys out of graduate schools in their late twenties, smart as hell, and hard working, but at least half of them do not know a thing initially. They get on a board of directors and end up getting on-the-job training. Sometimes, they can be very counter productive. The problem is that they are so bright. If they were stupid, they would be easy to deal with — you'd just blow them away. But you can't. They've got a gem of an idea or they have unshakable curiosity and you'll end up conducting a lecture and a training session.

Every venture guy thinks he is a strategist. I disagree with a number of venture philosophies and one of them is "strategic thinking." So many of them have been educated in the two or three top business schools that they all think alike — not necessarily correctly, but alike. I don't believe that a small business should search for the perfect strategy. By sorting out the unattractive alternatives, you will be left with six or seven viable strategies — pick one and execute the hell out of it. Success in small business is not in having the perfect strategy; it is in the execution of a fundamentally sound strategy.

The venture people who are particularly good in the strategic sense have a very deep knowledge of a particular market. You cannot come up with a workable strategy without such understanding. If you are dealing with a lot of companies and industries, I don't care how bright you think you are, you cannot have an in-depth knowledge of all of them. Some venture capitalists can be very helpful in particular companies, but they cannot be all things to all people. The match between the knowledge and skill of the venture investors and the operating management is very important.

The Kiss Principle ("Keep it simple, stupid!")

Managing a small business has enough problems and we do not need the complexities that often are introduced by venture investors. I have frequently wondered why venture capitalists put a whole bunch of terms and conditions in a deal. Some things are logical, such as preemptive rights, registration rights, board seats or observer positions. There is a tendency, however, on the part of lawyers of venture capitalists, to put in many other things which complicate a deal.

I think control is overplayed by entrepreneurs. No matter who has control — whatever that means — if there isn't an accommodation so that the "control" and the "non-control" can get together at some point, the business is in trouble and you have a more fundamental problem than control. The guy that runs the business has control, even if he doesn't own any stock. The entrepreneur that always searches and reaches for control either doesn't understand reality or has an immense ego, or both. From my point of view, I don't really worry too much about control, because if I don't like what they want me to do, I will leave and go do something else.

I run companies for people, if they don't like the way I run it they ought to get somebody else. I have no problem with that at all. I always tell some of the key investors, the day you don't like the way I am doing things, tell me. I am not going to be upset and will help you find my replacement and I can get another job. I get aggravated at managements that are only concerned about preserving their own position. What else is the issue of control except for that concern?

I think the relevance of control is not control but rather that it implies you have a bigger percentage. But what does this have to do with your ability to run a company's day-to-day operations? I would rather own 1% of something than 10% of nothing.

Structuring and pricing a deal should be kept as simple as possible. Pricing in an early-stage deal is not particularly important, except as it affects future relationships. When potential buyers in a second round financing say "I wish I had been around three years ago when the price was $1.00 rather than now at $6.00," I say "Hey you are not going to make the big bread on the spread between $1.00 and $6.00. If that is what you are satisfied with, I better not do the deal. You should be looking for the spread between $6 and $100." Pricing in second and later round financings is more important and it is clearer because you have something to measure it against. You can compare it to other companies in similar businesses or similar size companies in different businesses or both of these. What can you really evaluate a startup against?

My experience with Modicon was nice and simple, just common stock and we managed to stay that way. Hendrix, when I arrived, was complicated with all sorts of structures. There were too many venture capitalists in the company with diverse objectives. You had to deal with each separately. Each would sit around the table and negotiate the deal. First, venture capital Firm A needed a high interest rate and you would give it to them. Then venture capital Firm B needed a lower conversion, so you would give it to them. Someone else needed registration rights or other provisions and on and on and on. By the time it finally worked out you had a very complex deal with crazy anti-dilution provisions. We had common stock, three types of preferred stock and convertible debentures. Everybody had different agreements, and I couldn't go to the bathroom without checking with somebody.

Finally, I tossed in the towel and wrote my investors a letter which said "Dear People: I am not paying interest; we don't have the money. We are loaned up at the bank and drastically need a recapitalization." While my first suggestion was turned down, we finally arrived at another alternative which was accepted by the stockholders in the longest running stockholder meeting in the world — about four months. When the smoke blew away I had two fresh venture investors, the more disenchanted of the old investors were out and I had gained a simplified capital structure. From that point on we were able to work our way through business problems without creating investor dissatisfaction.

I would much rather operate through a lead investor than with a big group of investors. A lead investor, however, must truly be a lead and have the confidence of other investors. In one of my situations there was a lead investor but the followers came to the board meetings with their assistants. The board meetings were incredible — 15 to 18 people there. Even this would have been OK if they would have just observed. The unfortunate thing is that most venture capitalists are smart, they have good ideas and have large egos, so the meeting ends up being a graduate seminar. The company may be dying but they will argue about some theoretical idea. Having venture capitalists on the board is fine and often constructive, but too many of them can be counter-productive.

Many venture capitalists do not take board seats but instead come as observers. The trouble with an observer role is that they have to realize they are there to observe. At one of my first Hendrix board meetings I had to rent a hall to fit everybody in and that became a little bit awkward. We had everyone and their brothers with a right to come and bring a friend, so it wasn't one on one; it was two or three or four on one. When we would have a vote I would occasionally see a hand up there that didn't belong and say "hey wait a minute, you don't get a vote," and the hand would disappear. Actually, the observer role can work and be very effective if people contribute at the right time and in the right place. Under any business structures and with any relationship it is the effort put out to make things work that will build lasting relationships.

The Venture Capitalists/Entrepreneur Relationship

Getting venture capital is like getting married — you wake up the next morning and the honeymoon is over. In a venture-backed situation the honeymoon is generally a very short period — it usually ends at the closing.

Too many entrepreneurs forget who owns the company. The stockholders own the company. The chief executive is an owner only in the sense of his stock ownership and he must subjugate himself as an employee to himself as a stockholder and to the other stockholders. While he may be president, perhaps chief executive officer, he is still an employee. Those other people, some of whom are venture capitalists, own the company and they can tell him whatever they want him to do.

The venture capitalists, by-in-large, have a very important fiduciary responsibility. They are responsible for investing their client's money for financial gain and they have a right to expect a certain level of performance. I don't find that offensive at all, but I think some entrepreneurs do. If your stockholder venture capitalists want to sell the company and you don't, then it is reasonable to argue. If your argument is based on future growth, maybe you have a valid point. But, if it is because you don't want to work for a big company, I think you are way off base.

I did not want to sell Modicon to anyone at that particular time. The company was moving nicely and I felt we had far more to gain by remaining independent. Some owners, however, had other considerations and this was their prerogative. This was an opportunity for them to realize substantial financial gains and why should management stand in their way? Gould was an excellent choice overall, as long as the desire was to sell. As a matter of fact, I enjoyed working for Gould and was given additional responsibilities that would not have been available to me with Modicon as an independent company. The small business narcotic, however, brought me back to Hendrix.

If a venture investor had a strong conviction differing from my own, I would argue with them as I would argue with any boss — if I felt it important. If my boss finally said "I want it done such and so," I would then decide whether I could do it or not. If no was the answer, I would say you ought to get someone else who can do it, because I can't support your position. I don't present that as a threat to the venture capitalists, just a statement of fact. If a venture capitalist feels so strongly about a particular strategy and cannot sell the idea to management, then he ought to change the management and get someone else to do it his way. But it is a mistake for the venture capitalist to get into that mode, especially since egos must be bruised in admitting a mistake in selecting the original management.

A venture capitalist must sell his ideas and not all of them are willing to do that. They are in a poor position to produce edicts since they are not going to be the ones to execute the strategy or the ideas — this is management's responsibility. They ought to play more of a board member role, dealing with general strategies not details.

I get especially annoyed at directors' meetings where a venture capitalist confuses director and stockholder roles. As a director he has an individual responsibility to the company and all stockholders, not to the venture fund. If he wants to be a stockholder and argue from a stockholder's point of view he ought to call a stockholder meeting. You cannot mix these two roles. Good people, to a large degree, can divorce or separate their venture investment objectives from the company's objectives. My response to this problem is to point out that at a board meeting, you only get one vote whether you own 10% or 99% or nothing. If you want a stockholders meeting go call one. If you want to run the whole company then buy the company and do whatever you want.

The magic of successfully dealing with venture capitalists is mutual confidence. They have to have confidence in you and, if so, 95% of the problems never occur. How do you develop this confidence? It is doing what you say you are going to do. A cynic might say that venture capitalists are only concerned with numbers and, perhaps, this may be true in a minor way because how else can the score be kept. It is more important, however, that you can accurately predict the course of the business than it is to make an immediate profit. Reliable forecasting gives the venture capitalist confidence in your ability to understand your markets, your technology and your business.

An entrepreneur or a chief executive has to understand his employees, his markets, his technology and his responsibilities. But he also has to understand his stockholders and venture capitalists have objectives which must be considered. If you want venture capital then you have to accept the fact that venture capitalists have objectives which are independent of your individual empire. If one doesn't want to be subjected to those factors, don't get the venture money. If you are smart, go get the money somewhere else.

Entrepreneurs make a mistake when they say "give me his money and I can get along with him." A state of siege between management and owners will hurt a company's development. But, in the final analysis, if the company is dying and needs the money, take the money, because living badly is better than dying. If you can't live with the owners, then it may be best to find new management that can work with them so your ownership position may be built into greater value while you do something else. It is easier to change management than to change stockholders. A company is in business to be successful, and it is the relationships between people that make this happen.

Relationship Between Venture Capitalist and Entrepreneur

Brook H. Byers

Brook H. Byers *is a general partner of Kleiner Perkins Caufield & Byers in San Francisco, California. He has been a venture capital investor since 1972. He has worked in management positions for three publicly owned, venture-backed companies in publishing and electronics. He received a BEE from Georgia Tech and an MBA from the Stanford Graduate School of Business. KPC&B manages a very large venture capital fund and has a portfolio of over 90 high technology company investments in computers, electronics, telecommunications and health care.*

Venture capital portfolio monitoring might be compared to farming; that is, there are many different techniques employed between seed planting and the harvest. No single method is perfect because characteristics, such as the strength of the plant, soil condition, the abilities of the farmer, and the weather in current season, must be considered in each case. The venture capital investor must decide for each investment what to do in the years between the intensive period of analysis and negotiation leading to an investment and the future period when capital may be withdrawn and a return on investment realized. This decision depends on the type of involvement an investor seeks; some prefer to rely on management reports and periodic company visits, while others prefer to become "working partners" with management.

Our preference at KPC&B is one of "significant involvement" — giving business counsel and emotional support to the company management and receiving enhancement of our investment and personal satisfaction in return.

Factors Affecting Monitoring

Each investment deserves a unique monitoring approach, which depends on several key factors affecting our relationship with the company, including:

- the length of time we plan to be invested
- the company's need for assistance
- management's willingness to accept advice
- the portion of our total capitalization invested in the company
- our expertise relative to the company's needs
- our time commitments and the company's location
- the competence of co-investors, and
- the degree of potential influence on the company because of both percentage of ownership and, very importantly, personal relationships with management

Based on such factors, we tailor a monitoring method for each investment by using a combination of the following roles: member of the board of directors, interim officer, ad hoc volunteer, active entrepreneur, fire extinguisher, project consultant, counselor and lecturer. The tailored combination changes significantly over the life of the investment.

Four Examples of This Approach

Venture capital investment decisions are complex and allow for a variety of entrepreneurial situations to be attractive. Diversity by technology as well as by stage of development is an objective of a well-managed venture investment firm. Described below are four examples of how relationships between our firm and four ventures evolved.

First Example: Tandem Computers, Inc.

Tandem represents an example of extreme involvement on the part of the venture capital investors; that is, our firm recognized a unique market opportunity for fault tolerant computers and our firm "incubated" the company internally in 1974. Two of our partners left our firm to be president and vice president of finance, respectively, and another became chairman of the board. All three partners had extensive prior experience in the computer industry as managers. The enormous opportunity justified the investment of both seed capital and partners and the result has been one of the most successful venture capital investments in history. Tandem became a publicly held company in 1977 and the company has continued to grow dramatically, resulting in our stock being worth over 100 times our initial investment.

Second Example: Hybritech, Inc.

Hybritech represented a situation where a brilliant scientist perceived a unique opportunity but needed management assistance immediately. In order to capitalize on the lead time provided by the scientist's insight and technology, one of our partners launched the company in 1978 as acting president to prove the commerciality of the process and to recruit a permanent president with experience in that industry. Our partner then became chairman of the board and continued to advise the management team he helped assemble on strategic and policy matters, leaving operating issues to the team. This process allowed the venture a fast start, insured fundamental strategies compatible with our firm's philosophies for high growth companies, and the partner returned to full time venture capital activity. Hybritech became a publicly held company in 1981 and the value of the firm's holding has appreciated over 100 times our initial investment.

Third Example: Caremark
(formerly Home Health Care of America, Inc.)

This company is a case where an excellent management team needed capital in 1978 to exploit a unique market opportunity within a narrow "time window." The strategy for success called for a very rapid build up of the venture and aggressive geographic expansion. We invested with just such an aggressive posture and placed two of our partners on the board of directors to assist in the orderly execution of the plan. This venture, as will most others, encountered difficult periods, including a founder who was not compatible with company goals, emergence of competition, and stresses from rapid growth. Our role has been to assist in key strategic decisions, in recruiting officers and in financing the successful build up. The company became a publicly held company in 1982 and our firm's holdings have appreciated over 50 times our initial investment.

Fourth Example: LSI Logic Corporation

LSI Logic was a typical situation where we participated in 1981 in the startup financing of an exciting venture along with other venture capital firms. One of our partners went on the board of directors, as did another venture capital investor. The company pioneered a revolution in the semiconductor industry through the development of design development tools to make application-specific integrated circuits. Because of a seasoned management team and a fast execution of product development, our involvement has been advisory in nature with specific assistance in financing and customer situations. LSI Logic became a success and went public in 1983 at a price 25 times our initial investment cost.

Benefits of This Approach

We use the "significant involvement" approach to monitoring primarily because we believe it gives us greater investment success. However, many other benefits accrue to us, including:

1. greater personal satisfaction in having taken an active role in the growth of a new business
2. further professional training in business and technology from the "scar tissue" of being involved
3. being "in pace" with the company when business challenges occur and well informed advice is sought by management
4. intimate familiarity with the investment when later financings or mergers are proposed, and
5. the ability to attract venture capital investors (and their capital) from other geographical regions, who desire an involved "watchdog" investor

The benefits of "significant involvement" accrue to our companies and aid in our investment success because we provide:

1. experience in explosive growth businesses
2. a sounding board for top management on a personal level with non-employees
3. broad contacts for diversification, networking between our portfolio companies, foreign marketing expertise, banking contacts and consultants with special skills
4. independence for specific projects, such as strategic plans, acquisitions, compensation plans, and top management screening
5. arrangements for orderly private equity financings
6. communications with the investment community before and after a public offering, and
7. assistance in recruiting an excellent top management team

Problems of This Approach

We sometimes experience problems because of our "significant involvement" monitoring method. Among these problems are the following:

1. Involvement requires time, which can mean harder work by investors or an increase in staff — usually the former, however, because of the small team nature of the venture capital business.
2. Some managers are slow to accept significant investor involvement, viewing it as an intrusion upon their authority.
3. Once trust is established with management and the involvement is mutually satisfying, some entrepreneurs begin to expect unlimited support by the investor which makes it difficult to distinguish non-recurring problems (appropriate for our approach) from recurring problems (the operating responsibilities of management).

4. "Quiet" investment partners sometimes place a *de facto* responsibility for the investment on active investors.

5. An investor, because of significant involvement, is often obligated to participate in later equity financings, because such participation will determine the success of the offering, even though one might personally prefer not to participate further than a present investment level.

6. An involved investor can lose objectivity about an investment and make mistakes in the timing of selling.

Summary

We believe that investing capital in venture situations, combined with involved assistance as described in this article, offers both above average investment returns and better chances for survival of new companies in their difficult early years. Our investment record has proven this to be true, and the personal satisfaction we have derived, along with the satisfying and close relationships with outstanding entrepreneurs, makes it a magnificent way to do business.

An Entrepreneur's Guide to Financing the High Technology Company

Thomas H. Bruggere

Thomas H. Bruggere *is president and chief executive officer of Mentor Graphics Corporation, Beaverton, Oregon. He founded the company in 1981 to produce products for the electronics portion of the computer-aided design industry. Mr. Bruggere has 10 years of management experience including software engineering and product management and development with Tektronix, Inc. from 1977-1981, and with Burroughs Corporation from 1972-1977. He obtained a BS in mathematics from the University of California at Santa Barbara, an MS in computer science from the University of Wisconsin, and an MBA from Pepperdine University.*

Introduction

Raising money for a startup firm is like getting your first date — it can seem like an impossible task, it is hard to take the first step and it is the start of an effort you must continue for the rest of your (company's) life in order to be successful. Just like that first date, the attitudes, strategies and personal abilities you take into the effort will be instrumental in determining your ultimate degree of success.

The financial guidance a new high technology company may receive will be imprecise and inconsistent. There have been successful companies that have financed themselves every way imaginable. However, there are certain things one should pay attention to in order to maximize a company's chance for success. What follows is one entrepreneur's reflections on where to look for the problems and the opportunities. So let us start at the beginning.

Getting up the Nerve

Most would-be entrepreneurs worry about one question: what product should I build? The question of raising money is usually not addressed until after the decision is made to strike out on one's own. Because of the optimistic and confident nature of an entrepreneur, it is often just assumed that financing will be available.

At this stage, the individuals are mostly concerned with getting out of the nest of their existing company. A great deal of energy is put into the product technology because, after all, that is the hinge point for success, is it not? And, hence, that is what will bring the financial world to the door, is it not?

Not necessarily. A good product is certainly important, but it is not the most important thing to consider when starting the company. People are the most important ingredient at this or any other stage. Investors put their money into people, people, people and finally, product/market matches. Good people will make a mediocre product successful, while poor people will fall short with even a vastly superior product. Remember, if you really do have a good product idea, you are going to have competition; the bigger the market potential, the tougher the competition. Also, regardless of your experience or success, you will face difficult problems. Your ability to successfully meet the competition and to overcome these problems will depend upon the quality of your people.

So, good people are what will make the company successful, and investors know this. If you want to make it easier to finance the company, pay attention to the people in the company from the beginning. If you are having trouble raising money initially, take a hard, introspective look at the people in the company. You may need to make some changes.

Asking the Question

Now that you have your product idea refined and good people committed, you are almost ready to ask for the money. First, however, you must decide what to ask for, and whom to ask.

What to Ask For

A business plan will be needed which will include pro forma financial statements indicating how much money you will need to make the company profitable. You must decide how much of that money you want to raise now, and how much you are willing to raise later, hopefully at a higher price. A typical financial plan calls for $50 million in sales in five years with 10% after tax earnings.

The general financial stages of a startup company are prototype development, product development, successful marketing and expansion. Obviously, the further along your company is, the less business risk an investor is taking, and the greater the price you can charge for your stock. Most high technology companies raise enough money in their initial financing to take them through the product development stage. This strategy allows the company to prove that the product can be built and that someone will buy it.

It is not uncommon for a company to run out of money before the product development is completed. For this reason, you should try to get investors in the first financing who can and will put up more money if things do not go as planned. You should also raise more money than you think you need in order to give yourself a buffer. A good rule is to always take 50% more money than you think you need to achieve your plan.

Whom to Ask
The sources of money for the startup company are almost everywhere. Personal finances, relatives, banks, individuals, investment banks, venture capitalists and many other sources may be available to you if you just know where to look. But, all money is not created equal, so you must know what to look for.

Any time you bring an investor or group of investors into your company, you should ask yourself (and them), "what will they bring to my company?" The answer may be guidance, prestige, contacts, high valuation, etc. Make certain that there is a good match between what your company needs and what the investors bring. And always get the highest quality investors you can attract. Top quality investors will attract other investors to your company and provide a much smoother financing plan.

How can you tell a quality investor? There are some simple tests, and they all attempt to determine how the investors will help you. Ask in whom else they have invested: if they have a very successful track record of investing, they probably can help you be successful too. Find out how well known they are; the financial community is very close knit, and reputations are often well deserved.

Determine how long they stay invested in a company; you want early investors with "deep pockets" who can continue investing in subsequent financings. You don't, however, want someone with "short arms" who will not reach down into those pockets to help you in rough times. Finally, ask how they have helped other companies. This will give you some idea how they might help your company.

Next, you should try to match the type of investor to what your company needs. For example, a startup company usually needs consultive help from venture capital types, to adequate lines of credit at the bank. The following priority ranking of what a company needs is broken down by its financial stage.

Prototype/Product Development
Company Need: Active participation in guidance, product strategy, recruiting contacts, management team development

Best Investors: Venture capital, knowledgeable individuals

Successful Marketing
Company Need: Customer contacts, prestige, sales strategy, sales recruitment, less price sensitivity

Best Investors: Venture capital, investment bankers, large funds

Market Expansion
Company Need: Low price sensitivity, customer contacts, prestige, credibility

Best Investors: Large funds, general public

Venture capital investors are the most popular source of initial capital. Good ones will help nurture a company by providing counseling, insights learned from previous investments, access to potential employees, prestige and often customer contacts. They are, however, often the most price sensitive: a typical initial funding is $1 million to $5 million for 30% to 60% of your company.

Beware of the plethora of inexperienced venture capitalists. A number of venture capital funds are managed by people who are either inexperienced in helping a company or spread too thin to have the time to provide help. Always ask what the venture capitalists will bring to your company besides money, and what other companies they have been involved with — both as investors and as board members.

Investment banking firms can provide a limited private or public offering for your company. This can be an easy way to raise money by selling stock to relatively sophisticated institutional or individual investors who will probably not take an active role in the company. This group of investors will generally pay a higher price than a venture capitalist but will usually contribute little or no operating experience to the company.

For initial financings of the company, this method of financing is less attractive than venture capital unless the company already has significant operating experience. As with venture capitalists, investment bankers span a wide range of capability, prestige and experience. Always ask about their most recent offerings and be concerned about the type of investors with whom they will try to place your stock. Unsophisticated or impatient investors may not be very supportive if your company stumbles.

Banks will loan you money if you pledge assets as collateral. If the company has assets (inventory, accounts receivable, etc.), bank debt is an excellent way to generate cash. If, however, you are just getting started, your only assets may be your house, etc. While many companies have gotten started this way, banks are not venture investors (they currently cannot even own stock), and may not be patient when things don't go as planned. In general, it is best not to use banks to finance your startup other than through traditional leases and debt. However, it is important to develop a close, supportive relationship with a good bank from the beginning.

Family, friends and personal finances have started many high technology companies. You certainly should plan on a personal investment, however small. If you do finance your company this way, remember two things: 1) growing the company too slowly because of inadequate capital may cost market share and ultimately the long term viability of your company, and 2) friends and relatives probably don't bring operating experience or accountability to the company. You must, then, get these elsewhere.

One Example

Mentor Graphics is a public company in the fast growing computer aided engineering (CAE) industry. It was initially funded in 1981 by three venture capital firms: Venrock Associates, Greylock Management and Sutter Hill Ventures. It received three private rounds of financing totaling $10 million before raising $52 million in a public offering in January 1984. The figure below shows the stages of funding for Mentor Graphics as an example including the price paid per share by the investors and the total dollars raised.

Building the Relationship

Plan on an ongoing effort to raise money. If your company is successful, you will need capital for expansion. If it is not, you may need it for survival. In any event, you should have a long term financing plan. And don't hesitate to raise money just to have a reserve. These "war chests" have caused many companies to survive rough times while their under capitalized competition failed.

Also, because financing your company is an ongoing process, you should always be working at it. Don't wait until you need money to go out and tell your company's story. The more informed investors are about what you do, the better able you may be to raise money. (And besides, the best time to raise money is usually when you don't need it.)

For example, there are numerous financing seminars you can participate in whether your company is public or private. And because information on the financial "grapevine" travels quickly, a little exposure goes a long way. Also, always keep in mind that the better you tell your story (form and substance), the more attractive your company may be to an investor.

If the goal is to go public, you should plan your investor strategy accordingly. All else being equal, the strongest initial public offerings will come to companies with the most prestigious backers. (Of course, a strong sales/earnings story will always get people's attention in an initial public offering (IPO).

With either strategy, pay attention to your investors, (especially bankers). Keep them regularly informed of progress (at least quarterly), and treat them as an asset of the company. Their support in subsequent financings will be important to you.

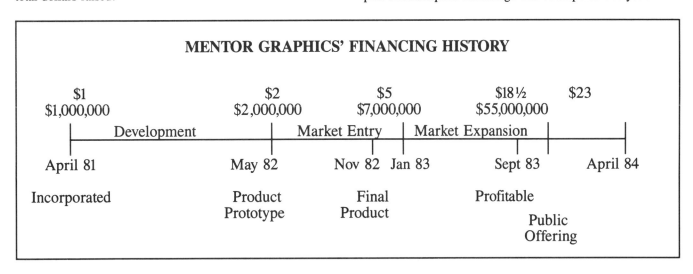

MENTOR GRAPHICS' FINANCING HISTORY

$1	$2	$5	$18½	$23
$1,000,000	$2,000,000	$7,000,000	$55,000,000	

Development — Market Entry — Market Expansion

| April 81 | May 82 | Nov 82 | Jan 83 | Sept 83 | April 84 |

Incorporated — Product Prototype — Final Product — Profitable — Public Offering

The Marriage

The climax of your financing efforts may be a public offering or being acquired. Investors will look for these goals in your plan because that is the way they will get their investment back. This is when it is most important to have a good investment banker and a supportive group of previous investors.

There are a variety of reasons why a company should go public. A public offering will provide a significant source of lower cost capital for the company. It may also enhance the credibility and prestige of your company in the eyes of customers and employees. And it will give early investors and employees some potential liquidity. Besides, the "war chest" of money you raise may give you an important edge over competitors.

On the other hand, being a public company will place new stresses on the company. It will focus you on managing for quarter to quarter increases in earnings, often at the sake of long term strategy. There will be a significant draw on management's time to deal with the financial community. And you may no longer have inexpensive stock to offer employees. In addition to all these problems, you will also have to begin to satisfy the paperwork required for public reporting results.

So it's very important to evaluate when you should take your company public. Your company should be growing in a market that is growing. It is also best to be at a significant sales level and to be profitable so you will be taken seriously by investors, always try to do an offering when the stock market is strong or you may be in for some disappointments. Most important, be certain you have the infrastructure within your company to manage a public company.

The amount of money you raise during an offering will depend largely on your company's need for cash. However, you will also want to consider your competitors' resources since they will probably be trying to out pace you. Also, the price of the stock will be a factor since it will determine the overall dilution of the offering. Finally, listen to the advice of your investment bankers since they will have a good measure on what is possible in a given stock market.

If you have done everything right, many of your existing investors, especially the later stage ones, will show their support by increasing their investment at the public offering. The worst thing you can have is existing investors selling most of their stock at the initial public offering. Naturally, potential new investors are unsettled when they see the people who know the most about the company selling out. However, if you have gotten good investors all along, you will be in good shape at the public offering.

The process of going public may seem so confusing and expensive as to be formidable. But with a good investment banker, it can be an easy and rewarding pinnacle for your company.

Summary

In summary, there are two important lessons that most successful high technology companies have learned about financings:

1. A continuing supply of funds will be needed, so it is important to have a planned investment strategy that brings in investors who will continue to support the company through both good and bad times.

2. Investors are backing people more than anything else, so it is important to be very introspective about the strengths and weaknesses of the key people in the company and to make changes when necessary.

With these lessons in mind, financing your high technology company should be approached with enthusiasm and confidence. Now is always the right time to get started.

Creating Successful Venture-Backed Companies*

Thomas J. Davis, Jr. and Charles P. Stetson, Jr.

Thomas J. Davis, Jr. is a founding general partner of the Mayfield Fund, a 15 year old venture capital firm now managing the fifth Mayfield Partnership. He is a former founding partner of the legendary Davis & Rock venture capital partnership which operated from 1961 to 1968. Mr. Davis is a graduate of Harvard College, Harvard Law School and the Stanford Business School Executive Development Program.

Charles P. Stetson, Jr. is a limited partner of Mayfield Fund. He manages a small private venture fund and specializes in strategic guidance for emerging companies.

Introduction

While much attention has been focused on the glamour and wealth surrounding the most successful venture-backed companies, little, if any, attention has been devoted to why these companies are successful. Venture-backed companies have achieved extraordinary growth in revenues, earnings, jobs and the creation of wealth for employees and investors over the last 25 years when compared with any other group of companies. This success raises many questions:

- Why do venture-backed companies achieve so much in so short a period of time?

- What is distinctive about the managements of these companies?

- Why are the personal attributes of the managers and their understanding of the business more important than the product to the venture capitalist?

- What does the experienced venture capitalist contribute besides money?

- What kind of environment is needed to foster high growth?

This article will examine a number of successful venture-backed companies from the perspective of success, which by dictionary definition includes "the attainment of wealth . . . or eminence."** Accordingly, the authors, in drawing on their experience in investing in over 100 companies and interviews with management and other prominent venture capitalists, will be focusing particularly on those that have achieved extraordinary success, as measured by an outstanding return on investment

* A longer version of this article appears in the Winter Edition, 1985, of the *Journal of Business Strategy*, Volume 5 Number 3.

** Webster's Dictionary

and recognition as an industry leader. The role of management as well as the role of the experienced venture capitalists in these companies will be examined focusing on what is unusual and distinctive in their inter-relationship. The article concludes with a summary of the principles behind the management practices that have contributed to their success.

Criteria for Success

Venture-backed companies have been very successful compared to the average publicly held company. Since 1973, the average stock appreciation of large companies, as measured by the Standard & Poor's 400 Index, was 1.4 times. During the same period, the average venture-backed company's stock traded in the public market, as measured by the *VENTURE CAPITAL 100 Index,* appreciated over 6.4 times. In addition, venture-backed companies have had a significantly higher growth rate in revenues, pre-tax earnings and number of employees when compared to the average, public company (Exhibit I). This article focuses on those companies in the Mayfield Fund and its predecessor that have achieved an outstanding success: returns to investors over 10 times and in one instance over 37 times the original investment (Exhibit II).

These companies are all recognized as leaders in their respective industry with dominant or near-dominant market share. They have created long-term values as opposed to short-lived phenomena. In addition, they have been pioneers in new markets, attracting other new companies that have tried to copy them. Each of these companies acknowledges the value-added contributions of their venture capitalists.

Criteria for Investment

The basic objective of the venture capitalist is to select the right team and the right business. Many business plans are reviewed from a variety of people and industries. According to the records that venture capitalists keep themselves, out of a hundred proposals received, seven or eight will merit a serious look, in view of compatibility with the venture firm's objectives, capital needed, stage of investment and expertise and background of the venture capitalist. From those, two to four may be funded.

In the investment process, it is important to appraise the quality of the management team focusing on the caliber of the individuals — their experience, talent and character as human beings first, then as managers and lastly as engineers, marketers or financial officers. Some qualities are measurable: such as, an individual's achievements in business and education and the reputation of the support group (attorneys, accountants). Reference checks can quantify the experience, talent and depth of the management team. Tandem's original team consisted of 15 experienced people primarily from Hewlett-Packard. Usually there are three or four. Some aspects, such as the personal attributes of the management team, are appraised subjectively.

In terms of the business to be undertaken, understanding the marketplace, the product needed, and product and distribution requirements are all vitally important to be successful. The business plan is a good starting point to explore the management team's knowledge of potential customer's needs and where a market niche can be established rapidly. An ideal market opportunity is usually one where there is a compelling need for a product or service and customers will pay a higher price because there is no other product presently available for the value. This is a defensible market position established with proprietary resources. The market for a company's product should have an immediate potential of $100 to $200 million with an above-average growth rate of 30% to 50%. Smaller markets and markets with lower growth rates limit the opportunity for extraordinary growth. On the other side, the entrepreneur whose goal is to have one percent of IBM's general computer market has generally been viewed as unpromising and without real merit. Larger companies with substantially greater financial, technical and marketing resources make it difficult to establish a defensible market position. The success of Equatorial Communications stands out against much larger, but unprofitable companies in the data communications-by-satellite business. In large part, Equatorial's success has been due to a superior understanding of global telecommunications trends and positioning the company to take advantage of these trends in a market segment with virtually no competition.

In reviewing the business plan with management, the venture capitalist tries to assess how the management team will capitalize on its opportunity. Sometimes new directions can evolve. When David Lee, a founder of Qume, presented his ideas for a new computer printer company, Paul Wythes of Sutter Hill Ventures helped him refine the original business concept so that the new company could better address the market with a proprietary product that was faster, more versatile and a higher quality than the current market leader. In a highly competitive $80 million market, Qume captured 22% of the market in a year and a half.

The final part of the investment process is to examine the projected financial statements. For a company that is just being formed, projections are based on an evaluation of the potential market and the talent of the management team to achieve success in a market niche. The valuation is a matter of judgment. With little or no revenue or earnings history that can be a good guideline, initial valuations are based more on such intangibles as the creativity of the management team.

In making the investment decision, the factors discussed above are very important. However, intuition frequently plays an important role. This could be as straight-forward as one venture capitalist telling his partner about Genentech, one of the original biotechnology companies and an acknowledged leader in the field. The partner, after hearing about the business plan, management team and potential products, stated, "With what this industry will do to change the world, it can never be the same and we have to be a part of the changes. We must invest." This instinct has been rewarded many times. More often, it is a positive feeling about the management team and the personal attributes of the individuals that is most important.

Once an investment decision has been made, the objective of the venture capitalist and management is to make the portfolio company successful — that is to create wealth and eminence. Hence, for the venture capitalist, the first and foremost goal is to be supportive, to ensure the survival and growth of the company and not to harm the company.

Profile of Management

Most management teams of successful venture-backed companies have had no prior experience in building a successful company from inception to maturity. One reason for this is that the venture capital industry is only 25 years old. With most successful venture-backed companies taking seven to 10 years at a minimum to reach maturity, successful managers, mostly as a result of the sale of the company to a much larger company, are only now beginning to recycle and become the key people in new management teams. Bob Schroeder left a large midwestern manufacturer to become president of Qume in 1973 at the age of 35. He is now president of International Power Technology. Vern Anderson, former president of Vidar and former chairman of Silicon Graphics, is now chairman of Ridge Computers.

The backgrounds of the members of the management teams at these companies have certain things in common. Many come from large, well-established companies where they have held middle management positions and responsibilities for new products. Few are senior officers. Typically, these managers have found that they are blocked from launching new products that they feel strongly about. When their ideas result in new products, they do not receive adequate compensation or stock ownership to build wealth. Also, they are not being recognized in other ways by their company for their contributions. Accordingly, many managers leave before reaching senior management positions, armed with a number of ideas about new market needs to be fulfilled. They are willing to take the risk associated with a new venture for the many rewards. Substantially all the managers of these new companies are under 45 years of age when founding the company. Most are in their mid-thirties to early forties with some even younger. Since many managers do not have graduate business school degrees, the management practices are based on personal work experience — some positive and some negative.

The resulting management practices, of which the most visible are flexible work hours, Friday afternoon beer busts, company swimming pools and sabbaticals, and employee ownership have been adopted in different degrees at the most successful venture-backed companies. Some of these practices have been adapted from companies recognized for being well-managed such as Hewlett-Packard and IBM. Other practices have been developed out of a need to do things differently. Consequently, these practices are in sharp contrast with the management practices at traditional companies (Exhibit III).

At the venture-backed companies, the orientation is towards people. A large company chief executive officer, speaking at a recent Los Angeles management conference, articulated the system of managing that entrepreneurs are seeking to change. He proudly described his management system. Every morning on his desk, he had the most recent sales and gross margin numbers for each division prepared, analyzed and summarized by two recent MBA graduates. The CEO proclaimed that he visited each plant at least once every two years! In describing the product development process, he spent an hour emphasizing the importance of market statistics, and not one second on the need to have the right people to develop and market a new product. In fact, not once in his long speech did this CEO mention individuals or human attributes and their importance.

Contribution of the Venture Capitalist
In assessing the role of the venture capitalist with a portfolio company, the value-added contribution is experience. He has

been through it so many times and can anticipate the needs of the company as it grows. For example, managing creative people so they are productive as a team was an issue in the early 1960s that venture capitalists and managements were very concerned about. Vern Anderson, as the young president of Vidar in the early 1960s, spent many late hours discussing this issue with one of his venture capitalist board members. One solution was flexible hours; another, the sabbatical to deal with the stress and burn out of employees. Both at the time were very revolutionary.

To be supportive, the experienced venture capitalist must do what he does best for the company. This includes participating in the selection of people to promote from within or finding additional talent to develop the management team. In the case of Qume, it was finding Bob Schroeder to be president. From having worked with as many as 100 companies, venture capitalists have a broad range of resources and can seek out those people who can be most helpful in developing the business. It could be assisting in developing the right support group such as bankers, attorneys and accountants or ensuring enough potential deep pocket investors for future financings. The lead investor generally takes the responsibility for adding knowledgeable investors who are frequently other venture capitalists with complementary skills and philosophies. This was particularly important for Genentech where the technology is so difficult to grasp.

In view of the long-term relationship being initiated (seven to 10 years), the venture capitalist and management team need to be compatible in management practices and the philosophy and values underlying these practices. A key point is that the experienced venture capitalist must feel positively that a "we - we" type of relationship can be established with the management team as opposed to a "we - they." In a "we - we" relationship, everyone has the same goals and is committed to working together to achieve them. If the venture capitalist is looking for a quick pay out and the management wants long-term growth first, then an adversarial relationship results ("we - they").

A relationship between management and venture capitalist based on mutual respect, inter-dependence and a responsibility to each other as the shareholders of the company is the most important issue. While it is management's responsibility to shape the company, the experienced venture capitalist can and does contribute at each stage. Both must work together to achieve the creation of wealth and eminence each expects, based on an understanding that transcends any written agreement. It is important to recognize that issues will arise as the company matures and this common understanding of the responsibilities of each to the company is necessary for success.

Creating an Environment for Success

Early Stage

The importance of setting the right environment cannot be over-emphasized. The challenge of building a successful company that will have over $100 million in sales with strong profits within seven to 10 years is an enormous task. The new company has everything going against it — no name recognition, no history of production, no established customers.

In the formation and early stages of development, the focus of the new company is on the market and understanding the needs of potential customers. It is very people-oriented, that is, the customers' needs, rather than product-oriented, that is, engineering-oriented. In the case of LSI Logic, it was responding to the need of customers to design their own silicon chips. In Tandem's case, it was the recognition of the need for transaction-oriented, real time, non-fail operations that set the stage for a doubling of sales each year for many years. A common theme is that companies work hard to establish the loyalty of their customers by addressing their needs.

Once the task is defined, the next challenge is to put the people in place. Bob Schroeder stresses that the first 15 people hired and the board of directors establish the character of the company. Thus, in addition to attracting experienced and talented people for key positions, the quality of the people hired is critical as they determine the quality of the company and ultimately the quality of its products.

Because experienced venture capitalists understand that the right people are vital to achieve the company's strategy and goals, they frequently assist in recruiting and interviewing key employees and directors. Talented engineers and executives are very aware of the successful companies that venture capitalists have backed. This adds credibility to the new company.

Once the team, support group and investors are in place, the new company needs help establishing credibility with customers and vendors. The experience and contacts of the venture capitalist often lead to a first big order. During the formative stage, discussions among the management group, between management and the support group and between management and venture capitalists are extensive and very time consuming. Even at this stage, the venture capitalist should stay out of operations so that management can manage. One venture capitalist described it this way. In New York, when a taxicab driver asked which route he preferred to go from uptown to the Wall Street area, he replied that he was going to read the paper, but would be very upset if the driver went via Newark.

Growth Stage

After the company has been successfully launched and revenues are beginning to build, the focus of management shifts. The key task becomes to build growth profitably, but the emphasis is still on people. A major restraint to growth is the lack of the right people in place. "People are the unique resource," contends Jim Patterson at Quantum.

Many of the managements of these venture-backed companies are near perfectionists in filling key positions. At Quantum, for example, management will not compromise on a second choice for a job position. In fact, one critical job position remained open for six months until the right person could be found. Watkins Johnson postponed entry into a closely related field for almost a year until they could recruit an outstanding person to manage the new activity.

A major attraction is the financial reward. In the United States, only a few employees at senior levels at more traditional companies have the opportunity to become wealthy through stock ownership. Talented and experienced people can be attracted to venture-backed companies if they are rewarded for their efforts and have a chance for significant appreciation in net worth. For example, Equatorial Communications, which has attained a market value of $200 million in five years, has employee ownership of 21% or employee equity of $42 million. Employee stock ownership is generally broad-based at these successful companies (Exhibit IV).

Non-monetary compensation provides an important part of the incentives at these high growth companies: the personal dignity resulting from performance with a minimum of supervision; a choice in lifestyles resulting from setting one's own work span during the day or night; and, the free access to the officers to register suggestions and complaints.

All of the managements at these companies believe that each employee has the right to be heard and should be fairly treated. The presidents support this principle and may become involved in any dispute in an endeavor to insure fairness to all. This fosters a high degree of loyalty among employees. They take pride in their company and are willing to work harder and longer.

One of the key concerns at this stage is to keep control of the direction of the company. The informal, person to person, communication that existed when the company was smaller can be lost. Communication is the key. Informal networks between engineers, salesmen and assembly line workers and management are encouraged. The Friday afternoon "beer bust" at many successful firms is an occasion where these networks and relationships are nurtured and flourish. At these sessions there is no rank. You will see, for instance, the manager of production chatting with the most recently hired assembly worker or junior engineer. These informal sessions create a comaraderie and foster mutual respect and a better appreciation of people and their skills.

With good communication among employees and between employees and customers, ideas about improving the quality of the product or new products can be implemented more quickly. The company can more readily respond to changes in the market. Substantially all of these successful venture-backed companies achieved their growth by internal development with product families as opposed to acquisition.

Communication becomes a mechanism for growth. It keeps everyone focused on the corporate objectives, with politics and uncertainty kept at a minimum. In many of these companies, the computer work station has become the company bulletin board and message center. Thus, through technology, any company as it grows larger can keep communicating.

In the middle stage of the development period, many of the early stage efforts of the venture capitalist continue. The role is still to be supportive. However, the emphasis generally shifts from survival to growth.

As a company grows, there are many times of difficulty where the lead investor or venture capitalist who is a board member can be invaluable. This occurred in the second and third rounds of private financing for Tandem Computers when potential investors and management became deadlocked on price. One of the venture capitalists was extremely impressed with the capability of management. He stepped in at management's price and other investors promptly followed. If he had not, Tandem might not have received the funds to maintain its growth. The funds invested by venture capitalists at each stage enable companies to grow faster and more efficiently.

In looking at growth, the experienced venture capitalist usually watches the evolution of the market closely. Because he sees so many proposals, he is frequently aware of new developments. His perspective of the market can be very helpful to the management team and its marketing group. Focusing on the changing markets is increasingly important as the time frame of product life cycles has shortened from what was frequently 10 years in the 1970s to three years in the 1980s in many industries. With shortened product life cycles, a company needs to position itself so that it is at the optimum point on the product cycle curve as quickly as possible. That is the position of maximum momentum to achieve dominant or near-dominant market share. It is also important to have the next product in position faster so that the shortened cycle will be repeated.

Later Stage

When the company is becoming mature, the challenge for management becomes keeping the system working efficiently. What is certain is that there will still be major problems to overcome. In high growth situations, errors in management show up much faster and with less warning. Like the champion golfer who knows that on any given day, he will have about five bad shots that he will have to recover from, the champion management team focuses on being able to respond to the unanticipated problems the company will face. The management team that resembles a weekend golfer does not have the experience to respond consistently.

A company that has studied the problem of high growth, and has been the most systematic in their training and articulate about the process, is Tandem. Management has set as an objective revenues of $1 billion. They must attract the right, next 9,000 employees to a base of 1,000 to achieve this goal, assuming that revenue per employee can be maintained at $100,000.

In order that all employees from managers to production workers understand the corporate objectives and how the value of their stock ownership is tied to these objectives, Tandem management initiated a two-day indoctrination course. The course illustrated each department's contribution to the bottom line and how delays in production, over-inventorying and not managing accounts receivable can be quantified and have a serious impact on the company's stock valuation and thus the employees' worth.

In addition to maintaining high productivity per employee, Tandem has achieved low turnover. Turnover over several years has been around 4% versus 21% for electronic companies generally. By focusing on these two numbers, the company minimizes costly retraining and supervision. The concept is to refrain from over-managing and instead increase an employee's sense of responsibility for a job. All employees are encouraged to participate in creating company policy. An assembly worker at the Tandem plant in Austin, Texas, suggested that each terminal should include the name of the employee who built it. A follow-up postcard to the customer creates direct communication, should any problems occur. In this way, the employee can assume responsibility for the quality of the workmanship and has accountability to the customer.

At Tandem, Jim Treybig has frequently said a company is either growing or dying. In the classic economic analysis of Joseph Schumpeter, each market ultimately dies as new products are introduced which revolutionize the market. Tandem is focusing on creating those next products with input from customers. The importance of those products is that they ensure growth.

Without them, the company will stagnate, the stock valuation will decline and talented employees, who see their net worth not increasing rapidly, will leave.

The challenge at this stage is intensified by the fact that, at some point, the company will sell its stock to the public. There is a significant, but sometimes difficult to quantify, change in the characteristics of ownership. A publicly held company must now deal with the pressures of the marketplace where there is typically a premium for short-term performance. One company has implemented a communications program for its 10 largest stockholders without violating the rules concerning insider information, so that there is frequent contact to ensure no surprises and an emphasis on long-term values. Another issue is that many employees who are now reasonably well off because of the public offering, could leave. The challenge for management is to continue to provide the environment where they will feel challenged and want to stay.

During the long-term relationship between management and venture capitalist, the venture capitalist draws on his experience as a resource to management in helping them chart a course, but he does not force it on the company.

Management still initiates most of the key decisions, such as when to go public or sell the company. At Qume it was the recommendation of the management to be acquired, based on a concern over adequate capitalization to meet another new product launch by NEC, the Japanese electronics company.

At Quantum, the venture capitalist introduced the company to a major investment banking firm that only recently began to underwrite promising new venture-backed companies. The introduction and credibility of the venture capitalist were very helpful in making the investment banker comfortable with the initial public offering. The venture capitalist may also find an acquisition opportunity. For Watkins Johnson, the venture capitalist introduced a company that Watkins Johnson subsequently acquired because the businesses were complementary and the management teams had a similar philosophy. For these introductions, there were no special fees; they were viewed as the responsibility of the venture capitalist to the company.

Underlying Principles

Establishing the proper attitude or philosophy is far more important than particular management practices, including any practices of managing by the numbers, however carefully conceived. The attitude or philosophy is based upon values shared by all the employees. People from large companies who investigate this form of management invariably focus on the specific practices and then endeavor to apply them without having created the shared values without which the practices are of dubious

value. Thus, it is important to understand the underlying principles and environment that these new management teams have created.

In summary, management assists all employees, singly and in groups, to create shared values. These values are based on trust. As a basis for trust, it is fundamental that integrity be shared throughout the organization — by management, the employees and the venture capitalists.

Integrity weeds out bad management practices and dishonesty; improves communications; and builds loyalty and trust. On the other hand, if there is a lack of integrity, bad management can drive out good, as managers hire in their own image. At one company each potential employee is carefully screened for integrity. The corporate policy is that the company will not hire anyone who does not have this value no matter how talented the individual.

Bob Schroeder says that integrity cannot be measured on a scale. "It's binary: you either have it or you don't. And you'd better have it, talk about it and symbolize it so it becomes a bedrock part of the shared values." While president of Qume, Schroeder twice received wine from vendors, despite a written policy against personal gifts. He sent the wine back with a polite note saying it was against corporate policy — and sent it through Qume's shipping department, with special crating required. In a short time most employees heard of those incidents and became aware of management's philosophy and practice. At International Power Technology, Schroeder has made a big point of buying a copy of microcomputer software for each user, honoring the license agreements under which most software is sold. Some people's initial reaction is that that's a waste of money, because the company already has the software in as many copies as it wants. But they came to realize that the issue is integrity and there can be no compromise. "Management must look for ways to symbolize integrity so it becomes part of the legend," says Schroeder.

Conclusion

Management, through character and leadership, creates the growth and success of a company. Management is like the football coach providing inspiration and guidance to build a superior world class team out of seemingly ordinary, but talented people. Everyone on the field has to take responsibility for their performance and truly share the desire to win and be successful.

To be a member of a winning team can be fun. Fun in this context means having an enjoyable, stimulating, dignified, challenging and productive place to work. This has its origins in the nature of the founders and has been perpetuated through recruitment practices rather than management edict. When the tasks are challenging and one's peers and supervisors are talented and everyone is treated with respect, then work can be fun.

The key to success will not prove to be organizational gimmicks, large or small, or Japanese-type circles or segregation of individuals into teams of champions or bootleggers while the rest of the employees are treated as infirms. The key will prove to be the emphasis on the dignity of each employee and treating each person as capable of quality work on a sustained basis because the individual is an adult, responsible, precious human being.

This revolutionary concept of management, its practices and underlying principles, is a significant change from the traditional management practices, including those of scientific management. The authors believe that the new relationship between management and employees working together for productivity that is quality-oriented rather than quantity-oriented may be creating a revolution as profound as that of the Industrial Revolution in Leeds and Manchester in the last century in England.

EXHIBIT I

Comparison of Growth and Current Valuation

	Latest 12 Months Revenue (In Millions)	Growth in Employ-ment Dec. 1982 to Dec. 1983	Pre-Tax Earnings As % of Latest 12 Months Revenue	Years Since Founding	Price/ Earnings 6/30/84	Market Price/ Book Value 6/30/84
1. Companies Discussed						
Equatorial Communications	$ 25.5	81.3%	18.5%	6	61.4	5.0
Genentech	54.2	79.4%	3.0	8	313.6	5.0
LSI Logic	58.0	348.2%	28.4	5	23.0	1.9
Quantum	79.9	11.1%	27.5	4	13.9	2.8
Qume*	54.0	N.A.	21.2	5	N.A.	N.A.
Scientific Data Systems*	100.6	10.0%	19.4	5	56.6	N.A.
Tandem	497.1	15.0%	10.4	10	32.6	2.7
Vidar*	12.5	−9.2%	15.1	9	31.6	6.5
		Growth of Revenue				
2. Venture Companies**	57%	37%	N.A.		22.0	N.A.
3. Standard & Poor's 400 Index	8.2%	0%	9.3%		11.7	1.41
4. Dow Jones Industrials	5%	−1.0%	N.A.		11.7	1.22

* Latest year before acquisition

** Based on study by Venture Economics of 80 venture-backed companies for period 1981 to 1982. These companies were funded in the 1975 to 1980 period.

*** Based on current price/earnings for Venture Capital 100 Index (June 30, 1984).

N.A. Not Available

EXHIBIT II

Comparison of Returns on Investment
As of June 30, 1984

	Times Return(*)	Year of First Investment
1. Companies Discussed		
Equatorial Communications	15.7	1978
Genentech	17.5[1]	1977
LSI Logic	19.5	1981
Quantum	10.7	1980
Qume[2]	26.1[3]	1975
Tandem	37.6[4]	1975
Vidar[2]	33	1960
2 Venture 100[5]	6.4	1973
3. Value Line Composite	1.7	1973
4. S&P 400	1.4	1974

* Times return is calculated by dividing the price at June 30, 1984 by the price per share of the investments (usually several) prior to public offering, allowing for stock splits. Data is based on Mayfield Funds and prior investments of Tommy Davis.

[1] The first partnership received a 45 to 1 return on investment.

[2] Vidar and Qume were valued at the date sold.

[3] Sutter Hill Ventures, the lead investor, received a 90 to 1 return on investment.

[4] The founding investors received a 175 to 1 return on investment.

[5] Source: *VENTURE CAPITAL JOURNAL.*

N.A.   Not Available

EXHIBIT III

Comparison of Management Practices

The Role of Management	Traditional Company	Successful Venture-Backed Company
1. Emphasis on understanding customer needs in product development	Low	High
2. Management emphasis	On the numbers	On people
3. Employee stock ownership	Low: senior management has largest stake; many employees no ownership	High; all employees own stock to some extent
4. Decision making	Hierarchical structure. Organization chart is a pyramid.	Team approach. Everyone has a valuable input.
5. Supervision of employees	High	Low
6. Work environment	Structured	Unstructured
7. Relationship between senior management and workers in the factory	Tends to be adversarial. Management versus labor.	Very positive, open relationship
8. Diversification	Open; leading to conglomerates.	Restricted to product families and areas of expertise.
9. Communication	Top down	Bottom up
10. Productivity	Quantitative	Qualitative

EXHIBIT IV

Employee Ownership in Venture-Backed Companies
As of June 30, 1984*

	# of Employees	% of Employees Owning Stock and Options**	% of the Company Owned by Employees Through Stock and Options**	Market Value of Employees Stock and Options*** (In Millions)
Equatorial Communications	242	34.7%	18.2%	$ 46.0
Genentech	622	84.7	20[E]	$ 99.1
LSI Logic	700	N.A.	21.6	$ 78.4
Quantum	673	68.3	9.2	$ 17.6
Tandem	5,268	100[1]	16.3	$178.7
Vidar	470	31.3	50.1	$ 14.0

*   Except for Vidar data is at time of sale. Data for Qume and Scientific Data Systems is not available.

**   Based on stock and options known to the Company. Some employees may own stock held in a brokerage firm name and thus would not be counted.

***   Options are issued at a current market price and stock initially issued at nominal value so that employees holding stock have significant appreciation.

[1]   Tandem periodically distributes a bonus option to each employee and in May 1984 issued options on 100 shares to each employee.

N.A.   Not Available

[E]   Estimated

When and How to go Public

The public marketplace is an uncertain friend for the small, growing company. In the 1960s virtually any company could raise money by "going public." This environment shifted radically in the 1970s, and by 1975 public financing was almost impossible for the small company. From 1979 to 1982 the public marketplace became progressively more receptive to new issues culminating in 1983 with the most active new issue market in recent history. In 1984, after the disappointing performance of many companies which went public in 1983, the public market was chilly toward new offerings. It still remains, however, a source of capital for those companies which have achieved some success and can demonstrate growth potential.

The decision to go public can be both tantalizing and traumatic. Although it may extend unfettered capital to a growing firm, it also exposes the embryonic business to a level of public scrutiny that may be more problematic than the watchful eyes of private investors. The public market is unforgiving in its business evaluation and slow to regain its confidence. A company experiencing its early growing pains may not be able to withstand public examination and pressure, and therefore it is imperative that management carefully examine the advantages and disadvantages of "going public" before succumbing to the lure of the public market. The venture capitalists' tactic of waiting for their portfolio companies to display the strengths of a viable independent business, before they recommend a public offering, should also be kept in mind by prospective entrepreneurs.

The following articles discuss "going public" as a viable alternative for the small company in need of growth capital and highlight the pitfalls awaiting the newly public company. In addition to presenting guidelines for dealing with investment bankers both before and after the public offering, these articles also offer useful advice for the public company assuming the new role of dealing with stockholders.

In the second article, a successful communications specialist offers some valuable insight into relaying your company's story to customers, to analysts and to the media — an important part of every company's marketing program.

It should be recognized that a newly public company will not normally be abandoned by its venture capital investors, because these investors rarely sell their ownership positions in a public offering. They continue to offer guidance and, in fact, achieve their greatest financial gains after a portfolio company attains success in the public marketplace.

Public Financing for Smaller Companies

Peter Whitmore Wallace

Peter Wallace is a principal of Hambrecht & Quist Incorporated, San Francisco, California. His background includes more than 20 years in investment banking and venture capital; before that he was manager of product development at Raychem Corporation. Hambrecht & Quist is an investment banker primarily serving emerging companies with substantial growth potential. The firm provides a full range of investment banking services to its corporate clients and is not only a leading underwriter of securities for emerging growth companies, but is also a major factor in the venture capital financing of early-stage companies.

Introduction

Over the past few years, we have seen an increased strengthening of demand in the marketplace for the offerings of smaller companies going public for the first time. Public financing has become a viable alternative for the well-managed smaller company exhibiting an above average growth rate and having the prospect for continued growth over the years ahead.

Hambrecht & Quist has specialized in raising money for the emerging high growth rate companies, generally in technology-related businesses. Over the past five years we have managed or co-managed more than 150 public offerings for a total of more than $4 billion. Looking back at the new issue market, in 1969 there were over 1,000 new offerings, which raised an estimated $2.6 billion for the issuing companies. The pace declined steadily in the next few years until in 1975 there were six initial offerings, which raised a total of $34 million, and the level remained low for the next couple of years, with a steady increase year to year starting in 1978. Despite the disruptions in the economy caused by inflation, high interest rates, and the recent recession, the public market has generally remained viable for the better quality smaller companies, where investors are looking for growth opportunities that will create equity gains at a rate substantially above that of inflation. It is important to recognize that the availability of the public market at any given point in time is highly dependent upon a variety of conditions, including the general state of the economy, inflationary trends, interest rates, and so on. In this article, we will presume the existence of a receptive public market and will deal with the factors to be considered by corporate management in assessing the merits of public financing as one of several alternatives. We will consider the principal criteria of the marketplace, the advantages and disadvantages of a public offering from the point of view of the issuing company, the process of selection of an underwriter and a description of the typical sequence of events that occur in the process of "going public" once the decision has been made.

Criteria of the Marketplace

From the "hot markets" and "concept companies" of the late 1960s we have seen a development in the sophistication of the criteria by which the marketplace evaluates young growing companies with respect to their stock issues. We have also seen the emergence of the institutional buyers (banks, pension funds, money managers, investment advisors) as the leading factor in the new issue market, in contrast to the previous dependence of that market upon the individual or "retail" buyer. The result has been a more analytical approach, a higher degree of selectivity, and a more consistent set of long-term objectives.

The primary goal, of course, is the achievement of a steadily increasing equity value through growth in sales and earnings. Particularly in periods of high inflation rates and high interest rates, a company must exhibit an above average growth potential in order to interest the investor, who sees alternative uses for his capital in low-risk, high-yield debt investments, and who needs to achieve "something extra" to compensate him for the risk of tying up his capital in a small, unseasoned company. In the past few years, many of the companies that have been coming to market with initial public offerings have been capable of consistent annual growth rates in the range of 30% to 50%, and in some cases have exceeded 100% with the prospect for continuation of that rate for at least a year or two more. In general, these companies have achieved an annual revenue rate that typically is at least in the $15 million to $20 million range and in some cases has been a great deal higher. Again, speaking in generalities, net income is usually above an annual rate of $1 million.

While there are many exceptions to the foregoing criteria (particularly in the smaller issues, often sold on a "best efforts" basis rather than in a firm underwriting), the ability to sustain after-market interest in the stock of a newly public company is significantly diminished when a company has not achieved the size, profitability, and growth outlined above.

Underwriters Criteria

For an investment banker to manage a successful offering, he must be sensitive to the requirements of the marketplace that he is serving. Accordingly, when an underwriter is approaching a potential corporate client he will be keeping in mind the market criteria described, while at the same time recognizing additional fundamental criteria that must be met in order for him to offer the stock with confidence, make a trading market in the securities, and continue to recommend purchases by his clients in the after-market.

Clearly the underwriter must be enthusiastic about the basic business in which the corporate client is engaged. For instance, if a company has had a superb growth record but its industry will be negatively affected by technology changes, increased major competition, recession-induced problems, or by other factors that will change the fundamental outlook, the underwriter will then think carefully about the wisdom of managing a stock offering for the company in question. An overriding consideration, in any event, is the quality of the people who are running the company. An investment banker must assess the capability, integrity, intelligence, "toughness," and desire to achieve, as well as the general objectives of the management group as a key part of his decision to proceed with an offering.

The quality of the financial record is also of major importance. The Securities and Exchange Commission (SEC) requires a summary of operation for the past five years and audited income statements for the past three years (with exceptions for companies whose existence has been of a shorter duration).

Public Offering from the Issuer's Viewpoint

The question of whether or not to go public is not trivial. Once a company has taken the step to offer shares of its stock to the public marketplace, it becomes subject to a degree of regulatory and market scrutiny from which it was previously insulated. This in turn will create additional demands upon management time and will inevitably play a part in operating decisions.

Let's take a look at the basic advantages and disadvantages of a public offering. On the plus side would be the following:

1. If a company is acceptable to the public market, its securities will generally command a higher price than in a private equity placement. This means that equity capital can be raised with minimal dilution.

2. Once a company's securities have become seasoned in the public market, the mechanism is in place for further public financings to bring in additional equity capital as needed to support a continuing growth program.

3. A viable public market creates liquidity, which can be important for shareholders in general and particularly for founders and managers who may have substantial holdings in the company's stock.

4. The public marketplace provides an objective and credible measure of the value of the company's stock, which is of importance in attracting new management talent through equity participation, in motivating employee shareholders, and in providing for acquisitions a medium of exchange with a readily acceptable valuation.

5. Being publicly held can increase a company's stature or image to its customers, suppliers, bankers, and others.

On the negative side of the ledger would be the following:

1. Going public requires a detailed disclosure of the company's affairs in its offering prospectus. This reveals to competitors, customers, employees, and the public-at-large many details of the company's business and ownership that it may feel more comfortable keeping to itself.

2. A public company is subjected to reporting requirements by the SEC that will mean, in general, the preparation of a public document on a quarterly basis. In addition, the requirements of the stock market and the public investors for continuing information about the company's affairs will mean the initiation of a formal management program to furnish periodic reports and maintain communication with analysts, portfolio managers, major shareholders, and a variety of others.

3. The expectations of a public shareholder group will put considerable emphasis on maintenance of a smooth pattern of operations and growth. Deviations from an established growth trend line that can be accommodated readily within a private company in order to focus on a particular development effort, a special marketing program, or other unusual expenditure are much more difficult to communicate to the public in a way that will avoid resultant fluctuations in the price of the stock.

4. Finally, the costs of the offering itself are not insignificant. In addition to the underwriter's compensation, or "spread," there are expenses of attorneys, auditors, financial printers,

and a number of additional costs all of which can add up to $250,000 or more even for a small offering. These costs obviously have to be weighed against the benefits of a public offering as compared with other methods of financing.

Selection of an Investment Banker

The investment banker who is chosen to be the company's managing underwriter performs a variety of roles. Immediately in connection with the public offering he will organize a syndicate of other investment bankers to achieve appropriate distribution of the company's stock, both on a geographical basis and to provide a balance between institutional and individual stockholders. Once the stock has been issued to the public, the managing underwriter assumes responsibility for a continued sponsorship of the corporate client to the financial community. This includes making a market in the company's stock, providing analytical reports by the securities research department, organizing presentations to groups of investors and potential investors, and generally assisting the corporation in establishing a strong following within the financial community. Among the characteristics that a company should look for in selecting an investment banker are the following:

Reputation. The stature and professional reputation of the investment banker within the financial community. This will affect the ability to form a strong syndicate of firms, and it will influence the quality of investors who can be attracted to the offering.

Experience. The investment banker's experience in underwriting issues of companies in the same or similar industries. This will be important in the degree of credibility accorded the underwriter's presence by the investment community. It will also influence his ability to price the issue accurately.

Research capability. Because the managing underwriter will be looked to by the financing community as a primary source of information about the newly public company, it is important that the selected investment banking firm have experienced analysts closely following the industry in which the company does its business. The reputation of an individual analyst on ''the street'' can have a strong effect on the degree of interest that can be sustained in the company's stock.

Market-making capability. When a company first issues stock to the public, the shares will be traded on the ''over-the-counter'' market. A number of investment banking firms will become the market-makers in this new stock. The role of the managing underwriter is generally to provide leadership in the market-making function and to provide sufficient depth on both the buy and the sell side of the market so that it will insure liquidity for even large shareholders. This requires the investment banking firm to devote sufficient capital to the market-making activity so that meaningful long or short positions can be maintained in the day-to-day market-making activities.

Distribution capability. Different investment banking firms have different client bases, some emphasizing institutional accounts, others primarily dealing with individuals, still others having an international emphasis as opposed to domestic, and so forth. A company should determine whether the investment banker can, in fact, distribute the company's stock effectively to a client base that can serve as a strong element of ongoing market interest in the stock.

In general, a company manager seeking an investment banker should take the time to be sure he is comfortable not only with the people with whom he will be directly involved initially, but also with those who will have ongoing responsibility for market-making, research, sales sponsorship, and so forth. He should talk with the managements of other corporate clients of the proposed investment banker and find out first hand what their experience has been and how they feel about a long-term relationship with the particular underwriter. The process of selection of an investment banker is that of selecting a particular kind of professional who can provide a variety of services over a long period of time.

Typical Sequence of Events

While each individual case has its own characteristics and its own time schedule, a typical pattern might be as follows: The XYZ Company has reached a point in its growth where it recognizes the need for additional capital to finance growth in the year or two ahead. The company may have been in business for a number of years and private investors who provided the initial capital are interested in seeing some degree of liquidity and a measure of value on their shares. In a series of meetings, the XYZ directors determine that it is appropriate for the company to seek a public offering. The management is directed to discuss this possibility with a number of underwriters and to ask those who appear to be both suitable and interested to make formal presentations to the board of directors. The proposed underwriters will each make visits to the company to become acquainted with management and operations prior to submitting their proposals. Finally a selection is made by the board and management of the company and the formal process commences.

When the preparation of the underwriting is to begin, an "all hands" meeting is held involving the company management, the managing underwriter, company counsel, underwriter's counsel, and auditors. At this time, a time schedule is laid out for the demanding task of preparing the registration statement to be filed with the SEC as well as the subsequent events that will involve the marketing of the proposed issue. A part of the registration statement is the prospectus, which will be distributed publicly, and which describes the company's history and operations in some detail. The preparation of the registration materials will typically take 30 to 60 days, a time period that may be extended, if necessary, to accommodate the completion of an audit.

Once the registration statement is filed with the SEC, the preliminary prospectuses are printed and the marketing process commences. At this time, the underwriter will invite other investment banking firms into the underwriting syndicate, and the final syndicate may be composed of 50 to 70 firms. As these firms accept positions in the syndicate their salesmen begin to talk with clients and furnish them with prospectuses. Meanwhile, the managing underwriter will typically organize a series of presentations by company management in various key cities where significant institutional or individual investor interest can be found. Perhaps a half dozen to a dozen cities will be visited over a period of one to two weeks.

At the same time the SEC processes the registration and ultimately responds (usually within thirty to forty days) with a series of comments, questions, or requests for additional information.

The prospectus is then modified as needed to conform with the SEC request, and when the SEC is satisfied with the content, it will permit the issue to become effective.

Immediately prior to the offering becoming effective, the underwriter and the company have the last of a series of price discussions and set the price of the offering, which will then be incorporated into an amended prospectus. The revised prospectus with the price amendment then becomes a final prospectus that is printed and distributed after the offering has become effective. As soon as the offering is effective, sales can be confirmed by the members of the syndicate to their clients. Prior to effectiveness, they can do nothing more than take indications of interest.

The final step will be the closing, generally five business days after the offering becomes effective. At this time, the money changes hands and the offering is completed.

Conclusion

The public marketplace should be considered as one of several valid alternatives for the small growing company. There are, however, both advantages and disadvantages to a public offering and these should be weighed carefully before attempting to go forward. The proper selection of the investment banker who will be managing underwriter for the issue is of key importance not only to the success of the issue, but perhaps even more important, to the maintenance of long-term interest in the stock once it becomes publicly held. Finally, market timing is important because the availability of the public market to smaller companies can change from time to time with changes in the economy and with changes in investor attitudes toward the stock market.

Public Relations for Emerging High Technology Companies

Regis McKenna

Regis McKenna is chairman and founder of Regis McKenna Inc., headquartered in Palo Alto, California with branch offices in Portland, Oregon; Phoenix, Arizona; Boston, Massachusetts; Orange County, California; London, England; Munich, Germany; and Paris, France. Mr. McKenna's firm specializes in providing marketing and communications strategy for small technology-based companies. He describes his role as primarily one of helping these emerging businesses and technologies evolve by developing marketing strategies and market positioning. Intel Corporation, Apple Computer and Tandem are some of the firm's clients. Mr. McKenna founded the firm in 1970 after 10 years of experience in editorial sales and marketing communications.

Public relations has an image problem all its own. It has come to represent all the fluff, and little of the substance, of business. In too many companies, PR departments are formed to control and manage the flow of information to the press. This practice tends to distort the meaning and purpose of public relations.

I regard public relations as a much more strategic endeavor. Relatively few people with whom you communicate will have direct knowledge of your product. Most people, including potential employees, potential customers, investors, analysts, and journalists indirectly gain their experience by what they hear or read. You must convey many messages about your business to everyone who is vital to you.

These messages must evoke a certain quality. Your customers are looking for more than a generic product. They want to do business with a technology leader, an innovator, a supplier known for excellence and reliability. They want to deal with well-managed companies with reputations for advanced or reliable products, as well as good support and service.

You can run ads and proclaim your virtues to the world, but I do not believe that is how you communicate your qualities with any degree of credibility.

Don't Just Inform, Communicate

It is essential to understand communication — and how it is distinct from information. "Strategic communication" develops or changes attitudes and opinions among people in target markets. To communicate strategically, you must understand something about the minds of the people you want to reach. In other words, you can communicate only with those people with whom you are more or less in tune. And it takes an educational process to achieve that meshing.

So public relations is an educational process directed toward intermediaries in business and industry, who influence market attitudes and opinions. It is directed communication, rather than distributed information.

What is Public Relations and What Can It Do For You?

No single definition for public relations exists because the field is as complex as communications itself. What is important to remember is that public relations is by nature educational. It is 90% strategy and only 10% tactics, or methods.

Let's look at what public relations can do for high-growth, entrepreneurial companies.

First and foremost, an early program of public relations helps establish credibility in the eyes of customers and investors. Most technological companies are in high-growth markets, and their buyers are faced with increasingly complex decisions. Customers want security. They want to know if a company will be around to support a product. It is the number one question on their minds when doing business with a new firm. This raises other questions concerning capitalization, management competition and long-range strategy.

The second, and perhaps equally important benefit, is the feedback and learning you acquire by talking to key journalists, analysts, and industry observers. These people provide a mirror that reflects how the world sees you. In many cases companies must change how they conduct business before they can change their public image.

Third, a sound public relations program is the most economical form of communications to your market. It is certainly the quickest way to achieve a degree of credibility in an industry where the window of opportunity does not stay open long.

And fourth, public relations is the best method of relating the individual qualities of your business and position in the most plausible manner.

The fact is that many entrepreneurial companies and products have been made distinctive through a good and early public relations effort.

Working With the Media

Let's look at the nature of media and press relations, which tends to be the focus of most public relations programs.

Ten years ago I kept an envelope in my desk drawer that contained hundreds of rejected integrated circuit chips. When an editor visited me, I would scatter a few chips on my desk, explain how they were made, and describe the complexity and computing power of these miniature devices.

Five years ago, my Apple computer become the center of discussion. Since then, more has been written about what the personal computer can do, will do, and won't do than any other electronic product in history.

Today my terminal, personal computer, and pictures of microcomputers attract little attention from visiting journalists. They want to discuss topics of a more universal nature.

These topics revolve around such questions as:

- Will America's electronics industry endure the Japanese?
- Who will survive the shake-out in personal computers and biotechnology?
- How widespread is the theft of American trade secrets?
- How will the AT&T divestiture affect the telecommunications industry?
- Is there too much venture capital?
- Will Europe and Japan develop a venture capital business?

Perspectives on the High Technology Environment

High technology is in itself of worldwide concern and those of us working within its boundaries are caught up in the media's striving for unusual coverage of these industries. Let's look at the events of the past few years that influenced the media's perspectives.

Within the past 10 years:

- The microprocessor put electronic intelligence into such everyday items as automobiles, telephones, banking terminals, microwave ovens, and small computers.
- The personal computer and its software became tools that brought to most journalists first-hand experience with technology.
- A few entrepreneurial high technology companies achieved spectacular growth, thus calling attention to their tech-

nologies. These companies and their competition became recognized on Wall Street, and their founders acted as spokesmen for the industries.

- As automobile, steel, and other older industries developed troubles, journalists began looking for new American industry success stories.
- Pac Man and other video games became the high technology passion of society, then just as quickly became symbols of the risk and vulnerability of all "hi tech" businesses (even though these products were not really high technology).
- Genetic engineering and other feats of biotechnology fulfilled many commercial possibilities, but public expectations soon exceeded the technolgies' short-term capabilities.
- The Japanese high technology challenge became evident, making headlines worldwide. (I have read so much about Japanese quality, management techniques and fifth-generation computers that I am convinced that their PR is as good as their 64K RAMs.)
- Since the U.S. government dropped its anti trust suit against IBM, that company has become the dominant driving standard in the small computer marketplace.

In the wake of all these events, it is difficult to put in proper perspective a new software package, instrument, CAE/CAM or CAD product, chip, specialized computer, or even another startup.

High Technology and the Media

The business and news media have evolved from the simple reporting of products and markets to analyzing industry and business issues.

The press follow and reflect industry maturity. When the general news press first encounter an industry, their stories are (from the industry perspective), naive and superficial, with all issues presented in black and white. As the business and general news press continue to cover an area, they also learn, grow, and begin to dig into the "news behind the news." The media then acquire journalists who specialize in technology.

Different product and performance positioning are necessary when dealing with business and general news press than would be successful with the trade press. In fact, when products are discussed in the business press, often they are put in the context of "The Office of the Future," "The Factory of the Future." The press are fascinated by glimpses of what lies ahead. And when the press get specific, they concentrate on popular applications and markets that are not quite yet here.

The news and business media have discovered technology only in the past few years. *Business Week* now allots approximately 20% percent of its issues to high technology. *The Wall Street Journal* has a weekly technology column and 10 to 20 items per week on technology-related issues and business. *Fortune* regularly runs major articles on technology. *Forbes, Newsweek* and *Time* now have computer editors on their staffs.

We will see increased emphasis on high technology businesses and issues. The industry will become more diverse, fragmented, complex, and difficult to understand; yet, there will be more information available about every facet of every industry. Journalists will need more help to make order out of the confusion. This, of course, will become an opportunity for some and obstacle for others.

The press, like your business, is competitive. We perhaps have been more aware of the jockeying for position in the trade press, and less aware of the growing competitive nature of the business press in technology-related areas.

Electronic News was the first newspaper-like journal in the electronics industry. It is loved or hated but read regularly by most managers in the electronics business. People who in one breath would discredit its reliability would also be the first to complain if their story did not get sufficient coverage. *Electronic News* was started by people whose background was newspapers, not electronics. Rather than delve into products, they covered the people changes, business activities, distribution, and the ups and downs of markets and companies. They brought human interest into technology.

And *Electronic News* had the important knack of capsulizing the news. It is fast-reading, with concise industry round-up, views, and "he said, you said" reporting — all aimed at serving a reader with little time to read. *Time* magazine built its success on this style.

The benefit of this type of coverage is that it spreads the news to non-technical management, distributors, industry, and financial analysts — making it possible to have knowledge about the industry without being an engineer.

One day in 1968, when I worked for National Semiconductor, I was taking a cab from the Plaza to *Electronic News*. The cab driver started asking me questions about what I was doing in New York City. I worked for an electronics company. Where? In California. Which one? A small company you probably never heard of. What's the name? National Semiconductor. The cab driver then said, "Ahhh, Sporck's gang." I picked myself up off the floor and then got a lecture on the perils of going into competition with TI. It turned out that his son was an engineer and sent him copies of *Electronic News.*

In the late 1960's, Lew Young moved back to *Business Week* from *Electronics* magazine as editor-in-chief, taking Bob Henkel with him. Both had business news backgrounds but were not engineers. Their previous associations with high technology moved them to increase *Business Week's* high technology coverage. Their Information Processing section led not only to new readers but to a new advertising market as well.

Not that their editorial work was directed toward advertisers; their editor focused on the market, which created a following.

Magazines and newspapers are not innovative; they follow trends rather than lead them. Few will risk turning to a new direction too early. But there are exceptions — *Fortune's* in-depth coverage of certain technologies and *Business Week's* capsulized views of a business or market. For most other business journals, however, technology is a foreign language. The journalist has to be convinced of the viability, value, and reliability of what you represent.

Technology is the future. It is where the stories are. Revenues will derive from technology and competition will create ever increasing attention from the broader news and business media.

Understanding the Media

When covering technology, journalists seek their own level of capability, comfort, and understanding. The way you communicate with one journalist will not suffice with others.

Here are some important characteristics to remember about the press:

1. The journalist is an intermediary, with different objectives from your own. The journalist does not consider his or her work as extensions of your positional activities.

2. The First Amendment guarantees freedom of the press. This is taken quite seriously by trade, business and news journalists.

3. The press is not a substitute for advertising. The notion that a story is free advertising is degrading to a journalist. This attitude will also mislead you in your approach and in your methods of reaching the press.

4. One-on-one communication is the most effective way of reaching a journalist. Although thousands of press releases are generated and mailed each week, less than 10% are printed. *Business Week* estimates that they receive at least 10,000 press releases a week. Yet releases do not form the basis of their stories. *Business Week, Forbes, Fortune,* and *Time,* for example, do not use press release material in their articles. *The Wall Street Journal,* and *The New York Times* use only those releases where the information concerns a

"matter of record" for the public market, such as a dividend announcement. Because the press is competitive and because of the variation of interest and understanding among the media, press conferences are of little value. They convey information but they do not communicate.

5. The trade press is often forgotten in comparison with the glamour of *Time* or *Fortune,* but it is still the backbone of high technology communication strategy.

6. The press network consists of many sources — industry and financial analysts, consultants, third-party references, major potential or actual customers, and other experts. In this complex technical world, the journalist looks to these analysts and experts to sort out fact from fiction. It is the word-of-mouth in these market groups that helps validate your presentation. It is very important to establish relationships with this group. You may also consider regularly previewing new products, strategies, and market changes with the key groups in your industry before going to the world-at-large.

7. The 90 to 10 rule applies. 90% of the world's views are controlled by the 10% of opinion makers. To build a position in any industry requires establishing relationships with a core of influential people. Whether consisting of employees, financial or industry analysts, or journalists, each group contains a few whose opinions and work dominate that group. A good job of public relations demands that you develop relationships with a relatively few people.

Emerging Companies and the Emerging Press

With this background, I think it is now appropriate that I address the question of "How do emerging companies deal with the emerging press?"

The answer, I believe, lies more with communication strategy and style and less with tactics. It rests with an understanding of the journalist and the way information is credibly communicated in a marketplace.

Between 1980 and 1984, over 1,000 new high technology companies were formed. In that same period roughly 30,000 new technology-based products were launched. Not all were successful, of course.

There has been much written about why products and companies fail. One of the most important criteria for success, assuming the product has intrinsic value, is rapid market penetration and positioning.

New companies initially gain ground as a result of product differentiation, rather than market or corporate strength. As companies grow, their positioning strength moves from product position to market position to corporate position.

The most important quality a growing company needs for rapid market access and to move up the positioning ladder is credibility. Credibility can be gained by inference, reference, or evidence.

- *Inference* is often used by startups to gain recognition. I tell budding entrepreneurs that who invests in their company is more important than how much is invested. I have no doubt that the business press's initial interest in Genentech was stimulated by Kleiner & Perkins' involvement. Similarly that Venrock, Art Rock, and Capital Management interests in Apple Computer provided "larger than reality" credibility. The quality of your investors, board of directors, and background of your first employees present you to the media marketplace.

- *Reference* is the most important promotional tool an emerging company can use — word-of-mouth. Do you realize that almost all computers, from personal to mainframes, are bought because of reference or word-of-mouth? All service-based businesses are built on word-of-mouth. And in all segments of the high technology industry there are networks of analysts, industry experts, peripheral and supporting product producers, and journalists who spread the word. Journalists understand and rely on word-of-mouth to determine your credibility.

- *Evidence* is the third factor that builds credibility. Satisfied customers are essential. But the most visible reinforcement for your business is growth and profits. This falls under the category of "If you're so good, why aren't you making money?" Other kinds of evidence exist, of course. These are clearly differentiated product performance, market share growth, significant product and technology, contacts, joint ventures, and licenses. But obviously, you are judged by the tangible evidence.

A Few Recommendations

1. *Good public relations,* as with other elements of the marketing mix, begins (with analysis of product and market positioning, competitive strategy and planning. To communicate your individuality to the media requires much homework. You should make clear differentiation of your product and market, analyze your competitive strengths and weaknesses, and define the developed market opportunity. The message you need to deliver to the market will evolve from

this exercise. This analysis is important not only for new companies and first-time products, but for all growing companies. In this fast-paced business, competitive positions change continually. Only by continued competitive analysis can you evolve a differentiated position.

2. *Think before you speak.* In any given week, a journalist talks to a wide spectrum of business and industry people, forming opinions of success or failure, competence or weakness. You are on stage in that context. Your knowledge of the business, the industry, the competition, the future, and your strategy for success plays an important role in how you and your company are perceived.

3. *Active public relations is an investment.* Many public relations companies fulfill well their job of regularly and personally informing major customers and a few financial analysts. But developing relationships takes time. Your interaction with key journalists and analysts will gain significant equity as you invest the time.

4. *Negative press does occur.* As one politician told me, "Never pick a fight with someone who buys his ink by the barrel." The press won't go away, you have to re-think your strategy and continue selling. In negative situations, your character and style will communicate business than any issue.

5. *Look beyond products.* For the business journalist, your activities within the present and future business environment is more important than your product. While you may begin with the limited positioning resources of product advantages, all industry-seasoned journalists know that a technology advantage is short-lived. Credibility is gained

through communication of a long-term strategy for success as well as your marketing and corporate strengths.

6. *Good public relations is an education process,* not an event. Pressing the media for an immediate article generally will not succeed. Most major business stories take months, even years, to evolve. The cover of any one of the major trade publications can require four to six months of lead time.

7. *Education — not influence.* Journalists and analysts do not want undue influence on their opinion. They want to buy, not be sold. You must develop long-term relationships where you and the journalist or the analyst come to understand each other's businesses, objectives, and methods. I suggest you treat key journalists and analysts as you would major customers, i.e., establish relationships at all levels, regularly educate, and maintain frequent contact.

8. Finally, the most important thing an emerging company can do is *preserve its individuality.* Image is just another word for character, and corporate character derives from those who form and drive the company. To put layers of people between you, your management, and the journalist will result in the opposite of what you want to achieve. The proverbial work month applies to communications as well as software development. The more people you put on the project the lower the productivity.

Communication seems so simple. Yet few companies communicate well. Effective public relations takes time and the interest of top management. It takes competitive strategy and planning. It takes time to develop relationships. It takes constant reinforcement and it takes an understanding of the market. But such an effort will reward you with a credible market position for attracting investors, new employees and market acceptance of your future products.

This article was derived from a speech Mr. McKenna gave in November 1982 at the Kleiner, Perkins, Caufield & Byers President's Day Symposium in San Francisco for their portfolio company operating executive officers.

Directories

United States Venture Capital Companies

This Directory contains information on over 700 venture capital companies located in the United States and Canada. Although this information has been compiled largely on the basis of questionnaires received from these companies — without an independent verification as to their accuracy — we believe that the data presented portrays the interests and structure of these venture firms.

Names of officers or partners are shown for the independent venture firms, but only appropriate officers are listed for investment banking operations, commercial banks, insurance companies and operating companies with venture activities. Each company has indicated the officer or person that should be contacted about new financing proposals.

Venture firms have been categorized by type of organization (i.e. private venture firm, SBIC, subsidiary of operating company, etc.). Differences between these types of firms are described in the articles of this book. "Affiliation" refers to the existence of a parent firm or an involved partner or organization. Describing the venture activities of investment banking firms and specialized consultants is complicated by the fact that some firms listed will act as intermediaries to assist in raising capital and will also invest in projects with their own capital or that of selected clients. In most cases, such investment will be made only when the individual firm is instrumental in handling the private placement activity.

We have indicated a venture firm's membership in one of the major venture capital industry's trade associations. These associations are: the American Association of Minority Enterprise Small Business Investment Companies (AAMESBIC); the National Association of Small Business Investment Companies (NASBIC); the National Venture Capital Association (NVCA); and the Western Association of Venture Capitalists (WAVC). The emergence of these organizations has been a significant development for the venture capital industry because it has fostered cooperation within a previously very individualistic industry. Membership in the industry associations is generally open to venture capital organizations and individual venture capitalists that are responsible for investing private capital in young companies on a professional basis.

Entries in the directory show project preferences and each firm's normal extent of involvement. Most venture capital firms indicated their minimum and preferred sizes of investment, although acting as the lead investor, many of the firms will often assist in raising money for larger projects. While specific project financings may total $10 million to $15 million, an individual venture firm may invest only $250,000 to $1 million. Investment bankers and consultants, however, generally described the minimum and preferred size of the total private placement — not the amount the investment banking or consulting firm is interested in investing. In some cases, both of these amounts are indicated.

While many firms have indicated a general interest in all types of financing, some prefer to finance either early-stage projects (seed, startup and first-stage financing) or expansion financings (second- and third-stage financing) or buyout or acquisition financings. Firms oriented only toward buyout or acquisition financing usually are interested in situations where the investment group assumes a controlling position in the project. The types of financing, categorized by stage of development of the project, can be defined as follows:

Early-Stage Financing

- *Seed Financing* — a relatively small amount of capital provided to an inventor or entrepreneur to prove a concept and qualify for startup capital. This would generally involve product development and market research. And also, if outcomes are positive, the building of a management team and the development of a business plan.

- *Research and Development Financing* — a tax advantaged partnership set up to finance product development for startup as well as more mature companies. Investors secure tax writeoffs for their investments as well as a later share of the profits if the product development is successful.

- *Startup* — financing provided to companies for use in completing product development and initial marketing. Companies may be in the process of being organized or they may have been in business a short time (one year or less), but have not sold their product commercially. Usually, such firms will have made market studies, assembled the key management, developed a business plan and generally be ready to do business.

- *First-Stage Financing* — financing provided to companies that have expended their initial capital (often in developing and market testing a prototype), and require funds to initiate full scale manufacturing and sales.

Expansion Financing

- *Second-Stage Financing* — working capital for the initial expansion of a company which is producing and shipping, and has growing accounts receivable and inventories. Although the company has clearly made progress, it may not yet be showing a profit.

- *Third-Stage or Mezzanine Financing* — funds provided for major expansion of a company whose sales volume is increasing, and that is breaking even or profitable. These

funds are utilized for further plant expansion, marketing, working capital, or development of an improved product.

- *Bridge Financing* — financing for a company expecting to go public within six months to a year. Often bridge financing is structured so that it can be repaid from the proceeds of a public underwriting. It can also involve restructuring of major stockholder positions through secondary transactions. Restructuring would be undertaken if there were early investors who wanted to reduce or liquidate their positions, or if management had changed and the stockholdings of the former management, their relatives and associates, were to be bought out to relieve a potential oversupply of stock when public.

Acquisition/Buyout Financing

- *Acquisition Financing* — funds provided to a firm to finance its acquisition of another company.

- *Management/Leveraged Buyout* — funds provided to enable an operating management group to acquire a product line or business (which may be at any stage of development), from either a public or private company; often these companies are closely held or family owned. Management/leveraged buyouts usually involve revitalizing an operation, with entrepreneurial management acquiring a significant equity interest.

The venture companies have also indicated their criteria for minimum operating standards of new financing proposals (standards such as annual sales and profit and loss status). This feature of the directory is designed to indicate the range of interests of the venture firms, but the minimum does not mean that most of a venture company's financings will be of this nature. Except in the case of those firms entirely oriented to startups or first-stage projects, this information indicates only that the venture firm will primarily consider projects that meet these minimum standards.

Although a venture company's geographic preference for investment projects is listed, this information does not necessarily limit a firm to a specific area because many times a venture capitalist may participate in a financing of a geographically distant company if a local venture investor also participates. In fact, very often a venture capitalist interested in a geographically distant company may attempt to interest a venture capitalist located near the company being considered. In addition, many of the larger firms have offices on both the East and West coasts.

Information regarding a venture firm's industry preferences is included in the listing. There is also an index of industry preferences included following the directory section. While this data provides a guide to the preferences of a venture firm, most venture companies will range outside these expressed interests if they find a project that is particularly appealing. Thus, these descriptions should not be taken as representing the sole interests of a venture firm. The industries listed in the questionnaire were as follows:

Communications
Cable television
Commercial communications
Data communications
Satellite and microwave communications
Telephone related

Computer Related
Computer graphics and CAD/CAM and CAE
Computer mainframes
Computer services
Memory devices
Micro and minicomputers
Office automation
Scanning-related
Software-applications
Software-artificial intelligence
Software-systems
Specialized turnkey systems
Terminals

Consumer
Computer stores/related services
Consumer products
Consumer services
Food and beverage products
Franchise businesses
Hotels and resort areas
Leisure and recreational products
Restaurants
Retailing

Distribution
Communications equipment
Computer equipment
Consumer products
Electronics equipment
Food products
Industrial products
Medical products

Electronic Components and Instrumentation
Analytical and scientific instrumentation
Component fabrication and testing equipment
Electronic components
Fiber optics
Laser related
Semiconductors

Energy/Natural Resources
Alternative energy
Coal related
Drilling and exploration services
Energy conservation
Minerals
Oil and gas exploration and production
Technology related products/equipment

Genetic Engineering
Gene splicing and manufacturing equipment
Monoclonal antibodies & hybridomas
Recombinant DNA (agriculture and industrial)
Recombinant DNA (medical)

Industrial Products and Equipment
Chemicals
Controls and sensors
Equipment and machinery
Other industrial automation
Plastics
Robotics/vision systems
Specialty materials

Medical/Health Related
Diagnostic equipment
Diagnostic test products
Disposable products
Drugs and medicines
Hospital and clinical labs
Medical services
Therapeutic equipment

Other

Agriculture, forestry, fishing

Education related

Finance and insurance

Publishing

Real estate

Specialty consulting

Transportation

A number of companies did not list any industry preferences, while others specified industries that are not included in the preceding list. Also, some venture firms noted business areas that they would not consider for investments.

Other operating characteristics of a venture firm are noted under the heading "Additional Information." These characteristics may include the year the firm was founded, number and dollar amount of investments made in the first half of 1985, and the usual method of compensation. Methods of compensation indicate whether the venture firm charges closing fees, placement fees, contingent fees, and so forth. This information provides clues about the way the firm operates, but such policies may not be followed in all cases, since each financing tends to be somewhat different.

HICKORY VENTURE CAPITAL CORPORATION

200 West Court Square #624
Huntsville, AL 35801
205-539-1931

Officers
J. Thomas Noojin, Chm. & Pres.
Floyd W. Collins, Exec. V.P.
George P. Lewis, V.P.

Whom to Contact
J. Thomas Noojin
Floyd W. Collins

Type of Firm
SBIC

Affiliation
First Tennessee Bank N.A. (parent)

Industry Association Membership
NASBIC

Project Preferences
Will function either as deal originator or
investor in deals created by others
Type of Financing:
Startup
First-stage
Second-stage
Later-stage expansion
Leveraged buyout
Minimum Investment: $250,000
Preferred Investment: $500,000-$1 million
Minimum Operating Data:
Annual Sales—Nominal
P&L—Losses (profits projected after 2 years)

Geographical Preferences
Southeast
Southwest

Industry Preferences

Communications
Cable television
Commercial communications
Data communications
Satellite and microwave communications
Telephone related

Computer Related
Computer graphics, CAD/CAM and CAE
Computer mainframes
Computer services
Memory devices
Micro and mini computers
Office automation
Scanning related
Software-applications
Software-artificial intelligence
Software-systems
Specialized turnkey systems
Terminals
Consumer
Retailing
Distribution
Communications equipment
Industrial products
Medical products
Electronic Components and Instrumentation
Analytical and scientific instrumentation
Component fabrication and testing
equipment
Electronic components
Fiber optics
Laser related
Semiconductors
Energy/Natural Resources
Alternative energy
Technology related products/equipment
Genetic Engineering
Monoclonal antibodies and hybridomas
Recombinant DNA (agricultural and
industrial)
Recombinant DNA (medical)
Industrial Products and Equipment
Chemicals
Controls and sensors
Equipment and machinery
Other industrial automation
Robotics/vision systems
Specialty materials
Medical/Health Related
Diagnostic equipment
Diagnostic test products
Disposable products
Drugs and medicines
Hospital and clinical labs
Medical services
Therapeutic equipment

Additional Information
Year Founded—1985
Capital Under Management—$12 million
Investments(1985-1st 6 months)—3
Invested(1985-1st 6 months)—$900,000
Method of Compensation—Return on
investment is of primary concern; do not
charge fees

PRIVATE CAPITAL CORPORATION

The Complete Health Building
2160 Highland Avenue
Birmingham, AL 35205
205-251-0152

Other Office
220 East 10th Street
Post Office Box 66
Anniston, AL 36202
205-236-4041

Officers
William W. Featheringill, Pres. (Birmingham)
William P. Acker III, V.P. (Birmingham)

Whom to Contact
Either of the above

Type of Firm
Private venture capital firm investing
own capital

Industry Association Membership
NASBIC

Project Preferences
Prefer role as deal originator but will also
invest in deals created by others
Type of Financing:
Startup
First-stage
Second-stage
Later-stage expansion
Leveraged buyout
Minimum Investment: $250,000
Preferred Investment: $500,000-$1 million
Minimum Operating Data:
Annual Sales—Over $3 million
P&L—Break even

Geographical Preferences
Southeast
Gulf States

Industry Preferences

Communications
Cable television
Commercial communications
Data communications
Satellite and microwave communications
Telephone related
Computer Related
Computer graphics, CAD/CAM and CAE
Specialized turnkey systems
Distribution
Communications equipment
Computer equipment
Consumer products
Electronics equipment
Food products
Industrial products
Medical products
Energy/Natural Resources
Technology related products/equipment
Industrial Products and Equipment
Plastics
Medical/Health Related
Diagnostic equipment
Diagnostic test products
Disposable products
Drugs and medicines
Hospital and clinical labs
Medical services
Therapeutic equipment
Will Not Consider
Commodities
Personal or professional service businesses

Additional Information
Year Founded—1973
Investments(1985-1st 6 months)—1
Invested(1985-1st 6 months)—$2.9 million
Method of Compensation—Return on
  investment is most important, but also
  charge for closing fees, service fees, etc.

CAMELBACK CAPITAL CORPORATION

123 North Centennial Way #103
Mesa, AZ 85201
602-834-4954

Officers
John G. Bartol, Chm.
Robert F. Pothier, Pres.

Whom to Contact
John G. Bartol

Type of Firm
Private venture capital firm investing
own capital

Project Preferences
Prefer role as deal originator
Type of Financing:
Second-stage
Minimum Investment: Less than $100,000
Preferred Investment: $100,000-$250,000
Minimum Operating Data:
Annual Sales—$500,000
P&L—Break even

Geographical Preference
Southwest

Industry Preferences
None

Additional Information
Year Founded—1979
Capital Under Management—$750,000
Method of Compensation—Return on
investment is of primary concern; do not
charge fees

EL DORADO INVESTMENT CO.

411 North Central Avenue
Station 1820
Phoenix, AZ 85003
602-250-2869

Manager
Greg S. Anderson

Type of Firm
Venture capital subsidiary or affiliate of
non-financial corporation

Affiliation
AZP Group Inc. (parent)

Project Preferences
Prefer role in deals created by others
Type of Financing:
First-stage
Second-stage
Later-stage expansion
Leveraged buyout

Minimum Investment: $500,000
Preferred Investment: $500,000-$1 million
Minimum Operating Data:
Annual Sales—Nominal
P&L—Losses (profits projected after 2 years)

Geographical Preference
National

Industry Preferences

Communications
Cable television
Commercial communications
Data communications
Satellite and microwave communications
Telephone related
Computer Related
Computer graphics, CAD/CAM and CAE
Computer mainframes
Computer services
Memory devices
Micro and mini computers
Office automation
Scanning related
Software-applications
Software-artificial intelligence
Software-systems
Specialized turnkey systems
Terminals
Consumer
Computer stores/related services
Consumer products
Consumer services
Food and beverage products
Franchise businesses
Hotels and resort areas
Leisure and recreational products
Restaurants
Retailing
Distribution
Communications equipment
Computer equipment
Consumer products
Electronics equipment
Food products
Industrial products
Medical products
Electronic Components and Instrumentation
Analytical and scientific instrumentation
Component fabrication and testing
equipment
Electronic components
Fiber optics
Laser related
Semiconductors
Energy/Natural Resources
Alternative energy
Coal related
Drilling and exploration services
Energy conservation
Minerals
Oil and gas exploration and production
Technology related products/equipment

Genetic Engineering
Gene splicing and manufacturing equipment
Monoclonal antibodies and hybridomas
Recombinant DNA (agricultural and
industrial)
Recombinant DNA (medical)
Industrial Products and Equipment
Chemicals
Controls and sensors
Energy management
Equipment and machinery
Other industrial automation
Plastics
Robotics/vision systems
Specialty materials
Medical/Health Related
Diagnostic equipment
Diagnostic test products
Disposable products
Drugs and medicines
Hospital and clinical labs
Medical services
Therapeutic equipment
Will Not Consider
Real estate

Additional Information
Year Founded—1983
Capital Under Management—$25 million
Investments(1985-1st 6 months)—2
Method of Compensation—Return on
investment is of primary concern; do not
charge fees

FBS VENTURE CAPITAL CO.

6900 East Camelback Road #452
Scottsdale, AZ 85251
602-941-2160

Other Offices
7515 Wayzata Boulevard
Minneapolis, MN 55426
612-544-2754

3000 Pearl Street #206
Boulder, CO 80301
303-442-6885

Officers
William B. McKee, Pres. (Arizona)
R. Randy Stolworthy, V.P. (Arizona)
Stephen W. Buchanan, Inv. Officer (Arizona)
W. Ray Allen, Exec. V.P. (Minnesota)
John H. Bullion, V.P. (Minnesota)
Brian P. Johnson, V.P. (Colorado)

Whom to Contact
Stephen W. Buchanan
John H. Bullion
Brian P. Johnson

Type of Firm
Private venture capital firm investing
own capital
SBIC

Affiliation
First Bank Systems, Inc. of Minneapolis
(limited partner)

Industry Association Membership
NASBIC

Project Preferences
Will function either as deal originator or
investor in deals created by others
Type of Financing:
Seed
Startup
First-stage
Second-stage
Leveraged buyout
Minimum Investment: Less than $100,000
Preferred Investment: $100,000-$250,000
Minimum Operating Data:
Annual Sales—Nominal
P&L—Losses (profits projected after 1 year)

Geographical Preference
Arizona
Colorado
Minnesota

Industry Preferences

Communications
Data communications
Satellite and microwave communications
Computer Related
Computer graphics, CAD/CAM and CAE
Micro and mini computers
Software-applications
**Electronic Components and
Instrumentation**
Analytical and scientific instrumentation
Component fabrication and testing
equipment
Fiber optics
Laser related
Industrial Products and Equipment
Chemicals
Medical/Health Related
Diagnostic equipment
Diagnostic test products
Will Not Consider
Natural resources
Real estate

Additional Information
Year Founded—1960
Capital Under Management—$20 million
Investments(1985-1st 6 months)—6
Invested(1985-1st 6 months)—Over $1 million
Method of Compensation—Return on
investment is of primary concern; do not
charge fees

GREYHOUND CAPITAL MANAGEMENT CORPORATION

Greyhound Tower #1408
Phoenix, AZ 85077
602-222-8816

Other Office
8 New England Executive Park
Burlington, MA 01803
617-272-8110

Officers
E. Allen Henson, Pres. (Arizona)
David A. Bays, V.P. (Arizona)
Del R. Lawin, Dir. Tech. Analysis (Arizona)
John S. Reedy, Mgr. Portfolio/Analysis
(Arizona)
William W. Bauman, Inv. Analyst (Arizona)
John B. Schroeder, Dir. Venture Inv.
(Massachusetts)

Whom to Contact
David A. Bays

Type of Firm
Venture capital subsidiary or affiliate of
non-financial corporation

Affiliation
The Greyhound Corporation (parent)

Project Preferences
Will function either as deal originator or
investor in deals created by others
Type of Financing:
Startup
First-stage
Second-stage
Later-stage expansion
Minimum Investment: $250,000
Preferred Investment: $500,000-$1 million
Minimum Operating Data:
Annual Sales—Nominal
P&L—Losses (profits projected after 2 years)

Geographical Preference
National

Industry Preferences

Communications
Telephone related
Computer Related
Computer graphics, CAD/CAM and CAE
Computer mainframes
Computer services
Memory devices
Micro and mini computers
Office automation
Software-applications
Software-artificial intelligence
Software-systems
Specialized turnkey systems
Terminals

**Electronic Components and
Instrumentation**
Fiber optics
Laser related
Industrial Products and Equipment
Robotics/vision systems

Additional Information
Year Founded—1979
Capital Under Management—$15 million
Investments(1985-1st 6 months)—8
Invested(1985-1st 6 months)—$3 million
Method of Compensation—Return on
investment is of primary concern; do not
charge fees

VNB CAPITAL CORPORATION

15 East Monroe #1200
Phoenix, AZ 85004
602-261-1577

Officers
James G. Gardner, Pres.
John M. Holliman, III, Mgn. Dir.

Whom to Contact
John M. Holliman, III

Type of Firm
SBIC
Venture capital subsidiary of
commercial bank

Affiliation
Valley National Bank of Arizona
(parent)

Industry Association Membership
NASBIC

Project Preferences
Will function either as deal originator or
investor in deals created by others
Type of Financing:
Second-stage
Later-stage expansion
Leveraged buyout
Minimum Investment: $250,000
Preferred Investment: $250,000-$500,000
Minimum Operating Data:
Annual Sales—$3 million
P&L—Losses (profits projected after 1 year)

Geographical Preferences
Within two hours of office
Southwest

Industry Preferences

Communications
Cable television
Commercial communications
Data communications
Satellite and microwave communications
Telephone related
Computer Related
Proprietary peripherals
**Electronic Components and
  Instrumentation**
Analytical and scientific instrumentation
Component fabrication and testing
  equipment
Electronic components
Fiber optics
Laser related
Semiconductors
Energy/Natural Resources
Technology related products/equipment
Industrial Products and Equipment
Chemicals
Controls and sensors
Energy management
Equipment and machinery
Other industrial automation
Plastics
Robotics/vision systems
Specialty materials
Medical/Health Related
Diagnostic equipment
Diagnostic test products
Disposable products
Drugs and medicines
Hospital and clinical labs
Medical services
Therapeutic equipment
Will Not Consider
Professional services
Retailing

Additional Information

Year Founded—1984
Capital Under Management—$15 million
Method of Compensation—Return on
  investment is most important, but also
  charge for closing fees, service fees, etc.

WESCOT CAPITAL CORPORATION

1601 North Seventh Street
Phoenix, AZ 85006
602-254-3944

Post Office Box 5190
Phoenix, AZ 85010

Partner

Karl Eller, Gen. Ptnr.
F. Wesley Clelland III, Gen. Ptnr.
Scott Eller, Gen. Ptnr.
Pamela Mason, Assoc.

Whom to Contact

F. Wesley Clelland III
Scott Eller
Pamela Mason

Type of Firm

Private venture capital firm investing
  own capital

Affiliation

SunVen Partners (limited partnership)
Hambrecht & Quist (general partner)

Project Preferences

Will function either as deal originator or
  investor in deals created by others
Type of Financing:
Seed
Research and development partnerships
Startup
First-stage
Second-stage
Later-stage expansion
Leveraged buyout
Minimum Investment: $250,000
Preferred Investment: $500,000-$1 million
Minimum Operating Data:
Annual Sales—Nominal

Geographical Preferences

Southwest
National

Industry Preferences

Communications
Cable television
Commercial communications
Data communications
Radio and television stations
Satellite and microwave communications
Telephone related
Computer Related
Computer graphics, CAD/CAM and CAE
Distribution
Computer equipment
Medical products
**Electronic Components and
  Instrumentation**
Various

Genetic Engineering
Various
Industrial Products and Equipment
Chemicals
Equipment and machinery
Other industrial automation
Robotics/vision systems
Specialty materials
Medical/Health Related
Diagnostic equipment
Diagnostic test products
Disposable products
Drugs and medicines
Hospital and clinical labs
Medical services
Therapeutic equipment
Other
Advertising
Publishing
Transportation
Will Not Consider
Agriculture
Consumer products
Oil and gas
Real estate

Additional Information

Year Founded—1984
Capital Under Management—$21 million
Investments(1985-1st 6 months)—5
Invested(1985-1st 6 months)—$2.5 million
Method of Compensation—Return on
  investment is of primary concern; do not
  charge fees

STEPHENS INC.

114 East Capitol Avenue
Post Office Box 3507
Little Rock, AR 72201
501-374-4361

Officers

Jon E.M. Jacoby, V.P.
Doug Martin, Assoc.
Felton Lamb, Jr., Assoc.

Whom to Contact

Doug Martin
Felton Lamb, Jr.

Type of Firm

Investment banking or merchant banking
firm investing own capital or funds of
partners or clients

Project Preferences

Will function either as deal originator or
investor in deals created by others
Type of Financing:
Second-stage
Leveraged buyout
Minimum Investment: $100,000
Preferred Investment: $250,000-$500,000
Minimum Operating Data:
Annual Sales—Nominal
P&L—Break even

Geographical Preference

None

Industry Preferences

Communications
Cable television
Commercial communications
Data communications
Satellite and microwave communications
Telephone related
Computer Related
Computer graphics, CAD/CAM and CAE
Computer mainframes
Computer services
Memory devices
Micro and mini computers
Office automation
Scanning related
Software-applications
Software-artificial intelligence
Software-systems
Specialized turnkey systems
Terminals

Consumer
Computer stores/related services
Consumer products
Consumer services
Food and beverage products
Franchise businesses
Hotels and resort areas
Leisure and recreational products
Restaurants
Retailing
Distribution
Communications equipment
Computer equipment
Consumer products
Electronics equipment
Food products
Industrial products
Medical products
**Electronic Components and
Instrumentation**
Analytical and scientific instrumentation
Component fabrication and testing
equipment
Electronic components
Fiber optics
Laser related
Semiconductors
Energy/Natural Resources
Alternative energy
Coal related
Drilling and exploration services
Energy conservation
Minerals
Oil and gas exploration and production
Technology related products/equipment
Genetic Engineering
Gene splicing and manufacturing equipment
Monoclonal antibodies and hybridomas
Recombinant DNA (agricultural and
industrial)
Recombinant DNA (medical)
Industrial Products and Equipment
Chemicals
Controls and sensors
Energy management
Equipment and machinery
Other industrial automation
Plastics
Robotics/vision systems
Specialty materials
Medical/Health Related
Diagnostic equipment
Diagnostic test products
Disposable products
Drugs and medicines
Hospital and clinical labs
Medical services
Therapeutic equipment

Other
Agriculture, forestry, fishing
Education related
Finance and insurance
Publishing
Real estate
Specialty consulting
Transportation
Will Not Consider
Company that are solely defense contractors

Additional Information

Year Founded—1933
Capital Under Management—$10 million
Investments(1985-1st 6 months)—2
Invested(1985-1st 6 months)—$5 million
Method of Compensation—Return on
investment is most important, but also
charge for closing fees, service fees, etc.

ACCEL PARTNERS

One Embarcadero Center
San Francisco, CA 94111
415-989-5656

Other Offices

One Palmer Square
Princeton, NJ 08542
609-683-4500

2020 Hogback Road
Ann Arbor, MI 48104
313-971-5234

Managing Partners

Dixon R. Doll
Arthur C. Patterson
James R. Swartz

Whom to Contact

Any of the above

Type of Firm

Private venture capital firm investing
own capital

Industry Association Memberships

NASBIC
NVCA
WAVC

Project Preferences

Will function either as deal originator or
investor in deals created by others
Type of Financing:
Seed
Research and development partnerships
Startup
First-stage
Second-stage
Later-stage expansion
Minimum Investment: Less than $100,000
Preferred Investment: No preference
Minimum Operating Data:
Annual Sales—Nominal
P&L—Losses (profits projected after 2 years)

Geographical Preference

None

Industry Preferences

Communications
Cable television
Commercial communications
Data communications
Local area networks
Satellite and microwave communications
Telephone related

Computer Related
Computer graphics, CAD/CAM and CAE
Computer mainframes
Computer services
Memory devices
Micro and mini computers
Office automation
Scanning related
Software-applications
Software-artificial intelligence
Software-systems
Specialized turnkey systems
Terminals
Consumer
Consumer services
Distribution
Communications equipment
Computer equipment
Consumer products
Electronics equipment
Food products
Industrial products
Medical products
**Electronic Components and
Instrumentation**
Analytical and scientific instrumentation
Component fabrication and testing
equipment
Electronic components
Fiber optics
Laser related
Semiconductors
Energy/Natural Resources
Alternative energy
Coal related
Drilling and exploration services
Energy conservation
Minerals
Oil and gas exploration and production
Technology related products/equipment
Genetic Engineering
Gene splicing and manufacturing equipment
Monoclonal antibodies and hybridomas
Recombinant DNA (agricultural and
industrial)
Recombinant DNA (medical)
Industrial Products and Equipment
Chemicals
Controls and sensors
Energy management
Equipment and machinery
Other industrial automation
Plastics
Robotics/vision systems
Specialty materials

Medical/Health Related
Diagnostic equipment
Diagnostic test products
Disposable products
Drugs and medicines
Hospital and clinical labs
Medical services
Therapeutic equipment

Additional Information

Year Founded—1983
Capital Under Management—$100 million
Investments(1985-1st 6 months)—14
Invested(1985-1st 6 months)—$6 million
Method of Compensation—Return on
investment is of primary concern; do not
charge fees

ADLER & COMPANY

375 Park Avenue #3303
New York, NY 10152
212-759-2800

Other Office

1245 Oakmead Parkway #103
Sunnyvale, CA 94086
408-720-8700

Partners

Frederick R. Adler, Mgn. Gen. Ptnr.
(New York)
Joy London, Gen. Ptnr. (New York)
David I. Caplan, Gen. Ptnr. (California)
Yuval Binur, Gen. Ptnr. (New York)
Daniel C. O'Neill, Venture Mgr. (California)
John B. Harlow II, Venture Mgr. (New York)
David J. Blumberg, Venture Mgr. (New York)

Whom to Contact

Any of the above

Type of Firm

Private venture capital firm investing
own capital

Industry Association Memberships

NASBIC
NVCA

Project Preferences

Will function either as deal originator or
investor in deals created by others

Type of Financing:
Seed
Research and development partnerships
Startup
First-stage
Second-stage
Later-stage expansion
Leveraged buyout
Minimum Investment: $100,000
Preferred Investment: No preference
Minimum Operating Data:
Annual Sales—Nominal
P&L—Losses (profits projected after 1 year)

Geographical Preference
None

Industry Preferences

Communications
Commercial communications
Data communications
Satellite and microwave communications
Telephone related
Computer Related
Computer graphics, CAD/CAM and CAE
Computer mainframes
Computer services
Memory devices
Micro and mini computers
Office automation
Scanning related
Software-applications
Software-artificial intelligence
Software-systems
Specialized turnkey systems
Terminals
Consumer
Computer stores/related services
Consumer products
Consumer services
Distribution
Communications equipment
Computer equipment
Consumer products
Electronics equipment
Food products
Industrial products
Medical products
**Electronic Components and
Instrumentation**
Analytical and scientific instrumentation
Component fabrication and testing
equipment
Electronic components
Fiber optics
Laser related
Semiconductors
Energy/Natural Resources
Technology related products/equipment

Genetic Engineering
Gene splicing and manufacturing equipment
Monoclonal antibodies and hybridomas
Recombinant DNA (agricultural and
industrial)
Recombinant DNA (medical)
Industrial Products and Equipment
Chemicals
Controls and sensors
Energy management
Equipment and machinery
Other industrial automation
Plastics
Robotics/vision systems
Specialty materials
Medical/Health Related
Diagnostic equipment
Diagnostic test products
Disposable products
Drugs and medicines
Hospital and clinical labs
Medical services
Therapeutic equipment

Additional Information
Year Founded—1965
Capital Under Management—$300 million
Investments(1985-1st 6 months)—16
Invested(1985-1st 6 months)—$15 million
Method of Compensation—Return on
investment is of primary concern; do not
charge fees

ADVANCED TECHNOLOGY
VENTURES

1000 El Camino Real #210
Menlo Park, CA 94025
415-321-8601

Other Office
Ten Post Office Square #1230
Boston, MA 02109
617-423-4050

Partners
Ralph J. Nunziato, Mgn. Ptnr.
Albert E. Paladino, Mgn. Ptnr.
Ivan E. Sutherland, Gen. Ptnr.
Robert C. Ammerman, Gen. Ptnr.
Jos C. Henkens, Gen. Ptnr.
Robert G. Loewy, Gen. Ptnr.
William R. Sutherland, Special Ptnr.
Robert F. Sproull, Special Ptnr.

Whom to Contact
Albert E. Paladino (Massachusetts)
Robert C. Ammerman (Massachusetts)
Ralph J. Nunziato (California)
Jos C. Henkens (California)

Type of Firm
Private venture capital firm investing
own capital

Affiliations
Advanced Technology Ventures, Bermuda
Advanced Technology Ventures II

Industry Association Membership
NVCA

Project Preferences
Will function either as deal originator or
investor in deals created by others
Type of Financing:
Seed
Startup
First-stage
Second-stage
Minimum Investment: Less than $100,000
Preferred Investment: $500,000-$1 million
Minimum Operating Data:
Annual Sales—Nominal
P&L—Losses (profits projected after 2 years)

Geographical Preference
None

Industry Preferences

Communications
Commercial communications
Data communications
Satellite and microwave communications
Telephone related
Computer Related
Computer graphics, CAD/CAM and CAE
Computer mainframes
Computer services
Memory devices
Micro and mini computers
Office automation
Scanning related
Software-applications
Software-artificial intelligence
Software-systems
Specialized turnkey systems
Terminals

Distribution
Communications equipment
Computer equipment
Consumer products
Electronics equipment
Food products
Industrial products
Medical products
**Electronic Components and
 Instrumentation**
Analytical and scientific instrumentation
Component fabrication and testing
 equipment
Electronic components
Fiber optics
Laser related
Semiconductors
Energy/Natural Resources
Alternative energy
Coal related
Technology related products/equipment
Genetic Engineering
Gene splicing and manufacturing equipment
Monoclonal antibodies and hybridomas
Recombinant DNA (agricultural and
 industrial)
Recombinant DNA (medical)
Industrial Products and Equipment
Chemicals
Controls and sensors
Energy management
Equipment and machinery
Other industrial automation
Plastics
Robotics/vision systems
Specialty materials
Medical/Health Related
Diagnostic equipment
Diagnostic test products
Drugs and medicines
Therapeutic equipment
Other
Agriculture, forestry, fishing

Additional Information
Year Founded—1979
Capital Under Management—$73.5 million
Investments(1985-1st 6 months)—5
Invested(1985-1st 6 months)—$2.3 million
Method of Compensation—Return on
 investment is of primary concern; do not
 charge fees

ALAFI CAPITAL COMPANY

Post Office Box 7338
Berkeley, CA 94707
415-653-7425

General Partner
Moshe Alafi

Type of Firm
Private venture capital firm investing
 own capital

Affiliation
Monsanto Company (limited partner)

Industry Association Membership
WAVC

Project Preferences
Prefer role as deal originator but will also
 invest in deals created by others
Type of Financing:
Seed
Startup
Second-stage
Minimum Investment: $250,000
Preferred Investment: $500,000-$1 million
Minimum Operating Data:
Annual Sales—Nominal
P&L—Break even

Geographical Preferences
West Coast
National

Industry Preferences

**Electronic Components and
 Instrumentation**
Analytical and scientific instrumentation
Electronic components
Fiber optics
Laser related
Semiconductors
Energy/Natural Resources
Energy conservation
Genetic Engineering
Gene splicing and manufacturing equipment
Monoclonal antibodies and hybridomas
Recombinant DNA (agricultural and
 industrial)
Recombinant DNA (medical)
Industrial Products and Equipment
Chemicals
Controls and sensors
Specialty materials

Medical/Health Related
Diagnostic equipment
Drugs and medicines
Hospital and clinical labs
Medical services
Therapeutic equipment

Additional Information
Year Founded—1984
Capital Under Management—$24 million
Investments(1985-1st 6 months)—3
Invested(1985-1st 6 months)—$12 million
Method of Compensation—Return on
 investment is of primary concern; do not
 charge fees

ALPHA PARTNERS

2200 Sand Hill Road #250
Menlo Park, CA 94025
415-854-7024

General Partners
Wallace F. Davis
Brian J. Grossi
Glenn E. Penisten
Ruth Scott
Samuel Urcis

Whom to Contact
Wallace F. Davis

Type of Firm
Private venture capital firm investing
 own capital

Project Preferences
Prefer role as deal originator
Type of Financing:
Seed
Minimum Operating Data:
Annual Sales—Nominal
P&L—Losses (profits projected after 2 years)

Geographical Preference
San Francisco Bay Area

Industry Preferences

Communications
Commercial communications
Data communications
Satellite and microwave communications
Telephone related

Computer Related
Computer graphics, CAD/CAM and CAE
Computer mainframes
Computer services
Memory devices
Micro and mini computers
Office automation
Software-applications
Software-artificial intelligence
Software-systems
Terminals
**Electronic Components and
  Instrumentation**
Analytical and scientific instrumentation
Component fabrication and testing
  equipment
Electronic components
Fiber optics
Laser related
Semiconductors
Genetic Engineering
Monoclonal antibodies and hybridomas
Recombinant DNA (agricultural and
  industrial)
Recombinant DNA (medical)
Industrial Products and Equipment
Chemicals
Equipment and machinery
Robotics/vision systems
Medical/Health Related
Diagnostic equipment
Diagnostic test products
Disposable products
Drugs and medicines
Medical services
Therapeutic equipment

Additional Information
Year Founded—1982
Capital Under Management—$40 million
Investments(1985-1st 6 months)—1
Invested(1985-1st 6 months)—$650,000
Method of Compensation—Return on
  investment is of primary concern; do not
  charge fees

ARSCOTT, NORTON & ASSOCIATES

375 Forest Avenue
Palo Alto, CA 94301
415-853-0766

Partners
David G. Arscott, Gen. Ptnr.
Dean C. Campbell, Gen. Ptnr.
Leal F. Norton, Gen. Ptnr.
Al Cuthbert, Assoc.

Whom to Contact
Any general partner

Type of Firm
Private venture capital firm investing
  own capital

Industry Association Memberships
NVCA
WAVC

Project Preferences
Will function either as deal originator or
  investor in deals created by others
Type of Financing:
Seed
Startup
First-stage
Second-stage
Later-stage expansion
Leveraged buyout
Preferred Investment: $500,000-$1 million
Minimum Operating Data:
Annual Sales—Nominal
P&L—Losses (profits projected after 3 years)

Geographical Preference
National

Industry Preferences

Communications
Cable television
Commercial communications
Data communications
Satellite and microwave communications
Telephone related

Computer Related
Computer graphics, CAD/CAM and CAE
Computer mainframes
Computer services
Memory devices
Micro and mini computers
Office automation
Scanning related
Software-applications
Software-artificial intelligence
Software-systems
Specialized turnkey systems
Terminals
**Electronic Components and
  Instrumentation**
Analytical and scientific instrumentation
Component fabrication and testing
  equipment
Electronic components
Fiber optics
Laser related
Semiconductors
Genetic Engineering
Gene splicing and manufacturing equipment
Monoclonal antibodies and hybridomas
Recombinant DNA (agricultural and
  industrial)
Recombinant DNA (medical)
Industrial Products and Equipment
Chemicals
Controls and sensors
Energy management
Equipment and machinery
Other industrial automation
Plastics
Robotics/vision systems
Specialty materials
Medical/Health Related
Diagnostic equipment
Diagnostic test products
Disposable products
Drugs and medicines
Hospital and clinical labs
Medical services
Therapeutic equipment
Will Not Consider
Real estate

Additional Information
Year Founded—1975
Capital Under Management—$75 million
Method of Compensation—Return on investment is of primary concern; do not charge fees

---

ASSET MANAGEMENT COMPANY

2275 East Bayshore Road
Palo Alto, CA 94303
415-494-7400

General Partners
Franklin P. Johnson, Jr.
Craig C. Taylor
John F. Shoch
Daniel P. Flamen

Whom to Contact
Any of the above

Type of Firm
Private venture capital management firm

Industry Association Memberships
NVCA
WAVC

Project Preferences
Prefer role as deal originator but will also invest in deals created by others
Type of Financing:
Seed
Startup
First-stage
Minimum Investment: $100,000
Preferred Investment: $500,000-$1 million
Minimum Operating Data:
Annual Sales—Nominal
P&L—Losses (profits projected after 2 years)

Geographical Preferences
Northwest
Southwest
Rocky Mountains
West Coast

Industry Preferences

Communications
Data communications
Telephone related

Computer Related
Computer graphics, CAD/CAM and CAE
Computer mainframes
Computer services
Memory devices
Micro and mini computers
Office automation
Scanning related
Software-applications
Software-artificial intelligence
Software-systems
Specialized turnkey systems
Terminals
Consumer
Retailing
Electronic Components and Instrumentation
Analytical and scientific instrumentation
Component fabrication and testing equipment
Electronic components
Fiber optics
Laser related
Semiconductors
Genetic Engineering
Food related
Gene splicing and manufacturing equipment
Monoclonal antibodies and hybridomas
Recombinant DNA (agricultural and industrial)
Recombinant DNA (medical)
Industrial Products and Equipment
Chemicals
Specialty materials
Medical/Health Related
Diagnostic equipment
Diagnostic test products
Disposable products
Drugs and medicines
Other
Education related
Will Not Consider
Motion pictures
Real estate

Additional Information
Year Founded—1965
Capital Under Management—$95 million
Investments(1985-1st 6 months)—9
Invested(1985-1st 6 months)—$5.4 million
Method of Compensation—Return on investment is of primary concern; do not charge fees

---

ASSOCIATES VENTURE CAPITAL CORPORATION

425 California Street #2203
San Francisco, CA 94104
415-956-1444

Officers
Walter P. Strycker, Pres.
Harold T. McCormick, V.P.

Whom to Contact
Walter P. Strycker

Type of Firm
Private venture capital firm investing own capital
MESBIC
Consulting firm evaluating and analyzing venture projects and arranging private placements

Affiliation
Majorven Associates (parent)

Industry Association Membership
AAMESBIC

Project Preferences
Prefer role as deal originator but will also invest in deals created by others
Type of Financing:
Leveraged buyout
Minimum Operating Data:
Annual Sales—Nominal
P&L—Losses (profits projected after 1 year)
Annual Sales (LBO)—$25 million-$400 million

Geographical Preference
None

Industry Preferences

Communications
Cable television
Commercial communications
Data communications
Satellite and microwave communications
Telephone related
Computer Related
Computer services
Memory devices
Micro and mini computers
Scanning related
Consumer
Consumer products

Distribution
Communications equipment
Computer equipment
Consumer products
Electronics equipment
Industrial products
Medical products
Electronic Components and Instrumentation
Analytical and scientific instrumentation
Component fabrication and testing equipment
Electronic components
Fiber optics
Laser related
Semiconductors
Energy/Natural Resources
Alternative energy
Coal related
Drilling and exploration services
Energy conservation
Minerals
Oil and gas exploration and production
Technology related products/equipment
Genetic Engineering
Gene splicing and manufacturing equipment
Monoclonal antibodies and hybridomas
Recombinant DNA (agricultural and industrial)
Recombinant DNA (medical)
Industrial Products and Equipment
Energy management
Equipment and machinery
Medical/Health Related
Diagnostic equipment
Diagnostic test products
Disposable products
Drugs and medicines
Hospital and clinical labs
Medical services
Therapeutic equipment

Additional Information
Year Founded—1978
Capital Under Management—$2 million
Investments(1985-1st 6 months)—2
Invested(1985-1st 6 months)—$200,000
Method of Compensation—Return on investment is most important, but also charge for closing fees, service fees, etc.

AVALON VENTURES

1020 Prospect Street #405
La Jolla, CA 92037
619-454-3803

Managing General Partner
Kevin J. Kinsella

Type of Firm
Private venture capital firm investing own capital
Consulting firm evaluating, analyzing and organizing venture projects and arranging private placements

Project Preferences
Prefer role as deal originator
Type of Financing:
Seed
Research and development partnerships
Startup
Minimum Investment: $250,000
Preferred Investment: Over $1 million

Geographical Preference
None

Industry Preferences
None

Additional Information
Year Founded—1983
Method of Compensation—Return on investment is of primary concern; do not charge fees

AVI MANAGEMENT, INC.

3000 Sand Hill Road
Building 3, #280
Menlo Park, CA 94025
415-854-4470

Officers
Peter L. Wolken, Pres.
Chuck K. Chan, V.P.
David Sturdevant, V.P.

Whom to Contact
Any of the above

Type of Firm
Private venture capital firm investing own capital

Industry Association Membership
WAVC

Project Preferences
Will function either as deal originator or investor in deals created by others
Type of Financing:
Seed
Startup
First-stage
Minimum Investment: $100,000
Preferred Investment: $250,000-$500,000
Minimum Operating Data:
Annual Sales—Nominal

Geographical Preference
Silicon Valley

Industry Preferences

Communications
Data communications
Computer Related
Computer graphics, CAD/CAM and CAE
Computer mainframes
Computer services
Memory devices
Micro and mini computers
Office automation
Scanning related
Software-applications
Software-artificial intelligence
Software-systems
Specialized turnkey systems
Terminals
Electronic Components and Instrumentation
Analytical and scientific instrumentation
Component fabrication and testing equipment
Electronic components
Fiber optics
Laser related
Semiconductors
Industrial Products and Equipment
Controls and sensors
Equipment and machinery
Other industrial automation
Robotics/vision systems
Semiconductor production equipment
Will Not Consider
Consumer related businesses

Additional Information
Year Founded—1982
Capital Under Management—$19 million
Investments(1985-1st 6 months)—4
Invested(1985-1st 6 months)—$800,000
Method of Compensation—Return on investment is of primary concern; do not charge fees

BANCORP VENTURE CAPITAL, INC.

2633 Cherry Avenue
Signal Hill, CA 90806
213-595-1177

Officers
Paul R. Blair, Pres.
Ron C. Miracle, Inv. Analyst

Whom to Contact
Either of the above

Type of Firm
SBIC

Affiliations
Home Interstate Bancorp (parent-stockholder)
First Trust Bank (parent-stockholder)
County Bank and Trust (parent-stockholder)

Industry Association Membership
NASBIC

Project Preferences
Prefer role as deal originator but will also
    invest in deals created by others
Type of Financing:
Second-stage
Later-stage expansion
Leveraged buyout
Minimum Investment: $500,000
Preferred Investment: $500,000-$3 million
Preferred Investment (LBO):
    $500,000-$3 million
Minimum Operating Data:
Annual Sales—$1.5 million
P&L—Break even
Annual Sales (LBO)—$2 million and over

Geographical Preference
West Coast

Industry Preferences

Communications
Cable television
Commercial communications
Data communications
Satellite and microwave communications
Telephone related

Computer Related
Computer graphics, CAD/CAM and CAE
Computer mainframes
Computer services
Memory devices
Micro and mini computers
Office automation
Scanning related
Software-applications
Software-artificial intelligence
Software-systems
Specialized turnkey systems
Terminals
Consumer
Consumer products
Food and beverage products
Leisure and recreational products
Distribution
Communications equipment
Computer equipment
Consumer products
Electronics equipment
Food products
Industrial products
Medical products
**Electronic Components and
    Instrumentation**
Analytical and scientific instrumentation
Component fabrication and testing
    equipment
Electronic components
Fiber optics
Laser related
Semiconductors
Energy/Natural Resources
Technology related products/equipment
Industrial Products and Equipment
Chemicals
Controls and sensors
Energy management
Equipment and machinery
Other industrial automation
Plastics
Robotics/vision systems
Specialty materials
Medical/Health Related
Diagnostic equipment
Diagnostic test products
Disposable products
Drugs and medicines
Therapeutic equipment

Additional Information
Year Founded—1984

BANKAMERICA CAPITAL CORPORATION

555 California Street
Department 3908
San Francisco, CA 94104
415-622-2230

Officers
Robert W. Gibson, Pres.
Patrick J. Topolski, V.P.

Whom to Contact
Either of the above

Type of Firm
SBIC

Affiliation
Bank of America

Industry Association Memberships
NASBIC
NVCA
WAVC

Project Preferences
Will function either as deal originator or
    investor in deals created by others
Type of Financing:
Leveraged buyout
Second-stage and later financings
Minimum Investment: $250,000
Preferred Investment: $250,000-$500,000
Preferred Investment (LBO): Open
Minimum Operating Data:
Annual Sales—$500,000
P&L—Losses (profits projected after 2 years)
Annual Sales (LBO)—$20 million and over

Geographical Preference
West Coast

Industry Preferences

Communications
Cable television
Commercial communications
Data communications
Satellite and microwave communications
Telephone related

Computer Related
Computer graphics, CAD/CAM and CAE
Computer mainframes
Computer services
Memory devices
Micro and mini computers
Office automation
Scanning related
Software-applications
Software-artificial intelligence
Software-systems
Specialized turnkey systems
Terminals
Consumer
Consumer products
Retailing
Distribution
Communications equipment
Computer equipment
Consumer products
Electronics equipment
Food products
Industrial products
Medical products
Electronic Components and Instrumentation
Analytical and scientific instrumentation
Component fabrication and testing equipment
Electronic components
Fiber optics
Laser related
Semiconductors
Industrial Products and Equipment
Chemicals
Controls and sensors
Energy management
Equipment and machinery
Other industrial automation
Plastics
Robotics/vision systems
Specialty materials
Medical/Health Related
Diagnostic equipment
Diagnostic test products
Disposable products
Drugs and medicines
Hospital and clinical labs
Medical services
Therapeutic equipment

Additional Information
Year Founded—1959
Capital Under Management—$150 million
Investments(1985-1st 6 months)—7
Invested(1985-1st 6 months)—$6.5 million
Method of Compensation—Return on investment is of primary concern; do not charge fees

BARTLETT SCHLUMBERGER CAPITAL CORPORATION

140 East Carrillo Street
Santa Barbara, CA 93101
805-963-6511

James L. Bartlett III, Pres.
Harry Short, V.P.
Robert W. Brown, V.P.
Frank H. Robinson

See NEW YORK for full listing

BAY PARTNERS

1927 Landings Drive #B
Mountain View, CA 94043
415-961-5800

General Partners
John Freidenrich, Gen. Ptnr.
W. Charles Hazel, Gen. Ptnr.
John E. Bosch, Gen. Ptnr.

Whom to Contact
Any of the above

Type of Firm
Private venture capital firm investing own capital

Project Preferences
Will function either as deal originator or investor in deals created by others
Type of Financing:
Startup
First-stage
Second-stage
Minimum Investment: $500,000
Preferred Investment: $500,000-$1 million
Minimum Operating Data:
Annual Sales—Nominal
P&L—Losses (profits projected after 2 years)

Geographical Preference
West Coast

Industry Preferences

Communications
Data communications
Computer Related
Computer graphics, CAD/CAM and CAE
Micro and mini computers
Software-applications
Genetic Engineering
Gene splicing and manufacturing equipment
Industrial Products and Equipment
Other industrial automation

Medical/Health Related
Diagnostic equipment

Additional Information
Year Founded—1976
Capital Under Management—$60 million
Investments(1985-1st 6 months)—4
Invested(1985-1st 6 months)—$2.8 million
Method of Compensation—Return on investment is of primary concern; do not charge fees

BAY VENTURE GROUP

One Embarcadero Center #3303
San Francisco, CA 94111
415-989-7680

General Partners
William R. Chandler
Charles Slutzkin
Peter Sturtevant

Whom to Contact
William R. Chandler

Type of Firm
SBIC

Industry Association Memberships
NASBIC
WAVC

Project Preferences
Prefer role as deal originator but will also invest in deals created by others
Type of Financing:
Seed
Startup
Minimum Investment: Less than $100,000
Preferred Investment: $250,000-$500,000

Geographical Preference
Within two hours of office

Industry Preferences

Communications
Telephone related
Computer Related
Computer graphics, CAD/CAM and CAE
Micro and mini computers
Office automation
Scanning related
Software-applications
Software-artificial intelligence
Software-systems
Specialized turnkey systems

**Electronic Components and
Instrumentation**
Analytical and scientific instrumentation
Fiber optics
Laser related
Semiconductors
Genetic Engineering
Gene splicing and manufacturing equipment
Monoclonal antibodies and hybridomas
Recombinant DNA (agricultural and
industrial)
Recombinant DNA (medical)
Industrial Products and Equipment
Controls and sensors
Equipment and machinery
Other industrial automation
Robotics/vision systems
Medical/Health Related
Diagnostic equipment
Diagnostic test products
Disposable products
Drugs and medicines
Therapeutic equipment

Additional Information
Year Founded—1981
Capital Under Management—$4 million
Investments(1985-1st 6 months)—5
Invested(1985-1st 6 months)—$350,000
Method of Compensation—Return on
investment is of primary concern; do not
charge fees

BECKMAN INSTRUMENTS, INC.

2500 Harbor Boulevard
Post Office Box 3100
Fullerton, CA 92634
714-871-4848

Officers
Louis T. Rosso, Pres.
George F. Kilmain, V.P.
Nathaniel Brenner, Mgr., Corporate Planning

Type of Firm
Venture capital subsidiary or affiliate of
non-financial corporation

Affiliation
SmithKline Beckman Corporation (parent)

Project Preferences
Will function either as deal originator or
investor in deals created by others
Type of Financing:
Startup
First-stage

Minimum Investment: Less than $100,000
Preferred Investment: $250,000-$500,000
Minimum Operating Data:
Annual Sales—Nominal

Geographical Preference
None

Industry Preferences

**Electronic Components and
Instrumentation**
Analytical and scientific instrumentation
Genetic Engineering
Gene splicing and manufacturing equipment
Recombinant DNA (medical)
Medical/Health Related
Diagnostic equipment
Diagnostic test products

Additional Information
Year Founded—1935

BENEFIT CAPITAL, INC.

11661 San Vicente Boulevard
Suite 1000
Los Angeles, CA 90049
213-820-8767

Officers
Robert W. Smiley, Chm. & CEO
Bruce G. Rossiter, Pres. & Dir.
John S. Cary, Sr. Assoc.
Allan M. Dawson, Assoc.
Nancy Schirber, Assoc.

Whom to Contact
Bruce G. Rossiter

Type of Firm
Investment banking or merchant banking
firm investing own capital or funds of
partners or clients
Consulting firm evaluating and analyzing
venture projects and arranging private
placements

Project Preferences
Prefer role as deal originator
Type of Financing:
Second-stage
Later-stage expansion
Leveraged buyout
Minimum Investment: $500,000
Preferred Investment: $500,000-$1 million
Preferred Investment (LBO):
$1 million-$5 million

Minimum Operating Data:
Annual Sales—Over $3 million
P&L—Profits NBT over $250,000
Annual Sales (LBO)—$5 million-$100 million

Geographical Preferences
West Coast
National

Industry Preferences

Communications
Cable television
Commercial communications
Data communications
Satellite and microwave communications
Telephone related
Computer Related
Computer graphics, CAD/CAM and CAE
Computer mainframes
Computer services
Memory devices
Micro and mini computers
Office automation
Scanning related
Software-applications
Software-artificial intelligence
Software-systems
Specialized turnkey systems
Terminals
Consumer
Computer stores/related services
Consumer products
Consumer services
Food and beverage products
Franchise businesses
Hotels and resort areas
Leisure and recreational products
Restaurants
Retailing
Distribution
Communications equipment
Computer equipment
Consumer products
Electronics equipment
Food products
Industrial products
Medical products
**Electronic Components and
Instrumentation**
Analytical and scientific instrumentation
Component fabrication and testing
equipment
Electronic components
Fiber optics
Laser related
Semiconductors

Genetic Engineering
Gene splicing and manufacturing equipment
Monoclonal antibodies and hybridomas
Recombinant DNA (agricultural and industrial)
Recombinant DNA (medical)
Industrial Products and Equipment
Chemicals
Controls and sensors
Energy management
Equipment and machinery
Other industrial automation
Plastics
Robotics/vision systems
Specialty materials
Medical/Health Related
Diagnostic equipment
Diagnostic test products
Disposable products
Drugs and medicines
Hospital and clinical labs
Medical services
Therapeutic equipment
Will Not Consider
Energy-related businesses
Entertainment
Real estate

Additional Information
Year Founded—1984
Investments(1985-1st 6 months)—1
Invested(1985-1st 6 months)—$1 million
Method of Compensation—Function primarily in service area; receive contingent fee in cash or equity
Professional fee required whether or not deal closes

BERLINER ASSOCIATES

535 Middlefield Road #240
Menlo Park, CA 94025
415-324-1231

Managing Directors
David L. Berliner
Martha L. Berliner

Whom to Contact
David L. Berliner

Type of Firm
Private venture capital firm investing own capital

Industry Association Membership
WAVC

Project Preferences
Prefer role in deals created by others
Type of Financing:
Seed
Startup
First-stage
Leveraged buyout
Minimum Investment: $100,000
Preferred Investment: $250,000-$500,000
Minimum Operating Data:
Annual Sales—Nominal

Geographical Preferences
Within two hours of office
West Coast

Industry Preferences

Distribution
Medical products
Electronic Components and Instrumentation
Analytical and scientific instrumentation
Laser related
Genetic Engineering
Gene splicing and manufacturing equipment
Monoclonal antibodies and hybridomas
Recombinant DNA (agricultural and industrial)
Recombinant DNA (medical)
Industrial Products and Equipment
Chemicals
Medical/Health Related
Diagnostic equipment
Diagnostic test products
Disposable products
Drugs and medicines
Hospital and clinical labs
Medical services
Therapeutic equipment

Additional Information
Year Founded—1977
Method of Compensation—Return on investment is of primary concern; do not charge fees

---

BESSEMER VENTURE PARTNERS

3000 Sand Hill Road
Building 3, #225
Menlo Park, CA 94025
415-854-2200

Other Offices
630 Fifth Avenue
New York, NY 10111
212-708-9300

83 Walnut Street
Wellesley Hills, MA 02181
617-237-6050

General Partners
William T. Burgin (New York & Massachusetts)
Neill H. Brownstein (California)
Robert H. Buescher (New York)
Robert B. Field (California)
James H. Furneaux (Massachusetts)
G. Felda Hardymon (Massachusetts)

Whom to Contact
Any of the above

Type of Firm
Private venture capital firm investing own capital

Affiliation
Bessemer Securities Corporation (sole limited partner)

Industry Association Memberships
NVCA
WAVC

Project Preferences
Will function either as deal originator or investor in deals created by others
Type of Financing:
Seed
Research and development partnerships
Startup
First-stage
Second-stage
Later-stage expansion
Leveraged buyout
Preferred Investment: No preference

Geographical Preference
National

Industry Preferences
None

Additional Information
Year Founded—1970
Capital Under Management—$100 million
Investments(1985-1st 6 months)—5
Invested(1985-1st 6 months)—$3 million
Method of Compensation—Return on
   investment is of primary concern; do not
   charge fees

BNP VENTURE CAPITAL CORP.

3000 Sand Hill Road
Building 1, #125
Menlo Park, CA 94025
415-854-1084

Officers
Edgerton Scott II, Pres.
Claude Ossart, Dir.

Whom to Contact
Edgerton Scott II

Type of Firm
SBIC

Affiliation
Banque Nationale de Paris (parent)

Project Preferences
Prefer role in deals created by others
Type of Financing:
First-stage
Second-stage
Leveraged buyout
Minimum Investment: $100,000
Preferred Investment: $100,000-$400,000
Minimum Operating Data:
Annual Sales—Nominal
P&L—Losses (profits projected after 1 year)

Geographical Preference
West Coast

Industry Preferences

Communications
Cable television
Commercial communications
Data communications
Satellite and microwave communications
Telephone related

Computer Related
Computer graphics, CAD/CAM and CAE
Computer mainframes
Computer services
Memory devices
Micro and mini computers
Office automation
Scanning related
Software-applications
Software-artificial intelligence
Software-systems
Specialized turnkey systems
Terminals
Distribution
Communications equipment
Computer equipment
Electronics equipment
**Electronic Components and
   Instrumentation**
Analytical and scientific instrumentation
Component fabrication and testing
   equipment
Electronic components
Fiber optics
Laser related
Semiconductors
Energy/Natural Resources
Alternative energy
Energy conservation
Technology related products/equipment
Genetic Engineering
Gene splicing and manufacturing equipment
Monoclonal antibodies and hybridomas
Recombinant DNA (agricultural and
   industrial)
Recombinant DNA (medical)
Industrial Products and Equipment
Chemicals
Controls and sensors
Energy management
Equipment and machinery
Other industrial automation
Plastics
Robotics/vision systems
Specialty materials
Medical/Health Related
Diagnostic equipment
Diagnostic test products
Disposable products
Drugs and medicines
Hospital and clinical labs
Medical services
Therapeutic equipment

Additional Information
Year Founded—1984
Capital Under Management—$5 million
Investments(1985-1st 6 months)—5
Invested(1985-1st 6 months)—$1 million
Method of Compensation—Return on
   investment is of primary concern; do not
   charge fees

BRENTWOOD ASSOCIATES

11661 San Vicente Boulevard
Suite 707
Los Angeles, CA 90049
213-826-6581

Other Offices
601 California Street #450
San Francisco, CA 94108
415-788-4893

c/o Hobbs Associates
Post Office Box 686
Corona del Mar, CA 92625
714-546-0961

Partners
George M. Crandell, Gen. Ptnr.
   (Los Angeles)
Roger C. Davisson, Gen. Ptnr. (Los Angeles)
B. Kipling Hagopian, Gen. Ptnr.
   (Los Angeles)
G. Bradford Jones, Gen. Ptnr. (Los Angeles)
Timothy M. Pennington, Gen. Ptnr.
   (Los Angeles)
Frederick J. Warren, Gen. Ptnr.
   (Los Angeles)
Toby Schreiber, Representative
   (San Francisco)
Linder C. Hobbs, Representative
   (Corona del Mar)
William M. Barnum, Principal (Los Angeles)
Brian P. McDermott, Principal (Los Angeles)

Whom to Contact
Brian P. McDermott
William Barnum
Toby Schreiber
Linder C. Hobbs

Type of Firm
Private venture capital firm investing
   own capital
SBIC

Industry Association Memberships
NASBIC
NVCA
WAVC

Project Preferences

Will function either as deal originator or investor in deals created by others

Type of Financing:
Seed
Startup
First-stage
Second-stage
Leveraged buyout
Minimum Investment: $250,000
Preferred Investment: Over $1 million
Preferred Investment (LBO):
$1 million and over
Minimum Operating Data:
Annual Sales—Nominal
P&L—Losses (profits projected after 2 years)
Annual Sales (LBO)—$50 million

Geographical Preference

West Coast (startups)
USA (later stages)

Industry Preferences

Communications
Broadcast properties (LBO)
Cable television (LBO)
Commercial communications
Data communications
Satellite and microwave communications
Computer Related
Computer graphics, CAD/CAM and CAE
Computer mainframes
Computer services
Memory devices
Micro and mini computers
Office automation
Scanning related
Software-applications
Software-artificial intelligence
Software-systems
Specialized turnkey systems
Terminals
Consumer
Selected businesses (LBO)
Distribution
(Interest in distribution is limited
to LBO opportunities)
Communications equipment
Computer equipment
Consumer products
Electronics equipment
Food products
Industrial products
Medical products

Electronic Components and Instrumentation
Analytical and scientific instrumentation
Component fabrication and testing equipment
Electronic components
Fiber optics
Laser related
Semiconductors
Energy/Natural Resources
Technology related products/equipment
Genetic Engineering
Gene splicing and manufacturing equipment
Monoclonal antibodies and hybridomas
Recombinant DNA (agricultural and industrial)
Recombinant DNA (medical)
Industrial Products and Equipment
Equipment and machinery
Other industrial automation
Robotics/vision systems
Medical/Health Related
Diagnostic equipment
Diagnostic test products
Drugs and medicines
Therapeutic equipment
Other
LBO candidates: stable businesses with a strong cash flow
Will Not Consider
Entertainment
Non-proprietary services
Oil and gas exploration and production
Real estate
LBO candidates subject to a high degree of technological obsolescence

Additional Information

Year Founded—1972
Capital Under Management—$280 million
Investments(1985-1st 6 months)—30
Invested(1985-1st 6 months)—$27 million
Method of Compensation—Return on investment is of primary concern; do not charge fees

---

BRYAN AND EDWARDS

3000 Sand Hill Road
Building 2, #215
Menlo Park, CA 94025
415-854-1555

Other Office

600 Montgomery Street
35th Floor
San Francisco, CA 94111
415-421-9990

Partners

John M. Bryan (San Francisco)
William C. Edwards (Menlo Park)
Alan R. Brudos (San Francisco/Menlo Park)
Robert W. Ledoux (San Francisco)
Guy H. Conger (Menlo Park)

Whom to Contact

Robert W. Ledoux
Guy H. Conger

Type of Firm

Private venture capital firm investing own capital

Industry Association Memberships

NASBIC
NVCA
WAVC

Project Preferences

Will function either as deal originator or investor in deals created by others
Type of Financing:
Startup
First-stage
Second-stage
Leveraged buyout
Minimum Investment: $100,000
Preferred Investment: $250,000-$750,000
Minimum Operating Data:
Annual Sales—Nominal
P&L—Losses (profits projected after 2 years)

Geographical Preferences

Within two hours of office
West Coast

Industry Preferences

Communications
Data communications
Satellite and microwave communications
Telephone related

Computer Related
Computer graphics, CAD/CAM and CAE
Computer mainframes
Computer services
Memory devices
Micro and mini computers
Office automation
Scanning related
Software-applications
Software-artificial intelligence
Software-systems
Specialized turnkey systems
Terminals
Electronic Components and Instrumentation
Analytical and scientific instrumentation
Component fabrication and testing equipment
Electronic components
Fiber optics
Laser related
Semiconductors
Energy/Natural Resources
Technology related products/equipment
Genetic Engineering
Gene splicing and manufacturing equipment
Monoclonal antibodies and hybridomas
Recombinant DNA (agricultural and industrial)
Recombinant DNA (medical)
Industrial Products and Equipment
Robotics/vision systems
Medical/Health Related
Diagnostic equipment
Diagnostic test products
Disposable products
Drugs and medicines
Medical services
Therapeutic equipment
Other
Finance and insurance
Will Not Consider
Real estate
Restaurants

Additional Information
Year Founded—1962
Investments(1985-1st 6 months)—16
Invested(1985-1st 6 months)—$3.5 million
Method of Compensation—Return on investment is of primary concern; do not charge fees

BURR, EGAN, DELEAGE & CO.

Three Embarcadero Center #2560
San Francisco, CA 94111
415-362-4022

East Coast Office
One Post Office Square #3800
Boston, MA 02109
617-482-8020

Partners
Craig L. Burr, Ptnr. (Massachusetts)
William P. Egan, Ptnr. (Massachusetts)
Jean Deleage, Ptnr. (California)
Brion Applegate, Ptnr. (California)
Shirley Cerrudo, Ptnr. (California)
Jean-Bernard Schmidt, Ptnr. (California)
Thomas E. Winter, Ptnr. (California)
Jonathan A. Flint, V.P. (Massachusetts)
Esther B. Sharp, V.P. (Massachusetts)
Annette M. Bianchi, Assoc. (California)

Whom to Contact
Jean Deleage (California)
Thomas E. Winter (California)
Craig L. Burr (Massachusetts)
William P. Egan (Massachusetts)

Type of Firm
Private venture capital firm investing own capital

Industry Association Membership
NVCA

Project Preferences
Prefer role as deal originator but will also invest in deals created by others
Type of Financing:
Startup
First-stage
Second-stage
Later-stage expansion
Leveraged buyout
Minimum Investment: $750,000
Preferred Investment: Over $1 million
Preferred Investment (LBO): $1 million and over

Geographical Preference
National

Industry Preferences

Communications
Cable television
Commercial communications
Data communications
Satellite and microwave communications
Telephone related

Computer Related
Computer graphics, CAD/CAM and CAE
Computer mainframes
Memory devices
Micro and mini computers
Software-applications
Software-systems
Consumer
Computer stores/related services
Retailing
Distribution
Communications equipment
Electronics equipment
Medical products
Electronic Components and Instrumentation
Analytical and scientific instrumentation
Component fabrication and testing equipment
Electronic components
Fiber optics
Laser related
Semiconductors
Energy/Natural Resources
Technology related products/equipment
Genetic Engineering
Gene splicing and manufacturing equipment
Monoclonal antibodies and hybridomas
Recombinant DNA (agricultural and industrial)
Recombinant DNA (medical)
Industrial Products and Equipment
Chemicals
Controls and sensors
Energy management
Equipment and machinery
Other industrial automation
Plastics
Robotics/vision systems
Specialty materials
Medical/Health Related
Diagnostic equipment
Diagnostic test products
Disposable products
Drugs and medicines
Hospital and clinical labs
Medical services
Therapeutic equipment
Will Not Consider
Real estate

Additional Information
Year Founded—1979
Capital Under Management—$200 million
Investments(1985-1st 6 months)—19
Invested(1985-1st 6 months)—$12 million
Method of Compensation—Return on investment is of primary concern; do not charge fees

BUSINESS OPPORTUNITY BUILDERS

2916 West Main Street
Visalia, CA 93277
209-733-4296

Other Offices

208 Newell Drive
Fortuna, CA 95540
707-725-9423

1617 East 17th Street #23
Santa Ana, CA 92701
714-541-8388

Officers

Robert D. Shipman, Chm. & Pres. (Visalia)
Merle Bechtold, Secy. & Treas. (Visalia)
William Fink, V.P. Marketing (Fortuna)
Kenneth Carter, V.P. Leasing (Santa Ana)

Whom to Contact

Robert D. Shipman

Type of Firm

Private venture capital firm investing
own capital
Consulting firm evaluating and analyzing
venture projects and arranging private
placements

Project Preferences

Prefer role as deal originator but will also
invest in deals created by others
Type of Financing:
Seed
First-stage
Second-stage
Leveraged buyout
Minimum Investment: $100,000
Preferred Investment: $100,000-$250,000
Minimum Operating Data:
Annual Sales—Nominal
P&L—Losses (profits projected after 3 years)

Geographical Preference

None

Industry Preferences

Communications

Cable television
Commercial communications
Data communications
Satellite and microwave communications
Telephone related

Consumer

Computer stores/related services
Consumer products
Consumer services
Food and beverage products
Franchise businesses
Hotels and resort areas
Leisure and recreational products
Restaurants
Retailing

Distribution

Communications equipment
Computer equipment
Consumer products
Electronics equipment
Food products
Industrial products
Medical products

Electronic Components and Instrumentation

Analytical and scientific instrumentation
Component fabrication and testing
equipment
Electronic components
Fiber optics
Laser related
Semiconductors

Energy/Natural Resources

Alternative energy
Coal related
Drilling and exploration services
Energy conservation
Minerals
Oil and gas exploration and production
Technology related products/equipment

Genetic Engineering

Gene splicing and manufacturing equipment
Monoclonal antibodies and hybridomas
Recombinant DNA (agricultural and
industrial)
Recombinant DNA (medical)

Industrial Products and Equipment

Chemicals
Controls and sensors
Energy management
Equipment and machinery
Other industrial automation
Plastics
Robotics/vision systems
Specialty materials

Medical/Health Related

Diagnostic equipment
Diagnostic test products
Disposable products
Drugs and medicines
Hospital and clinical labs
Medical services
Therapeutic equipment

Other

Agriculture, forestry, fishing
Education related
Finance and insurance
Publishing
Real estate
Specialty consulting
Transportation

Additional Information

Year Founded—1983
Method of Compensation—Return on
investment is most important, but also
charge for closing fees, service fees, etc.
Professional fee required whether or
not deal closes

CABLE, HOWSE & COZADD, INC.

3000 Sand Hill Road
Building 1, #190
Menlo Park, CA 94025
415-854-3340

Other Offices

999 Third Avenue #4300
Seattle, WA 98104
206-583-2700

1800 One Main Place
101 Southwest Main
Portland, OR 97204
503-248-9646

General Partners

Thomas J. Cable (Washington)
Elwood D. Howse, Jr. (Washington)
Bennett A. Cozadd (Washington)
Michael A. Ellison (Washington)
Wayne C. Wager (Washington)
James B. Glavin (Washington)
L. Barton Alexander (Oregon)
Gregory H. Turnbull (California)

Whom to Contact

Wayne C. Wager

Type of Firm

Private venture capital firm investing
own capital

Industry Association Memberships

NVCA
WAVC

Project Preferences

Prefer role as deal originator but will also
invest in deals created by others

Type of Financing:
Startup
First-stage
Second-stage
Later-stage expansion
Minimum Investment: $500,000
Preferred Investment: $1 million-$2.5 million
Minimum Operating Data:
Annual Sales—Nominal
P&L—Losses (profits projected after 3 years)

Geographical Preferences
Northwest
East Coast
West Coast

Industry Preferences

Communications
Data communications
Telephone related
Computer Related
Computer graphics, CAD/CAM and CAE
Computer mainframes
Computer services
Memory devices
Software-applications
Software-artificial intelligence
Software-systems
Specialized turnkey systems
**Electronic Components and
  Instrumentation**
Analytical and scientific instrumentation
Component fabrication and testing
  equipment
Electronic components
Fiber optics
Laser related
Semiconductors
Genetic Engineering
Monoclonal antibodies and hybridomas
Recombinant DNA (agricultural and
  industrial)
Recombinant DNA (medical)
Industrial Products and Equipment
Chemicals
Other industrial automation
Plastics
Robotics/vision systems
Specialty materials
Medical/Health Related
Diagnostic equipment
Drugs and medicines
Medical services
Therapeutic equipment
Will Not Consider
Natural resource exploration or extraction
Real estate

Additional Information
Year Founded—1977
Capital Under Management—$132 million
Investments(1985-1st 6 months)—23
Invested(1985-1st 6 months)—$10.3 million
Method of Compensation—Return on
  investment is of primary concern; do not
  charge fees

CALIFORNIA CAPITAL INVESTORS, LTD.

11812 San Vicente Boulevard
Los Angeles, CA 90049
213-820-7222

Partners
Arthur H. Bernstein, Gen. Ptnr.
Lynda Gibson, Inv. Analyst
Craig Colodny, Assoc.
Katherine Keck Moses, Inv. Officer

Whom to Contact
Lynda S. Gibson

Type of Firm
SBIC

Industry Association Membership
NASBIC

Project Preferences
Will function either as deal originator or
  investor in deals created by others
Type of Financing:
Second-stage
Later-stage expansion
Leveraged buyout
Minimum Investment: $150,000
Preferred Investment: $150,000-$300,000
Minimum Operating Data:
Annual Sales—$1.5 million
P&L—Break even

Geographical Preferences
Within two hours of office
West Coast

Industry Preferences

Communications
Cable television
Satellite and microwave communications
Computer Related
Various

Consumer
Consumer products
Consumer services
Food and beverage products
Franchise businesses
Leisure and recreational products
Distribution
Electronics equipment
Industrial products
**Electronic Components and
  Instrumentation**
Component fabrication and testing
  equipment
Fiber optics
Energy/Natural Resources
Oil and gas exploration and production
Industrial Products and Equipment
Chemicals
Medical/Health Related
Diagnostic equipment
Disposable products
Other
Transportation
Will Not Consider
Entertainment industry related
Retailing

Additional Information
Year Founded—1981
Capital Under Management—$6 million
Investments(1985-1st 6 months)—4
Invested(1985-1st 6 months)—$300,000
Method of Compensation—Return on
  investment is most important, but also
  charge for closing fees, service fees, etc.

CARLYLE CAPITAL CORPORATION

444 South Flower Street #4650
Los Angeles, CA 90017
213-689-9235

Officers
Raymond A. Doig, Pres.
Dennis C. Stanfill, Chm.

Whom to Contact
Raymond A. Doig

Type of Firm
Private venture capital firm investing
  own capital

Affiliation
Managed by Stanfill Doig & Co., Inc.

Project Preferences

Will function either as deal originator or investor in deals created by others

Type of Financing:
Second-stage
Later-stage expansion
Leveraged buyout
Minimum Investment: $500,000
Preferred Investment: $3 million-$5 million
Minimum Operating Data:
Annual Sales—$1.5 million
P&L—Break even

Industry Preferences

Communications
Radio and television stations
Consumer
Hotels and resort areas
Leisure and recreational products
Other
Publishing

Additional Information

Year Founded—1983
Capital Under Management—$34 million
Investments(1985-1st 6 months)—1
Invested(1985-1st 6 months)—$4.1 million
Method of Compensation—Return on investment is of primary concern; do not charge fees

---

CATALYST TECHNOLOGIES

1287 Lawrence Station Road
Sunnyvale, CA 94089
408-745-1110

Partners

Nolan K. Bushnell
John B. Anderson
Perry D. Odak
Lawrence Calof

Whom to Contact

John B. Anderson

Type of Firm

Private venture capital firm investing own capital

Project Preferences

Prefer role as deal originator but will also invest in deals created by others
Type of Financing:
Seed
Startup
Minimum Investment: Less than $100,000
Preferred Investment: $100,000-$250,000

Minimum Operating Data:

Annual Sales—Nominal
P&L—Losses (profits projected after 2 years)

Geographical Preference

Sunnyvale, CA

Industry Preferences

Communications
Cable television
Commercial communications
Data communications
Satellite and microwave communications
Telephone related
Computer Related
Micro and mini computers
Office automation
Consumer
Consumer products
Leisure and recreational products
Electronic Components and Instrumentation
Laser related
Industrial Products and Equipment
Robotics/vision systems
Will Not Consider
Medical related businesses
Energy related businesses

Additional Information

Year Founded—1983
Capital Under Management—$4.5 million
Investments(1985-1st 6 months)—3
Invested(1985-1st 6 months)—$300,000
Method of Compensation—Return on investment is most important, but also charge for closing fees, service fees, etc.

CFB VENTURE CAPITAL CORPORATION

Post Office Box 109
San Diego, CA 92112
619-230-3304

Officers

Yoshiaki Shibusawa, Pres.
Richard J. Roncaglia, V.P.
Fumito Tomisaka, Sr. Inv. Analyst

Whom to Contact

Richard J. Roncaglia

Type of Firm

SBIC

Affiliation

California First Bank (parent)

Industry Association Membership

NASBIC

Project Preferences

Will function either as deal originator or investor in deals created by others

Type of Financing:
Second-stage
Leveraged buyout
Minimum Investment: $100,000
Preferred Investment: $100,000-$250,000
Minimum Operating Data:
Annual Sales—Nominal
P&L—Break even

Geographical Preference

West Coast

Industry Preferences

Communications
Cable television
Commercial communications
Data communications
Satellite and microwave communications
Telephone related
Computer Related
Computer graphics, CAD/CAM and CAE
Computer mainframes
Computer services
Memory devices
Micro and mini computers
Office automation
Scanning related
Software-applications
Software-artificial intelligence
Software-systems
Specialized turnkey systems
Terminals
Electronic Components and Instrumentation
Analytical and scientific instrumentation
Component fabrication and testing equipment
Electronic components
Fiber optics
Laser related
Semiconductors
Energy/Natural Resources
Alternative energy
Coal related
Drilling and exploration services
Energy conservation
Minerals
Oil and gas exploration and production
Technology related products/equipment

Genetic Engineering
Gene splicing and manufacturing equipment
Monoclonal antibodies and hybridomas
Recombinant DNA (agricultural and
    industrial)
Recombinant DNA (medical)
Industrial Products and Equipment
Chemicals
Controls and sensors
Energy management
Equipment and machinery
Other industrial automation
Plastics
Robotics/vision systems
Specialty materials
Medical/Health Related
Diagnostic equipment
Diagnostic test products
Disposable products
Drugs and medicines
Hospital and clinical labs
Medical services
Therapeutic equipment

Additional Information

Year Founded—1983
Capital Under Management—$2 million
Investments(1985-1st 6 months)—2
Method of Compensation—Return on
    investment is of primary concern; do not
    charge fees

R.H. CHAPPELL COMPANY

One Lombard Street
San Francisco, CA 94111
415-397-5094

Officers

Robert H. Chappell, Pres.
N. Colin Lind, V.P.
Michael T. Hsieh, Assoc.
R. Craig Lind, Assoc.

Whom to Contact

Michael T. Hsieh

Type of Firm

Investment banking or merchant banking
    firm investing own capital or funds of
    partners or clients

Industry Association Membership

WAVC

Project Preferences

Prefer role as deal originator but will also
    invest in deals created by others

Type of Financing:
Seed
Startup
First-stage
Second-stage
Leveraged buyout
Minimum Investment: Less than $100,000
Preferred Investment: Over $500,000
Minimum Operating Data:
Annual Sales—Nominal
P&L—Losses (profits projected after 2 years)

Geographical Preferences

Within two hours of office
West Coast

Industry Preferences

Communications
Cable television
Commercial communications
Data communications
Satellite and microwave communications
Telephone related
Computer Related
Computer graphics, CAD/CAM and CAE
Computer mainframes
Computer services
Memory devices
Micro and mini computers
Office automation
Scanning related
Software-applications
Software-artificial intelligence
Software-systems
Specialized turnkey systems
Terminals
Consumer
Computer stores/related services
Consumer products
Consumer services
Food and beverage products
Franchise businesses
Hotels and resort areas
Leisure and recreational products
Restaurants
Retailing
**Electronic Components and
    Instrumentation**
Analytical and scientific instrumentation
Component fabrication and testing
    equipment
Electronic components
Fiber optics
Laser related
Semiconductors

Industrial Products and Equipment
Chemicals
Controls and sensors
Energy management
Equipment and machinery
Other industrial automation
Plastics
Robotics/vision systems
Specialty materials
Medical/Health Related
Diagnostic equipment
Diagnostic test products
Disposable products
Drugs and medicines
Hospital and clinical labs
Medical services
Therapeutic equipment
Other
Agriculture, forestry, fishing
Education related
Finance and insurance
Publishing
Real estate
Specialty consulting
Transportation

Additional Information

Year Founded—1980
Capital Under Management—$14 million
Investments(1985-1st 6 months)—8
Invested(1985-1st 6 months)—$8 million
Method of Compensation—Return on
    investment is most important, but also
    charge for closing fees, service fees, etc.

CHARTER VENTURES

525 University Avenue #1500
Palo Alto, CA 94301
415-325-6953

Partners

Johnson Cha
A. Barr Dolan

Whom to Contact

A. Barr Dolan

Type of Firm

Private venture capital firm investing
    own capital

Affiliation

Charter Venture Capital, management firm

Industry Association Membership

WAVC

Project Preferences

Will function either as deal originator or investor in deals created by others

Type of Financing:
Seed
Startup
First-stage
Second-stage
Leveraged buyout
Minimum Investment: $100,000
Preferred Investment: $250,000-$500,000
Minimum Operating Data:
Annual Sales—Nominal

Geographical Preference

None

Industry Preferences

Communications
Cable television
Commercial communications
Data communications
Satellite and microwave communications
Telephone related
Computer Related
Computer graphics, CAD/CAM and CAE
Computer mainframes
Computer services
Memory devices
Micro and mini computers
Office automation
Scanning related
Software-applications
Software-artificial intelligence
Software-systems
Specialized turnkey systems
Terminals
Electronic Components and Instrumentation
Analytical and scientific instrumentation
Component fabrication and testing equipment
Electronic components
Fiber optics
Laser related
Semiconductors
Energy/Natural Resources
Technology related products/equipment
Genetic Engineering
Gene splicing and manufacturing equipment
Monoclonal antibodies and hybridomas
Recombinant DNA (agricultural and industrial)
Recombinant DNA (medical)

Industrial Products and Equipment
Chemicals
Controls and sensors
Energy management
Equipment and machinery
Other industrial automation
Plastics
Robotics/vision systems
Specialty materials
Medical/Health Related
Diagnostic equipment
Diagnostic test products
Disposable products
Drugs and medicines
Hospital and clinical labs
Medical services
Therapeutic equipment
Other
Agriculture, forestry, fishing
Will Not Consider
Motion pictures

Additional Information

Year Founded—1982
Investments(1985-1st 6 months)—8
Method of Compensation—Return on investment is of primary concern; do not charge fees

---

CHATHAM VENTURE CORPORATION

333 West Santa Clara Street
Suite 800
San Jose, CA 95113
408-947-4062

William D. Jobe

See MASSACHUSETTS for full listing

CHURCHILL INTERNATIONAL

444 Market Street #2501
San Francisco, CA 94111
415-398-7677

Other Office

545 Middlefield Road
Menlo Park, CA 94025
415-328-4401

Nine Riverside Road
Weston, MA 02193
617-893-6555

Officers

Louis L. Davis, Chm. (San Francisco)
Robert C. Weeks, Pres. (Menlo Park)
Michael J. Schall, CFO (Menlo Park)
Roy G. Helsing, V.P. (Weston)
Franz Helbig, Inv. Dir. (West Berlin)
Bing Budiarto, Inv. Dir. (Menlo Park)
Janet Effland, Mgn. Dir. (Menlo Park)
Christopher Spray, Inv. Dir. (Weston)
David Ruth, Inv. Dir. (Weston)
Julie B. Dunbar, Mgr. Corp. Communications (Weston)

Whom to Contact

Julie B. Dunbar

Type of Firm

Investment banking or merchant banking firm investing own capital or funds of partners or clients
Private partnership

Industry Association Memberships

NASBIC
NVCA

Project Preferences

Will function either as deal originator or investor in deals created by others
Type of Financing:
Seed
Startup
Second-stage
Later-stage expansion
Minimum Investment: $250,000
Preferred Investment: $250,000-$1 million

Geographical Preference

None

Industry Preferences

Communications
Data communications
Satellite and microwave communications

Computer Related
Computer graphics, CAD/CAM and CAE
Computer mainframes
Computer services
Memory devices
Micro and mini computers
Office automation
Scanning related
Software-applications
Software-artificial intelligence
Software-systems
Specialized turnkey systems
Terminals
Electronic Components and Instrumentation
Analytical and scientific instrumentation
Component fabrication and testing equipment
Electronic components
Fiber optics
Laser related
Semiconductors
Genetic Engineering
Recombinant DNA (agricultural and industrial)
Industrial Products and Equipment
Chemicals
Controls and sensors
Energy management
Equipment and machinery
Other industrial automation
Plastics
Robotics/vision systems
Specialty materials
Medical/Health Related
Diagnostic equipment
Will Not Consider
Energy related businesses
Real estate
Non high technology

Additional Information
Year Founded—1978
Capital Under Management—$100 million
Investments(1985-1st 6 months)—18 (U.S. only)
Invested(1985-1st 6 months)—$7.5 million (U.S. only)
Method of Compensation—Return on investment is of primary concern; do not charge fees

CITICORP VENTURE CAPITAL, LTD.

Two Embarcadero Place
2200 Geng Road #203
Palo Alto, CA 94303
415-424-8000

Other Offices
153 East 53rd Street
28th Floor
New York, NY 10043
212-559-1116

717 North Harwood
Suite 2920, LB 87
Dallas, TX 75201
214-880-9670

Officers/California
David A. Wegmann, V.P.
J. Matthew Mackowski, V.P.
Larry J. Wells, V.P.
Allen G. Rosenberg, V.P.

Whom to Contact
Any of the above

Type of Firm
SBIC
Venture capital subsidiary of commercial bank

Affiliation
Citicorp, holding company for Citibank, N.A. (parent)

Industry Association Memberships
NASBIC
NVCA
WAVC

Project Preferences
Will function either as deal originator or investor in deals created by others
Type of Financing:
Seed
Startup
First-stage
Second-stage
Later-stage expansion
Leveraged buyout
Minimum Investment: $500,000
Preferred Investment: $1 million-$2 million
Preferred Investment (LBO): $5 million and over
Minimum Operating Data:
Annual Sales—Nominal
P&L—Losses (profits projected after 3 years)
Annual Sales (LBO)—$10 million and over

Geographical Preferences
Within two hours of office
Southwest
Rocky Mountains
West Coast

Industry Preferences

Communications
Commercial communications
Data communications
Satellite and microwave communications
Telephone related
Computer Related
Computer graphics, CAD/CAM and CAE
Computer mainframes
Computer services
Memory devices
Micro and mini computers
Office automation
Software-applications
Software-systems
Terminals
Consumer
Franchise businesses
Restaurants
Retailing
Electronic Components and Instrumentation
Analytical and scientific instrumentation
Electronic components
Laser related
Semiconductors
Genetic Engineering
Monoclonal antibodies and hybridomas
Recombinant DNA (agricultural and industrial)
Recombinant DNA (medical)
Research and manufacturing equipment
Industrial Products and Equipment
Controls and sensors
Equipment and machinery
Other industrial automation
Robotics/vision systems
Medical/Health Related
Diagnostic equipment
Drugs and medicines
Hospital and clinical labs
Medical services
Therapeutic equipment
Will Not Consider
Agriculture
Entertainment industries, including motion pictures
Finance companies
Insurance
Publishing
Real estate

Additional Information

Year Founded—1968
Capital Under Management—$170 million
Investments(1985-1st 6 months)—36
Invested(1985-1st 6 months)—$22 million
Method of Compensation—Return on investment is of primary concern; do not charge fees

CITY VENTURES, INC.

1880 Century Park East #413
Los Angeles, CA 90067
213-550-0416

Officers

Neill B. Lawton, Pres.
Anita M. Lenz, Inv. Mgr.
Saundra W. Kirshner, Inv. Officer

Whom to Contact

Any of the above

Type of Firm

SBIC

Affiliation

City National Bank, Beverly Hills, CA (parent)

Industry Association Membership

NVCA

Project Preferences

Will function either as deal originator or investor in deals created by others
Type of Financing:
Second-stage
Later-stage expansion
Leveraged buyout
Minimum Investment: $100,000
Preferred Investment: $250,000-$500,000
Preferred Investment (LBO):
$250,000 and over
Minimum Operating Data:
Annual Sales—$2 million
P&L—Break even
Annual Sales (LBO)—$5 million

Geographical Preference

None

Industry Preferences

Communications
Cable television
Commercial communications
Data communications
Satellite and microwave communications
Telephone related
Electronic Components and Instrumentation
Analytical and scientific instrumentation
Electronic components
Fiber optics
Laser related
Energy/Natural Resources
Energy conservation
Technology related products/equipment
Genetic Engineering
Recombinant DNA (agricultural and industrial)
Industrial Products and Equipment
Chemicals
Controls and sensors
Energy management
Equipment and machinery
Low technology manufacturing
Other industrial automation
Plastics
Robotics/vision systems
Service firms-industrial/commercial
Specialty materials
Medical/Health Related
Diagnostic equipment
Diagnostic test products
Disposable products
Drugs and medicines
Hospital and clinical labs
Medical services
Therapeutic equipment
Other
Industrial/commercial service firms
Will Not Consider
Entertainment production
Oil and gas related
Real estate
Restaurants or food service
Retailing
Textiles
Trucking
Wholesaling

Additional Information

Year Founded—1982
Capital Under Management—$2 million
Investments(1985-1st 6 months)—5
Invested(1985-1st 6 months)—$400,000
Method of Compensation—Return on investment is most important, but also charge for closing fees, service fees, etc.

COGENERATION CAPITAL FUND

300 Tamal Plaza #190
Corte Madera, CA 94925
415-924-3525

Partners

Howard W. Cann, Mgn. Gen. Ptnr.
Roy N. Bergmann, Gen. Ptnr.
Alan L. Hills, Gen. Ptnr.
Jonathan S. Saiger, Gen. Ptnr.
Michael C. Werner, Gen. Ptnr.

Whom to Contact

Howard W. Cann
Jonathan S. Saiger

Type of Firm

SBIC

Affiliation

Cogeneration Capital Associates Incorporated (fund manager)

Industry Association Membership

NASBIC

Project Preferences

Will function either as deal originator or investor in deals created by others
Type of Financing:
Startup
First-stage
Second-stage
Leveraged buyout
Minimum Investment: $250,000
Preferred Investment: $250,000-$500,000
Preferred Investment (LBO):
$250,000-$500,000
Minimum Operating Data:
Annual Sales—Nominal
P&L—Losses (profits projected after 2 years)

Geographical Preference

None

Industry Preferences

Energy/Natural Resources
Alternative energy

Additional Information

Year Founded—1984
Capital Under Management—$5 million
Investments(1985-1st 6 months)—3
Invested(1985-1st 6 months)—$2.25 million
Method of Compensation—Return on investment is most important, but also charge for closing fees, service fees, etc.

CONCORD PARTNERS

600 Montgomery Street
San Francisco, CA 94111
415-362-2400

E. Payson Smith, Jr., Gen. Ptnr.
Stephen M. Wilson, Assoc.
Philip M. Young, Gen. Ptnr.

See NEW YORK for full listing

CONTINENTAL CAPITAL VENTURES

555 California Street #5070
San Francisco, CA 94104
415-989-2020

Other Office
3000 Sand Hill Road
Building 1, #135
Menlo Park, CA 94025
415-854-6633

General Partners
Frank G. Chambers (San Francisco)
William A. Boeger, III (Menlo Park/
San Francisco)
Lawrance A. Brown, Jr. (Menlo Park/
San Francisco)
Donald R. Scheuch (Menlo Park/
San Francisco)

Whom to Contact
Frank G. Chambers
William A. Boeger, III

Type of Firm
Private venture capital firm investing
own capital

Industry Association Memberships
NVCA
WAVC

Project Preferences
Will function either as deal originator or
investor in deals created by others
Type of Financing:
Seed
Startup
First-stage
Second-stage
Minimum Investment: $250,000
Preferred Investment: $500,000-$1 million
Minimum Operating Data:
Annual Sales—Nominal
P&L—Losses (profits projected after 2 years)

Geographical Preference
West Coast

Industry Preferences

Communications
Data communications
Computer Related
Computer graphics, CAD/CAM and CAE
Computer services
Memory devices
Office automation
Software-applications
Software-artificial intelligence
Software-systems
Specialized turnkey systems
**Electronic Components and
Instrumentation**
Analytical and scientific instrumentation
Component fabrication and testing
equipment
Electronic components
Fiber optics
Laser related
Semiconductors
Genetic Engineering
Gene splicing and manufacturing equipment
Monoclonal antibodies and hybridomas
Recombinant DNA (agricultural and
industrial)
Recombinant DNA (medical)
Industrial Products and Equipment
Chemicals
Controls and sensors
Energy management
Equipment and machinery
Other industrial automation
Plastics
Robotics/vision systems
Specialty materials
Medical/Health Related
Diagnostic equipment
Diagnostic test products
Disposable products
Drugs and medicines
Hospital and clinical labs
Medical services
Therapeutic equipment
Will Not Consider
Motion pictures
Oil and gas
Real estate

Additional Information
Year Founded—1959
Method of Compensation—Return on
investment is of primary concern; do not
charge fees

CROCKER CAPITAL

111 Sutter Street #600
San Francisco, CA 94104
415-399-7889

Officer
Charles Crocker, Pres.

Type of Firm
Private venture capital firm investing
own capital
SBIC

Industry Association Membership
WAVC

Project Preferences
Will function either as deal originator or
investor in deals created by others
Type of Financing:
Seed
Research and development partnerships
Startup
Later-stage expansion
Leveraged buyout
Minimum Investment: $100,000
Preferred Investment: $250,000-$500,000
Minimum Operating Data:
Annual Sales—Nominal

Geographical Preference
West Coast

Industry Preferences

Communications
Satellite and microwave communications
Telephone related
Computer Related
Computer graphics, CAD/CAM and CAE
Computer mainframes
Computer services
Memory devices
Micro and mini computers
Office automation
Scanning related
Software-applications
Software-artificial intelligence
Software-systems
Specialized turnkey systems
Terminals
Distribution
Communications equipment
Computer equipment
Consumer products
Electronics equipment
Food products
Industrial products
Medical products

Electronic Components and Instrumentation
Analytical and scientific instrumentation
Component fabrication and testing equipment
Electronic components
Fiber optics
Laser related
Semiconductors
Genetic Engineering
Gene splicing and manufacturing equipment
Monoclonal antibodies and hybridomas
Recombinant DNA (agricultural and industrial)
Recombinant DNA (medical)
Industrial Products and Equipment
Chemicals
Controls and sensors
Energy management
Equipment and machinery
Other industrial automation
Plastics
Robotics/vision systems
Specialty materials
Medical/Health Related
Diagnostic equipment
Diagnostic test products
Disposable products
Drugs and medicines
Hospital and clinical labs
Medical services
Therapeutic equipment

Additional Information
Year Founded—1970
Investments(1985-1st 6 months)—3
Method of Compensation—Return on investment is of primary concern; do not charge fees

---

CROCKER VENTURES, INC.

One Montgomery Street
San Francisco, CA 94104
415-983-3636

Officer
Jordan Burkart, V.P. & Mgr.

Type of Firm
SBIC

Affiliation
Crocker National Bank (parent)

Industry Association Membership
NASBIC

Project Preferences
Prefer role in deals created by others
Type of Financing:
Startup
First-stage
Second-stage
Leveraged buyout
Minimum Investment: Less than $100,000
Preferred Investment: $100,000-$250,000

Geographical Preference
West Coast

Industry Preferences
None

Additional Information
Year Founded—1979
Capital Under Management—$1 million
Method of Compensation—Return on investment is of primary concern; do not charge fees

---

CROSSPOINT INVESTMENT CORPORATION

1951 Landings Drive
Mountain View, CA 94043
415-964-3545

Directors
Max S. Simpson, Pres.
John B. Mumford, V.P.
Kenneth A. Eldred, Secy.

Whom to Contact
Max S. Simpson

Type of Firm
SBIC

Affiliation
Crosspoint Financial Corporation (parent)

Industry Association Memberships
NASBIC
WAVC

Project Preferences
Will function either as deal originator or investor in deals created by others
Type of Financing:
Later-stage expansion
Leveraged buyout
Minimum Investment: $100,000
Preferred Investment: $100,000-$250,000

Minimum Operating Data:
Annual Sales—$500,000
P&L—Break even

Geographical Preference
West Coast

Industry Preferences

Communications
Commercial communications
Data communications
Computer Related
Computer graphics, CAD/CAM and CAE
Office automation
Distribution
Industrial products
Medical products
Electronic Components and Instrumentation
Analytical and scientific instrumentation
Electronic components
Industrial Products and Equipment
Controls and sensors
Robotics/vision systems
Medical/Health Related
Diagnostic equipment
Medical services
Will Not Consider
Motion pictures
Real estate
Retail

Additional Information
Year Founded—1979
Capital Under Management—$2.5 million
Investments(1985-1st 6 months)—3
Invested(1985-1st 6 months)—$300,000
Method of Compensation—Return on investment is of primary concern; do not charge fees

CROSSPOINT VENTURE PARTNERS

1951 Landings Drive
Mountain View, CA 94043
415-964-0100

Other Office

4600 Campus Drive #103
Newport Beach, CA 92660
714-852-1611

Partners

John B. Mumford, Mgn. Gen. Ptnr.
  (Mountain View)
James F. Willenborg, Mgn. Gen. Ptnr.
  (Mountain View)
Robert A. Hoff, Gen. Ptnr. (Newport Beach)
Frederick J. Dotzler, Gen. Ptnr.
  (Mountain View)
William P. Cargile, Gen. Ptnr.
  (Mountain View)
Roger J. Barry, Gen. Ptnr. (Mountain View)
David J. Blecki, Special Ltd. Ptnr.
  (Mountain View)

Whom to Contact

Any of the above

Type of Firm

Private venture capital firm investing
  own capital

Industry Association Memberships

NVCA
WAVC

Project Preferences

Prefer role as deal originator
Type of Financing:
Seed
Startup
Research and development partnerships
  (equity only)
Minimum Investment: Less than $100,000
Preferred Investment: $500,000-$1 million
Minimum Operating Data:
Annual Sales—Nominal
P&L—Losses (profits projected after 2 years)

Geographical Preferences

Northwest
Southwest
Midwest
Rocky Mountains
West Coast

Industry Preferences

Communications
Data communications
Satellite and microwave communications
Telephone related
Computer Related
Computer graphics, CAD/CAM and CAE
Computer mainframes
Computer services
Memory devices
Micro and mini computers
Office automation
Scanning related
Software-applications
Software-artificial intelligence
Software-systems
Specialized turnkey systems
Terminals
Distribution
Communications equipment
Computer equipment
Electronics equipment
Industrial products
Medical products
**Electronic Components and
  Instrumentation**
Analytical and scientific instrumentation
Component fabrication and testing
  equipment
Electronic components
Fiber optics
Laser related
Semiconductors
Genetic Engineering
Gene splicing and manufacturing equipment
Monoclonal antibodies and hybridomas
Recombinant DNA (agricultural and
  industrial)
Recombinant DNA (medical)
Industrial Products and Equipment
Controls and sensors
Other industrial automation
Robotics/vision systems
Medical/Health Related
Diagnostic equipment
Diagnostic test products
Disposable products
Drugs and medicines
Hospital and clinical labs
Medical services
Therapeutic equipment

Additional Information

Year Founded—1972
Capital Under Management—$65 million
Investments(1985-1st 6 months)—14
Invested(1985-1st 6 months)—$8 million
Method of Compensation—Return on
  investment is of primary concern; do not
  charge fees

THE CYPRESS FUND

2740 Sand Hill Road
Menlo Park, CA 94025
415-854-4193

Partners

Byron K. Adams, Jr., Gen. Ptnr.
Jonathan M. Hamren, Gen. Ptnr.
Val E. Vaden, Assoc.

Whom to Contact

Any of the above

Type of Firm

Private venture capital firm investing
  own capital

Industry Association Membership

WAVC

Project Preferences

Prefer role as deal originator but will also
  invest in deals created by others
Type of Financing:
Seed
Startup
First-stage
Leveraged buyout
Minimum Investment: $500,000
Preferred Investment: Over $1 million
Minimum Operating Data:
Annual Sales—Nominal

Geographical Preference

National

Industry Preferences

Communications
Commercial communications
Data communications
Satellite and microwave communications
Telephone related
Computer Related
Computer graphics, CAD/CAM and CAE
Computer mainframes
Computer services
Memory devices
Micro and mini computers
Office automation
Software-applications
Software-artificial intelligence
Software-systems
Specialized turnkey systems
Consumer
Consumer products
Consumer services
Retailing

Distribution
Communications equipment
Computer equipment
Consumer products
Electronics equipment
Food products
Industrial products
Medical products
**Electronic Components and
  Instrumentation**
Analytical and scientific instrumentation
Component fabrication and testing
  equipment
Electronic components
Fiber optics
Laser related
Semiconductors
Genetic Engineering
Gene splicing and manufacturing equipment
Monoclonal antibodies and hybridomas
Recombinant DNA (agricultural and
  industrial)
Recombinant DNA (medical)
Industrial Products and Equipment
Other industrial automation
Plastics
Robotics/vision systems
Specialty materials
Medical/Health Related
Diagnostic equipment
Diagnostic test products
Disposable products
Drugs and medicines
Hospital and clinical labs
Medical services
Therapeutic equipment

Additional Information
Year Founded—1985
Method of Compensation—Return on
  investment is of primary concern; do not
  charge fees

DEVEREAUX CAPITAL
CORPORATION

760 Market Street #315
San Francisco, CA 94102
415-781-8390

Officer
David Younge, Pres.

Type of Firm
Private venture capital firm investing
  own capital

Project Preferences
Prefer role as deal originator
Type of Financing:
Seed
Startup
First-stage
Second-stage
Leveraged buyout
Minimum Investment: Less than $100,000
Preferred Investment: Less than $100,000
Minimum Operating Data:
Annual Sales—Nominal
P&L—Break even

Geographical Preference
Within two hours of office

Industry Preferences

Communications
Telephone related
Consumer
Computer stores/related services
Consumer products
Consumer services
Food and beverage products
Franchise businesses
Hotels and resort areas
Leisure and recreational products
Restaurants
Retailing
Distribution
Consumer products
Food products
Industrial products
Industrial Products and Equipment
Chemicals
Specialty materials
Other
Education related
Publishing
Real estate
Transportation
Will Not Consider
Computer related businesses
High technology related businesses

Additional Information
Year Founded—1983
Capital Under Management—$2.5 million
Investments(1985-1st 6 months)—10
Invested(1985-1st 6 months)—$1 million
Method of Compensation—Return on
  investment is of primary concern; do not
  charge fees

DIEHL & COMPANY

1201 Dove Street
Newport Beach, CA 92660
714-955-2000

Officers
Russell R. Diehl
Michael Henton
Jack Norberg
Richard Stasand
Jeff Howes

Whom to Contact
Russell R. Diehl

Type of Firm
Investment banking or merchant banking
  firm investing own capital or funds of
  partners or clients

Project Preferences
Will function either as deal originator or
  investor in deals created by others
Type of Financing:
Second-stage
Leveraged buyout
Minimum Investment: $100,000
Preferred Investment: $100,000-$250,000
Preferred Investment (LBO): $10 million
Minimum Operating Data:
Annual Sales—$3 million
P&L—Break even
Annual Sales (LBO)—$30 million

Geographical Preferences
Within two hours of office
West Coast

Industry Preferences

Communications
Commercial communications
Data communications
Satellite and microwave communications
Telephone related
Computer Related
Computer graphics, CAD/CAM and CAE
Office automation
Software-artificial intelligence
Distribution
Communications equipment
Computer equipment
Electronics equipment
Industrial products
Medical products

Electronic Components and
  Instrumentation
Analytical and scientific instrumentation
Component fabrication and testing
  equipment
Electronic components
Fiber optics
Laser related
Semiconductors
Industrial Products and Equipment
Controls and sensors
Specialty materials
Medical/Health Related
Diagnostic equipment
Diagnostic test products
Disposable products
Drugs and medicines
Hospital and clinical labs
Medical services
Therapeutic equipment
Other
Finance and insurance
Will Not Consider
Real estate

Additional Information
Year Founded—1978
Capital Under Management—Over $10 million
Investments(1985-1st 6 months)—2
Method of Compensation—Return on
  investment is most important, but also
  charge for closing fees, service fees, etc.

DOUGERY, JONES & WILDER

2003 Landings Drive
Mountain View, CA 94043
415-968-4820

Other Office
5420 LBJ Freeway
Two Lincoln Centre #1100
Dallas, TX 75240
214-960-0077

Officers
John R. Dougery (California)
David A. Jones (California)
Henry L.B. Wilder (California)
Gerald P. Schoonhoven (California)
A. Lawson Howard (Texas)

Whom to Contact
Any of the above

Type of Firm
Private venture capital firm investing
  own capital

Industry Association Memberships
NVCA
WAVC

Project Preferences
Will function either as deal originator or
  investor in deals created by others
Type of Financing:
Seed
Startup
First-stage
Second-stage
Later-stage expansion
Leveraged buyout
Minimum Investment: $100,000
Preferred Investment: $500,000-$1 million
Preferred Investment (LBO): $3 million
Minimum Operating Data:
Annual Sales—Nominal
P&L—Losses (profits projected after 2 years)
Annual Sales (LBO)—$25 million and up

Geographical Preferences
Northwest
Southwest
West Coast

Industry Preferences

Communications
Data communications
Satellite and microwave communications
Telephone related
Computer Related
Computer graphics, CAD/CAM and CAE
Computer mainframes
Computer services
Memory devices
Micro and mini computers
Office automation
Scanning related
Software-applications
Software-artificial intelligence
Software-systems
Specialized turnkey systems
Terminals
Distribution
Communications equipment
Computer equipment
Electronics equip.ment
Industrial products
Medical products
**Electronic Components and
  Instrumentation**
Analytical and scientific instrumentation
Component fabrication and testing
  equipment
Electronic components
Fiber optics
Laser related
Semiconductors

Energy/Natural Resources
Alternative energy
Coal related
Drilling and exploration services
Energy conservation
Minerals
Oil and gas exploration and production
Technology related products/equipment
Genetic Engineering
Gene splicing and manufacturing equipment
Monoclonal antibodies and hybridomas
Recombinant DNA (agricultural and
  industrial)
Recombinant DNA (medical)
Industrial Products and Equipment
Chemicals
Controls and sensors
Energy management
Equipment and machinery
Other industrial automation
Plastics
Robotics/vision systems
Specialty materials
Medical/Health Related
Diagnostic equipment
Diagnostic test products
Disposable products
Drugs and medicines
Hospital and clinical labs
Medical services
Therapeutic equipment
Will Not Consider
Real estate
Motion pictures

Additional Information
Year Founded—1981
Capital Under Management—$86 million
Method of Compensation—Return on
  investment is of primary concern; do not
  charge fees

DREXEL BURNHAM LAMBERT INC./
THE LAMBDA FUNDS

1400 Civic Drive
Walnut Creek, CA 94596
415-945-8500

Jack Ross

See NEW YORK for full listing

THE EARLY STAGES COMPANY, INC.

244 California Street #300
San Francisco, CA 94111
415-986-5700

Partners
William P. Lanphear, IV, Ptnr.
Frank W. (Woody) Kuehn, Ptnr.
Morton Miller, Ptnr.
Micheline L. Chau, Assoc.

Whom to Contact
Frank W. (Woody) Kuehn

Type of Firm
Private venture capital firm investing
own capital

Industry Association Membership
WAVC

Project Preferences
Will function either as deal originator or
investor in deals created by others
Type of Financing:
First-stage
Second-stage
Leveraged buyout
Minimum Investment: $250,000
Preferred Investment: $250,000-$500,000
Minimum Operating Data:
Annual Sales—Nominal
P&L—Losses (profits projected after 2 years)

Geographical Preferences
West Coast
National

Industry Preferences

Communications
Telephone related
Computer Related
Software-applications
Software-systems
Consumer
Computer stores/related services
Consumer products
Consumer services
Food and beverage products
Franchise businesses
Leisure and recreational products
Restaurants
Retailing

Distribution
Communications equipment
Computer equipment
Consumer products
Electronics equipment
Food products
Industrial products
Medical products
Medical/Health Related
Diagnostic equipment
Diagnostic test products
Disposable products
Drugs and medicines
Hospital and clinical labs
Medical services
Therapeutic equipment
Will Not Consider
Motion pictures
Oil and gas
Real estate

Additional Information
Year Founded—1981
Capital Under Management—$12.75 million
Investments(1985-1st 6 months)—5
Invested(1985-1st 6 months)—$1 million
Method of Compensation—Return on
investment is of primary concern; do not
charge fees

EG&G VENTURE PARTNERS

700 East El Camino Real #270
Mountain View, CA 94040
415-967-2822

Other Office
45 William Street
Wellesley, MA 02181
617-237-5100

General Partners
John J. Rado
Andres Busher
Gerald Diamond

Whom to Contact
Any of the above

Type of Firm
Venture capital subsidiary or affiliate of
non-financial corporation

Affiliation
EG&G, Inc.

Industry Association Membership
WAVC

Project Preferences
Will function either as deal originator or
investor in deals created by others
Type of Financing:
Seed
Startup
First-stage
Second-stage
Later-stage expansion
Minimum Investment: $500,000
Preferred Investment: $500,000-$1 million
Minimum Operating Data:
Annual Sales—Nominal
P&L—Losses (profits projected after 2 years)

Geographical Preference
National

Industry Preferences

Communications
Data communications
Satellite and microwave communications
Telephone related
Computer Related
Computer graphics, CAD/CAM and CAE
Computer mainframes
Computer services
Memory devices
Micro and mini computers
Office automation
Scanning related
Software-applications
Software-artificial intelligence
Software-systems
Specialized turnkey systems
Terminals
**Electronic Components and
Instrumentation**
Analytical and scientific instrumentation
Component fabrication and testing
equipment
Electronic components
Fiber optics
Laser related
Semiconductors
Energy/Natural Resources
Technology related products/equipment
Genetic Engineering
Gene splicing and manufacturing equipment
Monoclonal antibodies and hybridomas
Recombinant DNA (agricultural and
industrial)
Recombinant DNA (medical)

Industrial Products and Equipment
Controls and sensors
Energy management
Equipment and machinery
Other industrial automation
Plastics
Robotics/vision systems
Specialty materials
Medical/Health Related
Diagnostic equipment
Diagnostic test products
Disposable products
Drugs and medicines
Hospital and clinical labs
Medical services
Therapeutic equipment

Additional Information
Year Founded—1985
Capital Under Management—$47.5 million
Method of Compensation—Return on
investment is of primary concern; do not
charge fees

EMC II VENTURE PARTNERS

1500 Imperial Bank Tower
701 B Street
San Diego, CA 92101
619-239-6866

General Partners
Bradley B. Gordon, Gen. Ptnr.
Alan J. Grant, Gen. Ptnr.
Ray W. McKewon, Gen. Ptnr.
Hans W. Schoepflin, Gen. Ptnr.
L. Kip Hallman III, Assoc.

Whom to Contact
Any of the above

Type of Firm
Private venture capital firm investing
own capital

Project Preferences
Prefer role as deal originator but will also
invest in deals created by others
Type of Financing:
Seed
Research and development partnerships
Startup
First-stage
Second-stage
Leveraged buyout
Minimum Investment: $250,000
Preferred Investment: $250,000-$1.5 million

Minimum Operating Data:
Annual Sales—Nominal
P&L—Losses (profits projected after 2 years)

Geographical Preferences
Southwest
West Coast
International joint ventures and financing

Industry Preferences

Communications
Cable television
Commercial communications
Data communications
Satellite and microwave communications
Telephone related
Computer Related
Computer graphics, CAD/CAM and CAE
Computer mainframes
Computer services
Memory devices
Micro and mini computers
Office automation
Scanning related
Software-applications
Software-artificial intelligence
Software-systems
Specialized turnkey systems
Terminals
Consumer
Computer stores/related services
Consumer products
Consumer services
Food and beverage products
Franchise businesses
Hotels and resort areas
Leisure and recreational products
Restaurants
Retailing
Distribution
Communications equipment
Computer equipment
Consumer products
Electronics equipment
Food products
Industrial products
Medical products
**Electronic Components and
Instrumentation**
Analytical and scientific instrumentation
Component fabrication and testing
equipment
Electronic components
Fiber optics
Laser related
Semiconductors

Energy/Natural Resources
Alternative energy
Coal related
Drilling and exploration services
Energy conservation
Minerals
Oil and gas exploration and production
Technology related products/equipment
Genetic Engineering
Gene splicing and manufacturing equipment
Monoclonal antibodies and hybridomas
Recombinant DNA (agricultural and
industrial)
Recombinant DNA (medical)
Industrial Products and Equipment
Chemicals
Controls and sensors
Energy management
Equipment and machinery
Other industrial automation
Plastics
Robotics/vision systems
Specialty materials
Medical/Health Related
Diagnostic equipment
Diagnostic test products
Disposable products
Drugs and medicines
Hospital and clinical labs
Medical services
Therapeutic equipment
Other
Agriculture, forestry, fishing
Education related
Finance and insurance
Publishing
Real estate
Specialty consulting
Transportation

Additional Information
Year Founded—1980
Capital Under Management—$20 million
Investments(1985-1st 6 months)—2
Invested(1985-1st 6 months)—$1 million
Method of Compensation—Return on
investment is of primary concern; do not
charge fees

EMPRISE MANAGEMENT

1333 Lawrence Expressway #150
Santa Clara, CA 95051
408-246-5500

Partners

Donald de Renne, Gen. Ptnr.
Patrick W. Latta, Gen. Ptnr.
J. Michael Loscavio, Ptnr.
William H. Rusher, Jr., Ptnr.

Whom to Contact

Donald de Renne

Type of Firm

Private firm evaluating and analyzing venture
 projects and providing startup resources to
 build companies

Project Preferences

Prefer role as deal originator
Type of Financing:
Seed
Research and development partnerships
Startup

Geographical Preference

Within two hours of office

Industry Preferences

Communications
Cable television
Commercial communications
Data communications
Satellite and microwave communications
Telephone related
Computer Related
Computer graphics, CAD/CAM and CAE
Computer mainframes
Micro and mini computers
Office automation
Scanning related
Software-applications
Software-artificial intelligence
Software-systems
Specialized turnkey systems
Consumer
Consumer products
Food and beverage products
Leisure and recreational products
**Electronic Components and
 Instrumentation**
Analytical and scientific instrumentation
Component fabrication and testing
 equipment
Electronic components
Fiber optics
Laser related
Semiconductors

Energy/Natural Resources
Alternative energy
Energy conservation
Technology related products/equipment
Industrial Products and Equipment
Controls and sensors
Energy management
Equipment and machinery
Other industrial automation
Robotics/vision systems
Specialty materials
Medical/Health Related
Diagnostic equipment
Diagnostic test products
Disposable products
Drugs and medicines
Therapeutic equipment
Other
Special interest in new markets or industries
Will Not Consider
Financial services
Real estate
Retail

Additional Information

Year Founded—1984
Method of Compensation—Equity return
 on investment

ENTERPRISE PARTNERS

5000 Birch Street #6200
Newport Beach, CA 92660
714-833-3650

Other Office

7855 Ivanhoe Avenue #300
La Jolla, CA 92037
619-454-8833

General Partners

Charles D. Martin (Newport Beach)
James H. Berglund (La Jolla)

Whom to Contact

Either of the above

Type of Firm

Private venture capital firm investing
 own capital

Affiliation

Hambrecht & Quist (co-sponsor)
Mayfield Fund (co-sponsor)

Project Preferences

Prefer role as deal originator but will also
 invest in deals created by others

Type of Financing:
Seed
Startup
First-stage
Second-stage
Later-stage expansion
Leveraged buyout
Minimum Investment: $100,000
Preferred Investment: $500,000-$1 million
Minimum Operating Data:
Annual Sales—Nominal
P&L—Losses (profits projected after 3 years)

Geographical Preference

Southern California
Southwest

Industry Preferences

Communications
Cable television
Commercial communications
Data communications
Satellite and microwave communications
Telephone related
Computer Related
Computer graphics, CAD/CAM and CAE
Computer mainframes
Computer services
Memory devices
Micro and mini computers
Office automation
Scanning related
Software-applications
Software-artificial intelligence
Software-systems
Specialized turnkey systems
Terminals
**Electronic Components and
 Instrumentation**
Analytical and scientific instrumentation
Component fabrication and testing
 equipment
Electronic components
Fiber optics
Laser related
Semiconductors
Genetic Engineering
Gene splicing and manufacturing equipment
Monoclonal antibodies and hybridomas
Recombinant DNA (agricultural and
 industrial)
Recombinant DNA (medical)

Industrial Products and Equipment
Chemicals
Controls and sensors
Energy management
Equipment and machinery
Other industrial automation
Plastics
Robotics/vision systems
Specialty materials
Medical/Health Related
Diagnostic equipment
Diagnostic test products
Disposable products
Drugs and medicines
Hospital and clinical labs
Medical services
Therapeutic equipment
Will Not Consider
Real estate
Oil and gas

Additional Information

Year Founded—1985
Capital Under Management—$29 million
Investments(1985-1st 6 months)—2
Invested(1985-1st 6 months)—$1.5 million
Method of Compensation—Carried interest
in return on investment

ENTERPRISE VENTURE CAPITAL CORP.

1922 The Alameda #306
San Jose, CA 95126
408-249-3507

Officers

Ernest de La Ossa, Pres.
Douglas S. Milroy, Secy. & Ops. Mgr.

Whom to Contact

Douglas S. Milroy

Type of Firm

SBIC

Industry Association Membership

NASBIC

Project Preferences

Will function either as deal originator or
investor in deals created by others
Type of Financing:
Second-stage
Later-stage expansion
Minimum Investment: $100,000
Preferred Investment: $100,000-$250,000

Minimum Operating Data:
Annual Sales—Nominal
P&L—Break even

Geographical Preference

West Coast

Industry Preferences

Communications
Cable television
Commercial communications
Data communications
Satellite and microwave communications
Telephone related
Computer Related
Computer graphics, CAD/CAM and CAE
Computer mainframes
Computer services
Memory devices
Micro and mini computers
Office automation
Scanning related
Software-applications
Software-artificial intelligence
Software-systems
Specialized turnkey systems
Terminals
Electronic Components and Instrumentation
Analytical and scientific instrumentation
Component fabrication and testing
equipment
Electronic components
Fiber optics
Laser related
Semiconductors
Industrial Products and Equipment
Chemicals
Controls and sensors
Energy management
Equipment and machinery
Other industrial automation
Plastics
Robotics/vision systems
Specialty materials
Will Not Consider
Biotechnology
Motion pictures
Oil related businesses

Additional Information

Year Founded—1983
Capital Under Management—$1.5 million
Method of Compensation—Return on
investment is of primary concern; do not
charge fees

EQUIS, INC.

Three Embarcadero Center
San Francisco, CA 94111
415-362-4181

Officer

R.G. (Bob) Perring, Pres.

Type of Firm

SBIC

Project Preferences

Will function either as deal originator or
investor in deals created by others
Type of Financing:
Seed
Startup
First-stage
Second-stage
Later-stage expansion
Leveraged buyout
Minimum Investment: $100,000
Preferred Investment: $100,000-$1 million
Preferred Investment (LBO):
$100,000-$1 million
Minimum Operating Data:
Annual Sales—Nominal
P&L—Losses (profits projected after 3 years)

Geographical Preference

None

Industry Preferences

Communications
Cable television
Commercial communications
Data communications
Satellite and microwave communications
Telephone related
Computer Related
Computer graphics, CAD/CAM and CAE
Computer mainframes
Computer services
Memory devices
Micro and mini computers
Office automation
Scanning related
Software-applications
Software-artificial intelligence
Software-systems
Specialized turnkey systems
Terminals

**Electronic Components and
Instrumentation**
Analytical and scientific instrumentation
Component fabrication and testing
equipment
Electronic components
Fiber optics
Laser related
Semiconductors
Genetic Engineering
Gene splicing and manufacturing equipment
Monoclonal antibodies and hybridomas
Recombinant DNA (agricultural and
industrial)
Recombinant DNA (medical)
Industrial Products and Equipment
Chemicals
Controls and sensors
Energy management
Equipment and machinery
Other industrial automation
Plastics
Robotics/vision systems
Specialty materials
Medical/Health Related
Diagnostic equipment
Diagnostic test products
Disposable products
Drugs and medicines
Hospital and clinical labs
Medical services
Therapeutic equipment

Additional Information
Year Founded—1985
Method of Compensation—Return on
investment is of primary concern; do not
charge fees

EQUITY CAPITAL SERVICE

3015 Fulgham
Visalia, CA 93277
209-733-4296

Partners
Robert D. Shipman
Bill Brumley

Whom to Contact
Robert D. Shipman

Type of Firm
Consulting firm evaluating and analyzing
venture projects and arranging private
placements
Also invest own capital and capital of clients

Project Preferences
Prefer role as deal originator but will also
invest in deals created by others
Type of Financing:
Seed
Startup
First-stage
Second-stage
Leveraged buyout
Minimum Investment: Less than $100,000
Preferred Investment: $250,000-$500,000
Minimum Operating Data:
Annual Sales—Nominal
P&L—Break even

Geographical Preferences
West Coast
National

Industry Preferences

Communications
Cable television
Commercial communications
Data communications
Satellite and microwave communications
Telephone related
Computer Related
Computer graphics, CAD/CAM and CAE
Computer mainframes
Computer services
Memory devices
Micro and mini computers
Office automation
Scanning related
Software-applications
Software-artificial intelligence
Software-systems
Specialized turnkey systems
Terminals
Consumer
Franchise businesses
Hotels and resort areas
Leisure and recreational products
Restaurants
Distribution
Communications equipment
Computer equipment
Electronics equipment
Industrial products
Medical products
**Electronic Components and
Instrumentation**
Analytical and scientific instrumentation
Component fabrication and testing
equipment
Electronic components
Fiber optics
Laser related
Semiconductors

Energy/Natural Resources
Alternative energy
Oil and gas exploration and production
Technology related products/equipment
Genetic Engineering
Gene splicing and manufacturing equipment
Monoclonal antibodies and hybridomas
Recombinant DNA (agricultural and
industrial)
Recombinant DNA (medical)
Industrial Products and Equipment
Chemicals
Controls and sensors
Energy management
Equipment and machinery
Other industrial automation
Plastics
Robotics/vision systems
Specialty materials
Medical/Health Related
Diagnostic equipment
Diagnostic test products
Disposable products
Drugs and medicines
Hospital and clinical labs
Medical services
Therapeutic equipment
Other
Agriculture, forestry, fishing
Transportation

Additional Information
Year Founded—1985
Method of Compensation—Function primarily
in service area; receive contingent fee in
cash or equity
Professional fee required whether or
not deal closes

EUROPEAN-AMERICAN
SECURITIES, INC.

333 Market Street #3200
San Francisco, CA 94105
415-982-5200

Officer
Lawrence E. Nerheim, Chm. & CEO

Type of Firm
Investment banking or merchant banking
firm investing own capital or funds of
partners or clients

Affiliation
EAS Corporation (subsidiary)

Project Preferences
Will function either as deal originator or
 investor in deals created by others
Type of Financing:
Second-stage
Later-stage expansion
Leveraged buyout
Minimum Investment: $500,000
Preferred Investment: $500,000-$1 million
Preferred Investment (LBO):
 $1 million and over
Minimum Operating Data:
Annual Sales—$1.5 million
P&L—Break even
Annual Sales (LBO)—$1.5 million and over

Geographical Preference
None

Industry Preferences

Consumer
Consumer products
Food and beverage products
Distribution
Medical products
Energy/Natural Resources
Alternative energy
Other
Finance and insurance
Real estate

Additional Information
Year Founded—1973
Capital Under Management—$6.25 million
Investments(1985-1st 6 months)—4
Invested(1985-1st 6 months)—$5 million
Method of Compensation—Return on
 investment is most important, but also
 charge for closing fees, service fees, etc.

FAIRFIELD VENTURE PARTNERS

650 Town Center Drive #810
Costa Mesa, CA 92626
714-754-5717

Other Office
1275 Summer Street
Stamford, CT 06905
203-358-0255

Partners
Pedro A. Castillo, Mgn. Ptnr. (Connecticut)
Oakes Ames, Gen. Ptnr. (Connecticut)
Edmund M. Olivier, Gen. Ptnr. (California)
Randall R. Lunn, Gen. Ptnr. (California)
Eugene E. Pettinelli, Gen. Ptnr. (Connecticut)
Thomas D. Berman, Assoc. (Connecticut)
Lawrence A. Bock, Assoc. (California)

Whom to Contact
Any of the above

Type of Firm
Private venture capital firm investing
 own capital

Industry Association Membership
NVCA

Project Preferences
Will function either as deal originator or
 investor in deals created by others
Type of Financing:
Seed
Startup
First-stage
Second-stage
Later-stage expansion
Leveraged buyout
Minimum Investment: $100,000
Preferred Investment: Over $750,000
Minimum Operating Data:
Annual Sales—Nominal
P&L—Losses (profits projected after 2 years)

Geographical Preferences
Within two hours of office
Northeast
West Coast

Industry Preferences

Communications
Commercial communications
Data communications
Satellite and microwave communications
Telephone related
Computer Related
Computer graphics, CAD/CAM and CAE
Computer mainframes
Computer services
Memory devices
Micro and mini computers
Office automation
Scanning related
Software-applications
Software-artificial intelligence
Software-systems
Specialized turnkey systems
Distribution
Medical products
**Electronic Components and
 Instrumentation**
Analytical and scientific instrumentation
Component fabrication and testing
equipment
Electronic components
Fiber optics
Laser related
Semiconductors

Genetic Engineering
Gene splicing and manufacturing equipment
Monoclonal antibodies and hybridomas
Recombinant DNA (agricultural and
 industrial)
Recombinant DNA (medical)
Industrial Products and Equipment
Advanced materials
Chemicals
Controls and sensors
Energy management
Other industrial automation
Robotics/vision systems
Specialty materials
Medical/Health Related
Diagnostic equipment
Diagnostic test products
Disposable products
Hospital and clinical labs
Medical services
Therapeutic equipment
Other
Finance and insurance
Publishing

Additional Information
Year Founded—1981
Capital Under Management—$100 million
Investments(1985-1st 6 months)—8
Invested(1985-1st 6 months)—$6.9 million
Method of Compensation—Return on
 investment is of primary concern; do not
 charge fees

FIRST AMERICAN CAPITAL FUNDING, INC.

9872 Chapman Avenue #216
Garden Grove, CA 92641
714-638-7171

Officer
Luu Trankiem, D.B.A., Pres.

Type of Firm
MESBIC

Industry Association Memberships
AAMESBIC
NASBIC

Project Preferences
Prefer role as deal originator but will also
 invest in deals created by others
Type of Financing:
Startup
First-stage
Second-stage
Later-stage expansion
Leveraged buyout

Minimum Investment: Less than $100,000
Preferred Investment: Less than $250,000
Minimum Operating Data:
Annual Sales—Nominal

Geographical Preference
West Coast

Industry Preferences

Consumer
Computer stores/related services
Consumer products
Consumer services
Food and beverage products
Franchise businesses
Hotels and resort areas
Leisure and recreational products
Restaurants
Retailing
Distribution
Communications equipment
Computer equipment
Consumer products
Electronics equipment
Food products
Industrial products
Medical products

Additional Information
Year Founded—1984
Method of Compensation—Return on
    investment is of primary concern; do not
    charge fees

FIRST CENTURY PARTNERSHIPS

350 California Street
San Francisco, CA 94104
415-955-1671

3000 Sand Hill Road
Building 3, #190
Menlo Park, CA 94025
415-854-7500

C. Sage Givens, Assoc. (San Francisco)
David T. Gleba, Inv. Analyst (San Francisco)
Steven P. Bird, Assoc. (Menlo Park)

See NEW YORK for full listing

GENERAL ELECTRIC VENTURE CAPITAL CORPORATION

3000 Sand Hill Road
Building 1, #230
Menlo Park, CA 94025
415-854-8092

Gregory P. Stapleton, Sr. V.P.
Robert W. McVicar, Sr. V.P.
Eric A. Young, V.P.
Stephen L. Waechter, V.P. & Treas.
David I. Nierenberg, Sr. V.P.
Mary C. Bechmann, Venture Analyst

See CONNECTICUT for full listing

GENESIS CAPITAL LIMITED PARTNERSHIP

20813 Stevens Creek Boulevard
Suite 101
Cupertino, CA 95014
408-446-9690

Gerald S. Casilli, Gen. Ptnr.

See WASHINGTON for full listing

GEOCAPITAL VENTURES

2092 Concourse Drive
San Jose, CA 95131
408-434-0590

James J. Harrison, Ptnr.

See NEW YORK for full listing

GIRARD CAPITAL, INC.

4320 La Jolla Village Drive
Suite #210
San Diego, CA 92122
619-457-5114

Officers
R.B. Woolley, Jr., Pres.
E. Sam Gudmundson, V.P.
Creighton Gallaway, V.P.
Irby R. McMichael, V.P.
Sanjay Subhedar, V.P.

Whom to Contact
E. Sam Gudmundson
Creighton Gallaway
Sanjay Subhedar

Type of Firm
Private venture capital firm investing
    own capital

Industry Association Membership
WAVC

Project Preferences
Prefer role as deal originator but will also
    invest in deals created by others
Type of Financing:
Seed
Startup
First-stage
Leveraged buyout
Minimum Investment: $500,000
Preferred Investment: $500,000-$1 million
Preferred Investment (LBO):
    $500,000-$10 million
Minimum Operating Data:
Annual Sales—Nominal
P&L—Losses (profits projected after 2 years)
Annual Sales (LBO)—$5 million-$50 million

Geographical Preference
Within two hours of office

Industry Preferences

Communications
Commercial communications
Data communications
Computer Related
Computer graphics, CAD/CAM and CAE
Computer mainframes
Memory devices
Micro and mini computers
Office automation
Scanning related
Software-applications
Software-artificial intelligence
Software-systems
Terminals
Distribution
Communications equipment
Computer equipment
Consumer products
Electronics equipment
Industrial products
Medical products
Electronic Components and Instrumentation
Analytical and scientific instrumentation
Component fabrication and testing
    equipment
Electronic components
Energy/Natural Resources
Technology related products/equipment

Genetic Engineering
Monoclonal antibodies and hybridomas
Recombinant DNA (agricultural and
    industrial)
Industrial Products and Equipment
Other industrial automation
Robotics/vision systems
Medical/Health Related
Diagnostic equipment
Diagnostic test products
Disposable products
Other
Finance and insurance
Real estate

Additional Information
Year Founded—1976
Capital Under Management—$15 million
Investments(1985-1st 6 months)—2
Invested(1985-1st 6 months)—$1.2 million
Method of Compensation—Return on
    investment is of primary concern; do not
    charge fees

BRUCE GLASPELL & ASSOCIATES

57 Post Street #513
San Francisco, CA 94104
415-781-1313

General Partner
Bruce Glaspell

Type of Firm
Investment banking or merchant banking
    firm investing own capital or funds of
    partners or clients

Project Preferences
Will function either as deal originator or
    investor in deals created by others
Type of Financing:
Seed
Startup
First-stage
Leveraged buyout
Minimum Investment: $250,000
Preferred Investment: $250,000-$500,000
Minimum Operating Data:
Annual Sales—Nominal
P&L—Losses (profits projected after 1 year)

Geographical Preference
None

Industry Preferences

Communications
Cable television
Commercial communications
Data communications
Satellite and microwave communications
Telephone related
Computer Related
Computer graphics, CAD/CAM and CAE
Computer mainframes
Computer services
Memory devices
Micro and mini computers
Office automation
Scanning related
Software-applications
Software-artificial intelligence
Software-systems
Specialized turnkey systems
Terminals
**Electronic Components and
    Instrumentation**
Analytical and scientific instrumentation
Component fabrication and testing
    equipment
Electronic components
Fiber optics
Laser related
Semiconductors
Energy/Natural Resources
Alternative energy
Coal related
Drilling and exploration services
Energy conservation
Minerals
Oil and gas exploration and production
Technology related products/equipment
Genetic Engineering
Gene splicing and manufacturing equipment
Monoclonal antibodies and hybridomas
Recombinant DNA (agricultural and
    industrial)
Recombinant DNA (medical)
Industrial Products and Equipment
Chemicals
Controls and sensors
Energy management
Equipment and machinery
Other industrial automation
Plastics
Robotics/vision systems
Specialty materials
Medical/Health Related
Diagnostic equipment
Diagnostic test products
Disposable products
Drugs and medicines
Hospital and clinical labs
Medical services
Therapeutic equipment

Other
Agriculture, forestry, fishing
Education related
Finance and insurance
Will Not Consider
Entertainment related businesses
Real estate

Additional Information
Year Founded—1972
Investments(1985-1st 6 months)—6
Invested(1985-1st 6 months)—$8 million
Method of Compensation—Return on
    investment is most important, but also
    charge for closing fees, service fees, etc.

GLENWOOD VENTURE
   MANAGEMENT

3000 Sand Hill Road
Building 3, #250
Menlo Park, CA 94025
415-854-8070

General Partners
Dag Tellefsen
John Hummer
Doug Broyles

Whom to Contact
Any of the above

Type of Firm
Private venture capital firm

Industry Association Memberships
NVCA
WAVC

Project Preferences
Prefer role as deal originator but will also
    invest in deals created by others
Type of Financing:
Seed
Startup
First-stage
Minimum Investment: Less than $100,000
Preferred Investment: $250,000-$500,000
Minimum Operating Data:
Annual Sales—Nominal

Geographical Preferences
Within two hours of office
West Coast

Industry Preferences

Communications
Satellite and microwave communications
Telephone related
Computer Related
Computer graphics, CAD/CAM and CAE
Computer mainframes
Computer services
Micro and mini computers
Office automation
Scanning related
Software-applications
Software-artificial intelligence
Software-systems
Specialized turnkey systems
Terminals
**Electronic Components and
Instrumentation**
Analytical and scientific instrumentation
Component fabrication and testing
equipment
Electronic components
Fiber optics
Laser related
Semiconductors
Genetic Engineering
Gene splicing and manufacturing equipment
Monoclonal antibodies and hybridomas
Recombinant DNA (agricultural and
industrial)
Recombinant DNA (medical)
Industrial Products and Equipment
Equipment and machinery
Plastics
Robotics/vision systems
Specialty materials
Medical/Health Related
Diagnostic equipment
Diagnostic test products
Disposable products
Drugs and medicines
Hospital and clinical labs
Medical services
Therapeutic equipment

Additional Information

Year Founded—1982
Capital Under Management—$17 million
Investments(1985-1st 6 months)—4
Invested(1985-1st 6 months)—$1.5 million
Method of Compensation—Return on
investment is of primary concern; do not
charge fees

GLYNN VENTURES

3000 Sand Hill Road
Building 2, #210
Menlo Park, CA 94025
415-854-2215

General Partners

John W. Glynn, Jr., Gen. Ptnr.
Jay Fredricks, Assoc.
Daryl Messinger, Assoc.

Whom to Contact

John W. Glynn, Jr.

Type of Firm

Private venture capital firm investing
own capital

Affiliation

New Enterprise Associates (special
limited partner)

Industry Association Membership

WAVC

Project Preferences

Prefer role in deals created by others
Type of Financing:
Startup
First-stage
Second-stage
Minimum Investment: $250,000
Preferred Investment: $500,000-$1 million
Minimum Operating Data:
Annual Sales—Nominal
P&L—Losses (profits projected after 2 years)

Geographical Preferences

Northeast
West Coast

Industry Preferences

Communications
Data communications
Satellite and microwave communications
Computer Related
Computer graphics, CAD/CAM and CAE
Computer mainframes
Computer services
Memory devices
Micro and mini computers
Office automation
Scanning related
Software-applications
Software-artificial intelligence
Software-systems
Specialized turnkey systems
Terminals

**Electronic Components and
Instrumentation**
Analytical and scientific instrumentation
Component fabrication and testing
equipment
Electronic components
Fiber optics
Laser related
Semiconductors
Medical/Health Related
Disposable products
Medical services

Additional Information

Year Founded—1983
Capital Under Management—$20 million
Investments(1985-1st 6 months)—2
Invested(1985-1st 6 months)—$600,000
Method of Compensation—Return on
investment is of primary concern; do not
charge fees

GRACE VENTURES CORPORATION

20300 Stevens Creek Boulevard
Suite 330
Cupertino, CA 95014
408-725-0774

Officers

Dr. Christian F. Horn, Pres.
Robert E. Pedigo, Exec. V.P.
Dr. Charles A. Bauer, V.P.
William B. Wittmeyer, V.P.
Susan A. Woods, Asst. V.P.

Whom to Contact

Any of the above

Type of Firm

Venture capital subsidiary or affiliate of
non-financial corporation

Affiliation

W.R. Grace & Co. (parent)

Industry Association Membership

NVCA

Project Preferences

Will function either as deal originator or
investor in deals created by others
Type of Financing:
Seed
Startup
First-stage
Second-stage
Later-stage expansion

Minimum Investment: $100,000
Preferred Investment: $500,000-$1 million
Minimum Operating Data:
Annual Sales—Nominal
P&L—Losses (profits projected after 2 years)

Geographical Preference
None

Industry Preferences

Communications
Data communications
Satellite and microwave communications
Computer Related
Computer graphics, CAD/CAM and CAE
Computer services
Memory devices
Office automation
Software-applications
Software-artificial intelligence
Software-systems
Distribution
Medical products
Electronic Components and Instrumentation
Analytical and scientific instrumentation
Component fabrication and testing equipment
Electronic components
Fiber optics
Laser related
Semiconductors
Industrial Products and Equipment
Chemicals
Controls and sensors
Energy management
Other industrial automation
Robotics/vision systems
Specialty materials
Medical/Health Related
Diagnostic equipment
Diagnostic test products
Disposable products
Medical services

Additional Information
Year Founded—1981
Capital Under Management—$50 million
Investments(1985-1st 6 months)—9
Invested(1985-1st 6 months)—$2.8 million
Method of Compensation—Return on investment is of primary concern; do not charge fees

GT CAPITAL MANAGEMENT, INC.

3000 Sand Hill Road
Building 4, #160
Menlo Park, CA 94025
415-856-6144

Officer
Kevin L. Cornwell, V.P.

Type of Firm
Venture investment unit of technology investment group

Affiliation
GT Management, Ltd. (parent)

Industry Association Membership
WAVC

Project Preferences
Prefer role in deals created by others
Type of Financing:
Startup
First-stage
Second-stage
Later-stage expansion
Minimum Investment: $100,000
Preferred Investment: $500,000-$1 million
Minimum Operating Data:
Annual Sales—Nominal
P&L—Losses (profits projected after 1 year)

Geographical Preference
West Coast

Industry Preferences

Communications
Data communications
Satellite and microwave communications
Telephone related
Computer Related
Computer graphics, CAD/CAM and CAE
Computer mainframes
Computer services
Memory devices
Micro and mini computers
Office automation
Scanning related
Software applications
Software-artificial intelligence
Software-systems
Specialized turnkey systems
Terminals
Distribution
Communications equipment
Computer equipment
Electronics equipment
Medical products

Electronic Components and Instrumentation
Analytical and scientific instrumentation
Component fabrication and testing equipment
Electronic components
Fiber optics
Laser related
Semiconductors
Energy/Natural Resources
Technology related products/equipment
Genetic Engineering
Gene splicing and manufacturing equipment
Monoclonal antibodies and hybridomas
Recombinant DNA (agricultural and industrial)
Recombinant DNA (medical)
Industrial Products and Equipment
Chemicals
Controls and sensors
Energy management
Equipment and machinery
Other industrial automation
Plastics
Robotics/vision systems
Specialty materials
Medical/Health Related
Diagnostic equipment
Diagnostic test products
Disposable products
Drugs and medicines
Hospital and clinical labs
Hospital information systems
Medical services
Therapeutic equipment

Additional Information
Year Founded—1979
Investments(1985-1st 6 months)—10
Invested(1985-1st 6 months)—$3.3 million
Method of Compensation—Return on investment is of primary concern; do not charge fees

HALLADOR, INC.

1435 River Park Drive #505
Post Office Box 15299
Sacramento, CA 95851
916-920-0191

Officers
David Hardie, Pres.
William T. Krieg, Exec. V.P.
George H. Bruns, Jr., Dir.

Whom to Contact
William T. Krieg

Type of Firm
Private venture capital firm investing own capital

Industry Association Membership
WAVC

Project Preferences
Prefer role in deals created by others
Type of Financing:
Startup
First-stage
Minimum Investment: Less than $100,000
Preferred Investment: $100,000-$250,000
Minimum Operating Data:
Annual Sales—$500,000
P&L—Losses (profits projected after 2 years)

Geographical Preference
West Coast

Industry Preferences

Computer Related
Computer services
Micro and mini computers
Office automation
Software-applications
Software-artificial intelligence
Software-systems
Terminals
Electronic Components and Instrumentation
Analytical and scientific instrumentation
Component fabrication and testing equipment
Electronic components
Energy/Natural Resources
Alternative energy
Drilling and exploration services
Energy conservation
Oil and gas exploration and production
Technology related products/equipment
Industrial Products and Equipment
Controls and sensors
Equipment and machinery
Robotics/vision systems
Other
Publishing

Additional Information
Year Founded—1979
Capital Under Management—$6 million
Investments(1985-1st 6 months)—5
Invested(1985-1st 6 months)—$1 million
Method of Compensation—Return on investment is of primary concern; do not charge fees

HAMBRECHT & QUIST VENTURE PARTNERS

One Post Street, Fourth Floor
San Francisco, CA 94104
415-393-9800

Other Offices
3000 Sand Hill Road
Building 2, #150
Menlo Park, CA 94025
415-854-8700

One Hollis Street #102
Wellesley, MA 02181
617-237-2099

2655 Le Jeune Road #513
Coral Gables, FL 33134
305-447-0423

Partners
John G. Balletto, Gen. Ptnr. (Menlo Park)
David P. Best, Gen. Ptnr. (San Francisco)
Daniel H. Case III, Gen. Ptnr.
  (San Francisco)
George M. Drysdale, Gen. Ptnr.
  (San Francisco)
Bob O. Evans, Gen. Ptnr. (San Francisco)
Kenneth L. Guernsey, Gen. Ptnr.
  (San Francisco)
William R. Hambrecht, Gen. Ptnr.
  (San Francisco)
Theodor H. Heinrichs, Gen. Ptnr.
  (San Francisco)
Clifford H. Higgerson, Gen. Ptnr.
  (San Francisco)
Ta-Lin Hsu, Gen. Ptnr. (San Francisco)
John R. Johnston, Gen. Ptnr.
  (San Francisco)
Robert J. Kunze, Mgn. Gen. Ptnr.
  (San Francisco)
Modesto A. Maidique, Gen. Ptnr.
  (Coral Gables)
Robert M. Morrill, Gen. Ptnr. (Wellesley)
Thomas J. O'Rourke, Gen. Ptnr.
  (Menlo Park)
Patrick J. Sansonnetti, Gen. Ptnr. (Wellesley)
Charles P. Waite, Jr., Gen. Ptnr.
  (San Francisco)
Allan M. Wolfe, Gen. Ptnr. (San Francisco)
Linda L. Hanson, CFO (San Francisco)

Whom to Contact
Any of the above

Type of Firm
Private venture capital firm

Affiliations
Hambrecht & Quist Group (general partner)
Hambrecht & Quist Incorporated (affiliated investment banking firm)

Industry Association Memberships
NVCA
WAVC

Project Preferences
Will function either as deal originator or investor in deals created by others
Type of Financing:
Research and development partnerships
Startup
First-stage
Second-stage
Later-stage expansion
Leveraged buyout
Minimum Investment: $250,000
Preferred Investment: $500,000-$5 million
Minimum Operating Data:
Annual Sales—Nominal
P&L—Losses (profits projected after 4 years)

Geographical Preferences
National
International, through joint ventures

Industry Preferences

Communications
Telephone related
Computer Related
Office automation
Electronic Components and Instrumentation
Analytical and scientific instrumentation
Component fabrication and testing equipment
Semiconductors
Energy/Natural Resources
Technology related products/equipment
Industrial Products and Equipment
Chemicals
Controls and sensors
Energy management
Equipment and machinery
Plastics
Robotics/vision systems
Specialty materials
Medical/Health Related
Various
Will Not Consider
Entertainment related businesses
Oil and gas exploration and production
Retail sales
Real estate

Additional Information
Year Founded—1968
Capital Under Management—$663 million
Investments(1985-1st 6 months)—76
Invested(1985-1st 6 months)—$51 million
Method of Compensation—Return on investment is of primary concern; do not charge fees

HAPP VENTURES

444 Castro Street #400
Mountain View, CA 94041
415-961-1115

Principal
William D. Happ

Type of Firm
Private venture capital firm investing own capital

Project Preferences
Will function either as deal originator or investor in deals created by others
Type of Financing:
Seed
Research and development partnerships
Startup
First-stage
Minimum Investment: $100,000
Preferred Investment: $500,000-$1 million
Minimum Operating Data:
Annual Sales—Nominal
P&L—Losses (profits projected after 3 years)

Geographical Preference
None

Industry Preferences

Communications
Various
Computer Related
Various
Electronic Components and Instrumentation
Various
Industrial Products and Equipment
Various
Medical/Health Related
Various

Additional Information
Year Founded—1982
Method of Compensation—Return on investment is of primary concern; do not charge fees

HARVEST VENTURES, INC.

3000 Sand Hill Road
Building 1, #205
Menlo Park, CA 94025
415-854-8400

Cloyd Marvin, Mgn. Dir.
Andrew Rachleff, Assoc.

See NEW YORK for full listing

HENRY & CO.

9191 Towne Centre Drive #230
San Diego, CA 92122
619-453-1655

Officers
Albert J. Henry, Chm. & CEO
F. David Hare, Pres.
Dan R. Hendrickson, Consultant
June M. Knaudt, Office Admin.

Whom to Contact
F. David Hare

Type of Firm
Private venture capital firm investing own capital

Industry Association Membership
WAVC

Project Preferences
Will function either as deal originator or investor in deals created by others
Type of Financing:
Second-stage
Minimum Investment: $500,000
Preferred Investment: $500,000-$1 million
Minimum Operating Data:
Annual Sales—$1.5 million
P&L—Losses (profits projected after 2 years)

Geographical Preferences
West Coast
Will consider other areas

Industry Preferences

Communications
Data communications
Computer Related
Computer graphics, CAD/CAM and CAE
Software-applications
Software-artificial intelligence
Software-systems
Specialized turnkey systems

Electronic Components and Instrumentation
Analytical and scientific instrumentation
Component fabrication and testing equipment
Electronic components
Fiber optics
Laser related
Semiconductors
Industrial Products and Equipment
Controls and sensors
Other industrial automation
Robotics/vision systems
Medical/Health Related
Diagnostic equipment
Diagnostic test products
Disposable products
Drugs and medicines
Medical services
Therapeutic equipment
Will Not Consider
Consumer products
Mining
Oil and gas
Real estate
Restaurants
Retail sales

Additional Information
Year Founded—1983
Capital Under Management—$21 million
Investments(1985-1st 6 months)—5
Invested(1985-1st 6 months)—$2.2 million
Method of Compensation—Return on investment is of primary concern; do not charge fees

LAWRENCE HERBST INVESTMENT TRUST FUND

Post Office Box 1659
Beverly Hills, CA 90213

Joe Tomlinson, V.P.

See TEXAS for full listing

HILLMAN VENTURES, INC.

2200 Sand Hill Road #240
Menlo Park, CA 94025
415-854-4653

Other Offices

450 Newport Center Drive #304
Newport Beach, CA 92660
714-644-7071

2000 Grant Building
Pittsburgh, PA 15219
412-281-2620

Officers

Philip S. Paul, Chm. & CEO (Menlo Park)
Stephen J. Banks, Pres. (Pittsburgh)
Kent L. Englemeier, V.P. (Pittsburgh)
Jay D. Glass, V.P. (Newport Beach)
Howard W. Geiger, Jr., V.P. (Menlo Park)
William J. O'Connor, Cntlr. (Pittsburgh)
Marc Yagjian, V.P. (Pittsburgh)

Whom to Contact

Any of the above

Type of Firm

Venture capital subsidiary of
non-financial corporation

Affiliation

The Hillman Company (parent)

Industry Association Membership

NVCA

Project Preferences

Will function either as deal originator or
investor in deals created by others
Type of Financing:
Seed
Research and development partnerships
Startup
First-stage
Second-stage
Later-stage expansion
Leveraged buyout
Minimum Investment: $100,000
Preferred Investment: $500,000-$1 million

Geographical Preference

None

Industry Preferences

Communications
Commercial communications
Data communications
Satellite and microwave communications
Telephone related

Computer Related
Computer graphics, CAD/CAM and CAE
Computer mainframes
Computer services
Memory devices
Micro and mini computers
Scanning related
Software-applications
Software-artificial intelligence
Software-systems
Terminals
Distribution
Communications equipment
Computer equipment
Electronics equipment
Industrial products
Medical products
**Electronic Components and
    Instrumentation**
Analytical and scientific instrumentation
Electronic components
Laser related
Optics technology
Semiconductors
Energy/Natural Resources
Alternative energy
Coal related
Technology related products/equipment
Genetic Engineering
Monoclonal antibodies and hybridomas
Recombinant DNA (agricultural and
    industrial)
Recombinant DNA (medical)
Research and manufacturing equipment
Industrial Products and Equipment
Advanced materials
Chemicals
Equipment and machinery
Other industrial automation
Plastics
Process equipment
Robotics/vision systems
Medical/Health Related
Diagnostic equipment
Drugs and medicines
Hospital and clinical labs
Medical services
Therapeutic equipment
Other
Finance and insurance

Additional Information

Method of Compensation—Return on
    investment is of primary concern; do not
    charge fees

HMS CAPITAL PARTNERS

425 First Street #F
Los Altos, CA 94022
415-948-1278

Partners

R.G. Grey
Frank R. Atkinson
Michael C. Hone

Whom to Contact

Any of the above

Type of Firm

Private limited partnership investing partners
    own money

Project Preferences

Prefer role as deal originator but will also
    invest in deals created by others
Type of Financing:
Seed
Startup
First-stage
Leveraged buyout
Preferred Investment: $500,000-$1 million
Minimum Operating Data:
Annual Sales—Nominal
P&L—Losses (profits projected after 1 year)

Geographical Preferences

Northwest
Southwest
Rocky Mountains
West Coast

Industry Preferences

Communications
Data communications
Satellite and microwave communications
Telephone related

Additional Information

Year Founded—1985
Capital Under Management—$25 million
Method of Compensation—Return on
    investment is of primary concern; do not
    charge fees

HOEBICH VENTURE MANAGEMENT, INC.

850 Hamilton Avenue
Palo Alto, CA 94301
415-326-5590

Other Office

5770 Croy Road
Morgan Hill, CA 95037

Officer

Christian Hoebich, Pres.

Type of Firm

Private venture capital firm investing
own capital

Project Preferences

Prefer role as deal originator but will also
invest in deals created by others
Type of Financing:
Seed
Startup
Minimum Investment: Less than $100,000
Preferred Investment: Less than $100,000
Minimum Operating Data:
Annual Sales—Nominal
P&L—Losses (profits projected after 2 years)

Geographical Preference

Within half an hour from office

Industry Preferences

Communications
Cable television
Commercial communications
Data communications
Satellite and microwave communications
Telephone related
Computer Related
Computer graphics, CAD/CAM and CAE
Computer mainframes
Computer services
Memory devices
Micro and mini computers
Office automation
Scanning related
Software-applications
Software-artificial Intelligence
Software-systems
Specialized turnkey systems
Terminals
Industrial Products and Equipment
Equipment and machinery
Other industrial automation
Robotics/vision systems
Other
Agriculture
Other

Additional Information

Year Founded—1972
Investments(1985-1st 6 months)—1
Method of Compensation—Function primarily
in service area; receive contingent fee in
cash or equity

HOLDING CAPITAL GROUP

2851 Alton Avenue
Irvine, CA 92714
714-863-0300

Bob E. Inman, Principal

See NEW YORK for full listing

HYTEC PARTNERS LTD.

1406 Burlingame Avenue #32
Burlingame, CA 94010
415-340-1616

Partners

John P. Breyer, Mgn. Gen. Ptnr.
Patrick J. McGovern, Gen. Ptnr.
Eva K. Breyer, Gen. Ptnr.

Whom to Contact

John P. Breyer

Type of Firm

Private venture capital firm investing
own capital

Industry Association Membership

WAVC

Project Preferences

Prefer deals created by others but will also
invest as deal originator
Type of Financing:
Startup
First-stage
Second-stage
Minimum Investment: $100,000
Preferred Investment: $100,000-$250,000
Minimum Operating Data:
Annual Sales—Nominal
P&L—Losses (profits projected after 2 years)

Geographical Preferences

Northwest
Southwest
West Coast

Industry Preferences

Communications
Data communications
Satellite and microwave communications
Telephone related
Computer Related
Computer graphics, CAD/CAM and CAE
Computer services
Memory devices
Micro and mini computers
Office automation
Scanning related
Software-applications
Software-artificial intelligence
Software-systems
Specialized turnkey systems
Terminals
Distribution
Communications equipment
Computer equipment
Electronics equipment
Industrial products
Medical products
Electronic Components and Instrumentation
Analytical and scientific instrumentation
Component fabrication and testing
equipment
Electronic components
Fiber optics
Laser related
Semiconductors
Genetic Engineering
Gene splicing and manufacturing equipment
Industrial Products and Equipment
Robotics/vision systems
Medical/Health Related
Diagnostic equipment
Diagnostic test products
Disposable products
Therapeutic equipment

Additional Information

Year Founded—1983
Capital Under Management—$5 million
Investments(1985-1st 6 months)—3
Invested(1985-1st 6 months)—$250,000
Method of Compensation—Return on
investment is of primary concern; do not
charge fees

IAI VENTURE PARTNERS

3000 Sand Hill Road
Bldg. 3, #210
Menlo Park, CA 94025
415-854-1955

Richard C. Pflager, Sr. V.P.

See MINNESOTA for full listing

INCO VENTURE CAPITAL MANAGEMENT

c/o International Nickel, Inc.
2099 Gateway Plaza #470
San Jose, CA 95112
408-993-9594

Richard G. Couch, Sr. V.P. & Principal

See NEW YORK for full listing

INDOSUEZ TECHNOLOGY GROUP

3000 Sand Hill Road
Building 4, #130
Menlo Park, CA 94025
415-854-0587

Partners
David E. Gold, Gen. Ptnr.
Philippe Sevin, Gen. Ptnr.
Gregory A. Nelson, Assoc.

Whom to Contact
Philippe Sevin
David E. Gold

Type of Firm
Private venture capital firm investing
own capital

Affiliation
Sequoia Capital (fund co-manager)
Banque Indosuez, Paris (fund sponsor)

Industry Association Membership
WAVC

Project Preferences
Will function either as deal originator or
investor in deals created by others
Type of Financing:
Seed
Startup
First-stage
Second-stage

Minimum Investment: Less than $100,000
Preferred Investment: $500,000-$1 million
Minimum Operating Data:
Annual Sales—Nominal

Geographical Preferences
Within two hours of office
West Coast

Industry Preferences

Communications
Data communications
Computer Related
Computer graphics, CAD/CAM and CAE
Computer mainframes
Computer services
Memory devices
Micro and mini computers
Office automation
Scanning related
Software-applications
Software-artificial intelligence
Software-systems
Specialized turnkey systems
Terminals
Distribution
Communications equipment
Computer equipment
Electronics equipment
**Electronic Components and
Instrumentation**
Analytical and scientific instrumentation
Component fabrication and testing
equipment
Electronic components
Fiber optics
Laser related
Semiconductors
Genetic Engineering
Gene splicing and manufacturing equipment
Monoclonal antibodies and hybridomas
Recombinant DNA (agricultural and
industrial)
Recombinant DNA (medical)
Industrial Products and Equipment
Other industrial automation
Robotics/vision systems
Medical/Health Related
Diagnostic equipment
Diagnostic test products
Disposable products
Drugs and medicines
Hospital and clinical labs
Medical services
Therapeutic equipment

Additional Information
Year Founded—1985
Capital Under Management—
Over $30 million
Investments(1985-1st 6 months)—10
Invested(1985-1st 6 months)—Over $4 million

INMAN & BOWMAN

Four Orinda Way
Building D, #150
Orinda, CA 94563
415-253-1611

General Partners
Grant M. Inman
D. Kirkwood Bowman

Whom to Contact
Either of the above

Type of Firm
Private venture capital firm investing
own capital

Industry Association Memberships
NVCA
WAVC

Project Preferences
Will function either as deal originator or
investor in deals created by others
Type of Financing:
Startup
First-stage
Minimum Investment: $250,000
Preferred Investment: $500,000-$1 million

Geographical Preference
West Coast

Industry Preferences

Communications
Commercial communications
Data communications
Satellite and microwave communications
Telephone related

Computer Related
Computer graphics, CAD/CAM and CAE
Computer mainframes
Computer services
Memory devices
Micro and mini computers
Office automation
Scanning related
Software-applications
Software-artificial intelligence
Software-systems
Specialized turnkey systems
Terminals
Electronic Components and Instrumentation
Analytical and scientific instrumentation
Component fabrication and testing equipment
Electronic components
Fiber optics
Laser related
Semiconductors
Medical/Health Related
Diagnostic equipment
Diagnostic test products
Disposable products
Drugs and medicines
Hospital and clinical labs
Medical services
Therapeutic equipment

Additional Information
Year Founded—1985
Capital Under Management—$43.5 million
Method of Compensation—Return on investment is of primary concern; do not charge fees

---

INSTITUTIONAL VENTURE PARTNERS

3000 Sand Hill Road
Building 2, #290
Menlo Park, CA 94025
415-854-0132

Partners
Reid W. Dennis, Mgn. Gen. Ptnr.
Sam D. Colella, Gen. Ptnr.
Mary Jane Elmore, Gen. Ptnr.
John K. Poitras, Gen. Ptnr.
T. Peter Thomas, Gen. Ptnr.
Mark J. Bronder, CFO

Whom to Contact
Sam D. Collela
Mary Jane Elmore
T. Peter Thomas

Type of Firm
Private venture capital firm investing own capital

Industry Association Memberships
NVCA
WAVC

Project Preferences
Will function either as deal originator or investor in deals created by others
Type of Financing:
Seed
Startup
First-stage
Second-stage
Minimum Investment: $500,000
Preferred Investment: $750,000-$1.5 million
Minimum Operating Data:
Annual Sales—Nominal
P&L—Losses (profits projected after 2 years)

Geographical Preference
Within two hours of office

Industry Preferences

Communications
Commercial communications
Data communications
Satellite and microwave communications
Telephone related
Computer Related
Computer graphics, CAD/CAM and CAE
Computer mainframes
Computer services
Memory devices
Micro and mini computers
Office automation
Scanning related
Software-applications
Software-artificial intelligence
Software-systems
Specialized turnkey systems
Terminals
Consumer
Computer stores/related services
Distribution
Communications equipment
Computer equipment
Electronics equipment
Medical products
Electronic Components and Instrumentation
Analytical and scientific instrumentation
Component fabrication and testing equipment
Electronic components
Fiber optics
Laser related
Semiconductors

Energy/Natural Resources
Technology related products/equipment
Genetic Engineering
Gene splicing and manufacturing equipment
Monoclonal antibodies and hybridomas
Recombinant DNA (agricultural and industrial)
Recombinant DNA (medical)
Industrial Products and Equipment
Controls and sensors
Other industrial automation
Robotics/vision systems
Specialty materials
Medical/Health Related
Diagnostic equipment
Diagnostic test products
Disposable products
Drugs and medicines
Will Not Consider
Consumer products
Extraction industries
Real estate
Service businesses

Additional Information
Year Founded—1980
Capital Under Management—$150 million
Investments(1985-1st 6 months)—15
Invested(1985-1st 6 months)—$12.7 million
Method of Compensation—Return on investment is of primary concern; do not charge fees

---

INTERSCOPE INVESTMENTS

10900 Wilshire Boulevard #1400
Los Angeles, CA 90024
213-208-8636

Officer
J. Murray Hill, II

Type of Firm
Private venture capital firm investing own capital

Industry Association Memberships
NVCA
WAVC

Project Preferences
Will function either as deal originator or investor in deals created by others

Type of Financing:
First-stage
Second-stage
Later-stage expansion
Leveraged buyout
Minimum Investment: Less than $100,000
Preferred Investment: $250,000-$1 million

Geographical Preference
None

Industry Preferences

Communications
Cable television
Commercial communications
Data communications
Satellite and microwave communications
Telephone related
Computer Related
Computer graphics, CAD/CAM and CAE
Computer mainframes
Computer services
Memory devices
Micro and mini computers
Office automation
Scanning related
Software-applications
Software-artificial intelligence
Software-systems
Specialized turnkey systems
Terminals
Consumer
Computer stores/related services
Consumer products
Consumer services
Food and beverage products
Franchise businesses
Hotels and resort areas
Leisure and recreational products
Restaurants
Retailing
Distribution
Communications equipment
Computer equipment
Consumer products
Electronics equipment
Food products
Industrial products
Medical products
Electronic Components and Instrumentation
Analytical and scientific instrumentation
Component fabrication and testing equipment
Electronic components
Fiber optics
Laser related
Semiconductors

Energy/Natural Resources
Alternative energy
Coal related
Drilling and exploration services
Energy conservation
Minerals
Oil and gas exploration and production
Technology related products/equipment
Genetic Engineering
Gene splicing and manufacturing equipment
Monoclonal antibodies and hybridomas
Recombinant DNA (agricultural and industrial)
Recombinant DNA (medical)
Industrial Products and Equipment
Chemicals
Controls and sensors
Energy management
Equipment and machinery
Other industrial automation
Plastics
Robotics/vision systems
Specialty materials
Medical/Health Related
Diagnostic equipment
Diagnostic test products
Disposable products
Drugs and medicines
Hospital and clinical labs
Medical services
Therapeutic equipment
Other
Agriculture, forestry, fishing
Education related
Finance and insurance
Publishing
Real estate
Specialty consulting
Transportation

Additional Information
Investments(1985-1st 6 months)—4
Invested(1985-1st 6 months)—$1.5 million
Method of Compensation—Return on investment is of primary concern; do not charge fees

INTERVEN PARTNERS

445 South Figueroa Street
Suite 2940
Los Angeles, CA 90071
213-622-1922

Other Office
227 Southwest Pine Street #200
Portland, OR 97204
503-223-4334

General Partners
David B. Jones (California)
Wayne B. Kingsley (Oregon)
Kenneth M. Deemer (California)
Jonathan E. Funk (California)
Keith R. Larson (California)

Whom to Contact
Wayne B. Kingsley
Jonathan E. Funk
Kenneth M. Deemer

Type of Firm
Private venture capital firm investing own capital

Industry Association Memberships
NASBIC
NVCA
WAVC

Project Preferences
Will function either as deal originator or investor in deals created by others
Type of Financing:
Seed
Startup
First-stage
Leveraged buyout
Minimum Investment: $500,000
Preferred Investment: $500,000-$1 million
Preferred Investment (LBO):
$1 million-$2 million
Minimum Operating Data:
Annual Sales—Nominal
P&L—Losses (profits projected after 2 years)
Annual Sales (LBO)—$15 million-$30 million

Geographical Preferences
Within two hours of office
Northwest
Southern California

Industry Preferences

Communications
Data communications

Computer Related
Computer graphics, CAD/CAM and CAE
Computer mainframes
Computer services
Memory devices
Micro and mini computers
Office automation
Scanning related
Software-applications
Software-artificial intelligence
Software-systems
Specialized turnkey systems
Terminals
Consumer
Consumer products
Consumer services
Food and beverage products
Retailing
**Electronic Components and
  Instrumentation**
Analytical and scientific instrumentation
Component fabrication and testing
  equipment
Electronic components
Fiber optics
Laser related
Semiconductors
Genetic Engineering
Gene splicing and manufacturing equipment
Monoclonal antibodies and hybridomas
Recombinant DNA (agricultural and
  industrial)
Recombinant DNA (medical)
Industrial Products and Equipment
Chemicals
Controls and sensors
Energy management
Equipment and machinery
Other industrial automation
Plastics
Robotics/vision systems
Specialty materials
Medical/Health Related
Diagnostic equipment
Diagnostic test products
Disposable products
Drugs and medicines
Hospital and clinical labs
Medical services
Therapeutic equipment
Will Not Consider
Energy/natural resources
Entertainment
Real estate

Additional Information

Year Founded—1985
Capital Under Management—$35 million
Method of Compensation—Return on
  investment is of primary concern; do not
  charge fees

INTERWEST PARTNERS

3000 Sand Hill Road
Building 3, #225
Menlo Park, CA 94025
415-854-8585

Other Offices

800 E. Sir Francis Drake Blvd.
Suite 3A
Larkspur, CA 94939
415-461-0361

One Galleria Tower #1375/LB 65
13355 Noel Road
Dallas, TX 75240
214-392-7279

General Partners

Eugene F. Barth (Menlo Park)
Berry Cash (Dallas)
Philip T. Gianos (Menlo Park)
Wallace R. Hawley (Menlo Park)
W. Scott Hedrick (Menlo Park & Larkspur)
Charles J. McMinn (Menlo Park)
Robert R. Momsen (Menlo Park & Larkspur)
Glenn A. Norem (Dallas)

Whom to Contact

Any of the above

Type of Firm

Private venture capital firm investing
  own capital

Industry Association Memberships

NVCA
WAVC

Project Preferences

Prefer role as deal originator but will also
  invest in deals created by others
Type of Financing:
Seed
Research and development partnerships
Startup
First-stage
Second-stage
Later-stage expansion
Leveraged buyout

Minimum Investment: $1 million
Preferred Investment: Over $1 million
Preferred Investment (LBO):
  $2 million-$5 million
Minimum Operating Data:
Annual Sales (LBO)—$10 million-$100 million

Geographical Preference

None

Industry Preferences

Communications
Data communications
Satellite and microwave communications
Telephone related
Computer Related
Computer graphics, CAD/CAM and CAE
Computer mainframes
Computer services
Memory devices
Micro and mini computers
Office automation
Scanning related
Software-applications
Software-artificial intelligence
Software-systems
Specialized turnkey systems
Terminals
Distribution
Communications equipment
Computer equipment
Consumer products
Electronics equipment
Food products
Industrial products
Medical products
**Electronic Components and
  Instrumentation**
Analytical and scientific instrumentation
Component fabrication and testing
  equipment
Electronic components
Semiconductors
Industrial Products and Equipment
Chemicals
Controls and sensors
Energy management
Equipment and machinery
Other industrial automation
Plastics
Robotics/vision systems
Specialty materials
Medical/Health Related
Diagnostic equipment
Diagnostic test products
Disposable products
Drugs and medicines
Hospital and clinical labs
Medical services
Therapeutic equipment

Other
Transportation
Will Not Consider
Oil and gas exploration and production
Real estate
Turnarounds

Additional Information
Year Founded—1979
Capital Under Management—$150 million
Investments(1985-1st 6 months)—30
Invested(1985-1st 6 months)—$4.2 million
Method of Compensation—Return on
investment is of primary concern; do not
charge fees

INVESTORS IN INDUSTRY (3i)

3i CAPITAL

450 Newport Center Drive #250
Newport Beach, CA 92660
714-720-1421

See MASSACHUSETTS for full listing

INVESTORS IN INDUSTRY (3i)

3i VENTURES

450 Newport Center Drive #250
Newport Beach, CA 92660
714-720-1421

Other Offices
99 High Street #1530
Boston, MA 02110
617-542-8560

91 Waterloo Road
London SE1 8XP
England
01-928-7822

Officer
Geoff Taylor, Pres. (United Kingdom)

Whom to Contact
Frederick M. Haney (California)
Alexander P. Cilento (California)
Dorothy Langer (Massachusetts)

Type of Firm
Subsidiary of U.K. financial institution

Affiliation
Investors in Industry plc, London, England

Project Preferences
Will function either as deal originator or
investor in deals created by others
Type of Financing:
Seed
Startup
First-stage
Second-stage
Minimum Investment: $200,000
Preferred Investment: $500,000 and over
Minimum Operating Data:
Annual Sales—Nominal
P&L—Losses (profits projected after 4 years)

Geographical Preferences
National
U.K.

Industry Preferences

Communications
Cable television
Commercial communications
Data communications
Satellite and microwave communications
Telephone related
Computer Related
Computer graphics, CAD/CAM and CAE
Computer mainframes
Computer services
Memory devices
Micro and mini computers
Office automation
Scanning related
Software-applications
Software-artificial intelligence
Software-systems
Specialized turnkey systems
Terminals
Consumer
Computer stores/related services
Franchise businesses
Hotels and resort areas
Leisure and recreational products
Retailing
Distribution
Communications equipment
Computer equipment
Consumer products
Electronics equipment
Food products
Industrial products
Medical products

**Electronic Components and
Instrumentation**
Analytical and scientific instrumentation
Component fabrication and testing
equipment
Electronic components
Fiber optics
Laser related
Semiconductors
Genetic Engineering
Monoclonal antibodies and hybridomas
Recombinant DNA (agricultural and
industrial)
Recombinant DNA (medical)
Research and manufacturing equipment
Industrial Products and Equipment
Advanced materials
Controls and sensors
Equipment and machinery
Other industrial automation
Plastics
Robotics/vision systems
Specialty materials
Medical/Health Related
Diagnostic equipment
Diagnostic test products
Drugs and medicines
Hospital and clinical labs
Medical services
Other
Particular interest in transatlantic activities
Will Not Consider
Oil and gas
Real estate

IRVINE TECHNOLOGY FUND

4600 Campus Drive
Newport Beach, CA 92660
714-852-9000

Partners
Walter W. Cruttenden
H. D. Thoreau
J.C. MacRae
Gregory E. Presson

Whom to Contact
H.D. Thoreau

Type of Firm
Private venture capital firm investing
own capital
Also invest side by side family trust

Affiliation
Cruttenden & Co., Inc.

Project Preferences
Will function either as deal originator or investor in deals created by others
Type of Financing:
Seed
Research and development partnerships
Startup
First-stage
Second-stage
Leveraged buyout
Minimum Investment: Less than $100,000
Preferred Investment: $100,000-$250,000
Preferred Investment (LBO): $250,000
Minimum Operating Data:
Annual Sales—Nominal
P&L—Losses (profits projected after 1 year)
Annual Sales (LBO)—$5 million-$50 million

Geographical Preference
Southern California

Industry Preferences

Communications
Commercial communications
Data communications
Fiber optics related
Satellite and microwave communications
Telephone related
Computer Related
Computer graphics, CAD/CAM and CAE
Computer mainframes
Computer services
Memory devices
Micro and mini computers
Office automation
Scanning related
Software-applications
Software-artificial intelligence
Software-systems
Specialized turnkey systems
Terminals
Consumer
Computer stores/related services
Consumer products
Consumer services
Food and beverage products
Franchise businesses
Leisure and recreational products
Retailing
Distribution
Communications equipment
Computer equipment
Consumer products
Electronics equipment
Food products
Industrial products
Medical products

Electronic Components and Instrumentation
Analytical and scientific instrumentation
Component fabrication and testing equipment
Electronic components
Fiber optics
Laser related
Semiconductors
Genetic Engineering
Gene splicing and manufacturing equipment
Monoclonal antibodies and hybridomas
Recombinant DNA (agricultural and industrial)
Recombinant DNA (medical)
Industrial Products and Equipment
Chemicals
Controls and sensors
Equipment and machinery
Other industrial automation
Plastics
Robotics/vision systems
Specialty materials
Medical/Health Related
Diagnostic equipment
Diagnostic test products
Disposable products
Drugs and medicines
Hospital and clinical labs
Medical services
Therapeutic equipment
Will Not Consider
Real estate

Additional Information
Year Founded—1981
Capital Under Management—$10 million (includes family trust under management)
Investments(1985-1st 6 months)—3
Invested(1985-1st 6 months)—
Less than $1 million
Method of Compensation—Return on investment is of primary concern

---

IVANHOE VENTURE CAPITAL, LTD.

737 Pearl Street #201
La Jolla, CA 92037
619-454-8882

Partners
P. Frederick Wulff, Gen. Ptnr.
Alan R. Toffler, Mgn. Gen. Ptnr.

Whom to Contact
Either of the above

Type of Firm
SBIC

Project Preferences
Prefer role as deal originator but will also invest in deals created by others
Type of Financing:
Second-stage
Later-stage expansion
Leveraged buyout
Minimum Investment: $100,000
Preferred Investment: $100,000-$250,000
Preferred Investment (LBO): $100,000-$250,000
Minimum Operating Data:
Annual Sales—Nominal
P&L—Break even

Geographical Preference
West Coast

Industry Preferences

Communications
Cable television
Data communications
Satellite and microwave communications
Computer Related
Computer services
Software-systems
Specialized turnkey systems
Terminals
Consumer
Franchise businesses
Distribution
Communications equipment
Electronics equipment
Food products
Industrial products
Medical products
Electronic Components and Instrumentation
Analytical and scientific instrumentation
Fiber optics
Laser related
Energy/Natural Resources
Co-generation
Energy conservation
Technology related products/equipment
Genetic Engineering
Monoclonal antibodies and hybridomas
Recombinant DNA (agricultural and industrial)
Industrial Products and Equipment
Controls and sensors
Energy management
Specialty materials

Medical/Health Related
Diagnostic equipment
Diagnostic test products
Disposable products
Drugs and medicines
Hospital and clinical labs
Medical services
Therapeutic equipment
Other
Education related
Transportation
Will Not Consider
Oil or gas exploration
Real estate
Startup companies

Additional Information
Year Founded—1982
Capital Under Management—$1.5 million
Investments(1985-1st 6 months)—2
Invested(1985-1st 6 months)—$220,000
Method of Compensation—Return on
  investment is most important, but also
  charge for closing fees, service fees, etc.

JAFCO AMERICA VENTURES INC.

2180 Sand Hill Road #320
Menlo Park, CA 94025
415-854-0746

Officers
Shunsuke Fukuda, Pres.
Lionel P. Boissiere, Jr., Mgr., Tech.
  & Bus. Devel.

Whom to Contact
Either of the above

Type of Firm
U.S. subsidiary of Japanese venture
  capital organization

Affiliations
Japan Associated Finance Co. Ltd. (parent)
Nomura Group (majority shareholder of
  parent company)

Project Preferences
Will function either as deal originator or
  investor in deals created by others
Type of Financing:
Second-stage
Later-stage expansion
Minimum Investment: $250,000
Preferred Investment: $500,000-$1 million
Minimum Operating Data:
Annual Sales—Nominal
P&L—Losses (profits projected after 2 years)

Geographical Preferences
West Coast
National

Industry Preferences

Communications
Cable television
Commercial communications
Data communications
Satellite and microwave communications
Telephone related
Computer Related
Computer graphics, CAD/CAM and CAE
Computer mainframes
Computer services
Memory devices
Micro and mini computers
Office automation
Scanning related
Software-applications
Software-artificial intelligence
Software-systems
Specialized turnkey systems
Terminals
Consumer
Computer stores/related services
Consumer products
Consumer services
Food and beverage products
Franchise businesses
Hotels and resort areas
Leisure and recreational products
Restaurants
Retailing
Distribution
Communications equipment
Computer equipment
Consumer products
Electronics equipment
Food products
Medical products
**Electronic Components and
  Instrumentation**
Analytical and scientific instrumentation
Component fabrication and testing
  equipment
Electronic components
Fiber optics
Laser related
Semiconductors
Energy/Natural Resources
Technology related products/equipment
Genetic Engineering
Gene splicing and manufacturing equipment
Monoclonal antibodies and hybridomas
Recombinant DNA (agricultural and
  industrial)
Recombinant DNA (medical)

Industrial Products and Equipment
Controls and sensors
Equipment and machinery
Robotics/vision systems
Medical/Health Related
Diagnostic equipment
Diagnostic test products
Drugs and medicines
Hospital and clinical labs
Medical services
Therapeutic equipment
Other
Education related

Additional Information
Year Founded—1984
Investments(1985-1st 6 months)—3
Method of Compensation—Return on
  investment is most important, but also
  charge for closing fees, service fees, etc.

JULIAN, COLE AND STEIN

11777 San Vicente Boulevard
Suite 522
Los Angeles, CA 90049
213-826-8002

General Partners
James M. Julian
Charles R. Cole
David L. R. Stein

Whom to Contact
Any of the above

Type of Firm
Private venture capital firm investing
  own capital

Industry Association Membership
NVCA

Project Preferences
Prefer role as deal originator
Type of Financing:
Seed
Startup
Minimum Investment: $100,000
Preferred Investment: Over $1 million
Minimum Operating Data:
Annual Sales—Nominal
P&L—Losses (profits projected after 2 years)

Geographical Preference
Southern California
West Coast

Industry Preferences

Communications
Data communications
Satellite and microwave communications
Computer Related
Minisupercomputers
Superminicomputers
Electronic Components and Instrumentation
Analytical and scientific instrumentation
Component fabrication and testing equipment
Electronic components
Fiber optics
Laser related
Semiconductors
Genetic Engineering
Gene splicing and manufacturing equipment
Monoclonal antibodies and hybridomas
Recombinant DNA (agricultural and industrial)
Recombinant DNA (medical)
Industrial Products and Equipment
Controls and sensors
High technology products for factory automation
Other industrial automation
Robotics/vision systems
Medical/Health Related
Diagnostic equipment
Diagnostic test products
Disposable products
Will Not Consider
Consumer products
Entertainment related businesses
Oil and gas exploration and production
Real estate

Additional Information

Year Founded—1983
Capital Under Management—$38 million
Investments(1985-1st 6 months)—5
Invested(1985-1st 6 months)—$2.3 million
Method of Compensation—Return on investment is of primary concern; do not charge fees

KLEINER PERKINS CAUFIELD & BYERS

Four Embarcadero Center #3520
San Francisco, CA 94111
415-421-3110

Other Office

Two Embarcadero Place #205
2200 Geng Road
Palo Alto, CA 94303
415-424-1660

Partners

Thomas J. Perkins, Gen. Ptnr. (San Francisco)
Brook H. Byers, Gen. Ptnr. (San Francisco)
Frank J. Caufield, Gen. Ptnr. (San Francisco)
John Doerr, Gen. Ptnr. (San Francisco)
James P. Lally, Gen. Ptnr. (Palo Alto)
Floyd Kvamme, Gen Ptnr. (Palo Alto)
Mark Bailey, Assoc. (Palo Alto)
John Boyle, Assoc. (San Francisco)

Whom to Contact

Kelley Brown

Type of Firm

Private venture capital firm investing own capital

Project Preferences

Prefer role as deal originator but will also invest in deals created by others
Type of Financing:
Startup
First-stage
Minimum Investment: $500,000
Preferred Investment: $1 million-$2 million
Minimum Operating Data:
Annual Sales—Nominal
P&L—Losses (profits projected after 2 years)

Geographical Preference

West Coast

Industry Preferences

Communications
Data communications
Satellite and microwave communications
Telephone related
Computer Related
Computer graphics, CAD/CAM and CAE
Memory devices
Micro and mini computers
Office automation
Scanning related
Software-applications
Software-artificial intelligence
Software-systems
Distribution
Medical products
Electronic Components and Instrumentation
Analytical and scientific instrumentation
Component fabrication and testing equipment
Electronic components
Fiber optics
Laser related
Semiconductors
Genetic Engineering
Gene splicing and manufacturing equipment
Monoclonal antibodies and hybridomas
Recombinant DNA (agricultural and industrial)
Recombinant DNA (medical)
Industrial Products and Equipment
Other industrial automation
Robotics/vision systems
Medical/Health Related
Diagnostic equipment
Diagnostic test products
Drugs and medicines
Therapeutic equipment
Will Not Consider
Agriculture
Consumer products and services
Energy or natural resources, including oil and gas
Hotels or motels
Motion pictures
Resort areas
Real estate
Retailing

Additional Information

Year Founded—1972
Capital Under Management—$238 million
Investments(1985-1st 6 months)—22
Invested(1985-1st 6 months)—$16.4 million
Method of Compensation—Return on investment is of primary concern; do not charge fees

ROBERT B. LEISY, CONSULTANT

14408 East Whittier Blvd. #B-5
Whittier, CA 90605
213-698-4862

Post Office Box 4405
Whittier, CA 90607

Principal
Robert B. Leisy

Type of Firm
Consulting firm evaluating and analyzing
venture projects, performing market and
financial research, and conducting
professional training seminars in venture
capital investment for NASBIC

Affiliation
Industrial Market Research Co. (sister firm)

Industry Association Membership
NASBIC

Project Preferences
Will function either as deal originator or in
deals created by others
Type of Financing:
First-stage
Second-stage
Minimum Investment: $250,000
Preferred Investment: $250,000-$1 million

Geographical Preference
Southern California

Industry Preferences

Communications
Various
Computer Related
Various
Distribution
Various
**Electronic Components and
Instrumentation**
Various
Energy/Natural Resources
Various
Industrial Products and Equipment
Various
Other
Industrial or business-to-business products
or services
Specialty consulting

Will Not Consider
Entertainment
Real estate

Additional Information
Year Founded—1972
Method of Compensation—Professional fee

LOMBARD ASSOCIATES

Four Embarcadero Center #1980
San Francisco, CA 94111
415-981-3500

Officers
Charles P. Stetson, Jr., Mgn. Dir.
Patricia George, V.P.

Whom to Contact
Either of the above

Type of Firm
Private venture capital firm investing
own capital

Affiliation
Davis Skaggs Capital/Lombard Fund
(general partner)

Project Preferences
Prefer role as deal originator but will also
invest in deals created by others
Type of Financing:
First-stage
Second-stage
Later-stage expansion
Leveraged buyout
Minimum Investment: $100,000
Preferred Investment: $100,000-$250,000
Minimum Operating Data:
Annual Sales—Nominal
P&L—Break even

Geographical Preference
Within two hours of office

Industry Preferences

Communications
Data communications
Satellite and microwave communications
Telephone related

Computer Related
Computer graphics, CAD/CAM and CAE
Computer mainframes
Computer services
Memory devices
Micro and mini computers
Office automation
Scanning related
Software-applications
Software-artificial intelligence
Software-systems
Specialized turnkey systems
Terminals
**Electronic Components and
Instrumentation**
Analytical and scientific instrumentation
Component fabrication and testing
equipment
Electronic components
Fiber optics
Laser related
Semiconductors
Energy/Natural Resources
Alternative energy
Industrial Products and Equipment
Chemicals
Controls and sensors
Energy management
Equipment and machinery
Other industrial automation
Plastics
Robotics/vision systems
Specialty materials
Medical/Health Related
Diagnostic equipment
Diagnostic test products
Disposable products
Drugs and medicines
Hospital and clinical labs
Medical services
Therapeutic equipment
Other
Finance and insurance
Publishing

Additional Information
Year Founded—1978
Capital Under Management—$5.5 million
Method of Compensation—Return on
investment is most important, but also
charge for closing fees, service fees, etc.

DONALD L. LUCAS

3000 Sand Hill Road
Building 3, #210
Menlo Park, CA 94025
415-854-4223

Principal
Donald L. Lucas

Whom to Contact
Eileen Lepera

Type of Firm
Private venture capital firm investing
own capital

Industry Association Membership
WAVC

Project Preferences
Will function either as deal originator or
investor in deals created by others
Type of Financing:
Startup
First-stage
Second-stage
Minimum Investment: $500,000
Preferred Investment: Over $1 million
Minimum Operating Data:
Annual Sales—$500,000

Geographical Preferences
Southeast
Midwest
West Coast

Industry Preferences

Communications
Satellite and microwave communications
Computer Related
Computer graphics, CAD/CAM and CAE
Computer services
Hospital software
Software-applications
Software-systems
**Electronic Components and
Instrumentation**
Electronic components
Medical/Health Related
Health maintenance organizations

Additional Information
Year Founded—1967
Investments(1985-1st 6 months)—5
Method of Compensation—Return on
investment is of primary concern; do not
charge fees

MARWIT CAPITAL CORPORATION

180 Newport Center Drive #200
Newport Beach, CA 92660
714-640-6234

Officer
Martin W. Witte, Pres.

Whom to Contact
Martin W. Witte
A. Alpern

Type of Firm
Private venture capital firm investing
own capital
SBIC

Project Preferences
Prefer role as deal originator but will also
invest in deals created by others
Type of Financing:
Second-stage
Later-stage expansion
Leveraged buyout
Mergers and acquisitions
Minimum Investment: $250,000
$100,000 minimum for California
investments
Preferred Investment: $500,000-$1 million
Preferred Investment (LBO):
$500,000 and over
Minimum Operating Data:
Annual Sales—$1.5 million
P&L—Break even

Geographical Preference
None

Industry Preferences

Communications
Cable television
Telephone related
Computer Related
Computer services
Office automation
Software-systems
Consumer
Leisure and recreational products
Distribution
Industrial products
Medical products
Medical/Health Related
Various
Other
Construction
Finance and insurance
Publishing
Real estate

Will Not Consider
Retail sales
Startups
Companies with negative net worth

Additional Information
Year Founded—1962
Capital Under Management—Over $5 million
Investments(1985-1st 6 months)—5
Invested(1985-1st 6 months)—$2 million
Method of Compensation—Return on
investment is most important, but also
charge for closing fees, service fees, etc.

MATRIX PARTNERS, L.P.

224 West Brokaw Road
San Jose, CA 95110
408-298-0270

East Coast Office
One Post Office Square
Boston, MA 02109
617-482-7735

Partners
Paul J. Ferri, Gen. Ptnr. (Massachusetts)
Frederick K. Fluegel, Gen. Ptnr. (California)
F. Warren Hellman, Gen. Ptnr. (California)
W. Michael Humphreys, Gen. Ptnr.
(Massachusetts)
Glen McLaughlin, Gen. Ptnr. (California)
Timothy A. Barrows, Associate
(Massachusetts)

Whom to Contact
Any of the above

Type of Firm
Private venture capital firm investing
own capital

Industry Association Memberships
NVCA
WAVC

Project Preferences
Will function either as deal originator or
investor in deals created by others
Type of Financing:
Seed
Startup
First-stage
Leveraged buyout
Minimum Investment: $500,000
Preferred Investment: $500,000-$1 million
Minimum Operating Data:
Annual Sales—Nominal
P&L—Losses (profits projected after 2 years)

Geographical Preference
Within two hours of office

Industry Preferences

Communications
Cable television
Commercial communications
Data communications
Satellite and microwave communications
Computer Related
Computer graphics, CAD/CAM and CAE
Computer mainframes
Computer services
Memory devices
Micro and mini computers
Office automation
Scanning related
Software-applications
Software-systems
Specialized turnkey systems
**Electronic Components and
  Instrumentation**
Analytical and scientific instrumentation
Component fabrication and testing
  equipment
Fiber optics
Semiconductors
Medical/Health Related
Diagnostic equipment
Drugs and medicines
Hospital and clinical labs
Medical services
Will Not Consider
Natural resources
Real estate development

Additional Information
Year Founded—1982
Capital Under Management—$115 million
Investments(1985-1st 6 months)—7
Invested(1985-1st 6 months)—$3.7 million
Method of Compensation—Return on
  investment is of primary concern; do not
  charge fees

LEONARD MAUTNER ASSOCIATES

1434 Sixth Street #10
Santa Monica, CA 90401
213-393-9788

Officers
Leonard Mautner, Pres.
Milton Rosenberg, Assoc.

Whom to Contact
Leonard Mautner

Type of Firm
Consulting firm evaluating and analyzing
  venture projects and arranging private
  placements

Project Preferences
Prefer role as deal originator
Type of Financing:
Seed
Startup
First-stage
Minimum Investment: $100,000
Preferred Investment: $100,000-$250,000
Minimum Operating Data:
Annual Sales—Nominal

Geographical Preferences
Within two hours of office
West Coast

Industry Preferences

Communications
Data communications
Computer Related
Computer graphics, CAD/CAM and CAE
Computer mainframes
Computer services
Memory devices
Micro and mini computers
Office automation
Scanning related
Software-applications
Software-artificial intelligence
Software-systems
Specialized turnkey systems
Terminals
**Electronic Components and
  Instrumentation**
Analytical and scientific instrumentation
Fiber optics
Laser related
Industrial Products and Equipment
Robotics/vision systems
Medical/Health Related
Diagnostic equipment
Diagnostic test products
Disposable products

Additional Information
Year Founded—1969
Investments(1985-1st 6 months)—3
Method of Compensation—Return on
  investment is most important, but also
  charge for closing fees, service fees, etc.

MAYFIELD FUND

2200 Sand Hill Road #200
Menlo Park, CA 94025
415-854-5560

General Partners
Thomas J. Davis, Jr.
F. Gibson Myers, Jr.
Glenn M. Mueller
Norman A. Fogelsong
A. Grant Heidrich III
Michael J. Levinthal

Whom to Contact
Any of the above

Type of Firm
Private venture capital firm investing
  own capital

Industry Association Memberships
NVCA
WAVC

Project Preferences
Prefer role as deal originator
Type of Financing:
Seed
Startup
First-stage
Second-stage
Leveraged buyout
Minimum Investment: $250,000
Preferred Investment: Over $1 million
Minimum Operating Data:
Annual Sales—Nominal
P&L—Losses (profits projected after 2 years)

Geographical Preferences
West Coast
Rocky Mountains
Texas
Northwest

Industry Preferences

Communications
Data communications
Satellite and microwave communications
Telephone related

Computer Related
Computer graphics, CAD/CAM and CAE
Computer mainframes
Computer services
Memory devices
Micro and mini computers
Office automation
Software-applications
Software-artificial intelligence
Software-systems
Specialized turnkey systems
Terminals
Vertical market systems
Consumer
Computer stores/related services
Retailing
Distribution
Communications equipment
Computer equipment
Electronics equipment
Medical products
Electronic Components and Instrumentation
Analytical and scientific instrumentation
Component fabrication and testing equipment
Electronic components
Fiber optics
Laser related
Semiconductors
Genetic Engineering
Gene splicing and manufacturing equipment
Monoclonal antibodies and hybridomas
Recombinant DNA (agricultural and industrial)
Recombinant DNA (medical)
Industrial Products and Equipment
Catalytic chemistry
Chemicals
Controls and sensors
Other industrial automation
Robotics/vision systems
Medical/Health Related
Diagnostic equipment
Drugs and medicines
Hospital and clinical labs
Medical services
Therapeutic equipment
Will Not Consider
Motion pictures
Oil and gas
Real estate

Additional Information
Year Founded—1969
Capital Under Management—$200 million
Investments(1985-1st 6 months)—20
Invested(1985-1st 6 months)—$8.4 million
Method of Compensation—Return on investment is of primary concern; do not charge fees

MBW MANAGEMENT, INC.

350 Second Street #7
Los Altos, CA 94022
415-941-2392

Other Offices
365 South Street, Second Floor
Morristown, NJ 07906
201-285-5533

2000 Hogback Road #2
Ann Arbor, MI 48105
313-971-3100

333 East Main Street
Post Office Box 1431
Midland, MI 48641
517-631-2471

Officers
Philip E. McCarthy, Mgn. Dir. (Morristown)
Ian R.N. Bund, Mgn. Dir. (Ann Arbor)
James R. Weersing, Mgn. Dir. (Los Altos)
Richard M. Goff, V.P., Treas. & Secy. (Ann Arbor)
Robert J. Harrington, V.P. (Los Altos)
Herbert D. Doan (Midland)
James N. Hauslein, Inv. Analyst (Morristown)

Whom to Contact
Ian R.N. Bund
Philip E. McCarthy
James R. Weersing

Type of Firm
Private venture capital firm investing own capital
SBIC

Affiliations
MBW Venture Partners Limited Partnership (fund managed)
Michigan Investment Fund L.P. (fund managed)
Doan Resources Limited Partnership (fund managed)
Doan Associates (fund managed)

Project Preferences
Will function either as deal originator or investor in deals created by others
Type of Financing:
Startup
First-stage
Second-stage
Later-stage expansion
Leveraged buyout

Minimum Investment: $500,000
Preferred Investment: $500,000-$1 million
Preferred Investment (LBO): $1.5 million-$2 million
Minimum Operating Data:
Annual Sales (LBO)—$20 million-$100 million

Geographical Preference
None

Industry Preferences

Communications
Data communications
Computer Related
Computer graphics, CAD/CAM and CAE
Computer mainframes
Computer services
Memory devices
Micro and mini computers
Office automation
Scanning related
Software-applications
Software-artificial intelligence
Software-systems
Specialized turnkey systems
Terminals
Energy/Natural Resources
Alternative energy
Coal related
Drilling and exploration services
Energy conservation
Minerals
Oil and gas exploration and production
Technology related products/equipment
Genetic Engineering
Gene splicing and manufacturing equipment
Monoclonal antibodies and hybridomas
Recombinant DNA (agricultural and industrial)
Recombinant DNA (medical)
Industrial Products and Equipment
Other industrial automation
Robotics/vision systems
Medical/Health Related
Diagnostic equipment
Diagnostic test products
Disposable products
Drugs and medicines
Hospital and clinical labs
Medical services
Therapeutic equipment
Will Not Consider
Consumer products
Franchises
Real estate

Additional Information

Year Founded—1984
Capital Under Management—$125.6 million
Investments(1985-1st 6 months)—7
Invested(1985-1st 6 months)—$3.9 million
Method of Compensation—Return on
investment is of primary concern; do not
charge fees

MCCOWN DE LEEUW & CO.

3000 Sand Hill Road
Building 2, #220
Menlo Park, CA 94025
415-854-0850

Other Office

900 Third Avenue, 28th Floor
New York, NY 10022
212-418-6539

General Partners

George E. McCown (California)
David E. De Leeuw (New York)
Luis F. Solis, Assoc. (California)

Whom to Contact

Any of the above

Type of Firm

Private venture capital firm investing
own capital

Project Preferences

Prefer role as deal originator but will also
invest in deals created by others
Type of Financing:
Leveraged buyout
Preferred Investment (LBO):
$20 million-$75 million
Minimum Operating Data:
P&L—Profits NBT over $3 million
Annual Sales (LBO)—
$40 million-$200 million

Geographical Preference

National

Industry Preferences

None

Additional Information

Year Founded—1983
Method of Compensation—Return on
investment is most important, but also
charge for closing fees, service fees, etc.

MELCHOR VENTURE MANAGEMENT, INC.

170 State Street #220
Los Altos, CA 94022
415-941-6565

Officers

Jack L. Melchor, Pres.
Gregory S. Young, V.P.
Richard H. Frank, V.P.

Whom to Contact

Gregory S. Young
Richard H. Frank

Type of Firm

Private venture capital firm investing
own capital

Affiliation

Portola Venture Fund

Industry Association Membership

WAVC

Project Preferences

Prefer role as deal originator
Type of Financing:
Seed
Startup
First-stage
Minimum Investment: Less than $100,000
Preferred Investment: $250,000-$500,000
Minimum Operating Data:
Annual Sales—Nominal
P&L—Losses (profits projected after 2 years)

Geographical Preference

Within two hours of office

Industry Preferences

Communications
Commercial communications
Data communications
Satellite and microwave communications
Computer Related
Computer graphics, CAD/CAM and CAE
Computer mainframes
Computer services
Memory devices
Micro and mini computers
Office automation
Scanning related
Software-applications
Software-artificial intelligence
Software-systems
Specialized turnkey systems
Terminals
Electronic Components and Instrumentation
Analytical and scientific instrumentation
Component fabrication and testing
equipment
Electronic components
Fiber optics
Laser related
Semiconductors
Genetic Engineering
Gene splicing and manufacturing equipment
Monoclonal antibodies and hybridomas
Recombinant DNA (agricultural and
industrial)
Recombinant DNA (medical)
Industrial Products and Equipment
Controls and sensors
Other industrial automation
Robotics/vision systems
Medical/Health Related
Diagnostic equipment
Therapeutic equipment
Will Not Consider
Distribution
Natural resources
Real estate
Retail
Service businesses

Additional Information

Year Founded—1979
Capital Under Management—$20 million
Investments(1985-1st 6 months)—3
Invested(1985-1st 6 months)—$440,000
Method of Compensation—Return on
investment is of primary concern; do not
charge fees

MENLO VENTURES

3000 Sand Hill Road
Building 4, #100
Menlo Park, CA 94025
415-854-8540

Partners

H. DuBose Montgomery, Gen. Ptnr.
Ken E. Joy, Gen. Ptnr.
Richard P. Magnuson, Gen. Ptnr.
Douglas C. Carlisle, Gen. Ptnr.
Denise M. O'Leary, Assoc.
John W. Jarve, Assoc.

Whom to Contact

Any of the above

Type of Firm

Private venture capital firm investing
own capital

Industry Association Memberships
NASBIC
NVCA
WAVC

Project Preferences
Will function either as deal originator or
investor in deals created by others
Type of Financing:
Seed
Startup
First-stage
Second-stage
Later-stage expansion
Leveraged buyout
Minimum Investment: $250,000
Preferred Investment: Over $1 million
Preferred Investment (LBO):
$1 million-$5 million
Minimum Operating Data:
Annual Sales—Nominal
P&L—Losses (profits projected after 3 years)
Annual Sales (LBO)—Up to $150 million

Geographical Preference
National

Industry Preferences

Communications
Cable television
Commercial communications
Data communications
Satellite and microwave communications
Telephone related
Computer Related
Computer graphics, CAD/CAM and CAE
Computer mainframes
Computer services
Memory devices
Micro and mini computers
Office automation
Scanning related
Software-applications
Software-artificial intelligence
Software-systems
Specialized turnkey systems
Terminals
Consumer
Computer stores/related services
Consumer products
Consumer services
Food and beverage products
Franchise businesses
Leisure and recreational products
Restaurants
Retailing

Distribution
Communications equipment
Computer equipment
Consumer products
Electronics equipment
Food products
Industrial products
Medical products
**Electronic Components and
Instrumentation**
Analytical and scientific instrumentation
Component fabrication and testing
equipment
Electronic components
Fiber optics
Laser related
Semiconductors
Energy/Natural Resources
Technology related products/equipment
Genetic Engineering
Gene splicing and manufacturing equipment
Monoclonal antibodies and hybridomas
Recombinant DNA (agricultural and
industrial)
Recombinant DNA (medical)
Industrial Products and Equipment
Chemicals
Controls and sensors
Energy management
Equipment and machinery
Other industrial automation
Plastics
Robotics/vision systems
Specialty materials
Medical/Health Related
Diagnostic equipment
Diagnostic test products
Disposable products
Drugs and medicines
Hospital and clinical labs
Medical services
Therapeutic equipment
Other
Finance and insurance
Transportation

Additional Information
Year Founded—1976
Capital Under Management—$152 million
Investments(1985-1st 6 months)—9
Invested(1985-1st 6 months)—$9 million
Method of Compensation—Return on
investment is of primary concern; do not
charge fees

MERRILL, PICKARD, ANDERSON & EYRE

Two Palo Alto Square #425
Palo Alto, CA 94306
415-856-8880

General Partners
Steven L. Merrill
W. Jeffers Pickard
James C. Anderson
Chris A. Eyre
Stephen E. Coit

Whom to Contact
Any of the above

Type of Firm
Private venture capital firm investing
own capital

Industry Association Memberships
NASBIC
NVCA
WAVC

Project Preferences
Will function either as deal originator or
investor in deals created by others
Type of Financing:
Startup
First-stage
Second-stage
Leveraged buyout
Minimum Investment: $500,000
Preferred Investment: Over $1 million
Minimum Operating Data:
Annual Sales—Nominal
P&L—Losses (profits projected after 2 years)

Geographical Preferences
West Coast
Northeast

Industry Preferences

Communications
Commercial communications
Data communications
Satellite and microwave communications
Telephone related

Computer Related
Computer graphics, CAD/CAM and CAE
Computer mainframes
Computer services
Memory devices
Micro and mini computers
Office automation
Scanning related
Software-applications
Software-artificial intelligence
Software-systems
Specialized turnkey systems
Terminals
Distribution
Communications equipment
Computer equipment
Consumer products
Electronics equipment
Food products
Industrial products
Medical products
**Electronic Components and
Instrumentation**
Analytical and scientific instrumentation
Component fabrication and testing
equipment
Electronic components
Fiber optics
Laser related
Semiconductors
Genetic Engineering
Gene splicing and manufacturing equipment
Industrial Products and Equipment
Controls and sensors
Robotics/vision systems
Medical/Health Related
Diagnostic equipment
Diagnostic test products
Disposable products
Drugs and medicines
Hospital and clinical labs
Medical services
Therapeutic equipment
Will Not Consider
Finance companies
Real estate

Additional Information
Year Founded—1980
Capital Under Management—$90 million
Investments(1985-1st 6 months)—12
Invested(1985-1st 6 months)—$6.1 million
Method of Compensation—Return on
investment is of primary concern; do not
charge fees

METROPOLITAN VENTURE COMPANY, INC.

5757 Wilshire Boulevard #670
Los Angeles, CA 90036
213-938-3488

Officers
Rudolph J. Lowy, Chm.
Esther Lowy, Pres.

Whom to Contact
Esther Lowy

Type of Firm
SBIC

Project Preferences
Will function either as deal originator or
investor in deals created by others
Type of Financing:
Second-stage
Later-stage expansion
Leveraged buyout
Minimum Investment: Less than $100,000
Preferred Investment: $100,000-$250,000

Geographical Preference
Southwest

Industry Preferences

Distribution
Consumer products
Food products
Medical products
Other
Education related
Finance and insurance
Real estate
Specialty consulting

Additional Information
Year Founded—1980
Capital Under Management—$2 million
Investments(1985-1st 6 months)—4
Invested(1985-1st 6 months)—$395,000
Method of Compensation—Return on
investment is most important, but also
charge for closing fees, service fees, etc.

MICROTECHNOLOGY INVESTMENTS LTD.

46 Red Birch Court
Danville, CA 94526
415-838-9319

Other Office
3400 Comserv Drive
Eagan, MN 55122
612-681-7580

Officer
Marion Melvin Stuckey, Chm.

Type of Firm
Private venture capital firm investing
own capital

Affiliation
Control Data Corporation (shareholder)

Project Preferences
Will function either as deal originator or
investor in deals created by others
Type of Financing:
Startup
First-stage
Leveraged buyout
Minimum Investment: $100,000
Preferred Investment: $250,000-$500,000
Minimum Operating Data:
Annual Sales—Nominal
P&L—Losses (profits projected after 2 years)

Geographical Preferences
Midwest
West Coast

Industry Preferences

Communications
Data communications
Computer Related
Specialize in industry-specific business
application software for microcomputers
Consumer
Computer stores/related services
Distribution
Computer equipment
Will Not Consider
Non computer related businesses

Additional Information
Year Founded—1982
Investments(1985-1st 6 months)—2
Method of Compensation—Return on
investment is of primary concern; do not
charge fees

MOHR, DAVIDOW VENTURES

3000 Sand Hill Road
Building 4, #240
Menlo Park, CA 94025
415-854-7236

Partners
Lawrence G. Mohr, Jr., Gen. Ptnr.
William H. Davidow, Gen. Ptnr.
Peter A. Roshko, Assoc.

Whom to Contact
Any of the above

Type of Firm
Private venture capital firm investing own capital

Industry Association Membership
WAVC

Project Preferences
Prefer role as deal originator but will also invest in deals created by others
Type of Financing:
Seed
Research and development partnerships
Startup
First-stage
Second-stage
Minimum Investment: $250,000
Preferred Investment: $500,000-$1 million
Minimum Operating Data:
Annual Sales—Nominal

Geographical Preferences
Within two hours of office
West Coast

Industry Preferences

Communications
Commercial communications
Data communications
Satellite and microwave communications
Telephone related
Computer Related
Computer graphics, CAD/CAM and CAE
Computer mainframes
Computer services
Memory devices
Micro and mini computers
Office automation
Scanning related
Software-applications
Software-artificial intelligence
Software-systems
Specialized turnkey systems
Terminals

Electronic Components and Instrumentation
Analytical and scientific instrumentation
Component fabrication and testing equipment
Electronic components
Fiber optics
Laser related
Semiconductors
Industrial Products and Equipment
Chemicals
Controls and sensors
Energy management
Equipment and machinery
Other industrial automation
Plastics
Robotics/vision systems
Specialty materials
Medical/Health Related
Diagnostic equipment
Diagnostic test products
Disposable products
Drugs and medicines
Hospital and clinical labs
Medical services
Therapeutic equipment

Additional Information
Year Founded—1983
Method of Compensation—Return on investment is of primary concern; do not charge fees

---

MONTGOMERY ASSOCIATES INC.

600 Montgomery Street
Post Office Box 2230
San Francisco, CA 94126
415-421-4200

Officer
Allen P. McKee, Pres.

Type of Firm
Private venture capital firm investing own capital

Industry Association Membership
WAVC

Project Preferences
Prefer role as deal originator but will also invest in deals created by others
Type of Financing:
Seed
Startup
First-stage

Minimum Investment: Less than $100,000
Preferred Investment: $250,000-$500,000
Minimum Operating Data:
Annual Sales—Nominal
P&L—Losses (profits projected after 2 years)

Geographical Preference
Within two hours of office

Industry Preferences

Communications
Commercial communications
Satellite and microwave communications
Telephone related
Consumer
Consumer products
Consumer services
Food and beverage products
Franchise businesses
Hotels and resort areas
Leisure and recreational products
Electronic Components and Instrumentation
Analytical and scientific instrumentation
Component fabrication and testing equipment
Electronic components
Fiber optics
Laser related
Semiconductors
Energy/Natural Resources
Alternative energy
Minerals
Oil and gas exploration and production
Technology related products/equipment
Industrial Products and Equipment
Chemicals
Controls and sensors
Energy management
Equipment and machinery
Other industrial automation
Plastics
Robotics/vision systems
Specialty materials
Medical/Health Related
Diagnostic equipment
Medical services
Therapeutic equipment
Other
Real estate

Additional Information
Year Founded—1979
Capital Under Management—$4 million
Investments(1985-1st 6 months)—2
Invested(1985-1st 6 months)—$650,000
Method of Compensation—Return on investment is of primary concern; do not charge fees

MONTGOMERY BRIDGE FUNDS

600 Montgomery Street
San Francisco, CA 94111
415-627-2000

Other Office
Montgomery Securities
26 rue du Mont-Blanc
1201 Geneva, Switzerland

General Partner
Montgomery Securities
Thomas W. Weisel, Sr. Ptnr.
James L. Pelkey, Gen. Ptnr.
Linda S. Gordon, Gen. Ptnr.
Harold O. Shattuck, Sr. Assoc.
Syed Z. Shariq, Sr. Assoc.
Richard H. Kimball, Assoc.
Gwen J. Gepfert, Assoc.

Whom to Contact
James L. Pelkey
Linda S. Gordon

Type of Firm
Investment banking or merchant banking firm investing own capital or funds of partners or clients

Industry Association Membership
NVCA

Project Preferences
Will function either as deal originator or investor in deals created by others
Type of Financing:
Second-stage
Later-stage expansion
Minimum Investment: $500,000
Preferred Investment: Over $1 million
Minimum Operating Data:
Annual Sales—$500,000
P&L—Losses (profits projected after 1 year)

Geographical Preference
None

Industry Preferences

Computer Related
Computer integrated manufacturing
Other
Financial services
Will Not Consider
Oil and gas
Real estate

Additional Information
Year Founded—1969
Capital Under Management—$100 million
Investments(1985-1st 6 months)—10
Invested(1985-1st 6 months)—$6.3 million
Method of Compensation—Return on investment is of primary concern; do not charge fees

---

MONTGOMERY MEDICAL VENTURES

600 Montgomery Street
San Francisco, CA 94111
415-627-2000

General Partner
Montgomery Medical Partnership
Jack Olshansky, Ptnr.
Richard D. Propper, M.D., Ptnr.
Montgomery Securities, Ptnr.
Thomas W. Weisel, Sr. Ptnr.
W. Robert Friedman, Jr., Ptnr.
Stephen J. Sogin, Ph.D., Ptnr.
Steve Weiss, Assoc.
Alan Kittner, Assoc.
Stephen Wong, Assoc.

Whom to Contact
Richard D. Propper, M.D.
Jack Olshansky

Type of Firm
Investment banking or merchant banking firm investing own capital or funds of partners or clients

Industry Association Membership
NVCA

Project Preferences
Prefer role as deal originator but will also invest in deals created by others
Type of Financing:
Seed
Startup
First-stage
Minimum Investment: $500,000
Preferred Investment: $500,000-$1 million
Minimum Operating Data:
Annual Sales—Nominal

Geographical Preference
None

Industry Preferences

Distribution
Medical products
Genetic Engineering
Monoclonal antibodies and hybridomas
Recombinant DNA (medical)
Medical/Health Related
Diagnostic equipment
Diagnostic test products
Disposable products
Drugs and medicines
Hospital and clinical labs
Medical services
Therapeutic equipment
Will Not Consider
Non health care companies

Additional Information
Year Founded—1969
Capital Under Management—$50.6 million
Investments(1985-1st 6 months)—7
Invested(1985-1st 6 months)—$4 million
Method of Compensation—Return on investment is of primary concern; do not charge fees

---

NATIONAL INVESTMENT MANAGEMENT, INC.

23133 Hawthorne Boulevard #300
Torrance, CA 90505
213-373-8944

General Partners
Richard D. Robins
Kenneth R. Finn

Whom to Contact
Richard D. Robins

Type of Firm
Private venture capital firm investing own capital

Affiliation
Lombard Sycamore Fund (institutional partnership)

Project Preferences
Prefer role as deal originator
Type of Financing:
Later-stage expansion
Leveraged buyout
Minimum Investment: $250,000
Preferred Investment: $250,000-$500,000
Preferred Investment (LBO): $500,000
Minimum Operating Data:
Annual Sales—Over $3 million
P&L—Break even
Annual Sales (LBO)—$10 million-$100 million

Geographical Preference
National

Industry Preferences

Communications
Commercial communications
Data communications
Consumer
Consumer products
Food and beverage products
Leisure and recreational products
Retailing
Distribution
Building products
Electronics equipment
Food products
Industrial products
Medical products
Electronic Components and Instrumentation
Analytical and scientific instrumentation
Industrial Products and Equipment
Equipment and machinery
Other industrial automation
Specialty materials
Medical/Health Related
Diagnostic equipment
Diagnostic test products
Disposable products
Hospital and clinical labs
Medical services
Other
Office supplies manufacturing
Publishing

Additional Information
Year Founded—1977
Capital Under Management—$10 million
Investments(1985-1st 6 months)—2
Invested(1985-1st 6 months)—$750,000
Method of Compensation—Return on investment is of primary concern; do not charge fees

---

NELSON CAPITAL CORPORATION

10000 Santa Monica Boulevard
Suite 300
Los Angeles, CA 90067
213-556-1944

Norman Tulchin, Chm.

See NEW YORK for full listing

NEST VENTURE PARTNERS

1086 East Meadow Circle
Palo Alto, CA 94303
415-493-0921

General Partners
Joe D. Giulie
Gary W. Almond
Reid Rutherford

Whom to Contact
Gary W. Almond

Type of Firm
Private venture capital firm investing own capital

Project Preferences
Prefer role as deal originator
Type of Financing:
Seed
Startup
Leveraged buyout
Minimum Investment: Less than $100,000
Preferred Investment: $100,000-$250,000
Minimum Operating Data:
Annual Sales—Nominal

Geographical Preference
Within two hours of office

Industry Preferences

Communications
Commercial communications
Data communications
Satellite and microwave communications
Computer Related
Computer graphics, CAD/CAM and CAE
Computer services
Office automation
Scanning related
Software-applications
Software-artificial intelligence
Software-systems
Specialized turnkey systems
Consumer
Consumer products
Consumer services
Food and beverage products
Distribution
Communications equipment
Computer equipment
Consumer products
Electronics equipment
Food products
Industrial products
Medical products

Electronic Components and Instrumentation
Analytical and scientific instrumentation
Component fabrication and testing equipment
Electronic components
Fiber optics
Laser related
Energy/Natural Resources
Technology related products/equipment
Genetic Engineering
Monoclonal antibodies and hybridomas
Industrial Products and Equipment
Controls and sensors
Equipment and machinery
Plastics
Robotics/vision systems
Medical/Health Related
Diagnostic equipment
Diagnostic test products
Disposable products
Drugs and medicines
Medical services
Therapeutic equipment
Other
Education related

Additional Information
Year Founded—1983
Method of Compensation—Return on investment is of primary concern; do not charge fees

---

NEW ENTERPRISE ASSOCIATES

235 Montgomery Street #1025
San Francisco, CA 94104
415-956-1579

Other Offices

1119 Saint Paul Street
Baltimore, MD 21202
301-244-0115

3000 Sand Hill Road
Bldg. 2, #210
Menlo Park, CA 94025
415-854-2660

Partners

C. Richard Kramlich, Mgn. Gen. Ptnr.
  (San Francisco)
Cornelius C. Bond, Jr., Gen. Ptnr.
  (San Francisco)
C. Woodrow Rea, Jr., Gen. Ptnr.
  (Menlo Park)
Frank A. Bonsal, Jr., Gen. Ptnr. (Baltimore)
Arthur J. Marks, Gen. Ptnr. (Baltimore)
Curran W. Harvey, Special Ptnr. (Baltimore)
Raymond L. Bank, Assoc. (Baltimore)
Thomas C. McConnell, Assoc.
  (San Francisco)
John W. Glynn, Special Ptnr. (Menlo Park)
Howard D. Wolfe, Jr., Special Ptnr.
  (Baltimore)

Whom to Contact

Any of the above

Type of Firm

Private venture capital firm investing
  own capital

Affiliation

Southwest Enterprise Associates (affiliated
  venture capital partnership)

Industry Association Memberships

NVCA
WAVC

Project Preferences

Will function either as deal originator or
  investor in deals created by others
Type of Financing:
Seed
Startup
First-stage
Second-stage
Leveraged buyout

Minimum Investment: $250,000
Preferred Investment: $500,000-$1 million
Minimum Operating Data:
Annual Sales—Nominal
P&L—Losses (profits projected after 3 years)

Geographical Preferences

Southwest
East Coast
West Coast

Industry Preferences

Communications
Commercial communications
Data communications
Satellite and microwave communications
Telephone related
Computer Related
Computer graphics, CAD/CAM and CAE
Computer mainframes
Computer services
Memory devices
Office automation
Scanning related
Software-applications
Software-artificial intelligence
Software-systems
Specialized turnkey systems
Consumer
Computer stores/related services
Consumer products
Consumer services
Leisure and recreational products
Retailing
**Electronic Components and
  Instrumentation**
Analytical and scientific instrumentation
Component fabrication and testing
  equipment
Electronic components
Fiber optics
Government electronics
Laser related
Semiconductors
Genetic Engineering
Recombinant DNA (agricultural and
  industrial)
Industrial Products and Equipment
Robotics/vision systems
Specialty materials
Medical/Health Related
Diagnostic equipment
Diagnostic test products
Disposable products
Medical services
Other
Finance and insurance

Additional Information

Year Founded—1977
Capital Under Management—$213 million
Investments(1985-1st 6 months)—49
Invested(1985-1st 6 months)—$24.8 million
Method of Compensation—Return on
  investment is of primary concern; do not
  charge fees

NEW WEST VENTURES

4350 Executive Drive #206
San Diego, CA 92121
619-457-0722

Other Office

4600 Campus Drive #103
Newport Beach, CA 92660
714-756-8940

Partner

Tim Haidinger

Type of Firm

SBIC

Industry Association Membership

NASBIC

Project Preferences

Will function either as deal originator or
  investor in deals created by others
Type of Financing:
Second-stage
Later-stage expansion
Leveraged buyout
Minimum Investment: $500,000
Preferred Investment: Over $1 million
Preferred Investment (LBO): Over $1 million
Minimum Operating Data:
Annual Sales—$1.5 million
P&L—Break even
Annual Sales (LBO)—$5 million and over

Geographical Preference

None

Industry Preferences

Communications
Cable television
Commercial communications
Data communications
Satellite and microwave communications
Telephone related

Computer Related
Computer graphics, CAD/CAM and CAE
Computer mainframes
Computer services
Memory devices
Micro and mini computers
Office automation
Scanning related
Software-applications
Software-artificial intelligence
Software-systems
Specialized turnkey systems
Terminals
Consumer
Computer stores/related services
Consumer products
Franchise businesses
Leisure and recreational products
Restaurants
Retailing
Distribution
Communications equipment
Computer equipment
Consumer products
Electronics equipment
Food products
Industrial products
Medical products
Electronic Components and Instrumentation
Analytical and scientific instrumentation
Component fabrication and testing equipment
Electronic components
Fiber optics
Laser related
Semiconductors
Industrial Products and Equipment
Chemicals
Controls and sensors
Energy management
Equipment and machinery
Other industrial automation
Plastics
Robotics/vision systems
Specialty materials
Medical/Health Related
Diagnostic equipment
Diagnostic test products
Disposable products
Drugs and medicines
Hospital and clinical labs
Medical services
Therapeutic equipment
Other
Transportation
Will Not Consider
Motion pictures
Natural resources
Real estate

Additional Information
Year Founded—1982
Capital Under Management—$5 million
Investments(1985-1st 6 months)—6
Invested(1985-1st 6 months)—$1 million
Method of Compensation—Return on investment is of primary concern; do not charge fees

NEWTEK VENTURES
500 Washington Street #720
San Francisco, CA 94111
415-986-5711

Other Office
3000 Sand Hill Road
Building 4, #190
Menlo Park, CA 94025
415-854-5731

General Partners
Peter J. Wardle (San Francisco)
Barry M. Weinman (Menlo Park)

Whom to Contact
Either of the above

Type of Firm
Private venture capital firm investing own capital

Industry Association Membership
WAVC

Project Preferences
Will function either as deal originator or investor in deals created by others
Type of Financing:
Seed
Startup
First-stage
Second-stage
Leveraged buyout
Minimum Investment: Less than $100,000
Preferred Investment: $250,000-$500,000
Minimum Operating Data:
Annual Sales—Nominal
P&L—Break even

Geographical Preferences
West Coast
Southwest
Midwest
Rocky Mountains

Industry Preferences

Communications
Cable television
Commercial communications
Data communications
Satellite and microwave communications
Telephone related
Computer Related
Computer graphics, CAD/CAM and CAE
Computer mainframes
Computer services
Memory devices
Micro and mini computers
Office automation
Scanning related
Software-applications
Software-artificial intelligence
Software-systems
Specialized turnkey systems
Terminals
Electronic Components and Instrumentation
Analytical and scientific instrumentation
Component fabrication and testing equipment
Electronic components
Fiber optics
Laser related
Semiconductors
Energy/Natural Resources
Alternative energy
Technology related products/equipment
Genetic Engineering
Gene splicing and manufacturing equipment
Monoclonal antibodies and hybridomas
Recombinant DNA (agricultural and industrial)
Recombinant DNA (medical)
Industrial Products and Equipment
Controls and sensors
Energy management
Other industrial automation
Robotics/vision systems
Medical/Health Related
Diagnostic equipment
Diagnostic test products
Disposable products
Drugs and medicines
Hospital and clinical labs
Medical services
Therapeutic equipment
Will Not Consider
Consumer related businesses
Distribution businesses

Additional Information

Year Founded—1983
Capital Under Management—$24.3 million
Investments(1985-1st 6 months)—6
Invested(1985-1st 6 months)—$2.6 million
Method of Compensation—Return on investment is of primary concern; do not charge fees

NORTH AMERICAN VENTURES FUNDS

c/o International Nickel, Inc.
2099 Gateway Plaza
San Jose, CA 95110
408-993-9594

R. Couch, Sr. V.P.

See ONTARIO for full listing

OAK GROVE VENTURES

173 Jefferson Drive
Menlo Park, CA 94025
415-324-2276

Other Office

2234 Beach Street
San Francisco, CA 94123
415-563-6336

General Partners

Paul M. Cook
James J. Hornthal
Duane C. Montopoli

Whom to Contact

Duane C. Montopoli (Menlo Park)
James J. Hornthal (San Francisco)

Type of Firm

Private venture capital firm investing own capital

Industry Association Membership

WAVC

Project Preferences

Will function either as deal originator or investor in deals created by others
Type of Financing:
Seed
Startup
First-stage
Minimum Investment: $100,000
Preferred Investment: $300,000-$600,000

Minimum Operating Data:
Annual Sales—Nominal
P&L—Losses (profits projected after 2 years)

Geographical Preference

West Coast

Industry Preferences

Communications
Data communications
Satellite and microwave communications
Computer Related
Computer graphics, CAD/CAM and CAE
Computer services
Office automation
Software-systems
Distribution
Computer equipment
Electronic Components and Instrumentation
Analytical and scientific instrumentation
Fiber optics
Laser related
Genetic Engineering
Recombinant DNA (agricultural and industrial)
Recombinant DNA (medical)
Industrial Products and Equipment
Chemicals
Specialty materials
Medical/Health Related
Diagnostic equipment
Medical services
Will Not Consider
Energy
Real estate
Retail

Additional Information

Year Founded—1972
Capital Under Management—$15 million
Investments(1985-1st 6 months)—2
Invested(1985-1st 6 months)—$600,000
Method of Compensation—Return on investment is of primary concern; do not charge fees

OAK INVESTMENT PARTNERS

2055 Gateway Place #550
San Jose, CA 95110
408-286-5233

Catherine A. Pierson
Jeffrey D. West

See CONNECTICUT for full listing

ONSET

Four Palo Alto Square #270
Palo Alto, CA 94306
415-424-8725

General Partners

Terry L. Opdendyk
Robert F. Graham
David M. Kelley

Whom to Contact

Any of the above

Type of Firm

Private venture capital firm investing own capital

Affiliations

Mayfield Fund
New Enterprise Associates
Kleiner Perkins Caufield & Byers

Industry Association Membership

WAVC

Project Preferences

Prefer role as deal originator
Type of Financing:
Seed
Minimum Investment: $100,000
Preferred Investment: $250,000-$500,000
Minimum Operating Data:
Annual Sales—Nominal
P&L—Losses (profits projected after 2 years)

Geographical Preference

Within two hours of office

Industry Preferences

Communications
Commercial communications
Data communications
Satellite and microwave communications
Telephone related
Computer Related
Computer graphics, CAD/CAM and CAE
Computer mainframes
Computer services
Memory devices
Micro and mini computers
Office automation
Scanning related
Software-applications
Software-artificial intelligence
Software-systems
Specialized turnkey systems
Terminals

**Electronic Components and
  Instrumentation**
Analytical and scientific instrumentation
Component fabrication and testing
  equipment
Electronic components
Fiber optics
Laser related
Semiconductors
Energy/Natural Resources
Technology related products/equipment
Genetic Engineering
Gene splicing and manufacturing equipment
Monoclonal antibodies and hybridomas
Recombinant DNA (agricultural and
  industrial)
Recombinant DNA (medical)
Industrial Products and Equipment
Chemicals
Controls and sensors
Energy management
Equipment and machinery
Other industrial automation
Plastics
Robotics/vision systems
Specialty materials
Medical/Health Related
Diagnostic equipment
Diagnostic test products
Disposable products
Therapeutic equipment

Additional Information

Year Founded—1984
Capital Under Management—$5 million
Investments(1985-1st 6 months)—3
Invested(1985-1st 6 months)—$1 million
Method of Compensation—Return on
  investment is of primary concern; do not
  charge fees

ORANGE NASSAU

Westerley Place #540
1500 Quail Street
Newport Beach, CA 92660
714-752-7811

John W. Blackburn, V.P.
David P. Carmack, Inv. Analyst

See MASSACHUSETTS for full listing

OSCCO VENTURES

3000 Sand Hill Road
Building 4, #140
Menlo Park, CA 94025
415-854-2222

General Partners

F. Ward Paine
Stephen E. Halprin
James G. Rudolph

Whom to Contact

Any of the above

Type of Firm

Private venture capital firm investing
  own capital

Project Preferences

Prefer role as deal originator but will also
  invest in deals created by others
Type of Financing:
Seed
First-stage
Second-stage
Leveraged buyout
Minimum Investment: $100,000
Preferred Investment: $500,000-$1 million
Minimum Operating Data:
Annual Sales—Nominal
P&L—Losses (profits projected after 2 years)

Geographical Preferences

Within two hours of office
West Coast
Northwest
Southwest
Rocky Mountains

Industry Preferences

Communications
Cable television
Commercial communications
Data communications
Satellite and microwave communications
Telephone related

Computer Related
Computer graphics, CAD/CAM and CAE
Computer mainframes
Computer services
Memory devices
Micro and mini computers
Office automation
Scanning related
Software-applications
Software-artificial intelligence
Software-systems
Specialized turnkey systems
Terminals
**Electronic Components and
  Instrumentation**
Analytical and scientific instrumentation
Component fabrication and testing
  equipment
Electronic components
Fiber optics
Laser related
Semiconductors
Energy/Natural Resources
Alternative energy
Drilling and exploration services
Energy conservation
Technology related products/equipment
Genetic Engineering
Gene splicing and manufacturing equipment
Monoclonal antibodies and hybridomas
Recombinant DNA (agricultural and
  industrial)
Recombinant DNA (medical)
Industrial Products and Equipment
Chemicals
Controls and sensors
Energy management
Equipment and machinery
Other industrial automation
Plastics
Robotics/vision systems
Specialty materials
Will Not Consider
Consumer products
Real estate
Retail sales

Additional Information

Year Founded—1962
Capital Under Management—$30 million
Investments(1985-1st 6 months)—3
Invested(1985-1st 6 months)—$1.2 million

OXFORD VENTURE CORPORATION

233 Wilshire Boulevard #730
Santa Monica, CA 90401
213-458-3135

Other Office
Soundview Plaza
1266 Main Street
Stamford, CT 06902
203-964-0592

Partners
Kenneth W. Rind, Gen. Ptnr. (Connecticut)
Cornelius T. Ryan, Gen. Ptnr. (Connecticut)
William R. Lonergan, Gen. Ptnr.
   (Connecticut)
Francis X. Driscoll, Gen. Ptnr. (Connecticut)
Stevan A. Birnbaum, Gen. Ptnr. (California)
Janice K. DeLong, Assoc. (Connecticut)
Bonnie J. Renta, Res. Analyst (California)
Elizabeth B. Smith, Res. Asst. (Connecticut)

Whom to Contact
Janice K. Delong
Bonnie J. Renta

Type of Firm
Private venture capital firm investing
   own capital

Industry Association Memberships
NASBIC
NVCA

Project Preferences
Will function either as deal originator or
   investor in deals created by others
Type of Financing:
Startup
First-stage
Second-stage
Later-stage expansion
Leveraged buyout
Minimum Investment: $500,000
Preferred Investment: $500,000-$1 million
Minimum Operating Data:
Annual Sales—Nominal
P&L—Losses (profits projected after 3 years)

Geographical Preference
None

Industry Preferences

Communications
Cable television
Commercial communications
Data communications
Satellite and microwave communications
Telephone related

Computer Related
Computer graphics, CAD/CAM and CAE
Computer mainframes
Computer services
Memory devices
Micro and mini computers
Office automation
Scanning related
Software-applications
Software-artificial intelligence
Software-systems
Specialized turnkey systems
Terminals
Distribution
Communications equipment
Computer equipment
Consumer products
Electronics equipment
Food products
Industrial products
Medical products
**Electronic Components and
   Instrumentation**
Analytical and scientific instrumentation
Component fabrication and testing
   equipment
Electronic components
Fiber optics
Laser related
Semiconductors
Energy/Natural Resources
Alternative energy
Genetic Engineering
Gene splicing and manufacturing equipment
Monoclonal antibodies and hybridomas
Recombinant DNA (agricultural and
   industrial)
Recombinant DNA (medical)
Industrial Products and Equipment
Chemicals
Controls and sensors
Energy management
Equipment and machinery
Other industrial automation
Plastics
Robotics/vision systems
Specialty materials
Medical/Health Related
Diagnostic equipment
Diagnostic test products
Disposable products
Drugs and medicines
Hospital and clinical labs
Medical services
Therapeutic equipment

Additional Information
Year Founded—1981
Capital Under Management—$100 million
Investments(1985-1st 6 months)—10
Invested(1985-1st 6 months)—$3.7 million
Method of Compensation—Return on
   investment is of primary concern; do not
   charge fees

PACIFIC ASSET PARTNERS

655 Montgomery Street #1410
San Francisco, CA 94111
415-362-6117

General Partners
Bob Stafford
Bob Sutton
Tony Hooker

Whom to Contact
Bob Stafford

Type of Firm
Private venture capital firm investing
   own capital

Project Preferences
Prefer role in deals created by others
Type of Financing:
Later-stage expansion
Leveraged buyout
Purchases of secondary positions
Minimum Investment: Less than $100,000
Preferred Investment: $100,000-$250,000
Preferred Investment (LBO):
   $100,000-$250,000
Minimum Operating Data:
Annual Sales—Over $3 million
P&L—Break even
Annual Sales (LBO)—$10 million-$50 million

Geographical Preference
Within two hours of office

Industry Preferences
None

Additional Information
Year Founded—1983
Capital Under Management—$18 million
Investments(1985-1st 6 months)—4
Invested(1985-1st 6 months)—$450,000
Method of Compensation—Return on
   investment is of primary concern; do not
   charge fees

PACIFIC CAPITAL FUND

675 Mariner's Island Boulevard
Suite 103
San Mateo, CA 94404
415-574-4747

Officers
Jose B. Colayco, Chm.
Eduardo B. Cu Unjieng, Pres.
Gina Maria C. Guerrero, Inv. Officer

Whom to Contact
Gina Marie C. Guerrero

Type of Firm
MESBIC

Affiliations
PCF Holdings, Inc. (parent)
PCF Venture Capital Corporation

Industry Association Memberships
AAMESBIC
NASBIC

Project Preferences
Will function either as deal originator or
investor in deals created by others
Type of Financing:
First-stage
Second-stage
Later-stage expansion
Leveraged buyout
Minimum Investment: Less than $100,000
Preferred Investment: Less than $250,000
Minimum Operating Data:
Annual Sales—Nominal
P&L—Losses (profits projected after 1 year)

Geographical Preferences
Within two hours of office
West Coast

Industry Preferences

Communications
Commercial communications
Data communications
Computer Related
Memory devices
Consumer
Food and beverage products
Leisure and recreational products
Restaurants
Distribution
Consumer products
Food products
**Electronic Components and
Instrumentation**
Analytical and scientific instrumentation

Genetic Engineering
Gene splicing and manufacturing equipment
Monoclonal antibodies and hybridomas
Recombinant DNA (agricultural and
industrial)
Recombinant DNA (medical)
Medical/Health Related
Diagnostic equipment
Other
Finance and insurance

Additional Information
Year Founded—1981
Capital Under Management—$3 million
Method of Compensation—Return on
investment is most important, but also
charge for closing fees, service fees, etc.

PACIFIC VENTURE PARTNERS

3000 Sand Hill Road
Building 4, #175
Menlo Park, CA 94025
415-854-2266

General Partners
James C. Balderston
Rigdon Currie
Anthony T. Ellis

Whom to Contact
Any of the above

Type of Firm
Private venture capital firm investing
own capital

Project Preferences
Will function either as deal originator or
investor in deals created by others
Type of Financing:
Startup
First-stage
Second-stage
Leveraged buyout
Minimum Investment: $100,000
Preferred Investment: $250,000-$1 million
Minimum Operating Data:
Annual Sales—Nominal

Geographical Preference
West Coast

Industry Preferences

Communications
Commercial communications
Data communications
Satellite and microwave communications
Telephone related
Computer Related
Computer graphics, CAD/CAM and CAE
Computer mainframes
Computer services
Memory devices
Micro and mini computers
Office automation
Scanning related
Software-applications
Software-artificial intelligence
Software-systems
Specialized turnkey systems
Terminals
Distribution
Communications equipment
Computer equipment
Consumer products
Electronics equipment
Food products
Industrial products
Medical products
**Electronic Components and
Instrumentation**
Analytical and scientific instrumentation
Component fabrication and testing
equipment
Electronic components
Fiber optics
Laser related
Semiconductors
Genetic Engineering
Gene splicing and manufacturing equipment
Monoclonal antibodies and hybridomas
Recombinant DNA (agricultural and
industrial)
Recombinant DNA (medical)
Industrial Products and Equipment
Controls and sensors
Other industrial automation
Robotics/vision systems
Medical/Health Related
Diagnostic equipment
Diagnostic test products
Disposable products
Drugs and medicines
Hospital and clinical labs
Medical services
Therapeutic equipment

Additional Information

Year Founded—1983
Capital Under Management—$15.2 million
Investments(1985-1st 6 months)—12
Invested(1985-1st 6 months)—$1.5 million

PARAGON PARTNERS

3000 Sand Hill Road
Building 2, #190
Menlo Park, CA 94025
415-854-8000

Partners

Robert F. Kibble, Gen. Ptnr.
John S. Lewis, Gen. Ptnr.
Jess R. Marzak, Gen. Ptnr.
Palyn Partners, Gen. Ptnr.
  Maxwell O. Paley
  Robert J. Domenico
  Michael J. Flynn, Ph.D.
  George E. Rossmann, Ph.D

Whom to Contact

Any of the above

Type of Firm

Private venture capital firm investing
  own capital

Industry Association Memberships

NVCA
WAVC

Project Preferences

Prefer role as deal originator but will also
  invest in deals created by others
Type of Financing:
Seed
Startup
First-stage
Second-stage
Later-stage expansion
Leveraged buyout
Minimum Investment: $300,000
Preferred Investment: $750,000-$1.5 million
Minimum Operating Data:
Annual Sales—Nominal
P&L—Losses (profits projected after 2 years)

Geographical Preference

National

Industry Preferences

Communications

Commercial communications
Data communications
Satellite and microwave communications
Telephone related

Computer Related

Computer graphics, CAD/CAM and CAE
Computer mainframes
Computer services
Memory devices
Micro and mini computers
Office automation
Scanning related
Software-applications
Software-artificial intelligence
Software-systems
Specialized turnkey systems
Terminals

Consumer

Computer stores/related services
Consumer services

Distribution

Communications equipment
Computer equipment
Electronics equipment
Medical products

Electronic Components and Instrumentation

Analytical and scientific instrumentation
Component fabrication and testing
  equipment
Electronic components
Fiber optics
Laser related
Semiconductors

Energy/Natural Resources

Drilling and exploration services
Oil and gas exploration
Technology related products/equipment

Genetic Engineering

Gene splicing and manufacturing equipment
Monoclonal antibodies and hybridomas
Recombinant DNA (agricultural and
  industrial)
Recombinant DNA (medical)

Industrial Products and Equipment

Chemicals
Controls and sensors
Energy management
Equipment and machinery
Other industrial automation
Plastics
Robotics/vision systems
Specialty materials

Medical/Health Related

Diagnostic equipment
Diagnostic test products
Disposable products
Drugs and medicines
Hospital and clinical labs
Medical services
Therapeutic equipment

Will Not Consider

Entertainment
Financial or consulting services
Publishing
Real estate

Additional Information

Year Founded—1984
Capital Under Management—$40 million
Investments(1985-1st 6 months)—6
Invested(1985-1st 6 months)—$5.3 million
Method of Compensation—Return on
  investment is of primary concern; do not
  charge fees

PARIBAS TECHNOLOGY

101 California Street #3150
San Francisco, CA 94111
415-788-2929

Other Offices

3, rue d'Antin
75002 Paris
France
331-298-0560

Yurakucho Denki Building
1-7-1 Yurakucho Chiyoda-Ku
CPO Box 20
Tokyo 100-71, Japan
813-201-4335

Principals

Thomas G. McKinley (United States)
Vincent Worms (United States)
Michel Jaugey (France)
Robert Lattes (France)
Tadahisa Ota (Japan)

Whom to Contact

Any of the above

Type of Firm

Private venture capital firm investing
  own capital

Affiliation

Banque Paribas, France (special limited
  partner)

Industry Association Membership
WAVC

Project Preferences
Will function either as deal originator or investor in deals created by others
Type of Financing:
Seed
Startup
First-stage
Second-stage
Leveraged buyout
Minimum Investment: $250,000
Preferred Investment: $500,000-$1 million
Minimum Operating Data:
Annual Sales—Nominal

Geographical Preference
None

Industry Preferences

Communications
Cable television
Commercial communications
Data communications
Satellite and microwave communications
Telephone related
Computer Related
Computer graphics, CAD/CAM and CAE
Computer mainframes
Computer services
Memory devices
Micro and mini computers
Office automation
Software-applications
Software-systems
Terminals
Distribution
Communications equipment
Computer equipment
Electronic Components and Instrumentation
Analytical and scientific instrumentation
Electronic components
Fiber optics
Laser related
Semiconductors
Energy/Natural Resources
Technology related products/equipment
Genetic Engineering
Monoclonal antibodies and hybridomas
Recombinant DNA (agricultural and industrial)
Recombinant DNA (medical)
Research and manufacturing equipment
Industrial Products and Equipment
Other industrial automation
Robotics/vision systems
Specialty materials

Medical/Health Related
Diagnostic equipment
Drugs and medicines
Hospital and clinical labs
Medical services
Therapeutic equipment
Other
Education related
Will Not Consider
Real estate

Additional Information
Year Founded—1981
Capital Under Management—$75 million
Investments(1985-1st 6 months)—6
Invested(1985-1st 6 months)—$3 million
Method of Compensation—Return on investment is of primary concern; do not charge fees

---

ALAN PATRICOF ASSOCIATES, INC.

1245 Oakmead Parkway #105
Sunnyvale, CA 94086
408-737-8788

W.R. Bottoms, Sr. V.P.
Camilla Jackson, Assoc.

See NEW YORK for full listing

PCF VENTURE CAPITAL CORP.

675 Mariner's Island Boulevard
Suite 103
San Mateo, CA 94404
415-574-4747

Officers
Eduardo B. Cu Unjieng, Pres.
Gina Marie Guerrero, Inv. Assoc.

Whom to Contact
Either of the above

Type of Firm
SBIC

Affiliation
Pacific Capital Corporation (MESBIC sister company)

Industry Association Membership
NASBIC

Project Preferences
Will function either as deal originator or investor in deals created by others
Type of Financing:
Second-stage
Later-stage expansion
Leveraged buyout
Minimum Investment: Less than $100,000
Preferred Investment: $100,000-$250,000
Minimum Operating Data:
Annual Sales—$750,000
P&L—Losses (profits projected after 1 year)

Geographical Preference
California

Industry Preferences

Communications
Commercial communications
Data communications
Telephone related
Consumer
Consumer products
Consumer services
Food and beverage products
Franchise businesses
Leisure and recreational products
Restaurants
Distribution
Communications equipment
Consumer products
Electronics equipment
Food products
Industrial Products and Equipment
Controls and sensors
Equipment and machinery
Other industrial automation
Medical/Health Related
Disposable products
Therapeutic equipment
Other
Agriculture, forestry, fishing
Finance and insurance
Real estate

Additional Information
Year Founded—1982
Capital Under Management—$3 million
Method of Compensation—Return on investment is most important, but also charge for closing fees, service fees, etc.

PEREGRINE ASSOCIATES/ MONTGOMERY VENTURES

606 Wilshire Boulevard #602
Santa Monica, CA 90401
213-458-1441

20833 Stevens Creek Boulevard
Cupertino, CA 95014
408-996-7212

Partners
Robert Crane, Ltd. Ptnr. (Cupertino)
Frank LaHaye, Gen. Ptnr. (Cupertino)
Gene Miller, Gen. Ptnr. (Santa Monica)
John Spence, Ltd. Ptnr. (Santa Monica)

Whom to Contact
Robert Crane
John Spence

Type of Firm
Private venture capital firm investing own capital

Project Preferences
Will function either as deal originator or investor in deals created by others
Type of Financing:
Startup
First-stage
Second-stage
Later-stage expansion
Leveraged buyout
Minimum Investment: $100,000
Preferred Investment: Over $1 million
Minimum Operating Data:
Annual Sales—Nominal

Geographical Preferences
West Coast
Northeast
Northwest
Southwest
Rocky Mountains

Industry Preferences

Communications
Cable television
Commercial communications
Data communications
Satellite and microwave communications
Telephone related

Computer Related
Computer graphics, CAD/CAM and CAE
Computer mainframes
Computer services
Memory devices
Micro and mini computers
Office automation
Scanning related
Software-applications
Software-artificial intelligence
Software-systems
Specialized turnkey systems
Terminals
Distribution
Communications equipment
Computer equipment
Consumer products
Electronics equipment
Food products
Industrial products
Medical products
Electronic Components and Instrumentation
Analytical and scientific instrumentation
Component fabrication and testing equipment
Electronic components
Fiber optics
Laser related
Semiconductors
Genetic Engineering
Gene splicing and manufacturing equipment
Monoclonal antibodies and hybridomas
Recombinant DNA (agricultural and industrial)
Recombinant DNA (medical)
Industrial Products and Equipment
Chemicals
Controls and sensors
Energy management
Equipment and machinery
Other industrial automation
Plastics
Robotics/vision systems
Specialty materials
Medical/Health Related
Diagnostic equipment
Diagnostic test products
Disposable products
Drugs and medicines
Hospital and clinical labs
Medical services
Therapeutic equipment
Other
Finance and insurance

Additional Information
Year Founded—1981
Capital Under Management—$50 million
Investments(1985-1st 6 months)—7
Invested(1985-1st 6 months)—$6 million
Method of Compensation—Return on investment is of primary concern; do not charge fees

---

PRINCETON/MONTROSE PARTNERS

2331 Honolulu Avenue, #G
Montrose, CA 91020
818-957-1590

East Coast Office
101 Poor Farm Road
Princeton, NJ 08540
609-921-1590

Partners
Ronald R. Hahn, Mgn. Ptnr. (New Jersey)
Donald R. Stroben, Mgn. Ptnr. (California)
Charles I. Kosmont, Gen. Ptnr. (California)
Richard J. Defieux, Gen. Ptnr. (New Jersey)
Laura M. Latella, Analyst (New Jersey)

Whom to Contact
Any partner

Type of Firm
Private venture capital firm investing own capital

Project Preferences
Will function either as deal originator or investor in deals created by others
Type of Financing:
Seed
Startup
First-stage
Second-stage
Later-stage expansion
Leveraged buyout
Minimum Investment: $100,000
Preferred Investment: $500,000-$1 million
Preferred Investment (LBO):
$500,000-$1 million
Minimum Operating Data:
Annual Sales—Nominal
P&L—Losses (profits projected after 2 years)

Geographical Preference
None

Industry Preferences

Computer Related
Computer products related to agribusiness, energy, or natural resources
Consumer
Food and beverage products
Restaurants
Distribution
Food products
Electronic Components and Instrumentation
Analytical and scientific instrumentation
Companies related to agribusiness, energy or natural resources
Energy/Natural Resources
Alternative energy
Coal related
Energy assets
Energy conservation
Energy product storage, processing and distribution
Energy related process controls
Energy resource location and extraction
Minerals
Natural resource location and extraction
Natural resource processing and distribution
Natural resource related assets
Oil and gas services
Specialty raw materials
Genetic Engineering
Monoclonal antibodies and hybridomas
Recombinant DNA (agricultural and industrial)
Research and manufacturing equipment
Industrial Products and Equipment
Advanced materials
Industrial automation
Process control
Agribusiness Related
Agriculture, forestry, fishing
Animal health
Farm equipment
Food products
Food storage, processing and distribution
Genetic improvement of plants and animals

Additional Information

Year Founded—1981
Capital Under Management—$17 million
Investments(1985-1st 6 months)—4
Invested(1985-1st 6 months)—$1.6 million
Method of Compensation—Return on investment is of primary concern; do not charge fees

R & D PARTNERS, INC.

701 Welch Road #1119
Palo Alto, CA 94304
415-328-2525

General Partners

Norman Smothers
Elliot McLennan

Whom to Contact

Either of the above

Type of Firm

Specialists in R&D partnerships

Project Preferences

Will function either as deal originator or investor in deals created by others
Type of Financing:
Research and development partnerships
Minimum Investment: $250,000
Preferred Investment: Over $250,000
Minimum Operating Data:
Annual Sales—Nominal
P&L—Losses (profits projected after 2 years)

Geographical Preference

Within two hours of office

Industry Preferences

Communications
Cable television
Commercial communications
Data communications
Satellite and microwave communications
Telephone related
Computer Related
Computer graphics, CAD/CAM and CAE
Computer mainframes
Computer services
Memory devices
Micro and mini computers
Office automation
Scanning related
Software-applications
Software-artificial intelligence
Software-systems
Specialized turnkey systems
Terminals
Electronic Components and Instrumentation
Analytical and scientific instrumentation
Component fabrication and testing equipment
Electronic components
Fiber optics
Laser related
Semiconductors

Industrial Products and Equipment
Chemicals
Controls and sensors
Energy management
Equipment and machinery
Other industrial automation
Plastics
Robotics/vision systems
Specialty materials
Medical/Health Related
Diagnostic equipment
Diagnostic test products
Disposable products
Drugs and medicines
Hospital and clinical labs
Medical services
Therapeutic equipment
Other
Agriculture, forestry, fishing
Education related
Finance and insurance
Publishing
Real estate
Specialty consulting
Transportation

Additional Information

Year Founded—1983
Capital Under Management—$1.2 million
Method of Compensation—Function primarily in service area; receive contingent fee in cash or equity
Professional fee required whether or not deal closes

REPRISE CAPITAL CORPORATION

10000 Santa Monica Boulevard
Suite 300
Los Angeles, CA 90067
213-556-1944

Norman Tulchin, V.P.

See NEW YORK for full listing

RIORDAN VENTURE MANAGEMENT

300 South Grand #2900
Los Angeles, CA 90071
213-629-4824

General Partners
Richard J. Riordan
J. Christopher Lewis

Whom to Contact
J. Christopher Lewis

Type of Firm
Private venture capital firm investing
own capital

Project Preferences
Will function either as deal originator or
investor in deals created by others
Type of Financing:
Seed
Startup
First-stage
Second-stage
Later-stage expansion
Leveraged buyout
Minimum Investment: $100,000
Preferred Investment: $500,000-$1 million
Minimum Operating Data:
Annual Sales—Nominal

Geographical Preference
West Coast

Industry Preferences

Communications
Cable television
Commercial communications
Data communications
Satellite and microwave communications
Telephone related
Computer Related
Computer graphics, CAD/CAM and CAE
Computer mainframes
Computer services
Memory devices
Micro and mini computers
Office automation
Scanning related
Software-applications
Software-artificial intelligence
Software-systems
Specialized turnkey systems
Terminals
Consumer
Computer stores/related services
Consumer products
Consumer services
Food and beverage products
Franchise businesses
Hotels and resort areas
Leisure and recreational products
Restaurants
Retailing
Distribution
Communications equipment
Computer equipment
Consumer products
Electronics equipment
Food products
Industrial products
Medical products
**Electronic Components and
Instrumentation**
Analytical and scientific instrumentation
Component fabrication and testing
equipment
Electronic components
Fiber optics
Laser related
Semiconductors
Genetic Engineering
Gene splicing and manufacturing equipment
Monoclonal antibodies and hybridomas
Recombinant DNA (agricultural and
industrial)
Recombinant DNA (medical)
Medical/Health Related
Diagnostic equipment
Diagnostic test products
Disposable products
Drugs and medicines
Hospital and clinical labs
Medical services
Therapeutic equipment

Additional Information
Year Founded—Before 1974
Investments(1985-1st 6 months)—5
Invested(1985-1st 6 months)—$3 million
Method of Compensation—Return on
investment is of primary concern; do not
charge fees

ROBERTSON, COLMAN & STEPHENS

One Embarcadero Center #3100
31st Floor
San Francisco, CA 94111
415-781-9700

Other Offices
535 Madison Avenue
New York, NY 10022
212-319-8900

155 Federal Street
Boston, MA 02110
617-542-9393

6/7 Queen Street
London EC4N 1SP
England

General Partners
Sanford R. Robertson, Ptnr. (California)
Paul H. Stephens, Ptnr. (California)
Robert L. Cummings, Ptnr. (California)
Nywood Wu, Ptnr. (California)
R. Lee Douglas, Special Ltd. Ptnr.
(California)
Gary W. Masner, Sr. Assoc. (California)

Whom to Contact
Robert L. Cummings
Nywood Wu

Type of Firm
Investment banking firm investing
own capital or funds of partners or clients

Industry Association Memberships
NVCA
WAVC

Project Preferences
Will function either as deal originator or
investor in deals created by others
Type of Financing:
Startup
First-stage
Second-stage
Later-stage expansion
Leveraged buyout
Minimum Investment: $500,000
Preferred Investment: Over $1 million
Preferred Investment (LBO): $2 million
Minimum Operating Data:
Annual Sales—Nominal
P&L—Losses (profits projected after 2 years)
Annual Sales (LBO)—$10 million

Geographical Preference
None

Industry Preferences

Communications
Cable television
Commercial communications
Data communications
Satellite and microwave communications
Telephone related
Computer Related
Computer graphics, CAD/CAM and CAE
Computer mainframes
Computer services
Memory devices
Micro and mini computers
Office automation
Scanning related
Software-applications
Software-artificial intelligence
Software-systems
Specialized turnkey systems
Terminals
Consumer
Computer stores/related services
Consumer products
Consumer services
Food and beverage products
Franchise businesses
Hotels and resort areas
Leisure and recreational products
Restaurants
Retailing
Distribution
Communications equipment
Computer equipment
Consumer products
Electronics equipment
Food products
Industrial products
Medical products
**Electronic Components and
  Instrumentation**
Analytical and scientific instrumentation
Component fabrication and testing
  equipment
Electronic components
Fiber optics
Laser related
Semiconductors
Energy/Natural Resources
Alternative energy
Technology related products/equipment
Genetic Engineering
Monoclonal antibodies and hybridomas
Recombinant DNA (agricultural and
  industrial)
Recombinant DNA (medical)

Industrial Products and Equipment
Chemicals
Controls and sensors
Energy management
Equipment and machinery
Other industrial automation
Plastics
Robotics/vision systems
Specialty materials
Medical/Health Related
Diagnostic equipment
Diagnostic test products
Disposable products
Drugs and medicines
Hospital and clinical labs
Medical services
Therapeutic equipment
Other
Education related
Finance and insurance

Additional Information
Year Founded—1978
Capital Under Management—$150 million
Investments(1985-1st 6 months)—20
Invested(1985-1st 6 months)—$9 million
Method of Compensation—Return on
  investment is of primary concern; do not
  charge fees

ARTHUR ROCK & CO.

1635 Russ Building
San Francisco, CA 94104
415-981-3921

Officers
Arthur Rock, Principal
Marie Getchel, Assoc.

Whom to Contact
Marie Getchel

Type of Firm
Private venture capital firm investing
  own capital

Project Preferences
Will function either as deal originator or
  investor in deals created by others
Type of Financing:
Seed
Research and development partnerships
Startup
First-stage
Leveraged buyout

Minimum Investment: $100,000
Preferred Investment: $250,000-$1 million
Minimum Operating Data:
Annual Sales—Nominal

Geographical Preference
West Coast

Industry Preferences

Communications
Cable television
Commercial communications
Data communications
Satellite and microwave communications
Telephone related
Computer Related
Computer graphics, CAD/CAM and CAE
Computer mainframes
Computer services
Memory devices
Micro and mini computers
Office automation
Scanning related
Software-applications
Software-artificial intelligence
Software-systems
Specialized turnkey systems
Terminals
Consumer
Computer stores/related services
Consumer products
Consumer services
Food and beverage products
Franchise businesses
Hotels and resort areas
Leisure and recreational products
Restaurants
Retailing
Distribution
Communications equipment
Computer equipment
Consumer products
Electronics equipment
Food products
Industrial products
Medical products
**Electronic Components and
  Instrumentation**
Analytical and scientific instrumentation
Component fabrication and testing
  equipment
Electronic components
Fiber optics
Laser related
Semiconductors

Energy/Natural Resources
Alternative energy
Coal related
Drilling and exploration services
Energy conservation
Minerals
Oil and gas exploration and production
Technology related products/equipment
Genetic Engineering
Gene splicing and manufacturing equipment
Monoclonal antibodies and hybridomas
Recombinant DNA (agricultural and industrial)
Recombinant DNA (medical)
Industrial Products and Equipment
Chemicals
Controls and sensors
Energy management
Equipment and machinery
Other industrial automation
Plastics
Robotics/vision systems
Specialty materials
Medical/Health Related
Diagnostic equipment
Diagnostic test products
Disposable products
Drugs and medicines
Hospital and clinical labs
Medical services
Therapeutic equipment
Other
Agriculture, forestry, fishing
Education related
Finance and insurance
Publishing
Real estate
Specialty consulting
Transportation

Additional Information
Year Founded—1961
Method of Compensation—Return on investment is of primary concern; do not charge fees

ROGERS & WHITNEY

3000 Sand Hill Road
Building 2, #175
Menlo Park, CA 94025
415-854-2767

Partners
Roy L. Rogers
Thomas M. Whitney

Whom to Contact
Either of the above

Type of Firm
Private venture capital firm investing own capital

Industry Association Membership
WAVC

Project Preferences
Will function either as deal originator or investor in deals created by others
Type of Financing:
Seed
Startup
First-stage
Second-stage
Leveraged buyout
Minimum Investment: $100,000
Preferred Investment: $250,000-$500,000
Minimum Operating Data:
Annual Sales—Nominal
P&L—Losses (profits projected after 1 year)

Geographical Preferences
Within two hours of office
West Coast

Industry Preferences

Communications
Cable television
Commercial communications
Data communications
Satellite and microwave communications
Telephone related
Computer Related
Computer graphics, CAD/CAM and CAE
Computer mainframes
Computer services
Memory devices
Micro and mini computers
Office automation
Scanning related
Software-applications
Software-artificial intelligence
Software-systems
Specialized turnkey systems
Terminals
Electronic Components and Instrumentation
Analytical and scientific instrumentation
Component fabrication and testing equipment
Electronic components
Fiber optics
Laser related
Semiconductors
Energy/Natural Resources
Technology related products/equipment
Will Not Consider
Oil and gas
Real estate

Additional Information
Year Founded—1986 (Whitney Ventures, predecessor company, 1983)
Capital Under Management—$10 million
Investments(1985-1st 6 months)—6
Method of Compensation—Return on investment is of primary concern; do not charge fees

ROTHSCHILD, UNTERBERG, TOWBIN VENTURES

3000 Sand Hill Road
Building 3, #260
Menlo Park, CA 94025
415-854-2576

Officers
J. Michael Gullard, Chm. & Gen. Ptnr.
Thomas A. Tisch, Gen. Ptnr.

Whom to Contact
Either of the above

Type of Firm
Venture capital firm in partnership with an investment banking firm

Affiliation
L. F. Rothschild, Unterberg, Towbin (joint venture)

Industry Association Membership
WAVC

Project Preferences
Will function either as deal originator or investor in deals created by others
Type of Financing:
Startup
First-stage
Second-stage
Minimum Investment: $250,000
Preferred Investment: $500,000-$1 million
Minimum Operating Data:
P&L—Losses (profits projected after 2 years)

Geographical Preference
None

Industry Preferences

Communications
Commercial communications
Data communications
Satellite and microwave communications
Telephone related

Computer Related
Computer graphics, CAD/CAM and CAE
Computer mainframes
Computer services
Memory devices
Micro and mini computers
Office automation
Scanning related
Software-applications
Software-artificial intelligence
Software-systems
Specialized turnkey systems
Terminals
Electronic Components and Instrumentation
Analytical and scientific instrumentation
Component fabrication and testing equipment
Electronic components
Fiber optics
Laser related
Semiconductors
Energy/Natural Resources
Technology related products/equipment
Genetic Engineering
Gene splicing and manufacturing equipment
Monoclonal antibodies and hybridomas
Recombinant DNA (agricultural and industrial)
Special interest in research, production, clinical lab instrumentation
Industrial Products and Equipment
Controls and sensors
Equipment and machinery
Other industrial automation
Robotics/vision systems
Medical/Health Related
Diagnostic equipment
Diagnostic test products
Disposable products
Medical services
Therapeutic equipment
Will Not Consider
Consumer
Real estate
Retail

Additional Information
Year Founded—1984
Capital Under Management—$20 million
Investments(1985-1st 6 months)—2
Invested(1985-1st 6 months)—$800,000
Method of Compensation—Return on investment is of primary concern; do not charge fees

SAN JOAQUIN CAPITAL CORPORATION

1675 Chester Avenue #330
Post Office Box 2538
Bakersfield, CA 93303
805-323-7581

Officers
Chester W. Troudy, Pres.
Jimmie Icardo, Chm.
Robert Sheldon, M.D., Vice Chm.
John E. Boydstun, CFO
David Cerrina, Secy.

Whom to Contact
Chester W. Troudy

Type of Firm
SBIC

Industry Association Membership
NASBIC

Project Preferences
Will function either as deal originator or investor in deals created by others
Type of Financing:
Later-stage expansion
Leveraged buyout
Minimum Investment: $100,000
Preferred Investment: $250,000-$500,000
Minimum Operating Data:
Annual Sales—$3 million
Annual Sales (LBO)—$5 million and over

Geographical Preference
West Coast

Industry Preferences

Communications
Cable television
Commercial communications
Data communications
Satellite and microwave communications
Telephone related
Consumer
Computer stores/related services
Consumer products
Consumer services
Food and beverage products
Franchise businesses
Hotels and resort areas
Leisure and recreational products
Restaurants
Retailing

Electronic Components and Instrumentation
Analytical and scientific instrumentation
Component fabrication and testing equipment
Electronic components
Fiber optics
Laser related
Semiconductors
Industrial Products and Equipment
Chemicals
Controls and sensors
Energy management
Equipment and machinery
Other industrial automation
Plastics
Robotics/vision systems
Specialty materials
Other
Agriculture, forestry, fishing
Education related
Finance and insurance
Publishing
Real estate
Specialty consulting
Transportation

Additional Information
Year Founded—1962
Capital Under Management—$4 million
Investments(1985-1st 6 months)—3
Invested(1985-1st 6 months)—$300,000
Method of Compensation—Return on investment is most important, but also charge for closing fees, service fees, etc.

SAN JOSE CAPITAL/ SAN JOSE SBIC, INC.

100 Park Center Plaza #427
San Jose, CA 95113
408-293-7708

General Partners
Daniel Hochman
Robert T. Murphy

Whom to Contact
Either of the above

Type of Firm
Private venture capital firm investing own capital
SBIC

Affiliation
San Jose SBIC, Inc. (wholly-owned subsidiary)

Industry Association Memberships
NASBIC
WAVC

Project Preferences
Will function either as deal originator or
  investor in deals created by others
Type of Financing:
Research and development partnerships
Startup
First-stage
Leveraged buyout
Minimum Investment: $100,000
Preferred Investment: $250,000-$500,000
Minimum Operating Data:
Annual Sales—Nominal
P&L—Losses (profits projected after 2 years)

Geographical Preference
West Coast

Industry Preferences

Communications
Commercial communications
Data communications
Satellite and microwave communications
Telephone related
Computer Related
Computer graphics, CAD/CAM and CAE
Memory devices
Micro and mini computers
Office automation
Scanning related
Specialized turnkey systems
Terminals
**Electronic Components and
  Instrumentation**
Analytical and scientific instrumentation
Component fabrication and testing
  equipment
Electronic components
Fiber optics
Laser related
Semiconductors
Industrial Products and Equipment
Controls and sensors
Other industrial automation
Robotics/vision systems
Medical/Health Related
Diagnostic equipment
Diagnostic test products
Patient education systems
Will Not Consider
Consumer
Entertainment industry
Food service

Additional Information
Year Founded—1977
Capital Under Management—$8 million
Investments(1985-1st 6 months)—7
Invested(1985-1st 6 months)—$850,000
Method of Compensation—Return on
  investment is of primary concern; do not
  charge fees

SAND HILL VENTURE GROUP

3000 Sand Hill Road
Bldg. 4, #145
Menlo Park, CA 94025
415-854-9600

Partners
D. McCrea Graham II, Chm.
Stuart Evans, Ptnr.

Whom to Contact
Either of the above

Type of Firm
Private venture capital firm investing
  own capital

Industry Association Memberships
WAVC

Project Preferences
Prefer role as deal originator but will also
  invest in deals created by others
Type of Financing:
Seed
Startup
First-stage
Leveraged buyout
Minimum Investment: $100,000
Preferred Investment: $250,000-$500,000
Preferred Investment (LBO):
  $5 million-$10 million
Minimum Operating Data:
Annual Sales—Nominal
P&L—Losses (profits projected after 2 years)
Annual Sales (LBO)—$30 million-$50 million

Geographical Preferences
Northwest
Southwest
East Coast
West Coast

Industry Preferences

Communications
Cable television
Commercial communications
Data communications
Satellite and microwave communications
Telephone related
Computer Related
Computer graphics, CAD/CAM and CAE
Computer mainframes
Computer services
Memory devices
Micro and mini computers
Office automation
Scanning related
Software-applications
Software-artificial intelligence
Software-systems
Specialized turnkey systems
Terminals
Consumer
Consumer products
Consumer services
Hotels and resort areas
Leisure and recreational products
**Electronic Components and
  Instrumentation**
Analytical and scientific instrumentation
Component fabrication and testing
equipment
Electronic components
Fiber optics
Laser related
Semiconductors
Energy/Natural Resources
Alternative energy
Energy conservation
Technology related products/equipment
Industrial Products and Equipment
Controls and sensors
Energy management
Other industrial automation
Robotics/vision systems
Medical/Health Related
Diagnostic equipment
Diagnostic test products
Disposable products
Other
Finance and insurance
Real estate
Transportation

Additional Information
Year Founded—1983
Capital Under Management—$8.5 million
Method of Compensation—Return on
  investment is of primary concern; do not
  charge fees

SAS ASSOCIATES

515 South Figueroa
Sixth Floor
Los Angeles, CA 90071
213-624-4232

Officers

Bruce P. Emmeluth, Sr. V.P.
James E. Moore, V.P.
Robert W. Campbell, V.P.
Joseph E. Giansante, V.P.

Whom to Contact

Robert W. Campbell

Type of Firm

Private venture capital firm investing
own capital

Affiliation

Seidler Amdec Securities Inc.
(general partner)

Industry Association Memberships

NVCA
WAVC

Project Preferences

Will function either as deal originator or
investor in deals created by others
Type of Financing:
First-stage
Second-stage
Later-stage expansion
Leveraged buyout
Minimum Investment: $100,000
Preferred Investment: $100,000-$250,000
Minimum Operating Data:
Annual Sales—$500,000
P&L—Losses (profits projected after 2 years)

Geographical Preferences

Northwest
Southwest
Rocky Mountains
West Coast

Industry Preferences

Communications
Cable television
Commercial communications
Data communications
Satellite and microwave communications
Telephone related

Computer Related
Computer graphics, CAD/CAM and CAE
Computer mainframes
Computer services
Memory devices
Micro and mini computers
Office automation
Scanning related
Software-applications
Software-artificial intelligence
Software-systems
Specialized turnkey systems
Terminals
Consumer
Computer stores/related services
Consumer products
Consumer services
Food and beverage products
Franchise businesses
Hotels and resort areas
Leisure and recreational products
Restaurants
Retailing
Distribution
Communications equipment
Computer equipment
Medical products
**Electronic Components and
Instrumentation**
Analytical and scientific instrumentation
Component fabrication and testing
equipment
Electronic components
Fiber optics
Laser related
Semiconductors
Energy/Natural Resources
Alternative energy
Oil and gas exploration and production
Genetic Engineering
Gene splicing and manufacturing equipment
Monoclonal antibodies and hybridomas
Recombinant DNA (agricultural and
industrial)
Recombinant DNA (medical)
Industrial Products and Equipment
Controls and sensors
Other industrial automation
Robotics/vision systems
Medical/Health Related
Diagnostic equipment
Diagnostic test products
Disposable products
Drugs and medicines
Hospital and clinical labs
Medical services
Therapeutic equipment
Other
Specialty consulting

Will Not Consider

Entertainment
Real estate

Additional Information

Year Founded—1970
Method of Compensation—Return on
investment is of primary concern; do not
charge fees

SCHRODER VENTURE MANAGERS LIMITED

755 Page Mill Road
Building A, #280
Palo Alto, CA 94304
415-424-1144

Other Office

One State Street
New York, NY 10004
212-269-6500

Officers

David Walters, Mgn. Dir. (California)
Michael Hentschel, Dir. (California)
Jeffrey J. Collinson, Mgn. Dir. (New York)
Judith E. Schneider, Dir. (New York)
Robert J. Gailus, Assoc. (California)

Whom to Contact

Any of the above

Type of Firm

Venture capital subsidiary of British
merchant bank

Affiliation

Schroders PLC, United Kingdom (parent)

Industry Association Memberships

NVCA
WAVC

Project Preferences

Will function either as deal originator or
investor in deals created by others
Type of Financing:
Seed
Startup
First-stage
Second-stage
Later-stage expansion
Leveraged buyout
Minimum Investment: $100,000
Preferred Investment: $500,000-$1 million
Preferred Investment (LBO): $1 million

Minimum Operating Data:
Annual Sales—Nominal
P&L—Losses (profits projected after 2 years)
Annual Sales (LBO)—$50 million

Geographical Preference
National

Industry Preferences

Communications
Cable television
Commercial communications
Data communications
Satellite and microwave communications
Telephone related
Computer Related
Computer graphics, CAD/CAM and CAE
Computer mainframes
Computer services
Memory devices
Office automation
Scanning related
Software-applications
Software-artificial intelligence
Software-systems
Specialized turnkey systems
Consumer
Computer stores/related services
Consumer products
Consumer services
Food and beverage products
Franchise businesses
Hotels and resort areas
Leisure and recreational products
Restaurants
Retailing
Distribution
Consumer products
Food products
Industrial products
Medical products
**Electronic Components and
  Instrumentation**
Analytical and scientific instrumentation
Component fabrication and testing
  equipment
Electronic components
Fiber optics
Laser related
Semiconductors
Energy/Natural Resources
Technology related products/equipment
Genetic Engineering
Gene splicing and manufacturing
  equipment
Monoclonal antibodies and hybridomas
Recombinant DNA (agricultural and
  industrial)
Recombinant DNA (medical)

Industrial Products and Equipment
Chemicals
Controls and sensors
Energy management
Equipment and machinery
Other industrial automation
Plastics
Robotics/vision systems
Specialty materials
Medical/Health Related
Diagnostic equipment
Diagnostic test products
Disposable products
Drugs and medicines
Hospital and clinical labs
Medical services
Therapeutic equipment
Other
Education related
Finance and insurance
Publishing
Specialty consulting
Transportation
Will Not Consider
Oil and gas exploration
Real estate
Motion Pictures

Additional Information
Year Founded—1983
Capital Under Management—$37.5 million
Investments(1985-1st 6 months)—10
Invested(1985-1st 6 months)—$4.9 million
Method of Compensation—Return on
  investment is of primary concern; do not
  charge fees

SEAPORT VENTURES, INC.

770 B Street #420
San Diego, CA 92101
619-232-4069

Officers
Michael Stolper, Pres.
Carole Rhoades, V.P.

Whom to Contact
Either of the above

Type of Firm
SBIC

Project Preferences
Will function either as deal originator or
  investor in deals created by others

Type of Financing:
Second-stage
Later-stage expansion
Leveraged buyout
Minimum Investment: $100,000
Preferred Investment: $100,000-$250,000
Preferred Investment (LBO): $250,000
Minimum Operating Data:
Annual Sales—$1.5 million
P&L—Losses (profits projected after 2 years)
Annual Sales (LBO)—$7 million and over

Geographical Preference
None

Industry Preferences

Communications
Cable television
Data communications
Satellite and microwave communications
Computer Related
Computer graphics, CAD/CAM and CAE
Computer services
Memory devices
Consumer
Consumer products
Consumer services
Food and beverage products
Franchise businesses
Hotels and resort areas
Leisure and recreational products
Restaurants
Retailing
Distribution
Consumer products
Electronics equipment
Food products
Industrial products
Medical products
**Electronic Components and
  Instrumentation**
Analytical and scientific instrumentation
Electronic components
Fiber optics
Laser related
Energy/Natural Resources
Various
Genetic Engineering
Monoclonal antibodies and hybridomas
Industrial Products and Equipment
Chemicals
Controls and sensors
Energy management
Equipment and machinery
Other industrial automation
Plastics
Specialty materials

Medical/Health Related
Diagnostic equipment
Diagnostic test products
Disposable products
Drugs and medicines
Medical services
Therapeutic equipment
Other
Agriculture, forestry, fishing
Finance and insurance
Will Not Consider
Real estate related project financings

Additional Information
Year Founded—1982
Capital Under Management—$2.8 million
Investments(1985-1st 6 months)—4
Invested(1985-1st 6 months)—$775,000
Method of Compensation—Return on
    investment is of primary concern; do not
    charge fees

SECURITY PACIFIC CAPITAL CORP./ FIRST SBIC OF CALIFORNIA

650 Town Center Drive
17th Floor
Costa Mesa, CA 92626
714-556-1964

Other Offices
50 Milk Street, 15th Floor
Boston, MA 02109
617-542-7601

5 Palo Alto Square #938
Palo Alto, CA 94304
415-424-8011

155 North Lake Avenue #1010
Pasadena, CA 91109
818-304-3451

Post Office Box 512
Washington, PA 15301
412-223-0707

Officers
Timothy Hay, Pres. (Costa Mesa)
Gregory Forrest, Exec. V. P. (Costa Mesa)
Alvin Brizzard, First V.P. (Costa Mesa)
Dmitry Bosky, V.P. (Costa Mesa)
Everett Cox, V.P. (Costa Mesa)
John Geer, Mgn. Ptnr. (Costa Mesa)
Brian Jones, Mgn. Ptnr. (Costa Mesa)
James McGoodwin, Mgn. Ptnr. (Costa Mesa)
Michael Cronin, Mgn. Ptnr. (Boston)
James McElwee, Mgn. Ptnr. (Palo Alto)
John Padgett, Mgn. Ptnr. (Pasadena)
Tony Stevens, Mgn. Ptnr. (Pasadena)
Daniel Dye, Mgn. Ptnr. (Washington, PA)

Whom to Contact
John Geer
Brian Jones
James McGoodwin
Michael Cronin
Jim McElwee
John Padgett
Tony Stevens
Daniel Dye

Type of Firm
SBIC
Venture capital subsidiary of
    commercial bank

Affiliation
Security Pacific Corporation (parent)

Industry Association Memberships
NASBIC
NVCA
WAVC

Project Preferences
Will function either as deal originator or
    investor in deals created by others
Type of Financing:
Startup
First-stage
Second-stage
Later-stage expansion
Leveraged buyout
Minimum Investment: $100,000
Preferred Investment:
    $100,000 to $10 million
Preferred Investment (LBO):
    $1 million and over

Geographical Preference
None

Industry Preferences
None

Additional Information
Year Founded—1960
Capital Under Management—$200 million
Investments(1985-1st 6 months)—26
Invested(1985-1st 6 months)—$33 million
Method of Compensation—Return on
    investment is of primary concern; do not
    charge fees

SEQUOIA CAPITAL

3000 Sand Hill Road
Building 4, #280
Menlo Park, CA 94025
415-854-3927

Partner
Donald T. Valentine, Gen. Ptnr.
Gordon Russell, Gen. Ptnr.
Pierre R. Lamond, Gen. Ptnr.
Walter F. Baumgartner, Gen. Ptnr.
Nancy Olson, Assoc.

Whom to Contact
Any of the above

Type of Firm
Private venture capital firm investing
    own capital

Industry Association Memberships
NVCA
WAVC

Project Preferences
Will function either as deal originator or
    investor in deals created by others
Type of Financing:
Startup
First-stage
Minimum Investment: $250,000
Preferred Investment: Over $1 million
Minimum Operating Data:
Annual Sales—Nominal
P&L—Losses (profits projected after 2 years)

Geographical Preference
West Coast

Industry Preferences

Communications
Cable television
Commercial communications
Data communications
Satellite and microwave communications
Telephone related

Computer Related
Computer graphics, CAD/CAM and CAE
Computer mainframes
Computer services
Memory devices
Micro and mini computers
Office automation
Scanning related
Software-applications
Software-artificial intelligence
Software-systems
Specialized turnkey systems
Terminals
Electronic Components and Instrumentation
Analytical and scientific instrumentation
Component fabrication and testing equipment
Electronic components
Fiber optics
Laser related
Semiconductors
Medical/Health Related
Diagnostic equipment
Diagnostic test products
Disposable products
Drugs and medicines
Hospital and clinical labs
Medical services
Therapeutic equipment

Additional Information
Year Founded—1971
Capital Under Management—$200 million
Investments(1985-1st 6 months)—15
Invested(1985-1st 6 months)—$10 million
Method of Compensation—Return on investment is of primary concern; do not charge fees

SEVIN ROSEN MANAGEMENT COMPANY

1245 Oakmead Parkway #101
Sunnyvale, CA 94086
408-720-8590

Other Offices
13455 Noel Road #1670
Dallas, TX 75240
214-960-1744

200 Park Avenue #4503
New York, NY 10166
212-687-5115

Officers
L.J. Sevin, Pres. (Texas)
Benjamin M. Rosen, Chm. (New York)
Jon W. Bayless, Ptnr. (Texas)
Roger S. Borovoy, Ptnr. (California)
Stephen M. Dow, Ptnr. (California)
Dennis J. Gorman, CFO (Texas)

Whom to Contact
Any of the above (closest office)

Type of Firm
Private venture capital firm investing own capital

Industry Association Membership
NVCA

Project Preferences
Prefer role as deal originator
Type of Financing:
Seed
Startup
Minimum Investment: $500,000
Preferred Investment: $500,000-$1 million
Minimum Operating Data:
Annual Sales—Nominal
P&L—Losses (profits projected after 2 years)

Geographical Preferences
Southwest
East Coast
West Coast

Industry Preferences

Communications
Commercial communications
Data communications
Satellite and microwave communications
Telephone related
Computer Related
Computer graphics, CAD/CAM and CAE
Computer mainframes
Computer services
Memory devices
Micro and mini computers
Office automation
Scanning related
Software-applications
Software-artificial intelligence
Software-systems
Specialized turnkey systems
Terminals
Distribution
Communications equipment
Computer equipment

Electronic Components and Instrumentation
Analytical and scientific instrumentation
Fiber optics
Semiconductors
Genetic Engineering
Gene splicing and manufacturing equipment
Monoclonal antibodies and hybridomas
Recombinant DNA (agricultural and industrial)
Recombinant DNA (medical)
Industrial Products and Equipment
Controls and sensors
Robotics/vision systems
Will Not Consider
Consulting services
Consumer services
Oil and gas
Real estate
Transportation

Additional Information
Year Founded—1981
Capital Under Management—$300 million
Investments(1985-1st 6 months)—6
Invested(1985-1st 6 months)—$10 million
Method of Compensation—Return on investment is of primary concern; do not charge fees

SHEARSON LEHMAN BROTHERS INC.

One Bush Street
San Francisco, CA 94104
415-981-3680

See NEW YORK for full listing

SIERRA VENTURES MANAGEMENT COMPANY

3000 Sand Hill Road
Building 1, #280
Menlo Park, CA 94025
415-854-1000

Other Office

645 Madison Avenue #2100
New York, NY 10022
212-750-9420

Partners

Peter C. Wendell, Gen. Ptnr. (California)
Vincent H. Tobkin, Gen. Ptnr. (California)
Gilbert H. Lamphere, Gen. Ptnr. (New York)
Thomas A. Barron, Gen. Ptnr. (New York)
Jeffrey M. Drazan, V.P. (California)

Whom to Contact

Jeffrey M. Drazan

Type of Firm

Private venture capital firm investing
own capital
SBIC

Affiliations

Wood River Capital Corp. (technology
investment management)
Sierra Ventures (technology investment
management)
The Prospect Group (technology investment
management)

Industry Association Membership

NVCA

Project Preferences

Prefer role as deal originator but will also
invest in deals created by others
Type of Financing:
Seed
Startup
First-stage
Leveraged buyout
Minimum Investment: Less than $100,000
Preferred Investment: $500,000-$1 million
Preferred Investment (LBO):
$1 million-$20 million
Minimum Operating Data:
Annual Sales—Nominal
P&L—Losses (profits projected after 2 years)
Annual Sales (LBO)—$20 million-$150 million

Geographical Preferences

Northeast
West Coast

Industry Preferences

Communications
Commercial communications
Data communications
Satellite and microwave communications
Telephone related
Computer Related
Computer graphics, CAD/CAM and CAE
Computer mainframes
Computer services
Memory devices
Micro and mini computers
Office automation
Scanning related
Software-applications
Software-artificial intelligence
Software-systems
Specialized turnkey systems
Terminals
Distribution
Communications equipment
Computer equipment
**Electronic Components and
Instrumentation**
Analytical and scientific instrumentation
Component fabrication and testing
equipment
Electronic components
Fiber optics
Laser related
Semiconductors
Genetic Engineering
Gene splicing and manufacturing equipment
Monoclonal antibodies and hybridomas
Recombinant DNA (agricultural and
industrial)
Recombinant DNA (medical)
Medical/Health Related
Diagnostic equipment
Diagnostic test products
Disposable products
Drugs and medicines
Hospital and clinical labs
Medical services
Therapeutic equipment
Other
Database services
Technology-related services

Additional Information

Year Founded—1978 (Wood River)
Capital Under Management—$100 million
(includes all funds managed)
Investments(1985-1st 6 months)—7
Invested(1985-1st 6 months)—$6.5 million
Method of Compensation—Return on
investment is of primary concern; do not
charge fees

SIGMA PARTNERS

2099 Gateway #310
San Jose, CA 95110
408-279-6300

Other Office

342 Green Street
Northboro, MA 01532
617-393-7396

Partners

J. Burgess Jamieson, Gen Ptnr.
C. Bradford Jeffries, Ltd. Ptnr.
Gardner C. Hendrie, Advisor (Massachusetts)
Clifford L. Haas, Assoc.

Whom to Contact

Any of the above

Type of Firm

Private venture capital firm investing
own capital

Industry Association Membership

WAVC

Project Preferences

Will function either as deal originator or
investor in deals created by others
Type of Financing:
Seed
Startup
First-stage
Second-stage
Leveraged buyout
Minimum Investment: $500,000
Preferred Investment: $500,000-$1 million
Preferred Investment (LBO):
$1 million-$2 million
Minimum Operating Data:
Annual Sales—Nominal
P&L—Losses (profits projected after 2 years)
Annual Sales (LBO)—$10 million and over

Geographical Preferences

West Coast
Northwest
Rocky Mountains
USA

Industry Preferences

Communications
Commercial communications
Data communications
Satellite and microwave communications
Telephone related

Computer Related
Computer graphics, CAD/CAM and CAE
Computer mainframes
Computer services
Memory devices
Micro and mini computers
Office automation
Scanning related
Software-applications
Software-artificial intelligence
Software-systems
Specialized turnkey systems
Terminals
**Electronic Components and
Instrumentation**
Analytical and scientific instrumentation
Component fabrication and testing
equipment
Electronic components
Fiber optics
Laser related
Semiconductors
Industrial Products and Equipment
Controls and sensors
Equipment and machinery
Other industrial automation
Robotics/vision systems
Medical/Health Related
Diagnostic equipment
Will Not Consider
Agriculture
Financial services
Natural resources
Real estate

Additional Information

Year Founded—1984
Capital Under Management—$44 million
Investments(1985-1st 6 months)—2
Invested(1985-1st 6 months)—$1.7 million
Method of Compensation—Return on
investment is of primary concern; do not
charge fees

SOFINNOVA, INC.

Three Embarcadero #2560
San Francisco, CA 94111
415-362-4021

Other Office
51 rue Saint Georges
75009 Paris
France
14-280-6870

Officers
Jean-Bernard Schmidt, Pres. (United States)
Jacques Vallee, V.P. (United States)
Jean Fonteneau, V.P. (France)

Whom to Contact
Any of the above

Type of Firm
Private venture capital firm investing
own capital

Affiliation
Sofinnova S.A., France (parent)

Industry Association Membership
WAVC

Project Preferences
Will function either as deal originator or
investor in deals created by others
Type of Financing:
Startup
First-stage
Second-stage
Minimum Investment: $100,000
Preferred Investment: $250,000-$500,000
Minimum Operating Data:
Annual Sales—Nominal
P&L—Losses (profits projected after 2 years)

Geographical Preference
None

Industry Preferences

Communications
Data communications
Satellite and microwave communications

Computer Related
Computer graphics, CAD/CAM and CAE
Computer mainframes
Computer services
Memory devices
Micro and mini computers
Office automation
Scanning related
Software-applications
Software-artificial intelligence
Software-systems
Specialized turnkey systems
Terminals
Distribution
Communications equipment
Computer equipment
Electronics equipment
Medical products
**Electronic Components and
Instrumentation**
Analytical and scientific instrumentation
Component fabrication and testing
equipment
Electronic components
Fiber optics
Laser related
Semiconductors
Genetic Engineering
Gene splicing and manufacturing equipment
Monoclonal antibodies and hybridomas
Recombinant DNA (agricultural and
industrial)
Recombinant DNA (medical)
Industrial Products and Equipment
Robotics/vision systems
Medical/Health Related
Diagnostic equipment
Diagnostic test products
Disposable products
Drugs and medicines
Hospital and clinical labs
Medical services
Therapeutic equipment

Additional Information

Year Founded—1976
Investments(1985-1st 6 months)—4
Invested(1985-1st 6 months)—$1.1 million
Method of Compensation—Return on
investment is of primary concern; do not
charge fees

SOUTHERN CALIFORNIA VENTURES

9920 La Cienega Boulevard #510
Inglewood, CA 90301
213-216-0544

Other Office

2102 Business Center Drive
Suite 218
Irvine, CA 92715
714-752-9341

Partners

B. Allen Lay, Gen. Ptnr. (Inglewood)
Jay Raskin, Gen. Ptnr. (Inglewood)
Robert W. Johnson, Principal (Irvine)

Whom to Contact

Any of the above

Type of Firm

Private venture capital firm investing
own capital

Industry Association Membership

WAVC

Project Preferences

Prefer role as deal originator but will also
invest in deals created by others
Type of Financing:
Seed
Startup
First-stage
Leveraged buyout
Minimum Investment: Less than $100,000
Preferred Investment: $250,000-$1 million
Minimum Operating Data:
Annual Sales—Nominal
P&L—Losses (profits projected after 2 years)

Geographical Preferences

Within two hours of office
Southern California

Industry Preferences

Other
Seek high value-added proprietary products
and services
Will Not Consider
Consumer products
Entertainment businesses
Natural resources extraction
Real estate
Restaurants
Retail

Additional Information

Year Founded—1983
Capital Under Management—$15 million
Investments(1985-1st 6 months)—5
Invested(1985-1st 6 months)—$1.7 million
Method of Compensation—Return on
investment is of primary concern; do not
charge fees

SPACE VENTURES

see United Business Ventures, Inc.
Newport Beach, CA

THE SPROUT GROUP

5300 Stevens Creek Boulevard
Suite 320
San Jose, CA 95129
408-554-1515

Lloyd D. Ruth, Gen. Ptnr.
Keith B. Geeslin
Jon R. Stone

See NEW YORK for full listing

STANFORD UNIVERSITY ENDOWMENT FUND

Treasurer's Office
209 Hamilton Avenue
Palo Alto, CA 94301
415-326-5782

Officer

Rodney H. Adams, Treas.

Type of Firm

Endowment investment fund

Industry Association Membership

WAVC

Project Preferences

Prefer role in deals created by others,
as coinvestor
Type of Financing:
Startup
First-stage
Second-stage
Minimum Investment: $250,000
Preferred Investment: $250,000-$500,000
Minimum Operating Data:
Annual Sales—Nominal
P&L—Losses (profits projected after 1 year)

Geographical Preference

West Coast

Industry Preferences

Communications
Cable television
Commercial communications
Data communications
Satellite and microwave communications
Telephone related
Computer Related
Computer graphics, CAD/CAM and CAE
Computer mainframes
Computer services
Memory devices
Micro and mini computers
Office automation
Software-applications
Software-artificial intelligence
Software-systems
Terminals
**Electronic Components and
Instrumentation**
Analytical and scientific instrumentation
Electronic components
Laser related
Optics technology
Semiconductors
Genetic Engineering
Gene splicing and manufacturing equipment
Monoclonal antibodies and hybridomas
Recombinant DNA (agricultural and
industrial)
Recombinant DNA (medical)
Industrial Products and Equipment
Chemicals
Controls and sensors
Energy management
Equipment and machinery
Other industrial automation
Plastics
Robotics/vision systems
Specialty materials
Medical/Health Related
Diagnostic equipment
Diagnostic test products
Drugs and medicines
Hospital and clinical labs
Medical services
Therapeutic equipment

Additional Information

Year Founded—1891
Capital Under Management—$90 million
Investments(1985-1st 6 months)—3
Invested(1985-1st 6 months)—
$750,000-$1 million
Method of Compensation—Return on
investment is of primary concern; do not
charge fees

THE STERLING GROUP, INC.

2200 Green Street
San Francisco, CA 94123
415-922-0768

Cameron Adair, Principal

See TEXAS for full listing

SUTTER HILL VENTURES

Two Palo Alto Square #700
Palo Alto, CA 94306
415-493-5600

General Partners
Paul M. Wythes
David L. Anderson
G. Leonard Baker, Jr.
William H. Younger, Jr.

Whom to Contact
Any of the above

Type of Firm
Private venture capital firm investing
own capital

Affiliation
Genstar Corp. (limited partner)

Industry Association Memberships
NVCA
WAVC

Project Preferences
Will function either as deal originator or
investor in deals created by others
Type of Financing:
Seed
Startup
First-stage
Second-stage
Purchase of secondary positions
Minimum Investment: $100,000
Preferred Investment: Over $1 million
Minimum Operating Data:
Annual Sales—Nominal

Geographical Preference
National

Industry Preferences

Communications
Commercial communications
Data communications
Satellite and microwave communications
Telephone related

Computer Related
Computer graphics, CAD/CAM and CAE
Computer mainframes
Computer services
Memory devices
Micro and mini computers
Office automation
Scanning related
Software-applications
Software-artificial intelligence
Software-systems
Specialized turnkey systems
Terminals
Distribution
Communications equipment
Computer equipment
Industrial products
Medical products
Electronic Components and Instrumentation
Analytical and scientific instrumentation
Component fabrication and testing
equipment
Electronic components
Fiber optics
Laser related
Semiconductors
Genetic Engineering
Gene splicing and manufacturing equipment
Monoclonal antibodies and hybridomas
Recombinant DNA (agricultural and
industrial)
Recombinant DNA (medical)
Industrial Products and Equipment
Chemicals
Controls and sensors
Energy management
Equipment and machinery
Other industrial automation
Plastics
Robotics/vision systems
Specialty materials
Medical/Health Related
Diagnostic equipment
Diagnostic test products
Disposable products
Drugs and medicines
Hospital and clinical labs
Medical services
Therapeutic equipment
Will Not Consider
Asset intensive businesses
Real estate

Additional Information
Year Founded—1962
Capital Under Management—
Over $500 million
Investments(1985-1st 6 months)—12
Invested(1985-1st 6 months)—$5.3 million
Method of Compensation—Return on
investment is of primary concern; do not
charge fees

TA ASSOCIATES

435 Tasso Street #200
Palo Alto, CA 94301
415-328-1210

Jeffrey T. Chambers, Gen. Ptnr.
Jacqueline C. Morby, Gen. Ptnr.
Michael C. Child, V.P.
Peter B. Kelly, Inv. Analyst
Paul A. White, Inv. Analyst

See MASSACHUSETTS for full listing

TAYLOR & TURNER

220 Montgomery Street
Penthouse #10
San Francisco, CA 94104
415-398-6821

Other Offices
Rotan Mosle Technology Partners, Ltd.
3800 RepublicBank Center
700 Louisiana
Houston, TX 77002
713-236-3180

VenWest Partners
Westinghouse Electric Building
Gateway Center
Pittsburgh, PA 15222
412-642-5858

General Partners
William H. Taylor II
Marshall C. Turner, Jr.

Whom to Contact
William H. Taylor II (California)
Marshall C. Turner, Jr. (California)
John V. Jaggers (Texas)

Type of Firm
Private venture capital firm investing
own capital

Affiliations

Rotan Mosle Technology Partners, Ltd., Houston (co-investing fund with Taylor & Turner as general partner)

VenWest Partners, Pittsburgh (co-investing fund with Taylor & Turner as general partner)

Industry Association Memberships

NASBIC

NVCA

Project Preferences

Will function either as deal originator or investor in deals created by others

Type of Financing:

Seed

Startup

First-stage

Second-stage

Later-stage expansion

Minimum Investment: Less than $100,000

Preferred Investment: $500,000-$1 million

Minimum Operating Data:

Annual Sales—Nominal

P&L—Losses (profits projected after 3 years)

Geographical Preference

None

Industry Preferences

Communications

Data communications

Satellite and microwave communications

Computer Related

Computer graphics, CAD/CAM and CAE

Computer mainframes

Computer services

Memory devices

Micro and mini computers

Office automation

Scanning related

Software-applications

Software-artificial intelligence

Software-systems

Specialized turnkey systems

Terminals

Electronic Components and Instrumentation

Analytical and scientific instrumentation

Electronic components

Fiber optics

Laser related

Semiconductors

Energy/Natural Resources

Technology related products/equipment

Genetic Engineering

Gene splicing and manufacturing equipment

Monoclonal antibodies and hybridomas

Recombinant DNA (agricultural and industrial)

Recombinant DNA (medical)

Industrial Products and Equipment

Advanced materials

Chemicals

Controls and sensors

Equipment and machinery

Other industrial automation

Plastics

Process controls

Robotics/vision systems

Specialty materials

Medical/Health Related

Diagnostic equipment

Diagnostic test products

Disposable products

Drugs and medicines

Hospital and clinical labs

Medical services

Therapeutic equipment

Other

Military/aerospace

Technology applied to vertical markets

Will Not Consider

Construction

Natural resources exploration

Real estate

Additional Information

Year Founded—1982

Capital Under Management—$18.5 million

Investments(1985-1st 6 months)—8

Invested(1985-1st 6 months)—$1.8 million

Method of Compensation—Return on investment is of primary concern; do not charge fees

---

TECHNOLOGY FUNDING

2000 Alameda de las Pulgas

Suite 250

San Mateo, CA 94403

415-345-2200

Partners

Charles R. Kokesh, Mgn. Gen. Ptnr.

Frank R. Pope, Gen. Ptnr.

John A. Griner, Gen. Ptnr.

Eugene J. Fischer, Gen. Ptnr.

Donald O. Vogt, Gen. Ptnr.

Paul D. Quadros, Sr. V.P.

Cowsy Wadia, V.P.

Whom to Contact

Eugene J. Fischer

John A. Griner

Type of Firm

Private venture capital group investing capital raised in public markets

Industry Association Membership

WAVC

Project Preferences

Will function either as deal originator or investor in deals created by others

Type of Financing:

First-stage

Second-stage

Later-stage expansion

Minimum Investment: $250,000

Preferred Investment: $500,000-$1 million

Minimum Operating Data:

Annual Sales—Nominal

P&L—Losses (profits projected after 2 years)

Geographical Preferences

West Coast

Northeast

Rocky Mountains

Industry Preferences

Communications

Data communications

Computer Related

Computer graphics, CAD/CAM and CAE

Computer mainframes

Computer services

Medical related

Memory devices

Micro and mini computers

Office automation

Software-applications

Software-artificial intelligence

Software-systems

Specialized turnkey systems

Electronic Components and Instrumentation

Fiber optics

Industrial Products and Equipment

Controls and sensors

Other industrial automation

Robotics/vision systems

Specialty materials

Medical/Health Related

Diagnostic equipment

Diagnostic test products

Disposable products

Will Not Consider

Consumer products

Genetic engineering

Natural resources

Capital intensive businesses

Additional Information

Year Founded—1979
Capital Under Management—$57 million
Investments(1985-1st 6 months)—13
Invested(1985-1st 6 months)—$5.4 million
Method of Compensation—Return on
    investment is of primary concern; do not
    charge fees

TECHNOLOGY PARTNERS

1550 Tiburon Boulevard #A
Belvedere, CA 94920
415-435-1935

Other Office

257 East Main Steet
Barrington, IL 60010
312-381-2510

Officers

William Hart, Mgn. Gen. Ptnr. (California)
Peter J. Gillespie (Illinois)

Type of Firm

Private venture capital firm investing
    own capital

Industry Association Membership

WAVC

Project Preferences

Prefer role as deal originator
Type of Financing:
Seed
Startup
Minimum Investment: Less than $100,000
Preferred Investment: $200,000-$400,000
Minimum Operating Data:
Annual Sales—Nominal
P&L—Losses (profits projected after 2 years)

Geographical Preference

National

Industry Preferences

Communications
Various
Computer Related
Various
Consumer
Technology based consumer products
    and services
Distribution
Communications equipment
Computer equipment
Electronics equipment
Industrial products

**Electronic Components and
    Instrumentation**
Various
Energy/Natural Resources
Technology related products/equipment
Genetic Engineering
Various
Industrial Products and Equipment
Controls and sensors
Energy management
Equipment and machinery
Other industrial automation
Plastics
Robotics/vision systems
Specialty materials
Medical/Health Related
Technology based products

Additional Information

Year Founded—1980
Capital Under Management—$10 million
Investments(1985-1st 6 months)—3
Invested(1985-1st 6 months)—$500,000
Method of Compensation—Return on
    investment is of primary concern; do not
    charge fees

TECHNOLOGY VENTURE INVESTORS

3000 Sand Hill Road
Building 4, #210
Menlo Park, CA 94025
415-854-7472

Partners

James J. Bochnowski, Ptnr.
Robert C. Kagle, Ptnr.
James A. Katzman, Ptnr.
David F. Marquardt, Ptnr.
Burton J. McMurtry, Ptnr.
Mark Wilson, Admin. Ptnr.

Whom to Contact

Any of the above

Type of Firm

Private venture capital firm investing
    own capital

Industry Association Memberships

NVCA
WAVC

Project Preferences

Prefer role as deal originator
Type of Financing:
Seed
Startup
First-stage
Second-stage
Later-stage expansion
Minimum Investment: $500,000
Preferred Investment: $1 million-$1.5 million
Minimum Operating Data:
Annual Sales—Nominal
P&L—Losses (profits projected after 2 years)

Geographical Preferences

West Coast
Northwest
Southwest
Midwest
Rocky Mountains

Industry Preferences

Communications
Commercial communications
Data communications
Satellite and microwave communications
Telephone related
Computer Related
Computer graphics, CAD/CAM and CAE
Computer mainframes
Computer services
Memory devices
Micro and mini computers
Office automation
Scanning related
Software-applications
Software-artificial intelligence
Software-systems
Specialized turnkey systems
Terminals
Consumer
Computer stores/related services
Consumer products
Distribution
Communications equipment
Computer equipment
Consumer products
Electronics equipment
Medical products
**Electronic Components and
    Instrumentation**
Analytical and scientific instrumentation
Component fabrication and testing
    equipment
Electronic components
Fiber optics
Laser related
Semiconductors

Genetic Engineering
Gene splicing and manufacturing equipment
Monoclonal antibodies and hybridomas
Recombinant DNA (agricultural and industrial)
Recombinant DNA (medical)
Industrial Products and Equipment
Controls and sensors
Equipment and machinery
Other industrial automation
Robotics/vision systems
Medical/Health Related
Diagnostic equipment
Diagnostic test products
Drugs and medicines
Therapeutic equipment

Additional Information
Year Founded—1980
Capital Under Management—$152 million
Investments(1985-1st 6 months)—18
Invested(1985-1st 6 months)—$13.9 million
Method of Compensation—Return on investment is of primary concern; do not charge fees

THORN EMI VENTURE FUND LIMITED
2750 Systron Drive
Concord, CA 94518
415-671-6786

Other Office
131 Via Bonita
Alamo, CA 94507
415-838-2045

General Partner
John Arrol

Type of Firm
Venture capital subsidiary or affiliate of non-financial corporation

Affiliation
THORN EMI plc (parent)

Project Preferences
Will function either as deal originator or investor in deals created by others
Type of Financing:
Startup
First-stage
Second-stage

Preferred Investment: $100,000-$400,000
Minimum Operating Data:
Annual Sales—Nominal

Geographical Preference
West Coast

Industry Preferences
Communications
Data communications
Satellite and microwave communications
Computer Related
Computer graphics, CAD/CAM and CAE
Memory devices
Office automation
Scanning related
Software-applications
Software-artificial intelligence
Software-systems
Electronic Components and Instrumentation
Analytical and scientific instrumentation
Component fabrication and testing equipment
Electronic components
Fiber optics
Laser related
Semiconductor equipment
Semiconductors
Test and measurement equipment
Industrial Products and Equipment
Controls and sensors
Robotics/vision systems
Other
Inertial guidance systems
Will Not Consider
Minerals exploration
Real estate
Restaurants
Retail

Additional Information
Year Founded—1983
Investments(1985-1st 6 months)—3
Invested(1985-1st 6 months)—$543,000
Method of Compensation—Return on investment is of primary concern; do not charge fees

3i VENTURES
450 Newport Center Drive #250
Newport Beach, CA 92660
714-720-1421

See INVESTORS IN INDUSTRY (3i)

UNION VENTURE CORPORATION
225 South Lake Avenue
Pasadena, CA 91101
213-236-6292

Other Office
18300 Von Karmen Avenue
Irvine, CA 92713
714-553-7130

Officers
Brent T. Rider, Pres. (Los Angeles)
John W. Ulrich, V.P. (Irvine)
Christopher L. Rafferty, V.P. (Los Angeles)
Jeffrey A. Watts, Sr. Inv. Officer (Los Angeles)
Lee R. McCracken, Inv. Officer (Irvine)
Thomas H. Peterson, Inv. Officer (Los Angeles)

Whom to Contact
Thomas H. Peterson

Type of Firm
SBIC
Venture capital subsidiary of commercial bank

Affiliations
Union Bank (parent)
Standard Chartered Bank (parent)

Industry Association Memberships
NASBIC
NVCA
WAVC

Project Preferences
Will function either as deal originator or investor in deals created by others
Type of Financing:
Startup
First-stage
Second-stage
Leveraged buyout
Minimum Investment: $500,000
Preferred Investment: $500,000-$1 million
Minimum Operating Data:
Annual Sales—Nominal
P&L—Losses (profits projected after 2 years)

Geographical Preference
None

Industry Preferences

Communications
Cable television
Commercial communications
Data communications
Satellite and microwave communications
Telephone related
Computer Related
Computer graphics, CAD/CAM and CAE
Computer mainframes
Computer services
Memory devices
Micro and mini computers
Office automation
Scanning related
Software-applications
Software-artificial intelligence
Software-systems
Specialized turnkey systems
Terminals
Distribution
Communications equipment
Computer equipment
Electronics equipment
Industrial products
Medical products
Electronic Components and Instrumentation
Analytical and scientific instrumentation
Component fabrication and testing equipment
Electronic components
Fiber optics
Laser related
Semiconductors
Genetic Engineering
Gene splicing and manufacturing equipment
Monoclonal antibodies and hybridomas
Recombinant DNA (agricultural and industrial)
Recombinant DNA (medical)
Industrial Products and Equipment
Chemicals
Controls and sensors
Energy management
Equipment and machinery
Other industrial automation
Plastics
Robotics/vision systems
Specialty materials

Medical/Health Related
Diagnostic equipment
Diagnostic test products
Disposable products
Drugs and medicines
Hospital and clinical labs
Medical services
Therapeutic equipment
Will Not Consider
Agriculture
Construction
Entertainment businesses
Fashion
Finance
Insurance
Mining
Motion pictures
Oil and gas exploration and producton
Real estate

Additional Information
Year Founded—1967
Capital Under Management—$22 million
Investments(1985-1st 6 months)—10
Invested(1985-1st 6 months)—$2.9 million

UNITED BUSINESS VENTURES, INC.

3931 MacArthur Boulevard #212
Newport Beach, CA 92660
714-851-0855

Officer
Leslie R. Brewer, Pres.

Type of Firm
Venture capital subsidiary of commercial bank
MESBIC

Affiliation
United Bank S.S.B.

Industry Association Membership
NASBIC

Project Preferences
Will function either as deal originator or investor in deals created by others
Type of Financing:
Startup
First-stage
Second-stage
Leveraged buyout
Minimum Investment: $100,000
Preferred Investment: $250,000-$500,000

Minimum Operating Data:
Annual Sales—$1.5 million
P&L—Profits NBT over $200,000

Geographical Preferences
Southwest
West Coast

Industry Preferences

Electronic Components and Instrumentation
Analytical and scientific instrumentation
Component fabrication and testing equipment
Electronic components
Fiber optics
Laser related
Semiconductors
Industrial Products and Equipment
Chemicals
Controls and sensors
Energy management
Equipment and machinery
Other industrial automation
Plastics
Robotics/vision systems
Specialty materials
Medical/Health Related
Diagnostic equipment
Diagnostic test products
Disposable products
Drugs and medicines
Hospital and clinical labs
Medical services
Therapeutic equipment

Additional Information
Year Founded—1977
Investments(1985-1st 6 months)—3
Invested(1985-1st 6 months)—$1.5 million
Method of Compensation—Return on investment is most important, but also charge for closing fees, service fees, etc.

U.S. VENTURE PARTNERS

2180 Sand Hill Road #300
Menlo Park, CA 94025
415-854-9080

Partners
William K. Bowes, Jr., Gen. Ptnr.
Robert Sackman, Gen. Ptnr.
Stuart G. Moldaw, Gen. Ptnr.
Roderick C.M. Hall, Gen. Ptnr.
H. Joseph Horowitz, Gen. Ptnr.
Bruce J. Boehm, Gen. Ptnr.
Jane H. Martin, Gen. Ptnr.
Steven M. Krausz, Assoc.
Nancy E. Glaser, Assoc.

Whom to Contact
Any of the above

Type of Firm
Private venture capital firm investing
own capital

Industry Association Memberships
NVCA
WAVC

Project Preferences
Will function either as deal originator or
investor in deals created by others
Type of Financing:
Seed
Startup
First-stage
Second-stage
Later-stage expansion
Minimum Investment: $100,000
Preferred Investment: $750,000 and over
Minimum Operating Data:
Annual Sales—Nominal
P&L—Losses (profits projected after 3 years)

Geographical Preferences
West Coast
Northwest
East Coast

Industry Preferences

Communications
Cable television
Commercial communications
Data communications
Satellite and microwave communications
Telephone related

Computer Related
Computer graphics, CAD/CAM and CAE
Memory devices
Micro and mini computers
Office automation
Software-applications
Software-systems
Terminals
Consumer
Consumer products
Food and beverage products
Franchise businesses
Distribution
Communications equipment
Consumer products
Electronics equipment
Specialty retailing
**Electronic Components and
  Instrumentation**
Analytical and scientific instrumentation
Electronic components
Optics technology
Semiconductors
Genetic Engineering
Gene splicing and manufacturing equipment
Monoclonal antibodies and hybridomas
Recombinant DNA (agricultural and
  industrial)
Recombinant DNA (medical)
Industrial Products and Equipment
Robotics/vision systems
Specialty materials
Medical/Health Related
Diagnostic equipment
Drugs and medicines
Other
Publishing
Will Not Consider
Oil and gas
Real estate

Additional Information
Year Founded—1981
Capital Under Management—$158.5 million
Investments(1985-1st 6 months)—17
Invested(1985-1st 6 months)—$8 million
Method of Compensation—Return on
  investment is of primary concern; do not
  charge fees

VAN KASPER & COMPANY

50 California Street #2350
San Francisco, CA 94111
415-391-5600

Officers
F. Van Kasper, Chm. & Pres.
Stephen R. Adams, Sr. V.P.
Jack A. Sullivan, Sr. V.P.
Hugh H. Gordon, Sr. V.P.
Bernard M. Goldsmith, Dir.,
  Corporate Finance
Kathleen Smythe de Urquieta, Sr. Assoc.
Peter Cole, Sr. Assoc.

Whom to Contact
Bernard M. Goldsmith
Kathleen Smythe de Urquieta
Peter Cole

Project Preferences
Prefer role as deal originator but will also
  invest in deals created by others
Type of Financing:
Second-stage
Later-stage expansion
Leveraged buyout
Minimum Investment: $100,000
Preferred Investment: $100,000-$250,000
Minimum Operating Data:
Annual Sales—$1.5 million
P&L—Break even

Geographical Preference
West Coast

Industry Preferences

Communications
Commercial communications
Data communications
Satellite and microwave communications
Computer Related
Computer graphics, CAD/CAM and CAE
Memory devices
Scanning related
Specialized turnkey systems
**Electronic Components and
  Instrumentation**
Analytical and scientific instrumentation
Electronic components
Fiber optics
Laser related
Semiconductors
Industrial Products and Equipment
Controls and sensors
Equipment and machinery
Medical/Health Related
Diagnostic equipment
Disposable products

Will Not Consider
Motion pictures
Natural resources
Real estate
Research and development ventures

Additional Information
Year Founded—1978
Capital Under Management—$3 million
Investments(1985-1st 6 months)—4
Invested(1985-1st 6 months)—$625,000
Method of Compensation—Function primarily
in service area; receive contingent fee in
cash or equity

VANGUARD ASSOCIATES

300 Hamilton Avenue #500
Palo Alto, CA 94301
415-324-8400

General Partners
Jack M. Gill
David H. Rammler
Douglas G. DeVivo

Whom to Contact
Any of the above

Type of Firm
Private venture capital firm investing
own capital

Industry Association Membership
WAVC

Project Preferences
Prefer role as deal originator but will also
invest in deals created by others
Type of Financing:
Seed
Startup
Minimum Investment: $250,000
Preferred Investment: $500,000-$1 million
Minimum Operating Data:
Annual Sales—Nominal
P&L—Losses (profits projected after 2 years)

Geographical Preference
West Coast

Industry Preferences

Communications
Data communications
Satellite and microwave communications
Telephone related

Computer Related
Computer graphics, CAD/CAM and CAE
Computer mainframes
Computer services
Memory devices
Micro and mini computers
Office automation
Scanning related
Software-applications
Software-artificial intelligence
Software-systems
Specialized turnkey systems
Terminals
**Electronic Components and
Instrumentation**
Analytical and scientific instrumentation
Laser related
Genetic Engineering
Gene splicing and manufacturing equipment
Monoclonal antibodies and hybridomas
Recombinant DNA (agricultural and
industrial)
Recombinant DNA (medical)
Industrial Products and Equipment
Chemicals
Controls and sensors
Robotics/vision systems
Medical/Health Related
Diagnostic equipment
Diagnostic test products
Disposable products
Drugs and medicines
Hospital and clinical labs
Medical services
Therapeutic equipment
Other
Agriculture, forestry, fishing
Finance and insurance

Additional Information
Year Founded—1981
Capital Under Management—$40 million
Investments(1985-1st 6 months)—8
Invested(1985-1st 6 months)—$3 million
Method of Compensation—Return on
investment is most important, but also
charge management fee

VENCA PARTNERS

235 Montgomery Street #810
San Francisco, CA 94104
415-781-4944

General Partner
Carolynn Gandolfo

Type of Firm
Private venture capital firm investing
own capital

Project Preferences
Will function either as deal originator or
investor in deals created by others
Type of Financing:
Startup
First-stage
Leveraged buyout
Minimum Investment: Less than $100,000
Preferred Investment: $250,000-$500,000
Minimum Operating Data:
Annual Sales—Nominal

Geographical Preferences
Rocky Mountains
West Coast

Industry Preferences

Communications
Commercial communications
Satellite and microwave communications
Telephone related
Computer Related
Computer graphics, CAD/CAM and CAE
Computer services
Office automation
Software-artificial intelligence
**Electronic Components and
Instrumentation**
Fiber optics
Genetic Engineering
Gene splicing and manufacturing equipment
Monoclonal antibodies and hybridomas
Recombinant DNA (agricultural and
industrial)
Recombinant DNA (medical)
Medical/Health Related
Diagnostic equipment
Diagnostic test products
Disposable products
Drugs and medicines
Hospital and clinical labs
Medical services
Therapeutic equipment

Will Not Consider
Financial institutions
Oil and gas exploration and production
Real estate
Stage, motion picture and television
   production

Additional Information
Year Founded—1983
Capital Under Management—$2 million
Method of Compensation—Return on
   investment is of primary concern; do not
   charge fees

VENROCK ASSOCIATES

Two Palo Alto Square #528
Palo Alto, CA 94306
415-493-5577

Anthony Sun, Gen. Ptnr.

See NEW YORK for full listing

VENTANA GROWTH FUND

1660 Hotel Circle North #612
San Diego, CA 92108
619-291-2757

Other Office
19600 Fairchild #150
Irvine, CA 92715
714-476-2204

Partners
F. D. Townsen, Sr. Gen. Ptnr.
Kenneth B. Tingey, Gen. Ptnr.

Whom to Contact
Kenneth B. Tingey

Type of Firm
Private venture capital firm investing
   own capital

Project Preferences
Prefer role as deal originator but will also
   invest in deals created by others
Type of Financing:
Seed
Startup
First-stage
Second-stage
Minimum Investment: $100,000
Preferred Investment: $100,000-$500,000

Minimum Operating Data:
Annual Sales—Nominal
P&L—Losses (profits projected after 2 years)

Geographical Preference
Within two hours of office

Industry Preferences

Communications
Data communications
Satellite and microwave communications
Telephone related
Computer Related
Computer graphics, CAD/CAM and CAE
Computer mainframes
Computer services
Memory devices
Micro and mini computers
Office automation
Scanning related
Software-applications
Software-artificial intelligence
Software-systems
Specialized turnkey systems
Terminals
Consumer
Computer stores/related services
Consumer products
Consumer services
Franchise businesses
Retailing
Distribution
Communications equipment
Computer equipment
Consumer products
Electronics equipment
Food products
Industrial products
Medical products
**Electronic Components and
   Instrumentation**
Analytical and scientific instrumentation
Component fabrication and testing
   equipment
Electronic components
Fiber optics
Laser related
Semiconductors
Energy/Natural Resources
Alternative energy
Coal related
Energy conservation
Technology related products/equipment
Genetic Engineering
Gene splicing and manufacturing equipment
Monoclonal antibodies and hybridomas
Recombinant DNA (agricultural and
   industrial)
Recombinant DNA (medical)

Industrial Products and Equipment
Chemicals
Controls and sensors
Energy management
Equipment and machinery
Other industrial automation
Plastics
Robotics/vision systems
Specialty materials
Medical/Health Related
Diagnostic equipment
Diagnostic test products
Disposable products
Drugs and medicines
Hospital and clinical labs
Medical services
Therapeutic equipment
Other
Agriculture, forestry, fishing
Education related
Finance and insurance
Publishing
Specialty consulting
Transportation
Will Not Consider
Investments in limited partnerships
Real estate

Additional Information
Year Founded—1982
Capital Under Management—$8.75 million
Investments(1985-1st 6 months)—4
Invested(1985-1st 6 months)—$425,000
Method of Compensation—Return on
   investment is of primary concern; do not
   charge fees

VENTURE GROWTH ASSOCIATES

3000 Sand Hill Road
Building 3, #125
Menlo Park, CA 94025
415-854-8001

Managing Partners
James R. Berdell
William H. Welling

Whom to Contact
Either of the above

Type of Firm
Private venture capital firm investing
   own capital

Industry Association Membership
WAVC

Project Preferences

Will function either as deal originator or
  investor in deals created by others
Type of Financing:
Seed
Research and development partnerships
First-stage
Second-stage
Later-stage expansion
Minimum Investment: $250,000
Preferred Investment: $500,000-$1 million
Minimum Operating Data:
Annual Sales—Nominal
P&L—Losses (profits projected after 2 years)

Geographical Preference

West Coast

Industry Preferences

Communications
Data communications
Satellite and microwave communications
Telephone related
Computer Related
Computer graphics, CAD/CAM and CAE
Computer mainframes
Computer services
Memory devices
Micro and mini computers
Office automation
Software-applications
Software-artificial intelligence
Software-systems
Specialized turnkey systems
Distribution
Electrical components
Electronics equipment
**Electronic Components and
  Instrumentation**
Analytical and scientific instrumentation
Electronic components
Semiconductor manufacturing equipment
Semiconductor materials
Semiconductors
Industrial Products and Equipment
Robotics/vision systems
Medical/Health Related
Diagnostic equipment
Diagnostic test products
Therapeutic equipment
Other
Education related

Additional Information

Year Founded—1982
Capital Under Management—$30 million
Investments(1985-1st 6 months)—5
Invested(1985-1st 6 months)—$3 million
Method of Compensation—Return on
  investment is of primary concern; do not
  charge fees

VISTA CAPITAL CORPORATION

701 "B" Street #760
San Diego, CA 92101
619-236-1900

Officers

Frederick J. Howden, Jr., Chm.
Leslie S. Buck, Pres.
Gregory D. Howard, V.P.

Whom to Contact

Any of the above

Type of Firm

SBIC

Affiliation

Vista Partners Inc. (fund manager)

Industry Association Membership

NASBIC

Project Preferences

Will function either as deal originator or
  investor in deals created by others
Type of Financing:
Research and development partnerships
Startup
First-stage
Second-stage
Later-stage expansion
Leveraged buyout
Minimum Investment: $500,000
Preferred Investment: $500,000-$1 million
Minimum Operating Data:
Annual Sales—$500,000
P&L—Losses (profits projected after 2 years)
Annual Sales (LBO)—$5 million-$30 million

Geographical Preferences

Within two hours of office
West Coast

Industry Preferences

Communications
Commercial communications
Data communications
Telephone related

Computer Related
Computer graphics, CAD/CAM and CAE
Computer mainframes
Computer services
Memory devices
Micro and mini computers
Office automation
Scanning related
Software-applications
Software-artificial intelligence
Software-systems
Specialized turnkey systems
Terminals
Consumer
Computer stores/related services
Distribution
Communications equipment
Computer equipment
Electronics equipment
Medical products
**Electronic Components and
  Instrumentation**
Analytical and scientific instrumentation
Component fabrication and testing
  equipment
Electronic components
Fiber optics
Laser related
Semiconductors
Genetic Engineering
Gene splicing and manufacturing equipment
Monoclonal antibodies and hybridomas
Recombinant DNA (agricultural and
  industrial)
Recombinant DNA (medical)
Industrial Products and Equipment
Chemicals
Controls and sensors
Energy management
Equipment and machinery
Other industrial automation
Plastics
Robotics/vision systems
Specialty materials
Medical/Health Related
Diagnostic equipment
Diagnostic test products
Disposable products
Drugs and medicines
Hospital and clinical labs
Medical services
Therapeutic equipment
Other
Agriculture, forestry, fishing
Finance and insurance
Publishing
Transportation

Additional Information

Year Founded—1983
Method of Compensation—Return on investment is most important, but also charge for closing fees, service fees, etc.

VISTA VENTURES

610 Newport Center Drive #400
Newport Beach, CA 92660
714-720-1416

See CONNECTICUT for full listing

WALDEN CAPITAL PARTNERS/ WALDEN VENTURES/ WALDEN INVESTORS

303 Sacramento Street #400
San Francisco, CA 94111
415-391-7225

Other Office

901 147th Place NE
Bellevue, WA 98007
206-643-7572

General Partners

George S. Sarlo (California)
Arthur S. Berliner (California)
Lip-Bu Tan (California)
Theodore M. Wight (Washington)

Whom to Contact

Arthur S. Berliner

Type of Firm

Private venture capital firm investing own capital
SBIC

Project Preferences

Will function either as deal originator or investor in deals created by others
Type of Financing:
Seed
Research and development partnerships
Startup
First-stage
Second-stage
Later-stage expansion
Minimum Investment: $250,000
Preferred Investment: $500,000-$1 million
Minimum Operating Data:
Annual Sales—Nominal

Geographical Preferences

West Coast
USA

Industry Preferences

Communications
Cable television
Commercial communications
Data communications
Satellite and microwave communications
Telephone related
Computer Related
Computer graphics, CAD/CAM and CAE
Computer mainframes
Computer services
Memory devices
Micro and mini computers
Office automation
Scanning related
Software-applications
Software-artificial intelligence
Software-systems
Specialized turnkey systems
Terminals
Consumer
Computer stores/related services
Consumer products
Consumer services
Food and beverage products
Franchise businesses
Hotels and resort areas
Leisure and recreational products
Restaurants
Retailing
Distribution
Communications equipment
Computer equipment
Consumer products
Electronics equipment
Food products
Industrial products
Medical products
Electronic Components and Instrumentation
Analytical and scientific instrumentation
Component fabrication and testing equipment
Electronic components
Fiber optics
Laser related
Semiconductors
Energy/Natural Resources
Alternative energy
Coal related
Drilling and exploration services
Energy conservation
Minerals
Oil and gas exploration and production
Technology related products/equipment

Genetic Engineering
Gene splicing and manufacturing equipment
Monoclonal antibodies and hybridomas
Recombinant DNA (agricultural and industrial)
Recombinant DNA (medical)
Industrial Products and Equipment
Chemicals
Controls and sensors
Energy management
Equipment and machinery
Other industrial automation
Plastics
Robotics/vision systems
Specialty materials
Medical/Health Related
Diagnostic equipment
Diagnostic test products
Disposable products
Drugs and medicines
Hospital and clinical labs
Medical services
Therapeutic equipment
Other
Agriculture, forestry, fishing
Education related
Finance and insurance
Publishing
Specialty consulting
Transportation
Will Not Consider
Real estate

Additional Information

Year Founded—1975
Capital Under Management—$40 million
Investments(1985-1st 6 months)—8
Invested(1985-1st 6 months)—$2.8 million
Method of Compensation—Return on investment is of primary concern; do not charge fees

---

WALLNER & CO.

215 Coast Boulevard
La Jolla, CA 92037
619-454-3805

Partners

Nicholas Wallner, Ptnr.
Peter S. Redfield, Ptnr.
Willard C. McNitt, Ptnr.
Frederick J. Oshay, Ptnr.
Gary M. Acquavella, Assoc.

Whom to Contact

Any of the above

Type of Firm
Private venture capital firm investing
   own capital
Private investment/leveraged buyout group

Project Preferences
Prefer role as deal originator but will also
   invest in deals created by others
Type of Financing:
Second-stage
Leveraged buyout
Minimum Investment: $100,000
Preferred Investment: No preference
Preferred Investment (LBO):
   $1 million and over
Minimum Operating Data:
Annual Sales (LBO)—$10 million and over

Geographical Preference
None

Industry Preferences

Consumer
Computer stores/related services
Consumer products
Consumer services
Food and beverage products
Franchise businesses
Hotels and resort areas
Leisure and recreational products
Restaurants
Retailing
Distribution
Communications equipment
Computer equipment
Consumer products
Electronics equipment
Food products
Industrial products
Medical items
Medical products
Industrial Products and Equipment
Chemicals
Controls and sensors
Energy management
Equipment and machinery
Other industrial automation
Plastics
Robotics/vision systems
Specialty materials
Medical/Health Related
Disposable products
Medical services
Other
Distribution & manufacturing companies with
   strong asset bases
Publishing
Real estate
Transportation

Will Not Consider
Research and development businesses

Additional Information
Year Founded—1974
Method of Compensation—Return on
investment is most important, but also
   charge for closing fees, management fees,
   service fees, etc.

WEISS, PECK & GREER VENTURE PARTNERS, L.P.

555 California Street #4760
San Francisco, CA 94104
415-622-6864

Other Offices
One New York Plaza, 30th Floor
New York, NY 10004
212-908-9500

265 Franklin Street
Boston, MA 02110
617-439-4630

Partners
Philip Greer, Mgn. Gen. Ptnr. (New York)
Robert J. Loarie, Gen. Ptnr. (California)
Ralph T. Linsalata, Gen. Ptnr.
   (Massachusetts)
John C. Savage, Gen. Ptnr. (California)
Eugene M. Weber, Gen. Ptnr. (California)
Gunnar Hurtig III, Gen. Ptnr. (California)

Whom to Contact
Eugene M. Weber
Ralph T. Linsalata

Type of Firm
Private venture capital firm investing
   own capital

Affiliations
Weiss, Peck & Greer (special limited partner)
WestVen

Industry Association Memberships
NVCA
WAVC

Project Preferences
Prefer role as deal originator but will also
   invest in deals created by others
Type of Financing:
Startup
First-stage
Second-stage
Leveraged buyout

Minimum Investment: $500,000
Preferred Investment: Over $1 million
Preferred Investment (LBO):
   $2 million and over
Minimum Operating Data:
Annual Sales—Nominal
P&L—Losses (profits projected after 2 years)
Annual Sales (LBO)—$25 million-$100 million

Geographical Preference
None

Industry Preferences

Communications
Commercial communications
Data communications
Satellite and microwave communications
Telephone related
Computer Related
Computer graphics, CAD/CAM and CAE
Computer mainframes
Computer services
Memory devices
Micro and mini computers
Office automation
Scanning related
Software-applications
Software-artificial intelligence
Software-systems
Specialized turnkey systems
Terminals
Consumer
Consumer products
Consumer services
Food and beverage products
Franchise businesses
Restaurants
Retailing
Distribution
Communications equipment
Computer equipment
Consumer products
Electronics equipment
Food products
Industrial products
Medical products
**Electronic Components and
   Instrumentation**
Analytical and scientific instrumentation
Component fabrication and testing
   equipment
Electronic components
Fiber optics
Laser related
Semiconductors
Energy/Natural Resources
Technology related products/equipment

Genetic Engineering
Gene splicing and manufacturing equipment
Monoclonal antibodies and hybridomas
Recombinant DNA (agricultural and
 industrial)
Recombinant DNA (medical)
Industrial Products and Equipment
Chemicals
Controls and sensors
Energy management
Equipment and machinery
Other industrial automation
Plastics
Robotics/vision systems
Specialty materials
Medical/Health Related
Diagnostic equipment
Diagnostic test products
Disposable products
Drugs and medicines
Hospital and clinical labs
Medical services
Therapeutic equipment
Other
Finance and insurance
Publishing
Transportation

Additional Information
Year Founded—1971
Capital Under Management—$260 million
Investments(1985-1st 6 months)—8
Invested(1985-1st 6 months)—$9 million
Method of Compensation—Return on
 investment is of primary concern; do not
 charge fees

J.H. WHITNEY & CO.

3000 Sand Hill Road
Building 1 #270
Menlo Park, CA 94025
415-854-0500

Other Office
630 Fifth Avenue #3200
New York, NY 10111
212-757-0500

Partners
Benno C. Schmidt, Mgn. Ptnr. (New York)
Don E. Ackerman, Gen. Ptnr. (New York)
Michael C. Brooks, Gen. Ptnr. (New York)
John W. Larson, Gen. Ptnr. (California)
Harry A. Marshall, Gen. Ptnr. (California)
David T. Morgenthaler II, Gen. Ptnr.
 (California)
Russell E. Planitzer, Gen. Ptnr. (New York)
Edward V. Ryan, Gen. Ptnr. (New York)

Whom to Contact
Any of the above

Type of Firm
Private venture capital firm investing
 own capital

Industry Association Membership
NVCA

Project Preferences
Prefer role as deal originator but will also
 invest in deals created by others
Type of Financing:
Seed
Startup
First-stage
Second-stage
Leveraged buyout
Minimum Investment: $1 million
Preferred Investment: Over $1 million

Geographical Preference
None

Industry Preferences

Communications
Cable television
Commercial communications
Data communications
Satellite and microwave communications
Telephone related
Computer Related
Computer graphics, CAD/CAM and CAE
Computer mainframes
Computer services
Memory devices
Micro and mini computers
Office automation
Scanning related
Software-applications
Software-artificial intelligence
Software-systems
Specialized turnkey systems
Terminals
Consumer
Retailing
Distribution
Communications equipment
Consumer products
Electronics equipment
Medical products

**Electronic Components and
 Instrumentation**
Analytical and scientific instrumentation
Component fabrication and testing
 equipment
Electronic components
Fiber optics
Laser related
Semiconductors
Energy/Natural Resources
Technology related products/equipment
Genetic Engineering
Gene splicing and manufacturing equipment
Monoclonal antibodies and hybridomas
Recombinant DNA (agricultural and
 industrial)
Recombinant DNA (medical)
Industrial Products and Equipment
Chemicals
Controls and sensors
Energy management
Equipment and machinery
Other industrial automation
Plastics
Robotics/vision systems
Specialty materials
Medical/Health Related
Diagnostic equipment
Diagnostic test products
Disposable products
Drugs and medicines
Hospital and clinical labs
Medical services
Therapeutic equipment
Will Not Consider
Agribusiness
Entertainment
Real estate
Service

Additional Information
Year Founded—1946
Method of Compensation—Return on
 investment is of primary concern; do not
 charge fees

WOODSIDE FUND

850 Woodside Drive
Woodside, CA 94062
415-368-5545

Partners

Vincent M. Occhipinti, Gen. Ptnr.
V. Frank Mendicino, Gen. Ptnr.
Robert E. Larson, Gen. ptnr.
Charles E. Greb, Gen. Ptnr.
Thomas R. Blakeslee, Ptnr.
William M. Hassebrock, Ptnr.
Craig L. Davidson, Assoc.

Whom to Contact

Any of the above

Type of Firm

Private venture capital firm investing
own capital

Project Preferences

Prefer role as deal originator but will also
invest in deals created by others
Type of Financing:
Seed
Startup
First-stage
Second-stage
Later-stage expansion
Minimum Investment: $100,000
Preferred Investment: $250,000-$500,000
Minimum Operating Data:
Annual Sales—Nominal
P&L—Losses (profits projected after 2 years)

Geographical Preferences

Within two hours of office
West Coast

Industry Preferences

Communications
Commercial communications
Data communications
Satellite and microwave communications
Telephone related
Computer Related
Computer graphics, CAD/CAM and CAE
Computer mainframes
Computer services
Memory devices
Micro and mini computers
Office automation
Scanning related
Software-applications
Software-artificial intelligence
Software-systems
Specialized turnkey systems

Consumer
Consumer products
Consumer services
Franchise businesses
Leisure and recreational products
Restaurants
Retailing
Distribution
Electronics equipment
Industrial products
Medical products
**Electronic Components and
Instrumentation**
Analytical and scientific instrumentation
Component fabrication and testing
equipment
Electronic components
Fiber optics
Laser related
Semiconductors
Energy/Natural Resources
Alternative energy
Technology related products/equipment
Industrial Products and Equipment
Chemicals
Controls and sensors
Energy management
Equipment and machinery
Other industrial automation
Plastics
Robotics/vision systems
Specialty materials
Medical/Health Related
Diagnostic equipment
Diagnostic test products
Disposable products
Drugs and medicines
Hospital and clinical labs
Medical services
Therapeutic equipment
Will Not Consider
Cable television
Motion pictures
Oil, gas or mineral exploration
Real estate

Additional Information

Year Founded—1983
Method of Compensation—Return on
investment is of primary concern; do not
charge fees

XEROX VENTURE CAPITAL

2029 Century Park E. #740
Los Angeles, CA 90067
213-278-7940

Al Talbot, Principal
Stephen P. Taylor, Asso.

See CONNECTICUT for full listing

ZIMMERMANN, WILSON & COMPANY, INC.

533 Carmel Rancho Center #6
Carmel, CA 93923
408-625-0404

Officers

Stephan F.P. Zimmermann, Pres.
Robert Medearis, Assoc.
Carlos Crisp, Assoc.

Whom to Contact

Stephan F.P. Zimmermann

Type of Firm

Consulting firm evaluating and analyzing
venture projects and arranging private
placements
Investment management company
representing direct investors

Affiliations

Carmel Venture Consultants Ltd. (associated
consultant co.)
Carmen Park Capital Group (associated
investment partners)

Project Preferences

Prefer role as deal originator but will also
invest in deals created by others
Type of Financing:
Second-stage
Later-stage expansion
Leveraged buyout
Minimum Investment: $500,000
Preferred Investment: Over $1 million
Minimum Operating Data:
Annual Sales—$500,000
P&L—Losses (profits projected after 2 years)

Geographical Preference

West Coast

Industry Preferences

Communications
Cable television
Commercial communications
Data communications
Satellite and microwave communications
Telephone related
Computer Related
Computer graphics, CAD/CAM and CAE
Computer mainframes
Computer services
Memory devices
Micro and mini computers
Office automation
Scanning related
Software-applications
Software-artificial intelligence
Software-systems
Specialized turnkey systems
Terminals
Consumer
Consumer products
Food and beverage products
Franchise businesses
Leisure and recreational products
**Electronic Components and
  Instrumentation**
Analytical and scientific instrumentation
Component fabrication and testing
  equipment
Electronic components
Fiber optics
Laser related
Semiconductors
Industrial Products and Equipment
Controls and sensors
Equipment and machinery
Other industrial automation
Robotics/vision systems
Specialty materials
Medical/Health Related
Diagnostic equipment
Diagnostic test products
Disposable products
Drugs and medicines
Hospital and clinical labs
Medical services
Therapeutic equipment
Will Not Consider
Motion pictures
Oil and gas drilling
Real estate
Tax-oriented transactions

Additional Information

Year Founded—1976
Investments(1985-1st 6 months)—2
Invested(1985-1st 6 months)—$2.5 million
Method of Compensation—Return on
  investment is most important, but also
  charge for closing fees, service fees, etc.

BOETTCHER VENTURE CAPITAL PARTNERS, L.P.

828 17th Street #216
Denver, CO 80202
303-628-8365

Officers
Foye F. Black, Jr., V.P. & Mgr.
Michael C. Franson, V.P.

Whom to Contact
Either of the above

Type of Firm
Investment banking or merchant banking firm investing own capital or funds of partners or clients

Affiliation
Boettcher & Co., Inc. (managing general partner)

Project Preferences
Will function either as deal originator or investor in deals created by others
Type of Financing:
First-stage
Second-stage
Later-stage expansion
Leveraged buyout
Minimum Investment: $100,000
Preferred Investment: $250,000-$500,000
Minimum Operating Data:
Annual Sales—Nominal
P&L—Break even

Geographical Preferences
Rocky Mountains
West Coast
Northwest

Industry Preferences

Communications
Cable television
Commercial communications
Data communications
Satellite and microwave communications
Telephone related

Computer Related
Computer graphics, CAD/CAM and CAE
Computer mainframes
Computer services
Memory devices
Micro and mini computers
Office automation
Scanning related
Software-applications
Software-artificial intelligence
Software-systems
Specialized turnkey systems
Terminals

Consumer
Computer stores/related services
Consumer products
Consumer services
Food and beverage products
Franchise businesses
Hotels and resort areas
Leisure and recreational products
Restaurants
Retailing

Distribution
Communications equipment
Computer equipment
Consumer products
Electronics equipment
Food products
Industrial products
Medical products

Electronic Components and Instrumentation
Analytical and scientific instrumentation
Component fabrication and testing equipment
Electronic components
Fiber optics
Laser related
Semiconductors

Energy/Natural Resources
Drilling and exploration services
Oil and gas exploration and production
Technology related products/equipment

Industrial Products and Equipment
Controls and sensors
Equipment and machinery
Robotics/vision systems

Medical/Health Related
Diagnostic equipment
Diagnostic test products
Disposable products
Drugs and medicines
Hospital and clinical labs
Medical services
Therapeutic equipment

Other
Publishing
Will Not Consider
Financial institutions
Insurance
Real estate

Additional Information
Year Founded—1984
Capital Under Management—$10.7 million
Investments(1985-1st 6 months)—4
Invested(1985-1st 6 months)—$1.2 million
Method of Compensation—Return on investment is of primary concern; do not charge fees

---

CENTENNIAL BUSINESS DEVELOPMENT FUND, LTD.

1999 Broadway #2100
Denver, CO 80202
303-298-9066

Post Office Box 13977
Denver, CO 80201

General Partners
David Bullwinkle
William D. Stanfill
Steven C. Halstedt
G. Jackson Tankersley Jr.

Whom to Contact
David Bullwinkle
William D. Stanfill

Type of Firm
Private venture capital firm investing own capital in later stage, venture capital backed companies

Affiliation
The Centennial Fund, Ltd.
Centennial Fund II, L.P.

Project Preferences
Will function either as deal originator or investor in deals created by others
Type of Financing:
Later-stage expansion
Leveraged buyout
Minimum Investment: $250,000
Preferred Investment: $500,000-$1 million
Minimum Operating Data:
Annual Sales—Over $10 million
P&L—Break even

Geographical Preference
National

Industry Preferences

Communications
Cable television
Commercial communications
Data communications
Satellite and microwave communications
Telephone related
Computer Related
Computer graphics, CAD/CAM and CAE
Computer mainframes
Computer services
Memory devices
Micro and mini computers
Office automation
Scanning related
Software-applications
Software-artificial intelligence
Software-systems
Specialized turnkey systems
Terminals
Consumer
Computer stores/related services
Consumer products
Consumer services
Food and beverage products
Franchise businesses
Hotels and resort areas
Leisure and recreational products
Restaurants
Retailing
Distribution
Communications equipment
Computer equipment
Consumer products
Electronics equipment
Food products
Industrial products
Medical products
Electronic Components and Instrumentation
Analytical and scientific instrumentation
Component fabrication and testing equipment
Electronic components
Fiber optics
Laser related
Semiconductors
Energy/Natural Resources
Alternative energy
Coal related
Drilling and exploration services
Energy conservation
Minerals
Technology related products/equipment

Genetic Engineering
Gene splicing and manufacturing equipment
Monoclonal antibodies and hybridomas
Recombinant DNA (agricultural and industrial)
Recombinant DNA (medical)
Industrial Products and Equipment
Chemicals
Controls and sensors
Energy management
Equipment and machinery
Other industrial automation
Plastics
Robotics/vision systems
Specialty materials
Medical/Health Related
Diagnostic equipment
Diagnostic test products
Disposable products
Drugs and medicines
Hospital and clinical labs
Medical services
Therapeutic equipment
Other
Education related
Finance and insurance
Publishing
Specialty consulting
Transportation
Will Not Consider
Real estate and project financing

Additional Information
Year Founded—1983
Capital Under Management—$12 million
Method of Compensation—Return on investment is of primary concern; do not charge fees

---

THE CENTENNIAL FUND, LTD./ CENTENNIAL FUND II, L.P.

1999 Broadway #2100
Denver, CO 80202
303-298-9066

Post Office Box 13977
Denver, CO 80201

Partners
Charles T. Closson, Gen. Ptnr.
Steven C. Halstedt, Gen. Ptnr.
G. Jackson Tankersley, Jr., Gen. Ptnr.
Mark Dubovoy, V.P. & Ptnr.
Craig A.T. Jones, Inv. Officer
George Still, Inv. Officer

Whom to Contact
Any of the above

Type of Firm
Private venture capital firm investing own capital

Affiliation
Larimer and Co.
Centennial Business Development Fund

Industry Association Memberships
NASBIC
NVCA

Project Preferences
Prefer role as deal originator but will also invest in deals created by others
Type of Financing:
Seed
Startup
First-stage
Leveraged buyout
Minimum Investment: $100,000
Preferred Investment: $500,000-$1 million
Minimum Operating Data:
Annual Sales—Nominal
P&L—Losses (profits projected after 2 years)

Geographical Preferences
Rocky Mountains
National (communications only)

Industry Preferences

Communications
Cable television
Commercial communications
Data communications
Satellite and microwave communications
Telephone related
Computer Related
Computer graphics, CAD/CAM and CAE
Computer mainframes
Computer services
Memory devices
Micro and mini computers
Office automation
Software-artificial intelligence
Software-systems
Terminals
Consumer
Consumer products
Consumer services
Electronic Components and Instrumentation
Analytical and scientific instrumentation
Electronic components
Fiber optics
Laser related
Semiconductors

Energy/Natural Resources
Alternative energy
Technology related products/equipment
Genetic Engineering
Monoclonal antibodies and hybridomas
Recombinant DNA (agricultural and
   industrial)
Recombinant DNA (medical)
Research and manufacturing equipment
Industrial Products and Equipment
Advanced materials
Chemicals
Controls and sensors
Equipment and machinery
Other industrial automation
Plastics
Robotics/vision systems
Medical/Health Related
Diagnostic equipment
Disposable products
Drugs and medicines
Hospital and clinical labs
Medical services
Therapeutic equipment
Will Not Consider
Construction
Energy extraction
Real estate

Additional Information
Year Founded—1981
Capital Under Management—$70 million
Investments(1985-1st 6 months)—18
Invested(1985-1st 6 months)—$5 million
Method of Compensation—Return on
   investment is of primary concern; do not
   charge fees

CHAMBERS FINANCIAL CORP.

720 South Colorado Boulevard
Suite 940
Denver, CO 80222
303-759-4860

Officers
Brad C. Ayers, Pres.
Robert S. Froug, V.P.
Leslee Moon Soderstrom, Analyst

Whom to Contact
Any of the above

Type of Firm
Private venture capital firm investing
   own capital

Affiliation
Prominvest SA, Brussels (exchange deals)

Industry Association Membership
NASBIC

Project Preferences
Prefer role as deal originator
Type of Financing:
Seed
Startup
Minimum Investment: Less than $100,000
Preferred Investment: $100,000-$250,000
Minimum Operating Data:
Annual Sales—Nominal
P&L—Break even

Geographical Preference
None

Industry Preferences

Communications
Cable television
Commercial communications
Data communications
Satellite and microwave communications
Telephone related
Computer Related
Computer services
Memory devices
Scanning related
Software-artificial intelligence
Consumer
Consumer products
Consumer services
Leisure and recreational products
**Electronic Components and
   Instrumentation**
Analytical and scientific instrumentation
Component fabrication and testing
   equipment
Electronic components
Fiber optics
Laser related
Semiconductors
Energy/Natural Resources
Alternative energy
Technology related products/equipment
Industrial Products and Equipment
Chemicals
Controls and sensors
Energy management
Equipment and machinery
Other industrial automation
Plastics
Robotics/vision systems
Specialty materials

Medical/Health Related
Diagnostic equipment
Diagnostic test products
Disposable products
Drugs and medicines
Hospital and clinical labs
Medical services
Therapeutic equipment
Other
Finance and insurance

Additional Information
Year Founded—1983
Capital Under Management—$1 million
Investments(1985-1st 6 months)—1
Invested(1985-1st 6 months)—$200,000
Method of Compensation—Return on
   investment is most important, but also
   charge for closing fees, service fees, etc.

COLORADO GROWTH CAPITAL, INC.

1600 Broadway #2125
Denver, CO 80202
303-831-0205

Officer
Nicholas H.C. Davis, Chm. & Pres.
Debra Chavez, Inv. Analyst

Whom to Contact
Debra Chavez

Type of Firm
SBIC

Industry Association Membership
NASBIC

Project Preferences
Will function either as deal originator or
   investor in deals created by others
Type of Financing:
Second-stage
Leveraged buyout
Minimum Investment: Less than $100,000
Preferred Investment: $100,000-$250,000
Minimum Operating Data:
Annual Sales—$500,000
P&L—Break even

Geographical Preference
Rocky Mountains

Industry Preferences

Distribution
Communications equipment
Computer equipment
Electronics equipment
**Electronic Components and
 Instrumentation**
Analytical and scientific instrumentation
Component fabrication and testing
 equipment
Electronic components
Semiconductors
Industrial Products and Equipment
Equipment and machinery
Other industrial automation
Robotics/vision systems
Medical/Health Related
Diagnostic equipment
Therapeutic equipment
Other
Manufacturing of patented or proprietary
 products with national market potential
Will Not Consider
High technology
Real estate
Retail
Services
Startup companies

Additional Information

Year Founded—1979
Capital Under Management—$1.6 million
Method of Compensation—Return on
 investment is of primary concern; do not
 charge fees

COLORADO VENTURE CAPITAL
CORPORATION

885 Arapahoe Avenue
Boulder, CO 80302
303-449-9018

Officers
Paul D. Whittle, Chm. & CEO
Clifford C. Thygesen, Pres.
Patrick J. Sweeney, V.P.

Whom to Contact
Patrick J. Sweeney

Type of Firm
Publicly held business development
 company

Project Preferences
Will function either as deal originator or
 investor in deals created by others
Type of Financing:
Second-stage
Leveraged buyout
Minimum Investment: $100,000
Preferred Investment: $100,000-$250,000
Minimum Operating Data:
Annual Sales—Nominal
P&L—Break even

Geographical Preference
Rocky Mountains

Industry Preferences

Communications
Data communications
Satellite and microwave communications
**Electronic Components and
 Instrumentation**
Analytical and scientific instrumentation
Component fabrication and testing
 equipment
Electronic components
Fiber optics
Laser related
Semiconductors
Industrial Products and Equipment
Controls and sensors
Energy management
Equipment and machinery
Other industrial automation
Robotics/vision systems
Specialty materials
Medical/Health Related
Diagnostic equipment
Diagnostic test products
Disposable products
Drugs and medicines
Hospital and clinical labs
Medical services
Therapeutic equipment
Will Not Consider
Mining
Oil and gas
Real estate

Additional Information
Year Founded—1981
Capital Under Management—$4 million
Method of Compensation—Return on
 investment is of primary concern; do not
 charge fees

COLUMBINE VENTURE FUND, LTD.

5613 DTC Parkway #510
Englewood, CO 80111
303-694-3222

General Partners
Mark Kimmel
Sherman J. Muller
Duane D. Pearsall
Terry E. Winters

Whom to Contact
Any of the above

Type of Firm
Private venture capital firm investing
 own capital

Industry Association Memberships
NASBIC
NVCA

Project Preferences
Prefer role as deal originator but will also
 invest in deals created by others
Type of Financing:
Seed
Research and development partnerships
Startup
First-stage
Minimum Investment: Less than $100,000
Preferred Investment: $250,000-$750,000
Minimum Operating Data:
Annual Sales—Nominal
P&L—Losses (profits projected after 2 years)

Geographical Preferences
Within two hours of office
Rocky Mountains

Industry Preferences

Communications
Data communications
Satellite and microwave communications
Computer Related
Computer graphics, CAD/CAM and CAE
Memory devices
Terminals
**Electronic Components and
 Instrumentation**
Analytical and scientific instrumentation
Component fabrication and testing
 equipment
Electronic components
Fiber optics
Laser related
Semiconductors
Energy/Natural Resources
Technology related products/equipment

Genetic Engineering
Gene splicing and manufacturing equipment
Monoclonal antibodies and hybridomas
Recombinant DNA (agricultural and industrial)
Recombinant DNA (medical)
Industrial Products and Equipment
Chemicals
Controls and sensors
Energy management
Equipment and machinery
Other industrial automation
Plastics
Robotics/vision systems
Specialty materials
Medical/Health Related
Diagnostic equipment
Diagnostic test products
Disposable products
Drugs and medicines
Therapeutic equipment
Will Not Consider
Construction
Oil and gas exploration and production
Real estate
Retailing

Additional Information
Year Founded—1983
Capital Under Management—$34.5 million
Investments(1985-1st 6 months)—5
Invested(1985-1st 6 months)—$3 million
Method of Compensation—Return on investment is of primary concern; do not charge fees

CVM EQUITY FUND I, LTD.

2995 Wilderness Place
Boulder, CO 80301
303-440-4055

Partners
William E. Coleman
R.D. Bloomer
R.C. Mercure, Jr.

Whom to Contact
William E. Coleman
R.D. Bloomer

Type of Firm
Private venture capital firm investing own capital

Project Preferences
Will function either as deal originator or investor in deals created by others
Type of Financing:
Startup
First-stage
Leveraged buyout
Minimum Investment: Less than $100,000
Preferred Investment: Less than $100,000
Minimum Operating Data:
P&L—Losses (profits projected after 3 years)

Geographical Preference
Rocky Mountains

Industry Preferences

Communications
Data communications
Computer Related
Computer graphics, CAD/CAM and CAE
Computer mainframes
Computer services
Memory devices
Micro and mini computers
Office automation
Scanning related
Software-applications
Software-artificial intelligence
Software-systems
Specialized turnkey systems
Terminals
Consumer
Consumer products
Consumer services
Distribution
Communications equipment
Computer equipment
Consumer products
Electronics equipment
Industrial products
Medical products
Electronic Components and Instrumentation
Analytical and scientific instrumentation
Component fabrication and testing equipment
Electronic components
Fiber optics
Laser related
Energy/Natural Resources
Technology related products/equipment
Genetic Engineering
Monoclonal antibodies and hybridomas
Recombinant DNA (medical)
Industrial Products and Equipment
Chemicals
Controls and sensors
Plastics
Robotics/vision systems
Specialty materials

Medical/Health Related
Diagnostic equipment
Diagnostic test products
Disposable products
Drugs and medicines
Hospital and clinical labs
Medical services
Therapeutic equipment
Other
Specialty consulting

Additional Information
Year Founded—1983
Capital Under Management—$1.7 million
Investments(1985-1st 6 months)—8
Invested(1985-1st 6 months)—$420,000
Method of Compensation—Return on investment is most important, but also charge for closing fees, service fees, etc.

DAIN BOSWORTH INCORPORATED

1225 17th Street #1800
Denver, CO 80202
303-294-7223

Robert Weisman, V.P.

See MINNESOTA for full listing

FBS VENTURE CAPITAL CO.

3000 Pearl Street #206
Boulder, CO 80301
303-442-6885

Brian P. Johnson, V.P.

See ARIZONA for full listing

GRAYSTONE CAPITAL, LTD.

1600 Stout Street #1920
Denver, CO 80202
303-573-8866

Officers
Gregory Pusey, Mgn. Dir. (special limited partner)
Christopher A. Crane, Dir. (special limited partner)

Whom to Contact
Christopher A. Crane

Type of Firm
Private venture capital firm investing own capital

Affiliation
Revden Corp. (general partner)

Project Preferences
Will function either as deal originator or investor in deals created by others
Type of Financing:
Seed
Leveraged buyout
Preferred Investment: Less than $100,000
Minimum Operating Data:
Annual Sales—Nominal
P&L—Losses (profits projected after 2 years)

Geographical Preference
None

Industry Preferences

Computer Related
Computer graphics, CAD/CAM and CAE
Computer services
Office automation
Consumer
Computer stores/related services
Consumer products
Consumer services
Food and beverage products
Distribution
Computer equipment
Consumer products
Food products
Medical products
Electronic Components and Instrumentation
Analytical and scientific instrumentation
Energy/Natural Resources
Alternative energy
Drilling and exploration services
Minerals
Oil and gas exploration and production
Industrial Products and Equipment
Chemicals
Controls and sensors
Energy management
Robotics/vision systems
Medical/Health Related
Diagnostic equipment
Diagnostic test products
Disposable products
Drugs and medicines
Hospital and clinical labs
Medical services
Therapeutic equipment

Other
Real estate
Specialty consulting
Transportation

Additional Information
Year Founded—1983
Capital Under Management—$2 million
Investments(1985-1st 6 months)—7
Invested(1985-1st 6 months)—$40,000
Method of Compensation—Return on investment is of primary concern; do not charge fees

---

HILL & KIRBY

885 Arapahoe Avenue
Boulder, CO 80302
303-442-5151

General Partners
John G. Hill
Paul J. Kirby
Thomas G. Washing

Whom to Contact
Any of the above

Type of Firm
Private venture capital firm investing own capital

Affiliation
Mayfield Fund (special limited partner)

Industry Association Membership
NVCA

Project Preferences
Will function either as deal originator or investor in deals created by others
Type of Financing:
Seed
Startup
First-stage
Second-stage
Leveraged buyout
Minimum Investment: $250,000
Preferred Investment: $500,000-$1 million
Minimum Operating Data:
Annual Sales—Nominal
P&L—Losses (profits projected after 2 years)

Geographical Preferences
Within two hours of office
Rocky Mountains
Northwest
Southwest
Midwest
West Coast

Industry Preferences

Communications
Data communications
Computer Related
Computer graphics, CAD/CAM and CAE
Computer mainframes
Computer services
Memory devices
Micro and mini computers
Office automation
Scanning related
Software-applications
Software-artificial intelligence
Software-systems
Specialized turnkey systems
Terminals
Distribution
Communications equipment
Computer equipment
Electronics equipment
Electronic Components and Instrumentation
Analytical and scientific instrumentation
Component fabrication and testing equipment
Electronic components
Fiber optics
Laser related
Semiconductors

Additional Information
Year Founded—1982
Capital Under Management—$51 million
Investments(1985-1st 6 months)—7
Invested(1985-1st 6 months)—$4.7 million
Method of Compensation—Return on investment is of primary concern; do not charge fees

---

INTERMOUNTAIN TECHNOLOGY VENTURES, L.P.

1113 Spruce #300
Boulder, CO 80302
303-443-1023

General Partner
K. Dieter Heidrich

Type of Firm
Private venture capital firm investing own capital

Affiliations
Weiss, Peck & Greer
Matrix Partners, L.P.

Project Preferences
Will function either as deal originator or investor in deals created by others
Type of Financing:
Seed
Startup
First-stage
Second-stage
Minimum Investment: Less than $100,000
Preferred Investment: $100,000-$250,000
Minimum Operating Data:
Annual Sales—Nominal
P&L—Losses (profits projected after 2 years)

Geographical Preferences
Rocky Mountains
Southwest

Industry Preferences

Communications
Commercial communications
Data communications
Networking
Satellite and microwave communications
Telephone related
Computer Related
Computer graphics, CAD/CAM and CAE
Computer mainframes
Computer services
Memory devices
Micro and mini computers
Office automation
Scanning related
Software-applications
Software-artificial intelligence
Software-systems
Specialized turnkey systems
Terminals
Distribution
Communications equipment
Computer equipment
Electronics equipment
Electronic Components and Instrumentation
Analytical and scientific instrumentation
Electronic components
Fiber optics
Laser related
Genetic Engineering
Gene splicing and manufacturing equipment
Recombinant DNA (agricultural and industrial)
Recombinant DNA (medical)
Industrial Products and Equipment
Controls and sensors
Equipment and machinery
Other industrial automation
Robotics/vision systems
Medical/Health Related
Diagnostic equipment
Diagnostic test products
Disposable products
Drugs and medicines
Hospital and clinical labs
Medical services
Therapeutic equipment

Additional Information
Year Founded—1984
Capital Under Management—$6 million
Investments(1985-1st 6 months)—2
Invested(1985-1st 6 months)—$300,000
Method of Compensation—Return on investment is of primary concern; do not charge fees

---

INVESTMENT SECURITIES OF COLORADO, INC.

4605 Denice Drive
Englewood, CO 80111
303-796-9192

Officer
Vern D. Kornelsen, Pres.

Type of Firm
Investment banking or merchant banking firm investing own capital or funds of partners or clients

Project Preferences
Prefer role as deal originator
Type of Financing:
Seed
Startup
First-stage
Minimum Investment: Less than $100,000
Preferred Investment: $250,000 or less
Minimum Operating Data:
Annual Sales—Nominal
P&L—Losses (profits projected after 2 years)

Geographical Preferences
Within two hours of office
Rocky Mountains

Industry Preferences

Communications
Data communications
Electronic Components and Instrumentation
Analytical and scientific instrumentation
Component fabrication and testing equipment
Electronic components
Fiber optics
Laser related
Semiconductors
Genetic Engineering
Gene splicing and manufacturing equipment
Monoclonal antibodies and hybridomas
Industrial Products and Equipment
Chemicals
Controls and sensors
Other industrial automation
Medical/Health Related
Diagnostic equipment
Diagnostic test products
Disposable products
Drugs and medicines
Hospital and clinical labs
Medical services
Therapeutic equipment

Additional Information
Year Founded—1969
Investments(1985-1st 6 months)—3
Invested(1985-1st 6 months)—$350,000
Method of Compensation—Return on investment is most important, but also charge for closing fees, service fees, etc.

THE MASTERS FUND

1426 Pearl Street SW #211
Boulder, CO 80302
303-443-2460

Partners
Carl D. Carman
Martin J. Chizzick

Whom to Contact
Either of the above

Type of Firm
Private venture capital firm investing own capital

Project Preferences

Prefer role as deal originator but will also
 invest in deals created by others
Type of Financing:
Seed
Startup
First-stage
Minimum Investment: $250,000
Preferred Investment: $250,000-$500,000
Minimum Operating Data:
Annual Sales—Nominal
P&L—Losses (profits projected after 2 years)

Geographical Preferences

Rocky Mountains
West Coast

Industry Preferences

Communications
Data communications
Computer Related
Memory devices
Office automation
Software-applications
Software-systems
Medical/Health Related
Diagnostic equipment

Additional Information

Year Founded—1983
Capital Under Management—$12 million
Investments(1985-1st 6 months)—7
Invested(1985-1st 6 months)—$706,000
Method of Compensation—Return on
 investment is of primary concern; do not
 charge fees

PERNOVO INC.

1877 Broadway #405
Boulder, CO 80302
303-442-1171

Other Office

Post Office Box 1264
Helsingborg, Sweden 25112
042-183-500

Officers

Nils Lindeblad, Pres. (United States)
Stig Eklund, Pres. (Sweden)

Type of Firm

Venture capital subsidiary or affiliate of
 non-financial corporation

Affiliation

Perstorp AB, Sweden (parent)

Industry Association Membership

NASBIC

Project Preferences

Prefer role as deal originator but will also
 invest in deals created by others
Type of Financing:
Startup
First-stage
Second-stage
Later-stage expansion
Leveraged buyout
Minimum Investment: $100,000
Preferred Investment: $500,000-$1 million
Minimum Operating Data:
Annual Sales—$500,000
P&L—Break even

Geographical Preference

None

Industry Preferences

Distribution
Medical products
**Electronic Components and
 Instrumentation**
Analytical and scientific instrumentation
Component fabrication and testing
 equipment
Fiber optics
Laser related
Energy/Natural Resources
Technology related products/equipment
Genetic Engineering
Gene splicing and manufacturing equipment
Monoclonal antibodies and hybridomas
Recombinant DNA (agricultural and
 industrial)
Recombinant DNA (medical)
Industrial Products and Equipment
Chemicals
Controls and sensors
Other industrial automation
Plastics
Robotics/vision systems
Specialty materials
Medical/Health Related
Diagnostic equipment
Diagnostic test products
Disposable products
Drugs and medicines
Hospital and clinical labs

Additional Information

Year Founded—1973
Capital Under Management—$10 million
Investments(1985-1st 6 months)—30
Method of Compensation—Return on
 investment is of primary concern; do not
 charge fees

THE ROCKIES FUND, INC.

8400 East Prentice Avenue #569
Englewood, CO 80111
303-793-3060

Officers

James H. Galbreath, Chm. & Pres.
Edgar J. Pfohl, V.P. & Secy.
Michael J. Scanlan, V.P. & Treas.

Whom to Contact

Edgar J. Pfohl

Type of Firm

Publicly traded business development
corporation

Affiliation

Galbreath Financial (fund manager and
 investment advisor)

Project Preferences

Prefer role as deal originator
Type of Financing:
Later-stage expansion
Leveraged buyout
Minimum Investment: $100,000
Preferred Investment: $100,000-$250,000
Minimum Operating Data:
Annual Sales—$1.5 million
P&L—Break even

Geographical Preference

Rocky Mountains

Industry Preferences

Communications
Cable television
Commercial communications
Data communications
Satellite and microwave communications
Telephone related

Computer Related
Computer graphics, CAD/CAM and CAE
Computer mainframes
Computer services
Memory devices
Micro and mini computers
Office automation
Scanning related
Software-applications
Software-artificial intelligence
Software-systems
Specialized turnkey systems
Terminals
Consumer
Will consider on a select basis
Distribution
Communications equipment
Computer equipment
Consumer products
Electronics equipment
Food products
Industrial products
Medical products
**Electronic Components and
   Instrumentation**
Analytical and scientific instrumentation
Component fabrication and testing
   equipment
Electronic components
Fiber optics
Laser related
Semiconductors
Energy/Natural Resources
Alternative energy
Technology related products/equipment
Genetic Engineering
Gene splicing and manufacturing equipment
Monoclonal antibodies and hybridomas
Recombinant DNA (agricultural and
   industrial)
Recombinant DNA (medical)
Industrial Products and Equipment
Chemicals
Controls and sensors
Energy management
Equipment and machinery
Other industrial automation
Plastics
Robotics/vision systems
Specialty materials
Medical/Health Related
Diagnostic equipment
Diagnostic test products
Disposable products
Drugs and medicines
Hospital and clinical labs
Medical services
Therapeutic equipment

Other
Agriculture, forestry, fishing
Education related
Finance and insurance
Publishing
Real estate
Specialty consulting
Transportation
Will Not Consider
Commodity-based businesses
Recreation-oriented businesses

Additional Information
Year Founded—1983
Capital Under Management—$3 million
Investments(1985-1st 6 months)—4
Invested(1985-1st 6 months)—$301,000
Method of Compensation—Return on
   investment is most important, but also
   charge for closing fees, service fees, etc.

ROCKY MOUNTAIN VENTURES, LTD.

1100 Tenth Street
Greeley, CO 80632
303-356-1200

Norman M. Dean, V.P.
Thomas A. Rapp, Jr., V.P.

See MONTANA for full listing

STEPHENSON MERCHANT BANKING

100 Garfield Street
Denver, CO 80206
303-837-1700

Partners
A. Emmet Stephenson, Jr., Sr. Ptnr.
Thomas Kent Mitchell, Dir.

Whom to Contact
Thomas Kent Mitchell

Type of Firm
Private venture capital firm investing
   own capital

Industry Association Memberships
NASBIC
NVCA

Project Preferences
Will function either as deal originator or
   investor in deals created by others
Type of Financing:
Later-stage expansion
Leveraged buyout
Minimum Investment: Less than $100,000
Preferred Investment: $500,000-$1 million
Preferred Investment (LBO):
   $500,000-$5 million
Minimum Operating Data:
Annual Sales—Over $3 million
P&L—Profits NBT over $200,000
Annual Sales (LBO)—$5 million-$50 million

Geographical Preferences
Within two hours of office
Rocky Mountains
Northwest
Southwest
East Coast
West Coast

Industry Preferences

Communications
Cable television
Commercial communications
Data communications
Satellite and microwave communications
Consumer
Consumer products
Distribution
Communications equipment
Consumer products
Food products
Industrial products
Medical products
Wholesalers
Industrial Products and Equipment
Controls and sensors
Equipment and machinery
Other industrial automation
Plastics
Medical/Health Related
Diagnostic equipment
Diagnostic test products
Disposable products
Therapeutic equipment
Other
Asbestos abatement
Finance and insurance
Luxury retirement communities
Mobile homes
Publishing
Water related businesses

Additional Information

Year Founded—1969
Capital Under Management—$100 million
Investments(1985-1st 6 months)—3
Method of Compensation—Return on investment is most important, but also charge for closing fees, service fees, etc.

UBD CAPITAL, INC.

1700 Broadway
Denver, CO 80274
303-863-6329

Officers

Richard B. Wigton, Pres.
William Rundorff, Secy. & Treas.

Whom to Contact

Richard B. Wigton

Type of Firm

SBIC
Venture capital subsidiary of commercial bank

Affiliation

United Bank of Denver (parent)

Industry Association Membership

NASBIC

Project Preferences

Prefer role as deal originator but will also invest in deals created by others
Type of Financing:
Second-stage
Later-stage expansion
Leveraged buyout
Minimum Investment: $100,000
Preferred Investment: $100,000-$250,000
Minimum Operating Data:
Annual Sales—$500,000
P&L—Break even
Annual Sales (LBO)—Over $2 million

Geographical Preference

Rocky Mountains

Industry Preferences

Communications
Cable television
Commercial communications
Data communications
Consumer
Consumer products
Consumer services
Leisure and recreational products

Distribution

Communications equipment
Computer equipment
Consumer products
Electronics equipment
Food products
Industrial products
Medical products
Energy/Natural Resources
Alternative energy
Coal related
Drilling and exploration services
Energy conservation
Minerals
Oil and gas exploration and production
Technology related products/equipment
Industrial Products and Equipment
Chemicals
Controls and sensors
Energy management
Equipment and machinery
Other industrial automation
Plastics
Robotics/vision systems
Specialty materials

Additional Information

Year Founded—1985
Capital Under Management—$1 million
Method of Compensation—Return on investment is of primary concern; do not charge fees

---

VENTURE ASSOCIATES LTD.

1337 Eighteenth Street #150
Denver, CO 80202
303-297-8670

30, rue Saint-Pierre
CH-1700 Fribourg
Switzerland
037-231-912

Officers

James B. Arkebauer, Pres.
Peter A. Thompson, V.P.
Charles W. Fusfield, Assoc.

Whom to Contact

James B. Arkebauer (Colorado)

Type of Firm

Private venture capital firm financing through private placement and public offering funding

Project Preferences

Prefer role as deal originator
Type of Financing:
Startup
First-stage
Second-stage
Minimum Investment: $100,000 (private placements)
Preferred Investment: $500,000-$3 million (public offerings)
Minimum Operating Data:
Annual Sales—Nominal
P&L—Losses (profits projected after 1 year)

Geographical Preference

None

Industry Preferences

Communications
Cable television
Commercial communications
Data communications
Satellite and microwave communications
Telephone related
Computer Related
Computer graphics, CAD/CAM and CAE
Computer mainframes
Computer services
Memory devices
Micro and mini computers
Office automation
Scanning related
Software-applications
Software-artificial intelligence
Software-systems
Specialized turnkey systems
Terminals
Consumer
Computer stores/related services
Consumer products
Consumer services
Food and beverage products
Franchise businesses
Hotels and resort areas
Leisure and recreational products
Restaurants
Retailing
Distribution
Communications equipment
Computer equipment
Consumer products
Electronics equipment
Food products
Industrial products
Medical products

Electronic Components and Instrumentation
Analytical and scientific instrumentation
Component fabrication and testing equipment
Electronic components
Fiber optics
Laser related
Semiconductors
Energy/Natural Resources
Alternative energy
Coal related
Drilling and exploration services
Energy conservation
Minerals
Oil and gas exploration and production
Technology related products/equipment
Genetic Engineering
Gene splicing and manufacturing equipment
Monoclonal antibodies and hybridomas
Recombinant DNA (agricultural and industrial)
Recombinant DNA (medical)
Industrial Products and Equipment
Chemicals
Controls and sensors
Energy management
Equipment and machinery
Other industrial automation
Plastics
Robotics/vision systems
Specialty materials
Medical/Health Related
Diagnostic equipment
Diagnostic test products
Disposable products
Drugs and medicines
Hospital and clinical labs
Medical services
Therapeutic equipment
Other
Agriculture, forestry, fishing
Education related
Finance and insurance
Publishing
Specialty consulting
Transportation
Will Not Consider
Real estate

Additional Information
Year Founded—1982
Investments(1985-1st 6 months)—2
Invested(1985-1st 6 months)—$3.2 million
Method of Compensation—Function primarily in service area; receive contingent fee in cash or equity

WESTERN STATES VENTURES, INC.

2120 Hollowbrook Drive #200
Colorado Springs, CO 80918
303-598-8465

Officers
William H. Critchfield, Pres.
Barry A. Weiner, Secy.
Kevin E. Cronk, CFO & Analyst

Whom to Contact
William H. Critchfield
Kevin E. Cronk

Type of Firm
Business development company

Project Preferences
Will function either as deal originator or investor in deals created by others
Type of Financing:
Seed
Startup
First-stage
Leveraged buyout
Minimum Investment: Less than $100,000
Preferred Investment: $250,000 or less
Minimum Operating Data:
Annual Sales—Nominal

Geographical Preferences
Southwest
Rocky Mountains

Industry Preferences

Communications
Satellite and microwave communications
Telephone related
Computer Related
Computer graphics, CAD/CAM and CAE
Computer services
Software-applications
Software-systems
Consumer
Consumer products
Consumer services
Franchise businesses
Restaurants
Distribution
Communications equipment
Computer equipment
Electronics equipment
Medical products
Electronic Components and Instrumentation
Analytical and scientific instrumentation
Electronic components
Fiber optics

Energy/Natural Resources
Oil and gas exploration and production
Technology related products/equipment
Genetic Engineering
Monoclonal antibodies and hybridomas
Recombinant DNA (medical)
Industrial Products and Equipment
Chemicals
Energy management
Robotics/vision systems
Medical/Health Related
Diagnostic equipment
Diagnostic test products
Disposable products
Drugs and medicines
Hospital and clinical labs
Medical services
Therapeutic equipment
Other
Education related

Additional Information
Year Founded—1983
Capital Under Management—$500,000
Investments(1985-1st 6 months)—1
Invested(1985-1st 6 months)—$25,000
Method of Compensation—Return on investment is most important, but also charge for closing fees, service fees, etc.

WOODY CREEK CAPITAL, INC.

1375 Walnut #225
Boulder, CO 80302
303-444-6000

Other Office
Woody Creek Capital
c/o Williams Resources, Inc.
320 South Boston #831
Tulsa, OK 74103
918-582-5811

Officers
Wayne W. Goss, Chm. (Colorado)
Joseph A. Zebrowski, Jr., Pres. (Oklahoma)

Whom to Contact
Either of the above

Type of Firm
Private venture capital firm investing own capital and funds of an affiliated private trust

Project Preferences

Prefer role as deal originator but will also
    invest in deals created by others

Type of Financing:

Leveraged buyout

Preferred Investment: $100,000-$500,000

Minimum Operating Data:

Annual Sales—Nominal

Geographical Preferences

Rocky Mountains

Southwest

Industry Preferences

Computer Related

Software-artificial intelligence

Energy/Natural Resources

Alternative energy

Coal related

Drilling and exploration services

Energy conservation

Minerals

Oil and gas exploration and production

Technology related products/equipment

Industrial Products and Equipment

Chemicals

Energy management

Robotics/vision systems

Additional Information

Year Founded—1982

ABACUS VENTURES

283 Greenwich Avenue
Greenwich, CT 06830
203-629-4991

General Partners
Yung Wong
Charles T. Lee

Whom to Contact
Either of the above

Type of Firm
Private venture capital firm investing
own capital

Project Preferences
Will function either as deal originator or
investor in deals created by others
Type of Financing:
Seed
Startup
First-stage
Second-stage
Minimum Investment: $250,000
Preferred Investment: $500,000-$1 million
Minimum Operating Data:
Annual Sales—Nominal
P&L—Losses (profits projected after 2 years)

Geographical Preference
National

Industry Preferences

Communications
Cable television
Commercial communications
Data communications
Satellite and microwave communications
Telephone related
Computer Related
Telecommunications related
**Electronic Components and
Instrumentation**
Telecommunications related
Industrial Products and Equipment
Telecommunications related

Additional Information
Year Founded—1985
Capital Under Management—$20 million
Method of Compensation—Return on
investment is of primary concern; do not
charge fees

THE BABCOCK GROUP

49 Locust Avenue
Post Office Box 1022
New Canaan, CT 06840
203-972-3579

Officers
Warner K. Babcock, Pres.
Piers L. Curry

Whom to Contact
Warner K. Babcock

Type of Firm
Private venture capital firm investing
own capital
Consulting firm evaluating and analyzing
venture projects and arranging private
placements

Affiliations
Babcock Ventures
Babcock Development Group
Warner King Babcock & Associates

Industry Association Membership
NASBIC

Project Preferences
Will function either as deal originator or
investor in deals created by others
Type of Financing:
Seed
Startup
First-stage
Leveraged buyout
Minimum Investment: Less than $100,000

Geographical Preference
None

Industry Preferences

Industrial Products and Equipment
Chemicals
Equipment and machinery
OEM coatings and specialty coatings
Plastics
Specialty materials
Coating Technologies
Architectural protective
Corrosion protective
Coatings for medical devices or disposables
Electrically conductive, insulating
Medical coatings for skin
Moisture protective
Pipeline coatings
Vapor deposition

Will Not Consider
Non coating related businesses

Additional Information
Year Founded—1985

BEACON PARTNERS

71 Strawberry Hill Avenue #614
Stamford, CT 06902
203-348-8858

Partners
Leonard Vignola
Chuck Murphy
Jack Katzen

Whom to Contact
Leonard Vignola

Type of Firm
Consulting firm evaluating and analyzing
venture projects and arranging private
placements

Industry Association Membership
NASBIC

Project Preferences
Prefer role as deal originator
Type of Financing:
First-stage
Second-stage
Leveraged buyout
Special emphasis on turnarounds
and workouts
Minimum Investment: $100,000
Preferred Investment: $500,000-$1 million
Preferred Investment (LBO): $1 million
Minimum Operating Data:
Annual Sales—$500,000
P&L—Losses (profits projected after 2 years)
Annual Sales (LBO)—$1 million-$10 million

Geographical Preferences
Northeast
Midwest

Industry Preferences

Communications
Cable television
Commercial communications
Data communications
Satellite and microwave communications
Telephone related

Computer Related
Computer graphics, CAD/CAM and CAE
Computer mainframes
Computer services
Memory devices
Micro and mini computers
Office automation
Scanning related
Software-applications
Software-artificial intelligence
Software-systems
Specialized turnkey systems
Terminals
Consumer
Consumer products
Franchise businesses
Distribution
Communications equipment
Food products
Medical products
**Electronic Components and
  Instrumentation**
Analytical and scientific instrumentation
Component fabrication and testing
  equipment
Electronic components
Fiber optics
Laser related
Semiconductors
Genetic Engineering
Monoclonal antibodies and hybridomas
Recombinant DNA (agricultural and
  industrial)
Industrial Products and Equipment
Chemicals
Controls and sensors
Energy management
Equipment and machinery
Other industrial automation
Plastics
Robotics/vision systems
Specialty materials
Medical/Health Related
Diagnostic equipment
Diagnostic test products
Disposable products
Drugs and medicines
Hospital and clinical labs
Medical services
Therapeutic equipment
Other
Publishing
Real estate
Specialty consulting

Additional Information
Year Founded—1975
Method of Compensation—Function primarily
  in service area; receive contingent fee in
  cash or equity
Professional fee required whether or
  not deal closes

BRIDGE CAPITAL ADVISORS, INC.

Cityplace
185 Asylum Street
Hartford, CT 06103
203-275-6700

Hoyt J. Goodrich, Mgn. Dir.

See NEW YORK for full listing

CAPITAL IMPACT CORPORATION

961 Main Street
Bridgeport, CT 06601
203-384-5670

Officers
Kevin S. Tierney, Pres.
John J. Cuticelli, Jr., Sr. V.P.
Joann M. Haines, V.P.
Francis P. Murray, Inv. Officer

Whom to Contact
Joann M. Haines
John J. Cuticelli, Jr.
Francis P. Murray

Type of Firm
SBIC
Venture capital subsidiary of
  commercial bank

Affiliation
Citytrust Bancorp (parent)

Industry Association Membership
NASBIC

Project Preferences
Will function either as deal originator or
  investor in deals created by others
Type of Financing:
Second-stage
Later-stage expansion
Leveraged buyout
Minimum Investment: Less than $100,000
Preferred Investment: $250,000-$500,000
Minimum Operating Data:
P&L—Break even

Geographical Preferences
Northeast
National

Industry Preferences

Consumer
Consumer products
Franchise businesses
Restaurants
Retailing
Distribution
Consumer products
Food products
Industrial products
**Electronic Components and
  Instrumentation**
Analytical and scientific instrumentation
Industrial Products and Equipment
Chemicals
Controls and sensors
Energy management
Equipment and machinery
General manufacturing
Other industrial automation
Plastics
Specialty materials
Other
Real estate
Transportation
Will Not Consider
Startups

Additional Information
Year Founded—1985
Capital Under Management—$7 million
Investments(1985-1st 6 months)—70
Invested(1985-1st 6 months)—$5 million
Method of Compensation—Return on
  investment is most important, but also
  charge for closing fees, service fees, etc.

CAPITAL RESOURCE COMPANY OF CONNECTICUT (LP)

699 Bloomfield Avenue
Bloomfield, CT 06002
203-243-1114

Partners
I. Martin Fierberg
Janice M. Romanowski
Philip D. Feltman
Morris Morgenstein
Michael Konover
Francis Caplan

Whom to Contact
Janice M. Romanowski
I. Martin Fierberg

Type of Firm
SBIC

Industry Association Membership
NASBIC

Project Preferences
Prefer role in deals created by others
Type of Financing:
Second-stage
Leveraged buyout
Minimum Investment: Less than $100,000
Preferred Investment: Less than $250,000
Minimum Operating Data:
Annual Sales—$500,000
P&L—Break even

Geographical Preference
Northeast

Industry Preferences

Communications
Telephone related
Computer Related
Computer graphics, CAD/CAM and CAE
Distribution
Medical products
Other
Transportation

Additional Information
Year Founded—1978
Capital Under Management—$5 million
Method of Compensation—Return on investment is of primary concern; do not charge fees

CIGNA VENTURE CAPITAL INCORPORATED

Cigna Capital Advisers, Inc.
S-307
Hartford, CT 06152
203-726-7598

See DELAWARE for full listing

ELF TECHNOLOGIES, INC.

High Ridge Park
Post Office Box 10037
Stamford, CT 06904
203-358-8120

Officers
Michel Ronc, Pres.
John Mahar, Exec. V.P.
Christine Civiale, Asst. V.P.
François Nicoly, Asst. V.P.

Whom to Contact
John Mahar

Type of Firm
Venture capital subsidiary or affiliate of non-financial corporation

Affiliation
Société Nationale Elf Aquitaine (parent)

Industry Association Memberships
NASBIC
NVCA

Project Preferences
Will function either as deal originator or investor in deals created by others
Type of Financing:
Seed
Startup
First-stage
Second-stage
Minimum Investment: $100,000
Preferred Investment: $250,000-$500,000
Minimum Operating Data:
Annual Sales—Nominal
P&L—Losses (profits projected after 2 years)

Geographical Preference
National

Industry Preferences

Computer Related
Computer graphics, CAD/CAM and CAE
Memory devices
Scanning related
Software-artificial intelligence
Electronic Components and Instrumentation
Fiber optics
Laser related
Energy/Natural Resources
Alternative energy
Drilling and exploration services
Energy conservation
Oil and gas exploration and production
Technology related products/equipment
Genetic Engineering
Monoclonal antibodies and hybridomas
Recombinant DNA (agricultural and industrial)
Recombinant DNA (medical)
Industrial Products and Equipment
Chemicals
Energy management
Plastics
Robotics/vision systems
Specialty materials
Medical/Health Related
Diagnostic test products
Drugs and medicines
Other
Agriculture
Other

Additional Information
Year Founded—1980
Capital Under Management—$50 million
Investments(1985-1st 6 months)—8
Invested(1985-1st 6 months)—$1.3 million
Method of Compensation—Return on investment is of primary concern; do not charge fees

FAIRCHESTER ASSOCIATES

1266 Main Street
Soundview Plaza
Stamford, CT 06902
203-357-0714

Other Office

515 One Piedmont Center
Atlanta, GA 30305
404-231-1550

Officers

William R. Knobloch, Pres. (Stamford)
Carl W. Knobloch, Jr., V.P. (Atlanta)

Whom to Contact

William R. Knobloch

Type of Firm

Private venture capital firm investing
own capital

Project Preferences

Prefer role as deal originator
Type of Financing:
Second-stage
Leveraged buyout
Minimum Investment: $250,000
Preferred Investment: $250,000-$500,000
Minimum Operating Data:
Annual Sales—$1.5 million
P&L—Must be profitable

Geographical Preferences

Northeast
Southeast
East Coast

Industry Preferences

Distribution
Medical products
**Electronic Components and
Instrumentation**
Analytical and scientific instrumentation
Component fabrication and testing
equipment
Electronic components
Fiber optics
Laser related
Semiconductors
Energy/Natural Resources
Alternative energy
Coal related
Drilling and exploration services
Energy conservation
Minerals
Oil and gas exploration and production
Technology related products/equipment

Industrial Products and Equipment
Controls and sensors
Energy management
Equipment and machinery
Medical/Health Related
Diagnostic equipment
Diagnostic test products
Disposable products
Drugs and medicines
Hospital and clinical labs
Medical services
Therapeutic equipment
Other
Agriculture, forestry, fishing
Finance and insurance
Publishing

Additional Information

Year Founded—1958
Capital Under Management—$10 million
Investments(1985-1st 6 months)—2
Invested(1985-1st 6 months)—$500,000
Method of Compensation—Return on
investment is of primary concern; do not
charge fees

FAIRFIELD VENTURE PARTNERS

1275 Summer Street
Stamford, CT 06905
203-358-0255

Other Office

650 Town Center Drive #810
Costa Mesa, CA 92626
714-754-5717

Partners

Pedro A. Castillo, Mgn. Ptnr. (Connecticut)
Oakes Ames, Gen. Ptnr. (Connecticut)
Edmund M. Olivier, Gen. Ptnr. (California)
Randall R. Lunn, Gen. Ptnr. (California)
Eugene E. Pettinelli, Gen. Ptnr. (Connecticut)
Thomas D. Berman, Assoc. (Connecticut)
Lawrence A. Bock, Assoc. (California)

Whom to Contact

Any of the above

Type of Firm

Private venture capital firm investing
own capital

Industry Association Membership

NVCA

Project Preferences

Will function either as deal originator or
investor in deals created by others
Type of Financing:
Seed
Startup
First-stage
Second-stage
Later-stage expansion
Leveraged buyout
Minimum Investment: $100,000
Preferred Investment: Over $750,000
Minimum Operating Data:
Annual Sales—Nominal
P&L—Losses (profits projected after 2 years)

Geographical Preferences

Within two hours of office
Northeast
West Coast

Industry Preferences

Communications
Commercial communications
Data communications
Satellite and microwave communications
Telephone related
Computer Related
Computer graphics, CAD/CAM and CAE
Computer mainframes
Computer services
Memory devices
Micro and mini computers
Office automation
Scanning related
Software-applications
Software-artificial intelligence
Software-systems
Specialized turnkey systems
Distribution
Medical products
**Electronic Components and
Instrumentation**
Analytical and scientific instrumentation
Component fabrication and testing
equipment
Electronic components
Fiber optics
Laser related
Semiconductors
Genetic Engineering
Gene splicing and manufacturing equipment
Monoclonal antibodies and hybridomas
Recombinant DNA (agricultural and
industrial)
Recombinant DNA (medical)

Industrial Products and Equipment
Chemicals
Controls and sensors
Energy management
Other industrial automation
Robotics/vision systems
Specialty materials
Medical/Health Related
Diagnostic equipment
Diagnostic test products
Disposable products
Hospital and clinical labs
Medical services
Therapeutic equipment
Other
Finance and insurance
Publishing

Additional Information
Year Founded—1981
Capital Under Management—$100 million
Investments(1985-1st 6 months)—8
Invested(1985-1st 6 months)—$6.9 million
Method of Compensation—Return on
   investment is of primary concern; do not
   charge fees

FIRST CONNECTICUT SBIC

177 State Street
Bridgeport, CT 06604
203-366-4726

Officers
James M. Breiner, Chm. & Treas.
David Engelson, Pres.
Steven Breiner, Exec. V.P.
Lawrence Yurdin, Exec. V.P.

Whom to Contact
Any of the above

Type of Firm
SBIC

Industry Association Membership
NASBIC

Project Preferences
Prefer role as deal originator
Type of Financing:
Second-stage
Leveraged buyout
Minimum Investment: Less than $100,000
Preferred Investment: $100,000-$250,000
Minimum Operating Data:
Annual Sales—Nominal
P&L—Losses (profits projected after 2 years)

Geographical Preferences
Within two hours of office
Northeast

Industry Preferences
None
Will Not Consider
Computer related companies
High technology startups

Additional Information
Year Founded—1960
Capital Under Management—$34 million
Invested(1985-1st 6 months)—$11 million
Method of Compensation—Return on
   investment is most important, but also
   charge for closing fees, service fees, etc.

GEMINI ASSOCIATES

16 Pitkin Street
East Hartford, CT 06108
203-528-9674

Officer
G. Stanton Geary, Pres.

Type of Firm
Consulting firm evaluating and analyzing
   venture projects and arranging private
   placements

Project Preferences
Prefer role as deal originator
Type of Financing:
Startup
First-stage
Second-stage
Minimum Investment: $250,000
Preferred Investment: $250,000-$500,000
Minimum Operating Data:
Annual Sales—Nominal
P&L—Losses (profits projected after 2 years)

Geographical Preference
Within two hours of office

Industry Preferences

Communications
Central station fire and burglar
   alarm companies
Security systems
Computer Related
Software-applications
Software-systems

Consumer
Computer stores/related services
Consumer products
Consumer services
Food and beverage products
Franchise businesses
Hotels and resort areas
Leisure and recreational products
Restaurants
Specialty foods
Distribution
Security products
Medical/Health Related
Hospital and clinical labs
Medical services

Additional Information
Year Founded—1971
Method of Compensation—Professional fee
   required whether or not deal closes

GENERAL ELECTRIC VENTURE CAPITAL CORPORATION

3135 Easton Turnpike
Fairfield, CT 06431
203-373-3333

Other Offices
33 Riverside Avenue
Westport, CT 06880
203-373-2154

3000 Sand Hill Road
Building 1, #230
Menlo Park, CA 94025
415-854-8092

Exchange Place, Floor 14
Boston, MA 02109
617-227-7922

Officers
Harry T. Rein, Pres. & CEO (Fairfield)
James J. Fitzpatrick, Sr. V.P. (Westport)
Gregory P. Stapleton, Sr. V.P. (Menlo Park)
Robert W. McVicar, Sr. V.P. (Menlo Park)
Eric A. Young, V.P. (Menlo Park)
Stephen L. Waechter, V.P. & Treas. (Fairfield)
Andrew C. Bangser, V.P. (Boston)
Preston H. Abbott, Secy. & Counsel
   (Fairfield)
David I. Nierenberg, Sr. V.P. (Menlo Park)
Lane C. DeCamp, V.P. (Westport)
Roxane I. Googin, Venture Analyst (Fairfield)
Mary C. Bechmann, Venture Analyst
   (Menlo Park)

Whom to Contact
Lane C. DeCamp
Roxane I. Googin
Mary C. Bechmann

Type of Firm
Venture capital subsidiary or affiliate of non-financial corporation

Affiliation
General Electric Company

Industry Association Membership
NVCA

Project Preferences
Will function either as deal originator or investor in deals created by others
Type of Financing:
Seed
Research and development partnerships
Startup
First-stage
Second-stage
Later-stage expansion
Minimum Investment: $100,000
Preferred Investment: $500,000 and over
Minimum Operating Data:
Annual Sales—Nominal
P&L—Losses (profits projected after 2 years)

Geographical Preference
None

Industry Preferences

Communications
Cable television
Commercial communications
Data communications
Satellite and microwave communications
Telephone related
Computer Related
Computer graphics, CAD/CAM and CAE
Computer mainframes
Computer services
Memory devices
Micro and mini computers
Office automation
Scanning related
Software-applications
Software-artificial intelligence
Software-systems
Specialized turnkey systems
Terminals
Consumer
Computer stores/related services
Consumer products
Consumer services

Distribution
Communications equipment
Computer equipment
Consumer products
Electronics equipment
Industrial products
Medical products
Electronic Components and Instrumentation
Analytical and scientific instrumentation
Component fabrication and testing equipment
Electronic components
Fiber optics
Laser related
Semiconductors
Energy/Natural Resources
Alternative energy
Technology related products/equipment
Genetic Engineering
Gene splicing and manufacturing equipment
Monoclonal antibodies and hybridomas
Recombinant DNA (agricultural and industrial)
Recombinant DNA (medical)
Industrial Products and Equipment
Chemicals
Controls and sensors
Energy management
Equipment and machinery
Other industrial automation
Plastics
Robotics/vision systems
Specialty materials
Medical/Health Related
Diagnostic equipment
Diagnostic test products
Disposable products
Drugs and medicines
Hospital and clinical labs
Medical services
Therapeutic equipment
Other
Agriculture, forestry, fishing
Education related
Finance and insurance
Will Not Consider
Non-technology based
Real estate

Additional Information
Year Founded—1968
Investments(1985-1st 6 months)—18
Invested(1985-1st 6 months)—$19 million
Method of Compensation—Return on investment is of primary concern; do not charge fees

---

GRAYROCK CAPITAL INC.

36 Grove Street
New Canaan, CT 06840
203-966-8392

Other Office
2 International Boulevard
Rexdale, Ontario
Canada M9W 1A2
416-675-4808

Officers
W.J. Gluck, Pres.
D.P. Driscoll, V.P.

Whom to Contact
W.J. Gluck (Connecticut)
D.P. Driscoll (Ontario)

Type of Firm
Venture capital subsidiary or affiliate of non-financial corporation

Affiliation
The Molson Companies Limited (parent)

Industry Association Memberships
NASBIC
NVCA

Project Preferences
Prefer role as deal originator but will also invest in deals created by others
Type of Financing:
Startup
First-stage
Second-stage
Later-stage expansion
Leveraged buyout
Minimum Investment: $100,000
Preferred Investment: $250,000-$500,000
Minimum Operating Data:
Annual Sales—$500,000
P&L—Losses (profits projected after 2 years)

Geographical Preferences
Northwest
East Coast
Midwest
West Coast
Near major metropolitan areas

Industry Preferences

Communications
Cable television
Commercial communications
Data communications
Satellite and microwave communications
Telephone related

Computer Related
Computer services
Office automation
Consumer
Computer stores/related services
Consumer products
Consumer services
Food and beverage products
Franchise businesses
Hotels and resort areas
Leisure and recreational products
Restaurants
Retailing
Distribution
Communications equipment
Computer equipment
Consumer products
Electronics equipment
Food products
Industrial products
Medical products
**Electronic Components and
  Instrumentation**
Fiber optics
Laser related
Energy/Natural Resources
Oil and gas exploration and production
Technology related products/equipment
Genetic Engineering
Gene splicing and manufacturing equipment
Monoclonal antibodies and hybridomas
Recombinant DNA (agricultural and
  industrial)
Recombinant DNA (medical)
Industrial Products and Equipment
Chemicals
Other industrial automation
Robotics/vision systems
Medical/Health Related
Diagnostic equipment
Diagnostic test products
Disposable products
Drugs and medicines
Hospital and clinical labs
Medical services
Therapeutic equipment
Other
Publishing
Will Not Consider
Software
Capital intensive businesses

Additional Information
Year Founded—1981
Capital Under Management—$30 million
Investments(1985-1st 6 months)—5
Invested(1985-1st 6 months)—$1.7 million

GTE CORPORATION

One Stamford Forum
Stamford, CT 06904
203-965-2117

Officer
Herbert F. Balzuweit, V.P.
  Business Development

Type of Firm
Corporate development department of GTE

Project Preferences
Prefer role in deals created by others
Type of Financing:
Later-stage expansion
Leveraged buyout
Preferred Investment: Over $1 million
Minimum Operating Data:
Annual Sales—Nominal

Geographical Preference
None

Industry Preferences

Communications
Data communications
Satellite and microwave communications
Telephone related
**Electronic Components and
  Instrumentation**
Electronic components
Laser related
Optics technology
Industrial Products and Equipment
Connectors
Hard surface coatings
Lighting: electronic ballasts
Precision materials: metals and ceramics

JAMES B. KOBAK & COMPANY

774 Hollow Tree Ridge Road
Darien, CT 06820
203-655-8764

Officer
James B. Kobak

Type of Firm
Consulting firm evaluating and analyzing
  venture projects and arranging private
  placements

Project Preferences
Will function either as deal originator or
  investor in deals created by others
Preferred Investment: Less than $100,000

Industry Preferences

Other
Publishing

Additional Information
Year Founded—1971

MARKETCORP VENTURE ASSOCIATES, L.P.

285 Riverside Avenue
Westport, CT 06880
203-222-1000

General Partners
E. Bulkeley Griswold
Rick Kurz
James W. Larson

Whom to Contact
Any of the above

Type of Firm
Private venture capital firm investing
  own capital

Affiliation
Marketing Corporation of America,
  Westport, CT (parent)

Project Preferences
Prefer role as deal originator but will also
  invest in deals created by others
Type of Financing:
Seed
Research and development partnerships
Later-stage expansion
Leveraged buyout
Minimum Investment: $250,000
Preferred Investment: $500,000-$1 million
Preferred Investment (LBO):
  $2 million-$5 million
Minimum Operating Data:
Annual Sales (LBO)—$20 million-$50 million

Geographical Preferences
Northeast
East Coast
Midwest

Industry Preferences

Communications
Cable television
Radio and television
Telephone related

Consumer
Consumer electronics
Non-food packaged goods
Distribution
Consumer products
Food products
**Electronic Components and
 Instrumentation**
Consumer electronics
Genetic Engineering
Recombinant DNA (agricultural and
 industrial)
Medical/Health Related
Home health care
Other
Publishing

Additional Information
Year Founded—1984
Capital Under Management—$66 million
Investments(1985-1st 6 months)—9
Invested(1985-1st 6 months)—$4 million
Method of Compensation—Return on
 investment is of primary concern; do not
 charge fees

MEMHARD INVESTMENT BANKERS, INC.

Post Office Box 617
Old Greenwich, CT 06870
203-637-5494

Officers
Richard C. Memhard, Pres.
Laura Memhard Fleming, Treas.
R. Scott Memhard, V.P.

Whom to Contact
Any of the above

Type of Firm
Investment banking or merchant banking
 firm investing own capital or funds of
 partners or clients
Consulting firm evaluating and analyzing
 venture projects and arranging private
 placements

Project Preferences
Prefer role as deal originator
Type of Financing:
Startup
First-stage
Second-stage
Later-stage expansion
Leveraged buyout
Minimum Investment: $500,000
Preferred Investment: $500,000-$1 million

Minimum Operating Data:
Annual Sales—Nominal
P&L—Losses (profits projected after 2 years)

Geographical Preferences
Southeast
East Coast
Midwest

Industry Preferences

Communications
Cable television
Satellite and microwave communications
Telephone related
Computer Related
Computer graphics, CAD/CAM and CAE
Computer services
Office automation
Consumer
Computer stores/related services
Consumer services
Food and beverage products
Hotels and resort areas
Distribution
Communications equipment
Computer equipment
Electronics equipment
Industrial products
**Electronic Components and
 Instrumentation**
Analytical and scientific instrumentation
Electronic components
Fiber optics
Laser related
Semiconductors
Energy/Natural Resources
Alternative energy
Energy conservation
Oil and gas exploration and production
Industrial Products and Equipment
Chemicals
Controls and sensors
Equipment and machinery
Robotics/vision systems
Specialty materials
Medical/Health Related
Diagnostic equipment
Hospital and clinical labs
Therapeutic equipment
Other
Agriculture, forestry, fishing
Education related
Finance and insurance
Publishing
Real estate

Additional Information
Year Founded—1973
Capital Under Management—$1 million
Investments(1985-1st 6 months)—2
Invested(1985-1st 6 months)—$700,000
Method of Compensation—Return on
 investment is most important, but also
 charge for closing fees, service fees, etc.
Function primarily in service area; receive
 contingent fee in cash or equity

MIP EQUITY FUND

Mip Equity Fund
47 Layfayette Place
Greenwich, CT 06830
203-661-6342

Other Office
Bezuidenhoutseweg 27
2594 The Hague
The Netherlands
070-814-891

Officers
A.B. DeBoer, Chm. & CEO
 (The Netherlands)
J. Blaak, Exec. V.P. (The Netherlands)
P. Steyhouwer, Exec. V.P. (The Netherlands)
Dan Piliero, Dir., U.S. Ops/Sr. V.P. (U.S.)
Hans Hylkema, Sr. Proj. Mgr.
 (The Netherlands)
Roel Van der Hayde, Proj. Mgr.
 (The Netherlands)

Whom to Contact
Dan Piliero
J. Blaak

Type of Firm
Private venture capital firm investing
 own capital
May provide subordinated convertible loans
 and help secure government grants for
 companies investing in The Netherlands

Industry Association Membership
NVCA

Project Preferences
Prefer role in deals created by others
Type of Financing:
Second-stage
Later-stage expansion
Minimum Investment: $1 million
Minimum Operating Data:
Annual Sales—Over $3 million
P&L—Must be profitable

Geographical Preference

Company may be located anywhere,
but investment must be made in
The Netherlands

Industry Preferences

Communications
Cable television
Commercial communications
Data communications
Satellite and microwave communications
Telephone related
Computer Related
Computer graphics, CAD/CAM and CAE
Computer mainframes
Computer services
Memory devices
Micro and mini computers
Office automation
Scanning related
Software-applications
Software-artificial intelligence
Software-systems
Specialized turnkey systems
Terminals
Distribution
Communications equipment
Computer equipment
Consumer products
Electronics equipment
Food products
Industrial products
Medical products
**Electronic Components and
Instrumentation**
Analytical and scientific instrumentation
Component fabrication and testing
equipment
Electronic components
Fiber optics
Laser related
Semiconductors
Energy/Natural Resources
Alternative energy
Coal related
Drilling and exploration services
Energy conservation
Minerals
Oil and gas exploration and production
Technology related products/equipment
Genetic Engineering
Gene splicing and manufacturing equipment
Monoclonal antibodies and hybridomas
Recombinant DNA (agricultural and
industrial)
Recombinant DNA (medical)

Industrial Products and Equipment
Chemicals
Controls and sensors
Energy management
Equipment and machinery
Other industrial automation
Plastics
Robotics/vision systems
Specialty materials
Medical/Health Related
Diagnostic equipment
Diagnostic test products
Disposable products
Drugs and medicines
Hospital and clinical labs
Medical services
Therapeutic equipment
Other
Agriculture, forestry, fishing
Education related
Finance and insurance
Publishing
Real estate
Specialty consulting
Transportation

Additional Information

Year Founded—1981
Capital Under Management—$400 million
Investments(1985-1st 6 months)—12
Invested(1985-1st 6 months)—$130 million
Method of Compensation—Return on
investment is of primary concern; do not
charge fees

NEW YORK SECURITIES CO.,
INCORPORATED

Two Rocaton Road
Darien, CT 06820
203-655-7488

Other Office

575 Madison Avenue
New York, NY 10022
212-605-0421

Officer

F. Kenneth Melis, Chm. (Connecticut)

Type of Firm

Investment banking or merchant banking
firm investing own capital or funds of
partners or clients

Affiliation

New York Securities Placement Corporation

Project Preferences

Prefer role as deal originator
Type of Financing:
First-stage
Leveraged buyout
Minimum Investment: $100,000
Minimum Operating Data:
Annual Sales—Nominal

Geographical Preference

Northeast

Industry Preferences

Communications
Cable television
Computer Related
Computer services
Distribution
Computer equipment
Energy/Natural Resources
Alternative energy
Medical/Health Related
Diagnostic equipment
Diagnostic test products
Disposable products
Drugs and medicines
Hospital and clinical labs
Medical services
Therapeutic equipment
Other
Agriculture, forestry, fishing
Finance and insurance

Additional Information

Year Founded—1962
Investments(1985-1st 6 months)—1
Invested(1985-1st 6 months)—$60,000

NORTHEASTERN CAPITAL CORP.

61 High Street
East Haven, CT 06512
203-469-7901

Officer

Louis W. Mingione, Pres. & Exec. Dir.

Type of Firm

SBIC

Industry Association Membership
NASBIC

Project Preferences
Will function either as deal originator or
 investor in deals created by others
Type of Financing:
Second-stage
Later-stage expansion
Leveraged buyout
Preferred Investment: Less than $100,000
Minimum Operating Data:
Annual Sales—Nominal
P&L—Losses (profits projected after 1 year)

Geographical Preference
East Coast

Industry Preferences

Computer Related
Computer services
Software-applications
Software-systems
Consumer
Computer stores/related services
Consumer products
Consumer services
Food and beverage products
Franchise businesses
Hotels and resort areas
Leisure and recreational products
Retailing
Distribution
Communications equipment
Computer equipment
Consumer products
Electronics equipment
Food products
Industrial products
Medical products
Medical/Health Related
Diagnostic equipment
Diagnostic test products
Disposable products
Drugs and medicines
Hospital and clinical labs
Medical services
Therapeutic equipment
Other
Insurance
Real estate
Specialty consulting
Transportation

Additional Information
Year Founded—1961
Capital Under Management—$1.6 million
Investments(1985-1st 6 months)—4
Invested(1985-1st 6 months)—$100,000
Method of Compensation—Return on
 investment is most important, but also
 charge for closing fees, service fees, etc.

OAK INVESTMENT PARTNERS

257 Riverside Avenue
Westport, CT 06880
203-226-8346

Other Office
2055 Gateway Place #550
San Jose, CA 95110
408-286-5233

Contacts
Bandel L. Carano, Assoc. (Connecticut)
Edward F. Glassmeyer (Connecticut)
Stewart H. Greenfield (Connecticut)
Carla P. Haugen (Connecticut)
Michael D. Kaufman (Connecticut)
Ann Huntress Lamont (Connecticut)
Ginger M. More (Connecticut)
Catherine A. Pierson (California)
Ronald J. Verrilli, CFO (Connecticut)
Karen C. Vinjamuri (Connecticut)
Jeffrey D. West (California)

Type of Firm
Private venture capital firm investing
 own capital

Industry Association Membership
NVCA

Project Preferences
Prefer role as deal originator
Type of Financing:
Startup
First-stage
Second-stage
Later-stage expansion
Leveraged buyout
Minimum Investment: $500,000
Preferred Investment: Over $1 million

Geographical Preference
None

Industry Preferences

Communications
Data communications
Satellite and microwave communications
Telephone related
Computer Related
Computer graphics, CAD/CAM and CAE
Computer services
Expert systems
**Electronic Components and
 Instrumentation**
Fiber optics
Laser related
Semiconductors
Genetic Engineering
Gene splicing and manufacturing equipment
Monoclonal antibodies and hybridomas
Recombinant DNA (agricultural and
 industrial)
Recombinant DNA (medical)
Industrial Products and Equipment
Controls and sensors
Other industrial automation
Medical/Health Related
Diagnostic equipment
Diagnostic test products
Medical services

Additional Information
Year Founded—1978
Capital Under Management—$235 million
Investments(1985-1st 6 months)—20
Invested(1985-1st 6 months)—$16 million
Method of Compensation—Return on
 investment is of primary concern; do not
 charge fees

ORIEN VENTURES

36 Grove Street
New Canaan, CT 06840
203-972-3400

Partner
George R. Kalan, Mgn. Gen. Ptnr.

Type of Firm
Private venture capital firm investing
 own capital

Affiliation
Vista Ventures (affiliated company)

Project Preferences

Will function either as deal originator or investor in deals created by others

Type of Financing:
Startup
First-stage
Second-stage
Later-stage expansion
Leveraged buyout
Minimum Investment: $100,000
Preferred Investment: $500,000-$1 million
Minimum Operating Data:
Annual Sales—Nominal
P&L—Losses (profits projected after 3 years)

Geographical Preference

None

Industry Preferences

Communications
Data communications
Satellite and microwave communications
Telephone related
Computer Related
Computer graphics, CAD/CAM and CAE
Computer mainframes
Computer services
Micro and mini computers
Office automation
Scanning related
Software-artificial intelligence
Software-systems
Specialized turnkey systems
Terminals
Electronic Components and Instrumentation
Analytical and scientific instrumentation
Component fabrication and testing equipment
Electronic components
Fiber optics
Laser related
Semiconductors
Genetic Engineering
Gene splicing and manufacturing equipment
Monoclonal antibodies and hybridomas
Recombinant DNA (agricultural and industrial)
Recombinant DNA (medical)
Industrial Products and Equipment
Chemicals
Controls and sensors
Energy management
Equipment and machinery
Other industrial automation
Plastics
Robotics/vision systems
Specialty materials

Medical/Health Related
Diagnostic equipment
Diagnostic test products
Disposable products
Drugs and medicines
Hospital and clinical labs
Medical services
Therapeutic equipment
Other
Agriculture, forestry, fishing
Will Not Consider
Financial intermediaries
Real estate

Additional Information

Year Founded—1985
Capital Under Management—$30 million

OXFORD VENTURE CORPORATION

Soundview Plaza
1266 Main Street
Stamford, CT 06902
203-964-0592

Other Office

233 Wilshire Boulevard #730
Santa Monica, CA 90401
213-458-3135

Partners

Kenneth W. Rind, Gen. Ptnr. (Connecticut)
Cornelius T. Ryan, Gen. Ptnr. (Connecticut)
William R. Lonergan, Gen. Ptnr. (Connecticut)
Francis X. Driscoll, Gen. Ptnr. (Connecticut)
Stevan A. Birnbaum, Gen. Ptnr. (California)
Janice K. DeLong, Assoc. (Connecticut)
Bonnie J. Renta, Res. Analyst (California)
Elizabeth B. Smith, Res. Asst. (Connecticut)

Whom to Contact

Janice K. Delong
Bonnie J. Renta

Type of Firm

Private venture capital firm investing own capital

Industry Association Memberships

NASBIC
NVCA

Project Preferences

Will function either as deal originator or investor in deals created by others

Type of Financing:
Startup
First-stage
Second-stage
Later-stage expansion
Leveraged buyout
Minimum Investment: $500,000
Preferred Investment: $500,000-$1 million
Minimum Operating Data:
Annual Sales—Nominal
P&L—Losses (profits projected after 3 years)

Geographical Preference

None

Industry Preferences

Communications
Cable television
Commercial communications
Data communications
Satellite and microwave communications
Telephone related
Computer Related
Computer graphics, CAD/CAM and CAE
Computer mainframes
Computer services
Memory devices
Micro and mini computers
Office automation
Scanning related
Software-applications
Software-artificial intelligence
Software-systems
Specialized turnkey systems
Terminals
Distribution
Communications equipment
Computer equipment
Electronics equipment
Medical products
Electronic Components and Instrumentation
Analytical and scientific instrumentation
Component fabrication and testing equipment
Electronic components
Fiber optics
Laser related
Semiconductors
Energy/Natural Resources
Alternative energy
Genetic Engineering
Gene splicing and manufacturing equipment
Monoclonal antibodies and hybridomas
Recombinant DNA (agricultural and industrial)
Recombinant DNA (medical)

Industrial Products and Equipment
Chemicals
Controls and sensors
Energy management
Equipment and machinery
Other industrial automation
Plastics
Robotics/vision systems
Specialty materials
Medical/Health Related
Diagnostic equipment
Diagnostic test products
Disposable products
Drugs and medicines
Hospital and clinical labs
Medical services
Therapuetic equipment

Additional Information
Year Founded—1981
Capital Under Management—$100 million
Investments(1985-1st 6 months)—10
Invested(1985-1st 6 months)—$3.7 million
Method of Compensation—Return on
  investment is of primary concern; do not
  charge fees

THE PITTSFORD GROUP

42 Greenwich Hills Drive
Greenwich, CT 36830
203-531-0322

See NEW YORK for full listing

PRIME CAPITAL MANAGEMENT CO., INC.

One Landmark Square #800
Stamford, CT 06901
203-964-0642

Officers
Theodore H. Elliott, Jr., Chm.
Dean E. Fenton, Pres.
H. Thomas Gnuse, V.P.

Whom to Contact
Dean E. Fenton

Type of Firm
Private venture capital firm investing
  own capital

Industry Association Membership
NVCA

Project Preferences
Will function either as deal originator or
  investor in deals created by others
Type of Financing:
Startup
First-stage
Minimum Investment: $250,000
Preferred Investment: $250,000-$500,000
Minimum Operating Data:
Annual Sales—Nominal

Geographical Preferences
Northeast
East Coast

Industry Preferences

Communications
Cable television
Commercial communications
Data communications
Satellite and microwave communications
Telephone related
Computer Related
Computer graphics, CAD/CAM and CAE
Computer mainframes
Computer services
Memory devices
Micro and mini computers
Office automation
Scanning related
Software-applications
Software-artificial intelligence
Software-systems
Specialized turnkey systems
Terminals
Consumer
Computer stores/related services
Distribution
Communications equipment
Computer equipment
Electronics equipment
Industrial products
Medical products
**Electronic Components and
  Instrumentation**
Analytical and scientific instrumentation
Component fabrication and testing
  equipment
Electronic components
Fiber optics
Laser related
Semiconductors
Energy/Natural Resources
Alternative energy
Energy conservation
Technology related products/equipment

Genetic Engineering
Gene splicing and manufacturing equipment
Monoclonal antibodies and hybridomas
Recombinant DNA (agricultural and
  industrial)
Recombinant DNA (medical)
Industrial Products and Equipment
Controls and sensors
Energy management
Equipment and machinery
Other industrial automation
Robotics/vision systems
Medical/Health Related
Diagnostic equipment
Diagnostic test products
Will Not Consider
Non high technology companies

Additional Information
Year Founded—1981
Capital Under Management—$26.2 million
Method of Compensation—Return on
  investment is of primary concern; do not
  charge fees

REGIONAL FINANCIAL ENTERPRISES

36 Grove Street
New Canaan, CT 06840
203-966-2800

Other Office
315 East Eisenhower Parkway
Suite 300
Ann Arbor, MI 48104
313-769-0941

Partners
Robert M. Williams, Ptnr. (Connecticut)
George E. Thomassy III, Ptnr. (Connecticut)
Howard C. Landis, Ptnr. (Connecticut)
Robert R. Sparacino, Ptnr. (Connecticut)
John V. Titsworth, Ptnr. (Connecticut)
James P. O'Neill, Ptnr. (Connecticut)
Barry P. Walsh, Assoc. (Michigan)

Whom to Contact
Any of the above

Type of Firm
Private venture capital firm investing
  own capital
SBIC

Industry Association Memberships
NASBIC
NVCA

Project Preferences

Prefer role as deal originator but will also invest in deals created by others

Type of Financing:
Startup
First-stage
Second-stage
Later-stage expansion
Leveraged buyout
Minimum Investment: $500,000
Preferred Investment: Over $1 million
Preferred Investment (LBO):
$1 million-$4 million
Minimum Operating Data:
Annual Sales—Nominal
P&L—Losses (profits projected after 2 years)
Annual Sales (LBO)—
$20 million-$100 million

Geographical Preference

National

Industry Preferences

Communications
Cable television
Commercial communications
Data communications
Satellite and microwave communications
Telephone related
Computer Related
Computer graphics, CAD/CAM and CAE
Computer services
Memory devices
Office automation
Scanning related
Software-applications
Software-artificial intelligence
Software-systems
Specialized turnkey systems
Consumer
Retailing
Distribution
Communications equipment
Computer equipment
Consumer products
Electronics equipment
Food products
Industrial products
Medical products
Electronic Components and Instrumentation
Analytical and scientific instrumentation
Component fabrication and testing equipment
Electronic components
Fiber optics
Laser related
Semiconductors

Genetic Engineering
Gene splicing and manufacturing equipment
Monoclonal antibodies and hybridomas
Recombinant DNA (agricultural and industrial)
Recombinant DNA (medical)
Industrial Products and Equipment
Chemicals
Controls and sensors
Robotics/vision systems
Specialty materials
Medical/Health Related
Diagnostic equipment
Diagnostic test products
Disposable products
Drugs and medicines
Hospital and clinical labs
Medical services
Therapeutic equipment
Other
Publishing
Transportation

Additional Information

Year Founded—1980
Capital Under Management—$130 million
Investments(1985-1st 6 months)—13
Invested(1985-1st 6 months)—$8.6 million
Method of Compensation—Return on investment is of primary concern; do not charge fees

---

SAUGATUCK CAPITAL COMPANY

999 Summer Street
Stamford, CT 06905
203-348-6669

Officers

Frank J. Hawley, Jr.
Alexander H. Dunbar
Norman W. Johnson

Whom to Contact

Any of the above

Type of Firm

Private venture capital firm investing own capital

Affiliation

Hawley and Associates

Industry Association Memberships

NASBIC
NVCA

Project Preferences

Prefer role as deal originator but will also invest in deals created by others

Type of Financing:
Second-stage
Later-stage expansion
Leveraged buyout
Minimum Investment: $500,000
Preferred Investment: $500,000-$1 million
Preferred Investment (LBO):
$1 million-$3 million
Minimum Operating Data:
Annual Sales—$1.5 million
P&L—Break even

Geographical Preference

None

Industry Preferences

Communications
Cable television
Commercial communications
Data communications
Satellite and microwave communications
Telephone related
Consumer
Consumer services
Food and beverage products
Leisure and recreational products
Distribution
Communications equipment
Consumer products
Food products
Industrial products
Medical products
Industrial Products and Equipment
Chemicals
Controls and sensors
Energy management
Equipment and machinery
Other industrial automation
Plastics
Robotics/vision systems
Specialty materials
Medical/Health Related
Alcohol & substance abuse centers
Diagnostic equipment
Diagnostic test products
Disposable products
Drugs and medicines
Hospital and clinical labs
Long-term care companies
Medical services
Psychiatric care centers
Therapeutic equipment
Other
Finance and insurance
Transportation

Additional Information

Year Founded—1982
Capital Under Management—$55 million
Investments(1985-1st 6 months)—5
Invested(1985-1st 6 months)—$7 million
Method of Compensation—Return on
investment is of primary concern; do not
charge fees

DONALD C. SEIBERT

Post Office Box 740
Old Greenwich, CT 06870
203-637-1704

Owner

Donald C. Seibert

Type of Firm

Private venture capital firm investing
own capital

Project Preferences

Will function either as deal originator or
investor in deals created by others
Type of Financing:
Seed
Startup
First-stage
Second-stage
Leveraged buyout
Minimum Investment: Less than $100,000
Preferred Investment: Less than $100,000
Minimum Operating Data:
Annual Sales—Nominal
P&L—Break even

Geographical Preference

None

Industry Preferences

Communications
Cable television
Commercial communications
Data communications
Satellite and microwave communications
Telephone related
Computer Related
Computer graphics, CAD/CAM and CAE
Computer mainframes
Computer services
Memory devices
Micro and mini computers
Office automation
Software-applications
Software-systems
Terminals

**Electronic Components and
Instrumentation**
Analytical and scientific instrumentation
Electronic components
Laser related
Optics technology
Semiconductors
Energy/Natural Resources
Minerals
Oil and gas
Industrial Products and Equipment
Industrial automation
Process controls
Robotics/vision systems
Medical/Health Related
Diagnostic equipment
Drugs and medicines
Hospital and clinical labs
Medical services
Therapeutic equipment

Additional Information

Year Founded—1968
Capital Under Management—$3 million
Method of Compensation—Return on
investment is of primary concern; do not
charge fees

SWEDISH INDUSTRIAL
DEVELOPMENT CORPORATION

545 Steamboat Road
Greenwich, CT 06830
203-661-2500

Officer

Tord Carmel, Pres.

Type of Firm

Venture capital subsidiary or affiliate of
non-financial corporation

Affiliation

Procordia AB, Sweden (parent)

Project Preferences

Will function either as deal originator or
investor in deals created by others
Type of Financing:
Second-stage
Minimum Investment: Less than $100,000
Preferred Investment: $100,000-$250,000
Minimum Operating Data:
Annual Sales—Nominal
P&L—Break even

Geographical Preference

National

Industry Preferences

Computer Related
Computer services
Software-artificial intelligence
Software-systems
Consumer
Food and beverage products
Genetic Engineering
Gene splicing and manufacturing equipment
Monoclonal antibodies and hybridomas
Recombinant DNA (agricultural and
industrial)
Recombinant DNA (medical)
Medical/Health Related
Drugs and medicines

Additional Information

Year Founded—1969
Method of Compensation—Return on
investment is of primary concern; do not
charge fees

TECHNOLOGY TRANSITIONS, INC.

One State Street #1950
Hartford, CT 06103
203-246-8142

Officers

Peter L. Scott, Chm.
Stanley F. Alfeld, Pres.
Richard B. Curtiss, V.P.
Stewart H. Rodman, V.P.
Timothy L. Haviland, Cntlr.

Whom to Contact

Stanley F. Alfeld
Richard B. Curtiss
Stewart H. Rodman

Type of Firm

Private venture capital firm investing
own capital

Project Preferences

Prefer role as deal originator but will also
invest in deals created by others
Type of Financing:
Seed
Research and development partnerships
Startup
First-stage
Second-stage
Minimum Investment: $250,000
Preferred Investment: $500,000-$1 million
Minimum Operating Data:
Annual Sales—Nominal
P&L—Losses (profits projected after 3 years)

Geographical Preferences

Northeast
Southeast
Southwest
East Coast
West Coast

Industry Preferences

Communications
Various
Computer Related
Computer graphics, CAD/CAM and CAE
Micro and mini computer based systems
Office automation
Software
**Electronic Components and
  Instrumentation**
Analytical and scientific instrumentation
Fiber optics
Laser related
Industrial Products and Equipment
Controls and sensors
Other industrial automation
Robotics/vision systems
Specialty materials
Medical/Health Related
Diagnostic equipment
Other
Aerospace and defense systems
Will Not Consider
Non high technology businesses

Additional Information

Year Founded—1984
Capital Under Management—$40 million
Investments(1985-1st 6 months)—10
Invested(1985-1st 6 months)—$3 million
Method of Compensation—Return on
investment

VENTECH PARTNERS, L.P.

30 Tower Lane
Avon Park South
Avon, CT 06001
203-677-0183

Other Office

200 Park Avenue #2525
New York, NY 10017
212-692-9177

General Partners

Samuel F. McKay (Connecticut)
Richard L. King (New York)

Whom to Contact

Samuel F. McKay
Richard L. King

Type of Firm

Private venture capital firm investing
  own capital

Project Preferences

Prefer role as deal originator but will also
  invest in deals created by others
Type of Financing:
Startup
First-stage
Second-stage
Minimum Investment: $250,000
Preferred Investment: $500,000-$1 million
Minimum Operating Data:
Annual Sales—Nominal
P&L—Losses (profits projected after 2 years)

Geographical Preference

None

Industry Preferences

Communications
Cable television
Commercial communications
Data communications
Satellite and microwave communications
Telephone related
Computer Related
Computer graphics, CAD/CAM and CAE
Computer mainframes
Computer services
Memory devices
Micro and mini computers
Office automation
Scanning related
Software-applications
Software-artificial intelligence
Software-systems
Specialized turnkey systems
Terminals
Distribution
Communications equipment
Computer equipment
Consumer products
Electronics equipment
Food products
Industrial products
Medical products
**Electronic Components and
  Instrumentation**
Analytical and scientific instrumentation
Component fabrication and testing
  equipment
Electronic components
Fiber optics
Laser related
Semiconductors

Energy/Natural Resources
Technology related products/equipment
Genetic Engineering
Gene splicing and manufacturing equipment
Monoclonal antibodies and hybridomas
Recombinant DNA (agricultural and
  industrial)
Recombinant DNA (medical)
Industrial Products and Equipment
Chemicals
Controls and sensors
Energy management
Equipment and machinery
Other industrial automation
Plastics
Robotics/vision systems
Specialty materials
Medical/Health Related
Diagnostic equipment
Diagnostic test products
Disposable products
Drugs and medicines
Hospital and clinical labs
Medical services
Therapeutic equipment

Additional Information

Year Founded—1982
Capital Under Management—$29 million
Investments(1985-1st 6 months)—6
Invested(1985-1st 6 months)—$2 million
Method of Compensation—Return on
  investment is of primary concern; do not
  charge fees

VISTA TECHNOLOGY
VENTURES, INC.

2410 Long Ridge Road
Stamford, CT 06903
203-322-0091
203-326-2751

Officers

Irwin Rudich, Pres.
Rose S. Rudich, V.P.

Whom to Contact

Irwin Rudich

Type of Firm

Private venture capital firm investing
  own capital
Investment banking or merchant banking
  firm investing own capital or funds of
  partners or clients
Consulting firm evaluating and analyzing
  venture projects and arranging private
  placements

Project Preferences
Prefer role as deal originator
Type of Financing:
Research and development partnerships
First-stage
Second-stage
Leveraged buyout
Minimum Investment: $500,000
Preferred Investment: $500,000-$1 million
Minimum Operating Data:
Annual Sales—Nominal
P&L—Losses (profits projected after 1 year)

Geographical Preferences
Within two hours of office
Northeast

Industry Preferences

Communications
Cable television
Commercial communications
Data communications
Satellite and microwave communications
Telephone related
Computer Related
Computer graphics, CAD/CAM and CAE
Computer mainframes
Computer services
Memory devices
Micro and mini computers
Office automation
Scanning related
Software-applications
Software-artificial intelligence
Software-systems
Specialized turnkey systems
Terminals
**Electronic Components and
   Instrumentation**
Analytical and scientific instrumentation
Component fabrication and testing
   equipment
Electronic components
Fiber optics
Laser related
Semiconductors
Genetic Engineering
Gene splicing and manufacturing equipment
Monoclonal antibodies and hybridomas
Recombinant DNA (agricultural and
   industrial)
Recombinant DNA (medical)

Industrial Products and Equipment
Chemicals
Controls and sensors
Energy management
Equipment and machinery
Other industrial automation
Plastics
Robotics/vision systems
Specialty materials
Medical/Health Related
Diagnostic equipment
Diagnostic test products
Disposable products
Drugs and medicines
Hospital and clinical labs
Medical services
Therapeutic equipment
Other
Publishing
Will Not Consider
Consumer retail

Additional Information
Year Founded—1969
Investments(1985-1st 6 months)—1
Invested(1985-1st 6 months)—$500,000
Method of Compensation—Return on
   investment is most important, but also
   charge for closing fees, service fees, etc.

VISTA VENTURES

36 Grove Street
New Canaan, CT 06840
203-972-3400

Other Offices
610 Newport Center Drive #400
Newport Beach, CA 92660
714-720-1416

Vista Ventures Ltd.
18 Hand Court
London WC1
England
01-242-1360

Partners
Gerald B. Bay, Mgn. Gen. Ptnr.
   (Connecticut)
Robert P. Cummins, Gen. Ptnr. (Connecticut)
Edwin Snape, Gen. Ptnr. (Connecticut)
John F. Tomlin, Gen. Ptnr. (Connecticut)
Gregory F. Zaic, Special Ltd. Ptnr.
   (Connecticut)
Robert C. Fleming, Assoc. (Connecticut)

Whom to Contact
Any of the above

Type of Firm
Private venture capital firm investing
   own capital

Affiliations
Vista Ventures Ltd. (affiliated company)
Orien Ventures (affiliated company)

Industry Association Memberships
NASBIC
NVCA

Project Preferences
Will function either as deal originator or
   investor in deals created by others
Type of Financing:
Seed
Startup
First-stage
Second-stage
Later-stage expansion
Leveraged buyout
Minimum Investment: $250,000
Preferred Investment: $500,000-$1 million
Minimum Operating Data:
Annual Sales—Nominal

Geographical Preference
None

Industry Preferences

Communications
Cable television
Commercial communications
Data communications
Satellite and microwave communications
Telephone related
Computer Related
Computer graphics, CAD/CAM and CAE
Computer mainframes
Computer services
Memory devices
Micro and mini computers
Office automation
Scanning related
Software-applications
Software-artificial intelligence
Software-systems
Specialized turnkey systems
Terminals
**Electronic Components and
   Instrumentation**
Analytical and scientific instrumentation
Component fabrication and testing
   equipment
Electronic components
Fiber optics
Laser related
Semiconductors

Genetic Engineering
Gene splicing and manufacturing equipment
Monoclonal antibodies and hybridomas
Recombinant DNA (agricultural and
  industrial)
Recombinant DNA (medical)
Industrial Products and Equipment
Chemicals
Controls and sensors
Energy management
Equipment and machinery
Other industrial automation
Plastics
Robotics/vision systems
Specialty materials
Medical/Health Related
Diagnostic equipment
Diagnostic test products
Disposable products
Drugs and medicines
Hospital and clinical labs
Medical services
Therapeutic equipment
Other
Agriculture, forestry, fishing

Additional Information
Year Founded—1980
Capital Under Management—$100 million
Investments(1985-1st 6 months)—11
Invested(1985-1st 6 months)—$3.5 million
Method of Compensation—Return on
  investment is of primary concern; do not
  charge fees

NEAL WEHR & ASSOCIATES

85 Quarry Dock Road
Branford, CT 06405
203-481-9225

Owner
Neal Wehr

Type of Firm
Consulting firm evaluating and analyzing
  venture projects and arranging private
  placements

Project Preferences
Prefer role as deal originator
Type of Financing:
Later-stage expansion
Leveraged buyout
Minimum Investment: $100,000
Preferred Investment: $250,000-$500,000
Preferred Investment (LBO): $50,000
Minimum Operating Data:
Annual Sales—$4 million
P&L—Break even

Geographical Preference
Northeast

Industry Preferences

Distribution
Communications equipment
Computer equipment
Consumer products
Electronics equipment
Food products
Industrial products
Medical products
Wholesaling
**Industrial Products and
  Equipment**
Chemicals
Controls and sensors
Energy management
Equipment and machinery
General manufacturing
Other industrial automation
Plastics
Robotics/vision systems
Specialty materials
Other
Education related
Publishing
Specialty consulting
Will Not Consider
High technology businesses

Additional Information
Year Founded—1975
Method of Compensation—Function primarily
  in service area; receive contingent fee in
  cash or equity

WHITEHEAD ASSOCIATES

15 Valley Drive
Greenwich, CT 06830
203-629-4633

Officers
Edwin C. Whitehead, Chm.
Joseph A. Orlando, Pres.
William E. Engbers, V.P.

Whom to Contact
William E. Engbers
Joseph A. Orlando

Type of Firm
Private venture capital firm investing
  own capital

Industry Association Memberships
NASBIC
NVCA

Project Preferences
Will function either as deal originator or
  investor in deals created by others
Type of Financing:
Seed
Startup
First-stage
Second-stage
Leveraged buyout
Minimum Investment: Less than $100,000
Preferred Investment: $500,000-$1 million
Minimum Operating Data:
Annual Sales—Nominal
P&L—Losses (profits projected after 5 years)

Geographical Preference
National

Industry Preferences

Communications
Commercial communications
Data communications
Computer Related
Scanning related
Software-artificial intelligence
Specialized turnkey systems
**Electronic Components and
  Instrumentation**
Analytical and scientific instrumentation
Component fabrication and testing
  equipment
Electronic components
Fiber optics
Laser related

Energy/Natural Resources
Technology related products/equipment
Genetic Engineering
Gene splicing and manufacturing equipment
Monoclonal antibodies and hybridomas
Recombinant DNA (agricultural and industrial)
Recombinant DNA (medical)
Industrial Products and Equipment
Controls and sensors
Robotics/vision systems
Medical/Health Related
Diagnostic equipment
Diagnostic test products
Disposable products
Drugs and medicines
Hospital and clinical labs
Medical devices
Medical services
Medical related computers and software
Therapeutic equipment

Additional Information
Year Founded—1980
Investments(1985-1st 6 months)—10
Method of Compensation—Return on investment is of primary concern; do not charge fees

XEROX VENTURE CAPITAL

800 Long Ridge Road
Post Office Box 1600
Stamford, CT 06904
203-329-8700

Other Office
2029 Century Park E. #740
Los Angeles, CA 90067
213-278-7940

Officers
Richard J. Hayes, Sr. Principal (Connecticut)
Lawrence R. Robinson III, Principal (Connecticut)
Al Talbot, Principal (California)
Worth Z. Ludwick, Assoc. (Connecticut)
Stephen P. Taylor, Assoc. (California)

Whom to Contact
Lawrence R. Robinson, III
Al Talbot

Type of Firm
Venture capital subsidiary or affiliate of non-financial corporation

Affiliation
Xerox Corp.

Project Preferences
Will function either as deal originator or investor in deals created by others
Type of Financing:
Startup
First-stage
Second-stage
Minimum Investment: $100,000
Preferred Investment: $500,000-$1 million
Minimum Operating Data:
Annual Sales—$500,000

Geographical Preference
None

Industry Preferences

Communications
Data communications
Computer Related
Computer graphics, CAD/CAM and CAE
Computer mainframes
Computer services
Memory devices
Micro and mini computers
Office automation
Software-applications
Software-systems
Terminals
Electronic Components and Instrumentation
Analytical and scientific instrumentation
Electronic components
Fiber optics
Laser related
Semiconductors

Additional Information
Year Founded—1975

CIGNA VENTURE CAPITAL INCORPORATED

Brandywine Office Building
One Beaver Valley Road
Wilmington, DE 19850

Fund Advisor
Cigna Capital Advisers, Inc.
S-307
Hartford, CT 06152
203-726-7598

Officer
Richard H. Forde, V.P., Fund Advisor
(Connecticut)

Type of Firm
Insurance company

Affiliation
Cigna Corporation (parent)

Project Preferences
Prefer role in deals created by others
Type of Financing:
Second-stage
Later-stage expansion
Leveraged buyout
Minimum Investment: $250,000
Preferred Investment: $500,000
Minimum Operating Data:
Annual Sales—Nominal
P&L—Losses (profits projected after 2 years)

Geographical Preference
National

Industry Preferences

Communications
Cable television
Commercial communications
Data communications
Satellite and microwave communications
Telephone related
Computer Related
Computer graphics, CAD/CAM and CAE
Memory devices
Micro and mini computers
Office automation
Specialized turnkey systems
Consumer
Leisure and recreational products
Distribution
Communications equipment
Computer equipment
Electronics equipment
Medical products

Electronic Components and Instrumentation
Analytical and scientific instrumentation
Electronic components
Fiber optics
Industrial Products and Equipment
Chemicals
Controls and sensors
Energy management
Other industrial automation
Robotics/vision systems
Medical/Health Related
Diagnostic equipment
Diagnostic test products
Disposable products
Drugs and medicines
Hospital and clinical labs
Medical services
Therapeutic equipment
Other
Publishing
Transportation

Additional Information
Year Founded—1969
Capital Under Management—$125 million
Investments(1985-1st 6 months)—6
Invested(1985-1st 6 months)—$12.5 million
Method of Compensation—Return on investment is of primary concern; do not charge fees

ALLIED CAPITAL CORPORATION

1625 I Street NW
Washington, DC 20006
202-331-1112

Other Office

111 East Las Olas Boulevard
Post Office Box 14758
Fort Lauderdale, FL 33301
305-763-8484

Officers

George C. Williams, Chm.
(Washington, D.C.)
David Gladstone, Pres. (Washington, D.C.)
Brooks H. Browne, Sr. V.P.
(Washington, D.C.)
Jonathan J. Ledecky, V.P. (Washington, D.C.)
Edwin H. Spina (Florida)
Clyde D. Garrett, II, V.P. (Washington, D.C.)
Cabell Williams, III, V.P. (Washington, D.C.)
Kathleen T. Ryan, Asst. V.P.
(Washington, D.C.)
Marion E.M. Erickson, Asst. Secy.
(Washington, D.C.)

Whom to Contact

David Gladstone
Jonathan J. Ledecky
Brooks H. Browne
Edwin H. Spina

Type of Firm

Public venture capital fund

Affiliation

Allied-North American (joint venture with
North American Company Ltd.)

Industry Association Membership

NASBIC

Project Preferences

Will function either as deal originator or
investor in deals created by others
Type of Financing:
First-stage
Second-stage
Later-stage expansion
Leveraged buyout
Minimum Investment: $100,000
Preferred Investment: $500,000-$1.5 million
Minimum Operating Data:
Annual Sales—$500,000
P&L—Break even

Geographical Preferences

Northeast
Southeast
East Coast
Midwest
Gulf States

Industry Preferences

Communications
Cable television
Commercial communications
Data communications
Satellite and microwave communications
Telephone related
Computer Related
Computer graphics, CAD/CAM and CAE
Computer mainframes
Computer services
Memory devices
Micro and mini computers
Office automation
Scanning related
Software-applications
Software-artificial intelligence
Software-systems
Specialized turnkey systems
Terminals
Consumer
Computer stores/related services
Consumer products
Consumer services
Food and beverage products
Franchise businesses
Hotels and resort areas
Leisure and recreational products
Restaurants
Retailing
Distribution
Communications equipment
Computer equipment
Consumer products
Electronics equipment
Food products
Industrial products
Medical products
**Electronic Components and
Instrumentation**
Analytical and scientific instrumentation
Component fabrication and testing
equipment
Electronic components
Fiber optics
Laser related
Semiconductors
Energy/Natural Resources
Alternative energy
Energy conservation
Technology related products/equipment
Genetic Engineering
Gene splicing and manufacturing equipment

Industrial Products and Equipment
Chemicals
Controls and sensors
Energy management
Equipment and machinery
Other industrial automation
Plastics
Robotics/vision systems
Specialty materials
Medical/Health Related
Diagnostic equipment
Diagnostic test products
Disposable products
Drugs and medicines
Hospital and clinical labs
Medical services
Therapeutic equipment
Other
Transportation

Additional Information

Year Founded—1958
Capital Under Management—$100 million
Method of Compensation—Return on
investment is of primary concern; do not
charge fees

AMERICAN ADVANCE VENTURES, L.P.

2000 L Street NW #702
Washington, DC 20036
202-887-5379

Other Office

2851 Fillmore Street
San Francisco, CA 94123
415-921-1797

Partners

E. Stevens Potts (District of Columbia)
Donald E. Bowman (District of Columbia)
Philip J. Gioia (California)

Whom to Contact

E. Stevens Potts

Type of Firm

Private venture capital firm investing
own capital

Project Preferences

Prefer role as deal originator but will also
invest in deals created by others
Type of Financing:
Seed
Startup
First-stage

Minimum Investment: $250,000
Preferred Investment: $800,000
Minimum Operating Data:
Annual Sales—Nominal
P&L—Losses (profits projected after 1 year)

Geographical Preference
National

Industry Preferences

Aerospace
Various
Communications
Telecommunications
Electronic Components and Instrumentation
Defense electronics
Energy/Natural Resources
Energy related
Medical/Health Related
Biotechnology
Medical technology
Other
Military technology

Additional Information
Year Founded—1985
Method of Compensation—Return on investment is most important, but also charge for closing fees, service fees, etc.

AMERICAN SECURITY CAPITAL CORP.

730 15th Street NW
Washington, DC 20013
202-624-4843

Officer
Brian K. Mercer, V.P. & Mgr.

Type of Firm
SBIC
Venture capital subsidiary of commercial bank

Affiliations
American Security Corporation (parent)
American Security Bank (affiliate)

Industry Association Membership
NASBIC

Project Preferences
Prefer role in deals created by others
Type of Financing:
Second-stage
Later-stage expansion
Leveraged buyout
Minimum Investment: $100,000
Preferred Investment: $250,000-$500,000
Minimum Operating Data:
Annual Sales—Over $1 million
P&L—Break even

Geographical Preference
East Coast

Industry Preferences
Communications
Cable television
Commercial communications
Data communications
Satellite and microwave communications
Computer Related
Software-systems
Electronic Components and Instrumentation
Analytical and scientific instrumentation
Component fabrication and testing equipment
Laser related
Industrial Products and Equipment
Chemicals
Controls and sensors
Energy management
Equipment and machinery
Other industrial automation
Plastics
Robotics/vision systems
Specialty materials
Medical/Health Related
Medical services

Additional Information
Year Founded—1984
Capital Under Management—$2.5 million
Investments(1985-1st 6 months)—4
Invested(1985-1st 6 months)—$800,000
Method of Compensation—Return on investment is most important, but also charge for closing fees, service fees, etc.

CORPORATE FINANCE OF WASHINGTON, INC.

1326 R Street NW #2
Washington, DC 20009
202-328-9053

Officer
Peter W. Gavian, Pres.

Type of Firm
Consulting firm evaluating and analyzing venture projects and arranging private placements

Project Preferences
Prefer role as deal originator
Type of Financing:
First-stage
Second-stage
Later-stage expansion
Leveraged buyout
Minimum Investment: $250,000
Preferred Investment: Over $1 million
Minimum Operating Data:
Annual Sales—$500,000
P&L—Break even

Geographical Preference
Within two hours of office

Industry Preferences

Communications
Cable television
Commercial communications
Data communications
Satellite and microwave communications
Telephone related
Computer Related
Computer graphics, CAD/CAM and CAE
Computer mainframes
Computer services
Memory devices
Micro and mini computers
Office automation
Scanning related
Software-applications
Software-artificial intelligence
Software-systems
Specialized turnkey systems
Terminals
Distribution
Communications equipment
Computer equipment
Consumer products
Electronics equipment
Food products
Industrial products
Medical products

**Electronic Components and
Instrumentation**
Analytical and scientific instrumentation
Component fabrication and testing
equipment
Electronic components
Fiber optics
Laser related
Semiconductors
Genetic Engineering
Gene splicing and manufacturing equipment
Monoclonal antibodies and hybridomas
Recombinant DNA (agricultural and
industrial)
Recombinant DNA (medical)
Industrial Products and Equipment
Chemicals
Controls and sensors
Energy management
Equipment and machinery
Other industrial automation
Plastics
Robotics/vision systems
Specialty materials
Medical/Health Related
Diagnostic equipment
Diagnostic test products
Disposable products
Drugs and medicines
Hospital and clinical labs
Medical services
Prosthetics
Therapeutic equipment

Additional Information
Year Founded—1976
Method of Compensation—Function primarily
in service area; receive contingent fee in
cash or equity

DC BANCORP VENTURE CAPITAL CO.

1801 K Street NW
Washington, DC 20006
202-955-6970

Officer
Allan A. Weissburg, Pres.

Type of Firm
SBIC

Industry Association Membership
NASBIC

Project Preferences
Will function either as deal originator or
investor in deals created by others

Type of Financing:
First-stage
Second-stage
Leveraged buyout
Minimum Investment: $100,000
Preferred Investment: $100,000-$500,000
Minimum Operating Data:
Annual Sales—Nominal
P&L—Losses (profits projected after 1 year)

Geographical Preference
Within two hours of office

Industry Preferences

Communications
Cable television
Commercial communications
Data communications
Satellite and microwave communications
Telephone related
Computer Related
Computer services
Office automation
Consumer
Computer stores/related services
Consumer products
Consumer services
Food and beverage products
Franchise businesses
Hotels and resort areas
Leisure and recreational products
Restaurants
Retailing
Distribution
Communications equipment
Computer equipment
Consumer products
Electronics equipment
Food products
Industrial products
Medical products
Energy/Natural Resources
Energy conservation
Industrial Products and Equipment
Energy management
Medical/Health Related
Diagnostic equipment
Diagnostic test products
Disposable products
Drugs and medicines
Hospital and clinical labs
Medical services
Therapeutic equipment
Other
Education related
Specialty consulting

Additional Information
Year Founded—1985
Capital Under Management—$1.5 million
Method of Compensation—Return on
investment is of primary concern; do not
charge fees

EWING CAPITAL, INC.

1110 Vermont Avenue NW #1170
Washington, DC 20005
202-463-8787

Officer
Samuel D. Ewing, Jr., Pres.

Type of Firm
Investment banking or merchant banking
firm investing own capital or funds of
partners or clients

Project Preferences
Prefer role as deal originator
Type of Financing:
First-stage
Second-stage
Later-stage expansion
Minimum Investment: $500,000
Preferred Investment: $500,000-$1 million
Minimum Operating Data:
Annual Sales—Nominal
P&L—Losses (profits projected after 2 years)

Geographical Preference
None
Industry Preferences

Communications
Broadcasting
Commercial communications
Satellite and microwave communications
Computer Related
Office automation
Software-applications
Software-systems
Consumer
Consumer products
Distribution
Communications equipment
Computer equipment
Electronics equipment
Industrial products
**Electronic Components and
Instrumentation**
Analytical and scientific instrumentation
Industrial Products and Equipment
Equipment and machinery

Other
Finance and insurance
Real estate
Specialty consulting

Additional Information
Year Founded—1981

FULCRUM VENTURE CAPITAL CORPORATION

2021 K Street NW #701
Washington, DC 20006
202-833-9590

Officers
Divakar R. Kamath, Pres.
Renate K. Todd, V.P.

Whom to Contact
Divakar R. Kamath

Type of Firm
MESBIC

Industry Association Memberships
AAMESBIC
NASBIC

Project Preferences
Will function either as deal originator or
    investor in deals created by others
Type of Financing:
Second-stage
Later-stage expansion
Leveraged buyout
Minimum Investment: $100,000
Preferred Investment: $250,000-$500,000
Preferred Investment (LBO):
    $250,000-$500,000
Minimum Operating Data:
Annual Sales—$1 million
P&L—Break even
Annual Sales (LBO)—$3 million and over

Geographical Preference
None

Industry Preferences

Communications
Cable television
Commercial communications
Data communications
Satellite and microwave communications
Telephone related

Computer Related
Computer graphics, CAD/CAM and CAE
Computer mainframes
Computer services
Memory devices
Micro and mini computers
Office automation
Scanning related
Software-applications
Software-artificial intelligence
Software-systems
Specialized turnkey systems
Terminals
Distribution
Communications equipment
Computer equipment
Electronics equipment
Industrial products
Medical products
**Electronic Components and
    Instrumentation**
Analytical and scientific instrumentation
Component fabrication and testing
    equipment
Electronic components
Fiber optics
Laser related
Semiconductors
Energy/Natural Resources
Technology related products/equipment
Industrial Products and Equipment
Chemicals
Controls and sensors
Energy management
Equipment and machinery
Other industrial automation
Plastics
Robotics/vision systems
Specialty materials
Medical/Health Related
Diagnostic equipment
Diagnostic test products
Disposable products
Drugs and medicines
Hospital and clinical labs
Medical services
Therapeutic equipment
Other
Transportation

Additional Information
Year Founded—1978
Capital Under Management—$7 million
Investments(1985-1st 6 months)—4
Invested(1985-1st 6 months)—$750,000
Method of Compensation—Return on
    investment is most important, but also
    charge for closing fees, service fees, etc.

MIDDLE ATLANTIC VENTURES

655 15th Street NW #300
Washington, DC 20005
202-393-8550

Owner
William E. Simmons, Jr.

Type of Firm
Private venture capital firm investing
    own capital

Project Preferences
Prefer role as deal originator but will also
    invest in deals created by others
Type of Financing:
Second-stage
Leveraged buyout
Minimum Investment: Less than $100,000
Preferred Investment (LBO):
    $500,000 or less
Minimum Operating Data:
Annual Sales—Nominal
Annual Sales (LBO)—$10 million or less

Geographical Preference
Middle Atlantic States

Industry Preferences
None

Additional Information
Year Founded—1980

MINORITY BROADCAST INVESTMENT CORPORATION

1155 Connecticut Avenue NW
Suite 900
Washington, DC 20036
202-293-1166

Officers
Larry Edler, Pres.
Minta D. Branham, Asst. V.P.

Whom to Contact
Larry Edler

Type of Firm
MESBIC

Affiliation
Storer Communications, Inc. (parent)

Industry Association Membership
AAMESBIC

Project Preferences
Prefer role as deal originator but will also invest in deals created by others
Type of Financing:
Startup
First-stage
Second-stage
Later-stage expansion
Leveraged buyout
Minimum Investment: $100,000
Preferred Investment: $250,000-$500,000
Preferred Investment (LBO): $250,000-$300,000
Minimum Operating Data:
Annual Sales—$500,000
P&L—Break even
Annual Sales (LBO)—$1 million and over

Geographical Preference
None

Industry Preferences

Communications
Cable television
Commercial communications
Data communications
Satellite and microwave communications
Telephone related
Distribution
Communications equipment

Additional Information
Year Founded—1979

PIERCE INVESTMENT BANKING

1910 K Street NW
Washington, DC 20006
202-833-8031

Officers
John Pierce Clark, Mgn. Dir.
David Gregg III, Mgn. Dir.
Thomas Howser, Mgn. Dir.
Dr. David Cohn, Technical Advisor
John Stoppleman, Legal Advisor

Whom to Contact
John Clark
David Gregg III
Thomas Howser

Type of Firm
Investment banking or merchant banking firm investing own capital or funds of partners or clients

Affiliation
Tucker Anthony, R.L. Day (consulting client)

Project Preferences
Prefer role as deal originator but will also invest in deals created by others
Type of Financing:
Research and development partnerships
First-stage
Second-stage
Later-stage expansion
Leveraged buyout
Minimum Investment: $250,000
Preferred Investment: $500,000-$1 million
Minimum Operating Data:
Annual Sales—$1.5 million
P&L—Break even
Annual Sales (LBO)—Over $1 million

Geographical Preferences
Within two hours of office
East Coast

Industry Preferences

Communications
Cable television
Commercial communications
Data communications
Satellite and microwave communications
Telephone related
Computer Related
Computer graphics, CAD/CAM and CAE
Computer services
Micro and mini computers
Office automation
Scanning related
Software-applications
Software-artificial intelligence
Software-systems
Specialized turnkey systems
Consumer
Computer stores/related services
Consumer services
Food and beverage products
Franchise businesses
Retailing
Distribution
Communications equipment
Computer equipment
Electronics equipment
Industrial products
Medical products
Electronic Components and Instrumentation
Analytical and scientific instrumentation
Component fabrication and testing equipment
Electronic components
Fiber optics
Laser related

Energy/Natural Resources
Alternative energy
Drilling and exploration services
Energy conservation
Minerals
Oil and gas exploration and production
Technology related products/equipment
Genetic Engineering
Gene splicing and manufacturing equipment
Monoclonal antibodies and hybridomas
Recombinant DNA (agricultural and industrial)
Recombinant DNA (medical)
Industrial Products and Equipment
Controls and sensors
Equipment and machinery
Other industrial automation
Robotics/vision systems
Specialty materials
Medical/Health Related
Diagnostic equipment
Diagnostic test products
Hospital and clinical labs
Medical services
Therapeutic equipment
Other
Publishing

Additional Information
Year Founded—1978
Investments(1985-1st 6 months)—3
Invested(1985-1st 6 months)—$1 million
Method of Compensation—Return on investment is most important, but also charge for closing fees, service fees, etc.

PRINTON, KANE & CO.

1346 Connecticut Avenue NW
Washington, DC 20036
800-526-4952

See NEW JERSEY for full listing

SYNDICATED COMMUNICATIONS, INC.

1030 15th Street NW #203
Washington, DC 20005
202-293-9428

Officers

Herbert P. Wilkins, Pres.
Terry L. Jones, V.P.
Duane C. McKnight, V.P.
Edward Hayes, Secy.
Mildred R. Dickerson, Treas.
Johnetta B. Bond, Financial Analyst

Whom to Contact

Herbert P. Wilkins
Terry L. Jones
Duane C. McKnight
Johnetta B. Bond

Type of Firm

Private venture capital firm investing
own capital
MESBIC

Affiliation

Syncom Capital Corporation (subsidiary)

Industry Association Memberships

AAMESBIC
NASBIC

Project Preferences

Prefer role as deal originator but will also
invest in deals created by others
Type of Financing:
Startup
First-stage
Second-stage
Later-stage expansion
Leveraged buyout
Minimum Investment: $100,000
Preferred Investment: $250,000-$500,000
Minimum Operating Data:
Annual Sales—$500,000

Geographical Preference

None

Industry Preferences

Communications
Cable television
Commercial communications
Data communications
Satellite and microwave communications
Telephone related

Additional Information

Year Founded—1977
Capital Under Management—$8.7 million
Investments(1985-1st 6 months)—3
Invested(1985-1st 6 months)—$300,000
Method of Compensation—Return on
investment is most important, but also
charge for closing fees, service fees, etc.

U.S. VENTURE DEVELOPMENT CORPORATION

4801 Massachusetts Avenue #400
Washington, DC 20016
202-364-8890

Other Office

1326 R Street, NW #2
Washington, DC 20009
202-328-9053

Officers

C. Stevens Avery II, Chm. & Pres.
Peter W. Gavian, Vice-Chm.
Sheldon Huminik, Secy./Treas.

Whom to Contact

C. Stevens Avery II
Sheldon Huminik

Type of Firm

Business development company providing
managerial assistance and arranging
public offerings for its portfolio companies

Project Preferences

Prefer role as deal originator but will also
invest in deals created by others
Type of Financing:
Seed
Startup
First-stage
Leveraged buyout
Minimum Investment: Less than $100,000
Preferred Investment: Less than $100,000
Preferred Investment (LBO):
$1 million-$10 million
Minimum Operating Data:
Annual Sales—Nominal
P&L—Losses (profits projected after 2 years)
Annual Sales (LBO)—$5 million-$50 million

Geographical Preferences

Within two hours of office
East Coast

Industry Preferences

Communications
Cable television
Commercial communications
Data communications
Satellite and microwave communications
Telephone related
Computer Related
Computer services
Micro and mini computers
Office automation
Software-applications
Software-systems
Terminals
Consumer
Computer stores/related services
Consumer products
Distribution
Computer equipment
Consumer products
Electronics equipment
Medical products
Electronic Components and Instrumentation
Analytical and scientific instrumentation
Optics technology
Semiconductors
Energy/Natural Resources
Alternative energy
Energy conservation
Technology related products/equipment
Genetic Engineering
Monoclonal antibodies and hybridomas
Industrial Products and Equipment
Chemicals
Controls and sensors
Defense related products
Robotics/vision systems
Medical/Health Related
Diagnostic equipment
Diagnostic test products
Disposable products
Drugs and medicines
Hospital and clinical labs
Medical services
Therapeutic equipment
Other
Finance and insurance
Real estate
Will Not Consider
Brokerage firms
Insurance companies
Investment banking firms and investment
companies

Additional Information
Year Founded—1981
Capital Under Management—
  Less than $1 million
Investments(1985-1st 6 months)—3
Method of Compensation—Function primarily
  in service area; receive contingent fee in
  cash or equity

WACHTEL & CO., INC.

1101 14th Street NW
Washington, DC 20005
202-898-1144

Officers
Sidney B. Wachtel, Chm.
John D. Sanders, V.P.
Wendie L. Wachtel, V.P. & Secy.
Bonnie K. Wachtel, V.P. & Legal Counsel
Irma S. Wachtel, V.P. & Treas.

Whom to Contact
Any of the above

Type of Firm
Investment banking or merchant banking
  firm investing own capital or funds of
  partners or clients
Consulting firm evaluating and analyzing
  venture projects and arranging private
  placements

Project Preferences
Prefer role as deal originator but will also
  invest in deals created by others
Type of Financing:
Startup
First-stage
Second-stage
Later-stage expansion
Minimum Investment: Less than $100,000
Preferred Investment: $100,000-$250,000
Minimum Operating Data:
Annual Sales—Nominal
P&L—Break even

Geographical Preference
East Coast

Industry Preferences

Communications
Satellite and microwave communications
Telephone related

Computer Related
Computer graphics, CAD/CAM and CAE
Computer services
Micro and mini computers
Software-applications
Software-systems
Consumer
Computer stores/related services
Consumer services
Distribution
Communications equipment
Computer equipment
Consumer products
Electronics equipment
**Electronic Components and
  Instrumentation**
Analytical and scientific instrumentation
Component fabrication and testing
  equipment
Electronic components
Fiber optics
Laser related
Semiconductors
Industrial Products and Equipment
Robotics/vision systems
Medical/Health Related
Diagnostic equipment
Other
Education related
Finance and insurance
Specialty consulting
Will Not Consider
Capital-intensive businesses

Additional Information
Year Founded—1961
Capital Under Management—$15 million
Investments(1985-1st 6 months)—8
Invested(1985-1st 6 months)—$710,000
Method of Compensation—Function primarily
  in service area; receive contingent fee in
  cash or equity

ALLIED CAPITAL CORPORATION

111 East Las Olas Boulevard
Post Office Box 14758
Fort Lauderdale, FL 33301
305-763-8484

Edwin H. Spina

See DISTRICT OF COLUMBIA for full listing

ALLIED-NORTH AMERICAN COMPANY

111 East Las Olas Blvd.
Post Office Box 14758
Fort Lauderdale, FL 33302
305-763-8484

Other Office
Allied Capital Corporation
1625 I Street NW
Washington, DC 20006
202-331-1112

Officers
George C. Williams, Chm.
   (Washington, D.C.)
Charles L. Palmer, Pres. & CEO (Florida)
Edwin Harkness Spina, V.P. (Florida)

Whom to Contact
Charles L. Palmer
Edwin Harkness Spina

Type of Firm
Management company representing Allied
   Capital Corporation and North American
   Company Ltd.

Affiliation
Allied Capital Corporation (joint venture)
North American Company Ltd. (joint venture)

Project Preferences
Will function either as deal originator or
   investor in deals created by others
Type of Financing:
Startup
First-stage
Second-stage
Later-stage expansion
Leveraged buyout
Minimum Investment: $250,000
Preferred Investment: $500,000-$1 million
Preferred Investment (LBO):
   $500,000-$3 million
Minimum Operating Data:
Annual Sales (LBO)—$5 million-$100 million

Geographical Preferences
Southeast
National

Industry Preferences

Communications
Cable television
Commercial communications
Data communications
Satellite and microwave communications
Telephone related
Computer Related
Computer graphics, CAD/CAM and CAE
Computer mainframes
Computer services
Memory devices
Micro and mini computers
Office automation
Scanning related
Software-applications
Software-artificial intelligence
Software-systems
Specialized turnkey systems
Terminals
Consumer
Computer stores/related services
Consumer products
Consumer services
Food and beverage products
Franchise businesses
Hotels and resort areas
Leisure and recreational products
Restaurants
Retailing
Distribution
Communications equipment
Computer equipment
Consumer products
Electronics equipment
Food products
Industrial products
Medical products
**Electronic Components and
   Instrumentation**
Analytical and scientific instrumentation
Component fabrication and testing
   equipment
Electronic components
Fiber optics
Laser related
Semiconductors
Energy/Natural Resources
Alternative energy
Coal related
Drilling and exploration services
Energy conservation
Minerals
Oil and gas exploration and production
Technology related products/equipment

Genetic Engineering
Gene splicing and manufacturing equipment
Monoclonal antibodies and hybridomas
Recombinant DNA (agricultural and
   industrial)
Recombinant DNA (medical)
Industrial Products and Equipment
Chemicals
Controls and sensors
Energy management
Equipment and machinery
Other industrial automation
Plastics
Robotics/vision systems
Specialty materials
Medical/Health Related
Diagnostic equipment
Diagnostic test products
Disposable products
Drugs and medicines
Hospital and clinical labs
Medical services
Therapeutic equipment
Other
Agriculture, forestry, fishing
Education related
Finance and insurance
Publishing
Real estate
Specialty consulting
Transportation

Additional Information
Year Founded—1985
Capital Under Management—$52 million
Method of Compensation—Return on
   investment is most important, but also
   charge for closing fees, service fees, etc.

BUSINESS RESEARCH COMPANY

205 Worth Avenue
Post Office Box 2137
Palm Beach, FL 33480
305-832-2155

Managing Directors
George B. Kilborne
A. Donald Grosset

Whom to Contact
George B. Kilbourne

Type of Firm
Investment banking or merchant banking
   firm investing own capital or funds of
   partners or clients

Project Preferences
Will function either as deal originator or
investor in deals created by others
Type of Financing:
Later-stage expansion
Leveraged buyout
Minimum Investment: $500,000
Preferred Investment: Over $1 million
Preferred Investment (LBO): $2 million
Minimum Operating Data:
Annual Sales—Over $3 million
P&L—Break even
Annual Sales (LBO)—Over $15 million

Geographical Preferences
East Coast
Midwest

Industry Preferences

Communications
Cable television
Commercial communications
Consumer
Hotels and resort areas
Distribution
Industrial products
Industrial Products and Equipment
Chemicals
Controls and sensors
Energy management
Equipment and machinery
Other industrial automation
Plastics
Robotics/vision systems
Specialty materials
Other
Real estate

Additional Information
Year Founded—1961
Investments(1985-1st 6 months)—1
Method of Compensation—Return on
investment is most important, but also
charge for closing fees, service fees, etc.

CARIBANK CAPITAL CORP./ CARIBANK VENTURE CORP.

255 East Dania Beach Boulevard
Dania, FL 33004
305-925-2211

Officers
Michael E. Chaney, Pres.
Harold F. Messner, V.P.
Elaine E. Healy, Inv. Officer

Whom to Contact
Harold F. Messner
Elaine E. Healy

Type of Firm
SBIC
Venture capital subsidiary of
commercial bank

Project Preferences
Will function either as deal originator or
investor in deals created by others
Type of Financing:
Second-stage
Later-stage expansion
Leveraged buyout
Minimum Investment: Less than $100,000
Preferred Investment: $100,000-$250,000
Minimum Operating Data:
Annual Sales—Nominal

Geographical Preferences
Southeast
Southwest

Industry Preferences

Communications
Cable television
Commercial communications
Data communications
Satellite and microwave communications
Telephone related
Computer Related
Computer graphics, CAD/CAM and CAE
Computer mainframes
Computer services
Memory devices
Micro and mini computers
Office automation
Scanning related
Software-applications
Software-artificial intelligence
Software-systems
Specialized turnkey systems
Terminals

Electronic Components and Instrumentation
Analytical and scientific instrumentation
Component fabrication and testing
equipment
Electronic components
Fiber optics
Laser related
Semiconductors
Energy/Natural Resources
Alternative energy
Coal related
Drilling and exploration services
Energy conservation
Minerals
Oil and gas exploration and production
Technology related products/equipment
Will Not Consider
Real estate

Additional Information
Year Founded—1982
Capital Under Management—$4.5 million
Investments(1985-1st 6 months)—3
Invested(1985-1st 6 months)—$443,000
Method of Compensation—Return on
investment is of primary concern; do not
charge fees

ELECTRO-SCIENCE MANAGEMENT CORPORATION

600 Courtland Street #490
Orlando, FL 32804
305-645-1188

Officer
G.A. Herbert, V.P.

Type of Firm
Private venture capital firm investing
own capital

Project Preferences
Will function either as deal originator or
investor in deals created by others
Type of Financing:
Research and development partnerships
Startup
First-stage
Leveraged buyout
Minimum Investment: $100,000
Preferred Investment: $100,000-$250,000
Preferred Investment (LBO):
$100,000-$250,000
Minimum Operating Data:
Annual Sales—$1.5 million
P&L—Losses (profits projected after 1 year)
Annual Sales (LBO)—$1 million-$8 million

Geographical Preference
Southeast

Industry Preferences

Communications
Data communications
Satellite and microwave communications
Computer Related
Computer graphics, CAD/CAM and CAE
Computer mainframes
Computer services
Memory devices
Micro and mini computers
Office automation
Scanning related
Software-applications
Software-artificial intelligence
Software-systems
Specialized turnkey systems
Terminals
**Electronic Components and
 Instrumentation**
Analytical and scientific instrumentation
Component fabrication and testing
equipment
Fiber optics
Laser related
Industrial Products and Equipment
Controls and sensors
Energy management
Equipment and machinery
Other industrial automation
Robotics/vision systems
Medical/Health Related
Diagnostic equipment
Diagnostic test products
Therapeutic equipment

Additional Information
Year Founded—1969
Capital Under Management—$10 million
Investments(1985-1st 6 months)—4
Invested(1985-1st 6 months)—$500,000
Method of Compensation—Return on
investment is of primary concern; do not
charge fees

FIRST TAMPA CAPITAL CORP.

501 East Kennedy Boulevard
Suite 806
Tampa, FL 33602
813-221-2171

Officers
Thomas L. du Pont, Pres.
Trevor A. Rolfe, Secy.
Frank L. Morsani, Chm.
Larry S. Hyman, Financial & Inv. Mgr.

Whom to Contact
Thomas L. du Pont
Larry S. Hyman

Type of Firm
SBIC

Industry Association Membership
NASBIC

Project Preferences
Will function either as deal originator or
investor in deals created by others
Type of Financing:
First-stage
Leveraged buyout
Minimum Investment: $100,000
Preferred Investment: $100,000-$300,000
Minimum Operating Data:
Annual Sales—Nominal
P&L—Break even

Geographical Preference
Southeast

Industry Preferences

Communications
Cable television
Commercial communications
Data communications
Telephone related
Computer Related
Office automation
Scanning related
Consumer
Consumer products
Consumer services
Food and beverage products
Franchise businesses
Hotels and resort areas
Leisure and recreational products
Restaurants
Retailing

Distribution
Communications equipment
Consumer products
Electronics equipment
Industrial products
**Electronic Components and
 Instrumentation**
Electronic components
Fiber optics
Laser related
Energy/Natural Resources
Alternative energy
Energy conservation
Technology related products/equipment
Industrial Products and Equipment
Chemicals
Controls and sensors
Energy management
Equipment and machinery
Other industrial automation
Plastics
Robotics/vision systems
Specialty materials
Medical/Health Related
Diagnostic equipment
Disposable products
Drugs and medicines
Hospital and clinical labs
Medical services
Therapeutic equipment
Other
Education related
Publishing
Real estate
Specialty consulting
Transportation

Additional Information
Year Founded—1984
Capital Under Management—$2 million
Investments(1985-1st 6 months)—1
Invested(1985-1st 6 months)—$150,000
Method of Compensation—Return on
investment is most important, but also
charge for closing fees, service fees, etc.

HAMBRECHT & QUIST VENTURE PARTNERS

2655 Le Jeune Road #513
Coral Gables, FL 33134
305-447-0423

Modesto A. Maidique, Gen. Ptnr.

See CALIFORNIA for full listing

NORTH AMERICAN COMPANY LTD.

111 East Las Olas Boulevard
Post Office Box 14758
Fort Lauderdale, FL 33302
305-463-0681

Officer
Charles L. Palmer, Pres.

Type of Firm
Private venture capital firm investing
    own capital

Affiliation
Allied-North American Company
    (joint venture)

Industry Association Membership
NVCA

Project Preferences
Will function either as deal originator or
    investor in deals created by others
Type of Financing:
Startup
First-stage
Second-stage
Later-stage expansion
Leveraged buyout
Minimum Investment: $250,000
Preferred Investment: $500,000-$1 million
Preferred Investment (LBO):
    $500,000-$3 million
Minimum Operating Data:
Annual Sales (LBO)—$5 million-$100 million

Geographical Preferences
Southeast
National

Industry Preferences

Communications
Cable television
Commercial communications
Data communications
Satellite and microwave communications
Telephone related

Computer Related
Computer graphics, CAD/CAM and CAE
Computer mainframes
Computer services
Memory devices
Micro and mini computers
Office automation
Scanning related
Software-applications
Software-artificial intelligence
Software-systems
Specialized turnkey systems
Terminals
Consumer
Computer stores/related services
Consumer products
Consumer services
Food and beverage products
Franchise businesses
Hotels and resort areas
Leisure and recreational products
Restaurants
Retailing
Distribution
Communications equipment
Computer equipment
Consumer products
Electronics equipment
Food products
Industrial products
Medical products
Electronic Components and Instrumentation
Analytical and scientific instrumentation
Component fabrication and testing
    equipment
Electronic components
Fiber optics
Laser related
Semiconductors
Energy/Natural Resources
Alternative energy
Coal related
Drilling and exploration services
Energy conservation
Minerals
Oil and gas exploration and production
Technology related products/equipment
Genetic Engineering
Gene splicing and manufacturing equipment
Monoclonal antibodies and hybridomas
Recombinant DNA (agricultural and
    industrial)
Recombinant DNA (medical)

Industrial Products and Equipment
Chemicals
Controls and sensors
Energy management
Equipment and machinery
Other industrial automation
Plastics
Robotics/vision systems
Specialty materials
Medical/Health Related
Diagnostic equipment
Diagnostic test products
Disposable products
Drugs and medicines
Hospital and clinical labs
Medical services
Therapeutic equipment
Other
Agriculture, forestry, fishing
Education related
Finance and insurance
Publishing
Real estate
Specialty consulting
Transportation

Additional Information
Year Founded—1943
Capital Under Management—$38 million
Method of Compensation—Return on
    investment is most important, but also
    charge for closing fees, service fees, etc.

PRINTON, KANE & CO.

2000 Glades Road #202
Boca Raton, FL 33431
800-526-4952

See NEW JERSEY for full listing

PRO-MED CAPITAL, INC.

1380 Miami Gardens Drive NE
North Miami Beach, FL 33179
305-949-5900

Officers
Fredric M. Rosemore, Pres.
Lance B. Rosemore, V.P.

Whom to Contact
Either of the above

Type of Firm
SBIC

Affiliations

Western Financial Capital Corporation
(subsidiary)
First Western SBLC (subsidiary)

Project Preferences

Prefer role in deals created by others
Type of Financing:
Second-stage
Leveraged buyout
Minimum Investment: Less than $100,000
Preferred Investment: $100,000-$500,000
Minimum Operating Data:
Annual Sales—$500,000
P&L—Profitable

Geographical Preference

None

Industry Preferences

Communications
Commercial communications
Telephone related
Computer Related
Computer services
Office automation
Specialized turnkey systems
Consumer
Franchise businesses
Hotels and resort areas
Retailing
Distribution
Industrial products
Medical products
**Electronic Components and
Instrumentation**
Fiber optics
Laser related
Industrial Products and Equipment
Chemicals
Controls and sensors
Energy management
Equipment and machinery
Other industrial automation
Plastics
Robotics/vision systems
Specialty materials
Medical/Health Related
Diagnostic equipment
Diagnostic test products
Disposable products
Drugs and medicines
Hospital and clinical labs
Medical services
Therapeutic equipment
Other
Real estate

Additional Information

Year Founded—1979
Capital Under Management—$14 million
Investments(1985-1st 6 months)—32
Method of Compensation—Return on
investment is most important, but also
charge for closing fees, service fees, etc.

SOUTH ATLANTIC CAPITAL CORPORATION

220 East Madison #530
Tampa, FL 33602
813-229-7400

Partners

Donald W. Burton, Gen. Ptnr.
Richard J. Brandewie, Gen. Ptnr.
Sandra P. Barber, Admin. Ptnr.

Whom to Contact

Donald W. Burton
Richard J. Brandewie

Type of Firm

Private venture capital firm investing
own capital

Industry Association Memberships

NASBIC
NVCA

Project Preferences

Will function either as deal originator or
investor in deals created by others
Type of Financing:
First-stage
Second-stage
Later-stage expansion
Leveraged buyout
Minimum Investment: $250,000
Preferred Investment: $750,000

Geographical Preference

Southeast

Industry Preferences

None
Will Not Consider
Oil and gas
Real estate

Additional Information

Year Founded—1981
Capital Under Management—$17.5 million
Method of Compensation—Return on
investment is of primary concern; do not
charge fees

VENTURE CAPITAL MANAGEMENT CORPORATION

Post Office Box 2626
Satellite Beach, FL 32937
305-777-1969

Officer

Dr. Robert A. Adams, Pres.

Type of Firm

Private venture capital firm investing
own capital
Consulting firm evaluating and analyzing
venture projects and arranging private
placements

Project Preferences

Will function either as deal originator or
investor in deals created by others
Type of Financing:
First-stage
Second-stage
Leveraged buyout
Minimum Investment: $250,000
Preferred Investment: $250,000-$500,000
Minimum Operating Data:
Annual Sales—$500,000
P&L—Break even

Geographical Preference

None

Industry Preferences

Communications
Commercial communications
Satellite and microwave communications
Consumer
Consumer products
Food and beverage products
Hotels and resort areas
Leisure and recreational products
Distribution
Consumer products
Food products
Industrial products
Medical products

**Electronic Components and
   Instrumentation**
Analytical and scientific instrumentation
Component fabrication and testing
   equipment
Energy/Natural Resources
Alternative energy
Technology related products/equipment
Genetic Engineering
Gene splicing and manufacturing equipment
Monoclonal antibodies and hybridomas
Recombinant DNA (agricultural and
   industrial)
Recombinant DNA (medical)
Industrial Products and Equipment
Chemicals
Equipment and machinery
Plastics
Specialty materials
Medical/Health Related
Diagnostic equipment
Diagnostic test products
Disposable products
Drugs and medicines
Hospital and clinical labs
Medical services
Therapeutic equipment
Other
Agriculture, forestry, fishing
Microbiology
Real estate

Additional Information
Year Founded—1974
Investments(1985-1st 6 months)—1
Method of Compensation—Function primarily
   in service area; receive contingent fee in
   cash or equity

VENTURE MANAGEMENT
ASSOCIATES INC.

One Southeast Financial Center
Miami, FL 33131
305-375-6470

Officers
Clement L. Hofmann, Pres.
John H. Lamothe, V.P.
James R. Fitzsimons, Jr., V.P.
Anne E. Cario, Treas.

Whom to Contact
Any of the above

Type of Firm
SBIC
Venture capital subsidiary of
   commercial bank

Affiliation
Southeast Banking Corporation
   (limited partner)

Industry Association Membership
NASBIC

Project Preferences
Will function either as deal originator or
   investor in deals created by others
Type of Financing:
First-stage
Second-stage
Later-stage expansion
Leveraged buyout
Minimum Investment: $250,000
Preferred Investment: $500,000-$1 million
Minimum Operating Data:
Annual Sales—Nominal

Geographical Preference
Southeast

Industry Preferences

Communications
Commercial communications
Data communications
Satellite and microwave communications
Telephone related
Computer Related
Computer graphics, CAD/CAM and CAE
Computer mainframes
Computer services
Memory devices
Micro and mini computers
Office automation
Scanning related
Software-applications
Software-artificial intelligence
Software-systems
Specialized turnkey systems
Terminals
Consumer
Consumer products
Consumer services
Franchise businesses
**Electronic Components and
   Instrumentation**
Analytical and scientific instrumentation
Component fabrication and testing
   equipment
Electronic components
Fiber optics
Laser related
Semiconductors
Energy/Natural Resources
Technology related products/equipment

Genetic Engineering
Gene splicing and manufacturing equipment
Monoclonal antibodies and hybridomas
Recombinant DNA (agricultural and
   industrial)
Recombinant DNA (medical)
Industrial Products and Equipment
Controls and sensors
Equipment and machinery
Plastics
Robotics/vision systems
Medical/Health Related
Diagnostic equipment
Diagnostic test products
Disposable products
Drugs and medicines
Hospital and clinical labs
Medical services
Therapeutic equipment
Other
Finance and insurance

Additional Information
Year Founded—1968
Capital Under Management—$23 million
Investments(1985-1st 6 months)—9
Invested(1985-1st 6 months)—$1.4 million
Method of Compensation—Return on
   investment is of primary concern; do not
   charge fees

VENTURE OPPORTUNITIES
CORPORATION

444 Brickell Avenue #650
Miami, FL 33131
305-358-0359

Officers
A. Fred March, Pres.
Flora March, V.P.
Robert E. Dady, Esq., Secy.

Whom to Contact
A. Fred March

Type of Firm
Private venture capital firm investing
   own capital
MESBIC

Industry Association Memberships
AAMESBIC
NASBIC

Project Preferences

Prefer role as deal originator but will also invest in deals created by others

Type of Financing:
First-stage
Second-stage
Minimum Investment: Less than $100,000
Preferred Investment: $100,000-$250,000
Preferred Investment (LBO):
$1 million-$2 million
Minimum Operating Data:
Annual Sales—$1.5 million
P&L—Break even
Annual Sales (LBO)—$1.5 million-$3 million

Geographical Preferences

Southeast
Northeast
East Coast

Industry Preferences

Communications
Cable television
Commercial communications
Data communications
Satellite and microwave communications
Telephone related
Computer Related
Computer graphics, CAD/CAM and CAE
Computer mainframes
Computer services
Memory devices
Micro and mini computers
Office automation
Scanning related
Software-applications
Software-artificial intelligence
Software-systems
Specialized turnkey systems
Terminals
Consumer
Computer stores/related services
Consumer products
Consumer services
Food and beverage products
Franchise businesses
Retailing
Distribution
Communications equipment
Computer equipment
Consumer products
Electronics equipment
Food products
Industrial products
Medical products

Electronic Components and Instrumentation
Analytical and scientific instrumentation
Component fabrication and testing equipment
Electronic components
Fiber optics
Laser related
Semiconductors
Industrial Products and Equipment
Chemicals
Controls and sensors
Energy management
Equipment and machinery
Other industrial automation
Plastics
Robotics/vision systems
Specialty materials
Medical/Health Related
Diagnostic equipment
Diagnostic test products
Disposable products
Drugs and medicines
Hospital and clinical labs
Medical services
Therapeutic equipment
Other
Agriculture, forestry, fishing
Finance and insurance
Transportation
Will Not Consider
Real estate

Additional Information

Year Founded—1978
Capital Under Management—$3.5 million
Investments(1985-1st 6 months)—7
Invested(1985-1st 6 months)—$1 million
Method of Compensation—Return on investment is most important, but also charge for closing fees, service fees, etc.

WYNDMOOR ASSOCIATES, LTD.

5430 Pine Creek Drive
Orlando, FL 32811
305-423-0852

Joseph J. Williams

See PENNSYLVANIA for full listing

ADVANCED TECHNOLOGY DEVELOPMENT CENTER

430 10th Street NW # N-116
Atlanta, GA 30318
404-894-3575

Officers
Joe Pentecost, PhD, Acting Dir.
Howard Edwards, PhD, Assoc. Dir.
Lindsey Hopkins, Assoc. Dir.
Ben Hill, Research Scientist
Don Plummer, Research/Communications
Sandra Cutler, Indust. Devel./Research

Whom to Contact
Ben Hill
Lindsey Hopkins

Type of Firm
Incubator for advanced technology startups

Industry Association Membership
NASBIC

Project Preferences
Prefer role as deal originator
Type of Financing:
Seed
Research and development partnerships
Startup
First-stage
Second-stage
Later-stage expansion
Leveraged buyout
Minimum Investment: Less than $100,000
Preferred Investment: Over $1 million
Minimum Operating Data:
Annual Sales—Nominal
P&L—Losses (profits projected after 2 years)

Geographical Preferences
Within two hours of office
Georgia
Southeast

Industry Preferences

Communications
Communications products

Computer Related
Computer graphics, CAD/CAM and CAE
Computer mainframes
Computer services
Memory devices
Micro and mini computers
Office automation
Scanning related
Software-applications
Software-artificial intelligence
Software-systems
Specialized turnkey systems
Terminals
Consumer
Consumer products
Electronic Components and Instrumentation
Analytical and scientific instrumentation
Component fabrication and testing equipment
Electronic components
Fiber optics
Laser related
Semiconductors
Energy/Natural Resources
Technology related products/equipment
Genetic Engineering
Gene splicing and manufacturing equipment
Monoclonal antibodies and hybridomas
Recombinant DNA (agricultural and industrial)
Recombinant DNA (medical)
Industrial Products and Equipment
Chemicals
Controls and sensors
Energy management
Equipment and machinery
Other industrial automation
Plastics
Robotics/vision systems
Specialty materials
Medical/Health Related
Diagnostic equipment
Diagnostic test products
Disposable products
Drugs and medicines
Therapeutic equipment
Other
Agriculture, forestry, fishing

Additional Information
Year Founded—1980
Method of Compensation—Function in service area

ADVANCED TECHNOLOGY DEVELOPMENT FUND

430 10th Street NW #N114
Atlanta, GA 30318
404-875-4393

General Partners
Ronald W. White
Daniel D. Ross

Whom to Contact
Either of the above

Type of Firm
Private venture capital firm investing own capital

Project Preferences
Prefer role as deal originator but will also invest in deals created by others
Type of Financing:
Seed
Startup
First-stage
Minimum Investment: $100,000
Preferred Investment: $250,000-$500,000
Minimum Operating Data:
Annual Sales—Nominal
P&L—Losses (profits projected after 2 years)

Geographical Preference
Southeast

Industry Preferences

Communications
Cable television
Commercial communications
Data communications
Satellite and microwave communications
Telephone related
Computer Related
Computer graphics, CAD/CAM and CAE
Computer mainframes
Computer services
Memory devices
Micro and mini computers
Office automation
Scanning related
Software-applications
Software-artificial intelligence
Software-systems
Specialized turnkey systems
Terminals

Electronic Components and Instrumentation
Analytical and scientific instrumentation
Component fabrication and testing equipment
Electronic components
Fiber optics
Laser related
Semiconductors
Energy/Natural Resources
Drilling and exploration services
Energy conservation
Technology related products/equipment
Genetic Engineering
Gene splicing and manufacturing equipment
Monoclonal antibodies and hybridomas
Recombinant DNA (agricultural and industrial)
Recombinant DNA (medical)
Industrial Products and Equipment
Chemicals
Controls and sensors
Energy management
Equipment and machinery
Other industrial automation
Plastics
Robotics/vision systems
Specialty materials
Medical/Health Related
Diagnostic equipment
Diagnostic test products
Disposable products
Drugs and medicines
Hospital and clinical labs
Medical services
Therapeutic equipment

Additional Information

Year Founded—1983
Capital Under Management—$11 million
Investments(1985-1st 6 months)—8
Invested(1985-1st 6 months)—$1 million
Method of Compensation—Return on investment is of primary concern; do not charge fees

ARETÊ VENTURES, INC.

5995 Barfield Road #220
Atlanta, GA 30328
404-257-9548

George W. Levert, Jr.

See MARYLAND for full listing

CRESCENT MANAGEMENT COMPANY

5775 Peachtree-Dunwoody Road
Suite 640-D
Atlanta, GA 30342
404-252-8660

Officers

Walter M. Wellman, Chm.
John N. Thomas, Jr., Pres.

Whom to Contact

Either of the above

Type of Firm

Investment banking or merchant banking firm investing own capital or funds of partners or clients

Project Preferences

Will function either as deal originator or investor in deals created by others
Type of Financing:
First-stage
Second-stage
Leveraged buyout
Minimum Investment: $250,000
Preferred Investment: $250,000-$500,000
Minimum Operating Data:
Annual Sales—$500,000
P&L—Losses (profits projected after 1 year)

Geographical Preference

Southeast

Industry Preferences

Communications
Cable television
Commercial communications
Data communications
Satellite and microwave communications
Telephone related
Computer Related
Computer graphics, CAD/CAM and CAE
Will consider advanced companies in areas other than CAD/CAM
Consumer
Computer stores/related services
Consumer products
Consumer services
Food and beverage products
Franchise businesses
Hotels and resort areas
Leisure and recreational products
Restaurants
Retailing
Distribution
Communications equipment
Computer equipment
Consumer products
Electronics equipment
Food products
Industrial products
Medical products
Electronic Components and Instrumentation
Analytical and scientific instrumentation
Component fabrication and testing equipment
Electronic components
Fiber optics
Laser related
Semiconductors
Energy/Natural Resources
Technology related products/equipment
Industrial Products and Equipment
Chemicals
Controls and sensors
Energy management
Equipment and machinery
Other industrial automation
Plastics
Robotics/vision systems
Specialty materials
Medical/Health Related
Diagnostic equipment
Diagnostic test products
Disposable products
Drugs and medicines
Hospital and clinical labs
Medical services
Therapeutic equipment
Other
Agriculture, forestry, fishing
Education related
Finance and insurance
Publishing
Real estate
Specialty consulting
Transportation

Additional Information

Year Founded—1982
Capital Under Management—$7.3 million
Investments(1985-1st 6 months)—4
Invested(1985-1st 6 months)—$2 million
Method of Compensation—Return on investment is most important, but also charge annual management fee

FAIRCHESTER ASSOCIATES

515 One Piedmont Center
Atlanta, GA 30305
404-231-1550

Carl W. Knobloch, Jr., V.P.

See CONNECTICUT for full listing

GRUBB & COMPANY

1500 Tower Place
3340 Peachtree Road
Atlanta, GA 30026
404-237-6222

Officers
Stephen B. Grubb, Mgn. Dir.
David E. Thomas, Jr., Dir.

Whom to Contact
Either of the above

Type of Firm
Investment banking or merchant banking
firm investing own capital or funds of
partners or clients

Project Preferences
Prefer role as deal originator
Type of Financing:
Startup
First-stage
Second-stage
Later-stage expansion
Leveraged buyout
Minimum Investment: $250,000
Preferred Investment: $500,000-$1 million
Minimum Operating Data:
Annual Sales—Nominal
P&L—Losses (profits projected after 1 year)

Geographical Preferences
Southeast
Southwest

Industry Preferences
None

Additional Information
Year Founded—1982
Method of Compensation—Function primarily
in service area; receive contingent fee in
cash or equity

NORO-MOSELEY PARTNERS

100 Galleria Parkway #1240
Atlanta, GA 30339
404-955-0020

General Partners
Charles D. Moseley, Jr.
Jack R. Kelly, Jr.
Russell R. French

Whom to Contact
Any of the above

Type of Firm
Private venture capital firm investing
own capital

Project Preferences
Will function either as deal originator or
investor in deals created by others
Type of Financing:
First-stage
Second-stage
Later-stage expansion
Leveraged buyout
Minimum Investment: $500,000
Preferred Investment: Over $500,000
Minimum Operating Data:
Annual Sales—$1.5 million
P&L—Profits NBT over $250,000

Geographical Preference
Southeast

Industry Preferences

Communications
Cable television
Commercial communications
Data communications
Satellite and microwave communications
Telephone related
Computer Related
Computer graphics, CAD/CAM and CAE
Computer mainframes
Computer services
Memory devices
Micro and mini computers
Office automation
Scanning related
Software-applications
Software-artificial intelligence
Software-systems
Specialized turnkey systems
Terminals

Consumer
Computer stores/related services
Consumer products
Consumer services
Food and beverage products
Franchise businesses
Hotels and resort areas
Leisure and recreational products
Restaurants
Retailing
Distribution
Communications equipment
Computer equipment
Consumer products
Electronics equipment
Food products
Industrial products
Medical products
**Electronic Components and
Instrumentation**
Analytical and scientific instrumentation
Component fabrication and testing
equipment
Electronic components
Fiber optics
Laser related
Semiconductors
Industrial Products and Equipment
Chemicals
Controls and sensors
Energy management
Equipment and machinery
Other industrial automation
Plastics
Robotics/vision systems
Specialty materials
Medical/Health Related
Diagnostic equipment
Diagnostic test products
Disposable products
Drugs and medicines
Hospital and clinical labs
Medical services
Therapeutic equipment
Will Not Consider
Agriculture
Real estate

Additional Information
Year Founded—1983
Capital Under Management—$43.5 million
Investments(1985-1st 6 months)—4
Invested(1985-1st 6 months)—$2.5 million
Method of Compensation—Return on
investment is of primary concern; do not
charge fees

NORTH RIVERSIDE CAPITAL CORPORATION

5775-D Peachtree Dunwoody Road
Suite 650
Atlanta, GA 30342
404-252-1076

Officers
Thomas R. Barry, Pres.
Elizabeth G. Anderson, V.P.

Whom to Contact
Either of the above

Type of Firm
SBIC

Affiliation
Great American Management and
Investment, Inc. (parent)

Industry Association Membership
NASBIC

Project Preferences
Will function either as deal originator or
investor in deals created by others
Type of Financing:
Second-stage
Later-stage expansion
Leveraged buyout
Minimum Investment: $250,000
Preferred Investment: $500,000-$1 million
Preferred Investment (LBO):
$500,000-$750,000
Minimum Operating Data:
Annual Sales—$1.5 million
P&L—Break even
Annual Sales (LBO)—$5 million and over

Geographical Preference
None

Industry Preferences

Communications
Cable television
Commercial communications
Telephone related
Computer Related
Computer services
Micro and mini computers
Office automation
Scanning related
Software-applications
Consumer
Consumer products
Food and beverage products
Leisure and recreational products

Distribution
Communications equipment
Computer equipment
Consumer products
Electronics equipment
Industrial products
Medical products
Electronic Components and Instrumentation
Analytical and scientific instrumentation
Component fabrication and testing equipment
Electronic components
Fiber optics
Laser related
Energy/Natural Resources
Energy conservation
Minerals
Oil and gas exploration and production
Technology related products/equipment
Genetic Engineering
Gene splicing and manufacturing equipment
Monoclonal antibodies and hybridomas
Recombinant DNA (agricultural and industrial)
Recombinant DNA (medical)
Industrial Products and Equipment
Chemicals
Energy management
Equipment and machinery
Other industrial automation
Plastics
Robotics/vision systems
Medical/Health Related
Diagnostic equipment
Diagnostic test products
Disposable products
Drugs and medicines
Hospital and clinical labs
Medical services
Therapeutic equipment
Other
Real estate
Transportation

Additional Information
Year Founded—1984
Capital Under Management—$5 million
Investments(1985-1st 6 months)—4
Invested(1985-1st 6 months)—$1.7 million
Method of Compensation—Return on
investment is most important, but also
charge for closing fees, service fees, etc.

THE ROBINSON-HUMPHREY COMPANY INC.

3333 Peachtree Road NE
Atlanta, GA 30326
404-266-6000

Officers
Deborah L. Keel, First V.P.
Charles B. Shelton, Mgn. Dir.

Whom to Contact
Either of the above

Type of Firm
Investment banking firm structuring and
arranging private placements

Project Preferences
Prefer role as deal originator
Type of Financing:
First-stage
Second-stage
Later-stage expansion
Leveraged buyout
Minimum Investment: $1 million
Preferred Investment: Over $1 million
Minimum Operating Data:
Annual Sales—Nominal
P&L—Break even

Geographical Preference
Southeast

Industry Preferences

Communications
Cable television
Commercial communications
Data communications
Satellite and microwave communications
Telephone related
Computer Related
Computer graphics, CAD/CAM and CAE
Computer mainframes
Computer services
Memory devices
Micro and mini computers
Office automation
Scanning related
Software-applications
Software-artificial intelligence
Software-systems
Specialized turnkey systems
Terminals

Consumer
Computer stores/related services
Consumer products
Consumer services
Food and beverage products
Franchise businesses
Hotels and resort areas
Leisure and recreational products
Restaurants
Retailing
Distribution
Communications equipment
Computer equipment
Consumer products
Electronics equipment
Food products
Industrial products
Medical products
**Electronic Components and
   Instrumentation**
Analytical and scientific instrumentation
Component fabrication and testing
   equipment
Electronic components
Fiber optics
Laser related
Semiconductors
Energy/Natural Resources
Alternative energy
Coal related
Drilling and exploration services
Energy conservation
Minerals
Oil and gas exploration and production
Technology related products/equipment
Genetic Engineering
Gene splicing and manufacturing equipment
Monoclonal antibodies and hybridomas
Recombinant DNA (agricultural and
   industrial)
Recombinant DNA (medical)
Industrial Products and Equipment
Chemicals
Controls and sensors
Energy management
Equipment and machinery
Other industrial automation
Plastics
Robotics/vision systems
Specialty materials
Medical/Health Related
Diagnostic equipment
Diagnostic test products
Disposable products
Drugs and medicines
Hospital and clinical labs
Medical services
Therapeutic equipment

Other
Agriculture, forestry, fishing
Education related
Finance and insurance
Publishing
Real estate
Specialty consulting
Transportation

Additional Information
Method of Compensation—Function primarily
   in service area; receive contingent fee in
   cash or equity

**UTECH VENTURE CAPITAL
CORPORATION**

5995 Barfield Road #220
Atlanta, GA 30328
404-257-9548

George W. Levert, Secy./Treas. & Ltd. Ptnr.

See MARYLAND for full listing

BANCORP HAWAII SBIC, INC.

111 South King Street #1060
Honolulu, HI 96813
808-521-6411

Post Office Box 2900
Honolulu, HI 96846

Officers
H. Howard Stephenson, Chm.
James D. Evans, Jr., Pres.
Thomas T. Triggs, V.P. & Mgr.

Whom to Contact
Thomas T. Triggs

Type of Firm
SBIC
Venture capital subsidiary of
  commercial bank

Affiliations
Bancorp Hawaii, Inc. (parent)
Bank of Hawaii (affiliate)

Industry Association Membership
NASBIC

Project Preferences
Will function either as deal originator or
  investor in deals created by others
Type of Financing:
Second-stage
Later-stage expansion
Leveraged buyout
Minimum Investment: Less than $100,000
Preferred Investment: $50,000-$150,000
Minimum Operating Data:
Annual Sales—$500,000
P&L—Break even

Geographical Preference
Hawaii
West Coast

Industry Preferences
None

Additional Information
Year Founded—1984
Capital Under Management—$1 million
Investments(1985-1st 6 months)—5
Invested(1985-1st 6 months)—$450,000
Method of Compensation—Return on
  investment is of primary concern; do not
  charge fees

ABBOTT CAPITAL CORPORATION

9933 Lawler Avenue #125
Skokie, IL 60077
312-982-0404

Officers
Richard E. Lassar, Pres.
Michael Silverman

Whom to Contact
Richard E. Lassar

Type of Firm
Private venture capital firm investing
own capital

Industry Association Membership
NASBIC

Project Preferences
Will function either as deal originator or
investor in deals created by others
Type of Financing:
Second-stage
Later-stage expansion
Leveraged buyout
Minimum Investment: $250,000
Preferred Investment: $250,000-$500,000
Preferred Investment (LBO):
$500,000-$2.5 million
Minimum Operating Data:
Annual Sales—$500,000
P&L—Break even

Geographical Preference
Midwest

Industry Preferences

Communications
Telephone related
Consumer
Furniture
Distribution
Electronics equipment
Medical products
**Electronic Components and
Instrumentation**
Electronic components
Industrial Products and Equipment
Equipment and machinery
Medical/Health Related
Drugs and medicines
Will Not Consider
Plays or motion pictures
Publications
Retail shops

Additional Information
Year Founded—1970
Capital Under Management—$2.5 million
Investments(1985-1st 6 months)—3
Invested(1985-1st 6 months)—$75,000
Method of Compensation—Return on
investment is of primary concern; do not
charge fees

ALLSTATE INSURANCE COMPANY— VENTURE CAPITAL DIVISION

E-2, Allstate Plaza
Northbrook, IL 60062
312-291-5681

Officers
Louis G. Lower II, Group V.P.
Leonard A. Batterson, Sr. Inv. Mgr.
Donald R. Johnson, Inv. Mgr.
Robert L. Lestina, Inv. Mgr.
Oliver M. Darden, Sr. Inv. Analyst
Sharri E. Marcin, Sr. Inv. Analyst
Marcy H. Shockey, Sr. Inv. Analyst
Paul J. Renze, Inv. Analyst
Marc S. Sandroff, Inv. Analyst

Whom to Contact
Leonard A. Batterson

Type of Firm
Venture capital division of an insurance
company

Affiliations
Sears Roebuck and Company (parent)
Dean Witter Reynolds Inc. (subsidiary
of parent)
Coldwell Banker & Co. (subsidiary of parent)

Industry Association Memberships
NASBIC
NVCA
WAVC

Project Preferences
Will function either as deal originator or
investor in deals created by others
Type of Financing:
Startup
First-stage
Second-stage
Later-stage expansion
Leveraged buyout

Minimum Investment: $500,000
Preferred Investment: Over $1 million
Preferred Investment (LBO):
Over $5 million
Minimum Operating Data:
Annual Sales—Nominal
P&L—Losses (profits projected after 2 years)

Geographical Preference
None

Industry Preferences

Communications
Cable television
Commercial communications
Data communications
Satellite and microwave communications
Telephone related
Computer Related
Computer graphics, CAD/CAM and CAE
Computer mainframes
Computer services
Memory devices
Micro and mini computers
Office automation
Scanning related
Software-applications
Software-artificial intelligence
Software-systems
Specialized turnkey systems
Terminals
Consumer
Computer stores/related services
Consumer products
Consumer services
Food and beverage products
Franchise businesses
Leisure and recreational products
Restaurants
Distribution
Communications equipment
Electronics equipment
Industrial products
Medical products
**Electronic Components and
Instrumentation**
Analytical and scientific instrumentation
Component fabrication and testing
equipment
Electronic components
Fiber optics
Laser related
Semiconductors
Energy/Natural Resources
Alternative energy

Genetic Engineering
Gene splicing and manufacturing equipment
Monoclonal antibodies and hybridomas
Recombinant DNA (agricultural and
   industrial)
Recombinant DNA (medical)
Industrial Products and Equipment
Chemicals
Controls and sensors
Energy management
Equipment and machinery
Other industrial automation
Plastics
Robotics/vision systems
Specialty materials
Medical/Health Related
Diagnostic equipment
Diagnostic test products
Disposable products
Drugs and medicines
Hospital and clinical labs
Medical services
Therapeutic equipment
Other
Publishing
Will Not Consider
Products or services in competition with
   parent company or its subsidiaries

Additional Information
Year Founded—1958
Capital Under Management—$200 million
Investments(1985-1st 6 months)—26
Invested(1985-1st 6 months)—$14.6 million
Method of Compensation—Return on
   investment is of primary concern; do not
   charge fees

ALPHA CAPITAL VENTURE PARTNERS

Three First National Plaza
Suite 1400
Chicago, IL 60602
312-372-1556

General Partners
Andrew H. Kalnow
Daniel W. O'Connell

Whom to Contact
Either of the above

Type of Firm
SBIC

Industry Association Membership
NASBIC

Project Preferences
Will function either as deal originator or
   investor in deals created by others
Type of Financing:
First-stage
Second-stage
Later-stage expansion
Leveraged buyout
Minimum Investment: $250,000
Preferred Investment: $250,000-$500,000
Preferred Investment (LBO):
   $400,000-$750,000
Minimum Operating Data:
Annual Sales—$500,000
P&L—Break even
Annual Sales (LBO)—$5 million-$50 million

Geographical Preference
Midwest

Industry Preferences

Communications
Cable television
Commercial communications
Data communications
Satellite and microwave communications
Telephone related
Computer Related
Computer graphics, CAD/CAM and CAE
Computer services
Memory devices
Office automation
Scanning related
Software-applications
Software-artificial intelligence
Software-systems
Specialized turnkey systems
Terminals
Consumer
Computer stores/related services
Consumer products
Food and beverage products
Franchise businesses
Restaurants
Retailing
Distribution
Communications equipment
Computer equipment
Consumer products
Electronics equipment
Food products
Industrial products
Medical products

**Electronic Components and
   Instrumentation**
Analytical and scientific instrumentation
Component fabrication and testing
   equipment
Electronic components
Fiber optics
Laser related
Semiconductors
Energy/Natural Resources
Drilling and exploration services
Energy conservation
Oil and gas exploration and production
Technology related products/equipment
Genetic Engineering
Gene splicing and manufacturing equipment
Monoclonal antibodies and hybridomas
Recombinant DNA (agricultural and
   industrial)
Recombinant DNA (medical)
Industrial Products and Equipment
Chemicals
Controls and sensors
Energy management
Equipment and machinery
Other industrial automation
Plastics
Robotics/vision systems
Specialty materials
Medical/Health Related
Diagnostic equipment
Diagnostic test products
Disposable products
Drugs and medicines
Hospital and clinical labs
Medical services
Therapeutic equipment
Other
Publishing
Will Not Consider
Real estate

Additional Information
Year Founded—1983
Capital Under Management—$5 million
Method of Compensation—Return on
   investment is of primary concern; do not
   charge fees

AMERITECH DEVELOPMENT CORPORATION

Sears Tower #9720
Chicago, IL 60606
312-993-1900

Officers
Raymond Chin
David Kronfeld
Lou Sands
Thomas Touton
Jeff White
John Wray

Whom to Contact
Any of above

Type of Firm
Venture capital subsidiary or affiliate of non-financial corporation

Affiliations
American Information Technologies Corp.(parent)

Industry Association Membership
NVCA

Project Preferences
Will function either as deal originator or investor in deals created by others
Type of Financing:
Startup
First-stage
Second-stage
Later-stage expansion
Minimum Investment: $250,000
Preferred Investment: $500,000-$1 million
Minimum Operating Data:
Annual Sales—Nominal
P&L—Losses (profits projected after 2 years)

Geographical Preference
National

Industry Preferences

Communications
Cable television
Commercial communications
Data communications
Satellite and microwave communications
Telephone related
Anything related to the communications or information industries

Additional Information
Year Founded—1984
Capital Under Management—$10 million
Investments(1985-1st 6 months)—3
Invested(1985-1st 6 months)—$1.2 million
Method of Compensation—Return on investment is of primary concern; do not charge fees

AMOCO VENTURE CAPITAL CO.

200 East Randolph Drive
Chicago, IL 60601
312-856-6523

Officers
G.E. Stone, Pres.
D.S. Wood, V.P.

Whom to Contact
G.E. Stone

Type of Firm
MESBIC

Affiliation
Amoco Corp. (parent)

Industry Association Memberships
AAMESBIC
NASBIC

Project Preferences
Will function either as deal originator or investor in deals created by others
Type of Financing:
Startup
First-stage
Second-stage
Leveraged buyout
Minimum Investment: $100,000
Preferred Investment: $250,000-$500,000
Minimum Operating Data:
Annual Sales—Nominal
P&L—Break even

Geographical Preference
None

Industry Preferences

Electronic Components and Instrumentation
Analytical and scientific instrumentation
Component fabrication and testing equipment
Electronic components
Fiber optics
Laser related
Semiconductors
Energy/Natural Resources
Drilling and exploration services
Petroleum industry goods or services
Technology related products/equipment
Genetic Engineering
Gene splicing and manufacturing equipment
Monoclonal antibodies and hybridomas
Recombinant DNA (agricultural and industrial)
Recombinant DNA (medical)
Industrial Products and Equipment
Chemicals
Controls and sensors
Energy management
Equipment and machinery
Other industrial automation
Plastics
Robotics/vision systems
Specialty materials
Medical/Health Related
Diagnostic equipment
Diagnostic test products
Disposable products
Drugs and medicines
Hospital and clinical labs
Medical services
Therapeutic equipment
Will Not Consider
Real estate

Additional Information
Year Founded—1970
Capital Under Management—$7.5 million
Investments(1985-1st 6 months)—5
Invested(1985-1st 6 months)—$1 million
Method of Compensation—Return on investment is of primary concern; do not charge fees

WILLIAM BLAIR VENTURE PARTNERS

135 South LaSalle Street
Chicago, IL 60603
312-853-8250

Partners
James E. Crawford III, Ptnr.
Samuel B. Guren, Ptnr.
Scott F. Meadow, Ptnr.
Gregg S. Newmark, Assoc.

Whom to Contact
Any of the above

Type of Firm
Private venture capital firm investing
own capital

Affiliation
William Blair & Company (affiliate)

Industry Association Memberships
NASBIC
NVCA

Project Preferences
Will function either as deal originator or
investor in deals created by others
Type of Financing:
Startup
First-stage
Second-stage
Later-stage expansion
Leveraged buyout
Minimum Investment: $500,000
Preferred Investment: $750,000-$1.5 million
Preferred Investment (LBO):
Over $1 million
Minimum Operating Data:
Annual Sales—Nominal
P&L—Losses (profits projected after 2 years)
Annual Sales (LBO)—Over $10 million

Geographical Preference
National

Industry Preferences

Communications
Cable television
Commercial communications
Data communications
Satellite and microwave communications
Telephone related

Computer Related
Computer graphics, CAD/CAM and CAE
Computer mainframes
Computer services
Memory devices
Micro and mini computers
Office automation
Scanning related
Software-applications
Software-artificial intelligence
Software-systems
Specialized turnkey systems
Terminals
Consumer
Computer stores/related services
Consumer products
Consumer services
Food and beverage products
Franchise businesses
Hotels and resort areas
Leisure and recreational products
Restaurants
Retailing
Distribution
Communications equipment
Computer equipment
Consumer products
Electronics equipment
Food products
Industrial products
Medical products
Electronic Components and Instrumentation
Analytical and scientific instrumentation
Component fabrication and testing
equipment
Electronic components
Fiber optics
Laser related
Semiconductors
Energy/Natural Resources
Energy conservation
Technology related products/equipment
Genetic Engineering
Gene splicing and manufacturing equipment
Monoclonal antibodies and hybridomas
Recombinant DNA (agricultural and
industrial)
Recombinant DNA (medical)
Industrial Products and Equipment
Chemicals
Controls and sensors
Energy management
Equipment and machinery
Other industrial automation
Plastics
Robotics/vision systems
Specialty materials

Medical/Health Related
Diagnostic equipment
Diagnostic test products
Disposable products
Drugs and medicines
Hospital and clinical labs
Medical services
Therapeutic equipment
Other
Agriculture, forestry, fishing
Education related
Finance and insurance
Publishing
Specialty consulting
Transportation
Will Not Consider
Real estate

Additional Information
Year Founded—1982
Capital Under Management—$50 million
Investments(1985-1st 6 months)—5
Invested(1985-1st 6 months)—$3.7 million
Method of Compensation—Return on
investment is of primary concern; do not
charge fees

BUSINESS VENTURES INC.

20 North Wacker Drive #550
Chicago, IL 60606
312-346-1580

Officers
Marc B. Grayson, Chm.
Milton G. Lefton, Pres.
Terry G. Chapman, Secy.

Whom to Contact
Milton G. Lefton

Type of Firm
SBIC

Industry Association Membership
NASBIC

Project Preferences
Will function either as deal originator or
investor in deals created by others
Type of Financing:
First-stage
Leveraged buyout
Minimum Investment: Less than $100,000
Preferred Investment: $100,000-$250,000
Minimum Operating Data:
Annual Sales—$500,000
P&L—Break even

Geographical Preference

Chicago Metropolitan Area
Midwest

Industry Preferences

Communications
Cable television
Commercial communications
Data communications
Satellite and microwave communications
Telephone related
Computer Related
Computer graphics, CAD/CAM and CAE
Computer mainframes
Computer services
Memory devices
Micro and mini computers
Office automation
Scanning related
Software-applications
Software-artificial intelligence
Software-systems
Specialized turnkey systems
Terminals
Consumer
Computer stores/related services
Consumer products
Consumer services
Food and beverage products
Franchise businesses
Hotels and resort areas
Leisure and recreational products
Restaurants
Retailing
Distribution
Communications equipment
Computer equipment
Consumer products
Electronics equipment
Food products
Industrial products
Medical products
**Electronic Components and
  Instrumentation**
Analytical and scientific instrumentation
Component fabrication and testing
  equipment
Electronic components
Fiber optics
Laser related
Semiconductors
Energy/Natural Resources
Alternative energy
Coal related
Drilling and exploration services
Energy conservation
Minerals
Oil and gas exploration and production
Technology related products/equipment

Genetic Engineering
Gene splicing and manufacturing equipment
Monoclonal antibodies and hybridomas
Recombinant DNA (agricultural and
  industrial)
Recombinant DNA (medical)
Industrial Products and Equipment
Chemicals
Controls and sensors
Energy management
Equipment and machinery
Other industrial automation
Plastics
Robotics/vision systems
Specialty materials
Medical/Health Related
Diagnostic equipment
Diagnostic test products
Disposable products
Drugs and medicines
Hospital and clinical labs
Medical services
Therapeutic equipment
Other
Agriculture, forestry, fishing
Education related
Finance and insurance
Publishing
Real estate
Specialty consulting
Transportation

Additional Information

Year Founded—1983
Capital Under Management—$550,000
Investments(1985-1st 6 months)—1
Method of Compensation—Return on
  investment is most important, but also
  charge for closing fees, service fees, etc.

THE CAPITAL STRATEGY GROUP, INC.

20 North Wacker Drive
Chicago, IL 60606
312-444-1170

Officer

Eric E. von Bauer, Pres.

Type of Firm

Private venture capital firm investing
  own capital
Investment banking or merchant banking
  firm investing own capital or funds of
  partners or clients
Consulting firm evaluating and analyzing
  venture projects and arranging private
  placements

Project Preferences

Prefer role as deal originator
Type of Financing:
Seed
Research and development partnerships
Startup
First-stage
Second-stage
Later-stage expansion
Leveraged buyout
Minimum Investment: Less than $100,000
Preferred Investment: $100,000-$500,000
Minimum Operating Data:
Annual Sales—Nominal

Geographical Preference

Midwest

Industry Preferences

Communications
Cable television
Commercial communications
Data communications
Satellite and microwave communications
Telephone related
Computer Related
Computer graphics, CAD/CAM and CAE
Computer mainframes
Computer services
Memory devices
Micro and mini computers
Office automation
Scanning related
Software-applications
Software-artificial intelligence
Software-systems
Specialized turnkey systems
Terminals
Consumer
Computer stores/related services
Consumer products
Consumer services
Food and beverage products
Franchise businesses
Leisure and recreational products
Retailing
Distribution
Communications equipment
Computer equipment
Consumer products
Electronics equipment
Food products
Industrial products
Medical products

Electronic Components and Instrumentation
Analytical and scientific instrumentation
Component fabrication and testing equipment
Electronic components
Fiber optics
Laser related
Semiconductors
Industrial Products and Equipment
Chemicals
Controls and sensors
Energy management
Equipment and machinery
Other industrial automation
Plastics
Robotics/vision systems
Specialty materials
Medical/Health Related
Diagnostic equipment
Diagnostic test products
Disposable products
Drugs and medicines
Hospital and clinical labs
Medical services
Therapeutic equipment
Other
Education related
Finance and insurance
Publishing
Specialty consulting
Transportation

Additional Information
Year Founded—1981
Method of Compensation—Return on investment is most important, but also charge for closing fees, service fees, etc.
Also function in service area; receive contingent fee in cash or equity

CATERPILLAR VENTURE CAPITAL, INC.

100 Northeast Adams Street
Peoria, IL 61629
309-675-5503

Officers
Robert L. Powers, Pres.
Jack W. Dennis, Technical Mgr.
William B. Heming, Venture Mgr.

Whom to Contact
Robert L. Powers
William B. Heming

Type of Firm
Venture capital subsidiary or affiliate of non-financial corporation

Affiliation
Caterpillar Tractor Company (parent)

Industry Association Membership
NVCA

Project Preferences
Will function either as deal originator or investor in deals created by others
Type of Financing:
Seed
Startup
First-stage
Second-stage
Later-stage expansion
Leveraged buyout
Minimum Investment: $250,000
Preferred Investment: Over $1 million
Preferred Investment (LBO): Over $3 million
Minimum Operating Data:
Annual Sales—Over $3 million
Annual Sales (LBO)—Over $30 million

Geographical Preference
None

Industry Preferences

Computer Related
Computer graphics, CAD/CAM and CAE
Computer services
Micro and mini computers
Terminals
Distribution
Industrial products
Electronic Components and Instrumentation
Analytical and scientific instrumentation
Laser related
Energy/Natural Resources
Alternative energy
Industrial Products and Equipment
Chemicals
Controls and sensors
Energy management
Equipment and machinery
Other industrial automation
Robotics/vision systems
Specialty materials
Other
Agriculture, forestry, fishing

Additional Information
Year Founded—1984
Investments(1985-1st 6 months)—6
Method of Compensation—Return on investment is of primary concern; do not charge fees

CONTINENTAL ILLINOIS EQUITY CORPORATION

231 South LaSalle Street
Chicago, IL 60697
312-828-8021

Officers
John L. Hines, Pres.
William Putze, Sr. V.P.
Seth L. Pierrepont, V.P.
Judith Bultman Meyer, V.P.
Samuel C. Freitag, V.P.
Scott E. Smith, V.P.
Burton E. McGillivray, Inv. Officer
Edward K. Chandler, Inv. Officer

Whom to Contact
Any of the above

Type of Firm
Venture capital subsidiary of commercial bank

Affiliations
Continental Illinois Venture Corporation
Continental Illinois National Bank
Continental Illinois Corporation

Industry Association Membership
NVCA

Project Preferences
Will function either as deal originator or investor in deals created by others
Type of Financing:
Second-stage
Later-stage expansion
Leveraged buyout
Minimum Investment: $600,000 and over
Preferred Investment: $1 million-$10 million
Minimum Operating Data:
Annual Sales—Over $3 million
P&L—Profits NBT over $$500,000

Industry Preferences

Communications
Cable television
Commercial communications
Data communications
Satellite and microwave communications
Telephone related
Computer Related
Computer graphics, CAD/CAM and CAE
Computer mainframes
Computer services
Memory devices
Micro and mini computers
Office automation
Scanning related
Software-applications
Software-artificial intelligence
Software-systems
Specialized turnkey systems
Terminals
Consumer
Consumer products
Consumer services
Food and beverage products
Franchise businesses
Leisure and recreational products
Restaurants
Distribution
Communications equipment
Computer equipment
Consumer products
Electronics equipment
Food products
Industrial products
Medical products
Electronic Components and Instrumentation
Analytical and scientific instrumentation
Component fabrication and testing equipment
Electronic components
Fiber optics
Laser related
Semiconductors
Energy/Natural Resources
Technology related products/equipment
Genetic Engineering
Gene splicing and manufacturing equipment
Monoclonal antibodies and hybridomas
Recombinant DNA (agricultural and industrial)
Recombinant DNA (medical)
Industrial Products and Equipment
Chemicals
Controls and sensors
Energy management
Equipment and machinery
Other industrial automation
Plastics
Robotics/vision systems
Specialty materials

Medical/Health Related
Diagnostic equipment
Diagnostic test products
Disposable products
Drugs and medicines
Hospital and clinical labs
Medical services
Therapeutic equipment
Other
Publishing
Transportation
Will Not Consider
Real estate

Additional Information

Year Founded—1978
Capital Under Management—
  Over $50 million
Investments(1985-1st 6 months)—5
Invested(1985-1st 6 months)—$2.5 million
Method of Compensation—Return on investment is of primary concern; do not charge fees

---

CONTINENTAL ILLINOIS VENTURE CORPORATION

231 South LaSalle Street
Chicago, IL 60697
312-828-8021

Officers

John L. Hines, Pres.
William Putze, Sr. V.P.
Seth L. Pierrepont, V.P.
Judith Bultman Meyer, V.P.
Samuel C. Freitag, V.P.
Scott E. Smith, V.P.
Burton E. McGillivray, Inv. Officer
Edward K. Chandler, Inv. Officer

Whom to Contact

Any of the above

Type of Firm

SBIC
Venture capital subsidiary of commercial bank

Affiliations

Continental Illinois Equity Corporation
Continental Illinois National Bank
Continental Illinois Corporation

Industry Association Memberships

NASBIC
NVCA

Project Preferences

Will function either as deal originator or investor in deals created by others
Type of Financing:
Seed
Startup
First-stage
Second-stage
Later-stage expansion
Leveraged buyout
Minimum Investment: $300,000
Preferred Investment: $500,000-$1 million
Minimum Operating Data:
Annual Sales—Nominal
P&L—Losses (profits projected after 2 years)

Geographical Preference

National

Industry Preferences

Communications
Cable television
Commercial communications
Data communications
Satellite and microwave communications
Telephone related
Computer Related
Computer graphics, CAD/CAM and CAE
Computer mainframes
Computer services
Memory devices
Micro and mini computers
Office automation
Scanning related
Software-applications
Software-artificial intelligence
Software-systems
Specialized turnkey systems
Terminals
Consumer
Consumer products
Consumer services
Food and beverage products
Franchise businesses
Leisure and recreational products
Restaurants
Distribution
Communications equipment
Computer equipment
Consumer products
Electronics equipment
Food products
Industrial products
Medical products

**Electronic Components and
Instrumentation**
Analytical and scientific instrumentation
Component fabrication and testing
equipment
Electronic components
Fiber optics
Laser related
Semiconductors
Energy/Natural Resources
Technology related products/equipment
Genetic Engineering
Gene splicing and manufacturing equipment
Monoclonal antibodies and hybridomas
Recombinant DNA (agricultural and
industrial)
Recombinant DNA (medical)
Industrial Products and Equipment
Chemicals
Controls and sensors
Energy management
Equipment and machinery
Other industrial automation
Plastics
Robotics/vision systems
Specialty materials
Medical/Health Related
Diagnostic equipment
Diagnostic test products
Disposable products
Drugs and medicines
Hospital and clinical labs
Medical services
Therapeutic equipment
Other
Publishing
Transportation
Will Not Consider
Real estate

Additional Information
Year Founded—1970
Capital Under Management—$50 million
Investments(1985-1st 6 months)—8
Invested(1985-1st 6 months)—$2 million
Method of Compensation—Return on
investment is of primary concern; do not
charge fees

THE EARL KINSHIP CAPITAL CORPORATION

4711 Golf Road
Concourse 1, #801
Skokie, IL 60076
312-676-2131

Daniel C. Searle, V.P., Treas. & Dir.
William L. Searle, V.P., Asst. Secy. & Dir.
Wesley M. Dixon, Jr., V.P., Secy. & Dir.
Linda A. Shepro, Dir. Accounting & Taxes

See RHODE ISLAND for full listing

FIRST CHICAGO INVESTMENT ADVISORS

Three First National Plaza
Suite 0140
Chicago, IL 60098
312-732-4154

Officers
T. Bondurant French, V.P.
Michael I. Gallie, V.P.
Patrick A. McGivney, V.P.
David S. Timson, V.P.

Whom to Contact
Any of the above

Type of Firm
Commercial bank with trust investment
venture capital activity

Affiliation
First Chicago Corporation (parent)

Industry Association Membership
NVCA

Project Preferences
Will function either as deal originator or
investor in deals created by others
Type of Financing:
First-stage
Second-stage
Later-stage expansion
Leveraged buyout
Minimum Investment: $500,000
Preferred Investment: $500,000-$1 million
Minimum Operating Data:
Annual Sales—$500,000
P&L—Losses (profits projected after 2 years)

Geographical Preference
None

Industry Preferences

Communications
Commercial communications
Data communications
Telephone related
Computer Related
Computer graphics, CAD/CAM and CAE
Computer services
Office automation
Software-systems
Terminals
Distribution
Communications equipment
Computer equipment
Electronics equipment
Medical products
**Electronic Components and
Instrumentation**
Analytical and scientific instrumentation
Component fabrication and testing
equipment
Electronic components
Fiber optics
Laser related
Semiconductors
Industrial Products and Equipment
Controls and sensors
Other industrial automation
Medical/Health Related
Diagnostic equipment
Diagnostic test products
Disposable products
Drugs and medicines
Hospital and clinical labs
Medical services
Therapeutic equipment

Additional Information
Year Founded—1972
Capital Under Management—$157 million
Investments(1985-1st 6 months)—6
Invested(1985-1st 6 months)—$2.8 million
Method of Compensation—Return on
investment is of primary concern; do not
charge fees

FIRST CHICAGO VENTURE CAPITAL

Three First National Plaza
Suite 1330
Chicago, IL 60670
312-732-5400

Other Office

133 Federal Street
Boston, MA 02110
617-542-9185

Officers

John A. Canning, Jr., Pres. (Illinois)
Kent P. Dauten, V.P. (Illinois)
Kevin M. McCafferty, V.P. (Massachusetts)
Paul R. Wood, V.P. (Illinois)
William J. Hunckler III, V.P. (Illinois)
Gary J. Little, V.P. (Illinois)
Samuel M. Mencoff, Sr.Inv. Mgr. (Illinois)
Paul J. Finnegan, Sr. Inv. Mgr. (Illinois)
Randall S. Sturges, Inv. Mgr. (Illinois)
Thomas R. Reusche, Inv. Mgr. (Illinois)
Darius G. Nevin, Inv. Mgr. (Massachusetts)
Benjamin D. Chereskin, Inv. Mgr. (Illinois)
David F. Mosher, Inv. Mgr. (Massachusetts)
Robert A. Compton, Inv. Analyst
(Massachusetts)
James N. Perry, Jr., Inv. Analyst (Illinois)

Whom to Contact

John A. Canning, Jr.

Type of Firm

Venture capital subsidiary of
commercial bank

Affiliations

First Chicago Corporation
The First National Bank of Chicago

Industry Association Memberships

NASBIC
NVCA

Project Preferences

Will function either as deal originator or
investor in deals created by others
Type of Financing:
First-stage
Second-stage
Later-stage expansion
Leveraged buyout
Minimum Investment: $1 million
Preferred Investment: Over $2 million

Geographical Preference

None

Industry Preferences

Communications
Cable television
Commercial communications
Data communications
Outdoor advertising
Television and radio broadcasting
Computer Related
Computer graphics, CAD/CAM and CAE
Office automation
Software-systems
Consumer
Retailing
Distribution
Electronics equipment
Industrial products
Medical products
**Electronic Components and
Instrumentation**
Component fabrication and testing
equipment
Electronic components
Industrial Products and Equipment
Equipment and machinery
Medical/Health Related
Medical services
Nursing homes

Additional Information

Year Founded—1961
Capital Under Management—$400 million
Investments(1985-1st 6 months)—38
Invested(1985-1st 6 months)—$46 million
Method of Compensation—Return on
investment is of primary concern; do not
charge fees

FRONTENAC VENTURE COMPANY

208 South LaSalle Street #1900
Chicago, IL 60604
312-368-0044

General Partners

Martin J. Koldyke
Rodney L. Goldstein
David A.R. Dullum

Whom to Contact

Any of the above

Type of Firm

Private venture capital firm investing
own capital
SBIC

Industry Association Memberships

NASBIC
NVCA

Project Preferences

Will function either as deal originator or
investor in deals created by others
Type of Financing:
Seed
First-stage
Later-stage expansion
Leveraged buyout
Minimum Investment: $250,000
Preferred Investment: $750,000-$3 million

Geographical Preferences

Midwest
Rocky Mountains

Industry Preferences

Communications
Various
Computer Related
Computer graphics, CAD/CAM and CAE
Office automation
Software-systems
Consumer
Consumer products
Consumer services
Retailing
**Electronic Components and
Instrumentation**
Analytical and scientific instrumentation
Industrial Products and Equipment
Various
Medical/Health Related
Diagnostic equipment
Diagnostic test products
Drugs and medicines
Hospital and clinical labs
Medical services
Therapeutic equipment
Other
Publishing
Transportation

Additional Information

Year Founded—1971
Capital Under Management—$100 million
Investments(1985-1st 6 months)—8
Invested(1985-1st 6 months)—$3.5 million
Method of Compensation—Return on
investment is of primary concern

GATEWAY MID-AMERICA PARTNERS

135 South LaSalle #540
Chicago, IL 60603
312-782-3100

George K. Hendrick, Jr., Chm., Stifel
Venture

See MISSOURI for full listing

GOLDER, THOMA & CRESSEY

120 South LaSalle Street #630
Chicago, IL 60603
312-853-3322

Partners
Stanley C. Golder, Gen. Ptnr.
Carl D. Thoma, Gen. Ptnr.
Bryan C. Cressey, Gen. Ptnr.
Bruce V. Rauner, Gen. Ptnr.
Robert M. Chefitz, Sr. Assoc.
Ryan A. Kuhn, Sr. Assoc.
Terrance McGuire, Assoc.
William V. Glastris, Jr., Assoc.
Robert B. Campbell, Assoc.
John M. Pasquesi, Assoc.
John E. von Schlegell, Assoc.

Whom to Contact
Stanley C. Golder
Carl D. Thoma
Bryan C. Cressey
Bruce V. Rauner

Type of Firm
Private venture capital firm investing
own capital

Industry Association Memberships
NASBIC
NVCA

Project Preferences
Will function either as deal originator or
investor in deals created by others
Type of Financing:
First-stage
Second-stage
Later-stage expansion
Leveraged buyout
Minimum Investment: $500,000
Preferred Investment: $500,000-$2 million
Preferred Investment (LBO): $2 million
Minimum Operating Data:
Annual Sales—Nominal
P&L—Losses (profits projected after 2 years)
Annual Sales (LBO)—$15 million-$20 million

Geographical Preference
None

Industry Preferences

Communications
Cable television
Commercial communications
Data communications
Satellite and microwave communications
Telephone related
Computer Related
Computer services
Office automation
Consumer
Franchise businesses
Restaurants
Distribution
Communications equipment
Medical products
**Electronic Components and
Instrumentation**
Analytical and scientific instrumentation
Fiber optics
Genetic Engineering
Gene splicing and manufacturing equipment
Medical/Health Related
Diagnostic equipment
Drugs and medicines
Hospital and clinical labs
Medical services
Therapeutic equipment
Other
Publishing
Transportation
Will Not Consider
Real estate
Motion picture industry
Entertainment industry

Additional Information
Year Founded—1980
Capital Under Management—$160 million
Investments(1985-1st 6 months)—11
Invested(1985-1st 6 months)—$10.6 million
Method of Compensation—Return on
investment is of primary concern; do not
charge fees

GOLDMAN & CO.

800 East Northwest Highway
Palatine, IL 60067
312-359-5021

Officers
George N. Goldman, Chm.
Andrew I. Walzer, V.P.

Whom to Contact
Andrew I. Walzer

Type of Firm
Private venture capital firm investing
own capital
Investment banking or merchant banking
firm investing own capital or funds of
partners or clients

Affiliations
Goldman Securities, Inc. (subsidiary)
Exemplar Industries, Inc. (subsidiary)

Project Preferences
Prefer role as deal originator
Type of Financing:
Startup
Later-stage expansion
Leveraged buyout
Minimum Investment: $250,000
Preferred Investment: $500,000-$1 million
Preferred Investment (LBO):
Over $1 million
Minimum Operating Data:
Annual Sales—$500,000
P&L—Losses (profits projected after 2 years)
Annual Sales (LBO)—
$5 million to $100 million

Geographical Preferences
Midwest
National

Industry Preferences

Communications
Data communications
Satellite and microwave communications

Computer Related
Computer graphics, CAD/CAM and CAE
Computer mainframes
Computer security
Computer services
Memory devices
Micro and mini computers
Office automation
Scanning related
Software-applications
Software-artificial intelligence
Software-systems
Specialized turnkey systems
Terminals
Consumer
Hotels and resort areas
Leisure and recreational products
Retailing
**Electronic Components and
    Instrumentation**
Analytical and scientific instrumentation
Component fabrication and testing
    equipment
Electronic components
Fiber optics
Laser related
Semiconductors
Energy/Natural Resources
Alternative energy
Energy conservation
Technology related products/equipment
Genetic Engineering
Gene splicing and manufacturing equipment
Monoclonal antibodies and hybridomas
Recombinant DNA (agricultural and
    industrial)
Recombinant DNA (medical)
Industrial Products and Equipment
Energy management
Equipment and machinery
Glass and mirrors
Other industrial automation
Plastics
Specialty materials
Medical/Health Related
Diagnostic equipment
Diagnostic test products
Disposable products
Drugs and medicines
Hospital and clinical labs
Medical services
Therapeutic equipment
Other
Finance and insurance
Publishing
Real estate
Purchase with leaseback of multiple
    location real estate packages—especially
    real estate of alternative health care
    delivery companies
Manufactured housing communities

Additional Information
Year Founded—1959
Investments(1985-1st 6 months)—2
Invested(1985-1st 6 months)—$2.7 million
Method of Compensation—Return on
    investment is of primary concern; do not
    charge fees

HAYES & GRIFFITH VENTURE MANAGEMENT L.P.

115 South LaSalle Street
Suite 2130 East
Chicago, IL 60603
312-750-2707

Partners
James L. Currie, Mgn. Gen. Ptnr.
James E. Hayes, Gen. Ptnr.
H. Tom Griffith, Gen. Ptnr.
Myral Bernstein, Assoc.

Whom to Contact
James L. Currie

Type of Firm
Private venture capital firm investing
    own capital

Affiliation
Hayes & Griffith, Inc. (affiliate)

Project Preferences
Prefer role as deal originator but will also
    invest in deals created by others
Type of Financing:
Seed
Startup
Leveraged buyout
Minimum Investment: Less than $100,000
Preferred Investment: $250,000-$500,000
Minimum Operating Data:
Annual Sales—Nominal

Geographical Preference
Midwest

Industry Preferences

Medical/Health Related
Diagnostic equipment
Diagnostic test products
Disposable products
Drugs and medicines
Hospital and clinical labs
Medical services
Therapeutic equipment

Additional Information
Year Founded—1985
Capital Under Management—$8 million
Method of Compensation—Return on
    investment is of primary concern; do not
    charge fees

IEG VENTURE MANAGEMENT, INC.

401 North Michigan #2020
Chicago, IL 60611
312-644-0890

Officers
Francis I. Blair, Pres.
Marian M. Zamlynski, Ops. Mgr. & V.P.

Whom to Contact
Either of the above

Type of Firm
Private venture capital firm investing
    own capital

Industry Association Membership
NASBIC

Project Preferences
Prefer role as deal originator
Type of Financing:
Seed
Startup
First-stage
Second-stage
Minimum Investment: $100,000
Preferred Investment: $250,000-$500,000
Minimum Operating Data:
Annual Sales—Nominal

Geographical Preference
Midwest

Industry Preferences

Communications
Commercial communications
Data communications
Satellite and microwave communications
Telephone related
Computer Related
Computer mainframes
Computer services
Memory devices
Micro and mini computers
Office automation
Scanning related
Software-applications
Software-artificial intelligence
Software-systems
Specialized turnkey systems

Distribution
Communications equipment
Computer equipment
Electronics equipment
Industrial products
Medical products
**Electronic Components and
Instrumentation**
Analytical and scientific instrumentation
Electronic components
Fiber optics
Laser related
Energy/Natural Resources
Technology related products/equipment
Industrial Products and Equipment
Controls and sensors
Energy management
Equipment and machinery
Other industrial automation
Robotics/vision systems
Specialty materials
Medical/Health Related
Diagnostic equipment
Diagnostic test products
Disposable products
Drugs and medicines
Hospital and clinical labs
Medical services
Therapeutic equipment
Other
Agriculture, forestry, fishing
Transportation
Will Not Consider
Real estate
Natural resources

Additional Information
Year Founded—1983
Investments(1985-1st 6 months)—4
Invested(1985-1st 6 months)—$716,000
Method of Compensation—Return on
    investment is of primary concern; do not
    charge fees

LONGWORTH VENTURES

135 South LaSalle Street #616
Chicago, IL 60603
312-372-3888

General Partners
Lawrence G. Sucsy
Thomas Galuhn
Andrew Beaurline

Whom to Contact
Any of the above

Type of Firm
Private venture capital firm investing
    own capital

Affiliation
Sucsy, Fischer & Co.

Project Preferences
Will function either as deal originator or
    investor in deals created by others
Type of Financing:
Startup
First-stage
Second-stage
Later-stage expansion
Leveraged buyout
Minimum Investment: $100,000
Preferred Investment: $250,000-$500,000
Preferred Investment (LBO):
    $1 million-$2 million
Minimum Operating Data:
Annual Sales—Nominal
P&L—Losses (profits projected after 2 years)
Annual Sales (LBO)—$5 million-$75 million

Geographical Preference
None

Industry Preferences

Communications
Cable television
Commercial communications
Data communications
Satellite and microwave communications
Telephone related
Computer Related
Computer graphics, CAD/CAM and CAE
Computer mainframes
Computer services
Memory devices
Micro and mini computers
Office automation
Scanning related
Software-applications
Software-artificial intelligence
Software-systems
Specialized turnkey systems
Terminals
Consumer
Consumer products
Franchise businesses
Distribution
Communications equipment
Electronics equipment
Medical products

**Electronic Components and
    Instrumentation**
Analytical and scientific instrumentation
Component fabrication and testing
    equipment
Electronic components
Fiber optics
Laser related
Semiconductors
Energy/Natural Resources
Alternative energy
Services
Technology related products/equipment
Genetic Engineering
Monoclonal antibodies and hybridomas
Recombinant DNA (agricultural and
    industrial)
Recombinant DNA (medical)
Research and manufacturing equipment
Industrial Products and Equipment
Chemicals
Controls and sensors
Energy management
Equipment and machinery
Other industrial automation
Plastics
Robotics/vision systems
Specialty materials
Medical/Health Related
Diagnostic equipment
Diagnostic test products
Disposable products
Drugs and medicines
Hospital and clinical labs
Medical services
Therapeutic equipment
Other
Agriculture, forestry, fishing
Transportation
Will Not Consider
Mineral extraction
Real estate

Additional Information
Method of Compensation—Return on
    investment is of primary concern; do not
    charge fees

THE LUKEN COMPANY

135 South LaSalle Street #1012
Chicago, IL 60603
312-263-4015

Officer
Donald Luken, Pres.

Type of Firm
Investment banking or merchant banking firm investing own capital or funds of partners or clients
Consulting firm evaluating and analyzing venture projects and arranging private placements

Project Preferences
Prefer role as deal originator but will also invest in deals created by others
Type of Financing:
First-stage
Second-stage
Later-stage expansion
Leveraged buyout
Minimum Investment: $500,000
Preferred Investment: Over $1 million
Minimum Operating Data:
Annual Sales—Nominal
P&L—Losses (profits projected after 1 year)

Geographical Preferences
Midwest
Rocky Mountains

Industry Preferences

Communications
Commercial communications
Computer Related
Computer services
Computer-based training
Specialized turnkey systems
Consumer
Leisure and recreational products
Distribution
Communications equipment
Computer equipment
Electronics equipment
Industrial products
Medical products
Electronic Components and Instrumentation
Component fabrication and testing equipment
Electronic components
Energy/Natural Resources
Drilling and exploration services
Energy conservation
Technology related products/equipment

Industrial Products and Equipment
Controls and sensors
Energy management
Equipment and machinery
Other
Agriculture, forestry, fishing
Education related
Finance and insurance
Publishing
Real estate
Specialty consulting
Transportation

Additional Information
Year Founded—1980
Investments(1985-1st 6 months)—3
Invested(1985-1st 6 months)—$1.8 million
Method of Compensation—Function primarily in service area; receive contingent fee in cash or equity

---

MESIROW VENTURE CAPITAL

350 North Clark Street
Chicago, IL 60610
312-670-6000

Officers
James C. Tyree, Mgn. Dir.
William P. Sutter, Jr., V.P.
Michael J. Barrett, Inv. Analyst

Whom to Contact
James C. Tyree

Type of Firm
Private venture capital firm investing own capital
SBIC
Investment banking or merchant banking firm investing own capital or funds of partners or clients

Affiliation
Mesirow & Co. (parent)

Industry Association Membership
NASBIC

Project Preferences
Prefer role as deal originator but will also invest in deals created by others
Type of Financing:
Second-stage
Later-stage expansion
Leveraged buyout

Minimum Investment: $250,000
Preferred Investment: Over $1 million
Preferred Investment (LBO):
$1 million-$10 million
Minimum Operating Data:
Annual Sales—$3 million
P&L—Break even
Annual Sales (LBO)—Over $10 million

Geographical Preference
None

Industry Preferences

Communications
Cable television
Commercial communications
Data communications
Satellite and microwave communications
Telephone related
Consumer
Computer stores/related services
Consumer products
Consumer services
Food and beverage products
Franchise businesses
Hotels and resort areas
Leisure and recreational products
Restaurants
Retailing
Distribution
Communications equipment
Computer equipment
Consumer products
Electronics equipment
Food products
Industrial products
Medical products
Industrial Products and Equipment
Chemicals
Controls and sensors
Energy management
Equipment and machinery
Other industrial automation
Plastics
Robotics/vision systems
Specialty materials
Medical/Health Related
Diagnostic equipment
Diagnostic test products
Disposable products
Drugs and medicines
Hospital and clinical labs
Medical services
Therapeutic equipment
Other
Agriculture, forestry, fishing
Education related
Finance and insurance
Publishing
Transportation

Will Not Consider
Real estate

Additional Information
Year Founded—1981
Capital Under Management—$35 million
Investments(1985-1st 6 months)—5
Invested(1985-1st 6 months)—$12 million

NELSON CAPITAL CORPORATION

2340 Des Plaines Avenue
Des Plaines, IL 60018
312-296-2280

See NEW YORK for full listing

NORTH AMERICAN CAPITAL LTD.

55 West Monroe Street
35th Floor
Lincolnwood, IL 60603
312-781-1111

Officers
Jeffrey E. Grossman, Chm.
Gregory I. Kravitt, Pres.
Mindy B. Warshawsky, Assoc.

Whom to Contact
Gregory I. Kravitt
Mindy B. Warshawsky

Type of Firm
Private venture capital firm investing
own capital

Affiliation
Reliable Investors Corporation

Project Preferences
Prefer role as deal originator but will also
invest in deals created by others
Type of Financing:
Second-stage
Later-stage expansion
Leveraged buyout
Minimum Investment: $100,000
Preferred Investment: $500,000-$1 million
Preferred Investment (LBO):
$1 million-$5 million
Minimum Operating Data:
Annual Sales—$500,000
P&L—Break even

Geographical Preference
Midwest

Industry Preferences

Communications
Cable television
Commercial communications
Data communications
Telephone related
Computer Related
Software-applications
Specialized turnkey systems
Consumer
Computer stores/related services
Consumer products
Consumer services
Food and beverage products
Franchise businesses
Hotels and resort areas
Leisure and recreational products
Restaurants
Retailing
Distribution
Communications equipment
Computer equipment
Consumer products
Electronics equipment
Food products
Industrial products
Medical products
Industrial Products and Equipment
Chemicals
Controls and sensors
Energy management
Equipment and machinery
Other industrial automation
Plastics
Robotics/vision systems
Specialty materials
Medical/Health Related
Diagnostic equipment
Diagnostic test products
Disposable products
Drugs and medicines
Hospital and clinical labs
Medical services
Therapeutic equipment
Other
Agriculture, forestry, fishing
Education related
Finance and insurance
Publishing
Real estate
Specialty consulting
Transportation
Will Not Consider
Gambling
Relending or reinvesting

Additional Information
Year Founded—1980
Capital Under Management—$10 million
Investments(1985-1st 6 months)—2
Invested(1985-1st 6 months)—$1 million
Method of Compensation—Return on
investment is of primary concern; do not
charge fees

NORTHERN CAPITAL CORPORATION

50 South LaSalle Street
Chicago, IL 60675
312-444-5399

Officers
Robert L. Underwood, Pres.
Peter H. Kingman, Dir.

Whom to Contact
Robert L. Underwood

Type of Firm
SBIC
Venture capital subsidiary of
commercial bank

Affiliation
Northern Trust Co. (parent)
Northern Investment Corp. (affiliate with
common management)

Industry Association Memberships
NASBIC
NVCA

Project Preferences
Will function either as deal originator or
investor in deals created by others
Type of Financing:
Seed
Startup
First-stage
Second-stage
Later-stage expansion
Minimum Investment: $250,000
Preferred Investment: $500,000-$750,000
Minimum Operating Data:
Annual Sales—Nominal
P&L—Losses (profits projected after 3 years)

Geographical Preferences
Midwest
National

Industry Preferences

Communications
Telecommunications
Computer Related
Various
Consumer
Consumer services
Electronic Components and Instrumentation
Various
Medical/Health Related
Health care products and services
Other
Business services
Will Not Consider
Finance companies
General construction
Magazine publishing
Motion picture or television production
Real estate
Non-U.S. companies

Additional Information

Year Founded—1984
Capital Under Management—$5 million
Investments(1985-1st 6 months)—2
Invested(1985-1st 6 months)—$1 million
Method of Compensation—Return on investment is of primary concern; do not charge fees

---

PIVAN MANAGEMENT COMPANY

7840 Lincoln Avenue
Skokie, IL 60077
312-677-1142

Officers
David B. Pivan
Richard L. Nelson

Whom to Contact
David B. Pivan

Type of Firm
Private venture capital firm investing own capital
Consulting firm evaluating and analyzing venture projects and arranging private placements

Project Preferences
Will function either as deal originator or investor in deals created by others
Type of Financing:
First-stage
Leveraged buyout

Minimum Investment: $100,000
Preferred Investment: $100,000-$250,000
Minimum Operating Data:
Annual Sales—Nominal
P&L—Break even

Geographical Preference
Midwest

Industry Preferences

Communications
Commercial communications
Data communications
Telephone related
Computer Related
Computer graphics, CAD/CAM and CAE
Memory devices
Micro and mini computers
Office automation
Software-systems
Distribution
Communications equipment
Computer equipment
Electronics equipment
Electronic Components and Instrumentation
Analytical and scientific instrumentation
Component fabrication and testing equipment
Electronic components
Fiber optics
Laser related
Energy/Natural Resources
Technology related products/equipment
Industrial Products and Equipment
Other industrial automation
Robotics/vision systems
Will Not Consider
Consumer related businesses, including food production and distribution

Additional Information
Year Founded—1976
Capital Under Management—$2 million
Investments(1985-1st 6 months)—2
Invested(1985-1st 6 months)—$300,000
Method of Compensation—Return on investment is most important, but also may charge for closing fees, service fees, etc.

PRINCE VENTURE PARTNERS

One First National Plaza #4950
Chicago, IL 60603
312-726-2232

Other Office
767 Third Avenue, 36th Floor
New York, NY 10017
212-319-6620

General Partners
Angus M. Duthie
James W. Fordyce

Whom to Contact
Angus M. Duthie (Illinois)
James W. Fordyce (New York)

Type of Firm
Private venture capital firm investing own capital

Affiliation
F.H. Prince & Company, Inc. (limited partner)

Industry Association Membership
NVCA

Project Preferences
Will function either as deal originator or investor in deals created by others
Type of Financing:
Seed
Startup
First-stage
Leveraged buyout
Minimum Investment: $100,000
Preferred Investment: $250,000-$500,000
Minimum Operating Data:
Annual Sales—Nominal
P&L—Losses (profits projected after 3 years)

Geographical Preference
National

Industry Preferences

Communications
Data communications
Satellite and microwave communications
Telephone related

Computer Related
Computer graphics, CAD/CAM and CAE
Computer mainframes
Computer services
Memory devices
Micro and mini computers
Office automation
Scanning related
Software-applications
Software-artificial intelligence
Software-systems
Specialized turnkey systems
Terminals
Electronic Components and Instrumentation
Analytical and scientific instrumentation
Component fabrication and testing equipment
Electronic components
Fiber optics
Laser related
Semiconductors
Genetic Engineering
Gene splicing and manufacturing equipment
Monoclonal antibodies and hybridomas
Recombinant DNA (agricultural and industrial)
Recombinant DNA (medical)
Medical/Health Related
Diagnostic equipment
Diagnostic test products
Disposable products
Drugs and medicines
Hospital and clinical labs
Medical services
Therapeutic equipment

Additional Information
Year Founded—1978
Capital Under Management—$25 million
Investments(1985-1st 6 months)—5
Invested(1985-1st 6 months)—$1.3 million
Method of Compensation—Return on investment is of primary concern; do not charge fees

---

THE PRODUCTIVITY FUND

c/o First Analysis Management
150 South Wacker Drive #880
Chicago, IL 60606
312-372-3111

Partners
F. Oliver Nicklin, Gen. Ptnr.
Bret Maxwell, Gen. Ptnr.
Brian Hand, Assoc.
Mike Siemplenski, Assoc.
Larry Hickey, Assoc.
Julie Wlach, Assoc.

Whom to Contact
Bret Maxwell

Type of Firm
Private venture capital firm investing own capital

Project Preferences
Will function either as deal originator or investor in deals created by others
Type of Financing:
Seed
Startup
First-stage
Second-stage
Leveraged buyout
Minimum Investment: $100,000
Preferred Investment: $250,000-$500,000
Minimum Operating Data:
Annual Sales—Nominal

Geographical Preference
None

Industry Preferences

Communications
Data communications
Satellite and microwave communications
Telephone related
Computer Related
Computer graphics, CAD/CAM and CAE
Computer mainframes
Computer services
Memory devices
Micro and mini computers
Office automation
Scanning related
Software-applications
Software-artificial intelligence
Software-systems
Specialized turnkey systems
Terminals

Distribution
Communications equipment
Computer equipment
Consumer products
Industrial products
Electronic Components and Instrumentation
Analytical and scientific instrumentation
Component fabrication and testing equipment
Electronic components
Fiber optics
Laser related
Semiconductors
Energy/Natural Resources
Technology related products/equipment
Industrial Products and Equipment
Controls and sensors
Robotics/vision systems
Specialty materials
Other
Hazardous waste testing, processing and disposal
Service related businesses

Additional Information
Year Founded—1985
Capital Under Management—$15 million

REPRISE CAPITAL CORPORATION

2340 Des Plaines
Des Plaines, IL 60018
312-296-2280

See NEW YORK for full listing

SEARS INVESTMENT COMPANY

55 West Monroe Street
32nd Floor
Chicago, IL 60603
312-875-0415

Officers
James M. Smith, Sr. Portfolio Mgr.
Scott S. Pape, Inv. Analyst

Whom to Contact
Either of the above

Type of Firm
Pension fund

Affiliation
Sears, Roebuck & Co.

Project Preferences

Prefer role in deals created by others

Type of Financing:
First-stage
Second-stage
Later-stage expansion
Leveraged buyout
Minimum Investment: $200,000
Preferred Investment: $250,000-$500,000
Minimum Operating Data:
Annual Sales—Nominal
P&L—Losses (profits projected after 1 year)

Geographical Preference

None

Industry Preferences

None

Additional Information

Year Founded—1976
Capital Under Management—$65 million
Investments(1985-1st 6 months)—6
Invested(1985-1st 6 months)—$1.8 million
Method of Compensation—Return on
  investment is of primary concern; do not
  charge fees

SEIDMAN JACKSON FISHER & CO.

233 North Michigan Avenue
Suite 1812
Chicago, IL 60601
312-856-1812

Partners

David C. Seidman
Douglas L. Jackson
Margaret G. Fisher

Whom to Contact

Any of the above

Type of Firm

Private venture capital firm investing
  own capital

Industry Association Membership

NVCA

Project Preferences

Will function either as deal originator or
  investor in deals created by others
Type of Financing:
First-stage
Second-stage
Later-stage expansion
Leveraged buyout

Minimum Investment: $500,000
Preferred Investment: $500,000-$1 million
Minimum Operating Data:
Annual Sales—Nominal
P&L—Losses (profits projected after 1 year)

Geographical Preference

None

Industry Preferences

Communications
Commercial communications
Data communications
Satellite and microwave communications
Telephone related
Computer Related
Computer graphics, CAD/CAM and CAE
Computer mainframes
Computer services
Memory devices
Micro and mini computers
Office automation
Scanning related
Software-applications
Software-artificial intelligence
Software-systems
Specialized turnkey systems
Terminals
Distribution
Communications equipment
Computer equipment
Consumer products
Electronics equipment
Food products
Industrial products
Medical products
**Electronic Components and
  Instrumentation**
Analytical and scientific instrumentation
Component fabrication and testing
  equipment
Electronic components
Fiber optics
Laser related
Semiconductors
Energy/Natural Resources
Technology related products/equipment
Industrial Products and Equipment
Chemicals
Controls and sensors
Energy management
Equipment and machinery
Other industrial automation
Plastics
Robotics/vision systems
Specialty materials

Medical/Health Related
Diagnostic equipment
Diagnostic test products
Disposable products
Drugs and medicines
Hospital and clinical labs
Medical services
Therapeutic equipment

Additional Information

Year Founded—1981
Capital Under Management—$45.5 million
Investments(1985-1st 6 months)—11
Invested(1985-1st 6 months)—$3.3 million
Method of Compensation—Return on
  investment is of primary concern; do not
  charge fees

SHELL FINANCIAL CORPORATION

40 Skokie Boulevard
Northbrook, IL 60062
312-498-3400

Other Office

730 North Franklin Street #700
Chicago, IL 60610
312-943-1676

Officers

Adam E. Robins, Pres. & Dir.
Sheldon H. Ginsburg, Dir.
Perry J. Snyderman, Dir.

Whom to Contact

Adam E. Robins

Type of Firm

Private venture capital firm investing
  own capital
Investment banking or merchant banking
  firm investing own capital or funds of
  partners or clients

Affiliation

Shell Equities Corporation (affiliate)

Project Preferences

Will function either as deal originator or
  investor in deals created by others
Type of Financing:
Seed
Startup
First-stage
Second-stage
Later-stage expansion
Leveraged buyout

Minimum Investment: $250,000
Preferred Investment: $250,000-$3 million
Preferred Investment (LBO):
    $250,000-$3 million
Minimum Operating Data:
Annual Sales—Nominal
P&L—Losses (profits projected after 1 year)
Annual Sales (LBO)—$500,000 and over

Geographical Preferences
Midwest
National

Industry Preferences

Communications
Cable television
Commercial communications
Consumer
Consumer products
Food and beverage products
Franchise businesses
Hotels and resort areas
Leisure and recreational products
Retailing
Distribution
Consumer products
Electronics equipment
Food products
Industrial products
Medical products
Industrial Products and Equipment
Traditional manufacturing
Medical/Health Related
Medical services
Other
Finance and insurance
Publishing
Real estate
Waste management
Will Not Consider
High technology businesses

Additional Information
Year Founded—1983
Investments(1985-1st 6 months)—9
Method of Compensation—Function primarily
    in service area; receive contingent fee in
    cash or equity

SQUARE D COMPANY

Executive Plaza
Palatine, IL 60067
312-397-2600

Officers
D.L. Knauss, Chm.
D.E. Wilson, Secy. & CFO
A.G. Mueller, V.P., Corp. Development
W.E. Craft, Group Cntlr.

Whom to Contact
A.G. Mueller
W.E. Craft

Type of Firm
Venture capital subsidiary or affiliate of
    non-financial corporation

Project Preferences
Prefer role in deals created by others
Type of Financing:
Seed
Startup
First-stage
Minimum Investment: Under $1 million
Preferred Investment: $250,000-$500,000
Minimum Operating Data:
Annual Sales—Nominal
P&L—Losses (profits projected after 2 years)

Geographical Preference
None

Industry Preferences

Communications
Data communications
Computer Related
Computer graphics, CAD/CAM and CAE
Software-artificial intelligence
Software-systems
**Electronic Components and
    Instrumentation**
Analytical and scientific instrumentation
Electronic components
Fiber optics
Laser related
Semiconductors
Industrial Products and Equipment
Controls and sensors
Other industrial automation
Robotics/vision systems
Specialty materials

Additional Information
Year Founded—1984

SUCSY, FISCHER & CO.

135 South LaSalle Street #616
Chicago, IL 60603
312-346-4545

Officers
Lawrence G. Sucsy
Paul F. Fischer

Whom to Contact
Either of the above

Type of Firm
Investment banking or merchant banking
    firm investing own capital or funds of
    partners or clients
Consulting firm evaluating and analyzing
    venture projects and arranging private
    placements

Affiliation
Longworth Ventures

Project Preferences
Will function either as deal originator or
    investor in deals created by others
Type of Financing:
Startup
First-stage
Second-stage
Later-stage expansion
Leveraged buyout
Minimum Investment: $100,000
Preferred Investment: $250,000-$500,000
Preferred Investment (LBO):
    $1 million-$10 million
Minimum Operating Data:
Annual Sales—Nominal
P&L—Losses (profits projected after 2 years)
Annual Sales (LBO)—$5 million-$75 million

Geographical Preference
Midwest

Industry Preferences

Communications
Cable television
Commercial communications
Data communications
Satellite and microwave communications
Telephone related

Computer Related
Computer graphics, CAD/CAM and CAE
Computer mainframes
Computer services
Memory devices
Micro and mini computers
Office automation
Scanning related
Software-applications
Software-artificial intelligence
Software-systems
Specialized turnkey systems
Terminals
Consumer
Consumer products
Franchise businesses
Distribution
Communications equipment
Computer equipment
Electronics equipment
Medical products
Electronic Components and Instrumentation
Analytical and scientific instrumentation
Component fabrication and testing equipment
Electronic components
Fiber optics
Laser related
Semiconductors
Energy/Natural Resources
Alternative energy
Services
Technology related products/equipment
Genetic Engineering
Monoclonal antibodies and hybridomas
Recombinant DNA (agricultural and industrial)
Recombinant DNA (medical)
Research and manufacturing equipment
Industrial Products and Equipment
Chemicals
Controls and sensors
Energy management
Equipment and machinery
Other industrial automation
Plastics
Robotics/vision systems
Specialty materials
Medical/Health Related
Diagnostic equipment
Disposable products
Drugs and medicines
Hospital and clinical labs
Therapeutic equipment

Other
Agriculture, forestry, fishing
Finance and insurance
Graphic arts
Packaging
Transportation

Additional Information
Year Founded—1972
Method of Compensation—Function primarily in service area; receive contingent fee in cash or equity

TECHNOLOGY PARTNERS

257 East Main Steet
Barrington, IL 60010
312-381-2510

Peter J. Gillespie

See CALIFORNIA for full listing

VANGUARD CAPITAL CORPORATION

One Northbrook Place, #200
Five Revere Drive
Northbrook, IL 60062
312-272-3636

Officer
Kenneth M. Arenberg, Pres.

Type of Firm
Private venture capital firm investing own capital

Industry Association Membership
NVCA

Project Preferences
Will function either as deal originator or investor in deals created by others
Type of Financing:
Seed
Preferred Investment: Less than $100,000
Minimum Operating Data:
Annual Sales—Nominal

Geographical Preference
Illinois

Industry Preferences
Marketing oriented companies
Spin-offs

Additional Information
Year Founded—1961
Method of Compensation—Return on investment is of primary concern; do not charge fees

CIRCLE VENTURES, INC.

20 North Meridian Street
Indianapolis, IN 46204
317-636-7242

Officers
Robert J. Salyers, Pres.
Samuel B. Sutphin II, V.P. & Inv. Mgr.
Larry R. Smith, Secy. & Treas.

Whom to Contact
Samuel B. Sutphin II

Type of Firm
SBIC

Affiliations
Raffensperger, Hughes & Co., Inc.
Eastside Community Investments, Inc.

Industry Association Membership
NASBIC

Project Preferences
Will function either as deal originator or
   investor in deals created by others
Type of Financing:
First-stage
Second-stage
Later-stage expansion
Leveraged buyout
Minimum Investment: $50,000
Preferred Investment: $75,000-$175,000
Minimum Operating Data:
Annual Sales—Nominal
P&L—Losses (profits projected after 1 year)

Geographical Preference
Indiana only

Industry Preferences

Communications
Cable television
Commercial communications
Data communications
Satellite and microwave communications
Telephone related
Computer Related
Computer services
Office automation
Software-applications
Consumer
Computer stores/related services
Consumer products
Food and beverage products
Franchise businesses

Distribution
Communications equipment
Computer equipment
Consumer products
Electronics equipment
Food products
Industrial products
Medical products
**Electronic Components and
   Instrumentation**
Analytical and scientific instrumentation
Component fabrication and testing
   equipment
Electronic components
Fiber optics
Laser related
Genetic Engineering
Gene splicing and manufacturing equipment
Monoclonal antibodies and hybridomas
Recombinant DNA (agricultural and
   industrial)
Recombinant DNA (medical)
Industrial Products and Equipment
Chemicals
Controls and sensors
Equipment and machinery
Other industrial automation
Plastics
Robotics/vision systems
Specialty materials
Medical/Health Related
Diagnostic equipment
Diagnostic test products
Disposable products
Drugs and medicines
Other
Publishing
Will Not Consider
Real estate

Additional Information
Year Founded—1983
Capital Under Management—$1 million
Investments(1985-1st 6 months)—2
Invested(1985-1st 6 months)—$145,000
Method of Compensation—Return on
   investment is of primary concern; do not
   charge fees

CORPORATION FOR INNOVATION DEVELOPMENT

One North Capitol Avenue #520
Indianapolis, IN 46204
317-635-7325

Officers
Marion C. Dietrich, Pres. & CEO
Donald K. Taylor, V.P.
M. Archie Leslie, V.P.

Whom to Contact
Donald K. Taylor
M. Archie Leslie

Type of Firm
Private venture capital firm investing
   own capital

Industry Association Membership
NASBIC

Project Preferences
Will function either as deal originator or
   investor in deals created by others
Type of Financing:
Startup
First-stage
Second-stage
Later-stage expansion
Leveraged buyout
Minimum Investment: $100,000
Preferred Investment: $250,000-$500,000

Geographical Preference
Indiana only

Industry Preferences

Communications
Data communications
Satellite and microwave communications
Telephone related
Computer Related
Computer graphics, CAD/CAM and CAE
Computer services
Memory devices
Micro and mini computers
Office automation
Software-applications
Software-systems
Consumer
Retailing
**Electronic Components and
   Instrumentation**
Analytical and scientific instrumentation
Electronic components
Laser related
Semiconductors

Energy/Natural Resources
Alternative energy
Energy conservation
Genetic Engineering
Monoclonal antibodies and hybridomas
Industrial Products and Equipment
Chemicals
Controls and sensors
Energy management
Equipment and machinery
Other industrial automation
Plastics
Robotics/vision systems
Specialty materials
Medical/Health Related
Diagnostic equipment
Diagnostic test products
Disposable products
Drugs and medicines
Hospital and clinical labs
Medical services
Therapeutic equipment
Will Not Consider
Real estate

Additional Information
Year Founded—1982
Capital Under Management—$10 million
Method of Compensation—Return on
  investment is of primary concern; do not
  charge fees

EQUITY RESOURCE COMPANY, INC.

One Plaza Place
Post Office Box 839
South Bend, IN 46624
219-237-5255

Officers
Richard T. Doermer, Chm.
Richard A. Rosenthal, Pres.
Michael J. Hammes, V.P. & Secy.
Marvin V. Basse, V.P. & Treas.

Whom to Contact
Michael J. Hammes

Type of Firm
SBIC

Affiliations
St. Joseph Bank and Trust of South Bend
Summit Bank and Trust of Fort Wayne

Industry Association Membership
NASBIC

Project Preferences
Will function either as deal originator or
  investor in deals created by others
Type of Financing:
Second-stage
Later-stage expansion
Leveraged buyout
Minimum Investment: Less than $100,000
Preferred Investment: $100,000-$250,000
Minimum Operating Data:
Annual Sales—Nominal
P&L—Break even

Geographical Preference
Within two hours of office

Industry Preferences
None

Additional Information
Year Founded—1983
Capital Under Management—$2 million
Investments(1985-1st 6 months)—1
Invested(1985-1st 6 months)—$100,000
Method of Compensation—Return on
  investment is of primary concern; do not
  charge fees

1ST SOURCE CAPITAL CORPORATION

100 North Michigan
South Bend, IN 46601
219-236-2180

Officers
Christopher J. Murphy III, Pres.
A.S. Burkart, V.P.
Eugene L. Cavanaugh, Jr., V.P.

Whom to Contact
Eugene L. Cavanaugh, Jr.

Type of Firm
SBIC

Affiliation
1st Source Bank, South Bend,
  Indiana (parent)

Industry Association Membership
NASBIC

Project Preferences
Will function either as deal originator or
  investor in deals created by others

Type of Financing:
Second-stage
Later-stage expansion
Leveraged buyout
Minimum Investment: $100,000
Preferred Investment: $100,000-$350,000
Minimum Operating Data:
Annual Sales—$500,000
P&L—Profits NBT over $200,000

Geographical Preference
Midwest

Industry Preferences

Communications
Cable television
Commercial communications
Data communications
Satellite and microwave communications
Telephone related
Computer Related
Computer graphics, CAD/CAM and CAE
Office automation
Consumer
Computer stores/related services
Consumer products
Leisure and recreational products
Distribution
Communications equipment
Computer equipment
Consumer products
Electronics equipment
Food products
Industrial products
Medical products
**Electronic Components and
  Instrumentation**
Analytical and scientific instrumentation
Component fabrication and testing
  equipment
Electronic components
Fiber optics
Laser related
Semiconductors
Industrial Products and Equipment
Chemicals
Controls and sensors
Energy management
Equipment and machinery
Other industrial automation
Plastics
Robotics/vision systems
Specialty materials

Medical/Health Related
Diagnostic equipment
Diagnostic test products
Disposable products
Drugs and medicines
Hospital and clinical labs
Medical services
Therapeutic equipment
Other
Transportation

Additional Information
Year Founded—1983
Capital Under Management—$1.8 million
Investments(1985-1st 6 months)—1
Invested(1985-1st 6 months)—$250,000
Method of Compensation—Return on
  investment is most important, but also
  charge for closing fees, service fees, etc.

HERITAGE VENTURE GROUP, INC.

2400 One Indiana Square
Indianapolis, IN 46204
317-635-5696

Officers
Arthur A. Angotti, Pres.
Thomas W. Binford, Chm.
Stephen M. Robbins, V.P. & Treas.
Julia M. Rogers, Secy.

Whom to Contact
Arthur A. Angotti

Type of Firm
SBIC

Industry Association Membership
NASBIC

Project Preferences
Will function either as deal originator or
  investor in deals created by others
Type of Financing:
Second-stage
Later-stage expansion
Leveraged buyout
Minimum Investment: $100,000
Preferred Investment: $250,000-$500,000
Minimum Operating Data:
Annual Sales—Nominal
P&L—Break even

Geographical Preferences
Midwest
National

Industry Preferences

Communications
Radio and television broadcasting
Satellite and microwave communications
Telephone related
Will Not Consider
Real estate

Additional Information
Year Founded—1981
Capital Under Management—Over $3 million
Method of Compensation—Return on
  investment is most important, but also
  charge for closing fees, service fees, etc.

MIDDLEWEST VENTURES, L.P.

20 North Meridian Street
Indianapolis, IN 46204
317-631-8822

Partners
Charles L. Rees, Mgn. Gen. Ptnr.
Thomas A. Hiatt, Gen. Ptnr.
Joseph H. Broeker, Gen. Ptnr.

Whom to Contact
Any of the above

Type of Firm
Private venture capital firm investing
  own capital

Affiliation
Raffensperger, Hughes & Co., Inc.
  (general partner)

Project Preferences
Prefer role as deal originator but will also
  invest in deals created by others
Type of Financing:
Seed
Startup
First-stage
Leveraged buyout
Minimum Investment: $250,000
Preferred Investment: $500,000-$1 million
Preferred Investment (LBO): $1 million
Minimum Operating Data:
Annual Sales—Nominal
P&L—Losses (profits projected after 2 years)

Geographical Preference
National

Industry Preferences

Communications
Cable television
Commercial communications
Data communications
Satellite and microwave communications
Telephone related
Computer Related
Computer graphics, CAD/CAM and CAE
Computer services
Office automation
Scanning related
Software-applications
Software-artificial intelligence
Software-systems
Specialized turnkey systems
Distribution
Electronics equipment
Food products
Industrial products
Medical products
**Electronic Components and
  Instrumentation**
Analytical and scientific instrumentation
Component fabrication and testing
  equipment
Fiber optics
Laser related
Genetic Engineering
Gene splicing and manufacturing equipment
Monoclonal antibodies and hybridomas
Recombinant DNA (agricultural and
  industrial)
Recombinant DNA (medical)
Industrial Products and Equipment
Controls and sensors
Equipment and machinery
Other industrial automation
Plastics
Robotics/vision systems
Specialty materials
Medical/Health Related
Diagnostic equipment
Diagnostic test products
Disposable products
Hospital and clinical labs
Medical services
Therapeutic equipment

Additional Information
Year Founded—1985
Method of Compensation—Return on
  investment is of primary concern; do not
  charge fees

MILLER VENTURE PARTNERS

235 Washington Street
Post Office Box 808
Columbus, IN 47202
812-376-3331

Partners
William I. Miller, Gen. Ptnr.
Ira G. Peppercorn, Sr. Inv. Mgr.

Whom to Contact
Ira G. Peppercorn

Type of Firm
Private venture capital firm investing
own capital

Affiliation
Irwin Management Co. (affiliate)

Project Preferences
Prefer role as deal originator but will also
invest in deals created by others
Type of Financing:
Seed
Startup
Minimum Investment: $100,000
Preferred Investment: $100,000-$250,000

Geographical Preferences
Within three hours of office
Midwest

Industry Preferences

Computer Related
Computer graphics, CAD/CAM and CAE
Scanning related
Distribution
Communications equipment
Electronics equipment
Food products
Industrial products
Medical products
**Electronic Components and
Instrumentation**
Analytical and scientific instrumentation
Component fabrication and testing
equipment
Fiber optics
Laser related
Energy/Natural Resources
Alternative energy
Energy conservation
Technology related products/equipment

Genetic Engineering
Gene splicing and manufacturing equipment
Monoclonal antibodies and hybridomas
Recombinant DNA (agricultural and
industrial)
Recombinant DNA (medical)
Industrial Products and Equipment
Chemicals
Controls and sensors
Energy management
Equipment and machinery
Other industrial automation
Plastics
Robotics/vision systems
Specialty materials
Medical/Health Related
Diagnostic equipment
Diagnostic test products
Disposable products
Drugs and medicines
Therapeutic equipment

Additional Information
Year Founded—1985
Capital Under Management—$2.7 million
Method of Compensation—Return on
investment is of primary concern; do not
charge fees

WHITE RIVER CAPITAL CORPORATION

500 Washington Street
Post Office Box 929
Columbus, IN 47202
812-376-1759

Officers
John A. Nash, Chm.
Thomas D. Washburn, Vice Chm.
David J. Blair, Pres. & Secy.
Timothy L. Murphy, Treas. & Asst. Secy.

Whom to Contact
David J. Blair

Type of Firm
SBIC

Affiliations
Irwin Union Corporation (parent)
Corporation For Innovation Development

Industry Association Membership
NASBIC

Project Preferences
Will function either as deal originator or
investor in deals created by others

Type of Financing:
Second-stage
Later-stage expansion
Leveraged buyout
Minimum Investment: $100,000
Preferred Investment: $100,000-$250,000
Minimum Operating Data:
Annual Sales—$500,000
P&L—Losses (profits projected after 1 year)

Geographical Preferences
Within two hours of office
Midwest

Industry Preferences

Communications
Cable television
Telephone related
Computer Related
Computer graphics, CAD/CAM and CAE
Office automation
Software-applications
Consumer
Consumer products
Consumer services
Retailing
Distribution
Computer equipment
Medical products
**Electronic Components and
Instrumentation**
Analytical and scientific instrumentation
Industrial Products and Equipment
Controls and sensors
Equipment and machinery
Other industrial automation
Robotics/vision systems
Medical/Health Related
Diagnostic equipment
Diagnostic test products
Disposable products
Drugs and medicines
Hospital and clinical labs
Medical services
Therapeutic equipment
Will Not Consider
Real estate

Additional Information
Year Founded—1982
Capital Under Management—$2 million
Investments(1985-1st 6 months)—2
Invested(1985-1st 6 months)—$50,000
Method of Compensation—Return on
investment is of primary concern; do not
charge fees

R.W. ALLSOP & ASSOCIATES

Corporate Center East #210
2750 First Avenue NE
Cedar Rapids, IA 52402
319-363-8971

Other Offices

815 East Mason Street #1501
Post Office Box 1368
Milwaukee, WI 53201
414-271-6510

111 West Port Plaza #600
St. Louis, MO 63146
314-434-1688

35 Corporate Woods #244
9101 West 110th Street
Overland Park, KS 66210
913-451-3719

Partners

Robert W. Allsop, Gen. Ptnr. (Iowa)
Paul D. Rhines, Gen. Ptnr. (Iowa)
Gregory B. Bultman, Gen. Ptnr. (Wisconsin)
Robert L. Kuk, Gen. Ptnr. (Missouri)
Larry C. Maddox, Gen. Ptnr. (Kansas)
James D. Thorp, Assoc. (Iowa)

Whom to Contact

Any of the above

Type of Firm

Private venture capital firm investing
own capital

Industry Association Memberships

NASBIC
NVCA

Project Preferences

Will function either as deal originator or
investor in deals created by others
Type of Financing:
First-stage
Second-stage
Later-stage expansion
Leveraged buyout
Minimum Investment: $500,000
Preferred Investment: $500,000-$1 million
Preferred Investment (LBO):
$1 million-$2 million
Minimum Operating Data:
Annual Sales—$1.5 million
P&L—Break even
Annual Sales (LBO)—$10 million-$50 million

Geographical Preference

National

Industry Preferences

Communications
Cellular radio equipment
Commercial communications
Data communications
Data compression, storage and transmission
equipment
Satellite and microwave communications
Telephone related
Computer Related
Computer graphics, CAD/CAM and CAE
Computer services
Office automation
Scanning related
Consumer
Consumer products
Consumer services
Distribution
Communications equipment
Electronics equipment
Food products
Industrial products
Medical products
**Electronic Components and
Instrumentation**
Analytical and scientific instrumentation
Component fabrication and testing
equipment
Electronic components
Fiber optics
Laser related
Genetic Engineering
Gene splicing and manufacturing equipment
Industrial Products and Equipment
Chemicals
Controls and sensors
Equipment and machinery
Other industrial automation
Robotics/vision systems
Specialty materials
Medical/Health Related
Diagnostic equipment
Diagnostic test products
Disposable products
Drugs and medicines
Hospital and clinical labs
Hospital management
Medical instruments
Medical services
Therapeutic equipment
Will Not Consider
Real estate

Additional Information

Year Founded—1981
Capital Under Management—$45 million
Investments(1985-1st 6 months)—10
Invested(1985-1st 6 months)—$2 million
Method of Compensation—Return on
investment is of primary concern; do not
charge fees

IOWA VENTURE CAPITAL FUND, L.P.

300 American Building
Cedar Rapids, IA 52401
319-363-8249

Other Offices

Commerce Tower #2724
911 Main Street
Kansas City, MO 64105
816-842-0114

600 East Mason Street
Milwaukee, WI 53202
414-276-3839

Officers

Jerry M. Burrows, Pres. (Iowa)
Donald E. Flynn, Exec. V.P. (Iowa)
David R. Schroder, V.P. (Iowa)
Kevin F. Mullane, V.P. (Missouri)
Steven J. Massey, V.P. (Wisconsin)

Whom to Contact

Jerry M. Burrows
Donald E. Flynn
David R. Schroder

Type of Firm

Private venture capital firm investing
own capital

Affiliation

InvestAmerica Venture Group, Inc.
(fund manager)

Project Preferences

Will function either as deal originator or
investor in deals created by others
Type of Financing:
First-stage
Second-stage
Later-stage expansion
Leveraged buyout
Minimum Investment: $100,000
Preferred Investment: $250,000-$500,000
Minimum Operating Data:
Annual Sales—Nominal

Geographical Preference
Midwest

Industry Preferences

Communications
Cable television
Commercial communications
Data communications
Satellite and microwave communications
Telephone related
Computer Related
Computer graphics, CAD/CAM and CAE
Computer mainframes
Computer services
Memory devices
Micro and mini computers
Office automation
Scanning related
Software-applications
Software-artificial intelligence
Software-systems
Specialized turnkey systems
Terminals
Distribution
Communications equipment
Computer equipment
Consumer products
Electronics equipment
Food products
Industrial products
Medical products
**Electronic Components and
    Instrumentation**
Analytical and scientific instrumentation
Component fabrication and testing
    equipment
Electronic components
Fiber optics
Laser related
Semiconductors
Genetic Engineering
Gene splicing and manufacturing equipment
Monoclonal antibodies and hybridomas
Recombinant DNA (agricultural and
    industrial)
Recombinant DNA (medical)
Industrial Products and Equipment
Chemicals
Controls and sensors
Energy management
Equipment and machinery
Other industrial automation
Plastics
Robotics/vision systems
Specialty materials

Medical/Health Related
Diagnostic equipment
Diagnostic test products
Disposable products
Drugs and medicines
Hospital and clinical labs
Medical services
Therapeutic equipment

Additional Information
Year Founded—1985
Capital Under Management—$15 million
Method of Compensation—Return on
    investment is of primary concern; do not
    charge fees

MORAMERICA CAPITAL
CORPORATION

300 American Building
Cedar Rapids, IA 52401
319-363-8249

Other Offices
Commerce Tower #2724
911 Main Street
Kansas City, MO 64105
816-842-0114

600 East Mason Street
Milwaukee, WI 53202
414-276-3839

Officers
Jerry M. Burrows, Pres. (Iowa)
Donald E. Flynn, Exec. V.P. (Iowa)
David R. Schroder, V.P. (Iowa)
Kevin F. Mullane, V.P. (Missouri)
Steven J. Massey, V.P. (Wisconsin)

Whom to Contact
Any of the above

Type of Firm
SBIC

Affiliations
MorAmerica Financial Corporation (parent)
InvestAmerica Venture Group, Inc.
    (fund manager)

Industry Association Membership
NASBIC

Project Preferences
Will function either as deal originator or
    investor in deals created by others

Type of Financing:
First-stage
Second-stage
Later-stage expansion
Leveraged buyout
Minimum Investment: $250,000
Preferred Investment: $250,000-$500,000
Minimum Operating Data:
Annual Sales—Nominal

Geographical Preference
None

Industry Preferences

Communications
Cable television
Commercial communications
Data communications
Satellite and microwave communications
Telephone related
Computer Related
Computer graphics, CAD/CAM and CAE
Computer mainframes
Computer services
Memory devices
Micro and mini computers
Office automation
Scanning related
Software-applications
Software-artificial intelligence
Software-systems
Specialized turnkey systems
Terminals
Distribution
Communications equipment
Computer equipment
Consumer products
Electronics equipment
Food products
Industrial products
Medical products
**Electronic Components and
    Instrumentation**
Analytical and scientific instrumentation
Component fabrication and testing
    equipment
Electronic components
Fiber optics
Laser related
Semiconductors
Genetic Engineering
Gene splicing and manufacturing equipment
Monoclonal antibodies and hybridomas
Recombinant DNA (agricultural and
    industrial)
Recombinant DNA (medical)

Industrial Products and Equipment
Chemicals
Controls and sensors
Energy management
Equipment and machinery
Other industrial automation
Plastics
Robotics/vision systems
Specialty materials
Medical/Health Related
Diagnostic equipment
Diagnostic test products
Disposable products
Drugs and medicines
Hospital and clinical labs
Medical services
Therapeutic equipment

Additional Information
Year Founded—1959
Capital Under Management—$35 million
Investments(1985-1st 6 months)—10
Invested(1985-1st 6 months)—$2.5 million
Method of Compensation—Return on
investment is of primary concern; do not
charge fees

PAPPAJOHN CAPITAL RESOURCES

2116 Financial Center
Des Moines, IA 50309
515-244-5746

Officer
John Pappajohn, Pres.

Type of Firm
Private venture capital firm investing
own capital

Project Preferences
Prefer role as deal originator
Type of Financing:
Seed
Startup
First-stage
Leveraged buyout
Minimum Investment: Less than $100,000
Preferred Investment: $100,000-$250,000
Minimum Operating Data:
Annual Sales—Nominal
P&L—Losses (profits projected after 2 years)

Geographical Preference
None

Industry Preferences

Medical/Health Related
Diagnostic equipment
Diagnostic test products
Disposable products
Drugs and medicines
Hospital and clinical labs
Medical services
Therapeutic equipment

Additional Information
Year Founded—1969
Capital Under Management—$16 million
Investments(1985-1st 6 months)—5
Method of Compensation—Return on
investment is of primary concern; do not
charge fees

UNITED INVESTMENT GROUPS, INC.

508 North Second Street
Fairfield, IA 52556
515-472-8296

Officers
Clyde Cleveland, Pres.
Kevin Twohy, Sr. V.P.
Zane G. Safrit, Dir., Project Development

Whom to Contact
Zane G. Safrit

Type of Firm
Private venture capital firm investing
own capital

Project Preferences
Prefer role in deals created by others
Type of Financing:
Research and development partnerships
Second-stage
Later-stage expansion
Minimum Investment: $500,000
Minimum Operating Data:
P&L—Profits NBT over $200,000

Geographical Preference
None

Industry Preferences

Communications
Data communications

Computer Related
Computer graphics, CAD/CAM and CAE
Computer services
Micro and mini computers
Office automation
Scanning related
Software-artificial intelligence
Specialized turnkey systems
Terminals
Consumer
Consumer products
Food and beverage products
Franchise businesses
Distribution
Communications equipment
Industrial products
Medical products
**Electronic Components and
Instrumentation**
Analytical and scientific instrumentation
Component fabrication and testing
equipment
Fiber optics
Laser related
Energy/Natural Resources
Alternative energy
Technology related products/equipment
Genetic Engineering
Monoclonal antibodies and hybridomas
Recombinant DNA (medical)
Industrial Products and Equipment
Controls and sensors
Energy management
Other industrial automation
Robotics/vision systems
Specialty materials
Medical/Health Related
Diagnostic equipment
Diagnostic test products
Disposable products
Medical services
Therapeutic equipment
Other
Publishing

Additional Information
Year Founded—1982
Capital Under Management—$18 million
Method of Compensation—Return on
investment is most important, but also
charge for closing fees, service fees, etc.

R.W. ALLSOP & ASSOCIATES

35 Corporate Woods #244
9101 West 110th Street
Overland Park, KS 66210
913-451-3719

Other Offices
Corporate Center East #210
2750 First Avenue NE
Cedar Rapids, IA 52402
319-363-8971

815 East Mason Street #1501
Post Office Box 1368
Milwaukee, WI 53201
414-271-6510

111 West Port Plaza #600
St. Louis, MO 63146
314-434-1688

Partners
Robert W. Allsop, Gen. Ptnr. (Iowa)
Paul D. Rhines, Gen. Ptnr. (Iowa)
Gregory B. Bultman, Gen. Ptnr. (Wisconsin)
Robert L. Kuk, Gen. Ptnr. (Missouri)
Larry C. Maddox, Gen. Ptnr. (Kansas)
James D. Thorp, Gen. Ptnr. (Iowa)

Whom to Contact
Any of the above

Type of Firm
Private venture capital firm investing
own capital

Industry Association Memberships
NASBIC
NVCA

Project Preferences
Will function either as deal originator or
investor in deals created by others
Type of Financing:
First-stage
Second-stage
Later-stage expansion
Leveraged buyout
Minimum Investment: $500,000
Preferred Investment: $500,000-$1 million
Preferred Investment (LBO):
$1 million-$2 million
Minimum Operating Data:
Annual Sales—$1.5 million
P&L—Break even
Annual Sales (LBO)—$10 million-$50 million

Geographical Preference
National

Industry Preferences
Communications
Cellular radio equipment
Commercial communications
Data communications
Data compression, storage and transmission
equipment
Satellite and microwave communications
Telephone related
Computer Related
Computer graphics, CAD/CAM and CAE
Computer services
Office automation
Scanning related
Consumer
Consumer products
Consumer services
Distribution
Communications equipment
Electronics equipment
Food products
Industrial products
Medical products
**Electronic Components and
Instrumentation**
Analytical and scientific instrumentation
Component fabrication and testing
equipment
Electronic components
Fiber optics
Laser related
Genetic Engineering
Gene splicing and manufacturing equipment
Industrial Products and Equipment
Chemicals
Controls and sensors
Equipment and machinery
Other industrial automation
Robotics/vision systems
Specialty materials
Medical/Health Related
Diagnostic equipment
Diagnostic test products
Disposable products
Drugs and medicines
Hospital and clinical labs
Hospital management
Medical instruments
Medical services
Therapeutic equipment
Will Not Consider
Real estate

Additional Information
Year Founded—1981
Capital Under Management—$45 million
Investments(1985-1st 6 months)—10
Invested(1985-1st 6 months)—$2 million
Method of Compensation—Return on
investment is of primary concern; do not
charge fees

337

BLUEGRASS CAPITAL CORP.

1815 Plantside Drive
Post Office Box 35000
Louisville, KY 40232
502-499-1004

Officer

Charles S. Arensberg

Type of Firm

Private venture capital firm investing
own capital

Affiliation

Venture Management Associates Inc.
(sister company)

Project Preferences

Prefer role as deal originator but will also
invest in deals created by others
Type of Financing:
Second-stage
Later-stage expansion
Leveraged buyout
Minimum Investment: Less than $100,000
Preferred Investment: $100,000-$250,000
Minimum Operating Data:
Annual Sales—$3 million
P&L—Losses (profits projected after 2 years)

Geographical Preference

Midwest

Industry Preferences

Communications
Commercial communications
Consumer
Consumer products
Consumer services
Furniture
Retailing
Distribution
Consumer products
Industrial products
Medical products
Industrial Products and Equipment
Ceramics/refractories
Equipment and machinery
Other industrial automation
Plastics
Robotics/vision systems
Specialty materials
Medical/Health Related
Eyecare
Other
Education related
Optics and optics chains

Additional Information

Year Founded—1985
Capital Under Management—Over $1 million
Investments(1985-1st 6 months)—1
Invested(1985-1st 6 months)—$170,000
Method of Compensation—Return on
investment is of primary concern; do not
charge fees

KENTUCKY HIGHLANDS CORPORATION

911 North Main Street
Post Office Box 928
London, KY 40741
606-864-5175

Officers

Steven C. Meng, Vice Chm. & CEO
L. Raymond Moncrief, COO

Whom to Contact

L. Raymond Moncrief

Type of Firm

Private venture capital firm investing
own capital
SBIC

Affiliation

Mountain Ventures, Inc. (wholly owned
SBIC subsidiary)

Industry Association Membership

NASBIC

Project Preferences

Prefer role as deal originator but will also
invest in deals created by others
Type of Financing:
Startup
First-stage
Second-stage
Leveraged buyout
Minimum Investment: Less than $100,000
Preferred Investment: $250,000-$500,000
Minimum Operating Data:
Annual Sales—$500,000
P&L—Break even

Geographical Preference

Eastern Kentucky

Industry Preferences

Communications
Commercial communications
Computer Related
Computer services
Office automation
Consumer
Consumer products
Consumer services
Distribution
Industrial products
Medical products
**Electronic Components and
Instrumentation**
Component fabrication and testing
equipment
Energy/Natural Resources
Technology related products/equipment
Industrial Products and Equipment
Chemicals
Controls and sensors
Energy management
Equipment and machinery
Other industrial automation
Plastics
Robotics/vision systems
Specialty materials
Medical/Health Related
Diagnostic equipment
Diagnostic test products
Medical services

Additional Information

Year Founded—1968
Capital Under Management—$9.9 million
Investments(1985-1st 6 months)—2
Invested(1985-1st 6 months)—$240,000
Method of Compensation—Return on
investment is of primary concern; do not
charge fees

LAWRENCE HERBST INVESTMENT TRUST FUND

Post Office Box 741
Lake Charles, LA 70602

See TEXAS for full listing

LOUISIANA EQUITY CAPITAL CORPORATION

451 Florida Street
Post Office Box 1511
Baton Rouge, LA 70821
504-389-4421

Officers
Melvin L. Rambin, Pres.
Jack McDonald, Inv. Officer
Thomas J. Adamek, Inv. Analyst

Whom to Contact
Jack McDonald

Type of Firm
SBIC
Venture capital subsidiary of commercial bank

Affiliation
Louisiana Bancshares, Inc.
Louisiana National Bank

Industry Association Membership
NASBIC

Project Preferences
Will function either as deal originator or investor in deals created by others
Type of Financing:
First-stage
Second-stage
Later-stage expansion
Leveraged buyout
Minimum Investment: $250,000
Preferred Investment: $250,000-$500,000
Minimum Operating Data:
Annual Sales—Nominal

Geographical Preferences
Southeast
Southwest

Industry Preferences

Communications
Cable television
Commercial communications
Data communications
Satellite and microwave communications
Telephone related

Computer Related
Computer graphics, CAD/CAM and CAE
Computer mainframes
Computer services
Memory devices
Micro and mini computers
Office automation
Scanning related
Software-applications
Software-artificial intelligence
Software-systems
Specialized turnkey systems
Terminals
Electronic Components and Instrumentation
Analytical and scientific instrumentation
Component fabrication and testing equipment
Electronic components
Fiber optics
Laser related
Semiconductors
Energy/Natural Resources
Alternative energy
Drilling and exploration services
Energy conservation
Technology related products/equipment
Genetic Engineering
Gene splicing and manufacturing equipment
Monoclonal antibodies and hybridomas
Recombinant DNA (agricultural and industrial)
Recombinant DNA (medical)
Industrial Products and Equipment
Chemicals
Controls and sensors
Energy management
Equipment and machinery
Other industrial automation
Plastics
Robotics/vision systems
Specialty materials
Medical/Health Related
Diagnostic equipment
Diagnostic test products
Drugs and medicines
Hospital and clinical labs
Medical services
Therapeutic equipment

Additional Information
Year Founded—1974
Capital Under Management—$8.2 million
Investments(1985-1st 6 months)—4
Invested(1985-1st 6 months)—$1.7 million
Method of Compensation—Return on investment is most important

SOUTHGATE VENTURE PARTNERS I/ SOUTHGATE VENTURE PARTNERS II

Cotton Exchange Building #702
New Orleans, LA 70130
504-525-2112

William D. Humphries, Ptnr.

See NORTH CAROLINA for full listing

WALNUT STREET CAPITAL COMPANY

231 Carondelet Street #702
New Orleans, LA 70130
504-525-2112

Managing General Partner
William D. Humphries

Type of Firm
SBIC

Affiliation
Southgate Venture Partners (joint venture)

Project Preferences
Will function either as deal originator or investor in deals created by others
Type of Financing:
Startup
First-stage
Second-stage
Later-stage expansion
Leveraged buyout
Minimum Investment: $100,000
Minimum Operating Data:
Annual Sales—Nominal

Geographical Preference
None

Industry Preferences
None

Additional Information
Year Founded—1982
Method of Compensation—Return on investment is most important, but also charge for closing fees, service fees, etc.

MAINE CAPITAL CORPORATION

70 Center Street
Portland, ME 04101
207-772-1001

Officers
Albert W. Moore, Chm.
David M. Coit, Pres.

Whom to Contact
David M. Coit

Type of Firm
SBIC

Industry Association Membership
NASBIC

Project Preferences
Prefer role as deal originator but will also invest in deals created by others
Type of Financing:
Startup
First-stage
Second-stage
Later-stage expansion
Leveraged buyout
Minimum Investment: Less than $100,000
Preferred Investment: $100,000-$250,000
Minimum Operating Data:
Annual Sales—Nominal
P&L—Losses (profits projected after 1 year)
Annual Sales (LBO)—Over $2 million

Geographical Preference
Maine only

Industry Preferences

Communications
Cable television
Commercial communications
Data communications
Satellite and microwave communications
Telephone related
Computer Related
Computer graphics, CAD/CAM and CAE
Computer mainframes
Computer services
Memory devices
Micro and mini computers
Office automation
Scanning related
Software-applications
Software-artificial intelligence
Software-systems
Specialized turnkey systems
Terminals

Consumer
Consumer products
Consumer services
Food and beverage products
Franchise businesses
Leisure and recreational products
Distribution
Communications equipment
Computer equipment
Consumer products
Electronics equipment
Food products
Industrial products
Medical products
Electronic Components and Instrumentation
Analytical and scientific instrumentation
Component fabrication and testing equipment
Electronic components
Fiber optics
Laser related
Semiconductors
Energy/Natural Resources
Alternative energy
Energy conservation
Technology related products/equipment
Genetic Engineering
Gene splicing and manufacturing equipment
Monoclonal antibodies and hybridomas
Recombinant DNA (agricultural and industrial)
Recombinant DNA (medical)
Industrial Products and Equipment
Chemicals
Controls and sensors
Energy management
Equipment and machinery
Other industrial automation
Plastics
Robotics/vision systems
Specialty materials
Medical/Health Related
Diagnostic equipment
Diagnostic test products
Disposable products
Drugs and medicines
Hospital and clinical labs
Medical services
Therapeutic equipment
Other
Education related
Finance and insurance
Publishing

Additional Information
Year Founded—1980
Capital Under Management—$2 million
Investments(1985-1st 6 months)—5
Invested(1985-1st 6 months)—$300,000
Method of Compensation—Return on investment is of primary concern; do not charge fees

ABS VENTURES LIMITED PARTNERSHIPS

135 East Baltimore Street
Baltimore, MD 21202
301-727-1700

Partners
Bruns H. Grayson, Mgn. Ptnr.
Arthur H. Reidel, Ptnr.
Edward T. Anderson, Principal
Robert Walkingshaw, Principal
John H.N. Fisher, Assoc.

Whom to Contact
Any of the above

Type of Firm
Private venture capital firm investing
own capital

Affiliation
Alex. Brown & Sons (general partner
of funds)

Industry Association Membership
NVCA

Project Preferences
Will function either as deal originator or
investor in deals created by others
Type of Financing:
Startup
First-stage
Second-stage
Later-stage expansion
Leveraged buyout
Minimum Investment: $500,000
Preferred Investment: $500,000-$1 million
Minimum Operating Data:
Annual Sales—Nominal
P&L—Losses (profits projected after 2 years)

Geographical Preference
None

Industry Preferences

Communications
Cable television
Commercial communications
Data communications
Satellite and microwave communications

Computer Related
Computer graphics, CAD/CAM and CAE
Computer mainframes
Computer services
Memory devices
Micro and mini computers
Office automation
Scanning related
Software-applications
Software-artificial intelligence
Software-systems
Specialized turnkey systems
Terminals
Consumer
Franchise businesses
Restaurants
Retailing
Distribution
Communications equipment
Computer equipment
Electronics equipment
Medical products
Electronic Components and Instrumentation
Analytical and scientific instrumentation
Component fabrication and testing
equipment
Electronic components
Fiber optics
Laser related
Semiconductors
Energy/Natural Resources
Technology related products/equipment
Genetic Engineering
Gene splicing and manufacturing equipment
Monoclonal antibodies and hybridomas
Recombinant DNA (agricultural and
industrial)
Recombinant DNA (medical)
Industrial Products and Equipment
Controls and sensors
Equipment and machinery
Other industrial automation
Robotics/vision systems
Medical/Health Related
Diagnostic equipment
Diagnostic test products
Disposable products
Drugs and medicines
Hospital and clinical labs
Medical services
Therapeutic equipment

Additional Information
Year Founded—1982
Capital Under Management—$107 million
Investments(1985-1st 6 months)—16
Invested(1985-1st 6 months)—$7.9 million
Method of Compensation—Return on
investment is of primary concern; do not
charge fees

ARETÊ VENTURES, INC.

4330 East West Highway #916
Bethesda, MD 20814
301-951-4499

Other Offices
711 West 40th Street #420
Baltimore, MD 21211
301-243-5551

5995 Barfield Road #220
Atlanta, GA 30328
404-257-9548

Officers
Robert W. Shaw, Jr., Pres. (Bethesda)
George W. Levert, Jr., Dir. (Atlanta)
John C. Weiss III, Dir. (Baltimore)

Whom to Contact
Any of the above

Type of Firm
Private venture capital firm investing
own capital
Consulting firm evaluating and analyzing
venture projects and arranging private
placements

Affiliation
Utech Venture Capital Corporation
Aretê Consulting Group, Inc.

Project Preferences
Will function either as deal originator or
investor in deals created by others
Type of Financing:
Startup
First-stage
Leveraged buyout
Minimum Investment: $100,000
Preferred Investment: $250,000—$1 million
Minimum Operating Data:
Annual Sales—$500,000
P&L—Break even

Geographical Preferences

East Coast
National
Will lead only on the East Coast

Industry Preferences

Energy/Natural Resources
Alternative energy
Coal related
Energy conservation
Technology related products/equipment
Communications
Data communications
Computer Related
Computer graphics, CAD/CAM and CAE
Office automation
Scanning related
Software-artificial intelligence
Distribution
Electronics equipment
Industrial products
Electronic Components and Instrumentation
Analytical and scientific instrumentation
Component fabrication and testing equipment
Industrial Products and Equipment
Controls and sensors
Energy management
Equipment and machinery
Specialty materials
Other
Specialty consulting
Utech will invest only in electric or gas utility related businesses

Additional Information

Year Founded—1983
Capital Under Management—$20 million
Method of Compensation—Return on investment is most important, but also charge for closing fees, service fees, etc.

BROVENTURE CAPITAL MANAGEMENT

16 West Madison Street
Baltimore, MD 21201
301-727-4520

Partners

William M. Gust, II
Harvey C. Branch
Philip D. English

Whom to Contact

William M. Gust, II
Harvey C. Branch

Type of Firm

Private venture capital firm investing own capital

Industry Association Membership

NVCA

Project Preferences

Will function either as deal originator or investor in deals created by others
Type of Financing:
Startup
First-stage
Second-stage
Leveraged buyout
Minimum Investment: $500,000
Preferred Investment: $500,000-$1 million
Minimum Operating Data:
Annual Sales—Nominal
P&L—Losses (profits projected after 2 years)

Geographical Preferences

Southeast
National

Industry Preferences

Communications
Data communications
Satellite and microwave communications
Telephone related
Computer Related
Computer graphics, CAD/CAM and CAE
Computer mainframes
Computer services
Memory devices
Micro and mini computers
Office automation
Scanning related
Software-applications
Software-artificial intelligence
Software-systems
Specialized turnkey systems
Terminals
Electronic Components and Instrumentation
Analytical and scientific instrumentation
Component fabrication and testing equipment
Electronic components
Fiber optics
Laser related
Semiconductors
Energy/Natural Resources
Technology related products/equipment
Genetic Engineering
Gene splicing and manufacturing equipment
Monoclonal antibodies and hybridomas
Recombinant DNA (agricultural and industrial)
Recombinant DNA (medical)

Industrial Products and Equipment
Chemicals
Controls and sensors
Energy management
Equipment and machinery
Other industrial automation
Plastics
Robotics/vision systems
Specialty materials
Medical/Health Related
Diagnostic equipment
Diagnostic test products
Disposable products
Drugs and medicines
Hospital and clinical labs
Medical services
Therapeutic equipment
Will Not Consider
Real estate
Oil and gas

Additional Information

Year Founded—1965
Capital Under Management— Over $20 million
Method of Compensation—Return on investment is of primary concern; do not charge fees

---

EMERGING GROWTH PARTNERS

400 East Pratt Street #610
Baltimore, MD 21202
301-332-1021

Partners

Howard P. Colhoun, Gen. Ptnr.
Robert E. Hall, Gen. Ptnr.
Peter S. Welles, Gen. Ptnr.
W. Andrew Grubbs, Gen. Ptnr.
Duncan J. Evered, Assoc.

Whom to Contact

Howard P. Colhoun

Type of Firm

Private venture capital firm investing funds of partners

Affiliation

Wellington Management Co.

Project Preferences

Will function either as deal originator or investor in deals created by others
Type of Financing:
First-stage
Second-stage
Leveraged buyout

Minimum Investment: $500,000
Preferred Investment: $500,000-$1 million
Minimum Operating Data:
Annual Sales—Nominal

Geographical Preference
National

Industry Preferences

Communications
Cable television
Commercial communications
Data communications
Satellite and microwave communications
Telephone related
Computer Related
Computer graphics, CAD/CAM and CAE
Computer mainframes
Computer services
Memory devices
Micro and mini computers
Office automation
Scanning related
Software-applications
Software-artificial intelligence
Software-systems
Specialized turnkey systems
Terminals
Consumer
Computer stores/related services
Consumer products
Consumer services
Food and beverage products
Franchise businesses
Hotels and resort areas
Leisure and recreational products
Restaurants
Retailing
Distribution
Communications equipment
Computer equipment
Consumer products
Electronics equipment
Food products
Industrial products
Medical products
**Electronic Components and
Instrumentation**
Analytical and scientific instrumentation
Component fabrication and testing
equipment
Electronic components
Fiber optics
Laser related
Semiconductors

Energy/Natural Resources
Alternative energy
Coal related
Drilling and exploration services
Energy conservation
Minerals
Oil and gas exploration and production
Technology related products/equipment
Genetic Engineering
Gene splicing and manufacturing equipment
Monoclonal antibodies and hybridomas
Recombinant DNA (agricultural and
industrial)
Recombinant DNA (medical)
Industrial Products and Equipment
Chemicals
Controls and sensors
Energy management
Equipment and machinery
Other industrial automation
Plastics
Robotics/vision systems
Specialty materials
Medical/Health Related
Diagnostic equipment
Diagnostic test products
Disposable products
Drugs and medicines
Hospital and clinical labs
Medical services
Therapeutic equipment

Additional Information
Year Founded—1982
Capital Under Management—$100 million

FIRST FINANCIAL MANAGEMENT SERVICES, INC.

7316 Wisconsin Avenue #215
Bethesda, MD 20814
301-951-9670

Officer
Kendall W. Wilson, Pres.

Type of Firm
Private venture capital firm investing
own capital
Consulting firm evaluating and analyzing
venture projects and arranging private
placements

Affiliation
Venture Technology, Inc. (merged in 1983)

Project Preferences
Will function either as deal originator or
investor in deals created by others
Type of Financing:
Startup
Minimum Investment: $100,000
Preferred Investment: $100,000-$250,000
Minimum Operating Data:
Annual Sales—Nominal
P&L—Break even

Geographical Preference
Within two hours of office

Industry Preferences

Communications
Commercial communications
Data communications
Telephone related
Computer Related
Computer services
Micro and mini computers
Office automation
Scanning related
Software-applications
Software-systems
Specialized turnkey systems
Terminals
Consumer
Consumer products
Consumer services
Leisure and recreational products
Distribution
Communications equipment
Computer equipment
Consumer products
Electronics equipment
Food products
Industrial products
Medical products
**Electronic Components and
Instrumentation**
Analytical and scientific instrumentation
Component fabrication and testing
equipment
Electronic components
Fiber optics
Laser related
Semiconductors
Energy/Natural Resources
Alternative energy
Coal related
Energy conservation
Technology related products/equipment
Genetic Engineering
Gene splicing and manufacturing equipment
Monoclonal antibodies and hybridomas
Recombinant DNA (agricultural and
industrial)
Recombinant DNA (medical)

Industrial Products and Equipment
Chemicals
Controls and sensors
Energy management
Equipment and machinery
Other industrial automation
Plastics
Robotics/vision systems
Specialty materials
Medical/Health Related
Diagnostic equipment
Diagnostic test products
Disposable products
Drugs and medicines
Hospital and clinical labs
Medical services
Therapeutic equipment
Other
Agriculture, forestry, fishing
Education related
Specialty consulting
Transportation
Will Not Consider
Banking
Real estate
Restaurants
Retail

Additional Information
Year Founded—1983
Method.of Compensation—Return on
   investment is most important, but also
   charge for closing fees, service fees, etc.

FIRST MARYLAND CAPITAL, INC.

107 West Jefferson Street
Rockville, MD 20850
301-251-6630

Officers
Joseph A. Kenary, Pres.
Webb C. Hayes, IV, V.P.
H. Greig Cummings, Jr., V.P.
Paul B. Kern, Jr., Secy. & Treas.
Mary Anne Roby, Asst. Secy.

Whom to Contact
Joseph A. Kenary

Type of Firm
SBIC

Industry Association Membership
NASBIC

Project Preferences
Will function either as deal originator or
   investor in deals created by others

Type of Financing:
First-stage
Minimum Investment: Less than $100,000
Preferred Investment: Less than $100,000
Minimum Operating Data:
Annual Sales—Nominal
P&L—Break even

Geographical Preference
East Coast

Industry Preferences

Communications
Commercial communications
Consumer
Consumer products
Consumer services
Medical/Health Related
Equipment and services

Additional Information
Year Founded—1984
Capital Under Management—$625,000
Investments(1985-1st 6 months)—1
Invested(1985-1st 6 months)—$100,000
Method of Compensation—Return on
   investment is of primary concern

GREATER WASHINGTON INVESTORS, INC.

5454 Wisconsin Avenue #1315
Chevy Chase, MD 20815
301-656-0626

Officers
Don A. Christensen, Pres.
Martin S. Pinson, Sr. V.P.
Cyril W. Draffin, Jr., V.P.
Jeffrey T. Griffin, V.P.

Whom to Contact
Cyril W. Draffin, Jr.

Type of Firm
SBIC

Industry Association Memberships
NASBIC
NVCA

Project Preferences
Will function either as deal originator or
   investor in deals created by others

Type of Financing:
First-stage
Second-stage
Later-stage expansion
Leveraged buyout
Minimum Investment: $250,000
Preferred Investment: $250,000-$500,000
Minimum Operating Data:
Annual Sales—Nominal
P&L—Losses (profits projected after 1 year)

Geographical Preferences
East Coast
Midwest

Industry Preferences

Communications
Data communications
Satellite and microwave communications
Telephone related
Computer Related
Computer graphics, CAD/CAM and CAE
Computer mainframes
Computer services
Memory devices
Micro and mini computers
Office automation
Scanning related
Software-applications
Software-artificial intelligence
Software-systems
Specialized turnkey systems
Terminals
Consumer
Computer stores/related services
**Electronic Components and
   Instrumentation**
Analytical and scientific instrumentation
Component fabrication and testing
   equipment
Electronic components
Fiber optics
Laser related
Semiconductors
Genetic Engineering
Recombinant DNA (agricultural and
   industrial)
Industrial Products and Equipment
Chemicals
Controls and sensors
Energy management
Equipment and machinery
Other industrial automation
Plastics
Robotics/vision systems
Specialty materials

Medical/Health Related
Biotechnology
Diagnostic equipment
Diagnostic test products
Disposable products
Drugs and medicines
Hospital and clinical labs
Medical services
Therapeutic equipment
Will Not Consider
Real estate
Retail/consumer oriented businesses

Additional Information
Year Founded—1959
Capital Under Management—$29 million
Investments(1985-1st 6 months)—14
Invested(1985-1st 6 months)—$2.2 million
Method of Compensation—Return on
investment is of primary concern; do not
charge fees

GROTECH PARTNERS, L.P.

100 Light Street, 9th Floor
Baltimore, MD 21202
301-752-4600

Frank A. Adams, Gen. Ptnr.
E. Rogers Novak, Jr., Gen. Ptnr.

See PENNSYLVANIA for full listing

MERIDIAN VENTURES

21 West Road
Baltimore, MD 21204
301-296-1000

General Partners
Earl L. Linehan
Michael J. Batza, Jr.
Roger C. Lipitz

Whom to Contact
Earl L. Linehan

Type of Firm
Private venture capital firm investing
own capital

Affiliations
Meridian Inc.
Meridian Healthcare

Project Preferences
Prefer role as deal originator but will also
invest in deals created by others
Type of Financing:
Seed
First-stage
Leveraged buyout
Minimum Investment: $100,000
Preferred Investment: $500,000-$1 million
Preferred Investment (LBO):
$1 million-$2 million

Geographical Preference
Northeast

Industry Preferences

Industrial Products and Equipment
Equipment and machinery
Medical/Health Related
Medical services
Other
Finance and insurance
Publishing
Real estate

Additional Information
Year Founded—1982
Capital Under Management—$7 million
Method of Compensation—Return on
investment is of primary concern; do not
charge fees

NEW ENTERPRISE ASSOCIATES

1119 Saint Paul Street
Baltimore, MD 21202
301-244-0115

Other Offices
235 Montgomery Street #1025
San Francisco, CA 94104
415-956-1579

3000 Sand Hill Road
Bldg. 2, #210
Menlo Park, CA 94025
415-854-2660

Partners
C. Richard Kramlich, Mgn. Gen. Ptnr.
(San Francisco)
Cornelius C. Bond, Jr., Gen. Ptnr.
(San Francisco)
C. Woodrow Rea, Jr., Gen. Ptnr.
(Menlo Park)
Frank A. Bonsal, Jr., Gen. Ptnr. (Baltimore)
Arthur J. Marks, Gen. Ptnr. (Baltimore)
Curran W. Harvey, Special Ptnr. (Baltimore)

Raymond L. Bank, Assoc. (Baltimore)
Thomas C. McConnell, Assoc.
(San Francisco)
John W. Glynn, Special Ptnr. (Menlo Park)
Howard D. Wolfe, Jr., Special Ptnr.
(Baltimore)

Whom to Contact
Any of the above

Type of Firm
Private venture capital firm investing
own capital

Affiliation
Southwest Enterprise Associates (affiliated
venture capital partnership)

Industry Association Memberships
NVCA
WAVC

Project Preferences
Will function either as deal originator or
investor in deals created by others
Type of Financing:
Seed
Startup
First-stage
Second-stage
Leveraged buyout
Minimum Investment: $250,000
Preferred Investment: $500,000-$1 million
Minimum Operating Data:
Annual Sales—Nominal
P&L—Losses (profits projected after 3 years)

Geographical Preferences
Southwest
East Coast
West Coast

Industry Preferences

Communications
Commercial communications
Data communications
Satellite and microwave communications
Telephone related
Computer Related
Computer graphics, CAD/CAM and CAE
Computer mainframes
Computer services
Memory devices
Office automation
Scanning related
Software-applications
Software-artificial intelligence
Software-systems
Specialized turnkey systems

Consumer
Computer stores/related services
Consumer products
Consumer services
Leisure and recreational products
Retailing
**Electronic Components and
Instrumentation**
Analytical and scientific instrumentation
Electronic components
Fiber optics
Government electronics
Laser related
Semiconductors
Genetic Engineering
Recombinant DNA (agricultural and
industrial)
Industrial Products and Equipment
Robotics/vision systems
Specialty materials
Medical/Health Related
Diagnostic equipment
Diagnostic test products
Disposable products
Medical services
Other
Finance and insurance

Additional Information
Year Founded—1977
Capital Under Management—$213 million
Investments(1985-1st 6 months)—49
Invested(1985-1st 6 months)—$24.8 million
Method of Compensation—Return on
investment is of primary concern; do not
charge fees

T. ROWE PRICE THRESHOLD
FUND, L.P.

100 East Pratt Street
Baltimore, MD 21202
301-547-2179

Officers
Edward J. Mathias, Mgn. Ptnr.
Jonathan M. Greene, Chm. Inv. Comm.

Whom to Contact
Jonathan M. Greene

Type of Firm
Private venture capital limited partnership

Affiliation
T. Rowe Price Associates, Inc.
(general partner)

Industry Association Membership
NVCA

Project Preferences
Prefer role in deals created by others
Type of Financing:
Second-stage
Later-stage expansion
Leveraged buyout
Minimum Investment: $500,000
Preferred Investment: Over $1 million
Minimum Operating Data:
Annual Sales—Over $3 million
P&L—Losses (profits projected after 1 year)

Geographical Preference
National

Industry Preferences
None

Additional Information
Year Founded—1983
Capital Under Management—$75 million
Investments(1985-1st 6 months)—8
Invested(1985-1st 6 months)—$10 million
Method of Compensation—Return on
investment is of primary concern; do not
charge fees

SUBURBAN CAPITAL CORPORATION

6610 Rockledge Drive
Bethesda, MD 20817
301-493-7025

Officers
Henry (Pete) Linsert, Pres.
Steve Dubin, V.P.
Doris Finch, Venture Officer

Whom to Contact
Henry (Pete) Linsert
Steve Dubin

Type of Firm
SBIC
Venture capital subsidiary of
commercial bank

Affiliation
Suburban Bank (parent)

Industry Association Membership
NASBIC

Project Preferences
Will function either as deal originator or
investor in deals created by others
Type of Financing:
First-stage
Second-stage
Later-stage expansion
Leveraged buyout
Minimum Investment: $250,000
Preferred Investment: $250,000-$500,000
Minimum Operating Data:
Annual Sales—Nominal
P&L—Losses (profits projected after 1 year)

Geographical Preferences
Within two hours of office
Northeast
Southeast
Southwest
East Coast

Industry Preferences

Communications
Cable television
Commercial communications
Data communications
Satellite and microwave communications
Telephone related
Computer Related
Software-applications
Distribution
Computer equipment
**Electronic Components and
Instrumentation**
Analytical and scientific instrumentation
Component fabrication and testing
equipment
Electronic components
Fiber optics
Laser related
Semiconductors
Energy/Natural Resources
Alternative energy
Genetic Engineering
Gene splicing and manufacturing equipment
Monoclonal antibodies and hybridomas
Recombinant DNA (agricultural and
industrial)
Recombinant DNA (medical)
Industrial Products and Equipment
Plastics
Robotics/vision systems
Medical/Health Related
Diagnostic test products
Medical services

Additional Information
Year Founded—1983
Capital Under Management—$8 million
Investments(1985-1st 6 months)—6
Invested(1985-1st 6 months)—$2 million
Method of Compensation—Return on
investment is of primary concern; do not
charge fees

UTECH VENTURE CAPITAL CORPORATION

c/o Arete Ventures
4330 East West Highway #916
Bethesda, MD 20814
301-951-4499

Other Offices
5995 Barfield Road #220
Atlanta, GA 30328
404-257-9548

711 West 40th Street #420
Baltimore, MD 21211
301-243-5551

One New York Plaza
New York, NY 10004
212-908-9539

Officers
Robert W. Shaw, Jr., Pres. & Gen. Ptnr.
(Bethesda)
George W. Levert, Secy./Treas. & Ltd. Ptnr.
(Atlanta)
Michael T. Eckhart, Ltd. Ptnr. & Consultant
(Bethesda)
John C. Weiss III, Ltd. Ptnr. (Baltimore)
Philip B. Smith, Ltd. Ptnr. & Consultant
(New York)

Whom to Contact
Any of the above

Type of Firm
Private venture capital firm investing
own capital

Affiliation
Aretê Ventures, Inc.

Project Preferences
Will function either as deal originator or
investor in deals created by others
Type of Financing:
Startup
First-stage
Leveraged buyout

Minimum Investment: $100,000
Preferred Investment: $250,000-$1 million
Minimum Operating Data:
Annual Sales—$500,000
P&L—Break even

Geographical Preference
East Coast (lead investor)
National

Industry Preferences

Energy/Natural Resources
Alternative energy
Coal related
Energy conservation
Technology related products/equipment
Communications
Data communications
Computer Related
Computer graphics, CAD/CAM and CAE
Office automation
Scanning related
Software-artificial intelligence
Distribution
Electronics equipment
Industrial products
Electronic Components and Instrumentation
Analytical and scientific instrumentation
Component fabrication and testing
equipment
Industrial Products and Equipment
Controls and sensors
Energy management
Equipment and machinery
Robotics/vision systems
Specialty materials
All investments must relate to the electric or
gas utility industry

Additional Information
Year Founded—1985
Capital Under Management—$20 million
Method of Compensation—Return on
investment

ACQUIVEST GROUP, INC.

10 Speen Street, 2nd Floor
Framingham, MA 01701
617-875-3242

Officers
S. John Loscocco, Pres.
Richard L. Baird, V.P.

Whom to Contact
S. John Loscocco

Type of Firm
Private venture capital firm investing
own capital

Project Preferences
Prefer role as deal originator
Type of Financing:
Later-stage expansion
Leveraged buyout
Financing for acquisition and development
Minimum Investment: $1 million
Preferred Investment: Over $3 million
Preferred Investment (LBO):
Over $10 million
Minimum Operating Data:
Annual Sales—$1.5 million
P&L—Break even

Geographical Preferences
Within two hours of office
(exceptions considered)

Industry Preferences

Communications
(established businesses only)
Data communications
Telephone related
Computer Related
(established businesses only)
Computer services
Software-applications
Consumer
Consumer products
Consumer services
Food and beverage products
Hotels and resort areas
Leisure and recreational products
Retailing
Distribution
Consumer products
Food products
Industrial products
Medical products

**Electronic Components and
Instrumentation**
Electronic components
Fiber optics
Semiconductors
Energy/Natural Resources
Alternative energy
Services only
Technology related products/equipment
Genetic Engineering
Gene splicing and manufacturing equipment
Monoclonal antibodies and hybridomas
Recombinant DNA (agricultural and
industrial)
Recombinant DNA (medical)
Scale-up of laboratory bioproducts, including
amino acids, enzymes, antibiotics
Industrial Products and Equipment
(Traditional technologies only)
Controls and sensors
Equipment and machinery
Specialty chemicals
Specialty materials
Traditional manufacturing
Medical/Health Related
Disposable products
Drugs and medicines
Health and nutrition products and services
Therapeutic equipment
Other
Bioprocessing and related projects
Education related
Finance and insurance
Publishing
Real estate

Additional Information
Year Founded—1960
Method of Compensation—Return on
investment is of primary concern; do not
charge fees

ADAMS HARKNESS & HILL, INC.

One Liberty Square
Boston, MA 02109
617-423-6688

Officers
T. L. Stebbins, Exec. V.P.
John C. Sullivan, V.P.
Timothy J. McMahon, Assoc.

Whom to Contact
Any of the above

Type of Firm
Investment banking or merchant banking
firm investing own capital or funds of
partners or clients

Project Preferences
Prefer role as deal originator
Type of Financing:
Second-stage
Later-stage expansion
Leveraged buyout
Minimum Investment: $1 million
Preferred Investment: Over $1 million
Preferred Investment (LBO):
$2 million and over
Minimum Operating Data:
Annual Sales—$3 million
P&L—Break even
Annual Sales (LBO)—$5 million and over

Geographical Preference
Northeast

Industry Preferences
None

Additional Information
Method of Compensation—Function primarily
in service area; receive contingent fee in
cash or equity

ADVANCED TECHNOLOGY
VENTURES

10 Post Office Square #1230
Boston, MA 02109
617-423-4050

Other Office
1000 El Camino Real #210
Menlo Park, CA 94025
415-321-8601

Partners
Ralph J. Nunziato, Mgn. Ptnr.
Albert E. Paladino, Mgn. Ptnr.
Ivan E. Sutherland, Gen. Ptnr.
Robert C. Ammerman, Gen. Ptnr.
Jos C. Henkens, Gen. Ptnr.
Robert G. Loewy, Gen. Ptnr.
William R. Sutherland, Special Ptnr.
Robert F. Sproull, Special Ptnr.

Whom to Contact
Albert E. Paladino (Massachusetts)
Robert C. Ammerman (Massachusetts)
Ralph J. Nunziato (California)
Jos C. Henkens (California)

Type of Firm
Private venture capital firm investing own capital

Affiliations
Advanced Technology Ventures, Bermuda
Advanced Technology Ventures II

Industry Association Membership
NVCA

Project Preferences
Will function either as deal originator or investor in deals created by others
Type of Financing:
Seed
Startup
First-stage
Second-stage
Minimum Investment: Less than $100,000
Preferred Investment: $500,000-$1 million
Minimum Operating Data:
Annual Sales—Nominal
P&L—Losses (profits projected after 2 years)

Geographical Preference
None

Industry Preferences

Communications
Commercial communications
Data communications
Satellite and microwave communications
Telephone related
Computer Related
Computer graphics, CAD/CAM and CAE
Computer mainframes
Computer services
Memory devices
Micro and mini computers
Office automation
Scanning related
Software-applications
Software-artificial intelligence
Software-systems
Specialized turnkey systems
Terminals
Distribution
Communications equipment
Computer equipment
Consumer products
Electronics equipment
Industrial products
Medical products

Electronic Components and Instrumentation
Analytical and scientific instrumentation
Component fabrication and testing equipment
Electronic components
Fiber optics
Laser related
Semiconductors
Energy/Natural Resources
Alternative energy
Coal related
Technology related products/equipment
Genetic Engineering
Gene splicing and manufacturing equipment
Monoclonal antibodies and hybridomas
Recombinant DNA (agricultural and industrial)
Recombinant DNA (medical)
Industrial Products and Equipment
Chemicals
Controls and sensors
Energy management
Equipment and machinery
Other industrial automation
Plastics
Robotics/vision systems
Specialty materials
Medical/Health Related
Diagnostic equipment
Diagnostic test products
Drugs and medicines
Therapeutic equipment
Other
Agriculture, forestry, fishing

Additional Information
Year Founded—1979
Capital Under Management—$73.5 million
Investments(1985-1st 6 months)—5
Invested(1985-1st 6 months)—$2.3 million
Method of Compensation—Return on investment is of primary concern; do not charge fees

---

AEGIS FUND LIMITED PARTNERSHIP

One Cranberry Hill
Lexington, MA 02173
617-338-5655

General Partners
John H. Carter
Walter J. Levison
Steven J. Roth
Clifton C. Smith

Whom to Contact
Any of the above

Type of Firm
Private venture capital firm investing own capital

Project Preferences
Will function either as deal originator or investor in deals created by others
Type of Financing:
Seed
Startup
First-stage
Minimum Investment: $250,000
Preferred Investment: $300,000-$600,000
Minimum Operating Data:
Annual Sales—Nominal
P&L—Losses (profits projected after 2 years)

Geographical Preference
Within 75 miles of Boston

Industry Preferences

Communications
Data communications
Satellite and microwave communications
Telephone related
Computer Related
Computer graphics, CAD/CAM and CAE
Computer services
Memory devices
Micro and mini computers
Office automation
Software-applications
Software-artificial intelligence
Software-systems
Consumer
Consumer services
Food and beverage products
Restaurants
Distribution
Computer equipment
Consumer products
Microcomputer software
Electronic Components and Instrumentation
Analytical and scientific instrumentation
Electronic components
Laser related
Optics technology
Semiconductors
Energy/Natural Resources
Alternative energy
Energy conservation
Genetic Engineering
Monoclonal antibodies and hybridomas
Recombinant DNA (agricultural and industrial)
Recombinant DNA (medical)

Industrial Products and Equipment
Advanced materials
Other industrial automation
Robotics/vision systems
Medical/Health Related
Clinical chemistry
Diagnostic equipment
Diagnostic test products
Drugs and medicines
Hospital and clinical labs
Medical services
Therapeutic equipment

Additional Information
Year Founded—1983
Capital Under Management—$26 million
Investments(1985-1st 6 months)—6
Invested(1985-1st 6 months)—$2.3 million
Method of Compensation—Return on
investment is of primary concern; do not
charge fees

AENEAS VENTURE CORPORATION

70 Federal Street
Boston, MA 02110
617-423-4250

Officers
Walter Cabot, Pres. & Ptnr.
Scott Sperling, V.P. & Mgn. Ptnr.
Donald Beane, V.P. & Ptnr.
Nils Peterson, V.P. & Ptnr.
Michael Thonis, V.P. & Ptnr.
J. Anthony (Tony) Downer, Assoc.
Marilyn Hayward, Inv. Analyst
Kenneth Purcell, Inv. Analyst
Max Herrnstein, Res. Analyst

Whom to Contact
Kenneth Purcell

Type of Firm
Endowment fund

Affiliation
Harvard Management Company, Inc. (parent)

Industry Association Membership
NVCA

Project Preferences
Will function either as deal originator or
investor in deals created by others
Type of Financing:
First-stage
Second-stage
Later-stage expansion
Leveraged buyout

Minimum Investment: $500,000
Preferred Investment: $750,000-$1.5 million
Preferred Investment (LBO):
$1 million-$10 million
Minimum Operating Data:
Annual Sales—Nominal
P&L—Losses (profits projected after 2 years)
Annual Sales (LBO)—Over $15 million

Geographical Preference
None

Industry Preferences

Communications
Cable television
Commercial communications
Data communications
Satellite and microwave communications
Telephone related
Computer Related
Computer graphics, CAD/CAM and CAE
Computer mainframes
Computer services
Memory devices
Micro and mini computers
Office automation
Scanning related
Software-applications
Software-artificial intelligence
Software-systems
Specialized turnkey systems
Terminals
Consumer
Computer stores/related services
Consumer products
Consumer services
Food and beverage products
Franchise businesses
Hotels and resort areas
Leisure and recreational products
Restaurants
Retailing
Distribution
Communications equipment
Computer equipment
Consumer products
Electronics equipment
Food products
Industrial products
Medical products
**Electronic Components and
Instrumentation**
Analytical and scientific instrumentation
Component fabrication and testing
equipment
Electronic components
Fiber optics
Laser related
Semiconductors

Energy/Natural Resources
Alternative energy
Coal related
Drilling and exploration services
Energy conservation
Minerals
Oil and gas exploration and production
Technology related products/equipment
Genetic Engineering
Gene splicing and manufacturing equipment
Monoclonal antibodies and hybridomas
Recombinant DNA (agricultural and
industrial)
Recombinant DNA (medical)
Industrial Products and Equipment
Chemicals
Controls and sensors
Energy management
Equipment and machinery
Other industrial automation
Plastics
Robotics/vision systems
Specialty materials
Medical/Health Related
Diagnostic equipment
Diagnostic test products
Disposable products
Drugs and medicines
Hospital and clinical labs
Medical services
Therapeutic equipment
Other
Agriculture, forestry, fishing
Education related
Finance and insurance
Publishing
Real estate
Specialty consulting
Transportation

Additional Information
Year Founded—1974
Capital Under Management—
Over $500 million
Investments(1985-1st 6 months)—14
Invested(1985-1st 6 months)—$16 million

AMERICAN RESEARCH & DEVELOPMENT INC.

45 Milk Street, 7th Floor
Boston, MA 02109
617-423-7500

Partners
Charles J. Coulter, Mgn. Gen. Ptnr.
R. Courtney Whitin, Jr., Gen. Ptnr.
George W. McKinney III, Gen. Ptnr.
Francis J. Hughes, Jr., Gen. Ptnr.
A. Wade Blackman, Jr., Gen. Ptnr.
J. Luc Beaubien, Assoc.
Susan V. Pote, Admin. Mgr.

Whom to Contact
Susan V. Pote

Type of Firm
Private venture capital firm investing
own capital

Industry Association Membership
NVCA

Project Preferences
Will function either as deal originator or
investor in deals created by others
Type of Financing:
Seed
Startup
First-stage
Second-stage
Leveraged buyout
Minimum Investment: Less than $100,000
Preferred Investment: $500,000-$1 million
Minimum Operating Data:
Annual Sales—Nominal
P&L—Losses (profits projected after 2 years)

Geographical Preferences
Northeast
National

Industry Preferences

Communications
Telephone related
Voice and data communications

Computer Related
Computer graphics, CAD/CAM and CAE
Computer mainframes
Computer services
Memory devices
Micro and mini computers
Office automation
Scanning related
Software-applications
Software-artificial intelligence
Software-systems
Specialized turnkey systems
Terminals
Distribution
Communications equipment
Computer equipment
Electronics equipment
Industrial products
Medical products
**Electronic Components and
Instrumentation**
Analytical and scientific instrumentation
Component fabrication and testing
equipment
Electronic components
Fiber optics
Laser related
Semiconductors
Energy/Natural Resources
Alternative energy
Coal related
Energy conservation
Technology related products/equipment
Genetic Engineering
Gene splicing and manufacturing equipment
Monoclonal antibodies and hybridomas
Recombinant DNA (agricultural and
industrial)
Recombinant DNA (medical)
Industrial Products and Equipment
Chemicals
Controls and sensors
Energy management
Equipment and machinery
Other industrial automation
Plastics
Robotics/vision systems
Specialty materials
Medical/Health Related
Diagnostic test products
Therapeutic equipment

Additional Information
Year Founded—1946
Capital Under Management—$60 million
Method of Compensation—Return on
investment is most important, but also
charge for closing fees, service fees, etc.

AMPERSAND MANAGEMENT COMPANY

265 Franklin Street #1501
Boston, MA 02110
617-439-8300

see Paine Webber Venture
Management Company
Boston, MA

ANALOG DEVICES ENTERPRISES

Two Technology Way
Post Office Box 280
Norwood, MA 02062
617-329-1855

Officers
Lawrence T. Sullivan, Gen. Mgr.
Robert A. Boole, Dir. Venture Analysis
Pierre Dogan, Mgr. Venture Analysis
John Hudson, Cntlr.

Whom to Contact
Robert A. Boole

Type of Firm
Venture capital subsidiary or affiliate of
non-financial corporation

Affiliation
Analog Devices, Inc.

Project Preferences
Prefer role as deal originator but will also
invest in deals created by others
Type of Financing:
Startup
First-stage
Second-stage
Minimum Investment: $500,000
Preferred Investment: Over $1 million
Minimum Operating Data:
Annual Sales—Nominal
P&L—Losses (profits projected after 2 years)

Geographical Preference
None

Industry Preferences

Computer Related
Computer graphics, CAD/CAM and CAE
Parallel architecture computers
Scientific computers
Software-applications
Software-artificial intelligence
Software-systems
Specialized turnkey systems
Electronic Components and Instrumentation
Analytical and scientific instrumentation
Component fabrication and testing equipment
Digital signal processing
Electronic components
Fiber optics
Semiconductors
Industrial Products and Equipment
Controls and sensors
Other industrial automation
Robotics/vision systems

Additional Information

Year Founded—1980
Capital Under Management—$35 million
Investments(1985-1st 6 months)—7
Invested(1985-1st 6 months)—$5.3 million
Method of Compensation—Return on investment is of primary concern; do not charge fees

APPLIED TECHNOLOGY INVESTORS, INC.

55 Wheeler Street
Cambridge, MA 02138
617-354-4107

Other Office
55 Broadway
One Exchange Plaza, 23rd Floor
New York, NY 10006
212-425-9799

General Partners
Frederick B. Bamber (Massachusetts)
Thomas L. Flaherty (New York)
Michael Mayers (New York)

Whom to Contact
Any of the above

Type of Firm
Private venture capital firm investing own capital

Project Preferences
Will function either as deal originator or investor in deals created by others
Type of Financing:
Seed
Startup
First-stage
Second-stage
Leveraged buyout
Minimum Investment: $100,000
Preferred Investment: $250,000-$500,000
Minimum Operating Data:
Annual Sales—Nominal
P&L—Losses (profits projected after 2 years)

Geographical Preference
National

Industry Preferences

Communications
Cable television
Commercial communications
Data communications
Satellite and microwave communications
Telephone related
Computer Related
Computer graphics, CAD/CAM and CAE
Computer mainframes
Computer services
Memory devices
Micro and mini computers
Office automation
Scanning related
Software-applications
Software-artificial intelligence
Software-systems
Specialized turnkey systems
Terminals
Electronic Components and Instrumentation
Analytical and scientific instrumentation
Component fabrication and testing equipment
Electronic components
Fiber optics
Laser related
Semiconductors
Industrial Products and Equipment
Robotics/vision systems
Medical/Health Related
Diagnostic equipment
Diagnostic test products

Additional Information
Year Founded—1983
Investments(1985-1st 6 months)—6
Invested(1985-1st 6 months)—$800,000
Method of Compensation—Return on investment is of primary concern; do not charge fees

BAIN CAPITAL

Two Copley Place
Boston, MA 02116
617-572-3000

Other Office
6720 Wemberly Way
McLean, VA 22101
703-448-8188

Partners
W. Mitt Romney, Gen. Ptnr.
T. Coleman Andrews, Gen. Ptnr. (Virginia)
Robert F. White, Principal
Geoffrey S. Rehnert, Assoc.
Joshua Bekenstein, Assoc.
L. Scott Foushee, Analyst
Adam Kirsch, Analyst

Whom to Contact
Robert F. White (Massachusetts)
Geoffrey S. Rehnert (Massachusetts)
Joshua Bekenstein (Massachusetts)

Type of Firm
Venture capital subsidiary or affiliate of non-financial corporation

Affiliation
Bain & Company

Project Preferences
Will function either as deal originator or investor in deals created by others
Type of Financing:
First-stage
Second-stage
Later-stage expansion
Leveraged buyout
Minimum Investment: $500,000
Preferred Investment: Over $500,000
Preferred Investment (LBO):
Over $1 million
Minimum Operating Data:
Annual Sales—Nominal
Annual Sales (LBO)—Over $10 million

Geographical Preference
None

Industry Preferences

Communications
Cable television
Commercial communications
Data communications
Satellite and microwave communications
Telephone related
Consumer
Computer stores/related services
Consumer products
Consumer services
Food and beverage products
Franchise businesses
Hotels and resort areas
Leisure and recreational products
Restaurants
Retailing
Distribution
Communications equipment
Computer equipment
Consumer products
Electronics equipment
Food products
Industrial products
Medical products
Electronic Components and Instrumentation
Analytical and scientific instrumentation
Component fabrication and testing equipment
Electronic components
Fiber optics
Laser related
Semiconductors
Industrial Products and Equipment
Chemicals
Controls and sensors
Energy management
Equipment and machinery
Other industrial automation
Plastics
Robotics/vision systems
Specialty materials
Medical/Health Related
Diagnostic equipment
Diagnostic test products
Disposable products
Drugs and medicines
Hospital and clinical labs
Medical services
Therapeutic equipment

Other
Agriculture, forestry, fishing
Education related
Finance and insurance
Publishing
Real estate
Specialty consulting
Transportation
Will Not Consider
Businesses in the research and development stage

Additional Information
Year Founded—1984
Capital Under Management—$38 million
Investments(1985-1st 6 months)—6
Invested(1985-1st 6 months)—$7 million
Method of Compensation—Return on investment is of primary concern; do not charge fees

---

BANCBOSTON CAPITAL, INC.

100 Federal Street
Boston, MA 02110
617-434-4012

Officers
Frederick M. Fritz, Pres.
Mary J. Reilly, V.P.
John C. Whistler, Inv. Officer
David C. Richardson, Inv. Assoc.

Whom to Contact
Frederick M. Fritz

Type of Firm
Venture capital subsidiary of commercial bank

Affiliation
Bank of Boston Corporation (parent)

Project Preferences
Will function either as deal originator or investor in deals created by others
Type of Financing:
Later-stage expansion
Leveraged buyout
Minimum Investment: $1 million
Preferred Investment: $2 million-$10 million
Preferred Investment (LBO):
Over $15 million

Geographical Preference
National

Industry Preferences
None

Will Not Consider
Agriculture
Energy
Real estate

Additional Information
Year Founded—1974
Capital Under Management—$50 million
Investments(1985-1st 6 months)—1
Invested(1985-1st 6 months)—$1 million

BANCBOSTON VENTURES INC.

100 Federal Street
Boston, MA 02110
617-434-2442

Officers
Paul F. Hogan, Pres.
Jeffrey W. Wilson, V.P.
Diana H. Frazier, V.P.
Stephen J. O'Leary, Inv. Officer
Robert M. Freedman, Inv. Officer
Cheryl L. Krane, Portfolio Admin.

Whom to Contact
Any of the above

Type of Firm
Private venture capital firm investing own capital
SBIC
Venture capital subsidiary of commercial bank

Affiliation
Bank of Boston Corporation (parent)

Industry Association Memberships
NASBIC
NVCA

Project Preferences
Will function either as deal originator or investor in deals created by others
Type of Financing:
Seed
Startup
First-stage
Second-stage
Later-stage expansion
Leveraged buyout
Minimum Investment: $250,000
Preferred Investment: $500,000-$1 million
Minimum Operating Data:
Annual Sales—Nominal
P&L—Losses (profits projected after 2 years)

Geographical Preferences

Northeast
Southwest
East Coast
West Coast

Industry Preferences

Communications
Cable television
Commercial communications
Data communications
Satellite and microwave communications
Telephone related
Computer Related
Computer graphics, CAD/CAM and CAE
Computer mainframes
Computer services
Memory devices
Micro and mini computers
Office automation
Scanning related
Software-applications
Software-artificial intelligence
Software-systems
Specialized turnkey systems
Terminals
Distribution
Communications equipment
Computer equipment
Consumer products
Electronics equipment
Food products
Industrial products
Medical products
**Electronic Components and
  Instrumentation**
Analytical and scientific instrumentation
Component fabrication and testing
  equipment
Electronic components
Fiber optics
Laser related
Semiconductors
Genetic Engineering
Gene splicing and manufacturing equipment
Monoclonal antibodies and hybridomas
Recombinant DNA (agricultural and
  industrial)
Recombinant DNA (medical)
Industrial Products and Equipment
Chemicals
Controls and sensors
Energy management
Equipment and machinery
Other industrial automation
Plastics
Robotics/vision systems
Specialty materials

Medical/Health Related
Diagnostic equipment
Diagnostic test products
Disposable products
Drugs and medicines
Hospital and clinical labs
Medical services
Therapeutic equipment
Other
Agriculture, forestry, fishing
Will Not Consider
Insurance
Oil and gas
Real estate

Additional Information

Year Founded—1959
Capital Under Management—$35 million
Investments(1985-1st 6 months)—12
Invested(1985-1st 6 months)—$3 million
Method of Compensation—Return on
  investment is of primary concern; do not
  charge fees

BATTERY VENTURES, L.P.

60 Batterymarch Street
Boston, MA 02110
617-542-7710

Partner

Robert G. Barrett, Gen. Ptnr.
Richard D. Frisbie, Gen. Ptnr.
Howard Anderson, Gen. Ptnr.
Oliver D. Curme, Assoc.

Whom to Contact

Robert G. Barrett
Richard D. Frisbie
Oliver D. Curme

Type of Firm

Private venture capital firm investing
  own capital

Affiliation

The Yankee Group, a technology
  research firm

Industry Association Memberships

NASBIC
NVCA

Project Preferences

Will function either as deal originator or
  investor in deals created by others

Type of Financing:

Seed
Startup
First-stage
Second-stage
Later-stage expansion
Leveraged buyout
Minimum Investment: Less than $100,000
Preferred Investment: $500,000-$1 million
Minimum Operating Data:
Annual Sales—Nominal
P&L—Losses (profits projected after 2 years)

Geographical Preference

None

Industry Preferences

Communications
Cable television
Commercial communications
Data communications
Satellite and microwave communications
Telephone related
Computer Related
Computer graphics, CAD/CAM and CAE
Computer mainframes
Computer services
Memory devices
Micro and mini computers
Office automation
Scanning related
Software-applications
Software-artificial intelligence
Software-systems
Specialized turnkey systems
Terminals
Distribution
Communications equipment
Computer equipment
**Electronic Components and
  Instrumentation**
Advanced video technology
Analytical and scientific instrumentation
Electronic components
Fiber optics
Laser related
Optics technology
Semiconductors
Industrial Products and Equipment
Controls and sensors
Other industrial automation
Process control
Robotics/vision systems
Will Not Consider
Medical
Genetic engineering

Additional Information
Year Founded—1983
Capital Under Management—$35 million
Investments(1985-1st 6 months)—6
Invested(1985-1st 6 months)—$3 million
Method of Compensation—Return on
investment is of primary concern; do not
charge fees

R.C. BERNER & CO.

65 William Street
Wellesley, MA 02181
617-237-9472

Officers
Robert C. Berner, Pres.
H.S. Berner, Treas.
A.M. Albrecht, Asst. to Pres.

Whom to Contact
Robert C. Berner

Type of Firm
Consulting firm evaluating and analyzing
venture projects and arranging private
placements
Finder and intermediary

Affiliations
BKS Associates Venture Investment Co.
Communication Engineering Co.,
Technical Consultants

Project Preferences
Prefer role in deals created by others
Type of Financing:
Later-stage expansion
Leveraged buyout
Minimum Investment: $500,000
Preferred Investment: $500,000-$1 million
Preferred Investment (LBO): $2.5 million
Minimum Operating Data:
Annual Sales—Over $3 million
P&L—Profits NBT over $200,000
Annual Sales (LBO)—$10 million-$30 million

Geographical Preferences
National
Europe

Industry Preferences

Communications
Commercial communications
Data communications
Telephone related

Computer Related
Computer graphics, CAD/CAM and CAE
Computer services
Memory devices
Micro and mini computers
Office automation
Software-applications
Software-artificial intelligence
Software-systems
Terminals
Consumer
Consumer products
Consumer services
Food and beverage products
Hotels and resort areas
Leisure and recreational products
Retailing
Distribution
Communications equipment
Computer equipment
Consumer products
Electronics equipment
Food products
Industrial products
Medical products
**Electronic Components and
Instrumentation**
Analytical and scientific instrumentation
Component fabrication and testing
equipment
Electronic components
Fiber optics
Laser related
Semiconductors
Industrial Products and Equipment
Chemicals
Controls and sensors
Equipment and machinery
Other industrial automation
Plastics
Robotics/vision systems
Specialty materials
Medical/Health Related
Diagnostic equipment
Diagnostic test products
Disposable products
Drugs and medicines
Hospital and clinical labs
Medical services
Therapeutic equipment
Other
Education related
Finance and insurance

Additional Information
Year Founded—1966

BESSEMER VENTURE PARTNERS

83 Walnut Street
Wellesley Hills, MA 02181
617-237-6050

Other Offices
630 Fifth Avenue
New York, NY 10111
212-708-9300

3000 Sand Hill Road
Building 3, #225
Menlo Park, CA 94025
415-854-2200

General Partners
William T. Burgin (New York &
Massachusetts)
Neill H. Brownstein (California)
Robert H. Buescher (New York)
Robert B. Field (California)
James H. Furneaux (Massachusetts)
G. Felda Hardymon (Massachusetts)

Whom to Contact
Any of the above

Type of Firm
Private venture capital firm investing
own capital

Affiliation
Bessemer Securities Corporation
(sole limited partner)

Industry Association Memberships
NVCA
WAVC

Project Preferences
Will function either as deal originator or
investor in deals created by others
Type of Financing:
Seed
Research and development partnerships
Startup
First-stage
Second-stage
Later-stage expansion
Leveraged buyout
Preferred Investment: No preference

Geographical Preference
National

Industry Preferences
None

Additional Information

Year Founded—1970
Capital Under Management—$100 million
Investments(1985-1st 6 months)—5
Invested(1985-1st 6 months)—$3 million
Method of Compensation—Return on
   investment is of primary concern; do not
   charge fees

BOSTON CAPITAL VENTURES

One Devonshire Place #2913
Boston, MA 02109
617-227-6550

General Partners

A. Dana Callow, Jr.
Donald J. Steiner
H.J. von der Goltz

Whom to Contact

Any of the above

Type of Firm

Private venture capital firm investing
   own capital

Industry Association Membership

NVCA

Project Preferences

Prefer role as deal originator but will also
   invest in deals created by others
Type of Financing:
Startup
First-stage
Second-stage
Leveraged buyout
Minimum Investment: $250,000
Preferred Investment: $500,000-$1 million
Minimum Operating Data:
Annual Sales—Nominal
P&L—Losses (profits projected after 1 year)

Geographical Preferences

Northeast
East Coast

Industry Preferences

Communications
Commercial communications
Data communications
Satellite and microwave communications
Telephone related

Computer Related
Computer graphics, CAD/CAM and CAE
Computer mainframes
Computer services
Memory devices
Micro and mini computers
Office automation
Scanning related
Software-applications
Software-artificial intelligence
Software-systems
Specialized turnkey systems
Terminals
Consumer
Consumer services
Leisure and recreational products
Distribution
Communications equipment
Computer equipment
Consumer products
Electronics equipment
Food products
Industrial products
Medical products
**Electronic Components and
   Instrumentation**
Analytical and scientific instrumentation
Component fabrication and testing
   equipment
Electronic components
Fiber optics
Laser related
Semiconductors
Energy/Natural Resources
Alternative energy
Energy conservation
Technology related products/equipment
Genetic Engineering
Gene splicing and manufacturing equipment
Monoclonal antibodies and hybridomas
Recombinant DNA (agricultural and
   industrial)
Recombinant DNA (medical)
Industrial Products and Equipment
Chemicals
Controls and sensors
Energy management
Equipment and machinery
Other industrial automation
Plastics
Robotics/vision systems
Specialty materials
Medical/Health Related
Diagnostic equipment
Diagnostic test products
Disposable products
Drugs and medicines
Hospital and clinical labs
Medical services
Therapeutic equipment

Other
Finance and insurance
Publishing
Transportation

Additional Information

Year Founded—1982
Capital Under Management—$20 million
Investments(1985-1st 6 months)—2
Invested(1985-1st 6 months)—$1 million
Method of Compensation—Return on
   investment is of primary concern; do not
   charge fees

THE BOSTON VENTURE FUND, INC.

33 Bedford Street #7
Lexington, MA 02173
617-862-0269

Officer

Thomas Schinkel, Pres.

Type of Firm

Private venture capital firm investing
   own capital

Project Preferences

Will function either as deal originator or
   investor in deals created by others
Type of Financing:
Startup
First-stage
Minimum Investment: Less than $100,000
Preferred Investment: $250,000-$500,000
Minimum Operating Data:
Annual Sales—Nominal

Geographical Preference

Northeast

Industry Preferences

Communications
Cable television
Commercial communications
Data communications
Satellite and microwave communications
Telephone related
Computer Related
Computer graphics, CAD/CAM and CAE
Software-artificial intelligence

Electronic Components and Instrumentation
Analytical and scientific instrumentation
Component fabrication and testing equipment
Electronic components
Fiber optics
Laser related
Semiconductors
Genetic Engineering
Gene splicing and manufacturing equipment
Monoclonal antibodies and hybridomas
Recombinant DNA (agricultural and industrial)
Recombinant DNA (medical)
Industrial Products and Equipment
Robotics/vision systems
Medical/Health Related
Diagnostic equipment
Diagnostic test products
Disposable products
Drugs and medicines
Hospital and clinical labs
Medical services
Therapeutic equipment

Additional Information

Year Founded—1982
Investments(1985-1st 6 months)—8
Method of Compensation—Return on investment is of primary concern; do not charge fees

BOSTON VENTURES LIMITED PARTNERSHIP/BOSTON VENTURES MANAGEMENT, INC.

45 Milk Street, Fifth Floor
Boston, MA 02109
617-292-8125

Officers

William F. Thompson, Pres. & Dir.
Richard C. Wallace, Dir.
Roy F. Coppedge III, Dir.
Anthony J. Bolland, Dir.
James M. Wilson, Dir.
Martha Crowninshield

Whom to Contact

Any of the above

Type of Firm

Private venture capital firm investing own capital
Investment banking or merchant banking firm investing own capital or funds of partners or clients

Affiliation

Boston Ventures Management is the investment advisor for Boston Ventures Limited Partnership

Project Preferences

Prefer role as deal originator
Type of Financing:
Later-stage expansion
Leveraged buyout
Minimum Investment: Over $2 million
Preferred Investment: $5 million-$10 million
Preferred Investment (LBO): $10 million-$15 million
Minimum Operating Data:
Annual Sales—Over $10 million
P&L—Profits NBT over $2 million
Annual Sales (LBO)—$25 million-$1 billion

Geographical Preferences

None
United Kingdom

Industry Preferences

Communications
Cable television
Commercial communications
Data communications
Satellite and microwave communications
Telephone related
Consumer
Consumer products
Consumer services
Food and beverage products
Franchise businesses
Hotels and resort areas
Leisure and recreational products
Restaurants
Retailing
Distribution
Communications equipment
Consumer products
Food products
Medical products
Medical/Health Related
Disposable products
Drugs and medicines
Hospital and clinical labs
Medical services
Other
Finance and insurance
Publishing
Will Not Consider
Energy
High technology
Real estate development

Additional Information

Year Founded—1983
Capital Under Management—$114 million
Investments(1985-1st 6 months)—4
Invested(1985-1st 6 months)—$27.7 million
Method of Compensation—Return on investment is most important, but also charge for closing fees, service fees, etc.

BRISTOL INVESTMENT TRUST

842A Beacon Street
Boston, MA 02215
617-566-5212

Officers

Bernard G. Berkman, Trustee
Stephen V. O'Donnell, Jr., Trust Officer

Whom to Contact

Either of the above

Type of Firm

Private venture capital firm investing own capital

Project Preferences

Prefer role as deal originator but will also invest in deals created by others
Type of Financing:
First-stage
Second-stage
Later-stage expansion
Leveraged buyout
Minimum Investment: Less than $100,000
Preferred Investment: Less than $100,000
Minimum Operating Data:
Annual Sales—Nominal

Geographical Preference

Northeast

Industry Preferences

Consumer
Food and beverage products
Franchise businesses
Hotels and resort areas
Leisure and recreational products
Restaurants
Retailing
Distribution
Consumer products
Food products
Medical products
Medical/Health Related
Hospital and clinical labs
Medical services

Other
Finance and insurance
Real estate

Additional Information
Year Founded—1966
Method of Compensation—Return on
investment is of primary concern; do not
charge fees

BURR, EGAN, DELEAGE & CO.

One Post Office Square #3800
Boston, MA 02109
617-482-8020

West Coast Office
Three Embarcadero Center #2560
San Francisco, CA 94111
415-362-4022

Partners
Craig L. Burr, Ptnr. (Massachusetts)
William P. Egan, Ptnr. (Massachusetts)
Jean Deleage, Ptnr. (California)
Brion Applegate, Ptnr. (California)
Shirley Cerrudo, Ptnr. (California)
Jean-Bernard Schmidt, Ptnr. (California)
Thomas E. Winter, Ptnr. (California)
Jonathan A. Flint, V.P. (Massachusetts)
Esther B. Sharp, V.P. (Massachusetts)
Annette M. Bianchi, Assoc. (California)

Whom to Contact
Craig L. Burr
William P. Egan
Jean Deleage
Thomas E. Winter

Type of Firm
Private venture capital firm investing
own capital

Industry Association Membership
NVCA

Project Preferences
Prefer role as deal originator but will also
invest in deals created by others
Type of Financing:
Startup
First-stage
Second-stage
Later-stage expansion
Leveraged buyout
Minimum Investment: $750,000
Preferred Investment: Over $1 million
Preferred Investment (LBO):
$1 million and over

Geographical Preference
National

Industry Preferences

Communications
Cable television
Commercial communications
Data communications
Satellite and microwave communications
Telephone related
Computer Related
Computer graphics, CAD/CAM and CAE
Computer mainframes
Memory devices
Micro and mini computers
Software-applications
Software-systems
Consumer
Computer stores/related services
Retailing
Distribution
Communications equipment
Electronics equipment
Medical products
**Electronic Components and
Instrumentation**
Analytical and scientific instrumentation
Component fabrication and testing
equipment
Electronic components
Fiber optics
Laser related
Semiconductors
Energy/Natural Resources
Technology related products/equipment
Genetic Engineering
Gene splicing and manufacturing equipment
Monoclonal antibodies and hybridomas
Recombinant DNA (agricultural and
industrial)
Recombinant DNA (medical)
Industrial Products and Equipment
Chemicals
Controls and sensors
Energy management
Equipment and machinery
Other industrial automation
Plastics
Robotics/vision systems
Specialty materials
Medical/Health Related
Diagnostic equipment
Diagnostic test products
Disposable products
Drugs and medicines
Hospital and clinical labs
Medical services
Therapeutic equipment
Will Not Consider
Real estate

Additional Information
Year Founded—1979
Capital Under Management—$200 million
Investments(1985-1st 6 months)—19
Invested(1985-1st 6 months)—$12 million
Method of Compensation—Return on
investment is of primary concern; do not
charge fees

CHARLES RIVER VENTURES

67 Batterymarch Street
Boston, MA 02110
617-482-9370

General Partners
Richard M. Burnes, Jr., Gen. Ptnr.
John T. Neises, Gen. Ptnr.
Robert F. Higgins, Gen. Ptnr.
Donald W. Feddersen, Gen. Ptnr.
Paul A. Maeder, Assoc.

Whom to Contact
Any of the above

Type of Firm
Private venture capital firm investing
own capital

Industry Association Membership
NVCA

Project Preferences
Prefer role as deal originator but will also
invest in deals created by others
Type of Financing:
Startup
Second-stage
Later-stage expansion
Leveraged buyout
Minimum Investment: $500,000
Minimum Operating Data:
Annual Sales—Nominal
P&L—Losses (profits projected after 2 years)

Geographical Preference
None

Industry Preferences

Communications
Cable television
Commercial communications
Data communications
Satellite and microwave communications
Telephone related

Computer Related
Computer graphics, CAD/CAM and CAE
Computer mainframes
Computer services
Memory devices
Micro and mini computers
Office automation
Scanning related
Software-applications
Software-artificial intelligence
Software-systems
Specialized turnkey systems
Terminals
Electronic Components and Instrumentation
Analytical and scientific instrumentation
Component fabrication and testing equipment
Electronic components
Fiber optics
Laser related
Semiconductors
Genetic Engineering
Gene splicing and manufacturing equipment
Monoclonal antibodies and hybridomas
Recombinant DNA (agricultural and industrial)
Recombinant DNA (medical)
Industrial Products and Equipment
Controls and sensors
Energy management
Robotics/vision systems
Medical/Health Related
Diagnostic equipment
Diagnostic test products
Disposable products
Drugs and medicines
Hospital and clinical labs
Medical services
Therapeutic equipment
Will Not Consider
Real estate

Additional Information
Year Founded—1970
Capital Under Management— Over $140 million
Investments(1985-1st 6 months)—6
Invested(1985-1st 6 months)—$6 million
Method of Compensation—Return on investment is of primary concern; do not charge fees

CHATHAM VENTURE CORPORATION

450 Bedford Street
Lexington, MA 02173
617-863-0970

Other Office
333 West Santa Clara Street
Suite 800
San Jose, CA 95113
408-947-4062

Partners
Euan C. Malcolmson (Massachusetts)
Stephen J. Gaal (Massachusetts)
William D. Jobe (California)

Whom to Contact
Any of the above

Type of Firm
Private venture capital firm investing own capital

Affiliations
Japhet U.S. Venture Capital Fund Ltd.
Chatham Venture Partners L.P.

Project Preferences
Will function either as deal originator or investor in deals created by others
Type of Financing:
Seed
Startup
First-stage
Second-stage
Later-stage expansion
Minimum Investment: $250,000
Preferred Investment: $500,000-$1 million
Minimum Operating Data:
Annual Sales—Nominal
P&L—Losses (profits projected after 2 years)

Geographical Preference
National

Industry Preferences

Communications
Data communications
Satellite and microwave communications
Telephone related

Computer Related
Computer graphics, CAD/CAM and CAE
Computer mainframes
Computer services
Micro and mini computers
Office automation
Software-applications
Software-artificial intelligence
Software-systems
Specialized turnkey systems
Electronic Components and Instrumentation
Analytical and scientific instrumentation
Fiber optics
Laser related
Industrial Products and Equipment
Robotics/vision systems

Additional Information
Year Founded—1981
Capital Under Management—$23.5 million
Investments(1985-1st 6 months)—5
Invested(1985-1st 6 months)—$1.7 million
Method of Compensation—Return on investment is of primary concern; do not charge fees

CHURCHILL INTERNATIONAL

Nine Riverside Road
Weston, MA 02193
617-893-6555

Roy G. Helsing, V.P.
Christopher Spray, Inv. Dir.
David Ruth, Inv. Dir.
Julie B. Dunbar, Mgr. Corp. Communications

See CALIFORNIA for full listing

CLAFLIN CAPITAL MANAGEMENT, INC.

185 Devonshire Street
Boston, MA 02110
617-426-6505

General Partners
Thomas M. Claflin II
Lloyd C. Dahmen
John O. Flender
Joseph Stavenhagen

Whom to Contact
Any of the above

Type of Firm
Private venture capital firm investing own capital

Project Preferences

Prefer role as deal originator
Type of Financing:
Seed
Startup
First-stage
Minimum Investment: Less than $100,000
Preferred Investment: $100,000-$250,000
Minimum Operating Data:
Annual Sales—Nominal
P&L—Losses (profits projected after 1 year)

Geographical Preference

Northeast

Industry Preferences

Communications
Data communications
Satellite and microwave communications
Computer Related
Computer graphics, CAD/CAM and CAE
Software-applications
Software-systems
Terminals
Consumer
Specialized consumer products
Electronic Components and Instrumentation
Analytical and scientific instrumentation
Electronic components
Medical/Health Related
Medical services
Other
Direct response marketing
Will Not Consider
Natural resources
Real estate
Research and development projects
Companies requiring more than $1.5 million to reach positive cash flow

Additional Information

Year Founded—1978
Capital Under Management—$29 million
Investments(1985-1st 6 months)—5
Invested(1985-1st 6 months)—$1.2 million
Method of Compensation—Return on investment is of primary concern; do not charge fees

COMMONWEALTH PARTNERS

881 Commonwealth Avenue #540
Boston, MA 02215
617-353-4550

General Partner

Charles W. Smith

Type of Firm

Private venture capital firm investing own capital

Affiliation

Boston University Community Technology Foundation

Industry Association Membership

NVCA

Project Preferences

Prefer role in deals created by others
Type of Financing:
Startup
First-stage
Minimum Investment: $100,000
Minimum Operating Data:
Annual Sales—Nominal
P&L—Losses (profits projected after 3 years)

Geographical Preference

National

Industry Preferences

Communications
Cable television
Commercial communications
Data communications
Satellite and microwave communications
Telephone related
Computer Related
Office automation
Software-systems
Consumer
Consumer products
Distribution
Electronics equipment
Medical products
Electronic Components and Instrumentation
Analytical and scientific instrumentation
Laser related
Optics technology
Genetic Engineering
Monoclonal antibodies and hybridomas
Industrial Products and Equipment
Other industrial automation
Process control
Robotics/vision systems

Medical/Health Related
Diagnostic equipment
Drugs and medicines
Medical services

Additional Information

Year Founded—1984
Capital Under Management—$2.7 million
Investments(1985-1st 6 months)—6
Invested(1985-1st 6 months)—$220,000
Method of Compensation—Return on investment is of primary concern; do not charge fees

COPLEY VENTURE PARTNERS

Federal Reserve Plaza
Boston, MA 02210
617-722-6030

Partners

Julius Jensen III, Mgn. Gen. Ptnr.
David J. Ryan, Gen. Ptnr.
Mary Ellen Eagan, Research Assoc.

Whom to Contact

Julius Jensen III
David J. Ryan

Type of Firm

Private venture capital firm investing own capital

Project Preferences

Will function either as deal originator or investor in deals created by others
Type of Financing:
Startup
First-stage
Second-stage
Minimum Investment: $250,000
Preferred Investment: $500,000-$1 million
Minimum Operating Data:
Annual Sales—Nominal
P&L—Losses (profits projected after 2 years)

Geographical Preference

None

Industry Preferences

Communications
Commercial communications
Data communications
Satellite and microwave communications
Telephone related

Computer Related
Computer graphics, CAD/CAM and CAE
Computer mainframes
Computer services
Memory devices
Micro and mini computers
Office automation
Scanning related
Software-applications
Software-artificial intelligence
Software-systems
Specialized turnkey systems
Terminals
Consumer
Franchise businesses
Retailing
Distribution
Communications equipment
Medical products
**Electronic Components and
Instrumentation**
Analytical and scientific instrumentation
Component fabrication and testing
equipment
Electronic components
Fiber optics
Laser related
Semiconductors
Genetic Engineering
Monoclonal antibodies and hybridomas
Industrial Products and Equipment
Other industrial automation
Robotics/vision systems
Medical/Health Related
Diagnostic equipment
Diagnostic test products
Disposable products
Drugs and medicines
Hospital and clinical labs
Medical services
Therapeutic equipment
Other
Finance and insurance

Additional Information
Year Founded—1985
Method of Compensation—Return on
investment is of primary concern; do not
charge fees

EASTECH MANAGEMENT COMPANY, INC.

One Liberty Square
Ninth Floor
Boston, MA 02109
617-338-0200

Partners
G. Bickley Stevens II, Gen. Ptnr.
Fontaine K. Richardson, Gen. Ptnr.
Michael H. Shanahan

Whom to Contact
Michael H. Shanahan

Type of Firm
Private venture capital firm investing
own capital

Project Preferences
Prefer role as deal originator
Type of Financing:
Startup
First-stage
Second-stage
Minimum Investment: $500,000
Preferred Investment: $500,000-$1 million
Minimum Operating Data:
Annual Sales—Nominal
P&L—Losses (profits projected after 2 years)

Geographical Preferences
Within two hours of office
Northeast
East Coast

Industry Preferences
Communications
Data communications
Computer Related
Computer graphics, CAD/CAM and CAE
Computer mainframes
Computer services
Memory devices
Micro and mini computers
Office automation
Scanning related
Software-applications
Software-artificial intelligence
Software-systems
Specialized turnkey systems
Terminals
**Electronic Components and
Instrumentation**
Analytical and scientific instrumentation
Component fabrication and testing
equipment
Semiconductors

Will Not Consider
Agriculture, forestry, fishing
Entertainment
Finance and insurance
Natural resources
Oil and gas
Publishing
Real estate
Retail
Transportation

Additional Information
Year Founded—1981
Capital Under Management—$34.4 million
Investments(1985-1st 6 months)—8
Invested(1985-1st 6 months)—$1.8 million
Method of Compensation—Return on
investment is of primary concern; do not
charge fees

EG&G VENTURE PARTNERS

45 William Street
Wellesley, MA 02181
617-237-5100

See CALIFORNIA for full listing

ELRON TECHNOLOGIES, INC.

12 Oak Park Drive
Bedford, MA 01730
617-275-8990
617-275-9390

Other Office
1211 Avenue of the Americas
New York, NY 10036
212-819-1644

Officer
Carlos Zorea, Sr. V.P. (Massachusetts)

Type of Firm
Venture capital subsidiary or affiliate of
non-financial corporation

Affiliation
Elron Electronic Industries, Ltd.

Project Preferences
Will function either as deal originator or
investor in deals created by others

Type of Financing:
Seed
Startup
First-stage
Second-stage
Leveraged buyout
Minimum Investment: $250,000
Preferred Investment: $500,000-$1 million
Minimum Operating Data:
Annual Sales—Nominal

Geographical Preferences
National
Israel

Industry Preferences

Communications
Cable television
Commercial communications
Data communications
Satellite and microwave communications
Telephone related
Computer Related
Computer graphics, CAD/CAM and CAE
Computer mainframes
Computer services
Memory devices
Micro and mini computers
Office automation
Scanning related
Software-applications
Software-artificial intelligence
Software-systems
Specialized turnkey systems
Terminals
Electronic Components and Instrumentation
Analytical and scientific instrumentation
Component fabrication and testing
  equipment
Electronic components
Fiber optics
Laser related
Semiconductors
Industrial Products and Equipment
Robotics/vision systems
Medical/Health Related
Diagnostic equipment
Diagnostic test products
Disposable products
Drugs and medicines
Hospital and clinical labs
Medical services
Therapeutic equipment

Additional Information
Year Founded—1983
Method of Compensation—Return on
  investment is of primary concern; do not
  charge fees

FANEUIL HALL ASSOCIATES

One Boston Place, 16th Floor
Boston, MA 02108
617-723-1955

General Partner
David T. Riddiford

Type of Firm
Private venture capital firm investing
own capital

Industry Association Membership
NVCA

Project Preferences
Will function either as deal originator or
  investor in deals created by others
Type of Financing:
Seed
Startup
First-stage
Minimum Investment: $250,000
Preferred Investment: $250,000-$500,000
Minimum Operating Data:
Annual Sales—Nominal

Geographical Preferences
Northeast
Southeast
Southwest
East Coast

Industry Preferences

Communications
Commercial communications
Data communications
Satellite and microwave communications
Telephone related

Computer Related
Computer graphics, CAD/CAM and CAE
Computer mainframes
Computer services
Memory devices
Micro and mini computers
Office automation
Scanning related
Software-applications
Software-artificial intelligence
Software-systems
Specialized turnkey systems
Terminals
Electronic Components and Instrumentation
Analytical and scientific instrumentation
Component fabrication and testing
  equipment
Electronic components
Fiber optics
Laser related
Semiconductors
Genetic Engineering
Gene splicing and manufacturing equipment
Monoclonal antibodies and hybridomas
Recombinant DNA (agricultural and
  industrial)
Recombinant DNA (medical)
Industrial Products and Equipment
Chemicals
Controls and sensors
Energy management
Equipment and machinery
Other industrial automation
Plastics
Robotics/vision systems
Specialty materials
Medical/Health Related
Diagnostic equipment
Diagnostic test products
Disposable products
Drugs and medicines
Hospital and clinical labs
Medical services
Therapeutic equipment

Additional Information
Year Founded—1973
Capital Under Management—$6 million
Investments(1985-1st 6 months)—2
Invested(1985-1st 6 months)—$500,000
Method of Compensation—Return on
  investment is of primary concern; do not
  charge fees

FIDELITY VENTURE ASSOCIATES, INC.

82 Devonshire Street
Boston, MA 02109
617-570-6450

Officers
Samuel W. Bodman, Chm.
William R. Elfers, V.P.
Gordon F. Kingsley, V.P.
Thomas F. Stephenson, Pres.
Donald R. Young, Assoc.

Whom to Contact
Donald R. Young
William R. Elfers
Gordon F. Kingsley

Type of Firm
Private venture capital firm investing
own capital

Project Preferences
Prefer role as deal originator but will also
invest in deals created by others
Type of Financing:
Startup
First-stage
Second-stage
Later-stage expansion
Leveraged buyout
Minimum Investment: $250,000
Preferred Investment: $500,000-$1 million
Preferred Investment (LBO): $1 million
Minimum Operating Data:
Annual Sales—Nominal
P&L—Losses (profits projected after 3 years)
Annual Sales (LBO)—$10 million and over

Geographical Preference
None

Industry Preferences

Communications
Cable television
Commercial communications
Data communications
Satellite and microwave communications
Telephone related

Computer Related
Computer graphics, CAD/CAM and CAE
Computer mainframes
Computer services
Memory devices
Micro and mini computers
Office automation
Scanning related
Software-applications
Software-artificial intelligence
Software-systems
Specialized turnkey systems
Terminals

Consumer
Computer stores/related services
Consumer products
Consumer services
Food and beverage products
Franchise businesses
Hotels and resort areas
Leisure and recreational products
Restaurants
Retailing

Distribution
Communications equipment
Computer equipment
Consumer products
Electronics equipment
Food products
Industrial products
Medical products

Electronic Components and Instrumentation
Analytical and scientific instrumentation
Component fabrication and testing
equipment
Electronic components
Fiber optics
Laser related
Semiconductors

Energy/Natural Resources
Alternative energy
Coal related
Drilling and exploration services
Energy conservation
Minerals
Oil and gas exploration and production
Technology related products/equipment

Genetic Engineering
Gene splicing and manufacturing equipment
Monoclonal antibodies and hybridomas
Recombinant DNA (agricultural and
industrial)
Recombinant DNA (medical)

Industrial Products and Equipment
Chemicals
Controls and sensors
Energy management
Equipment and machinery
Other industrial automation
Plastics
Robotics/vision systems
Specialty materials

Medical/Health Related
Diagnostic equipment
Diagnostic test products
Disposable products
Drugs and medicines
Hospital and clinical labs
Medical services
Therapeutic equipment

Other
Agriculture, forestry, fishing
Education related
Publishing
Transportation

Additional Information
Year Founded—1969
Capital Under Management—
$50 million and over
Investments(1985-1st 6 months)—8
Invested(1985-1st 6 months)—$3 million
Method of Compensation—Return on
investment is of primary concern; do not
charge fees

FIN-TECH

36 Washington Street
Wellesley Hills, MA 02181
617-237-7762

Partners
William Wolfson
Robert L. Massard

Whom to Contact
Either of the above

Type of Firm
Private venture capital firm investing
own capital

Project Preferences
Will function either as deal originator or
investor in deals created by others
Type of Financing:
Seed
Startup
First-stage
Leveraged buyout

Minimum Investment: Less than $100,000
Preferred Investment: $100,000-$250,000
Minimum Operating Data:
Annual Sales—Nominal
P&L—Losses (profits projected after 2 years)

Geographical Preference
Northeast

Industry Preferences

Communications
Data communications
Telephone related
Computer Related
Computer graphics, CAD/CAM and CAE
Computer mainframes
Computer services
Memory devices
Micro and mini computers
Office automation
Scanning related
Software-applications
Software-artificial intelligence
Software-systems
Specialized turnkey systems
Terminals
**Electronic Components and
   Instrumentation**
Analytical and scientific instrumentation
Component fabrication and testing
   equipment
Electronic components
Fiber optics
Laser related
Semiconductors
Energy/Natural Resources
Technology related products/equipment
Industrial Products and Equipment
Controls and sensors
Energy management
Equipment and machinery
Other industrial automation
Robotics/vision systems
Medical/Health Related
Diagnostic equipment

Additional Information
Year Founded—1967
Method of Compensation—Return on
   investment is of primary concern; do not
   charge fees

FIRST CHICAGO VENTURE CAPITAL

133 Federal Street
Boston, MA 02110
617-542-9185

Kevin M. McCafferty, V.P.
Darius G. Nevin, Inv. Mgr.
David F. Mosher, Inv. Mgr.
Robert F. Compton, Inv. Analyst

See ILLINOIS for full listing

FLEET VENTURE PARTNERS

60 State Street
Boston, MA 02109
617-367-6700

James A. Saalfield, Gen. Ptnr.

See RHODE ISLAND for full listing

FOSTER DYKEMA CABOT & CO., INC.

50 Milk Street
Boston, MA 02109
617-423-3900

Officers
Jere H. DyKema, Chm.
Robert E. Gibbons, Pres.
Frank H. Foster, Financial Analyst

Whom to Contact
Frank H. Foster
Robert E. Gibbons

Type of Firm
Investment banking or merchant banking
   firm investing own capital or funds of
   partners or clients
Consulting firm evaluating and analyzing
   venture projects and arranging private
   placements

Project Preferences
Prefer role as deal originator
Type of Financing:
Seed
Startup
First-stage
Second-stage
Leveraged buyout

Minimum Investment: $500,000
Preferred Investment: Over $1 million
Minimum Operating Data:
Annual Sales—Nominal
P&L—Losses (profits projected after 2 years)

Geographical Preference
Northeast

Industry Preferences
None

Additional Information
Year Founded—1964
Method of Compensation—Function primarily
   in service area; receive contingent fee in
   cash or equity

FOWLER, ANTHONY & CO.

20 Walnut Street
Wellesley, MA 02181
617-237-4201

Officer
John A. Quagliaroli, Pres.

Type of Firm
Private venture capital firm investing
   own capital
Consulting firm evaluating and analyzing
   venture projects and arranging private
   placements
Mergers and acquisitions

Project Preferences
Prefer role as deal originator but will also
   invest in deals created by others
Type of Financing:
Seed
Startup
First-stage
Second-stage
Later-stage expansion
Leveraged buyout
Minimum Investment: Less than $100,000
Preferred Investment: $250,000-$500,000
Minimum Operating Data:
Annual Sales—Nominal

Geographical Preference
Northeast

Industry Preferences

Communications
Cable television
Commercial communications
Data communications
Digital signal processing
Enhancement devices
Network control products
Satellite and microwave communications
Telephone related

Computer Related
Computer graphics, CAD/CAM and CAE
Computer services
Memory devices
Micro and mini computers
Office automation
Scanning related
Software-applications
Software-artificial intelligence
Software-systems
Specialized turnkey systems
Terminals

Consumer
Consumer products
Consumer services
Leisure and recreational products
Specialty retailing

Distribution
Communications equipment
Computer equipment
Electronics equipment
Industrial products
Medical products

Electronic Components and Instrumentation
Analytical and scientific instrumentation
Component fabrication and testing equipment
Electronic components
Fiber optics
Laser related
Other optics technology
Semiconductors

Energy/Natural Resources
Alternative energy
Technology related products/equipment

Genetic Engineering
Gene splicing and manufacturing equipment
Recombinant DNA (agricultural and industrial)

Industrial Products and Equipment
Chemicals
Controls and sensors
Equipment and machinery
Other industrial automation
Robotics/vision systems
Specialty materials

Medical/Health Related
Diagnostic equipment
Diagnostic test products
Disposable products
Drugs and medicines
Health maintenance organizations
Home health care
Hospital and clinical labs
Medical services
Therapeutic equipment

Other
Corporate information services
Electronic publishing
On-line database products and services
Publishing

Additional Information
Year Founded—1976
Investments(1985-1st 6 months)—2
Method of Compensation—Function primarily in service area; receive contingent fee in cash or equity

---

GENERAL ELECTRIC VENTURE CAPITAL CORPORATION

Exchange Place, Floor 14
Boston, MA 02109
617-227-7922

Andrew C. Bangser, V.P.

See CONNECTICUT for full listing

THE GENESIS VENTURE CAPITAL GROUP, INC.

100 Fifth Avenue
Waltham, MA 02154
617-890-4499

Officers
Arnold L. Mende, Pres.

Type of Firm
Investment banking or merchant banking firm investing own capital or funds of partners or clients

Project Preferences
Prefer role as deal originator but will also invest in deals created by others

Type of Financing:
Seed
Startup
First-stage
Second-stage
Later-stage expansion
Leveraged buyout
Minimum Investment: Less than $100,000
Preferred Investment: Over $1 million
Preferred Investment (LBO):
$1 million-$5 million
Minimum Operating Data:
Annual Sales—Nominal
P&L—Losses (profits projected after 1 year)
Annual Sales (LBO)—$5 million-$50 million

Geographical Preference
None

Industry Preferences

Communications
Data communications
Satellite and microwave communications

Computer Related
Computer graphics, CAD/CAM and CAE
Computer mainframes
Computer services
Memory devices
Micro and mini computers
Office automation
Scanning related
Software-applications
Software-artificial intelligence
Software-systems
Specialized turnkey systems
Terminals

Consumer
Computer stores/related services
Consumer products
Consumer services
Food and beverage products
Franchise businesses
Hotels and resort areas
Leisure and recreational products
Restaurants
Retailing

Distribution
Communications equipment
Computer equipment
Consumer products
Electronics equipment
Food products
Industrial products
Medical products

Electronic Components and Instrumentation
Analytical and scientific instrumentation
Component fabrication and testing equipment
Electronic components
Fiber optics
Laser related
Semiconductors
Industrial Products and Equipment
Chemicals
Controls and sensors
Energy management
Equipment and machinery
Other industrial automation
Plastics
Robotics/vision systems
Specialty materials
Other
Agriculture, forestry, fishing
Education related
Finance and insurance
Publishing
Real estate
Specialty consulting
Transportation

Additional Information
Year Founded—1970
Capital Under Management—$40 million
Investments(1985-1st 6 months)—3
Invested(1985-1st 6 months)—$2.5 million
Method of Compensation—Return on investment is most important, but also charge for closing fees, service fees, etc.

GLOBAL INVESTMENTS LIMITED PARTNERSHIP

600 Atlantic Avenue #2000
Boston, MA 02210
617-973-9680

Officers
Matthias Plum, Jr., Pres.
Bradford S. Wallace, Assoc.

Whom to Contact
Matthias Plum, Jr.

Type of Firm
Private venture capital firm investing own capital

Affiliation
General Investment & Development Co. (affiliate)

Project Preferences
Will function either as deal originator or investor in deals created by others
Type of Financing:
Seed
Startup
First-stage
Second-stage
Later-stage expansion
Leveraged buyout
Minimum Investment: Less than $100,000 (if follow-on round is anticipated)
Preferred Investment: $250,000-$500,000
Minimum Operating Data:
Annual Sales—Nominal
P&L—Losses (profits projected after 3 years)

Geographical Preference
Within two hours of office

Industry Preferences
None

Additional Information
Year Founded—1982
Investments(1985-1st 6 months)—4
Invested(1985-1st 6 months)—$1 million
Method of Compensation—Return on investment is of primary concern; do not charge fees

---

GREYHOUND CAPITAL MANAGEMENT CORPORATION

8 New England Executive Park
Burlington, MA 01803
617-272-8110

John B. Schroeder, Dir. Venture Inv.

See ARIZONA for full listing

GREYLOCK MANAGEMENT CORPORATION

One Federal Street
Boston, MA 02110
617-423-5525

Officers
Daniel S. Gregory, Chm.
Robert P. Henderson, Vice Chm.
Charles P. Waite, Pres.
Henry F. McCance, V.P. & Treas.
Howard E. Cox, Jr., V.P.
David N. Strohm, V.P.
William H. Helman, Assoc.

Whom to Contact
William H. Helman
Henry F. McCance
Howard E. Cox, Jr.
David N. Strohm

Type of Firm
Private venture capital partnerships investing own capital

Industry Association Membership
NVCA

Project Preferences
Will function either as deal originator or investor in deals created by others
Type of Financing:
Startup
First-stage
Second-stage
Later-stage expansion
Minimum Investment: $250,000
Preferred Investment: Over $1 million

Geographical Preference
National

Industry Preferences

Communications
Cable television
Commercial communications
Data communications
Satellite and microwave communications
Telephone related

Computer Related
Computer graphics, CAD/CAM and CAE
Computer mainframes
Computer services
Memory devices
Micro and mini computers
Office automation
Software-applications
Software-systems
Terminals
Distribution
Communications equipment
Computer equipment
Medical products
**Electronic Components and
 Instrumentation**
Analytical and scientific instrumentation
Electronic components
Fiber optics
Other optics technology
Semiconductors
Energy/Natural Resources
Services
Technology related products/equipment
Genetic Engineering
Monoclonal antibodies and hybridomas
Recombinant DNA (agricultural and
 industrial)
Recombinant DNA (medical)
Industrial Products and Equipment
Advanced materials
Chemicals
Equipment and machinery
Other industrial automation systems
Medical/Health Related
Diagnostic equipment
Diagnostic test products
Disposable products
Hospital and clinical labs
Medical services
Therapeutic equipment

Additional Information
Year Founded—1965
Capital Under Management—
 Over $150 million
Investments(1985-1st 6 months)—10
Invested(1985-1st 6 months)—$12 million
Method of Compensation—Return on
 investment is of primary concern; do not
 charge fees

HAMBRECHT & QUIST VENTURE PARTNERS

One Hollis Street #102
Wellesley, MA 02181
617-237-2099

Robert M. Morrill, Gen. Ptnr.
Patrick J. Sansonnetti, Gen. Ptnr.

See CALIFORNIA for full listing

HAMBRO INTERNATIONAL VENTURE FUND

One Boston Place #923
Boston, MA 02108
617-722-7055

Richard A. D'Amore, Gen. Ptnr.
Robert S. Sherman, Gen. Ptnr.

See NEW YORK for full listing

JOHN HANCOCK VENTURE CAPITAL MANAGEMENT, INC.

200 Clarendon Street
Post Office Box 111
Boston, MA 02117
617-421-6231

Officers
Edward W. Kane, Mgn. Dir.
D. Brooks Zug, Mgn. Dir.
William A. Johnston, Sr. Inv. Officer
Robert J. Lepkowski, Inv. Officer
Nancy C. Raulston, Inv. Officer
Laurie J. Thomsen, Asst. Inv. Officer
Frederick C. Maynard III, Inv. Analyst
Daniel Baldini, Inv. Analyst

Whom to Contact
Edward W. Kane
D. Brooks Zug

Type of Firm
Limited partnership

Affiliation
John Hancock Mutual Life Insurance
 Company (parent)

Industry Association Membership
NVCA

Project Preferences
Prefer role in deals created by others
Type of Financing:
Seed
Startup
First-stage
Second-stage
Later-stage expansion
Leveraged buyout
Minimum Investment: $500,000
Preferred Investment: $500,000-$1 million
Preferred Investment (LBO):
 $1 million-$3 million
Minimum Operating Data:
Annual Sales—Nominal
P&L—Losses (profits projected after 2 years)
Annual Sales (LBO)—$20 million-$100 million

Geographical Preference
None

Industry Preferences

Communications
Cable television
Commercial communications
Data communications
Satellite and microwave communications
Telephone related
Computer Related
Computer graphics, CAD/CAM and CAE
Computer mainframes
Computer services
Memory devices
Micro and mini computers
Office automation
Scanning related
Software-applications
Software-artificial intelligence
Software-systems
Specialized turnkey systems
Terminals
Consumer
Computer stores/related services
Consumer services
Franchise businesses
Retailing
Distribution
Communications equipment
Computer equipment
Consumer products
Electronics equipment
Medical products

Electronic Components and Instrumentation
Analytical and scientific instrumentation
Component fabrication and testing equipment
Electronic components
Fiber optics
Laser related
Semiconductors
Energy/Natural Resources
Technology related products/equipment
Genetic Engineering
Gene splicing and manufacturing equipment
Monoclonal antibodies and hybridomas
Recombinant DNA (agricultural and industrial)
Recombinant DNA (medical)
Industrial Products and Equipment
Energy management
Robotics/vision systems
Specialty materials
Medical/Health Related
Diagnostic equipment
Diagnostic test products
Disposable products
Drugs and medicines
Hospital and clinical labs
Medical services
Therapeutic equipment

Additional Information
Year Founded—1982
Method of Compensation—Return on investment is of primary concern; do not charge fees

---

HARBOUR FINANCIAL COMPANY

45 Milk Street
Boston, MA 02109
617-426-8106

Officer
John R. Schwanbeck, Pres.

Type of Firm
Investment banking or merchant banking firm investing own capital or funds of partners or clients

Project Preferences
Prefer role as deal originator but will also invest in deals created by others
Type of Financing:
Startup
First-stage
Second-stage
Leveraged buyout

Minimum Investment: $500,000
Preferred Investment: Over $1 million
Preferred Investment (LBO): $1 million
Minimum Operating Data:
Annual Sales—Nominal
P&L—Losses (profits projected after 2 years)
Annual Sales (LBO)—$15 million and over

Geographical Preference
Northeast

Industry Preferences

Communications
Data communications
Computer Related
Computer graphics, CAD/CAM and CAE
Computer mainframes
Computer services
Memory devices
Micro and mini computers
Office automation
Scanning related
Software-applications
Software-artificial intelligence
Software-systems
Specialized turnkey systems
Terminals
Electronic Components and Instrumentation
Analytical and scientific instrumentation
Component fabrication and testing equipment
Electronic components
Fiber optics
Laser related
Semiconductors
Genetic Engineering
Gene splicing and manufacturing equipment
Monoclonal antibodies and hybridomas
Recombinant DNA (agricultural and industrial)
Recombinant DNA (medical)
Industrial Products and Equipment
Chemicals
Controls and sensors
Energy management
Equipment and machinery
Other industrial automation
Plastics
Robotics/vision systems
Specialty materials
Medical/Health Related
Diagnostic equipment
Diagnostic test products
Disposable products
Drugs and medicines
Hospital and clinical labs
Medical services
Therapeutic equipment

Additional Information
Year Founded—1980
Method of Compensation—Function primarily in service area; receive contingent fee in cash or equity

---

HLM PARTNERS

10 Liberty Square
Boston, MA 02109
617-423-3530

General Partners
A.R. Haberkorn III
Judith P. Lawrie
James J. Mahoney, Jr.

Whom to Contact
Any of the above

Type of Firm
Private venture capital firm investing own capital

Project Preferences
Prefer role in deals created by others
Type of Financing:
Second-stage
Later-stage expansion
Minimum Investment: $500,000
Preferred Investment: $500,000-$1 million
Minimum Operating Data:
Annual Sales—Over $3 million
P&L—Losses (profits projected after 1 year)

Geographical Preference
None

Industry Preferences

Communications
Cable television
Commercial communications
Data communications
Satellite and microwave communications
Telephone related
Computer Related
Computer graphics, CAD/CAM and CAE
Computer mainframes
Computer services
Memory devices
Micro and mini computers
Office automation
Scanning related
Software-applications
Software-artificial intelligence
Software-systems
Specialized turnkey systems
Terminals

Consumer
Computer stores/related services
Consumer products
Consumer services
Food and beverage products
Franchise businesses
Hotels and resort areas
Leisure and recreational products
Restaurants
Retailing
Distribution
Communications equipment
Computer equipment
Consumer products
Electronics equipment
Food products
Industrial products
Medical products
Electronic Components and Instrumentation
Analytical and scientific instrumentation
Component fabrication and testing equipment
Electronic components
Fiber optics
Laser related
Semiconductors
Energy/Natural Resources
Alternative energy
Coal related
Drilling and exploration services
Energy conservation
Minerals
Oil and gas exploration and production
Technology related products/equipment
Genetic Engineering
Gene splicing and manufacturing equipment
Monoclonal antibodies and hybridomas
Recombinant DNA (agricultural and industrial)
Recombinant DNA (medical)
Industrial Products and Equipment
Chemicals
Controls and sensors
Energy management
Equipment and machinery
Other industrial automation
Plastics
Robotics/vision systems
Specialty materials
Medical/Health Related
Diagnostic equipment
Diagnostic test products
Disposable products
Drugs and medicines
Hospital and clinical labs
Medical services
Therapeutic equipment

Other
Education related
Finance and insurance
Publishing
Specialty consulting
Transportation

Additional Information
Year Founded—1984
Capital Under Management—$100 million
Method of Compensation—Return on investment is of primary concern; do not charge fees

---

INVESTORS IN INDUSTRY (3i)

3i CAPITAL

99 High Street #1530
Boston, MA 02110
617-542-8560

Other Office
450 Newport Center Drive #250
Newport Beach, CA 92660
714-720-1421

Officers
David R. Shaw, Pres.
Thomas A. Ballantyne, V.P.
Kevin J. Dougherty, V.P.
William N. Holm, Jr., V.P.
David Warnock, V.P.
Peter J. Bollier, Treas.

Whom to Contact
Any of the above (Massachusetts)

Type of Firm
Subsidiary of U.K. financial institution

Affiliation
Investors in Industry plc, London, England

Project Preferences
Will function either as deal originator or investor in deals created by others
Type of Financing:
Second-stage
Later-stage expansion
Leveraged buyout
Purchase of secondary positions
Minimum Investment: $500,000
Preferred Investment: Over $1 million
Minimum Operating Data:
Annual Sales—$1.5 million
P&L—Break even

Geographical Preferences
East Coast
West Coast

Industry Preferences

Communications
Cable television
Commercial communications
Data communications
Satellite and microwave communications
Telephone related
Computer Related
Computer graphics, CAD/CAM and CAE
Computer mainframes
Computer services
Micro and mini computers
Office automation
Software-applications
Software-systems
Consumer
Consumer products
Consumer services
Food and beverage products
Franchise businesses
Leisure and recreational products
Retailing
Distribution
Communications equipment
Consumer products
Electronics equipment
Food products
Industrial products
Medical products
Electronic Components and Instrumentation
Analytical and scientific instrumentation
Electronic components
Semiconductors
Energy/Natural Resources
Services
Genetic Engineering
Monoclonal antibodies and hybridomas
Research and manufacturing equipment
Industrial Products and Equipment
Advanced materials
Chemicals
Equipment and machinery
Other industrial automation
Plastics
Process control
Medical/Health Related
Diagnostic equipment
Hospital and clinical labs
Medical services

Other
Agriculture, forestry, fishing
Publishing
Transportation
Particular interest in transatlantic activities
Will Not Consider
Real estate

INVESTORS IN INDUSTRY (3i)

3i VENTURES

99 High Street #1530
Boston, MA 02110
617-542-8560

See CALIFORNIA for full listing

ARTHUR D. LITTLE ENTERPRISES, INC.

20 Acorn Park
Cambridge, MA 02140
617-864-5770

Officers
Walter J. Cairns, Pres.
Paul J. Ballantine, Treas.

Whom to Contact
Either of the above

Type of Firm
Venture capital subsidiary or affiliate of non-financial corporation

Affiliation
Arthur D. Little, Inc. (parent)

Project Preferences
Prefer role as deal originator but will also invest in deals created by others
Type of Financing:
Seed
Startup
First-stage
Second-stage
Minimum Investment: $250,000
Preferred Investment: $300,000-$600,000
Minimum Operating Data:
Annual Sales—Nominal
P&L—Losses (profits projected after 1 year)

Geographical Preference
Within two hours of office

Industry Preferences

Communications
Data communications
Telephone related
Computer Related
Computer graphics, CAD/CAM and CAE
Computer mainframes
Computer services
Memory devices
Micro and mini computers
Office automation
Scanning related
Software-applications
Software-artificial intelligence
Software-systems
Specialized turnkey systems
Terminals
Consumer
Consumer products
Leisure and recreational products
Electronic Components and Instrumentation
Analytical and scientific instrumentation
Component fabrication and testing equipment
Electronic components
Fiber optics
Laser related
Semiconductors
Energy/Natural Resources
Alternative energy
Coal related
Energy conservation
Technology related products/equipment
Genetic Engineering
Gene splicing and manufacturing equipment
Monoclonal antibodies and hybridomas
Recombinant DNA (agricultural and industrial)
Recombinant DNA (medical)
Industrial Products and Equipment
Chemicals
Controls and sensors
Energy management
Equipment and machinery
Other industrial automation
Plastics
Robotics/vision systems
Specialty materials
Medical/Health Related
Diagnostic equipment
Diagnostic test products
Disposable products
Drugs and medicines
Hospital and clinical labs
Medical services
Therapeutic equipment
Other
Agriculture, forestry, fishing
Education related
Transportation

Additional Information
Year Founded—1984
Capital Under Management—$15 million
Investments(1985-1st 6 months)—3
Invested(1985-1st 6 months)—$1.5 million
Method of Compensation—Return on investment is most important, but also charge for closing fees, service fees, etc.

MASSACHUSETTS COMMUNITY DEVELOPMENT FINANCE CORP.

131 State Street
Boston, MA 02109
617-742-0366

Officers
Charles T. Grigsby, Pres.
Nancy Nye, V.P.
Judith Cranna, Inv. Officer
Anne Kesson-Lowell, Inv. Analyst

Whom to Contact
Any of the above

Type of Firm
State-owned venture capital company

Project Preferences
Will function either as deal originator or investor in deals created by others
Type of Financing:
Startup
First-stage
Second-stage
Later-stage expansion
Leveraged buyout
Minimum Investment: $100,000
Preferred Investment: $100,000-$250,000

Geographical Preference
Massachusetts only

Industry Preferences

Industrial Products and Equipment
Manufacturing

Additional Information
Year Founded—1975
Capital Under Management—$10 million
Investments(1985-1st 6 months)—4
Invested(1985-1st 6 months)—$475,000
Method of Compensation—Return on investment is of primary concern

MASSACHUSETTS TECHNOLOGY DEVELOPMENT CORPORATION

84 State Street #500
Boston, MA 02109
617-723-4920

Officers
John F. Hodgman, Pres.
Robert J. Crowley, V.P.
Susan Master-Karnik, Dir. Finance
Laura Morrissette, Inv. Analyst
Jeffrey Davison, Inv. Analyst
Gary Katz, Inv. Analyst
Barbara Plantholt, Consultant

Whom to Contact
John F. Hodgman
Robert J. Crowley

Type of Firm
Independent state agency providing venture capital financing to new and expanding technology companies in Massachusetts

Industry Association Membership
NASBIC

Project Preferences
Will function either as deal originator or investor in deals created by others
Type of Financing:
Startup
First-stage
Minimum Investment: Less than $100,000
Preferred Investment: $100,000-$250,000
Minimum Operating Data:
Annual Sales—Nominal

Geographical Preference
Massachusetts only

Industry Preferences

Communications
Commercial communications
Data communications
Satellite and microwave communications
Telephone related

Computer Related
Computer graphics, CAD/CAM and CAE
Computer mainframes
Computer services
Memory devices
Micro and mini computers
Office automation
Scanning related
Software-applications
Software-artificial intelligence
Software-systems
Specialized turnkey systems
Terminals
Consumer
Consumer products
Distribution
Electronics equipment
Electronic Components and Instrumentation
Analytical and scientific instrumentation
Component fabrication and testing equipment
Electronic components
Fiber optics
Laser related
Semiconductors
Energy/Natural Resources
Alternative energy
Genetic Engineering
Recombinant DNA (agricultural and industrial)
Recombinant DNA (medical)
Industrial Products and Equipment
Chemicals
Controls and sensors
Energy management
Equipment and machinery
Other industrial automation
Plastics
Robotics/vision systems
Specialty materials
Medical/Health Related
Diagnostic equipment
Diagnostic test products
Therapeutic equipment
Other
Agriculture, forestry, fishing
Will Not Consider
Non technology-based industries

Additional Information
Year Founded—1978
Capital Under Management—$10 million
Investments(1985-1st 6 months)—7
Invested(1985-1st 6 months)—$1 million
Method of Compensation—Return on investment is of primary concern; do not charge fees

MATRIX PARTNERS, L.P.

One Post Office Square
Boston, MA 02109
617-482-7735

West Coast Office
224 West Brokaw Road
San Jose, CA 95110
408-298-0270

Partners
Paul J. Ferri, Gen. Ptnr. (Massachusetts)
Frederick K. Fluegel, Gen. Ptnr. (California)
F. Warren Hellman, Gen. Ptnr. (California)
W. Michael Humphreys, Gen. Ptnr. (Massachusetts)
Glen McLaughlin, Gen. Ptnr. (California)
Timothy A. Barrows, Associate (Massachusetts)

Whom to Contact
Any of the above

Type of Firm
Private venture capital firm investing own capital

Industry Association Membership
NVCA

Project Preferences
Will function either as deal originator or investor in deals created by others
Type of Financing:
Startup
First-stage
Second-stage
Leveraged buyout
Minimum Investment: $250,000
Preferred Investment: $500,000-$1 million
Minimum Operating Data:
Annual Sales—Nominal

Geographical Preference
None

Industry Preferences

Communications
Cable television
Commercial communications
Data communications
Satellite and microwave communications

Computer Related
Computer graphics, CAD/CAM and CAE
Computer mainframes
Computer services
Micro and mini computers
Office automation
Scanning related
Software-applications
Software-systems
Specialized turnkey systems
Electronic Components and Instrumentation
Analytical and scientific instrumentation
Component fabrication and testing equipment
Fiber optics
Semiconductors
Medical/Health Related
Diagnostic equipment
Drugs and medicines
Hospital and clinical labs
Medical services
Will Not Consider
Natural resources
Real estate development

Additional Information

Year Founded—1982
Capital Under Management—$115 million
Investments(1985-1st 6 months)—7
Invested(1985-1st 6 months)—$3.7 million
Method of Compensation—Return on investment is of primary concern; do not charge fees

MCGOWAN, LECKINGER, BERG

10 Forbes Road
Braintree, MA 02184
617-849-0020

Partners

James A. McGowan, Gen. Ptnr.
Robert T. Leckinger, Gen. Ptnr.
Stan Berg, Gen. Ptnr.
Frank Casal, Assoc.
Murt Hunt, Assoc.

Whom to Contact

Any of the above

Type of Firm

Co-investment agreement with First Capital Corporation of Chicago

Affiliation

First Capital Corporation of Chicago

Project Preferences

Prefer role as deal originator but will also invest in deals created by others
Type of Financing:
First-stage
Second-stage
Later-stage expansion
Leveraged buyout
Minimum Investment: $500,000
Preferred Investment: $500,000-$10 million
Minimum Operating Data:
Annual Sales—Nominal

Geographical Preference

National

Industry Preferences

Consumer
Retailing
Will Not Consider
Non-retail businesses

Additional Information

Year Founded—1984
Capital Under Management—$20 million
Investments(1985-1st 6 months)—3
Method of Compensation—Return on investment is of primary concern

MEMORIAL DRIVE TRUST

20 Acorn Park
Cambridge, MA 02140
617-864-5770

Officer

J.E. de Valpine, Admin. & CEO
Schorr Berman, Inv. Officer
Jay V. Senerchia, Inv. Officer
Paul D. Shuwall, Inv. Officer

Whom to Contact

Schorr Berman
Jay V. Senerchia
Paul D. Shuwall

Type of Firm

Private venture capital firm investing own capital

Industry Association Membership

NVCA

Project Preferences

Will function either as deal originator or investor in deals created by others

Type of Financing:

Second-stage
Leveraged buyout
Minimum Investment: $750,000
Preferred Investment: $1 million or more
Minimum Operating Data:
Annual Sales—Nominal

Geographical Preference

None

Industry Preferences

Communications
Cable television
Commercial communications
Data communications
Satellite and microwave communications
Telephone related
Computer Related
Artificial intelligence hardware and software
Computer graphics, CAD/CAM and CAE
Computer mainframes
Computer services
Computer-integrated manufacturing
Memory devices
Micro and mini computers
Office automation
Scanning related
Software-applications
Software-systems
Specialized turnkey systems
Terminals
Electronic Components and Instrumentation
Analytical and scientific instrumentation
Component fabrication and testing equipment
Electronic components
Fiber optics
Laser related
Semiconductors
Energy/Natural Resources
Coal related
Drilling and exploration services
Energy conservation
Oil and gas exploration and production
Technology related products/equipment
Genetic Engineering
Recombinant DNA (agricultural and industrial)
Recombinant DNA (medical)
Industrial Products and Equipment
Chemicals
Controls and sensors
Energy management
Equipment and machinery
Other industrial automation
Plastics
Robotics/vision systems
Specialty materials

Medical/Health Related
Diagnostic equipment
Drugs and medicines
Hospital and clinical labs
Other
Agriculture, forestry, fishing
Transportation

Additional Information
Year Founded—1951
Capital Under Management—$300 million
Investments(1985-1st 6 months)—12
Invested(1985-1st 6 months)—$6 million
Method of Compensation—Return on
   investment is of primary concern; do not
   charge fees

MORGAN, HOLLAND FUND L.P.

One Liberty Square
Boston, MA 02109
617-423-1765

Partners
James F. Morgan, Gen. Ptnr.
Daniel J. Holland, Gen. Ptnr.
Robert L. Rosbe, Jr., Gen. Ptnr.
Jay Delahanty, Gen. Ptnr.
Edwin M. Kania, Jr., Assoc.

Whom to Contact
Jay Delahanty
Robert L. Rosbe, Jr.
Edwin M. Kania, Jr.

Type of Firm
Private venture capital firm investing
   own capital

Industry Association Memberships
NASBIC
NVCA

Project Preferences
Will function either as deal originator or
   investor in deals created by others
Type of Financing:
Startup
First-stage
Second-stage
Later-stage expansion
Leveraged buyout
Minimum Investment: $100,000
Preferred Investment: $500,000-$1 million
Minimum Operating Data:
Annual Sales—Nominal
P&L—Losses (profits projected after 2 years)

Geographical Preference
National

Industry Preferences

Communications
Data communications
Satellite and microwave communications
Telephone related
Computer Related
Computer graphics, CAD/CAM and CAE
Computer mainframes
Computer services
Memory devices
Micro and mini computers
Office automation
Scanning related
Software-applications
Software-artificial intelligence
Software-systems
Specialized turnkey systems
Terminals
Distribution
Medical products
**Electronic Components and
   Instrumentation**
Analytical and scientific instrumentation
Component fabrication and testing
   equipment
Electronic components
Fiber optics
Laser related
Semiconductors
Energy/Natural Resources
Alternative energy
Drilling and exploration services
Technology related products/equipment
Genetic Engineering
Gene splicing and manufacturing equipment
Monoclonal antibodies and hybridomas
Recombinant DNA (agricultural and
   industrial)
Recombinant DNA (medical)
Industrial Products and Equipment
Chemicals
Controls and sensors
Equipment and machinery
Other industrial automation
Plastics
Robotics/vision systems
Specialty materials
Medical/Health Related
Diagnostic equipment
Diagnostic test products
Disposable products
Drugs and medicines
Hospital and clinical labs
Medical services
Therapeutic equipment

Other
Agriculture, forestry, fishing
Education related
Transportation
Will Not Consider
Real estate
Oil and gas exploration

Additional Information
Year Founded—1982
Capital Under Management—$58.5 million
Method of Compensation—Return on
   investment is of primary concern; do not
   charge fees

NEW ENGLAND CAPITAL
CORPORATION

One Washington Mall
Seventh Floor
Boston, MA 02108
617-722-6400

Officers
Z. David Patterson, Exec. V.P.
Stuart D. Pompian, V.P.
Thomas C. Tremblay, V.P.

Whom to Contact
Stuart D. Pompian
Thomas C. Tremblay

Type of Firm
SBIC
Venture capital subsidiary of
   commercial bank

Affiliation
Bank of New England Corporation (parent)

Industry Association Memberships
NASBIC
NVCA

Project Preferences
Will function either as deal originator or
   investor in deals created by others
Type of Financing:
Second-stage
Leveraged buyout
Growth capital
Minimum Investment: $250,000
Preferred Investment: $500,000-$1 million
Minimum Operating Data:
Annual Sales—$500,000
P&L—Break even
Annual Sales (LBO)—$2 million-$50 million

Geographical Preference
Northeast

Industry Preferences

Communications
Cable television
Commercial communications
Data communications
Telephone related
Computer Related
Computer graphics, CAD/CAM and CAE
Computer services
Memory devices
Micro and mini computers
Office automation
Scanning related
Software-applications
Software-artificial intelligence
Software-systems
Specialized turnkey systems
Terminals
Distribution
Communications equipment
Industrial products
Medical products
**Electronic Components and
   Instrumentation**
Analytical and scientific instrumentation
Component fabrication and testing
   equipment
Electronic components
Fiber optics
Laser related
Semiconductors
Industrial Products and Equipment
Chemicals
Controls and sensors
Energy management
Equipment and machinery
Other industrial automation
Plastics
Robotics/vision systems
Specialty materials
Medical/Health Related
Diagnostic equipment
Diagnostic test products
Disposable products
Drugs and medicines
Hospital and clinical labs
Medical services
Therapeutic equipment
Will Not Consider
Entertainment
Real estate

Additional Information
Year Founded—1961
Capital Under Management—$15 million
Investments(1985-1st 6 months)—6
Invested(1985-1st 6 months)—$2.3 million
Method of Compensation—Return on
   investment is of primary concern; do not
   charge fees

NEW ENGLAND MESBIC, INC.

50 Kearney Road #3
Needham, MA 02194
617-449-2066

Officers
Dr. Etang Chen, Pres.
Dr. San-Lang Lien, Treas.
Chris Chen, Mgr.

Whom to Contact
Dr. Etang Chen

Type of Firm
MESBIC

Project Preferences
Will function either as deal originator or
   investor in deals created by others
Type of Financing:
Second-stage
Leveraged buyout
Minimum Investment: $100,000
Preferred Investment: $100,000-$250,000
Minimum Operating Data:
Annual Sales—Nominal
P&L—Break even

Geographical Preferences
Within two hours of office
Northeast

Industry Preferences

Communications
Cable television
Commercial communications
Data communications
Satellite and microwave communications
Telephone related

Computer Related
Computer graphics, CAD/CAM and CAE
Computer mainframes
Computer services
Memory devices
Micro and mini computers
Office automation
Scanning related
Software-applications
Software-artificial intelligence
Software-systems
Specialized turnkey systems
Terminals
Consumer
Computer stores/related services
Consumer products
Consumer services
Food and beverage products
Franchise businesses
Hotels and resort areas
Leisure and recreational products
Restaurants
Retailing
Distribution
Communications equipment
Computer equipment
Consumer products
Electronics equipment
Food products
Industrial products
Medical products
**Electronic Components and
   Instrumentation**
Analytical and scientific instrumentation
Component fabrication and testing
   equipment
Electronic components
Fiber optics
Laser related
Semiconductors
Energy/Natural Resources
Technology related products/equipment
Genetic Engineering
Monoclonal antibodies and hybridomas
Industrial Products and Equipment
Chemicals
Controls and sensors
Energy management
Equipment and machinery
Other industrial automation
Plastics
Robotics/vision systems
Specialty materials
Medical/Health Related
Diagnostic equipment
Diagnostic test products
Disposable products
Drugs and medicines
Hospital and clinical labs
Medical services
Therapeutic equipment

Other
Publishing

Additional Information
Year Founded—1982
Capital Under Management—$1.7 million
Investments(1985-1st 6 months)—7
Invested(1985-1st 6 months)—$500,000
Method of Compensation—Return on
 investment is of primary concern; do not
 charge fees

ORANGE NASSAU

260 Franklin Street
Boston, MA 02110
617-451-6220

Other Offices
One Galleria Tower #635
13355 Noel Road
Dallas, TX 75240
214-385-9685

Westerley Place #540
1500 Quail Street
Newport Beach, CA 92660
714-752-7811

Officers
Joost E. Tjaden, Mgn. Dir. (Massachusetts)
Richard D. Tadler, V.P. (Massachusetts)
Linda S. Linsalata, V.P. (Massachussetts)
John W. Blackburn, V.P. (California)
Gregory B. Peters, Assoc. (Massachusetts)
Martin J. Silver, Assoc. (Texas)
F. Dan Blanchard, Assoc. (Texas)
Benjamin G. Dawson, Inv. Analyst
 (Massachusetts)
David P. Carmack, Inv. Analyst (California)

Whom to Contact
Any of the above

Type of Firm
Venture capital subsidiary of financial
 operating company

Affiliations
The Orange Nassau Group, The Hague,
 The Netherlands
Alpha Associes S.A, Paris, France
Southeast Asean Venture Investment
 Company, Singapore
Bever Investments C.V., The Hague,
 The Netherlands

Industry Association Memberships
NASBIC
NVCA

Project Preferences
Prefer role as deal originator
Type of Financing:
Startup
First-stage
Second-stage
Later-stage expansion
Leveraged buyout
Minimum Investment: $500,000
Preferred Investment: $500,000-$1 million
Minimum Operating Data:
Annual Sales—Nominal

Geographical Preference
None

Industry Preferences

Communications
Cable television
Commercial communications
Data communications
Satellite and microwave communications
Telephone related
Computer Related
Computer graphics, CAD/CAM and CAE
Computer mainframes
Computer services
Memory devices
Micro and mini computers
Office automation
Scanning related
Software-applications
Software-artificial intelligence
Software-systems
Specialized turnkey systems
Terminals
Consumer
Computer stores/related services
Consumer products
Consumer services
Distribution
Communications equipment
Computer equipment
Consumer products
Electronics equipment
Industrial products
Medical products

**Electronic Components and
 Instrumentation**
Analytical and scientific instrumentation
Component fabrication and testing
 equipment
Electronic components
Fiber optics
Laser related
Optics technology
Semiconductors
Energy/Natural Resources
Energy conservation
Technology related products/equipment
Genetic Engineering
Gene splicing and manufacturing equipment
Monoclonal antibodies and hybridomas
Recombinant DNA (agricultural and
 industrial)
Recombinant DNA (medical)
Industrial Products and Equipment
Chemicals
Controls and sensors
Energy management
Equipment and machinery
Other industrial automation
Plastics
Process control
Robotics/vision systems
Specialty materials
Medical/Health Related
Diagnostic equipment
Diagnostic test products
Disposable products
Drugs and medicines
Hospital and clinical labs
Medical services
Therapeutic equipment
Will Not Consider
Real estate

Additional Information
Year Founded—1980
Method of Compensation—Return on
 investment is of primary concern; do not
 charge fees

PAINE WEBBER MANAGEMENT COMPANY

265 Franklin Street #1501
Boston, MA 02110
617-439-8300

Partners
Richard A. Charpie, Mgn. Gen. Ptnr.
William C. Mills III, Mgn. Gen. Ptnr.
Merlin D. Schulze, Mgn. Gen. Ptnr.
Charles D. Yie, Assoc.
Marcia D. Jacobs, Assoc.

Whom to Contact
Richard A. Charpie
William C. Mills III
Charles D. Yie
Marcia D. Jacobs

Type of Firm
Venture capital subsidiary of a financial
institution investing funds of limited
partners

Affiliations
PaineWebber Inc. (parent)
Ampersand Management Company
(predecessor)

Industry Association Membership
NVCA

Project Preferences
Will function either as deal originator or
investor in deals created by others
Type of Financing:
Startup
First-stage
Second-stage
Later-stage expansion
Leveraged buyout
Minimum Investment: $500,000
Preferred Investment: $500,000-$1 million
Minimum Operating Data:
Annual Sales—Nominal

Geographical Preferences
Northeast
Near major metropolitan area

Industry Preferences

Communications
Commercial communications
Data communications
Satellite and microwave communications
Telephone related

Computer Related
Computer graphics, CAD/CAM and CAE
Computer mainframes
Computer services
Memory devices
Micro and mini computers
Office automation
Scanning related
Software-applications
Software-artificial intelligence
Software-systems
Specialized turnkey systems
Terminals
Electronic Components and Instrumentation
Analytical and scientific instrumentation
Component fabrication and testing
equipment
Electronic components
Fiber optics
Laser related
Semiconductors
Genetic Engineering
Gene splicing and manufacturing equipment
Monoclonal antibodies and hybridomas
Recombinant DNA (agricultural and
industrial)
Recombinant DNA (medical)
Industrial Products and Equipment
Chemicals
Controls and sensors
Energy management
Equipment and machinery
Other industrial automation
Plastics
Robotics/vision systems
Specialty materials
Medical/Health Related
Diagnostic equipment
Diagnostic test products
Disposable products
Drugs and medicines
Hospital and clinical labs
Medical services
Therapeutic equipment
Will Not Consider
Agriculture
Natural resources
Oil and gas
Real estate

Additional Information
Year Founded—Ampersand (predecessor
company) 1970
Capital Under Management—$54 million
Investments(1985-1st 6 months)—9
Invested(1985-1st 6 months)—$3.5 million
Method of Compensation—Return on
investment is of primary concern; do not
charge fees

PALMER PARTNERS

300 Unicorn Park Drive
Woburn, MA 01801
617-933-5445

Partners
William H. Congleton, Gen. Ptnr.
Stephen J. Ricci, Gen. Ptnr.
John A. Shane, Gen. Ptnr.
Karen S. Camp, Ptnr.
Michael T. Fitzgerald, Ptnr.
Alison J. Seavey, Ptnr.

Whom to Contact
Any of the above

Type of Firm
Private venture capital firm investing
own capital

Industry Association Membership
NVCA

Project Preferences
Will function either as deal originator or
investor in deals created by others
Type of Financing:
Seed
Startup
First-stage
Second-stage
Later-stage expansion
Minimum Investment: $100,000
Preferred Investment: $500,000-$1 million
Minimum Operating Data:
Annual Sales—Nominal
P&L—Losses (profits projected after 2 years)

Geographical Preference
None

Industry Preferences
None
Will Not Consider
Real estate

Additional Information
Year Founded—1972
Capital Under Management—$32 million
Investments(1985-1st 6 months)—3
Invested(1985-1st 6 months)—$600,000
Method of Compensation—Return on
investment is of primary concern; do not
charge fees

PLANT RESOURCES VENTURE FUNDS

124 Mount Auburn Street #310
Cambridge, MA 02138
617-492-3900

Principals
John R. Hesse, Mgn. Gen. Ptnr.
Richard C. McGinity, Gen. Ptnr.
Richard O. von Werssowetz, Gen. Ptnr.
Christopher D. Earl, Scientific Assoc.

Whom to Contact
Richard C. McGinity
Richard O. von Werssowetz
John R. Hesse

Type of Firm
Private venture capital firm investing
own capital

Project Preferences
Prefer role as deal originator but will also
invest in deals created by others
Type of Financing:
Startup
First-stage
Minimum Investment: $250,000
Preferred Investment: $500,000-$1 million
Minimum Operating Data:
Annual Sales—Nominal
P&L—Losses (profits projected after 2 years)

Geographical Preference
National

Industry Preferences

**Animal and Plant Related Technologies
and Products**
Agriculture, aquaculture and forestry
Animal reproduction and nutrition
Animal diagnostics
Biological fertilizers
Crop additives and protectants
Plant growth regulators
Consumer
Consumer products in horticulture
and agriculture
Food products
Distribution
Mail order of plants, seeds, food and
similar products
Technologically improved agriculture or plant
related products

Genetic Engineering
Agricultural applications of cellular and
molecular biology
Genetically improved seeds, plants,
and trees
Laboratory equipment
Monoclonal antibodies and hybridomas
Recombinant DNA (agricultural and
industrial)
Industrial Products and Equipment
Advanced food processing equipment
Biological waste treatment processes
and products
Food additives
Waste treatment and recovery systems
Other
Equipment used in food, chemical and
agricultural research
Specialized farm financing, management
and services
Will Not Consider
Communications
Energy
Medical/human health related

Additional Information
Year Founded—1981
Capital Under Management—$57.8 million
Investments(1985-1st 6 months)—5
Invested(1985-1st 6 months)—$1.5 million
Method of Compensation—Return on
investment is most important, but also
charge for closing fees, service fees, etc.

RAYTHEON VENTURES

100 Hayden Avenue
Lexington, MA 02173
617-860-4703

Officers
David R.A. Steadman, Pres.
Clyde E. Rettig, V.P.

Whom to Contact
Either of the above

Type of Firm
Venture capital subsidiary or affiliate of
non-financial corporation

Affiliation
Raytheon Company (parent)

Project Preferences
Will function either as deal originator or
investor in deals created by others

Type of Financing:
Startup
First-stage
Second-stage
Later-stage expansion
Minimum Investment: $250,000
Preferred Investment: $500,000-$1 million
Minimum Operating Data:
Annual Sales—Nominal
P&L—Losses (profits projected after 3 years)

Geographical Preference
None

Industry Preferences

Communications
Satellite and microwave communications
Computer Related
Computer graphics, CAD/CAM and CAE
Memory devices
Micro and mini computers
Scanning related
Software-artificial intelligence
Software-systems
**Electronic Components and
Instrumentation**
Analytical and scientific instrumentation
Component fabrication and testing
equipment
Electronic components
Fiber optics
Laser related
Semiconductors
Energy/Natural Resources
Alternative energy
Coal related
Drilling and exploration services
Energy conservation
Minerals
Oil and gas exploration and production
Technology related products/equipment
Industrial Products and Equipment
Controls and sensors
Other industrial automation
Robotics/vision systems
Specialty materials
Medical/Health Related
Diagnostic equipment
Diagnostic test products

Additional Information
Method of Compensation—Return on
investment is of primary concern; do not
charge fees

REGENT FINANCIAL CORP.

10 Commercial Wharf West
Boston, MA 02110
617-723-4820

Officer
Jason S. Rosenberg, Pres.

Type of Firm
Private venture capital firm investing
own capital

Project Preferences
Prefer role in deals created by others
Type of Financing:
Second-stage
Leveraged buyout
Minimum Investment: Less than $100,000
Preferred Investment: $100,000-$250,000
Minimum Operating Data:
Annual Sales—$1.5 million
P&L—Break even

Geographical Preference
Northeast

Industry Preferences

Communications
Data communications
Satellite and microwave communications
Telephone related
Computer Related
Computer graphics, CAD/CAM and CAE
Computer services
Memory devices
Office automation
Scanning related
Software-applications
Software-artificial intelligence
Software-systems
Consumer
Consumer services
Distribution
Consumer products
Industrial products
Medical products
Other
Real estate

Additional Information
Year Founded—1966
Capital Under Management—Over $3 million
Invested(1985-1st 6 months)—$1.5 million
Method of Compensation—Return on
investment is most important, but also
charge for closing fees, service fees, etc.

ROBERTSON, COLMAN & STEPHENS

155 Federal Street
Boston, MA 02110
617-542-9393

See CALIFORNIA for full listing

SCHOONER CAPITAL CORPORATION

77 Franklin Street
Boston, MA 02110
617-357-9031

Officers
Vincent J. Ryan, Pres.
Bernice E. Bradin, V.P.
Garry B. Watzke, V.P. & Gen. Cnsl.
Cynthia C. Heller, Treas.

Whom to Contact
Bernice E. Bradin

Type of Firm
Private venture capital firm investing
own capital

Project Preferences
Will function either as deal originator or
investor in deals created by others
Type of Financing:
Startup
First-stage
Leveraged buyout
Equity for project financing
Minimum Investment: $250,000
Preferred Investment: $250,000-$500,000
Minimum Operating Data:
Annual Sales—Nominal
P&L—Positive cash flow

Geographical Preference
National

Industry Preferences

Communications
Cable television
Paging
**Electronic Components and
Instrumentation**
Fiber optics
Industrial Products and Equipment
Robotics/vision systems
Other
Biotechnology related to agriculture
Service industries
Specialty consulting

Renewable Energy/Load Management
Biomass
Cogeneration
District heating
Geothermal
Hydroelectric
Waste

Additional Information
Year Founded—1968
Method of Compensation—Return on
investment is most important, but also
charge for closing fees, service fees, etc.

SECURITY PACIFIC CAPITAL CORP./FIRST SBIC OF CALIFORNIA

50 Milk Street, 15th Floor
Boston, MA 02109
617-542-7601

Michael Cronin, Mgn. Ptnr.

See CALIFORNIA for full listing

SIGMA PARTNERS

342 Green Street
Northboro, MA 01532
617-393-7396

Gardner C. Hendrie

See CALIFORNIA for full listing

THE SPROUT GROUP

One Center Plaza, Sixth Floor
Boston, MA 02108
617-570-8720

Larry E. Reeder, Gen. Ptnr.
C. Edward Hazen, V.P., DLJ Capital Corp.

See NEW YORK for full listing

SUBRO VENTURES CORPORATION

40 Grove Street
Wellesley, MA 02181
617-237-4727

Officers
Stuart H. Watson, Pres.
Robert H. Lacey, V.P., Fin.

Whom to Contact
Stuart H. Watson

Type of Firm
Private venture capital firm investing
own capital

Project Preferences
Prefer role in deals created by others
Type of Financing:
Seed
First-stage
Second-stage
Minimum Investment: Less than $100,000
Preferred Investment: Less than $250,000
Minimum Operating Data:
Annual Sales—Nominal

Geographical Preference
East Coast

Industry Preferences

Communications
Commercial communications
Satellite and microwave communications
Telephone related
Computer Related
Software-applications
Software-systems
Consumer
Restaurants
Distribution
Communications equipment
Food products
Medical products
**Electronic Components and
Instrumentation**
Optics technology
Energy/Natural Resources
Alternative energy
Energy conservation
Technology related products/equipment
Genetic Engineering
Recombinant DNA (agricultural and
industrial)
Industrial Products and Equipment
Robotics/vision systems

Medical/Health Related
Diagnostic equipment
Drugs and medicines
Hospital and clinical labs
Medical services
Therapeutic equipment
Other
Agriculture, forestry, fishing
Education related
Finance and insurance
Publishing
Real estate
Specialty consulting
Transportation

Additional Information
Year Founded—1983
Method of Compensation—Return on
investment is of primary concern; do not
charge fees

SUMMIT VENTURES

One Boston Place #912
Boston, MA 02108
617-742-5500

Partners
E. Roe Stamps, IV, Mgn. Ptnr.
Stephen G. Woodsum, Mgn. Ptnr.
Thomas A. Avery, Gen. Ptnr.
Jacques Eldin, V.P.
John A. Genest, V.P.
Gregory M. Avis, Sr. Assoc.
Lawrence W. Lepard, Sr. Assoc.
Martin J. Mannion, Sr. Assoc.
Michel Payan, Sr. Assoc.
Craig Y. Lee, Assoc.
Eric Shealy, Assoc.

Whom to Contact
Any of the above

Type of Firm
Private venture capital firm investing
own capital

Project Preferences
Prefer role as deal originator but will also
invest in deals created by others
Type of Financing:
Startup
First-stage
Second-stage
Later-stage expansion
Leveraged buyout

Minimum Investment: $1 million
Preferred Investment: $2 million-$4 million
Preferred Investment (LBO):
$1 million and over
Minimum Operating Data:
Annual Sales—Nominal

Geographical Preference
United States
Canada

Industry Preferences

Communications
Cable television
Commercial communications
Data communications
Satellite and microwave communications
Telephone related
Television stations
Computer Related
Computer graphics, CAD/CAM and CAE
Computer mainframes
Computer services
Micro and mini computer related
Office automation
Software-applications
Software-artificial intelligence
Software-systems
Specialized turnkey systems
Consumer
Restaurants
**Electronic Components and
Instrumentation**
Analytical and scientific instrumentation
Component fabrication and testing
equipment
Electronic components
Fiber optics
Laser related
Industrial Products and Equipment
Chemicals
Controls and sensors
Energy management
Equipment and machinery
Other industrial automation
Robotics/vision systems
Specialty materials
Medical/Health Related
Diagnostic equipment
Diagnostic test products
Disposable products
Drugs and medicines
Hospital and clinical labs
Medical services
Therapeutic equipment
Will Not Consider
Consumer products
Real estate
Restaurants

Additional Information

Year Founded—1984
Capital Under Management—$160 million
Investments(1985-1st 6 months)—7
Invested(1985-1st 6 months)—$15 million
Method of Compensation—Return on
  investment is of primary concern; do not
  charge fees

TA ASSOCIATES

45 Milk Street
Boston, MA 02109
617-338-0800

Other Offices

435 Tasso Street #200
Palo Alto, CA 94301
415-328-1210

Partners

C. Kevin Landry, Mgn. Ptnr. (Massachusetts)
Jeffrey T. Chambers, Gen. Ptnr. (California)
Robert W. Daly, Ptnr. (Massachusetts)
Donald J. Kramer, Ptnr. (Massachusetts)
P. Andrews McLane, Gen. Ptnr.
  (Massachusetts)
Jacqueline C. Morby, Gen. Ptnr.
  (Massachusetts)
Michael C. Child, V.P. (California)
John L. Bunce, Jr., Assoc. (Massachusetts)
Brian J. Conway, Assoc. (Massachusetts)
Nabil El-Hage, Assoc. (Massachusetts)
Henry Koerner, Assoc. (Massachusetts)
Linda C. Wisnewski, Assoc. (Massachusetts)
Peter B. Kelly, Inv. Analyst (California)
Leighton B. Welch, Inv. Analyst
  (Massachusetts)
Paul A. White, Inv. Analyst (California)

Whom to Contact

John L. Bunce, Jr.
Jeffrey T. Chambers
Michael C. Child
Brian J. Conway
Robert W. Daly
Nabil El-Hage
Donald J. Kramer
Henry Koerner
Linda C. Wisnewski

Type of Firm

Private venture capital firm investing
  own capital

Affiliation

Advent Capital Company (affiliated SBIC)

Industry Association Memberships

NASBIC
NVCA

Project Preferences

Prefer role as deal originator but will also
  invest in deals created by others

Type of Financing:
Seed
Startup
First-stage
Second-stage
Later-stage expansion
Leveraged buyout
Minimum Investment: $1 million
Preferred Investment: $3 million
Minimum Operating Data:
Annual Sales—Nominal

Geographical Preference

None

Industry Preferences

Communications
Cable television
Commercial communications
Data communications
Satellite and microwave communications
Telephone related
Computer Related
Computer graphics, CAD/CAM and CAE
Computer mainframes
Computer services
Memory devices
Micro and mini computers
Office automation
Scanning related
Software-applications
Software-artificial intelligence
Software-systems
Specialized turnkey systems
Terminals
Consumer
Computer stores/related services
Consumer products
Consumer services
Food and beverage products
Franchise businesses
Hotels and resort areas
Leisure and recreational products
Restaurants
Retailing

Electronic Components and
  Instrumentation
Analytical and scientific instrumentation
Component fabrication and testing
  equipment
Electronic components
Fiber optics
Laser related
Semiconductors
Energy/Natural Resources
Technology related products/equipment
Genetic Engineering
Gene splicing and manufacturing equipment
Monoclonal antibodies and hybridomas
Recombinant DNA (agricultural and
  industrial)
Recombinant DNA (medical)
Industrial Products and Equipment
Chemicals
Controls and sensors
Energy management
Equipment and machinery
Other industrial automation
Plastics
Robotics/vision systems
Specialty materials
Medical/Health Related
Diagnostic equipment
Diagnostic test products
Disposable products
Drugs and medicines
Hospital and clinical labs
Medical services
Therapeutic equipment

Additional Information

Year Founded—1963
Capital Under Management—$510 million
Investments(1985-1st 6 months)—30
Invested(1985-1st 6 months)—$62 million
Method of Compensation—Return on
  investment is of primary concern; do not
  charge fees

3i CAPITAL

99 High Street #1530
Boston, MA 02110
617-542-8560

See INVESTORS IN INDUSTRY (3i)

TRANSATLANTIC CAPITAL CORPORATION

185 Devonshire Street
Seventh Floor
Boston, MA 02110
617-482-0015

Officer
John O. Flender, Pres. & Treas.

Type of Firm
SBIC

Affiliation
Transatlantic Investment Corporation
(sister private venture capital firm)

Industry Association Membership
NASBIC

Project Preferences
Will function either as deal originator or
investor in deals created by others
Type of Financing:
Startup
First-stage
Second-stage
Leveraged buyout
Minimum Investment: $100,000
Preferred Investment: $250,000-$500,000
Minimum Operating Data:
Annual Sales—Nominal
P&L—Losses (profits projected after 2 years)

Geographical Preference
Within two hours of office

Industry Preferences

Communications
Cable television
Commercial communications
Data communications
Satellite and microwave communications
Telephone related
Computer Related
Computer graphics, CAD/CAM and CAE
Computer mainframes
Computer services
Memory devices
Micro and mini computers
Office automation
Scanning related
Software-applications
Software-artificial intelligence
Software-systems
Specialized turnkey systems
Terminals

Electronic Components and Instrumentation
Analytical and scientific instrumentation
Component fabrication and testing equipment
Electronic components
Fiber optics
Laser related
Semiconductors
Genetic Engineering
Gene splicing and manufacturing equipment
Monoclonal antibodies and hybridomas
Recombinant DNA (agricultural and industrial)
Recombinant DNA (medical)
Industrial Products and Equipment
Chemicals
Controls and sensors
Energy management
Equipment and machinery
Other industrial automation
Plastics
Robotics/vision systems
Specialty materials
Medical/Health Related
Diagnostic equipment
Diagnostic test products
Disposable products
Drugs and medicines
Hospital and clinical labs
Medical services
Therapeutic equipment
Will Not Consider
Financial institutions
Real estate

Additional Information
Year Founded—1979
Capital Under Management—$6.5 million
Investments(1985-1st 6 months)—1
Invested(1985-1st 6 months)—$150,000
Method of Compensation—Return on investment is of primary concern; do not charge fees

---

TRANSPORTATION CAPITAL CORP.

566 Commonwealth Avenue
Boston, MA 02215
617-262-9701

Jon Hirsch, Asst. V.P.

See NEW YORK for full listing

TURNER REVIS ASSOCIATES

14 Union Wharf
Boston, MA 02109
617-227-9734

General Partners
John G. Turner
Kenneth J. Revis

Whom to Contact
Either of the above

Type of Firm
Venture capital fund investing funds of major bank

Affiliation
Co-investment agreement with First Chicago Venture Capital

Project Preferences
Prefer role as deal originator but will also invest in deals created by others
Type of Financing:
Seed
Startup
First-stage
Minimum Investment: $250,000
Preferred Investment: $250,000-$500,000
Minimum Operating Data:
Annual Sales—Nominal
P&L—Losses (profits projected after 2 years)

Geographical Preference
Massachusetts

Industry Preferences

Computer Related
Computer graphics, CAD/CAM and CAE
Computer mainframes
Computer services
Memory devices
Micro and mini computers
Scanning related
Scanning related
Software-applications
Software-artificial intelligence
Software-systems
Specialized turnkey systems
Terminals
Electronic Components and Instrumentation
Analytical and scientific instrumentation
Component fabrication and testing equipment
Electronic components
Fiber optics
Laser related
Semiconductors

Industrial Products and Equipment
Controls and sensors
Other industrial automation
Robotics/vision systems
Will Not Consider
Consumer
Distribution
Energy/natural resources
Genetic engineering
Medical/health related
Real estate

Additional Information
Year Founded—1983
Capital Under Management—$12 million
Investments(1985-1st 6 months)—8
Invested(1985-1st 6 months)—$3 million
Method of Compensation—Return on investment is of primary concern; do not charge fees

ULIN, MORTON, BRADLEY & WELLING

75 Federal Street
Boston, MA 02110
617-423-0003

Officers
Peter A. Ulin, Mgn. Dir.
Perry W. Morton, Mgn. Dir.
W. Lambert Welling, Mgn. Dir.
Murray M. Beach
Nicholas Holland

Whom to Contact
W. Lambert Welling

Type of Firm
Investment banking or merchant banking firm investing own capital or funds of partners or clients
Consulting firm evaluating and analyzing venture projects and arranging private placements

Project Preferences
Will function either as deal originator or investor in deals created by others
Type of Financing:
First-stage
Second-stage
Later-stage expansion
Leveraged buyout
Minimum Investment: $1 million
Preferred Investment: Over $1 million
Preferred Investment (LBO):
$1.5 million and over

Minimum Operating Data:
Annual Sales—Nominal
P&L—Losses (profits projected after 1 year)
Annual Sales (LBO)—
$15 million-$100 million

Geographical Preference
None

Industry Preferences
None

Additional Information
Year Founded—1984
Method of Compensation—Function primarily in service area; receive contingent fee in cash or equity

UNC VENTURES

195 State Street #700
Boston, MA 02109
617-723-8300

Partners
Edward Dugger III, Mgn. Ptnr.
James W. Norton, Jr., Ptnr.

Whom to Contact
Edward Dugger III

Type of Firm
Private venture capital firm investing own capital
Invest in companies in which ethnic minorities have substantial ownership

Affiliations
UNC Ventures, Inc.
UNC Ventures II, L.P.
UNC Associates, Inc.

Project Preferences
Will function either as deal originator or investor in deals created by others
Type of Financing:
Startup
First-stage
Second-stage
Later-stage expansion
Leveraged buyout
Minimum Investment: $250,000
Preferred Investment: $500,000-$1 million
Minimum Operating Data:
Annual Sales—$500,000
P&L—Break even

Geographical Preference
National

Industry Preferences

Communications
Commercial communications
Data communications
Telephone related
Computer Related
Computer graphics, CAD/CAM and CAE
Memory devices
Office automation
Scanning related
Software-applications
Software-artificial intelligence
Terminals
Consumer
Franchise businesses
Electronic Components and Instrumentation
Component fabrication and testing equipment
Electronic components
Fiber optics
Laser related
Energy/Natural Resources
Coal related
Industrial Products and Equipment
Controls and sensors
Robotics/vision systems
Medical/Health Related
Diagnostic equipment
Diagnostic test products
Other
Agriculture, forestry, fishing
Finance and insurance
Real estate
Specialty consulting

Additional Information
Year Founded—1971
Capital Under Management—$30 million
Investments(1985-1st 6 months)—3
Invested(1985-1st 6 months)—$2.5 million
Method of Compensation—Return on investment is most important, but also charge for closing fees, service fees, etc.

UST CAPITAL CORP.

40 Court Street
Boston, MA 02108
617-542-6300

Officer
C.W. Dick, V.P.

Type of Firm
SBIC

Affiliation
United States Trust Company (parent)

Industry Association Membership
NASBIC

Project Preferences
Will function either as deal originator or
  investor in deals created by others
Type of Financing:
Seed
Startup
First-stage
Second-stage
Minimum Investment: $100,000
Preferred Investment: $100,000-$250,000

Geographical Preference
Northeast

Industry Preferences

Communications
Cable television
Commercial communications
Data communications
Satellite and microwave communications
Telephone related
Computer Related
Computer graphics, CAD/CAM and CAE
Computer mainframes
Computer services
Memory devices
Micro and mini computers
Office automation
Scanning related
Software-applications
Software-artificial intelligence
Software-systems
Specialized turnkey systems
Terminals
Consumer
Consumer products
Consumer services
Distribution
Consumer products
**Electronic Components and
  Instrumentation**
Analytical and scientific instrumentation
Component fabrication and testing
  equipment
Electronic components
Fiber optics
Laser related
Semiconductors
Industrial Products and Equipment
Controls and sensors

Medical/Health Related
Diagnostic equipment
Diagnostic test products
Disposable products
Drugs and medicines
Hospital and clinical labs
Medical services
Therapeutic equipment
Will Not Consider
Finance companies
Real estate

Additional Information
Year Founded—1961
Capital Under Management—$3.6 million
Investments(1985-1st 6 months)—4
Invested(1985-1st 6 months)—$300,000
Method of Compensation—Return on
  investment is of primary concern; do not
  charge fees

THE VENTURE CAPITAL FUND OF
NEW ENGLAND

100 Franklin Street
Boston, MA 02110
617-451-2575

Partners
Richard A. Farrell, Gen. Ptnr.
Harry J. Healer, Jr., Gen. Ptnr.
E. Janice Leeming, Assoc.

Whom to Contact
Any of the above

Type of Firm
Private venture capital firm investing
  own capital

Industry Association Memberships
NASBIC
NVCA

Project Preferences
Will function either as deal originator or
  investor in deals created by others
Type of Financing:
Startup
First-stage
Second-stage
Leveraged buyout
Minimum Investment: $100,000
Preferred Investment: $250,000-$500,000
Preferred Investment (LBO):
  $500,000-$1 million

Minimum Operating Data:
Annual Sales—Nominal
P&L—Losses (profits projected after 2 years)
Annual Sales (LBO)—$5 million-$8 million

Geographical Preference
Northeast

Industry Preferences

Communications
Cable television
Commercial communications
Data communications
Radio and television broadcasting
Satellite and microwave communications
Telephone related
Computer Related
Computer graphics, CAD/CAM and CAE
Computer mainframes
Computer services
Memory devices
Micro and mini computers
Office automation
Scanning related
Software-applications
Software-artificial intelligence
Software-systems
Specialized turnkey systems
Terminals
Consumer
Consumer products
Leisure and recreational products
Distribution
Communications equipment
Computer equipment
Consumer products
Electronics equipment
Industrial products
Medical products
Recreation and leisure products
Sports equipment
**Electronic Components and
  Instrumentation**
Analytical and scientific instrumentation
Component fabrication and testing
  equipment
Electronic components
Fiber optics
Laser related
Semiconductors
Energy/Natural Resources
Alternative energy
Energy conservation
Technology related products/equipment
Genetic Engineering
Gene splicing and manufacturing equipment
Monoclonal antibodies and hybridomas

Industrial Products and Equipment
Controls and sensors
Equipment and machinery
Other industrial automation
Robotics/vision systems
Specialty materials
Medical/Health Related
Diagnostic equipment
Therapeutic equipment
Other
Education related
Finance and insurance
Publishing
Specialty consulting

Additional Information
Year Founded—1980
Capital Under Management—$19.2 million
Investments(1985-1st 6 months)—9
Invested(1985-1st 6 months)—$1.4 million
Method of Compensation—Return on
investment is of primary concern; do not
charge fees

VENTURE FOUNDERS CORPORATION

One Cranberry Hill
Lexington, MA 02173
617-863-0900

Other Offices
Venture Founders Ltd. (VFL)
39 The Green, South Bar Street
Banbury, Oxon
England OX16 9AE
0295-65881

BeneVenture Founders Management N.V.
(BeneVent)
Excelsiorlaan 21, Bus 4
1930 Zaventem, Brussels
Belgium
02-720-5023

V.F. (Europe) Ltd. (VF Euro)
Old Bank House, 42 Hardgate
Haddington, East Lothian
Scotland EH41 3JS
062-082-4561

Partners and Officers
Alexander L.M. Dingee, Jr., Pres.
& Gen. Ptnr. (United States)
Edward H. Getchell, V.P.
& Gen. Ptnr. (United States)
Gregory A. Hulecki (United States)
John O. Peterson, V.P. (United States)
David T. Riddiford, Gen. Ptnr. (United States)
Leonard E. Smollen, Exec. V.P.
& Gen. Ptnr. (United States)
Ross Yeiter, Treas. & Gen. Ptnr.
(United States)
Michael H. Zeldin, V.P. of Technology
(United States)
Joseph M. Frye, Jr., Gen. Ptnr. & Dir.
(United States & Europe)
Robert J. Ashmead, Dir. VFL
(United Kingdom)
Jos B. Peeters, Mgr. BeneVent (Belgium)
David A.H. Younger, Chm. VF Euro
(United Kingdom)

Whom to Contact
Gregory A. Hulecki
Ross Yeiter
Joseph M. Frye, Jr.
Robert J. Ashmead
Jos B. Peeters
David A.H. Younger

Type of Firm
Private venture capital firm investing
own capital

Industry Association Memberships
NASBIC
NVCA

Project Preferences
Prefer role as deal originator but will also
invest in deals created by others
Type of Financing:
Seed
Research and development partnerships
Startup
First-stage
Minimum Investment: Less than $100,000
Preferred Investment: $100,000-$750,000
Minimum Operating Data:
Annual Sales—Nominal
P&L—Losses (profits projected after 2 years)

Geographical Preferences
East Coast
Canada
United Kingdom
Benelux countries
Europe

Industry Preferences

Communications
Data communications
Telephone related
Computer Related
Computer graphics, CAD/CAM and CAE
Computer mainframes
Computer services
Memory devices
Micro and mini computers
Office automation
Scanning related
Software-applications
Software-artificial intelligence
Software-systems
Specialized turnkey systems
Terminals
Distribution
Automated purchase and distribution of
consumer products
Medical products
**Electronic Components and
Instrumentation**
Analytical and scientific instrumentation
Component fabrication and testing
equipment
Electronic components
Fiber optics
Laser related
Semiconductors
Energy/Natural Resources
Energy cost reduction technologies
Energy interconversion
Genetic Engineering
Biochemical technologies (including DNA,
RNA and proteins)
Recombinant DNA (agriculture and
veterinary)
Industrial Products and Equipment
Controls and sensors
Energy management
Equipment and machinery
Other industrial automation
Plastics
Robotics/vision systems
Specialty materials
Medical/Health Related
Diagnostic equipment
Therapeutic equipment
Will Not Consider
Finance and lending
Gambling
Hotels or restaurants
Local retail or other regionally restricted
businesses
Motion pictures
Oil, gas or mineral exploration
Promotional businesses
Publishing, including magazines
Real estate, general construction
or development

Additional Information
Year Founded—1973
Capital Under Management—$65 million
Investments(1985-1st 6 months)—14
Invested(1985-1st 6 months)—$3.8 million
Method of Compensation—Return on investment is of primary concern; do not charge fees

VIMAC CORPORATION

12 Arlington Street
Boston, MA 02116
617-267-2785

Officers
Max J. Steinmann, Pres.
Bottina Keller, Secy. & Treas.
James W. Walsh, Atty.
Dr. Eduard Burkhard, Consultant
Dr. Calvin A. Page, Consultant
John S. Morse, Consultant

Whom to Contact
Max J. Steinmann

Type of Firm
Consulting firm evaluating and analyzing venture projects and arranging private placements

Industry Association Membership
NVCA

Project Preferences
Prefer role as deal originator but will also invest in deals created by others
Type of Financing:
Seed
First-stage
Minimum Investment: $100,000
Preferred Investment: $250,000
Minimum Operating Data:
Annual Sales—Nominal
P&L—Losses (profits projected after 2 years)

Geographical Preferences
Northeast
East Coast
West Coast

Industry Preferences

Computer Related
Computer services
Office automation
Software-applications
Software-systems
Specialized turnkey systems

Distribution
Computer equipment

Additional Information
Year Founded—1982
Capital Under Management—$4.5 million
Investments(1985-1st 6 months)—2
Invested(1985-1st 6 months)—$600,000
Method of Compensation—Return on investment is of primary concern; do not charge fees

WEISS, PECK & GREER VENTURE PARTNERS, L.P.

265 Franklin Street
Boston, MA 02110
617-439-4630

Ralph T. Linsalata, Gen. Ptnr.

See CALIFORNIA for full listing

WS & G VENTURES, INC.

60 State Street
Boston, MA 02109
617-227-7200

Officers
Alexandra Moses, Pres.
Paulette Speight, Treas.

Whom to Contact
Alexandra Moses

Type of Firm
Investment bank investing own capital or affiliates' funds, and evaluating venture projects and private placements

Affiliation
Widett, Slater & Goldman, P.C. (joint venture)

Project Preferences
Prefer role as deal originator but will also invest in deals created by others
Type of Financing:
Seed
Research and development partnerships
Startup
First-stage
Second-stage
Later-stage expansion
Leveraged buyout
Minimum Investment: $250,000
Preferred Investment: $250,000 and over

Minimum Operating Data:
Annual Sales—Nominal
P&L—Losses (profits projected after 2 years)

Geographical Preference
None

Industry Preferences

Communications
Commercial communications
Data communications
Computer Related
Computer graphics, CAD/CAM and CAE
Computer mainframes
Computer services
Memory devices
Micro and mini computers
Office automation
Scanning related
Software-applications
Software-artificial intelligence
Software-systems
Specialized turnkey systems
Terminals
Consumer
Consumer products
Consumer services
Franchise businesses
Distribution
Communications equipment
Computer equipment
Consumer products
Electronics equipment
Food products
Industrial products
Medical products
Electronic Components and Instrumentation
Analytical and scientific instrumentation
Component fabrication and testing equipment
Electronic components
Fiber optics
Laser related
Semiconductors
Energy/Natural Resources
Technology related products/equipment
Genetic Engineering
Gene splicing and manufacturing equipment
Monoclonal antibodies and hybridomas
Recombinant DNA (agricultural and industrial)
Recombinant DNA (medical)

Industrial Products and Equipment
Chemicals
Controls and sensors
Energy management
Equipment and machinery
Other industrial automation
Plastics
Robotics/vision systems
Specialty materials
Medical/Health Related
Diagnostic equipment
Diagnostic test products
Disposable products
Drugs and medicines
Hospital and clinical labs
Medical services
Therapeutic equipment

Additional Information
Method of Compensation—Function primarily
in service area; receive contingent fee in
cash or equity

ZERO STAGE CAPITAL EQUITY FUND, L.P.

156 Sixth Street
Cambridge, MA 02142
617-876-5355

Partners
Paul M. Kelley, Mgn. Gen. Ptnr.
Gordon B. Baty, Gen. Ptnr.
Edward B. Roberts, Gen. Ptnr.
Jerome Goldstein, Gen. Ptnr.
Joseph P. Lombard, Special Ptnr.

Whom to Contact
Paul M. Kelley

Type of Firm
Private venture capital firm investing
own capital

Affiliation
First Stage Capital Equity Fund, L.P.

Project Preferences
Prefer role as deal originator but will also
invest in deals created by others
Type of Financing:
Seed
Minimum Investment: Less than $100,000
Preferred Investment: $100,000-$250,000
Minimum Operating Data:
Annual Sales—Nominal

Geographical Preference
None

Industry Preferences

Communications
Cable television
Commercial communications
Data communications
Satellite and microwave communications
Telephone related
Computer Related
Computer graphics, CAD/CAM and CAE
Computer mainframes
Computer services
Memory devices
Micro and mini computers
Office automation
Scanning related
Software-applications
Software-artificial intelligence
Software-systems
Specialized turnkey systems
Terminals
Distribution
Communications equipment
Computer equipment
Consumer products
Electronics equipment
Food products
Industrial products
Medical products
Electronic Components and Instrumentation
Analytical and scientific instrumentation
Component fabrication and testing
equipment
Electronic components
Fiber optics
Laser related
Semiconductors
Energy/Natural Resources
Alternative energy
Coal related
Energy conservation
Genetic Engineering
Gene splicing and manufacturing equipment
Monoclonal antibodies and hybridomas
Recombinant DNA (agricultural and
industrial)
Recombinant DNA (medical)
Industrial Products and Equipment
Chemicals
Controls and sensors
Energy management
Equipment and machinery
Other industrial automation
Plastics
Robotics/vision systems
Specialty materials

Medical/Health Related
Diagnostic equipment
Diagnostic test products
Disposable products
Drugs and medicines
Hospital and clinical labs
Medical services
Therapeutic equipment
Other
Agriculture, forestry, fishing
Will Not Consider
Oil and gas exploration and production
Real estate
Retail

Additional Information
Year Founded—1982
Capital Under Management—$5 million
Investments(1985-1st 6 months)—5
Invested(1985-1st 6 months)—$725,000
Method of Compensation—Return on
investment is of primary concern; do not
charge fees

ZERO STAGE CAPITAL II—CENTRAL PENNSYLVANIA

Zero Stage Equity Fund, L.P.
156 Sixth Street
Cambridge, MA 02142
617-876-5355

Dennis R. Costello, Gen. Ptnr.

See PENNSYLVANIA for full listing

ACCEL PARTNERS

2020 Hogback Road
Ann Arbor, MI 48104
313-971-5234

Other Offices
One Palmer Square
Princeton, NJ 08542
609-683-4500

One Embarcadero Center
San Francisco, CA 94111
415-989-5656

Managing Partners
Dixon R. Doll
Arthur C. Patterson
James R. Swartz

Whom to Contact
Any of the above

Type of Firm
Private venture capital firm investing
own capital

Industry Association Memberships
NASBIC
NVCA
WAVC

Project Preferences
Will function either as deal originator or
investor in deals created by others
Type of Financing:
Seed
Research and development partnerships
Startup
First-stage
Second-stage
Later-stage expansion
Minimum Investment: Less than $100,000
Preferred Investment: No preference
Minimum Operating Data:
Annual Sales—Nominal
P&L—Losses (profits projected after 2 years)

Geographical Preference
None

Industry Preferences

Communications
Cable television
Commercial communications
Data communications
Local area networks
Satellite and microwave communications
Telephone related

Computer Related
Computer graphics, CAD/CAM and CAE
Computer mainframes
Computer services
Memory devices
Micro and mini computers
Office automation
Scanning related
Software-applications
Software-artificial intelligence
Software-systems
Specialized turnkey systems
Terminals
Consumer
Consumer services
Distribution
Communications equipment
Computer equipment
Consumer products
Electronics equipment
Food products
Industrial products
Medical products
**Electronic Components and
Instrumentation**
Analytical and scientific instrumentation
Component fabrication and testing
equipment
Electronic components
Fiber optics
Laser related
Semiconductors
Energy/Natural Resources
Alternative energy
Coal related
Drilling and exploration services
Energy conservation
Minerals
Oil and gas exploration and production
Technology related products/equipment
Genetic Engineering
Gene splicing and manufacturing equipment
Monoclonal antibodies and hybridomas
Recombinant DNA (agricultural and
industrial)
Recombinant DNA (medical)
Industrial Products and Equipment
Chemicals
Controls and sensors
Energy management
Equipment and machinery
Other industrial automation
Plastics
Robotics/vision systems
Specialty materials

Medical/Health Related
Diagnostic equipment
Diagnostic test products
Disposable products
Drugs and medicines
Hospital and clinical labs
Medical services
Therapeutic equipment

Additional Information
Year Founded—1983
Capital Under Management—$100 million
Investments(1985-1st 6 months)—14
Invested(1985-1st 6 months)—$6 million
Method of Compensation—Return on
investment is of primary concern; do not
charge fees

COMERICA CAPITAL CORPORATION

30150 Telegraph #245
Birmingham, MI 48010
313-258-5801

Officers
John D. Berkaw, Pres.
Debra A. Ball, Asst. V.P.

Whom to Contact
Either of the above

Type of Firm
SBIC
Venture capital subsidiary of
commercial bank

Affiliation
Comerica Inc., Detroit (parent)

Industry Association Membership
NASBIC

Project Preferences
Will function either as deal originator or
investor in deals created by others
Type of Financing:
Startup
First-stage
Second-stage
Later-stage expansion
Minimum Investment: $250,000
Preferred Investment: $500,000-$1 million
Minimum Operating Data:
Annual Sales—Nominal
P&L—Losses (profits projected after 2 years)

Geographical Preferences
Midwest
National

Industry Preferences

Communications
Cable television
Data communications
Satellite and microwave communications
Telephone related
Computer Related
Computer graphics, CAD/CAM and CAE
Computer services
Memory devices
Micro and mini computers
Office automation
Scanning related
Software-applications
Software-artificial intelligence
Software-systems
Specialized turnkey systems
**Electronic Components and
  Instrumentation**
Analytical and scientific instrumentation
Component fabrication and testing
  equipment
Electronic components
Laser related
Semiconductors
Energy/Natural Resources
Alternative energy
Technology related products/equipment
Industrial Products and Equipment
Chemicals
Controls and sensors
Equipment and machinery
Other industrial automation
Robotics/vision systems
Specialty materials
Medical/Health Related
Diagnostic equipment
Diagnostic test products
Hospital and clinical labs
Medical services
Therapeutic equipment
Will Not Consider
Real estate

Additional Information
Year Founded—1981
Investments(1985-1st 6 months)—2
Invested(1985-1st 6 months)—$530,000
Method of Compensation—Return on
  investment is of primary concern; do not
  charge fees

DEARBORN CAPITAL CORPORATION

Post Office Box 1729
Dearborn, MI 48121
313-337-8577

Officers
Michael L. LaManes, Pres.
Gary L. Ferguson, V.P.

Whom to Contact
Either of the above

Type of Firm
MESBIC

Affiliation
Ford Motor Company (parent)

Industry Association Membership
AAMESBIC

Project Preferences
Prefer role as deal originator but will also
  invest in deals created by others
Type of Financing:
Second-stage
Later-stage expansion
Leveraged buyout
Minimum Investment: Less than $100,000
Preferred Investment: $100,000-$250,000
Minimum Operating Data:
Annual Sales—$500,000
P&L—Losses (profits projected after 1 year)

Geographical Preference
National

Industry Preferences

**Electronic Components and
  Instrumentation**
Analytical and scientific instrumentation
Electronic components
Industrial Products and Equipment
Automotive industry related products
  and services
Chemicals
Controls and sensors
Equipment and machinery
Other industrial automation
Plastics
Robotics/vision systems
Specialty materials
Will Not Consider
Any product or service not related to the
  automotive industry

Additional Information
Year Founded—1978
Method of Compensation—Return on
  investment is of primary concern; do not
  charge fees

HOUSTON & ASSOCIATES, INC.

1625 Woodward Avenue #220
Bloomfield Hills, MI 48013
313-332-1625

Other Office
Nine Hickory Hollow
Birmingham, MI 48010
313-645-1860

Officers
E. James Houston, Jr., Pres.
Ann D. Houston, Secy.

Whom to Contact
E. James Houston, Jr.

Type of Firm
Consulting firm evaluating and analyzing
  venture projects and arranging private
  placements

Affiliation
Xylem Corporation (affiliated via ownership)

Project Preferences
Prefer role as deal originator but will also
  invest in deals created by others
Type of Financing:
Startup
First-stage
Second-stage
Leveraged buyout
Minimum Investment: Less than $100,000
Preferred Investment: Less than $250,000
Preferred Investment (LBO):
  Less than $5 million
Minimum Operating Data:
Annual Sales—Nominal
P&L—Losses (profits projected after 2 years)

Geographical Preference
Midwest

Industry Preferences

Communications
Cable television
Commercial communications
Telephone related
Computer Related
Computer services
Micro and mini computers
Software-applications
Software-systems
Consumer
Computer stores/related services
Consumer products
Consumer services
Food and beverage products
Franchise businesses
Hotels and resort areas
Leisure and recreational products
Restaurants
Retailing
Distribution
Communications equipment
Computer equipment
Consumer products
Electronics equipment
Food products
Industrial products
Medical products
Electronic Components and Instrumentation
Electronic components
Energy/Natural Resources
Coal related
Minerals
Industrial Products and Equipment
Chemicals
Controls and sensors
Energy management
Equipment and machinery
Other industrial automation
Plastics
Robotics/vision systems
Specialty materials
Medical/Health Related
Hospital and clinical labs
Medical services
Other
Agriculture, forestry, fishing
Publishing
Specialty consulting

Additional Information

Year Founded—1971
Capital Under Management—$1 million
Method of Compensation—Professional fee required whether or
    not deal closes

INNER-CITY CAPITAL ACCESS CENTER, INC.

1505 Woodward Avenue #700
Detroit, MI 48226
313-961-2470

Officers

Walter M. McMurtry, Jr., Pres.
Harbans S. Dang, Treas. & Secy.

Whom to Contact

Either of the above

Type of Firm

MESBIC

Affiliations

Inner-City Business Improvement Forum (parent)
Southeastern Michigan Business Development Center (sister company)

Industry Association Membership

AAMESBIC

Project Preferences

Will function either as deal originator or investor in deals created by others
Type of Financing:
First-stage
Second-stage
Later-stage expansion
Leveraged buyout
Minimum Investment: Less than $100,000
Preferred Investment: $100,000-$250,000
Minimum Operating Data:
Annual Sales—$500,000
P&L—Break even

Geographical Preference

Midwest

Industry Preferences

Communications
Commercial communications
Consumer
Consumer products
Consumer services
Food and beverage products
Franchise businesses
Distribution
Consumer products
Food products
Industrial products
Genetic Engineering
Research and manufacturing equipment
Industrial Products and Equipment
Equipment and machinery
Other industrial automation

Medical/Health Related
Medical services
Other
Transportation
Will Not Consider
Real estate

Additional Information

Year Founded—1979
Capital Under Management—$1 million
Method of Compensation—Return on investment is most important, but also charge for closing fees, service fees, etc.

L. J. JOHNSON & COMPANY

2705 Lowell Road
Ann Arbor, MI 48103
313-996-8033

Officer

L.J. Johnson, Pres.

Type of Firm

Private venture capital firm investing own capital
Consulting firm evaluating and analyzing venture projects and arranging private placements

Project Preferences

Prefer role as deal originator but will also invest in deals created by others
Type of Financing:
Seed
Research and development partnerships
Startup
Leveraged buyout
Minimum Investment: $250,000
Preferred Investment: $500,000-$1 million
Minimum Operating Data:
Annual Sales—$500,000
P&L—Break even

Geographical Preference

None

Industry Preferences

Computer Related
Computer graphics, CAD/CAM and CAE
Computer mainframes
Computer services
Memory devices
Micro and mini computers
Scanning related
Scanning related
Software-applications
Software-artificial intelligence
Software-systems
Specialized turnkey systems
Terminals
Distribution
Communications equipment
Computer equipment
Consumer products
Electronics equipment
Food products
Industrial products
Medical products
Industrial Products and Equipment
Robotics/vision systems
Other
Finance and insurance

Additional Information

Year Founded—1979
Method of Compensation—Return on
  investment is most important, but also
  charge for closing fees, service fees, etc.
Function primarily in service area; receive
  contingent fee in cash or equity

MBW MANAGEMENT, INC.

2000 Hogback Road #2
Ann Arbor, MI 48105
313-971-3100

Other Offices

350 Second Street #7
Los Altos, CA 94022
415-941-2392

365 South Street, Second Floor
Morristown, NJ 07906
201-285-5533

333 East Main Street
Post Office Box 1431
Midland, MI 48641
517-631-2471

Officers

Philip E. McCarthy, Mgn. Dir. (Morristown)
Ian R.N. Bund, Mgn. Dir. (Ann Arbor)
James R. Weersing, Mgn. Dir. (Los Altos)
Richard M. Goff, V.P., Treas. & Secy.
  (Ann Arbor)
Robert J. Harrington, V.P. (Los Altos)
Herbert D. Doan (Midland)
James N. Hauslein, Inv. Analyst (Morristown)

Whom to Contact

Ian R.N. Bund
Philip E. McCarthy
James R. Weersing

Type of Firm

Private venture capital firm investing
  own capital
SBIC

Affiliations

MBW Venture Partners Limited Partnership
  (fund managed)
Michigan Investment Fund L.P.
  (fund managed)
Doan Resources Limited Partnership
  (fund managed)
Doan Associates (fund managed)

Project Preferences

Will function either as deal originator or
  investor in deals created by others
Type of Financing:
Startup
First-stage
Second-stage
Later-stage expansion
Leveraged buyout
Minimum Investment: $500,000
Preferred Investment: $500,000-$1 million
Preferred Investment (LBO):
  $1.5 million-$2 million
Minimum Operating Data:
Annual Sales (LBO)—$20 million-$40 million

Geographical Preference

None

Industry Preferences

Communications
Data communications

Computer Related
Computer graphics, CAD/CAM and CAE
Computer mainframes
Computer services
Memory devices
Micro and mini computers
Office automation
Scanning related
Software-applications
Software-artificial intelligence
Software-systems
Specialized turnkey systems
Terminals
**Electronic Components and
  Instrumentation**
Analytical and scientific instrumentation
Component fabrication and testing
  equipment
Electronic components
Fiber optics
Laser related
Semiconductors
Genetic Engineering
Gene splicing and manufacturing equipment
Monoclonal antibodies and hybridomas
Recombinant DNA (agricultural and
  industrial)
Recombinant DNA (medical)
Industrial Products and Equipment
Other industrial automation
Robotics/vision systems
Medical/Health Related
Diagnostic equipment
Diagnostic test products
Disposable products
Drugs and medicines
Hospital and clinical labs
Medical services
Therapeutic equipment
Will Not Consider
Consumer products
Franchises
Real estate

Additional Information

Year Founded—1984
Capital Under Management—$125.6 million
Investments(1985-1st 6 months)—7
Invested(1985-1st 6 months)—$3.9 million
Method of Compensation—Return on
  investment is of primary concern; do not
  charge fees

METRO-DETROIT INVESTMENT COMPANY

30777 Northwestern #300
Farmington Hills, MI 48018
313-851-6300

Officers
William J. Fowler, Pres.
Michael J. George, V.P. & Secy.
George Caracostas, V.P.

Whom to Contact
William J. Fowler

Type of Firm
MESBIC

Affiliation
Melody Distributing Co. (parent)

Industry Association Memberships
AAMESBIC
NASBIC

Project Preferences
Prefer role in deals created by others
Type of Financing:
First-stage
Second-stage
Minimum Investment: $100,000
Preferred Investment: $100,000-$250,000
Minimum Operating Data:
Annual Sales—$500,000
P&L—Losses (profits projected after 1 year)

Geographical Preferences
Within two hours of office
Midwest

Industry Preferences

Distribution
Communications equipment
Electronics equipment
Medical products
Industrial Products and Equipment
Equipment and machinery
Plastics
Specialty materials
Medical/Health Related
Diagnostic equipment
Diagnostic test products
Hospital and clinical labs
Medical services
Therapeutic equipment
Will Not Consider
Consumer products
Restaurants
Retailing

Additional Information
Year Founded—1978
Capital Under Management—$8 million
Investments(1985-1st 6 months)—25
Invested(1985-1st 6 months)—$1.6 million
Method of Compensation—Return on investment is most important, but also charge for closing fees, service fees, etc.

MICHIGAN CAPITAL AND SERVICE, INC./NBD EQUITY CORP.

500 First National Building
201 South Main Street
Ann Arbor, MI 48104
313-663-0702

Officers
Joseph F. Conway, Pres.
James A. Parsons, V.P. & Secy.
Carlene D. Dettleff, Asst. Secy./Asst. Treas.
Jeffrey C. Atkinson, Inv. Mgr.
Mary L. Campbell, Inv. Mgr.

Whom to Contact
Any of the above

Type of Firm
SBIC
Venture capital subsidiary of commercial bank

Affiliation
NBD Bancorp, Inc. (parent)

Industry Association Memberships
NASBIC
NVCA

Project Preferences
Will function either as deal originator or investor in deals created by others
Type of Financing:
Seed
Startup
First-stage
Second-stage
Later-stage expansion
Leveraged buyout
Minimum Investment: $250,000
Preferred Investment: $500,000-$1 million
Preferred Investment (LBO): $1 million
Minimum Operating Data:
Annual Sales—Nominal
P&L—Losses (profits projected after 2 years)
Annual Sales (LBO)—$20 million-$500 million

Geographical Preferences
Midwest
Midwest as lead; throughout U.S. as participant

Industry Preferences

Communications
Broadcasting
Cable television
Commercial communications
Data communications
Satellite and microwave communications
Telephone related
Computer Related
Computer graphics, CAD/CAM and CAE
Computer mainframes
Computer services
Memory devices
Micro and mini computers
Office automation
Scanning related
Software-applications
Software-artificial intelligence
Software-systems
Specialized turnkey systems
Terminals
Electronic Components and Instrumentation
Analytical and scientific instrumentation
Component fabrication and testing equipment
Electronic components
Fiber optics
Laser related
Semiconductors
Energy/Natural Resources
Alternative energy
Technology related products/equipment
Industrial Products and Equipment
Controls and sensors
Equipment and machinery
Other industrial automation
Robotics/vision systems
Specialty materials
Medical/Health Related
Diagnostic equipment
Diagnostic test products
Hospital and clinical labs
Medical services
Therapeutic equipment
Will Not Consider
Finance businesses
Real estate
Restaurants

Additional Information
Year Founded—1966
Capital Under Management—$25.2 million
Investments(1985-1st 6 months)—15
Invested(1985-1st 6 months)—$3.8 million
Method of Compensation—Return on investment is of primary concern; do not charge fees

MICHIGAN TECH CAPITAL CORP.

Technology Park, 1700 Duncan
Post Office Box 529
Hubbell, MI 49934
906-487-2643

Officers
Edward J. Koepel, Pres.
Clark L. Pellegrini, V.P. & Treas.
Richard E. Tieder, V.P. & Secy.

Whom to Contact
Any of the above

Type of Firm
SBIC

Affiliations
Michigan Tech Ventures, Inc.
Michigan Technological University

Industry Association Membership
NASBIC

Project Preferences
Will function either as deal originator or investor in deals created by others
Type of Financing:
Startup
Minimum Investment: Less than $100,000
Preferred Investment: Less than $100,000
Minimum Operating Data:
Annual Sales—$500,000
P&L—Losses (profits projected after 2 years)

Geographical Preference
Midwest

Industry Preferences
Computer Related
Computer graphics, CAD/CAM and CAE
Software-applications
Software-systems
Electronic Components and Instrumentation
Analytical and scientific instrumentation
Energy/Natural Resources
Minerals

Genetic Engineering
Recombinant DNA (agricultural and industrial)
Industrial Products and Equipment
Chemicals
Controls and sensors
Energy management
Equipment and machinery
Other industrial automation
Plastics
Robotics/vision systems
Specialty materials

Additional Information
Year Founded—1982

REGIONAL FINANCIAL ENTERPRISES

315 East Eisenhower Parkway
Suite 300
Ann Arbor, MI 48104
313-769-0941

Barry P. Walsh, Assoc.

See CONNECTICUT for full listing

TAURUS FINANCIAL GROUP, INC.

601 South Norton Road
Corunna, MI 48817
517-743-5729

Officers
Robert G. Machala, Pres.
Cory B. Weston, V.P.
Robin Mitchell, V.P.

Whom to Contact
Robert G. Machala

Type of Firm
Consulting firm evaluating and analyzing venture projects and arranging private placements

Affiliation
Taurus Mortage Corp.

Project Preferences
Will function either as deal originator or investor in deals created by others

Type of Financing:
First-stage
Second-stage
Later-stage expansion
Leveraged buyout
Preferred Investment: Over $1 million
Preferred Investment (LBO): Over $1 million
Minimum Operating Data:
Annual Sales (LBO)—Over $1 million

Geographical Preference
None

Industry Preferences
Communications
Cable television
Commercial communications
Data communications
Satellite and microwave communications
Telephone related
Computer Related
Computer graphics, CAD/CAM and CAE
Computer mainframes
Computer services
Memory devices
Micro and mini computers
Office automation
Scanning related
Software-applications
Software-artificial intelligence
Software-systems
Specialized turnkey systems
Terminals
Consumer
Computer stores/related services
Consumer products
Consumer services
Food and beverage products
Franchise businesses
Hotels and resort areas
Leisure and recreational products
Restaurants
Retailing
Distribution
Communications equipment
Computer equipment
Consumer products
Electronics equipment
Food products
Industrial products
Medical products
Electronic Components and Instrumentation
Analytical and scientific instrumentation
Component fabrication and testing equipment
Electronic components
Fiber optics
Laser related
Semiconductors

Energy/Natural Resources
Alternative energy
Coal related
Drilling and exploration services
Energy conservation
Minerals
Oil and gas exploration and production
Technology related products/equipment
Genetic Engineering
Gene splicing and manufacturing equipment
Monoclonal antibodies and hybridomas
Recombinant DNA (agricultural and
  industrial)
Recombinant DNA (medical)
Industrial Products and Equipment
Chemicals
Controls and sensors
Energy management
Equipment and machinery
Other industrial automation
Plastics
Robotics/vision systems
Specialty materials
Medical/Health Related
Diagnostic equipment
Diagnostic test products
Disposable products
Drugs and medicines
Hospital and clinical labs
Medical services
Therapeutic equipment
Other
Agriculture, forestry, fishing
Education related
Finance and insurance
Publishing
Real estate
Specialty consulting
Transportation
Will Not Consider
Graphic arts
Motion pictures

Additional Information
Year Founded—1966
Method of Compensation—Function primarily
  in service area; receive contingent fee in
  cash or equity

ALTAIR VENTURES, INC.

1221 Nicollet Mall #216
Minneapolis, MN 55403
612-342-2903

Officer

Phillip L. Hendershott, Chm. & CEO

Type of Firm

Private venture capital firm investing
own capital

Project Preferences

Prefer role as deal originator
Type of Financing:
Startup
First-stage
Second-stage
Later-stage expansion
Leveraged buyout
Minimum Investment: Less than $100,000
Preferred Investment: Less than $1 million
Preferred Investment (LBO):
$250,000-$1 million
Minimum Operating Data:
Annual Sales—Nominal
P&L—Losses (profits projected after 2 years)
Annual Sales (LBO)—$5 million-$250 million

Geographical Preference

Midwest

Industry Preferences

Computer Related
Computer graphics, CAD/CAM and CAE
Consumer
Consumer products
Consumer services
Food and beverage products
Leisure and recreational products
Retailing
Distribution
Consumer products
Food products
Industrial products
Industrial Products and Equipment
Chemicals
Controls and sensors
Equipment and machinery
Other industrial automation
Plastics
Robotics/vision systems
Specialty materials
Other
Education related
Finance and insurance
Transportation

Additional Information

Year Founded—1984
Capital Under Management—$550,000
Investments(1985-1st 6 months)—1
Invested(1985-1st 6 months)—$50,000
Method of Compensation—Return on
investment is most important, but also
charge for closing fees, service fees, etc.

CHERRY TREE VENTURES

640 Northland Executive Center
3600 West 80th Street
Minneapolis, MN 55431
612-893-9012

Partners

Tony J. Christianson, Gen. Ptnr.
Gordon F. Stofer, Gen. Ptnr.
Thomas W. Jackson, Assoc.
John C. Bergstrom, Inv. Analyst

Whom to Contact

Thomas W. Jackson
John C. Bergstrom

Type of Firm

Private venture capital firm investing
own capital

Industry Association Memberships

NASBIC
NVCA

Project Preferences

Will function either as deal originator or
investor in deals created by others
Type of Financing:
Seed
Research and development partnerships
Startup
First-stage
Second-stage
Leveraged buyout
Minimum Investment: Less than $100,000
Preferred Investment: $500,000-$1 million
Minimum Operating Data:
Annual Sales—Nominal

Geographical Preference

Within two hours of office

Industry Preferences

Communications
Commercial communications
Data communications
Telephone related
Computer Related
Computer graphics, CAD/CAM and CAE
Computer services
Micro and mini computers
Office automation
Scanning related
Software-applications
Software-artificial intelligence
Software-systems
Consumer
Consumer services
Franchise businesses
Restaurants
Retailing
Distribution
Communications equipment
Computer equipment
Electronics equipment
Medical products
**Electronic Components and
Instrumentation**
Analytical and scientific instrumentation
Fiber optics
Laser related
Genetic Engineering
Monoclonal antibodies and hybridomas
Recombinant DNA (agricultural and
industrial)
Recombinant DNA (medical)
Medical/Health Related
Diagnostic equipment
Diagnostic test products
Disposable products
Drugs and medicines
Hospital and clinical labs
Medical services
Therapeutic equipment
Other
Education related
Finance and insurance
Publishing
Will Not Consider
Real estate

Additional Information

Year Founded—1982
Capital Under Management—$40 million
Investments(1985-1st 6 months)—13
Invested(1985-1st 6 months)—$2 million
Method of Compensation—Return on
investment is of primary concern; do not
charge fees

CONTROL DATA CAPITAL CORPORATION

3601 West 77th Street
Minneapolis, MN 55435
612-921-4118

Officers
D.C. Curtis, Jr., Pres.
T.F. Hunt, Jr., V.P.
R.R. Burns, V.P.
D.R. Pickerell, Secy./Treas.
T.A. Ehlinger, Asst. Secy.

Whom to Contact
D.C. Curtis

Type of Firm
SBIC

Affiliation
Control Data Corporation (parent)

Industry Association Memberships
AAMESBIC
NASBIC

Project Preferences
Prefer role as deal originator but will also invest in deals created by others
Type of Financing:
Startup
First-stage
Minimum Investment: $250,000
Preferred Investment: $250,000-$500,000
Minimum Operating Data:
Annual Sales—Nominal
P&L—Losses (profits projected after 2 years)

Geographical Preference
National

Industry Preferences

Communications
Data communications
Telephone related
Computer Related
Computer graphics, CAD/CAM and CAE
Computer mainframes
Computer services
Memory devices
Micro and mini computers
Office automation
Scanning related
Software-applications
Software-artificial intelligence
Software-systems
Specialized turnkey systems
Terminals

Industrial Products and Equipment
Controls and sensors
Energy management
Other industrial automation
Robotics/vision systems
Medical/Health Related
Diagnostic equipment
Diagnostic test products
Therapeutic equipment
Will Not Consider
Construction
Consumer products
Entertainment
Real estate
Retailing

Additional Information
Year Founded—1977
Capital Under Management—$22 million
Investments(1985-1st 6 months)—6
Invested(1985-1st 6 months)—$461,000
Method of Compensation—Return on investment is of primary concern; do not charge fees

---

CONTROL DATA COMMUNITY VENTURES FUND, INC.

3601 West 77th Street
Minneapolis, MN 55435
612-921-4352

Officer
Thomas F. Hunt, Jr., Pres.

Type of Firm
MESBIC

Affiliation
Control Data Corporation (parent)

Industry Association Membership
AAMESBIC

Project Preferences
Will function either as deal originator or investor in deals created by others
Type of Financing:
First-stage
Second-stage
Later-stage expansion
Leveraged buyout
Minimum Investment: $250,000
Preferred Investment: $250,000-$500,000
Minimum Operating Data:
Annual Sales—$500,000
P&L—Break even

Geographical Preference
None

Industry Preferences

Communications
Cable television
Commercial communications
Data communications
Satellite and microwave communications
Telephone related
Computer Related
Computer graphics, CAD/CAM and CAE
Computer mainframes
Computer services
Memory devices
Micro and mini computers
Office automation
Scanning related
Software-applications
Software-artificial intelligence
Software-systems
Specialized turnkey systems
Terminals
Consumer
Consumer products
Consumer services
Distribution
Communications equipment
Computer equipment
Consumer products
Electronics equipment
Food products
Industrial products
Medical products
Electronic Components and Instrumentation
Analytical and scientific instrumentation
Component fabrication and testing equipment
Electronic components
Fiber optics
Laser related
Semiconductors
Energy/Natural Resources
Technology related products/equipment
Genetic Engineering
Gene splicing and manufacturing equipment
Monoclonal antibodies and hybridomas
Recombinant DNA (agricultural and industrial)
Recombinant DNA (medical)
Industrial Products and Equipment
Chemicals
Controls and sensors
Energy management
Equipment and machinery
Other industrial automation
Plastics
Robotics/vision systems
Specialty materials

Medical/Health Related
Diagnostic equipment
Diagnostic test products
Disposable products
Drugs and medicines
Hospital and clinical labs
Medical services
Therapeutic equipment
Other
Education related
Transportation
Will Not Consider
Construction
Real estate

Additional Information
Year Founded—1979
Capital Under Management—$7.5 million
Investments(1985-1st 6 months)—4
Invested(1985-1st 6 months)—$615,000
Method of Compensation—Return on
   investment is most important, but also
   charge for closing fees, service fees, etc.

DAIN BOSWORTH INCORPORATED

100 Dain Tower
Minneapolis, MN 55402
612-371-7700

Other Offices
First Interstate Center #1500
999 Third Avenue
Seattle, WA 98104
206-621-3112

1225 17th Street #1800
Denver, CO 80202
303-294-7223

Officers
James Stearns, V.P. (Washington)
Robert Weisman, V.P. (Colorado)
Michael Norton, V.P. (Minnesota)

Whom to Contact
Any of the above

Type of Firm
Investment bank evaluating and analyzing
   venture projects and arranging private
   placements

Project Preferences
Prefer role as deal originator
Type of Financing:
Research and development partnerships
Second-stage
Later-stage expansion
Leveraged buyout
Minimum Investment: $1 million
Minimum Operating Data:
Annual Sales—Nominal
P&L—Losses (profits projected after 1 year)

Geographical Preferences
Midwest
Northwest
Rocky Mountains

Industry Preferences

Communications
Cable television
Commercial communications
Data communications
Satellite and microwave communications
Telephone related
Computer Related
Computer graphics, CAD/CAM and CAE
Computer mainframes
Computer services
Memory devices
Micro and mini computers
Office automation
Scanning related
Software-applications
Software-artificial intelligence
Software-systems
Specialized turnkey systems
Terminals
Consumer
Computer stores/related services
Consumer products
Consumer services
Food and beverage products
Franchise businesses
Hotels and resort areas
Leisure and recreational products
Restaurants
Retailing
Distribution
Communications equipment
Computer equipment
Consumer products
Electronics equipment
Food products
Industrial products
Medical products

**Electronic Components and
   Instrumentation**
Analytical and scientific instrumentation
Component fabrication and testing
   equipment
Electronic components
Fiber optics
Laser related
Semiconductors
Energy/Natural Resources
Alternative energy
Coal related
Drilling and exploration services
Energy conservation
Minerals
Oil and gas exploration and production
Technology related products/equipment
Genetic Engineering
Gene splicing and manufacturing equipment
Monoclonal antibodies and hybridomas
Recombinant DNA (agricultural and
   industrial)
Recombinant DNA (medical)
Industrial Products and Equipment
Chemicals
Controls and sensors
Energy management
Equipment and machinery
Other industrial automation
Plastics
Robotics/vision systems
Specialty materials
Medical/Health Related
Diagnostic equipment
Diagnostic test products
Disposable products
Drugs and medicines
Hospital and clinical labs
Medical services
Therapeutic equipment
Other
Agriculture, forestry, fishing
Education related
Finance and insurance
Publishing
Real estate
Specialty consulting
Transportation

Additional Information
Year Founded—1909
Method of Compensation—Professional fee
   required whether or not deal closes

FBS VENTURE CAPITAL CO.

7515 Wayzata Boulevard
Minneapolis, MN 55426
612-544-2754

W. Ray Allen, Exec. V.P.
John Bullion, V.P.

See ARIZONA for full listing

FIRST MIDWEST CAPITAL CORPORATION

1010 Plymouth Building
12 South Sixth Street
Minneapolis, MN 55402
612-339-9391

Officers
Alan K. Ruvelson, Pres.
Walter L. Tiffin, V.P. & Treas.
Patricia A. Montgomery, Secy.
James C. Harris, Asst. Secy.

Whom to Contact
Alan K. Ruvelson
Walter L. Tiffin

Type of Firm
SBIC

Industry Association Membership
NASBIC

Project Preferences
Will function either as deal originator or
  investor in deals created by others
Type of Financing:
First-stage
Second-stage
Later-stage expansion
Leveraged buyout
Minimum Investment: $100,000
Preferred Investment: $100,000-$250,000
Minimum Operating Data:
Annual Sales—Nominal
P&L—Losses (profits projected after 2 years)

Geographical Preference
Midwest

Industry Preferences

Communications
Cable television
Commercial communications
Data communications
Satellite and microwave communications
Telephone related

Computer Related
Computer graphics, CAD/CAM and CAE
Computer mainframes
Computer services
Memory devices
Micro and mini computers
Office automation
Scanning related
Software-applications
Software-artificial intelligence
Software-systems
Specialized turnkey systems
Terminals
Consumer
Consumer products
Retailing
Distribution
Communications equipment
Consumer products
Electronics equipment
Food products
Industrial products
Medical products
**Electronic Components and
  Instrumentation**
Analytical and scientific instrumentation
Component fabrication and testing
  equipment
Electronic components
Fiber optics
Laser related
Semiconductors
Industrial Products and Equipment
Chemicals
Controls and sensors
Energy management
Equipment and machinery
Other industrial automation
Plastics
Robotics/vision systems
Specialty materials
Medical/Health Related
Diagnostic equipment
Diagnostic test products
Disposable products
Drugs and medicines
Hospital and clinical labs
Medical services
Therapeutic equipment
Other
Transportation
Will Not Consider
Real estate

Additional Information
Year Founded—1959
Method of Compensation—Return on
  investment is of primary concern; do not
  charge fees

THE 530 FUNDS

430 International Centre
900 Second Avenue South
Minneapolis, MN 55402
612-342-0001

Partner
Michael I. Rosen
Richard E. Gilbert
Burton G. Ross

Whom to Contact
Michael I. Rosen

Type of Firm
Private venture capital firm investing
  own capital

Affiliation
Resource Bank & Trust (parent of one of
  general partners)

Project Preferences
Will function either as deal originator or
  investor in deals created by others
Type of Financing:
First-stage
Second-stage
Later-stage expansion
Leveraged buyout
Minimum Investment: Less than $100,000
Preferred Investment: $100,000-$250,000
Preferred Investment (LBO):
  $150,000-$250,000
Minimum Operating Data:
Annual Sales—$500,000
P&L—Losses (profits projected after 2 years)

Geographical Preference
None

Industry Preferences

Communications
Cable television
Commercial communications
Data communications
Satellite and microwave communications
Telephone related
Computer Related
Office automation
Software-applications
Consumer
Consumer products
Consumer services
Food and beverage products
Franchise businesses
Leisure and recreational products
Retailing

Distribution
Consumer products
Food products
Industrial products
Medical products
**Electronic Components and
  Instrumentation**
Analytical and scientific instrumentation
Component fabrication and testing
  equipment
Electronic components
Fiber optics
Laser related
Semiconductors
Industrial Products and Equipment
Chemicals
Controls and sensors
Energy management
Equipment and machinery
Other industrial automation
Plastics
Robotics/vision systems
Specialty materials
Medical/Health Related
Diagnostic equipment
Diagnostic test products
Disposable products
Drugs and medicines
Hospital and clinical labs
Medical services
Nursing homes, aggregate housing,
  elderly housing
Therapeutic equipment
Other
Agriculture, forestry, fishing
Education related
Finance and insurance
Publishing
Real estate
Specialty consulting
Transportation

Additional Information

Year Founded—1982
Capital Under Management—$7 million
Method of Compensation—Return on
  investment is of primary concern; do not
  charge fees

IAI VENTURE PARTNERS

1100 Dain Tower
Post Office Box 1160
Minneapolis, MN 55402
612-371-7780

Other Offices

3000 Sand Hill Road
Bldg. 3, #210
Menlo Park, CA 94025
415-854-1955

Officers

Noel P. Rahn, CEO (Minnesota)
Mitchell Dann, V.P. (Minnesota)
Richard C. Pflager, Sr. V.P. (California)

Whom to Contact

Mitchell Dann
Richard C. Pflager

Type of Firm

Private venture capital firm investing
  own capital

Affiliation

Investment Advisers, Inc. (general partner)

Project Preferences

Will function either as deal originator or
  investor in deals created by others
Type of Financing:
Seed
Startup
First-stage
Second-stage
Later-stage expansion
Leveraged buyout
Minimum Investment: $100,000
Preferred Investment: $500,000-$1 million
Minimum Operating Data:
Annual Sales—Nominal
P&L—Losses (profits projected after 2 years)

Geographical Preference

None

Industry Preferences

Communications
Cable television
Commercial communications
Data communications
Satellite and microwave communications
Telephone related

Computer Related
Computer graphics, CAD/CAM and CAE
Computer mainframes
Computer services
Memory devices
Micro and mini computers
Office automation
Scanning related
Software-applications
Software-artificial intelligence
Software-systems
Specialized turnkey systems
Terminals
Distribution
Communications equipment
Computer equipment
Consumer products
Electronics equipment
Food products
Industrial products
Medical products
**Electronic Components and
  Instrumentation**
Analytical and scientific instrumentation
Component fabrication and testing
  equipment
Electronic components
Fiber optics
Laser related
Semiconductors
Genetic Engineering
Gene splicing and manufacturing equipment
Monoclonal antibodies and hybridomas
Recombinant DNA (agricultural and
  industrial)
Recombinant DNA (medical)
Industrial Products and Equipment
Chemicals
Controls and sensors
Energy management
Equipment and machinery
Other industrial automation
Plastics
Robotics/vision systems
Specialty materials
Medical/Health Related
Diagnostic equipment
Diagnostic test products
Disposable products
Drugs and medicines
Hospital and clinical labs
Medical services
Therapeutic equipment
Other
Agriculture, forestry, fishing
Education related
Finance and insurance
Publishing
Real estate
Specialty consulting
Transportation

Additional Information
Year Founded—1983
Capital Under Management—$50.2 million
Investments(1985-1st 6 months)—5
Invested(1985-1st 6 months)—$878,000

IMPACT SEVEN, INC.

511 11th Avenue South
Post Office Box 77
Minneapolis, MN 55415
612-338-6473

Dileep Rao, V.P.

See WISCONSIN for full listing

MEDICAL INDUSTRIAL CAPITAL, INC.

1201 Marquette Avenue #400
Minneapolis, MN 55403
612-332-5130

Officers
George Heenan, Chm. & CEO
Timothy I. Maudlin, Pres. & COO
Fred A. Barnette, Jr., V.P.
Jeffrey E. Figgatt, V.P. & Inv. Officer
Mary Ann Kennedy, Dir., Financial Services

Whom to Contact
Jeffrey E. Figgatt

Type of Firm
Private venture capital firm investing
own capital

Project Preferences
Prefer role as deal originator but will also
invest in deals created by others
Type of Financing:
Seed
Research and development partnerships
Startup
First-stage
Minimum Investment: Less than $100,000
Preferred Investment: $250,000-$500,000

Geographical Preference
Minnesota
Texas
Selected other major medical centers

Industry Preferences

Genetic Engineering
Monoclonal antibodies and hybridomas
Recombinant DNA (medical)
Research and manufacturing equipment
Medical/Health Related
Diagnostic equipment
Diagnostic test products
Disposable products
Drugs and medicines
Hospital and clinical labs
Medical devices
Medical services
Medically-related computers and software
Therapeutic equipment
Will Not Consider
Non medically related businesses

Additional Information
Year Founded—1974
Capital Under Management—$6 million
Investments(1985-1st 6 months)—6
Method of Compensation—Return on
investment is of primary concern; do not
charge fees

MICROTECHNOLOGY INVESTMENTS LTD.

3400 Comserv Drive
Eagan, MN 55122
612-681-7580

See CALIFORNIA for full listing

MINNESOTA SEED CAPITAL, INC.

1660 South Highway 100
Parkdale Plaza #146
Minneapolis, MN 55416
612-545-5684

Officers
Richard C. Gottier, Pres., CEO & Gen. Ptnr.
Thomas M. Neitge, V.P. & Secy.
Thomas K. Rice, Ph.D., V.P.

Whom to Contact
Thomas M. Neitge
Thomas K. Rice, Ph.D.

Type of Firm
Private venture capital firm investing
own capital

Project Preferences
Will function either as deal originator or
investor in deals created by others
Type of Financing:
Seed
Startup
First-stage
Minimum Investment: Less than $100,000
Preferred Investment: $250,000-$500,000
Minimum Operating Data:
Annual Sales—Nominal

Geographical Preference
Minnesota only

Industry Preferences

Communications
Data communications
Satellite and microwave communications
Computer Related
Networks
Software-applications
Electronic Components and Instrumentation
Analytical and scientific instrumentation
Component fabrication and testing
equipment
Laser related
Energy/Natural Resources
Technology related products/equipment
Genetic Engineering
Gene splicing and manufacturing equipment
Monoclonal antibodies and hybridomas
Recombinant DNA (agricultural and
industrial)
Recombinant DNA (medical)
Industrial Products and Equipment
Plastics
Robotics/vision systems
Medical/Health Related
Diagnostic equipment
Diagnostic test products
Disposable products
Therapeutic equipment
Other
Education related

Additional Information
Year Founded—1980
Capital Under Management—$11.5 million
Invoctments(1985-1st 6 months)—6
Invested(1985-1st 6 months)—$300,000
Method of Compensation—Return on
investment is of primary concern; do not
charge fees

NORTH STAR VENTURES, INC.

100 South Fifth Street #2200
Minneapolis, MN 55402
612-333-1133

Officers
Terrence W. Glarner, Pres.
David W. Stassen, V.P.
Keith M. Eastman, V.P.

Whom to Contact
Terrence W. Glarner

Type of Firm
SBIC

Industry Association Memberships
NASBIC
NVCA

Project Preferences
Will function either as deal originator or
investor in deals created by others
Type of Financing:
First-stage
Second-stage
Later-stage expansion
Minimum Investment: $250,000
Preferred Investment: $250,000-$500,000
Minimum Operating Data:
Annual Sales—$500,000
P&L—Break even

Geographical Preference
None

Industry Preferences

Communications
Data communications
Computer Related
Computer graphics, CAD/CAM and CAE
Computer mainframes
Computer services
Memory devices
Micro and mini computers
Office automation
Scanning related
Software-applications
Software-artificial intelligence
Software-systems
Specialized turnkey systems
Terminals

**Electronic Components and
Instrumentation**
Component fabrication and testing
equipment
Electronic components
Fiber optics
Laser related
Semiconductors
Energy/Natural Resources
Minerals
Genetic Engineering
Gene splicing and manufacturing equipment
Monoclonal antibodies and hybridomas
Recombinant DNA (agricultural and
industrial)
Recombinant DNA (medical)
Industrial Products and Equipment
Controls and sensors
Equipment and machinery
Robotics/vision systems
Medical/Health Related
Diagnostic equipment
Diagnostic test products
Disposable products
Drugs and medicines
Therapeutic equipment
Will Not Consider
Real estate

Additional Information
Year Founded—1974
Capital Under Management—$25 million
Investments(1985-1st 6 months)—20
Invested(1985-1st 6 months)—$2 million
Method of Compensation—Return on
investment is of primary concern; do not
charge fees

NORTHLAND CAPITAL CORPORATION

Missabe Building #613
227 West First Street
Duluth, MN 55802
218-722-0545

Officer
George G. Barnum, Jr., Pres.

Type of Firm
SBIC

Industry Association Membership
NASBIC

Project Preferences
Will function either as deal originator or
investor in deals created by others
Type of Financing:
First-stage
Second-stage
Later-stage expansion
Leveraged buyout
Minimum Investment: Less than $100,000
Preferred Investment: $100,000-$250,000
Minimum Operating Data:
Annual Sales—Nominal
P&L—Losses (profits projected after 2 years)

Geographical Preference
None

Industry Preferences

Communications
Cable television
Commercial communications
Data communications
Satellite and microwave communications
Telephone related
Computer Related
Computer graphics, CAD/CAM and CAE
Computer mainframes
Computer services
Memory devices
Micro and mini computers
Office automation
Scanning related
Software-applications
Software-artificial intelligence
Software-systems
Specialized turnkey systems
Terminals
Consumer
Hotels and resort areas
**Electronic Components and
Instrumentation**
Analytical and scientific instrumentation
Component fabrication and testing
equipment
Electronic components
Fiber optics
Laser related
Semiconductors
Medical/Health Related
Diagnostic equipment
Diagnostic test products
Disposable products
Drugs and medicines
Hospital and clinical labs
Medical services
Therapeutic equipment
Other
Agriculture, forestry, fishing

Additional Information
Year Founded—1967
Capital Under Management—$2 million
Investments(1985-1st 6 months)—3
Invested(1985-1st 6 months)—$400,000
Method of Compensation—Return on investment is most important, but also charge for closing fees, service fees, etc.

NORWEST VENTURE CAPITAL MANAGEMENT, INC.

2800 Piper Jaffray Tower
Minneapolis, MN 55402
612-372-8770

Other Offices
1300 SW Fifth #3018
Portland, OR 97201
503-223-6622

Officers
Robert F. Zicarelli, Chm. (Minnesota)
Daniel J. Haggerty, Pres. (Minnesota)
Douglas E. Johnson, V.P. (Minnesota)
Timothy A. Stepanek, V.P. (Minnesota)
Leonard J. Brandt, V.P. (Minnesota)
John P. Whaley, V.P. (Minnesota)
John E. Lindahl, V.P. (Minnesota)
John L. Thomson, V.P. (Minnesota)
Anthony J. Miadich, V.P. (Oregon)
Dale R. Vogel, V.P. (Oregon)
Stephen J. Schewe, Assoc. (Minnesota)
Michael I. Cohen, Assoc. (Minnesota)
Brian C. Lee, Assoc. (Minnesota)
Ernie C. Parizeau, Assoc. (Minnesota)
Richard B. Keller II, Assoc. (Oregon)

Whom to Contact
Douglas E. Johnson
Anthony J. Miadich

Type of Firm
Private venture capital firm investing own capital
SBIC

Affiliation
Norwest Corporation (holding company)

Project Preferences
Will function either as deal originator or investor in deals created by others
Type of Financing:
Startup
First-stage
Second-stage
Later-stage expansion
Leveraged buyout

Minimum Investment: $250,000
Preferred Investment: Over $1 million

Geographical Preference
National

Industry Preferences
Communications
Cable television
Commercial communications
Data communications
Satellite and microwave communications
Telephone related
Consumer
Computer stores/related services
Consumer products
Consumer services
Food and beverage products
Franchise businesses
Hotels and resort areas
Leisure and recreational products
Restaurants
Retailing
Distribution
Communications equipment
Computer equipment
Consumer products
Electronics equipment
Food products
Industrial products
Medical products
Electronic Components and Instrumentation
Analytical and scientific instrumentation
Component fabrication and testing equipment
Electronic components
Fiber optics
Laser related
Semiconductors
Energy/Natural Resources
Alternative energy
Coal related
Drilling and exploration services
Energy conservation
Minerals
Oil and gas exploration and production
Technology related products/equipment
Genetic Engineering
Gene splicing and manufacturing equipment
Monoclonal antibodies and hybridomas
Recombinant DNA (agricultural and industrial)
Recombinant DNA (medical)

Industrial Products and Equipment
Chemicals
Controls and sensors
Energy management
Equipment and machinery
Other industrial automation
Plastics
Robotics/vision systems
Specialty materials
Medical/Health Related
Diagnostic equipment
Diagnostic test products
Disposable products
Drugs and medicines
Hospital and clinical labs
Medical services
Therapeutic equipment
Will Not Consider
Real estate

Additional Information
Year Founded—1961
Capital Under Management—$270 million
Investments(1985-1st 6 months)—30
Invested(1985-1st 6 months)—$13 million
Method of Compensation—Return on investment is of primary concern; do not charge fees

PATHFINDER VENTURE CAPITAL FUNDS

7300 Metro Boulevard #585
Minneapolis, MN 55435
612-835-1121

Partners
Jack K. Ahrens II, Gen. Ptnr.
Marvin L. Bookin, Gen. Ptnr.
Norman Dann, Gen. Ptnr.
Andrew J. Greenshields, Gen. Ptnr.
Gary A. Stoltz, Gen. Ptnr.
J. Todd Johnson, Assoc.
Kenneth H. Levin, Assoc.

Whom to Contact
Any of the above

Type of Firm
Private venture capital firm investing own capital

Affiliation
Pathfinder Ventures, Inc. (management company)

Industry Association Memberships
NASBIC
NVCA

Project Preferences

Will function either as deal originator or investor in deals created by others

Type of Financing:
Startup
First-stage
Second-stage
Later-stage expansion
Leveraged buyout
Minimum Investment: $100,000
Preferred Investment: $500,000-$1.5 million
Preferred Investment (LBO):
$1 million-$2 million
Minimum Operating Data:
Annual Sales—Nominal
P&L—Losses (profits projected after 2 years)

Geographical Preferences

National
Near major metropolitan areas

Industry Preferences

Communications
Data communications
Satellite and microwave communications
Telephone related
Computer Related
Computer graphics, CAD/CAM and CAE
Computer mainframes
Computer services
Memory devices
Micro and mini computers
Office automation
Scanning related
Software-applications
Software-artificial intelligence
Software-systems
Specialized turnkey systems
Terminals
Electronic Components and Instrumentation
Analytical and scientific instrumentation
Component fabrication and testing equipment
Electronic components
Fiber optics
Laser related
Semiconductors
Genetic Engineering
Gene splicing and manufacturing equipment
Monoclonal antibodies and hybridomas
Recombinant DNA (agricultural and industrial)
Recombinant DNA (medical)

Industrial Products and Equipment
Chemicals
Controls and sensors
Energy management
Equipment and machinery
Other industrial automation
Plastics
Robotics/vision systems
Specialty materials
Medical/Health Related
Diagnostic equipment
Diagnostic test products
Disposable products
Drugs and medicines
Hospital and clinical labs
Medical services
Therapeutic equipment
Will Not Consider
Consumer
Distribution
Energy/natural resources
Finance and insurance
Publishing
Real estate
Transportation

Additional Information

Year Founded—1980
Capital Under Management—$72.6 million
Investments(1985-1st 6 months)—7
Invested(1985-1st 6 months)—$1.8 million
Method of Compensation—Return on investment is of primary concern; do not charge fees

---

PIPER JAFFRAY VENTURES, LTD.

Piper Jaffray Tower
Post Office Box 28
Minneapolis, MN 55440
612-342-6314

Other Office

1600 IBM Building
Seattle, WA 98101
206-223-3800

Officers

R. Hunt Greene, Pres. (Minnesota)
Gary L. Takacs (Washington)
Frank B. Bennett (Minnesota)
Douglas R. Whitaker (Minnesota)

Whom to Contact

Frank B. Bennett
Douglas R. Whitaker
Gary L. Takacs

Type of Firm

Investment banking or merchant banking firm investing own capital or funds of partners or clients

Industry Association Memberships

NASBIC
NVCA

Project Preferences

Will function either as deal originator or investor in deals created by others
Type of Financing:
Startup
First-stage
Second-stage
Later-stage expansion
Leveraged buyout

Geographical Preference

None

Industry Preferences

None

Additional Information

Year Founded—1895

SHARED VENTURES, INC.

6550 York Avenue S.
Minneapolis, MN 55435
612-925-3411

Officers

Howard Weiner, Pres.
Frederick L. Weiner, V.P.

Whom to Contact

Either of the above

Type of Firm

SBIC

Industry Association Membership

NASBIC

Project Preferences

Will function either as deal originator or investor in deals created by others
Type of Financing:
Startup
First-stage
Leveraged buyout
Minimum Investment: Less than $100,000
Preferred Investment: $100,000-$250,000

Minimum Operating Data:
Annual Sales—Nominal
P&L—Losses (profits projected after 2 years)

Geographical Preference
Midwest

Industry Preferences

Consumer
Food and beverage products
Franchise businesses
Leisure and recreational products
Restaurants
Retailing
Distribution
Communications equipment
Computer equipment
Consumer products
Electronics equipment
Food products
Industrial products
Medical products
Electronic Components and
Instrumentation
Analytical and scientific instrumentation
Component fabrication and testing
  equipment
Electronic components
Fiber optics
Laser related
Semiconductors
Industrial Products and Equipment
Controls and sensors
Equipment and machinery
Other industrial automation
Plastics
Robotics/vision systems
Specialty materials
Medical/Health Related
Diagnostic equipment
Diagnostic test products
Disposable products
Drugs and medicines
Hospital and clinical labs
Medical services
Therapeutic equipment
Other
Education related
Publishing
Transportation

Additional Information
Year Founded—1981

THRESHOLD VENTURES, INC.

430 Oak Grove Street #303
Minneapolis, MN 55403
612-874-7199

Officers
T. Denny Sanford, CEO
John Shannon, V.P.

Whom to Contact
John Shannon

Type of Firm
SBIC

Industry Association Membership
NASBIC

Project Preferences
Prefer role as deal originator but will also
  invest in deals created by others
Type of Financing:
Startup
First-stage
Second-stage
Later-stage expansion
Leveraged buyout
Minimum Investment: $100,000
Preferred Investment: $100,000-$250,000
Minimum Operating Data:
Annual Sales—Nominal

Geographical Preferences
Midwest
Southeast
Northwest

Industry Preferences

Communications
Cable television
Commercial communications
Radio and television
Telephone related
Computer Related
Computer graphics, CAD/CAM and CAE
Computer mainframes
Computer services
Memory devices
Micro and mini computers
Office automation
Scanning related
Software-applications
Software-artificial intelligence
Software-systems
Specialized turnkey systems
Terminals

Consumer
Computer stores/related services
Consumer products
Consumer services
Food and beverage products
Franchise businesses
Hotels and resort areas
Leisure and recreational products
Restaurants
Retailing
Distribution
Computer equipment
Electronics equipment
Food products
Industrial products
Medical products
Electronic Components and
Instrumentation
Analytical and scientific instrumentation
Component fabrication and testing
  equipment
Electronic components
Fiber optics
Laser related
Semiconductors
Genetic Engineering
Recombinant DNA (medical)
Industrial Products and Equipment
Chemicals
Plastics
Robotics/vision systems
Specialty materials
Medical/Health Related
Drugs and medicines
Other
Finance and insurance
Outdoor advertising
Publishing

Additional Information
Year Founded—1983
Capital Under Management—Over $1 million
Investments(1985-1st 6 months)—9
Method of Compensation—Return on
  investment is most important, but also
  charge for closing fees, service fees, etc.

INVESAT CAPITAL CORPORATION

162 East Amite Street
Jackson, MS 39201
601-969-3242

Post Office Box 3288
Jackson, MS 39207

Officer
John R. Bise, Pres.

Type of Firm
Private venture capital firm investing
   own capital

Industry Association Membership
NASBIC

Project Preferences
Will function either as deal originator or
   investor in deals created by others
Type of Financing:
Second-stage
Later-stage expansion
Leveraged buyout
Minimum Investment: $100,000
Preferred Investment: $250,000-$500,000
Preferred Investment (LBO): $300,000
Minimum Operating Data:
Annual Sales—$500,000
P&L—Break even

Geographical Preference
Southeast

Industry Preferences

Communications
Cable television
Telephone related
Computer Related
Software-applications
Specialized turnkey systems
Consumer
Consumer products
Consumer services
Food and beverage products
Franchise businesses
Hotels and resort areas
Leisure and recreational products
Distribution
Communications equipment
Electronics equipment
Industrial products
Medical products
**Electronic Components and
   Instrumentation**
Analytical and scientific instrumentation
Laser related

Energy/Natural Resources
Energy conservation
Technology related products/equipment
Industrial Products and Equipment
Controls and sensors
Energy management
Medical/Health Related
Diagnostic equipment
Diagnostic test products
Disposable products
Drugs and medicines
Hospital and clinical labs
Medical services
Therapeutic equipment

Additional Information
Year Founded—1974
Capital Under Management—$7.5 million
Method of Compensation—Return on
   investment is of primary concern; do not
   charge fees

R.W. ALLSOP & ASSOCIATES

111 West Port Plaza #600
St. Louis, MO 63146
314-434-1688

Other Offices

Corporate Center East #210
2750 First Avenue NE
Cedar Rapids, IA 52402
319-363-8971

815 East Mason Street #1501
Post Office Box 1368
Milwaukee, WI 53201
414-271-6510

35 Corporate Woods #244
9101 West 110th Street
Overland Park, KS 66210
913-451-3719

Partners

Robert W. Allsop, Gen. Ptnr. (Iowa)
Paul D. Rhines, Gen. Ptnr. (Iowa)
Gregory B. Bultman, Gen. Ptnr. (Wisconsin)
Robert L. Kuk, Gen. Ptnr. (Missouri)
Larry C. Maddox, Gen. Ptnr. (Kansas)
James D. Thorp, Assoc. (Iowa)

Whom to Contact

Any of the above

Type of Firm

Private venture capital firm investing own capital

Industry Association Memberships

NASBIC
NVCA

Project Preferences

Will function either as deal originator or investor in deals created by others
Type of Financing:
First-stage
Second-stage
Later-stage expansion
Leveraged buyout
Minimum Investment: $500,000
Preferred Investment: $500,000-$1 million
Preferred Investment (LBO):
$1 million-$2 million
Minimum Operating Data:
Annual Sales—$1.5 million
P&L—Break even
Annual Sales (LBO)—$10 million-$50 million

Geographical Preference

National

Industry Preferences

Communications
Cellular radio equipment
Commercial communications
Data communications
Data compression, storage and transmission equipment
Satellite and microwave communications
Telephone related
Computer Related
Computer graphics, CAD/CAM and CAE
Computer services
Office automation
Scanning related
Consumer
Consumer products
Consumer services
Distribution
Communications equipment
Electronics equipment
Food products
Industrial products
Medical products
Electronic Components and Instrumentation
Analytical and scientific instrumentation
Component fabrication and testing equipment
Electronic components
Fiber optics
Laser related
Genetic Engineering
Gene splicing and manufacturing equipment
Industrial Products and Equipment
Chemicals
Controls and sensors
Equipment and machinery
Other industrial automation
Robotics/vision systems
Specialty materials
Medical/Health Related
Diagnostic equipment
Diagnostic test products
Disposable products
Drugs and medicines
Hospital and clinical labs
Hospital management
Medical instruments
Medical services
Therapeutic equipment
Will Not Consider
Real estate

Additional Information

Year Founded—1981
Capital Under Management—$45 million
Investments(1985-1st 6 months)—10
Invested(1985-1st 6 months)—$2 million
Method of Compensation—Return on investment is of primary concern; do not charge fees

---

CAPITAL FOR BUSINESS, INC.

11 South Meramec #800
St. Louis, MO 63105
314-854-7427

Other Office

720 Main Street
Kansas City, MO 64105
816-234-2381

Officers

James B. Hebenstreit, Pres. (St. Louis)
Bart Bergman, V.P. (Kansas City)
William O. Cannon, V.P. (St. Louis)

Whom to Contact

William O. Cannon
Bart Bergman

Type of Firm

SBIC

Affiliation

Commerce Bancshares, Inc. (majority parent)

Industry Association Membership

NASBIC

Project Preferences

Will function either as deal originator or investor in deals created by others
Type of Financing:
Research and development partnerships
First-stage
Second-stage
Later-stage expansion
Leveraged buyout
Minimum Investment: $200,000
Preferred Investment: $250,000-$750,000
Minimum Operating Data:
Annual Sales—$500,000
P&L—Break even

Geographical Preference

Missouri and contiguous states

Industry Preferences

Communications
Cable television
Commercial communications
Data communications
Satellite and microwave communications
Telephone related
Computer Related
Computer graphics, CAD/CAM and CAE
Computer services
Memory devices
Micro and mini computers
Office automation
Scanning related
Software-applications
Software-artificial intelligence
Software-systems
Specialized turnkey systems
Terminals
Consumer
Consumer products
Consumer services
Distribution
Communications equipment
Computer equipment
Electronics equipment
Industrial products
Medical products
**Electronic Components and
  Instrumentation**
Analytical and scientific instrumentation
Component fabrication and testing
  equipment
Electronic components
Fiber optics
Laser related
Semiconductors
Genetic Engineering
Gene splicing and manufacturing equipment
Monoclonal antibodies and hybridomas
Recombinant DNA (agricultural and
  industrial)
Recombinant DNA (medical)
Industrial Products and Equipment
Chemicals
Controls and sensors
Energy management
Equipment and machinery
Other industrial automation
Plastics
Robotics/vision systems
Specialty materials
Medical/Health Related
Diagnostic equipment
Diagnostic test products
Disposable products
Drugs and medicines
Hospital and clinical labs
Medical services
Therapeutic equipment

Other
Education related
Publishing
Transportation

Additional Information

Year Founded—1959
Capital Under Management—$10 million
Investments(1985-1st 6 months)—7
Invested(1985-1st 6 months)—$3 million
Method of Compensation—Return on
  investment is most important, but also
  charge for closing fees, service fees, etc.

GATEWAY MID-AMERICA PARTNERS

500 North Broadway #1575
St. Louis, MO 63102
314-342-2243

Other Office

135 South LaSalle #540
Chicago, IL 60603
312-782-3100

Officers

Richard F. Ford, Mgn. Ptnr. (Missouri)
John S. McCarthy, Gen. Ptnr. (Missouri)
Peter A. Brooke, Mgn. Ptnr., Advent Int'l
  (Massachusetts)
George K. Hendrick, Jr., Chm., Stiefel
  Venture (Illinois)
Edward L. Morris, Pres., Stiefel Venture
  (Missouri)

Whom to Contact

Any of the above

Type of Firm

Private venture capital firm investing
  own capital

Affiliations

Stiefel Venture Corp. (general partner)
Advent International Corporation (special
  limited partner)
Moshe Alafi (special limited partner)

Industry Association Membership

NASBIC

Project Preferences

Will function either as deal originator or
  investor in deals created by others
Type of Financing:
First-stage
Second-stage
Leveraged buyout

Minimum Investment: $250,000
Preferred Investment: $500,000-$1 million
Minimum Operating Data:
Annual Sales—$500,000
P&L—Break even

Geographical Preference

Midwest

Industry Preferences

Communications
Cable television
Commercial communications
Data communications
Satellite and microwave communications
Telephone related
Computer Related
Computer graphics, CAD/CAM and CAE
Computer mainframes
Computer services
Memory devices
Micro and mini computers
Office automation
Scanning related
Software-applications
Software-artificial intelligence
Software-systems
Specialized turnkey systems
Terminals
**Electronic Components and
  Instrumentation**
Analytical and scientific instrumentation
Component fabrication and testing
  equipment
Electronic components
Fiber optics
Laser related
Semiconductors
Genetic Engineering
Gene splicing and manufacturing equipment
Monoclonal antibodies and hybridomas
Recombinant DNA (agricultural and
  industrial)
Recombinant DNA (medical)
Industrial Products and Equipment
Controls and sensors
Equipment and machinery
Other industrial automation
Robotics/vision systems
Medical/Health Related
Diagnostic equipment
Diagnostic test products
Disposable products
Drugs and medicines
Hospital and clinical labs
Medical services
Therapeutic equipment

Will Not Consider

Agriculture
Oil exploration
Real estate

Additional Information

Year Founded—1984
Capital Under Management—$15 million
Investments(1985-1st 6 months)—8
Invested(1985-1st 6 months)—$3 million
Method of Compensation—Return on
    investment is of primary concern; do not
    charge fees

HARBOUR GROUP INVESTMENTS

7701 Forsyth Boulevard #550
St. Louis, MO 63105
314-727-5550

Officers

Sam Fox, Chm.
Ralph S. Lobdell, Exec. V.P.
Robert W. Hull, V.P.
Peter S. Finley, V.P.

Whom to Contact

Ralph S. Lobdell
Robert W. Hull
Peter S. Finley

Type of Firm

Investment banking or merchant banking
    firm investing own capital or funds of
    partners or clients

Project Preferences

Prefer role as deal originator but will also
    invest in deals created by others
Type of Financing:
Leveraged buyout
Preferred Investment (LBO):
    $2 million-$7 million
Minimum Operating Data:
P&L—Profits NBT over $2 million
Annual Sales (LBO)—$15 million and over

Geographical Preference

None

Industry Preferences

Consumer
Consumer products
Food and beverage products

Distribution
Communications equipment
Computer equipment
Consumer products
Electronics equipment
Food products
Industrial products
Medical products
**Electronic Components and
    Instrumentation**
Analytical and scientific instrumentation
Component fabrication and testing
    equipment
Electronic components
Fiber optics
Laser related
Semiconductors
Industrial Products and Equipment
Chemicals
Controls and sensors
Energy management
Equipment and machinery
Other industrial automation
Plastics
Robotics/vision systems
Specialty materials
Traditional manufacturing operations
Medical/Health Related
Diagnostic equipment
Diagnostic test products
Disposable products
Therapeutic equipment
Other
Transportation
Will Not Consider
Capital intensive high technology companies
Consulting
Finance and insurance

Additional Information

Year Founded—1984
Capital Under Management—$35 million
Investments(1985-1st 6 months)—1
Invested(1985-1st 6 months)—$3 million
Method of Compensation—Return on
    investment is of primary concern; do not
    charge fees

INTECH GROUP, INC.

130 South Bemiston #703
Clayton, MO 63105
314-863-3888

Officer

William W. Canfield, Pres.

Type of Firm

Private venture capital firm investing
    own capital

Project Preferences

Prefer role as deal originator
Type of Financing:
Startup
First-stage
Second-stage
Minimum Investment: $100,000
Preferred Investment: $250,000-$500,000
Minimum Operating Data:
Annual Sales—$1 million
P&L—Break even

Geographical Preferences

Southeast
Southwest
Midwest
Rocky Mountains

Industry Preferences

Communications
Data communications
Computer Related
Computer graphics, CAD/CAM and CAE
Computer services
Software-applications
Software-artificial intelligence
Specialized turnkey systems

Additional Information

Year Founded—1983
Capital Under Management—$1.5 million
Investments(1985-1st 6 months)—1
Invested(1985-1st 6 months)—$250,000
Method of Compensation—Return on
    investment is most important, but also
    charge for closing fees, service fees, etc.

INTERCAPCO WEST, INC.

7800 Bonhomme Avenue
Clayton, MO 63105
314-863-0600

Officers
Thomas E. Phelps, Chm.
Mark J. Lincoln, Pres.

Whom to Contact
Mark J. Lincoln

Type of Firm
SBIC

Industry Association Membership
NASBIC

Project Preferences
Will function either as deal originator or
    investor in deals created by others
Type of Financing:
Later-stage expansion
Leveraged buyout
Minimum Investment: $100,000
Preferred Investment: $250,000-$500,000
Minimum Operating Data:
Annual Sales—$1.5 million
P&L—Break even

Geographical Preferences
Within two hours of office
Midwest

Industry Preferences
None

Additional Information
Year Founded—1976
Capital Under Management—$2.5 million
Investments(1985-1st 6 months)—2
Invested(1985-1st 6 months)—$150,000
Method of Compensation—Return on
    investment is most important, but also
    charge for closing fees, service fees, etc.

IOWA VENTURE CAPITAL FUND, L.P.

Commerce Tower #2724
911 Main Street
Kansas City, MO 64105
816-842-0114

Other Offices
300 American Building
Cedar Rapids, IA 52401
319-363-8249

600 East Mason Street
Milwaukee, WI 53202
414-276-3839

Officers
Jerry M. Burrows, Pres. (Iowa)
Donald E. Flynn, Exec. V.P. (Iowa)
David R. Schroder, V.P. (Cedar Rapids)
Kevin F. Mullane, V.P. (Missouri)
Steven J. Massey, V.P. (Wisconsin)

Whom to Contact
Jerry M. Burrows
Donald E. Flynn
David R. Schroder

Type of Firm
Private venture capital firm investing
    own capital

Affiliation
InvestAmerica Venture Group, Inc.
    (fund manager)

Project Preferences
Will function either as deal originator or
    investor in deals created by others
Type of Financing:
First-stage
Second-stage
Later-stage expansion
Leveraged buyout
Minimum Investment: $100,000
Preferred Investment: $250,000-$500,000
Minimum Operating Data:
Annual Sales—Nominal

Geographical Preference
Midwest

Industry Preferences

Communications
Cable television
Commercial communications
Data communications
Satellite and microwave communications
Telephone related

Computer Related
Computer graphics, CAD/CAM and CAE
Computer mainframes
Computer services
Memory devices
Micro and mini computers
Office automation
Scanning related
Software-applications
Software-artificial intelligence
Software-systems
Specialized turnkey systems
Terminals
Distribution
Communications equipment
Computer equipment
Consumer products
Electronics equipment
Food products
Industrial products
Medical products
**Electronic Components and
    Instrumentation**
Analytical and scientific instrumentation
Component fabrication and testing
    equipment
Electronic components
Fiber optics
Laser related
Semiconductors
Genetic Engineering
Gene splicing and manufacturing equipment
Monoclonal antibodies and hybridomas
Recombinant DNA (agricultural and
    industrial)
Recombinant DNA (medical)
Industrial Products and Equipment
Chemicals
Controls and sensors
Energy management
Equipment and machinery
Other industrial automation
Plastics
Robotics/vision systems
Specialty materials
Medical/Health Related
Diagnostic equipment
Diagnostic test products
Disposable products
Drugs and medicines
Hospital and clinical labs
Medical services
Therapeutic equipment

Additional Information
Year Founded—1985
Capital Under Management—$15 million
Method of Compensation—Return on
    investment is of primary concern; do not
    charge fees

MORAMERICA CAPITAL CORPORATION

Commerce Tower #2724
911 Main Street
Kansas City, MO 64105
816-842-0114

Other Offices

300 American Building
Cedar Rapids, IA 52401
319-363-8249

600 East Mason Street
Milwaukee, WI 53202
414-276-3839

Officers

Jerry M. Burrows, Pres. (Iowa)
Donald E. Flynn, Exec. V.P. (Iowa)
David R. Schroder, V.P. (Iowa)
Kevin F. Mullane, V.P. (Missouri)
Steven J. Massey, V.P. (Wisconsin)

Whom to Contact

Any of the above

Type of Firm

SBIC

Affiliations

MorAmerica Financial Corporation (parent)
InvestAmerica Venture Group, Inc.
  (fund manager)

Industry Association Membership

NASBIC

Project Preferences

Will function either as deal originator or
  investor in deals created by others
Type of Financing:
First-stage
Second-stage
Later-stage expansion
Leveraged buyout
Minimum Investment: $250,000
Preferred Investment: $250,000-$500,000
Minimum Operating Data:
Annual Sales—Nominal

Geographical Preference

None

Industry Preferences

Communications
Cable television
Commercial communications
Data communications
Satellite and microwave communications
Telephone related
Computer Related
Computer graphics, CAD/CAM and CAE
Computer mainframes
Computer services
Memory devices
Micro and mini computers
Office automation
Scanning related
Software-applications
Software-artificial intelligence
Software-systems
Specialized turnkey systems
Terminals
Distribution
Communications equipment
Computer equipment
Consumer products
Electronics equipment
Food products
Industrial products
Medical products
Electronic Components and Instrumentation
Analytical and scientific instrumentation
Component fabrication and testing
  equipment
Electronic components
Fiber optics
Laser related
Semiconductors
Genetic Engineering
Gene splicing and manufacturing equipment
Monoclonal antibodies and hybridomas
Recombinant DNA (agricultural and
  industrial)
Recombinant DNA (medical)
Industrial Products and Equipment
Chemicals
Controls and sensors
Energy management
Equipment and machinery
Other industrial automation
Plastics
Robotics/vision systems
Specialty materials
Medical/Health Related
Diagnostic equipment
Diagnostic test products
Disposable products
Drugs and medicines
Hospital and clinical labs
Medical services
Therapeutic equipment

Additional Information

Year Founded—1959
Capital Under Management—$35 million
Investments(1985-1st 6 months)—10
Invested(1985-1st 6 months)—$2.5 million
Method of Compensation—Return on
  investment is of primary concern; do not
  charge fees

UNITED MISSOURI CAPITAL CORP.

Tenth and Grand
Kansas City, MO 64106
816-556-7333

Officers

William J. Bolt, Jr., Pres.
Joseph M. Kessinger, Exec. V.P. & Mgr.
David Miller, Secy.
William Teiwes, Treas.

Whom to Contact

Joseph M. Kessinger

Type of Firm

SBIC

Industry Association Membership

NASBIC

Project Preferences

Prefer role as deal originator
Type of Financing:
Second-stage
Leveraged buyout
Minimum Investment: $100,000
Preferred Investment: $100,000-$500,000
Minimum Operating Data:
Annual Sales—$500,000
P&L—Break even

Geographical Preference

Midwest

Industry Preferences

Communications
Data communications
Computer Related
Office automation
Specialized turnkey systems
Consumer
Consumer products
Consumer services

Distribution
Communications equipment
Consumer products
Food products
Industrial products
**Electronic Components and
  Instrumentation**
Analytical and scientific instrumentation
Fiber optics
Industrial Products and Equipment
Chemicals
Controls and sensors
Energy management
Equipment and machinery
Other industrial automation
Plastics
Robotics/vision systems
Specialty materials
Medical/Health Related
Diagnostic equipment
Drugs and medicines
Hospital and clinical labs
Medical services
Other
Publishing

Additional Information
Year Founded—1984
Capital Under Management—$2.5 million
Method of Compensation—Return on
  investment is of primary concern; do not
  charge fees

DEVELOPMENT CORPORATION OF MONTANA

350 North Last Chance Gulch
Norwest Bank Building
Post Office Box 196
Helena, MT 59624
406-442-3850

Officer

Richard L. Bourke, Pres.

Type of Firm

Private venture capital firm investing
own capital

Project Preferences

Will function either as deal originator or
investor in deals created by others
Type of Financing:
Seed
Research and development partnerships
Startup
First-stage
Second-stage
Later-stage expansion
Minimum Investment: Less than $100,000
Preferred Investment: Less than $100,000
Minimum Operating Data:
Annual Sales—Nominal
P&L—Losses (profits projected after 1 year)

Geographical Preference

Montana

Industry Preferences

Communications
Cable television
Commercial communications
Data communications
Satellite and microwave communications
Telephone related
Computer Related
Computer graphics, CAD/CAM and CAE
Computer mainframes
Computer services
Memory devices
Micro and mini computers
Office automation
Scanning Related
Software-applications
Software-artificial intelligence
Software-systems
Specialized turnkey systems
Terminals

Consumer
Computer stores/related services
Consumer products
Consumer services
Food and beverage products
Franchise businesses
Hotels and resort areas
Leisure and recreational products
Restaurants
Retailing
Distribution
Communications equipment
Computer equipment
Consumer products
Electronics equipment
Food products
Industrial products
Medical products
Electronic Components and Instrumentation
Analytical and scientific instrumentation
Component fabrication and testing
equipment
Electronic components
Fiber optics
Laser related
Semiconductors
Energy/Natural Resources
Alternative energy
Coal related
Drilling and exploration services
Energy conservation
Minerals
Oil and gas exploration and production
Technology related products/equipment
Genetic Engineering
Gene splicing and manufacturing equipment
Monoclonal antibodies and hybridomas
Recombinant DNA (agricultural and
industrial)
Recombinant DNA (medical)
Industrial Products and Equipment
Chemicals
Controls and sensors
Energy management
Equipment and machinery
Other industrial automation
Plastics
Robotics/vision systems
Specialty materials
Medical/Health Related
Diagnostic equipment
Diagnostic test products
Disposable products
Drugs and medicines
Hospital and clinical labs
Medical services
Therapeutic equipment

Other
Education related
Publishing
Real estate
Specialty consulting
Transportation
Will Not Consider
Agricultural operations
Residential real estate

Additional Information

Year Founded—1970
Capital Under Management—$2.3 million
Investments(1985-1st 6 months)—1
Invested(1985-1st 6 months)—$75,000
Method of Compensation—Return on
investment is most important, but also
charge for closing fees, service fees, etc.

ROCKY MOUNTAIN VENTURES, LTD.

315 Securities Building
Billings, MT 59101
406-256-1984

Other Office

1100 Tenth Street
Greeley, CO 80632
303-356-1200

Officers

James H. Koessler, Pres. (Montana)
E.E. Kuhns, Chm. (Montana)
Robert M. Brown, V.P. (Montana)
Norman M. Dean, V.P. (Colorado)
Thomas A. Rapp, Jr., V.P. (Colorado)

Whom to Contact

James H. Koessler
Norman M. Dean

Type of Firm

SBIC

Affiliations

Rocky Mountain Capital, Ltd.
(sister company)
Venture Capital Corporation of Montana
(sister company)

Industry Association Membership

NASBIC

Project Preferences

Will function either as deal originator or
investor in deals created by others

Type of Financing:
Second-stage
Later-stage expansion
Leveraged buyout
Minimum Investment: $100,000
Preferred Investment: $100,000-$250,000
Preferred Investment (LBO): $200,000
Minimum Operating Data:
Annual Sales—Nominal
P&L—Losses (profits projected after 1 year)

Geographical Preference
Rocky Mountains

Industry Preferences
None
Will Not Consider
Construction
Farming and ranching
Mining

Additional Information
Year Founded—1983
Capital Under Management—$1 million
Investments(1985-1st 6 months)—3
Invested(1985-1st 6 months)—$500,000
Method of Compensation—Return on
    investment is most important, but also
    charge for closing fees, service fees, etc.

GRANITE STATE CAPITAL, INC.

10 Fort Eddy Road
Concord, NH 03301
603-228-9090

Officers
W. Robert Felder, Pres.
Richard Carey, Treas.
Russell F. Hilliard, Secy.
Albert Hall III, Interim Mgr.

Whom to Contact
Albert Hall III

Type of Firm
SBIC

Affiliation
New Hampshire Business Development
  Corporation (parent)

Industry Association Membership
NASBIC

Project Preferences
Prefer role in deals created by others
Type of Financing:
First-stage
Second-stage
Later-stage expansion
Leveraged buyout
Minimum Investment: $100,000
Preferred Investment: $100,000-$250,000
Minimum Operating Data:
Annual Sales—$500,000
P&L—Break even

Geographical Preference
Northeast

Industry Preferences

Communications
Cable television
Commercial communications
Data communications
Satellite and microwave communications
Telephone related

Computer Related
Computer graphics, CAD/CAM and CAE
Computer mainframes
Computer services
Memory devices
Micro and mini computers
Office automation
Scanning related
Software-applications
Software-artificial intelligence
Software-systems
Specialized turnkey systems
Terminals
Consumer
Computer stores/related services
Consumer products
Consumer services
Food and beverage products
Franchise businesses
Hotels and resort areas
Leisure and recreational products
Restaurants
Retailing
Distribution
Communications equipment
Computer equipment
Consumer products
Electronics equipment
Food products
Industrial products
Medical products
**Electronic Components and
  Instrumentation**
Analytical and scientific instrumentation
Component fabrication and testing
  equipment
Electronic components
Fiber optics
Laser related
Semiconductors
Genetic Engineering
Gene splicing and manufacturing equipment
Monoclonal antibodies and hybridomas
Recombinant DNA (agricultural and
  industrial)
Recombinant DNA (medical)
Industrial Products and Equipment
Chemicals
Controls and sensors
Energy management
Equipment and machinery
Other industrial automation
Plastics
Robotics/vision systems
Specialty materials

Medical/Health Related
Diagnostic equipment
Diagnostic test products
Disposable products
Drugs and medicines
Hospital and clinical labs
Medical services
Therapeutic equipment
Other
Agriculture, forestry, fishing
Education related
Finance and insurance
Publishing
Real estate
Specialty consulting
Transportation

Additional Information
Year Founded—1983
Capital Under Management—$1 million
Method of Compensation—Return on
  investment is most important, but also
  charge for closing fees, service fees, etc.

HAMPSHIRE CAPITAL CORPORATION

500 Spaulding Turnpike
Post Office Box 3010
Portsmouth, NH 03801
603-431-7755

Officer
Philip G. Baker, Pres.

Type of Firm
SBIC

Affiliation
Business Investment Advisory Corporation
  (investment advisor)

Industry Association Membership
NASBIC

Project Preferences
Prefer role as deal originator but will also
  invest in deals created by others
Type of Financing:
Startup
First-stage
Second-stage
Leveraged buyout
Minimum Investment: Less than $100,000
Preferred Investment: Less than $100,000
Preferred Investment (LBO): $100,000
Minimum Operating Data:
Annual Sales—Nominal
P&L—Break even

Geographical Preferences
East Coast
U.S. Virgin Islands

Industry Preferences

Communications
Telephone related
Consumer
Computer stores/related services
Consumer products
Consumer services
Food and beverage products
Franchise businesses
Hotels and resort areas
Leisure and recreational products
Restaurants
Retailing
Distribution
Communications equipment
Computer equipment
Consumer products
Electronics equipment
Food products
Industrial products
Medical products
Other
Agriculture, forestry, fishing
Education related
Finance and insurance
Publishing
Real estate
Specialty consulting
Transportation
Will Not Consider
High technology businesses

Additional Information
Year Founded—1979
Capital Under Management—$500,000
Method of Compensation—Return on
 investment is most important, but also
 charge for closing fees, service fees, etc.

HARVARD VENTURE CAPITAL

27 Loop Road
Post Office Box 746
Merrimack, NH 03054
603-429-0858

Partners
Michael G. Angel, Mgn. Ptnr.
John D. Keith, Gen. Ptnr.

Whom to Contact
Michael G. Angel

Type of Firm
Private venture capital firm investing
 own capital

Affiliation
The Harvard Group (parent)

Industry Association Membership
NVCA

Project Preferences
Will function either as deal originator or
 investor in deals created by others
Type of Financing:
Seed
Research and development partnerships
Startup
First-stage
Leveraged buyout
Minimum Investment: $100,000
Preferred Investment: $100,000-$500,000
Minimum Operating Data:
Annual Sales—Nominal
P&L—Break even

Geographical Preferences
Within two hours of office
Northeast

Industry Preferences

Other
Real estate
Specialty consulting

Additional Information
Year Founded—1983
Capital Under Management—$25 million
Investments(1985-1st 6 months)—5
Invested(1985-1st 6 months)—$10 million
Method of Compensation—Return on
 investment is of primary concern; do not
 charge fees

LOTUS CAPITAL CORPORATION

875 Elm Street
Manchester, NH 03101
603-668-8802

Officers
Richard J. Ash, Pres.
David J. Towner, V.P., Treas. & Secy.

Whom to Contact
Richard J. Ash

Type of Firm
Private venture capital firm investing
 own capital
SBIC

Affiliation
Roan Venture (incubator company managed
 by Lotus Capital)

Industry Association Membership
NASBIC

Project Preferences
Prefer role as deal originator but will also
 invest in deals created by others
Type of Financing:
First-stage
Second-stage
Later-stage expansion
Leveraged buyout
Minimum Investment: Less than $100,000
Preferred Investment: $100,000-$500,000
Preferred Investment (LBO): $200,000
Minimum Operating Data:
Annual Sales—Nominal
P&L—Break even

Geographical Preference
Northeast

Industry Preferences

Communications
Cable television
Commercial communications
Data communications
Satellite and microwave communications
Telephone related
Computer Related
Computer graphics, CAD/CAM and CAE
Office automation
Scanning related
Distribution
Communications equipment
Electronics equipment
Industrial products
Medical products
**Electronic Components and
 Instrumentation**
Analytical and scientific instrumentation
Fiber optics
Laser related
Energy/Natural Resources
Drilling and exploration services
Oil and gas exploration and production
Technology related products/equipment
Genetic Engineering
Monoclonal antibodies and hybridomas
Recombinant DNA (agricultural and
 industrial)
Recombinant DNA (medical)

Industrial Products and Equipment
Chemicals
Controls and sensors
Energy management
Equipment and machinery
Other industrial automation
Plastics
Robotics/vision systems
Specialty materials
Medical/Health Related
Diagnostic equipment
Diagnostic test products
Disposable products
Drugs and medicines
Geriatric areas
Hospital and clinical labs
Medical services
Therapeutic equipment
Other
Education related
Finance and insurance
Specialty consulting
Will Not Consider
Computer software

WYNDMOOR ASSOCIATES, LTD.

10 Parkway
Hanover, NH 03755
603-643-6346

W. Bradley McConky

See PENNSYLVANIA for full listing

ACCEL PARTNERS

One Palmer Square
Princeton, NJ 08542
609-683-4500

Other Offices

2020 Hogback Road
Ann Arbor, MI 48104
313-971-5234

One Embarcadero Center
San Francisco, CA 94111
415-989-5656

Managing Partners

Dixon R. Doll
Arthur C. Patterson
James R. Swartz

Whom to Contact

Any of the above

Type of Firm

Private venture capital firm investing
own capital

Industry Association Memberships

NASBIC
NVCA
WAVC

Project Preferences

Will function either as deal originator or
investor in deals created by others
Type of Financing:
Seed
Research and development partnerships
Startup
First-stage
Second-stage
Later-stage expansion
Minimum Investment: Less than $100,000
Preferred Investment: No preference
Minimum Operating Data:
Annual Sales—Nominal
P&L—Losses (profits projected after 2 years)

Geographical Preference

None

Industry Preferences

Communications
Cable television
Commercial communications
Data communications
Local area networks
Satellite and microwave communications
Telephone related

Computer Related
Computer graphics, CAD/CAM and CAE
Computer mainframes
Computer services
Memory devices
Micro and mini computers
Office automation
Scanning related
Software-applications
Software-artificial intelligence
Software-systems
Specialized turnkey systems
Terminals
Consumer
Consumer services
Distribution
Communications equipment
Computer equipment
Consumer products
Electronics equipment
Food products
Industrial products
Medical products
**Electronic Components and
  Instrumentation**
Analytical and scientific instrumentation
Component fabrication and testing
  equipment
Electronic components
Fiber optics
Laser related
Semiconductors
Energy/Natural Resources
Alternative energy
Coal related
Drilling and exploration services
Energy conservation
Minerals
Oil and gas exploration and production
Technology related products/equipment
Genetic Engineering
Gene splicing and manufacturing equipment
Monoclonal antibodies and hybridomas
Recombinant DNA (agricultural and
  industrial)
Recombinant DNA (medical)
Industrial Products and Equipment
Chemicals
Controls and sensors
Energy management
Equipment and machinery
Other industrial automation
Plastics
Robotics/vision systems
Specialty materials

Medical/Health Related
Diagnostic equipment
Diagnostic test products
Disposable products
Drugs and medicines
Hospital and clinical labs
Medical services
Therapeutic equipment

Additional Information

Year Founded—1983
Capital Under Management—$100 million
Investments(1985-1st 6 months)—14
Invested(1985-1st 6 months)—$6 million
Method of Compensation—Return on
  investment is of primary concern; do not
  charge fees

BRADFORD ASSOCIATES

22 Chambers Street
Princeton, NJ 08540
609-921-3880

Partners

Bradford Mills, Gen. Ptnr.
Winston J. Churchill, Gen. Ptnr.
Herbert Salzman, Mgn. Dir.

Whom to Contact

Any of the above

Type of Firm

Private venture capital firm investing
own capital
Investment firm investing own capital or
funds of partners and clients

Affiliation

Bessemer Securities Corporation (partner)

Industry Association Membership

NVCA

Project Preferences

Prefer role as deal originator but will also
invest in deals created by others
Type of Financing:
Second-stage
Later-stage expansion
Leveraged buyout
Minimum Investment: $1 million
Preferred Investment: $4 million and over
Preferred Investment (LBO): $4 million
Minimum Operating Data:
Annual Sales—Over $3 million
P&L—Profits NBT over $2 million
Annual Sales (LBO)—$20 million and over

Geographical Preferences
Northeast
Southeast
East Coast
Midwest

Industry Preferences

Communications
Telephone related
Consumer
Consumer products
Leisure and recreational products
Retailing
Distribution
Industrial products
Electronic Components and Instrumentation
Analytical and scientific instrumentation
Energy/Natural Resources
Drilling and exploration services
Minerals
Oil and gas exploration and production
Industrial Products and Equipment
Chemicals
Controls and sensors
Equipment and machinery
Light manufacturing
Office supplies
Medical/Health Related
Diagnostic equipment
Disposable products
Hospital and clinical labs
Medical services
Other
Filtration media
Will Not Consider
Banking
High-technology industries
Real estate

Additional Information
Year Founded—1974
Capital Under Management—$43 million
Investments(1985-1st 6 months)—2
Invested(1985-1st 6 months)—$13 million
Method of Compensation—Return on investment is most important, but also charge for closing fees, service fees, etc.

DOMAIN ASSOCIATES

One Palmer Square
Princeton, NJ 08542
609-683-5656

Partners
James C. Blair
Jennifer H. Lobo
Jesse Treu

Whom to Contact
Either of the above

Type of Firm
Private venture capital firm investing own capital

Affiliation
Biotechnology Investments Ltd., managed by N.M. Rothschild & Sons Ltd. (advisor to venture capital fund)

Project Preferences
Will function either as deal originator or investor in deals created by others
Type of Financing:
Seed
Startup
First-stage
Second-stage
Leveraged buyout
Minimum Investment: $500,000 (unless seed financing)
Preferred Investment: Over $1 million
Minimum Operating Data:
Annual Sales—Nominal
P&L—Losses (profits projected after 2 years)

Geographical Preference
None

Industry Preferences

Electronic Components and Instrumentation
Analytical and scientific instrumentation
Genetic Engineering
Gene splicing and manufacturing equipment
Monoclonal antibodies and hybridomas
Recombinant DNA (agricultural and industrial)
Recombinant DNA (medical)
Industrial Products and Equipment
Chemicals
Controls and sensors
Specialty materials

Medical/Health Related
Diagnostic equipment
Diagnostic test products
Disposable products
Drugs and medicines
Hospital and clinical labs
Therapeutic equipment

Additional Information
Year Founded—1985
Capital Under Management—$100 million
Investments(1985-1st 6 months)—7
Invested(1985-1st 6 months)—$3.1 million

D.S. VENTURES, INC.

350 Mount Kemble Avenue
CN 1931
Morristown, NJ 07960
201-267-1000

Frank C. Briden, V.P.

See TEXAS for full listing

DSV PARTNERS

221 Nassau Street
Princeton, NJ 08542
609-924-4420

Partners
James R. Bergman, Gen. Ptnr.
Morton Collins, Gen. Ptnr.
Robert S. Hillas, Gen. Ptnr.
John K. Clarke, Assoc.
James J. Millar, Assoc.

Whom to Contact
Any of the above

Type of Firm
Private venture capital firm investing own capital

Industry Association Membership
NVCA

Project Preferences
Will function either as deal originator or investor in deals created by others
Type of Financing:
Seed
Research and development partnerships
Startup
First-stage
Second-stage

417

Minimum Investment: $100,000
Preferred Investment: $500,000-$1 million
Minimum Operating Data:
Annual Sales—Nominal
P&L—Losses (profits projected after 3 years)

Geographical Preference
None

Industry Preferences

Communications
Data communications
Satellite and microwave communications
Computer Related
Computer graphics, CAD/CAM and CAE
Computer mainframes
Computer services
Memory devices
Micro and mini computers
Office automation
Scanning related
Software-applications
Software-artificial intelligence
Software-systems
Terminals
Electronic Components and Instrumentation
Analytical and scientific instrumentation
Component fabrication and testing equipment
Electronic components
Fiber optics
Semiconductors
Energy/Natural Resources
Alternative energy
Energy conservation
Technology related products/equipment
Industrial Products and Equipment
Chemicals
Controls and sensors
Other industrial automation
Robotics/vision systems
Medical/Health Related
Diagnostic equipment
Diagnostic test products
Drugs and medicines
Hospital and clinical labs
Medical services
Therapeutic equipment
Will Not Consider
Real estate

Additional Information
Year Founded—1968
Capital Under Management—$100 million
Investments(1985-1st 6 months)—11
Invested(1985-1st 6 months)—$2.5 million
Method of Compensation—Return on investment is of primary concern; do not charge fees

---

EDELSON TECHNOLOGY PARTNERS

Park 80 West, Plaza Two
Saddle Brook, NJ 07662
201-843-4474

Partners
Harry Edelson, Mgn. Ptnr.
Raymond Bosso, Ptnr.
Anthony Buffa, Ptnr.
Carol Maurizi, Assoc.

Whom to Contact
Harry Edelson

Type of Firm
Private venture capital firm investing own capital

Affiliation
Amerinex (joint venture)

Project Preferences
Will function either as deal originator or investor in deals created by others
Type of Financing:
Startup
First-stage
Second-stage
Later-stage expansion
Leveraged buyout
Minimum Investment: $250,000
Preferred Investment: $500,000-$1 million
Preferred Investment (LBO): $2 million
Minimum Operating Data:
Annual Sales—Nominal
P&L—Losses (profits projected after 2 years)
Annual Sales (LBO)—$10 million-$100 million

Geographical Preference
None

Industry Preferences

Communications
Cable television
Commercial communications
Data communications
Satellite and microwave communications
Telephone related
Computer Related
Computer graphics, CAD/CAM and CAE
Computer mainframes
Computer services
Memory devices
Micro and mini computers
Office automation
Scanning related
Software-applications
Software-artificial intelligence
Software-systems
Specialized turnkey systems
Terminals
Consumer
Entertainment
Leisure and recreational products
Distribution
Communications equipment
Computer equipment
Electronics equipment
Industrial products
Medical products
Electronic Components and Instrumentation
Electronic components
Fiber optics
Laser related
Semiconductors
Energy/Natural Resources
Technology related products/equipment
Genetic Engineering
Gene splicing and manufacturing equipment
Monoclonal antibodies and hybridomas
Recombinant DNA (agricultural and industrial)
Recombinant DNA (medical)
Industrial Products and Equipment
Controls and sensors
Robotics/vision systems
Medical/Health Related
Diagnostic equipment
Diagnostic test products
Disposable products
Other
Publishing

Additional Information
Year Founded—1984
Capital Under Management—$36 million
Investments(1985-1st 6 months)—6
Invested(1985-1st 6 months)—$6 million
Method of Compensation—Return on investment is of primary concern; do not charge fees

ESLO CAPITAL CORPORATION

2401 Morris Avenue #220
Union, NJ 07083
201-687-4920

Officers
Leo Katz, Pres.
Estelle Katz, Secy.

Whom to Contact
Leo Katz

Type of Firm
SBIC

Industry Association Membership
NASBIC

Project Preferences
Will function either as deal originator or
  investor in deals created by others
Type of Financing:
Second-stage
Leveraged buyout
Minimum Investment: Less than $100,000
Preferred Investment: $100,000-$250,000
Minimum Operating Data:
Annual Sales—$500,000
P&L—Break even

Geographical Preferences
Northeast
Southeast

Industry Preferences

Communications
Cable television
Commercial communications
Data communications
Satellite and microwave communications
Telephone related
Computer Related
Computer graphics, CAD/CAM and CAE
Computer mainframes
Computer services
Memory devices
Micro and mini computers
Office automation
Scanning related
Software-applications
Software-artificial intelligence
Software-systems
Specialized turnkey systems
Terminals

Consumer
Computer stores/related services
Consumer products
Consumer services
Food and beverage products
Franchise businesses
Hotels and resort areas
Leisure and recreational products
Restaurants
Retailing
Distribution
Communications equipment
Computer equipment
Consumer products
Electronics equipment
Food products
Industrial products
Medical products
**Electronic Components and
  Instrumentation**
Analytical and scientific instrumentation
Component fabrication and testing
  equipment
Electronic components
Fiber optics
Laser related
Semiconductors
Energy/Natural Resources
Alternative energy
Coal related
Drilling and exploration services
Energy conservation
Minerals
Oil and gas exploration and production
Technology related products/equipment
Industrial Products and Equipment
Chemicals
Controls and sensors
Energy management
Equipment and machinery
Other industrial automation
Plastics
Robotics/vision systems
Specialty materials
Medical/Health Related
Diagnostic equipment
Diagnostic test products
Disposable products
Drugs and medicines
Hospital and clinical labs
Medical services
Therapeutic equipment
Other
Education related
Finance and insurance
Publishing
Real estate
Specialty consulting
Transportation

Additional Information
Year Founded—1979
Capital Under Management—$2 million
Investments(1985-1st 6 months)—7
Invested(1985-1st 6 months)—$800,000
Method of Compensation—Return on
  investment is most important, but also
  charge for closing fees, service fees, etc.

GENERAL INSTRUMENT CORP.

225 Alwood Road
Clifton, NJ 07012
201-779-3000

Officer
Gerard Johnson, V.P. & CFO

Whom to Contact
James R. Rulmyr

Type of Firm
Venture capital subsidiary or affiliate of
  non-financial corporation

Affiliation
General Instrument Corp. (parent)

Project Preferences
Will function either as deal originator or
  investor in deals created by others
Type of Financing:
Seed
Research and development partnerships
Startup
First-stage
Second-stage
Later-stage expansion
Leveraged buyout
Preferred Investment: No preference

Geographical Preference
None

Industry Preferences

Communications
Cable television
Commercial communications
Data communications
Satellite and microwave communications
Telephone related

Computer Related
Computer graphics, CAD/CAM and CAE
Memory devices
Micro and mini computers
Office automation
Software-artificial intelligence
Specialized turnkey systems
Terminals
**Electronic Components and
  Instrumentation**
Electronic components
Fiber optics
Semiconductors
Industrial Products and Equipment
Controls and sensors
Energy management
Other industrial automation

Additional Information
Year Founded—1981
Capital Under Management—$30 million
Investments(1985-1st 6 months)—4
Invested(1985-1st 6 months)—$7 million
Method of Compensation—Return on
  investment is of primary concern; do not
  charge fees

INNOVEN GROUP

Park 80 West, Plaza One
Saddle Brook, NJ 07662
201-845-4900

Officers
Gerald A. Lodge, Chief Exec.
Raun J. Rasmussen, Pres.

Whom to Contact
Either of the above

Type of Firm
Private venture capital firm investing
  own capital

Affiliations
Emerson Electric Company
Monsanto Company
Anheuser-Busch Companies

Industry Association Membership
NVCA

Project Preferences
Will function either as deal originator or
  investor in deals created by others

Type of Financing:
Seed
Startup
First-stage
Second-stage
Later-stage expansion
Leveraged buyout
Minimum Investment: $100,000
Preferred Investment: $500,000-$1 million
Minimum Operating Data:
Annual Sales—Nominal
P&L—Losses (profits projected after 2 years)

Geographical Preference
East Coast

Industry Preferences

Communications
Commercial communications
Data communications
Satellite and microwave communications
Computer Related
Computer graphics, CAD/CAM and CAE
Computer mainframes
Computer services
Memory devices
Micro and mini computers
Office automation
Scanning related
Software-applications
Software-artificial intelligence
Software-systems
Specialized turnkey systems
Terminals
Consumer
Computer stores/related services
Consumer products
Consumer services
Food and beverage products
Franchise businesses
Hotels and resort areas
Leisure and recreational products
Restaurants
Retailing
Distribution
Consumer products
Food products
**Electronic Components and
  Instrumentation**
Analytical and scientific instrumentation
Component fabrication and testing
  equipment
Electronic components
Fiber optics
Laser related
Semiconductors
Energy/Natural Resources
Technology related products/equipment

Genetic Engineering
Gene splicing and manufacturing equipment
Monoclonal antibodies and hybridomas
Recombinant DNA (agricultural and
  industrial)
Recombinant DNA (medical)
Industrial Products and Equipment
Chemicals
Controls and sensors
Energy management
Equipment and machinery
Other industrial automation
Plastics
Robotics/vision systems
Specialty materials
Medical/Health Related
Diagnostic equipment
Diagnostic test products
Disposable products
Drugs and medicines
Hospital and clinical labs
Medical services
Therapeutic equipment
Will Not Consider
Banking
Insurance
Leasing
Real estate

Additional Information
Year Founded—1972
Capital Under Management—$60 million
Investments(1985-1st 6 months)—7
Invested(1985-1st 6 months)—$2.5 million
Method of Compensation—Return on
  investment is of primary concern; do not
  charge fees

INVESTMENT PARTNERS
OF AMERICA

732 West Eighth Street
Plainfield, NJ 07060
201-561-3622

Other Office
c/o Conboy, Hewitt, O'Brien &
  Boardman
100 Park Avenue
New York, NY 10017

Partners
Frank J. Abella, Jr., Mgn. Ptnr. (New Jersey)
Donald Stuart Bab, Gen. Ptnr. (New York)

Whom to Contact
Either of the above

Type of Firm
Private venture capital firm investing
own capital
Investment banking or merchant banking
firm investing own capital or funds of
partners or clients
Consulting firm evaluating and analyzing
venture projects and arranging private
placements

Project Preferences
Prefer role as deal originator but will also
invest in deals created by others
Type of Financing:
Research and development partnerships
Second-stage
Preferred Investment: $500,000-$1 million
Minimum Operating Data:
Annual Sales—Over $3 million
P&L—Break even

Geographical Preferences
Within two hours of office
Northeast
East Coast

Industry Preferences

Communications
Data communications
Military telecommunications
Consumer
Consumer products
Consumer services
Food and beverage products
Leisure and recreational products
Distribution
Communications equipment
Food products
Industrial products
**Electronic Components and
Instrumentation**
Analytical and scientific instrumentation
Component fabrication and testing
equipment
Electronic components
Energy/Natural Resources
Alternative energy
Coal related
Drilling and exploration services
Energy conservation
Minerals
Oil and gas exploration and production
Technology related products/equipment
Industrial Products and Equipment
Chemicals
Controls and sensors
Equipment and machinery
Plastics
Robotics/vision systems
Specialty materials

Medical/Health Related
Disposable products
Hospital and clinical labs
Other
Agriculture, forestry, fishing
Finance and insurance
Specialty consulting
Will Not Consider
Commodities
Real estate

Additional Information
Year Founded—1984
Investments(1985-1st 6 months)—6
Invested(1985-1st 6 months)—Over $2 million
Method of Compensation—Return on
investment is most important, but also
charge for closing fees, service fees, etc.

JOHNSON & JOHNSON DEVELOPMENT CORPORATION

One Johnson & Johnson Plaza
New Brunswick, NJ 08933
201-524-6407

Officers
C.M. Anderson, Pres.
L.A. Cahill, Dir. New Bus. Development
W.B. Deibler, Dir. New Ventures

Whom to Contact
Any of the above

Type of Firm
Venture capital subsidiary or affiliate of
non-financial corporation

Affiliation
Johnson & Johnson (parent)

Project Preferences
Will function either as deal originator or
investor in deals created by others
Type of Financing:
Seed
Startup
First-stage
Preferred Investment: No preference
Minimum Operating Data:
Annual Sales—Nominal

Geographical Preference
None

Industry Preferences

Consumer
Health care related consumer products
**Electronic Components and
Instrumentation**
Laser related
Genetic Engineering
Monoclonal antibodies and hybridomas
Recombinant DNA (medical)
Medical/Health Related
Diagnostic equipment
Drugs and medicines
Will Not Consider
Health care facilities
Non health care related businesses

Additional Information
Year Founded—1973
Method of Compensation—Licensing of
products and technology for marketing by
Johnson & Johnson is of primary concern:
do not charge fees.

JOHNSTON ASSOCIATES, INC.

181 Cherry Valley Road
Princeton, NJ 08540
609-924-3131

Officers
Robert B. Stockman, V.P.
Robert F. Johnston, Pres.

Whom to Contact
Any of the above

Type of Firm
Private venture capital firm investing
own capital

Industry Association Membership
NVCA

Project Preferences
Prefer role as deal originator
Type of Financing:
Seed
Leveraged buyout
Minimum Investment: $250,000
Preferred Investment: $250,000-$500,000
Minimum Operating Data:
Annual Sales—Nominal

Geographical Preferences
Within two hours of office
Northeast

Industry Preferences

Genetic Engineering
Monoclonal antibodies and hybridomas
Recombinant DNA (medical)
Medical/Health Related
Diagnostic equipment
Hospital and clinical labs
Medical services
Therapeutic equipment
Other
Toxic waste processing

Additional Information

Year Founded—1967
Investments(1985-1st 6 months)—2
Invested(1985-1st 6 months)—$500,000
Method of Compensation—Return on
 investment is of primary concern; do not
 charge fees

MBW MANAGEMENT, INC.

365 South Street, Second Floor
Morristown, NJ 07906
201-285-5533

Other Offices

2000 Hogback Road
Ann Arbor, MI 48105
313-971-3100

350 Second Street #7
Los Altos, CA 94022
415-941-2392

333 East Main Street
Post Office Box 1431
Midland, MI 48641
517-631-2471

Officers

Philip E. McCarthy, Mgn. Dir. (Morristown)
Ian R.N. Bund, Mgn. Dir. (Ann Arbor)
James R. Weersing, Mgn. Dir. (Los Altos)
Richard M. Goff, V.P., Treas. & Secy.
 (Ann Arbor)
Robert J. Harrington, V.P. (Los Altos)
Herbert D. Doan (Midland)
James N. Hauslein, Inv. Analyst (Morristown)

Whom to Contact

Ian R.N. Bund
Philip E. McCarthy
James R. Weersing

Type of Firm

Private venture capital firm investing
 own capital
SBIC

Affiliations

MBW Venture Partners Limited Partnership
 (fund managed)
Michigan Investment Fund L.P.
 (fund managed)
Doan Resources Limited Partnership
 (fund managed)
Doan Associates (fund managed)

Project Preferences

Will function either as deal originator or
 investor in deals created by others
Type of Financing:
Startup
First-stage
Second-stage
Later-stage expansion
Leveraged buyout
Minimum Investment: $500,000
Preferred Investment: $500,000-$1 million
Preferred Investment (LBO):
 $1.5 million-$2 million
Minimum Operating Data:
Annual Sales (LBO)—
 $20 million-$100 million

Geographical Preference
None

Industry Preferences

Communications
Data communications
Computer Related
Computer graphics, CAD/CAM and CAE
Computer mainframes
Computer services
Memory devices
Micro and mini computers
Office automation
Scanning related
Software-applications
Software-artificial intelligence
Software-systems
Specialized turnkey systems
Terminals
**Electronic Components and
 Instrumentation**
Analytical and scientific instrumentation
Component fabrication and testing
 equipment
Electronic components
Fiber optics
Laser related
Semiconductors

Genetic Engineering
Gene splicing and manufacturing equipment
Monoclonal antibodies and hybridomas
Recombinant DNA (agricultural and
 industrial)
Recombinant DNA (medical)
Industrial Products and Equipment
Other industrial automation
Robotics/vision systems
Medical/Health Related
Diagnostic equipment
Diagnostic test products
Disposable products
Drugs and medicines
Hospital and clinical labs
Medical services
Therapeutic equipment
Will Not Consider
Consumer products
Franchises
Real estate

Additional Information

Year Founded—1984
Capital Under Management—$125.6 million
Investments(1985-1st 6 months)—7
Invested(1985-1st 6 months)—$3.9 million
Method of Compensation—Return on
 investment is of primary concern; do not
 charge fees

MED-TECH VENTURES, INC.

201 Tabor Road
Morris Plains, NJ 07950
201-540-3457

Officers

Fred G. Weiss, Pres.
H. Kirk Merritt, V.P.
O.W. McGillicuddy, Dir.

Whom to Contact
Any of the above

Type of Firm
Venture capital subsidiary or affiliate of
 non-financial corporation

Affiliation
Warner-Lambert Company

Project Preferences
Will function either as deal originator or
 investor in deals created by others

Type of Financing:
Startup
First-stage
Second-stage
Later-stage expansion
Minimum Investment: $250,000
Preferred Investment: $500,000-$1 million

Geographical Preference
None

Industry Preferences

Consumer
Consumer products
Distribution
Consumer products
Medical products
Electronic Components and Instrumentation
Analytical and scientific instrumentation
Fiber optics
Medical/Health Related
Drugs and medicines
Medical services
Therapeutic equipment
Will Not Consider
Energy/natural resources
Finance
Industrial
Real estate

Additional Information
Year Founded—1983
Capital Under Management—$25 million
Method of Compensation—Return on investment is of primary concern; do not charge fees

---

MONMOUTH CAPITAL CORPORATION

125 Wyckoff Road
Post Office Box 335
Eatontown, NJ 07724
201-542-4927

Officers
Eugene W. Landy, Pres.
Ralph B. Patterson, Exec. V.P.
Ernest V. Bencivenga, Secy. & Treas.

Whom to Contact
Ralph B. Patterson

Type of Firm
SBIC

Industry Association Membership
NASBIC

Project Preferences
Will function either as deal originator or investor in deals created by others
Type of Financing:
Second-stage
Later-stage expansion
Leveraged buyout
Minimum Investment: $50,000
Preferred Investment: $100,000-$250,000
Preferred Investment (LBO): $400,000
Minimum Operating Data:
Annual Sales—Nominal
P&L—Break even

Geographical Preference
Northeast

Industry Preferences

Communications
Cable television
Commercial communications
Data communications
Satellite and microwave communications
Telephone related
Consumer
Computer stores/related services
Consumer products
Consumer services
Food and beverage products
Franchise businesses
Hotels and resort areas
Leisure and recreational products
Restaurants
Retailing
Distribution
Communications equipment
Computer equipment
Consumer products
Electronics equipment
Food products
Industrial products
Medical products
Electronic Components and Instrumentation
Analytical and scientific instrumentation
Component fabrication and testing equipment
Electronic components
Fiber optics
Laser related
Semiconductors

Industrial Products and Equipment
Chemicals
Controls and sensors
Energy management
Equipment and machinery
Other industrial automation
Plastics
Robotics/vision systems
Specialty materials

Additional Information
Year Founded—1961
Capital Under Management—$10 million
Investments(1985-1st 6 months)—2
Invested(1985-1st 6 months)—$600,000
Method of Compensation—Return on investment is most important, but also charge for closing fees, service fees, etc.

P.F. INVESTMENTS CO.

c/o Pengad
Post Office Box 99
Bayonne, NJ 07002
201-436-5625

General Partner
Donald B. Pierson

Type of Firm
Private venture capital firm investing own capital

Project Preferences
Prefer role as deal originator but will also invest in deals created by others
Type of Financing:
Seed
Startup
Leveraged buyout
Minimum Investment: Less than $100,000
Preferred Investment: $100,000-$250,000
Minimum Operating Data:
Annual Sales—Nominal
P&L—Losses (profits projected after 2 years)

Geographical Preferences
Within two hours of office
Northeast

Industry Preferences

Communications
Data communications
Telephone related

Computer Related
Computer graphics, CAD/CAM and CAE
Computer mainframes
Computer services
Memory devices
Micro and mini computers
Office automation
Scanning related
Software-applications
Software-artificial intelligence
Software-systems
Specialized turnkey systems
Terminals
Consumer
Consumer services
Distribution
Communications equipment
Computer equipment
Industrial products
Industrial Products and Equipment
Controls and sensors
Energy management
Equipment and machinery
Other
Real estate
Specialty consulting
Will Not Consider
Low technology industries

Additional Information
Year Founded—1966
Capital Under Management—$3.2 million
Investments(1985-1st 6 months)—3
Invested(1985-1st 6 months)—$450,000
Method of Compensation—Return on
  investment is of primary concern; do not
  charge fees

PRINCETON/MONTROSE PARTNERS

101 Poor Farm Road
Princeton, NJ 08540
609-921-1590

West Coast Office
2331 Honolulu Avenue #G
Montrose, CA 91020
818-957-3623

Partners
Ronald R. Hahn, Mgn. Ptnr. (New Jersey)
Donald R. Stroben, Mgn. Ptnr. (California)
Charles I. Kosmont, Gen. Ptnr. (California)
Richard J. Defieux, Gen. Ptnr. (New Jersey)
Laura M. Latella, Analyst (New Jersey)

Whom to Contact
Any partner

Type of Firm
Private venture capital firm investing
  own capital

Project Preferences
Will function either as deal originator or
  investor in deals created by others
Type of Financing:
Seed
Startup
First-stage
Second-stage
Later-stage expansion
Leveraged buyout
Minimum Investment: $100,000
Preferred Investment: $500,000-$1 million
Preferred Investment (LBO):
  $500,000-$1 million
Minimum Operating Data:
Annual Sales—Nominal
P&L—Losses (profits projected after 2 years)

Geographical Preference
None

Industry Preferences

Computer Related
Computer products related to agribusiness,
  energy, or natural resources
Consumer
Food and beverage products
Restaurants
Distribution
Food products
**Electronic Components and
  Instrumentation**
Analytical and scientific instrumentation
Companies related to agribusiness, energy
  or natural resources
Energy/Natural Resources
Alternative energy
Coal related
Energy assets
Energy conservation
Energy product storage, processing and
  distribution
Energy related process controls
Energy resource location and extraction
Minerals
Natural resource location and extraction
Natural resource processing and distribution
Natural resource related assets
Oil and gas services
Specialty raw materials
Genetic Engineering
Monoclonal antibodies and hybridomas
Recombinant DNA (agricultural and
  industrial)
Research and manufacturing equipment

Industrial Products and Equipment
Advanced materials
Industrial automation
Process controls
Agribusiness Related
Agriculture, forestry, fishing
Animal health
Farm equipment
Food products
Food storage, processing and distribution
Genetic improvement of plants and animals

Additional Information
Year Founded—1981
Capital Under Management—$17 million
Investments(1985-1st 6 months)—8
Invested(1985-1st 6 months)—$1.6 million
Method of Compensation—Return on
  investment is of primary concern; do not
  charge fees

PRINTON, KANE & CO.

830 Morris Turnpike
Short Hills, NJ 07078
201-467-9300

Other Offices
590 Madison Avenue #312
New York, NY 10222
800-526-4952

1346 Connecticut Avenue NW
Washington, DC 20036
800-526-4952

90 State Street #1418
Albany, NY 12207
800-526-4952

2000 Glades Road #202
Boca Raton, FL 33431
800-526-4952

Partners
Thomas F. Kane, Ptnr. (New Jersey)
John R. Parker, Ptnr. (New Jersey)
Robert L. Rose, Dir., Corporate Finance
  (New Jersey)

Whom to Contact
Robert L. Rose

Type of Firm
Investment banking or merchant banking
  firm investing own capital or funds of
  partners or clients

Project Preferences

Prefer role as deal originator but will also invest in deals created by others

Type of Financing:
Seed
Research and development partnerships
Startup
First-stage
Second-stage
Later-stage expansion
Leveraged buyout
Minimum Investment: $100,000
Preferred Investment: $500,000-$1 million
Minimum Operating Data:
Annual Sales—Nominal

Geographical Preference
None

Industry Preferences

Communications
Cable television
Commercial communications
Data communications
Satellite and microwave communications
Telephone related
Computer Related
Computer graphics, CAD/CAM and CAE
Computer mainframes
Computer services
Memory devices
Micro and mini computers
Office automation
Scanning related
Software-applications
Software-artificial intelligence
Software-systems
Specialized turnkey systems
Terminals
Electronic Components and Instrumentation
Analytical and scientific instrumentation
Component fabrication and testing equipment
Electronic components
Fiber optics
Laser related
Semiconductors
Energy/Natural Resources
Alternative energy
Coal related
Drilling and exploration services
Energy conservation
Minerals
Oil and gas exploration and production
Technology related products/equipment

Medical/Health Related
Diagnostic equipment
Diagnostic test products
Disposable products
Drugs and medicines
Hospital and clinical labs
Medical services
Therapeutic equipment

Additional Information
Year Founded—1972
Method of Compensation—Return on investment is most important, but also charge for closing fees, service fees, etc.

RICHARDSON & MCGRATH ASSOCIATES

104 Algonquin
Oakland, NJ 07436
201-337-9608

See NEW YORK for full listing

UNICORN VENTURES LTD./ UNICORN VENTURES II, L.P.

14 Commerce Drive
Cranford, NJ 07016
201-276-7880

General Partners
Frank P. Diassi
Arthur Bugs Baer

Whom to Contact
Either of the above

Type of Firm
SBIC

Industry Association Membership
NASBIC

Project Preferences
Will function either as deal originator or investor in deals created by others
Type of Financing:
Startup
First-stage
Second-stage
Later-stage expansion
Leveraged buyout
Minimum Investment: $250,000
Preferred Investment: $500,000-$1 million
Minimum Operating Data:
Annual Sales—$500,000

Geographical Preference
National

Industry Preferences

Communications
Cable television
Commercial communications
Data communications
Satellite and microwave communications
Telephone related
Computer Related
Computer graphics, CAD/CAM and CAE
Computer mainframes
Computer services
Memory devices
Micro and mini computers
Office automation
Scanning related
Software-applications
Software-artificial intelligence
Software-systems
Specialized turnkey systems
Terminals
Consumer
Computer stores/related services
Consumer products
Consumer services
Food and beverage products
Franchise businesses
Hotels and resort areas
Leisure and recreational products
Restaurants
Retailing
Distribution
Communications equipment
Computer equipment
Consumer products
Electronics equipment
Food products
Industrial products
Medical products
Electronic Components and Instrumentation
Analytical and scientific instrumentation
Component fabrication and testing equipment
Electronic components
Fiber optics
Laser related
Semiconductors
Energy/Natural Resources
Alternative energy
Coal related
Drilling and exploration services
Energy conservation
Minerals
Oil and gas exploration and production
Technology related products/equipment

Genetic Engineering
Gene splicing and manufacturing equipment
Monoclonal antibodies and hybridomas
Recombinant DNA (agricultural and industrial)
Recombinant DNA (medical)
Industrial Products and Equipment
Chemicals
Controls and sensors
Energy management
Equipment and machinery
Other industrial automation
Plastics
Robotics/vision systems
Specialty materials
Medical/Health Related
Diagnostic equipment
Diagnostic test products
Disposable products
Drugs and medicines
Hospital and clinical labs
Medical services
Therapeutic equipment
Other
Agriculture, forestry, fishing
Education related
Finance and insurance
Publishing
Real estate
Specialty consulting
Transportation
Will Not Consider
Entertainment

Additional Information
Year Founded—1981
Capital Under Management—$35 million
Investments(1985-1st 6 months)—9
Invested(1985-1st 6 months)—$3 million
Method of Compensation—Return on investment is of primary concern; do not charge fees

---

VENTURTECH

210 Main Street
Post Office Box 210
Gladstone, NJ 07934
201-234-2373

General Partners
F. Duffield Meyercord
E. Max Charlet
David C. Costine

Whom to Contact
E. Max Charlet
David C. Costine

Type of Firm
Private venture capital firm investing own capital

Project Preferences
Prefer role as deal originator but will also invest in deals created by others
Type of Financing:
Startup
First-stage
Second-stage
Minimum Investment: $250,000
Preferred Investment: $500,000-$1 million
Minimum Operating Data:
Annual Sales—Nominal

Geographical Preference
None

Industry Preferences

Communications
Data communications
Local area networks
Satellite and microwave communications
Computer Related
Computer graphics, CAD/CAM and CAE
Computer services
Memory devices
Office automation
Scanning related
Software-applications
Software-artificial intelligence
Software-systems
Specialized turnkey systems
Terminals
Electronic Components and Instrumentation
Analytical and scientific instrumentation
Component fabrication and testing equipment
Electronic components
Fiber optics
Gallium arsenide
Image processing
Laser related
Semiconductors (custom chips)
Space technology
Industrial Products and Equipment
Controls and sensors
Factory automation
Robotics/vision systems
Medical/Health Related
Diagnostic equipment
Diagnostic test products

Additional Information
Year Founded—1973
Method of Compensation—Return on investment is of primary concern; do not charge fees

426

ASSOCIATED SOUTHWEST INVESTORS INC.

124 Tenth Street NW
Albuquerque, NM 87102
505-842-5955

Officer
John R. Rice, Pres.

Type of Firm
MESBIC

Industry Association Memberships
AAMESBIC
NASBIC

Project Preferences
Will function either as deal originator or
investor in deals created by others
Type of Financing:
Startup
First-stage
Second-stage
Later-stage expansion
Leveraged buyout
Minimum Investment: $100,000
Preferred Investment: $250,000-$500,000
Minimum Operating Data:
Annual Sales—Nominal
P&L—Losses (profits projected after 2 years)

Geographical Preference
Southwest

Industry Preferences

Communications
Cable television
Commercial communications
Computer Related
Office automation
Consumer
Consumer products
Food and beverage products
Distribution
Communications equipment
Computer equipment
Consumer products
Electronics equipment
Food products
Industrial products
Medical products
**Electronic Components and
Instrumentation**
Analytical and scientific instrumentation
Fiber optics
Laser related
Energy/Natural Resources
Alternative energy
Technology related products/equipment

Genetic Engineering
Gene splicing and manufacturing equipment
Monoclonal antibodies and hybridomas
Recombinant DNA (agricultural and
industrial)
Recombinant DNA (medical)
Industrial Products and Equipment
Chemicals
Controls and sensors
Energy management
Equipment and machinery
Other industrial automation
Plastics
Robotics/vision systems
Specialty materials
Medical/Health Related
Diagnostic equipment
Diagnostic test products
Disposable products
Drugs and medicines
Hospital and clinical labs
Medical services
Therapeutic equipment
Will Not Consider
Real estate

Additional Information
Year Founded—1971
Capital Under Management—$2.5 million
Investments(1985-1st 6 months)—3
Invested(1985-1st 6 months)—$500,000
Method of Compensation—Return on
investment is most important, but also
charge for closing fees, service fees, etc.

EQUITY CAPITAL CORPORATION

231 Washington Avenue #2
Santa Fe, NM 87501
505-988-4273

Officers
Jerry A. Henson, Pres.
Ralph H. Scheuer, Secy.
John C. Tubbs, Treas.

Whom to Contact
Jerry A. Henson

Type of Firm
SBIC

Industry Association Membership
NASBIC

Project Preferences
Will function either as deal originator or
investor in deals created by others

Type of Financing:
Second-stage
Later-stage expansion
Leveraged buyout
Minimum Investment: $100,000
Preferred Investment: $100,000-$250,000
Minimum Operating Data:
Annual Sales—$500,000
P&L—Break even

Geographical Preference
Southwest

Industry Preferences
None

Additional Information
Year Founded—1984
Capital Under Management—$1.4 million
Investments(1985-1st 6 months)—3
Invested(1985-1st 6 months)—$212,000

MEADOWS RESOURCES, INC.

1650 University Boulevard NE
Suite 500
Albuquerque, NM 87102
505-768-6200

Officers
James G. Jennings, Jr., Pres.
Max H. Maerki, V.P.
Charles R. Mollo, V.P.
Janice L. Breeze, Inv. Mgr.
John G. Farah, Venture Mgr.
William D. Kouba, Venture Mgr.
Jack Winter, Venture Mgr.
Carol D. Radosevich, Venture Mgr.
Beth K. Petronis, Venture Mgr.
Christopher Worthing, Inv. Mgr.

Whom to Contact
Any investment/venture manager

Type of Firm
Diversification subsidiary of a parent
company with a venture capital portfolio

Affiliation
Public Service Company of New Mexico

Industry Association Memberships
NASBIC
NVCA

Project Preferences
Will function either as deal originator or
investor in deals created by others

Type of Financing:
Second-stage
Later-stage expansion
Leveraged buyout
Minimum Investment: Less than $100,000
Preferred Investment: $500,000-$1 million
Preferred Investment (LBO):
    $3 million-$10 million

Geographical Preferences
Southwest
East Coast
West Coast

Industry Preferences

Communications
Cable television
Commercial communications
Data communications
Satellite and microwave communications
Telephone related
Computer Related
Computer graphics, CAD/CAM and CAE
Computer mainframes
Computer services
Memory devices
Micro and mini computers
Office automation
Scanning related
Software-applications
Software-artificial intelligence
Software-systems
Specialized turnkey systems
Terminals
**Electronic Components and
    Instrumentation**
Analytical and scientific instrumentation
Component fabrication and testing
    equipment
Electronic components
Fiber optics
Laser related
Semiconductors
Genetic Engineering
Gene splicing and manufacturing equipment
Monoclonal antibodies and hybridomas
Recombinant DNA (agricultural and
    industrial)
Recombinant DNA (medical)
Medical/Health Related
Diagnostic equipment
Diagnostic test products
Disposable products
Drugs and medicines
Hospital and clinical labs
Medical services
Therapeutic equipment
Other
Finance and insurance
Real estate

Additional Information
Year Founded—1981
Capital Under Management—$25 million
Investments(1985-1st 6 months)—6
Invested(1985-1st 6 months)—$5.2 million
Method of Compensation—Return on
    investment is of primary concern; do not
    charge fees

NEW MEXICO ENERGY RESEARCH
AND DEVELOPMENT INSTITUTE

1220 South St. Francis Drive
Pinon Building, #358
Santa Fe, NM 87501
505-827-5886

Officers
Larry Icerman, Dir.
Emily Miller, Bus. Analyst
Robert Rea, Asst. Dir. Project Devel.

Whom to Contact
Any of the above

Type of Firm
State-sponsored seed capital program for
    energy-related technology development
    in New Mexico

Project Preferences
Will function either as deal originator or
    investor in deals created by others
Type of Financing:
Seed
Minimum Investment: Less than $100,000
Preferred Investment: $100,000-$250,000
Minimum Operating Data:
Annual Sales—Nominal

Geographical Preference
New Mexico (must be located here or be
    willing to relocate for R&D and ultimate
    production)

Industry Preferences

Energy/Natural Resources
Alternative energy
Coal related
Drilling and exploration services
Energy conservation
Minerals
Oil and gas exploration and production
Technology related products/equipment
Will Not Consider
Non energy related businesses

Additional Information
Year Founded—1981
Capital Under Management—$4.9 million
Investments(1985-1st 6 months)—8
Invested(1985-1st 6 months)—$517,000
Method of Compensation—Establishment of
    new businesses in New Mexico is most
    important; a provision for royalties is also
    in R&D contract

SANTA FE PRIVATE EQUITY FUNDS

524 Camino del Monte Sol
Sante Fe, NM 87501
505-983-1769

Partners
A. David Silver, Mgn. Gen. Ptnr.
Larry H. Coleman, Ph.D., Gen. Ptnr.
Kay Tsunemori, Assoc.
Kyle A. Lefkoff, Assoc.
Angela H. Peck, Assoc.

Whom to Contact
Any of the above

Type of Firm
Private venture capital firm investing
    own capital

Project Preferences
Will function either as deal originator or
    investor in deals created by others
Type of Financing:
Startup
First-stage
Minimum Investment: $250,000
Preferred Investment: $500,000-$1 million
Minimum Operating Data:
Annual Sales—Nominal
P&L—Losses (profits projected after 2 years)

Geographical Preference
None

Industry Preferences

Communications
Data communications
Computer Related
Computer graphics, CAD/CAM and CAE
Computer mainframes
Computer services
Memory devices
Micro and mini computers
Office automation
Software-applications
Software-systems
Terminals

Distribution
Computer equipment
Medical products
**Electronic Components and
 Instrumentation**
Analytical and scientific instrumentation
Laser related
Genetic Engineering
Research and manufacturing equipment
Medical/Health Related
Diagnostic equipment
Drugs and medicines
Hospital and clinical labs
Medical services
Therapeutic equipment
Will Not Consider
Extractive industries
Energy

Additional Information

Year Founded—1983
Capital Under Management—$50 million
Investments(1985-1st 6 months)—6
Invested(1985-1st 6 months)—$5 million
Method of Compensation—Return on
 investment is of primary concern; do not
 charge fees

ACKLEY CAPITAL CORPORATION

58 North Main Street
Honeoye Falls, NY 14472
716-624-2024

Officers

Edward J. Ackley, Gen. Ptnr. & Pres.
Bruce W. Marche, Ptnr. & Fin. Mgr.
J. William Reeves, Ptnr. & Secy.
Ronald P. Hotte, Ptnr.
James S. Johnson, Ptnr.
John M. Greenwood, Ptnr.
Holly B. Peer, Proj. Coordinator

Whom to Contact

Edward J. Ackley
Holly B. Peer

Type of Firm

Private venture capital firm investing
own capital

Project Preferences

Prefer role as deal originator but will also
invest in deals created by others
Type of Financing:
Seed
Startup
Minimum Investment: Less than $100,000
Preferred Investment: Less than $100,000
Minimum Operating Data:
Annual Sales—Nominal
P&L—Losses (profits projected after 2 years)

Geographical Preference

None

Industry Preferences

Communications
Cable television
Commercial communications
Data communications
Satellite and microwave communications
Telephone related
Computer Related
Computer graphics, CAD/CAM and CAE
Computer mainframes
Computer services
Memory devices
Micro and mini computers
Office automation
Scanning related
Software-applications
Software-artificial intelligence
Software-systems
Specialized turnkey systems
Terminals

**Electronic Components and
Instrumentation**
Analytical and scientific instrumentation
Component fabrication and testing
equipment
Electronic components
Fiber optics
Laser related
Semiconductors
Energy/Natural Resources
Alternative energy
Coal related
Drilling and exploration services
Energy conservation
Minerals
Oil and gas exploration and production
Technology related products/equipment
Genetic Engineering
Gene splicing and manufacturing equipment
Monoclonal antibodies and hybridomas
Recombinant DNA (agricultural and
industrial)
Recombinant DNA (medical)
Industrial Products and Equipment
Chemicals
Controls and sensors
Energy management
Equipment and machinery
Other industrial automation
Plastics
Robotics/vision systems
Specialty materials
Medical/Health Related
Diagnostic equipment
Diagnostic test products
Disposable products
Drugs and medicines
Hospital and clinical labs
Medical services
Therapeutic equipment
Other
Finance and insurance
Will Not Consider
Retail

Additional Information

Year Founded—1983
Investments(1985-1st 6 months)—1
Invested(1985-1st 6 months)—$100,000

ADLER & COMPANY

375 Park Avenue #3303
New York, NY 10152
212-759-2800

Other Office

1245 Oakmead Parkway #103
Sunnyvale, CA 94086
408-720-8700

Partners

Frederick R. Adler, Mgn. Gen. Ptnr.
(New York)
Joy London, Gen. Ptnr. (New York)
David I. Caplan, Gen. Ptnr. (California)
Yuval Binur, Gen. Ptnr. (New York)
Daniel C. O'Neill, Venture Mgr. (California)
John B. Harlow II, Venture Mgr. (New York)
David J. Blumberg, Venture Mgr. (New York)

Whom to Contact

Any of the above

Type of Firm

Private venture capital firm investing
own capital

Industry Association Memberships

NASBIC
NVCA

Project Preferences

Will function either as deal originator or
investor in deals created by others
Type of Financing:
Seed
Research and development partnerships
Startup
First-stage
Second-stage
Later-stage expansion
Leveraged buyout
Minimum Investment: $100,000
Preferred Investment: No preference
Minimum Operating Data:
Annual Sales—Nominal
P&L—Losses (profits projected after 1 year)

Geographical Preference

None

Industry Preferences

Communications
Commercial communications
Data communications
Satellite and microwave communications
Telephone related
Computer Related
Computer graphics, CAD/CAM and CAE
Computer mainframes
Computer services
Memory devices
Micro and mini computers
Office automation
Scanning related
Software-applications
Software-artificial intelligence
Software-systems
Specialized turnkey systems
Terminals
Consumer
Computer stores/related services
Consumer products
Consumer services
Distribution
Communications equipment
Computer equipment
Consumer products
Electronics equipment
Food products
Industrial products
Medical products
Electronic Components and Instrumentation
Analytical and scientific instrumentation
Component fabrication and testing
   equipment
Electronic components
Fiber optics
Laser related
Semiconductors
Energy/Natural Resources
Technology related products/equipment
Genetic Engineering
Gene splicing and manufacturing equipment
Monoclonal antibodies and hybridomas
Recombinant DNA (agricultural and
   industrial)
Recombinant DNA (medical)
Industrial Products and Equipment
Chemicals
Controls and sensors
Energy management
Equipment and machinery
Other industrial automation
Plastics
Robotics/vision systems
Specialty materials

Medical/Health Related
Diagnostic equipment
Diagnostic test products
Disposable products
Drugs and medicines
Hospital and clinical labs
Medical services
Therapeutic equipment

Additional Information
Year Founded—1965
Capital Under Management—$300 million
Investments(1985-1st 6 months)—16
Invested(1985-1st 6 months)—$15 million
Method of Compensation—Return on
   investment is of primary concern; do not
   charge fees

ADLER & SHAYKIN

375 Park Avenue
New York, NY 10152
212-319-2800

Other Office
1631 Locust Street
Philadelphia, PA 19103
215-985-9999

Partners
Frederick R. Adler, Mgn. Ptnr. (New York)
Leonard P. Shaykin, Mgn. Ptnr. (New York)
Philip H. Behr, Sr. Ptnr. (Pennsylvania)
John J. Murphy, Ptnr. (New York)
Michael P. Bruce, Ptnr. (New York)
John G. Quigley, Ptnr. (New York)
Linda J. Wachner, Principal (New York)
Janet L. Daly, Controller (New York)

Whom to Contact
John J. Murphy
Philip H. Behr

Type of Firm
Investment fund arranging and participating
   in management leveraged buyouts

Project Preferences
Prefer role as deal originator but will also
   invest in deals created by others
Type of Financing:
Leveraged buyout
Minimum Investment: $1 million
Preferred Investment:
   $2 million to $20 million
Preferred Investment (LBO):
   $5 million and over
Minimum Operating Data:
Annual Sales (LBO)—Over $20 million

Geographical Preference
National

Industry Preferences

Communications
Cable television
Commercial communications
Data communications
Satellite and microwave communications
Telephone related
Computer Related
Computer graphics, CAD/CAM and CAE
Computer mainframes
Computer services
Memory devices
Micro and mini computers
Office automation
Scanning related
Software-applications
Software-artificial intelligence
Software-systems
Specialized turnkey systems
Terminals
Consumer
Computer stores/related services
Consumer products
Consumer services
Food and beverage products
Franchise businesses
Hotels and resort areas
Leisure and recreational products
Restaurants
Retailing
Distribution
Communications equipment
Computer equipment
Consumer products
Electronics equipment
Food products
Industrial products
Medical products
Industrial Products and Equipment
Chemicals
Controls and sensors
Energy management
Equipment and machinery
Other industrial automation
Plastics
Robotics/vision systems
Specialty materials
Will Not Consider
Real estate
Startup and early state companies
Turnarounds

Additional Information
Year Founded—1983
Capital Under Management—$125 million
Investments(1985-1st 6 months)—2
Invested(1985-1st 6 months)—$6 million
Method of Compensation—Return on
  investment is most important, but also
  charge for closing fees, service fees, etc.

ALEPH NULL CORPORATION

One Old Country Road
Post Office Box 25
Carle Place, NY 11514
516-742-9527

Officers
Herman Fialkov, Pres.
Jay M. Fialkov, V.P.
Richard E. Kopelman, V.P.
Arthur Schwartz, Assoc.

Whom to Contact
Herman Fialkov

Type of Firm
Private venture capital firm investing
  own capital

Project Preferences
Prefer role as deal originator but will also
  invest in deals created by others
Type of Financing:
Seed
Minimum Investment: Less than $100,000
Preferred Investment: $100,000-$250,000
Minimum Operating Data:
Annual Sales—Nominal

Geographical Preference
Within two hours of office

Industry Preferences

Communications
Commercial communications
Data communications
Satellite and microwave communications
Telephone related
Computer Related
Computer services
Software-applications
Software-artificial intelligence
Software-systems
Consumer
Food and beverage products
Distribution
Food products

**Electronic Components and
  Instrumentation**
Fiber optics
Laser related
Semiconductors
Medical/Health Related
Diagnostic equipment
Diagnostic test products
Disposable products
Drugs and medicines
Hospital and clinical labs
Medical services
Therapeutic equipment

Additional Information
Year Founded—1979
Capital Under Management—$5 million
Investments(1985-1st 6 months)—4
Invested(1985-1st 6 months)—$325,000

ALIMANSKY VENTURE GROUP INC.

790 Madison Avenue #705
New York, NY 10021
212-472-0502

Officers
Burt Alimansky, Exec. Mgn. Dir.
Philip N. Sussman, Mgn. Dir.
Allan R. Feldman, Assoc.
Adrian Horne, Assoc.
Teed J. Welsh, Assoc.
Sarah D. Robins, Asst.

Whom to Contact
Burt Alimansky
Philip N. Sussman
Sarah D. Robins

Type of Firm
Investment banking or merchant banking
  firm investing own capital or funds of
  partners or clients
Consulting firm evaluating and analyzing
  venture projects and arranging private
  placements

Affiliation
Alimansky Planning Group (affiliate)

Industry Association Membership
NASBIC

Project Preferences
Prefer role as deal originator but will also
  invest in deals created by others

Type of Financing:
Seed
Research and development partnerships
Startup
First-stage
Second-stage
Later-stage expansion
Leveraged buyout
Minimum Investment: Less than $100,000
Preferred Investment: Over $1 million
Preferred Investment (LBO): Over $500,000
Minimum Operating Data:
Annual Sales—Nominal
P&L—Losses (profits projected after 2 years)
Annual Sales (LBO)—$3 million and over

Geographical Preference
None

Industry Preferences

Communications
Cable television
Commercial communications
Data communications
Satellite and microwave communications
Telephone related
Computer Related
Computer graphics, CAD/CAM and CAE
Computer mainframes
Computer services
Memory devices
Micro and mini computers
Office automation
Scanning related
Software-applications
Software-artificial intelligence
Software-systems
Specialized turnkey systems
Terminals
Consumer
Computer stores/related services
Consumer products
Consumer services
Food and beverage products
Franchise businesses
Hotels and resort areas
Leisure and recreational products
Restaurants
Retailing
Distribution
Communications equipment
Computer equipment
Consumer products
Electronics equipment
Food products
Industrial products
Medical products

Electronic Components and Instrumentation
Analytical and scientific instrumentation
Component fabrication and testing equipment
Electronic components
Fiber optics
Laser related
Semiconductors
Energy/Natural Resources
Alternative energy
Energy conservation
Technology related products/equipment
Genetic Engineering
Gene splicing and manufacturing equipment
Monoclonal antibodies and hybridomas
Recombinant DNA (agricultural and industrial)
Recombinant DNA (medical)
Industrial Products and Equipment
Chemicals
Controls and sensors
Energy management
Equipment and machinery
Other industrial automation
Plastics
Robotics/vision systems
Specialty materials
Medical/Health Related
Diagnostic equipment
Diagnostic test products
Disposable products
Drugs and medicines
Hospital and clinical labs
Medical services
Therapeutic equipment
Other
Agriculture, forestry, fishing
Education related
Finance and insurance
Publishing
Specialty consulting
Transportation
Will Not Consider
Oil and gas
Real estate

Additional Information
Year Founded—1980
Method of Compensation—Return on investment is most important, but also charge for closing fees, service fees, etc.

AMERICAN COMMERCIAL CAPITAL CORP.

310 Madison Avenue
New York, NY 10017
212-986-3305

Officer
Gerald J. Grossman, Pres.

Type of Firm
SBIC

Industry Association Membership
NASBIC

Project Preferences
Will function either as deal originator or investor in deals created by others
Type of Financing:
Later-stage expansion
Leveraged buyout
Minimum Investment: $100,000
Preferred Investment: $100,000-$250,000
Minimum Operating Data:
Annual Sales—$1.5 million
P&L—Profitable

Geographical Preference
Northeast

Industry Preferences

Communications
Cable television
Commercial communications
Telephone related
Consumer
Computer stores/related services
Consumer products
Consumer services
Food and beverage products
Franchise businesses
Hotels and resort areas
Leisure and recreational products
Restaurants
Retailing
Distribution
Communications equipment
Computer equipment
Consumer products
Electronics equipment
Food products
Industrial products
Medical products

Electronic Components and Instrumentation
Analytical and scientific instrumentation
Component fabrication and testing equipment
Electronic components
Fiber optics
Laser related
Semiconductors
Industrial Products and Equipment
Chemicals
Controls and sensors
Energy management
Equipment and machinery
Other industrial automation
Plastics
Robotics/vision systems
Specialty materials
Medical/Health Related
Diagnostic equipment
Diagnostic test products
Disposable products
Drugs and medicines
Hospital and clinical labs
Medical services
Therapeutic equipment
Other
Education related
Finance and insurance
Publishing
Real estate
Transportation

Additional Information
Year Founded—1981
Capital Under Management—$4 million
Investments(1985-1st 6 months)—10
Invested(1985-1st 6 months)—$1 million
Method of Compensation—Return on investment is of primary concern; do not charge fees

AMERICAN CORPORATE SERVICES

515 Madison Avenue #1225
New York, NY 10022
212-688-9691

Other Offices
Eames House, Church Street
Rudgwick, West Sussex RH12 3EE
England
040-372-2851

250 Scarlett Road #1811
Toronto, Ontario
Canada
416-762-2139

Officers
Sanford R. Simon, Pres. (United States)
Keith C. Langworthy, V.P. (United States)
Norman Wellen, Sr. V.P. (United States)
Michael R. Simon, V.P. (United States)
Christopher Normand, Dir. (England)
Gerald Murray, Assoc. (Canada)

Whom to Contact
Michael R. Simon
Christopher Normand

Type of Firm
Investment banking or merchant banking
firm investing own capital or funds of
partners or clients

Industry Association Membership
NASBIC

Project Preferences
Prefer role as deal originator but will also
invest in deals created by others
Type of Financing:
First-stage
Second-stage
Later-stage expansion
Leveraged buyout
Minimum Investment: $100,000
Preferred Investment: $250,000-$500,000
Minimum Operating Data:
Annual Sales—Nominal
P&L—Break even

Geographical Preference
None

Industry Preferences

Communications
Cable television
Commercial communications
Data communications
Satellite and microwave communications
Telephone related
Computer Related
Computer graphics, CAD/CAM and CAE
Computer mainframes
Computer services
Memory devices
Micro and mini computers
Office automation
Scanning related
Software-applications
Software-artificial intelligence
Software-systems
Specialized turnkey systems
Terminals
Consumer
Food and beverage products
**Electronic Components and
Instrumentation**
Analytical and scientific instrumentation
Component fabrication and testing
equipment
Electronic components
Fiber optics
Laser related
Semiconductors
Industrial Products and Equipment
Chemicals
Controls and sensors
Energy management
Equipment and machinery
Other industrial automation
Plastics
Robotics/vision systems
Specialty materials
Medical/Health Related
Hospital and clinical labs
Medical services
Other
Publishing

Additional Information
Year Founded—1972
Capital Under Management—$4 million
Investments(1985-1st 6 months)—3
Invested(1985-1st 6 months)—$800,000
Method of Compensation—Return on
investment is most important, but also
charge for closing fees, service fees, etc.

AMEV CAPITAL CORP.

One World Trade Center
50th Floor
New York, NY 10048
212-775-9100

Officers
Martin S. Orland, Pres.
Robert S. Whyte, V.P.

Whom to Contact
Any of the above

Type of Firm
SBIC

Affiliation
AMEV Holdings Inc. (parent)

Project Preferences
Prefer role as deal originator but will also
invest in deals created by others
Type of Financing:
Second-stage
Later-stage expansion
Leveraged buyout
Minimum Investment: $500,000
Preferred Investment: $500,000-$1 million
Preferred Investment (LBO): $750,000
Minimum Operating Data:
Annual Sales—Over $3 million
P&L—Profits NBT over $200,000

Geographical Preference
None

Industry Preferences

Communications
Cable television
Data communications
Satellite and microwave communications
Telephone related
Computer Related
Office automation
Software-applications
Specialized turnkey systems
Consumer
Consumer products
Food and beverage products
Hotels and resort areas
Leisure and recreational products
Retailing
Distribution
Communications equipment
Consumer products
Electronics equipment
Food products
Industrial products
Medical products

Electronic Components and Instrumentation
Analytical and scientific instrumentation
Component fabrication and testing equipment
Electronic components
Fiber optics
Energy/Natural Resources
Alternative energy
Industrial Products and Equipment
Chemicals
Equipment and machinery
Plastics
Medical/Health Related
Diagnostic equipment
Disposable products
Hospital and clinical labs
Medical services
Therapeutic equipment
Other
Education related
Transportation

Additional Information
Year Founded—1979
Capital Under Management—$13 million
Investments(1985-1st 6 months)—3
Invested(1985-1st 6 months)—$2.1 million
Method of Compensation—Return on investment is of primary concern; do not charge fees

---

APPLIED TECHNOLOGY INVESTORS, INC.

55 Broadway
One Exchange Plaza, 23rd Floor
New York, NY 10006
212-425-9799

Thomas L. Flaherty, Gen. Ptnr.
Michael Mayers, Gen. Ptnr.

See MASSACHUSETTS for full listing

ATHENA VENTURE PARTNERS L.P.

375 Park Avenue #3303
New York, NY 10152
212-759-2800

Other Office
13 Rozanis Street
Tel Aviv
Israel 61393
  03-484-902

Partners
Frederick R. Adler, Mgn. Ptnr.
  (United States)
Dan Tolkowsky, Mgn. Ptnr. (Israel)
Gideon Tolkowsky, Ptnr. (Israel)
Gill Cogan, Ptnr. (Israel)

Whom to Contact
Any of the above

Type of Firm
Private venture capital firm investing own capital

Project Preferences
Will function either as deal originator or investor in deals created by others
Type of Financing:
Seed
Startup
First-stage
Second-stage
Preferred Investment: $1 million-$2 million
Minimum Operating Data:
Annual Sales—Nominal
P&L—Losses (profits projected after 3 years)

Geographical Preferences
National
Israel
United Kingdom
France

Industry Preferences

Communications
Data communications
Satellite and microwave communications
Telephone related

Computer Related
Computer graphics, CAD/CAM and CAE
Computer mainframes
Computer services
Memory devices
Micro and mini computers
Office automation
Scanning related
Software-applications
Software-artificial intelligence
Software-systems
Specialized turnkey systems
Terminals
Electronic Components and Instrumentation
Analytical and scientific instrumentation
Component fabrication and testing equipment
Electronic components
Fiber optics
Laser related
Semiconductors
Energy/Natural Resources
Alternative energy
Genetic Engineering
Gene splicing and manufacturing equipment
Monoclonal antibodies and hybridomas
Recombinant DNA (agricultural and industrial)
Recombinant DNA (medical)
Industrial Products and Equipment
Chemicals
Controls and sensors
Energy management
Equipment and machinery
Other industrial automation
Plastics
Robotics/vision systems
Specialty materials
Medical/Health Related
Diagnostic equipment
Diagnostic test products
Disposable products
Drugs and medicines
Hospital and clinical labs
Medical services
Therapeutic equipment
Other
Agriculture, forestry, fishing

Additional Information
Year Founded—1985
Method of Compensation—Return on investment is of primary concern; do not charge fees

BARTLETT SCHLUMBERGER CAPITAL CORPORATION

375 Park Avenue
New York, NY 10152
212-319-7500

Other Office

140 East Carrillo Street
Santa Barbara, CA 93101
805-963-6511

Officers

James L. Bartlett III, Pres. (New York
  & California)
Marvin Maslow, Exec. V.P. (New York)
Harry Short, V.P. (California)
Robert W. Brown, V.P. (California)
Steven Worzman, V.P. (New York)
Frank H. Robinson (California)

Whom to Contact

Steven Worzman
Robert W. Brown

Type of Firm

Private investment firm providing mezzanine
  financings for companies with sales
  between $5 million and $50 million
Type of Financing:
Later-stage expansion
Leveraged buyout
Minimum Investment: $1 million
Preferred Investment: $3 million-$5 million
Minimum Operating Data:
Annual Sales—$5 million
P&L—Profitable

Geographical Preference

National

Industry Preferences

Communications
Cable television
Commercial communications
Data communications
Satellite and microwave communications
Telephone related
Consumer
Computer stores/related services
Consumer products
Consumer services
Food and beverage products
Franchise businesses
Hotels and resort areas
Leisure and recreational products
Restaurants
Retailing

Distribution
Communications equipment
Computer equipment
Consumer products
Electronics equipment
Food products
Industrial products
Medical products
**Electronic Components and
  Instrumentation**
Analytical and scientific instrumentation
Component fabrication and testing
  equipment
Electronic components
Fiber optics
Laser related
Semiconductors
Energy/Natural Resources
Alternative energy
Coal related
Drilling and exploration services
Energy conservation
Minerals
Oil and gas exploration and production
Technology related products/equipment
Genetic Engineering
Gene splicing and manufacturing equipment
Monoclonal antibodies and hybridomas
Recombinant DNA (agricultural and
  industrial)
Recombinant DNA (medical)
Industrial Products and Equipment
Chemicals
Controls and sensors
Energy management
Equipment and machinery
Other industrial automation
Plastics
Robotics/vision systems
Specialty materials
Medical/Health Related
Diagnostic equipment
Diagnostic test products
Disposable products
Drugs and medicines
Hospital and clinical labs
Medical services
Therapeutic equipment
Other
Agriculture, forestry, fishing
Education related
Finance and insurance
Publishing
Real estate
Specialty consulting
Transportation

Additional Information

Year Founded—1973

BESSEMER VENTURE PARTNERS

630 Fifth Avenue
New York, NY 10111
212-708-9300

Other Offices

3000 Sand Hill Road
Building 3, #225
Menlo Park, CA 94025
415-854-2200

83 Walnut Street
Wellesley Hills, MA 02181
617-237-6050

General Partners

William T. Burgin (New York &
  Massachusetts)
Neill H. Brownstein (California)
Robert H. Buescher (New York)
Robert B. Field (California)
James H. Furneaux (Massachusetts)
G. Felda Hardymon (Massachusetts)

Whom to Contact

Any of the above

Type of Firm

Private venture capital firm investing
  own capital

Affiliation

Bessemer Securities Corporation (sole
  limited partner)

Industry Association Memberships

NVCA
WAVC

Project Preferences

Prefer role as deal originator but will also
  invest in deals created by others
Type of Financing:
Seed
Research and development partnerships
Startup
First-stage
Second-stage
Later-stage expansion
Leveraged buyout
Preferred Investment: No preference

Geographical Preference

National

Industry Preferences

None

Additional Information
Year Founded—1970
Capital Under Management—$100 million
Investments(1985-1st 6 months)—5
Invested(1985-1st 6 months)—$3 million
Method of Compensation—Return on
   investment is of primary concern; do not
   charge fees

BRAINTREE MANAGEMENT LTD.

59 South Greeley Avenue
Chappaqua, NY 10514
914-238-5221

Officer
George Newlin, Pres.

Type of Firm
Investment banking or merchant banking
   firm investing own capital or funds of
   partners or clients
Consulting firm evaluating and analyzing
   venture projects and arranging private
   placements

Project Preferences
Will function either as deal originator or
   investor in deals created by others
Type of Financing:
Startup
Second-stage
Leveraged buyout
Minimum Investment: Less than $100,000
Preferred Investment: $250,000-$500,000
Minimum Operating Data:
Annual Sales—Nominal
P&L—Losses (profits projected after 2 years)

Geographical Preference
Northeast

Industry Preferences

Communications
Commercial communications
Telephone related
Consumer
Consumer products
Consumer services
Food and beverage products
Franchise businesses
Hotels and resort areas
Leisure and recreational products
Distribution
Industrial products
Medical products

**Electronic Components and
   Instrumentation**
Analytical and scientific instrumentation
Industrial Products and Equipment
Equipment and machinery
Robotics/vision systems
Specialty materials
Medical/Health Related
Diagnostic equipment
Diagnostic test products
Disposable products
Drugs and medicines
Hospital and clinical labs
Medical services
Therapeutic equipment
Other
Education related
Finance and insurance
Publishing
Real estate

Additional Information
Year Founded—1976
Method of Compensation—Function primarily
   in service area; receive contingent fee in
   cash or equity

BRIDGE CAPITAL ADVISORS, INC.

50 Broadway
New York, NY 10004
212-514-6700

Other Office
Cityplace
185 Asylum Street
Hartford, CT 06103
203-275-6700

Officers
Donald P. Remey, Mgn. Dir. (New York)
Hoyt J. Goodrich, Mgn. Dir. (New York &
   Connecticut)
Geoffrey H. Wadsworth, V.P. (New York)

Whom to Contact
Any of the above

Type of Firm
Private investment firm investing
   own capital
Private, limited partnership investment firm
   investing own capital in expansion
   financing using debt with equity kickers

Affiliation
Bridge Capital Investors (limited partnership
   managed by Bridge Capital Advisors)

Industry Association Membership
NVCA

Project Preferences
Prefer role as deal originator but will also
   invest in deals created by others
Type of Financing:
Later-stage expansion
Minimum Investment: $1 million
Preferred Investment: Over $1 million
Minimum Operating Data:
Annual Sales—Over $5 million
P&L—Profitable

Geographical Preferences
Northeast
East Coast

Industry Preferences

Communications
Cable television
Commercial communications
Data communications
Satellite and microwave communications
Telephone related
Computer Related
Computer services
Memory devices
Micro and mini computers
Office automation
Scanning related
Specialized turnkey systems
Terminals
Consumer
Computer stores/related services
Consumer products
Consumer services
Food and beverage products
Franchise businesses
Hotels and resort areas
Leisure and recreational products
Restaurants
Retailing
Distribution
Communications equipment
Computer equipment
Consumer products
Electronics equipment
Food products
Industrial products
Medical products
**Electronic Components and
   Instrumentation**
Analytical and scientific instrumentation
Component fabrication and testing
   equipment
Electronic components
Fiber optics
Laser related
Semiconductors

Industrial Products and Equipment
Chemicals
Controls and sensors
Energy management
Equipment and machinery
Other industrial automation
Plastics
Robotics/vision systems
Specialty materials
Medical/Health Related
Diagnostic equipment
Diagnostic test products
Disposable products
Drugs and medicines
Hospital and clinical labs
Medical services
Therapeutic equipment
Other
Agriculture, forestry, fishing
Education related
Finance and insurance
Publishing
Specialty consulting
Transportation
Will Not Consider
Oil and gas
Real estate

Additional Information
Year Founded—1983
Capital Under Management—$51 million
Method of Compensation—Return on
    investment is of primary concern; do not
    charge fees

BT CAPITAL CORPORATION

280 Park Avenue
New York, NY 10017
212-850-1920

Officers
Carl Muller, Chm.
James G. Hellmuth, Deputy Chm.
Noel E. Urben, Pres.
Keith R. Fox, V.P.
Michael Nugent, V.P.
Martha Cassidy, V.P.
William Drake, Asst. V.P.
Adrienne Halper, Asst. V.P.
Melanie Okun, Asst. V.P.

Whom to Contact
James G. Hellmuth
Noel E. Urben
Keith R. Fox
Michael Nugent

Type of Firm
SBIC
Venture capital subsidiary of
    commercial bank

Affiliation
Bankers Trust New York Corporation (parent)

Industry Association Membership
NASBIC

Project Preferences
Will function either as deal originator or
    investor in deals created by others
Type of Financing:
Later-stage expansion
Leveraged buyout
Minimum Investment: $1 million
Preferred Investment: $3 million-$5 million
Minimum Operating Data:
Annual Sales—Over $3 million
P&L—Profits NBT over $500,000

Geographical Preference
None

Industry Preferences

Communications
Cable television
Consumer
Consumer products
Consumer services
Restaurants
Retailing
Distribution
Industrial products
**Electronic Components and
    Instrumentation**
Electronic components
Energy/Natural Resources
Energy conservation
Industrial Products and Equipment
Chemicals
Controls and sensors
Energy management
Equipment and machinery
Other industrial automation
Plastics
Robotics/vision systems
Specialty materials
Medical/Health Related
Diagnostic equipment
Disposable products
Other
Education related
Publishing
Textiles

Will Not Consider
Startups
High technology

Additional Information
Year Founded—1974
Capital Under Management—$75 million
Investments(1985-1st 6 months)—4
Invested(1985-1st 6 months)—$12 million
Method of Compensation—Return on
    investment is most important, but also
    charge for closing fees, service fees, etc.

BUFFALO CAPITAL CORPORATION

Mount Morris Road
Geneseo, NY 14454
716-243-4310

Other Office
30 Rockefeller Plaza #4350
New York, NY 10112
212-489-7600

Officers
J.H. Hickman III, Chm. (Geneseo)
Arthur R. Taylor, Dir. (New York)
Michael Palmer, Dir. (New York)
Gretchen L. Hickman, V.P. (Geneseo)
John H. Hickman IV, V.P. (Geneseo)
Linda A. McLaughlin, Exec. Asst. (Geneseo)

Whom to Contact
J.H. Hickman III

Type of Firm
Investment banking or merchant banking
    firm investing own capital or funds of
    partners or clients

Affiliations
The Hickman Corp., Geneseo (parent)
Arthur R. Taylor & Co., New York (affiliate)
Saudi Arabian Investment Co., Jeddah
    (affiliate)

Project Preferences
Prefer role as deal originator
Type of Financing:
Startup
First-stage
Second-stage
Later-stage expansion
Leveraged buyout
Minimum Investment: $100,000
Preferred Investment: $250,000-$500,000
Minimum Operating Data:
Annual Sales—Nominal
P&L—Break even

Geographical Preferences
Northeast
Southeast
East Coast
Canada

Industry Preferences

Communications
Cable television
Commercial communications
Data communications
Satellite and microwave communications
Telephone related
Television stations
Computer Related
Bar code technology
Computer graphics, CAD/CAM and CAE
Computer mainframes
Computer services
Memory devices
Micro and mini computers
Office automation
Scanning related
Software-applications
Software-artificial intelligence
Software-systems
Specialized turnkey systems
Terminals
Consumer
Computer stores/related services
Consumer products
Consumer services
Food and beverage products
Franchise businesses
Hotels and resort areas
Leisure and recreational products
Restaurants
Retailing
Distribution
Communications equipment
Computer equipment
Consumer products
Electronics equipment
Food products
Industrial products
Medical products
**Electronic Components and
  Instrumentation**
Analytical and scientific instrumentation
Component fabrication and testing
  equipment
Electronic components
Fiber optics
Laser related
Semiconductors

Energy/Natural Resources
Alternative energy
Coal related
Drilling and exploration services
Energy conservation
Minerals
Oil and gas exploration and production
Technology related products/equipment
Genetic Engineering
Gene splicing and manufacturing equipment
Monoclonal antibodies and hybridomas
Recombinant DNA (agricultural and
  industrial)
Recombinant DNA (medical)
Industrial Products and Equipment
Chemicals
Controls and sensors
Energy management
Equipment and machinery
Other industrial automation
Plastics
Robotics/vision systems
Specialty materials
Medical/Health Related
Diagnostic equipment
Diagnostic test products
Disposable products
Drugs and medicines
Hospital and clinical labs
Medical services
Therapeutic equipment
Other
Agriculture, forestry, fishing
Education related
Finance and insurance
Publishing
Real estate
Specialty consulting
Transportation

Additional Information
Year Founded—1969
Capital Under Management—
  Over $25 million
Investments(1985-1st 6 months)—3
Invested(1985-1st 6 months)—$1.3 million
Method of Compensation—Return on
  investment is most important, but also
  charge for closing fees, service fees, etc.

CHEMICAL VENTURE CAPITAL CORP./ CHEMICAL EQUITY INC.

277 Park Avenue
New York, NY 10172
212-310-4949

Officers
Steven J. Gilbert, Pres. & CEO
Michael J. Feldman
Jeffrey C. Walker
Barry Schwimmer
David Jaffe
Nathaniel Henshaw
John Kirtley

Whom to Contact
Any of the above

Type of Firm
SBIC
Venture capital subsidiary of
  commercial bank

Affiliation
Chemical New York Corporation (parent)

Industry Association Memberships
NASBIC
NVCA

Project Preferences
Will function either as deal originator or
  investor in deals created by others
Type of Financing:
Seed
Startup
First-stage
Second-stage
Later-stage expansion
Leveraged buyout
Minimum Investment: $500,000
Preferred Investment: Over $1 million
Preferred Investment (LBO):
  Less than $15 million
Minimum Operating Data:
Annual Sales—Nominal
P&L—Losses (profits projected after 2 years)

Geographical Preference
None

Industry Preferences

Communications
Cable television
Commercial communications
Data communications
Satellite and microwave communications
Telephone related

Computer Related
Computer services
Office automation
Software-artificial intelligence
Software-systems
Specialized turnkey systems
Consumer
Computer stores/related services
Consumer products
Consumer services
Food and beverage products
Franchise businesses
Hotels and resort areas
Leisure and recreational products
Restaurants
Retailing
Distribution
Communications equipment
Computer equipment
Consumer products
Electronics equipment
Food products
Industrial products
Medical products
**Electronic Components and
   Instrumentation**
Analytical and scientific instrumentation
Component fabrication and testing
   equipment
Electronic components
Fiber optics
Laser related
Semiconductors
Industrial Products and Equipment
Chemicals
Controls and sensors
Energy management
Equipment and machinery
Other industrial automation
Plastics
Robotics/vision systems
Specialty materials
Medical/Health Related
Diagnostic equipment
Diagnostic test products
Disposable products
Drugs and medicines
Hospital and clinical labs
Medical services
Therapeutic equipment
Other
Agriculture, forestry, fishing
Education related
Finance and insurance
Publishing
Real estate
Specialty consulting
Transportation

Additional Information
Year Founded—1984
Capital Under Management—$100 million
Investments(1985-1st 6 months)—7
Invested(1985-1st 6 months)—$3.7 million
Method of Compensation—Return on
   investment is of primary concern; do not
   charge fees

CITICORP VENTURE CAPITAL, LTD.

Citicorp Center
153 East 53rd Street, 28th Fl.
New York, NY 10043
212-559-1127

Other Offices
717 North Harwood
Suite 2920, LB 87
Dallas, TX 75201
214-880-9670

2 Embarcadero Place, #203
2200 Geng Road
Palo Alto, CA 94303
415-424-8000

Officers/New York
William T. Comfort, Chm.
Peter G. Gerry, Pres.
Guy de Chazal, V.P.
Stanley Nitzburg, V.P.
John R. Whitman, V.P.
David F. Thomas, V.P.
Richard M. Cashin, V.P.
Kilin To, V.P.
Stephen C. Sherril, Asst. V.P.
Bruce C. Bruckmann, Asst. V.P.
Scott G. Fossel, Asst. V.P.
Richard C. Mayberry, Asst. V.P.

Whom to Contact
Peter G. Gerry

Type of Firm
SBIC
Venture capital subsidiary of bank
   holding company

Affiliation
Citicorp (parent)

Industry Association Memberships
NASBIC
NVCA
WAVC

Project Preferences
Will function either as deal originator or
   investor in deals created by others
Type of Financing:
Startup
First-stage
Second-stage
Later-stage expansion
Leveraged buyout
Minimum Investment: $500,000
Preferred Investment: $500,000-$1 million
Preferred Investment (LBO):
   $3 million-$10 million
Minimum Operating Data:
Annual Sales—Depends on stage
   of financing
Annual Sales (LBO)—$100 million and over

Geographical Preference
None

Industry Preferences
None

Additional Information
Year Founded—1968
Capital Under Management—$500 million
Investments(1985-1st 6 months)—36
Invested(1985-1st 6 months)—$22.1 million
Method of Compensation—Return on
   investment is of primary concern; do not
   charge fees

CMNY CAPITAL COMPANY, INC.

77 Water Street
New York, NY 10005
212-437-7078

Vice Presidents
Robert Davidoff
Jeffrey Kenner
David Gruber
Robert Marks

Whom to Contact
Robert Davidoff

Type of Firm
SBIC

Affiliation
Carl Marks and Company, Inc. (affiliate)

Industry Association Memberships
NASBIC
NVCA

Project Preferences
Will function either as deal originator or
investor in deals created by others
Type of Financing:
First-stage
Second-stage
Later-stage expansion
Leveraged buyout
Minimum Investment: $100,000
Preferred Investment: $250,000-$500,000
Minimum Operating Data:
Annual Sales—Nominal

Geographical Preference
None

Industry Preferences

Communications
Cable television
Commercial communications
Data communications
Satellite and microwave communications
Telephone related
Computer Related
Computer graphics, CAD/CAM and CAE
Computer mainframes
Computer services
Memory devices
Micro and mini computers
Office automation
Scanning related
Software-applications
Software-artificial intelligence
Software-systems
Specialized turnkey systems
Terminals
Consumer
Computer stores/related services
Consumer products
Consumer services
Food and beverage products
Franchise businesses
Leisure and recreational products
Retailing
Distribution
Communications equipment
Computer equipment
Consumer products
Electronics equipment
Food products
Industrial products
Medical products

**Electronic Components and
Instrumentation**
Analytical and scientific instrumentation
Component fabrication and testing
equipment
Electronic components
Fiber optics
Laser related
Semiconductors
Energy/Natural Resources
Drilling and exploration services
Oil and gas exploration and production
Technology related products/equipment
Industrial Products and Equipment
Chemicals
Controls and sensors
Energy management
Equipment and machinery
Other industrial automation
Plastics
Robotics/vision systems
Specialty materials
Medical/Health Related
Diagnostic equipment
Diagnostic test products
Disposable products
Drugs and medicines
Hospital and clinical labs
Medical services
Therapeutic equipment
Other
Education related
Finance and insurance
Publishing
Specialty consulting

Additional Information
Year Founded—1962
Capital Under Management—$45 million
Investments(1985-1st 6 months)—15
Invested(1985-1st 6 months)—$1.7 million
Method of Compensation—Return on
investment is of primary concern; do not
charge fees

COFINAM INCORPORATED

1270 Avenue of the Americas
19th Floor
New York, NY 10020
212-265-1400

Officers
Jean Karoubi, Pres.
Jerrold M. Newman, V.P.
Anne Hessler, Inv. Analyst

Whom to Contact
Jerrold M. Newman

Type of Firm
Private venture capital firm investing
own capital
Investment banking or merchant banking
firm investing own capital or funds of
partners or clients

Project Preferences
Will function either as deal originator or
investor in deals created by others
Type of Financing:
Later-stage expansion
Leveraged buyout
Minimum Investment: $200,000
Preferred Investment: $250,000-$1 million
Preferred Investment (LBO):
$250,000-$750,000
Minimum Operating Data:
Annual Sales—$3 million
P&L—Profits NBT over $250,000
Annual Sales (LBO)—$3 million-$75 million

Geographical Preferences
East Coast
(would consider other areas)

Industry Preferences

Consumer
Consumer products
Consumer services
Food and beverage products
Franchise businesses
Hotels and resort areas
Leisure and recreational products
Restaurants
Retailing
Distribution
Consumer products
Food products
Medical/Health Related
Disposable products
Other
Real estate

Additional Information
Year Founded—1982
Capital Under Management—$15 million
Investments(1985-1st 6 months)—2
Invested(1985-1st 6 months)—$2.4 million
Method of Compensation—Return on
investment is most important, but may
charge for closing fees, service fees, etc.

COLEMAN VENTURES, INC.

5909 Northern Boulevard
East Norwich, NY 11732
516-626-3642

Officers
Gregory S. Coleman, Pres.
Roger V. Coleman, V.P.

Whom to Contact
Gregory S. Coleman

Type of Firm
Private venture capital firm investing
own capital
Consulting firm evaluating and analyzing
venture projects and arranging private
placements

Project Preferences
Will function either as deal originator or
investor in deals created by others
Type of Financing:
Seed
Startup
Minimum Investment: Less than $100,000
Preferred Investment: $100,000-$500,000
Minimum Operating Data:
Annual Sales—Nominal
P&L—Break even

Geographical Preferences
Within two hours of office
Northeast
East Coast

Industry Preferences

Communications
Telephone related
Computer Related
Computer services
Micro and mini computers
Software-applications
Software-systems
Consumer
Computer stores/related services
Consumer products
Consumer services
Food and beverage products
Franchise businesses
Hotels and resort areas
Leisure and recreational products
Restaurants
Retailing

**Electronic Components and
Instrumentation**
Electronic components
Fiber optics
Laser related
Semiconductors
Energy/Natural Resources
Alternative energy
Photovoltaic energy-solar
Industrial Products and Equipment
Chemicals
Energy management
Plastics
Medical/Health Related
Therapeutic equipment
Other
Agriculture, forestry, fishing
Education related
Publishing
Real estate
Will Not Consider
Distribution industry

Additional Information
Year Founded—1965
Capital Under Management—$5 million
Investments(1985-1st 6 months)—4
Invested(1985-1st 6 months)—$600,000
Method of Compensation—Return on
investment is of primary concern; do not
charge fees

CONCORD PARTNERS

535 Madison Avenue
New York, NY 10022
212-906-7100

Other Office
600 Montgomery Street
San Francisco, CA 94111
415-362-2400

Partners
Charles L. Lea, Jr., Gen. Ptnr. (New York)
Edgar A. Miller, Gen. Ptnr. (New York)
Thomas L. Piper III, Gen. Ptnr. (New York)
Roland D. Underhill, Gen. Ptnr. (New York)
E. Payson Smith, Jr., Gen. Ptnr. (California)
John B. Clinton, Gen. Ptnr. (New York)
Philip M. Young, Gen. Ptnr. (California)
Peter A. Leidel, Assoc. (New York)
Marilyn G. Breslow, Assoc. (New York)
Stephen M. Wilson, Assoc. (California)

Whom to Contact
Any of the above

Type of Firm
Private venture capital firm investing
own capital

Affiliation
Dillon, Read & Co., Inc.

Industry Association Membership
NVCA

Project Preferences
Will function either as deal originator or
investor in deals created by others
Type of Financing:
Startup
First-stage
Second-stage
Leveraged buyout
Minimum Investment: $250,000
Preferred Investment: $700,000 and over
Preferred Investment (LBO):
$1.5 million and over
Minimum Operating Data:
Annual Sales—Nominal
P&L—Losses (profits projected after 3 years)

Geographical Preference
None

Industry Preferences

Communications
Cable television
Commercial communications
Data communications
Satellite and microwave communications
Telephone related
Computer Related
Computer graphics, CAD/CAM and CAE
Computer mainframes
Computer services
Memory devices
Micro and mini computers
Office automation
Scanning related
Software-applications
Software-artificial intelligence
Software-systems
Specialized turnkey systems
Terminals
Distribution
Communications equipment
Electronics equipment
Medical products

Electronic Components and Instrumentation
Analytical and scientific instrumentation
Component fabrication and testing equipment
Electronic components
Fiber optics
Laser related
Semiconductors
Energy/Natural Resources
Alternative energy
Coal related
Drilling and exploration services
Energy conservation
Oil and gas exploration and production
Technology related products/equipment
Genetic Engineering
Gene splicing and manufacturing equipment
Monoclonal antibodies and hybridomas
Recombinant DNA (agricultural and industrial)
Recombinant DNA (medical)
Industrial Products and Equipment
Chemicals
Controls and sensors
Energy management
Equipment and machinery
Other industrial automation
Plastics
Robotics/vision systems
Specialty materials
Medical/Health Related
Diagnostic equipment
Drugs and medicines
Hospital and clinical labs
Medical services
Other
Finance and insurance

Additional Information
Year Founded—1981
Capital Under Management—$115 million
Investments(1985-1st 6 months)—9
Invested(1985-1st 6 months)—$6.5 million
Method of Compensation—Return on investment is of primary concern; do not charge fees

CROYDEN CAPITAL CORPORATION

45 Rockefeller Plaza #2165
New York, NY 10111
212-974-0184

Officers
Victor L. Hecht, Pres.
Harry Freund, Chm.
Jay Goldsmith, Co-Chm.
Donald Cecil, Dir.

Whom to Contact
Victor L. Hecht

Type of Firm
SBIC

Industry Association Membership
NASBIC

Project Preferences
Will function either as deal originator or investor in deals created by others
Type of Financing:
First-stage
Second-stage
Later-stage expansion
Leveraged buyout
Minimum Investment: $100,000
Preferred Investment: $250,000-$500,000
Preferred Investment (LBO): $250,000
Minimum Operating Data:
Annual Sales—$1 million
P&L—Break even
Annual Sales (LBO)—$10 million-$25 million

Geographical Preferences
Northeast
Southeast
East Coast
National

Industry Preferences

Communications
Cable television
Commercial communications
Data communications
Radio and television
Satellite and microwave communications
Telephone related
Consumer
Consumer products
Consumer services
Franchise businesses
Leisure and recreational products
Retailing

Distribution
Communications equipment
Computer equipment
Consumer products
Electronics equipment
Food products
Industrial products
Medical products
Electronic Components and Instrumentation
Analytical and scientific instrumentation
Component fabrication and testing equipment
Electronic components
Fiber optics
Laser related
Semiconductors
Industrial Products and Equipment
Chemicals
Controls and sensors
Energy management
Equipment and machinery
Other industrial automation
Plastics
Robotics/vision systems
Specialty materials
Medical/Health Related
Diagnostic equipment
Diagnostic test products
Disposable products
Drugs and medicines
Hospital and clinical labs
Medical services
Therapeutic equipment
Other
Publishing
Transportation
Will Not Consider
Entertainment
Finance, insurance or other lending concerns

Additional Information
Year Founded—1984
Method of Compensation—Return on investment is most important, but also charge for closing fees, service fees, etc.

CW GROUP, INC.

1041 Third Avenue
New York, NY 10021
212-308-5266

Officers

Walter Channing, Jr.
Barry Weinberg
Charles M. Hartman
William Lomicka

Whom to Contact

Any of the above

Type of Firm

Private venture capital firm investing
own capital

Industry Association Membership

NVCA

Project Preferences

Prefer role as deal originator but will also
invest in deals created by others
Type of Financing:
Seed
Startup
First-stage
Second-stage
Leveraged buyout
Minimum Investment: Less than $100,000
Preferred Investment: $500,000-$2 million
Minimum Operating Data:
Annual Sales—Nominal
P&L—Losses (profits projected after 3 years)

Geographical Preference

None

Industry Preferences

Genetic Engineering
Gene splicing and manufacturing equipment
Monoclonal antibodies and hybridomas
Recombinant DNA (agricultural and
industrial)
Recombinant DNA (medical)
Medical/Health Related
Diagnostic equipment
Diagnostic services
Diagnostic test products
Disposable products
Drugs and medicines
Hospital and clinical labs
Medical services
Nursing homes
Rehabilitation and step-down facilities

Additional Information

Year Founded—1982
Capital Under Management—$50 million
Investments(1985-1st 6 months)—7
Invested(1985-1st 6 months)—$4.1 million
Method of Compensation—Return on
investment is of primary concern; do not
charge fees

DAVIS GROUP

Post Office Box 6491
FDR Station
New York, NY 10022
212-977-8482

Other Office

1431 Cherokee Trail, Box 59
Knoxville, TN 37920
615-579-5180

Officers

Roger W. Davis, Chm.
M.L.D. Thompson, Ptnr.
Edward C. Herbert, Ptnr.

Whom to Contact

Roger W. Davis (New York)

Type of Firm

Investment banking or merchant banking
firm investing own capital or funds of
partners or clients
Consulting firm evaluating and analyzing
venture projects and arranging private
placements

Project Preferences

Prefer role as deal originator but will also
invest in deals created by others
Type of Financing:
Startup
First-stage
Leveraged buyout
Minimum Investment: Less than $100,000
Preferred Investment: No preference
Minimum Operating Data:
Annual Sales—Nominal
P&L—Break even

Geographical Preference

None

Industry Preferences

Communications
Satellite and microwave communications

Consumer
Consumer products
Consumer services
Food and beverage products
Leisure and recreational products
Distribution
Food products
Medical products
Genetic Engineering
Monoclonal antibodies and hybridomas
Recombinant DNA (agricultural and
industrial)
Recombinant DNA (medical)
Research and manufacturing equipment
Industrial Products and Equipment
Equipment and machinery
Plastics
Medical/Health Related
Diagnostic equipment
Drugs and medicines
Hospital and clinical labs
Medical services
Therapeutic equipment
Other
Agriculture, forestry, fishing
Education related
Publishing
Real estate
Specialize in troubled companies
Specialty consulting
Transportation

Additional Information

Year Founded—1969
Method of Compensation—Return on
investment is most important, but also
charge for closing fees, service fees, etc.

CHARLES DE THAN GROUP

51 East 67th Street
New York, NY 10021
212-988-5108

Officer

Charles de Than

Type of Firm

Consulting firm and investment broker
evaluating and analyzing venture projects
and arranging private placements
Investment broker engaged in money
management and analyzing merger and
acquisition projects

Project Preferences

Will function as deal originator, broker, or
investor in deals created by others

Type of Financing:
Startup
First-stage
Second-stage
Later-stage expansion
Leveraged buyout
Minimum Investment: $100,000
Preferred Investment: No preference
Preferred Investment (LBO):
   $1 million and over
Minimum Operating Data:
Annual Sales—$1 million
Annual Sales (LBO)—$10 million and over

Geographical Preference
None

Industry Preferences
None

Additional Information
Year Founded—1970

DEMUTH, FOLGER & TERHUNE

One Exchange Plaza
at 55 Broadway
New York, NY 10006
212-509-5580

General Partners
Donald F. DeMuth
Thomas W. Folger
J. Michael Terhune

Whom to Contact
Any of the above

Type of Firm
Private venture capital firm investing
   own capital

Industry Association Membership
NVCA

Project Preferences
Will function either as deal originator or
   investor in deals created by others
Type of Financing:
Seed
Startup
First-stage
Second-stage
Later-stage expansion
Leveraged buyout
Minimum Investment: $500,000
Preferred Investment: Over $1 million
Preferred Investment (LBO):
   $2 million-$4 million

Minimum Operating Data:
Annual Sales—Nominal
P&L—Losses (profits projected after 2 years)

Geographical Preference
None

Industry Preferences

Communications
Cable television
Commercial communications
Data communications
Satellite and microwave communications
Telephone related
Computer Related
Computer graphics, CAD/CAM and CAE
Computer mainframes
Computer services
Memory devices
Micro and mini computers
Office automation
Scanning related
Software-applications
Software-artificial intelligence
Software-systems
Specialized turnkey systems
Terminals
Distribution
Communications equipment
Computer equipment
Electronics equipment
Medical products
**Electronic Components and
   Instrumentation**
Analytical and scientific instrumentation
Component fabrication and testing
   equipment
Electronic components
Fiber optics
Laser related
Semiconductors
Energy/Natural Resources
Technology related products/equipment
Industrial Products and Equipment
Controls and sensors
Energy management
Equipment and machinery
Other industrial automation
Robotics/vision systems
Specialty materials
Medical/Health Related
Diagnostic equipment
Diagnostic test products
Disposable products
Drugs and medicines
Hospital and clinical labs
Medical services
Therapeutic equipment

Additional Information
Year Founded—1983
Investments(1985-1st 6 months)—6
Invested(1985-1st 6 months)—$4 million
Method of Compensation—Return on
   investment is of primary concern; do not
   charge fees

DREXEL BURNHAM LAMBERT INC./
THE LAMBDA FUNDS

55 Broad Street
New York, NY 10004
212-480-3965

Other Office
1400 Civic Drive
Walnut Creek, CA 94596
415-945-8500

Officers
Anthony M. Lamport, Mgn. Dir.
Richard J. Dumler, First V.P.
Frank Kline, Jr., V.P.
Alexa Mahnken, Analyst

Whom to Contact
Alexa Mahnken (New York)
Jack Ross (California)

Type of Firm
Investment banking or merchant banking
   firm investing own capital or funds of
   partners or clients

Industry Association Membership
NVCA

Project Preferences
Will function either as deal originator or
   investor in deals created by others
Type of Financing:
First-stage
Second-stage
Later-stage expansion
Leveraged buyout
Minimum Investment: $400,000
Preferred Investment: $500,000-$1 million
Preferred Investment (LBO):
   $500,000-$500 million
Minimum Operating Data:
Annual Sales—Nominal
P&L—Losses (profits projected after 2 years)
Annual Sales (LBO)—$5 million-$1 billion

Geographical Preferences
National
Canada

Industry Preferences

Communications
Cable television
Data communications
Telephone related
Computer Related
Computer graphics, CAD/CAM and CAE
Computer services
Office automation
Software-applications
Software-systems
Specialized turnkey systems
Consumer
Consumer services
Distribution
Communications equipment
Computer equipment
Electronics equipment
Industrial products
Medical products
Electronic Components and Instrumentation
Analytical and scientific instrumentation
Component fabrication and testing equipment
Electronic components
Fiber optics
Laser related
Semiconductors
Industrial Products and Equipment
Chemicals
Controls and sensors
Equipment and machinery
Other industrial automation
Plastics
Specialty materials
Medical/Health Related
Diagnostic equipment
Diagnostic test products
Disposable products
Drugs and medicines
Hospital and clinical labs
Medical services
Therapeutic equipment
Other
Education related
Finance and insurance
Publishing
Will Not Consider
Airlines
Entertainment
Natural resources
Real estate
R&D partnerships

Additional Information

Year Founded—1979
Capital Under Management—$40 million
Investments(1985-1st 6 months)—10
Invested(1985-1st 6 months)—$5.4 million
Method of Compensation—Return on investment is of primary concern; do not charge fees

---

EBERSTADT FLEMING INC.

Two World Trade Center
32nd Floor
New York, NY 10048
212-912-7000

Officers

Jack W. Lasersohn, Dir.
Andrew H. Chapman, V.P.
Michael E. Norton, V.P.

Whom to Contact

Jack W. Lasersohn

Type of Firm

Private venture capital firm investing own capital
Investment banking or merchant banking firm investing own capital or funds of partners or clients

Affiliation

Robert Fleming & Co. Ltd. (parent)

Project Preferences

Prefer role as deal originator but will also invest in deals created by others
Type of Financing:
Seed
Startup
First-stage
Second-stage
Leveraged buyout
Minimum Investment: Less than $100,000
Preferred Investment: $500,000-$1 million
Minimum Operating Data:
Annual Sales—Nominal
P&L—Losses (profits projected after 4 years)

Geographical Preference

None

Industry Preferences

Communications
Cable television
Commercial communications
Data communications
Satellite and microwave communications
Telephone related
Computer Related
Computer graphics, CAD/CAM and CAE
Computer mainframes
Computer services
Memory devices
Micro and mini computers
Office automation
Scanning related
Software-applications
Software-artificial intelligence
Software-systems
Specialized turnkey systems
Terminals
Electronic Components and Instrumentation
Analytical and scientific instrumentation
Component fabrication and testing equipment
Electronic components
Fiber optics
Laser related
Semiconductors
Genetic Engineering
Gene splicing and manufacturing equipment
Monoclonal antibodies and hybridomas
Recombinant DNA (agricultural and industrial)
Recombinant DNA (medical)
Industrial Products and Equipment
Controls and sensors
Robotics/vision systems
Specialty materials
Medical/Health Related
Diagnostic equipment
Diagnostic test products
Disposable products
Drugs and medicines
Hospital and clinical labs
Medical services
Therapeutic equipment

Additional Information

Year Founded—1932
Capital Under Management—$70 million
Investments(1985-1st 6 months)—12
Invested(1985-1st 6 months)—$13 million
Method of Compensation—Return on investment is of primary concern; do not charge fees

ELK ASSOCIATES FUNDING CORPORATION

600 Third Avenue #3810
New York, NY 10016
212-972-8550

Officers
Gary C. Granoff, Pres.
Ellen M. Walker, V.P. & Gen. Counsel
Margaret Chance, Secy.

Whom to Contact
Gary C. Granoff

Type of Firm
MESBIC

Industry Association Memberships
AAMESBIC
NASBIC

Project Preferences
Will function either as deal originator or
investor in deals created by others
Type of Financing:
Second-stage
Later-stage expansion
Leveraged buyout
Minimum Investment: Less than $100,000
Preferred Investment: $100,000-$250,000
Minimum Operating Data:
Annual Sales—$1.5 million
P&L—Profits NBT over $50,000

Geographical Preference
Northeast

Industry Preferences

Consumer
Computer stores/related services
Consumer products
Consumer services
Food and beverage products
Franchise businesses
Hotels and resort areas
Leisure and recreational products
Restaurants
Retailing
Distribution
Communications equipment
Computer equipment
Consumer products
Electronics equipment
Food products
Industrial products
Medical products
Other
Transportation

Additional Information
Year Founded—1980
Capital Under Management—$14 million
Investments(1985-1st 6 months)—50
Invested(1985-1st 6 months)—$3.5 million
Method of Compensation—Return on
investment is most important, but also
charge for closing fees, service fees, etc.

EQUICO CAPITAL CORPORATION

1290 Avenue of the Americas
New York, NY 10019
212-397-8660

Officer
Duane E. Hill, Pres. & CEO

Type of Firm
MESBIC

Industry Association Memberships
AAMESBIC
NASBIC

Project Preferences
Will function either as deal originator or
investor in deals created by others
Type of Financing:
Second-stage
Later-stage expansion
Leveraged buyout
Minimum Investment: $100,000
Preferred Investment: $250,000-$500,000
Preferred Investment (LBO):
$300,000-$750,000
Minimum Operating Data:
Annual Sales—$1.5 million
P&L—Break even
Annual Sales (LBO)—Over $5 million

Geographical Preference
None

Industry Preferences

Communications
Cable television
Telephone related

Computer Related
Computer graphics, CAD/CAM and CAE
Computer mainframes
Computer services
Memory devices
Micro and mini computers
Office automation
Scanning related
Software-applications
Software-artificial intelligence
Software-systems
Specialized turnkey systems
Terminals
Consumer
Consumer products
Consumer services
Leisure and recreational products
Distribution
Communications equipment
Computer equipment
Consumer products
Electronics equipment
Food products
Industrial products
Medical products
**Electronic Components and
Instrumentation**
Analytical and scientific instrumentation
Component fabrication and testing
equipment
Electronic components
Fiber optics
Laser related
Semiconductors
Medical/Health Related
Diagnostic equipment
Diagnostic test products
Disposable products
Drugs and medicines
Hospital and clinical labs
Medical services
Therapeutic equipment

Additional Information
Year Founded—1971
Capital Under Management—$20 million
Investments(1985-1st 6 months)—4
Invested(1985-1st 6 months)—$1.4 million
Method of Compensation—Return on
investment is most important, but also
charge for closing fees, service fees, etc.

EUCLID PARTNERS CORPORATION

50 Rockefeller Plaza
New York, NY 10020
212-489-1770

Partners
Milton J. Pappas
A. Bliss McCrum, Jr.
Jeffrey T. Hamilton

Whom to Contact
Any of the above

Type of Firm
Private venture capital firm investing
own capital

Affiliation
Euclid Partners II, L.P.

Project Preferences
Will function either as deal originator or
investor in deals created by others
Type of Financing:
Startup
First-stage
Second-stage
Later-stage expansion
Leveraged buyout
Minimum Investment: $250,000
Preferred Investment: $500,000-$1 million
Minimum Operating Data:
Annual Sales—Nominal

Geographical Preference
None

Industry Preferences

Communications
Data communications
Telephone related
Computer Related
Computer graphics, CAD/CAM and CAE
Computer mainframes
Computer services
Memory devices
Micro and mini computers
Office automation
Scanning related
Software-applications
Software-artificial intelligence
Software-systems
Specialized turnkey systems
Terminals

**Electronic Components and
Instrumentation**
Analytical and scientific instrumentation
Component fabrication and testing
equipment
Electronic components
Fiber optics
Laser related
Semiconductors
Energy/Natural Resources
Drilling and exploration services
Oil and gas exploration and production
Technology related products/equipment
Genetic Engineering
Gene splicing and manufacturing equipment
Monoclonal antibodies and hybridomas
Recombinant DNA (agricultural and
industrial)
Recombinant DNA (medical)
Industrial Products and Equipment
Chemicals
Controls and sensors
Energy management
Equipment and machinery
Other industrial automation
Plastics
Robotics/vision systems
Specialty materials
Medical/Health Related
Diagnostic equipment
Diagnostic test products
Disposable products
Therapeutic equipment

Additional Information
Year Founded—1970
Capital Under Management—$22 million
Investments(1985-1st 6 months)—7
Invested(1985-1st 6 months)—$4.4 million
Method of Compensation—Return on
investment is of primary concern; do not
charge fees

EVERLAST CAPITAL CORP.

350 Fifth Avenue #2805
New York, NY 10118
212-695-3910

Officers
Sung K. Kang, Pres.
Yung Duk Hahn, V.P.
Frank Segreto, V.P.
Song J. Kang, Secy.
June W. Lee, Dir.

Whom to Contact
Sung K. Kang
Frank Segreto

Type of Firm
MESBIC

Industry Association Memberships
AAMESBIC
NASBIC

Project Preferences
Prefer role as deal originator but will also
invest in deals created by others
Type of Financing:
Startup
First-stage
Later-stage expansion
Leveraged buyout
Minimum Investment: $250,000
Preferred Investment: $500,000-$1 million
Minimum Operating Data:
Annual Sales—Nominal
P&L—Break even

Geographical Preferences
Within two hours of office
Northeast

Industry Preferences

Consumer
Computer stores/related services
Consumer products
Consumer services
Food and beverage products
Franchise businesses
Hotels and resort areas
Leisure and recreational products
Restaurants
Retailing
Other
Agriculture, forestry, fishing

Additional Information
Year Founded—1984
Capital Under Management—$3.8 million
Investments(1985-1st 6 months)—75
Invested(1985-1st 6 months)—$2.5 million

FAIRFIELD EQUITY CORPORATION

200 East 42nd Street
New York, NY 10017
212-867-0150

Officers
Matthew A. Berdon, Pres.
Samuel L. Highleyman, V.P.
Alfred Hollander, V.P.
Joel Handel, Secy.

Whom to Contact
Matthew A. Berdon

Type of Firm
SBIC

Project Preferences
Will function either as deal originator or
    investor in deals created by others
Type of Financing:
Second-stage
Leveraged buyout
Minimum Investment: Less than $100,000
Preferred Investment: $100,000-$250,000
Minimum Operating Data:
Annual Sales—$1.5 million
P&L—Profits NBT over $250,000

Geographical Preference
Northeast

Industry Preferences

Communications
Cable television
Commercial communications
Data communications
Satellite and microwave communications
Telephone related
Consumer
Computer stores/related services
Consumer products
Consumer services
Food and beverage products
Franchise businesses
Hotels and resort areas
Leisure and recreational products
Restaurants
Retailing
Industrial Products and Equipment
Chemicals
Controls and sensors
Energy management
Equipment and machinery
Other industrial automation
Plastics
Robotics/vision systems
Specialty materials

Other
Agriculture, forestry, fishing
Education related
Finance and insurance
Publishing
Real estate
Specialty consulting
Transportation

Additional Information
Year Founded—1959
Capital Under Management—$3 million
Investments(1985-1st 6 months)—4
Invested(1985-1st 6 months)—$500,000
Method of Compensation—Return on
    investment is of primary concern; do not
    charge fees

FERRANTI HIGH TECHNOLOGY INC.

515 Madison Avenue #1225
New York, NY 10022
212-688-9828

Other Office
Millbank Tower, Millbank
London SW1P 4QS
England
    01-834-6611

Officers
Sanford R. Simon, Pres. (United States)
Keith C. Langworthy, V.P. (United States)
Michael R. Simon, V.P. (United States)
Harry Dutson, Dir. (England)

Whom to Contact
Michael R. Simon
Harry Dutson

Type of Firm
SBIC

Affiliation
Ferranti plc, England (parent)

Industry Association Membership
NASBIC

Project Preferences
Will function either as deal originator or
    investor in deals created by others
Type of Financing:
First-stage
Second-stage
Later-stage expansion
Minimum Investment: $100,000
Preferred Investment: $250,000-$500,000

Minimum Operating Data:
Annual Sales—Nominal
P&L—Break even

Geographical Preference
None

Industry Preferences

Communications
Cable television
Commercial communications
Data communications
Satellite and microwave communications
Telephone related
Computer Related
Computer graphics, CAD/CAM and CAE
Computer mainframes
Computer services
Memory devices
Micro and mini computers
Office automation
Scanning related
Software-applications
Software-artificial intelligence
Software-systems
Specialized turnkey systems
Terminals
**Electronic Components and
    Instrumentation**
Analytical and scientific instrumentation
Component fabrication and testing
    equipment
Electronic components
Fiber optics
Laser related
Semiconductors
Industrial Products and Equipment
Controls and sensors
Other industrial automation
Robotics/vision systems
Specialty materials

Additional Information
Year Founded—1982
Capital Under Management—$5 million
Investments(1985-1st 6 months)—3
Invested(1985-1st 6 months)—$800,000
Method of Compensation—Return on
    investment is of primary concern; do not
    charge fees

FIRST AMERICA-ISRAEL TECHNOLOGY L.P. (FAIT)

685 Fifth Avenue
New York, NY 10022
212-486-6670

Other Office

10 Bavli Street
Tel Aviv
Israel, 62331
03-462-533

Managing Directors

Arie Genger (United States/Israel)
Thomas Hardy (United States/Israel)

Whom to Contact

Thomas Hardy

Type of Firm

Private venture capital firm investing
own capital

Project Preferences

Will function either as deal originator or
investor in deals created by others
Type of Financing:
Second-stage
Later-stage expansion
Leveraged buyout
Minimum Investment: $500,000
Preferred Investment: $500,000-$1 million
Minimum Operating Data:
P&L—Break even

Geographical Preference

Investment opportunity must demonstrate
link between Israel and the United States
Will invest in both Israeli and United States
entities

Industry Preferences

None

Additional Information

Year Founded—1985
Method of Compensation—Return on
investment is of primary concern; do not
charge fees

FIRST BOSTON CORPORATION

12 East 49th Street
New York, NY 10017
212-909-2000

Other Office

Park Avenue Plaza
New York, NY 10055
212-909-2000

Officers

W.E. Mayer, Mgn. Dir.
J.L. Freeman, Mgn. Dir.
F.P. Jenkins, Jr., Mgn. Dir.
Denis Newman, Mgn. Dir.
G.B. Weiksner, Mgn. Dir.
Brian Young, Mgn. Dir.
J.M. Parker, V.P.
H.W. Bogle, Assoc.
J.F. Kenny, Jr., Assoc.
B.C. Kerester, Analyst
W.B. McCarthy, Jr., V.P.
A.M. Ziolkowski, V.P.

Whom to Contact

B.C. Kerester

Type of Firm

Investment banking or merchant banking
firm investing own capital or funds of
partners or clients

Affiliation

First Boston Corporation

Industry Association Membership

NVCA

Project Preferences

Will function either as deal originator or
investor in deals created by others
Type of Financing:
Startup
First-stage
Second-stage
Leveraged buyout
Minimum Investment: $100,000
Preferred Investment: $500,000-$1 million

Geographical Preference

None

Industry Preferences

Communications
Cable television
Commercial communications
Data communications
Satellite and microwave communications
Telephone related

Computer Related
Computer graphics, CAD/CAM and CAE
Computer mainframes
Computer services
Memory devices
Micro and mini computers
Office automation
Scanning related
Software-applications
Software-artificial intelligence
Software-systems
Specialized turnkey systems
Terminals
Consumer
Food and beverage products
**Electronic Components and
   Instrumentation**
Analytical and scientific instrumentation
Component fabrication and testing
   equipment
Electronic components
Fiber optics
Laser related
Semiconductors
Medical/Health Related
Diagnostic equipment
Diagnostic test products
Disposable products
Drugs and medicines
Hospital and clinical labs
Medical services
Therapeutic equipment
Other
Real estate

Additional Information

Year Founded—1981
Capital Under Management—$67 million
Investments(1985-1st 6 months)—12
Invested(1985-1st 6 months)—$8.4 million
Method of Compensation—Return on
   investment is of primary concern; do not
   charge fees

FIRST CENTURY PARTNERSHIPS

1345 Avenue of the Americas
New York, NY 10105
212-698-6382

Other Offices

350 California Street
San Francisco, CA 94104
415-955-1671

3000 Sand Hill Road
Building 3, #190
Menlo Park, CA 94025
415-854-7500

Officers

John S. Dulaney, Chm. & Ptnr. (New York)
Michael J. Myers, Pres. & Ptnr. (New York)
David S. Lobel, V.P. & Ptnr. (New York)
Roberto Buaron, V.P. & Ptnr. (New York)
C. Sage Givens, Assoc. (San Francisco)
Steven P. Bird, Assoc. (Menlo Park)
Lisa Roumell, Assoc. (New York)
Geoffrey Y. Yang, Assoc. (New York)
David T. Gleba, Inv. Analyst (San Francisco)

Whom to Contact

David S. Lobel
Roberto Buaron
C. Sage Givens
Steven P. Bird

Type of Firm

Venture capital affiliate of investment firm

Affiliations

Smith-Barney Venture Corp. (manager)
Smith-Barney, Inc. (parent)

Industry Association Membership

NVCA

Project Preferences

Prefer role as deal originator but will also
invest in deals created by others
Type of Financing:
Seed
Startup
First-stage
Second-stage
Later-stage expansion
Leveraged buyout
Minimum Investment: $500,000
Preferred Investment: $1 million
Preferred Investment (LBO): $2 million
Minimum Operating Data:
Annual Sales—Nominal
P&L—Losses (profits projected after 3 years)
Annual Sales (LBO)—$30 million-$200 million

Geographical Preference

National

Industry Preferences

Communications

Commercial communications
Data communications
Satellite and microwave communications
Telephone related

Computer Related

Computer graphics, CAD/CAM and CAE
Computer mainframes
Computer services
Memory devices
Micro and mini computers
Office automation
Scanning related
Software-applications
Software-artificial intelligence
Software-systems
Specialized turnkey systems
Terminals

Consumer

Computer stores/related services
Consumer products
Consumer services
Franchise businesses
Retailing

Distribution

Communications equipment
Computer equipment
Consumer products
Electronics equipment
Food products
Industrial products
Medical products

Electronic Components and Instrumentation

Analytical and scientific instrumentation
Component fabrication and testing
equipment
Defense electronics
Electronic components
Fiber optics
Laser related
Semiconductors

Energy/Natural Resources

Drilling and exploration services
Oil and gas exploration and production
Technology related products/equipment

Genetic Engineering

Gene splicing and manufacturing equipment
Monoclonal antibodies and hybridomas
Recombinant DNA (agricultural and
industrial)
Recombinant DNA (medical)

Industrial Products and Equipment

Chemicals
Controls and sensors
Energy management
Equipment and machinery
Other industrial automation
Plastics
Robotics/vision systems
Specialty materials

Medical/Health Related

Diagnostic equipment
Diagnostic test products
Disposable products
Drugs and medicines
Hospital and clinical labs
Medical services
Therapeutic equipment

Other

Finance and insurance
Transportation

Will Not Consider

Banking
Brokerage
Consulting
Real estate

Additional Information

Year Founded—1972
Capital Under Management—
Over $150 million
Investments(1985-1st 6 months)—7
Invested(1985-1st 6 months)—$6 million
Method of Compensation—Return on
investment is of primary concern; do not
charge fees

FIRST ROCHESTER CAPITAL CORPORATION

16 East Main Street
Rochester, NY 14450
716-263-3583

Partners

John Mooney
David Hessler

Whom to Contact

Either of the above

Type of Firm

Private venture capital firm investing
own capital

Affiliations

Genesee Ventures
KG Capital Corporation

Industry Association Membership

NASBIC

Project Preferences

Will function either as deal originator or
investor in deals created by others

Type of Financing:
Seed
Startup
First-stage
Second-stage
Later-stage expansion
Minimum Investment: Less than $100,000
Preferred Investment: $100,000-$250,000
Minimum Operating Data:
Annual Sales—Nominal
P&L—Losses (profits projected after 2 years)

Geographical Preference
Northeast

Industry Preferences

Communications
Data communications
Telephone related
Computer Related
Computer graphics, CAD/CAM and CAE
Computer mainframes
Computer services
Memory devices
Micro and mini computers
Office automation
Scanning related
Software-applications
Software-artificial intelligence
Software-systems
Specialized turnkey systems
Terminals
Distribution
Communications equipment
Computer equipment
Consumer products
Electronics equipment
Food products
Industrial products
Medical products
Electronic Components and Instrumentation
Analytical and scientific instrumentation
Component fabrication and testing equipment
Electronic components
Fiber optics
Laser related
Semiconductors
Energy/Natural Resources
Alternative energy
Technology related products/equipment
Genetic Engineering
Gene splicing and manufacturing equipment
Monoclonal antibodies and hybridomas
Recombinant DNA (agricultural and industrial)
Recombinant DNA (medical)

Industrial Products and Equipment
Controls and sensors
Equipment and machinery
Other industrial automation
Robotics/vision systems
Medical/Health Related
Diagnostic equipment
Diagnostic test products
Disposable products
Drugs and medicines
Hospital and clinical labs
Medical services
Therapeutic equipment

Additional Information
Year Founded—1983
Capital Under Management—$1.75 million
Investments(1985-1st 6 months)—1
Invested(1985-1st 6 months)—$150,000
Method of Compensation—Return on investment is of primary concern; do not charge fees

---

FLEET VENTURE PARTNERS

430 Park Avenue
New York, NY 10022

Habib Y. Gorgi, Gen. Ptnr.

See RHODE ISLAND for full listing

FOSTER MANAGEMENT COMPANY

437 Madison Avenue
New York, NY 10022
212-753-4810

Officers
John H. Foster, Pres.
Michael J. Connelly, Exec. V.P.
Timothy E. Foster, V.P.
John C. Garbarino, V.P.

Whom to Contact
Michael J. Connelly

Type of Firm
Private venture capital firm investing own capital

Industry Association Memberships
NASBIC
NVCA

Project Preferences
Prefer role as deal originator but will also invest in deals created by others
Type of Financing:
Startup
First-stage
Second-stage
Later-stage expansion
Leveraged buyout
Minimum Investment: $500,000
Preferred Investment: Over $1 million
Preferred Investment (LBO):
$3 million-$15 million
Minimum Operating Data:
Annual Sales—Nominal
P&L—Losses (profits projected after 3 years)

Geographical Preference
None

Industry Preferences

Communications
Cable television
Radio and television broadcasting
Service companies
Consumer
Consumer services
Food and beverage products
Distribution
Medical products
Medical/Health Related
Hospital and clinical labs
Medical insurance products
Medical services
Outpatient facilities
Other
Finance and insurance
Transportation

Additional Information
Year Founded—1972
Capital Under Management—$100 million
Investments(1985-1st 6 months)—5
Invested(1985-1st 6 months)—$5.5 million
Method of Compensation—Return on investment is of primary concern; do not charge fees

FOUNDERS EQUITY, INC.

477 Madison Avenue
New York, NY 10022
212-319-5900

Officers
Warren H. Haber, Chm.
Joel Friedman, V.P.
John L. Teeger, Pres.
Kevin B. McCollum, V.P.
Donn L. Hartley, V.P.

Whom to Contact
John L. Teeger
Donn L. Hartley

Type of Firm
Investment banking or merchant banking
firm investing own capital or funds of
partners or clients

Affiliations
Founders Property (affiliate)
Founders Capital (division)

Project Preferences
Prefer role as deal originator but will also
invest in deals created by others
Type of Financing:
Later-stage expansion
Leveraged buyout
Minimum Investment: Over $1 million
Preferred Investment: Over $3 million
Preferred Investment (LBO):
Over $10 million
Minimum Operating Data:
Annual Sales—Over $3 million
P&L—Profits NBT over $2 million
Annual Sales (LBO)—Over $15 million

Geographical Preference
None

Industry Preferences

Communications
Newspapers
Radio
Computer Related
Computer graphics, CAD/CAM and CAE
Software-applications
Consumer
Consumer products
Consumer services
Franchise businesses
Leisure and recreational products
Restaurants
Retailing

Distribution
Communications equipment
Computer equipment
Consumer products
Electronics equipment
Food products
Industrial products
Medical products
Value-added distributors preferred
**Electronic Components and
  Instrumentation**
Analytical and scientific instrumentation
Component fabrication and testing
  equipment
Electronic components
Industrial Products and Equipment
Automotive aftermarket products
Chemicals
Controls and sensors
Energy management
Equipment and machinery
Other industrial automation
Plastics
Remanufacturers/rebuilders of
  industrial products
Robotics/vision systems
Specialty materials
Medical/Health Related
Diagnostic equipment
Diagnostic test products
Therapeutic equipment
Will Not Consider
Commodity oriented products

Additional Information
Year Founded—1969
Investments(1985-1st 6 months)—1
Invested(1985-1st 6 months)—$18 million
Method of Compensation—Return on
  investment is most important, but also
  charge for closing fees, service fees, etc.

FRANCIS X. DRISCOLL
ASSOCIATES, INC.

8 Hansen Lane
Huntington Station, NY 11746
516-423-8432

Officers
Francis X. Driscoll, Pres.
Joan M. Driscoll, V.P. & Treas.
Richard Testa, Secy.
Justin L. Driscoll, Assoc.

Whom to Contact
Francis X. Driscoll
Justin L. Driscoll

Type of Firm
Private venture capital firm investing
  own capital

Project Preferences
Will function either as deal originator or
  investor in deals created by others
Type of Financing:
Seed
Startup
First-stage
Second-stage
Leveraged buyout
Minimum Investment: Less than $100,000
Preferred Investment: Less than $100,000
Minimum Operating Data:
Annual Sales—Nominal
P&L—Break even

Geographical Preference
None

Industry Preferences

Communications
Cable television
Commercial communications
Data communications
Satellite and microwave communications
Telephone related
Computer Related
Computer graphics, CAD/CAM and CAE
Computer mainframes
Computer services
Memory devices
Micro and mini computers
Office automation
Scanning related
Software-applications
Software-artificial intelligence
Software-systems
Specialized turnkey systems
Terminals
Consumer
Computer stores/related services
Consumer products
Consumer services
Food and beverage products
Franchise businesses
Hotels and resort areas
Leisure and recreational products
Restaurants
Retailing
Distribution
Communications equipment
Computer equipment
Consumer products
Electronics equipment
Food products
Industrial products
Medical products

Electronic Components and Instrumentation
Analytical and scientific instrumentation
Component fabrication and testing equipment
Electronic components
Fiber optics
Laser related
Semiconductors
Energy/Natural Resources
Alternative energy
Coal related
Drilling and exploration services
Energy conservation
Minerals
Oil and gas exploration and production
Technology related products/equipment
Genetic Engineering
Gene splicing and manufacturing equipment
Monoclonal antibodies and hybridomas
Recombinant DNA (agricultural and industrial)
Recombinant DNA (medical)
Industrial Products and Equipment
Chemicals
Controls and sensors
Energy management
Equipment and machinery
Other industrial automation
Plastics
Robotics/vision systems
Specialty materials
Medical/Health Related
Diagnostic equipment
Diagnostic test products
Disposable products
Drugs and medicines
Hospital and clinical labs
Medical services
Therapeutic equipment
Other
Agriculture, forestry, fishing
Education related
Finance and insurance
Publishing
Real estate
Specialty consulting
Transportation

Additional Information
Year Founded—1983
Capital Under Management—$1 million
Investments(1985-1st 6 months)—4
Invested(1985-1st 6 months)—$100,000
Method of Compensation—Return on investment is of primary concern; do not charge fees

THE FRANKLIN CORPORATION

1185 Avenue of the Americas
New York, NY 10036
212-719-4844

Officers
Herman E. Goodman, Chm.
Alan L. Farkas, Pres.
James S. Eisberg, Gen. Counsel
Elliot Gorman, Cntlr.

Whom to Contact
Alan L. Farkas

Type of Firm
SBIC

Project Preferences
Will function either as deal originator or investor in deals created by others
Type of Financing:
Second-stage
Later-stage expansion
Leveraged buyout
Minimum Investment: $250,000
Preferred Investment: $500,000-$1 million
Minimum Operating Data:
Annual Sales—$500,000
P&L—Break even

Geographical Preferences
Northeast
National

Industry Preferences

Communications
Commercial communications
Computer Related
Computer graphics, CAD/CAM and CAE
Computer services
Consumer
Consumer products
Leisure and recreational products
Retailing
Distribution
Communications equipment
Computer equipment
Electronics equipment
Industrial products
Electronic Components and Instrumentation
Analytical and scientific instrumentation
Component fabrication and testing equipment
Electronic components
Fiber optics
Laser related

Industrial Products and Equipment
Chemicals
Controls and sensors
Equipment and machinery
Other
Education related
Real estate
Transportation

Additional Information
Year Founded—1959
Capital Under Management—$28 million
Investments(1985-1st 6 months)—8
Invested(1985-1st 6 months)—$1.7 million
Method of Compensation—Return on investment is most important, but also charge for closing fees, service fees, etc.

FRESHSTART VENTURE CAPITAL CORPORATION

313 West 53rd Street
New York, NY 10019
212-265-2249

Officers
Zindel Zelmanovitch, Pres.
Pearl Greenbaum, V.P.
Neil Greenbaum, Secy.
Michael Moskowitz, Secy. & Treas.

Whom to Contact
Zindel Zelmanovitch

Type of Firm
MESBIC

Project Preferences
Prefer role as deal originator but will also invest in deals created by others
Type of Financing:
Second-stage
Minimum Investment: Less than $100,000
Preferred Investment: Less than $100,000
Minimum Operating Data:
Annual Sales—$500,000

Geographical Preference
Northeast

Industry Preferences

Communications
Commercial communications
Radio broadcasting
Consumer
Food and beverage products
Restaurants
Retailing

Distribution
Communications equipment
Industrial products

Additional Information
Year Founded—1982

FUNDEX CAPITAL CORPORATION

525 Northern Boulevard
Great Neck, NY 11021
516-466-8550

Officers
Howard F. Sommer, Pres.
Martin Albert, V.P.

Whom to Contact
Howard F. Sommer

Type of Firm
SBIC

Industry Association Membership
NASBIC

Project Preferences
Prefer role as deal originator but will also
    invest in deals created by others
Type of Financing:
Startup
First-stage
Second-stage
Later-stage expansion
Leveraged buyout
Minimum Investment: Less than $100,000
Preferred Investment: $100,000-$250,000
Minimum Operating Data:
Annual Sales—Nominal
P&L—Break even

Geographical Preferences
Northeast
Southeast

Industry Preferences

Communications
Cable television
Commercial communications
Data communications
Satellite and microwave communications
Telephone related

Computer Related
Computer graphics, CAD/CAM and CAE
Computer mainframes
Computer services
Memory devices
Micro and mini computers
Office automation
Scanning related
Software-applications
Software-artificial intelligence
Software-systems
Specialized turnkey systems
Terminals
Consumer
Computer stores/related services
Consumer products
Consumer services
Food and beverage products
Franchise businesses
Hotels and resort areas
Leisure and recreational products
Restaurants
Retailing
Distribution
Communications equipment
Computer equipment
Consumer products
Electronics equipment
Food products
Industrial products
Medical products
**Electronic Components and
    Instrumentation**
Analytical and scientific instrumentation
Component fabrication and testing
    equipment
Electronic components
Fiber optics
Laser related
Semiconductors
Energy/Natural Resources
Alternative energy
Coal related
Drilling and exploration services
Energy conservation
Minerals
Oil and gas exploration and production
Technology related products/equipment
Genetic Engineering
Gene splicing and manufacturing equipment
Monoclonal antibodies and hybridomas
Recombinant DNA (agricultural and
    industrial)
Recombinant DNA (medical)

Industrial Products and Equipment
Chemicals
Controls and sensors
Energy management
Equipment and machinery
Other industrial automation
Plastics
Robotics/vision systems
Specialty materials
Medical/Health Related
Diagnostic equipment
Diagnostic test products
Disposable products
Drugs and medicines
Hospital and clinical labs
Medical services
Therapeutic equipment
Other
Agriculture, forestry, fishing
Education related
Finance and insurance
Publishing
Real estate
Specialty consulting
Transportation

Additional Information
Year Founded—1978
Capital Under Management—$4 million
Investments(1985-1st 6 months)—9
Invested(1985-1st 6 months)—$1.1 million
Method of Compensation—Return on
    investment is most important, but also
    charge for closing fees, service fees, etc.

GENESEE VENTURES

16 East Main Street
Rochester, NY 14614
716-263-3584

Partners
John Mooney
Bernard Kozel
Frederick Schwertz
David Hessler

Whom to Contact
Any of the above

Type of Firm
Private venture capital firm investing
    own capital

Affiliations
First Rochester Capital Corporation
KG Capital Corporation

Industry Association Membership
NASBIC

Project Preferences
Will function either as deal originator or
   investor in deals created by others
Type of Financing:
Seed
Startup
First-stage
Second-stage
Later-stage expansion
Leveraged buyout
Minimum Investment: Less than $100,000
Preferred Investment: $250,000-$500,000
Minimum Operating Data:
Annual Sales—Nominal
P&L—Losses (profits projected after 2 years)

Geographical Preference
Northeast

Industry Preferences

Communications
Data communications
Telephone related
Computer Related
Computer graphics, CAD/CAM and CAE
Computer mainframes
Computer services
Memory devices
Micro and mini computers
Office automation
Scanning related
Software-applications
Software-artificial intelligence
Software-systems
Specialized turnkey systems
Terminals
Distribution
Communications equipment
Computer equipment
Consumer products
Electronics equipment
Food products
Industrial products
Medical products
**Electronic Components and
   Instrumentation**
Analytical and scientific instrumentation
Component fabrication and testing
   equipment
Electronic components
Fiber optics
Laser related
Semiconductors
Energy/Natural Resources
Alternative energy
Technology related products/equipment

Genetic Engineering
Gene splicing and manufacturing equipment
Monoclonal antibodies and hybridomas
Recombinant DNA (agricultural and
   industrial)
Recombinant DNA (medical)
Industrial Products and Equipment
Controls and sensors
Energy management
Equipment and machinery
Other industrial automation
Robotics/vision systems
Specialty materials
Medical/Health Related
Diagnostic equipment
Diagnostic test products
Disposable products
Drugs and medicines
Hospital and clinical labs
Medical services
Therapeutic equipment

Additional Information
Year Founded—1984
Method of Compensation—Return on
   investment is of primary concern; do not
   charge fees

GEOCAPITAL VENTURES

655 Madison Avenue
New York, NY 10021
212-935-0111

Other Office
2092 Concourse Drive
San Jose, CA 95131
408-434-0590

Partners
Stephen J. Clearman (New York)
James J. Harrison (California)
Irwin Lieber (New York)

Whom to Contact
Any of the above

Type of Firm
Private venture capital firm investing
   own capital

Project Preferences
Prefer role as deal originator but will also
   invest in deals created by others
Type of Financing:
Seed
Startup
First-stage
Leveraged buyout

Minimum Investment: Less than $100,000
Preferred Investment: $250,000-$500,000
Minimum Operating Data:
Annual Sales—Nominal
P&L—Losses (profits projected after 1 year)
Annual Sales (LBO)—$15 million-$40 million

Geographical Preference
None

Industry Preferences

Communications
Data communications
Computer Related
Computer services
Software-applications
Software-artificial intelligence
Software-systems
Specialized turnkey systems
**Electronic Components and
   Instrumentation**
Component fabrication and testing
   equipment
Medical/Health Related
Diagnostic equipment
Diagnostic test products
Disposable products
Drugs and medicines
Hospital and clinical labs
Medical services
Therapeutic equipment

Additional Information
Year Founded—1984
Capital Under Management—$20 million
Investments(1985-1st 6 months)—3
Invested(1985-1st 6 months)—$1 million
Method of Compensation—Return on
   investment is of primary concern; do not
   charge fees

GLOBUS GROWTH GROUP

44 West 24th Street
New York, NY 10010
212-243-1000

Officers
Stephen E. Globus, Chm.
Richard D. Globus, Pres.

Whom to Contact
Stephen E. Globus

Type of Firm
Public venture capital company

Project Preferences
Prefer role as deal originator
Type of Financing:
Seed
Research and development partnerships
Startup
First-stage
Minimum Investment: Less than $100,000
Preferred Investment: $100,000-$250,000
Minimum Operating Data:
Annual Sales—Nominal
P&L—Losses (profits projected after 2 years)

Geographical Preference
Northeast

Industry Preferences

Computer Related
Computer graphics, CAD/CAM and CAE
Computer services
Consumer
Consumer services
Distribution
Medical products
Genetic Engineering
Gene splicing and manufacturing equipment
Monoclonal antibodies and hybridomas
Recombinant DNA (agricultural and industrial)
Recombinant DNA (medical)
Medical/Health Related
Diagnostic equipment
Diagnostic test products
Disposable products
Drugs and medicines
Hospital and clinical labs
Medical services
Therapeutic equipment
Other
Agriculture, forestry, fishing
Finance and insurance
Service related companies
Will Not Consider
Computer hardware manufacture
Food and beverage products
Oil exploration and production
Real estate
Restaurants

Additional Information
Year Founded—1981
Investments(1985-1st 6 months)—3
Invested(1985-1st 6 months)—$2 million
Method of Compensation—Function primarily in service area; receive contingent fee in cash or equity

ARTHUR P. GOULD & CO.

One Wilshire Drive
Lake Success, NY 11020
516-773-3000

Officers
Arthur P. Gould, Pres.
Andrew Gould, V.P.
Ira Wolff, V.P.

Whom to Contact
Ira Wolff

Type of Firm
Investment banking or merchant banking firm investing own capital or funds of partners or clients
Consulting firm evaluating and analyzing venture projects and arranging private placements

Project Preferences
Prefer role as deal originator
Type of Financing:
Research and development partnerships
First-stage
Second-stage
Later-stage expansion
Leveraged buyout
Minimum Investment: $500,000
Preferred Investment: Over $1 million
Preferred Investment (LBO):
$5 million and over
Minimum Operating Data:
Annual Sales—Nominal
P&L—Losses (profits projected after 3 years)
Annual Sales (LBO)—$20 million and over

Geographical Preference
None

Industry Preferences

Communications
Cable television
Commercial communications
Data communications
Satellite and microwave communications
Telephone related
Computer Related
Computer graphics, CAD/CAM and CAE
Computer mainframes
Computer services
Memory devices
Micro and mini computers
Scanning related
Software-artificial intelligence
Specialized turnkey systems

Consumer
Consumer products
Food and beverage products
Franchise businesses
Leisure and recreational products
Restaurants
Retailing
Distribution
Communications equipment
Computer equipment
Consumer products
Electronics equipment
Food products
Industrial products
Medical products
Electronic Components and Instrumentation
Analytical and scientific instrumentation
Component fabrication and testing equipment
Electronic components
Fiber optics
Laser related
Semiconductors
Energy/Natural Resources
Alternative energy
Energy conservation
Oil and gas exploration and production
Technology related products/equipment
Genetic Engineering
Gene splicing and manufacturing equipment
Monoclonal antibodies and hybridomas
Recombinant DNA (agricultural and industrial)
Recombinant DNA (medical)
Industrial Products and Equipment
Chemicals
Controls and sensors
Energy management
Equipment and machinery
Other industrial automation
Plastics
Robotics/vision systems
Specialty materials
Medical/Health Related
Diagnostic equipment
Diagnostic test products
Disposable products
Drugs and medicines
Hospital and clinical labs
Medical services
Therapeutic equipment
Other
Agriculture, forestry, fishing
Finance and insurance
Real estate

Additional Information

Year Founded—1967
Method of Compensation—Function primarily
in service area; receive contingent fee in
cash or equity

THE GREENHOUSE MANAGEMENT CORPORATION

Four Cedar Swamp Road
Glen Cove, NY 11542
516-759-1972

Officers

Solomon Manber, Chm.
Evelyn Berezin, Pres.
John Labiak, V.P. & Treas.

Whom to Contact

Evelyn Berezin

Type of Firm

Private venture capital firm investing
own capital

Affiliation

Vanguard Ventures, Inc. (parent)

Project Preferences

Will function either as deal originator or
investor in deals created by others
Type of Financing:
Seed
Research and development partnerships
Startup
First-stage
Minimum Investment: $250,000
Preferred Investment: $250,000-$500,000
Minimum Operating Data:
Annual Sales—Nominal
P&L—Losses (profits projected after 2 years)

Geographical Preference

Within two hours of office

Industry Preferences

Communications
Data communications
Satellite and microwave communications
Telephone related
Computer Related
Computer mainframes
Computer services
Software-applications
Software-artificial intelligence
Software-systems

Electronic Components and Instrumentation
Analytical and scientific instrumentation
Component fabrication and testing
equipment
Electronic components
Laser related
Semiconductors
Genetic Engineering
Gene splicing and manufacturing equipment
Monoclonal antibodies and hybridomas
Recombinant DNA (agricultural and
industrial)
Recombinant DNA (medical)
Medical/Health Related
Diagnostic equipment
Diagnostic test products
Disposable products
Drugs and medicines
Hospital and clinical labs
Medical services
Therapeutic equipment

Additional Information

Year Founded—1981
Investments(1985-1st 6 months)—5
Invested(1985-1st 6 months)—$882,000
Method of Compensation—Return on
investment is most important, but also
charge for closing fees, service fees, etc.

HAMBRO INTERNATIONAL VENTURE FUND

17 East 71st Street
New York, NY 10021
212-288-7778

Other Office

One Boston Place #923
Boston, MA 02108
617-722-7055

Partners

Edwin A. Goodman, Gen. Ptnr. (New York)
Anders K. Brag, Gen. Ptnr. (New York)
Richard A. D'Amore, Gen. Ptnr.
(Massachusetts)
Robert S. Sherman, Gen. Ptnr.
(Massachusetts)
Arthur C. Spinner, Gen. Ptnr. (New York)
Frances N. Janis, Assoc. (New York)

Whom to Contact

Any of the above

Type of Firm

Private venture capital firm investing
own capital

Affiliation

Boston Hambro Corp.

Industry Association Memberships

NASBIC
NVCA

Project Preferences

Will function either as deal originator or
investor in deals created by others
Type of Financing:
Seed
Startup
First-stage
Second-stage
Leveraged buyout
Minimum Investment: $250,000
Preferred Investment: $500,000-$1 million
Minimum Operating Data:
Annual Sales—Nominal

Geographical Preference

None

Industry Preferences

Communications
Data communications
Satellite and microwave communications
Computer Related
Computer graphics, CAD/CAM and CAE
Computer mainframes
Office automation
Software-applications
Software-systems
Specialized turnkey systems
Consumer
Consumer products
Consumer services
Retailing
Distribution
Communications equipment
Consumer products
Electronics equipment
Electronic Components and Instrumentation
Fiber optics
Laser related
Industrial Products and Equipment
Other industrial automation
Robotics/vision systems
Specialty materials
Medical/Health Related
Diagnostic equipment
Medical services

Additional Information
Year Founded—1982
Capital Under Management—$60 million
Investments(1985-1st 6 months)—11
Invested(1985-1st 6 months)—$4.3 million
Method of Compensation—Return on investment is of primary concern; do not charge fees

HANOVER CAPITAL CORPORATION

505 Park Avenue
New York, NY 10022
212-838-5893

Officers
Robert L. Frome, Pres.
Patricia Donahue, Secy. & Treas.
Bernard Karluk, Assoc.

Whom to Contact
Patricia Donahue

Type of Firm
Private venture capital firm investing own capital

Project Preferences
Prefer role as deal originator
Type of Financing:
Second-stage
Leveraged buyout
Minimum Investment: $100,000
Preferred Investment: $500,000-$1 million
Preferred Investment (LBO): $750,000
Minimum Operating Data:
Annual Sales—$1.5 million
P&L—Break even

Geographical Preferences
Northeast
Southeast
West Coast
Texas

Industry Preferences

Communications
Cable television
Commercial communications
Data communications
Satellite and microwave communications
Telephone related
Consumer
Consumer products
Consumer services
Food and beverage products
Retailing

Distribution
Communications equipment
Consumer products
Electronics equipment
Food products
Industrial products
Medical products
Industrial Products and Equipment
Factory automation
Other industrial automation
Robotics/vision systems
Medical/Health Related
Diagnostic equipment
Diagnostic test products
Disposable products
Drugs and medicines
Hospital and clinical labs
Medical services
Therapeutic equipment
Other
Finance and insurance
Publishing

Additional Information
Year Founded—1983
Method of Compensation—Return on investment is most important, but also charge for closing fees, service fees, etc.
Function primarily in service area; receive contingent fee in cash or equity

HARRISON CAPITAL INC.

2000 Westchester Avenue
White Plains, NY 10650
914-253-7084

Officers
E.W. Wolahan, Pres.
E.J. Steigauf, V.P.
J.D. Keough, V.P.
J.A. Hewitt, V.P.
E.T. Carroll, Financial Analyst

Whom to Contact
E.J. Steigauf
E.T. Carroll

Type of Firm
Venture capital subsidiary or affiliate of non-financial corporation

Industry Association Membership
NASBIC

Project Preferences
Will function either as deal originator or investor in deals created by others

Type of Financing:
Startup
First-stage
Second-stage
Later-stage expansion
Minimum Investment: $100,000
Preferred Investment: $500,000-$1 million
Minimum Operating Data:
Annual Sales—$3 million
P&L—Losses (profits projected after 2 years)

Geographical Preference
None

Industry Preferences

Communications
Cable television
Commercial communications
Data communications
Satellite and microwave communications
Telephone related
Computer Related
Computer graphics, CAD/CAM and CAE
Computer mainframes
Computer services
Memory devices
Micro and mini computers
Office automation
Scanning related
Software-applications
Software-artificial intelligence
Software-systems
Specialized turnkey systems
Terminals
Distribution
Communications equipment
Computer equipment
Electronics equipment
Industrial products
Electronic Components and Instrumentation
Analytical and scientific instrumentation
Component fabrication and testing equipment
Electronic components
Fiber optics
Laser related
Semiconductors
Energy/Natural Resources
Alternative energy
Coal related
Drilling and exploration services
Energy conservation
Minerals
Oil and gas exploration and production
Technology related products/equipment

Genetic Engineering
Gene splicing and manufacturing equipment
Monoclonal antibodies and hybridomas
Recombinant DNA (agricultural and industrial)
Recombinant DNA (medical)
Industrial Products and Equipment
Chemicals
Controls and sensors
Energy management
Equipment and machinery
Other industrial automation
Plastics
Robotics/vision systems
Specialty materials

Additional Information
Year Founded—1980
Method of Compensation—Return on investment is of primary concern; do not charge fees

HARVEST VENTURES, INC.

767 Third Avenue
New York, NY 10017
212-838-7776

Other Office
3000 Sand Hill Road
Building 1, #205
Menlo Park, CA 94025
415-854-8400

Officers
Harvey Wertheim, Mgn. Dir. (New York)
Harvey Mallement, Mgn. Dir. (New York)
Cloyd Marvin, Mgn. Dir. (California)
Andrew Rachleff, Assoc. (California)

Whom to Contact
Harvey Wertheim
Harvey Mallement
Cloyd Marvin

Type of Firm
SBIC
Private venture capital firm investing own capital plus capital of institutional and corporate limited partners

Project Preferences
Will function either as deal originator or investor in deals created by others
Type of Financing:
First-stage
Second-stage
Later-stage expansion
Leveraged buyout

Minimum Investment: $500,000
Preferred Investment: $500,000-$1 million
Preferred Investment (LBO):
$500,000-$1 million
Minimum Operating Data:
Annual Sales—Nominal
P&L—Losses (profits projected after 2 years)
Annual Sales (LBO)—$10 million-$50 million

Geographical Preference
None

Industry Preferences

Communications
Cable television
Commercial communications
Data communications
Satellite and microwave communications
Telephone related
Computer Related
Computer graphics, CAD/CAM and CAE
Computer mainframes
Computer services
Memory devices
Micro and mini computers
Office automation
Scanning related
Software-applications
Software-artificial intelligence
Software-systems
Specialized turnkey systems
Terminals
Consumer
Computer stores/related services
Franchise businesses
Leisure and recreational products
Restaurants
Distribution
Communications equipment
Computer equipment
Electronics equipment
Industrial products
Medical products
Electronic Components and Instrumentation
Analytical and scientific instrumentation
Component fabrication and testing equipment
Electronic components
Fiber optics
Laser related
Semiconductors
Energy/Natural Resources
Technology related products/equipment
Genetic Engineering
Gene splicing and manufacturing equipment
Monoclonal antibodies and hybridomas
Recombinant DNA (agricultural and industrial)
Recombinant DNA (medical)

Industrial Products and Equipment
Chemicals
Controls and sensors
Energy management
Equipment and machinery
Other industrial automation
Plastics
Robotics/vision systems
Specialty materials
Medical/Health Related
Diagnostic equipment
Diagnostic test products
Disposable products
Drugs and medicines
Hospital and clinical labs
Medical services
Therapeutic equipment
Other
Finance and insurance

Additional Information
Year Founded—1976
Capital Under Management—$68 million
Investments(1985-1st 6 months)—13
Invested(1985-1st 6 months)—$5.2 million
Method of Compensation—Return on investment is of primary concern; do not charge fees

LAWRENCE HERBST INVESTMENT TRUST FUND

R.D. #1 Post Office Box 5
Rock Stream, NY 14878

John Popowich, Treas.
Ruth Gray, Admin. Asst.

See TEXAS for full listing

HI-TECH VENTURE CONSULTANTS, INC.

471 West Broadway
New York, NY 10012
212-982-4485

Officers
Robert A. Friedenberg, Pres./Management
Ralph L. Hensler, Pres./Tech. Assessment

Type of Firm
Consulting firm evaluating and analyzing venture projects and arranging private placements

Project Preferences
Will function either as deal originator or as finder in deals created by others
Type of Financing:
Seed
Startup
First-stage
Second-stage

Geographical Preference
Northeast

Industry Preferences

Communications
Data communications
Local area networks
Telephone related
Teletext
Videotex
Voice-video transmission
Computer Related
Computer graphics, CAD/CAM and CAE
Computer services
Memory devices
Micro and mini computers
Office automation
Peripherals
Software-artificial intelligence
Electronic Components and Instrumentation
Analytical and scientific instrumentation
Laser related
Optics technology
Semiconductors
Energy/Natural Resources
Alternative energy
Energy conservation
Technology related products/equipment
Waste reprocessing
Industrial Products and Equipment
Controls and sensors
Environmental products and services
Other industrial automation
Robotics/vision systems
Medical/Health Related
Diagnostic equipment
Medical services

Additional Information
Year Founded—1983
Method of Compensation—Function primarily in service area; receive contingent fee in cash or equity

---

HOLDING CAPITAL GROUP

685 Fifth Avenue, 14th Floor
New York, NY 10022
212-486-6670

Other Offices
2851 Alton Avenue
Irvine, CA 92714
714-863-0300

7136 South Yale #208
Tulsa, OK 74136
918-492-8524

2440 Parkside
Irving, TX 75061
214-252-2799

Principals
S.A. Spencer (New York)
Arie Genger (New York)
James W. Donaghy (New York)
Bob E. Inman (California)
Christopher B. Shanklin (Oklahoma)
William C. Martin (Texas)

Whom to Contact
James W. Donaghy
Bob E. Inman
William C. Martin
Christopher B. Shanklin

Type of Firm
Private venture capital firm investing own capital
SBIC

Project Preferences
Prefer role as deal originator but will also invest in deals created by others
Type of Financing:
Later-stage expansion
Leveraged buyout
Minimum Investment: $100,000
Preferred Investment: Over $1 million
Preferred Investment (LBO): $5 million and over
Minimum Operating Data:
P&L—Profits NBT over $500,000

Geographical Preference
None

Industry Preferences
None

Additional Information
Year Founded—1975
Investments(1985-1st 6 months)—30
Method of Compensation—Return on investment is most important, but also charge for closing fees, service fees, etc.

HUTTON VENTURE INVESTMENT PARTNERS INC.

One Battery Park Plaza #1801
New York, NY 10004
212-742-3722

Officers
James E. McGrath, Pres.
James F. Wilson, Inv. Mgr.
Timothy E. Noll, Inv. Mgr.
Margaret G. Chung, Inv. Analyst

Whom to Contact
James E. McGrath

Type of Firm
Investment banking or merchant banking firm investing own capital or funds of partners or clients

Affiliation
The E.F. Hutton Group, Inc. (parent)

Industry Association Membership
NVCA

Project Preferences
Prefer role as deal originator but will also invest in deals created by others
Type of Financing:
Seed
Startup
First-stage
Leveraged buyout
Minimum Investment: $250,000
Preferred Investment: $500,000-$1 million
Minimum Operating Data:
Annual Sales—Nominal
P&L—Losses (profits projected after 2 years)

Geographical Preference
None

Industry Preferences

Communications
Data communications
Satellite and microwave communications
Telephone related

Computer Related
Computer graphics, CAD/CAM and CAE
Computer mainframes
Computer services
Memory devices
Software-artificial intelligence
Distribution
Electronics equipment
Medical products
**Electronic Components and
   Instrumentation**
Analytical and scientific instrumentation
Component fabrication and testing
   equipment
Electronic components
Fiber optics
Laser related
Semiconductors
Energy/Natural Resources
Technology related products/equipment
Genetic Engineering
Monoclonal antibodies and hybridomas
Recombinant DNA (agricultural and
   industrial)
Industrial Products and Equipment
Controls and sensors
Robotics/vision systems
Medical/Health Related
Diagnostic equipment
Diagnostic test products
Disposable products
Drugs and medicines
Hospital and clinical labs
Medical services
Therapeutic equipment

Additional Information
Year Founded—1981
Capital Under Management—$25 million
Investments(1985-1st 6 months)—5
Invested(1985-1st 6 months)—$2 million
Method of Compensation—Return on
   investment is of primary concern; do not
   charge fees

HYCLIFF CAPITAL L.P.

1211 Avenue of the Americas
New York, NY 10036
212-921-7755

Partners
Robert A. Bernhard
David N. Nutt

Whom to Contact
David N. Nutt

Type of Firm
Private venture capital firm investing
   own capital

Project Preferences
Will function either as deal originator or
   investor in deals created by others
Type of Financing:
Seed
Later-stage expansion
Leveraged buyout
Minimum Investment: $100,000
Preferred Investment: $250,000-$500,000
Minimum Operating Data:
Annual Sales—Over $3 million
P&L—Break even

Geographical Preference
Northeast

Industry Preferences

Communications
Cable television
Commercial communications
Data communications
Satellite and microwave communications
Telephone related
Computer Related
Computer graphics, CAD/CAM and CAE
Computer mainframes
Computer services
Memory devices
Micro and mini computers
Office automation
Scanning related
Software-applications
Software-artificial intelligence
Software-systems
Specialized turnkey systems
Terminals
Consumer
Consumer products
Retailing
Distribution
Computer equipment
Electronics equipment
Medical products
**Electronic Components and
   Instrumentation**
Analytical and scientific instrumentation
Component fabrication and testing
   equipment
Electronic components
Fiber optics
Laser related
Semiconductors

Genetic Engineering
Gene splicing and manufacturing equipment
Monoclonal antibodies and hybridomas
Recombinant DNA (agricultural and
   industrial)
Recombinant DNA (medical)
Industrial Products and Equipment
Robotics/vision systems
Medical/Health Related
Diagnostic equipment
Diagnostic test products
Disposable products
Drugs and medicines
Hospital and clinical labs
Medical services
Therapeutic equipment
Other
Publishing

Additional Information
Year Founded—1983
Investments(1985-1st 6 months)—5
Method of Compensation—Return on
   investment is most important, but also
   charge for closing fees, service fees, etc.

INCO VENTURE CAPITAL
MANAGEMENT

One New York Plaza, 37th Floor
New York, NY 10004
212-612-5620

Other Office
c/o International Nickel, Inc.
2099 Gateway Plaza #470
San Jose, CA 95112
408-993-9594

Officers
Stuart F. Feiner, Pres. & Mgn. Principal
   (New York)
Richard G. Couch, Sr. V.P. & Principal
   (California)
George Middlemas, Sr. V.P. & Principal
   (New York)
A. Douglas Peabody, Sr. V.P. & Principal
   (New York)

Whom to Contact
Any of the above

Type of Firm
Venture capital subsidiary or affiliate of
   non-financial corporation

Affiliations

Inco Limited (parent)
Inco United States, Inc. (U.S.
  holding company)
Inco Securities Corporation (holding
  company for venture investments)
North American Ventures Funds
North American Partners Limited
  Partnerships

Industry Association Membership

WAVC

Project Preferences

Will function either as deal originator or
  investor in deals created by others

Type of Financing:
Seed
Research and development partnerships
Startup
First-stage
Second-stage
Leveraged buyout
Minimum Investment: $250,000
Preferred Investment: $500,000-$1 million
Minimum Operating Data:
Annual Sales—Nominal
P&L—Losses (profits projected after 4 years)

Geographical Preference

None

Industry Preferences

Communications
Cable television
Commercial communications
Data communications
Satellite and microwave communications
Telephone related
Computer Related
Computer graphics, CAD/CAM and CAE
Computer services
Memory devices
Office automation
Scanning related
Software-applications
Software-artificial intelligence
Software-systems
Specialized turnkey systems
Consumer
Consumer products
Distribution
Communications equipment
Computer equipment
Consumer products
Electronics equipment
Medical products

**Electronic Components and
  Instrumentation**
Analytical and scientific instrumentation
Component fabrication and testing
  equipment
Electronic components
Fiber optics
Laser related
Semiconductors
Energy/Natural Resources
Alternative energy
Technology related products/equipment
Genetic Engineering
Gene splicing and manufacturing equipment
Monoclonal antibodies and hybridomas
Recombinant DNA (agricultural and
  industrial)
Recombinant DNA (medical)
Industrial Products and Equipment
Controls and sensors
Energy management
Other industrial automation
Robotics/vision systems
Specialty materials
Medical/Health Related
Diagnostic equipment
Diagnostic test products
Disposable products
Drugs and medicines
Medical services
Therapeutic equipment
Other
Education related
Will Not Consider
Real estate

Additional Information

Year Founded—1974
Capital Under Management—Over $100
  million, including co-managed funds
Investments(1985-1st 6 months)—15
Invested(1985-1st 6 months)—$1.3 million
Method of Compensation—Return on
  investment is of primary concern; do not
  charge fees

INTERFID LTD.

1 Dag Hammarskjold Plaza
New York, NY 10017
212-832-2324

Officers

Amos Kaminski, Pres.
James Hart, V.P.
Wayne Anderson, Admin. V.P.
Uzi Yair, Assoc.
James Brown, Assoc.

Whom to Contact

James Hart
Uzi Yair

Type of Firm

Investment banking or merchant banking
  firm investing own capital or funds of
  partners or clients
Consulting firm evaluating and analyzing
  venture projects and arranging private
  placements

Affiliation

Privest I & II, N.V., Netherlands Antilles
  (funds advised)

Project Preferences

Will function either as deal originator or
  investor in deals created by others
Type of Financing:
Startup
Second-stage
Later-stage expansion
Leveraged buyout
Minimum Investment: $250,000
Preferred Investment: Over $750,000
Preferred Investment (LBO):
  $750,000-$2.5 million
Minimum Operating Data:
Annual Sales—$1.5 million
P&L—Losses (profits projected after 1 year)
Annual Sales (LBO)—$10 million-$50 million

Geographical Preferences

Northeast
National

Industry Preferences

Communications
Broadcasting
Cable television
Data communications
Satellite and microwave communications
Telephone related

463

Computer Related
Computer services
Office automation
Scanning related
Software-applications
Software-systems
Terminals
Consumer
Computer stores/related services
Consumer products
Consumer services
Food and beverage products
Franchise businesses
Leisure and recreational products
Retailing
Distribution
Communications equipment
Computer equipment
Consumer products
Electronics equipment
Food products
Industrial products
Medical products
**Electronic Components and
  Instrumentation**
Analytical and scientific instrumentation
Component fabrication and testing
  equipment
Electronic components
Fiber optics
Laser related
Semiconductors
Genetic Engineering
Monoclonal antibodies and hybridomas
Recombinant DNA (agricultural and
  industrial)
Industrial Products and Equipment
Chemicals
Controls and sensors
Energy management
Equipment and machinery
Other industrial automation
Plastics
Robotics/vision systems
Specialty materials
Medical/Health Related
Diagnostic equipment
Diagnostic test products
Disposable products
Hospital and clinical labs
Therapeutic equipment
Other
Agriculture, forestry, fishing
Real estate
Transportation

Additional Information
Year Founded—1984
Capital Under Management—$19 million
Investments(1985-1st 6 months)—4
Invested(1985-1st 6 months)—$2.1 million
Method of Compensation—Return on
  investment is most important, but also
  charge for closing fees, service fees, etc.

INTERNATIONAL TECHNOLOGY VENTURES, INC.

535 Madison Avenue, 19th Floor
New York, NY 10022
212-371-5895

Officers
John Soden, Pres.

Type of Firm
Private venture capital firm investing
  own capital

Affiliation
Ing. C. Olivetti & C., S.P.A. (limited and
  general partner in venture capital fund)

Industry Association Membership
NVCA

Project Preferences
Prefer role as deal originator but will also
  invest in deals created by others
Type of Financing:
Seed
Startup
First-stage
Second-stage
Minimum Investment: $250,000
Preferred Investment: $500,000-$1 million
Minimum Operating Data:
Annual Sales—Nominal
P&L—Losses (profits projected after 2 years)

Geographical Preference
None

Industry Preferences

Communications
Data communications
Satellite and microwave communications
Telephone related

Computer Related
Computer graphics, CAD/CAM and CAE
Computer mainframes
Computer services
Memory devices
Micro and mini computers
Office automation
Scanning related
Software-applications
Software-artificial intelligence
Software-systems
Specialized turnkey systems
Terminals
Consumer
Computer stores/related services
Distribution
Communications equipment
Computer equipment
Electronics equipment
**Electronic Components and
  Instrumentation**
Analytical and scientific instrumentation
Component fabrication and testing
  equipment
Electronic components
Fiber optics
Laser related
Semiconductors
Industrial Products and Equipment
Other industrial automation
Will Not Consider
Agriculture
Energy/natural resorces
Genetic engineering
Medical/health related
Real estate
Transportation

Additional Information
Year Founded—1983 (Olivetti corporate
  venture capital fund founded in 1979)
Capital Under Management—$43 million
Investments(1985-1st 6 months)—7
Invested(1985-1st 6 months)—$5 million
Method of Compensation—Return on
  investment is of primary concern; do not
  charge fees

INVESTECH, L.P.

515 Madison Avenue #2400
New York, NY 10022
212-308-5811

General Partners
Sheldon F. Claar
Seymour L. Goldblatt
Carl S. Hutman
Tancred V. Schiavoni

Whom to Contact
Carl S. Hutman
Tancred V. Schiavoni

Type of Firm
Private venture capital firm investing
own capital

Project Preferences
Will function either as deal originator or
investor in deals created by others
Type of Financing:
Seed
Research and development partnerships
Startup
First-stage
Second-stage
Later-stage expansion
Buyout or acquisition
Purchases of secondary positions
Minimum Investment: $200,000
Preferred Investment: $500,000-$1 million
Minimum Operating Data:
Annual Sales—Nominal
P&L—Losses (profits projected after 2 years)

Geographical Preference
None

Industry Preferences

Communications
Antennas
Front-end processors
Local area networks
Telephone related
Computer Related
Computer graphics, CAD/CAM and CAE
Displays
Memory devices
Micro and mini computers
Office automation
Printers
Software-applications
Software-artificial intelligence
Software-systems
Voice technology
Distribution
Communications equipment
Computer equipment
Computer software
Electronics equipment
Industrial products
Medical products
Electronic Components and Instrumentation
Laser related
Optics technology
Semiconductors
Sensors and transducers
Energy/Natural Resources
Alternative storage media
Conversion efficiency improvements
Geo-search instrumentation
Prime movers
Technology related products/equipment
Genetic Engineering
Monoclonal antibodies and hybridomas
Recombinant DNA (agricultural and industrial)
Recombinant DNA (medical)
Research and manufacturing equipment
Industrial Products and Equipment
Bio-process systems
Controls and sensors
Energy management
Other industrial automation
Quality control systems
Robotics/vision systems
Specialty materials
Vision sensing and control
Medical/Health Related
Diagnostic equipment
Drugs and medicines
Hospital and clinical labs
Prosthetic devices
Therapeutic equipment
Other
Security devices

Additional Information
Year Founded—1981
Capital Under Management—$27.5 million
Method of Compensation—Return on
investment is of primary concern; do not
charge fees

INVESTMENT PARTNERS OF AMERICA

c/o Conboy, Hewitt, O'Brien & Boardman
100 Park Avenue
New York, NY 10017

Donald Stuart Bab, Gen. Ptnr.

See NEW JERSEY for full listing

IRVING CAPITAL CORPORATION
ITC CAPITAL CORPORATION

1290 Avenue of the Americas
Third Floor
New York, NY 10019
212-408-4800

Officers
J. Andrew McWethy, E.V.P. & Gen. Mgr.
Barry A. Solomon, V.P.
Stephen A. Tuttle, V.P.
Kathleen M. Snyder, Asst. Secy.

Whom to Contact
Any of the above

Type of Firm
SBIC
Venture capital subsidiary of
commercial bank

Affiliations
Irving Trust Company (parent)
Irving Bank Corporation (parent)

Industry Association Membership
NASBIC

Project Preferences
Will function either as deal originator or
investor in deals created by others
Type of Financing:
Second-stage
Later-stage expansion
Leveraged buyout
Minimum Investment: $500,000
Preferred Investment: Over $1 million
Preferred Investment (LBO):
$1 million-$10 million
Minimum Operating Data:
Annual Sales—$1.5 million
P&L—Profits NBT over $100,000
Annual Sales (LBO)—$10 million-$100 million

Geographical Preference
National

Industry Preferences

Communications
Cable television
Commercial communications
Data communications
Satellite and microwave communications
Telephone related
Computer Related
Computer graphics, CAD/CAM and CAE
Computer mainframes
Computer services
Memory devices
Micro and mini computers
Office automation
Scanning related
Software-applications
Software-artificial intelligence
Software-systems
Specialized turnkey systems
Terminals
Consumer
Retailing
Distribution
Communications equipment
Computer equipment
Consumer products
Electronics equipment
Food products
Industrial products
Medical products
**Electronic Components and
  Instrumentation**
Analytical and scientific instrumentation
Component fabrication and testing
  equipment
Electronic components
Fiber optics
Laser related
Semiconductors
Industrial Products and Equipment
Chemicals
Controls and sensors
Energy management
Equipment and machinery
Other industrial automation
Plastics
Robotics/vision systems
Specialty materials
Medical/Health Related
Diagnostic equipment
Diagnostic test products
Disposable products
Drugs and medicines
Hospital and clinical labs
Medical services
Therapeutic equipment
Will Not Consider
Real estate

Additional Information
Year Founded—1976
Capital Under Management—$25 million
Investments(1985-1st 6 months)—3
Invested(1985-1st 6 months)—$2.3 million
Method of Compensation—Return on
  investment is of primary concern; do not
  charge fees

KEY VENTURE CAPITAL CORP.

60 State Street
Albany, NY 12180
518-447-3181

Officers
John M. Lang, Pres.
Mark R. Hursty, Exec. V.P.
Richard C. Van Auken, Asst. V.P.

Whom to Contact
Mark R. Hursty

Type of Firm
SBIC

Affiliation
Key Corp. (parent)

Project Preferences
Will function either as deal originator or
  investor in deals created by others
Type of Financing:
First-stage
Second-stage
Later-stage expansion
Leveraged buyout
Minimum Investment: $100,000
Preferred Investment: $100,000-$250,000

Geographical Preference
Northeast

Industry Preferences

**Electronic Components and
  Instrumentation**
Analytical and scientific instrumentation
Component fabrication and testing
  equipment
Electronic components
Fiber optics
Laser related
Semiconductors

Additional Information
Year Founded—1983
Capital Under Management—$4 million
Investments(1985-1st 6 months)—8
Invested(1985-1st 6 months)—$1.2 million
Method of Compensation—Return on
  investment is of primary concern; do not
  charge fees

KG CAPITAL CORPORATION

3100 Monroe Avenue
Rochester, NY 14618
716-586-6015

General Partners
Bernard Kozel, Pres.
Dr. Frederick A. Schwertz, V.P.

Whom to Contact
Either of the above

Type of Firm
Limited partnership

Affiliations
First Rochester Capital Corporation
Genesee Ventures

Project Preferences
Will function either as deal originator or
  investor in deals created by others
Type of Financing:
Startup
First-stage
Second-stage
Minimum Investment: $100,000
Minimum Operating Data:
Annual Sales—Nominal

Geographical Preference
None

Industry Preferences

Communications
Data communications
Graphic arts
Satellite and microwave communications
Telephone related
Computer Related
Software-applications
Software-systems
**Electronic Components and
  Instrumentation**
Electronic components
Semiconductors

Industrial Products and Equipment
Advanced materials
Chemicals
Machine tools
Robotics/vision systems
Will Not Consider
Service companies

Additional Information
Year Founded—1981
Capital Under Management—$1.2 million
Method of Compensation—Return on investment is of primary concern; do not charge fees

---

LAIDLAW ADAMS & PECK INC.

275 Madison Avenue
New York, NY 10016
212-210-5790

Officers
Robert H. Clayton, Jr., Chm.
Bart Gutekunst, Mgn. Dir.
Gary J. Fine, First V.P.
Christopher J. Ryan, V.P.
Richard Beberman, Assoc.

Whom to Contact
Bart Gutekunst

Type of Firm
Investment banking or merchant banking firm investing own capital or funds of partners or clients
Consulting firm evaluating and analyzing venture projects and arranging private placements

Project Preferences
Prefer role as deal originator but will also invest in deals created by others
Type of Financing:
Second-stage
Later-stage expansion
Leveraged buyout
Minimum Investment: $1 million
Preferred Investment: Over $1 million
Minimum Operating Data:
Annual Sales—$3 million
P&L—Break even

Geographical Preference
None

Industry Preferences

Communications
Cable television
Commercial communications
Data communications
Satellite and microwave communications
Telephone related
Computer Related
Computer graphics, CAD/CAM and CAE
Computer mainframes
Computer services
Memory devices
Micro and mini computers
Office automation
Scanning related
Software-applications
Software-artificial intelligence
Software-systems
Specialized turnkey systems
Terminals
Consumer
Computer stores/related services
Consumer products
Consumer services
Food and beverage products
Franchise businesses
Hotels and resort areas
Leisure and recreational products
Restaurants
Retailing
Distribution
Communications equipment
Computer equipment
Consumer products
Electronics equipment
Food products
Industrial products
Medical products
Electronic Components and Instrumentation
Analytical and scientific instrumentation
Component fabrication and testing equipment
Electronic components
Fiber optics
Laser related
Semiconductors
Energy/Natural Resources
Alternative energy
Coal related
Drilling and exploration services
Energy conservation
Minerals
Oil and gas exploration and production
Technology related products/equipment
Genetic Engineering
Gene splicing and manufacturing equipment
Monoclonal antibodies and hybridomas
Recombinant DNA (agricultural and industrial)
Recombinant DNA (medical)

Industrial Products and Equipment
Chemicals
Controls and sensors
Energy management
Equipment and machinery
Other industrial automation
Plastics
Robotics/vision systems
Specialty materials
Medical/Health Related
Diagnostic equipment
Diagnostic test products
Disposable products
Drugs and medicines
Hospital and clinical labs
Medical services
Therapeutic equipment
Other
Agriculture, forestry, fishing
Education related
Finance and insurance
Publishing
Real estate
Specialty consulting
Transportation

Additional Information
Year Founded—1842

LAWRENCE VENTURE ASSOCIATES

One New York Plaza
New York, NY 10004
212-908-9553

Other Office
3401 West End Avenue #680
Nashville, TN 37203
615-383-0982

Partners
Larry J. Lawrence, Mgn. Gen. Ptnr. (New York)
Richard W. Smith, Gen. Ptnr. (New York)
Philip B. Smith, Gen. Ptnr. (New York)
Jack Tyrrell, Gen. Ptnr. (Tennessee)
W. Patrick Ortale III, Gen. Ptnr. (Tennessee)
Thomas A. Gallagher, Assoc. (Tennessee)

Whom to Contact
Any of the above

Type of Firm
Private venture capital firm investing own capital

Project Preferences
Will function either as deal originator or investor in deals created by others

Type of Financing:
Startup
First-stage
Second-stage
Later-stage expansion
Leveraged buyout
Minimum Investment: $500,000
Preferred Investment: $500,000-$1 million
Minimum Operating Data:
Annual Sales—Nominal
P&L—Losses (profits projected after 2 years)

Geographical Preference
National

Industry Preferences

Communications
Data communications
Satellite and microwave communications
Computer Related
Computer graphics, CAD/CAM and CAE
Computer mainframes
Computer services
Memory devices
Micro and mini computers
Office automation
Scanning related
Software-applications
Software-artificial intelligence
Software-systems
Specialized turnkey systems
Terminals
Distribution
Electronics equipment
Medical products
Electronic Components and Instrumentation
Analytical and scientific instrumentation
Component fabrication and testing equipment
Electronic components
Fiber optics
Laser related
Optics technology
Semiconductors
Energy/Natural Resources
Alternative energy
Services
Industrial Products and Equipment
Advanced materials
Medical/Health Related
Diagnostic equipment
Diagnostic test products
Disposable products
Drugs and medicines
Hospital and clinical labs
Medical services
Therapeutic equipment

Additional Information
Method of Compensation—Return on investment is of primary concern; do not charge fees

---

MANUFACTURERS HANOVER VENTURE CAPITAL CORPORATION

140 East 45th Street
New York, NY 10017
212-808-0109

Officers
Thomas J. Sandleitner, Pres.
Edward L. Koch III, V.P.
Kevin P. Falvey, V.P.
Bryan J. Carey, Sr. Inv. Mgr.
Kathleen P. Prime, Inv. Analyst

Whom to Contact
Kevin P. Falvey
Bryan J. Carey
Kathleen P. Prime

Type of Firm
Venture capital subsidiary of commercial bank

Affiliation
Manufacturers Hanover Corporation

Industry Association Membership
NASBIC

Project Preferences
Will function either as deal originator or investor in deals created by others
Type of Financing:
First-stage
Second-stage
Later-stage expansion
Leveraged buyout
Minimum Investment: $500,000
Preferred Investment: $500,000-$1 million
Preferred Investment (LBO):
$10 million or less

Geographical Preference
None

Industry Preferences

Communications
Cable television
Commercial communications
Data communications
Satellite and microwave communications
Telephone related

Computer Related
Computer graphics, CAD/CAM and CAE
Computer mainframes
Computer services
Memory devices
Micro and mini computers
Office automation
Software-applications
Software-systems
Terminals
Consumer
Computer stores/related services
Consumer products
Consumer services
Food and beverage products
Franchise businesses
Retailing
Distribution
Communications equipment
Computer equipment
Consumer products
Electronics equipment
Food products
Industrial products
Medical products
Electronic Components and Instrumentation
Analytical and scientific instrumentation
Component fabrication and testing equipment
Electronic components
Fiber optics
Laser related
Semiconductors
Energy/Natural Resources
Alternative energy
Coal related
Drilling and exploration services
Energy conservation
Minerals
Oil and gas exploration and production
Technology related products/equipment
Industrial Products and Equipment
Chemicals
Controls and sensors
Energy management
Equipment and machinery
Other industrial automation
Plastics
Robotics/vision systems
Specialty materials
Medical/Health Related
Diagnostic equipment
Diagnostic test products
Disposable products
Drugs and medicines
Hospital and clinical labs
Medical services
Therapeutic equipment

Additional Information
Year Founded—1981
Capital Under Management—$110 million
Investments(1985-1st 6 months)—5
Invested(1985-1st 6 months)—$3 million
Method of Compensation—Return on investment is of primary concern; do not charge fees

MCCOWN DE LEEUW & CO.

900 Third Avenue, 28th Floor
New York, NY 10022
212-418-6539

David E. De Leeuw, Gen. Ptnr.

See CALIFORNIA for full listing

MECOX CAPITAL, INC.

415 Madison Avenue
New York, NY 10017
212-750-5100

Affiliate's Office
Energy and Technology Investment
Consultants, SA
13, rue de Florissant
1206 Geneva, Switzerland
022- 31-2050

Officers
Dr. Aris P. Christodoulou, Pres.
  (United States)
Bruno Lepinoy, Affiliate (Switzerland)

Whom to Contact
Either of the above

Type of Firm
Investment banking or merchant banking firm investing own capital or funds of partners or clients
Consulting firm evaluating and analyzing venture projects and arranging private placements
Private venture capital firm arranging investment projects on behalf of itself and clients

Affiliation
Energy and Technology Investment Consultants, SA (joint venture)

Project Preferences
Prefer role as deal originator
Type of Financing:
Second-stage
Leveraged buyout
Mergers and acquisitions
Minimum Investment: Less than $100,000
Preferred Investment: $100,000-$250,000
Preferred Investment (LBO):
  $100,000-$300,000
Minimum Operating Data:
Annual Sales—$500,000
P&L—Losses (profits projected after 1 year)

Geographical Preference
None

Industry Preferences

Consumer
Consumer products
Cosmetics, toiletries and personal care products
Food and beverage products
Distribution
Consumer products
Medical products
Electronic Components and Instrumentation
Analytical and scientific instrumentation
Energy/Natural Resources
Technology related products/equipment
Genetic Engineering
Reagent chemicals and supplies
Industrial Products and Equipment
Chemicals
Microencapsulation
Plastics
Pollution control
Specialty materials
Medical/Health Related
Biomaterials
Diagnostic equipment
Diagnostic test products
Disposable products
Drug delivery
Drugs and medicines
Hospital and clinical labs
Medical services
Therapeutic equipment
Other
Specialty consulting

Additional Information
Year Founded—1980
Method of Compensation—Return on investment is most important, but also charge for closing fees, service fees, etc.
Professional fee required whether or not deal closes

ML VENTURE PARTNERS I, L.P.

717 Fifth Avenue, 22nd Floor
New York, NY 10022
212-980-0410

Officers
George Kokkinakis, Chm. & Ptnr.
Stephen J. Warner, Pres. & Ptnr.
George L. Sing, V.P. & Ptnr.
R. Stephen McCormack, V.P. & Ptnr.
Robert Finzi, V.P.
Walter Perlstein, V.P.

Whom to Contact
Any of the above

Type of Firm
Public venture capital partnership investing own capital

Affiliation
Merrill Lynch & Co.

Industry Association Membership
NVCA

Project Preferences
Will function either as deal originator or investor in deals created by others
Type of Financing:
Startup
First-stage
Second-stage
Minimum Investment: $500,000
Preferred Investment: $750,000 and over
Minimum Operating Data:
Annual Sales—Nominal
P&L—Losses (profits projected after 3 years)

Geographical Preference
National

Industry Preferences

Communications
Commercial communications
Data communications
Satellite and microwave communications
Telephone related-PBX

Computer Related
Artificial intelligence
Computer graphics, CAD/CAM and CAE
Computer mainframes
Computer services
Electronic technical publishing
Memory devices
Micro and mini computers
Office automation
Scanning related
Software-applications
Software-artificial intelligence
Software-systems
Specialized turnkey systems
Terminals
Electronic Components and Instrumentation
Analytical and scientific instrumentation
Component fabrication and testing equipment
Electronic components
Fiber optics
Laser related
Semiconductors
Genetic Engineering
Gene splicing and manufacturing equipment
Monoclonal antibodies and hybridomas
Other agricultural genetics
Recombinant DNA (agricultural and industrial)
Recombinant DNA (medical)
Industrial Products and Equipment
Other industrial automation
Robotics/vision systems
Medical/Health Related
Diagnostic equipment
Diagnostic test products
Disposable products
Drugs and medicines
Hospital and clinical labs
Medical services
Therapeutic equipment
Will Not Consider
Franchising
Real estate
Retail

Additional Information
Year Founded—1982
Capital Under Management—$60 million
Investments(1985-1st 6 months)—7
Invested(1985-1st 6 months)—$4 million
Method of Compensation—Return on investment is of primary concern; do not charge fees

MORGAN STANLEY & CO., INC.

1251 Avenue of the Americas
New York, NY 10020
212-974-4000

Officers
William F. Murdy, Principal
Grant Behrman, V.P.
Susan Carter, Assoc.
Virginia Turezyn, Assoc.
Earl Hebin, Assoc.

Whom to Contact
William F. Murdy
Grant Behrman
Susan Carter

Type of Firm
Investment banking or merchant banking firm investing own capital or funds of partners or clients

Project Preferences
Will function either as deal originator or investor in deals created by others
Type of Financing:
Second-stage
Later-stage expansion
Leveraged buyout
Minimum Investment: $500,000
Preferred Investment: $500,000-$1 million
Minimum Operating Data:
Annual Sales—Nominal
P&L—Losses (profits projected after 2 years)

Geographical Preference
National

Industry Preferences

Communications
Cable television
Commercial communications
Data communications
Satellite and microwave communications
Telephone related
Computer Related
Computer graphics, CAD/CAM and CAE
Computer mainframes
Computer services
Memory devices
Micro and mini computers
Office automation
Scanning related
Software-applications
Software-artificial intelligence
Software-systems
Specialized turnkey systems
Terminals

Consumer
Computer stores/related services
Consumer products
Consumer services
Food and beverage products
Franchise businesses
Retailing
Distribution
Communications equipment
Computer equipment
Consumer products
Electronics equipment
Food products
Industrial products
Medical products
Electronic Components and Instrumentation
Analytical and scientific instrumentation
Component fabrication and testing equipment
Electronic components
Fiber optics
Laser related
Semiconductors
Genetic Engineering
Gene splicing and manufacturing equipment
Monoclonal antibodies and hybridomas
Recombinant DNA (agricultural and industrial)
Recombinant DNA (medical)
Industrial Products and Equipment
Controls and sensors
Equipment and machinery
Robotics/vision systems
Medical/Health Related
Diagnostic equipment
Diagnostic test products
Disposable products
Drugs and medicines
Hospital and clinical labs
Medical services
Therapeutic equipment

Additional Information
Year Founded—1981
Method of Compensation—Return on investment is most important, but also charge for closing fees, service fees, etc.

N.A.B. NORDIC INVESTORS LTD.

c/o DnC Capital Corp.
600 Fifth Avenue
New York, NY 10020
212-315-6532

Officers
Jack A. Prizzi, Sr. V.P.
Michael Ionata, Asst. V.P.

Whom to Contact
Jack A. Prizzi
Michael Ionata

Type of Firm
Private venture capital firm investing
own capital

Affiliation
DnC Capital Corp. (investment advisor and
general partner)

Industry Association Memberships
NASBIC
NVCA

Project Preferences
Will function either as deal originator or
investor in deals created by others
Type of Financing:
First-stage
Second-stage
Later-stage expansion
Leveraged buyout
Minimum Investment: $250,000
Preferred Investment: $250,000-$500,000
Minimum Operating Data:
Annual Sales—$500,000
P&L—Break even

Geographical Preference
None

Industry Preferences

Communications
Cable television
Commercial communications
Data communications
Satellite and microwave communications
Telephone related

Computer Related
Computer graphics, CAD/CAM and CAE
Computer services
Memory devices
Micro and mini computers
Office automation
Scanning related
Software-applications
Software-artificial intelligence
Software-systems
Specialized turnkey systems
Terminals
Distribution
Communications equipment
Computer equipment
Consumer products
Electronics equipment
Food products
Industrial products
Medical products
**Electronic Components and
Instrumentation**
Analytical and scientific instrumentation
Component fabrication and testing
equipment
Electronic components
Fiber optics
Laser related
Semiconductors
Energy/Natural Resources
Alternative energy
Energy conservation
Technology related products/equipment
Genetic Engineering
Gene splicing and manufacturing equipment
Monoclonal antibodies and hybridomas
Recombinant DNA (agricultural and
industrial)
Recombinant DNA (medical)
Industrial Products and Equipment
Chemicals
Controls and sensors
Energy management
Equipment and machinery
Other industrial automation
Plastics
Robotics/vision systems
Specialty materials
Medical/Health Related
Diagnostic equipment
Diagnostic test products
Disposable products
Drugs and medicines
Hospital and clinical labs
Medical services
Therapeutic equipment

Other
Transportation
Will Not Consider
Retail
Real estate
Oil and gas
Consulting

Additional Information
Year Founded—1983
Capital Under Management—$10 million
Investments(1985-1st 6 months)—3
Invested(1985-1st 6 months)—$500,000
Method of Compensation—Return on
investment is of primary concern; do not
charge fees

NAZEM & CO., L.P.

600 Madison Avenue, 14th Floor
New York, NY 10022
212-644-6433

Partners
Fred F. Nazem, Mgn. Gen. Ptnr.
Peter G. Imperiale, Gen. Ptnr.
Edward F. Hummer, Assoc.
Ramon V. Reyes, Assoc.
Philip E. Barak, Assoc. & CFO

Whom to Contact
Fred F. Nazem
Peter G. Imperiale

Type of Firm
Private venture capital firm investing
own capital and capital of limited partners

Affiliation
Nazem & Lieber (private venture capital
partnership)

Project Preferences
Prefer role as deal originator but will also
invest in deals created by others
Type of Financing:
Seed
Startup
First-stage
Second-stage
Leveraged buyout
Minimum Investment: $250,000
Preferred Investment: Over $500,000
Preferred Investment (LBO):
$1 million-$2 million
Minimum Operating Data:
Annual Sales—Nominal
P&L—Losses (profits projected after 2 years)
Annual Sales (LBO)—$25 million-$75 million

Geographical Preferences
Southwest
East Coast
West Coast

Industry Preferences

Communications
Data communications
Integrated voice and data
Network processors
Satellite and microwave communications
Computer Related
Computer graphics, CAD/CAM and CAE
Computer mainframes
Computer services
Software-applications
Software-artificial intelligence
Software-systems
Specialized turnkey systems
Distribution
Medical products
Electronic Components and Instrumentation
Analytical and scientific instrumentation
Component fabrication and testing
  equipment
Fiber optics
Laser related
Semiconductors
Genetic Engineering
Gene splicing and manufacturing equipment
Monoclonal antibodies and hybridomas
Recombinant DNA (agricultural and
  industrial)
Recombinant DNA (medical)
Industrial Products and Equipment
Chemicals
Controls and sensors
Material sciences
Other industrial automation
Robotics/vision systems
Specialty materials
Medical/Health Related
Diagnostic equipment
Diagnostic test products
Disposable products
Drugs and medicines
Hospital and clinical labs
Medical services
Therapeutic equipment

Additional Information
Year Founded—1976
Method of Compensation—Return on
  investment is of primary concern; do not
  charge fees

NELSON CAPITAL CORPORATION

591 Stewart Avenue
Garden City, NY 11530
516-222-2555

Other Offices
10000 Santa Monica Boulevard
Suite 300
Los Angeles, CA 90067
213-556-1944

2340 Des Plaines Avenue
Des Plaines, IL 60018
312-296-2280

Officers
Irwin B. Nelson, Pres. (New York)
Norman Tulchin, Chm. (California)

Whom to Contact
Either of the above

Type of Firm
SBIC

Industry Association Membership
NASBIC

Project Preferences
Prefer role as deal originator but will also
  invest in deals created by others
Type of Financing:
Later-stage expansion
Leveraged buyout
Minimum Investment: $250,000
Preferred Investment: $500,000-$1 million
Minimum Operating Data:
Annual Sales—$1.5 million
P&L—Break even

Geographical Preference
National

Industry Preferences

Communications
Telephone related
Computer Related
Computer graphics, CAD/CAM and CAE
Computer mainframes
Computer services
Memory devices
Micro and mini computers
Office automation
Scanning related
Software-applications
Software-artificial intelligence
Software-systems
Specialized turnkey systems
Terminals

Consumer
Computer stores/related services
Consumer products
Consumer services
Food and beverage products
Franchise businesses
Hotels and resort areas
Leisure and recreational products
Distribution
Communications equipment
Computer equipment
Consumer products
Electronics equipment
Food products
Industrial products
Medical products
Electronic Components and Instrumentation
Analytical and scientific instrumentation
Component fabrication and testing
  equipment
Electronic components
Fiber optics
Laser related
Semiconductors
Energy/Natural Resources
Alternative energy
Industrial Products and Equipment
Chemicals
Controls and sensors
Energy management
Equipment and machinery
Other industrial automation
Plastics
Robotics/vision systems
Specialty materials
Other
Education related
Publishing
Real estate
Transportation
Will Not Consider
Apparel

Additional Information
Year Founded—1973
Capital Under Management—$2.1 million
Investments(1985-1st 6 months)—4
Invested(1985-1st 6 months)—$350,000
Method of Compensation—Return on
  investment is most important, but also
  charge for closing fees, service fees, etc.

472

NEW YORK SECURITIES CO., INCORPORATED

575 Madison Avenue
New York, NY 10022
212-605-0421

See CONNECTICUT for full listing

NORSTAR VENTURE CAPITAL, INC.

One Norstar Plaza
Albany, NY 12201
518-447-4050

Officers
Raymond A. Lancaster, Pres.
Joseph L. Reinhart, Assoc.
Stephen Puricelli, Assoc.

Whom to Contact
Any of the above

Type of Firm
Venture capital subsidiary of bank
holding company

Affiliation
Norstar Bancorp (parent)

Industry Association Memberships
NASBIC
NVCA

Project Preferences
Will function either as deal originator or
investor in deals created by others
Type of Financing:
Seed
Startup
First-stage
Second-stage
Leveraged buyout
Minimum Investment: $250,000
Preferred Investment: $500,000-$750,000
Minimum Operating Data:
Annual Sales—Nominal

Geographical Preference
East Coast

Industry Preferences
None

Additional Information
Year Founded—1984
Method of Compensation—Return on
investment is of primary concern; do not
charge fees

NORTH AMERICAN VENTURES FUNDS

c/o Inco Venture Capital Mgt.
One New York Plaza
New York, NY 10004
212-612-5620

S. Feiner, Chm.
A.D. Peabody, V.P.
G.M. Middlemas, Sr. V.P.

See ONTARIO for full listing

NORTH STREET CAPITAL CORP.

250 North Street RA-6S
White Plains, NY 10625
914-335-7901

Officers
Ralph L. McNeal, Sr., Pres.
Eric B. Weeks, Cntlr.

Whom to Contact
Ralph L. McNeal, Sr.

Type of Firm
MESBIC

Affiliation
General Foods Corporation (parent)

Industry Association Memberships
AAMESBIC
NASBIC

Project Preferences
Will function either as deal originator or
investor in deals created by others
Type of Financing:
Second-stage
Leveraged buyout
Minimum Investment: $250,000
Preferred Investment: $500,000-$1 million
Minimum Operating Data:
Annual Sales—$500,000
P&L—Losses (profits projected after 2 years)

Geographical Preference
National

Industry Preferences
None
Will Not Consider
Individual franchises
Consulting

Additional Information
Year Founded—1971
Capital Under Management—$2 million
Investments(1985-1st 6 months)—2
Invested(1985-1st 6 months)—$500,000
Method of Compensation—Return on
investment is most important, but also
charge for closing fees, service fees, etc.

NORTHWOOD VENTURES

420 Madison Avenue, 13th Floor
New York, NY 10017
212-935-4679

General Partner
Peter G. Schiff

Type of Firm
Private venture capital firm investing
own capital

Industry Association Membership
NVCA

Project Preferences
Will function either as deal originator or
investor in deals created by others
Type of Financing:
Startup
First-stage
Second-stage
Leveraged buyout
Minimum Investment: Less than $100,000
Preferred Investment: $100,000-$500,000
Minimum Operating Data:
Annual Sales—Nominal
P&L—Losses (profits projected after 2 years)

Geographical Preferences
Northeast
National

Industry Preferences

Communications
Cable television
Commercial communications
Data communications
Satellite and microwave communications
Telephone related

Computer Related
Computer graphics, CAD/CAM and CAE
Computer mainframes
Computer services
Memory devices
Micro and mini computers
Office automation
Scanning related
Software-applications
Software-artificial intelligence
Software-systems
Specialized turnkey systems
Terminals
Consumer
Computer stores/related services
Consumer products
Consumer services
Restaurants
Retailing
**Electronic Components and
   Instrumentation**
Analytical and scientific instrumentation
Component fabrication and testing
   equipment
Electronic components
Fiber optics
Laser related
Semiconductors
Energy/Natural Resources
Drilling and exploration services
Oil and gas exploration and production
Technology related products/equipment
Medical/Health Related
Diagnostic equipment
Diagnostic test products
Disposable products
Other
Agriculture, forestry, fishing
Education related
Finance and insurance
Publishing
Specialty consulting
Will Not Consider
Real estate

Additional Information
Year Founded—1983
Capital Under Management—$5 million
Investments(1985-1st 6 months)—7
Invested(1985-1st 6 months)—$575,000
Method of Compensation—Return on
   investment is of primary concern; do not
   charge fees

OLIVETTI PARTNERS C.V.

see International Technology Ventures, Inc.
New York, NY

ALAN PATRICOF ASSOCIATES, INC.

545 Madison Avenue
New York, NY 10022
212-753-6300

Other Offices
1245 Oakmead Parkway #105
Sunnyvale, CA 94086
408-737-8788

24 Upper Brook Street
London, W1Y 1PD, England
01-493-3633

67 Rue de Monceau
75008 Paris, France
01-563-3513

Officers
Alan J. Patricof, Chm. (New York)
Robert G. Faris, Pres. (New York)
Lewis Solomon, Exec. V.P. (New York)
W.R. Bottoms, Sr. V.P. (California)
John C. Baker, V.P. (New York)
Jonathan Ben-Cnaan, Mgn. Dir. (New York)
Ronald M. Cohen, Exec. Chm. (England)
Maurice Tchenio, Mgn. Dir. (France)
Camilla Jackson, Assoc. (California)
Charles Cheskiewicz, Assoc. (New York)
Eugene Levy, Assoc. (New York)
Adrian Beecroft, Dir. (England)
Peter Englander, Dir. (England)
Jonathan Stuart, Assoc. (England)

Whom to Contact
Any of the above

Type of Firm
Private venture capital firm investing
   own capital

Affiliation
MMG Patricof & Co. Inc. (corporate
   finance affiliate)

Industry Association Memberships
NVCA
WAVC

Project Preferences
Prefer role as deal originator but will also
   invest in deals created by others
Type of Financing:
Seed
Startup
First-stage
Second-stage
Later-stage expansion
Leveraged buyout

Minimum Investment: $250,000
Preferred Investment: Over $1 million
Minimum Operating Data:
Annual Sales—Nominal
P&L—Losses (profits projected after 2 years)

Geographical Preference
None

Industry Preferences

Communications
Cable television
Commercial communications
Data communications
Satellite and microwave communications
Telephone related
Computer Related
Computer graphics, CAD/CAM and CAE
Computer mainframes
Computer services
Memory devices
Micro and mini computers
Office automation
Scanning related
Software-applications
Software-artificial intelligence
Software-systems
Specialized turnkey systems
Terminals
Consumer
Computer stores/related services
Consumer products
Consumer services
Food and beverage products
Franchise businesses
Hotels and resort areas
Leisure and recreational products
Restaurants
Retailing
Distribution
Communications equipment
Computer equipment
Consumer products
Electronics equipment
Food products
Industrial products
Medical products
**Electronic Components and
   Instrumentation**
Analytical and scientific instrumentation
Component fabrication and testing
   equipment
Electronic components
Fiber optics
Laser related
Semiconductors

Energy/Natural Resources
Alternative energy
Coal related
Drilling and exploration services
Energy conservation
Minerals
Oil and gas exploration and production
Technology related products/equipment
Genetic Engineering
Gene splicing and manufacturing equipment
Monoclonal antibodies and hybridomas
Recombinant DNA (agricultural and
    industrial)
Recombinant DNA (medical)
Industrial Products and Equipment
Chemicals
Controls and sensors
Energy management
Equipment and machinery
Other industrial automation
Plastics
Robotics/vision systems
Specialty materials
Medical/Health Related
Diagnostic equipment
Diagnostic test products
Disposable products
Drugs and medicines
Hospital and clinical labs
Medical services
Therapeutic equipment
Other
Agriculture, forestry, fishing
Education related
Finance and insurance
Publishing
Specialty consulting
Transportation
Will Not Consider
Special projects without a continuing
    business life

Additional Information
Year Founded—1969
Capital Under Management—
$200 million U.S.; £40 million (U.K.);
FF100 million (France)
Investments(1985-1st 6 months)—23
Invested(1985-1st 6 months)—$16 million
Method of Compensation—Return on
    investment is of primary concern, do not
    charge fees

PENNTECH PAPERS, INC.

Three Barker Avenue
White Plains, NY 10601
914-997-1600

Officer
Theodore T. Mason, V.P. Corp. Dev.

Type of Firm
Paper manufacturing company seeking
    investments leading to potential acquisition

Project Preferences
Prefer role as deal originator
Type of Financing:
Second-stage
Later-stage expansion
Leveraged buyout
Preferred Investment: Variable, leading
    to acquisition
Minimum Operating Data:
Annual Sales—$500,000
P&L—Break even

Geographical Preference
Northeast

Industry Preferences

Energy/Natural Resources
Alternative energy
Energy conservation
Pulp and paper industry related
Technology related products/equipment
Industrial Products and Equipment
Controls and sensors
Equipment and machinery
Pulp and paper industry related
Specialty materials

Additional Information
Year Founded—1969
Method of Compensation—Return on
    investment is of primary concern; do not
    charge fees

PENNWOOD CAPITAL CORPORATION

9 West 57th Street
New York, NY 10019
212-753-1600

Principals
Marc C. Ostrow
James J. Fuld, Jr.

Whom to Contact
Either of the above

Type of Firm
Private venture capital firm investing
    own capital
Investment banking or merchant banking
    firm investing own capital or funds of
    partners or clients

Project Preferences
Prefer role as deal originator
Type of Financing:
Leveraged buyout
Preferred Investment (LBO):
    $10 million-$50 million
Minimum Operating Data:
Annual Sales—Over $3 million
P&L—Profits NBT over $1.5 million

Geographical Preference
National

Industry Preferences

Consumer
Consumer products
Consumer services
Food and beverage products
Leisure and recreational products
Retailing
Distribution
Consumer products
Electronics equipment
Food products
Industrial products
Medical products
**Electronic Components and
    Instrumentation**
Electronic components
Industrial Products and Equipment
Chemicals
Equipment and machinery
Other industrial automation
Plastics
Will Not Consider
High technology

Additional Information
Year Founded—1979

PIONEER VENTURES CO.

113 East 55th Street
New York, NY 10022
212-980-9094

General Partners
N.A. McConnell
J.G. Niven
R. Scott Asen

Whom to Contact
J.G. Niven
R. Scott Asen

Type of Firm
Private venture capital firm investing
own capital
SBIC
MESBIC

Affiliation
Pioneer III
Pioneer IV

Industry Association Memberships
NASBIC
NVCA

Project Preferences
Will function either as deal originator or
investor in deals created by others
Type of Financing:
Startup
First-stage
Second-stage
Leveraged buyout
Minimum Investment: $300,000
Preferred Investment: $500,000-$1 million
Minimum Operating Data:
Annual Sales—Nominal
P&L—Losses (profits projected after 2 years)

Geographical Preference
National

Industry Preferences

Communications
Commercial communications
Consumer
Consumer products
Cooking schools
Food and beverage products
Franchise businesses
Distribution
Medical products
**Electronic Components and
Instrumentation**
Laser related
Optics technology

Energy/Natural Resources
Alternative energy
Drilling and exploration services
Minerals
Genetic Engineering
Recombinant DNA (agricultural and
industrial)
Medical/Health Related
Diagnostic equipment
Health maintenance organizations
Hospital and clinical labs
Implants
Surgical centers
Therapeutic equipment
Other
Agriculture, forestry, fishing
Education related
Publishing
Real estate
Will Not Consider
Finance companies
Insurance companies
Weapons

Additional Information
Year Founded—1972
Capital Under Management—
Over $50 million
Method of Compensation—Return on
investment is of primary concern; do not
charge fees

THE PITTSFORD GROUP

Eight Lodge Pole Road
Pittsford, NY 14534
716-223-3523

Other Office
42 Greenwich Hills Drive
Greenwich, CT 06830
203-531-0322

Officers
Logan M. Cheek III (New York)
C.C. Hipkins, Jr. (Connecticut)
William R. Rassman, M.D. (New York)

Whom to Contact
Logan M. Cheek III

Type of Firm
Private venture capital firm investing
own capital

Affiliation
Pittsford Capital Partners 1985 L.P.

Project Preferences
Will function either as deal originator or
investor in deals created by others
Type of Financing:
Startup
First-stage
Second-stage
Later-stage expansion
Leveraged buyout
Minimum Investment: $100,000
Preferred Investment: $250,000-$500,000
Preferred Investment (LBO):
$500,000 and over
Minimum Operating Data:
Annual Sales—Nominal
P&L—Losses (profits projected after 2 years)
Annual Sales (LBO)—$5 million-$10 million

Geographical Preferences
Middle Atlantic
Northeast
National

Industry Preferences

Distribution
Medical products
Genetic Engineering
Gene splicing and manufacturing equipment
Monoclonal antibodies and hybridomas
Recombinant DNA (agricultural and
industrial)
Recombinant DNA (medical)
Medical/Health Related
Computer hardware and software related to
the medical industry
Diagnostic equipment
Diagnostic test products
Disposable products
Drugs and medicines
Hospital and clinical labs
Information sciences related to the
medical industry
Medical services
Therapeutic equipment

Additional Information
Year Founded—1975
Capital Under Management—$25 million
Investments(1985-1st 6 months)—9
Invested(1985-1st 6 months)—$5.5 million
Method of Compensation—Return on
investment is of primary concern; do not
charge fees

J.B. POINDEXTER & CO.

Three East 54th Street
New York, NY 10022
212-888-8900

Partners

Peter S.H. Grubstein, Gen. Ptnr.
James P. Kressler, Gen. Ptnr.
John B. Poindexter, Gen. Ptnr.
Edwin T. Veith, Gen. Ptnr.
Joel-Tomas Citron, Consultant
Douglas E. Rodriguez, Consultant

Whom to Contact

Joel-Tomas Citron
Peter S.H. Grubstein
Douglas E. Rodriguez

Type of Firm

Long term, equity investment firm investing
own capital

Project Preferences

Prefer role as deal originator
Type of Financing:
Leveraged buyout
Minimum Investment: $500,000
Preferred Investment: Over $1 million
Preferred Investment (LBO):
$500,000-$5 million
Minimum Operating Data:
P&L—Break even
Annual Sales (LBO)—$25 million-$350 million

Geographical Preference

National

Industry Preferences

Communications
Telephone related
Computer Related
Office automation
Consumer
Consumer products
Food and beverage products
Leisure and recreational products
Retailing
Distribution
Communications equipment
Consumer products
Electronics equipment
Food products
Industrial products
Medical products

**Electronic Components and
Instrumentation**
Analytical and scientific instrumentation
Component fabrication and testing
equipment
Electronic components
Laser related
Industrial Products and Equipment
Chemicals
Controls and sensors
Equipment and machinery
Other industrial automation
Plastics
Specialty materials
Medical/Health Related
Diagnostic equipment
Disposable products
Other
Transportation
Will Not Consider
Natural resources
Real estate
Turnarounds

Additional Information

Year Founded—1985
Method of Compensation—Return on
investment is most important, but also
charge for closing fees, service fees, etc.

PRINCE VENTURE PARTNERS

767 Third Avenue, 36th Floor
New York, NY 10017
212-319-6620

James W. Fordyce

See ILLINOIS for full listing

PRINTON, KANE & CO.

590 Madison Avenue #312
New York, NY 10222
800-526-4952

90 State Street #1418
Albany, NY 12207
800-526-4952

See NEW JERSEY for full listing

THE PROSPECT GROUP, INC.

645 Madison Avenue
New York, NY 10022
212-758-8500

Officers

W. Wallace McDowell, Jr., Chm.
Thomas A. Barron, Pres.
Gilbert Lamphere, Vice Chm.

Whom to Contact

Any of the above

Type of Firm

Private venture capital firm investing
own capital

Affiliations

Wood River Capital Corp. (subsidiary)
Danville Resources (affiliate)
Sierra Ventures (affiliate)

Industry Association Membership

NASBIC

Project Preferences

Prefer role as deal originator but will also
invest in deals created by others
Type of Financing:
Seed
Startup
First-stage
Leveraged buyout
Minimum Investment: $500,000
Preferred Investment: Over $500,000
Preferred Investment (LBO):
$5 million and over
Minimum Operating Data:
Annual Sales—Nominal
P&L—Losses (profits projected after 2 years)
Annual Sales (LBO)—$50 million-$500 million

Geographical Preference

None

Industry Preferences

Communications
Cable television
Commercial communications
Data communications
Satellite and microwave communications
Telephone related

Computer Related
Computer graphics, CAD/CAM and CAE
Computer mainframes
Computer services
Memory devices
Micro and mini computers
Office automation
Scanning related
Software-applications
Software-artificial intelligence
Software-systems
Specialized turnkey systems
Terminals
Consumer
Computer stores/related services
Consumer products
Consumer services
Food and beverage products
Franchise businesses
Hotels and resort areas
Leisure and recreational products
Restaurants
Retailing
Distribution
Communications equipment
Computer equipment
Consumer products
Electronics equipment
Food products
Industrial products
Medical products
**Electronic Components and
  Instrumentation**
Analytical and scientific instrumentation
Component fabrication and testing
  equipment
Electronic components
Fiber optics
Laser related
Semiconductors
Genetic Engineering
Gene splicing and manufacturing equipment
Monoclonal antibodies and hybridomas
Recombinant DNA (agricultural and
  industrial)
Recombinant DNA (medical)
Industrial Products and Equipment
Chemicals
Controls and sensors
Energy management
Equipment and machinery
Other industrial automation
Plastics
Robotics/vision systems
Specialty materials

Medical/Health Related
Diagnostic equipment
Diagnostic test products
Disposable products
Drugs and medicines
Hospital and clinical labs
Medical services
Therapeutic equipment
Other
Agriculture, forestry, fishing
Education related
Finance and insurance
Publishing
Transportation

Additional Information
Year Founded—1981
Capital Under Management—
  Over $100 million
Method of Compensation—Return on
  investment is of primary concern; do not
  charge fees

PRUDENTIAL VENTURE CAPITAL MANAGEMENT

717 Fifth Avenue
New York, NY 10022
212-753-0901

Officers
William S. Field, Chm.
Robert A. Knox, Pres.
Mark Rossi, V.P.
Paul Hirschbiel, Dir.
Dana O'Brien, Dir.
Martha L. Robinson, Dir.
Greg L. Schumaker

Whom to Contact
Any of the above

Type of Firm
Private partnership investing own capital
Private venture capital firm investing own
  capital and managing venture capital
  investments for Prudential Insurance Co.

Affiliation
Prudential Insurance Co. (parent)

Industry Association Membership
NVCA

Project Preferences
Will function either as deal originator or
  investor in deals created by others

Type of Financing:
Later-stage expansion
Leveraged buyout
Minimum Investment: $2 million
Preferred Investment: $2 million-$4 million
Preferred Investment (LBO):
  $2 million-$5 million
Minimum Operating Data:
Annual Sales—Over $3 million
Annual Sales (LBO)—$15 million-$150 million

Geographical Preference
None

Industry Preferences

Communications
Cable television
Commercial communications
Data communications
Satellite and microwave communications
Telephone related
Computer Related
Computer graphics, CAD/CAM and CAE
Computer mainframes
Computer services
Memory devices
Office automation
Scanning related
Software-applications
Software-artificial intelligence
Software-systems
Consumer
Computer stores/related services
Consumer products
Consumer services
Food and beverage products
Retailing
Distribution
Communications equipment
Consumer products
Electronics equipment
Food products
Industrial products
Medical products
**Electronic Components and
  Instrumentation**
Analytical and scientific instrumentation
Component fabrication and testing
  equipment
Electronic components
Fiber optics
Laser related
Semiconductors
Energy/Natural Resources
Technology related products/equipment
Industrial Products and Equipment
Equipment and machinery
Plastics
Robotics/vision systems
Specialty materials

Medical/Health Related
Diagnostic equipment
Diagnostic test products
Disposable products
Drugs and medicines
Hospital and clinical labs
Medical services
Other
Publishing

Additional Information
Year Founded—1982
Capital Under Management—$250 million
Investments(1985-1st 6 months)—6
Invested(1985-1st 6 months)—$13 million
Method of Compensation—Return on
    investment is of primary concern; do not
    charge fees

QUESTEC ENTERPRISES, INC.

328 Main Street
Huntington, NY 11743
516-351-1222

Officers
William P. Sharpe, Pres.
Charles L. Lassen, V.P.

Whom to Contact
Either of the above

Type of Firm
Venture capital subsidiary or affiliate of
    non-financial corporation

Affiliation
Kollmorgen Corporation (parent)

Project Preferences
Will function either as deal originator or
    investor in deals created by others
Type of Financing:
Startup
First-stage
Second-stage
Minimum Investment: Less than $100,000
Preferred Investment: $500,000-$1 million
Minimum Operating Data:
Annual Sales—Nominal
P&L—Losses (profits projected after 2 years)

Geographical Preference
None

Industry Preferences

Communications
Satellite and microwave communications

Computer Related
Computer graphics, CAD/CAM and CAE
Scanning related
Software-applications
Software-artificial intelligence
Software-systems
Specialized turnkey systems
**Electronic Components and
    Instrumentation**
Analytical and scientific instrumentation
Component fabrication and testing
    equipment
Electronic components
Fiber optics
Laser related
Energy/Natural Resources
Alternative energy
Coal related
Energy conservation
Oil and gas exploration and production
Technology related products/equipment
Genetic Engineering
Gene splicing and manufacturing equipment
Monoclonal antibodies and hybridomas
Recombinant DNA (agricultural and
    industrial)
Industrial Products and Equipment
Chemicals
Controls and sensors
Equipment and machinery
Other industrial automation
Plastics
Robotics/vision systems
Specialty materials
Medical/Health Related
Diagnostic test products
Other
Agriculture, forestry, fishing
Education related
Publishing
Specialty consulting
Will Not Consider
Consumer products
Property

Additional Information
Year Founded—1983
Capital Under Management—$12 million
Investments(1985-1st 6 months)—3
Invested(1985-1st 6 months)—$2.4 million
Method of Compensation—Return on
    investment is of primary concern; do not
    charge fees

QUINCY PARTNERS

Post Office Box 154
Glen Head, NY 11545
212-355-7830

Officer
Donald J. Sutherland, Pres.

Type of Firm
Private venture capital firm investing
    own capital

Project Preferences
Prefer role as deal originator
Type of Financing:
Leveraged buyout
Preferred Investment: Over $1 million
Minimum Operating Data:
Annual Sales—Over $3 million
P&L—Profitable
Annual Sales (LBO)—$15 million-$50 million

Geographical Preference
National

Industry Preferences
None

Additional Information
Year Founded—1970
Method of Compensation—Return on
    investment is most important, but also
    charge for closing fees, service fees, etc.

RAIN HILL GROUP, INC.

90 Broad Street
New York, NY 10004
212-483-9162

Officers
Richard A. Cawley, Pres.
Robin George, V.P.

Whom to Contact
Diane Lupi

Type of Firm
Service company retained by large industrial
    interests seeking technology-based
    business opportunities

Project Preferences
None

Geographical Preference
None

Industry Preferences

Communications
Cable television
Commercial communications
Data communications
Satellite and microwave communications
Telephone related
Computer Related
Computer graphics, CAD/CAM and CAE
Computer mainframes
Computer services
Memory devices
Micro and mini computers
Office automation
Scanning related
Software-applications
Software-artificial intelligence
Software-systems
Specialized turnkey systems
Terminals
Consumer
Computer stores/related services
Consumer products
Consumer services
Food and beverage products
Franchise businesses
Hotels and resort areas
Leisure and recreational products
Restaurants
Retailing
Distribution
Communications equipment
Computer equipment
Consumer products
Electronics equipment
Food products
Industrial products
Medical products
**Electronic Components and
   Instrumentation**
Analytical and scientific instrumentation
Component fabrication and testing
   equipment
Electronic components
Fiber optics
Laser related
Semiconductors
Energy/Natural Resources
Technology related products/equipment
Genetic Engineering
Gene splicing and manufacturing equipment
Monoclonal antibodies and hybridomas
Recombinant DNA (agricultural and
   industrial)
Recombinant DNA (medical)

Industrial Products and Equipment
Chemicals
Controls and sensors
Energy management
Equipment and machinery
Manufacturing and process technology
Other industrial automation
Plastics
Robotics/vision systems
Specialty materials
Medical/Health Related
Diagnostic equipment
Diagnostic test products
Disposable products
Drugs and medicines
Hospital and clinical labs
Medical services
Therapeutic equipment
Will Not Consider
Leasing companies
Public utilities
Real estate

Additional Information
Year Founded—1976
Method of Compensation—No fees

RAND CAPITAL CORPORATION

1300 Rand Building
Buffalo, NY 14203
716-853-0802

Officers
George F. Rand III, Chm.
Donald A. Ross, Pres., CEO & Treas.
Keith B. Wiley, V.P. & Secy.
Thomas J. Bernard, V.P.

Whom to Contact
Keith B. Wiley

Type of Firm
Private venture capital firm investing
   own capital
SBIC

Industry Association Membership
NASBIC

Project Preferences
Will function either as deal originator or
   investor in deals created by others
Type of Financing:
Seed
Research and development partnerships
Startup
Second-stage
Leveraged buyout

Preferred Investment: $250,000-$500,000
Minimum Operating Data:
Annual Sales—$1.5 million
P&L—Break even

Geographical Preferences
Northeast
Southeast

Industry Preferences

Communications
Cable television
Commercial communications
Data communications
Satellite and microwave communications
Telephone related
Computer Related
Computer graphics, CAD/CAM and CAE
Computer mainframes
Computer services
Memory devices
Micro and mini computers
Office automation
Scanning related
Software-applications
Software-artificial intelligence
Software-systems
Specialized turnkey systems
Terminals
Distribution
Communications equipment
Computer equipment
Consumer products
Electronics equipment
Food products
Industrial products
Medical products
**Electronic Components and
   Instrumentation**
Analytical and scientific instrumentation
Component fabrication and testing
   equipment
Electronic components
Fiber optics
Laser related
Semiconductors
Energy/Natural Resources
Alternative energy
Coal related
Drilling and exploration services
Energy conservation
Minerals
Oil and gas exploration and production
Technology related products/equipment
Genetic Engineering
Gene splicing and manufacturing equipment
Monoclonal antibodies and hybridomas
Recombinant DNA (agricultural and
   industrial)
Recombinant DNA (medical)

Industrial Products and Equipment
Chemicals
Controls and sensors
Energy management
Equipment and machinery
Other industrial automation
Plastics
Robotics/vision systems
Specialty materials
Medical/Health Related
Diagnostic equipment
Diagnostic test products
Disposable products
Drugs and medicines
Hospital and clinical labs
Medical services
Therapeutic equipment

Additional Information
Year Founded—1969
Capital Under Management—$10 million
Investments(1985-1st 6 months)—3
Invested(1985-1st 6 months)—$600,000
Method of Compensation—Return on
    investment is most important, but also
    charge for closing fees, service fees, etc.

REGULUS INTERNATIONAL CAPITAL CO. INC.

10 Rockefeller Plaza
New York, NY 10020
212-582-7715

Officer
Lee H. Miller

Type of Firm
Private venture capital firm investing
    own capital

Project Preferences
Prefer role as deal originator
Type of Financing:
Seed
Startup
First-stage
Leveraged buyout
Minimum Investment: Less than $100,000
Preferred Investment: $250,000-$500,000
Minimum Operating Data:
Annual Sales—Nominal
P&L—Losses (profits projected after 1 year)

Geographical Preference
East Coast

Industry Preferences

Industrial Products and Equipment
Plastics
Specialty materials
Other
Agriculture, forestry, fishing
Coatings
Packaging
Paper
Printing & converting
Publishing

Additional Information
Year Founded—1975
Method of Compensation—Return on
    investment is of primary concern; do not
    charge fees

REPRISE CAPITAL CORPORATION

591 Stewart Avenue
Garden City, NY 11530
516-222-1028

Other Offices
10000 Santa Monica Boulevard
Suite 300
Los Angeles, CA 90067
213-556-1944

2340 Des Plaines
Des Plaines, IL 60018
312-296-2280

Officers
Stanley Tulchin, Chm. (New York)
Irwin B. Nelson, Pres. (New York)
Norman Tulchin, V.P. (California)

Whom to Contact
Any of the above

Type of Firm
Private venture capital firm investing
    own capital

Industry Association Membership
NASBIC

Project Preferences
Prefer role as deal originator
Type of Financing:
Turn around situations
Minimum Investment: $100,000
Preferred Investment: $250,000-$500,000
Minimum Operating Data:
Annual Sales—Over $3 million
P&L—Losses (profits projected after 1 year)

Geographical Preference
National

Industry Preferences

Computer Related
Office automation
Specialized turnkey systems
Consumer
Consumer products
Consumer services
Food and beverage products
Hotels and resort areas
Leisure and recreational products
Distribution
Communications equipment
Computer equipment
Consumer products
Electronics equipment
Food products
Industrial products
Medical products
Industrial Products and Equipment
Chemicals
Controls and sensors
Energy management
Equipment and machinery
Other industrial automation
Plastics
Robotics/vision systems
Specialty materials
Medical/Health Related
Disposable products
Other
Education related
Finance and insurance
Publishing
Real estate
Transportation
Will Not Consider
Apparel
Retail

Additional Information
Year Founded—1984
Capital Under Management—$50 million
Investments(1985-1st 6 months)—3
Invested(1985-1st 6 months)—$600,000
Method of Compensation—Return on
    investment is most important, but also
    charge for closing fees, service fees, etc.

REVERE AE CAPITAL FUND, INC.

745 Fifth Avenue, 19th Floor
New York, NY 10151
212-888-6800

Officers

Gregor Medinger, Chm.
Clinton Reynolds, Pres.
Joseph C. White, Portfolio Mgr.
Dora S. Chiu, Portfolio Mgr.

Whom to Contact

Clinton Reynolds
Joseph C. White
Dora S. Chiu

Type of Firm

Public venture capital firm investing
own capital

Affiliation

AE Capital Management (investment advisor)

Project Preferences

Will function either as deal originator or
investor in deals created by others
Type of Financing:
Later-stage expansion
Leveraged buyout
Minimum Investment: $1 million
Preferred Investment: Over $1 million
Preferred Investment (LBO):
$1 million-$2 million
Minimum Operating Data:
Annual Sales—Over $3 million
P&L—Break even
Annual Sales (LBO)—Over $10 million

Geographical Preferences

Northeast
Southeast
East Coast
West Coast

Industry Preferences

Communications
Cable television
Commercial communications
Data communications
Satellite and microwave communications
Telephone related

Consumer
Computer stores/related services
Consumer products
Consumer services
Food and beverage products
Franchise businesses
Hotels and resort areas
Leisure and recreational products
Restaurants
Retailing
Distribution
Communications equipment
Computer equipment
Consumer products
Electronics equipment
Food products
Industrial products
Medical products
**Electronic Components and
Instrumentation**
Analytical and scientific instrumentation
Component fabrication and testing
equipment
Electronic components
Energy/Natural Resources
Alternative energy
Energy conservation
Technology related products/equipment
Industrial Products and Equipment
Chemicals
Controls and sensors
Energy management
Equipment and machinery
Other industrial automation
Plastics
Robotics/vision systems
Specialty materials
Medical/Health Related
Diagnostic equipment
Diagnostic test products
Disposable products
Drugs and medicines
Hospital and clinical labs
Medical services
Therapeutic equipment
Other
Education related
Finance and insurance
Publishing
Specialty consulting
Transportation
Will Not Consider
Mining
Oil and gas exploration and production
Real estate

Additional Information

Year Founded—1971
Capital Under Management—$38 million
Investments(1985-1st 6 months)—2
Invested(1985-1st 6 months)—$3 million
Method of Compensation—Return on
investment is of primary concern; do not
charge fees

RICHARDSON & MCGRATH ASSOCIATES

Rockefeller Center #1401
New York, NY 10185
212-517-9011

Other Offices

500 Seneca Parkway
Rochester, NY 14613
716-254-8543

104 Algonquin
Oakland, NJ 07436
201-337-9608

Partners

John J. Richardson, Gen. Ptnr.
(New York City)
M.H. McGrath, Mgn. Dir. (New York City)

Whom to Contact

Either of the above

Type of Firm

Private venture capital firm investing
own capital
Consulting firm evaluating and analyzing
venture projects and arranging private
placements

Project Preferences

Will function either as deal originator or
investor in deals created by others
Type of Financing:
Startup
First-stage
Minimum Investment: $100,000
Preferred Investment: $100,000-$250,000
Minimum Operating Data:
Annual Sales—Nominal
P&L—Losses (profits projected after 3 years)

Geographical Preference

None

Industry Preferences

Consumer
Consumer products
Consumer services
Food and beverage products
Retailing
Distribution
Consumer products
Food products
Industrial products
Medical products
Genetic Engineering
Gene splicing and manufacturing equipment
Monoclonal antibodies and hybridomas
Recombinant DNA (agricultural and
    industrial)
Recombinant DNA (medical)
Industrial Products and Equipment
Chemicals
Specialty materials
Medical/Health Related
Diagnostic equipment
Diagnostic test products
Disposable products
Drugs and medicines
Health maintainence organizations
Hospital and clinical labs
Medical services
Nursing homes
Preferred provider organizations
Therapeutic equipment
Other
Agriculture
Animal health
Specialty consulting
Will Not Consider
Real estate

Additional Information

Year Founded—1983
Method of Compensation—Function primarily
    in service area; receive contingent fee in
    cash or equity

ROBERTSON, COLMAN & STEPHENS

535 Madison Avenue
New York, NY 10022
212-319-8900

See CALIFORNIA for full listing

ROTHSCHILD VENTURES INC.

One Rockefeller Plaza
New York, NY 10020
212-757-6000

Officers

Robert S Pirie, Chm.
Jess L. Belser, Pres. & CEO
Aniello A. Bianco, Exec. V.P.
Douglas S. Luke, Jr., Sr. V.P.
Ivan L. Wolff, Sr. V.P.
Robert A. Bettigole, V.P.
Bonnie L. Howard, Assoc.
Patrick F. Latterell, Assoc.
Kathryn A. Minckler, Assoc.

Whom to Contact

Jess L. Belser

Type of Firm

Investment banking or merchant banking
    firm investing own capital or funds of
    partners or clients

Affiliation

Rothschild Inc. (parent)

Industry Association Memberships

NASBIC
NVCA

Project Preferences

Prefer role as deal originator but will also
    invest in deals created by others
Type of Financing:
Seed
Research and development partnerships
Startup
First-stage
Second-stage
Later-stage expansion
Minimum Investment: $250,000
Preferred Investment: Over $1 million
Minimum Operating Data:
Annual Sales—Nominal
P&L—Losses (profits projected after 3 years)

Geographical Preference

None

Industry Preferences

Communications
Cable television
Commercial communications
Data communications
Satellite and microwave communications
Telephone related

Computer Related
Computer graphics, CAD/CAM and CAE
Computer mainframes
Computer services
Memory devices
Micro and mini computers
Office automation
Scanning related
Software-applications
Software-artificial intelligence
Software-systems
Specialized turnkey systems
Terminals
Consumer
Computer stores/related services
Consumer products
Consumer services
Distribution
Communications equipment
Computer equipment
Consumer products
Electronics equipment
Food products
Industrial products
Medical products
**Electronic Components and
    Instrumentation**
Analytical and scientific instrumentation
Component fabrication and testing
    equipment
Electronic components
Fiber optics
Laser related
Semiconductors
Energy/Natural Resources
Minerals
Technology related products/equipment
Genetic Engineering
Gene splicing and manufacturing equipment
Monoclonal antibodies and hybridomas
Recombinant DNA (agricultural and
    industrial)
Recombinant DNA (medical)
Industrial Products and Equipment
Chemicals
Controls and sensors
Energy management
Equipment and machinery
Material sciences
Other industrial automation
Plastics
Robotics/vision systems
Specialty materials
Medical/Health Related
Diagnostic equipment
Diagnostic test products
Disposable products
Drugs and medicines
Hospital and clinical labs
Medical services
Therapeutic equipment

Other
Education related
Finance and insurance
Transportation

Additional Information
Year Founded—1945

ROUNDHILL CAPITAL

44 Wall Street
New York, NY 10005
212-747-0066

Officers
J. Morton Davis, Pres.
Kevin Kimberlin, V.P.

Whom to Contact
Kevin Kimberlin

Type of Firm
Private venture capital firm investing
 own capital
SBIC
Investment banking or merchant banking
 firm investing own capital or funds of
 partners or clients

Affiliation
D.H. Blair & Co. (parent)

Project Preferences
Will function either as deal originator or
 investor in deals created by others
Type of Financing:
First-stage
Second-stage
Leveraged buyout
Minimum Investment: $250,000
Preferred Investment: Over $1 million
Minimum Operating Data:
Annual Sales—Nominal
P&L—Losses (profits projected after 2 years)

Geographical Preference
National

Industry Preferences

Communications
Cable television
Commercial communications
Data communications
Satellite and microwave communications
Telephone related

Computer Related
Computer graphics, CAD/CAM and CAE
Computer mainframes
Computer services
Memory devices
Micro and mini computers
Office automation
Scanning related
Software-applications
Software-artificial intelligence
Software-systems
Specialized turnkey systems
Terminals
Consumer
Computer stores/related services
Consumer products
Consumer services
Food and beverage products
Franchise businesses
Hotels and resort areas
Leisure and recreational products
Restaurants
Retailing
Distribution
Medical products
**Electronic Components and
 Instrumentation**
Analytical and scientific instrumentation
Component fabrication and testing
 equipment
Electronic components
Fiber optics
Laser related
Semiconductors
Genetic Engineering
Gene splicing and manufacturing equipment
Monoclonal antibodies and hybridomas
Recombinant DNA (agricultural and
 industrial)
Recombinant DNA (medical)
Industrial Products and Equipment
Chemicals
Controls and sensors
Energy management
Equipment and machinery
Other industrial automation
Plastics
Robotics/vision systems
Specialty materials
Medical/Health Related
Diagnostic equipment
Diagnostic test products
Disposable products
Drugs and medicines
Hospital and clinical labs
Medical services
Therapeutic equipment
Other
Finance and insurance
Publishing

Additional Information
Year Founded—1979
Capital Under Management—$20 million
Investments(1985-1st 6 months)—5
Invested(1985-1st 6 months)—$1.5 million
Method of Compensation—Return on
 investment is of primary concern; do not
 charge fees

SALOMON BROTHERS INC

One New York Plaza
New York, NY 10004
212-747-6293

Officer
Melvin W. Ellis, V.P.

Type of Firm
Investment banking or merchant banking
 firm investing own capital and funds of
 partners

Affiliation
Salomon Inc (parent)

Industry Association Memberships
NASBIC
NVCA

Project Preferences
Will function either as deal originator or
 investor in deals created by others
Type of Financing:
Startup
First-stage
Second-stage
Minimum Investment: $500,000
Preferred Investment: $500,000-$1 million
Minimum Operating Data:
Annual Sales—Nominal
P&L—Losses (profits projected after 2 years)

Geographical Preference
None

Industry Preferences

Communications
Cable television
Commercial communications
Data communications
Satellite and microwave communications
Telephone related

Computer Related
Computer graphics, CAD/CAM and CAE
Computer mainframes
Computer services
Memory devices
Micro and mini computers
Office automation
Scanning related
Software-applications
Software-artificial intelligence
Software-systems
Specialized turnkey systems
Terminals
**Electronic Components and
  Instrumentation**
Analytical and scientific instrumentation
Component fabrication and testing
  equipment
Electronic components
Fiber optics
Laser related
Semiconductors
Energy/Natural Resources
Technology related products/equipment
Genetic Engineering
Gene splicing and manufacturing equipment
Monoclonal antibodies and hybridomas
Recombinant DNA (agricultural and
  industrial)
Recombinant DNA (medical)
Industrial Products and Equipment
Chemicals
Controls and sensors
Energy management
Equipment and machinery
Other industrial automation
Plastics
Robotics/vision systems
Specialty materials
Medical/Health Related
Diagnostic equipment
Diagnostic test products
Disposable products
Drugs and medicines
Hospital and clinical labs
Medical services
Therapeutic equipment

Additional Information
Year Founded—1985
Capital Under Management—$40 million
Method of Compensation—Return on
  investment is of primary concern; do not
  charge fees

SCHRODER VENTURE MANAGERS LIMITED

One State Street
New York, NY 10004
212-269-6500

Other Office
755 Page Mill Road
Building A, #280
Palo Alto, CA 94304
415-424-1144

Officers
David Walters, Mgn. Dir. (California)
Michael Hentschel, Dir. (California)
Jeffrey J. Collinson, Mgn. Dir. (New York)
Judith E. Schneider, Dir. (New York)
Robert J. Gailus, Assoc. (California)

Whom to Contact
Any of the above

Type of Firm
Venture capital subsidiary of British
  merchant bank

Affiliation
Schroders PLC, United Kingdom (parent)

Industry Association Memberships
NVCA
WAVC

Project Preferences
Will function either as deal originator or
  investor in deals created by others
Type of Financing:
Seed
Startup
First-stage
Second-stage
Later-stage expansion
Leveraged buyout
Minimum Investment: $100,000
Preferred Investment: $500,000-$1 million
Preferred Investment (LBO): $1 million
Minimum Operating Data:
Annual Sales—Nominal
P&L—Losses (profits projected after 2 years)
Annual Sales (LBO)—$50 million

Geographical Preference
National

Industry Preferences

Communications
Cable television
Commercial communications
Data communications
Satellite and microwave communications
Telephone related
Computer Related
Computer graphics, CAD/CAM and CAE
Computer mainframes
Computer services
Memory devices
Office automation
Scanning related
Software-applications
Software-artificial intelligence
Software-systems
Specialized turnkey systems
Consumer
Computer stores/related services
Consumer products
Consumer services
Food and beverage products
Franchise businesses
Hotels and resort areas
Leisure and recreational products
Restaurants
Retailing
Distribution
Consumer products
Food products
Industrial products
Medical products
**Electronic Components and
  Instrumentation**
Analytical and scientific instrumentation
Component fabrication and testing
  equipment
Electronic components
Fiber optics
Laser related
Semiconductors
Energy/Natural Resources
Technology related products/equipment
Genetic Engineering
Gene splicing and manufacturing equipment
Monoclonal antibodies and hybridomas
Recombinant DNA (agricultural and
  industrial)
Rocombinant DNA (medical)
Industrial Products and Equipment
Chemicals
Controls and sensors
Energy management
Equipment and machinery
Other industrial automation
Plastics
Robotics/vision systems
Specialty materials

Medical/Health Related
Diagnostic equipment
Diagnostic test products
Disposable products
Drugs and medicines
Hospital and clinical labs
Medical services
Therapeutic equipment
Other
Education related
Finance and insurance
Publishing
Specialty consulting
Transportation
Will Not Consider
Oil and gas exploration
Real estate
Motion Pictures

Additional Information
Year Founded—1983
Capital Under Management—$37.5 million
Investments(1985-1st 6 months)—10
Invested(1985-1st 6 months)—$4.9 million
Method of Compensation—Return on
  investment is of primary concern; do not
  charge fees

SEVIN ROSEN MANAGEMENT COMPANY

200 Park Avenue #4503
New York, NY 10166
212-687-5115

Other Offices
13455 Noel Road #1670
Dallas, TX 75240
214-960-1744

1245 Oakmead Parkway #101
Sunnyvale, CA 94086
408-720-8590

Officers
L.J. Sevin, Pres. (Texas)
Benjamin M. Rosen, Chm. (New York)
Jon W. Bayless, Ptnr. (Texas)
Roger S. Borovoy, Ptnr. (California)
Stephen M. Dow, Ptnr. (California)
Dennis J. Gorman, CFO (Texas)

Whom to Contact
Any of the above (closest office)

Type of Firm
Private venture capital firm investing
  own capital

Industry Association Membership
NVCA

Project Preferences
Prefer role as deal originator
Type of Financing:
Seed
Startup
Minimum Investment: $500,000
Preferred Investment: $500,000-$1 million
Minimum Operating Data:
Annual Sales—Nominal
P&L—Losses (profits projected after 2 years)

Geographical Preferences
Southwest
East Coast
West Coast

Industry Preferences

Communications
Commercial communications
Data communications
Satellite and microwave communications
Telephone related
Computer Related
Computer graphics, CAD/CAM and CAE
Computer mainframes
Computer services
Memory devices
Micro and mini computers
Office automation
Scanning related
Software-applications
Software-artificial intelligence
Software-systems
Specialized turnkey systems
Terminals
Distribution
Communications equipment
Computer equipment
**Electronic Components and
  Instrumentation**
Analytical and scientific instrumentation
Fiber optics
Semiconductors
Genetic Engineering
Gene splicing and manufacturing equipment
Monoclonal antibodies and hybridomas
Recombinant DNA (agricultural and
  industrial)
Recombinant DNA (medical)
Industrial Products and Equipment
Controls and sensors
Robotics/vision systems

Will Not Consider
Consulting services
Consumer services
Oil and gas
Real estate
Transportation

Additional Information
Year Founded—1981
Capital Under Management—$300 million
Investments(1985-1st 6 months)—6
Invested(1985-1st 6 months)—$10 million
Method of Compensation—Return on
  investment is of primary concern; do not
  charge fees

SHEARSON LEHMAN BROTHERS INC.

American Express Tower
World Financial Center
New York, NY 10285
212-298-2893

Other Offices
One Bush Street
San Francisco, CA 94104
415-981-3680

Officers
Jim C. Cowart
Edward J. Smith
Jonathan Meyers
Frederick Frank
Robert McCabe
Jody Owen
David Ogens

Whom to Contact
Any of the above

Type of Firm
Investment banking or merchant banking
  firm investing own capital or funds of
  partners or clients

Affiliations
Summit Ventures (joint venture)
Robinson-Humphrey (subsidiary)
AVA Partners (affiliate)

Project Preferences
Will function either as deal originator or
  investor in deals created by others
Type of Financing:
First-stage
Second-stage
Later-stage expansion
Leveraged buyout

Minimum Investment: $100,000
Preferred Investment: $100,000 and over
Preferred Investment (LBO):
 $500,000-$15 million
Minimum Operating Data:
Annual Sales—Nominal

Geographical Preference
None

Industry Preferences

Communications
Cable television
Commercial communications
Data communications
Satellite and microwave communications
Telephone related
Computer Related
Computer graphics, CAD/CAM and CAE
Computer mainframes
Computer services
Memory devices
Micro and mini computers
Office automation
Scanning related
Software-applications
Software-artificial intelligence
Software-systems
Specialized turnkey systems
Terminals
Distribution
Communications equipment
Computer equipment
Electronics equipment
Industrial products
Medical products
Energy/Natural Resources
Technology related products/equipment
Industrial Products and Equipment
Controls and sensors
Other industrial automation
Specialty materials
Medical/Health Related
Diagnostic equipment
Diagnostic test products
Disposable products
Drugs and medicines
Hospital and clinical labs
Medical services
Therapeutic equipment
Will Not Consider
Financial services

Additional Information
Year Founded—1860

SIERRA VENTURES MANAGEMENT COMPANY

645 Madison Avenue #2100
New York, NY 10022
212-750-9420

Other Office
3000 Sand Hill Road
Building 1, #280
Menlo Park, CA 94025
415-854-1000

Partners
Peter C. Wendell, Gen. Ptnr. (California)
Vincent H. Tobkin, Gen. Ptnr. (California)
Gilbert H. Lamphere, Gen. Ptnr. (New York)
Thomas A. Barron, Gen. Ptnr. (New York)
Jeffrey M. Drazan, V.P. (California)

Whom to Contact
Jeffrey M. Drazan

Type of Firm
Private venture capital firm investing
 own capital
SBIC

Affiliations
Wood River Capital Corp. (technology
 investment management)
Sierra Ventures (technology investment
 management)
The Prospect Group (technology investment
 management)

Industry Association Membership
NVCA

Project Preferences
Prefer role as deal originator but will also
 invest in deals created by others
Type of Financing:
Seed
Startup
First-stage
Leveraged buyout
Minimum Investment: Less than $100,000
Preferred Investment: $500,000-$1 million
Preferred Investment (LBO):
 $1 million-$20 million
Minimum Operating Data:
Annual Sales—Nominal
P&L—Losses (profits projected after 2 years)
Annual Sales (LBO)—$20 million-$150 million

Geographical Preferences
Northeast
West Coast

Industry Preferences

Communications
Commercial communications
Data communications
Satellite and microwave communications
Telephone related
Computer Related
Computer graphics, CAD/CAM and CAE
Computer mainframes
Computer services
Memory devices
Micro and mini computers
Office automation
Scanning related
Software-applications
Software-artificial intelligence
Software-systems
Specialized turnkey systems
Terminals
Distribution
Communications equipment
Computer equipment
**Electronic Components and
 Instrumentation**
Analytical and scientific instrumentation
Component fabrication and testing
 equipment
Electronic components
Fiber optics
Laser related
Semiconductors
Genetic Engineering
Gene splicing and manufacturing equipment
Monoclonal antibodies and hybridomas
Recombinant DNA (agricultural and
 industrial)
Recombinant DNA (medical)
Medical/Health Related
Diagnostic equipment
Diagnostic test products
Disposable products
Drugs and medicines
Hospital and clinical labs
Medical services
Therapeutic equipment
Other
Database services
Technology-related services

Additional Information
Year Founded—1978 (Wood River)
Capital Under Management—$100 million
 (includes all funds managed)
Investments(1985-1st 6 months)—7
Invested(1985-1st 6 months)—$6.5 million
Method of Compensation—Return on
 investment is of primary concern; do not
 charge fees

MARTIN SIMPSON & CO.

150 Broadway #1606
New York, NY 10038
212-406-5200

Officers

Robert S. Anderson, V.P.
Robert C. Dunne, V.P.
Martin B.C. Simpson, Pres.
C.M. Brancato, V.P.
F. Halpern, V.P.
L.S. Doty, V.P.
R.F. Reed, V.P.
P. Rogers, V.P.

Whom to Contact

Robert S. Anderson

Type of Firm

Investment banking or merchant banking
firm investing own capital or funds of
partners or clients

Project Preferences

Will function either as deal originator or
investor in deals created by others
Type of Financing:
Seed
Startup
First-stage
Second-stage
Leveraged buyout
Minimum Investment: $100,000
Preferred Investment: $500,000 and over
Minimum Operating Data:
Annual Sales—Nominal
P&L—Losses (profits projected after 2 years)

Geographical Preferences

Northeast
Southeast
East Coast
Midwest

Industry Preferences

Communications
Data communications
Satellite and microwave communications
Telephone related

Computer Related
Computer graphics, CAD/CAM and CAE
Computer mainframes
Computer services
Memory devices
Micro and mini computers
Office automation
Scanning related
Software-applications
Software-artificial intelligence
Software-systems
Specialized turnkey systems
Terminals
Distribution
Communications equipment
Computer equipment
Electronics equipment
Industrial products
Medical products
**Electronic Components and
Instrumentation**
Analytical and scientific instrumentation
Component fabrication and testing
equipment
Electronic components
Fiber optics
Laser related
Semiconductors
Genetic Engineering
Gene splicing and manufacturing equipment
Monoclonal antibodies and hybridomas
Recombinant DNA (agricultural and
industrial)
Recombinant DNA (medical)
Industrial Products and Equipment
Controls and sensors
Energy management
Equipment and machinery
Other industrial automation
Medical/Health Related
Diagnostic equipment
Diagnostic test products
Disposable products
Drugs and medicines
Hospital and clinical labs
Medical services
Therapeutic equipment
Other
Real estate
Will Not Consider
Automotive industry
Energy
Entertainment
Motion pictures

Additional Information

Year Founded—1973
Investments(1985-1st 6 months)—2
Invested(1985-1st 6 months)—$3 million
Method of Compensation—Return on
investment is most important, but also
charge for closing fees, service fees, etc.

ALLAN E. SKORA ASSOCIATES

49 West 12th Street
Executive Suite
New York, NY 10011
212-691-9895

Officer

Allan E. Skora, Pres.

Type of Firm

Private venture capital firm investing
own capital
Investment banking or merchant banking
firm investing own capital or funds of
partners or clients
Consulting firm evaluating and analyzing
venture projects and arranging private
placements

Affiliations

Entertainment Funding Group (subsidiary)
Marine Development Group (subsidiary)

Project Preferences

Will function either as deal originator or
investor in deals created by others
Type of Financing:
Seed
Research and development partnerships
Startup
First-stage
Second-stage
Later-stage expansion
Leveraged buyout
Merger/acquisition financing
Technology transfer and licensing
Minimum Investment: Less than $100,000
Preferred Investment: Over $1 million
Minimum Operating Data:
Annual Sales—Nominal
P&L—Losses (profits projected after 3 years)
Annual Sales (LBO)—$10 million-$150 million

Geographical Preferences

National
Europe
Other international

Industry Preferences

Communications
Cable television
Commercial communications
Data communications
Home satellite technology
Satellite and microwave communications
Telephone related
Computer Related
Computer graphics, CAD/CAM and CAE
Computer services
Micro and mini computers
Office automation
Scanning related
Software-applications
Software-artificial intelligence
Software-systems
Terminals
Consumer
Computer stores/related services
Consumer products
Food and beverage products
Franchise businesses
Hotels and resort areas
Leisure and recreational products
Modular housing
Restaurants
Video disks and tapes
Distribution
Communications equipment
Computer equipment
Consumer products
Food products
Medical products
Motion pictures
Electronic Components and Instrumentation
Analytical and scientific instrumentation
Component fabrication and testing equipment
Electronic components
Laser related
Optics technology
Security devices and systems
Energy/Natural Resources
Alternative energy
Coal related
Cogeneration
Energy conservation
Minerals
Oil and gas exploration and production
Strategic metals
Technology related products/equipment
Waste to energy projects

Genetic Engineering
Gene splicing and manufacturing equipment
Monoclonal antibodies and hybridomas
Recombinant DNA (agricultural and industrial)
Recombinant DNA (medical)
Research and manufacturing equipment
Industrial Products and Equipment
Chemicals
Controls and sensors
Energy management
Other industrial automation
Plastics
Robotics/vision systems
Specialty materials
Waste chemical recyling
Medical/Health Related
Dental technology
Diagnostic equipment
Diagnostic test products
Disposable products
Drugs and medicines
Hospital and clinical labs
Medical services
Microbiology
Therapeutic equipment
Other
Education related
Environmental technology
Finance and insurance
Motion pictures and entertainment
Pollution control
Printing and graphics technology
Publishing
Real estate
Specialty consulting
Transportation
Waste management and recycling

Additional Information
Year Founded—1976
Investments(1985-1st 6 months)—11
Invested(1985-1st 6 months)—$4.2 million
Method of Compensation—Return on investment is of primary concern; do not charge fees

S/L HEALTH CARE VENTURES

1250 Broadway, 25th Floor
New York, NY 10024
212-714-1470

Partners
Wallace H. Steinberg, Gen. Ptnr.
Richard P. Lyman, Gen. Ptnr.
Harold R. Werner, Gen. Ptnr.
Joanne E. Conklin, V.P. New Business Devel.
Mona I. Geller, V.P. New Business Devel.
Robert Friedman, Venture Capital Assoc.

Whom to Contact
Harold R. Werner

Type of Firm
Private venture capital firm investing own capital

Project Preferences
Prefer role as deal originator
Type of Financing:
Startup
First-stage
Minimum Investment: $500,000
Preferred Investment: $1 million
Minimum Operating Data:
Annual Sales—Nominal

Geographical Preference
None

Industry Preferences

Genetic Engineering
Monoclonal antibodies and hybridomas
Recombinant DNA (medical)
Medical/Health Related
Any high technology health care products
Diagnostic test products
Disposable products
Drugs and medicines
Medical services
Therapeutic equipment

Additional Information
Year Founded—1986
Capital Under Management $40 million
Method of Compensation—Return on investment is of primary concern; do not charge fees

THE SPROUT GROUP

140 Broadway
New York, NY 10005
212-504-3600

Other Offices

One Center Plaza, Sixth Floor
Boston, MA 02108
617-570-8720

5300 Stevens Creek Boulevard
Suite 320
San Jose, CA 95129
408-554-1515

Partners

Richard E. Kroon, Mgn. Ptnr. (New York)
Peter T. Grauer, Gen. Ptnr. (New York)
Janet A. Hickey, Gen. Ptnr. (New York)
David L. Mordy, Gen. Ptnr. (New York)
Lloyd D. Ruth, Gen. Ptnr. (New York & California)
Larry E. Reeder, Gen. Ptnr. (Massachusetts)
Keith B. Geeslin (California)
C. Edward Hazen, V.P., DLJ Capital Corp. (Massachusetts)
Russell B. Pyne (New York)
Jon R. Stone (California)

Whom to Contact

Richard E. Kroon
Larry E. Reeder
Keith B. Geeslin
Jon R. Stone

Type of Firm

Private venture capital firm investing own capital
Investment banking or merchant banking firm investing own capital or funds of partners or clients

Affiliation

Donaldson, Lufkin & Jenrette, Inc. (parent)

Industry Association Memberships

NASBIC
NVCA

Project Preferences

Prefer role as deal originator but will also invest in deals created by others
Type of Financing:
Seed
Research and development partnerships
Startup
First-stage
Later-stage expansion
Leveraged buyout

Minimum Investment: $500,000
Preferred Investment: $500,000-$1.5 million
Preferred Investment (LBO):
  $1.5 million-$6 million
Minimum Operating Data:
Annual Sales—Nominal
P&L—Losses (profits projected after 3 years)
Annual Sales (LBO)—Over $100 million

Geographical Preference

National

Industry Preferences

Communications
Data communications
Telephone related
Computer Related
Computer graphics, CAD/CAM and CAE
Computer services
Micro and mini computers
Office automation
Scanning related
Software-artificial intelligence
Specialized turnkey systems
Consumer
Computer stores/related services
Consumer products
Consumer services
Retailing
Distribution
Communications equipment
Computer equipment
Consumer products
Electronics equipment
Food products
Industrial products
Medical products
Electronic Components and Instrumentation
Analytical and scientific instrumentation
Component fabrication and testing equipment
Electronic components
Fiber optics
Laser related
Semiconductors
Energy/Natural Resources
Technology related products/equipment
Genetic Engineering
Gene splicing and manufacturing equipment
Monoclonal antibodies and hybridomas
Recombinant DNA (agricultural and industrial)
Recombinant DNA (medical)

Industrial Products and Equipment
Chemicals
Controls and sensors
Energy management
Equipment and machinery
Other industrial automation
Plastics
Robotics/vision systems
Specialty materials
Medical/Health Related
Diagnostic equipment
Diagnostic test products
Disposable products
Drugs and medicines
Hospital and clinical labs
Medical services
Therapeutic equipment
Other
Finance and insurance
Will Not Consider
Commodity products
Entertainment
Fashion driven businesses
High cost medical technologies
Low gross margin technologies
Natural resource exploration
Package goods startups
Publishing startups
Real estate

Additional Information

Year Founded—1969
Capital Under Management—$175 million
Investments(1985-1st 6 months)—7
Invested(1985-1st 6 months)—$8 million
Method of Compensation—Return on investment is most important

---

SRK MANAGEMENT COMPANY

126 East 56th Street
New York, NY 10022
212-371-0900

Officers

Sidney R. Knafel
Victoria Hamilton
Michael S. Willner
Donald A. Kent

Whom to Contact

Sidney R. Knafel
Victoria Hamilton

Type of Firm

Private venture capital firm investing own capital

Affiliation
Insight Communications Company

Project Preferences
Will function either as deal originator or
   investor in deals created by others
Type of Financing:
Seed
Startup
First-stage
Leveraged buyout
Minimum Investment: $100,000
Preferred Investment: $250,000-$1 million
Minimum Operating Data:
Annual Sales—Nominal
P&L—Losses (profits projected after 1 year)

Geographical Preference
None

Industry Preferences

Communications
Cable television
Commercial communications
Data communications
Satellite and microwave communications
Telephone related
Computer Related
Micro and mini computers
Scanning related
Software-applications
Software-artificial intelligence
Software-systems
**Electronic Components and
   Instrumentation**
Analytical and scientific instrumentation
Component fabrication and testing
   equipment
Electronic components
Genetic Engineering
Gene splicing and manufacturing equipment
Medical/Health Related
Diagnostic equipment
Diagnostic test products
Disposable products
Therapeutic equipment
Will Not Consider
Consumer goods
Real estate

Additional Information
Year Founded—1981
Investments(1985-1st 6 months)—7
Invested(1985-1st 6 months)—$2.5 million
Method of Compensation—Return on
   investment is of primary concern; do not
   charge fees

TESSLER & CLOHERTY, INC.

420 Madison Avenue #1101
New York, NY 10017
212-752-8010

General Partners
Daniel Tessler, Chm.
Patricia Cloherty, Pres.

Whom to Contact
Either of the above

Type of Firm
Private venture capital firm investing
   own capital
SBIC

Affiliation
Fifty-Third Street Ventures, L.P. (SBIC)

Industry Association Membership
NASBIC

Project Preferences
Will function either as deal originator or
   investor in deals created by others
Type of Financing:
Startup
First-stage
Second-stage
Leveraged buyout
Minimum Investment: $250,000
Preferred Investment: $500,000-$1 million
Minimum Operating Data:
Annual Sales—Nominal
P&L—Losses (profits projected after 2 years)

Geographical Preference
National

Industry Preferences

Communications
Broadcasting
Cable television
Commercial communications
Data communications
Satellite and microwave communications
Telephone related

Computer Related
Computer graphics, CAD/CAM and CAE
Computer mainframes
Computer services
Memory devices
Micro and mini computers
Office automation
Scanning related
Software-applications
Software-artificial intelligence
Software-systems
Specialized turnkey systems
Terminals
**Electronic Components and
   Instrumentation**
Analytical and scientific instrumentation
Component fabrication and testing
   equipment
Electronic components
Fiber optics
Laser related
Semiconductors
Energy/Natural Resources
Oil field services
Oil production tools
Industrial Products and Equipment
Chemicals
Controls and sensors
Energy management
Equipment and machinery
Other industrial automation
Plastics
Robotics/vision systems
Specialty materials
Medical/Health Related
Diagnostic equipment
Diagnostic test products
Disposable products
Drugs and medicines
Hospital and clinical labs
Medical services
Therapeutic equipment
Other
Publishing
Will Not Consider
Motion pictures
Oil, gas or mineral exploration
Real estate or land development

Additional Information
Year Founded—1980
Capital Under Management—$18 million
Method of Compensation—Return on
   investment is of primary concern; do not
   charge fees

TRANSPORTATION CAPITAL CORP.

60 East 42nd Street
New York, NY 10165
212-697-4885

Other Office
566 Commonwealth Avenue
Boston, MA 02215
617-262-9701

Officers
Paul M. Thorner, V.P.
Melvin L. Hirsch, Pres. (New York)
Robert H. Silver, V.P. (New York)
Dorothy T. Hirsch, Treas. (New York)
Jon Hirsch, Asst. V.P. (Massachusetts)
Sally Hagwood, Asst. Treas. (New York)
Margaret Shiroky, Asst. Secy. (New York)
Paul M. Thorner, V.P. (Massachusetts)
Susan R. Hirsch, V.P (New York)

Whom to Contact
Robert H. Silver

Type of Firm
MESBIC

Industry Association Membership
NASBIC

Project Preferences
Prefer role as deal originator but will also
  invest in deals created by others
Type of Financing:
Startup
Later-stage expansion
Leveraged buyout
Minimum Investment: Less than $100,000
Preferred Investment: $100,000-$250,000
Minimum Operating Data:
Annual Sales—Nominal
P&L—Break even

Geographical Preference
Northeast

Industry Preferences

Other
Transportation
Will Not Consider
Non transportation related businesses

Additional Information
Year Founded—1979
Capital Under Management—$23 million
Investments(1985-1st 6 months)—101
Invested(1985-1st 6 months)—$6 million
Method of Compensation—Return on
  investment is of primary concern; do not
  charge fees

UTECH VENTURE CAPITAL CORPORATION

One New York Plaza
New York, NY 10004
212-908-9539

Philip B. Smith, Ltd. Ptnr. & Consultant

See MARYLAND for full listing

VEGA CAPITAL CORP.

720 White Plains Road
Scarsdale, NY 10583
914-472-8550

Officers
Victor Harz, Pres.
Ronald A. Linden, V.P.

Whom to Contact
Ronald A. Linden

Type of Firm
SBIC

Industry Association Membership
NASBIC

Project Preferences
Will function either as deal originator or
  investor in deals created by others
Type of Financing:
Second-stage
Later-stage expansion
Leveraged buyout
Minimum Investment: $100,000
Preferred Investment: $200,000-$2 million
Minimum Operating Data:
Annual Sales—$1.5 million
P&L—Break even

Geographical Preference
None

Industry Preferences

Distribution
Communications equipment
Computer equipment
Consumer products
Electronics equipment
Food products
Industrial products
Medical products
Electronic Components and Instrumentation
Analytical and scientific instrumentation
Component fabrication and testing
  equipment
Electronic components
Fiber optics
Laser related
Semiconductors
Industrial Products and Equipment
Chemicals
Controls and sensors
Energy management
Equipment and machinery
Other industrial automation
Plastics
Robotics/vision systems
Specialty materials
Medical/Health Related
Diagnostic equipment
Diagnostic test products
Disposable products
Drugs and medicines
Hospital and clinical labs
Medical services
Therapeutic equipment
Other
Agriculture, forestry, fishing
Real estate
Transportation

Additional Information
Year Founded—1968
Capital Under Management—$10 million
Investments(1985-1st 6 months)—4
Invested(1985-1st 6 months)—$870,000
Method of Compensation—Return on
  investment is most important, but also
  charge for closing fees, service fees, etc.

VENCON MANAGEMENT, INC.

301 West 53rd Street #10F
New York, NY 10019
212-581-8787

Officers
Irvin Barash, Pres.
Ellen Fischer, Research Analyst

Whom to Contact
Irvin Barash

Type of Firm
Private venture capital firm investing
    own capital

Project Preferences
Prefer role as deal originator but will also
    invest in deals created by others
Type of Financing:
Seed
Startup
First-stage
Leveraged buyout
Minimum Investment: $250,000
Preferred Investment: $500,000-$1 million
Preferred Investment (LBO): $1 million
Minimum Operating Data:
Annual Sales—Nominal
P&L—Losses (profits projected after 1 year)
Annual Sales (LBO)—$10 million-$50 million

Geographical Preference
National

Industry Preferences

**Electronic Components and
    Instrumentation**
Semiconductors
Energy/Natural Resources
Alternative energy
Technology related products/equipment
Genetic Engineering
Gene splicing and manufacturing equipment
Monoclonal antibodies and hybridomas
Recombinant DNA (agricultural and
    industrial)
Recombinant DNA (medical)
Industrial Products and Equipment
Chemicals
Controls and sensors
Energy management
Equipment and machinery
Other industrial automation
Plastics
Robotics/vision systems
Specialty materials

Medical/Health Related
Diagnostic equipment
Diagnostic test products
Disposable products
Drugs and medicines
Hospital and clinical labs
Medical services
Therapeutic equipment
Other
Agriculture, forestry, fishing
Will Not Consider
Distribution
Retail

Additional Information
Year Founded—1972
Capital Under Management—$3 million

VENROCK ASSOCIATES

30 Rockefeller Plaza #5508
New York, NY 10112
212-247-3700

Other Office
Two Palo Alto Square #528
Palo Alto, CA 94306
415-493-5577

General Partners
Peter O. Crisp (New York)
Anthony B. Evnin (New York)
David R. Hathaway (New York)
Ted H. McCourtney, Jr. (New York)
Henry S. Smith (New York)
Anthony Sun (California)

Whom to Contact
Any of the above

Type of Firm
Private venture capital firm investing
    own capital

Affiliation
Rockefeller Family Office, New York City

Industry Association Membership
NVCA

Project Preferences
Will function either as deal originator or
    investor in deals created by others

Type of Financing:
Seed
Research and development partnerships
Startup
First-stage
Second-stage
Leveraged buyout
Minimum Investment: $500,000
Preferred Investment: $500,000-$1 million
Minimum Operating Data:
Annual Sales—Nominal

Geographical Preference
None

Industry Preferences

Communications
Various
Computer Related
Various
**Electronic Components and
    Instrumentation**
Various
Genetic Engineering
Various
Medical/Health Related
Various

Additional Information
Year Founded—1969 (Rockefeller
    involvement since 1932)
Capital Under Management—
    Over $150 million

VENTECH PARTNERS, L.P.

200 Park Avenue #2525
New York, NY 10017
212-692-9177

Other Office
30 Tower Lane
Avon Park South
Avon, CT 06001
203-677-0183

General Partners
Samuel F. McKay (Connecticut)
Richard L. King (New York)

Whom to Contact
Samuel F. McKay
Richard L. King

Type of Firm
Private venture capital firm investing
    own capital

Project Preferences

Prefer role as deal originator but will also invest in deals created by others

Type of Financing:
Startup
First-stage
Second-stage
Minimum Investment: $250,000
Preferred Investment: $500,000-$1 million
Minimum Operating Data:
Annual Sales—Nominal
P&L—Losses (profits projected after 2 years)

Geographical Preference
None

Industry Preferences

Communications
Cable television
Commercial communications
Data communications
Satellite and microwave communications
Telephone related
Computer Related
Computer graphics, CAD/CAM and CAE
Computer mainframes
Computer services
Memory devices
Micro and mini computers
Office automation
Scanning related
Software-applications
Software-artificial intelligence
Software-systems
Specialized turnkey systems
Terminals
Distribution
Communications equipment
Computer equipment
Consumer products
Electronics equipment
Food products
Industrial products
Medical products
Electronic Components and Instrumentation
Analytical and scientific instrumentation
Component fabrication and testing equipment
Electronic components
Fiber optics
Laser related
Semiconductors
Energy/Natural Resources
Technology related products/equipment

Genetic Engineering
Gene splicing and manufacturing equipment
Monoclonal antibodies and hybridomas
Recombinant DNA (agricultural and industrial)
Recombinant DNA (medical)
Industrial Products and Equipment
Chemicals
Controls and sensors
Energy management
Equipment and machinery
Other industrial automation
Plastics
Robotics/vision systems
Specialty materials
Medical/Health Related
Diagnostic equipment
Diagnostic test products
Disposable products
Drugs and medicines
Hospital and clinical labs
Medical services
Therapeutic equipment

Additional Information

Year Founded—1982
Capital Under Management—$29 million
Investments(1985-1st 6 months)—6
Invested(1985-1st 6 months)—$2 million
Method of Compensation—Return on investment is of primary concern; do not charge fees

---

THE VENTURE CAPITAL FUND OF AMERICA

509 Madison Avenue #1406
New York, NY 10022
212-838-5577

Partners
Dayton T. Carr, Gen. Ptnr.
Arnaud J. Isnard, Assoc.
Bromwell Ault, Special Ltd. Ptnr.

Whom to Contact
Any of the above

Type of Firm
Private venture capital firm investing own capital

Project Preferences
Will function either as deal originator or investor in deals created by others

Type of Financing:
Startup
First-stage
Second-stage
Later-stage expansion
Leveraged buyout
Minimum Investment: $100,000
Preferred Investment: $300,000-$600,000
Minimum Operating Data:
Annual Sales—Nominal

Geographical Preference
National

Industry Preferences

Communications
Commercial communications
Satellite and microwave communications
Telephone related
Computer Related
Computer graphics, CAD/CAM and CAE
Computer services
Memory devices
Software-applications
Software-systems
Consumer
Consumer products
Consumer services
Distribution
Consumer products
Medical products
Electronic Components and Instrumentation
Analytical and scientific instrumentation
Electronic components
Laser related
Optics technology
Energy/Natural Resources
Alternative energy
Coal related
Energy conservation
Minerals
Oil and gas services
Genetic Engineering
Monoclonal antibodies and hybridomas
Recombinant DNA (agricultural and industrial)
Recombinant DNA (medical)
Research and manufacturing equipment
Industrial Products and Equipment
Chemicals
Equipment and machinery
Industrial automation
Plastics
Process control
Robotics/vision systems
Specialty materials

Medical/Health Related
Diagnostic equipment
Drugs and medicines
Hospital and clinical labs
Medical services
Therapeutic equipment
Other
Agriculture, forestry, fishing
Education related
Transportation
Will Not Consider
Publishing
Real estate
Tax shelters

Additional Information
Year Founded—1983
Method of Compensation—Return on
investment is of primary concern; do not
charge fees

VERONIS, SUHLER & ASSOCIATES

515 Madison Avenue
New York, NY 10022
212-935-4990

Officers
John J. Veronis, Chm.
John S. Suhler, Pres.
James E. Boddorf, Exec. V.P.
J. Michael Hadley, Sr. V.P.
Marvin L. Shapiro, Affiliate
Jeffrey T. Stevenson, V.P.
Paul E. Hale, V.P.
David C. Lamb, Assoc.
Robert L. Stone, Assoc.
Anna M. Syrett, Research Dir.

Whom to Contact
Any officer or associate

Type of Firm
Investment banking or merchant banking
firm investing own capital or funds of
partners or clients

Affiliation
Communications Investment Partners
(general partners own Veronis, Suhler
& Associates)

Project Preferences
Prefer role as deal originator
Type of Financing:
Leveraged buyout
Minimum Investment: $1 million
Preferred Investment: Over $1 million

Geographical Preference
None

Industry Preferences

Communications
Cable television
Radio and television broadcasting
Other
Publishing

Additional Information
Year Founded—1981

WARBURG, PINCUS VENTURES, INC.

466 Lexington Avenue
10th Floor
New York, NY 10017
212-878-0600

Officers
Lionel I. Pincus, Chm.
John L. Vogelstein, Pres.
Nissan Boury, Mgn. Dir.
Christopher W. Brody, Mgn. Dir.
Stephen W. Fillo, Mgn. Dir.
Andrew Gaspar, Mgn. Dir.
Henry Kressel, Mgn. Dir.
Sidney Lapidus, Mgn. Dir.
Barbara L. Manfrey, Mgn. Dir.
Rodman W. Moorhead, III, Mgn. Dir.
Ernest H. Pomerantz, Mgn. Dir.
Charles A. Steinberg, Mgn. Dir.
John Friedman, V.P.
Jeffrey A. Harris, V.P.
Adam Solomon, V.P.
Edward McKinley, Assoc.
Howard Newman, Assoc.
Ian M. Smith, Assoc.
Peter Stalker, Assoc.
Michelle McNally, Assoc.

Whom to Contact
Christopher W. Brody
Stephen W. Fillo
Sidney Lapidus
Rodman W. Moorhead

Type of Firm
Private venture capital firm investing
own capital

Affiliations
Warburg, Pincus Capital Partners (venture
capital fund)
Warburg, Pincus Capital Corp. (venture
capital fund)

Industry Association Membership
NVCA

Project Preferences
Prefer role as deal originator but will also
invest in deals created by others
Type of Financing:
Seed
Research and development partnerships
Startup
First-stage
Second-stage
Later-stage expansion
Leveraged buyout
Minimum Investment: $500,000
Preferred Investment: Over $1 million
Minimum Operating Data:
Annual Sales—Nominal
Annual Sales—Potential $100 million
sales in 5-8 years
P&L—Losses (profits projected after 2 years)
Annual Sales (LBO)—$50 million and over

Geographical Preference
National

Industry Preferences

Communications
Cable television
Commercial communications
Data communications
Satellite and microwave communications
Telephone related
Computer Related
Computer graphics, CAD/CAM and CAE
Computer mainframes
Computer services
Memory devices
Micro and mini computers
Office automation
Scanning related
Software-applications
Software-artificial intelligence
Software-systems
Specialized turnkey systems
Terminals
Consumer
Computer stores/related services
Consumer products
Consumer services
Food and beverage products
Franchise businesses
Hotels and resort areas
Leisure and recreational products
Restaurants
Retailing

Distribution
Communications equipment
Computer equipment
Consumer products
Electronics equipment
Food products
Industrial products
Medical products
**Electronic Components and
Instrumentation**
Analytical and scientific instrumentation
Component fabrication and testing
equipment
Electronic components
Fiber optics
Laser related
Semiconductors
Energy/Natural Resources
Alternative energy
Coal related
Drilling and exploration services
Energy conservation
Minerals
Oil and gas exploration and production
Technology related products/equipment
Genetic Engineering
Gene splicing and manufacturing equipment
Monoclonal antibodies and hybridomas
Recombinant DNA (agricultural and
industrial)
Recombinant DNA (medical)
Industrial Products and Equipment
Chemicals
Controls and sensors
Energy management
Equipment and machinery
Other industrial automation
Plastics
Robotics/vision systems
Specialty materials
Medical/Health Related
Diagnostic equipment
Diagnostic test products
Disposable products
Drugs and medicines
Hospital and clinical labs
Medical services
Therapeutic equipment
Other
Agriculture, forestry, fishing
Education related
Finance and insurance
Publishing
Real estate
Specialty consulting
Transportation
Will Not Consider
Gambling

Additional Information
Year Founded—1966
Capital Under Management—$500 million
Investments(1985-1st 6 months)—25
Invested(1985-1st 6 months)—$26 million
Method of Compensation—Return on
investment is of primary concern; do not
charge fees

WEISS, PECK & GREER VENTURE PARTNERS, L.P.

One New York Plaza, 30th Floor
New York, NY 10004
212-908-9500

Other Offices
555 California Street #4760
San Francisco, CA 94104
415-622-6864

265 Franklin Street
Boston, MA 02110
617-439-4630

Partners
Philip Greer, Mgn. Gen. Ptnr. (New York)
Robert J. Loarie, Gen. Ptnr. (California)
Ralph T. Linsalata, Gen. Ptnr.
(Massachusetts)
John C. Savage, Gen. Ptnr. (California)
Eugene M. Weber, Gen. Ptnr. (California)
Gunnar Hurtig III, Gen. Ptnr. (California)

Whom to Contact
Eugene M. Weber
Ralph T. Linsalata

Type of Firm
Private venture capital firm investing
own capital

Affiliations
Weiss, Peck & Greer (special limited partner)
WestVen

Industry Association Memberships
NVCA
WAVC

Project Preferences
Prefer role as deal originator but will also
invest in deals created by others
Type of Financing:
Startup
First-stage
Second-stage
Leveraged buyout

Minimum Investment: $500,000
Preferred Investment: Over $1 million
Preferred Investment (LBO):
$2 million and over
Minimum Operating Data:
Annual Sales—Nominal
P&L—Losses (profits projected after 2 years)
Annual Sales (LBO)—$25 million-$100 million

Geographical Preference
None

Industry Preferences

Communications
Commercial communications
Data communications
Satellite and microwave communications
Telephone related
Computer Related
Computer graphics, CAD/CAM and CAE
Computer mainframes
Computer services
Memory devices
Micro and mini computers
Office automation
Scanning related
Software-applications
Software-artificial intelligence
Software-systems
Specialized turnkey systems
Terminals
Consumer
Consumer products
Consumer services
Food and beverage products
Franchise businesses
Restaurants
Retailing
Distribution
Communications equipment
Computer equipment
Consumer products
Electronics equipment
Food products
Industrial products
Medical products
**Electronic Components and
Instrumentation**
Analytical and scientific instrumentation
Component fabrication and testing
equipment
Electronic components
Fiber optics
Laser related
Semiconductors
Energy/Natural Resources
Technology related products/equipment

Genetic Engineering
Gene splicing and manufacturing equipment
Monoclonal antibodies and hybridomas
Recombinant DNA (agricultural and
  industrial)
Recombinant DNA (medical)
Industrial Products and Equipment
Chemicals
Controls and sensors
Energy management
Equipment and machinery
Other industrial automation
Plastics
Robotics/vision systems
Specialty materials
Medical/Health Related
Diagnostic equipment
Diagnostic test products
Disposable products
Drugs and medicines
Hospital and clinical labs
Medical services
Therapeutic equipment
Other
Finance and insurance
Publishing
Transportation

Additional Information
Year Founded—1971
Capital Under Management—$260 million
Investments(1985-1st 6 months)—8
Invested(1985-1st 6 months)—$9 million
Method of Compensation—Return on
  investment is of primary concern; do not
  charge fees

WELSH, CARSON, ANDERSON & STOWE

45 Wall Street
New York, NY 10005
212-422-3232

General Partners
Patrick J. Welsh
Russell L. Carson
Bruce K. Anderson
Richard H. Stowe
Charles G. Moore
Andrew M. Paul
William W. Neal

Whom to Contact
Any of the above

Type of Firm
Private venture capital firm investing
  own capital

Industry Association Membership
NVCA

Project Preferences
Will function either as deal originator or
  investor in deals created by others
Type of Financing:
Startup
First-stage
Second-stage
Leveraged buyout
Minimum Investment: $1 million
Preferred Investment: Over $1 million
Minimum Operating Data:
Annual Sales—Nominal
P&L—Losses (profits projected after 3 years)

Geographical Preference
National

Industry Preferences

Communications
Data communications
Satellite and microwave communications
Telephone related
Computer Related
Computer graphics, CAD/CAM and CAE
Computer services
Memory devices
Micro and mini computers
Office automation
Software-applications
Software-systems
Electronic Components and Instrumentation
Analytical and scientific instrumentation
Fiber optics
Semiconductors
Industrial Products and Equipment
Controls and sensors
Other industrial automation
Robotics/vision systems
Medical/Health Related
Diagnostic equipment
Medical services
Therapeutic equipment
Will Not Consider
Real estate

Additional Information
Year Founded—1979
Capital Under Management—$325 million
Invested(1985-1st 6 months)—$27.3 million
Method of Compensation—Return on
  investment is of primary concern; do not
  charge fees

WERTHEIM & CO.

200 Park Avenue
New York, NY 10166
212-578-0200

Officers
Frederick A. Klingenstein, Chm.
Robert F. Shapiro, Pres.
James A. Harmon, Vice Chm.
Thomas C. Darling, V.P.

Whom to Contact
Thomas C. Darling

Type of Firm
Investment banking or merchant banking
  firm investing own capital or funds of
  partners or clients

Project Preferences
Will function either as deal originator or
  investor in deals created by others
Type of Financing:
Research and development partnerships
Startup
First-stage
Leveraged buyout
Minimum Investment: $100,000
Preferred Investment: $250,000-$1 million

Geographical Preference
None

Industry Preferences

Communications
Commercial communications
Data communications
Satellite and microwave communications
Computer Related
Computer graphics, CAD/CAM and CAE
Computer services
Software-applications
Software-systems
Specialized turnkey systems
Consumer
Consumer products
Consumer services
Retailing
Distribution
Consumer products
Industrial products
Electronic Components and Instrumentation
Analytical and scientific instrumentation
Electronic components
Laser related
Energy/Natural Resources
Oil and gas exploration and production

Genetic Engineering
Recombinant DNA (agricultural and
    industrial)
Recombinant DNA (medical)
Industrial Products and Equipment
Chemicals
Controls and sensors
Robotics/vision systems
Specialty materials
Medical/Health Related
Diagnostic equipment
Diagnostic test products
Medical services
Therapeutic equipment
Other
Publishing
Real estate

Additional Information

Year Founded—1927
Method of Compensation—Return on
    investment is of primary concern; do not
    charge fees

J. H. WHITNEY & CO.

630 Fifth Avenue #3200
New York, NY 10111
212-757-0500

Other Office

3000 Sand Hill Road
Building 1, #270
Menlo Park, CA 94025
415-854-0500

Partners

Benno C. Schmidt, Mgn. Ptnr. (New York)
Don E. Ackerman, Gen. Ptnr. (New York)
Michael C. Brooks, Gen. Ptnr. (New York)
John W. Larson, Gen. Ptnr. (California)
Harry A. Marshall, Gen. Ptnr. (California)
David T. Morgenthaler II, Gen. Ptnr.
    (California)
Russell E. Planitzer, Gen. Ptnr. (New York)
Edward V. Ryan, Gen. Ptnr. (New York)

Whom to Contact

Any of the above

Type of Firm

Private venture capital firm investing
    own capital

Industry Association Membership

NVCA

Project Preferences

Prefer role as deal originator but will also
    invest in deals created by others
Type of Financing:
Seed
Startup
First-stage
Second-stage
Leveraged buyout
Minimum Investment: $1 million
Preferred Investment: Over $1 million

Geographical Preference

None

Industry Preferences

Communications
Cable television
Commercial communications
Data communications
Satellite and microwave communications
Telephone related
Computer Related
Computer graphics, CAD/CAM and CAE
Computer mainframes
Computer services
Memory devices
Micro and mini computers
Office automation
Scanning related
Software-applications
Software-artificial intelligence
Software-systems
Specialized turnkey systems
Terminals
Consumer
Retailing
Distribution
Communications equipment
Consumer products
Electronics equipment
Medical products
**Electronic Components and
    Instrumentation**
Analytical and scientific instrumentation
Component fabrication and testing
    equipment
Electronic components
Fiber optics
Laser related
Semiconductors
Energy/Natural Resources
Technology related products/equipment
Genetic Engineering
Gene splicing and manufacturing equipment
Monoclonal antibodies and hybridomas
Recombinant DNA (agricultural and
    industrial)
Recombinant DNA (medical)

Industrial Products and Equipment
Chemicals
Controls and sensors
Energy management
Equipment and machinery
Other industrial automation
Plastics
Robotics/vision systems
Specialty materials
Medical/Health Related
Diagnostic equipment
Diagnostic test products
Disposable products
Drugs and medicines
Hospital and clinical labs
Medical services
Therapeutic equipment

Additional Information

Year Founded—1946
Method of Compensation—Return on
    investment is of primary concern; do not
    charge fees

WINFIELD CAPITAL CORPORATION

237 Mamaroneck Avenue
White Plains, NY 10605
914-949-2600

Officers

Stanley Pechman, Pres.
Martin Bring, Treas.
Robert Fischer, Secy.

Whom to Contact

Stanley Pechman

Type of Firm

SBIC

Industry Association Membership

NASBIC

Project Preferences

Will function either as deal originator or
    investor in deals created by others
Type of Financing:
Later-stage expansion
Leveraged buyout
Minimum Investment: $100,000
Preferred Investment: $100,000 and over
Minimum Operating Data:
Annual Sales—$1.5 million
P&L—Break even

Geographical Preferences

Southeast
East Coast

Industry Preferences
None
Will Not Consider
High technology startups

Additional Information
Year Founded—1972
Capital Under Management—$8 million
Investments(1985-1st 6 months)—6
Invested(1985-1st 6 months)—$1 million
Method of Compensation—Return on
  investment is of primary concern; do not
  charge fees

WOLFENSOHN ASSOCIATES L.P.

425 Park Avenue
New York, NY 10022
212-909-8100

Partners
James D. Wolfensohn, Gen. Ptnr.
Dr. Harold Brown, Gen. Ptnr.
Stuart W. Ray, Gen. Ptnr.
Samuel J. Moss, Gen. Ptnr.
Denise M. Gilbert, Assoc.
Peter Levin, Assoc.
Robert S. Shriver, Assoc.

Whom to Contact
Stuart W. Ray
Samuel J. Moss

Type of Firm
Private venture capital firm investing
  own capital

Affiliation
James D. Wolfensohn Incorporated (fund
manager)

Project Preferences
Will function either as deal originator or
  investor in deals created by others
Type of Financing:
Seed
Research and development partnerships
Startup
First-stage
Second-stage
Later-stage expansion
Leveraged buyout
Minimum Investment: $1 million
Preferred Investment: Over $1 million
Minimum Operating Data:
Annual Sales—Nominal
P&L—Losses (profits projected after 2 years)

Geographical Preference
National

Industry Preferences

Communications
Data communications
Satellite and microwave communications
Telephone related
Computer Related
Computer graphics, CAD/CAM and CAE
Computer mainframes
Computer services
Memory devices
Micro and mini computers
Office automation
Scanning related
Software-applications
Software-artificial intelligence
Software-systems
Specialized turnkey systems
Terminals
**Electronic Components and
  Instrumentation**
Analytical and scientific instrumentation
Component fabrication and testing
  equipment
Electronic components
Fiber optics
Laser related
Semiconductors
Energy/Natural Resources
Coal related
Technology related products/equipment
Genetic Engineering
Gene splicing and manufacturing equipment
Monoclonal antibodies and hybridomas
Recombinant DNA (agricultural and
  industrial)
Recombinant DNA (medical)
Industrial Products and Equipment
Controls and sensors
Other industrial automation
Robotics/vision systems
Specialty materials
Medical/Health Related
Diagnostic equipment
Diagnostic test products
Disposable products
Drugs and medicines
Hospital and clinical labs
Medical services
Therapeutic equipment

Additional Information
Year Founded—1984
Capital Under Management—$90 million
Investments(1985-1st 6 months)—2
Invested(1985-1st 6 months)—$3 million
Method of Compensation—Return on
  investment is of primary concern; do not
  charge fees

HERBERT YOUNG SECURITIES, INC.

98 Cuttermill Road
Great Neck, NY 11021
516-487-8300

Officers
Herbert D. Levine, Pres.
Melvin Norman, V.P.
Lionel Malamed, V.P.
Clara Y. Levine, Secy.

Whom to Contact
Herbert D. Levine

Type of Firm
Investment banking or merchant banking
  firm investing own capital or funds of
  partners or clients

Project Preferences
Prefer role as deal originator but will also
  invest in deals created by others

Geographical Preference
None

Industry Preferences

Communications
Cable television
Commercial communications
Data communications
Satellite and microwave communications
Telephone related
Computer Related
Computer graphics, CAD/CAM and CAE
Computer mainframes
Computer services
Memory devices
Micro and mini computers
Office automation
Scanning related
Software-applications
Software-artificial intelligence
Software-systems
Specialized turnkey systems
Terminals

Consumer
Food and beverage products
Leisure and recreational products
Distribution
Communications equipment
Computer equipment
Electronics equipment
Food products
Medical products
**Electronic Components and
  Instrumentation**
Analytical and scientific instrumentation
Component fabrication and testing
  equipment
Electronic components
Fiber optics
Laser related
Photovoltaics
Semiconductors
Energy/Natural Resources
Alternative energy
Coal related
Drilling and exploration services
Energy conservation
Minerals
Oil and gas exploration and production
Technology related products/equipment
Genetic Engineering
Gene splicing and manufacturing equipment
Monoclonal antibodies and hybridomas
Recombinant DNA (agricultural and
  industrial)
Recombinant DNA (medical)
Industrial Products and Equipment
Chemicals
Controls and sensors
Energy management
Equipment and machinery
Other industrial automation
Plastics
Robotics/vision systems
Specialty materials
Medical/Health Related
Diagnostic equipment
Diagnostic test products
Disposable products
Drugs and medicines
Hospital and clinical labs
Medical services
Therapeutic equipment

Additional Information

Year Founded—1959
Method of Compensation—Function primarily
  in service area; receive contingent fee in
  cash or equity

CAROLINA VENTURE CAPITAL CORP.

137 East Franklin Street #404
Post Office Box 646
Chapel Hill, NC 27514
919-929-3003

Other Office
14 Archer Road
Hilton Head Island, SC 29928
803-842-3101

Officer
Thomas H. Harvey, Pres.

Type of Firm
SBIC

Industry Association Membership
NASBIC

Project Preferences
Will function either as deal originator or
investor in deals created by others
Type of Financing:
First-stage
Second-stage
Later-stage expansion
Leveraged buyout
Minimum Investment: $100,000
Preferred Investment: $100,000-$250,000
Minimum Operating Data:
Annual Sales—Nominal
P&L—Break even

Geographical Preference
Southeast

Industry Preferences

Communications
Commercial communications
Consumer
Leisure and recreational products
Distribution
Communications equipment
Other
Real estate

Additional Information
Year Founded—1980
Capital Under Management—$2 million
Investments(1985-1st 6 months)—3
Invested(1985-1st 6 months)—$275,000
Method of Compensation—Return on
investment is of primary concern; do not
charge fees

FALCON CAPITAL CORPORATION

311 South Evans Street
Greenville, NC 27834
919-752-5918

Officers
Dr. P.S. Prasad, Pres.
Rajiv Dutta, V.P.
Gary A. Herring, Secy.

Whom to Contact
Rajiv Dutta

Type of Firm
SBIC

Industry Association Membership
NASBIC

Project Preferences
Prefer role in deals created by others
Type of Financing:
Second-stage
Later-stage expansion
Leveraged buyout
Minimum Investment: Less than $100,000
Preferred Investment: Less than $100,000
Minimum Operating Data:
Annual Sales—$500,000
P&L—Break even

Geographical Preferences
Southeast
East Coast

Industry Preferences

Consumer
Consumer products
Franchise businesses
Hotels and resort areas
Distribution
Medical products
Medical/Health Related
Diagnostic equipment
Diagnostic test products
Disposable products
Drugs and medicines
Hospital and clinical labs
Medical services
Therapeutic equipment

Additional Information
Year Founded—1964
Investments(1985-1st 6 months)—4
Invested(1985-1st 6 months)—$280,000
Method of Compensation—Return on
investment is most important, but also
charge for closing fees, service fees, etc.

HERITAGE CAPITAL CORPORATION

2290 First Union Plaza
Charlotte, NC 28282
704-334-2867

Officers
H.B. McManaway, Jr., Pres.
W.R. Starnes, V.P.
G. Kinsey Roper, V.P.

Whom to Contact
Any of the above

Type of Firm
SBIC

Affiliation
Ruddick Corporation (parent)

Industry Association Membership
NASBIC

Project Preferences
Will function either as deal originator or
investor in deals created by others
Type of Financing:
First-stage
Second-stage
Leveraged buyout
Minimum Investment: $100,000
Preferred Investment: $250,000-$500,000
Minimum Operating Data:
Annual Sales—$500,000

Geographical Preference
Primarily southeast

Industry Preferences
None
Will Not Consider
Businesses ineligible for SBIC funding

Additional Information
Year Founded—1962
Method of Compensation—Return on
investment is of primary concern; do not
charge fees

INTERSOUTH PARTNERS

2634 Chapel Hill Boulevard
Suite 322
Durham, NC 27707
919-493-2359

Post Office Box 13546
Research Triangle Park, NC 27709

Partners
Dennis J. Dougherty, Gen. Ptnr.
Roy O. Rodwell, Gen. Ptnr.
Joseph A. Velk, Assoc.

Whom to Contact
Any of the above

Type of Firm
Private venture capital firm investing
own capital

Project Preferences
Will function either as deal originator or
investor in deals created by others
Type of Financing:
Seed
Startup
First-stage
Second-stage
Later-stage expansion
Leveraged buyout
Minimum Investment: $250,000
Preferred Investment: $500,000-$1 million
Preferred Investment (LBO):
$500,000 and over
Minimum Operating Data:
Annual Sales—Nominal
P&L—Losses (profits projected after 2 years)
Annual Sales (LBO)—$5 million and over

Geographical Preference
Southeast

Industry Preferences

Communications
Cable television
Commercial communications
Data communications
Satellite and microwave communications
Telephone related

Computer Related
Computer graphics, CAD/CAM and CAE
Computer mainframes
Computer services
Memory devices
Micro and mini computers
Office automation
Scanning related
Software-applications
Software-artificial intelligence
Software-systems
Specialized turnkey systems
Terminals
Consumer
Computer stores/related services
Consumer products
Consumer services
Food and beverage products
Franchise businesses
Leisure and recreational products
Retailing
Distribution
Communications equipment
Computer equipment
Consumer products
Electronics equipment
Food products
Industrial products
Medical products
**Electronic Components and
Instrumentation**
Analytical and scientific instrumentation
Component fabrication and testing
equipment
Electronic components
Fiber optics
Laser related
Semiconductors
Energy/Natural Resources
Technology related products/equipment
Genetic Engineering
Gene splicing and manufacturing equipment
Monoclonal antibodies and hybridomas
Recombinant DNA (agricultural and
industrial)
Recombinant DNA (medical)
Industrial Products and Equipment
Chemicals
Controls and sensors
Energy management
Equipment and machinery
Other industrial automation
Plastics
Robotics/vision systems
Specialty materials

Medical/Health Related
Diagnostic equipment
Diagnostic test products
Disposable products
Drugs and medicines
Hospital and clinical labs
Medical services
Therapeutic equipment
Will Not Consider
Entertainment
Financial institutions
Oil and gas exploration
Real estate
Restaurants

Additional Information
Year Founded—1985

KITTY HAWK CAPITAL, LTD.

2030 One Tryon Center
Charlotte, NC 28284
704-333-3777

General Partners
Walter H. Wilkinson, Jr.
W. Chris Hegele

Whom to Contact
W. Chris Hegele

Type of Firm
SBIC

Industry Association Membership
NASBIC

Project Preferences
Will function either as deal originator or
investor in deals created by others
Type of Financing:
Startup
First-stage
Second-stage
Later-stage expansion
Leveraged buyout
Minimum Investment: $100,000
Preferred Investment: $100,000-$250,000
Minimum Operating Data:
Annual Sales—Nominal
P&L—Losses (profits projected after 2 years)

Geographical Preferences
Southeast
Northeast

Industry Preferences

Communications
Commercial communications
Data communications
Satellite and microwave communications
Telephone related
Computer Related
Computer services
Office automation
Software-applications
Specialized turnkey systems
Distribution
Communications equipment
Computer equipment
Electronics equipment
Industrial products
Medical products
Electronic Components and
Instrumentation
Analytical and scientific instrumentation
Component fabrication and testing
    equipment
Electronic components
Laser related
Semiconductors
Industrial Products and Equipment
Chemicals
Controls and sensors
Energy management
Equipment and machinery
Other industrial automation
Plastics
Robotics/vision systems
Specialty materials
Medical/Health Related
Diagnostic equipment
Diagnostic test products
Disposable products
Drugs and medicines
Hospital and clinical labs
Medical services
Therapeutic equipment
Other
Publishing
Will Not Consider
Single location retailing

Additional Information

Year Founded—1980
Capital Under Management—$5.5 million
Investments(1985-1st 6 months)—4
Invested(1985-1st 6 months)—$300,000
Method of Compensation—Return on
    investment is of primary concern; do not
    charge fees

NCNB VENTURE CORP.

One NCNB Plaza
Post Office Box 120
Charlotte, NC 28255
704-374-5723

Officers

S. Epes Robinson, Pres.
Michael F. Elliot, V.P.

Whom to Contact

Either of the above

Type of Firm

SBIC
Venture capital subsidiary of
    commercial bank

Affiliation

NCNB National Bank (parent)

Industry Association Membership

NASBIC

Project Preferences

Will function either as deal originator or
    investor in deals created by others
Type of Financing:
Startup
First-stage
Second-stage
Leveraged buyout
Minimum Investment: $250,000
Preferred Investment: $500,000-$1 million
Preferred Investment (LBO):
    $500,000-$1 million
Minimum Operating Data:
Annual Sales—Nominal
P&L—Losses (profits projected after 1 year)
Annual Sales (LBO)—$10 million or over

Geographical Preference

Southeast

Industry Preferences

Communications
Commercial communications
Data communications
Computer Related
Computer graphics, CAD/CAM and CAE
Computer services
Micro and mini computers
Office automation
Scanning related
Software-applications
Software-systems
Specialized turnkey systems

Distribution
Communications equipment
Electronics equipment
Food products
Industrial products
Medical products
Electronic Components and
Instrumentation
Analytical and scientific instrumentation
Component fabrication and testing
    equipment
Electronic components
Fiber optics
Laser related
Genetic Engineering
Gene splicing and manufacturing equipment
Industrial Products and Equipment
Controls and sensors
Equipment and machinery
Other industrial automation
Medical/Health Related
Diagnostic equipment
Diagnostic test products
Disposable products
Medical services
Therapeutic equipment
Other
Education related
Publishing

Additional Information

Year Founded—1984
Capital Under Management—$7.5 million
Investments(1985-1st 6 months)—4
Invested(1985-1st 6 months)—$1.5 million
Method of Compensation—Return on
    investment is of primary concern; do not
    charge fees

SOUTHGATE VENTURE PARTNERS I/
SOUTHGATE VENTURE PARTNERS II

227 North Tryon Street #201
Charlotte, NC 28202
704-372-1410

Other Office

Cotton Exchange Building #702
New Orleans, LA 70130
504-525-2112

Partners

Alexander B. Wilkins, Jr., Gen. Ptnr.
William D. Humphries, Ptnr.

Whom to Contact

Alexander B. Wilkins (North Carolina)
William D. Humphries (Louisiana)

Type of Firm
Private venture capital firm investing
own capital

Affiliations
Delta Capital, Incorporated (100%
owned affiliate)
Walnut Street Capital (25% owned affiliate)

Industry Association Membership
NASBIC

Project Preferences
Will function either as deal originator or
investor in deals created by others
Type of Financing:
Startup
First-stage
Second-stage
Later-stage expansion
Leveraged buyout
Minimum Investment: $100,000
Preferred Investment: $100,000-$500,000
Minimum Operating Data:
P&L—Break even

Geographical Preferences
Southeast
Southwest
West Coast
Northeast

Industry Preferences
None

Additional Information
Year Founded—1983
Capital Under Management—$22 million
Method of Compensation—Return on
investment is of primary concern; do not
charge fees

TRIVEST VENTURE FUND

1300 St. Mary's Street #210
Raleigh, NC 27605
919-834-9984

Kennedy C. O'Herron, Gen. Ptnr.

See PENNSYLVANIA for full listing

VENTURE CAPITALISTS INC.

1801 East Fifth Street
Post Office Box 36759
Charlotte, NC 28236
704-333-5360

Officers
Frederick William Byrum, Pres.
Kimberly Ann Smith, Secy. & Treas.

Whom to Contact
Frederick William Byrum

Type of Firm
Private venture capital firm investing
own capital

Project Preferences
Will function either as deal originator or
investor in deals created by others
Type of Financing:
First-stage
Minimum Investment: $100,000
Preferred Investment: $100,000-$250,000

Geographical Preference
None

Industry Preferences

Communications
Cable television
Commercial communications
Data communications
Satellite and microwave communications
Computer Related
Computer graphics, CAD/CAM and CAE
Computer mainframes
Computer services
Memory devices
Micro and mini computers
Office automation
Scanning related
Software-applications
Software-artificial intelligence
Software-systems
Specialized turnkey systems
Terminals
Distribution
Communications equipment
Medical products
**Electronic Components and
Instrumentation**
Fiber optics
Semiconductors

Genetic Engineering
Gene splicing and manufacturing equipment
Monoclonal antibodies and hybridomas
Recombinant DNA (agricultural and
industrial)
Recombinant DNA (medical)
Industrial Products and Equipment
Controls and sensors
Medical/Health Related
Diagnostic equipment
Diagnostic test products
Disposable products
Drugs and medicines
Hospital and clinical labs
Medical services
Therapeutic equipment
Other
Agriculture, forestry, fishing
Publishing

Additional Information
Year Founded—1983
Capital Under Management—$638,000

VENTURE FIRST ASSOCIATES

2422 Reynolda Road
Winston-Salem, NC 27106
919-722-9600

General Partners
M. Campbell Cawood
J. Douglass Mullins
B. Otto Wheeley

Whom to Contact
Any of the above

Type of Firm
Private venture capital firm investing
own capital

Industry Association Membership
NVCA

Project Preferences
Will function either as deal originator or
investor in deals created by others
Type of Financing:
Seed
Startup
First-stage
Minimum Investment: $250,000
Preferred Investment: $500,000-$1 million
Minimum Operating Data:
Annual Sales—Nominal
P&L—Losses (profits projected after 1 year)

Geographical Preference

Southeast

Industry Preferences

Communications
Commercial communications
Data communications
Computer Related
Computer graphics, CAD/CAM and CAE
Computer services
Memory devices
Micro and mini computers
Office automation
Scanning related
Software-artificial intelligence
Specialized turnkey systems
Terminals
Consumer
Consumer products
Consumer services
Distribution
Communications equipment
Consumer products
Electronics equipment
Food products
Industrial products
Medical products
**Electronic Components and
 Instrumentation**
Analytical and scientific instrumentation
Component fabrication and testing
 equipment
Electronic components
Fiber optics
Laser related
Genetic Engineering
Gene splicing and manufacturing equipment
Monoclonal antibodies and hybridomas
Recombinant DNA (agricultural and
 industrial)
Recombinant DNA (medical)
Industrial Products and Equipment
Chemicals
Controls and sensors
Equipment and machinery
Robotics/vision systems
Specialty materials
Medical/Health Related
Diagnostic equipment
Diagnostic test products
Disposable products
Drugs and medicines
Hospital and clinical labs
Medical services
Therapeutic equipment
Other
Agriculture, forestry, fishing

Additional Information

Year Founded—1984
Capital Under Management—$13.2 million
Investments(1985-1st 6 months)—3
Invested(1985-1st 6 months)—$1.1 million
Method of Compensation—Return on
 investment is of primary concern; do not
 charge fees

BASIC SEARCH COMPANY

10 West Streetsboro Street
Park Place, #301
Hudson, OH 44236
216-656-2442

Officer

Burton D. Morgan, Pres.

Type of Firm

Private venture capital firm investing
own capital

Project Preferences

Prefer role as deal originator but will also
invest in deals created by others
Type of Financing:
Seed
Leveraged buyout
Minimum Investment: Less than $100,000
Preferred Investment: Less than $100,000
Minimum Operating Data:
Annual Sales—$1.5 million
P&L—Losses (profits projected after 1 year)

Geographical Preference

Midwest

Industry Preferences

Communications
Satellite and microwave communications
Computer Related
Memory devices
Software-applications
Consumer
Consumer products
Consumer services
Franchise businesses
Hotels and resort areas
Distribution
Communications equipment
Industrial products
Medical products
**Electronic Components and
Instrumentation**
Analytical and scientific instrumentation
Electronic components
Laser related
Semiconductors
Energy/Natural Resources
Alternative energy
Coal related
Drilling and exploration services
Genetic Engineering
Gene splicing and manufacturing equipment
Industrial Products and Equipment
Chemicals
Equipment and machinery
Plastics

Medical/Health Related
Diagnostic equipment
Hospital and clinical labs
Medical services
Therapeutic equipment
Other
Agriculture, forestry, fishing
Publishing
Real estate
Transportation

Additional Information

Year Founded—1970
Capital Under Management—$10 million
Investments(1985-1st 6 months)—6
Invested(1985-1st 6 months)—$400,000
Method of Compensation—Return on
investment is of primary concern; do not
charge fees

BRANTLEY VENTURE PARTNERS, INC.

20776 Brantley Road
Shaker Heights, OH 44122
216-371-1118

General Partner

Robert P. Pinkas

Type of Firm

Private venture capital firm investing
own capital

Affiliation

DSV Partners (general partner)

Project Preferences

Prefer role as deal originator but will also
invest in deals created by others
Type of Financing:
Seed
Startup
First-stage
Minimum Investment: $100,000
Preferred Investment: $250,000-$500,000
Minimum Operating Data:
Annual Sales—Nominal

Geographical Preference

Midwest

Industry Preferences

Communications
Cable television
Commercial communications
Data communications
Satellite and microwave communications
Telephone related
Computer Related
Computer graphics, CAD/CAM and CAE
Computer mainframes
Computer services
Memory devices
Micro and mini computers
Office automation
Scanning related
Software-applications
Software-artificial intelligence
Software-systems
Specialized turnkey systems
Terminals
Consumer
Computer stores/related services
**Electronic Components and
Instrumentation**
Analytical and scientific instrumentation
Component fabrication and testing
equipment
Electronic components
Fiber optics
Laser related
Semiconductors
Genetic Engineering
Gene splicing and manufacturing equipment
Monoclonal antibodies and hybridomas
Recombinant DNA (agricultural and
industrial)
Recombinant DNA (medical)
Industrial Products and Equipment
Chemicals
Controls and sensors
Other industrial automation
Robotics/vision systems
Specialty materials
Medical/Health Related
Diagnostic equipment
Diagnostic test products
Disposable products
Drugs and medicines
Hospital and clinical labs
Medical services
Therapeutic equipment

Additional Information

Year Founded—1986
Method of Compensation—Return on
investment is of primary concern; do not
charge fees

CAPITAL FUNDS CORPORATION

127 Public Square
Cleveland, OH 44114
216-622-8628

Officers
Carl G. Nelson, V.P. & Chief Inv. Officer
David B. Chilcote, Asst. V.P.

Whom to Contact
Either of the above

Type of Firm
SBIC
Venture capital subsidiary of
commercial bank

Affiliation
Society National Bank, Cleveland, Ohio

Industry Association Membership
NASBIC

Project Preferences
Will function either as deal originator or
investor in deals created by others
Type of Financing:
First-stage
Second-stage
Leveraged buyout
Minimum Investment: $100,000
Preferred Investment: $250,000-$500,000
Minimum Operating Data:
Annual Sales—$1.5 million

Geographical Preference
Ohio and neighboring states

Industry Preferences

Communications
Cable television
Commercial communications
Data communications
Satellite and microwave communications
Telephone related
Computer Related
Computer graphics, CAD/CAM and CAE
Scanning related
Software-applications
Software-systems
Industrial Products and Equipment
Plastics
Robotics/vision systems
Specialty materials

Additional Information
Year Founded—1960
Capital Under Management—$4 million
Investments(1985-1st 6 months)—4
Invested(1985-1st 6 months)—$800,000
Method of Compensation—Return on
investment is of primary concern; do not
charge fees

CARDINAL DEVELOPMENT FUND

40 South Third Street #460
Columbus, OH 43215
614-464-5557

Officers
Richard Bannon, Ptnr.
J. Thomas Walker, Ptnr.
John Holscher, V.P.
Richard Focht, V.P.
Katharine Presutti, Mgr.

Whom to Contact
Any of the above

Type of Firm
Private venture capital firm investing
own capital

Industry Association Membership
NVCA

Project Preferences
Will function either as deal originator or
investor in deals created by others
Type of Financing:
Startup
First-stage
Second-stage
Later-stage expansion
Leveraged buyout
Minimum Investment: $250,000
Preferred Investment: $500,000-$1 million
Minimum Operating Data:
Annual Sales—Nominal
P&L—Losses (profits projected after 2 years)

Geographical Preference
None

Industry Preferences

Communications
Data communications
Telephone related

Computer Related
Computer graphics, CAD/CAM and CAE
Computer mainframes
Computer services
Memory devices
Micro and mini computers
Office automation
Software-applications
Software-systems
Terminals
Consumer
Computer stores/related services
Consumer products
Consumer services
Food and beverage products
Franchise businesses
Hotels and resort areas
Leisure and recreational products
Restaurants
Distribution
Communications equipment
Computer equipment
Consumer products
Electronics equipment
Food products
Industrial products
Medical products
**Electronic Components and
Instrumentation**
Analytical and scientific instrumentation
Electronic components
Fiber optics
Laser related
Semiconductors
Energy/Natural Resources
Technology related products/equipment
Genetic Engineering
Monoclonal antibodies and hybridomas
Recombinant DNA (agricultural and
industrial)
Recombinant DNA (medical)
Research and manufacturing equipment
Industrial Products and Equipment
Chemicals
Controls and sensors
Equipment and machinery
Plastics
Medical/Health Related
Diagnostic equipment
Diagnostic test products
Disposable products
Drugs and medicines
Hospital and clinical labs
Medical services
Therapeutic equipment
Other
Finance and insurance
Publishing

Will Not Consider
Resource recovery of any kind

Additional Information
Year Founded—1982
Capital Under Management—Over $30 million
Method of Compensation—Return on investment is of primary concern; do not charge fees

---

CLARION CAPITAL CORPORATION

1801 East 12th Street #201
Cleveland, OH 44114
216-687-1096

Officers
Morton A. Cohen, Chm.
Roger W. Eaglen, V.P.
Michael L. Boeckman, V.P.

Whom to Contact
Roger W. Eaglen
Morton A. Cohen

Type of Firm
SBIC

Affiliation
First City Financial Corp., Ltd., Canada (controlling shareholder)

Industry Association Membership
NASBIC

Project Preferences
Will function either as deal originator or investor in deals created by others
Type of Financing:
Startup
First-stage
Second-stage
Minimum Investment: $250,000
Preferred Investment: $250,000-$500,000
Minimum Operating Data:
Annual Sales—Nominal
P&L—Losses (profits projected after 3 years)

Geographical Preferences
Northeast
East Coast
Midwest
West Coast

Industry Preferences

Communications
Cable television
Cellular telephone
Commercial communications
Data communications
Satellite and microwave communications
Telephone related
Consumer
Franchise businesses
Distribution
Communications equipment
Electronics equipment
Industrial products
Medical products
Electronic Components and Instrumentation
Analytical and scientific instrumentation
Component fabrication and testing equipment
Electronic components
Fiber optics
Laser related
Semiconductors
Genetic Engineering
Genetic engineering support industries
Industrial Products and Equipment
Chemicals
Controls and sensors
Energy management
Equipment and machinery
Other industrial automation
Plastics
Robotics/vision systems
Specialty chemicals
Specialty materials
Medical/Health Related
Diagnostic equipment
Diagnostic test products
Disposable products
Drugs and medicines
Hospital and clinical labs
Medical services
Therapeutic equipment
Other
Publishing

Additional Information
Year Founded—1968
Capital Under Management—$17 million
Investments(1985-1st 6 months)—3
Invested(1985-1st 6 months)—$804,000
Method of Compensation—Return on investment is most important, but also charge for closing fees, service fees, etc.

THE DANA VENTURE CAPITAL CORPORATION

4500 Dorr Street
Post Office Box 1000
Toledo, OH 43697
419-535-4780

Officers
Gene C. Swartz, Pres.
Gary M. Golden, V.P.

Whom to Contact
Gene C. Swartz

Type of Firm
Venture capital subsidiary or affiliate of non-financial corporation

Affiliation
Dana Corporation (parent)

Project Preferences
Will function either as deal originator or investor in deals created by others
Type of Financing:
Seed
First-stage
Second-stage
Minimum Investment: $1 million
Preferred Investment: Over $1 million

Geographical Preference
None

Industry Preferences

Computer Related
Computer graphics, CAD/CAM and CAE
Computer services
Memory devices
Software-applications
Software-artificial intelligence
Software-systems
Distribution
Computer equipment
Industrial products
Medical products
Electronic Components and Instrumentation
Analytical and scientific instrumentation
Component fabrication and testing equipment
Electronic components
Fiber optics
Laser related
Semiconductors

Energy/Natural Resources
Alternative energy
Drilling and exploration services
Energy conservation
Minerals
Oil and gas exploration and production
Technology related products/equipment
Industrial Products and Equipment
Controls and sensors
Energy management
Equipment and machinery
Other industrial automation
Plastics
Specialty materials
Medical/Health Related
Diagnostic equipment
Diagnostic test products
Disposable products
Other
Education related

Additional Information
Year Founded—1982
Capital Under Management—$6 million
Method of Compensation—Return on
  investment is of primary concern; do not
  charge fees

FIRST CITY TECHNOLOGY VENTURES

35555 Curtis Boulevard
Eastlake, OH 44094
216-953-0555

Officers
Morton A. Cohen, Chm.
Roger W. Eaglen, V.P.
Michael L. Boeckman, V.P.

Whom to Contact
Roger W. Eaglen
Morton A. Cohen

Type of Firm
Private venture capital firm investing
  own capital

Affiliation
First City Financial Corp., Ltd., Canada
  (controlling shareholder)

Project Preferences
Will function either as deal originator or
  investor in deals created by others
Type of Financing:
Startup
First-stage
Second-stage
Leveraged buyout

Minimum Investment: $250,000
Preferred Investment: $250,000-$500,000
Minimum Operating Data:
Annual Sales—Nominal
P&L—Losses (profits projected after 3 years)

Geographical Preferences
Northeast
East Coast
Midwest
West Coast
Canada

Industry Preferences

Communications
Cable television
Cellular telephone
Commercial communications
Data communications
Satellite and microwave communications
Telephone related
Consumer
Franchise businesses
Distribution
Communications equipment
Electronics equipment
Industrial products
Medical products
**Electronic Components and
  Instrumentation**
Analytical and scientific instrumentation
Component fabrication and testing
  equipment
Electronic components
Fiber optics
Laser related
Semiconductors
Genetic Engineering
Genetic engineering support industries
Industrial Products and Equipment
Chemicals
Controls and sensors
Energy management
Equipment and machinery
Other industrial automation
Plastics
Robotics/vision systems
Specialty materials
Other
Publishing

Additional Information
Year Founded—1982
Capital Under Management—$6 million
Investments(1985-1st 6 months)—4
Invested(1985-1st 6 months)—$1 million

FIRST OHIO CAPITAL CORPORATION

606 Madison Avenue
Post Office Box 2061
Toledo, OH 43604
419-259-7150

Officers
Michael J. Aust, V.P.
David J. McMacken, Inv. Analyst

Whom to Contact
Either of the above

Type of Firm
SBIC

Affiliation
First Ohio Bancshares, Inc. (parent)

Industry Association Membership
NASBIC

Project Preferences
Will function either as deal originator or
  investor in deals created by others
Type of Financing:
First-stage
Second-stage
Later-stage expansion
Leveraged buyout
Minimum Investment: $100,000
Preferred Investment: $200,000-$300,000
Minimum Operating Data:
Annual Sales—Nominal
P&L—Break even

Geographical Preference
Midwest

Industry Preferences

Computer Related
Memory devices
Office automation
Distribution
Communications equipment
Computer equipment
Consumer products
Electronics equipment
Industrial products
Medical products
**Electronic Components and
  Instrumentation**
Analytical and scientific instrumentation
Component fabrication and testing
  equipment
Electronic components

Industrial Products and Equipment
Chemicals
Controls and sensors
Energy management
Equipment and machinery
Other industrial automation
Plastics
Robotics/vision systems
Specialty materials
Medical/Health Related
Various

Additional Information
Year Founded—1982
Method of Compensation—Return on
investment is of primary concern; do not
charge fees

GRIES INVESTMENT COMPANY

720 Statler Office Tower
Cleveland, OH 44115
216-861-1146

Officers
Robert D. Gries, Pres.
Richard F. Brezic, V.P.

Whom to Contact
Either of the above

Type of Firm
SBIC

Industry Association Membership
NASBIC

Project Preferences
Will function either as deal originator or
investor in deals created by others
Type of Financing:
Startup
First-stage
Second-stage
Later-stage expansion
Leveraged buyout
Minimum Investment: Less than $100,000
Preferred Investment: $100,000-$250,000
Minimum Operating Data:
Annual Sales—Nominal

Geographical Preference
None

Industry Preferences
None

Additional Information
Year Founded—1964
Capital Under Management—
$2 million-$3 million
Investments(1985-1st 6 months)—3
Method of Compensation—Return on
investment is of primary concern; do not
charge fees

HEARTLAND GROUP, INC.

545 Hanna Building
Cleveland, OH 44115
216-696-6663

Officers
John Sherwin, Jr., Pres.
Douglas R. Elliott, Exec. V.P.
Peter D. Sachtjen, Mgn. Dir.
Thomas Ford, Mgn. Dir.

Whom to Contact
Douglas R. Elliot

Type of Firm
Private venture capital firm investing
own capital

Project Preferences
Prefer role as deal originator but will also
invest in deals created by others
Type of Financing:
Seed
Research and development partnerships
Startup
First-stage
Leveraged buyout
Minimum Investment: Less than $100,000
Preferred Investment: $100,000-$500,000
Minimum Operating Data:
Annual Sales—Nominal
P&L—Losses (profits projected after 3 years)

Geographical Preference
Midwest

Industry Preferences

Computer Related
Various
**Electronic Components and
Instrumentation**
Analytical and scientific instrumentation
Electronic components
Fiber optics
Energy/Natural Resources
Coal related
Energy and natural resource technologies

Genetic Engineering
Gene splicing and manufacturing equipment
Monoclonal antibodies and hybridomas
Recombinant DNA (agricultural and
industrial)
Recombinant DNA (medical)
Industrial Products and Equipment
Chemicals
Industrial products
Specialty materials
Medical/Health Related
Various
Other
Biotechnology

Additional Information
Year Founded—1985
Method of Compensation—Return on
investment is of primary concern; do not
charge fees

HOOK PARTNERS

815 National City Bank Bldg.
Cleveland, OH 44114
216-621-3142

General Partners
John B. Hook
Albert A. Augustus
David J. Hook

Whom to Contact
David J. Hook

Type of Firm
Private venture capital firm investing
own capital

Project Preferences
Will function either as deal originator or
investor in deals created by others
Type of Financing:
Startup
First-stage
Second-stage
Leveraged buyout
Minimum Investment: Less than $100,000
Preferred Investment: $100,000-$250,000
Minimum Operating Data:
Annual Sales—Nominal
P&L—Losses (profits projected after 2 years)

Geographical Preference
West Coast

Industry Preferences

Communications
Data communications
Satellite and microwave communications
Telephone related
Computer Related
Computer graphics, CAD/CAM and CAE
Computer mainframes
Memory devices
Micro and mini computers
Office automation
Scanning related
Software-applications
Software-artificial intelligence
Software-systems
Specialized turnkey systems
Terminals
Distribution
Communications equipment
Computer equipment
Electronics equipment
Medical products
Electronic Components and Instrumentation
Analytical and scientific instrumentation
Component fabrication and testing equipment
Electronic components
Fiber optics
Laser related
Semiconductors
Genetic Engineering
Gene splicing and manufacturing equipment
Monoclonal antibodies and hybridomas
Recombinant DNA (agricultural and industrial)
Recombinant DNA (medical)
Industrial Products and Equipment
Controls and sensors
Energy management
Other industrial automation
Robotics/vision systems
Medical/Health Related
Diagnostic equipment
Diagnostic test products
Therapeutic equipment

Additional Information

Year Founded—1979
Capital Under Management $15 million
Investments(1985-1st 6 months)—5
Invested(1985-1st 6 months)—$800,000
Method of Compensation—Return on investment is of primary concern; do not charge fees

LUBRIZOL ENTERPRISES, INC.

29400 Lakeland Boulevard
Wickliffe, OH 44092
216-943-4200

Officers

Donald L. Murfin, Pres.
Bruce H. Grasser, V.P.
David R. Anderson, V.P.
James R. Glynn, V.P. Finance & Treas.
Edward M. Kiggins, PhD.,
   Dir. Licensing/Technology
Arthur J. Chatroo, Esq., Gen. Counsel

Whom to Contact

Any officer

Type of Firm

Venture capital subsidiary or affiliate of non-financial corporation

Affiliation

The Lubrizol Corporation (parent)

Industry Association Memberships

NASBIC
NVCA

Project Preferences

Prefer role as deal originator but will also invest in deals created by others
Type of Financing:
Seed
Research and development partnerships
Startup
First-stage
Second-stage
Leveraged buyout
Minimum Investment: $500,000
Preferred Investment: Over $1 million
Minimum Operating Data:
Annual Sales—Nominal
P&L—Losses (profits projected after 4 years)

Geographical Preference

None

Industry Preferences

Industrial Products and Equipment
Biological science
Chemical science
Material science

Additional Information

Year Founded—1979
Capital Under Management—$60 million
Investments(1985-1st 6 months)—2
Invested(1985-1st 6 months)—$7.1 million
Method of Compensation—Return on investment is of primary concern; do not charge fees

MIAMI VALLEY CAPITAL, INC.

131 North Ludlow Street #315
Dayton, OH 45402
513-222-7222

Officers

Everett F. Telljohann, Pres.
W. Walker Lewis, Jr., Chm.

Whom to Contact

W. Walker Lewis, Jr.

Type of Firm

SBIC

Project Preferences

Prefer role as deal originator but will also invest in deals created by others
Type of Financing:
Startup
First-stage
Second-stage
Later-stage expansion
Leveraged buyout
Minimum Investment: Less than $100,000
Preferred Investment: $100,000-$250,000
Preferred Investment (LBO): $100,000
Minimum Operating Data:
Annual Sales—Nominal
P&L—Losses (profits projected after 1 year)
Annual Sales (LBO)—$2 million and over

Geographical Preference

Within one hour of office

Industry Preferences

Communications
Cable television
Computer Related
Applied systems
Computer graphics, CAD/CAM and CAE
Memory devices
Micro and mini computers
Office automation
Scanning related
Specialized turnkey systems
Terminals

Distribution
Communications equipment
Computer equipment
Consumer products
Electronics equipment
Food products
Industrial products
Medical products
Electronic Components and Instrumentation
Analytical and scientific instrumentation
Component fabrication and testing equipment
Electronic components
Fiber optics
Laser related
Semiconductors
Industrial Products and Equipment
Chemicals
Controls and sensors
Energy management
Equipment and machinery
Other industrial automation
Plastics
Robotics/vision systems
Specialty materials
Medical/Health Related
Applied technology
Diagnostic equipment
Diagnostic test products
Disposable products
Drugs and medicines
Hospital and clinical labs
Medical services
Therapeutic equipment

Additional Information
Year Founded—1980
Capital Under Management—$2.7 million
Method of Compensation—Return on investment is of primary concern; do not charge fees

MORGENTHALER VENTURES
700 National City Bank Bldg.
Cleveland, OH 44114
216-621-3070

Partners
David T. Morgenthaler, Mgn. Ptnr.
Robert D. Pavey, Gen. Ptnr.
Paul S. Brentlinger, Gen. Ptnr.
Robert C. Bellas, Jr., Gen. Ptnr.

Whom to Contact
Any of the above

Type of Firm
Private venture capital firm investing own capital

Industry Association Membership
NVCA

Project Preferences
Will function either as deal originator or investor in deals created by others
Type of Financing:
Startup
First-stage
Second-stage
Later-stage expansion
Leveraged buyout
Minimum Investment: $250,000
Preferred Investment: $500,000-$1 million
Preferred Investment (LBO):
 $1 million-$3 million
Minimum Operating Data:
Annual Sales—Nominal
P&L—Losses (profits projected after 3 years)
Annual Sales (LBO)—$25 million-$250 million

Geographical Preference
National

Industry Preferences

Communications
Commercial communications
Data communications
Satellite and microwave communications
Telephone related
Computer Related
Computer graphics, CAD/CAM and CAE
Computer mainframes
Computer services
Memory devices
Micro and mini computers
Office automation
Scanning related
Software-applications
Software-artificial intelligence
Software-systems
Specialized turnkey systems
Terminals
Consumer
Franchise businesses
Leisure and recreational products
Distribution
Communications equipment
Computer equipment
Electronics equipment
Medical products

Electronic Components and Instrumentation
Analytical and scientific instrumentation
Component fabrication and testing equipment
Electronic components
Fiber optics
Laser related
Semiconductors
Energy/Natural Resources
Technology related products/equipment
Genetic Engineering
Gene splicing and manufacturing equipment
Monoclonal antibodies and hybridomas
Recombinant DNA (agricultural and industrial)
Recombinant DNA (medical)
Industrial Products and Equipment
Chemicals
Controls and sensors
Energy management
Equipment and machinery
Other industrial automation
Plastics
Robotics/vision systems
Specialty materials
Medical/Health Related
Diagnostic equipment
Diagnostic test products
Disposable products
Drugs and medicines
Hospital and clinical labs
Medical services
Therapeutic equipment
Other
Agriculture, forestry, fishing

Additional Information
Year Founded—1971
Capital Under Management— Over $100 million
Investments(1985-1st 6 months)—5
Invested(1985-1st 6 months)—$1.75 million
Method of Compensation—Return on investment is of primary concern; do not charge fees

NATIONAL CITY CAPITAL CORPORATION/NATIONAL CITY VENTURE CORPORATION

623 Euclid Avenue
Post Office Box 73303-N
Cleveland, OH 44114
216-575-2487

Officers
Michael Sherwin, Pres.
Martha A. Barry, V.P.
John B. Naylor, V.P.

Whom to Contact
Martha A. Barry

Type of Firm
SBIC
Venture capital subsidiary of commercial bank

Affiliation
National City Corporation (parent)

Industry Association Membership
NASBIC

Project Preferences
Will function either as deal originator or investor in deals created by others
Type of Financing:
Second-stage
Later-stage expansion
Leveraged buyout
Minimum Investment: $250,000
Preferred Investment: $250,000-$500,000
Minimum Operating Data:
P&L—Losses (profits projected after 2 years)

Geographical Preference
None

Industry Preferences
None

Additional Information
Year Founded—1979
Capital Under Management—$20 million
Investments(1985-1st 6 months)—5
Invested(1985-1st 6 months)—$1.3 million
Method of Compensation—Return on investment is of primary concern

PRIMUS CAPITAL FUND

1375 East Ninth Street
One Cleveland Center, #2140
Cleveland, OH 44114
216-621-2185

Partners
Loyal Wilson, Mgn. Ptnr.
David A. DeVore, Principal
William C. Mulligan, Principal

Whom to Contact
Any of the above

Type of Firm
Private venture capital firm investing own capital

Industry Association Memberships
NASBIC
NVCA

Project Preferences
Prefer role as deal originator but will also invest in deals created by others
Type of Financing:
Seed
Startup
First-stage
Leveraged buyout
Minimum Investment: $250,000
Preferred Investment: $500,000-$1 million
Minimum Operating Data:
Annual Sales—Nominal
P&L—Losses (profits projected after 1 year)

Geographical Preference
Midwest

Industry Preferences

Communications
Cable television
Commercial communications
Data communications
Satellite and microwave communications
Telephone related
Computer Related
Computer graphics, CAD/CAM and CAE
Computer mainframes
Computer services
Memory devices
Micro and mini computers
Office automation
Scanning related
Software-applications
Software-artificial intelligence
Software-systems
Specialized turnkey systems
Terminals

Consumer
Consumer products
Consumer services
Food and beverage products
Retailing
Distribution
Communications equipment
Computer equipment
Consumer products
Electronics equipment
Food products
Industrial products
Medical products
Electronic Components and Instrumentation
Analytical and scientific instrumentation
Component fabrication and testing equipment
Electronic components
Fiber optics
Laser related
Semiconductors
Energy/Natural Resources
Technology related products/equipment
Genetic Engineering
Gene splicing and manufacturing equipment
Monoclonal antibodies and hybridomas
Recombinant DNA (agricultural and industrial)
Recombinant DNA (medical)
Industrial Products and Equipment
Chemicals
Controls and sensors
Energy management
Equipment and machinery
Other industrial automation
Plastics
Robotics/vision systems
Specialty materials
Medical/Health Related
Diagnostic equipment
Diagnostic test products
Disposable products
Drugs and medicines
Hospital and clinical labs
Medical services
Therapeutic equipment
Will Not Consider
Real estate
Mineral exploration
Agriculture

Additional Information
Year Founded—1984
Capital Under Management—$30 million
Investments(1985-1st 6 months)—4
Invested(1985-1st 6 months)—$2.2 million
Method of Compensation—Return on investment is of primary concern; do not charge fees

RIHT CAPITAL CORPORATION

796 Huntington Building
Cleveland, OH 44115
216-781-3655

Peter D. Van Oosterhout, Pres.

See RHODE ISLAND for full listing

SCIENTIFIC ADVANCES, INC.

601 West Fifth Avenue
Columbus, OH 43201
614-294-5541

Officers
Charles G. James, Pres.
Thomas W. Harvey, V.P.
Paul F. Purcell, V.P.
Daniel J. Shea, V.P.
William E. Tanner, Asst. Treas. & Cntlr.
Veronica Payer, Assoc.

Whom to Contact
Thomas W. Harvey
Paul F. Purcell
Daniel J. Shea

Type of Firm
Venture capital subsidiary or affiliate of
non-financial corporation

Affiliation
Battelle Memorial Institute (parent)

Industry Association Memberships
NASBIC
NVCA

Project Preferences
Will function either as deal originator or
investor in deals created by others
Type of Financing:
Startup
First-stage
Second-stage
Minimum Investment: $500,000
Preferred Investment: $500,000-$1 million
Minimum Operating Data:
Annual Sales—Nominal
P&L—Losses (profits projected after 2 years)

Geographical Preference
National

Industry Preferences

Communications
Data communications
Satellite and microwave communications
Telephone related
Computer Related
Computer graphics, CAD/CAM and CAE
Computer mainframes
Computer services
Memory devices
Micro and mini computers
Office automation
Scanning related
Software-applications
Software-artificial intelligence
Software-systems
Specialized turnkey systems
Terminals
Distribution
Communications equipment
Computer equipment
Industrial products
Medical products
**Electronic Components and
  Instrumentation**
Analytical and scientific instrumentation
Component fabrication and testing
  equipment
Electronic components
Fiber optics
Laser related
Semiconductors
Energy/Natural Resources
Alternative energy
Coal related
Energy conservation
Technology related products/equipment
Genetic Engineering
Gene splicing and manufacturing equipment
Monoclonal antibodies and hybridomas
Recombinant DNA (agricultural and
  industrial)
Recombinant DNA (medical)
Industrial Products and Equipment
Chemicals
Controls and sensors
Energy management
Equipment and machinery
Other industrial automation
Plastics
Robotics/vision systems
Specialty materials
Medical/Health Related
Diagnostic equipment
Diagnostic test products
Disposable products
Drugs and medicines
Hospital and clinical labs
Medical services
Therapeutic equipment

Will Not Consider
Non-technical

Additional Information
Year Founded—1962
Capital Under Management—$20 million
Investments(1985-1st 6 months)—4
Invested(1985-1st 6 months)—$1 million
Method of Compensation—Return on
  investment is of primary concern; do not
  charge fees

ALLIANCE BUSINESS INVESTMENT COMPANY

One Williams Center #2000
Tulsa, OK 74172
918-584-3581

Officers
Barry M. Davis, Pres.
Mark R. Blankenship, V.P.

Whom to Contact
Mark R. Blankenship

Type of Firm
SBIC

Industry Association Membership
NASBIC

Project Preferences
Prefer role as deal originator but will also invest in deals created by others
Type of Financing:
First-stage
Second-stage
Later-stage expansion
Minimum Investment: $250,000
Preferred Investment: $500,000-$1 million
Minimum Operating Data:
Annual Sales—$3 million
P&L—Profits NBT over $500,000

Geographical Preferences
Southwest
Midwest
National

Industry Preferences

Communications
Commercial communications
Data communications
Satellite and microwave communications
Computer Related
Computer graphics, CAD/CAM and CAE
Office automation
Software-applications
Consumer
Consumer products
Consumer services
Leisure and recreational products
Distribution
Communications equipment
Industrial products
Medical products
Electronic Components and Instrumentation
Fiber optics
Laser related
Semiconductors

Energy/Natural Resources
Alternative energy
Coal related
Energy conservation
Minerals
Oil and gas exploration and production
Technology related products/equipment
Genetic Engineering
Recombinant DNA (agricultural and industrial)
Recombinant DNA (medical)
Industrial Products and Equipment
Chemicals
Controls and sensors
Equipment and machinery
Other industrial automation
Plastics
Robotics/vision systems
Specialty materials
Medical/Health Related
Diagnostic equipment
Hospital and clinical labs
Medical services
Therapeutic equipment
Other
Transportation
Will Not Consider
Retail

Additional Information
Year Founded—1959
Capital Under Management—$12 million
Method of Compensation—Return on investment is of primary concern; do not charge fees

---

FIRST OKLAHOMA INVESTMENT CAPITAL CORPORATION

120 North Robinson Avenue
Suite 880-C
Oklahoma City, OK 73102
405-272-4470

Officers
David Pendley, Pres.
John Lewis, Sr. V.P.
Arthur J. Miller, V.P.

Whom to Contact
Arthur J. Miller

Type of Firm
SBIC
Venture capital subsidiary of commercial bank

Affiliation
First Oklahoma Bancorporation, Inc. (parent)

Industry Association Membership
NASBIC

Project Preferences
Will function either as deal originator or investor in deals created by others
Type of Financing:
Later-stage expansion
Leveraged buyout
Minimum Investment: $100,000
Preferred Investment: $250,000-$500,000
Preferred Investment (LBO):
$500,000-$1 million
Minimum Operating Data:
Annual Sales—$1.5 million
P&L—Profits NBT over $100,000
Annual Sales (LBO)—$500,000 and over

Geographical Preferences
Southwest
Other areas with lead investor

Industry Preferences

Communications
Cable television
Commercial communications
Data communications
Satellite and microwave communications
Telephone related
Consumer
Computer stores/related services
Consumer products
Consumer services
Food and beverage products
Franchise businesses
Hotels and resort areas
Leisure and recreational products
Restaurants
Retailing
Distribution
Communications equipment
Computer equipment
Consumer products
Electronics equipment
Food products
Industrial products
Medical products
Industrial Products and Equipment
Chemicals
Controls and sensors
Energy management
Equipment and machinery
Other industrial automation
Plastics
Robotics/vision systems
Specialty materials
Other
Finance and insurance
Publishing

Will Not Consider
Agriculture
Real estate

Additional Information
Year Founded—1978
Capital Under Management—$3 million
Investments(1985-1st 6 months)—1
Invested(1985-1st 6 months)—$250,000
Method of Compensation—Return on
investment is most important, but also
charge for closing fees, service fees, etc.

HOLDING CAPITAL GROUP

7136 South Yale #208
Tulsa, OK 74136
918-492-8524

Christopher B. Shanklin, Principal

See NEW YORK for full listing

TSF CAPITAL CORP.

2415 East Skelly Drive #102
Tulsa, OK 74105
918-749-5588

Officers
G. Douglas Fox, Chm.
Robert E. Craine, Jr., Pres.
Howard G. Barnett, Jr., Exec. V.P.

Whom to Contact
Robert E. Craine, Jr.

Type of Firm
Venture capital subsidiary or affiliate of
non-financial corporation

Affiliation
Tribune/Swab-Fox Companies, Inc. (parent)

Project Preferences
Will function either as deal originator or
investor in deals created by others
Type of Financing:
Startup
First-stage
Second-stage
Later-stage expansion
Leveraged buyout
Minimum Investment: $100,000
Preferred Investment: $250,000-$500,000
Preferred Investment (LBO): $400,000

Minimum Operating Data:
Annual Sales—Nominal
P&L—Losses (profits projected after 1 year)
Annual Sales (LBO)—$5 million and over

Geographical Preferences
Within three hours of office
Southwest
Rocky Mountains
Oklahoma-Texas mid-continent region

Industry Preferences

Communications
Data communications
Telephone related
Computer Related
Specialized turnkey systems
Consumer
Consumer services
Leisure and recreational products
Distribution
Communications equipment
Medical products
**Electronic Components and
Instrumentation**
Fiber optics
Laser related
Energy/Natural Resources
Technology related products/equipment
Industrial Products and Equipment
Controls and sensors
Plastics
Robotics/vision systems
Medical/Health Related
Diagnostic equipment
Diagnostic test products
Disposable products
Drugs and medicines
Hospital and clinical labs
Medical services
Therapeutic equipment
Other
Finance and insurance
Publishing
Transportation
Will Not Consider
Oil and gas exploration and development
Real estate

Additional Information
Year Founded—1983
Capital Under Management—$3 million
Investments(1985-1st 6 months)—6
Invested(1985-1st 6 months)—$1 million
Method of Compensation—Return on
investment is most important

WESTERN VENTURE CAPITAL CORP.

4880 South Lewis
Post Office Box 702680
Tulsa, OK 74170
918-749-7981

Officers
Joe D. Tippens, V.P.

Type of Firm
SBIC

Project Preferences
Will function either as deal originator or
investor in deals created by others
Type of Financing:
First-stage
Second-stage
Later-stage expansion
Leveraged buyout
Minimum Investment: $150,000
Preferred Investment: $250,000-$500,000
Preferred Investment (LBO):
$250,000-$1 million
Minimum Operating Data:
Annual Sales—Nominal
P&L—Losses (profits projected after 2 years)
Annual Sales (LBO)—$1 million-$5 million

Geographical Preferences
Within two hours of office
Southwest
Midwest
Rocky Mountains

Industry Preferences

Communications
Cable television
Commercial communications
Data communications
Satellite and microwave communications
Telephone related
Computer Related
Computer graphics, CAD/CAM and CAE
Computer mainframes
Computer services
Memory devices
Micro and mini computers
Office automation
Scanning related
Software-applications
Software-artificial intelligence
Software-systems
Specialized turnkey systems
Terminals

Consumer
Consumer products
Food and beverage products
Leisure and recreational products
Distribution
Communications equipment
Computer equipment
Consumer products
Electronics equipment
Food products
Industrial products
Medical products
Electronic Components and Instrumentation
Analytical and scientific instrumentation
Component fabrication and testing equipment
Electronic components
Fiber optics
Laser related
Energy/Natural Resources
Alternative energy
Coal related
Drilling and exploration services
Energy conservation
Minerals
Oil and gas exploration and production
Technology related products/equipment
Genetic Engineering
Gene splicing and manufacturing equipment
Monoclonal antibodies and hybridomas
Recombinant DNA (agricultural and industrial)
Recombinant DNA (medical)
Industrial Products and Equipment
Chemicals
Controls and sensors
Energy management
Equipment and machinery
Other industrial automation
Plastics
Robotics/vision systems
Specialty materials
Medical/Health Related
Diagnostic equipment
Diagnostic test products
Disposable products
Drugs and medicines
Hospital and clinical labs
Medical services
Therapeutic equipment
Other
Agriculture, forestry, fishing
Transportation
Will Not Consider
Food service
Motion pictures

Additional Information
Year Founded—1980
Capital Under Management—$5 million
Investments(1985-1st 6 months)—3
Invested(1985-1st 6 months)—$285,000

WOODY CREEK CAPITAL, INC.

c/o Williams Resources, Inc.
320 South Boston #831
Tulsa, OK 74103
918-582-5811

Joseph A. Zebrowski, Jr., Pres.

See COLORADO for full listing

CABLE, HOWSE & COZADD, INC.

1800 One Main Place
101 Southwest Main
Portland, OR 97204
503-248-9646

Other Offices
999 Third Avenue #4300
Seattle, WA 98104
206-583-2700

3000 Sand Hill Road
Building 1, #190
Menlo Park, CA 94025
415-854-3340

General Partners
Thomas J. Cable (Washington)
Elwood D. Howse, Jr. (Washington)
Bennett A. Cozadd (Washington)
Michael A. Ellison (Washington)
Wayne C. Wager (Washington)
James B. Glavin (Washington)
L. Barton Alexander (Oregon)
Gregory H. Turnbull (California)

Whom to Contact
Wayne C. Wager

Type of Firm
Private venture capital firm investing
own capital

Industry Association Memberships
NVCA
WAVC

Project Preferences
Prefer role as deal originator but will also
invest in deals created by others
Type of Financing:
Startup
First-stage
Second-stage
Later-stage expansion
Minimum Investment: $500,000
Preferred Investment: $1 million-$2.5 million
Minimum Operating Data:
Annual Sales—Nominal
P&L—Losses (profits projected after 3 years)

Geographical Preferences
Northwest
East Coast
West Coast

Industry Preferences

Communications
Data communications
Telephone related
Computer Related
Computer graphics, CAD/CAM and CAE
Computer mainframes
Computer services
Memory devices
Software-applications
Software-artificial intelligence
Software-systems
Specialized turnkey systems
**Electronic Components and
Instrumentation**
Analytical and scientific instrumentation
Component fabrication and testing
equipment
Electronic components
Fiber optics
Laser related
Semiconductors
Genetic Engineering
Monoclonal antibodies and hybridomas
Recombinant DNA (agricultural and
industrial)
Recombinant DNA (medical)
Industrial Products and Equipment
Chemicals
Other industrial automation
Plastics
Robotics/vision systems
Specialty materials
Medical/Health Related
Diagnostic equipment
Drugs and medicines
Medical services
Therapeutic equipment
Will Not Consider
Natural resource exploration or extraction
Real estate

Additional Information
Year Founded—1977
Capital Under Management—$132 million
Investments(1985-1st 6 months)—23
Invested(1985-1st 6 months)—$10.3 million
Method of Compensation—Return on
investment is of primary concern; do not
charge fees

THE EARL KINSHIP CORPORATION

10300 Southwest Greenburg Road
Suite 240
Portland, OR 97223
503-244-7307

John W. Dixon, Dir., West Coast Office

See RHODE ISLAND for full listing

INTERVEN PARTNERS

227 Southwest Pine Street #200
Portland, OR 97204
503-223-4334

Other Office
445 South Figueroa Street
Suite 2940
Los Angeles, CA 90071
213-622-1922

General Partners
David B. Jones (California)
Wayne B. Kingsley (Oregon)
Kenneth M. Deemer (California)
Jonathan E. Funk (California)
Keith R. Larson (California)

Whom to Contact
Wayne B. Kingsley
Jonathan E. Funk
Kenneth M. Deemer

Type of Firm
Private venture capital firm investing
own capital

Industry Association Memberships
NASBIC
NVCA
WAVC

Project Preferences
Will function either as deal originator or
investor in deals created by others
Type of Financing:
Seed
Startup
First-stage
Leveraged buyout
Minimum Investment: $500,000
Preferred Investment: $500,000-$1 million
Preferred Investment (LBO):
$1 million-$2 million
Minimum Operating Data:
Annual Sales—Nominal
P&L—Losses (profits projected after 2 years)
Annual Sales (LBO)—$15 million-$30 million

Geographical Preferences

Within two hours of office
Northwest
Southern California

Industry Preferences

Communications
Data communications
Computer Related
Computer graphics, CAD/CAM and CAE
Computer mainframes
Computer services
Memory devices
Micro and mini computers
Office automation
Scanning related
Software-applications
Software-artificial intelligence
Software-systems
Specialized turnkey systems
Terminals
Consumer
Consumer products
Consumer services
Food and beverage products
Retailing
Electronic Components and Instrumentation
Analytical and scientific instrumentation
Component fabrication and testing equipment
Electronic components
Fiber optics
Laser related
Semiconductors
Genetic Engineering
Gene splicing and manufacturing equipment
Monoclonal antibodies and hybridomas
Recombinant DNA (agricultural and industrial)
Recombinant DNA (medical)
Industrial Products and Equipment
Chemicals
Controls and sensors
Energy management
Equipment and machinery
Other industrial automation
Plastics
Robotics/vision systems
Specialty materials
Medical/Health Related
Diagnostic equipment
Diagnostic test products
Disposable products
Drugs and medicines
Hospital and clinical labs
Medical services
Therapeutic equipment

Will Not Consider

Energy/natural resources
Entertainment
Real estate

Additional Information

Year Founded—1985
Capital Under Management—$35 million
Method of Compensation—Return on investment is of primary concern; do not charge fees

---

NORWEST VENTURE CAPITAL MANAGEMENT, INC.

1300 SW Fifth #3018
Portland, OR 97201
503-223-6622

Other Office

2800 Piper Jaffray Tower
Minneapolis, MN 55402
612-372-8770

Officers

Robert F. Zicarelli, Chm. (Minnesota)
Daniel J. Haggerty, Pres. (Minnesota)
Douglas E. Johnson, V.P. (Minnesota)
Timothy A. Stepanek, V.P. (Minnesota)
Leonard J. Brandt, V.P. (Minnesota)
John P. Whaley, V.P. (Minnesota)
John E. Lindahl, V.P. (Minnesota)
John L. Thomson, Assoc. (Minnesota)
Anthony J. Miadich, V.P. (Oregon)
Dale R. Vogel, V.P. (Oregon)
Stephen J. Schewe, Assoc. (Minnesota)
Michael I. Cohen, Assoc. (Minnesota)
Brian C. Lee, Assoc. (Minnesota)
Ernie C. Parizeau, Assoc. (Minnesota)
Richard B. Keller II, Assoc. (Oregon)

Whom to Contact

Douglas E. Johnson
Anthony J. Miadich

Type of Firm

Private venture capital firm investing own capital

Affiliation

Norwest Corporation (holding company)

Project Preferences

Will function either as deal originator or investor in deals created by others

Type of Financing:

Startup
First-stage
Second-stage
Later-stage expansion
Leveraged buyout
Minimum Investment: $250,000
Preferred Investment: Over $1 million

Geographical Preference

National

Industry Preferences

Communications
Cable television
Commercial communications
Data communications
Satellite and microwave communications
Telephone related
Consumer
Computer stores/related services
Consumer products
Consumer services
Food and beverage products
Franchise businesses
Hotels and resort areas
Leisure and recreational products
Restaurants
Retailing
Distribution
Communications equipment
Computer equipment
Consumer products
Electronics equipment
Food products
Industrial products
Medical products
Electronic Components and Instrumentation
Analytical and scientific instrumentation
Component fabrication and testing equipment
Electronic components
Fiber optics
Laser related
Semiconductors
Energy/Natural Resources
Alternative energy
Coal related
Drilling and exploration services
Energy conservation
Minerals
Oil and gas exploration and production
Technology related products/equipment
Genetic Engineering
Gene splicing and manufacturing equipment
Monoclonal antibodies and hybridomas
Recombinant DNA (agricultural and industrial)
Recombinant DNA (medical)

Industrial Products and Equipment
Chemicals
Controls and sensors
Energy management
Equipment and machinery
Other industrial automation
Plastics
Robotics/vision systems
Specialty materials
Medical/Health Related
Diagnostic equipment
Diagnostic test products
Disposable products
Drugs and medicines
Hospital and clinical labs
Medical services
Therapeutic equipment
Will Not Consider
Real estate

Additional Information
Year Founded—1961
Capital Under Management—$270 million
Investments(1985-1st 6 months)—30
Invested(1985-1st 6 months)—$13 million
Method of Compensation—Return on investment is of primary concern; do not charge fees

---

ORIANS INVESTMENT COMPANY

529 SW Third Avenue #600
Portland, OR 97204
503-224-7885

Other Office
1111 Third Avenue #700
Seattle, WA 98101
206-467-0880

Officers
Robert J. Orians, Pres. (Oregon)
Dennis Bromka, Dir., Institutional Sales (Oregon)
J.H. Seely, Jr., Dir., Corporate Finance (Oregon)
James M. Key, V.P. (Washington)
Ernest Birchenough, V.P., Secy. & Treas. (Oregon)

Whom to Contact
Robert J. Orians
J.H. Seely, Jr.
James M. Key

Type of Firm
Investment banking or merchant banking firm investing own capital or funds of partners or clients

Affiliation
Orians Venture Partners (joint venture)

Project Preferences
Will function either as deal originator or investor in deals created by others
Type of Financing:
Seed
Startup
First-stage
Leveraged buyout
Minimum Investment: Less than $100,000
Preferred Investment: $250,000-$500,000
Minimum Operating Data:
Annual Sales—Nominal

Geographical Preference
West Coast

Industry Preferences

Communications
Cable television
Commercial communications
Data communications
Satellite and microwave communications
Telephone related
Computer Related
Computer graphics, CAD/CAM and CAE
Computer mainframes
Computer services
Memory devices
Micro and mini computers
Office automation
Scanning related
Software-applications
Software-artificial intelligence
Software-systems
Specialized turnkey systems
Terminals
Consumer
Consumer products
Food and beverage products
Leisure and recreational products
Electronic Components and Instrumentation
Analytical and scientific instrumentation
Component fabrication and testing equipment
Electronic components
Fiber optics
Laser related
Semiconductors
Genetic Engineering
Gene splicing and manufacturing equipment
Monoclonal antibodies and hybridomas
Recombinant DNA (agricultural and industrial)
Recombinant DNA (medical)

Industrial Products and Equipment
Chemicals
Controls and sensors
Energy management
Equipment and machinery
Other industrial automation
Plastics
Robotics/vision systems
Specialty materials
Medical/Health Related
Diagnostic equipment
Diagnostic test products
Disposable products
Drugs and medicines
Hospital and clinical labs
Medical services
Therapeutic equipment
Will Not Consider
Oil and gas
Real estate

Additional Information
Year Founded—1979
Capital Under Management—$6 million
Investments(1985-1st 6 months)—4
Invested(1985-1st 6 months)—$600,000
Method of Compensation—Return on investment is most important, but also charge for closing fees, service fees, etc.

RAINIER VENTURE PARTNERS

One Lincoln Center #440
10300 Southwest Greenburg Road
Portland, OR 97223
503-245-5900

Other Office
9725 Southeast 36th Street
Suite 300
Mercer Island, WA 98040
206-232-6720

Partners
John L. Moser (Washington)
George H. Clute (Washington)
W. Denman Van Ness (California)
Richard H. Drew (Oregon)

Whom to Contact
Any of the above

Type of Firm
Private venture capital firm investing own capital

Affiliation
Hambrecht & Quist

Industry Association Membership
WAVC

Project Preferences
Will function either as deal originator or
investor in deals created by others
Type of Financing:
Startup
First-stage
Second-stage
Later-stage expansion
Leveraged buyout
Minimum Investment: $250,000
Preferred Investment: $750,000-$1 million
Minimum Operating Data:
Annual Sales—Nominal
P&L—Losses (profits projected after 2 years)

Geographical Preferences
Northwest
West Coast

Industry Preferences

Communications
Data communications
Satellite and microwave communications
Telephone related
Computer Related
Computer graphics, CAD/CAM and CAE
Computer mainframes
Computer services
Memory devices
Micro and mini computers
Office automation
Scanning related
Software-applications
Software-artificial intelligence
Software-systems
Specialized turnkey ssytems
Terminals
**Electronic Components and
Instrumentation**
Analytical and scientific instrumentation
Component fabrication and testing
equipment
Electronic components
Fiber optics
Laser related
Semiconductors
Genetic Engineering
Gene splicing and manufacturing equipment
Monoclonal antibodies and hybridomas
Recombinant DNA (agricultural and
industrial)
Recombinant DNA (medical)

Industrial Products and Equipment
Chemicals
Controls and sensors
Energy management
Equipment and machinery
Other industrial automation
Plastics
Robotics/vision systems
Specialty materials
Medical/Health Related
Diagnostic equipment
Diagnostic test products
Disposable products
Drugs and medicines
Hospital and clinical labs
Medical services
Therapeutic equipment
Will Not Consider
Extractive industries
Financial intermediaries
Real estate

Additional Information
Year Founded—1982
Capital Under Management—$25.7 million
Method of Compensation—Return on
investment is of primary concern; do not
charge fees

ROSENFELD & CO.

1211 Southwest Sixth Avenue
Portland, OR 97204
503-228-3255

Principal
William W. Rosenfeld, Jr.

Type of Firm
Investment banking or merchant banking
firm investing own capital or funds of
partners or clients

Project Preferences
Prefer role as deal originator
Type of Financing:
First-stage
Second-stage
Later-stage expansion
Leveraged buyout
Minimum Investment: $250,000
Preferred Investment: Over $1 million
Preferred Investment (LBO): Over $1 million
Minimum Operating Data:
Annual Sales—$1.5 million
P&L—Profits NBT over $100,000
Annual Sales (LBO)—$5 million and over

Geographical Preference
Within two hours of office

Industry Preferences

Consumer
Consumer products
Food and beverage products
Leisure and recreational products
Distribution
Food products
Industrial products
Medical products
**Electronic Components and
Instrumentation**
Analytical and scientific instrumentation
Component fabrication and testing
equipment
Energy/Natural Resources
Forest products, timberlands
Industrial Products and Equipment
Chemicals
Controls and sensors
Energy management
Equipment and machinery
Other industrial automation
Plastics
Robotics/vision systems
Specialty materials
Medical/Health Related
Diagnostic equipment
Diagnostic test products
Disposable products
Drugs and medicines
Hospital and clinical labs
Medical services
Therapeutic equipment
Other
Agriculture, forestry, fishing
Education related
Finance and insurance
Publishing

Additional Information
Year Founded—1977
Capital Under Management—$1 million
Investments(1985-1st 6 months)—2
Invested(1985-1st 6 months)—$750,000
Method of Compensation—Function primarily
in service area; receive contingent fee in
cash or equity

SHAW VENTURE PARTNERS

851 SW Sixth Avenue
Portland, OR 97204
503-228-4884

Partners
Ralph R. Shaw, Gen. Ptnr.
Herbert S. Shaw, Ltd. Ptnr.
Alan S. Dishlip, Ltd. Ptnr.
David Starr, Assoc.

Whom to Contact
Any of the above

Type of Firm
Private venture capital firm investing
own capital

Project Preferences
Will function either as deal originator or
investor in deals created by others
Type of Financing:
Startup
First-stage
Second-stage
Leveraged buyout
Minimum Investment: $250,000
Preferred Investment: $500,000-$1 million
Minimum Operating Data:
Annual Sales—Nominal
P&L—Losses (profits projected after 3 years)

Geographical Preferences
Northwest
West Coast
Other regions also considered

Industry Preferences

Communications
Commercial communications
Data communications
Satellite and microwave communications
Computer Related
Computer graphics, CAD/CAM and CAE
Computer mainframes
Computer services
Memory devices
Micro and mini computers
Office automation
Scanning related
Software-applications
Software-artificial intelligence
Software-systems
Specialized turnkey systems
Consumer
Consumer products
Consumer services
Leisure and recreational products

Distribution
Consumer products
Food products
Medical products
**Electronic Components and
Instrumentation**
Analytical and scientific instrumentation
Component fabrication and testing
equipment
Electronic components
Fiber optics
Laser related
Semiconductors
Energy/Natural Resources
Alternative energy
Energy conservation
Technology related products/equipment
Genetic Engineering
Monoclonal antibodies and hybridomas
Recombinant DNA (agricultural and
industrial)
Recombinant DNA (medical)
Industrial Products and Equipment
Chemicals
Controls and sensors
Energy management
Equipment and machinery
Other industrial automation
Plastics
Robotics/vision systems
Specialty materials
Medical/Health Related
Diagnostic equipment
Diagnostic test products
Disposable products
Drugs and medicines
Hospital and clinical labs
Medical services
Therapeutic equipment
Other
Agriculture, forestry, fishing
Education related
Finance and insurance
Publishing
Transportation
Will Not Consider
Real estate

Additional Information
Year Founded—1983
Capital Under Management—$35 million
Investments(1985-1st 6 months)—4
Invested(1985-1st 6 months)—$1.5 million
Method of Compensation—Return on
investment is of primary concern; do not
charge fees

ADLER & SHAYKIN

1631 Locust Street
Philadelphia, PA 19103
215-985-9999

Philip H. Behr, Sr. Ptnr.

See NEW YORK for full listing

ALLIANCE ENTERPRISE CORPORATION

1801 Market Street, 3rd Floor
Philadelphia, PA 19103
215-977-3925

Officers
William Priestley, Pres. & Chm.
Terrence Hicks, V.P.

Whom to Contact
Terrence Hicks

Type of Firm
MESBIC

Affiliation
Sun Co., Inc. (parent)

Industry Association Memberships
AAMESBIC
NASBIC

Project Preferences
Prefer role as deal originator but will also
invest in deals created by others
Type of Financing:
Second-stage
Leveraged buyout
Minimum Investment: $100,000
Preferred Investment (LBO): $200,000
Minimum Operating Data:
Annual Sales—$1.5 million
Annual Sales (LBO)—$5 million

Geographical Preferences
Northeast
Southwest

Industry Preferences

Communications
Cable television
Computer Related
Micro and mini computers
Software-applications
Software-artificial intelligence
Specialized turnkey systems

**Electronic Components and
Instrumentation**
Analytical and scientific instrumentation
Component fabrication and testing
equipment
Electronic components
Fiber optics
Laser related
Semiconductors
Energy/Natural Resources
Alternative energy
Coal related
Drilling and exploration services
Energy conservation
Minerals
Oil and gas exploration and production
Technology related products/equipment

Additional Information
Year Founded—1971
Method of Compensation—Return on
investment is most important, but also
charge for closing fees, service fees, etc.

ALUMINUM COMPANY OF AMERICA

1501 Alcoa Building
Pittsburgh, PA 15219
412-553-3884

Officers
Charles K. Ligon, V.P. Corporate Planning
Richard P. McCracken, Mgr. Inv. Analysis

Whom to Contact
Either of the above

Type of Firm
Industrial company investing own funds

Project Preferences
Prefer role in deals created by others
Type of Financing:
Second-stage
Later-stage expansion
Minimum Investment: $100,000
Preferred Investment: $500,000-$1 million
Minimum Operating Data:
Annual Sales—Nominal
P&L—Losses (profits projected after 2 years)

Geographical Preference
None

Industry Preferences

Communications
Satellite and microwave communications

Computer Related
Memory devices
Software-artificial intelligence
Consumer
Food and beverage products
**Electronic Components and
Instrumentation**
Analytical and scientific instrumentation
Component fabrication and testing
equipment
Electronic components
Fiber optics
Laser related
Semiconductors
Industrial Products and Equipment
Ceramics
Chemicals
Composites
Controls and sensors
Energy management
Equipment and machinery
High barrier packaging materials
Other industrial automation
Plastics
Robotics/vision systems
Separations materials and equipment
Specialty materials

Additional Information
Investments(1985-1st 6 months)—1
Invested(1985-1st 6 months)—$2 million

CEO VENTURE FUND

4516 Henry Street #402
Pittsburgh, PA 15213
412-687-3451

Partners
James Colker, Mgn. Ptnr.
William R. Newlin, Mgn. Ptnr.
Glen F. Chatfield, Gen. Ptnr.
Gene Yost, Gen. Ptnr.
Gary P. Golding, Exec. Fund Dir.

Whom to Contact
James Colker
William R. Newlin
Gary P. Golding

Type of Firm
Private venture capital firm investing
own capital

Affiliation
Parker/Hunter Incorporated, Pittsburgh
(investment advisors)

Project Preferences
Prefer role as deal originator but will also invest in deals created by others
Type of Financing:
Second-stage
Later-stage expansion
Leveraged buyout
Minimum Investment: $500,000
Preferred Investment: $500,000-$1 million
Minimum Operating Data:
Annual Sales—$1.5 million
P&L—Break even

Geographical Preferences
Within two hours of office
Southwestern Pennsylvania and surrounding states
National

Industry Preferences

Communications
Data communications
Computer Related
Computer graphics, CAD/CAM and CAE
Scanning related
Software-applications
Software-artificial intelligence
Software-systems
Specialized turnkey systems
Electronic Components and Instrumentation
Analytical and scientific instrumentation
Component fabrication and testing equipment
Electronic components
Fiber optics
Laser related
Semiconductors
Energy/Natural Resources
Technology related products/equipment
Genetic Engineering
Gene splicing and manufacturing equipment
Monoclonal antibodies and hybridomas
Recombinant DNA (agricultural and industrial)
Recombinant DNA (medical)
Industrial Products and Equipment
Basic metal and glass production
Chemicals
Controls and sensors
Energy management
Equipment and machinery
Other industrial automation
Plastics
Robotics/vision systems
Specialty materials
Medical/Health Related
Diagnostic equipment
Diagnostic test products
Therapeutic equipment

Additional Information
Year Founded—1985
Capital Under Management—$10 million
Method of Compensation—Return on investment is most important, but also charge for closing fees, service fees, etc.

CAPITAL CORP. OF AMERICA

225 South 15th Street #920
Philadelphia, PA 19102
215-732-1666

Officers
Martin M. Newman, Pres.
Barton M. Banks, Secy.

Whom to Contact
Martin M. Newman

Type of Firm
SBIC

Project Preferences
Prefer role as deal originator but will also invest in deals created by others
Type of Financing:
First-stage
Second-stage
Later-stage expansion
Leveraged buyout
Minimum Investment: Less than $100,000
Preferred Investment: $250,000-$500,000
Minimum Operating Data:
Annual Sales—$500,000

Geographical Preference
National

Industry Preferences

Communications
Cable television
Commercial communications
Data communications
Satellite and microwave communications
Telephone related
Computer Related
Computer graphics, CAD/CAM and CAE
Computer mainframes
Computer services
Memory devices
Micro and mini computers
Office automation
Scanning related
Software-applications
Software-artificial intelligence
Software-systems
Specialized turnkey systems
Terminals

Consumer
Hotels and resort areas
Distribution
Communications equipment
Computer equipment
Electronics equipment
Medical products
Electronic Components and Instrumentation
Analytical and scientific instrumentation
Component fabrication and testing equipment
Electronic components
Fiber optics
Laser related
Semiconductors
Industrial Products and Equipment
Chemicals
Controls and sensors
Energy management
Equipment and machinery
Medical/Health Related
Diagnostic equipment

Additional Information
Year Founded—1962
Capital Under Management—$5 million
Investments(1985-1st 6 months)—2
Invested(1985-1st 6 months)—$250,000
Method of Compensation—Return on investment is of primary concern; do not charge fees

---

CENTURY IV PARTNERS

1760 Market Street
Philadelphia, PA 19103
215-751-9444

Partners
Walter M. Aikman, Gen. Ptnr.
Charles A. Burton, Gen. Ptnr.
Thomas R. Morse, Sr. Assoc.
Michael Radow, Sr. Assoc.

Whom to Contact
Any of the above

Type of Firm
Private venture capital firm investing own capital

Industry Association Membership
NVCA

Project Preferences
Will function either as deal originator or investor in deals created by others

Type of Financing:
Startup
First-stage
Second-stage
Later-stage expansion
Leveraged buyout
Minimum Investment: $500,000
Preferred Investment: $500,000-$1 million
Minimum Operating Data:
Annual Sales—Nominal
P&L—Losses (profits projected after 2 years)

Geographical Preference
None

Industry Preferences

Communications
Cable television
Commercial communications
Data communications
Satellite and microwave communications
Telephone related
Computer Related
Computer graphics, CAD/CAM and CAE
Computer mainframes
Computer services
Memory devices
Micro and mini computers
Office automation
Scanning related
Software-applications
Software-artificial intelligence
Software-systems
Specialized turnkey systems
Terminals
Consumer
Computer stores/related services
Consumer products
Consumer services
Food and beverage products
Franchise businesses
Retailing
Distribution
Communications equipment
Computer equipment
Consumer products
Electronics equipment
Food products
Industrial products
Medical products
Electronic Components and Instrumentation
Analytical and scientific instrumentation
Component fabrication and testing equipment
Electronic components
Fiber optics
Laser related
Semiconductors

Energy/Natural Resources
Energy conservation
Technology related products/equipment
Genetic Engineering
Gene splicing and manufacturing equipment
Monoclonal antibodies and hybridomas
Recombinant DNA (agricultural and industrial)
Recombinant DNA (medical)
Research and manufacturing equipment
Industrial Products and Equipment
Chemicals
Controls and sensors
Energy management
Equipment and machinery
Other industrial automation
Plastics
Robotics/vision systems
Specialty materials
Medical/Health Related
Diagnostic equipment
Diagnostic test products
Disposable products
Drugs and medicines
Hospital and clinical labs
Medical services
Therapeutic equipment
Will Not Consider
Forestry, fishing
Minerals
Real estate

Additional Information
Year Founded—1983
Capital Under Management—$50 million
Investments(1985-1st 6 months)—7
Invested(1985-1st 6 months)—$4 million
Method of Compensation—Return on investment is of primary concern; do not charge fees

---

ERIE SMALL BUSINESS INVESTMENT COMPANY

32 West Eighth Street #615
Erie, PA 16501
814-453-7964

Officers
George R. Heaton, Pres. & Treas.
John E. Britton, Secy.
Thomas B. Hagen, Asst. Secy.
Joseph P. Scottino, Asst. Secy.
Jeffrey H. Heaton, Financial analyst

Whom to Contact
George R. Heaton
Jeffrey H. Heaton

Type of Firm
SBIC

Project Preferences
Will function either as deal originator or investor in deals created by others
Type of Financing:
Seed
Startup
First-stage
Second-stage
Leveraged buyout
Minimum Investment: $100,000
Preferred Investment: $100,000-$250,000
Preferred Investment (LBO): $100,000-$200,000
Minimum Operating Data:
Annual Sales—$1.5 million
P&L—Profits NBT over $200,000
Annual Sales (LBO)—$1.5 million and over

Geographical Preference
Northeast

Industry Preferences

Communications
Cable television
Commercial communications
Data communications
Satellite and microwave communications
Telephone related
Computer Related
Computer graphics, CAD/CAM and CAE
Computer mainframes
Computer services
Memory devices
Micro and mini computers
Office automation
Scanning related
Software-applications
Software-artificial intelligence
Software-systems
Specialized turnkey systems
Terminals
Consumer
Consumer products
Consumer services
Food and beverage products
Distribution
Communications equipment
Computer equipment
Consumer products
Electronics equipment
Food products
Industrial products
Medical products

**Electronic Components and
  Instrumentation**
Analytical and scientific instrumentation
Component fabrication and testing
  equipment
Electronic components
Fiber optics
Laser related
Semiconductors
Energy/Natural Resources
Alternative energy
Coal related
Drilling and exploration services
Energy conservation
Minerals
Oil and gas exploration and production
Technology related products/equipment
Industrial Products and Equipment
Chemicals
Controls and sensors
Energy management
Equipment and machinery
Other industrial automation
Plastics
Robotics/vision systems
Specialty materials
Medical/Health Related
Diagnostic equipment
Diagnostic test products
Disposable products
Drugs and medicines
Hospital and clinical labs
Medical services
Therapeutic equipment
Other
Publishing
Transportation

Additional Information
Year Founded—1985
Capital Under Management—$1.1 million
Method of Compensation—Return on
  investment is most important, but also
  charge for closing fees, service fees, etc.

**FIRST VALLEY CAPITAL
  CORPORATION**

Hamilton Financial Center #201
One Center Square
Allentown, PA 18101
215-776-6760

Officer
Matthew W. Thomas, Pres.

Type of Firm
SBIC

Affiliations
First Valley Bank
First Valley Corporation (Parent of
  First Valley Bank)

Industry Association Membership
NASBIC

Project Preferences
Will function either as deal originator or
  investor in deals created by others
Type of Financing:
Startup
First-stage
Leveraged buyout
Minimum Investment: Less than $100,000
Preferred Investment: Less than $100,000
Minimum Operating Data:
Annual Sales—Nominal
P&L—Losses (profits projected after 1 year)

Geographical Preference
Within two hours of office

Industry Preferences

Communications
Cable television
Telephone related
Computer Related
Computer graphics, CAD/CAM and CAE
Computer services
Software-applications
Consumer
Consumer products
Consumer services
Food and beverage products
Franchise businesses
Leisure and recreational products
Retailing
Distribution
Communications equipment
Medical products
**Electronic Components and
  Instrumentation**
Analytical and scientific instrumentation
Electronic components
Industrial Products and Equipment
Chemicals
Controls and sensors
Equipment and machinery
Other industrial automation
Plastics
Medical/Health Related
Diagnostic equipment
Diagnostic test products
Disposable products
Drugs and medicines
Hospital and clinical labs
Medical services
Therapeutic equipment

Other
Education related
Finance and insurance
Publishing
Will Not Consider
Hotels/motels
Real estate
Restaurants

Additional Information
Year Founded—1983
Capital Under Management—$600,000
Investments(1985-1st 6 months)—1
Invested(1985-1st 6 months)—$35,000
Method of Compensation—Return on
  investment is of primary concern; do not
  charge fees

FOSTIN CAPITAL CORP.

681 Andersen Drive
Pittsburgh, PA 15220
412-928-8900

Post Office Box 67
Pittsburgh, PA 15230

Officers
William F. Woods, Pres.
Thomas M. Levine, Exec. V.P.
David M. Martin, Treas.

Whom to Contact
Any of the above

Type of Firm
Private venture capital firm investing
  own capital
Investment banking or merchant banking
  firm investing own capital or funds of
  partners or clients

Affiliations
Foster Industries, Inc.
Foster Investment Company
Fostin Capital Associates

Industry Association Memberships
NASBIC
NVCA

Project Preferences
Will function either as deal originator or
  investor in deals created by others

Type of Financing:
Seed
Startup
First-stage
Second-stage
Leveraged buyout
Minimum Investment: $100,000
Preferred Investment: $500,000
Minimum Operating Data:
Annual Sales—Nominal
P&L—Losses (profits projected after 2 years)

Geographical Preference
National

Industry Preferences

Communications
Cable television
Commercial communications
Data communications
Satellite and microwave communications
Telephone related
Computer Related
Computer graphics, CAD/CAM and CAE
Computer mainframes
Computer services
Memory devices
Micro and mini computers
Office automation
Scanning related
Software-applications
Software-artificial intelligence
Software-systems
Specialized turnkey systems
Terminals
Consumer
Computer stores/related services
Consumer products
Consumer services
Food and beverage products
Franchise businesses
Leisure and recreational products
Restaurants
Distribution
Communications equipment
Computer equipment
Electronics equipment
Medical products
Electronic Components and Instrumentation
Analytical and scientific instrumentation
Component fabrication and testing equipment
Electronic components
Fiber optics
Laser related
Semiconductors

Genetic Engineering
Gene splicing and manufacturing equipment
Monoclonal antibodies and hybridomas
Recombinant DNA (agricultural and industrial)
Recombinant DNA (medical)
Industrial Products and Equipment
Chemicals
Controls and sensors
Equipment and machinery
Other industrial automation
Plastics
Robotics/vision systems
Specialty materials
Medical/Health Related
Diagnostic equipment
Diagnostic test products
Disposable products
Drugs and medicines
Hospital and clinical labs
Medical services
Therapeutic equipment

Additional Information
Year Founded—1982
Capital Under Management—$25 million
Investments(1985-1st 6 months)—11
Invested(1985-1st 6 months)—$1.9 million
Method of Compensation—Return on investment is of primary concern; do not charge fees

---

GENESIS SEED MANAGEMENT COMPANY

Five Great Valley Parkway #227
Malvern, PA 19355
215-648-3950

Other Office
Two Penn Center Plaza #410
Philadelphia, PA 19102
215-988-0010

Officers
Joel S. Lawson III, Chm. (Philadelphia)
Thomas A. Penn, Pres. (Malvern)

Whom to Contact
Thomas A. Penn

Type of Firm
Private venture capital firm investing own capital

Affiliation
Howard & Company (common ownership)

Project Preferences
Prefer role as deal originator but will also invest in deals created by others
Type of Financing:
Seed
Startup
First-stage
Minimum Investment: Less than $100,000
Preferred Investment: $250,000-$500,000
Minimum Operating Data:
Annual Sales—Nominal

Geographical Preference
Pennsylvania

Industry Preferences

Communications
Commercial communications
Data communications
Satellite and microwave communications
Telephone related
Computer Related
Computer graphics, CAD/CAM and CAE
Computer mainframes
Computer services
Memory devices
Micro and mini computers
Office automation
Scanning related
Software-applications
Software-artificial intelligence
Software-systems
Specialized turnkey systems
Terminals
Consumer
Consumer products
Consumer services
Food and beverage products
Franchise businesses
Distribution
Communications equipment
Computer equipment
Consumer products
Electronics equipment
Food products
Industrial products
Medical products
Electronic Components and Instrumentation
Analytical and scientific instrumentation
Component fabrication and testing equipment
Electronic components
Fiber optics
Laser related
Semiconductors
Energy/Natural Resources
Alternative energy
Technology related products/equipment

Genetic Engineering
Gene splicing and manufacturing equipment
Monoclonal antibodies and hybridomas
Recombinant DNA (agricultural and
industrial)
Recombinant DNA (medical)
Industrial Products and Equipment
Chemicals
Controls and sensors
Energy management
Equipment and machinery
Other industrial automation
Plastics
Robotics/vision systems
Specialty materials
Medical/Health Related
Diagnostic equipment
Diagnostic test products
Disposable products
Drugs and medicines
Hospital and clinical labs
Medical services
Therapeutic equipment
Other
Publishing
Transportation
Will Not Consider
Oil and gas exploration or production
Real estate
Restaurants
Retail businesses

Additional Information
Year Founded—1985
Capital Under Management—$5 million
Method of Compensation—Return on
investment is of primary concern; do not
charge fees

GREATER PHILADELPHIA VENTURE CAPITAL CORP.

225 South 15th Street #920
Philadelphia, PA 19102
215-732-3415

Officer
Martin M. Newman, Gen. Mgr.

Type of Firm
MESBIC

Project Preferences
Prefer role as deal originator but will also
invest in deals created by others

Type of Financing:
First-stage
Second-stage
Later-stage expansion
Leveraged buyout
Minimum Investment: Less than $100,000
Preferred Investment: $250,000-$500,000
Minimum Operating Data:
Annual Sales—$500,000

Geographical Preference
National

Industry Preferences

Communications
Cable television
Commercial communications
Data communications
Satellite and microwave communications
Telephone related
Computer Related
Computer graphics, CAD/CAM and CAE
Computer mainframes
Computer services
Memory devices
Micro and mini computers
Office automation
Scanning related
Software-applications
Software-artificial intelligence
Software-systems
Specialized turnkey systems
Terminals
Consumer
Hotels and resort areas
Distribution
Communications equipment
Computer equipment
Electronics equipment
Medical products
**Electronic Components and
Instrumentation**
Analytical and scientific instrumentation
Component fabrication and testing
equipment
Electronic components
Fiber optics
Laser related
Semiconductors
Industrial Products and Equipment
Chemicals
Controls and sensors
Energy management
Equipment and machinery
Medical/Health Related
Diagnostic equipment

Additional Information
Year Founded—1971
Capital Under Management—$5 million
Investments(1985-1st 6 months)—2
Invested(1985-1st 6 months)—$250,000

GROTECH PARTNERS, L.P.

Two Glenhardie Corporate Cntr.
1285 Drummers Lane #102
Wayne, PA 19087
215-964-1888

Other Office
100 Light Street, 9th Floor
Baltimore, MD 21202
301-752-4600

Partners
Edward F. Sager, Jr., Gen. Ptnr.
(Pennsylvania)
Frank A. Adams, Gen. Ptnr. (Maryland)
E. Rogers Novak, Jr., Gen. Ptnr. (Maryland)

Whom to Contact
Any of the above

Type of Firm
Private venture capital firm investing
own capital
Investment banking or merchant banking
firm investing own capital or funds of
partners or clients

Affiliation
Baker, Watts & Co. (general partner)

Project Preferences
Prefer role as deal originator but will also
invest in deals created by others
Type of Financing:
Second-stage
Later-stage expansion
Leveraged buyout
Minimum Investment: $250,000
Preferred Investment: $500,000-$1 million
Preferred Investment (LBO):
$1 million and over
Minimum Operating Data:
Annual Sales—$3 million
P&L—Profits NBT over $500,000
Annual Sales (LBO)—$10 million and over

Geographical Preference
Mid-Atlantic
East Coast

Industry Preferences

Communications
Cable television
Commercial communications
Data communications
Satellite and microwave communications
Telephone related
Computer Related
Computer graphics, CAD/CAM and CAE
Computer services
Memory devices
Micro and mini computers
Office automation
Software-applications
Software-artificial intelligence
Software-systems
Specialized turnkey systems
Terminals
Consumer
Computer stores/related services
Consumer products
Consumer services
Food and beverage products
Restaurants
Retailing
Distribution
Communications equipment
Computer equipment
Consumer products
Electronics equipment
Food products
Industrial products
Medical products
Electronic Components and Instrumentation
Analytical and scientific instrumentation
Component fabrication and testing equipment
Electronic components
Fiber optics
Laser related
Semiconductors
Energy/Natural Resources
Alternative energy
Drilling and exploration services
Energy conservation
Oil and gas exploration and production
Technology related products/equipment
Industrial Products and Equipment
Chemicals
Equipment and machinery
Other industrial automation
Plastics
Robotics/vision systems
Medical/Health Related
Diagnostic equipment
Drugs and medicines
Hospital and clinical labs
Medical services
Therapeutic equipment

Other
Finance and insurance

Additional Information
Year Founded—1984
Capital Under Management—Over $20 million
Investments(1985-1st 6 months)—4
Invested(1985-1st 6 months)—$2 million
Method of Compensation—Return on investment is of primary concern; do not charge fees

---

LAWRENCE HERBST INVESTMENT TRUST FUND

Post Office Box 1003
Milford, PA 18337

See TEXAS for full listing

HILLMAN VENTURES, INC.

2000 Grant Building
Pittsburgh, PA 15219
412-281-2620

Other Offices
2200 Sand Hill Road #240
Menlo Park, CA 94025
415-854-4653

450 Newport Center Drive #304
Newport Beach, CA 92660
714-644-7071

Officers
Philip S. Paul, Chm. & CEO (Menlo Park)
Stephen J. Banks, Pres. (Pittsburgh)
Kent L. Engelmeier, V.P. (Pittsburgh)
Jay D. Glass, V.P. (Newport Beach)
Howard W. Geiger, Jr., V.P. (Menlo Park)
William J. O'Connor, Cntlr. (Pittsburgh)
Marc Yagjian, V.P. (Pittsburgh)

Whom to Contact
Any of the above

Type of Firm
Venture capital subsidiary of non-financial corporation

Affiliation
The Hillman Company (parent)

Industry Association Membership
NVCA

Project Preferences
Will function either as deal originator or investor in deals created by others
Type of Financing:
Seed
Research and development partnerships
Startup
First-stage
Second-stage
Later-stage expansion
Leveraged buyout
Minimum Investment: $100,000
Preferred Investment: $500,000-$1 million

Geographical Preference
None

Industry Preferences

Communications
Commercial communications
Data communications
Satellite and microwave communications
Telephone related
Computer Related
Computer graphics, CAD/CAM and CAE
Computer mainframes
Computer services
Memory devices
Micro and mini computers
Scanning related
Software-applications
Software-artificial intelligence
Software-systems
Terminals
Distribution
Communications equipment
Computer equipment
Electronics equipment
Industrial products
Medical products
Electronic Components and Instrumentation
Analytical and scientific instrumentation
Electronic components
Laser related
Optics technology
Semiconductors
Energy/Natural Resources
Alternative energy
Coal related
Technology related products/equipment
Genetic Engineering
Monoclonal antibodies and hybridomas
Recombinant DNA (agricultural and industrial)
Recombinant DNA (medical)
Research and manufacturing equipment

Industrial Products and Equipment
Advanced materials
Chemicals
Equipment and machinery
Other industrial automation
Plastics
Process equipment
Robotics/vision systems
Medical/Health Related
Diagnostic equipment
Drugs and medicines
Hospital and clinical labs
Medical services
Therapeutic equipment
Other
Finance and insurance

Additional Information
Method of Compensation—Return on
investment is of primary concern; do not
charge fees

HOWARD & COMPANY

Two Penn Center Plaza
Philadelphia, PA 19102
215-988-0010

Officers
Graeme K. Howard, Jr., Ptnr.
Joel S. Lawson III, Mgn. Ptnr.
T. Patrick Hurley, Jr., Ptnr.
Michael A. Cuneo, Ptnr.
Gabriel F. Nagy, Sr. Consultant
Richard M. Corbin, Dir.

Whom to Contact
T. Patrick Hurley, Jr.
Michael A. Cuneo

Type of Firm
Corporate finance advisory firm evaluating
and analyzing venture projects and
arranging private placements

Project Preferences
Prefer role as deal originator
Type of Financing:
Second-stage
Later-stage expansion
Leveraged buyout
Minimum Investment: $500,000
Preferred Investment: $1 million-$5 million
Preferred Investment (LBO): $1 million
Minimum Operating Data:
Annual Sales—$5 million
P&L—Losses (profits projected after 2 years)
Annual Sales (LBO)—$10 million-$50 million

Geographical Preference
East Coast

Industry Preferences

Communications
Cable television
Commercial communications
Data communications
Satellite and microwave communications
Telephone related
Computer Related
Computer graphics, CAD/CAM and CAE
Computer services
Office automation
Software-applications
Software-systems
Specialized turnkey systems
Consumer
Computer stores/related services
Consumer products
Restaurants
Retailing
Distribution
Communications equipment
Computer equipment
Consumer products
Electronics equipment
Food products
Industrial products
Medical products
**Electronic Components and
Instrumentation**
Analytical and scientific instrumentation
Electronic components
Fiber optics
Laser related
Genetic Engineering
Gene splicing and manufacturing equipment
Industrial Products and Equipment
Controls and sensors
Equipment and machinery
Other industrial automation
Robotics/vision systems
Specialty materials
Medical/Health Related
Diagnostic equipment
Diagnostic test products
Disposable products
Drugs and medicines
Hospital and clinical labs
Medical services
Therapeutic equipment

Additional Information
Year Founded—1972
Method of Compensation—Professional fees

INNOVEST GROUP, INC.

1700 Market #1228
Philadelphia, PA 19103
215-564-3960

Officers
Richard E. Woosnam, Pres.
Nila K. Sendzik, V.P.
Christine A. Rogers

Whom to Contact
Richard E. Woosnam
Nila K. Sendzik

Type of Firm
Investment banking or merchant banking
firm investing own capital or funds of
partners or clients

Affiliation
Capital Management Corporation (subsidiary)

Project Preferences
Prefer role as deal originator but will also
invest in deals created by others
Type of Financing:
First-stage
Second-stage
Later-stage expansion
Leveraged buyout
Minimum Investment: $250,000
Preferred Investment: $500,000-$1 million
Minimum Operating Data:
Annual Sales—Nominal
P&L—Losses (profits projected after 1 year)

Geographical Preferences
Within two hours of office
Northeast
Southeast
East Coast

Industry Preferences

Communications
Commercial communications
Telephone related
Computer Related
Computer graphics, CAD/CAM and CAE
Computer services
Office automation
Distribution
Communications equipment
Electronics equipment
Industrial products
Medical products

Electronic Components and Instrumentation
Component fabrication and testing equipment
Electronic components
Laser related
Energy/Natural Resources
Alternative energy
Industrial Products and Equipment
Controls and sensors
Energy management
Equipment and machinery
Other industrial automation
Plastics
Robotics/vision systems
Medical/Health Related
Diagnostic equipment
Disposable products
Medical services
Therapeutic equipment
Other
Education related
Finance and insurance
Publishing
Real estate
Transportation

Additional Information
Year Founded—1971
Capital Under Management—$8 million
Investments(1985-1st 6 months)—1
Invested(1985-1st 6 months)—$250,000
Method of Compensation—Return on investment is most important, but also charge for closing fees, service fees, etc.

KEYSTONE VENTURE CAPITAL MANAGEMENT COMPANY

211 South Broad Street
Philadelphia, PA 19107
215-985-5519

Officers
G. Kenneth Macrae, Pres.
Robert A. Bezuch, Sr. V.P.
Timothy W. Cunningham, V.P.

Whom to Contact
Any of the above

Type of Firm
Private venture capital firm investing own capital

Affiliation
Butcher & Singer Inc. (general partner)

Industry Association Membership
NVCA

Project Preferences
Will function either as deal originator or investor in deals created by others
Type of Financing:
First-stage
Second-stage
Later-stage expansion
Leveraged buyout
Minimum Investment: $500,000
Preferred Investment: $500,000-$1 million
Minimum Operating Data:
Annual Sales—Nominal

Geographical Preference
Pennsylvania and adjacent states

Industry Preferences

Communications
Cable television
Commercial communications
Data communications
Satellite and microwave communications
Telephone related
Computer Related
Computer graphics, CAD/CAM and CAE
Computer mainframes
Computer services
Memory devices
Micro and mini computers
Office automation
Scanning related
Software-applications
Software-artificial intelligence
Software-systems
Specialized turnkey systems
Terminals
Consumer
Computer stores/related services
Consumer products
Consumer services
Food and beverage products
Franchise businesses
Leisure and recreational products
Restaurants
Retailing
Distribution
Communications equipment
Computer equipment
Consumer products
Electronics equipment
Food products
Industrial products
Medical products

Electronic Components and Instrumentation
Analytical and scientific instrumentation
Component fabrication and testing equipment
Electronic components
Fiber optics
Laser related
Semiconductors
Energy/Natural Resources
Alternative energy
Energy conservation
Technology related products/equipment
Industrial Products and Equipment
Chemicals
Controls and sensors
Energy management
Equipment and machinery
Other industrial automation
Plastics
Robotics/vision systems
Specialty materials
Medical/Health Related
Diagnostic equipment
Diagnostic test products
Disposable products
Drugs and medicines
Hospital and clinical labs
Medical services
Therapeutic equipment
Other
Transportation
Will Not Consider
Mining
Real estate
Foreign-based companies

Additional Information
Year Founded—1983
Method of Compensation—Return on investment is of primary concern; do not charge fees

---

KOPVENCO, INC.

Koppers Building #3100
Pittsburgh, PA 15219
412-227-2608

Officers
James A. Harris, Pres.
J. Roger Beidler, V.P. & Treas.
Dr. A.W. Lawrence, V.P.
R.R. Wingard, V.P.
H.J. Zeh, Jr., V.P.

Whom to Contact
James A. Harris
J. Roger Beidler

Type of Firm
Venture capital subsidiary or affiliate of non-financial corporation

Affiliation
Koppers Company, Inc. (parent)

Project Preferences
Will function either as deal originator or investor in deals created by others
Type of Financing:
Startup
First-stage
Second-stage
Leveraged buyout
Minimum Investment: No Limit
Preferred Investment: No preference
Minimum Operating Data:
Annual Sales—Nominal
P&L—Losses (profits projected after 3 years)

Geographical Preference
None

Industry Preferences

Electronic Components and Instrumentation
Fiber optics
Laser related
Energy/Natural Resources
Alternative energy
Coal related
Energy conservation
Minerals
Technology related products/equipment
Genetic Engineering
Recombinant DNA (agricultural and industrial)
Industrial Products and Equipment
Chemicals
Equipment and machinery
Other industrial automation
Robotics/vision systems
Specialty materials
Other
Agriculture, forestry, fishing
Transportation
Will Not Consider
Consumer products

Additional Information
Year Founded—1978
Capital Under Management
—Over $35 million
Investments(1985-1st 6 months)—5
Invested(1985-1st 6 months)—$1 million
Method of Compensation—Return on investment is of primary concern

NEPA MANAGEMENT CORP.

Ben Franklin Advanced
  Technology Center
Lehigh University
Bethlehem, PA 18015
215-865-6550

Officers
Frederick J. Beste III, Pres. & CEO
Myer M. Alperin, Chm.
David C. Hall, V.P.
L. Jack Bradt, Secy. & Treas.
Charles D. Snelling, Asst. Secy.

Whom to Contact
Frederick J. Beste, III
Glen R. Bressner

Type of Firm
Private venture capital firm investing own capital

Industry Association Membership
NASBIC

Project Preferences
Prefer role as deal originator but will also invest in deals created by others
Type of Financing:
Seed
Startup
First-stage
Second-stage
Leveraged buyout
Minimum Investment: Less than $100,000
Preferred Investment: $100,000-$750,000
Preferred Investment (LBO):
  $100,000-$750,000
Minimum Operating Data:
Annual Sales—Nominal
P&L—Losses (profits projected after 2 years)
Annual Sales (LBO)—$2 million-$50 million

Geographical Preference
Within two hours of office

Industry Preferences

Communications
Cable television
Commercial communications
Data communications
Satellite and microwave communications
Telephone related

Computer Related
Computer graphics, CAD/CAM and CAE
Computer mainframes
Computer services
Memory devices
Micro and mini computers
Office automation
Scanning related
Software-applications
Software-artificial intelligence
Software-systems
Specialized turnkey systems
Terminals
Consumer
Consumer products
Consumer services
Leisure and recreational products
Electronic Components and Instrumentation
Analytical and scientific instrumentation
Component fabrication and testing equipment
Electronic components
Fiber optics
Laser related
Semiconductors
Energy/Natural Resources
Alternative energy
Technology related products/equipment
Genetic Engineering
Gene splicing and manufacturing equipment
Monoclonal antibodies and hybridomas
Recombinant DNA (agricultural and industrial)
Recombinant DNA (medical)
Industrial Products and Equipment
Chemicals
Controls and sensors
Energy management
Equipment and machinery
Other industrial automation
Plastics
Robotics/vision systems
Specialty materials
Medical/Health Related
Diagnostic equipment
Diagnostic test products
Disposable products
Drugs and medicines
Hospital and clinical labs
Medical services
Therapeutic equipment

Additional Information
Year Founded—1984
Capital Under Management—$8 million
Investments(1985-1st 6 months)—2
Invested(1985-1st 6 months)—$430,000
Method of Compensation—Return on investment is of primary concern; do not charge fees

PENNSYLVANIA GROWTH INVESTMENT CORP.

1000 RIDC Plaza #311
Pittsburgh, PA 15238
412-963-9339

Officers
Wm. L. Mosenson, Pres.
Mary G. Dell, Exec. V.P.
R.J. Fleishman, Pres.
Karl F. Krieger, Treas.

Whom to Contact
Mary G. Dell
William L. Mosenson

Type of Firm
Private venture capital firm investing
own capital

Project Preferences
Prefer role as deal originator but will also
invest in deals created by others
Type of Financing:
Research and development partnerships
First-stage
Second-stage
Later-stage expansion
Leveraged buyout
Minimum Investment: $250,000
Preferred Investment: $250,000-$500,000
Minimum Operating Data:
Annual Sales—$500,000
P&L—Losses (profits projected after 2 years)

Geographical Preferences
Within two hours of office
Northeast
Southeast
East Coast
Midwest

Industry Preferences

Communications
Cable television
Commercial communications
Data communications
Telephone related
Computer Related
Computer graphics, CAD/CAM and CAE
Computer services
Scanning related
Software-applications
Software-artificial intelligence
Software-systems
Specialized turnkey systems

Consumer
Consumer products
Food and beverage products
Franchise businesses
Hotels and resort areas
Leisure and recreational products
Distribution
Communications equipment
Industrial products
Medical products
Electronic Components and Instrumentation
Analytical and scientific instrumentation
Component fabrication and testing
equipment
Electronic components
Fiber optics
Laser related
Semiconductors
Energy/Natural Resources
Technology related products/equipment
Industrial Products and Equipment
Chemicals
Controls and sensors
Equipment and machinery
Other industrial automation
Robotics/vision systems
Medical/Health Related
Diagnostic equipment
Diagnostic test products
Disposable products
Drugs and medicines
Hospital and clinical labs
Medical services
Therapeutic equipment
Other
Education related
Real estate
Will Not Consider
Mining
Oil and gas exploration and production
Restaurants
Retail businesses

Additional Information
Year Founded—1961
Method of Compensation—Return on
investment is of primary concern; do not
charge fees

PHILADELPHIA CITYWIDE DEVELOPMENT CORPORATION

100 South Broad Street #2032
Philadelphia, PA 19110
215-561-6600

Officers
Dean Rosencranz, Exec. V.P.
Thomas J. Patterson, Chm.
Stephen Muschanka, Venture Fund Mgr.

Whom to Contact
Stephen Muschanka

Type of Firm
Economic development corporation

Affiliations
Advanced Technology Center of
Southeastern Pennsylvania
(participating organization)
Philadelphia Small Business Venture Fund

Project Preferences
Will function either as deal originator or
investor in deals created by others
Type of Financing:
First-stage
Second-stage
Later-stage expansion
Minimum Investment: Less than $100,000
Preferred Investment: Less than $100,000
Minimum Operating Data:
Annual Sales—Nominal
P&L—Profitable after 1 year

Geographical Preference
Philadelphia

Industry Preferences
Businesses which are based on advanced
technology
Will Not Consider
Retail

Additional Information
Year Founded—1977
Capital Under Management—$3 million
Method of Compensation—Return on
investment is of primary concern; do not
charge fees

PHILADELPHIA INDUSTRIES, INC.

1401 Walnut Street
Second Floor
Philadelphia, PA 19102
215-569-9900

Officers
Jack Farber, Pres.
Steve Dubin, V.P. & Corp. Counsel
John J. Murray, V.P. Corp. Development
James G. Baxter, V.P. Finance
Margaret M. Quinn, V.P. & Secy.

Whom to Contact
John J. Murray

Type of Firm
Privately owned investment company
investing own capital

Affiliations
City Stores Company (subsidiary investment
company)
Bankers Securities Corporation (subsidiary
investment company)

Project Preferences
Prefer role as deal originator
Type of Financing:
Later-stage expansion
Leveraged buyout
Minimum Investment: $1 million
Preferred Investment: Over $1 million
Preferred Investment (LBO):
$10 million-$20 million
Minimum Operating Data:
Annual Sales—Over $3 million
P&L—Profits NBT over $1 million
Annual Sales (LBO)—$25 million-$50 million

Geographical Preference
Northeast

Industry Preferences

Communications
Cable television
Distribution
Communications equipment
Computer equipment
Consumer products
Electronics equipment
Food products
Industrial products
Medical products

Industrial Products and Equipment
Basic manufacturing
Chemicals
Equipment and machinery
Paper and metal conversion
Plastics
Specialty materials
Other
Direct mail marketing
Finance and insurance
Packaging
Printing
Specialty paper products
Will Not Consider
Computer hardware or software
Genetic engineering
Natural resource exploration
Real estate

Additional Information
Year Founded—1968
Capital Under Management—$50 million
Investments(1985-1st 6 months)—2
Invested(1985-1st 6 months)—$15 million
Method of Compensation—Return on
investment is most important, but also
charge for closing fees, service fees, etc.

PITTSBURGH SEED FUND PARTNERS

4516 Henry Street #102
Pittsburgh, PA 15213
412-687-5200

Other Office
Post Office Box 220
Laughlintown, PA 15655

General Partners
Thomas N. Canfield
L. Frank Demmler
J. Stuart Lovejoy
John R. Thorne

Whom to Contact
Any of the above

Type of Firm
Private venture capital firm investing
own capital

Project Preferences
Prefer role as deal originator
Type of Financing:
Seed
Startup
First-stage

Minimum Investment: $100,000
Preferred Investment: $250,000-$500,000
Minimum Operating Data:
Annual Sales—Nominal
P&L—Losses (profits projected after 3 years)

Geographical Preference
Southwest Pennsylvania

Industry Preferences

Communications
Data communications
Telephone related
Computer Related
Computer graphics, CAD/CAM and CAE
Computer services
Memory devices
Office automation
Scanning related
Software-applications
Software-artificial intelligence
Software-systems
Terminals
**Electronic Components and
Instrumentation**
Analytical and scientific instrumentation
Electronic components
Fiber optics
Laser related
Semiconductors
Energy/Natural Resources
Technology related products/equipment
Industrial Products and Equipment
Controls and sensors
Energy management
Equipment and machinery
Robotics/vision systems
Specialty materials
Medical/Health Related
Diagnostic equipment
Diagnostic test products
Disposable products
Medical services
Therapeutic equipment
Will Not Consider
Commodities
Energy exploration
Financial instruments
Real estate

Additional Information
Year Founded—1985
Capital Under Management—$8 million
Method of Compensation—Return on
investment is of primary concern; do not
charge fees

PNC VENTURE CAPITAL GROUP

PNB Building, 19th Floor
Fifth Avenue and Wood Street
Pittsburgh, PA 15222
412-355-2245

Officers
Gary J. Zentner, Pres.
David McL. Hillman, Exec. V.P. & Mgr.
Jeffrey H. Schutz, V.P.
Peter V. Del Presto, Inv. Analyst

Whom to Contact
Any of the above

Type of Firm
SBIC
Venture capital subsidiary of
  commercial bank

Affiliations
PNC Financial Corp. (parent)
PNC Merchant Banking Company

Industry Association Memberships
NASBIC
NVCA

Project Preferences
Will function either as deal originator or
  investor in deals created by others
Type of Financing:
First-stage
Second-stage
Later-stage expansion
Leveraged buyout
Minimum Investment: $150,000
Preferred Investment: $250,000-$500,000
Preferred Investment (LBO):
  $500,000-$1 million
Minimum Operating Data:
Annual Sales—Nominal
P&L—Losses (profits projected after 2 years)

Geographical Preferences
Northeast
Midwest

Industry Preferences

Communications
Cable television
Commercial communications

Computer Related
Computer graphics, CAD/CAM and CAE
Computer mainframes
Computer services
Memory devices
Micro and mini computers
Office automation
Scanning related
Software-applications
Software-artificial intelligence
Software-systems
Specialized turnkey systems
Terminals
Distribution
Communications equipment
Computer equipment
Electronics equipment
Industrial products
Medical products
**Electronic Components and
  Instrumentation**
Analytical and scientific instrumentation
Component fabrication and testing
  equipment
Electronic components
Fiber optics
Laser related
Semiconductors
Energy/Natural Resources
Coal related
Technology related products/equipment
Genetic Engineering
Gene splicing and manufacturing equipment
Industrial Products and Equipment
Chemicals
Controls and sensors
Energy management
Equipment and machinery
Other industrial automation
Plastics
Robotics/vision systems
Specialty materials
Medical/Health Related
Diagnostic equipment
Diagnostic test products
Disposable products
Drugs and medicines
Hospital and clinical labs
Medical services
Therapeutic equipment
Will Not Consider
Oil and gas exploration
Real estate

Additional Information
Year Founded—1981
Capital Under Management—$20 million
Investments(1985-1st 6 months)—5
Method of Compensation—Return on
  investment is of primary concern; do not
  charge fees

ROBINSON VENTURE PARTNERS

6507 Wilkins Avenue
Pittsburgh, PA 15217
412-661-1200

Partners
Stephen G. Robinson, Gen. Ptnr.
Donald M. Robinson, Gen. Ptnr.
Carol L. Robinson, Gen. Ptnr.
James M. Pekins, Inv. Analyst

Whom to Contact
Stephen G. Robinson

Type of Firm
Private venture capital firm investing
  own capital

Industry Association Membership
NVCA

Project Preferences
Will function either as deal originator or
  investor in deals created by others
Type of Financing:
Seed
Startup
First-stage
Second-stage
Leveraged buyout
Minimum Investment: Less than $100,000
Preferred Investment: $250,000-$500,000
Minimum Operating Data:
Annual Sales—Nominal
P&L—Losses (profits projected after 2 years)

Geographical Preferences
East Coast
Midwest

Industry Preferences

Communications
Cable television
Commercial communications
Data communications
Satellite and microwave communications
Telephone related

Computer Related
Computer graphics, CAD/CAM and CAE
Computer mainframes
Computer services
Memory devices
Micro and mini computers
Office automation
Scanning related
Software-applications
Software-artificial intelligence
Software-systems
Specialized turnkey systems
Terminals
Consumer
Retailing
Distribution
Communications equipment
Computer equipment
Consumer products
Electronics equipment
Food products
Industrial products
Medical products
Electronic Components and Instrumentation
Analytical and scientific instrumentation
Component fabrication and testing equipment
Electronic components
Fiber optics
Laser related
Semiconductors
Energy/Natural Resources
Technology related products/equipment
Genetic Engineering
Gene splicing and manufacturing equipment
Monoclonal antibodies and hybridomas
Recombinant DNA (agricultural and industrial)
Recombinant DNA (medical)
Industrial Products and Equipment
Chemicals
Controls and sensors
Energy management
Equipment and machinery
Other industrial automation
Plastics
Robotics/vision systems
Specialty materials
Medical/Health Related
Diagnostic equipment
Diagnostic test products
Disposable products
Drugs and medicines
Hospital and clinical labs
Medical services
Therapeutic equipment
Other
Education related

Additional Information

Year Founded—1982
Capital Under Management—Over $4 million
Investments(1985-1st 6 months)—2
Invested(1985-1st 6 months)—$925,000
Method of Compensation—Return on investment is of primary concern; do not charge fees

SAFEGUARD SCIENTIFICS INC.

630 Park Avenue
King of Prussia, PA 19406
215-265-4000

Officers

Warren V. Musser, Chm.
Adolf A. Paier, Pres.
Raymond H. Kraftson, V.P., Gen. Counsel, Secy.
Charles A. Root, V.P. Operations
Gerald M. Wilk, V.P. Finance
William T. Gillan, Treas.
Joseph F. Waterman, Dir. Corp. Development

Whom to Contact

Joseph F. Waterman

Type of Firm

Entrepreneurial company seeking alliances with emerging growth companies

Project Preferences

Prefer role as deal originator but will also invest in deals created by others
Type of Financing:
Second-stage
Leveraged buyout
Minimum Investment: $1 million
Preferred Investment: Over $2 million
Preferred Investment (LBO): $5 million and over
Minimum Operating Data:
Annual Sales—Over $3 million
P&L—Profitable
Annual Sales (LBO)—Over $10 million

Geographical Preference

None

Industry Preferences

Communications
Data communications
Satellite and microwave communications
Telephone related

Computer Related
Computer services
Micro and mini computers
Office automation
Scanning related
Software-applications
Software-artificial intelligence
Software-systems
Distribution
Communications equipment
Computer equipment
Electronics equipment
Electronic Components and Instrumentation
Component fabrication and testing equipment
Electronic components
Fiber optics
Laser related
Energy/Natural Resources
Energy conservation
Solar energy
Genetic Engineering
Monoclonal antibodies and hybridomas
Industrial Products and Equipment
Metal finishing
Other industrial automation
Robotics/vision systems
Other
Systems furniture

Additional Information

Year Founded—1953
Investments(1985-1st 6 months)—1
Invested(1985-1st 6 months)—$500,000
Method of Compensation—Return on investment is most important, but also charge for closing fees, service fees, etc.

SECURITY PACIFIC CAPITAL CORP./FIRST SBIC OF CALIFORNIA

Post Office Box 512
Washington, PA 15301
412-223-0707

Daniel Dye, Mgn. Ptnr.

See CALIFORNIA for full listing

SEED VENTURES, INC.

5 Great Valley Parkway #227
Malvern, PA 19355
215-648-3950

Officer
Thomas A. Penn, Pres.

Type of Firm
Consulting firm evaluating and analyzing
  venture projects and arranging private
  placements

Project Preferences
Prefer role as deal originator but will also
  invest in deals created by others
Type of Financing:
Seed
Startup
Leveraged buyout
Minimum Investment: $250,000
Preferred Investment: $500,000-$1 million
Preferred Investment (LBO):
  $10 million and over
Minimum Operating Data:
Annual Sales—Nominal
P&L—Losses (profits projected after 2 years)
Annual Sales (LBO)—$5 million and over

Geographical Preference
Northeast

Industry Preferences

Communications
Satellite and microwave communications
Computer Related
Micro and mini computers
Scanning related
Software-applications
Software-artificial intelligence
Software-systems
Consumer
Food and beverage products
Leisure and recreational products
Restaurants
**Electronic Components and
  Instrumentation**
Analytical and scientific instrumentation
Laser related
Semiconductors
Energy/Natural Resources
Alternative energy
Technology related products/equipment
Genetic Engineering
Gene splicing and manufacturing equipment

Industrial Products and Equipment
Controls and sensors
Energy management
Equipment and machinery
Other industrial automation
Robotics/vision systems
Specialty materials
Medical/Health Related
Diagnostic equipment
Diagnostic test products
Disposable products
Medical services
Therapeutic equipment

Additional Information
Year Founded—1985
Method of Compensation—Function primarily
  in service area; receive contingent fee in
  cash or equity

SOUTHEASTERN PENNSYLVANIA DEVELOPMENT FUND

One Penn Center at Suburban Station
Philadelphia, PA 19103
215-568-4677

Officers
Paul A. Mitchell, Pres.
Bryan E. Fischer, V.P.

Whom to Contact
Either of the above

Type of Firm
Long term secured lender

Project Preferences
Prefer role as deal originator but will also
  invest in deals created by others
Type of Financing:
Startup
First-stage
Second-stage
Later-stage expansion
Leveraged buyout
Minimum Investment: $100,000
Preferred Investment: $250,000-$500,000
Preferred Investment (LBO):
  $150,000-$600,000
Minimum Operating Data:
Annual Sales—$500,000
P&L—Break even
Annual Sales (LBO)—$500,000-$15 million

Geographical Preference
Southeastern Pennsylvania

Industry Preferences

Consumer
Computer stores/related services
Consumer products
Consumer services
Food and beverage products
Franchise businesses
Hotels and resort areas
Leisure and recreational products
Restaurants
Retailing
Industrial Products and Equipment
Chemicals
Controls and sensors
Energy management
Equipment and machinery
Other industrial automation
Plastics
Robotics/vision systems
Specialty materials

Additional Information
Year Founded—1963
Method of Compensation—Interest on
  loan principal

TDH II LIMITED

c/o K.S. Sweet Associates
259 Radnor Chester Road
Radnor, PA 19087
215-964-0112

c/o K.S. Sweet Associates
Post Office Box 259
Radnor, PA 19087

Partners
J.B. Doherty, Mgn. Gen. Ptnr.
Jarret B. Kling, Assoc. Gen. Ptnr.
Stephen W. Harris, Assoc.
Richard J. Loranger, Assoc.
Ellen J. Wiggins, Assoc.

Whom to Contact
Stephen W. Harris
Richard J. Loranger
Ellen J. Wiggins

Type of Firm
Private venture capital firm investing
  own capital

Affiliations
TDH Administrative Services, Inc. (corporate
  general partner)
TDH Inc. (affiliated predecessor)
TDH Capital Corporation (affiliated
  predecessor)

Project Preferences

Will function either as deal originator or investor in deals created by others
Type of Financing:
First-stage
Second-stage
Later-stage expansion
Leveraged buyout
Minimum Investment: $250,000
Preferred Investment: Over $1 million
Preferred Investment (LBO): $1.5 million
Minimum Operating Data:
Annual Sales—$500,000
P&L—Break even
Annual Sales (LBO)—$4 million-$50 million

Geographical Preference

None

Industry Preferences

Communications
Cable television
Commercial communications
Data communications
Satellite and microwave communications
Telephone related
Distribution
Communications equipment
Computer equipment
Consumer products
Electronics equipment
Food products
Industrial products
Medical products
Electronic Components and Instrumentation
Analytical and scientific instrumentation
Component fabrication and testing equipment
Electronic components
Fiber optics
Laser related
Semiconductors
Industrial Products and Equipment
Chemicals
Controls and sensors
Energy management
Equipment and machinery
Other industrial automation
Plastics
Robotics/vision systems
Specialty materials
Medical/Health Related
Diagnostic equipment
Diagnostic test products
Disposable products
Drugs and medicines
Hospital and clinical labs
Medical services
Therapeutic equipment

Additional Information

Year Founded—1971
Capital Under Management—$36 million
Investments(1985-1st 6 months)—6
Invested(1985-1st 6 months)—$3.5 million

TRIVEST VENTURE FUND

Post Office Box 36
Ligonier, PA 15658
412-471-0151

Other Office

1300 St. Mary's Street #210
Raleigh, NC 27605
919-834-9984

General Partners

Thomas W. Courtney
James H. Knowles, Jr.
Kennedy C. O'Herron

Whom to Contact

Thomas W. Courtney (Pennsylvania)
James H. Knowles, Jr. (Pennsylvania)
Floyd H. Moore, Jr. (Pennsylvania)
Kennedy C. O'Herron (North Carolina)
Clifford A. Clark (North Carolina)

Type of Firm

Private venture capital firm investing own capital

Project Preferences

Will function either as deal originator or investor in deals created by others
Type of Financing:
Startup
First-stage
Second-stage
Later-stage expansion
Leveraged buyout
Minimum Investment: $250,000
Preferred Investment: $250,000-$1 million

Geographical Preference

None

Industry Preferences

None

Additional Information

Year Founded—1984
Capital Under Management—$36.1 million
Investments(1985-1st 6 months)—4
Invested(1985-1st 6 months)—$2 million
Method of Compensation—Return on investment is of primary concern; do not charge fees

---

VENTURE ASSOCIATES

Two Penn Center Plaza #410
Philadelphia, PA 19102
215-988-0010

Officers

Michael A. Cuneo, Ptnr.
Richard M. Corbin, Dir.
George Groff
Steve N. Economou
Richard S. Gorodesky

Whom to Contact

Michael A. Cuneo

Type of Firm

Consulting firm evaluating and analyzing venture projects and arranging private placements

Project Preferences

Prefer role as deal originator
Type of Financing:
Seed
Startup
First-stage
Second-stage
Later-stage expansion
Leveraged buyout
Minimum Investment: $100,000
Preferred Investment: $250,000-$500,000
Preferred Investment (LBO): $1 million
Minimum Operating Data:
Annual Sales—Nominal
P&L—Losses (profits projected after 2 years)
Annual Sales (LBO)—$10 million-$50 million

Geographical Preference

East Coast

Industry Preferences

Communications
Data communications
Satellite and microwave communications
Telephone related

Computer Related
Computer graphics, CAD/CAM and CAE
Computer services
Office automation
Software-applications
Software-systems
Specialized turnkey systems
Consumer
Computer stores/related services
Consumer products
Restaurants
Retailing
Distribution
Communications equipment
Computer equipment
Consumer products
Electronics equipment
Food products
Industrial products
Medical products
**Electronic Components and
Instrumentation**
Analytical and scientific instrumentation
Electronic components
Fiber optics
Laser related
Genetic Engineering
Gene splicing and manufacturing equipment
Industrial Products and Equipment
Controls and sensors
Equipment and machinery
Other industrial automation
Robotics/vision systems
Specialty materials
Medical/Health Related
Diagnostic equipment
Diagnostic test products
Disposable products
Drugs and medicines
Hospital and clinical labs
Medical services
Therapeutic equipment

Additional Information
Year Founded—1982
Method of Compensation—Return on
  investment is of primary concern; do not
  charge fees

VENWEST PARTNERS

Westinghouse Electric Building
Gateway Center
Pittsburgh, PA 15222
412-642-5858

Other Office
Taylor and Turner
220 Montgomery St. Penthse. 10
San Francisco, CA 94104
415-398-6821

General Partners
John W. Brock, Jr., Pres. (Pittsburgh)
William H. Taylor II (California)
Marshall C. Turner, Jr. (California)

Whom to Contact
Any of the above

Type of Firm
Private venture capital firm investing
  own capital

Affiliation
Taylor & Turner, San Francisco

Project Preferences
Will function either as deal originator or
  investor in deals created by others
Type of Financing:
Seed
Startup
First-stage
Second-stage
Later-stage expansion
Minimum Investment: Less than $100,000
Preferred Investment: $500,000-$1 million
Minimum Operating Data:
Annual Sales—Nominal
P&L—Losses (profits projected after 2 years)

Geographical Preference
None

Industry Preferences

Communications
Data communications
Satellite and microwave communications

Computer Related
Computer graphics, CAD/CAM and CAE
Computer mainframes
Computer services
Memory devices
Micro and mini computers
Office automation
Scanning related
Software-applications
Software-artificial intelligence
Software-systems
Specialized turnkey systems
Terminals
Consumer
Consumer products
**Electronic Components and
Instrumentation**
Analytical and scientific instrumentation
Electronic components
Fiber optics
Laser related
Semiconductors
Energy/Natural Resources
Technology related products/equipment
Genetic Engineering
Gene splicing and manufacturing equipment
Monoclonal antibodies and hybridomas
Recombinant DNA (agricultural and
  industrial)
Recombinant DNA (medical)
Industrial Products and Equipment
Chemicals
Controls and sensors
Energy management
Equipment and machinery
Other industrial automation
Plastics
Process controls
Robotics/vision systems
Specialty materials
Medical/Health Related
Diagnostic equipment
Diagnostic test products
Disposable products
Drugs and medicines
Hospital and clinical labs
Medical services
Therapeutic equipment
Other
Military/aerospace

Additional Information

Year Founded—1983
Capital Under Management—$18.5 million
(with affiliates)
Investments(1985-1st 6 months)—12
Invested(1985-1st 6 months)—$1.8 million
Method of Compensation—Return on
investment is of primary concern; do not
charge fees

WYNDMOOR ASSOCIATES, LTD.

8600 Elliston Drive
Wyndmoor, PA 19118
215-233-3023

Other Offices

10 Parkway
Hanover, NH 03755
603-643-6346

5430 Pine Creek Drive
Orlando, FL 32811
305-423-0852

Principals

S. Penn Thomas (Pennsylvania)
Joseph J. Williams (Florida)
W. Bradley McConky (New Hampshire)

Whom to Contact

Any of the above

Type of Firm

Investment banking or merchant banking
firm investing own capital or funds of
partners or clients
Consulting firm evaluating and analyzing
venture projects and arranging private
placements

Project Preferences

Prefer role as deal originator
Type of Financing:
Leveraged buyout
Minimum Investment: $500,000
Preferred Investment: $500,000-$1 million
Minimum Operating Data:
Annual Sales—Nominal
P&L—Break even

Geographical Preferences

East Coast
West Coast
Near major metropolitan area

Industry Preferences

Communications
Satellite and microwave communications
Computer Related
Computer mainframes
Computer services
Micro and mini computers
Office automation
Software-applications
Software-systems
Terminals
Consumer
Computer stores/related services
Consumer products
Leisure and recreational products
Distribution
Communications equipment
Computer equipment
Consumer products
Electronics equipment
Food products
Industrial products
Medical products
**Electronic Components and
Instrumentation**
Analytical and scientific instrumentation
Electronic components
Semiconductors
Energy/Natural Resources
Energy conservation
Genetic Engineering
Research and manufacturing equipment
Industrial Products and Equipment
Advanced materials
Chemicals
Equipment and machinery
Other industrial automation
Plastics
Process controls
Medical/Health Related
Hospital and clinical labs
Medical services
Other
Agriculture, forestry, fishing
Publishing
Transportation
Will Not Consider
Restaurants
Furs
Gourmet foods

Additional Information

Year Founded—1984
Capital Under Management—$5.4 million
Investments(1985-1st 6 months)—3
Invested(1985-1st 6 months)—$1.5 million
Method of Compensation—Return on
investment is most important, but also
charge for closing fees, service fees, etc.
Professional fee required whether or
not deal closes

ZERO STAGE CAPITAL II—CENTRAL PENNSYLVANIA

416 Old Main
University Park, PA 16804
814-863-0532

Other Office

Zero Stage Equity Fund, L.P.
156 Sixth Street
Cambridge, MA 02142
617-876-5355

Partners

Paul M. Kelley, Mgn. Gen. Ptnr.
(Massachusetts)
Dennis R. Costello, Gen. Ptnr.
(Pennsylvania)
Gordon B. Baty, Gen. Ptnr. (Massachusetts)
Edward B. Roberts, Gen. Ptnr.
(Massachusetts)
Jerome Goldstein, Gen. Ptnr.
(Massachusetts)
Joseph P. Lombard, Special Ptnr.
(Massachusetts)

Whom to Contact

Dennis R. Costello

Type of Firm

Private venture capital firm investing
own capital

Project Preferences

Prefer role as deal originator but will also
invest in deals created by others
Type of Financing:
Seed
Minimum Investment: Less than $100,000
Preferred Investment: $100,000-$250,000
Minimum Operating Data:
Annual Sales—Nominal

Geographical Preference

Central/northern Pennsylvania

Industry Preferences

Communications
Cable television
Commercial communications
Data communications
Satellite and microwave communications
Telephone related
Computer Related
Computer graphics, CAD/CAM and CAE
Computer mainframes
Computer services
Memory devices
Micro and mini computers
Office automation
Scanning related
Software-applications
Software-artificial intelligence
Software-systems
Specialized turnkey systems
Terminals
Distribution
Communications equipment
Computer equipment
Consumer products
Electronics equipment
Food products
Industrial products
Medical products
Electronic Components and Instrumentation
Analytical and scientific instrumentation
Component fabrication and testing equipment
Electronic components
Fiber optics
Laser related
Semiconductors
Energy/Natural Resources
Alternative energy
Coal related
Energy conservation
Genetic Engineering
Gene splicing and manufacturing equipment
Monoclonal antibodies and hybridomas
Recombinant DNA (agricultural and industrial)
Recombinant DNA (medical)
Industrial Products and Equipment
Chemicals
Controls and sensors
Energy management
Equipment and machinery
Other industrial automation
Plastics
Robotics/vision systems
Specialty materials

Medical/Health Related
Diagnostic equipment
Diagnostic test products
Disposable products
Drugs and medicines
Hospital and clinical labs
Medical services
Therapeutic equipment
Other
Agriculture, forestry, fishing
Will Not Consider
Oil and gas exploration and development
Real estate
Retail

Additional Information

Year Founded—1985
Capital Under Management—Approximately $5 million
Method of Compensation—Return on investment is of primary concern; do not charge fees

DOMESTIC CAPITAL CORPORATION

815 Reservoir Avenue
Cranston, RI 02910
401-946-3310

Officer
Nathaniel B. Baker, Pres.

Type of Firm
SBIC

Industry Association Membership
NASBIC

Project Preferences
Will function either as deal originator or
investor in deals created by others
Type of Financing:
Second-stage
Later-stage expansion
Leveraged buyout
Minimum Investment: Less than $100,000
Preferred Investment: $100,000-$250,000
Preferred Investment (LBO):
$100,000-$300,000
Minimum Operating Data:
Annual Sales—$500,000
P&L—Break even
Annual Sales (LBO)—$1.5 million

Geographical Preference
Northeast

Industry Preferences

Communications
Cable television
Commercial communications
Data communications
Satellite and microwave communications
Telephone related
Consumer
Computer stores/related services
Consumer products
Consumer services
Food and beverage products
Franchise businesses
Hotels and resort areas
Leisure and recreational products
Restaurants
Retailing
Distribution
Communications equipment
Computer equipment
Consumer products
Electronics equipment
Food products
Industrial products
Medical products

**Electronic Components and
Instrumentation**
Analytical and scientific instrumentation
Component fabrication and testing
equipment
Electronic components
Fiber optics
Laser related
Semiconductors
Industrial Products and Equipment
Chemicals
Controls and sensors
Energy management
Equipment and machinery
Other industrial automation
Plastics
Robotics/vision systems
Specialty materials
Medical/Health Related
Diagnostic equipment
Diagnostic test products
Disposable products
Drugs and medicines
Hospital and clinical labs
Medical services
Therapeutic equipment
Other
Education related
Finance and insurance
Publishing
Real estate
Transportation

Additional Information
Year Founded—1984
Capital Under Management—$500,000
Investments(1985-1st 6 months)—3
Invested(1985-1st 6 months)—$200,000
Method of Compensation—Return on
investment is of primary concern; do not
charge fees

THE EARL KINSHIP CAPITAL CORPORATION

2401 Hospital Trust Tower
Post Office Box 248
Providence, RI 02903
401-831-4800

Other Offices
4711 Golf Road
Concourse 1, #801
Skokie, IL 60076
312-676-2131

10300 Southwest Greenburg Road
Suite 240
Portland, OR 97223
503-244-7307

Officers
Richard J. Ramsden, CEO, Pres. & Dir.
(Rhode Island)
Daniel C. Searle, V.P., Treas. & Dir (Illinois)
William L. Searle, V.P., Asst. Secy. & Dir.
(Illinois)
Wesley M. Dixon, Jr., V.P., Secy. & Dir.
(Illinois)

Whom to Contact
Richard J. Ramsden (Rhode Island)
Evangeline H. Rocha (Rhode Island)
Michael I. Block (Illinois)
John W. Dixon (Oregon)

Type of Firm
Private venture capital firm investing
own capital

Project Preferences
Will function either as deal originator or
investor in deals created by others
Type of Financing:
Research and development partnerships
Startup
Second-stage
Leveraged buyout
Minimum Investment: $1 million
Preferred Investment: $1 million-$2 million
Minimum Operating Data:
Annual Sales—Nominal
P&L—Losses (profits projected after 2 years)

Geographical Preference
National

Industry Preferences

Communications
Cable television
Computer Related
Computer graphics, CAD/CAM and CAE
Software-applications
Software-systems
Specialized turnkey systems
Consumer
Consumer products
Food and beverage products
Electronic Components and Instrumentation
Analytical and scientific instrumentation
Energy/Natural Resources
Hydroelectric projects
Oil and gas exploration and production
Genetic Engineering
Monoclonal antibodies and hybridomas
Medical/Health Related
Diagnostic equipment
Drugs and medicines
Medical services
Other
Finance and insurance
Real estate

Additional Information

Year Founded—1982
Capital Under Management—$60 million
Method of Compensation—Return on investment is of primary concern; do not charge fees

---

FLEET VENTURE PARTNERS

111 Westminster Street
Providence, RI 02903
401-278-6770

Other Office

60 State Street
Boston, MA 02109
617-367-6700

430 Park Avenue
New York, NY 10022

Partners

Robert M. Van Degna, Mgn. Ptnr. (Rhode Island)
James A. Saalfield, Gen. Ptnr. (Massachusetts)
Habib Y. Gorgi Gen. Ptnr. (New York)

Whom to Contact

Any of the above

Type of Firm

Venture capital affiliate of commercial bank
Coinvestor/marketing entity for affiliated venture firms

Affiliations

Fleet Growth Resources (general partner)
Fleet Financial Group (bank holding company, parent of Fleet Growth Resources and Fleet National Bank)
Fleet Venture Resources (SBIC subsidiary of Fleet National Bank)

Industry Association Memberships

NASBIC
NVCA

Project Preferences

Will function either as deal originator or investor in deals created by others
Type of Financing:
Seed
Startup
First-stage
Second-stage
Later-stage expansion
Leveraged buyout
Minimum Investment: $250,000
Preferred Investment: $500,000-$1 million
Preferred Investment (LBO): $1 million-$2 million
Minimum Operating Data:
Annual Sales—Nominal
P&L—Losses (profits projected after 3 years)
Annual Sales (LBO)—Less than $50 million

Geographical Preferences

Northeast
National (LBO)

Industry Preferences

Communications
Cable television
Commercial communications
Data communications
Radio and television broadcasting
Satellite and microwave communications
Telephone related
Consumer
Consumer products
Retailing
Electronic Components and Instrumentation
Analytical and scientific instrumentation
Component fabrication and testing equipment
Electronic components
Fiber optics
Laser related

Industrial Products and Equipment
Chemicals
Controls and sensors
Energy management
Equipment and machinery
Other industrial automation
Plastics
Robotics/vision systems
Specialty materials
Medical/Health Related
Diagnostic equipment
Diagnostic test products
Disposable products
Drugs and medicines
Hospital and clinical labs
Medical services
Therapeutic equipment

Additional Information

Year Founded—1967
Capital Under Management—$25 million
Investments(1985-1st 6 months)—4
Invested(1985-1st 6 months)—$1.6 million
Method of Compensation—Return on investment is of primary concern; fees charged in leveraged buyout financings

---

NARRAGANSETT CAPITAL CORPORATION

40 Westminster Street
Providence, RI 02903
401-751-1000

Officers

Arthur D. Little
Robert D. Manchester
Gregory P. Barber
Roger A. Vandenberg
William P. Lane

Whom to Contact

Gregory P. Barber
Roger A. Vandenberg

Type of Firm

Public venture capital firm investing own capital

Industry Association Memberships

NASBIC
NVCA

Project Preferences

Prefer role as deal originator
Type of Financing:
Leveraged buyout
Minimum Investment: $2 million
Preferred Investment: $5 million

Minimum Operating Data:
Annual Sales—$20 million
P&L—Must be profitable

Geographical Preference
None

Industry Preferences

Communications
Cable television

Additional Information
Year Founded—1959
Capital Under Management—$200 million
Investments(1985-1st 6 months)—5
Invested(1985-1st 6 months)—$25 million
Method of Compensation—Return on
    investment is most important, but also
    charge for closing fees, service fees, etc.

OLD STONE CAPITAL CORP.

One Old Stone Square
11th Floor
Providence, RI 02903
401-278-2559

Officer
Arthur C. Barton, Exec. V.P.

Type of Firm
SBIC
Venture capital subsidiary of a thrift
    institution

Affiliation
Old Stone Bank, a Federal Savings Bank
    (parent)

Industry Association Membership
NASBIC

Project Preferences
Prefer role as deal originator but will also
    invest in deals created by others
Type of Financing:
Later-stage expansion
Leveraged buyout
Minimum Investment: $100,000
Preferred Investment: $250,000-$500,000
Preferred Investment (LBO):
    $250 million-$750 million
Minimum Operating Data:
Annual Sales—$1.5 million
P&L—Break even

Geographical Preference
None

Industry Preferences

Communications
Cable television
Radio stations
Will Not Consider
High technology

RIHT CAPITAL CORPORATION

One Hospital Trust Plaza
Providence, RI 02903
401-278-8819

Other Office
796 Huntington Building
Cleveland, OH 44115
216-781-3655

Officers
Peter D. Van Oosterhout, Pres.
    (Rhode Island & Ohio)
Robert A. Comey, V.P. (Rhode Island)
Peter C. Canepa, V.P. (Rhode Island)

Whom to Contact
Any of the above

Type of Firm
SBIC
Venture capital subsidiary of
    commercial bank

Affiliation
Rhode Island Hospital Trust National Bank
    (parent)

Industry Association Membership
NASBIC

Project Preferences
Will function either as deal originator or
    investor in deals created by others
Type of Financing:
Second-stage
Later-stage expansion
Leveraged buyout
Minimum Investment: $100,000
Preferred Investment: $300,000-$750,000
Minimum Operating Data:
P&L—Break even

Geographical Preferences
Northeast
East Coast
Midwest
National

Industry Preferences

Communications
Cable television
Telephone related
Computer Related
Computer graphics, CAD/CAM and CAE
Office automation
Software-systems
Consumer
Hotels and resort areas
Leisure and recreational products
Distribution
Communications equipment
Computer equipment
Consumer products
Electronics equipment
Food products
Industrial products
Medical products
**Electronic Components and
    Instrumentation**
Analytical and scientific instrumentation
Component fabrication and testing
    equipment
Electronic components
Fiber optics
Laser related
Semiconductors
Energy/Natural Resources
Alternative energy
Coal related
Drilling and exploration services
Energy conservation
Minerals
Oil and gas exploration and production
Technology related products/equipment
Industrial Products and Equipment
Chemicals
Controls and sensors
Energy management
Equipment and machinery
Other industrial automation
Plastics
Robotics/vision systems
Specialty materials
Medical/Health Related
Diagnostic equipment
Diagnostic test products
Disposable products
Drugs and medicines
Hospital and clinical labs
Medical services
Therapeutic equipment
Other
Publishing
Real estate
Specialty consulting
Transportation

Additional Information

Year Founded—1982
Capital Under Management—$20.9 million
Investments(1985-1st 6 months)—14
Invested(1985-1st 6 months)—$2.1 million
Method of Compensation—Return on
    investment is of primary concern; do not
    charge fees

CAROLINA VENTURE CAPITAL CORP.

14 Archer Road
Hilton Head Island, SC 29928
803-842-3101

See NORTH CAROLINA for full listing

CHARLESTON CAPITAL CORPORATION

111 Church Street
Post Office Box 328
Charleston, SC 29402
803-723-6464

Officers
Henry Yaschik, Pres.
Thomas M. Ervin

Whom to Contact
Thomas M. Ervin

Type of Firm
SBIC

Industry Association Membership
NASBIC

Project Preferences
Prefer role as deal originator but will also
  invest in deals created by others
Type of Financing:
First-stage
Second-stage
Later-stage expansion
Leveraged buyout
Minimum Investment: Less than $100,000
Preferred Investment: $100,000-$250,000
Minimum Operating Data:
Annual Sales—Nominal
P&L—Break even

Geographical Preference
Southeast

Industry Preferences

Communications
Cable television
Commercial communications
Data communications
Satellite and microwave communications
Telephone related

Consumer
Computer stores/related services
Consumer products
Consumer services
Food and beverage products
Franchise businesses
Hotels and resort areas
Leisure and recreational products
Restaurants
Retailing
Distribution
Communications equipment
Computer equipment
Consumer products
Electronics equipment
Food products
Industrial products
Medical products
Industrial Products and Equipment
Chemicals
Controls and sensors
Energy management
Equipment and machinery
Other industrial automation
Plastics
Robotics/vision systems
Specialty materials
Other
Agriculture, forestry, fishing
Education related
Finance and insurance
Publishing
Real estate
Specialty consulting
Transportation
Will Not Consider
Projects ineligible for SBIC investment

Additional Information
Year Founded—1961
Capital Under Management—$2.3 million
Investments(1985-1st 6 months)—8
Invested(1985-1st 6 months)—$680,000
Method of Compensation—Return on
  investment is most important, but also
  charge for closing fees, service fees, etc.

REEDY RIVER VENTURES, INC.

400 Haywood Road
Post Office Box 17526
Greenville, SC 29606
803-297-9198

General Partners
John M. Sterling, Jr.
Tecumeh C. Hooper, Jr.

Whom to Contact
Either of the above

Type of Firm
SBIC

Industry Association Membership
NASBIC

Project Preferences
Will function either as deal originator or
  investor in deals created by others
Type of Financing:
Second-stage
Later-stage expansion
Leveraged buyout
Minimum Investment: $100,000
Preferred Investment: $100,000-$250,000
Preferred Investment (LBO): $350,000
Minimum Operating Data:
Annual Sales—$500,000
P&L—Losses (profits projected after 1 year)
Annual Sales (LBO)—$5 million and over

Geographical Preference
Southeast

Industry Preferences

Communications
Cable television
Commercial communications
Data communications
Satellite and microwave communications
Telephone related
Computer Related
Computer services
Office automation
Software-applications
Consumer
Computer stores/related services
Food and beverage products
Franchise businesses

Distribution
Communications equipment
Computer equipment
Consumer products
Electronics equipment
Food products
Industrial products
Medical products
**Electronic Components and
    Instrumentation**
Analytical and scientific instrumentation
Component fabrication and testing
    equipment
Electronic components
Fiber optics
Laser related
Semiconductors
Energy/Natural Resources
Alternative energy
Energy conservation
Industrial Products and Equipment
Chemicals
Controls and sensors
Energy management
Equipment and machinery
Other industrial automation
Plastics
Robotics/vision systems
Specialty materials
Medical/Health Related
Diagnostic equipment
Diagnostic test products
Disposable products
Drugs and medicines
Hospital and clinical labs
Medical services
Therapeutic equipment
Other
Real estate
Transportation

Additional Information

Year Founded—1981
Capital Under Management—$4 million
Investments(1985-1st 6 months)—2
Invested(1985-1st 6 months)—$400,000
Method of Compensation—Long term capital
    gain and current interest; also charge for
    closing fees, service fees, etc.

DAVIS GROUP

1431 Cherokee Trail, Box 59
Knoxville, TN 37920
615-579-5180

See NEW YORK for full listing

LAWRENCE VENTURE ASSOCIATES

3401 West End Avenue #680
Nashville, TN 37203
615-383-0982

Jack Tyrrell, Gen. Ptnr.
W. Patrick Ortale III, Gen. Ptnr.
Thomas A. Gallagher, Assoc.

See NEW YORK for full listing

MASSEY BURCH INVESTMENT GROUP, INC.

310 25th Avenue North
Nashville, TN 37203
615-329-9448

Officers
Jack C. Massey, Chm.
Lucius E. Burch III, Pres.
Frank B. Sheffield, V.P.
Donald M. Johnston, V.P.
E. Townes Duncan, V.P.
Robert C. Fisher, Jr., Inv. Analyst

Whom to Contact
Any of the above

Type of Firm
Investment banking or merchant banking firm investing own capital or funds of partners or clients

Affiliation
First Nashville Corp. (majority owned subsidiary)

Project Preferences
Prefer role as deal originator but will also invest in deals created by others
Type of Financing:
First-stage
Second-stage
Later-stage expansion
Leveraged buyout
Minimum Investment: $500,000
Preferred Investment: $500,000-$2 million

Minimum Operating Data:
Annual Sales—Nominal
P&L—Losses (profits projected after 2 years)

Geographical Preferences
Southeast
Southwest
Gulf States

Industry Preferences

Communications
Cable television
Commercial communications
Data communications
Satellite and microwave communications
Telephone related
Computer Related
Computer services
Software-applications
Software-artificial intelligence
Software-systems
Specialized turnkey systems
Consumer
Franchise businesses
Distribution
Medical products
Electronic Components and Instrumentation
Analytical and scientific instrumentation
Component fabrication and testing equipment
Electronic components
Fiber optics
Laser related
Semiconductors
Energy/Natural Resources
Alternative energy
Energy conservation
Technology related products/equipment
Genetic Engineering
Agriculture related
Biotechnology
Monoclonal antibodies and hybridomas
Industrial Products and Equipment
Controls and sensors
Energy management
Other industrial automation
Robotics/vision systems
Medical/Health Related
Diagnostic equipment
Diagnostic test products
Disposable products
Drugs and medicines
Hospital and clinical labs
Medical services
Therapeutic equipment

Other
Education related
Finance and insurance
Service related industries, particularly privatization opportunities

Additional Information
Year Founded—1968
Capital Under Management— Over $100 million
Investments(1985-1st 6 months)—7
Invested(1985-1st 6 months)—$10.3 million
Method of Compensation—Return on investment is most important, but also charge for closing fees, service fees, etc.

TENNESSEE EQUITY CAPITAL CORPORATION

1102 Stonewall Jackson
Nashville, TN 37220
615-373-4502

Officer
Walter S. Cohen, Chm.

Type of Firm
Private venture capital firm investing own capital
MESBIC

Industry Association Membership
NASBIC

Project Preferences
Prefer role as deal originator but will also invest in deals created by others
Type of Financing:
First-stage
Second-stage
Later-stage expansion
Leveraged buyout
Minimum Investment: Less than $100,000
Preferred Investment: $250,000-$500,000
Minimum Operating Data:
Annual Sales—$1.5 million
P&L—Break even
Annual Sales (LBO)—$2 million-$15 million

Geographical Preferences
National
Carribean Basin

Industry Preferences

Communications
Cable television
Data communications
Satellite and microwave communications
Telephone related
Consumer
Consumer products
Consumer services
Food and beverage products
Franchise businesses
Hotels and resort areas
Leisure and recreational products
Restaurants
Electronic Components and Instrumentation
Fiber optics
Laser related
Industrial Products and Equipment
Manufacture of consumer goods
Robotics/vision systems
Other
Finance and insurance
Publishing
Real estate
Specialty consulting
Will Not Consider
Commodity related businesses
Oil and gas
Precious metals

Additional Information

Year Founded—1978
Method of Compensation—Return on investment is most important, but also charge for closing fees, service fees, etc.

TENNESSEE VENTURE CAPITAL CORP.

162 Fourth Avenue North
Post Office Box 2567
Nashville, TN 37219
615-244-6935

Officer

Wendell Knox, Pres.

Type of Firm
MESBIC

Industry Association Membership
AAMESBIC

Project Preferences
Prefer role as deal originator but will also invest in deals created by others

Type of Financing:
Second-stage
Leveraged buyout
Minimum Investment: Less than $100,000
Preferred Investment: Less than $100,000
Minimum Operating Data:
Annual Sales—Nominal
P&L—Break even

Geographical Preference
Tennessee only

Industry Preferences

Communications
Data communications
Computer Related
Computer graphics, CAD/CAM and CAE
Computer mainframes
Computer services
Memory devices
Micro and mini computers
Office automation
Scanning related
Software-applications
Software-artificial intelligence
Software-systems
Specialized turnkey systems
Terminals
Distribution
Communications equipment
Computer equipment
Consumer products
Electronics equipment
Food products
Industrial products
Medical products
Electronic Components and Instrumentation
Analytical and scientific instrumentation
Component fabrication and testing equipment
Electronic components
Fiber optics
Laser related
Semiconductors
Energy/Natural Resources
Energy conservation
Technology related products/equipment
Industrial Products and Equipment
Chemicals
Controls and sensors
Energy management
Equipment and machinery
Other industrial automation
Plastics
Robotics/vision systems
Specialty materials

Medical/Health Related
Diagnostic equipment
Diagnostic test products
Disposable products
Drugs and medicines
Hospital and clinical labs
Medical services
Therapeutic equipment

Additional Information
Year Founded—1979
Capital Under Management—$1 million
Investments(1985-1st 6 months)—1
Invested(1985-1st 6 months)—$100,000
Method of Compensation—Return on investment is of primary concern; do not charge fees

---

VALLEY CAPITAL CORPORATION

Krystal Building #806
Chattanooga, TN 37402
615-265-1557

Officers
Lamar J. Partridge, Pres.
Ivena Faye Munger, Exec. Secy./Admin. Asst.

Whom to Contact
Ivena Faye Munger

Type of Firm
MESBIC

Industry Association Memberships
AAMESBIC
NASBIC

Project Preferences
Prefer role as deal originator but will also invest in deals created by others
Type of Financing:
Second-stage
Later-stage expansion
Leveraged buyout
Minimum Investment: Less than $100,000
Preferred Investment: $100,000-$250,000
Preferred Investment (LBO): $150,000
Minimum Operating Data:
Annual Sales—Nominal
P&L—Profits NBT over $50,000
Annual Sales (LBO)—$400,000 and over

Geographical Preference
Within 4 hours of office

Industry Preferences

Communications
Cable television
Commercial communications
Data communications
Satellite and microwave communications
Telephone related
Computer Related
Software-systems
Consumer
Computer stores/related services
Consumer products
Consumer services
Food and beverage products
Franchise businesses
Leisure and recreational products
Restaurants
Retailing
Distribution
Communications equipment
Computer equipment
Consumer products
Electronics equipment
Food products
Industrial products
Medical products
Electronic Components and Instrumentation
Electronic components
Energy/Natural Resources
Alternative energy
Coal related
Energy conservation
Industrial Products and Equipment
Chemicals
Controls and sensors
Energy management
Equipment and machinery
Other industrial automation
Plastics
Robotics/vision systems
Specialty materials
Medical/Health Related
Diagnostic equipment
Disposable products
Therapeutic equipment
Other
Transportation
Will Not Consider
Motion pictures
Promotion companies

Additional Information

Year Founded—1982
Capital Under Management—$1 million
Method of Compensation—Return on investment is most important, but also charge for closing fees, service fees, etc.

WEST TENNESSEE VENTURE CAPITAL CORPORATION

152 Beale Street
Post Office Box 300
Memphis, TN 38101
901-527-6091

Officers

Richard S. Moody, Chm.
Osbie L. Howard, Pres.
Peter R. Pettit, Secy.
Ernest Owens, Treas.
Bennie L. Marshall, Mgr.

Whom to Contact

Bennie L. Marshall

Type of Firm

MESBIC

Industry Association Memberships

AAMESBIC
NASBIC

Project Preferences

Will function either as deal originator or investor in deals created by others
Type of Financing:
First-stage
Second-stage
Later-stage expansion
Leveraged buyout
Minimum Investment: Less than $100,000
Preferred Investment: $100,000-$250,000
Preferred Investment (LBO): $150,000
Minimum Operating Data:
Annual Sales—Nominal
P&L—Break even
Annual Sales (LBO)—$500,000-$2 million

Geographical Preference

Southeast

Industry Preferences

Communications
Commercial communications
Telephone related

Computer Related
Computer graphics, CAD/CAM and CAE
Computer mainframes
Computer services
Memory devices
Micro and mini computers
Office automation
Scanning related
Software-applications
Software-artificial intelligence
Software-systems
Specialized turnkey systems
Terminals
Consumer
Franchise businesses
Distribution
Communications equipment
Computer equipment
Consumer products
Electronics equipment
Food products
Industrial products
Medical products
Electronic Components and Instrumentation
Analytical and scientific instrumentation
Component fabrication and testing equipment
Electronic components
Fiber optics
Laser related
Semiconductors
Genetic Engineering
Gene splicing and manufacturing equipment
Industrial Products and Equipment
Controls and sensors
Equipment and machinery
Medical/Health Related
Diagnostic equipment
Diagnostic test products
Disposable products
Drugs and medicines
Hospital and clinical labs
Medical services
Therapeutic equipment
Will Not Consider
Passive real estate deals

Additional Information

Year Founded—1982
Capital Under Management—$1.3 million
Investments(1985-1st 6 months)—4
Invested(1985-1st 6 months)—$495,000
Method of Compensation—Return on investment is most important, but also charge for closing fees, service fees, etc.

ALLIED BANCSHARES CAPITAL CORPORATION

Post Office Box 3326
Houston, TX 77253
713-226-1625

Officers
Philip A. Tuttle, Pres.
Mary D. Bass, Inv. Officer

Whom to Contact
Either of the above

Type of Firm
SBIC

Affiliation
Allied Bancshares, Inc. (parent—bank holding company)

Industry Association Membership
NASBIC

Project Preferences
Will function either as deal originator or investor in deals created by others
Type of Financing:
Second-stage
Leveraged buyout
Minimum Investment: $250,000
Preferred Investment: $500,000-$1 million
Minimum Operating Data:
Annual Sales—Nominal
P&L—Losses (profits projected after 2 years)

Geographical Preferences
Southwest
National

Industry Preferences

Communications
Cable television
Commercial communications
Data communications
Satellite and microwave communications
Telephone related
Computer Related
Computer graphics, CAD/CAM and CAE
Computer mainframes
Computer services
Memory devices
Micro and mini computers
Office automation
Scanning related
Software-applications
Software-artificial intelligence
Software-systems
Specialized turnkey systems
Terminals

Consumer
Computer stores/related services
Consumer products
Consumer services
Food and beverage products
Franchise businesses
Hotels and resort areas
Leisure and recreational products
Restaurants
Retailing
Distribution
Communications equipment
Computer equipment
Consumer products
Electronics equipment
Food products
Industrial products
Medical products
Electronic Components and Instrumentation
Analytical and scientific instrumentation
Component fabrication and testing equipment
Electronic components
Fiber optics
Laser related
Semiconductors
Energy/Natural Resources
Alternative energy
Coal related
Drilling and exploration services
Energy conservation
Minerals
Oil and gas exploration and production
Technology related products/equipment
Genetic Engineering
Gene splicing and manufacturing equipment
Monoclonal antibodies and hybridomas
Recombinant DNA (agricultural and industrial)
Recombinant DNA (medical)
Industrial Products and Equipment
Chemicals
Controls and sensors
Energy management
Equipment and machinery
Other industrial automation
Plastics
Robotics/vision systems
Specialty materials
Medical/Health Related
Diagnostic equipment
Diagnostic test products
Disposable products
Drugs and medicines
Hospital and clinical labs
Medical services
Therapeutic equipment

Other
Agriculture, forestry, fishing
Education related
Finance and insurance
Publishing
Real estate
Specialty consulting
Transportation

Additional Information
Year Founded—1979
Capital Under Management—$20 million
Investments(1985-1st 6 months)—4
Invested(1985-1st 6 months)—$1.9 million
Method of Compensation—Return on investment is most important, but also charge for closing fees, service fees, etc.

AMERICAP CORPORATION

One Shell Plaza
910 Louisiana, Third Floor
Houston, TX 77002
713-221-4909

Officers
Jim Hurn, Pres.
Ben Andrews, V.P.

Whom to Contact
Either of the above

Type of Firm
SBIC

Industry Association Membership
NASBIC

Project Preferences
Will function either as deal originator or investor in deals created by others
Type of Financing:
Leveraged buyout
Minimum Investment: $100,000
Preferred Investment: $100,000-$250,000
Minimum Operating Data:
Annual Sales—Nominal
P&L—Break even

Geographical Preferences
Southwest
Gulf States

Industry Preferences

Computer Related
Computer graphics, CAD/CAM and CAE
Computer mainframes
Computer services
Memory devices
Micro and mini computers
Scanning related
Scanning related
Software-applications
Software-artificial intelligence
Software-systems
Specialized turnkey systems
Terminals
Distribution
Communications equipment
Computer equipment
Consumer products
Electronics equipment
Food products
Industrial products
Medical products
Energy/Natural Resources
Technology related products/equipment
Industrial Products and Equipment
Equipment and machinery
Robotics/vision systems
Medical/Health Related
Diagnostic equipment
Diagnostic test products
Disposable products
Drugs and medicines
Hospital and clinical labs
Medical services
Therapeutic equipment

Additional Information
Year Founded—1983
Capital Under Management—$4 million
Method of Compensation—Return on
 investment is of primary concern; do not
 charge fees

BENTSEN INVESTMENT COMPANY

4600 Post Oak Place #100
Houston, TX 77027
713-627-9111

Officer
Lloyd M. Bentsen III, Chm.

Type of Firm
Private venture capital firm investing
 own capital
Investment banking or merchant banking
 firm investing own capital or funds of
 partners or clients

Affiliations
Triad Ventures Limited (co-managed venture
 capital fund)
Financial Services of Austin, Texas
 (joint venture)
MSI Capital of Dallas, Texas (joint venture)

Project Preferences
Prefer role as deal originator but will also
 invest in deals created by others
Type of Financing:
Second-stage
Later-stage expansion
Leveraged buyout
Minimum Investment: $500,000
Preferred Investment: $1 million-$2 million
Minimum Operating Data:
Annual Sales—$1.5 million
P&L—Break even

Geographical Preference
Texas

Industry Preferences
None

Additional Information
Year Founded—1979
Capital Under Management—
 Over $15 million (including affiliates)
Method of Compensation—Function primarily
 in service area; receive contingent fee in
 cash or equity

BRITTANY CAPITAL COMPANY

2424 LTV Tower
Dallas, TX 75201
214-742-5810

General Partners
Robert E. Clements
Steven S. Peden

Whom to Contact
Steven S. Peden

Type of Firm
SBIC

Industry Association Membership
NASBIC

Project Preferences
Will function either as deal originator or
 investor in deals created by others

Type of Financing:
Second-stage
Later-stage expansion
Leveraged buyout
Minimum Investment: $100,000
Preferred Investment: $100,000-$250,000

Geographical Preference
None

Industry Preferences
None

Additional Information
Year Founded—1969
Capital Under Management—$4 million
Investments(1985-1st 6 months)—4
Invested(1985-1st 6 months)—$500,000
Method of Compensation—Return on
 investment is of primary concern; do not
 charge fees

CAPITAL SOUTHWEST CORPORATION

12900 Preston Road #700
Dallas, TX 75230
214-233-8242

Officers
William R. Thomas, Pres. & Chm.
J. Bruce Duty, V.P./Secy./Treas.
Patrick F. Hamner, Inv. Assoc.

Whom to Contact
Any of the above

Type of Firm
Publicly held venture firm investing
 own capital

Affiliation
Capital Southwest Venture Corporation
 (wholly-owned SBIC)

Industry Association Memberships
NASBIC
NVCA

Project Preferences
Will function either as deal originator or
 investor in deals created by others
Type of Financing:
First-stage
Second-stage
Later-stage expansion
Minimum Investment: $300,000
Preferred Investment: $300,000-$2 million

Minimum Operating Data:
Annual Sales—$500,000
P&L—Losses (profits projected after 1 year)

Geographical Preference
None

Industry Preferences

Communications
Data communications
Telephone related
Computer Related
Computer graphics, CAD/CAM and CAE
Computer mainframes
Computer services
Memory devices
Micro and mini computers
Office automation
Scanning related
Software-applications
Software-artificial intelligence
Software-systems
Specialized turnkey systems
Terminals
Consumer
Consumer products
Food and beverage products
Retailing
Distribution
Communications equipment
Computer equipment
Consumer products
Electronics equipment
Food products
Industrial products
Medical products
Electronic Components and Instrumentation
Analytical and scientific instrumentation
Component fabrication and testing equipment
Electronic components
Fiber optics
Laser related
Semiconductors
Energy/Natural Resources
Minerals
Oil and gas exploration and production
Technology related products/equipment
Genetic Engineering
Recombinant DNA (agricultural and industrial)
Recombinant DNA (medical)

Industrial Products and Equipment
Chemicals
Controls and sensors
Energy management
Equipment and machinery
Other industrial automation
Plastics
Robotics/vision systems
Specialty materials
Medical/Health Related
Diagnostic equipment
Diagnostic test products
Disposable products
Drugs and medicines
Hospital and clinical labs
Medical services
Therapeutic equipment
Other
Publishing
Real estate
Transportation
Will Not Consider
Real estate

Additional Information
Year Founded—1961
Capital Under Management—$64 million
Invested(1985-1st 6 months)—$1.3 million
Method of Compensation—Return on investment is of primary concern; do not charge fees

---

BERRY CASH SOUTHWEST PARTNERSHIP

One Galleria Tower
13355 Noel Road #1375
Dallas, TX 75240
214-392-7279

Partners
H. Berry Cash, Gen. Ptnr.
Glenn A. Norem, Gen. Ptnr.
Nancy J. Schuele, Assoc.

Whom to Contact
Any of the above

Type of Firm
Private venture capital firm investing own capital

Affiliation
InterWest Partners

Industry Association Membership
NASBIC

Project Preferences
Will function either as deal originator or investor in deals created by others
Type of Financing:
Startup
First-stage
Minimum Investment: $500,000
Preferred Investment: $500,000-$1 million
Minimum Operating Data:
Annual Sales—Nominal
P&L—Losses (profits projected after 2 years)

Geographical Preferences
Southwest
Rocky Mountains
West Coast

Industry Preferences

Communications
Commercial communications
Data communications
Satellite and microwave communications
Telephone related
Computer Related
Computer graphics, CAD/CAM and CAE
Computer mainframes
Computer peripherals
Computer services
Memory devices
Micro and mini computers
Office automation
Scanning related
Software-applications
Software-systems
Specialized turnkey systems
Terminals
Electronic Components and Instrumentation
Analytical and scientific instrumentation
Component fabrication and testing equipment
Defense electronics
Electronic components
Laser related
Optics technology
Semiconductors
Genetic Engineering
Medical instrumentation
Industrial Products and Equipment
Controls and sensors
Equipment and machinery
Other industrial automation
Robotics/vision systems
Medical/Health Related
Diagnostic equipment
Diagnostic test products
Therapeutic equipment
Will Not Consider
Oil and gas exploration and production
Real estate

Additional Information
Year Founded—1983
Capital Under Management—$25 million
Investments(1985-1st 6 months)—5
Invested(1985-1st 6 months)—$2.5 million
Method of Compensation—Return on
 investment is of primary concern; do not
 charge fees

CHARTER VENTURE GROUP, INC.

2600 Citadel Plaza Drive #600
Houston, TX 77008
713-863-0704

Officer
Kent E. Smith, Pres.

Type of Firm
SBIC

Affiliation
Charter Bancshares, Inc. (parent)

Industry Association Membership
NASBIC

Project Preferences
Will function either as deal originator or
 investor in deals created by others
Type of Financing:
Second-stage
Later-stage expansion
Leveraged buyout
Minimum Investment: Less than $100,000
Preferred Investment: $100,000-$200,000
Minimum Operating Data:
Annual Sales—$500,000
P&L—Break even

Geographical Preference
Southwest

Industry Preferences

Communications
Cable television
Commercial communications
Data communications
Satellite and microwave communications
Telephone related

Computer Related
Computer graphics, CAD/CAM and CAE
Computer mainframes
Computer services
Memory devices
Micro and mini computers
Office automation
Scanning related
Software-applications
Software-artificial intelligence
Software-systems
Specialized turnkey systems
Terminals
Distribution
Communications equipment
Computer equipment
Consumer products
Electronics equipment
Food products
Industrial products
Medical products
Electronic Components and Instrumentation
Analytical and scientific instrumentation
Component fabrication and testing
 equipment
Electronic components
Fiber optics
Laser related
Semiconductors
Energy/Natural Resources
Technology related products/equipment
Genetic Engineering
Gene splicing and manufacturing equipment
Monoclonal antibodies and hybridomas
Recombinant DNA (agricultural and
 industrial)
Recombinant DNA (medical)
Industrial Products and Equipment
Chemicals
Controls and sensors
Energy management
Equipment and machinery
Other industrial automation
Plastics
Robotics/vision systems
Specialty materials
Medical/Health Related
Diagnostic equipment
Diagnostic test products
Disposable products
Drugs and medicines
Hospital and clinical labs
Medical services
Therapeutic equipment
Will Not Consider
Construction
Real estate

Additional Information
Year Founded—1980
Capital Under Management—$2 million
Investments(1985-1st 6 months)—3
Invested(1985-1st 6 months)—$85,000
Method of Compensation—Return on
 investment is of primary concern; do not
 charge fees

CITICORP VENTURE CAPITAL, LTD.

717 North Harwood
Suite 2920, LB 87
Dallas, TX 75201
214-880-9670

Other Offices
153 East 53rd Street
28th Floor
New York, NY 10043
212-559-1127

Two Embarcadero Place, #203
2200 Geng Road
Palo Alto, CA 94303
415-424-8000

Officers/Texas
Thomas F. McWilliams, V.P.
Newell V. Starks, Sr. Inv. Officer

Whom to Contact
Either of the above

Type of Firm
SBIC
Venture capital subsidiary of bank
 holding company

Affiliation
Citicorp (parent)

Industry Association Memberships
NASBIC
NVCA
WAVC

Project Preferences
Prefer role as deal originator but will also
 invest in deals created by others
Type of Financing:
Seed
Startup
First-stage
Second-stage
Later-stage expansion
Leveraged buyout

Preferred Investment: $1 million
Minimum Operating Data:
Annual Sales—Nominal

Geographical Preference
None

Industry Preferences

Communications
Cable television
Commercial communications
Data communications
Satellite and microwave communications
Telephone related
Computer Related
Computer graphics, CAD/CAM and CAE
Computer mainframes
Computer services
Micro and mini computers
Office automation
Software-applications
Software-systems
Terminals
Consumer
Food and beverage products
Distribution
Communications equipment
Electronics equipment
Food products
Industrial products
Medical products
Electronic Components and Instrumentation
Analytical and scientific instrumentation
Component fabrication and testing equipment
Electronic components
Fiber optics
Laser related
Semiconductors
Energy/Natural Resources
Drilling and exploration services
Energy conservation
Minerals
Technology related products/equipment
Genetic Engineering
Gene splicing and manufacturing equipment
Monoclonal antibodies and hybridomas
Recombinant DNA (agricultural and industrial)
Recombinant DNA (medical)
Industrial Products and Equipment
Chemicals
Controls and sensors
Energy management
Equipment and machinery
Other industrial automation
Plastics
Robotics/vision systems
Specialty materials

Medical/Health Related
Diagnostic equipment
Hospital and clinical labs
Medical services
Other
Agriculture, forestry, fishing
Education related
Finance and insurance
Publishing
Will Not Consider
Project-oriented investments
Tax-advantaged investments

Additional Information
Year Founded—1983 (Texas)
Capital Under Management—$500 million (all offices)
Method of Compensation—Return on investment is of primary concern; do not charge fees

---

COLLINS CAPITAL

2670 One Dallas Centre
Dallas, TX 75201
214-741-6666

Officers
Michael J. Collins, Pres.
Thomas U. Barton, COO
Andrew Weis, V.P.
Paula Stokey, V.P.

Whom to Contact
Thomas U. Barton

Type of Firm
Private venture capital firm investing own capital

Project Preferences
Prefer role in deals created by others
Type of Financing:
Seed
Startup
First-stage
Second-stage
Leveraged buyout
Minimum Investment: $250,000
Preferred Investment: $500,000-$1 million
Minimum Operating Data:
Annual Sales—Nominal
P&L—Losses (profits projected after 1 year)

Geographical Preference
None

Industry Preferences

Communications
Cable television
Commercial communications
Data communications
Satellite and microwave communications
Telephone related
Distribution
Communications equipment
Computer equipment
Consumer products
Electronics equipment
Food products
Industrial products
Medical products
Electronic Components and Instrumentation
Analytical and scientific instrumentation
Component fabrication and testing equipment
Electronic components
Fiber optics
Laser related
Semiconductors
Industrial Products and Equipment
Chemicals
Controls and sensors
Energy management
Equipment and machinery
Other industrial automation
Plastics
Robotics/vision systems
Specialty materials
Medical/Health Related
Diagnostic equipment
Diagnostic test products
Disposable products
Drugs and medicines
Hospital and clinical labs
Medical services
Therapeutic equipment

Additional Information
Year Founded—1978
Method of Compensation—Return on investment is of primary concern; do not charge fees

CRITERION VENTURE PARTNERS

333 Clay Street #4300
Houston, TX 77002
713-751-2400

Partners
David O. Wicks, Jr., Sr. Ptnr.
M. Scott Albert, Ptnr.
Crichton W. Brown, Assoc.

Whom to Contact
Any of the above

Type of Firm
Private venture capital firm investing
own capital

Affiliation
Criterion Investments, Inc. (corporate general
partner)

Industry Association Memberships
NASBIC
NVCA

Project Preferences
Will function either as deal originator or
investor in deals created by others
Type of Financing:
Startup
First-stage
Second-stage
Later-stage expansion
Leveraged buyout
Minimum Investment: $250,000
Preferred Investment: $500,000-$1 million
Minimum Operating Data:
Annual Sales—Nominal

Geographical Preferences
Southeast
Southwest

Industry Preferences

Communications
Cable television
Commercial communications
Data communications
NASA spin-off
Satellite and microwave communications
Telephone related

Computer Related
Computer graphics, CAD/CAM and CAE
Computer services
Memory devices
Micro and mini computers
Office automation
Scanning related
Software-applications
Software-artificial intelligence
Software-systems
Consumer
Consumer products
Consumer services
Retailing
Distribution
Communications equipment
Computer equipment
Consumer products
Electronics equipment
Industrial products
Medical products
**Electronic Components and
Instrumentation**
Analytical and scientific instrumentation
Component fabrication and testing
equipment
Electronic components
Fiber optics
Laser related
Semiconductors
Energy/Natural Resources
Alternative energy
Drilling and exploration services
Energy conservation
Technology related products/equipment
Genetic Engineering
Gene splicing and manufacturing equipment
Recombinant DNA (agricultural and
industrial)
Recombinant DNA (medical)
Industrial Products and Equipment
Controls and sensors
Energy management
Equipment and machinery
Other industrial automation
Robotics/vision systems
Specialty materials
Medical/Health Related
Diagnostic equipment
Diagnostic test products
Disposable products
Drugs and medicines
Hospital and clinical labs
Medical services
Therapeutic equipment
Other
Education related
Finance and insurance
Specialty consulting
Transportation

Will Not Consider
Oil and gas exploration
Real estate

Additional Information
Year Founded—1983
Capital Under Management—$20 million
Investments(1985-1st 6 months)—4
Invested(1985-1st 6 months)—$2 million
Method of Compensation—Return on
investment is of primary concern; do not
charge fees

CRUTCHFIELD & COMPANY

1000 Westlake High Drive #4B
Austin, TX 78746
512-327-6810

Officers
John H. Crutchfield, CEO
Geoffrey Andron, V.P.

Whom to Contact
Either of the above

Type of Firm
Private venture capital firm investing
own capital

Project Preferences
Will function either as deal originator or
investor in deals created by others
Type of Financing:
Seed
Research and development partnerships
Startup
First-stage
Leveraged buyout
Minimum Investment: $250,000
Preferred Investment: $250,000-$500,000
Minimum Operating Data:
Annual Sales—Nominal
P&L—Losses (profits projected after 3 years)

Geographical Preference
Within two hours of office

Industry Preferences

Communications
Cable television
Commercial communications
Data communications
Satellite and microwave communications
Telephone related

Computer Related
Computer graphics, CAD/CAM and CAE
Computer mainframes
Computer services
Memory devices
Micro and mini computers
Office automation
Scanning related
Software-applications
Software-artificial intelligence
Software-systems
Specialized turnkey systems
Terminals
**Electronic Components and
 Instrumentation**
Analytical and scientific instrumentation
Component fabrication and testing
 equipment
Electronic components
Fiber optics
Laser related
Semiconductors
Industrial Products and Equipment
Chemicals
Controls and sensors
Energy management
Equipment and machinery
Other industrial automation
Plastics
Robotics/vision systems
Specialty materials
Other
Motion picture and video production

Additional Information
Year Founded—1979
Capital Under Management—$7 million
Investments(1985-1st 6 months)—2
Invested(1985-1st 6 months)—$500,000
Method of Compensation—Return on
 investment is most important, but also
 charge for closing fees, service fees, etc.

CURTIN & CO., INCORPORATED

2050 Houston Natural Gas Bldg.
Houston, TX 77002
713-658-9806

Officers
John D. Curtin, Jr., Pres.
Stewart Cureton, Jr., V.P.
Charles Armbrust, V.P.

Whom to Contact
Any of the above

Type of Firm
Investment banking or merchant banking
 firm investing own capital or funds of
 partners or clients

Industry Association Membership
NVCA

Project Preferences
Will function either as deal originator or
 investor in deals created by others
Type of Financing:
Startup
First-stage
Second-stage
Leveraged buyout
Minimum Investment: $500,000
Preferred Investment: Over $1 million
Preferred Investment (LBO):
 $10 million and over
Minimum Operating Data:
Annual Sales—Nominal
P&L—Losses (profits projected after 2 years)
Annual Sales (LBO)—$10 million and over

Geographical Preference
Southwest

Industry Preferences

Communications
Cable television
Commercial communications
Data communications
Satellite and microwave communications
Telephone related
Computer Related
Computer graphics, CAD/CAM and CAE
Computer mainframes
Computer services
Memory devices
Micro and mini computers
Office automation
Scanning related
Software-applications
Software-artificial intelligence
Software-systems
Specialized turnkey systems
Terminals
Consumer
Consumer products
Consumer services
Food and beverage products
Leisure and recreational products
Restaurants
Retailing

Distribution
Communications equipment
Computer equipment
Consumer products
Electronics equipment
Food products
Industrial products
Medical products
**Electronic Components and
 Instrumentation**
Analytical and scientific instrumentation
Component fabrication and testing
 equipment
Electronic components
Fiber optics
Laser related
Semiconductors
Energy/Natural Resources
Alternative energy
Drilling and exploration services
Energy conservation
Oil and gas exploration and production
Technology related products/equipment
Industrial Products and Equipment
Chemicals
Controls and sensors
Energy management
Equipment and machinery
Other industrial automation
Plastics
Robotics/vision systems
Specialty materials
Medical/Health Related
Diagnostic equipment
Diagnostic test products
Disposable products
Drugs and medicines
Hospital and clinical labs
Medical services
Therapeutic equipment
Other
Education related
Finance and insurance
Publishing
Real estate
Specialty consulting
Transportation

Additional Information
Year Founded—1975
Method of Compensation—Return on
 investment is most important, but also
 charge for closing fees, service fees, etc.

DOUGERY, JONES & WILDER

5420 LBJ Freeway
Two Lincoln Centre #1100
Dallas, TX 75240
214-960-0077

A. Lawson Howard

See CALIFORNIA for full listing

D.S. VENTURES, INC.

351 Phelps Court
Post office Box 2300
Irving, TX 75061
214-659-7000

350 Mount Kemble Avenue
CN 1931
Morristown, NJ 07960
201-267-1000

Officers
Martin G. White, Pres. (Texas)
Frank C. Briden, V.P. (New Jersey)

Whom to Contact
Either of the above

Type of Firm
Venture capital subsidiary or affiliate of
non-financial corporation

Affiliation
Diamond Shamrock Corporation (parent)

Project Preferences
Will function either as deal originator or
investor in deals created by others
Type of Financing:
Seed
Startup
First-stage
Second-stage
Later-stage expansion
Minimum Investment: $100,000
Preferred Investment: $500,000-$1 million
Minimum Operating Data:
Annual Sales—Nominal

Geographical Preference
None

Industry Preferences

Distribution
Medical products

**Electronic Components and
 Instrumentation**
Analytical and scientific instrumentation
Electronic components
Fiber optics
Laser related
Semiconductors
Energy/Natural Resources
Coal related
Drilling and exploration services
Oil and gas exploration and production
Technology related products/equipment
Genetic Engineering
Monoclonal antibodies and hybridomas
Recombinant DNA (medical)
Industrial Products and Equipment
Ceramics
Chemicals
Controls and sensors
Plastics
Specialty materials
Medical/Health Related
Biopolymers
Diagnostic chemicals
Diagnostic test products
Disposable products
Medical services
Therapeutic equipment

Additional Information
Year Founded—1981
Capital Under Management—$5.5 million
Method of Compensation—Return on
investment is of primary concern; do not
charge fees

ENERGY CAPITAL CORPORATION

953 Esperson Building
Houston, TX 77002
713-236-0006

Officers
Herbert F. Poyner, Jr., Pres.
Donald R. Henderson, V.P., Asst. Secy.-Treas.
George Allman, Jr., Secy.-Treas.

Whom to Contact
Herbert F. Poyner

Type of Firm
SBIC

Industry Association Membership
NASBIC

Project Preferences
Prefer role as deal originator
Type of Financing:
First-stage
Leveraged buyout
Minimum Investment: $250,000
Preferred Investment: $500,000-$1 million
Preferred Investment (LBO):
$500,000-$1 million
Minimum Operating Data:
Annual Sales—Nominal

Geographical Preference
Gulf States

Industry Preferences

Energy/Natural Resources
Oil and gas development drilling
Oil and gas producing property acquisitions
Will Not Consider
Non oil or gas related industries

Additional Information
Year Founded—1980
Capital Under Management—$13 million
Method of Compensation—Return on
investment is of primary concern; do not
charge fees

ENTERPRISE CAPITAL
CORPORATION

3115 Allen Parkway #100
Houston, TX 77019
713-526-8070

Officers
Paul Z. Brochstein, Chm.
Fred S. Zeidman, Pres.
Fiore P. Talarico, Jr., CFO
Eta G. Paransky, Consultant

Whom to Contact
Fred S. Zeidman
Fiore P. Talarico, Jr.
Eta G. Paransky

Type of Firm
SBIC

Affiliation
Mainland Savings Association (parent)

Industry Association Membership
NASBIC

Project Preferences
Will function either as deal originator or
investor in deals created by others
Type of Financing:
First-stage
Second-stage
Leveraged buyout
Minimum Investment: $250,000
Preferred Investment: $500,000-$1 million
Minimum Operating Data:
Annual Sales—$500,000
P&L—Break even

Geographical Preference
None

Industry Preferences

Communications
Cable television
Commercial communications
Data communications
Satellite and microwave communications
Telephone related
Consumer
Consumer products
Distribution
Communications equipment
Computer equipment
Consumer products
Electronics equipment
Food products
Industrial products
Medical products
**Electronic Components and
Instrumentation**
Analytical and scientific instrumentation
Component fabrication and testing
equipment
Electronic components
Fiber optics
Laser related
Semiconductors
Genetic Engineering
Gene splicing and manufacturing equipment
Monoclonal antibodies and hybridomas
Recombinant DNA (agricultural and
industrial)
Recombinant DNA (medical)
Industrial Products and Equipment
Chemicals
Controls and sensors
Energy management
Equipment and machinery
Other industrial automation
Plastics
Robotics/vision systems
Specialty materials

Medical/Health Related
Diagnostic equipment
Diagnostic test products
Disposable products
Drugs and medicines
Hospital and clinical labs
Medical services
Therapeutic equipment
Other
Aerospace
Will Not Consider
Computer software
Non developmental real estate

Additional Information
Year Founded—1970
Investments(1985-1st 6 months)—7

FINANCIAL SERVICES-AUSTIN, INC.

301 West Sixth Street
Post Office Box 1987
Austin, TX 78767
512-472-7171

Officers
H.A. Abshier, Chm.
Brad Fowler, Pres.
Rex Gwinn, Sr. V.P.
Ward Greenwood, Sr. V.P.
G. Felder Thornhill, Exec. V.P.

Whom to Contact
Any of the above

Type of Firm
Investment banking or merchant banking
firm investing own capital or funds of
partners or clients

Affiliation
Triad Ventures Ltd. (associated venture
partnership)

Project Preferences
Prefer role as deal originator but will also
invest in deals created by others
Type of Financing:
Second-stage
Leveraged buyout
Minimum Investment: $500,000
Preferred Investment: $500,000-$1 million
Minimum Operating Data:
Annual Sales—$1.5 million

Geographical Preference
Southwest

Industry Preferences

Communications
Cable television
Commercial communications
Data communications
Satellite and microwave communications
Telephone related
Consumer
Computer stores/related services
Consumer products
Consumer services
Food and beverage products
Franchise businesses
Hotels and resort areas
Leisure and recreational products
Restaurants
Retailing
Distribution
Communications equipment
Computer equipment
Consumer products
Electronics equipment
Food products
Industrial products
Medical products
Energy/Natural Resources
Alternative energy
Coal related
Drilling and exploration services
Energy conservation
Minerals
Oil and gas exploration and production
Technology related products/equipment
Industrial Products and Equipment
Chemicals
Controls and sensors
Energy management
Equipment and machinery
Other industrial automation
Plastics
Robotics/vision systems
Specialty materials
Other
Agriculture, forestry, fishing
Education related
Finance and insurance
Publishing
Real estate
Specialty consulting
Transportation

Additional Information
Year Founded—1979
Method of Compensation—Return on
investment is most important, but also
charge for closing fees, service fees, etc.

FIRST DALLAS FINANCIAL COMPANY

3302 Southland Center
Dallas, TX 75201
214-922-0070

Officers
John T. McGuire, Pres.
C. Thomas May, Chm.

Whom to Contact
John T. McGuire

Type of Firm
Consulting firm evaluating and analyzing venture projects and arranging private placements

Affiliation
May Financial Corporation (parent)

Project Preferences
Prefer role as deal originator
Type of Financing:
Second-stage
Leveraged buyout
Preferred Investment: Over $1 million
Preferred Investment (LBO):
  $1 million and over
Minimum Operating Data:
Annual Sales—$1.5 million
P&L—Break even
Annual Sales (LBO)—$5 million and over

Geographical Preference
Southwest

Industry Preferences

Computer Related
Computer graphics, CAD/CAM and CAE
Office automation
Consumer
Computer stores/related services
Consumer products
Consumer services
Food and beverage products
Franchise businesses
Hotels and resort areas
Leisure and recreational products
Restaurants
Retailing
Distribution
Consumer products
Food products
Industrial products
Medical products
Energy/Natural Resources
Technology related products/equipment

Industrial Products and Equipment
Energy management
Equipment and machinery
Other industrial automation
Plastics
Other
Finance and insurance
Public warehousing
Transportation
Will Not Consider
Insurance
Real estate

Additional Information
Year Founded—1980
Invested(1985-1st 6 months)—$4 million
Method of Compensation—Function primarily in service area; receive contingent fee in cash or equity

THE FIRST HOUSTON (INTERNATIONAL) CORPORATION

1900 West Loop South #1100
Houston, TX 77027
713-850-1100

Officers
J.W. Harris, Pres.
Vernon G. Hafernik, Sr. V.P.
Robert W. McQueen, Chm.
Leon E. Roy, Vice Chm.

Whom to Contact
J.W. Harris

Type of Firm
Investment banking or merchant banking firm investing own capital or funds of partners or clients

Affiliation
F.H. Securities (subsidiary)

Project Preferences
Prefer role as deal originator
Type of Financing:
Research and development partnerships
Startup
First-stage
Minimum Investment: $500,000
Preferred Investment: $500,000-$1 million
Minimum Operating Data:
Annual Sales—Over $3 million
P&L—Profitable

Geographical Preference
Southwest

Industry Preferences

Electronic Components and Instrumentation
Analytical and scientific instrumentation
Electronic components
Fiber optics
Energy/Natural Resources
Technology related products/equipment

Additional Information
Year Founded—1979
Investments(1985-1st 6 months)—1
Invested(1985-1st 6 months)—$750,000
Method of Compensation—Function primarily in service area; receive contingent fee in cash or equity

GILL CAPITAL CORPORATION

615 Soledad
San Antonio, TX 78205
512-299-6514

Officers
William R. Cain, Pres.
Michael J. Meyer, Sr. V.P.
Judith Knight Shields, V.P.

Whom to Contact
Any of the above

Type of Firm
SBIC

Affiliation
Gill Savings Association (parent)

Industry Association Membership
NASBIC

Project Preferences
Will function either as deal originator or investor in deals created by others
Type of Financing:
Second-stage
Later-stage expansion
Leveraged buyout
Minimum Investment: $500,000
Preferred Investment: $500,000-$1 million
Minimum Operating Data:
Annual Sales—$1.5 million
P&L—Break even

Geographical Preferences
Southwest
National

Industry Preferences
None

Additional Information
Year Founded—1984
Capital Under Management—$15 million
(private capital)
Investments(1985-1st 6 months)—4
Invested(1985-1st 6 months)—$3.6 million
Method of Compensation—Return on
investment is of primary concern; do not
charge fees

LAWRENCE HERBST INVESTMENT TRUST FUND

Post Office Box 3842
Houston, TX 77253

Other Offices
Post Office Box 1659
Beverly Hills, CA 90213

Post Office Box 1003
Milford, PA 18337

Post Office Box 741
Lake Charles, LA 70602

R.D. #1 Post Office Box 5
Rock Stream, NY 14878

Officers
Dr. Lawrence Herbst, Pres. (Texas
& Louisiana)
Joe Tomlinson, V.P. (California)
John Popowich, Treas. (New York)
Ruth Gray, Admin. Asst. (New York)

Whom to Contact
Dr. Lawrence Herbst

Type of Firm
Venture capital subsidiary or affiliate of
non-financial corporation

Project Preferences
Will function either as deal originator or
investor in deals created by others
Type of Financing:
Seed
Research and development partnerships
Startup
First-stage
Second-stage
Leveraged buyout
Minimum Investment: Less than $100,000
Preferred Investment: $250,000-$500,000

Minimum Operating Data:
Annual Sales—Nominal
P&L—Break even

Geographical Preference
None

Industry Preferences
Communications
Cable television
Commercial communications
Data communications
Satellite and microwave communications
Telephone related
Computer Related
Computer graphics, CAD/CAM and CAE
Computer mainframes
Computer services
Memory devices
Micro and mini computers
Office automation
Scanning related
Software-applications
Software-artificial intelligence
Software-systems
Specialized turnkey systems
Terminals
Consumer
Computer stores/related services
Consumer products
Consumer services
Food and beverage products
Franchise businesses
Hotels and resort areas
Leisure and recreational products
Restaurants
Retailing
Distribution
Communications equipment
Computer equipment
Consumer products
Electronics equipment
Food products
Industrial products
Medical products
Electronic Components and Instrumentation
Analytical and scientific instrumentation
Component fabrication and testing
equipment
Electronic components
Fiber optics
Laser related
Semiconductors

Energy/Natural Resources
Alternative energy
Coal related
Drilling and exploration services
Energy conservation
Minerals
Oil and gas exploration and production
Technology related products/equipment
Genetic Engineering
Gene splicing and manufacturing equipment
Monoclonal antibodies and hybridomas
Recombinant DNA (agricultural and
industrial)
Recombinant DNA (medical)
Industrial Products and Equipment
Chemicals
Controls and sensors
Energy management
Equipment and machinery
Other industrial automation
Plastics
Robotics/vision systems
Specialty materials
Medical/Health Related
Diagnostic equipment
Diagnostic test products
Disposable products
Drugs and medicines
Hospital and clinical labs
Medical services
Therapeutic equipment
Other
Agriculture, forestry, fishing
Education related
Finance and insurance
Horse racing and breeding
Publishing
Real estate
Specialty consulting
Transportation

Additional Information
Year Founded—1966
Investments(1985-1st 6 months)—2
Method of Compensation—Professional fee
required whether or not deal closes

HOLDING CAPITAL GROUP

2440 Parkside
Irving, TX 75061
214-252-2799

William C. Martin, Principal

See NEW YORK for full listing

IDANTA PARTNERS

201 Main Street #3200
Fort Worth, TX 76102
817-338-2020

Partners
David J. Dunn, Mgn. Ptnr.
Dev Purkayastha, Gen. Ptnr.
Steven B. Dunn, Gen. Ptnr.

Whom to Contact
Dev Purkayastha
Steven B. Dunn

Type of Firm
Private venture capital firm investing
own capital

Industry Association Memberships
NVCA
WAVC

Project Preferences
Will function either as deal originator or
investor in deals created by others
Type of Financing:
Startup
First-stage
Second-stage
Leveraged buyout
Minimum Investment: $250,000
Preferred Investment: $500,000-$1 million
Minimum Operating Data:
Annual Sales—Nominal
P&L—Losses (profits projected after 2 years)

Geographical Preference
None

Industry Preferences
None
Will Not Consider
Oil and gas
Real estate

Additional Information
Year Founded—1971
Method of Compensation—Return on
investment is of primary concern; do not
charge fees

INTERCAPCO, INC.

1701 North Market Street #200
Dallas, TX 75202
214-748-5893

Officers
Richard H. Collins, Chm. & Mgn. Dir.
Linda G. Wilson, Cntlr. & Asst. Secy.

Whom to Contact
Linda G. Wilson

Type of Firm
SBIC

Industry Association Membership
NASBIC

Project Preferences
Will function either as deal originator or
investor in deals created by others
Type of Financing:
Second-stage
Later-stage expansion
Leveraged buyout
Minimum Investment: $100,000
Preferred Investment: $250,000-$500,000
Minimum Operating Data:
Annual Sales—$500,000
P&L—Break even

Geographical Preferences
Southwest
Midwest

Industry Preferences

Communications
Satellite and microwave communications
Telephone related
Computer Related
Computer services
Consumer
Hotels and resort areas
Distribution
Industrial products
Medical products
Energy/Natural Resources
Drilling and exploration services
Oil and gas exploration and production
Technology related products/equipment
Industrial Products and Equipment
Chemicals
Medical/Health Related
Drugs and medicines

Additional Information
Year Founded—1976
Capital Under Management—$13.5 million
Investments(1985-1st 6 months)—22
Method of Compensation—Return on
investment is most important, but also
charge for closing fees, service fees, etc.

INTERFIRST VENTURE CORPORATION

901 Main Street, 20th Floor
Post Office Box 83644
Dallas, TX 75283
214-977-3160

Officers
Jim O'Donnell, Pres.
Mark Masur, V.P.
Frank Young, V.P.
Sallee McDermitt, Inv. officer
Pat Whelan, Inv. Officer
Wendy Stanley, Assoc.

Whom to Contact
Any of the above

Type of Firm
Venture capital subsidiary of
commercial bank

Affiliation
InterFirst Corp.

Industry Association Membership
NASBIC

Project Preferences
Will function either as deal originator or
investor in deals created by others
Type of Financing:
Startup
First-stage
Second-stage
Later-stage expansion
Leveraged buyout
Minimum Investment: $500,000
Preferred Investment: $500,000 and over
Preferred Investment (LBO): $1.5 million
Minimum Operating Data:
Annual Sales—Nominal
P&L—Losses (profits projected after 2 years)
Annual Sales (LBO)—$20 million-$200 million

Geographical Preferences
Southeast
Southwest

Industry Preferences

Communications
Cable television
Commercial communications
Data communications
Satellite and microwave communications
Telephone related
Computer Related
Computer graphics, CAD/CAM and CAE
Computer mainframes
Computer services
Memory devices
Micro and mini computers
Office automation
Scanning related
Software-applications
Software-artificial intelligence
Software-systems
Specialized turnkey systems
Terminals
Consumer
Computer stores/related services
Consumer products
Consumer services
Food and beverage products
Franchise businesses
Hotels and resort areas
Leisure and recreational products
Restaurants
Retailing
Distribution
Communications equipment
Computer equipment
Consumer products
Electronics equipment
Food products
Industrial products
Medical products
Electronic Components and Instrumentation
Analytical and scientific instrumentation
Component fabrication and testing equipment
Electronic components
Fiber optics
Laser related
Semiconductors
Energy/Natural Resources
Technology related products/equipment
Industrial Products and Equipment
Chemicals
Controls and sensors
Energy management
Equipment and machinery
Other industrial automation
Plastics
Robotics/vision systems
Specialty materials

Medical/Health Related
Diagnostic equipment
Diagnostic test products
Disposable products
Drugs and medicines
Hospital and clinical labs
Medical services
Therapeutic equipment
Other
Transportation
Will Not Consider
Financial institutions
Real estate

Additional Information

Year Founded—1962
Capital Under Management—$40 million
Investments(1985-1st 6 months)—4
Invested(1985-1st 6 months)—$4 million
Method of Compensation—Return on investment is of primary concern; do not charge fees

---

INTERWEST PARTNERS

One Galleria Tower #1375/LB 65
13355 Noel Road
Dallas, TX 75240
214-392-7279

Berry Cash, Gen. Ptnr.
Glenn A. Norem, Gen. Ptnr.

See CALIFORNIA for full listing

ITEC SECURITIES CORPORATION

5311 Kirby Drive #1000
Houston, TX 77005
713-622-4334

Officer
Alex Budzinsky, Pres.

Type of Firm
Investment banking or merchant banking firm investing own capital or funds of partners or clients
Consulting firm evaluating and analyzing venture projects and arranging private placements

Affiliation
Itec Capital Corporation (parent)

Project Preferences
Prefer role as deal originator
Type of Financing:
First-stage
Second-stage
Leveraged buyout
Minimum Investment: $100,000
Preferred Investment: $250,000 and over
Minimum Operating Data:
Annual Sales—$500,000
P&L—Break even

Geographical Preference
Gulf States

Industry Preferences

Computer Related
Specialized turnkey systems
Consumer
Franchise businesses
Hotels and resort areas
Leisure and recreational products
Restaurants
Energy/Natural Resources
Alternative energy
Coal related
Oil and gas exploration and production
Genetic Engineering
Monoclonal antibodies and hybridomas
Industrial Products and Equipment
Controls and sensors
Energy management
Medical/Health Related
Diagnostic test products
Other
Finance and insurance
Real estate
Specialty consulting

Additional Information
Year Founded—1981
Method of Compensation—Function primarily in service area; receive contingent fee in cash or equity
Professional fee required whether or not deal closes

RICHARD JAFFE & CO., INC.

7318 Royal Circle
Dallas, TX 75230
214-739-1845

Officer
Richard R. Jaffe, Pres.

Type of Firm
Private venture capital firm investing
own capital

Project Preferences
Will function either as deal originator or
investor in deals created by others
Type of Financing:
First-stage
Minimum Investment: Less than $100,000
Preferred Investment: Less than $100,000
Minimum Operating Data:
Annual Sales—Nominal
P&L—Break even

Geographical Preference
Southwest

Industry Preferences

Computer Related
Computer services
Office automation
Scanning related
Consumer
Retirement housing related
Industrial Products and Equipment
Robotics/vision systems
Medical/Health Related
Medical services
Other
Real estate
Specialty consulting

Additional Information
Year Founded—1962
Capital Under Management—$3 million
Investments(1985-1st 6 months)—1
Invested(1985-1st 6 months)—$100,000
Method of Compensation—Return on
investment is most important, but also
charge for closing fees, service fees, etc.

LONE STAR CAPITAL, LTD.

2401 Fountainview #950
Houston, TX 77057
713-266-6616

Partners
Stuart Schube, Ptnr. (Houston)
Martin D. O'Malley, Assoc. (Houston)

Whom to Contact
Any of the above

Type of Firm
SBIC management company

Affiliations
Bow Lane Capital Corp. (SBIC under
management)
Wesbanc Ventures, Ltd. (SBIC under
management)

Industry Association Memberships
NASBIC
NVCA

Project Preferences
Prefer role as deal originator but will also
invest in deals created by others
Type of Financing:
Second-stage
Later-stage expansion
Leveraged buyout
Minimum Investment: $250,000
Preferred Investment: $500,000-$1 million
Minimum Operating Data:
Annual Sales—$500,000
P&L—Break even

Geographical Preference
None

Industry Preferences

Communications
Data communications
Satellite and microwave communications
Computer Related
Computer graphics, CAD/CAM and CAE
Computer services
Office automation
Scanning related
Software-applications
Specialized turnkey systems
Consumer
Retailing

Distribution
Communications equipment
Computer equipment
Consumer products
Electronics equipment
Food products
Industrial products
Medical products
**Electronic Components and
Instrumentation**
Analytical and scientific instrumentation
Component fabrication and testing
equipment
Electronic components
Fiber optics
Laser related
Semiconductors
Energy/Natural Resources
Alternative energy
Technology related products/equipment
Industrial Products and Equipment
Chemicals
Controls and sensors
Energy management
Equipment and machinery
Other industrial automation
Plastics
Robotics/vision systems
Specialty materials
Medical/Health Related
Diagnostic equipment
Diagnostic test products
Disposable products
Drugs and medicines
Hospital and clinical labs
Medical services
Therapeutic equipment

Additional Information
Year Founded—1979
Capital Under Management—$12 million
Investments(1985-1st 6 months)—9
Invested(1985-1st 6 months)—$966,000
Method of Compensation—Return on
investment is most important, but also
charge for closing fees, service fees, etc.

564

MAPLELEAF CAPITAL CORPORATION

55 Waugh Drive #710
Houston, TX 77007
713-880-4494

Officers
Edward M. Fink, Pres.
Bernadette Obermeier, Secy. & Treas.

Whom to Contact
Either of the above

Type of Firm
SBIC

Project Preferences
Will function either as deal originator or
  investor in deals created by others
Type of Financing:
Second-stage
Later-stage expansion
Leveraged buyout
Minimum Investment: $100,000
Preferred Investment: $250,000-$500,000
Minimum Operating Data:
Annual Sales—$500,000
P&L—Losses (profits projected after 2 years)

Geographical Preference
Southwest

Industry Preferences

Communications
Data communications
Medical technology
Consumer
Consumer products
Consumer services
Distribution
Consumer products
Industrial products
Medical products
Energy/Natural Resources
Technology related products/equipment
Industrial Products and Equipment
Other industrial automation
Robotics/vision systems
Medical/Health Related
Hospital and clinical labs
Medical services

Additional Information
Year Founded—1980
Capital Under Management—$5.5 million
Investments(1985-1st 6 months)—3
Invested(1985-1st 6 months)—$1.3 million
Method of Compensation—Return on
  investment is most important, but also
  charge for closing fees, service fees, etc.

MESBIC FINANCIAL CORPORATION OF DALLAS

12655 North Central Expressway
Suite 814
Dallas, TX 75243
214-637-0445

Officers
Donald R. Lawhorne, Pres.
Thomas G. Gerron, V.P. & Cntlr.
Gregory A. Campbell, V.P.

Whom to Contact
Thomas G. Gerron
Gregory A. Campbell

Type of Firm
MESBIC

Affiliation
MGI (wholly owned consulting subsidiary)

Industry Association Memberships
AAMESBIC
NASBIC

Project Preferences
Prefer role as deal originator but will also
  invest in deals created by others
Type of Financing:
Second-stage
Later-stage expansion
Leveraged buyout
Minimum Investment: Less than $100,000
Preferred Investment: $100,000-$250,000
Preferred Investment (LBO):
  $100,000-$200,000
Minimum Operating Data:
Annual Sales—$500,000
P&L—Break even
Annual Sales (LBO)—$2 million and over

Geographical Preference
North Texas
Southwest

Industry Preferences

Communications
Cable television
Commercial communications
Data communications
Satellite and microwave communications
Telephone related

Computer Related
Computer graphics, CAD/CAM and CAE
Computer mainframes
Computer services
Memory devices
Micro and mini computers
Office automation
Scanning related
Software-applications
Software-artificial intelligence
Software-systems
Specialized turnkey systems
Terminals
Consumer
Franchise businesses
Distribution
Communications equipment
Computer equipment
Consumer products
Electronics equipment
Food products
Industrial products
Medical products
Electronic Components and Instrumentation
Analytical and scientific instrumentation
Component fabrication and testing
  equipment
Electronic components
Fiber optics
Laser related
Semiconductors
Energy/Natural Resources
Technology related products/equipment
Industrial Products and Equipment
Chemicals
Controls and sensors
Energy management
Equipment and machinery
Other industrial automation
Plastics
Robotics/vision systems
Specialty materials
Medical/Health Related
Diagnostic equipment
Diagnostic test products
Disposable products
Drugs and medicines
Hospital and clinical labs
Medical services
Therapeutic equipment
Other
Publishing
Transportation
Will Not Consider
Oil drilling and exploration
Real estate

Additional Information

Year Founded—1970
Capital Under Management—$4.3 million
Investments(1985-1st 6 months)—1
Invested(1985-1st 6 months)—$70,000
Method of Compensation—Return on
investment is most important, but also
charge for closing fees, service fees, etc.

MID STATE CAPITAL CORPORATION

510 North Valley Mills Drive
Waco, TX 76710
817-776-9500

Post Office Box 7554
Waco, TX 76714

Officers

Smith E. Thomasson, Pres.
Matt Landry, V.P.
Pat Rominger, Secy.-Treas.

Whom to Contact

Smith E. Thomasson

Type of Firm

SBIC

Affiliation

United Bankes, Inc. (parent)

Industry Association Membership

NASBIC

Project Preferences

Will function either as deal originator or
investor in deals created by others
Type of Financing:
First-stage
Second-stage
Later-stage expansion
Leveraged buyout
Minimum Investment: Less than $100,000
Preferred Investment: $100,000-$250,000
Minimum Operating Data:
Annual Sales—$500,000
P&L—Break even

Geographical Preferences

Southwest
Midwest

Industry Preferences

Communications
Commercial communications
Data communications

Computer Related
Computer graphics, CAD/CAM and CAE
Computer mainframes
Computer services
Memory devices
Micro and mini computers
Office automation
Scanning related
Software-applications
Software-artificial intelligence
Software-systems
Specialized turnkey systems
Terminals
Consumer
Consumer products
Consumer services
Leisure and recreational products
Retailing
Distribution
Communications equipment
Computer equipment
Consumer products
Electronics equipment
Industrial products
Medical products
**Electronic Components and
Instrumentation**
Analytical and scientific instrumentation
Component fabrication and testing
equipment
Electronic components
Fiber optics
Laser related
Semiconductors
Industrial Products and Equipment
Controls and sensors
Equipment and machinery
Other industrial automation
Robotics/vision systems
Medical/Health Related
Diagnostic equipment
Diagnostic test products
Disposable products
Medical services
Therapeutic equipment
Other
Publishing
Real estate
Will Not Consider
Agriculture
Energy

Additional Information

Year Founded—1985
Capital Under Management—$1.4 million
Method of Compensation—Return on
investment is most important, but also
charge for closing fees, service fees, etc.

MSI CAPITAL CORPORATION

6510 Abrams Road #650
Dallas, TX 75231
214-341-1553

Lock Box 820036
Dallas, TX 75382

Officers

Nick Stanfield, Pres.
Phil Cerpanya, V.P.
Richard Wierzbicki, Inv. Analyst

Whom to Contact

Nick Stanfield

Type of Firm

Investment banking or merchant banking
firm investing own capital or funds of
partners or clients

Affiliation

Triad Ventures Ltd. (co-managed venture
capital fund)

Industry Association Membership

NVCA

Project Preferences

Will function either as deal originator or
investor in deals created by others
Type of Financing:
First-stage
Leveraged buyout
Minimum Investment: $250,000
Preferred Investment: $250,000-$500,000
Minimum Operating Data:
Annual Sales—Nominal
P&L—Break even

Geographical Preference

Texas

Industry Preferences

Communications
Cable television
Commercial communications
Data communications
Satellite and microwave communications
Telephone related

Computer Related
Computer graphics, CAD/CAM and CAE
Computer mainframes
Computer services
Memory devices
Micro and mini computers
Office automation
Scanning related
Software-applications
Software-artificial intelligence
Software-systems
Specialized turnkey systems
Terminals
Consumer
Consumer products
Consumer services
Leisure and recreational products
Retailing
Distribution
Communications equipment
Computer equipment
Consumer products
Electronics equipment
Food products
Industrial products
Medical products
Electronic Components and Instrumentation
Electronic components
Fiber optics
Laser related
Energy/Natural Resources
Drilling and exploration services
Technology related products/equipment
Industrial Products and Equipment
Chemicals
Controls and sensors
Energy management
Equipment and machinery
Other industrial automation
Plastics
Robotics/vision systems
Specialty materials
Medical/Health Related
Diagnostic equipment
Diagnostic test products
Disposable products
Drugs and medicines
Hospital and clinical labs
Medical services
Therapeutic equipment
Other
Finance and insurance
Publishing
Transportation
Will Not Consider
Professional partnerships
Real estate
Restaurants

Additional Information
Year Founded—1976
Capital Under Management—Over $5 million
Investments(1985-1st 6 months)—3
Invested(1985-1st 6 months)—$1.6 million
Method of Compensation—Return on investment is most important, but also charge for closing fees, service fees, etc.

MVENTURE CORP.

1704 Main Street #1901
Dallas, TX 75201
214-741-1469

Officers
Joseph B. Longino, Jr., Pres.
J. Wayne Gaylord, Exec. V.P.
Michael Brown, Inv. Officer
Thomas Bartlett, Inv. Officer
Erin Tierney, Inv. Officer

Whom to Contact
Any of the above

Type of Firm
SBIC
Venture capital subsidiary of commercial bank

Affiliations
MBank Dallas, N.A. (parent)
MCorp (parent bank holding company)

Industry Association Membership
NASBIC

Project Preferences
Will function either as deal originator or investor in deals created by others
Type of Financing:
First-stage
Second-stage
Later-stage expansion
Leveraged buyout
Minimum Investment: $250,000
Preferred Investment: $500,000-$1 million
Preferred Investment (LBO):
  $1 million-$2 million
Minimum Operating Data:
Annual Sales—Nominal
P&L—Losses (profits projected after 2 years)

Geographical Preference
Southwest

Industry Preferences

Communications
Cable television
Commercial communications
Data communications
Satellite and microwave communications
Telephone related
Computer Related
Computer graphics, CAD/CAM and CAE
Computer services
Memory devices
Office automation
Scanning related
Consumer
Consumer products
Consumer services
Food and beverage products
Distribution
Communications equipment
Computer equipment
Consumer products
Electronics equipment
Food products
Industrial products
Medical products
Electronic Components and Instrumentation
Analytical and scientific instrumentation
Component fabrication and testing equipment
Electronic components
Fiber optics
Laser related
Semiconductors
Energy/Natural Resources
Alternative energy
Coal related
Drilling and exploration services
Energy conservation
Minerals
Oil and gas exploration and production
Technology related products/equipment
Industrial Products and Equipment
Chemicals
Controls and sensors
Energy management
Equipment and machinery
Other industrial automation
Plastics
Robotics/vision systems
Specialty materials
Medical/Health Related
Diagnostic equipment
Diagnostic test products
Disposable products
Drugs and medicines
Hospital and clinical labs
Medical services
Therapeutic equipment

Other
Education related
Publishing
Transportation
Will Not Consider
Real estate
Seldom invest in retail operations

Additional Information
Year Founded—1976
Capital Under Management—$60 million
Investments(1985-1st 6 months)—13
Invested(1985-1st 6 months)—$12.7 million
Method of Compensation—Return on
  investment is most important, but also
  charge for closing fees, service fees, etc.

NEW BUSINESS RESOURCES II, INC.

4137 Billy Mitchell Road
Post Office Box 796
Addison, TX 75001
214-233-6631

Partners
Richard J. Hanschen
J.R. Hanschen
Bill Konrad

Whom to Contact
J.R. Hanschen
Bill Konrad

Type of Firm
Private venture capital firm investing
  own capital

Affiliation
Telpar, Inc. (incubator venture operating
  company)

Industry Association Membership
NVCA

Project Preferences
Prefer role as deal originator but will also
  invest in deals created by others
Type of Financing:
Seed
Startup
Later-stage expansion
Leveraged buyout
Minimum Investment: $250,000
Preferred Investment: $500,000-$1 million
Minimum Operating Data:
Annual Sales—Nominal
P&L—Losses (profits projected after 2 years)
Annual Sales (LBO)—$5 million

Geographical Preference
None

Industry Preferences

Communications
Data communications
Satellite and microwave communications
Computer Related
Computer graphics, CAD/CAM and CAE
Computer mainframes
Computer services
Memory devices
Micro and mini computers
Office automation
Scanning related
Software-applications
Software-artificial intelligence
Software-systems
Specialized turnkey systems
Terminals
**Electronic Components and
  Instrumentation**
Analytical and scientific instrumentation
Component fabrication and testing
  equipment
Electronic components
Fiber optics
Laser related
Semiconductors
Genetic Engineering
Gene splicing and manufacturing equipment
Industrial Products and Equipment
Robotics/vision systems
Specialty materials
Medical/Health Related
Diagnostic equipment
Diagnostic test products
Disposable products
Drugs and medicines
Hospital and clinical labs
Medical services
Therapeutic equipment

Additional Information
Year Founded—1969
Investments(1985-1st 6 months)—1
Invested(1985-1st 6 months)—$1.5 million
Method of Compensation—Return on
  investment is of primary concern; do not
  charge fees

OMEGA CAPITAL CORPORATION

755 South 11th Street
Beaumont, TX 77701
409-832-0221

Post Office Box 2173
Beaumont, TX 77704

Officers
Ted E. Moon, Jr., Pres.
Frank J. Ryan, Jr., Gen. Mgr.

Whom to Contact
Frank J. Ryan

Type of Firm
SBIC

Industry Association Membership
NASBIC

Project Preferences
Will function either as deal originator or
  investor in deals created by others
Type of Financing:
First-stage
Second-stage
Later-stage expansion
Leveraged buyout
Minimum Investment: Less than $100,000
Preferred Investment: $100,000-$250,000
Minimum Operating Data:
Annual Sales—Nominal
P&L—Losses (profits projected after 2 years)

Geographical Preferences
Southeast
Southwest
Rocky Mountains
Gulf States

Industry Preferences

Communications
Cable television
Consumer
Computer stores/related services
Consumer products
Consumer services
Food and beverage products
Franchise businesses
Hotels and resort areas
Leisure and recreational products
Restaurants
Retailing
Distribution
Consumer products
Industrial products

Energy/Natural Resources
Drilling and exploration services
Technology related products/equipment
Industrial Products and Equipment
Chemicals
Controls and sensors
Energy management
Equipment and machinery
Other industrial automation
Plastics
Robotics/vision systems
Specialty materials

Additional Information
Year Founded—1983
Capital Under Management—$1 million
Investments(1985-1st 6 months)—3
Invested(1985-1st 6 months)—$200,000
Method of Compensation—Return on
   investment is most important, but also
   charge for closing fees, service fees, etc.

ORANGE NASSAU

One Galleria Tower #635
13355 Noel Road
Dallas, TX 75240
214-385-9685

Martin J. Silver, Assoc.
F. Dan Blanchard, Assoc.

See MASSACHUSETTS for full listing

PORCARI, FEARNOW & ASSOCIATES

1900 West Loop South #1150
Houston, TX 77027
713-840-7500

Officers
Michael T. Fearnow, Chm. & CFO
Arthur J. Porcari, Pres. & CEO

Whom to Contact
Michael T. Fearnow

Type of Firm
Investment banking or merchant banking
   firm investing own capital or funds of
   partners or clients

Project Preferences
Will function either as deal originator or
   investor in deals created by others
Type of Financing:
Second-stage
Leveraged buyout

Minimum Investment: $500,000
Preferred Investment: $500,000-$1 million
Minimum Operating Data:
Annual Sales—$500,000
P&L—Break even

Geographical Preferences
Southwest
Gulf States

Industry Preferences

Consumer
Computer stores/related services
Consumer products
Consumer services
Food and beverage products
Franchise businesses
Hotels and resort areas
Leisure and recreational products
Restaurants
Retailing
Distribution
Communications equipment
Computer equipment
Consumer products
Electronics equipment
Food products
Industrial products
Medical products
Energy/Natural Resources
Alternative energy
Coal related
Drilling and exploration services
Energy conservation
Minerals
Oil and gas exploration and production
Technology related products/equipment

Additional Information
Year Founded—1978
Investments(1985-1st 6 months)—2
Invested(1985-1st 6 months)—$1.5 million
Method of Compensation—Return on
   investment is most important, but also
   charge for closing fees, service fees, etc.

REPUBLIC VENTURE GROUP, INC./REPUBLIC VENTURE CAPITAL CORP.

Pacific & St. Paul Streets
Dallas, TX 75201
214-922-5078

Post Office Box 225961
Dallas, TX 75265

Officers
Robert H. Wellborn, Pres.
William W. Richey, V.P.
Wayne C. Willcox, V.P.
Bart A. McLean, Inv. Officer
Sherry L. Richardson, Inv. Officer

Whom to Contact
Any of the above

Type of Firm
SBIC
Venture capital subsidiary of
   commercial bank

Affiliation
Republic Bank Dallas (parent)

Industry Association Memberships
NASBIC
NVCA

Project Preferences
Will function either as deal originator or
   investor in deals created by others
Type of Financing:
First-stage
Second-stage
Later-stage expansion
Leveraged buyout
Minimum Investment: $250,000
Preferred Investment: $500,000-$1 million
Preferred Investment (LBO):
   $500,000-$1 million
Minimum Operating Data:
Annual Sales—$500,000
P&L—Losses (profits projected after 2 years)

Geographical Preferences
Southwest
National

Industry Preferences

Communications
Cable television
Commercial communications
Data communications
Satellite and microwave communications
Telephone related

Computer Related
Computer graphics, CAD/CAM and CAE
Computer mainframes
Computer services
Memory devices
Micro and mini computers
Office automation
Scanning related
Software-applications
Software-artificial intelligence
Software-systems
Specialized turnkey systems
Terminals
Consumer
Consumer products
Food and beverage products
Electronic Components and Instrumentation
Analytical and scientific instrumentation
Component fabrication and testing equipment
Electronic components
Fiber optics
Laser related
Semiconductors
Energy/Natural Resources
Drilling and exploration services
Oil and gas exploration and production
Technology related products/equipment
Industrial Products and Equipment
Chemicals
Controls and sensors
Energy management
Equipment and machinery
Other industrial automation
Plastics
Robotics/vision systems
Specialty materials
Medical/Health Related
Diagnostic equipment
Diagnostic test products
Disposable products
Drugs and medicines
Hospital and clinical labs
Medical services
Therapeutic equipment
Other
Agriculture, forestry, fishing
Publishing
Transportation
Will Not Consider
Finance and insurance
Real estate

Additional Information
Year Founded—1961
Capital Under Management—$22 million
Investments(1985-1st 6 months)—6
Invested(1985-1st 6 months)—$1.4 million
Method of Compensation—Return on investment is of primary concern; do not charge fees

---

RETZLOFF CAPITAL CORPORATION

15000 Northwest Freeway #310
Post Office Box 41250
Houston, TX 77240
713-466-4690

Officers
James K. Hines, Pres.
George Martinez, Treas.
Steve Retzloff, Exec. V.P.
Diane S. Langdon, Secy.

Whom to Contact
James K. Hines

Type of Firm
SBIC

Affiliation
Retzloff Industries, Inc. (parent)

Project Preferences
Will function either as deal originator or investor in deals created by others
Type of Financing:
Startup
First-stage
Minimum Investment: $500,000
Preferred Investment: $500,000-$1 million

Geographical Preference
None

Industry Preferences
None

Additional Information
Year Founded—1983
Capital Under Management—$4.5 million
Investments(1985-1st 6 months)—4
Invested(1985-1st 6 months)—$825,000
Method of Compensation—Return on investment is most important, but also charge for closing fees, service fees, etc.

ROTAN MOSLE TECHNOLOGY PARTNERS, LTD.

3800 RepublicBank Center
700 Louisiana
Houston, TX 77002
713-236-3180

Other Office
Taylor & Turner
220 Montgomery Street
Penthouse #10
San Francisco, CA 94104
415-398-6821

Partners
John V. Jaggers, Pres.
William H. Taylor II
Marshall C. Turner, Jr.

Whom to Contact
John V. Jaggers (Texas)

Type of Firm
Private venture capital firm investing own capital

Affiliations
Taylor & Turner, San Francisco (co-investing fund with Taylor & Turner as general partner)
VenWest Partners, Pittsburgh (co-investing fund with Taylor & Turner as general partner)

Industry Association Memberships
NASBIC
NVCA

Project Preferences
Will function either as deal originator or investor in deals created by others
Type of Financing:
Seed
Startup
First-stage
Second-stage
Later-stage expansion
Minimum Investment: Less than $100,000
Preferred Investment: $500,000-$1 million
Minimum Operating Data:
Annual Sales—Nominal
P&L—Losses (profits projected after 2 years)

Geographical Preference
None

Industry Preferences

Communications
Data communications
Satellite and microwave communications
Computer Related
Computer graphics, CAD/CAM and CAE
Computer mainframes
Computer services
Memory devices
Micro and mini computers
Office automation
Scanning related
Software-applications
Software-artificial intelligence
Software-systems
Specialized turnkey systems
Terminals
Consumer
Consumer products
Electronic Components and Instrumentation
Analytical and scientific instrumentation
Electronic components
Fiber optics
Laser related
Semiconductors
Energy/Natural Resources
Technology related products/equipment
Genetic Engineering
Gene splicing and manufacturing equipment
Monoclonal antibodies and hybridomas
Recombinant DNA (agricultural and industrial)
Recombinant DNA (medical)
Industrial Products and Equipment
Advanced materials
Chemicals
Controls and sensors
Equipment and machinery
Other industrial automation
Plastics
Process controls
Robotics/vision systems
Specialty materials
Medical/Health Related
Diagnostic equipment
Diagnostic test products
Disposable products
Drugs and medicines
Hospital and clinical labs
Medical services
Therapeutic equipment
Other
Military/aerospace
Will Not Consider
Natural resource exploration
Real estate

Additional Information

Year Founded—1983
Capital Under Management—$18.5 million (with affiliates)
Investments(1985-1st 6 months)—8
Invested(1985-1st 6 months)—$1.8 million
Method of Compensation—Return on investment is of primary concern; do not charge fees

---

R. PATRICK ROWLES & CO., INC.

3336 Richmond Avenue #202
Houston, TX 77098
713-521-0388

Officers

R. Patrick Rowles, Pres.
Nancy Arbuckle, V.P.

Whom to Contact

Either of the above

Type of Firm

Consulting firm evaluating and analyzing venture projects and arranging private placements

Project Preferences

Prefer role as deal originator but will also invest in deals created by others
Type of Financing:
Startup
First-stage
Second-stage
Minimum Investment: Less than $100,000
Preferred Investment: $250,000-$500,000
Minimum Operating Data:
Annual Sales—Nominal
P&L—Break even

Geographical Preference

Southwest

Industry Preferences

Communications
Satellite and microwave communications
Computer Related
Computer graphics, CAD/CAM and CAE
Micro and mini computers
Software-applications
Software-artificial intelligence
Software-systems
Energy/Natural Resources
Technology related products/equipment

Genetic Engineering
Gene splicing and manufacturing equipment
Monoclonal antibodies and hybridomas
Recombinant DNA (agricultural and industrial)
Recombinant DNA (medical)
Industrial Products and Equipment
Energy management
Medical/Health Related
Diagnostic equipment
Diagnostic test products
Disposable products
Drugs and medicines
Other
Finance and insurance
Publishing

Additional Information

Year Founded—1981
Investments(1985-1st 6 months)—1
Invested(1985-1st 6 months)—$820,000
Method of Compensation—Return on investment is most important, but also charge for closing fees, service fees, etc.

RUST VENTURES, L.P.

114 West Seventh Street
Austin, TX 78701
512-479-0055

Partners

Jack R. Crosby, Gen. Ptnr.
Jeffery C. Garvey, Gen. Ptnr.
Kenneth P. DeAngelis, Gen. Ptnr.
Joseph C. Aragona, Ptnr.
William P. Wood, Ptnr.

Whom to Contact

Kenneth P. DeAngelis

Type of Firm

Private venture capital firm investing own capital

Affiliation

Rust Capital, Ltd. (SBIC affiliate under common management)

Project Preferences

Will function either as deal originator or investor in deals created by others
Type of Financing:
Startup
First-stage
Second-stage
Later-stage expansion
Leveraged buyout

Minimum Investment: $500,000
Preferred Investment: Over $1 million
Preferred Investment (LBO):
   $1.5-$2.5 million
Minimum Operating Data:
Annual Sales—Nominal
P&L—Losses (profits projected after 2 years)
Annual Sales (LBO)—Over $15 million

Geographical Preference
Southwest (early stage)
None (later stage & LBO)

Industry Preferences

Communications
Cable television
Data communications
Satellite and microwave communications
Telephone related
Computer Related
Office automation
Software-artificial intelligence
**Electronic Components and
   Instrumentation**
Analytical and scientific instrumentation
Electronic components
Fiber optics
Laser related
Semiconductors
Industrial Products and Equipment
Chemicals
Controls and sensors
Energy management
Equipment and machinery
Other industrial automation
Plastics
Robotics/vision systems
Specialty materials
Medical/Health Related
Medical services
Will Not Consider
Real estate

Additional Information
Year Founded—1979
Capital Under Management—$48.3 million
   (includes Rust Capital, Ltd.)
Method of Compensation—Return on
   investment is of primary concern;
   usually do not charge fees

SAN ANTONIO VENTURE GROUP, INC.

2300 West Commerce
San Antonio, TX 78209
512-223-3633

Officers
Domingo Bueno, Pres.
Mike Parish, Inv. Advisor
Tom Woodley, Inv. Advisor

Whom to Contact
Mike Parish

Type of Firm
SBIC

Affiliation
MESBIC of San Antonio (sister company)

Industry Association Membership
NASBIC

Project Preferences
Will function either as deal originator or
   investor in deals created by others
Type of Financing:
Second-stage
Later-stage expansion
Leveraged buyout
Minimum Investment: Less than $100,000
Preferred Investment: $100,000-$250,000
Minimum Operating Data:
Annual Sales—$500,000
P&L—Break even

Geographical Preference
San Antonio

Industry Preferences

Consumer
Consumer products
Consumer services
Food and beverage products
Leisure and recreational products
Restaurants
Retailing
Distribution
Communications equipment
Computer equipment
Consumer products
Electronics equipment
Food products
Industrial products
Medical products

Industrial Products and Equipment
Chemicals
Controls and sensors
Equipment and machinery
Plastics
Robotics/vision systems
Specialty materials
Medical/Health Related
Diagnostic equipment
Diagnostic test products
Disposable products
Drugs and medicines
Hospital and clinical labs
Medical services
Therapeutic equipment
Other
Transportation

Additional Information
Year Founded—1978
Capital Under Management—$1 million
Investments(1985-1st 6 months)—1
Invested(1985-1st 6 months)—$40,000
Method of Compensation—Return on
   investment is most important, but also
   charge for closing fees, service fees, etc.

SBI CAPITAL CORP.

6305 Beverly Hill
Houston, TX 77036
713-975-1188

Post Office Box 771668
Houston, TX 77215

Officer
William E. Wright, Pres.

Type of Firm
SBIC

Industry Association Membership
NASBIC

Project Preferences
Will function either as deal originator or
   investor in deals created by others
Type of Financing:
First-stage
Second-stage
Later-stage expansion
Leveraged buyout
Minimum Investment: $500,000
Preferred Investment: $250,000-$500,000
Minimum Operating Data:
Annual Sales—$1.5 million
P&L—Break even

Geographical Preference
Southwest

Industry Preferences

Computer Related
Computer graphics, CAD/CAM and CAE
Computer mainframes
Computer services
Memory devices
Micro and mini computers
Scanning related
Scanning related
Software-applications
Software-artificial intelligence
Software-systems
Specialized turnkey systems
Terminals
Electronic Components and Instrumentation
Analytical and scientific instrumentation
Component fabrication and testing equipment
Electronic components
Fiber optics
Laser related
Semiconductors
Energy/Natural Resources
Technology related products/equipment
Genetic Engineering
Gene splicing and manufacturing equipment
Monoclonal antibodies and hybridomas
Recombinant DNA (agricultural and industrial)
Recombinant DNA (medical)
Industrial Products and Equipment
Chemicals
Controls and sensors
Energy management
Equipment and machinery
Other industrial automation
Plastics
Robotics/vision systems
Specialty materials
Medical/Health Related
Diagnostic equipment
Diagnostic test products
Disposable products
Drugs and medicines
Hospital and clinical labs
Medical services
Therapeutic equipment

Additional Information
Year Founded—1980
Capital Under Management—$5 million
Investments(1985-1st 6 months)—4
Invested(1985-1st 6 months)—$528,000
Method of Compensation—Return on investment is of primary concern; do not charge fees

SEVIN ROSEN MANAGEMENT COMPANY

13455 Noel Road #1670
Dallas, TX 75240
214-960-1744

Other Offices
200 Park Avenue #4503
New York, NY 10166
212-687-5115

1245 Oakmead Parkway #101
Sunnyvale, CA 94086
408-720-8590

Officers
L.J. Sevin, Pres. (Texas)
Benjamin M. Rosen, Chm. (New York)
Jon W. Bayless, Ptnr. (Texas)
Roger S. Borovoy, Ptnr. (California)
Stephen M. Dow, Ptnr. (California)
Dennis J. Gorman, CFO (Texas)

Whom to Contact
Any of the above (closest office)

Type of Firm
Private venture capital firm investing own capital

Industry Association Membership
NVCA

Project Preferences
Prefer role as deal originator
Type of Financing:
Seed
Startup
Minimum Investment: $500,000
Preferred Investment: $500,000-$1 million
Minimum Operating Data:
Annual Sales—Nominal
P&L—Losses (profits projected after 2 years)

Geographical Preferences
Southwest
East Coast
West Coast

Industry Preferences

Communications
Commercial communications
Data communications
Satellite and microwave communications
Telephone related

Computer Related
Computer graphics, CAD/CAM and CAE
Computer mainframes
Computer services
Memory devices
Micro and mini computers
Office automation
Scanning related
Software-applications
Software-artificial intelligence
Software-systems
Specialized turnkey systems
Terminals
Distribution
Communications equipment
Computer equipment
Electronic Components and Instrumentation
Analytical and scientific instrumentation
Fiber optics
Semiconductors
Genetic Engineering
Gene splicing and manufacturing equipment
Monoclonal antibodies and hybridomas
Recombinant DNA (agricultural and industrial)
Recombinant DNA (medical)
Industrial Products and Equipment
Controls and sensors
Robotics/vision systems
Will Not Consider
Consulting services
Consumer services
Oil and gas
Real estate
Transportation

Additional Information
Year Founded—1981
Capital Under Management—$300 million
Investments(1985-1st 6 months)—6
Invested(1985-1st 6 months)—$10 million
Method of Compensation—Return on investment is of primary concern; do not charge fees

SOUTH TEXAS SMALL BUSINESS INVESTMENT COMPANY

One O'Connor Plaza
Victoria, TX 77901
512-573-5151

Officers
Kenneth L. Vickers, Pres.
Royce F. Church, V.P. & Gen. Mgr.
Richard T. Cullen, V.P.
E.K. Ponish, Secy.
Robert L. Coffey, Treas.

Whom to Contact
Kenneth L. Vickers
Royce F. Church

Type of Firm
SBIC
Venture capital subsidiary of
commercial bank

Affiliation
Victoria Bank and Trust Company (parent)

Project Preferences
Will function either as deal originator or
investor in deals created by others
Type of Financing:
Second-stage
Later-stage expansion
Leveraged buyout
Minimum Investment: Less than $100,000
Preferred Investment: $100,000-$250,000
Minimum Operating Data:
Annual Sales—Nominal
P&L—Profitable

Geographical Preference
Within two hours of office

Industry Preferences

Communications
Cable television
Commercial communications
Data communications
Satellite and microwave communications
Telephone related

Computer Related
Computer graphics, CAD/CAM and CAE
Computer mainframes
Computer services
Memory devices
Micro and mini computers
Office automation
Scanning related
Software-applications
Software-artificial intelligence
Software-systems
Specialized turnkey systems
Terminals
Consumer
Computer stores/related services
Consumer products
Consumer services
Food and beverage products
Franchise businesses
Hotels and resort areas
Leisure and recreational products
Restaurants
Retailing
Distribution
Communications equipment
Computer equipment
Consumer products
Electronics equipment
Food products
Industrial products
Medical products
Electronic Components and Instrumentation
Analytical and scientific instrumentation
Component fabrication and testing
equipment
Electronic components
Fiber optics
Laser related
Semiconductors
Energy/Natural Resources
Alternative energy
Coal related
Drilling and exploration services
Energy conservation
Minerals
Oil and gas exploration and production
Technology related products/equipment
Genetic Engineering
Gene splicing and manufacturing equipment
Monoclonal antibodies and hybridomas
Recombinant DNA (agricultural and
industrial)
Recombinant DNA (medical)

Industrial Products and Equipment
Chemicals
Controls and sensors
Energy management
Equipment and machinery
Other industrial automation
Plastics
Robotics/vision systems
Specialty materials
Medical/Health Related
Diagnostic equipment
Diagnostic test products
Disposable products
Drugs and medicines
Hospital and clinical labs
Medical services
Therapeutic equipment
Other
Agriculture, forestry, fishing
Education related
Finance and insurance
Publishing
Real estate
Specialty consulting
Transportation

Additional Information
Year Founded—1969
Capital Under Management—$2.7 million
Investments(1985-1st 6 months)—6
Invested(1985-1st 6 months)—$431,000
Return on investment is of primary concern;
do not charge fees

SOUTHWEST ENTERPRISE ASSOCIATES

5420 LBJ Freeway #1266
Lock Box 41
Dallas, TX 75240
214-991-1620

NEA Partners Southwest
235 Montgomery Street #1205
San Francisco, CA 94104
415-956-1579

Partners
C.V. Prothro, Mgn. Gen. Ptnr. (Texas)
C.R. Kramlich, Gen. Ptnr. (California)
H. Leland Murphy, Assoc. (Texas)

Whom to Contact
H. Leland Murphy

Type of Firm
Private venture capital firm investing
own capital

Affiliations
NEA Partners Southwest, L.P.
(general partner)
New Enterprise Associates (joint venture)

Project Preferences
Will function either as deal originator or
investor in deals created by others
Type of Financing:
Seed
Startup
First-stage
Minimum Investment: $500,000
Preferred Investment: $500,000-$1 million
Minimum Operating Data:
Annual Sales—Nominal

Geographical Preference
Southwest

Industry Preferences

Communications
Data communications
Telephone related
Computer Related
Computer mainframes
Memory devices
Micro and mini computers
Terminals
**Electronic Components and
Instrumentation**
Electronic components
Semiconductors
Will Not Consider
Agriculture
Energy related businesses
Real estate
Retailing

Additional Information
Year Founded—1983
Capital Under Management—$25 million
Investments(1985-1st 6 months)—6
Invested(1985-1st 6 months)—$2 million
Method of Compensation—Return on
investment is of primary concern; do not
charge fees

THE SOUTHWEST VENTURE PARTNERSHIPS

300 Convent #1400
San Antonio, TX 78205
512-227-1010

Other Office
5080 Spectrum Drive #610-E
Dallas, TX 75248
214-960-0404

Partners
Michael Bell, Gen. Ptnr. (San Antonio)
J. Edward McAteer, Gen. Ptnr. (Dallas)
Charles D. Grojean, Gen. Ptnr. (San Antonio)
Mark D. Buckner, CFO (San Antonio)
John L. Long, Jr., Assoc. (San Antonio)

Whom to Contact
Michael Bell
J. Edward McAteer
Charles D. Grojean

Type of Firm
Private venture capital firm investing
own capital

Affiliations
HixVen Partners, formerly Hixon Venture
Company (affiliate partnership)
Southwest Venture Management Company
(management company for partnerships)

Industry Association Memberships
NASBIC
NVCA

Project Preferences
Will function either as deal originator or
investor in deals created by others
Type of Financing:
First-stage
Second-stage
Leveraged buyout
Minimum Investment: $500,000
Preferred Investment: $500,000-$1 million
Minimum Operating Data:
Annual Sales—$500,000
P&L—Losses (profits projected after 2 years)

Geographical Preference
None

Industry Preferences

Communications
Cable television
Commercial communications
Data communications
Satellite and microwave communications
Telephone related
Computer Related
Computer graphics, CAD/CAM and CAE
Computer mainframes
Computer services
Memory devices
Micro and mini computers
Office automation
Scanning related
Software-applications
Software-artificial intelligence
Software-systems
Specialized turnkey systems
Terminals
Energy/Natural Resources
Alternative energy
Drilling and exploration services
Genetic Engineering
Gene splicing and manufacturing equipment
Monoclonal antibodies and hybridomas
Recombinant DNA (agricultural and
industrial)
Recombinant DNA (medical)
Medical/Health Related
Diagnostic equipment
Diagnostic test products
Disposable products
Drugs and medicines
Hospital and clinical labs
Medical services
Therapeutic equipment
Will Not Consider
Real estate

Additional Information
Year Founded—1975
Capital Under Management—$70 million
Investments(1985-1st 6 months)—12
Invested(1985-1st 6 months)—$4 million
Method of Compensation—Return on
investment is of primary concern; do not
charge fees

THE STERLING GROUP, INC.

Eight Greenway Plaza #702
Houston, TX 77046
713-877-8257

Other Office
2200 Green Street
San Francisco, CA 94123
415-922-0768

Principals
Gordon A. Cain (Texas)
Frank J. Hevrdejs (Texas)
Cameron Adair (California)
William C. Oehmig (Texas)

Whom to Contact
Frank J. Hevrdejs
Cameron Adair

Type of Firm
Investment banking firm investing own
capital or funds of clients

Affiliation
Sterling Financial Corporation (affiliate under
common ownership)

Industry Association Membership
NVCA

Project Preferences
Prefer role as deal originator
Type of Financing:
Leveraged buyout
Preferred Investment (LBO):
$1 million and over
Minimum Operating Data:
Annual Sales (LBO)—$3 million-$150 million

Geographical Preference
National

Industry Preferences

Consumer
Consumer products
Food and beverage products
Franchise businesses
Leisure and recreational products
Restaurants
Retailing
Distribution
Consumer products
Electronics equipment
Food products
Industrial products
Medical products

Industrial Products and Equipment
Chemicals
Equipment and machinery
Fertilizers
Plastics
Medical/Health Related
Disposable products
Drugs and medicines

Additional Information
Year Founded—1982
Capital Under Management—Over
$900 million in LBO transactions
completed to date
Method of Compensation—Return on
investment is most important, but also
charge for closing fees, service fees, etc.

STRATEGIC DEVELOPMENT & MARKETING CORPORATION

Four Forest Plaza #660
12222 Merit Drive
Dallas, TX 75251
214-991-1990

Officers
Shawn P. Clark, Pres.
D. Michael Cannady, Exec. V.P.
William O. Kling, V.P.
Dr. Phillip R. Ash, V.P.

Whom to Contact
D. Michael Cannady

Type of Firm
Consulting firm evaluating and analyzing
venture projects and arranging private
placements
Strategic marketing consultants investing
own resources and capital in situations
where marketing strategy is crucial

Project Preferences
Prefer role as deal originator but will also
invest in deals created by others
Type of Financing:
Seed
Research and development partnerships
Startup
First-stage
Leveraged buyout
Turnaround
Minimum Investment: Less than $100,000
Preferred Investment: Less than $100,000
Minimum Operating Data:
Annual Sales—Nominal
P&L—Losses (profits projected after 2 years)

Geographical Preferences
Southwest
National

Industry Preferences

Communications
Cable television
Commercial communications
Data communications
Satellite and microwave communications
Telephone related
Computer Related
Computer graphics, CAD/CAM and CAE
Computer mainframes
Computer services
Memory devices
Micro and mini computers
Office automation
Scanning related
Software-applications
Software-artificial intelligence
Software-systems
Specialized turnkey systems
Terminals
Consumer
Computer stores/related services
Consumer products
Consumer services
Food and beverage products
Franchise businesses
Hotels and resort areas
Leisure and recreational products
Restaurants
Retailing
Distribution
Communications equipment
Computer equipment
Consumer products
Electronics equipment
Food products
Industrial products
Medical products
Electronic Components and Instrumentation
Analytical and scientific instrumentation
Component fabrication and testing
equipment
Electronic components
Fiber optics
Laser related
Semiconductors
Energy/Natural Resources
Technology related products/equipment

Industrial Products and Equipment
Chemicals
Computer integrated manufacturing systems
Controls and sensors
Energy management
Equipment and machinery
Other industrial automation
Plastics
Robotics/vision systems
Specialty materials
Medical/Health Related
Diagnostic equipment
Diagnostic test products
Disposable products
Drugs and medicines
Hospital and clinical labs
Medical services
Therapeutic equipment
Other
Companies involved in rapidly changing
  market environments
Education related
Finance and insurance
Publishing
Specialty consulting
Transportation
Will Not Consider
Companies not market driven or in
  stable marketplaces

Additional Information
Year Founded—1981
Method of Compensation—Return on
  investment is most important, but also
  charge for closing fees, service fees, etc.
Professional fee required whether or
  not deal closes

STUART COMPANY

2421 One Main Place
Dallas, TX 75202
214-744-0750

Officer
Daniel B. Stuart

Type of Firm
Private venture capital firm investing
  own capital

Project Preferences
Will function either as deal originator or
  investor in deals created by others
Type of Financing:
Seed
Startup
Leveraged buyout

Minimum Investment: Less than $100,000
Preferred Investment: $100,000-$250,000
Preferred Investment (LBO):
  $1 million-$50 million
Minimum Operating Data:
Annual Sales—Nominal
P&L—Losses (profits projected after 1 year)
Annual Sales (LBO)—$20 million

Geographical Preferences
Southwest
Midwest

Industry Preferences

Communications
Various
Computer Related
Computer graphics, CAD/CAM and CAE
Computer services
Office automation
Software-applications
Software-artificial intelligence
Software-systems
Specialized turnkey systems
Consumer
Food and beverage products
Distribution
Medical products
Industrial Products and Equipment
Plastics
Specialty materials
Medical/Health Related
Diagnostic equipment
Medical services
Other
Education related

Additional Information
Year Founded—1976
Capital Under Management—$10 million
Investments(1985-1st 6 months)—2
Invested(1985-1st 6 months)—$10 million
Method of Compensation—Return on
  investment and consulting fees

SUNWESTERN MANAGEMENT, INC.

12221 Morit Drive #1680
Dallas, TX 75251
214-239-5650

Officers
Dan M. Krausse, Chm. & CEO
James F. Leary, Pres.
Tom H. Delimitros, Sr. V.P.
Thomas W. Wright, V.P.

Whom to Contact
James F. Leary

Type of Firm
Private venture capital firm investing
  own capital
SBIC

Industry Association Memberships
NASBIC
NVCA

Project Preferences
Prefer role as deal originator but will also
  invest in deals created by others
Type of Financing:
Seed
Startup
First-stage
Second-stage
Later-stage expansion
Leveraged buyout
Minimum Investment: $250,000
Preferred Investment: $500,000-$1 million
Preferred Investment (LBO): $1 million
Minimum Operating Data:
Annual Sales—Nominal
P&L—Losses (profits projected after 2 years)
Annual Sales (LBO)—$25 million

Geographical Preference
Southwest

Industry Preferences

Communications
Commercial communications
Data communications
Paging services
Telephone related
Computer Related
Computer graphics, CAD/CAM and CAE
Computer services
Office automation
Software-applications
Software-systems
Distribution
Communications equipment
Industrial products
Medical products
Energy/Natural Resources
Drilling and exploration services
Oil and gas exploration and production
Technology related products/equipment
Industrial Products and Equipment
Chemicals
Energy management
Plastics
Specialty materials
Medical/Health Related
Diagnostic equipment
Diagnostic test products
Disposable products

Other
Finance and insurance
Will Not Consider
Real estate
Restaurants

Additional Information
Year Founded—1982
Capital Under Management—$46 million
Investments(1985-1st 6 months)—12
Invested(1985-1st 6 months)—$6 million
Method of Compensation—Return on
  investment is of primary concern; do not
  charge fees

TENNECO VENTURES, INC.

1010 Milam #T-2919
Post Office Box 2511
Houston, TX 77001
713-757-8776

Officers
Richard L. Wambold, Pres.
Carl S. Stutts, V.P.
James J. Kozlowski, Dir. New
  Business Devel.

Whom to Contact
Either of the above

Type of Firm
Venture capital subsidiary or affiliate of
  non-financial corporation

Affiliation
Tenneco, Inc. (parent)

Industry Association Membership
NVCA

Project Preferences
Will function either as deal originator or
  investor in deals created by others
Type of Financing:
Startup
First-stage
Second-stage
Later-stage expansion
Leveraged buyout
Minimum Investment: $250,000
Preferred Investment: $500,000-$1 million

Geographical Preference
National

Industry Preferences

Communications
Data communications
Satellite and microwave communications
Telephone related
Computer Related
Computer graphics, CAD/CAM and CAE
Scanning related
Software-applications
Software-artificial intelligence
Software-systems
Specialized turnkey systems
Consumer
Food and beverage products
Retailing
Distribution
Food products
Industrial products
Medical products
**Electronic Components and
  Instrumentation**
Analytical and scientific instrumentation
Laser related
Energy/Natural Resources
Alternative energy
Drilling and exploration services
Energy conservation
Minerals
Technology related products/equipment
Genetic Engineering
Gene splicing and manufacturing equipment
Monoclonal antibodies and hybridomas
Recombinant DNA (agricultural and
  industrial)
Recombinant DNA (medical)
Industrial Products and Equipment
Chemicals
Controls and sensors
Energy management
Equipment and machinery
Other industrial automation
Plastics
Robotics/vision systems
Specialty materials
Medical/Health Related
Diagnostic equipment
Diagnostic test products
Disposable products
Drugs and medicines
Hospital and clinical labs
Medical services
Therapeutic equipment
Other
Agriculture, forestry, fishing
Publishing
Transportation
Will Not Consider
Real estate

Additional Information
Year Founded—1984
Capital Under Management—$30 million
Investments(1985-1st 6 months)—2
Invested(1985-1st 6 months)—$900,000
Method of Compensation—Return on
  investment is of primary concern; do not
  charge fees

TEXAS CAPITAL CORPORATION

1341 West Mockingbird #1250E
Dallas, TX 75247
214-638-0638

Officers
David G. Franklin, V.P.
Tom L. Beecroft, Asst. V.P.

Whom to Contact
Either of the above

Type of Firm
SBIC

Affiliation
TeleCom Corporation (parent)

Industry Association Membership
NASBIC

Project Preferences
Will function either as deal originator or
  investor in deals created by others
Type of Financing:
First-stage
Second-stage
Later-stage expansion
Leveraged buyout
Minimum Investment: $250,000
Preferred Investment: $250,000-$500,000
Preferred Investment (LBO):
  $300,000-$500,000
Minimum Operating Data:
Annual Sales—$3 million
P&L—Break even

Geographical Preference
Southwest

Industry Preferences

Communications
Cable television
Commercial communications
Data communications
Satellite and microwave communications
Telephone related

Computer Related
Computer graphics, CAD/CAM and CAE
Computer mainframes
Computer services
Memory devices
Micro and mini computers
Office automation
Scanning related
Software-applications
Software-artificial intelligence
Software-systems
Specialized turnkey systems
Terminals
Distribution
Communications equipment
Computer equipment
Consumer products
Electronics equipment
Food products
Industrial products
Medical products
Electronic Components and Instrumentation
Analytical and scientific instrumentation
Component fabrication and testing equipment
Electronic components
Fiber optics
Laser related
Semiconductors
Energy/Natural Resources
Technology related products/equipment
Industrial Products and Equipment
Chemicals
Controls and sensors
Energy management
Equipment and machinery
Other industrial automation
Plastics
Robotics/vision systems
Specialty materials
Medical/Health Related
Diagnostic equipment
Diagnostic test products
Disposable products
Drugs and medicines
Hospital and clinical labs
Medical services
Therapeutic equipment
Will Not Consider
Energy exploration
Real estate

Additional Information
Year Founded—1958
Capital Under Management—$15 million
Method of Compensation—Return on investment is of primary concern; do not charge fees

TEXAS COMMERCE INVESTMENT COMPANY

707 Travis Street
Post Office Box 2558
Houston, TX 77252
713-236-4719

Officers
Fred R. Lummis, V.P.
Frederic C. Hamilton, Jr., Asst. V.P.

Whom to Contact
Either of the above

Type of Firm
Venture capital subsidiary of commercial bank

Affiliation
Texas Commerce Bancshares, Inc. (parent)

Industry Association Membership
NASBIC

Project Preferences
Will function either as deal originator or investor in deals created by others
Type of Financing:
First-stage
Second-stage
Later-stage expansion
Leveraged buyout
Minimum Investment: $500,000
Preferred Investment: $500,000-$1 million
Preferred Investment (LBO): $500,000-$50 million
Minimum Operating Data:
Annual Sales—Nominal
P&L—Losses (profits projected after 2 years)
Annual Sales (LBO)—$10 million-$50 million

Geographical Preference
None

Industry Preferences

Communications
Cable television
Commercial communications
Data communications
Satellite and microwave communications
Telephone related

Computer Related
Computer graphics, CAD/CAM and CAE
Computer mainframes
Computer services
Memory devices
Micro and mini computers
Office automation
Scanning related
Software-applications
Software-artificial intelligence
Software-systems
Specialized turnkey systems
Terminals
Consumer
Consumer products
Consumer services
Food and beverage products
Leisure and recreational products
Distribution
Food products
Industrial products
Medical products
Electronic Components and Instrumentation
Fiber optics
Laser related
Energy/Natural Resources
Alternative energy
Coal related
Drilling and exploration services
Energy conservation
Minerals
Oil and gas exploration and production
Oil and gas exploration and production
Technology related products/equipment
Genetic Engineering
Gene splicing and manufacturing equipment
Monoclonal antibodies and hybridomas
Recombinant DNA (agricultural and industrial)
Recombinant DNA (medical)
Industrial Products and Equipment
Ceramics
Chemicals
Composites
Controls and sensors
Energy management
Equipment and machinery
Other industrial automation
Plastics
Robotics/vision systems
Specialty materials
Medical/Health Related
Diagnostic equipment
Diagnostic test products
Disposable products
Drugs and medicines
Hospital and clinical labs
Medical services
Therapeutic equipment

Other
Agriculture, forestry, fishing
Finance and insurance
Publishing
Transportation
Will Not Consider
Real estate
Motion pictures

Additional Information
Year Founded—1982
Capital Under Management—$10 million
Investments(1985-1st 6 months)—5
Invested(1985-1st 6 months)—$1.2 million
Method of Compensation—Return on
investment is of primary concern; do not
charge fees

TRIAD VENTURES LIMITED

301 West Sixth Street
Post Office Box 1987
Austin, TX 78767
512-472-7171

Partners
H.A. Abshier, Jr., Gen. Ptnr.
Lloyd Bentsen III, Gen. Ptnr.
Nick Stanfield, Gen. Ptnr.
Rex E. Gwinn, Sr. V.P.
W. Ward Greenwood, Sr. V.P.

Whom to Contact
Any of the above

Type of Firm
Regional general industry venture
capital fund

Affiliations
Triad Ventures Management, Ltd.
(general partner)
Bentsen Investment Company
(general partner)
Financial Services-Austin, Inc.
(general partner)
MSI Capital Corporation (general partner)

Project Preferences
Will function either as deal originator or
investor in deals created by others
Type of Financing:
Startup
First-stage
Second-stage
Later-stage expansion
Leveraged buyout
Minimum Investment: $250,000
Preferred Investment: $250,000-$500,000

Minimum Operating Data:
Annual Sales—$500,000
P&L—Losses (profits projected after 2 years)

Geographical Preference
Southwest

Industry Preferences

Communications
Cable television
Commercial communications
Data communications
Satellite and microwave communications
Telephone related
Computer Related
Computer graphics, CAD/CAM and CAE
Computer mainframes
Computer services
Memory devices
Micro and mini computers
Office automation
Scanning related
Software-applications
Software-artificial intelligence
Software-systems
Specialized turnkey systems
Terminals
Consumer
Computer stores/related services
Consumer products
Consumer services
Food and beverage products
Franchise businesses
Hotels and resort areas
Leisure and recreational products
Restaurants
Retailing
Distribution
Communications equipment
Computer equipment
Consumer products
Electronics equipment
Food products
Industrial products
Medical products
**Electronic Components and
Instrumentation**
Analytical and scientific instrumentation
Component fabrication and testing
equipment
Electronic components
Fiber optics
Laser related
Semiconductors
Energy/Natural Resources
Drilling and exploration services
Oil and gas exploration and production
Technology related products/equipment

Genetic Engineering
Gene splicing and manufacturing equipment
Monoclonal antibodies and hybridomas
Recombinant DNA (agricultural and
industrial)
Recombinant DNA (medical)
Industrial Products and Equipment
Chemicals
Controls and sensors
Energy management
Equipment and machinery
Other industrial automation
Plastics
Robotics/vision systems
Specialty materials
Medical/Health Related
Diagnostic equipment
Diagnostic test products
Disposable products
Drugs and medicines
Hospital and clinical labs
Medical services
Therapeutic equipment
Other
Education related
Finance and insurance
Publishing
Transportation

Additional Information
Year Founded—1984
Capital Under Management—$15.5 million
Investments(1985-1st 6 months)—3
Invested(1985-1st 6 months)—$1.6 million

T.V.P. ASSOCIATES

2777 Stemmons Freeway #1741
Dallas, TX 75207
214-689-4265

General Partners
James P. Leake
James Silcock

Whom to Contact
James Silcock

Type of Firm
Private venture capital firm investing
own capital

Affiliation
Lexington Capital Group, Inc. (management
company)

Project Preferences
Prefer role as deal originator but will also
invest in deals created by others

Type of Financing:
Seed
Startup
First-stage
Leveraged buyout
Minimum Investment: $100,000
Preferred Investment: $500,000-$1 million
Minimum Operating Data:
Annual Sales—Nominal
P&L—Losses (profits projected after 2 years)

Geographical Preferences
Southwest
National (telecommunications, only)

Industry Preferences

Communications
Commercial communications
Data communications
Satellite and microwave communications
Telephone related
Computer Related
Computer graphics, CAD/CAM and CAE
Computer services
Office automation
Software-applications
Software-artificial intelligence
Software-systems
Specialized turnkey systems
Distribution
Communications equipment
Electronics equipment
Electronic Components and Instrumentation
Analytical and scientific instrumentation
Component fabrication and testing equipment
Electronic components
Semiconductors
Energy/Natural Resources
Technology related products/equipment
Industrial Products and Equipment
Controls and sensors
Equipment and machinery
Specialty materials
Medical/Health Related
Diagnostic equipment
Diagnostic test products
Disposable products
Therapeutic equipment
Will Not Consider
Oil and gas exploration
Real estate

Additional Information
Year Founded—1983
Capital Under Management—$15 million
Investments(1985-1st 6 months)—3
Invested(1985-1st 6 months)—$1.2 million
Method of Compensation—Return on investment is of primary concern; do not charge fees

---

UNDERWOOD, NEUHAUS & CO., INC.

724 Travis Street
Houston, TX 77002
713-221-2413

Officers
Thomas M. Hargrove, 1st V.P.
Ben Ederer, Assoc.

Whom to Contact
Either of the above

Type of Firm
Investment banking or merchant banking firm investing own capital or funds of partners or clients
Consulting firm evaluating and analyzing venture projects and arranging private placements

Project Preferences
Prefer role as deal originator
Type of Financing:
First-stage
Second-stage
Later-stage expansion
Leveraged buyout
Minimum Investment: $1 million
Preferred Investment: Over $1 million
Minimum Operating Data:
Annual Sales—$1.5 million
P&L—Break even
Annual Sales (LBO)—$10 million

Geographical Preferences
Southwest
Gulf States

Industry Preferences

Communications
Cable television
Satellite and microwave communications
Computer Related
Computer services
Consumer
Consumer services
Food and beverage products
Leisure and recreational products

Distribution
Industrial products
Medical products
Energy/Natural Resources
Alternative energy
Drilling and exploration services
Energy conservation
Technology related products/equipment
Medical/Health Related
Diagnostic equipment
Diagnostic test products
Disposable products
Drugs and medicines
Hospital and clinical labs
Medical services
Therapeutic equipment
Will Not Consider
Real estate

Additional Information
Year Founded—1907
Method of Compensation—Function primarily in service area; receive contingent fee in cash or equity

---

UNITED MERCANTILE CAPITAL CORPORATION

444 Executive Center Boulevard
Suite 222
El Paso, TX 79902
915-533-6375

Post Office Box 66
El Paso, TX 79940

Officers
L. Joe Justice, Pres.
Patricia M. Justice, V.P.
Fred Davidoff, Secy.
Taffy D. Bagley, Asst. Secy.

Whom to Contact
L. Joe Justice

Type of Firm
SBIC

Affiliations
United Mercantile Corporation (holding company)
United Mercantile Life Insurance Company (subsidiary of holding company)

Industry Association Membership
NASBIC

Project Preferences

Prefer role as deal originator but will also
invest in deals created by others
Type of Financing:
Startup
Leveraged buyout
Minimum Investment: Less than $100,000
Preferred Investment: $125,000 or less
Minimum Operating Data:
Annual Sales—Nominal

Geographical Preference

West Texas
Southwest

Industry Preferences

Distribution
Wholesaling or other distribution
Industrial Products and Equipment
Manufacturing
Will Not Consider
Retail

Additional Information

Year Founded—1975
Capital Under Management—$1.8 million
Investments(1985-1st 6 months)—6
Invested(1985-1st 6 months)—$300,000
Method of Compensation—Return on
investment is most important, but also
charge for closing fees, service fees, etc.
Professional fee required whether or
not deal closes

WEST CENTRAL CAPITAL CORPORATION

440 Northlake Center #206
Dallas, TX 75238
214-348-3969

Officers

Howard W. Jacob, Pres.
Barbara C. Evans, V.P.

Whom to Contact

Barbara C. Evans

Type of Firm

Private venture capital firm investing
own capital

Project Preferences

Prefer role as deal originator
Type of Financing:
Second-stage
Later-stage expansion
Preferred Investment: Less than $100,000

Geographical Preference

Within two hours of office

Industry Preferences

Communications
Radio broadcasting
Distribution
Industrial products
Industrial Products and Equipment
Equipment and machinery
Medical/Health Related
Medical services
Other
Real estate

Additional Information

Year Founded—1964
Method of Compensation—Return on
investment is most important, but also
charge for closing fees, service fees, etc.

WOODLAND CAPITAL COMPANY

3007 Skyway Circle North
Irving, TX 75038
214-659-9500

Officers

Atlee M. Kohl, Chm.
Stewart D. Siebens, Pres.
Paul S. Coulis, Dir.
John B. Lane, Dir.

Whom to Contact

Stewart D. Siebens

Type of Firm

Private venture capital firm investing
own capital

Affiliation

Woodland Investment Company (parent)

Project Preferences

Prefer 80% ownership in private companies;
minimum of 5% in public companies
Minimum Investment: $100,000
Preferred Investment: $250,000-$500,000
Minimum Operating Data:
Annual Sales—$500,000
P&L—Break even

Geographical Preference

Sunbelt

Industry Preferences

Consumer
Food and beverage products
Franchise businesses
Retailing
Distribution
Consumer products
Electronics equipment
Food products
Medical products
**Electronic Components and
Instrumentation**
Electronic components
Medical/Health Related
Diagnostic equipment
Diagnostic test products
Medical services
Therapeutic equipment
Will Not Consider
Real estate

Additional Information

Year Founded—1979
Capital Under Management—$15 million
Investments(1985-1st 6 months)—2
Invested(1985-1st 6 months)—$750,000
Method of Compensation—Return on
investment is most important, but also
charge for closing fees, service fees, etc.

THE WOODLANDS VENTURE CAPITAL CORPORATION

2201 Timberloch Place
Post Office Box 4000
The Woodlands, TX 77380
713-363-7115

Officers

George P. Mitchell, Pres.
Michael H. Richmond, Sr. V.P.
Martin P. Sutter, Mgn. Dir.
J. Michael Schafer, Inv. Assoc.

Whom to Contact

Martin P. Sutter
J. Michael Schafer

Type of Firm

Venture capital subsidiary or affiliate of
non-financial corporation

Affiliation

Mitchell Energy & Development Corp.
(parent)

Project Preferences
Will function either as deal originator or
  investor in deals created by others
Type of Financing:
Startup
First-stage
Minimum Investment: $250,000
Preferred Investment: $250,000-$500,000
Minimum Operating Data:
Annual Sales—Nominal
P&L—Losses (profits projected after 3 years)

Geographical Preferences
Within two hours of office
National
No geographic preferences for medical
  related businesses

Industry Preferences

Genetic Engineering
Gene splicing and manufacturing equipment
Monoclonal antibodies and hybridomas
Recombinant DNA (agricultural and
  industrial)
Recombinant DNA (medical)
Medical/Health Related
Diagnostic equipment
Diagnostic test products
Disposable products
Drugs and medicines
Hospital and clinical labs
Medical services
Therapeutic equipment
Other
Businesses related to the Houston Research
  Center or The Woodlands Research Forest
Will Not Consider
Finance and insurance
Real estate

Additional Information
Year Founded—1984
Capital Under Management—$15 million
Investments(1985-1st 6 months)—3
Invested(1985-1st 6 months)—$1.1 million
Method of Compensation—Return on
  investment is of primary concern; do not
  charge fees

MERCHANT FUNDING CORPORATION

2010 Beneficial Tower
Salt Lake City, UT 84111
801-363-4463

Officers
Kent K. Christensen, Pres.
Anthony L. Camberlango, Dir.

Whom to Contact
Either of the above

Type of Firm
Private venture capital firm investing
own capital

Project Preferences
Prefer role as deal originator but will also
invest in deals created by others
Type of Financing:
First-stage
Second-stage
Leveraged buyout
Minimum Investment: $100,000
Preferred Investment: $250,000-$500,000
Minimum Operating Data:
Annual Sales—$500,000
P&L—Break even

Geographical Preference
Rocky Mountains

Industry Preferences

Communications
Cable television
Commercial communications
Data communications
Satellite and microwave communications
Telephone related
Consumer
Computer stores/related services
Consumer products
Consumer services
Food and beverage products
Franchise businesses
Hotels and resort areas
Leisure and recreational products
Restaurants
Retailing
Distribution
Communications equipment
Computer equipment
Consumer products
Electronics equipment
Food products
Industrial products
Medical products

Medical/Health Related
Diagnostic equipment
Diagnostic test products
Disposable products
Drugs and medicines
Hospital and clinical labs
Medical services
Therapeutic equipment
Other
Real estate

Additional Information
Year Founded—1984
Method of Compensation—Function primarily
in service area; receive contingent fee in
cash or equity

ATLANTIC VENTURE PARTNERS

7th & Franklin Streets #815
Richmond, VA 23219
804-644-5496

Post Office Box 1493
Richmond, VA 23212

Other Office
801 North Fairfax Street #404
Alexandria, VA 22314
703-548-6026

Officers
Robert H. Pratt, Gen. Ptnr. (Richmond)
Wallace L. Bennett, Gen. Ptnr. (Alexandria)
Edward C. McCarthy (Alexandria)

Whom to Contact
Robert H. Pratt
Wallace L. Bennett

Type of Firm
Private venture capital firm investing
own capital

Affiliation
Wheat, First Securities Inc. (parent)

Industry Association Memberships
NASBIC
NVCA

Project Preferences
Will function either as deal originator or
investor in deals created by others
Type of Financing:
First-stage
Second-stage
Later-stage expansion
Leveraged buyout
Minimum Investment: $250,000
Preferred Investment: $500,000-$1 million
Minimum Operating Data:
Annual Sales—Nominal
P&L—Losses (profits projected after 1 year)

Geographical Preference
Southeast

Industry Preferences

Communications
Cable television
Commercial communications
Data communications
Satellite and microwave communications
Telephone related

Computer Related
Computer graphics, CAD/CAM and CAE
Computer mainframes
Computer services
Memory devices
Micro and mini computers
Office automation
Scanning related
Software-applications
Software-artificial intelligence
Software-systems
Specialized turnkey systems
Terminals
Consumer
Computer stores/related services
Consumer products
Consumer services
Food and beverage products
Franchise businesses
Hotels and resort areas
Leisure and recreational products
Restaurants
Retailing
Distribution
Communications equipment
Computer equipment
Consumer products
Electronics equipment
Food products
Industrial products
Medical products
**Electronic Components and
Instrumentation**
Analytical and scientific instrumentation
Component fabrication and testing
equipment
Electronic components
Fiber optics
Laser related
Semiconductors
Energy/Natural Resources
Alternative energy
Coal related
Drilling and exploration services
Energy conservation
Minerals
Oil and gas exploration and production
Technology related products/equipment
Industrial Products and Equipment
Chemicals
Controls and sensors
Energy management
Equipment and machinery
Other industrial automation
Plastics
Robotics/vision systems
Specialty materials

Other
Education related
Finance and insurance
Publishing
Transportation

Additional Information
Year Founded—1981
Capital Under Management—$18 million
Investments(1985-1st 6 months)—8
Invested(1985-1st 6 months)—$3.6 million
Method of Compensation—Return on
investment is of primary concern; do not
charge fees

BAIN CAPITAL

6720 Wemberly Way
McLean, VA 22101
703-448-8188

T. Coleman Andrews, Gen. Ptnr.

See MASSACHUSETTS for full listing

BASIC INVESTMENT CORPORATION

6723 Whittier Avenue #201
McLean, VA 22102
703-356-4300

Officers
Frank Luwis, Pres.
Edward Sandler, Dir.

Whom to Contact
Edward Sandler

Type of Firm
MESBIC

Industry Association Membership
NASBIC

Project Preferences
Will function either as deal originator or
investor in deals created by others
Type of Financing:
Seed
Startup
First-stage
Second-stage
Later-stage expansion
Leveraged buyout

Minimum Investment: Less than $100,000
Preferred Investment: Less than $100,000
Minimum Operating Data:
Annual Sales—Nominal
P&L—Break even

Geographical Preferences
Within two hours of office
Southeast

Industry Preferences

Consumer
Franchise businesses
Hotels and resort areas

Additional Information
Year Founded—1983
Capital Under Management—$500,000
Method of Compensation—Return on
   investment is most important, but also
   charge for closing fees, service fees, etc.

HILLCREST GROUP

Nine South 12th Street
Post Office Box 1776
Richmond, VA 23214
804-643-7358

General Partners
A. Hugh Ewing
James B. Farinholt, Jr.
John P. Funkhouser

Whom to Contact
Any of the above

Type of Firm
SBIC

Affiliation
United Virginia Bank

Industry Association Membership
NASBIC

Project Preferences
Will function either as deal originator or
   investor in deals created by others
Type of Financing:
Second-stage
Later-stage expansion
Leveraged buyout
Minimum Investment: $200,000
Preferred Investment: $500,000
Preferred Investment (LBO): $500,000

Minimum Operating Data:
Annual Sales—$500,000
P&L—Losses (profits projected after 1 year)
Annual Sales (LBO)—$5 million and over

Geographical Preference
Southeast
Mid Atlantic States

Industry Preferences

Diversified
Will Not Consider
Financial
Real estate

Additional Information
Year Founded—1981
Capital Under Management—$8.6 million
Investments(1985-1st 6 months)—3
Invested(1985-1st 6 months)—$685,000
Method of Compensation—Return on
   investment is of primary concern; do not
   charge fees

METROPOLITAN CAPITAL CORPORATION

2550 Huntington Avenue
Alexandria, VA 22303
703-960-4698

Officers
J.B. Toomey, Pres. & CEO
H.P. Weinberg, V.P.
S.W. Austin, V.P. & Treas.
K.A. Idle, Secy.
C.S. Weber, Asst. Secy.

Whom to Contact
S.W. Austin

Type of Firm
SBIC

Affiliation
VSE Corporation (parent)

Industry Association Membership
NASBIC

Project Preferences
Prefer role in deals created by others
Type of Financing:
Second-stage
Later-stage expansion
Minimum Investment: $100,000
Preferred Investment: $100,000-$250,000

Minimum Operating Data:
Annual Sales—Nominal
P&L—Losses (profits projected after 1 year)

Geographical Preferences
Within two hours of office
Washington, D.C. metropolitan area

Industry Preferences

Communications
Data communications
Satellite and microwave communications
Computer Related
Computer graphics, CAD/CAM and CAE
Computer mainframes
Computer services
Memory devices
Micro and mini computers
Office automation
Scanning related
Software-applications
Software-artificial intelligence
Software-systems
Specialized turnkey systems
Terminals
Distribution
Communications equipment
Computer equipment
Electronics equipment
Industrial products
Medical products
**Electronic Components and
   Instrumentation**
Analytical and scientific instrumentation
Component fabrication and testing
   equipment
Electronic components
Fiber optics
Laser related
Semiconductors
Industrial Products and Equipment
Controls and sensors
Other industrial automation
Robotics/vision systems
Specialty materials
Medical/Health Related
Diagnostic equipment
Diagnostic test products

Additional Information
Year Founded—1970
Capital Under Management—$2.1 million
Investments(1985-1st 6 months)—3
Invested(1985-1st 6 months)—$565,000
Method of Compensation—Return on
   investment is most important, but also
   charge for closing fees, service fees, etc.

SOVRAN FUNDING CORPORATION

One Commercial Place
Sovran Center, Sixth Floor
Norfolk, VA 23510
804-441-4041

Officer
David A. King, Pres.

Type of Firm
SBIC

Affiliation
Sovran Financial Corporation

Project Preferences
Will function either as deal originator or
investor in deals created by others
Type of Financing:
Second-stage
Later-stage expansion
Leveraged buyout
Minimum Investment: $100,000
Preferred Investment: $250,000-$500,000
Preferred Investment (LBO): $500,000
Minimum Operating Data:
Annual Sales—$500,000
P&L—Break even
Annual Sales (LBO)—$5 million and over

Geographical Preferences
Within two hours of office
Southeast

Industry Preferences

Communications
Commercial communications
Data communications
Telephone related
Computer Related
Computer graphics, CAD/CAM and CAE
Computer mainframes
Computer services
Memory devices
Micro and mini computers
Office automation
Scanning related
Software-applications
Software-artificial intelligence
Software-systems
Specialized turnkey systems
Terminals
Consumer
Computer stores/related services
Food and beverage products
Franchise businesses
Restaurants

Distribution
Communications equipment
Computer equipment
Consumer products
Electronics equipment
Food products
Industrial products
Medical products
**Electronic Components and
Instrumentation**
Analytical and scientific instrumentation
Component fabrication and testing
equipment
Electronic components
Fiber optics
Laser related
Semiconductors
Energy/Natural Resources
Alternative energy
Genetic Engineering
Gene splicing and manufacturing equipment
Monoclonal antibodies and hybridomas
Recombinant DNA (agricultural and
industrial)
Recombinant DNA (medical)
Industrial Products and Equipment
Chemicals
Controls and sensors
Energy management
Equipment and machinery
Other industrial automation
Plastics
Robotics/vision systems
Specialty materials
Medical/Health Related
Diagnostic equipment
Diagnostic test products
Disposable products
Drugs and medicines
Hospital and clinical labs
Medical services
Therapeutic equipment

Additional Information
Year Founded—1985
Capital Under Management—$5 million
Investments(1985-1st 6 months)—1
Invested(1985-1st 6 months)—$1 million
Method of Compensation—Return on
investment is of primary concern; do not
charge fees

VENTURE AMERICA

2911 Huntermill Road #200
Oakton, VA 22124
703-281-5600

Partners
James R. Ball, Mgn. Ptnr.
Daniel E. Moore, Gen. Ptnr.

Whom to Contact
Either of the above

Type of Firm
Private venture capital firm investing
own capital
Consulting firm evaluating and analyzing
venture projects and arranging private
placements

Affiliation
Venture America Services Co. (wholly owned
entrepreneurial services company)

Project Preferences
Prefer role as deal originator
Type of Financing:
Seed
Research and development partnerships
Startup
Minimum Investment: Less than $100,000
Preferred Investment: Less than $100,000
Minimum Operating Data:
Annual Sales—Nominal
P&L—Losses (profits projected after 2 years)

Geographical Preferences
Within two hours of office
Northeast

Industry Preferences

Communications
Cable television
Commercial communications
Data communications
Satellite and microwave communications
Telephone related
Computer Related
Computer services
Office automation
Specialized turnkey systems

Consumer
Computer stores/related services
Consumer products
Consumer services
Food and beverage products
Franchise businesses
Hotels and resort areas
Leisure and recreational products
Restaurants
Retailing
Distribution
Communications equipment
Computer equipment
Consumer products
Electronics equipment
Food products
Industrial products
Medical products
Electronic Components and Instrumentation
Analytical and scientific instrumentation
Component fabrication and testing equipment
Electronic components
Fiber optics
Laser related
Semiconductors
Energy/Natural Resources
Alternative energy
Genetic Engineering
Gene splicing and manufacturing equipment
Monoclonal antibodies and hybridomas
Recombinant DNA (agricultural and industrial)
Recombinant DNA (medical)
Industrial Products and Equipment
Energy management
Other industrial automation
Plastics
Medical/Health Related
Diagnostic equipment
Diagnostic test products
Disposable products
Drugs and medicines
Hospital and clinical labs
Medical services
Therapeutic equipment
Other
Education related
Finance and insurance
Publishing
Specialty consulting

Additional Information
Year Founded—1984
Capital Under Management—$2.9 million
Investments(1985-1st 6 months)—5
Invested(1985-1st 6 months)—$500,000
Method of Compensation—Return on investment is most important, but also charge for closing fees, service fees, etc.

WHEAT, FIRST SECURITIES

707 East Main Street
Post Office Box 1357
Richmond, VA 23211
804-649-2311

Officers
James C. Wheat, Jr., Chm.
F. Carlyle Tiller, Pres.-WFS Financial Corp.
John L. McElroy, Jr., Vice-Chm.
Marshall B. Wishnak, Pres.-Wheat, First Secur.
R. Edward Morrissett, Jr., Exec. V.P.-Corp. Finance
Allen B. Rider III, Asst. V.P.-Corp. Finance

Whom to Contact
R. Edward Morrissett, Jr. (Virginia)
Allen B. Rider III

Type of Firm
Investment banking or merchant banking firm investing own capital or funds of partners or clients

Affiliations
WFS Financial Corp. (holding company)
Atlantic Venture Partners (venture capital subsidiary)
Seven Hills Partners (partnership)

Project Preferences
Prefer role as deal originator but will also invest in deals created by others
Type of Financing:
Second-stage
Later-stage expansion
Leveraged buyout
Minimum Investment: $1 million
Preferred Investment: Over $1 million
Minimum Operating Data:
Annual Sales—$1.5 million
P&L—Break even

Geographical Preferences
Southeast
East Coast

Industry Preferences

Communications
Cable television
Commercial communications
Data communications
Satellite and microwave communications
Telephone related
Computer Related
Computer graphics, CAD/CAM and CAE
Computer mainframes
Computer services
Memory devices
Micro and mini computers
Office automation
Scanning related
Software-applications
Software-artificial intelligence
Software-systems
Specialized turnkey systems
Terminals
Consumer
Computer stores/related services
Consumer products
Consumer services
Home furnishings
Leisure and recreational products
Distribution
Communications equipment
Computer equipment
Consumer products
Electronics equipment
Food products
Industrial products
Medical products
Electronic Components and Instrumentation
Analytical and scientific instrumentation
Component fabrication and testing equipment
Electronic components
Fiber optics
Laser related
Semiconductors
Energy/Natural Resources
Coal related
Technology related products/equipment
Industrial Products and Equipment
Chemicals
Controls and sensors
Energy management
Equipment and machinery
Other industrial automation
Plastics
Robotics/vision systems
Specialty materials
Medical/Health Related
Hospital and clinical labs

Other
Agriculture, forestry, fishing
Finance and insurance
Publishing
Real estate
Textiles
Transportation

Additional Information
Year Founded—1934
Method of Compensation—Function primarily
  in service area; receive contingent fee in
  cash or equity

CABLE, HOWSE & COZADD, INC.

999 Third Avenue #4300
Seattle, WA 98104
206-583-2700

Other Offices

1800 One Main Place
101 Southwest Main
Portland, OR 97204
503-248-9646

3000 Sand Hill Road
Building 1, #190
Menlo Park, CA 94025
415-854-3340

General Partners

Thomas J. Cable (Washington)
Elwood D. Howse, Jr. (Washington)
Bennett A. Cozadd (Washington)
Michael A. Ellison (Washington)
Wayne C. Wager (Washington)
James B. Glavin (Washington)
L. Barton Alexander (Oregon)
Gregory H. Turnbull (California)

Whom to Contact

Wayne C. Wager

Type of Firm

Private venture capital firm investing
own capital

Industry Association Memberships

NVCA
WAVC

Project Preferences

Prefer role as deal originator but will also
invest in deals created by others
Type of Financing:
Startup
First-stage
Second-stage
Later-stage expansion
Minimum Investment: $500,000
Preferred Investment: $1 million-$2.5 million
Minimum Operating Data:
Annual Sales—Nominal
P&L—Losses (profits projected after 3 years)

Geographical Preferences

Northwest
Rocky Mountains
West Coast

Industry Preferences

Communications
Data communications
Telephone related
Computer Related
Computer graphics, CAD/CAM and CAE
Computer mainframes
Computer services
Memory devices
Software-applications
Software-artificial intelligence
Software-systems
Specialized turnkey systems
**Electronic Components and
Instrumentation**
Analytical and scientific instrumentation
Component fabrication and testing
equipment
Electronic components
Fiber optics
Laser related
Semiconductors
Genetic Engineering
Monoclonal antibodies and hybridomas
Recombinant DNA (agricultural and
industrial)
Recombinant DNA (medical)
Industrial Products and Equipment
Chemicals
Other industrial automation
Plastics
Robotics/vision systems
Specialty materials
Medical/Health Related
Diagnostic equipment
Drugs and medicines
Medical services
Therapeutic equipment
Will Not Consider
Natural resource exploration or extraction
Real estate

Additional Information

Year Founded—1977
Capital Under Management—$132 million
Investments(1985-1st 6 months)—23
Invested(1985-1st 6 months)—$10.3 million
Method of Compensation—Return on
investment is of primary concern; do not
charge fees

CAPITAL RESOURCE CORPORATION

1001 Logan Building
Seattle, WA 98101
206-623-6550

Officer

T. Evans Wyckoff, Pres.

Type of Firm

SBIC

Project Preferences

Prefer role in deals created by others
Type of Financing:
First-stage
Second-stage
Leveraged buyout
Minimum Investment: Less than $100,000
Preferred Investment: $100,000-$250,000
Minimum Operating Data:
Annual Sales—$1.5 million

Geographical Preference

Within two hours of office

Industry Preferences

Communications
Cable television
Commercial communications
Data communications
Satellite and microwave communications
Telephone related
Computer Related
Computer graphics, CAD/CAM and CAE
Computer mainframes
Computer services
Memory devices
Micro and mini computers
Office automation
Scanning related
Software-applications
Software-artificial intelligence
Software-systems
Specialized turnkey systems
Terminals
**Electronic Components and
Instrumentation**
Analytical and scientific instrumentation
Component fabrication and testing
equipment
Electronic components
Fiber optics
Laser related
Semiconductors

Energy/Natural Resources
Alternative energy
Coal related
Drilling and exploration services
Energy conservation
Minerals
Oil and gas exploration and production
Technology related products/equipment
Industrial Products and Equipment
Chemicals
Controls and sensors
Energy management
Equipment and machinery
Other industrial automation
Plastics
Robotics/vision systems
Specialty materials

Additional Information
Year Founded—1980
Capital Under Management—$2 million
Investments(1985-1st 6 months)—3
Method of Compensation—Return on
investment is of primary concern; do not
charge fees

DAIN BOSWORTH INCORPORATED

First Interstate Center #1500
999 Third Avenue
Seattle, WA 98104
206-621-3112

James Stearns, V.P.

See MINNESOTA for full listing

GENESIS CAPITAL LIMITED PARTNERSHIP

Post Office Box 5065
Bellevue, WA 98009
206-454-7211

Other Office
20813 Stevens Creek Boulevard
Suite 101
Cupertino, CA 95014
408-446-9690

General Partners
David E. Kratter (Washington)
Gerald S. Casilli (California)

Whom to Contact
Either of the above

Type of Firm
Private venture capital firm investing
own capital

Project Preferences
Will function either as deal originator or
investor in deals created by others
Type of Financing:
Startup
First-stage
Second-stage
Minimum Investment: Less than $100,000
Preferred Investment: $250,000-$500,000
Minimum Operating Data:
Annual Sales—Nominal
P&L—Losses (profits projected after 3 years)

Geographical Preferences
Within two hours of office
West Coast

Industry Preferences

Communications
Data communications
Computer Related
Computer graphics, CAD/CAM and CAE
Computer services
Micro and mini computers
Office automation
Terminals
Electronic Components and Instrumentation
Analytical and scientific instrumentation
Electronic components
Fiber optics
Laser related
Semiconductors
Genetic Engineering
Research and manufacturing equipment
Industrial Products and Equipment
Advanced materials
Controls and sensors
Other industrial automation
Robotics/vision systems
Medical/Health Related
Diagnostic equipment
Will Not Consider
Oil and gas
Real estate
Restaurants

Additional Information
Year Founded—1982
Capital Under Management—$20 million
Method of Compensation—Return on
investment is of primary concern; do not
charge fees

GULL INDUSTRIES INC.

Post Office Box 24687
Seattle, WA 98124
206-624-5900

Officers
William True, Exec. V.P.
Claude Olson, V.P.

Whom to Contact
Claude Olson

Type of Firm
Private venture capital firm investing
own capital

Project Preferences
Will function either as deal originator or
investor in deals created by others
Type of Financing:
First-stage
Second-stage
Later-stage expansion
Minimum Investment: Less than $100,000
Preferred Investment: $100,000-$250,000
Minimum Operating Data:
Annual Sales—Nominal
P&L—Losses (profits projected after 2 years)

Geographical Preference
Northwest

Industry Preferences

Communications
Commercial communications
Data communications
Telephone related
Computer Related
Micro and mini computers
Office automation
Software-applications
Specialized turnkey systems
Consumer
Food and beverage products
Franchise businesses
Leisure and recreational products
Retailing
Distribution
Consumer products
Food products
Industrial products
Medical products
Electronic Components and Instrumentation
Analytical and scientific instrumentation
Fiber optics
Laser related

Energy/Natural Resources
Alternative energy
Technology related products/equipment
Industrial Products and Equipment
Controls and sensors
Other industrial automation
Robotics/vision systems
Medical/Health Related
Diagnostic equipment
Diagnostic test products
Disposable products
Medical services
Other
Agriculture, forestry, fishing
Education related
Finance and insurance
Publishing
Real estate
Specialty consulting
Transportation

Additional Information
Year Founded—1959
Capital Under Management—$1.5 million
Investments(1985-1st 6 months)—3
Invested(1985-1st 6 months)—$400,000
Method of Compensation—Return on
  investment is of primary concern; do not
  charge fees

ORIANS INVESTMENT COMPANY

1111 Third Avenue #700
Seattle, WA 98101
206-467-0880

James M. Key, V.P.

See OREGON for full listing

PACIFIC RIM VENTURES

514 South Skagit Street
Post Office Box 332
Burlington, WA 98233
206-755-9057

Officers
Robert L. Apter, Pres.
Diane Sawyer Apter, Sr. Ptnr.

Whom to Contact
Robert L. Apter

Type of Firm
Consulting firm evaluating and analyzing
  venture projects and arranging private
  placements
Private placements arranged for companies
  with potential to locate in Skagit County,
  Washington

Project Preferences
Prefer role as deal originator but will also
  invest in deals created by others
Type of Financing:
Seed
Startup
First-stage
Second-stage
Leveraged buyout
Minimum Investment: Less than $100,000
Preferred Investment: $100,000-$250,000
Preferred Investment (LBO):
  $1 million-$3 million
Minimum Operating Data:
Annual Sales—Nominal
P&L—Losses (profits projected after 2 years)

Geographical Preferences
Within two hours of office
Skagit County, Washington

Industry Preferences

Communications
Commercial communications
Data communications
Satellite and microwave communications
Computer Related
Computer graphics, CAD/CAM and CAE
Computer mainframes
Computer services
Memory devices
Micro and mini computers
Office automation
Scanning related
Software-applications
Software-artificial intelligence
Software-systems
Specialized turnkey systems
Terminals
Consumer
Consumer products
Food and beverage products
Leisure and recreational products
Distribution
Communications equipment
Computer equipment
Consumer products
Electronics equipment
Food products
Industrial products
Medical products

**Electronic Components and
  Instrumentation**
Analytical and scientific instrumentation
Component fabrication and testing
  equipment
Electronic components
Fiber optics
Laser related
Semiconductors
Energy/Natural Resources
Technology related products/equipment
Genetic Engineering
Gene splicing and manufacturing equipment
Monoclonal antibodies and hybridomas
Recombinant DNA (agricultural and
  industrial)
Recombinant DNA (medical)
Industrial Products and Equipment
Chemicals
Controls and sensors
Energy management
Equipment and machinery
Other industrial automation
Plastics
Robotics/vision systems
Specialty materials
Medical/Health Related
Diagnostic equipment
Diagnostic test products
Disposable products
Drugs and medicines
Hospital and clinical labs
Medical services
Therapeutic equipment
Other
Agriculture, forestry, fishing
Education related

Additional Information
Year Founded—1985
Method of Compensation—Return on
  investment is most important, but also
  charge for closing fees, service fees, etc.

THE PALMER GROUP LIMITED
  PARTNERSHIP

98 Union Building #410
Seattle, WA 98101
206-628-8980

Partners
Craig R. Palmer, Gen. Ptnr.
Michael Brownfield, Ptnr.

Whom to Contact
Craig R. Palmer

Type of Firm

Private venture capital firm investing own capital

Investment banking or merchant banking firm investing own capital or funds of partners or clients

Project Preferences

Prefer role as deal originator
Type of Financing:
Seed
Second-stage
Leveraged buyout
Mezzanine
Minimum Investment: $100,000
Minimum Operating Data:
Annual Sales—$1 million
P&L—Break even
Annual Sales (LBO)—$10 million

Geographical Preference

West Coast

Industry Preferences

None

Additional Information

Year Founded—1982
Method of Compensation—Return on investment is most important, but also charge for closing fees, service fees, etc.

PALMS & COMPANY, INC.

6702 139th Avenue NE #760
Redmond, WA 98502
206-885-4401

Officers

Peter J. Palms IV, Pres.
Carol A. Sarko, V.P.
Jody Ray Strugar, V.P.

Whom to Contact

Any of the above

Type of Firm

Private venture capital firm investing own capital

Investment banking or merchant banking firm investing own capital or funds of partners or clients

Consulting firm evaluating and analyzing venture projects and arranging private placements

Project Preferences

Prefer role as deal originator
Type of Financing:
Seed
Startup
First-stage
Second-stage
Later-stage expansion
Leveraged buyout
Minimum Investment: $250,000
Preferred Investment: $1 million-$100 million
Preferred Investment (LBO): $15 million
Minimum Operating Data:
Annual Sales—$500,000
P&L—Profits NBT over $$100,000
Annual Sales (LBO)—Over $5 million

Geographical Preferences

Northwest
West Coast
Alaska

Industry Preferences

Communications
Cable television
Computer Related
Voice activation
Consumer
Franchise businesses
Hotels and resort areas
Leisure and recreational products
Distribution
Consumer products
Industrial products
Medical products
Electronic Components and Instrumentation
Analytical and scientific instrumentation
Component fabrication and testing equipment
Electronic components
Laser related
Semiconductors
Energy/Natural Resources
Ethanol plants
Industrial Products and Equipment
Chemicals
Controls and sensors
Energy management
Equipment and machinery
Other industrial automation
Plastics
Robotics/vision systems
Specialty materials

Medical/Health Related
Diagnostic equipment
Diagnostic test products
Disposable products
Drugs and medicines
Hospital and clinical labs
Medical services
Therapeutic equipment
Other
Agriculture, forestry, fishing
Aviation
Finance and insurance
Motion pictures
Real estate
Time sharing developments
Transportation
Water parks and other theme parks
Will Not Consider
Research and development businesses

Additional Information

Year Founded—1968
Capital Under Management—$44 million
Investments(1985-1st 6 months)—6
Invested(1985-1st 6 months)—$500,000
Method of Compensation—Return on investment is most important, but also charge for closing fees, service fees, etc.

PEOPLES CAPITAL CORPORATION

2411 Fourth Avenue #400
Seattle, WA 98121
206-344-8105

Officer

Richard W. Maider, Pres.

Type of Firm

SBIC

Affiliation

Peoples National Bank of Washington (parent)

Industry Association Membership

NASBIC

Project Preferences

Prefer role in deals created by others
Type of Financing:
Second-stage
Leveraged buyout
Minimum Investment: $100,000
Preferred Investment: $100,000-$250,000
Minimum Operating Data:
Annual Sales—$1.5 million
P&L—Break even

Geographical Preference
Northwest

Industry Preferences

Communications
Cable television
Commercial communications
Data communications
Radio broadcasting
Satellite and microwave communications
Telephone related
Consumer
Food and beverage products
Distribution
Medical products
Electronic Components and Instrumentation
Analytical and scientific instrumentation
Component fabrication and testing equipment
Electronic components
Fiber optics
Laser related
Energy/Natural Resources
Alternative energy
Energy conservation
Technology related products/equipment
Genetic Engineering
Gene splicing and manufacturing equipment
Monoclonal antibodies and hybridomas
Recombinant DNA (agricultural and industrial)
Recombinant DNA (medical)
Industrial Products and Equipment
Controls and sensors
Medical/Health Related
Diagnostic equipment
Diagnostic test products
Will Not Consider
Software companies

Additional Information
Year Founded—1981
Capital Under Management—$1.7 million
Investments(1985-1st 6 months)—4
Invested(1985-1st 6 months)—$450,000
Method of Compensation—Return on investment is of primary concern; do not charge fees

---

PHOENIX PARTNERS I & II

One Union Square #2125
Seattle, WA 98101
206-624-8698

Partners
Stuart C. Johnston, Mgn. Gen. Ptnr.
John W. Keefe, Jr., Gen. Ptnr.

Whom to Contact
Stuart C. Johnston

Type of Firm
Private venture capital firm investing own capital

Project Preferences
Will function either as deal originator or investor in deals created by others
Type of Financing:
Startup
First-stage
Second-stage
Later-stage expansion
Leveraged buyout
Minimum Investment: $500,000
Preferred Investment: $500,000-$1 million
Preferred Investment (LBO): $1 million
Minimum Operating Data:
Annual Sales—$1.5 million
P&L—Break even
P&L—Losses (profits projected after 2 years)
Annual Sales (LBO)—$12 million and over

Geographical Preference
None

Industry Preferences

Computer Related
Computer graphics, CAD/CAM and CAE
Computer mainframes
Computer services
Memory devices
Micro and mini computers
Scanning related
Scanning related
Software-applications
Software-artificial intelligence
Software-systems
Specialized turnkey systems
Terminals
Distribution
Computer equipment

Electronic Components and Instrumentation
Analytical and scientific instrumentation
Component fabrication and testing equipment
Electronic components
Fiber optics
Laser related
Semiconductors
Industrial Products and Equipment
Controls and sensors
Robotics/vision systems

Additional Information
Year Founded—1982
Capital Under Management—$42 million
Investments(1985-1st 6 months)—4
Invested(1985-1st 6 months)—$3.2 million
Method of Compensation—Return on investment is of primary concern; do not charge fees

---

PIPER JAFFRAY VENTURES, LTD.

1600 IBM Building
Seattle, WA 98101
206-223-3800

Gary L. Takacs

See MINNESOTA for full listing

RAINIER VENTURE PARTNERS

9725 Southeast 36th Street
Suite 300
Mercer Island, WA 98040
206-232-6720

Other Office
One Lincoln Center #440
10300 Southwest Greenburg Road
Portland, OR 97223
503-245-5900

Partners
John L. Moser (Washington)
George H. Clute (Washington)
Richard H. Drew (Oregon)
W. Denman Van Ness (California)

Whom to Contact
Any of the above

Type of Firm
Private venture capital firm investing
own capital

Affiliation
Hambrecht & Quist

Industry Association Membership
WAVC

Project Preferences
Will function either as deal originator or
investor in deals created by others
Type of Financing:
Startup
First-stage
Second-stage
Later-stage expansion
Leveraged buyout
Minimum Investment: $250,000
Preferred Investment: $750,000-$1 million
Minimum Operating Data:
Annual Sales—Nominal
P&L—Losses (profits projected after 2 years)

Geographical Preferences
Northwest
West Coast

Industry Preferences

Communications
Data communications
Satellite and microwave communications
Telephone related
Computer Related
Computer graphics, CAD/CAM and CAE
Computer mainframes
Computer services
Memory devices
Micro and mini computers
Office automation
Scanning related
Software-applications
Software-artificial intelligence
Software-systems
Specialized turnkey systems
Terminals
**Electronic Components and
Instrumentation**
Analytical and scientific instrumentation
Component fabrication and testing
equipment
Electronic components
Fiber optics
Laser related
Semiconductors

Genetic Engineering
Gene splicing and manufacturing equipment
Monoclonal antibodies and hybridomas
Recombinant DNA (agricultural and
industrial)
Recombinant DNA (medical)
Industrial Products and Equipment
Chemicals
Controls and sensors
Energy management
Equipment and machinery
Other industrial automation
Plastics
Robotics/vision systems
Specialty materials
Medical/Health Related
Diagnostic equipment
Diagnostic test products
Disposable products
Drugs and medicines
Hospital and clinical labs
Medical services
Therapeutic equipment
Will Not Consider
Extractive industries
Financial intermediaries
Real estate

Additional Information
Year Founded—1982
Capital Under Management—$25.7 million
Method of Compensation—Return on
investment is of primary concern; do not
charge fees

UNION STREET CAPITAL CORPORATION

One Union Square #3000
600 University Street
Seattle, WA 98101
206-382-9138

Officers
John C.T. Conte, Jr., Pres.
Chandler H. Everett, V.P. & Treas.
Stanton J. Barnes, V.P. & Secy.
Michael J. O'Byrne, Dir. Tech., Mgt. Services
Alice J. Kling, Ph.D., Research Dir.

Whom to Contact
John C.T. Conte, Jr.
Chandler H. Everett
Stanton J. Barnes

Type of Firm
Private venture capital firm investing
own capital
Consulting firm evaluating and analyzing
venture projects and arranging private
placements

Project Preferences
Will function either as deal originator or
investor in deals created by others
Type of Financing:
First-stage
Second-stage
Later-stage expansion
Minimum Investment: $250,000
Preferred Investment: $250,000-$500,000
Minimum Operating Data:
Annual Sales—Nominal
P&L—Losses (profits projected after 2 years)

Geographical Preferences
West Coast
Pacific Northwest (Washington, Oregon,
Idaho, Alaska)

Industry Preferences
None
Will Not Consider
Real estate

Additional Information
Year Founded—1984
Method of Compensation—Return on
investment is most important, but also
charge for closing fees, service fees, etc.

WALDEN CAPITAL PARTNERS/ WALDEN VENTURES/WALDEN INVESTORS

901 147th Place NE
Bellevue, WA 98007
206-643-7572

Theodore M. Wight, Gen Ptnr.

See CALIFORNIA for full listing

R.W. ALLSOP & ASSOCIATES

815 East Mason Street #1501
Post Office Box 1368
Milwaukee, WI 53201
414-271-6510

Other Offices
Corporate Center East #210
2750 First Avenue NE
Cedar Rapids, IA 52402
319-363-8971

111 West Port Plaza #600
St. Louis, MO 63146
314-434-1688

35 Corporate Woods #244
9101 West 110th Street
Overland Park, KS 66210
913-451-3719

Partners
Robert W. Allsop, Gen. Ptnr. (Iowa)
Paul D. Rhines, Gen. Ptnr. (Iowa)
Gregory B. Bultman, Gen. Ptnr. (Wisconsin)
Robert L. Kuk, Gen. Ptnr. (Missouri)
Larry C. Maddox, Gen. Ptnr. (Kansas)
James D. Thorp, Assoc. (Iowa)

Whom to Contact
Any of the above

Type of Firm
Private venture capital firm investing
own capital

Industry Association Memberships
NASBIC
NVCA

Project Preferences
Will function either as deal originator or
investor in deals created by others
Type of Financing:
First-stage
Second-stage
Later-stage expansion
Leveraged buyout
Minimum Investment: $500,000
Preferred Investment: $500,000-$1 million
Preferred Investment (LBO):
$1 million-$2 million
Minimum Operating Data:
Annual Sales—$1.5 million
P&L—Break even
Annual Sales (LBO)—$10 million-$50 million

Geographical Preference
National

Industry Preferences

Communications
Cellular radio equipment
Commercial communications
Data communications
Data compression, storage and
transmission equipment
Satellite and microwave communications
Telephone related
Computer Related
Computer graphics, CAD/CAM and CAE
Computer services
Office automation
Scanning related
Consumer
Consumer products
Consumer services
Distribution
Communications equipment
Electronics equipment
Food products
Industrial products
Medical products
**Electronic Components and
Instrumentation**
Analytical and scientific instrumentation
Component fabrication and testing
equipment
Electronic components
Fiber optics
Laser related
Genetic Engineering
Gene splicing and manufacturing equipment
Industrial Products and Equipment
Chemicals
Controls and sensors
Equipment and machinery
Other industrial automation
Robotics/vision systems
Specialty materials
Medical/Health Related
Diagnostic equipment
Diagnostic test products
Disposable products
Drugs and medicines
Hospital and clinical labs
Hospital management
Medical instruments
Medical services
Therapeutic equipment
Will Not Consider
Real estate

Additional Information
Year Founded—1981
Capital Under Management—$45 million
Investments(1985-1st 6 months)—10
Invested(1985-1st 6 months)—$2 million
Method of Compensation—Return on
investment is of primary concern; do not
charge fees

ROBERT W. BAIRD, INC.

777 East Wisconsin Avenue
Milwaukee, WI 53201
414-765-3889

Officer
J.S. Anderson

Type of Firm
Investment banking and consulting firm
evaluating and analyzing projects and
arranging private placements

Project Preferences
Will function either as deal originator or
agent in deals created by others
Type of Financing:
Second-stage
Later-stage expansion
Leveraged buyout
Minimum Investment: $500,000
Preferred Investment: $500,000-$5 million
Minimum Operating Data:
Annual Sales—$1 million
P&L—Break even

Geographical Preference
Midwest

Industry Preferences
None

Additional Information
Method of Compensation—Function primarily
in service area; receive contingent fee in
cash or equity

IMPACT SEVEN, INC.

320 Industrial Road
Turtle Lake, WI 54889
715-986-4171

Other Offices

130 Second Street North
Wisconsin Rapids, WI 54494
715-421-0317

511 11th Avenue South
Post Office Box 77
Minneapolis, MN 55415
612-338-6473

Officers

William Bay, Pres. (Turtle Lake)
Dileep Rao, V.P. (Minneapolis)

Whom to Contact

Either of the above

Type of Firm

Community development corporation

Project Preferences

Will function either as deal originator or
investor in deals created by others
Type of Financing:
Startup
First-stage
Second-stage
Later-stage expansion
Leveraged buyout
Minimum Investment: Less than $100,000
Minimum Operating Data:
Annual Sales—$500,000
P&L—Break even

Geographical Preference

Wisconsin

Industry Preferences

None

Additional Information

Year Founded—1970
Capital Under Management—$5 million
Invested(1985-1st 6 months)—$1 million
Method of Compensation—Return on
investment is of primary concern; do not
charge fees

IOWA VENTURE CAPITAL FUND, L.P.

600 East Mason Street
Milwaukee, WI 53202
414-276-3839

Other Offices

300 American Building
Cedar Rapids, IA 52401
319-363-8249

Commerce Tower #2724
911 Main Street
Kansas City, MO 64105
816-842-0114

Officers

Jerry M. Burrows, Pres. (Iowa)
Donald E. Flynn, Exec. V.P. (Iowa)
David R. Schroder, V.P. (Iowa)
Kevin F. Mullane, V.P. (Missouri)
Steven J. Massey, V.P. (Wisconsin)

Whom to Contact

Jerry M. Burrows
Donald E. Flynn
David R. Schroder

Type of Firm

Private venture capital firm investing
own capital

Affiliation

InvestAmerica Venture Group, Inc.
(fund manager)

Project Preferences

Will function either as deal originator or
investor in deals created by others
Type of Financing:
First-stage
Second-stage
Later-stage expansion
Leveraged buyout
Minimum Investment: $100,000
Preferred Investment: $250,000-$500,000
Minimum Operating Data:
Annual Sales—Nominal

Geographical Preference

Midwest

Industry Preferences

Communications
Cable television
Commercial communications
Data communications
Satellite and microwave communications
Telephone related

Computer Related
Computer graphics, CAD/CAM and CAE
Computer mainframes
Computer services
Memory devices
Micro and mini computers
Office automation
Scanning related
Software-applications
Software-artificial intelligence
Software-systems
Specialized turnkey systems
Terminals
Distribution
Communications equipment
Computer equipment
Consumer products
Electronics equipment
Food products
Industrial products
Medical products
**Electronic Components and
Instrumentation**
Analytical and scientific instrumentation
Component fabrication and testing
equipment
Electronic components
Fiber optics
Laser related
Semiconductors
Genetic Engineering
Gene splicing and manufacturing equipment
Monoclonal antibodies and hybridomas
Recombinant DNA (agricultural and
industrial)
Recombinant DNA (medical)
Industrial Products and Equipment
Chemicals
Controls and sensors
Energy management
Equipment and machinery
Other industrial automation
Plastics
Robotics/vision systems
Specialty materials
Medical/Health Related
Diagnostic equipment
Diagnostic test products
Disposable products
Drugs and medicines
Hospital and clinical labs
Medical services
Therapeutic equipment

Additional Information
Year Founded—1985
Capital Under Management—$15 million
Method of Compensation—Return on
  investment is of primary concern; do not
  charge fees

LUBAR & CO., INCORPORATED

3060 First Wisconsin Center
Milwaukee, WI 53202
414-291-9000

Officers
Sheldon B. Lubar, Pres. & Chm.
James C. Rowe, V.P. & Treas.
William T. Donovan, V.P.
David J. Lubar, V.P.
Hillel Bachrach, V.P.

Whom to Contact
Any of the above

Type of Firm
Private venture capital firm investing
  own capital

Industry Association Membership
NVCA

Project Preferences
Prefer role as deal originator
Type of Financing:
Startup
Second-stage
Later-stage expansion
Leveraged buyout
Minimum Investment: $250,000
Preferred Investment: $500,000-$1 million
Minimum Operating Data:
P&L—Losses (profits projected after 1 year)

Geographical Preference
Midwest

Industry Preferences
None

Additional Information
Year Founded—1977
Capital Under Management—$10.5 million
Investments(1985-1st 6 months)—4
Invested(1985-1st 6 months)—$1.2 million
Method of Compensation—Return on
  investment is of primary concern; do not
  charge fees

M&I VENTURES CORPORATION

770 North Water Street
Milwaukee, WI 53202
414-765-7910

Officers
John T. Byrnes, Pres.
Daniel P. Howell, V.P.

Whom to Contact
Daniel P. Howell

Type of Firm
SBIC
Venture capital subsidiary of
  commercial bank

Affiliation
Marshall & Ilsley Corporation (parent)

Industry Association Membership
NASBIC

Project Preferences
Will function either as deal originator or
  investor in deals created by others
Type of Financing:
Startup
First-stage
Second-stage
Later-stage expansion
Leveraged buyout
Minimum Investment: $250,000
Preferred Investment: $250,000-$500,000
Preferred Investment (LBO):
  $250,000 and over
Minimum Operating Data:
Annual Sales—Nominal
P&L—Losses (profits projected after 2 years)
Annual Sales (LBO)—$5 million and over

Geographical Preferences
Midwest
Southwest

Industry Preferences

Computer Related
Office automation
Software-applications
Software-systems
Distribution
Consumer products
Electronics equipment
Food products
Industrial products
Medical products

**Electronic Components and
  Instrumentation**
Analytical and scientific instrumentation
Component fabrication and testing
  equipment
Electronic components
Laser related
Optics technology
Semiconductors
Genetic Engineering
Research and manufacturing equipment
Industrial Products and Equipment
Chemicals
Controls and sensors
Equipment and machinery
Other industrial automation
Plastics
Robotics
Specialty materials
Medical/Health Related
Diagnostic equipment
Diagnostic test products
Disposable products
Drugs and medicines
Hospital and clinical labs
Medical services
Therapeutic equipment
Other
Publishing
Will Not Consider
Real estate

Additional Information
Year Founded—1982
Method of Compensation—Return on
  investment is of primary concern; do not
  charge fees

MADISON CAPITAL CORPORATION

102 State Street
Madison, WI 53703
608-256-8185

Officers
Roth S. Schleck, Chm.
Roger H. Ganser, Pres. & CEO
G. Howard Phipps, V.P. & Secy.
Toby E. Sherry, Treas.

Whom to Contact
Roger H. Ganser

Type of Firm
SBIC

Industry Association Membership
NASBIC

Project Preferences

Will function either as deal originator or investor in deals created by others
Type of Financing:
Startup
First-stage
Second-stage
Later-stage expansion
Leveraged buyout
Minimum Investment: $100,000
Preferred Investment: $100,000-$250,000
Minimum Operating Data:
Annual Sales—Nominal
P&L—Losses (profits projected after 2 years)

Geographical Preference

Midwest

Industry Preferences

Communications
Commercial communications
Data communications
Computer Related
Computer graphics, CAD/CAM and CAE
Computer mainframes
Computer services
Memory devices
Micro and mini computers
Office automation
Scanning related
Software-applications
Software-artificial intelligence
Software-systems
Specialized turnkey systems
Terminals
Consumer
Consumer products
Consumer services
Distribution
Communications equipment
Computer equipment
Consumer products
Electronics equipment
Industrial products
Medical products
Electronic Components and Instrumentation
Analytical and scientific instrumentation
Component fabrication and testing equipment
Electronic components
Fiber optics
Laser related
Semiconductors
Energy/Natural Resources
Alternative energy
Technology related products/equipment

Genetic Engineering
Gene splicing and manufacturing equipment
Monoclonal antibodies and hybridomas
Recombinant DNA (agricultural and industrial)
Recombinant DNA (medical)
Industrial Products and Equipment
Chemicals
Controls and sensors
Energy management
Equipment and machinery
Other industrial automation
Plastics
Robotics/vision systems
Specialty materials
Medical/Health Related
Diagnostic equipment
Diagnostic test products
Disposable products
Drugs and medicines
Hospital and clinical labs
Medical services
Therapeutic equipment
Other
Agriculture, forestry, fishing
Education related
Finance and insurance
Any industry for leveraged buyouts
Will Not Consider
Publishing
Real estate
Restaurants

Additional Information

Year Founded—1982
Capital Under Management—$1.9 million
Method of Compensation—Return on investment is of primary concern; do not charge fees

---

MARINE VENTURE CAPITAL, INC.

111 East Wisconsin Avenue
Post Office Box 2033
Milwaukee, WI 53201
414-765-2274

Officers

H. Wayne Foreman, Pres.
Reed R. Prior, V.P.

Whom to Contact

Either of the above

Type of Firm

SBIC
Venture capital subsidiary of commercial bank

Affiliations

Marine Bank, N.A. (parent)
The Marine Corporation (bank holding company)

Project Preferences

Will function either as deal originator or investor in deals created by others
Type of Financing:
Second-stage
Later-stage expansion
Leveraged buyout
Minimum Investment: $250,000
Preferred Investment: $250,000-$500,000
Preferred Investment (LBO): $500,000
Minimum Operating Data:
Annual Sales—$1.5 million
P&L—Losses (profits projected after 1 year)
Annual Sales (LBO)—$5 million-$30 million

Geographical Preference

None

Industry Preferences

Industrial Products and Equipment
Chemicals
Controls and sensors
Energy management
Equipment and machinery
Factory automation
Other industrial automation
Plastics
Robotics/vision systems
Specialty materials
Medical/Health Related
Diagnostic equipment
Diagnostic test products
Disposable products
Drugs and medicines
Hospital and clinical labs
Medical services
Therapeutic equipment
Other
No industry preferences in financing leveraged buyouts
Will Not Consider
Financial institutions
Real estate

Additional Information

Year Founded—1983
Capital Under Management—$3 million
Method of Compensation—Return on investment is of primary concern; do not charge fees

---

MATRIX VENTURE FUNDS, INC.

808 North Third Street #400
Milwaukee, WI 53151
414-289-9893

Officer
Lawrence J. Kujawski, Pres.

Type of Firm
Consulting firm evaluating and analyzing
venture projects and arranging private
placements

Project Preferences
Prefer role as deal originator
Type of Financing:
Startup
First-stage
Leveraged buyout
Minimum Operating Data:
Annual Sales—Nominal
P&L—Break even

Geographical Preference
Midwest

Industry Preferences

Computer Related
Software-applications
Software-artificial intelligence
Software-systems
Consumer
Consumer products
Consumer services
**Electronic Components and
Instrumentation**
Analytical and scientific instrumentation
Component fabrication and testing
equipment
Industrial Products and Equipment
Controls and sensors
Energy management
Equipment and machinery
Other industrial automation
Plastics
Robotics/vision systems
Other
Publishing
Specialty consulting

Additional Information
Year Founded—1976

MORAMERICA CAPITAL CORPORATION

600 East Mason Street
Milwaukee, WI 53202
414-276-3839

Other Offices
300 American Building
Cedar Rapids, IA 52401
319-363-8249

Commerce Tower Building #2724
911 Main Street
Kansas City, MO 64105
816-842-0114

Officers
Jerry M. Burrows, Pres. (Iowa)
Donald E. Flynn, V.P. (Iowa)
David Schroder, V.P. (Iowa)
Kevin F. Mullane, V.P. (Missouri)
Steven Massey, V.P. (Wisconsin)

Whom to Contact
Any of the above

Type of Firm
SBIC

Affiliations
MorAmerica Financial Corporation (parent)
InvestAmerica Venture Group, Inc.
(fund manager)

Industry Association Membership
NASBIC

Project Preferences
Will function either as deal originator or
investor in deals created by others
Type of Financing:
First-stage
Second-stage
Later-stage expansion
Leveraged buyout
Minimum Investment: $250,000
Preferred Investment: $250,000-$500,000
Minimum Operating Data:
Annual Sales—Nominal

Geographical Preference
None

Industry Preferences

Communications
Cable television
Commercial communications
Data communications
Satellite and microwave communications
Telephone related

Computer Related
Computer graphics, CAD/CAM and CAE
Computer mainframes
Computer services
Memory devices
Micro and mini computers
Office automation
Scanning related
Software-applications
Software-artificial intelligence
Software-systems
Specialized turnkey systems
Terminals
Distribution
Communications equipment
Computer equipment
Consumer products
Electronics equipment
Food products
Industrial products
Medical products
**Electronic Components and
Instrumentation**
Analytical and scientific instrumentation
Component fabrication and testing equipment
Electronic components
Fiber optics
Laser related
Semiconductors
Genetic Engineering
Gene splicing and manufacturing equipment
Monoclonal antibodies and hybridomas
Recombinant DNA (agricultural and
industrial)
Recombinant DNA (medical)
Industrial Products and Equipment
Chemicals
Controls and sensors
Energy management
Equipment and machinery
Other industrial automation
Plastics
Robotics/vision systems
Specialty materials
Medical/Health Related
Diagnostic equipment
Diagnostic test products
Disposable products
Drugs and medicines
Hospital and clinical labs
Medical services
Therapeutic equipment

Additional Information
Year Founded—1959
Capital Under Management—$35 million
Investments(1985-1st 6 months)—10
Invested(1985-1st 6 months)—$2.5 million
Method of Compensation—Return on
investment is of primary concern; do not
charge fees

WIND POINT PARTNERS, L.P.

1525 Howe Street
Racine, WI 53403
414-631-4030

Partners
James E. Daverman, Gen. Ptnr.
Arthur DelVesco, Gen. Ptnr.
S. Curtis Johnson III, Gen. Ptnr.
Richard R. Kracum, Inv. Mgr.

Whom to Contact
Any of the above

Type of Firm
Private venture capital firm investing
own capital

Industry Association Membership
NVCA

Project Preferences
Will function either as deal originator or
investor in deals created by others
Type of Financing:
Startup
First-stage
Second-stage
Later-stage expansion
Leveraged buyout
Minimum Investment: $500,000
Preferred Investment: Over $1 million
Minimum Operating Data:
Annual Sales—Nominal
P&L—Losses (profits projected after 2 years)

Geographical Preference
None

Industry Preferences

Communications
Cable television
Data communications
Satellite and microwave communications
Telephone related
Computer Related
Computer graphics, CAD/CAM and CAE
Computer mainframes
Computer services
Memory devices
Micro and mini computers
Office automation
Scanning related
Software-applications
Software-artificial intelligence
Software-systems
Specialized turnkey systems
Terminals

Consumer
Consumer products
Consumer services
Food and beverage products
Franchise businesses
Distribution
Communications equipment
Consumer products
Electronics equipment
Food products
Industrial products
Medical products
Electronic Components and Instrumentation
Analytical and scientific instrumentation
Electronic components
Fiber optics
Laser related
Energy/Natural Resources
Alternative energy
Technology related products/equipment
Genetic Engineering
Monoclonal antibodies and hybridomas
Recombinant DNA (agricultural and industrial)
Recombinant DNA (medical)
Industrial Products and Equipment
Chemicals
Controls and sensors
Equipment and machinery
Other industrial automation
Robotics/vision systems
Specialty materials
Medical/Health Related
Diagnostic equipment
Diagnostic test products
Disposable products
Drugs and medicines
Hospital and clinical labs
Medical services
Therapeutic equipment
Other
Finance and insurance
Publishing
Real estate

Additional Information
Year Founded—1983
Capital Under Management—$36 million
Investments(1985-1st 6 months)—4
Invested(1985 1st 6 months)—$3 million
Method of Compensation—Return on
investment is of primary concern; do not
charge fees

THE WISCONSIN MESBIC, INC.

622 North Water Street #500
Milwaukee, WI 53202
414-278-0377

Officers
Charles A. McKinney, Chm.
William P. Beckett, Pres.

Whom to Contact
William P. Beckett

Type of Firm
MESBIC

Affiliation
22 shareholders are major corporations
doing business in Wisconsin

Industry Association Memberships
AAMESBIC
NASBIC

Project Preferences
Prefer role as deal originator but will also
invest in deals created by others
Type of Financing:
Startup
First-stage
Second-stage
Later-stage expansion
Leveraged buyout
Minimum Investment: $100,000
Preferred Investment (LBO):
$100,000-$200,000
Minimum Operating Data:
Annual Sales—Nominal
P&L—Losses (profits projected after 2 years)

Geographical Preference
Midwest

Industry Preferences
None
Will Not Consider
Real estate

Additional Information
Year Founded—1984
Capital Under Management—$1 million
Method of Compensation—Return on
investment is most important, but also
charge for closing fees, service fees, etc.

CAPITAL CORPORATION OF WYOMING, INC.

145 South Durbin Street #201
Post Office Box 3599
Casper, WY 82602
307-234-5438

Officers

Larry J. McDonald, Pres.
Lue Brown, V.P.
Scott Weaver, V.P.
Jean Hughley, Asst. V.P.

Whom to Contact

Scott Weaver

Type of Firm

SBIC

Affiliation

Wyoming Industrial Development Corporation
(parent)

Industry Association Membership

NASBIC

Project Preferences

Prefer role as deal originator but will also
invest in deals created by others
Type of Financing:
Startup
First-stage
Second-stage
Later-stage expansion
Leveraged buyout
Minimum Investment: Less than $100,000
Preferred Investment: $100,000-$250,000
Minimum Operating Data:
Annual Sales—Nominal
P&L—Break even

Geographical Preference

Wyoming only

Industry Preferences

Computer Related
Office automation
Consumer
Consumer products
Consumer services
Food and beverage products
Food processing
Leisure and recreational products

Distribution
Communications equipment
Computer equipment
Consumer products
Direct mail marketing and distribution
Electronics equipment
Food products
Industrial products
Medical products
Electronic Components and Instrumentation
Analytical and scientific instrumentation
Component fabrication and testing
equipment
Electronic components
Fiber optics
Laser related
Semiconductors
Energy/Natural Resources
Alternative energy
Coal related
Drilling and exploration services
Energy conservation
Minerals
Oil and gas exploration and production
Technology related products/equipment
Genetic Engineering
Recombinant DNA (agricultural and
industrial)
Industrial Products and Equipment
Chemicals
Controls and sensors
Energy management
Equipment and machinery
General manufacturing
Other industrial automation
Plastics
Robotics/vision systems
Specialty materials
Medical/Health Related
Diagnostic equipment
Diagnostic test products
Disposable products
Drugs and medicines
Hospital and clinical labs
Medical services
Therapeutic equipment
Other
Agriculture, forestry, fishing
Education related
Publishing
Transportation

Additional Information

Year Founded—1979
Capital Under Management—$13 million
Investments(1985-1st 6 months)—7
Invested(1985-1st 6 months)—$1 million
Method of Compensation—Return on
investment is most important, but also
charge for closing fees, service fees, etc.

Canadian Venture Capital Companies

The overview and directory of Canadian venture capital sources has been prepared in cooperation with Venture Economics Canada Limited. Venture Economics Canada Limited (VEC) was established in the spring of 1985 to track the investment activities of Canadian venture capitalists and to provide information services to institutional investors, corporations and venture capital firms. For information on these services, or on VEC's quarterly publication, Canadian Venture Capital, please contact Mary Macdonald (President), at Venture Economics Canada Limited, 7 Sultan Street, Toronto, Ontario, Canada M5S 1L6 Tel: (416) 960-5881.

Venture Capital in Canada

Mary Macdonald

Mary Macdonald *is president of Venture Economics Canada Limited, an affiliate
company of Venture Economics, Inc. Prior to establishing VEC in May 1985,
Ms. Macdonald was president of MPI Consulting Limited. She has consulted extensively
to corporate, institutional and public sector clients on venture capital activity in
Canada.*

Innovation and entrepreneurship are concepts which were slower to take root in reality in Canada than in the United States. Throughout the 1960's and most of the 1970's, significant differences in economic structure, market size, public policy, and prevailing attitudes resulted in an environment which was less conducive to the development of entrepreneurial investment opportunities and hence, to venture investment activity than in the U.S. While some of these fundamentals still present a challenge, the Canadian environment has changed significantly in the past five years. The importance of young innovative firms in achieving the necessary economic restructuring is now widely accepted and the potential for superior returns from venture investments is increasingly being recognized.

As a result, since 1980, there has been a dramatic increase in the quality and the quantity of available investment opportunities and an accompanying increase in capital commitments for venture investing. The investment activity tells the tale. Between 1975 and 1979, the Canadian venture industry made about 260 investments totaling approximately $100 million; between 1980 and 1984, the professional venture community invested almost $500 million in more than 600 firms in Canada and the U.S. This growth reflects an industry on the move.

The 1980's: The Fundamentals for Growth

Several factors coincided to pave the way for the growth in the Canadian venture industry. The economic reality of technology and its role in fostering productivity and competitiveness began to take hold. The rationalization of major industries and the increase in small technology, information and service firms encouraged entrepreneurs and management resources to develop growth enterprises. Canada began to experience success stories with young technology-based firms (e.g. Mitel and AES); government policy became more supportive of entrepreneurs in the development process. Together these factors contributed to a strengthening of investment opportunities.

On the capital side, some venture firms founded in the late 1960's and early 1970's began to demonstrate substantial returns on investment. A role model had also developed with the success of the U.S. venture capital industry, further demonstrating the advantages of pooled capital and professional venture management. Capital commitments to the Canadian venture industry began to grow again with more than $750 million committed to private venture investors and crown venture agencies (government-owned) between 1980 and 1984. Total capital under management now stands at an estimated $1.5 billion, not far off the standard 1:10 rule of thumb ratio normally used for Canada/U.S. comparisons.

Current Investment Trends

In 1984, Canadian venture investors disbursed almost $110 million and preliminary estimates indicate disbursements will exceed $125 million in 1985. Since its earliest days, the Canadian industry has actively participated in U.S. investment opportunities with U.S. investors. This international orientation has been a function of the investment opportunities available in the U.S., the window provided by the U.S. market on emerging opportunities, and the desire on the part of Canadian investors to increase their exposure to the more mature U.S. industry, thereby strengthening their own skills as venture investors. Of the total disbursements in 1984, 55% ($60 million) was invested in Canadian enterprises.

The industry distribution of these investments on a dollar basis was significantly different from that of the investments made by the U.S. venture industry in 1984, as evidenced by Figure 1. The Canadian investments were not as heavily concentrated in the computer, communications and electronics sectors. Instead, a greater share of invested capital was directed towards firms in industrial products, consumer related goods and services and other manufacturing and services.

However, when examined in terms of number of companies financed, the investment activity in computer related and communications-based firms in Canada is much higher than implied by the data on amounts invested. These trends suggest that Canadian investors tend to invest smaller amounts of capital in technology related investments and make larger capital commitments to firms oriented towards productivity related industrial products as well as consumer products and services. As a result, these investments should, overall, have less exposure to the dramatic cyclical swings experienced in the technology sector.

The distribution of dollars invested in Canadian firms in 1984 by stage of development was not very different from U.S. industry norms. Almost 32% of capital invested in Canada went to firms in seed, startup or other early stage (U.S. industry: 34%) and 52% went to firms needing second or third stage expansion financing (U.S. industry: 54%).

There was, however, a wide divergence from these industry norms in the distribution of investments made by Canadian venture capitalists in U.S. firms. In 1984, almost 54% of Canadian capital invested in the U.S. went to early stage firms, while only 22% went to companies in the expansion stage. This trend reflects the desire of Canadian investors to capitalize on early stage technology deals available in the U.S. and also to enhance their own familiarity with the nature and the management of these firms.

Cross Border Capital Flows: Strengthening Links

With the growing awareness in Canada over the past five years of the benefits of venture capital investments has come an increased interaction between the Canadian and U.S. markets. Some Canadian venture firms have formalized a relationship with a U.S. firm to participate in the U.S. market. Some Canadian corporations have also established venture capital subsidiaries in the U.S. for investment and/or strategic reasons. Genstar's Sutter Hill Ventures and Inco's New York based subsidiary are probably the two best known examples of this.

While the direction of these relationships to date has primarily been north to south, U.S. investors are starting to participate with their Canadian counterparts in Canadian opportunities. For example, the Palmer Organization has invested in a Canadian data acquisition products firm with Novacap Investments and Canadian Enterprise Development Corporation; Adler & Co. has joined Ventures West Technologies in the startup financing

of a Western Canadian firm working on the development of a supercomputer; and Venca Partners has invested with Ventures West Technologies in a Canadian biotechnology startup.

The relative maturity of the U.S. industry combined with the level of activity tends to dwarf the Canadian industry in comparison. However, the strong, steady development of investment opportunities, of capital commitments to venture investors, and of relationships between Canadian and U.S. investors is bound to lead to an increased interest in the Canadian market in years to come.

Where To From Here?

The level of activity in the Canadian industry could well be on the brink of another sizeable leap forward. In its budget released earlier this year, the federal government introduced specific measures to increase the attractiveness of investments in small and medium Canadian growth enterprises to pension fund investors. Under current regulations, Canadian pension funds can carry a maximum of 10% of their assets in foreign securities — a ceiling many funds consider to be too low. This ceiling has also served as an impediment of sorts to Canadian venture capitalists in that, by a quirk of Canadian tax law, pension fund investments in limited partnerships are deemed to be foreign property and hence counted as part of the 10% basket.

The new legislation proposes to allow pension funds to increase their allowable foreign holdings by $3 for every additional $1 they invest in small/medium Canadian enterprises (assets of $35 million or less). Furthermore, limited partnerships investing in such firms will no longer be deemed to be foreign property, enabling pension funds to participate in venture capital funds without trading off liquid foreign assets.

Although the legislation has not yet been enacted (and the regulations as they now stand present some fundamental difficulties), the new measures do reflect an increased awareness of the potential benefits of investments in young growth enterprises.

The entrepreneurial spirit is taking hold in Canada and is growing stronger in response to the increased availability of capital. The venture capital community is maturing and producing experienced venture capital investors in the process. Institutional investors, a critical source of capital in Canada, are recognizing the value of venture investments to their portfolio and committing capital accordingly. With these fundamentals in place, the Canadian venture capital industry unquestionably bears watching in the future.

Figure 1

Venture Capital Disbursements
By Industry: 1984

	% of Dollars Invested (in Can. & US) (in US)		% of Companies Financed (in Can. & US) (in US)	
	Canadian Investors	U.S. Investors	Canadian Investors	U.S. Investors
Computer Related	18%	43%	29%	40%
Communications	8	16	14	13
Other Electronics	4	13	5	12
Medical	2	8	6	11
Industrial Products	12	5	7	8
Consumer Related	9	6	12	5
Genetics	3	2	4	3
Energy	1	2	2	2
Other Manuf./Services	43	5	21	6
	100%	100%	100%	100%

AVF INVESTMENTS LTD.

300,1550—Eighth Street SW
Calgary, Alberta T2R 1K1
403-228-9152

Officers
Clifford M. James, Pres.
Robert W. Ruff, V.P. Finance & Admin.
James F. Perry, V.P. Ops.
John M. Todd, Consultant

Whom to Contact
Clifford M. James

Type of Firm
Private venture capital firm investing own
capital

Industry Association Membership
ACVCC

Project Preferences
Prefer role as deal originator but will also
invest in deals created by others
Type of Financing:
Startup
First-stage
Second-stage
Minimum Investment: $250,000
Preferred Investment: $500,000-$1 million
Minimum Operating Data:
Annual Sales—Nominal
P&L—Losses (profits projected after 2 years)

Geographical Preferences

Central Canada
Western Canada

Industry Preferences

Energy/Natural Resources
Alternative energy
Drilling and exploration services
Energy conservation
Minerals
Oil and gas exploration and production
Technology related products/equipment
Will Not Consider
Real estate

Additional Information
Year Founded—1980
Capital Under Management—$13.25 million
Investments(1985-1st 6 months)—3
Invested(1985-1st 6 months)—$810,000

AEONIAN CAPITAL CORPORATION

602—12th Avenue SW #400
Calgary, Alberta T2R 1J3
403-264-4394

Officers
C.A. Smith, Pres.
A.S. Burgess, V.P.

Whom to Contact
Either of the above

Type of Firm
Private venture capital firm investing own
capital

Industry Association Membership
ACVCC

Project Preferences
Will function either as deal originator or
investor in deals created by others
Type of Financing:
Startup
First-stage
Second-stage
Leveraged buyout
Minimum Investment: Less than $100,000
Preferred Investment: $100,000-$250,000
Minimum Operating Data:
Annual Sales—$500,000
P&L—Losses (profits projected after 1 year)

Geographical Preferences

National

Industry Preferences

Communications
Cable television
Commercial communications
Data communications
Satellite and microwave communications
Telephone related
Computer Related
Computer graphics, CAD/CAM and CAE
Computer mainframes
Computer services
Memory devices
Micro and mini computers
Office automation
Scanning related
Software-applications
Software-artificial intelligence
Software-systems
Specialized turnkey systems
Terminals

Consumer
Computer stores/related services
Consumer products
Consumer services
Food and beverage products
Franchise businesses
Hotels and resort areas
Leisure and recreational products
Restaurants
Retailing
Distribution
Communications equipment
Computer equipment
Consumer products
Electronics equipment
Food products
Industrial products
Medical products
**Electronic Components and
Instrumentation**
Analytical and scientific instrumentation
Component fabrication and testing
equipment
Electronic components
Fiber optics
Laser related
Semiconductors
Energy/Natural Resources
Alternative energy
Coal related
Drilling and exploration services
Energy conservation
Minerals
Oil and gas exploration and production
Technology related products/equipment
Genetic Engineering
Gene splicing and manufacturing equipment
Monoclonal antibodies and hybridomas
Recombinant DNA (agricultural and
industrial)
Recombinant DNA (medical)
Industrial Products and Equipment
Chemicals
Controls and sensors
Energy management
Equipment and machinery
Other industrial automation
Plastics
Robotics/vision systems
Specialty materials
Medical/Health Related
Diagnostic equipment
Diagnostic test products
Disposable products
Drugs and medicines
Hospital and clinical labs
Medical services
Therapeutic equipment

Other
Agriculture, forestry, fishing
Education related
Finance and insurance
Publishing
Real estate
Specialty consulting
Transportation

Additional Information
Year Founded—1982
Capital Under Management—$10 million
Investments(1985-1st 6 months)—1

ALTA-CAN TELECOM INC.

26H, 411—1 Street Southeast
Calgary, Alberta T2G 4Y5
403-231-8535

Officers
A.A. MacKinnon, Pres.
N.W. Clark, V.P.
D.F. Campbell, Dir. Finance

Whom to Contact
Any of the above

Type of Firm
Venture capital subsidiary or affiliate of
non-financial corporation

Affiliation
Alberta Government Telephones (sole
shareholder)

Industry Association Membership
ACVCC

Project Preferences
Prefer role as deal originator but will also
invest in deals created by others
Type of Financing:
Seed
Startup
First-stage
Second-stage
Later-stage expansion
Leveraged buyout
Minimum Investment: Less than $100,000
Preferred Investment: $250,000-$1 million
Minimum Operating Data:
Annual Sales—Nominal
P&L—Losses (profits projected after 4 years)

Geographical Preferences

Western Canada

Industry Preferences

Communications
Commercial communications
Data communications
Satellite and microwave communications
Telephone related
Computer Related
Computer graphics, CAD/CAM and CAE
Computer services
Memory devices
Office automation
Software-applications
Software-artificial intelligence
Software-systems
Specialized turnkey systems
**Electronic Components and
Instrumentation**
Analytical and scientific instrumentation
Component fabrication and testing
equipment
Electronic components
Fiber optics
Laser related
Semiconductors
Industrial Products and Equipment
Chemicals
Controls and sensors
Energy management
Equipment and machinery
Other industrial automation
Plastics
Robotics/vision systems
Specialty materials
Medical/Health Related
Diagnostic equipment
Diagnostic test products
Disposable products
Drugs and medicines
Hospital and clinical labs
Medical services
Therapeutic equipment
Will Not Consider
Non-technology situations
Areas with a high degree of government
regulation

Additional Information
Year Founded—1982
Capital Under Management—$15 million
Method of Compensation—Return on
investment is most important, but also
charge for closing fees, service fees, etc.

ALTAVENTURES

Edmonton Research Park
9411 20th Avenue
Edmonton, Alberta P6N 1E5
403-461-2974

Other Office
Post Office Box 1213
Ponoka, Alberta T0C 2H0
403-783-3453

Officers
E.A. Clarke, Pres. (Ponoka)
F.E. Brown, Chm. (Edmonton)

Whom to Contact
E.A. Clarke

Type of Firm
Private venture capital firm investing own
capital

Industry Association Membership
ACVCC

Project Preferences
Prefer role as deal originator
Type of Financing:
Seed
Startup
Leveraged buyout
Minimum Investment: Less than $100,000
Preferred Investment: $100,000-$250,000
Minimum Operating Data:
Annual Sales—Nominal
P&L—Losses (profits projected after 2 years)

Geographical Preferences

Alberta

Industry Preferences

Communications
Cable television
Commercial communications
Data communications
Satellite and microwave communications
Telephone related

Computer Related
Computer graphics, CAD/CAM and CAE
Computer mainframes
Computer services
Memory devices
Micro and mini computers
Office automation
Scanning related
Software-applications
Software-artificial intelligence
Software-systems
Specialized turnkey systems
Terminals
Electronic Components and Instrumentation
Analytical and scientific instrumentation
Component fabrication and testing equipment
Electronic components
Fiber optics
Laser related
Semiconductors
Energy/Natural Resources
Alternative energy
Coal related
Drilling and exploration services
Energy conservation
Minerals
Oil and gas exploration and production
Technology related products/equipment
Genetic Engineering
Gene splicing and manufacturing equipment
Monoclonal antibodies and hybridomas
Recombinant DNA (agricultural and industrial)
Recombinant DNA (medical)
Industrial Products and Equipment
Chemicals
Controls and sensors
Energy management
Equipment and machinery
Other industrial automation
Plastics
Robotics/vision systems
Specialty materials
Medical/Health Related
Diagnostic equipment
Diagnostic test products
Disposable products
Drugs and medicines
Hospital and clinical labs
Medical services
Therapeutic equipment
Other
Publishing
Transportation
Will Not Consider
Oil and gas exploration and development
Real estate development

Additional Information
Year Founded—1985
Capital Under Management—$1.5 million
Investments(1985-1st 6 months)—3
Invested(1985-1st 6 months)—$1.1 million
Method of Compensation—Return on investment is most important, but also charge for closing fees, service fees, etc.

CAPWEST CAPITAL SERVICES LTD.

10080 Jasper Avenue, #1102
Edmonton, Alberta T5J 1V9
403-426-7117

Officers
M.A. Miles, Pres.
H.H. Millar, V.P.
E. Pechet, V.P.
G. Van Schalkwyk, Dir.
Pamela S. Miles, V.P.

Whom to Contact
M.A. Miles
Pamela S. Miles

Type of Firm
Investment banking or merchant banking firm investing own capital or funds of partners or clients

Industry Association Membership
ACVCC

Project Preferences
Prefer role as deal originator but will also invest in deals created by others
Type of Financing:
Second-stage
Leveraged buyout
Minimum Investment: $250,000
Preferred Investment: $500,000-$1 million

Geographical Preferences

Western Canada

Industry Preferences

Communications
Cable television
Commercial communications
Data communications
Satellite and microwave communications
Telephone related

Consumer
Computer stores/related services
Consumer products
Consumer services
Food and beverage products
Franchise businesses
Hotels and resort areas
Leisure and recreational products
Restaurants
Retailing
Distribution
Communications equipment
Computer equipment
Consumer products
Electronics equipment
Food products
Industrial products
Medical products
Energy/Natural Resources
Alternative energy
Coal related
Drilling and exploration services
Energy conservation
Minerals
Oil and gas exploration and production
Technology related products/equipment
Industrial Products and Equipment
Chemicals
Controls and sensors
Energy management
Equipment and machinery
Other industrial automation
Plastics
Robotics/vision systems
Specialty materials
Medical/Health Related
Diagnostic equipment
Diagnostic test products
Disposable products
Drugs and medicines
Hospital and clinical labs
Medical services
Therapeutic equipment
Other
Agriculture, forestry, fishing
Education related
Finance and insurance
Publishing
Real estate
Specialty consulting
Transportation

Additional Information
Year Founded—1973

GOLD BAR DEVELOPMENTS LTD.

Post Office Box 3160
Edmonton, Alberta T5J 2G7
403-420-6666

Officers

Sandy A. Mactaggart, Pres.
Greg Greenough, V.P. & Gen. Mgr.
John Elias, V.P. Finance

Whom to Contact

John Elias

Type of Firm

Venture capital subsidiary or affiliate of
non-financial corporation

Affiliation

Maclab Enterprises, Inc.
(associated company)

Industry Association Membership

ACVCC

Project Preferences

Prefer role in deals created by others
Type of Financing:
Startup
First-stage
Second-stage
Minimum Investment: Less than $100,000
Preferred Investment: $100,000-$250,000
Minimum Operating Data:
Annual Sales—Nominal
P&L—Losses (profits projected after 2 years)

Geographical Preferences

None

Industry Preferences

Communications
Commercial communications
Data communications
Satellite and microwave communications
Telephone related
Computer Related
Computer graphics, CAD/CAM and CAE
Computer mainframes
Computer services
Memory devices
Micro and mini computers
Office automation
Scanning related
Software-applications
Software-artificial intelligence
Software-systems
Specialized turnkey systems
Terminals

**Electronic Components and
Instrumentation**
Analytical and scientific instrumentation
Component fabrication and testing
equipment
Electronic components
Fiber optics
Laser related
Semiconductors
Energy/Natural Resources
Technology related products/equipment
Genetic Engineering
Gene splicing and manufacturing equipment
Monoclonal antibodies and hybridomas
Recombinant DNA (agricultural and
industrial)
Recombinant DNA (medical)
Industrial Products and Equipment
Robotics/vision systems
Medical/Health Related
Diagnostic equipment
Diagnostic test products
Disposable products
Drugs and medicines
Hospital and clinical labs
Medical services
Therapeutic equipment

Additional Information

Year Founded—1957
Investments(1985-1st 6 months)—3
Invested(1985-1st 6 months)—$1.2 million
Method of Compensation—Return on
investment is of primary concern; do not
charge fees

VENCAP EQUITIES ALBERTA LTD.

816, 10025 Jasper Avenue
Edmonton, Alberta T5J 1S6
403-420-1171

Other Office

125—9 Avenue SE
Palliser Square Bldg. #2410
Calgary, Alberta T2G 0P6
403-237-8101

Officers

Derek Mather, Pres. & CEO
(Edmonton/Calgary)
R.A. (Sandy) Slator, V.P. & CFO (Edmonton)
Richard Rutherford, V.P. (Edmonton)
E.M. (Ted) Mills, Inv. Officer (Calgary)
Ian Monteith, Inv. Officer (Calgary)
W.R. (Bill) McKenzie, Inv. Officer (Edmonton)
O.S. (Oleh) Hnatiuk, Inv. Officer (Edmonton)
M.E. (Mike) Phillips, Inv. Officer (Edmonton)

Whom to Contact

Any of the above

Type of Firm

Private venture capital firm investing
own capital

Industry Association Membership

ACVCC

Project Preferences

Will function either as deal originator or
investor in deals created by others
Type of Financing:
Startup
First-stage
Second-stage
Later-stage expansion
Leveraged buyout
Minimum Investment: $500,000
Preferred Investment: Over $1 million
Minimum Operating Data:
Annual Sales—Nominal
P&L—Losses (profits projected after 3 years)

Geographical Preferences

Western Canada
Alberta

Industry Preferences

Communications
Cable television
Commercial communications
Data communications
Satellite and microwave communications
Telephone related
Computer Related
Computer graphics, CAD/CAM and CAE
Computer mainframes
Computer services
Memory devices
Micro and mini computers
Office automation
Scanning related
Software-applications
Software-artificial intelligence
Software-systems
Specialized turnkey systems
Terminals
Consumer
Computer stores/related services
Consumer products
Consumer services
Food and beverage products
Franchise businesses
Hotels and resort areas
Leisure and recreational products
Restaurants
Retailing

Distribution
Communications equipment
Computer equipment
Consumer products
Electronics equipment
Food products
Industrial products
Medical products
Electronic Components and Instrumentation
Analytical and scientific instrumentation
Component fabrication and testing equipment
Electronic components
Fiber optics
Laser related
Semiconductors
Energy/Natural Resources
Alternative energy
Coal related
Drilling and exploration services
Energy conservation
Minerals
Technology related products/equipment
Genetic Engineering
Gene splicing and manufacturing equipment
Monoclonal antibodies and hybridomas
Recombinant DNA (agricultural and industrial)
Recombinant DNA (medical)
Industrial Products and Equipment
Chemicals
Controls and sensors
Energy management
Equipment and machinery
Other industrial automation
Plastics
Robotics/vision systems
Specialty materials
Medical/Health Related
Diagnostic equipment
Diagnostic test products
Disposable products
Drugs and medicines
Hospital and clinical labs
Medical services
Therapeutic equipment
Other
Agriculture, forestry, fishing
Education related
Publishing
Transportation
Will Not Consider
Banking and finance
Oil and gas exploration
Real estate development

Additional Information
Year Founded—1983
Capital Under Management—$260 million
Investments(1985-1st 6 months)—8
Invested(1985-1st 6 months)—$19.2 million
Method of Compensation—Return on investment is of primary concern; do not charge fees

BAWLF MANAGEMENT

550 Burrard Street #410
Vancouver
British Columbia V6C 2J6
604-682-6336

Officers
Charles W. Bawlf, Pres.
Howard Jones, Assoc.

Whom to Contact
Charles W. Bawlf

Type of Firm
Private venture capital firm investing
own capital

Project Preferences
Will function either as deal originator or
investor in deals created by others
Type of Financing:
Second-stage
Leveraged buyout
Minimum Investment: $500,000
Preferred Investment: Over $1 million
Minimum Operating Data:
Annual Sales—$1.5 million
P&L—Break even

Geographical Preferences

Canada:
West
United States:
Northwest

Industry Preferences

Communications
Cable television
Commercial communications
Data communications
Satellite and microwave communications
Telephone related
Computer Related
Computer graphics, CAD/CAM and CAE
Computer mainframes
Computer services
Memory devices
Micro and mini computers
Office automation
Scanning related
Software-applications
Software-artificial intelligence
Software-systems
Specialized turnkey systems
Terminals

Consumer
Computer stores/related services
Consumer products
Consumer services
Food and beverage products
Franchise businesses
Hotels and resort areas
Leisure and recreational products
Restaurants
Retailing
Distribution
Communications equipment
Computer equipment
Consumer products
Electronics equipment
Food products
Industrial products
Medical products
**Electronic Components and
Instrumentation**
Analytical and scientific instrumentation
Component fabrication and testing
equipment
Electronic components
Fiber optics
Laser related
Semiconductors
Energy/Natural Resources
Alternative energy
Coal related
Drilling and exploration services
Energy conservation
Minerals
Oil and gas exploration and production
Technology related products/equipment
Genetic Engineering
Gene splicing and manufacturing equipment
Monoclonal antibodies and hybridomas
Recombinant DNA (agricultural and
industrial)
Recombinant DNA (medical)
Industrial Products and Equipment
Chemicals
Controls and sensors
Energy management
Equipment and machinery
Other industrial automation
Plastics
Robotics/vision systems
Specialty materials
Medical/Health Related
Diagnostic equipment
Diagnostic test products
Disposable products
Drugs and medicines
Hospital and clinical labs
Medical services
Therapeutic equipment

Other
Agriculture, forestry, fishing
Education related
Finance and insurance
Publishing
Real estate
Specialty consulting
Transportation

Additional Information
Year Founded—1974
Capital Under Management—$5 million
Investments(1985-1st 6 months)—3
Invested(1985-1st 6 months)—$2.5 million
Method of Compensation—Return on
investment is most important, but also
charge for closing fees, service fees, etc.

CANADA OVERSEAS INVESTMENTS LIMITED

1055 West Hastings Street
Guinness Tower, #1120
Vancouver
British Columbia V6E 2E9
604-681-7374

See ONTARIO for full listing

FEDERAL BUSINESS DEVELOPMENT BANK

900 West Hastings Street
Vancouver
British Columbia V6C 1E7
604-687-1300

W.J. Lichti, Portfolio Mgr.
J.D. Douglas, Portfolio Mgr.
A. Charnish, Portfolio Mgr.

See QUEBEC for full listing

VENTURES WEST TECHNOLOGIES

400-321 Water Street
Vancouver
British Columbia V6B 1B8
604-688-9495

Officers
M.J. Brown, Pres.
J.H. Farris, Exec. V.P.
J.M. Fletcher, V.P.
W.J. Boden, V.P.
V.J.E. Jones, V.P.
S. Znaimer, Sr. Inv. Officer
F.T. White, Assoc.

Whom to Contact
S. Znaimer

Type of Firm
Private venture capital firm investing
  own capital

Industry Association Membership
ACVCC

Project Preferences
Prefer role as deal originator but will also
  invest in deals created by others
Type of Financing:
Startup
First-stage
Later-stage expansion
Minimum Investment: $250,000
Preferred Investment: $500,000-$1 million
Minimum Operating Data:
Annual Sales—Nominal

Geographical Preferences

Central Canada
Western Canada

Industry Preferences

Communications
Commercial communications
Data communications
Radio broadcasting
Satellite and microwave communications
Telephone related
Computer Related
Computer graphics, CAD/CAM and CAE
Office automation
Software-applications
Software-artificial intelligence
Software-systems
Specialized turnkey systems
Consumer
Entertainment

**Electronic Components and
  Instrumentation**
Component fabrication and testing
  equipment
Electronic components
Fiber optics
Laser related
Semiconductor design
Energy/Natural Resources
Technology related products/equipment
Genetic Engineering
Gene splicing and manufacturing equipment
Monoclonal antibodies and hybridomas
Recombinant DNA (agricultural and
  industrial)
Recombinant DNA (medical)
Industrial Products and Equipment
Controls and sensors
Other industrial automation
Robotics/vision systems
Medical/Health Related
Hospital and clinical labs
Medical robotics
Other
Transportation
Will Not Consider
Real estate

Additional Information
Year Founded—1973
Capital Under Management—$34 million
Investments(1985-1st 6 months)—6
Invested(1985-1st 6 months)—$4 million
Method of Compensation—Return on
  investment is of primary concern; do not
  charge fees

ATLANTIC VENTURES TRUST

297 Waterloo Road
Fredericton
New Brunswick E3B 5P2
506-454-2762

William M. Jones

See NOVA SCOTIA for full listing

ATLANTIC VENTURES TRUST

137 Elizabeth Avenue
St. John's
Newfoundland A1B 1F2
709-726-9251

George E. Lee

See NOVA SCOTIA for full listing

ATLANTIC VENTURES TRUST

1246 Hollis Street
Halifax
Nova Scotia B3J 1T6
902-421-1595

Other Offices

297 Waterloo Road
Fredericton
New Brunswick E3B 5P2
506-454-2762

27½ Water Street
Charlottetown
Prince Edward Island C1A 1A2
902-892-8666

137 Elizabeth Avenue
St. John's
Newfoundland A1B 1F2
709-726-9251

Officers

Thomas J. Hayes, Pres. (Nova Scotia)
William M. Jones (New Brunswick)
Donald M. Deacon (Prince Edward Island)
George E. Lee (Newfoundland)

Whom to Contact

Thomas J. Hayes

Type of Firm

Private venture capital firm investing
own capital

Industry Association Membership

ACVCC

Project Preferences

Will function either as deal originator or
investor in deals created by others
Type of Financing:
First-stage
Second-stage
Leveraged buyout
Minimum Investment: $100,000
Preferred Investment: $100,000-$250,000
Minimum Operating Data:
Annual Sales—$500,000
P&L—Break even

Geographical Preferences

Eastern Canada

Industry Preferences

Communications
Cable television
Commercial communications
Data communications
Satellite and microwave communications
Telephone related
Computer Related
Computer graphics, CAD/CAM and CAE
Computer mainframes
Computer services
Memory devices
Micro and mini computers
Office automation
Scanning related
Software-applications
Software-artificial intelligence
Software-systems
Specialized turnkey systems
Terminals
Consumer
Computer stores/related services
Consumer products
Consumer services
Food and beverage products
Franchise businesses
Hotels and resort areas
Leisure and recreational products
Restaurants
Retailing
Distribution
Communications equipment
Computer equipment
Consumer products
Electronics equipment
Food products
Industrial products
Medical products
**Electronic Components and
Instrumentation**
Analytical and scientific instrumentation
Component fabrication and testing
equipment
Electronic components
Fiber optics
Laser related
Semiconductors
Energy/Natural Resources
Alternative energy
Coal related
Drilling and exploration services
Energy conservation
Minerals
Oil and gas exploration and production
Technology related products/equipment

Genetic Engineering
Gene splicing and manufacturing equipment
Monoclonal antibodies and hybridomas
Recombinant DNA (agricultural and
industrial)
Recombinant DNA (medical)
Industrial Products and Equipment
Chemicals
Controls and sensors
Energy management
Equipment and machinery
Other industrial automation
Plastics
Robotics/vision systems
Specialty materials
Medical/Health Related
Diagnostic equipment
Diagnostic test products
Disposable products
Drugs and medicines
Hospital and clinical labs
Medical services
Therapeutic equipment
Other
Agriculture, forestry, fishing
Education related
Publishing
Specialty consulting
Transportation
Will Not Consider
Finance and insurance
Real estate

Additional Information

Year Founded—1982
Capital Under Management—$6.7 million
Method of Compensation—Return on
investment is of primary concern; do not
charge fees

BG ACORN CAPITAL FUND

141 Adelaide Street West #601
Toronto, Ontario M5H 3L5
416-362-9009

Partners
Michael M. Boyd, Mgn. Ptnr.
E.C. (Ted) Higgins, Mgn. Ptnr.
Ted Anderson, Inv. Mgr.

Whom to Contact
Any of the above

Type of Firm
Private venture capital firm investing
own capital

Industry Association Membership
ACVCC

Project Preferences
Will function either as deal originator or
investor in deals created by others
Type of Financing:
Startup
First-stage
Second-stage
Leveraged buyout
Minimum Investment: $250,000
Preferred Investment: $500,000-$1 million
Preferred Investment (LBO):
$800,000-$1.5 million
Minimum Operating Data:
Annual Sales—$500,000
P&L—Break even
Annual Sales (LBO)—$10 million-$100 million

Geographical Preferences

National

Industry Preferences

Communications
Cable television
Commercial communications
Data communications
Satellite and microwave communications
Telephone related

Computer Related
Computer graphics, CAD/CAM and CAE
Computer mainframes
Computer services
Memory devices
Micro and mini computers
Office automation
Scanning related
Software-applications
Software-artificial intelligence
Software-systems
Specialized turnkey systems
Terminals
Consumer
Computer stores/related services
Consumer products
Consumer services
Food and beverage products
Franchise businesses
Hotels and resort areas
Leisure and recreational products
Restaurants
Retailing
Distribution
Communications equipment
Computer equipment
Consumer products
Electronics equipment
Food products
Industrial products
Medical products
**Electronic Components and
Instrumentation**
Analytical and scientific instrumentation
Component fabrication and testing
equipment
Electronic components
Fiber optics
Laser related
Semiconductors
Energy/Natural Resources
Alternative energy
Coal related
Drilling and exploration services
Energy conservation
Minerals
Oil and gas exploration and production
Technology related products/equipment

Genetic Engineering
Gene splicing and manufacturing equipment
Monoclonal antibodies and hybridomas
Recombinant DNA (agricultural and
industrial)
Recombinant DNA (medical)
Industrial Products and Equipment
Chemicals
Controls and sensors
Energy management
Equipment and machinery
Other industrial automation
Plastics
Robotics/vision systems
Specialty materials
Medical/Health Related
Diagnostic equipment
Diagnostic test products
Disposable products
Drugs and medicines
Hospital and clinical labs
Medical services
Therapeutic equipment
Other
Agriculture, forestry, fishing
Education related
Finance and insurance
Publishing
Transportation
Will Not Consider
Real estate

Additional Information
Year Founded—1984
Capital Under Management—$19 million
Investments(1985-1st 6 months)—11
Invested(1985-1st 6 months)—$4.5 million
Method of Compensation—Return on
investment is most important, but also
charge for closing fees, service fees, etc.

CAN-CHUNG VENTURES INC.

59 John Street
Mississauga
Ontario N1M 1C3
416-896-0700

Officers
Walter Wang, Chm.
Dr. George K. Lewis, Pres.

Whom to Contact
Walter Wang

Type of Firm
Private venture capital firm investing own capital

Project Preferences
Prefer role as deal originator
Type of Financing:
Startup
First-stage
Second-stage
Later-stage expansion
Leveraged buyout
Minimum Investment: $300,000
Preferred Investment: $300,000-$2 million
Minimum Operating Data:
Annual Sales—$3 million

Geographical Preferences

China

Industry Preferences

Communications
Telephone related
Consumer
Consumer products
Hotels and resort areas
Shoe manufacturing
Energy/Natural Resources
Alternative energy
Drilling and exploration services
Energy conservation
Minerals
Oil and gas exploration and production
Technology related products/equipment
Genetic Engineering
Recombinant DNA (agricultural and industrial)
Recombinant DNA (medical)
Industrial Products and Equipment
Automotive parts

Medical/Health Related
Diagnostic equipment
Diagnostic test products
Disposable products
Drugs and medicines
Hospital and clinical labs
Medical services
Therapeutic equipment
Other
Agriculture, forestry, fishing
Education related

Additional Information
Year Founded—1985
Method of Compensation—Return on investment is most important, but also charge for closing fees, service fees, etc.

CANADA OVERSEAS INVESTMENTS LIMITED

Royal Bank Pl., S. Tower #2901
Post Office Box 62
Toronto, Ontario M5J 2J2
416-865-0266

Other Office
1055 West Hastings Street
Guinness Tower, #1120
Vancouver
British Columbia V6E 2E9
604-681-7374

Officer
Michael M. Koerner, Pres.

Type of Firm
Private venture capital firm investing own capital

Affiliation
Sylva Investments Limited (parent)

Project Preferences
Will function either as deal originator or investor in deals created by others
Type of Financing:
Startup
First-stage
Second-stage
Leveraged buyout
Minimum Investment: $250,000
Preferred Investment: $250,000-$500,000
Minimum Operating Data:
Annual Sales—Over $3 million
P&L—Break even

Geographical Preferences

Canada:
East
West
United States:
Northeast

Industry Preferences

Communications
Cable television
Commercial communications
Data communications
Satellite and microwave communications
Computer Related
Computer graphics, CAD/CAM and CAE
Computer services
Memory devices
Office automation
Electronic Components and Instrumentation
Analytical and scientific instrumentation
Component fabrication and testing equipment
Electronic components
Energy/Natural Resources
Drilling and exploration services
Technology related products/equipment
Industrial Products and Equipment
Chemicals
Controls and sensors
Plastics
Other
Agriculture
Will Not Consider
Distribution
Merchandising
Real estate

Additional Information
Year Founded—1959
Investments(1985-1st 6 months)—4
Method of Compensation—Return on investment is of primary concern; do not charge fees

CANADIAN ENTERPRISE DEVELOPMENT CORPORATION

199 Bay Street #1100
Toronto, Ontario M5J 1I4, ON
416-366-7607

Officers
Gerald D. Sutton, Pres. (Ontario)
William J. Brown, V.P. (Ontario)
Daniel Nixon, V.P. (British Columbia)
Barbara Atchie, Secy. & Treas. (Ontario)

Whom to Contact
Gerald D. Sutton
William J. Brown
Daniel Nixon

Type of Firm
Private venture capital firm investing
own capital

Industry Association Membership
ACVCC

Project Preferences
Will function either as deal originator or
investor in deals created by others
Type of Financing:
Startup
First-stage
Leveraged buyout
Minimum Investment: $250,000
Preferred Investment: $500,000-$1 million
Preferred Investment (LBO):
$500,000-$1 million
Minimum Operating Data:
Annual Sales—Nominal
P&L—Losses (profits projected after 2 years)
Annual Sales (LBO)—$6 million-$12 million

Geographical Preferences

Canada:
National
United States:
Northeast
Northwest
East Coast
Midwest
West Coast

Industry Preferences

Communications
Cable television
Commercial communications
Data communications
Satellite and microwave communications
Telephone related

Computer Related
Computer graphics, CAD/CAM and CAE
Computer mainframes
Computer services
Memory devices
Micro and mini computers
Office automation
Scanning related
Software-applications
Software-artificial intelligence
Software-systems
Specialized turnkey systems
Terminals
Electronic Components and Instrumentation
Analytical and scientific instrumentation
Component fabrication and testing
equipment
Electronic components
Fiber optics
Laser related
Semiconductors
Energy/Natural Resources
Technology related products/equipment
Genetic Engineering
Gene splicing and manufacturing equipment
Monoclonal antibodies and hybridomas
Recombinant DNA (agricultural and
industrial)
Recombinant DNA (medical)
Industrial Products and Equipment
Chemicals
Controls and sensors
Energy management
Equipment and machinery
Other industrial automation
Plastics
Robotics/vision systems
Specialty materials
Medical/Health Related
Diagnostic equipment
Diagnostic test products
Disposable products
Drugs and medicines
Hospital and clinical labs
Medical services
Therapeutic equipment
Will Not Consider
Agriculture, forestry, fishing
Distribution
Finance
Natural resources
Real estate
Retailing

Additional Information
Year Founded—1962
Capital Under Management—$20 million
Investments(1985-1st 6 months)—7
Invested(1985-1st 6 months)—$1.7 million
Method of Compensation—Return on
investment is of primary concern; do not
charge fees

CORPORATE GROWTH ASSISTANCE LIMITED

19 York Ridge Road
Willowdale
Ontario M2P 1R8
416-927-7772

Officer
Millard S. Roth, Pres.

Type of Firm
Private venture capital firm investing
own capital

Affiliations
Business Ventureco Inc. (company
under management)
Two Futures Investment Corp. (company
under management)

Project Preferences
Prefer role as deal originator but will also
invest in deals created by others
Type of Financing:
Second-stage
Later-stage expansion
Leveraged buyout
Minimum Investment: $250,000
Preferred Investment: $500,000-$1 million
Preferred Investment (LBO): $3 million
Minimum Operating Data:
Annual Sales—$1.5 million
P&L—Break even
Annual Sales (LBO)—$20 million-$50 million

Geographical Preferences

Central Canada

Industry Preferences

Communications
Commercial communications
Computer Related
Memory devices
Software-artificial intelligence
Consumer
Leisure and recreational products

Distribution
Communications equipment
Electronics equipment
Food products
Medical products
**Electronic Components and
  Instrumentation**
Analytical and scientific instrumentation
Energy/Natural Resources
Energy conservation
Industrial Products and Equipment
Chemicals
Equipment and machinery
Medical/Health Related
Disposable products

Additional Information
Year Founded—1967
Capital Under Management—$6 million
Investments(1985-1st 6 months)—1
Invested(1985-1st 6 months)—$250,000
Method of Compensation—Return on
  investment is most important, but also
  charge for closing fees, service fees, etc.

FEDERAL BUSINESS DEVELOPMENT
BANK

250 University Avenue
Toronto, Ontario M5H 3E5
416-593-1144

G.R. Cornwall, Portfolio Mgr.
G.D. Fife, Portfolio Mgr.

See QUEBEC for full listing

GORDON CAPITAL CORPORATION

Toronto-Dominion Centre #5401
Post Office Box 67
Toronto, Ontario M5K 1E7
416-364-9393

Officer
A. Richard G. Reid, Mgr., Venture
Investments

Type of Firm
Investment banking or merchant banking
  firm investing own capital or funds of
  partners or clients

Industry Association Membership
ACVCC

Project Preferences
Prefer role as deal originator but will also
  invest in deals created by others
Type of Financing:
Second-stage
Later-stage expansion
Minimum Investment: $250,000
Preferred Investment: $500,000-$1 million
Minimum Operating Data:
Annual Sales—Over $3 million
P&L—Profitable

Geographical Preferences

Eastern Canada
Western Canada

Industry Preferences

Communications
Commercial communications
Data communications
Satellite and microwave communications
Telephone related
Computer Related
Micro and mini computers
Consumer
Consumer products
Food and beverage products
Distribution
Communications equipment
Consumer products
Food products
Industrial products
Medical products
**Electronic Components and
  Instrumentation**
Fiber optics
Laser related
Industrial Products and Equipment
Chemicals
Energy management
Equipment and machinery
Other industrial automation
Plastics
Robotics/vision systems
Medical/Health Related
Diagnostic equipment
Drugs and medicines
Hospital and clinical labs
Medical services
Other
Finance and insurance
Publishing
Transportation

Additional Information
Year Founded—1968
Capital Under Management—$50 million
Investments(1985-1st 6 months)—5
Invested(1985-1st 6 months)—$3 million
Method of Compensation—Return on
  investment is most important, but also
  charge for closing fees, service fees, etc.

GRAYROCK CAPITAL INC.

Two International Boulevard
Rexdale, Ontario M9W 1A2
416-675-4807

Other Office
36 Grove Street
New Canaan, CT 06840
203-966-8392

Officers
W.J. Gluck, Pres. (United States)
D.P. Driscoll, V.P. (Canada)

Whom to Contact
Either of the above

Type of Firm
Venture capital subsidiary or affiliate of
  non-financial corporation

Affiliation
The Molson Companies Limited (parent)

Industry Association Memberships
NASBIC
NVCA
ACVCC

Project Preferences
Prefer role as deal originator but will also
  invest in deals created by others
Type of Financing:
Startup
First-stage
Second-stage
Later-stage expansion
Leveraged buyout
Minimum Investment: $100,000
Preferred Investment: $250,000-$500,000
Minimum Operating Data:
Annual Sales—$500,000
P&L—Losses (profits projected after 2 years)

Geographical Preferences

Near major metropolitan area
Canada:
National
United States:
Northwest
East Coast
Midwest
West Coast

Industry Preferences

Communications
Cable television
Commercial communications
Data communications
Satellite and microwave communications
Telephone related
Computer Related
Computer services
Office automation
Consumer
Computer stores/related services
Consumer products
Consumer services
Food and beverage products
Franchise businesses
Hotels and resort areas
Leisure and recreational products
Restaurants
Retailing
Distribution
Communications equipment
Computer equipment
Consumer products
Electronics equipment
Food products
Industrial products
Medical products
Electronic Components and Instrumentation
Fiber optics
Laser related
Energy/Natural Resources
Oil and gas exploration and production
Technology related products/equipment
Genetic Engineering
Gene splicing and manufacturing equipment
Monoclonal antibodies and hybridomas
Recombinant DNA (agricultural and industrial)
Recombinant DNA (medical)
Industrial Products and Equipment
Chemicals
Other industrial automation
Robotics/vision systems

Medical/Health Related
Diagnostic equipment
Diagnostic test products
Disposable products
Drugs and medicines
Hospital and clinical labs
Medical services
Therapeutic equipment
Other
Publishing
Will Not Consider
Computer software
Capital intensive businesses

Additional Information

Year Founded—1981
Capital Under Management—$30 million
Investments(1985-1st 6 months)—5
Invested(1985-1st 6 months)—$1.7 million

GRIEVE HORNER AND ASSOCIATES INC.

20 Victoria Street #900
Toronto, Ontario M5C 2N8
416-362-7668

Partners

Anthony Brown
Alan Grieve
Ralph Horner

Whom to Contact

Any of the above

Type of Firm

Private venture capital firm investing own capital

Industry Association Membership

ACVCC

Project Preferences

Will function either as deal originator or investor in deals created by others
Type of Financing:
Startup
First-stage
Minimum Investment: $250,000
Preferred Investment: $250,000-$500,000
Minimum Operating Data:
Annual Sales—Nominal
P&L—Losses (profits projected after 3 years)

Geographical Preferences

Canada:
Central
United States:
Northeast
East Coast

Industry Preferences

Communications
Commercial communications
Data communications
Media and information products and services
Satellite and microwave communications
Telephone related
Computer Related
Data banks
Electronic information services
Software-applications
Software-artificial intelligence
Distribution
Communications equipment
Electronics equipment
Genetic Engineering
Recombinant DNA (agricultural and industrial)
Other
Information industries
Will Not Consider
Oil and gas exploration and production
Real estate

Additional Information

Year Founded—1976
Capital Under Management—$10 million
Investments(1985-1st 6 months)—3
Invested(1985-1st 6 months)—$2 million
Method of Compensation—Return on investment is of primary concern

HELIX INVESTMENTS LIMITED

401 Bay Street #2400
Toronto, Ontario M5H2Y4
416-367-1290

Officers
Donald C. Webster, Pres.
Michael J. Needham, Sr. V.P. & Secy.
Peter Tolnai, V.P.
Fred Sorkin, V.P.
Kenneth W. Soehner, Treas.

Whom to Contact
Any of the above

Type of Firm
Private venture capital firm investing
own capital

Industry Association Membership
ACVCC

Project Preferences
Prefer role as deal originator but will also
invest in deals created by others
Type of Financing:
Seed
Startup
First-stage
Second-stage
Leveraged buyout
Minimum Investment: $250,000
Preferred Investment: $1 million-$2 million
Minimum Operating Data:
Annual Sales—Nominal
P&L—Losses (profits projected after 2 years)

Geographical Preferences

North America

Industry Preferences

Communications
Telecommunications
Computer Related
Computer hardware and software
Other
Wide range of investment interests

Additional Information
Year Founded—1968
Capital Under Management—$95 million
Investments(1985-1st 6 months)—11
Invested(1985-1st 6 months)—$4.8 million
Method of Compensation—Return on
investment is of primary concern; do not
charge fees

IDEA CORPORATION

33 Yonge Street #800
Toronto, Ontario M5E 1V3
416-362-4400

Officers
Harold W. Blakley, Pres.
Bill Douglas, Sr. Mgr. Venture Inv.
Peter Love, Sr. Mgr. Venture Inv.
Bruno Maruzzo, Sr. Mgr. Tech. Assessment

Whom to Contact
Harold W. Blakley

Type of Firm
Government agency financing technological
developments

Industry Association Membership
ACVCC

Project Preferences
Prefer role as deal originator but will also
invest in deals created by others
Type of Financing:
Seed
Research and development partnerships
Startup
First-stage
Second-stage
Minimum Investment: Less than $100,000
Preferred Investment: No preference
Minimum Operating Data:
Annual Sales—Nominal

Geographical Preferences

Ontario

Industry Preferences

Communications
Data communications
Satellite and microwave communications
Telephone related
Computer Related
Computer graphics, CAD/CAM and CAE
Computer mainframes
Computer services
Memory devices
Micro and mini computers
Office automation
Scanning related
Software-applications
Software-artificial intelligence
Software-systems
Specialized turnkey systems
Terminals
Consumer
Consumer products

Distribution
Computer software
**Electronic Components and
Instrumentation**
Analytical and scientific instrumentation
Component fabrication and testing
equipment
Electronic components
Fiber optics
Laser related
Semiconductors
Energy/Natural Resources
Technology related products/equipment
Genetic Engineering
Gene splicing and manufacturing equipment
Monoclonal antibodies and hybridomas
Recombinant DNA (agricultural and
industrial)
Recombinant DNA (medical)
Industrial Products and Equipment
Chemicals
Controls and sensors
Energy management
Equipment and machinery
Other industrial automation
Plastics
Robotics/vision systems
Specialty materials
Medical/Health Related
Diagnostic equipment
Diagnostic test products
Drugs and medicines
Therapeutic equipment
Will Not Consider
Businesses where technological innovation
is not involved

Additional Information
Year Founded—1981
Capital Under Management—$60 million
Investments(1985-1st 6 months)—11
Invested(1985-1st 6 months)—$4.9 million
Method of Compensation—Return on
investment is of primary concern; do not
charge fees

KANATA GENESIS FUND LTD.

Eight Brewer Hunt Way
Kanata, Ontario K2K 2B5
613-592-6453

Officers
Brian Beninger, Pres.
Michael Beninger, Secy.
Irwin Nightingale, Treas.

Whom to Contact
Michael Beninger

Type of Firm
Public venture capital company

Affiliation
Benbaron Venture Corporation
(management company)

Industry Association Membership
ACVCC

Project Preferences
Prefer role as deal originator but will also
invest in deals created by others
Type of Financing:
Seed
Startup
First-stage
Minimum Investment: Less than $100,000
Preferred Investment: Less than $250,000
Minimum Operating Data:
Annual Sales—Nominal
P&L—Losses (profits projected after 2 years)

Geographical Preferences
Central Canada

Industry Preferences
Computer Related
Software-applications
Specialized turnkey systems
**Electronic Components and
Instrumentation**
Electronic components
Fiber optics
Laser related
Energy/Natural Resources
Technology related products/equipment

Additional Information
Year Founded—1982
Capital Under Management—$1.3 million
Investments(1985-1st 6 months)—1
Invested(1985-1st 6 months)—$50,000
Method of Compensation—Return on
investment is of primary concern; do not
charge fees

MIDDLEFIELD VENTURES LIMITED

First Canadian Place #5850
Post Office Box 192
Toronto, Ontario M5X 1A6
416-362-8602

Officers
D.L. (Sandy) Sinclair, Chm.
G.L. (Gordon) Leonard, Pres.
W.G. (Garth) Jestley, Exec. V.P.
R.M. (Richard) Harland, Inv. Officer
P.A. (Peter) Harbic, Inv. Officer

Whom to Contact
Any of the above

Type of Firm
Private venture capital firm investing
own capital

Industry Association Membership
ACVCC

Project Preferences
Will function either as deal originator or
investor in deals created by others
Type of Financing:
Second-stage
Later-stage expansion
Leveraged buyout
Minimum Investment: $250,000
Preferred Investment: $500,000-$1 million
Preferred Investment (LBO):
$1 million or less
Minimum Operating Data:
Annual Sales—$500,000
P&L—Break even

Geographical Preferences
National

Industry Preferences
Communications
Cable television
Commercial communications
Data communications
Satellite and microwave communications
Telephone related

Computer Related
Computer graphics, CAD/CAM and CAE
Computer mainframes
Computer services
Memory devices
Micro and mini computers
Office automation
Scanning related
Software-applications
Software-artificial intelligence
Software-systems
Specialized turnkey systems
Terminals
Consumer
Computer stores/related services
Consumer products
Consumer services
Food and beverage products
Franchise businesses
Hotels and resort areas
Leisure and recreational products
Restaurants
Retailing
Distribution
Communications equipment
Computer equipment
Consumer products
Electronics equipment
Food products
Industrial products
Medical products
**Electronic Components and
Instrumentation**
Analytical and scientific instrumentation
Component fabrication and testing
equipment
Electronic components
Fiber optics
Laser related
Semiconductors
Energy/Natural Resources
Alternative energy
Technology related products/equipment
Genetic Engineering
Gene splicing and manufacturing equipment
Monoclonal antibodies and hybridomas
Recombinant DNA (agricultural and
industrial)
Recombinant DNA (medical)
Industrial Products and Equipment
Chemicals
Controls and sensors
Energy management
Equipment and machinery
Other industrial automation
Plastics
Robotics/vision systems
Specialty materials

Medical/Health Related
Diagnostic equipment
Diagnostic test products
Disposable products
Drugs and medicines
Hospital and clinical labs
Medical services
Therapeutic equipment
Other
Agriculture, forestry, fishing
Education related
Publishing
Transportation
Will Not Consider
Capital intensive finance
Natural resource extraction
Real Estate

Additional Information
Year Founded—1985
Capital Under Management—$32 million
Investments(1985-1st 6 months)—3
Invested(1985-1st 6 months)—$2.4 million
Method of Compensation—Return on
   investment is of primary concern; do not
   charge fees

NORANDA ENTERPRISE LIMITED

90 Sparks Street #1128
Ottawa, Ontario K1P 5T8, ON
613-230-6205

Officers
D.C. Cameron, Pres.
L.R. Charlebois, V.P.
L.M. Copeland, Dir. Special Projects

Whom to Contact
Any of the above

Type of Firm
Venture capital subsidiary or affiliate of
   non-financial corporation

Affiliations
Noranda Inc. (parent)

Industry Association Membership
ACVCC

Project Preferences
Prefer role as deal originator but will also
   invest in deals created by others
Type of Financing:
First-stage
Second-stage
Later-stage expansion
Leveraged buyout

Minimum Investment: $500,000
Preferred Investment: Over $1 million
Minimum Operating Data:
Annual Sales—$500,000
P&L—Losses (profits projected after 2 years)

Geographical Preferences

Canada:
National
United States:
National

Industry Preferences

Communications
Cable television
Commercial communications
Data communications
Satellite and microwave communications
Telephone related
Computer Related
Computer graphics, CAD/CAM and CAE
Computer mainframes
Computer services
Memory devices
Micro and mini computers
Office automation
Scanning related
Software-applications
Software-artificial intelligence
Software-systems
Specialized turnkey systems
Terminals
**Electronic Components and
   Instrumentation**
Analytical and scientific instrumentation
Component fabrication and testing
   equipment
Electronic components
Fiber optics
Laser related
Semiconductors
Energy/Natural Resources
Alternative energy
Energy conservation
Technology related products/equipment
Genetic Engineering
Gene splicing and manufacturing equipment
Monoclonal antibodies and hybridomas
Recombinant DNA (agricultural and
   industrial)
Recombinant DNA (medical)
Industrial Products and Equipment
Chemicals
Controls and sensors
Energy management
Equipment and machinery
Other industrial automation
Plastics
Robotics/vision systems
Specialty materials

Medical/Health Related
Diagnostic equipment
Diagnostic test products
Disposable products
Drugs and medicines
Hospital and clinical labs
Medical services
Therapeutic equipment

Additional Information
Year Founded—1973
Method of Compensation—Return on
   investment is of primary concern; do not
   charge fees

NORTH AMERICAN VENTURES FUNDS

85 Bloor Street East #506
Toronto, Ontario M4W 1A9
416-967-5774

Other Offices
c/o Inco Venture Capital Management
One New York Plaza
New York, NY 10004
212-612-5620

c/o International Nickel, Inc.
2099 Gateway Plaza
San Jose, CA 95110
408-993-9594

Officers
S. Feiner, Chm. (New York)
G. Fells, Pres. (Ontario)
M. Kostuch, V.P. (Ontario)
A.D. Peabody, V.P. (New York)
G. Middlemas, V.P. (New York)
D. McCart, Inv. Officer (Ontario)
P. Standeven, V.P. (Ontario)
R. Couch, Sr. V.P. (California)

Whom to Contact
Any of the above

Type of Firm
Private venture capital firm investing
   own capital

Affiliations
Inco Limited, New York (shareholder in
   general partner)
SB Capital Corporation Ltd., Toronto
   (shareholder in general partner)

Industry Association Membership
ACVCC

Project Preferences

Will function either as deal originator or investor in deals created by others

Type of Financing:
Seed
Startup
First-stage
Second-stage
Leveraged buyout
Minimum Investment: Less than $100,000
Preferred Investment: $400,000-$1 million
Preferred Investment (LBO):
 $1 million-$2 million
Minimum Operating Data:
P&L—Losses (profits projected after 2 years)

Geographical Preferences

None

Industry Preferences

Communications
Cable television
Commercial communications
Data communications
Satellite and microwave communications
Telephone related
Computer Related
Computer graphics, CAD/CAM and CAE
Computer mainframes
Computer services
Memory devices
Micro and mini computers
Office automation
Scanning related
Software-applications
Software-artificial intelligence
Software-systems
Specialized turnkey systems
Terminals
Consumer
Computer stores/related services
Consumer services
Franchise businesses
Distribution
Communications equipment
Computer equipment
Consumer products
Electronics equipment
Industrial products
Medical products
Electronic Components and
 Instrumentation
Analytical and scientific instrumentation
Component fabrication and testing
 equipment
Electronic components
Fiber optics
Laser related
Semiconductors

Energy/Natural Resources
Alternative energy
Technology related products/equipment
Genetic Engineering
Gene splicing and manufacturing equipment
Monoclonal antibodies and hybridomas
Recombinant DNA (agricultural and
 industrial)
Recombinant DNA (medical)
Industrial Products and Equipment
Chemicals
Controls and sensors
Energy management
Equipment and machinery
Other industrial automation
Plastics
Robotics/vision systems
Specialty materials
Medical/Health Related
Diagnostic equipment
Diagnostic test products
Disposable products
Drugs and medicines
Hospital and clinical labs
Medical services
Therapeutic equipment
Other
Publishing
Transportation
Will Not Consider
Real estate

Additional Information

Year Founded—1981
Capital Under Management—$60 million
Method of Compensation—Return on
 investment is of primary concern; do not
 charge fees

NORTHERN TELECOM LIMITED

33 City Centre Drive
Mississauga
Ontario L5B 3A2
416-275-0960

Officers

Raymond J. Herpers, Gen. Mgr.
Esmond T. Goei, Dir.
James H. Boyle, Inv. Analyst

Whom to Contact

Any of the above

Type of Firm

Division of non-financial corporation

Industry Association Membership

ACVCC

Project Preferences

Will function either as deal originator or investor in deals created by others

Type of Financing:
Startup
First-stage
Second-stage
Later-stage expansion
Minimum Investment: $250,000
Preferred Investment: $500,000-$1 million
Minimum Operating Data:
Annual Sales—Nominal
P&L—Losses (profits projected after 2 years)

Geographical Preference

None

Industry Preferences

Communications
Cable television
Commercial communications
Data communications
Satellite and microwave communications
Telephone related
Computer Related
Computer graphics, CAD/CAM and CAE
Computer mainframes
Computer services
Memory devices
Micro and mini computers
Office automation
Scanning related
Distribution
Communications equipment
Computer equipment
Consumer products
Electronics equipment
Electronic Components and
 Instrumentation
Component fabrication and testing
 equipment
Electronic components
Fiber optics
Laser related
Semiconductors
Industrial Products and Equipment
Controls and sensors
Other industrial automation
Robotics/vision systems

Additional Information

Year Founded—1981
Investments(1985-1st 6 months)—6
Invested(1985-1st 6 months)—$6.8 million
Method of Compensation—Return on
 investment is of primary concern; do not
 charge fees

NOVACAP INVESTMENTS INC.

199 Bay Street #1100
Toronto, Ontario M5J 1L4

Abraham Rolnick, V.P.

See QUEBEC for full listing

ONTARIO CENTRE FOR RESOURCE MACHINERY TECHNOLOGY

127 Cedar Street, Fourth Floor
Sudbury, Ontario P3E 1B1
705-673-6606

Officers
John Dodge, Pres.
Patricia Taylor, Dir.-Finance & Admin.
John Wilson, Dir.-Technology Devel.
Wayne Rideout, Dir.-Business Devel.
Bob MacBean, Dir.- Venture Inv.

Whom to Contact
Any of the above

Type of Firm
Crown corporation funded under provincial
government
Ministry of Industry, Trade and Technology

Industry Association Membership
ACVCC

Project Preferences
Will function either as deal originator or
investor in deals created by others
Type of Financing:
Research and development partnerships
First-stage
Second-stage
Later-stage expansion
Minimum Investment: Less than $100,000
Preferred Investment: $250,000-$500,000
Minimum Operating Data:
Annual Sales—Nominal
P&L—Losses (profits projected after 2 years)

Geographical Preferences

Central Canada
Ontario

Industry Preferences

Energy/Natural Resources
Minerals
Oil and gas exploration and production
Technology related products/equipment

Other
Ontario based businesses providing at least
a portion of their products or services to
the resource sector

Additional Information
Year Founded—1982
Capital Under Management—$16.4 million
Investments(1985-1st 6 months)—6
Invested(1985-1st 6 months)—$1.3 million

ROYAL BANK VENTURE CAPITAL LIMITED

13th Floor, South Tower
Royal Bank Plaza
Toronto, Ontario M5J 2J5
416-974-6230

Officers
B.D. Marshall, Pres.
R.D.D. Forbes, Exec. V.P.
C.J. Cazabon, Mgr.-Investments
J. Sayegh, Mgr.-Investments

Whom to Contact
Any of the above

Type of Firm
Venture capital subsidiary of
commercial bank

Affiliation
James D. Wolfensohn & Co., New York
(partially funded by a Royal Bank
subsidiary)

Industry Association Membership
ACVCC

Project Preferences
Prefer role as deal originator but will also
invest in deals created by others
Type of Financing:
Second-stage
Later-stage expansion
Leveraged buyout
Minimum Investment: $250,000
Preferred Investment: $500,000-$1 million
Preferred Investment (LBO):
$1 million-$5 million
Minimum Operating Data:
Annual Sales—$500,000
Annual Sales (LBO)—$2 million and over

Geographical Preferences

National

Industry Preferences

Communications
Commercial communications
Data communications
Satellite and microwave communications
Telephone related
Computer Related
Computer graphics, CAD/CAM and CAE
Office automation
Scanning related
Software-applications
Software-artificial intelligence
Software-systems
Specialized turnkey systems
Terminals
Electronic Components and Instrumentation
Analytical and scientific instrumentation
Component fabrication and testing
equipment
Electronic components
Fiber optics
Laser related
Semiconductors
Energy/Natural Resources
Coal related
Drilling and exploration services
Energy conservation
Minerals
Oil and gas exploration and production
Technology related products/equipment
Industrial Products and Equipment
Chemicals
Controls and sensors
Energy management
Equipment and machinery
Other industrial automation
Plastics
Robotics/vision systems
Specialty materials
Medical/Health Related
Diagnostic equipment
Diagnostic test products
Disposable products
Drugs and medicines
Hospital and clinical labs
Medical services
Therapeutic equipment
Will Not Consider
Computer services
Financial services
Real estate

Additional Information
Year Founded—1969
Capital Under Management—$25 million
Investments(1985-1st 6 months)—10
Invested(1985-1st 6 months)—$3.5 million
Method of Compensation—Return on
investment is most important, but also
charge for closing fees, service fees, etc.

SB CAPITAL CORPORATION LTD.

85 Bloor Street East #506
Toronto, Ontario M4W 1A9
416-967-5439

Officers

G. Fells, Pres.
M. Kostuch, V.P.
P. Standeven, V.P.
D. McCart, Inv. Officer

Whom to Contact

Any of the above

Type of Firm

Private venture capital firm investing
own capital

Affiliations

North American Ventures Management
(affiliate)
North American Ventures Fund (fund
managed by affiliate)
North American Ventures Fund II (fund
managed by affiliate)

Industry Association Memberships

NASBIC
ACVCC

Project Preferences

Prefer role as deal originator but will also
invest in deals created by others
Type of Financing:
Seed
Startup
First-stage
Second-stage
Leveraged buyout
Minimum Investment: Less than $100,000
Preferred Investment: $100,000-$250,000
Minimum Operating Data:
Annual Sales—Nominal
P&L—Losses (profits projected after 1 year)

Geographical Preferences

Eastern Canada

Industry Preferences

Consumer
Computer stores/related services
Consumer services
Franchise businesses
Retailing

Distribution
Communications equipment
Computer equipment
Consumer products
Electronics equipment
Food products
Industrial products
Medical products
Other
Education related
Publishing
Will Not Consider
Real estate

Additional Information

Year Founded—1973
Method of Compensation—Return on
investment is of primary concern; do not
charge fees

SHARWOOD AND COMPANY

20 Victoria Street #900
Toronto, Ontario M5C 2N8
416-869-1598

Officers

Gordon R. Sharwood, Pres.
Kenneth L. Cutts, Exec. V.P.
Earl Duffy, Sr. V.P.
William H. Simmons, Sr. V.P.

Type of Firm

Investment banking or merchant banking
firm investing own capital or funds of
partners or clients
Consulting firm evaluating and analyzing
venture projects and arranging private
placements

Project Preferences

Will function either as deal originator or
investor in deals created by others
Type of Financing:
Second-stage
Later-stage expansion
Leveraged buyout
Minimum Investment: $500,000
Preferred Investment: Over $1 million
Preferred Investment (LBO):
$1 million and over
Minimum Operating Data:
Annual Sales—Over $3 million
Annual Sales (LBO)—$20 million-$30 million

Geographical Preferences

National

Industry Preferences

Communications
Cable television
Commercial communications
Data communications
Satellite and microwave communications
Telephone related
Computer Related
Computer graphics, CAD/CAM and CAE
Computer mainframes
Computer services
Memory devices
Micro and mini computers
Office automation
Scanning related
Software-applications
Software-artificial intelligence
Software-systems
Specialized turnkey systems
Terminals
Consumer
Computer stores/related services
Consumer products
Consumer services
Food and beverage products
Franchise businesses
Hotels and resort areas
Leisure and recreational products
Restaurants
Retailing
Distribution
Communications equipment
Computer equipment
Consumer products
Electronics equipment
Food products
Industrial products
Medical products
**Electronic Components and
Instrumentation**
Analytical and scientific instrumentation
Component fabrication and testing
equipment
Electronic components
Fiber optics
Laser related
Semiconductors
Energy/Natural Resources
Alternative energy
Coal related
Drilling and exploration services
Energy conservation
Minerals
Oil and gas exploration and production
Technology related products/equipment
Genetic Engineering
Gene splicing and manufacturing equipment
Monoclonal antibodies and hybridomas
Recombinant DNA (agricultural and
industrial)
Recombinant DNA (medical)

Industrial Products and Equipment
Chemicals
Controls and sensors
Energy management
Equipment and machinery
Other industrial automation
Plastics
Robotics/vision systems
Specialty materials
Medical/Health Related
Diagnostic equipment
Diagnostic test products
Disposable products
Drugs and medicines
Hospital and clinical labs
Medical services
Therapeutic equipment
Other
Agriculture, forestry, fishing
Education related
Finance and insurance
Publishing
Real estate
Specialty consulting
Transportation

Additional Information
Year Founded—1976
Method of Compensation—Function primarily
in service area; receive contingent fee in
cash or equity
Professional fee required whether or
not deal closes

T.D. CAPITAL GROUP LTD.

Toronto-Dominion Centre
Post Office Box 1
Toronto, Ontario M5K 1A2
416-982-5542

Officers
E.J. Collins, Pres.
I.D. Collier, V.P.
M.J. Hanley, Mgr.-Mergers/Acquisitions
L.E.R. Davis, Mgr.-Mergers/Acquisitions
J.C. Dryden, Mgr.-Inv.
D.M. Rolfe, Mgr.-Inv.
W.J. Patrick, Treas.

Whom to Contact
I.D. Collier

Type of Firm
Venture capital subsidiary of
commercial bank

Affiliation
The Toronto-Dominion Bank (parent)

Industry Association Membership
ACVCC

Project Preferences
Will function either as deal originator or
investor in deals created by others
Type of Financing:
Second-stage
Later-stage expansion
Leveraged buyout
Minimum Investment: $500,000
Preferred Investment: Over $1 million
Preferred Investment (LBO):
Over $2 million
Minimum Operating Data:
Annual Sales—$1.5 million

Geographical Preferences

None

Industry Preferences

Communications
Cable television
Commercial communications
Data communications
Satellite and microwave communications
Telephone related
Computer Related
Office automation
Consumer
Consumer products
Consumer services
Food and beverage products
Franchise businesses
Leisure and recreational products
Restaurants
Retailing
Distribution
Communications equipment
Computer equipment
Consumer products
Electronics equipment
Food products
Industrial products
Medical products
**Electronic Components and
Instrumentation**
Analytical and scientific instrumentation
Component fabrication and testing
equipment
Electronic components
Fiber optics
Laser related
Semiconductors
Energy/Natural Resources
Energy conservation
Technology related products/equipment

Industrial Products and Equipment
Chemicals
Controls and sensors
Energy management
Equipment and machinery
Other industrial automation
Plastics
Robotics/vision systems
Specialty materials
Medical/Health Related
Diagnostic equipment
Diagnostic test products
Disposable products
Drugs and medicines
Hospital and clinical labs
Medical services
Therapeutic equipment
Other
Education related
Finance and insurance
Publishing
Transportation

Additional Information
Year Founded—1968
Investments(1985-1st 6 months)—10
Invested(1985-1st 6 months)—$7.2 million
Method of Compensation—Return on
investment is most important, but also
charge for closing fees, service fees, etc.

TRIARCH CORPORATION LIMITED

120 Adelaide Street West #1120
Toronto, Ontario M5H 1V1
416-364-2271

Officer
J.F.C. Stewart

Type of Firm
Investment banking or merchant banking
firm investing own capital or funds of
partners or clients

Industry Association Membership
ACVCC

Project Preferences
Prefer role as deal originator but will also
invest in deals created by others
Type of Financing:
Later-stage expansion
Leveraged buyout
Minimum Operating Data:
Annual Sales—Over $10 million
P&L—Losses (profits projected after 1 year)
Annual Sales (LBO)—$10 million-$100 million

Geographical Preferences

None

Industry Preferences

Distribution
Communications equipment
Computer equipment
Consumer products
Electronics equipment
Industrial products
Medical products
**Electronic Components and
    Instrumentation**
Component fabrication and testing
    equipment
Energy/Natural Resources
Minerals
Oil and gas exploration and production
Industrial Products and Equipment
Chemicals
Controls and sensors
Specialty materials
Will Not Consider
Real estate

Additional Information

Year Founded—1953
Capital Under Management—$10 million
Method of Compensation—Return on
    investment is most important, but also
    charge for closing fees, service fees, etc.

VENGROWTH CAPITAL FUNDS

111 Richmond Street West #805
Toronto, Ontario M5H 2G4
416-947-9123

Partners

R. Earl Storie, Mgn. Ptnr.
Harry G. Mortimore, Mgn. Ptnr.
Andrew L. Gutman, Ptnr.
Mark H. Leonard, Inv. Mgr.

Whom to Contact

Any of the above

Type of Firm

Private venture capital firm investing
    own capital

Industry Association Membership

ACVCC

Project Preferences

Will function either as deal originator or
    investor in deals created by others

Type of Financing:

First-stage
Second-stage
Later-stage expansion
Leveraged buyout
Minimum Investment: $500,000
Preferred Investment: $500,000-$1 million
Preferred Investment (LBO):
    $1 million-$1.5 million
Minimum Operating Data:
Annual Sales—Nominal
P&L—Losses (profits projected after 2 years)
Annual Sales (LBO)—$10 million-$50 million

Geographical Preferences

None

Industry Preferences

Communications
Cable television
Commercial communications
Data communications
Satellite and microwave communications
Telephone related
Computer Related
Computer graphics, CAD/CAM and CAE
Computer services
Memory devices
Office automation
Scanning related
Software-applications
Specialized turnkey systems
Consumer
Consumer services
Food and beverage products
Retailing
Distribution
Communications equipment
Computer equipment
Consumer products
Electronics equipment
Food products
Industrial products
Medical products
**Electronic Components and
    Instrumentation**
Analytical and scientific instrumentation
Component fabrication and testing
    equipment
Electronic components
Fiber optics
Laser related
Energy/Natural Resources
Drilling and exploration services
Energy conservation
Oil and gas exploration and production
Technology related products/equipment

Genetic Engineering
Gene splicing and manufacturing equipment
Monoclonal antibodies and hybridomas
Recombinant DNA (agricultural and
    industrial)
Recombinant DNA (medical)
Industrial Products and Equipment
Chemicals
Controls and sensors
Energy management
Equipment and machinery
Other industrial automation
Plastics
Robotics/vision systems
Specialty materials
Medical/Health Related
Diagnostic equipment
Diagnostic test products
Disposable products
Drugs and medicines
Hospital and clinical labs
Medical services
Therapeutic equipment
Other
Agriculture, forestry, fishing
Education related
Finance and insurance
Publishing
Transportation
Will Not Consider
Real estate

Additional Information

Year Founded—1982
Capital Under Management—$34 million
Investments(1985-1st 6 months)—10
Invested(1985-1st 6 months)—$4.2 million
Method of Compensation—Return on
    investment is of primary concern; do not
    charge fees

ATLANTIC VENTURES TRUST

27½ Water Street
Charlottetown
Prince Edward Island C1A 1A2
902-892-8666

Donald M. Deacon

See NOVA SCOTIA for full listing

ALTAMIRA CAPITAL CORP.

475 Michel Jasmin
Dorval, Quebec H9P 1C2
514-631-2682

Officers
Eric E. Baker, Pres.
Robert Mee, V.P.
Christopher J. Winn, V.P. Finance

Whom to Contact
Any of the above

Type of Firm
Private venture capital firm investing
own capital

Industry Association Membership
ACVCC

Project Preferences
Prefer role as deal originator but will also
invest in deals created by others
Type of Financing:
First-stage
Leveraged buyout
Minimum Investment: $500,000
Preferred Investment: Over $1 million
Minimum Operating Data:
Annual Sales—$500,000
P&L—Losses (profits projected after 2 years)

Geographical Preferences

Canada:
National
United States:
Northeast

Industry Preferences

Communications
Commercial communications
Data communications
Satellite and microwave communications

Computer Related
Computer graphics, CAD/CAM and CAE
Memory devices
Micro and mini computers
Office automation
Scanning related
Software-artificial intelligence
Terminals
**Electronic Components and
Instrumentation**
Analytical and scientific instrumentation
Component fabrication and testing
equipment
Electronic components
Fiber optics
Laser related
Semiconductors
Genetic Engineering
Gene splicing and manufacturing equipment
Monoclonal antibodies and hybridomas
Recombinant DNA (agricultural and
industrial)
Recombinant DNA (medical)
Industrial Products and Equipment
Chemicals
Controls and sensors
Energy management
Equipment and machinery
Other industrial automation
Plastics
Robotics/vision systems
Specialty materials
Medical/Health Related
Diagnostic equipment
Diagnostic test products
Disposable products
Drugs and medicines
Hospital and clinical labs
Medical services
Therapeutic equipment
Will Not Consider
Natural resources
Real estate

Additional Information
Year Founded—1984
Capital Under Management—$25 million
Investments(1985-1st 6 months)—4
Method of Compensation—Return on
investment is of primary concern; do not
charge fees

CONSORTIUM INVESTMENT CORPORATION

One Westmount Square
Tenth Floor
Montreal, Quebec H3Z 2P9
514-931-5821

Officer
M.L. Lippman, Pres.

Type of Firm
Private venture capital firm investing
own capital

Project Preferences
Prefer role as deal originator but will also
invest in deals created by others
Type of Financing:
First-stage
Second-stage
Later-stage expansion
Leveraged buyout
Minimum Investment: Less than $100,000
Preferred Investment: No preference
Minimum Operating Data:
Annual Sales—$500,000

Geographical Preferences

Central Canada
No geographic preference for co-investments

Industry Preferences

Consumer
Consumer products
Consumer services
Food and beverage products
Franchise businesses
Leisure and recreational products
Distribution
Consumer products
Food products
Industrial products
Medical products
**Industrial Products and
Equipment**
Chemicals
Controls and sensors
Energy management
Equipment and machinery
Plastics
Robotics/vision systems
Specialty materials
Medical/Health Related
Diagnostic equipment
Disposable products
Drugs and medicines
Hospital and clinical labs
Therapeutic equipment

Other
Education related
Finance and insurance
Publishing
Real estate
Specialty consulting

Additional Information
Year Founded—1966
Capital Under Management—$20 million
Investments(1985-1st 6 months)—2
Invested(1985-1st 6 months)—$275,000
Method of Compensation—Return on investment is of primary concern; do not charge fees

FEDERAL BUSINESS DEVELOPMENT BANK

800 Place Victoria #4600
Post Office Box 335
Montreal, Quebec H4Z 1L4
514-283-2252

Other Offices
250 University Avenue
Toronto, Ontario M5H 3E5
416-593-1144

900 West Hastings Street
Vancouver
British Columbia V6C 1E7
604-687-1300

Officers
R.J.E. Lafond, Asst. V.P. (Quebec)
T.R. Bradbury, Sr. Mgr. (Quebec)
R.M. Jack, Sr. Mgr. (Quebec)
P.W. Giddings, Sr. Mgr. (Quebec)
D. Laporte, Sr. Mgr. (Quebec)
G.R. Cornwall, Portfolio Mgr. (Ontario)
G.D. Fife, Portfolio Mgr. (Ontario)
W.J. Lichti, Portfolio Mgr. (British Columbia)
J.D. Douglas, Portfolio Mgr. (British Columbia)
A. Charnish, Portfolio Mgr. (British Columbia)

Whom to Contact
Any of the above

Type of Firm
Investment banking division of federal government owned business development bank

Industry Association Membership
ACVCC

Project Preferences
Will function either as deal originator or investor in deals created by others
Type of Financing:
Startup
First-stage
Second-stage
Later-stage expansion
Leveraged buyout
Minimum Investment: Less than $100,000
Preferred Investment: $250,000-$15 million
Preferred Investment (LBO):
$200,000-$1 million
Minimum Operating Data:
Annual Sales—Nominal
P&L—Losses (profits projected after 2 years)

Geographical Preferences
National

Industry Preferences
None
Will Not Consider
Electronic and print mass media
Natural resource exploration and extraction
Real estate

Additional Information
Year Founded—1983
Capital Under Management—$47 million
Investments(1985-1st 6 months)—11
Invested(1985-1st 6 months)—$6.5 million
Method of Compensation—Return on investment is most important, but also charge for closing fees, service fees, etc.

ALEXIS NIHON CORPORATION

6380 Cote De Liesse
Montreal, Quebec H4T 1E3
514-731-3344

Officers
Paul Massicotte, Pres.
Donald R. Mitchicine, Secy.

Type of Firm
Private venture capital firm investing own capital

Project Preferences
Will function either as deal originator or investor in deals created by others
Type of Financing:
Second-stage
Later-stage expansion
Leveraged buyout
Minimum Investment: $100,000
Preferred Investment: $500,000 and over
Minimum Operating Data:
Annual Sales—$1.5 million

Geographical Preferences
Canada:
National
United States:
National

Industry Preferences
Communications
Commercial communications
Data communications
Computer Related
Computer graphics, CAD/CAM and CAE
Computer services
Micro and mini computers
Office automation
Software-applications
Software-artificial intelligence
Software-systems
Specialized turnkey systems
Terminals
Distribution
Communications equipment
Electronics equipment
Electronic Components and Instrumentation
Electronic components
Fiber optics
Laser related
Semiconductors
Energy/Natural Resources
Drilling and exploration services
Energy conservation
Oil and gas exploration and production
Technology related products/equipment
Industrial Products and Equipment
Controls and sensors
Energy management
Equipment and machinery
Other industrial automation
Robotics/vision systems
Specialty materials
Other
Finance and insurance
Publishing
Real estate
Specialty consulting
Transportation

Additional Information

Method of Compensation—Return on investment is most important, but also charge for closing fees, service fees, etc.

NOVACAP INVESTMENTS INC.

1981 McGill College #380
Montreal, Quebec H3A 3A9
514-282-1383

Other Office

199 Bay Street #1100
Toronto, Ontario M5J 1L4

Officers

Roger Décary, Chairman (Quebec)
Jean Béique, Vice Chm. (Quebec)
Marc Beauchamp, Pres. (Quebec)
Jacques Tousignant, V.P. (Quebec)
Abraham Rolnick, V.P. (Ontario)
Jean-Pierre Chartrand, V.P. (Quebec)
Richard Roy, Secy. (Quebec)

Whom to Contact

Marc Beauchamp
Jacques Tousignant
Jean-Pierre Chartrand
Abraham Rolnick

Type of Firm

Private venture capital firm investing own capital

Industry Association Membership

ACVCC

Project Preferences

Will function either as deal originator or investor in deals created by others
Type of Financing:
First-stage
Preferred Investment: $500,000-$1 million
Minimum Operating Data:
Annual Sales—$1.5 million
P&L—Break even

Geographical Preferences

Canada:
East
United States:
East Coast

Industry Preferences

Communications

Data communications
Satellite and microwave communications
Computer Related
Computer graphics, CAD/CAM and CAE
Computer mainframes
Computer services
Memory devices
Micro and mini computers
Office automation
Scanning related
Software-applications
Software-artificial intelligence
Software-systems
Specialized turnkey systems
Terminals
Consumer
Consumer products
Electronic Components and Instrumentation
Analytical and scientific instrumentation
Component fabrication and testing equipment
Electronic components
Fiber optics
Laser related
Semiconductors
Genetic Engineering
Gene splicing and manufacturing equipment
Monoclonal antibodies and hybridomas
Recombinant DNA (agricultural and industrial)
Recombinant DNA (medical)
Industrial Products and Equipment
Chemicals
Controls and sensors
Energy management
Equipment and machinery
Other industrial automation
Plastics
Robotics/vision systems
Specialty materials
Medical/Health Related
Diagnostic equipment
Diagnostic test products
Disposable products
Drugs and medicines
Hospital and clinical labs
Medical services
Therapeutic equipment
Other
Low technology industries
Will Not Consider
Natural resources extraction
Real estate
Service industries

Additional Information

Year Founded—1981
Capital Under Management—$20 million
Investments(1985-1st 6 months)—9
Method of Compensation—Return on investment is of primary concern; do not charge fees

---

PARCAP MANAGEMENT INC.

1000 Sherbrooke Street West
Suite 2310
Montreal, Quebec H3A 3G4
514-281-0073

Officers

Jean F. Morrissette, Pres.
Mario de Felice, V.P. Finance

Whom to Contact

Jean F. Morrissette

Type of Firm

Private venture capital firm investing own capital

Industry Association Membership

ACVCC

Project Preferences

Prefer role as deal originator but will also invest in deals created by others
Type of Financing:
Second-stage
Later-stage expansion
Leveraged buyout
Minimum Investment: $1 million
Preferred Investment: Over $1 million
Preferred Investment (LBO):
$5 million and over
Minimum Operating Data:
Annual Sales—Over $3 million
P&L—Profits NBT over $1 million

Geographical Preferences

Canada:
East
Central
United States:
Northeast

Industry Preferences

Communications
Cable television
Commercial communications
Data communications
Satellite and microwave communications
Telephone related

Consumer
Food and beverage products
Electronic Components and Instrumentation
Analytical and scientific instrumentation
Component fabrication and testing equipment
Electronic components
Fiber optics
Laser related
Semiconductors
Industrial Products and Equipment
Chemicals
Controls and sensors
Energy management
Equipment and machinery
Other industrial automation
Plastics
Robotics/vision systems
Specialty materials
Other
Finance and insurance

Additional Information
Year Founded—1983
Method of Compensation—Return on investment is most important, but also charge for closing fees, service fees, etc.

SOCIÉTÉ D'INVESTISSEMENT DESJARDINS

1, Complexe Desjardins
Post Office Box 760
Montreal, Quebec H5B 1B8
514-281-7676

Officers
Paul Gauthier, Pres. & Dir. General
Raymond Gagné, Sr. V.P., Corp. Services
Pierre Brunet, V.P., Investments
Bernard Paradis, V.P. Finance & Treas.
Viviane Leblanc, Asst. Treas.
Francine Durocher Monin, Asst. Secy.
Jean Matteau, Proj. Mgr. Corp. Services
Serge Desjardins, Economist, Corp. Services
Jocelyn Devost, Computer Analyst
Daniel Laporte, Proj. Mgr. Investments
Germain Benôit, Sr. Analyst

Whom to Contact
Pierre Brunet

Type of Firm
Development capital subsidiary of a savings and credit cooperative group

Affiliation
Desjardins Group, Lévis, Quebec

Project Preferences
Prefer role as deal originator but will also invest in deals created by others
Type of Financing:
Later-stage expansion
Leveraged buyout
Minimum Investment: $500,000
Preferred Investment: $500,000-$10 million
Preferred Investment (LBO): $500,000-$5 million
Minimum Operating Data:
Annual Sales—Over $3 million
P&L—Profits NBT over $500,000
Annual Sales (LBO)—$5 million and over

Geographical Preferences
Eastern Canada

Industry Preferences
Communications
Cable television
Commercial communications
Data communications
Satellite and microwave communications
Telephone related
Consumer
Consumer products
Food and beverage products
Distribution
Consumer products
Food products
Industrial products
Electronic Components and Instrumentation
Analytical and scientific instrumentation
Component fabrication and testing equipment
Electronic components
Fiber optics
Laser related
Semiconductors
Energy/Natural Resources
Energy conservation
Technology related products/equipment
Industrial Products and Equipment
Chemicals
Controls and sensors
Energy management
Equipment and machinery
Other industrial automation
Plastics
Robotics/vision systems
Specialty materials

Medical/Health Related
Diagnostic equipment
Diagnostic test products
Disposable products
Drugs and medicines
Hospital and clinical labs
Medical services
Therapeutic equipment
Other
Agriculture, forestry, fishing
Education related
Finance and insurance
Publishing
Real estate
Specialty consulting
Transportation
Will Not Consider
Natural resources

Additional Information
Year Founded—1971
Capital Under Management—$100 million
Investments(1985-1st 6 months)—2
Invested(1985-1st 6 months)—$4.5 million
Method of Compensation—Return on investment is of primary concern; do not charge fees

Small Company Underwriters

In 1985, 264 small companies raised almost $2 billion of new equity capital in underwritten public offerings. This was an increase from 1984, when 266 small businesses (shareholder equity of $10 million or under) raised $1.7 billion.

The public marketplace for small company underwritings has improved dramatically since the recession-impacted years of 1974 and 1975. In 1975 only four companies with a net worth of $5 million or under had public offerings and raised a meager $16.2 million. But it was only in 1981 that these smaller companies were able to surpass the $1.4 billion of underwritings set in 1969 — the heyday of the new issue market — when a record 698 companies tapped the equity market. In 1981, 306 of these small capitalization companies were able to raise $1.8 billion and although this exceeds 1969's amount, it is still far behind 1969's activity when adjusted for a 50% inflation rate. In 1982's relatively sluggish new issue market, 113 of these smaller-sized companies raised $619 million. In 1983 the new issue market for small companies soared to unprecedented heights, with 477 issuers in the net worth under $5 million category raising a record $3.7 billion, more capital than was raised by theses companies in the prior six years combined. The total for this subset of small companies fell back in 1984, as 224 firms offered $1.2 billion of new equity to the public. In 1985, 209 companies with a net worth of $5 million or less raised $1.32 billion.

The receptivity of the public stock market to new issues in 1983 set loose a deluge of small company public offerings. The initial reaction to the success of these offerings was ebullient. The initial indications of paper profits available for entrepreneurs and venture capitalists were impressive. But paper profits are not realized profits.

The venture capital industry experienced the effects of a changing public marketplace in 1983 from frenzied and heated in the first half to a gradual cooling down by year-end. Unrealistic expectations held early in 1983 by entrepreneurs, venture capitalists and investors created inflated market valuations which quickly dropped in the last half of the year as the companies began to experience difficulties in meeting the short-term expectations of the public investors. Although the frenetic pace of public offerings continued throughout 1983, by mid-year, new issues were being buffeted by a declining stock market and investors became wary.

Investor caution aside, the amount of new equity capital raised by small companies in 1983 should remain on the books as a record for some time to come although the number of issues coming to market that year did not quite catch the record 698 small company offerings tallied in 1969. By 1984 the volume of small company new issues had dropped off substantially from the prior year's inflated levels as investors licked the wounds suffered during the market downturn that began in the second half of 1983. By the end of 1984, the market began to experience a recovery.

Several factors have contributed to the generally favorable market for small company equity offerings prevalent in recent years. Streamlined registration procedures, the 1978 capital gains tax cut, initially impressive aftermarket performances, an improved climate for entrepreneurs and public acceptance of new, untested companies must also be taken into account in assessing the increased new issue activity. The new issue market, long the province of the individual investors, has also captured the attention of the large financial institutions and portfolio managers as well.

To illustrate the growth in small issue underwritings, at the end of the directory section we have included "Index of Offerings" charts. These charts depict the underwritings of companies with both a net worth of $5 million or less and $10 million or less for 1982 through 1985.

The following directory lists key information about investment banking firms active in underwriting issues for small companies (all of these companies have a net worth of $10 million or less and those with a net worth of $5 million or less are indicated by an asterisk).

The listings include data such as the names of key corporate finance personnel or principal officers and partners of the firm and information about each issue for these investment bankers underwrote in 1984 through the first nine months of 1985. Only "firm commitment" underwritings with a minimum offering price of $1.00 per share have been included. The following underwriting illustrates the information presented:

Entry	Explanation
D'Lites of America, Inc.	Name of company
Fast-service restaurants	Description of business
September 1984	Date of underwriting
$14.25 million under-written	Amount of underwriting
$1.035 million fee	Amount of underwriter's fee
$9.50 per share*	Price of issue
$.15 earnings per share last year	Earnings per share in fiscal year prior to offering

*or unit—many equity issuers offer a combination of securities together in a unit, usually common stock and warrants, or debentures and common stock or warrants.

This information should be helpful to companies contemplating a possible public offering by identifying underwriters with experience in similar businesses and by showing the terms of the underwritings. Trends in new issue underwriting can be discerned by examining the entries of investment banking firms that have been particularly active in underwriting securities for smaller companies.

The data for this directory was compiled by the editors of VENTURE CAPITAL JOURNAL and is presented each month in the JOURNAL's "New Issue Barometer."

ADVEST, INC.
Six Central Row
Hartford, CT 06103
203-525-1421

John Everets, Jr., Mgn. Dir./Corp. Fin.

Collins Industries, Inc.*
Manufactures specialty vehicles —
  ambulances, limosines, hearses etc.
November 1984
$11.96 million underwritten
$801,000 fee
$997 per unit
$.31 earnings per share last year

Computer Synergy, Inc.*
Markets integrated computer systems for
  acute care hospitals
April 1984
$3.23 million underwritten
$296,700 fee
$5 per share
$.18 earnings per share last year

Decor Corp.*
Operates graphic art retail stores in
  shopping malls
August 1985
$3.50 million underwritten
$245,000 fee
$7 per share
$.25 earnings per share last year

Display Components, Inc.*
Magnetic electron optical devices
July 1984
$1.8 million underwritten
$180,000 fee
$4 per share
$.75 earnings per share last year

Mars Stores, Inc.
A New England retail discount store chain
April 1985
$7.64 million underwritten
$383,500 fee
$12 per share
$.81 earnings per share last year

MOSCOM Corporation*
Manufactures microprocessor-based
  telecommunications products
August 1985
$8.61 million underwritten
$609,500 fee
$6 per share
$(.40) loss per share last year

Video Display Corporation*
Manufactures rebuilt and new CRTs
January 1985
$2.38 million underwritten
$210,000 fee
$5 per share
$.20 earnings per share last year

Vortec Corporation*
Rents and sells home health care items and
  industrial products
June 1985
$4.95 million underwritten
$383,620 fee
$9 per share
$.66 earnings per share last year

ALLEN & COMPANY INCORPORATED
711 Fifth Avenue
New York, NY 10022
212-832-8000

Herbert A. Allen, Pres.

Britton Lee, Inc.
Manufactures a hardware-based relational
  database management system
January 1985
$16.20 million underwritten
$1.242 million fee
$9 per share
$(.19) loss per share last year

DNA Plant Technology Corp.
Commercial crops and industrial/consumer
  products
January 1984
$12.65 million underwritten
$968,000 fee
$5.75 per share
$(.40) loss per share last year

**Environmental Testing and Certification
  Corporation**
Provides toxic waste management services
  to industry
April 1985
$15.84 million underwritten
$971,750 fee
$19 per share
$.17 earnings per share last year

ANTHONY INVESTMENT CO.
4831 East Turquoise Avenue
Paradise Valley, AZ 85253
602-948-8208

Anthony Silverman, President

Computer Superstores, Inc.*
Retails computer systems in NM, TX and AZ
February 1985
$1.05 million underwritten
$105,000 fee
$1 per unit
$.01 earnings per share last year

APPLE FINANCIAL CORPORATION
120 Broadway
New York, NY 10271
212-437-2670

Andrew Renert, V.P.

**American Video Teleconferencing
  Corporation***
Manufactures proprietary hard and software
  for teleconferencing
June 1985
$1.00 million underwritten
$100,000 fee
$1 per unit
$(.01) loss per share last year

ROBERT W. BAIRD & CO.
  INCORPORATED
First Wisconsin Center
777 E. Wisconsin Avenue
Milwaukee, WI 53202
414-765-3500

Bernard E. Adee, Corp. Fin.
Robert Leonhardt, Corp. Fin.
Charles Leurs, Corp. Fin.

Automated Systems, Inc.*
Fabricates sophisticated printed
  circuit boards
November 1984
$12.30 million underwritten
$864,000 fee
$10.25 per share
$.48 earnings per share last year

Electronic Tele-Communications, Inc.*
Manufactures electronic telecommunications
  equipment
September 1985
$4.00 million underwritten
$350,000 fee
$8 per share
$.32 earnings per share last year

BAKER, WATTS & CO.
100 Light Street
Baltimore, MD 21203
301-685-2600

L. Victor Seested, Ptnr.
G. Thomas Yeager, III, Ptnr.
Sewell S. Watts, III, Ptnr.

Microsemi Corporation
Makes discrete diodes and assemblies
March 1984
$4.4 million underwritten
$352,000 fee
$5.50 per share
$.22 earnings per share last year

BATEMAN EICHLER, HILL RICHARDS INCORPORATED
700 South Flower Street
Los Angeles, CA 90017
213-625-3545

James W. Lewis, Mgr./Corp. Fin.

DH Technology, Inc.*
Manufactures dot matrix print heads
May 1984
$9.113 million underwritten
$675,000 fee
$6.75 per share
$.61 earnings per share last year

Flow Systems, Inc.
Manufactures waterjet and abrasivejet
  cutting systems for automated applications
October 1984
$13.20 million underwritten
$825,000 fee
$12 per share
$.39 earnings per share last year

GEORGE K. BAUM & COMPANY
1004 Baltimore Avenue
Kansas City, MO 64105
816-474-1100

William H. Coughlin, Pres.
Jack Henning, Exec. V.P.
Craig L. Beach, V.P. & Treas.

American City Business Journals, Inc.*
Publishes and manages metropolitan weekly
  business newspapers
July 1985
$9.24 million underwritten
$739,200 fee
$10.50 per share
$.14 earnings per share last year

BEAR, STEARNS & CO.
55 Water Street
New York, NY 10041
212-929-1024

John H. Slade, Ptnr.
Marius Decker, Ptnr.
Alan C. Greenberg, Ptnr.

Aequitron Medical Incorporated*
Manufactures apnea-related medical
  electronic equipment
March 1984
$3.30 million underwritten
$283,125 fee
$4 per share
$.05 earnings per share last year

Carriage Industries, Inc.
Supplies carpet to OEMs of manufactured
  housing and recreational vehicles
August 1984
$6.30 million underwritten
$504,000 fee
$7 per share
$.95 earnings per share last year

Direct Action Marketing, Inc.*
Markets consumer products thru mail order/
  promotion for oil companies and
  credit cards
September 1984
$12.75 million underwritten
$960,000 fee
$8 per share
$1.13 earnings per share last year

**Engineered Systems & Development
  Corporation***
Manufactures equipment to make floppy
  disks used in computer with word
  processing
May 1984
$6.34 million underwritten
$487,500 fee
$3 per share
$.00 earnings per share last year

Fuddruckers, Inc.
Operates restaurants specializing in fresh,
  quality hamburgers
June 1984
$7.64 million underwritten
$533,000 fee
$12 per share
$.06 earnings per share last year

Lieberman Enterprises Incorporated
Distributes pre-recorded music and provides
  merchandizing services
November 1984
$18.00 million underwritten
$1.248 million fee
$15 per share
$2.52 earnings per share last year

National FSI, Inc.*
Provides systems for administering employee
  benefit plans
August 1985
$12.25 million underwritten
$900,000 fee
$12 per share
$.84 earnings per share last year

Optrotech Ltd.—Israel*
Manufactures electro-optical system for
  automated inspection of PC boards
August 1984
$9.63 million underwritten
$700,000 fee
$11 per share
$(.06) loss per share last year

Trio-Tech International*
Markets environmental test equipment for
  ceramic pack of semiconductors
December 1984
$4.55 million underwritten
$364,000 fee
$6 per share
$1.10 earnings per share last year

SANFORD C. BERNSTEIN & CO., INC.
767 5th Avenue
New York, NY 10153
212-486-5800

Zalman C. Bernstein, Chm.
Lewis A. Sanders, Pres.
Roger Hertog, Exec. V.P.

Sierra Health Services, Inc.*
Owns a health maintenance organization in
    Nevada.
April 1985
$18.75 million underwritten
$1.395 million fee
$12 per share
$.20 earnings per share last year

BIRR, WILSON & CO., INC.
155 Sansome Street
San Francisco, CA 94104
415-983-7700

William D. McCarthy, Sr. V.P. & CFO

All Seasons Resorts, Incorporated*
Markets memberships in system of outdoor
    resort campgrounds
March 1984
$3.58 million underwritten
$302,100 fee
$7 per share
$.47 earnings per share 1/17/83 (inception)
    through 10/31/83

Transtector Systems, Inc.*
Transient overvoltage protectors
July 1984
$4.538 million underwritten
$371,250 fee
$5.50 per share
$.20 earnings per share last year

BLACKSTOCK & CO., INC.
10 West Adams Street
Jacksonville, FL 32202
904-632-8000

Henry T. Blackstock, Pres.

Action Packets, Inc.*
Markets gift shop items
December 1984
$0.83 million underwritten
$82,500 fee
$6 per share
$.16 earnings per share for the year
    ended 4/30/84

American Home Patient Centers, Inc.*
Operates home health care centers in the
    Southern U.S.
January 1985
$2.43 million underwritten
$242,812 fee
$4.62 per share
$(.02) loss per share last year

Bio-Analytic Laboratories, Inc.*
Manufactures chemical solutions for medical
    tests and instrumentation
February 1984
$2.00 million underwritten
$200,000 fee
$5 per share
$(.12) loss per share last year

D.H. BLAIR & CO., INC.
44 Wall Street
New York, NY 10005
212-968-2016

Richard A. Brenner, Corp. Fin.
Morton Davis, Corp. Fin.

Advanced Communications, Inc.*
Business communication equipment
January 1984
$3.025 million underwritten
$302,500 fee
$5.50 per unit
$(.70) loss per share last year

American Shared Hospital Services*
Provides medical care providers with
    diagnostic imaging equipment
July 1984
$4.25 million underwritten
$425,000 fee
$5 per share
$.09 earnings per share for the three months
    ended 3/31/84

American Technical Ceramics Corp.
Manufactures multilayer ceramic and
    porcelain capacitors
June 1985
$7.26 million underwritten
$725,620 fee
$7 per share
$.60 earnings per share last year

Cardoi-Pace Medical, Inc.*
Manufactures the Durapulse heart
    pacemaker and accessories
January 1985
$4.30 million underwritten
$430,000 fee
$2 per unit
$(.27) loss per share last year

CitiSource Inc.*
Markets hand-held field force computers
September 1984
$3.68 million underwritten
$368,000 fee
$5 per share
$(.19) loss per share for the nine months
    ended 5/31/84

Cogenic Energy Systems Inc.*
Manufactures electrical cogeneration
    systems
March 1985
$5.00 million underwritten
$500,000 fee
$1,000 per unit
$.16 earnings per share for the nine months
    ended 10/31/84

Comtrex Systems Corporation*
Markets microprocessor-based point-of-sale
    terminals
July 1985
$4.80 million underwritten
$480,000 fee
$6 per share
$.60 earnings per share last year

CVD Equipment Corporation*
Produces furnaces for the processing of
    semiconductor materials
September 1985
$3.33 million underwritten
$332,500 fee
$4.75 per unit
$.24 earnings per share last year

Daltex Medical Sciences, Inc.*
Markets medical devices and
    pharmaceuticals that reduce cost of
    diagnosis and tests
September 1984
$6.00 million underwritten
$600,000 fee
$2 per share
$.04 earnings per share 7/28/83 (inception)
    to 7/31/84

Daxor Corporation*
Researches techniques for preservation of
    human sperm and embryos
March 1985
$5.60 million underwritten
$560,000 fee
$7 per unit
$.22 earnings per share last year

Dental Management Services, Inc.*
Establishes and maintains dental centers
January 1984
$3.0 million underwritten
$300,000 fee
$6 per unit
$(.30) loss per share last year

Endo-LASE, Inc.*
Distributes medical laser products
January 1984
$4.8 million underwritten
$480,000 fee
$6 per unit
$(.08) loss per share for the nine months
  ended 9/30/83

Eye Care Centers of America, Inc.*
Operates "Eye Pro Express" optical
  department stores
May 1985
$7.20 million underwritten
$720,000 fee
$3 per unit
$.10 earnings per share 10/24/84 (inception)
  to 12/31/84

**International Remote Imaging
  Systems, Inc.***
Manufactures an automated urinalysis
  workstation
September 1985
$3.60 million underwritten
$300,000 fee
$1000.00 per unit
$(.24) loss per share last year

Intervoice, Inc.*
Sells touchtone telephone access voice
  response systems
May 1985
$3.60 million underwritten
$360,000 fee
$3 per unit
$.12 earnings per share last year

Investment Technologies, Inc.*
Acquires marketing rights for online
  securities evaluation system
January 1985
$4.00 million underwritten
$400,000 fee
$1 per share
$(.15) loss per share 7/8/83 (inception)
  to 10/31/84

Kappa Networks, Inc.*
Manufactures electronic components
  and systems
August 1985
$3.60 million underwritten
$360,000 fee
$1000 per unit
$.65 earnings per share last year

Laser Corporation*
Manufactures lasers and subassemblies
  for OEMs
August 1984
$2.25 million underwritten
$220,500 fee
$4 per share
$.45 earnings per share last year

Marketing Systems of America, Inc.*
Sells marketing programs to increase sales
  volume of retailers
November 1984
$4.00 million underwritten
$400,000 fee
$2 per unit
$(.08) loss per share 12/6/83 (inception)
  to 6/30/84

**Martinez & Murphey Vestment
  Makers, Inc.***
A custom manufacturer of liturgical vesture
  for clergy and churches
April 1984
$2.16 million underwritten
$210,600 fee
$2 per unit
$(.06) loss per share last year

Medco Research Inc.*
Manages drug clinical studies for
  pharmaceutical companies
November 1984
$2.50 million underwritten
$250,000 fee
$2 per unit
$(.18) loss per share last year

National Business Communications Corp.*
Designs and markets private telephone
  systems in FL, GA, TN and AZ
January 1984
$3.60 million underwritten
$360,000 fee
$3 per unit
$.17 pro forma earnings per share for the six
  months ended 8/31/83

Pasta & Cheese, Inc.*
Manufactures a variety of premium pasta
  products and gourmet foods
March 1985
$5.00 million underwritten
$490,980 fee
$6 per share
$.18 earnings per share last year

Profit Technology, Incorporated*
Develops high technology products for
  corporate, governmental and educational
  markets
September 1984
$3.15 million underwritten
$315,000 fee
$2 per unit
$(.06) loss per share for the eleven months
  ended 7/31/84

Reid-Ashman, Inc.*
Manufactures positioning systems for
  semiconductor makers
April 1985
$3.08 million underwritten
$308,430 fee
$6 per share
$.45 earnings per share last year

SunResorts Ltd. N.V.
Operates Mullet Bay Resort in St. Maarten,
  Netherlands Antilles
September 1985
$8.40 million underwritten
$756,000 fee
$7 per unit
$.18 earnings per share last year

Techdyne, Inc.*
Manufactures electro-mechanical injection
  molded components
April 1985
$4.00 million underwritten
$400,000 fee
$6 per share
$.49 earnings per share last year

Telecalc, Inc.*
Designs computer-based information
  systems for phone management
August 1985
$2.55 million underwritten
$255,000 fee
$6 per share
$(.32) loss per share last year

Uniforce Temporary Personnel, Inc.*
Provides temporary personnel to employees
  in business and government
March 1984
$3.99 million underwritten
$399,000 fee
$7 per share
$.03 earnings per share last year

WILLIAM BLAIR & COMPANY
135 South LaSalle Street
Chicago, IL 60603
312-236-1600

E. David Coolidge, III, Mgr./Corp. Fin.

Central Sprinkler Corporation*
Manufactures automatic fire sprinkler heads
  and valves
May 1985
$8.29 million underwritten
$650,000 fee
$12.75 per share
$.67 earnings per share last year

Concord Computing Corporation*
System for check and credit card
  transactions
June 1984
$3.2 million underwritten
$260,000 fee
$8 per share
$.57 earnings per share last year

D'Lites of America, Inc.*
Franchises fast service restaurants featuring
  "lite" foods
September 1984
$14.25 million underwritten
$1.035 million fee
$9.50 per share
$.15 earnings per share last year

BLINDER, ROBINSON & CO., INC.
The Blinder Bldg.
6455 S. Yosemite, 9th Floor
Englewood, CO 80111
303-733-8200

Regis Dahl, Corp. Fin.

Martin Lawrence Limited Editions, Inc.*
Sells limited edition lithographs, sculptures
  and other art.
January 1985
$1.50 million underwritten
$150,000 fee
$2 per unit
$.06 earnings per share last year

BLUNT ELLIS & LOEWI
INCORPORATED
225 East Mason Street
Milwaukee, WI 53202
414-347-3400

Richard C. Fischer, Corp. Fin.

American City Business Journals, Inc.*
Publishes and manages metropolitan weekly
  business newspapers
July 1985
$9.24 million underwritten
$739,200 fee
$10 per share
$.14 earnings per share last year

Certified Collateral Corporation*
Provides computerized auto claim service to
  insurance companies
July 1985
$9.63 million underwritten
$700,000 fee
$14 per share
$(.04) loss per share last year

London House, Inc.*
Develops psychological test system providing
  immediate computerized scoring
April 1984
$4.41 million underwritten
$374,850 fee
$7 per share
$.16 earnings per share last year

MBI Business Centers Inc.*
(Formerly The Math Box, Inc.)
Sells microcomputers and related products
  through computer centers
January 1984
$4.32 million underwritten
$324,000 fee
$9 per share
$(.62) loss per share last year

Pawnee Industries, Inc.*
Manufactures custom extrusion
  thermoplastic sheet materials
July 1985
$5.14 million underwritten
$397,300 fee
$8 per share
$.39 earnings per share last year

BLYTH EASTMAN PAINE WEBBER
INCORPORATED
1221 Avenue of the Americas
New York, NY 10020
212-730-8500

Michael J. Johnston, Pres.
Roger W. Mehle, Exec. V.P.

Clear Channel Communications, Inc.*
Operates FM and AM radio stations
April 1984
$7.5 million underwritten
$562,500 fee
$10 per share
$1.01 earnings per share last year

Northern Data Systems, Inc.*
Integrated turnkey computer systems
August 1984
$6.0 million underwritten
$480,000 fee
$7.50 per share
$.40 earnings per share last year

BOETTCHER & COMPANY, INC.
828 17th Street, Box 54
Denver, CO 80201
303-628-8000

Robert L. Manning, Jr., Corp. Fin.

Horizon Air Industries, Inc.
A passenger airline serving the western
  continental U.S.
January 1984
$4.13 million underwritten
$375,000 fee
$5.50 per share
$(.37) loss per share last year
and
June 1985
$11.00 million underwritten
$852,50 fee
$10 per unit
$.69 earnings per share last year

Melridge, Inc.
A leading grower of hybrid bulbs and flowers
November 1984
$7.54 million underwritten
$486,000 fee
$8 per share
$.69 earnings per share last year

Sunworld International Airways, Inc.*
A passenger airline serving seven Western
  U.S. cities
June 1985
$7.75 million underwritten
$680,000 fee
$8 per share
$(.28) loss per share last year

Wiland Services, Inc.*
Provides data processing to direct mail
  marketers
August 1984
$5.313 million underwritten
$425,000 fee
$6.25 per share
$.27 earnings per share last year

BOND, RICHMAN & CO., INC.
28 Broadway
New York, NY 10004
212-344-5710

A.B. Bramnik, Pres.

The Learning Annex, Inc.*
Markets courses providing training in
  vocational skills and hobbies
August 1984
$2.89 million underwritten
$288,750 fee
$2 per unit
$(.08) loss per share last year

THE BONHAM COMPANY, INC.
1404 Union Bank Tower, P.O. Box 174
62 Commerce Street
Montgomery, Al 36104
205-264-6453

John Bonham, Pres.

**Magic Years Child Care & Learning
  Centers, Inc.***
Operates two child day-care centers in PA
August 1984
$1.20 million underwritten
$120,000 fee
$3 per unit
$(.02) loss per share last year

J.C. BRADFORD & CO.
170 Fourth Avenue N.
Nashville, TN 37219
615-748-9000

Robert Doolittle, Corp. Fin.

Steel Technologies Inc.
Processes flat rolled steel to close
  tolerances for industry
August 1985
$11.75 million underwritten
$910,000 fee
$11.75 per share
$.86 earnings per share last year

**BREAN MURRAY, FOSTER
  SECURITIES INC.**
67 Wall Street
New York, NY 10005
212-422-2300

Christopher Mortenson, Sr. V.P./Corp. Fin.

Thermedics Inc.
Markets a family of biomedical-grade plastics
May 1985
$4.69 million underwritten
$281,250 fee
$12 per share
$(.09) loss per share last year

BROADCHILD SECURITIES
(Division of D.H. Blair Investors Corp.)
One Whitehall Street
New York, NY 10004
212-248-0300

Carl Renov, Acting Pres.

Cardiopulmonary Technologies, Inc.*
Healthcare offices treating cardiac,
  respiratory and neuromuscular
December 1984
$3.00 million underwritten
$300,000 fee
$2.50 per unit
$(.03) loss per share last year

Quantum Diagnostics, Ltd.*
Manufactures and markets devices for use
  in medical diagnoses
July 1985
$3.00 million underwritten
$300,000 fee
$6 per unit
$(.16) loss per share last year

Satori Entertainment Corporation*
Distributes independently produced feature
  films and programs
December 1984
$2.50 million underwritten
$250,000 fee
$2 per share
$(.05) loss per share last year

Technogenetics Incorporated*
Markets products based on monoclonal and
  polyclonal antibodies
July 1984
$2.50 million underwritten
$250,000 fee
$2 per unit
$.00 earnings per share last year

**BRODIS SECURITIES
INCORPORATED**
One Great Neck Road, Box 2112
Great Neck, NY 11022
516-466-5566

Ronald Brodis, Principal

Cellular America, Inc.*
Operates cellular radio telephone systems
July 1984
$1.00 million underwritten
$100,000 fee
$1 per unit
$.00 earnings per share last year

BROOKEHILL EQUITIES, INC.
(Formerly Brookehill Capital
  Management Inc.)
One Battery Park
New York, NY 10004
212-460-0660

Robert deRose, Ptnr.
Walter S. Grossman, Ptnr.

Dental World Center, Inc.*
Provides services to company-managed and
  franchised dental centers
March 1984
$1.00 million underwritten
$100,000 fee
$2 per unit
$(.09) loss per share last year

ALEX. BROWN & SONS
135 East Baltimore Street
Baltimore, MD 21202
301-727-1700

Donald B. Hebb, Jr., Corp. Fin.

Autodesk, Inc.*
Develops CAD and drafting software for
 desktop computers
June 1985
$15.40 million underwritten
$1.12 million fee
$11 per share
$.30 earnings per share last year

Chili's Inc.*
Operates grill and bar restaurant chain
January 1984
$15.0 million underwritten
$1.05 million fee
$15 per share
$.55 earnings per share last year

Compression Labs, Incorporated
Manufactures video compression equipment
 for two-way color teleconferencing
April 1984
$12.76 million underwritten
$893,340 fee
$9 per share
$(.21) loss per share last year

Environmental Testing and Certification
 Corporation
Provides toxic waste management services
 to industry
April 1985
$15.84 million underwritten
$971,750 fee
$19 per share
$.17 earnings per share last year

Epsilon Data Management, Inc.*
Computer-based marketing services
January 1984
$12.075 million underwritten
$850,500 fee
$11.50 per share
$.44 earnings per share last year

Sylvan Learning Corporation
Franchises reading and math learning
 centers for children
July 1985
$7.65 million underwritten
$535,500 fee
$9 per share
$(.06) loss per share last year

VM Software Inc.*
Markets system software for use with the
 VM operating system
May 1985
$24.72 million underwritten
$1.73 million fee
$16 per share
$.52 earnings per share last year

WNS, Inc.
Retails home decoration accessories in
 regional shopping malls July 1985
$10.20 million underwritten
$731,000 fee
$12 per share
$.92 earnings per share last year

Zycad Corporation
Develops computers to increase CAD/CAM
 production for IC fabrication
June 1984
$30.00 million underwritten
$2.1 million fee
$15 per share
$.09 earnings per share last year

BURGESS & LEITH INCORPORATED
60 State Street
Boston, MA 02109
617-742-5900

A. Clinton Allen, III, Chm. & CEO
William M. Breed, Director

Sporto Corp.
Manufactures women's athletic/leisure
 fashion footwear
January 1984
$5.90 million underwritten
$472,000 fee
$7.38 per share
$.48 earnings per share last year

BURNS, PAULI & CO., INC.
515 Olive Street
St. Louis, MO 63101
314-436-7575

Eugene T. Burns, Pres.
Kenneth E. Nunn, Corp. Fin.

Engineered Support Systems, Inc.*
A military ground support equipment
 contractor
August 1985
$9.75 million underwritten
$780,000 fee
$10 per share
$.42 earnings per share last year

BUTCHER & SINGER INC.
Sovereign Development of the Midwest
P.O. Box 957
Philadelphia, PA 19105
215-985-5000

Henry P. Glendinning, Jr., Corp. Fin.

International Mobile Machines
 Corporation*
Developing advanced technologies in
 telecommunications
August 1985
$7.13 million underwritten
$605,625 fee
$7.12 per share
$(.78) loss per share last year

Robert Bruce Industries Inc.*
Manufactures men's sweaters distributed
 under brand names in the U.S.
November 1984
$6.00 million underwritten
$464,000 fee
$8 per share
$1.50 earnings per share last year

CABLE, HOWSE & RAGEN
999 3rd Avenue, #4300
Seattle, WA 98104
206-343-5000

Ross K. Chapin, Corp. Fin.

Develcon Electronics Ltd.
Data communications equipment
January 1984
$12.75 million underwritten
$860,000 fee
$19.125 per share
$.88 earnings per share last year

CAROLINA SECURITIES
 CORPORATION
North Carolina National Bank Building
Box 1071
Raleigh, NC 27602
919-032-3711

Glenn E. Anderson, Chm.
Garland S. Tucker III, Pres & CEO
Whitefield Lee, V.P./Corp. Fin.

Day Telecommunications, Inc.*
Manufactures microprocessor-based
 switching control terminals
January 1984
$2.85 million underwritten
$247,000 fee
$6 per share
$.27 pro forma earnings per share last year

Phoenix Medical Technology, Inc.*
Manufactures disposable medical products
including vinyl examination gloves
June 1984
$3.60 million underwritten
$324,000 fee
$6 per share
$.38 earnings per share last year

THE CHICAGO CORPORATION
208 South La Salle Street
Chicago, IL 60604
312-855-7600

Paul W. Oliver, Jr., Corp. Fin.
Phillip R. Clarke, III, Corp. Fin.

London House, Inc.*
Develops psychological tests
April 1984
$4.41 million underwritten
$374,850 fee
$7 per share
$.16 earnings per share last year

TCBY Enterprises, Inc.
Franchises and owns soft-serve frozen
yogurt stores
August 1985
$8.72 million underwritten
$54,450 fee
$19 per share
$.30 earnings per share last year

CITIWIDE SECURITIES CORP.
111 Broadway #2020
New York, NY 10006
212-608-4115

Paul M. Galant, Pres.

Business Computer Solutions, Inc.*
Develops business software for Wang and
compatible computers
February 1985
$4.14 million underwritten
$414,000 fee
$2.00 per unit
$(.02) loss per share for the nine months
ended 11/30/84

Cellcom Corp.*
Operates cellular mobile radio telephone
systems
March 1984
$4.88 million underwritten
$487,500 fee
$2 per unit
$.00 earnings per share last year

Polymuse, Inc.*
Consultants to the entertainment business
April 1984
$1.95 million underwritten
$195,000 fee
$6 per unit
$.05 earnings per share last year

Restech, Inc.*
Provides financial consulting to the
entertainment industry
August 1984
$0.75 million underwritten
$75,000 fee
$1 per share
$.00 earnings per share last year

**Teletrak Advanced Technology
Systems, Inc.***
Develops microcomputer-based real time
information management analysis systems
January 1984
$2.70 million underwritten
$270,000 fee
$1 per unit
$(.06) loss per share 1/5/83 (inception)
to 9/30/83

S.D.COHN & CO.
120 Broadway
New York, NY 10271
212-227-0300

Damon Testaverde, Sr. V.P.

Cardinal Entertainment Corporation
Produces action and youth oriented, low
budget feature films
March 1985
$3.00 million underwritten
$300,000 fee
$2 per unit
$(.13) loss per share 6/25/84 (inception)
to 12/31/84

Digital Transervice Corporation*
Markets high speed digital services via
networks and stations
May 1985
$6.00 million underwritten
$600,000 fee
$2 per share
$.00 earnings per share last year

**International Information Network
(Infoline, Inc.)***
Provides informational programs over
the telephone
December 1984
$2.50 million underwritten
$250,000 fee
$2 per share
$.01 pro forma earnings per share for the
ten months ended 10/31/84

Pictel Corporation*
Manufactures video compression equipment
for videoconferencing systems
October 1984
$4.40 million underwritten
$440,000 fee
$2 per share
$.00 earnings per share last year

Spectrum Microwave Corporation*
Manufactures microwave equipment for data
transmission over communications
networks
May 1984
$4.00 million underwritten
$400,000 fee
$2 per unit
$.00 earnings per share last year

Systems Technology Associates, Inc.*
Manufactures electronic switching equipment
for international phone service
March 1985
$2.50 million underwritten
$250,000 fee
$2 per share
$.19 earnings per share last year

COMITEAU LEVINE & CO., INC.
17 Battery Place
New York, NY 10005
212-943-8560

Allan M. Levine, Pres.

Entertainment Marketing, Incorporated*
Distributes consumer electronic products in
the southwest U.S.
July 1985
$3.00 million underwritten
$300,000 fee
$2 per share
$.04 earnings per share last year

Warner Computer Systems, Inc.*
Provides computer services to brokers,
  banks and insurance companies
February 1984
$1.70 million underwritten
$170,000 fee
$1 per share
$.01 earnings per share last year

COMMERCE CAPITAL INC.
646 NBC Center
Lincoln, NE 68508
402-474-1394

Dwaine Rogge, Pres.

Chief Automotive Systems, Inc.*
Manufactures a patented vehicle collision
  repair and realignment system
August 1984
$10.00 million underwritten
$820,000 fee
$10 per share
$1.15 earnings per share last year

CRAIG-HALLUM, INC.
133 South Seventh Street
Minneapolis, MN 55402
612-332-1212

James Young, Corp. Fin.
Mary Pihringer, Corp. Fin.
John Builion, Corp. Fin.
Ellie Winninghoff, Corp. Fin.

Check Technology Corporation*
Markets a computerized printing system for
  the finance industry
June 1985
$2.00 million underwritten
$200,000 fee
$1000 per unit
$(.31) loss per share last year

Dimensional Medicine, Inc.*
Developing medical imaging and graphics
  workstations
July 1985
$3.45 million underwritten
$345,000 fee
$3 per share
$(1.08) loss per share last year

G V Medical, Inc.*
Develops laser enhanced transluminal
  angioplaster catheter system
November 1984
$3.50 million underwritten
$350,000 fee
$5 per share
$(.56) loss per share for the nine months
  ended 9/30/84

CROWELL, WEEDON & CO.
One Wilshire Blvd.
Los Angeles, CA 90017
213-620-1850

Hal Harigan, Corp. Fin.
James W. Fox, Corp. Fin.

American Businessphones, Inc.*
Markets multi-featured telephone
  interconnect systems
December 1984
$3.60 million underwritten
$324,000 fee
$6 per share
$.56 earnings per share last year

DAIN BOSWORTH & CO.
100 Dain Tower
Minneapolis, MN 55402
612-371-2711

D.R. Coleman, Jr., Sr., V.P./Corp. Fin.

American Medcenters, Inc.*
Develops and manages health maintenance
  organizations
January 1985
$11.20 million underwritten
$840,000 fee
$8 per share
$.32 earnings per share last year

Bay Pacific Health Corporation*
A federally qualified, individual practice
  association HMO
November 1984
$4.95 million underwritten
$346,500 fee
$6 per share
$.12 pro forma earnings for the six months
  ended 6/30/84

Best Buy Co., Inc.*
Retails consumer electronic products in the
  Minneapolis area
April 1985
$10.13 million underwritten
$757,500 fee
$14 per share
$.21 earnings per share last year

Chief Automotive Systems, Inc.*
Manufactures a patented vehicle collision
  repair and realignment system
August 1984
$10.00 million underwritten
$820,000 fee
$10 per share
$1.15 earnings per share last year

Computer Depot, Inc.*
Sells PCs, software and related service
  through centers in department stores
July 1984
$9.00 million underwritten
$800,000 fee
$9 per share
$.22 earnings per share last year

**Expeditors International of
  Washington, Inc.***
Forwards international airfreight from
  Far East to the U.S.
September 1984
$6.75 million underwritten
$540,000 fee
$9 per unit
$.33 earnings per share last year

FilmTec Corp.*
Reverse osmosis membrane products
January 1984
$10.682 million underwritten
$751,688 fee
$13.50 per share
$.38 earnings per share last year

Flow Systems, Inc.*
Manufactures waterjet and abrasivejet
  cutting systems for automated applications
October 1984
$13.20 million underwritten
$825,000 fee
$12 per share
$.39 earnings per share last year

II Morrow Inc.*
Manufactures general aviation and marine
  navigation instruments
March 1984
$4.72 million underwritten
$378,000 fee
$9 per share
$.45 earnings per share last year

DAVENPORT & CO. OF VIRGINIA, INC.
801 E. Main Street
Richmond, VA 23219
804-780-2000

R. Walter Jones IV, Mgr. Corp. Fin.

The Peanut Shack of America, Inc.*
Franchises specialty retail food stores in U.S.
   shopping malls
August 1985
$4.31 million underwritten
$344,700 fee
$8 per share
$.32 earnings per share last year

R.G. DICKINSON & CO.
200 Des Moines Building
Des Moines, IA 50309
515-247-8100

Larry Cheeves, V.P./Corp. Fin.
William Bestman, Corp. Fin.

General Metal & Abrasives Company*
Reclaims and recycles previously used steel
   abrasive materials
December 1984
$2.16 million underwritten
$216,000 fee
$6.00 per share
$.55 earnings per share last year

Medical Imaging Centers of America, Inc.*
Operates free standing medical diagnostic
   imaging centers
August 1984
$3.50 million underwritten
$332,500 fee
$5 per unit
$(.16) pro forma loss per share last year

Urgent Care Centers of America, Inc.*
Manages a chain of minor medical
   treatment centers
February 1984
$13.00 million underwritten
$1.04 million fee
$5 per share
$(.35) loss per share for the nine months
   ended 11/30/83

Vipont Laboratories, Inc.*
Markets sanguinaria-based oral hygiene
   antiplaque products
July 1985
$6.88 million underwritten
$580,000 fee
$13.75 per share
$(1.62) loss per share last year

DIVERSIFIED EQUITIES CORP.
104 E. 40th Street, #401
New York, NY 10016
212-682-3838

Earthworm Tractor Company Incorporated*
Buys and sells new and used construction
   equipment in the U.S. and overseas
December 1984
$3.50 million underwritten
$350,000 fee
$1 per share
$(.12) loss per share last year

DONALDSON, LUFKIN & JENRETTE SECURITIES CORPORATION
140 Broadway
New York, NY 10005
212-902-2000

John S. Chalsty, Inv. Bkg.

Catalyst Energy Development Corporation
Operates electric and thermal energy
   power plants
May 1985
$16.00 million underwritten
$1.12 million fee
$10 per share
$.06 earnings per share last year

Data Translation, Inc.*
Manufactures data aquisition products for
   industry and scientific microcomputers
February 1985
$8.00 million underwritten
$600,000 fee
$10 per share
$.90 earnings per share last year

Duquesne Systems*
Designs software for IBM and compatible
   systems
January 1984
$8.625 million underwritten
$675,000 fee
$11.50 per share
$.49 earnings per share last year

Epsilon Data Management, Inc.*
Computer-based marketing services
January 1984
$12.075 million underwritten
$850,500 fee
$11.50 per share
$.44 earnings per share last year

S.A.Y. Industries, Inc.***
Manufactures plastic containers for motor oil
   and automotive chemicals
January 1984
$8.00 million underwritten
$624,000 fee
$10 per share
$.22 earnings per share last year

Star Technologies, Inc.
Manufactures high performance scientific
   computer systems
December 1984
$19.80 million underwritten
$1.694 million fee
$9 per share
$(.77) loss per share last year

DREXEL BURNHAM LAMBERT INCORPORATED
60 Broad Street
New York, NY 10004
212-480-6000

Frederick H. Joseph, Sr. Exec. V.P./Corp. Fin.

A.L. Laboratories, Incorporated*
Develops pharmaceutical, animal health and
   nutritional products
February 1984
$23.25 million underwritten
$1.8 million fee
$16 per share
$.08 earnings per share last year

Astrex, Inc.
Sells electro-mechanical devices used in
   electronic equipment
September 1985
$15.00 million underwritten
$600,000 fee
$1000.00 per share
$.96 earnings per share last year

Audio/Video Affiliates, Inc.
Sells home entertainment and consumer
   electrical products through retail stores
July 1984
$15.95 million underwritten
$1.233 million fee
$11 per share
$.68 earnings per share last year

Component Technology Corp.*
Manufactures critical tolerance and plastic
   subassemblies for OEMs
April 1985
$9.60 million underwritten
$648,000 fee
$12 per share
$.81 earnings per share last year

Durakon Industries, Inc.*
Produces pickup truckbed liners
August 1984
$10.5 million underwritten
$760,000 fee
$10.50 per share
$.36 earnings per share last year

Elan Corporation, plc*
Researches and develops drug delivery
  systems
January 1984
$13.2 million underwritten
$924,000 fee
$12 per unit
$.10 earnings per share last year

Environmental Processing, Inc.*
Tests and conditions semiconductor circuits
July 1984
$3.50 million underwritten
$262,500 fee
$5 per unit
$(.39) loss per share last year

Flow Systems, Inc.
Manufactures waterjet and abrasivejet
  cutting systems for automated applications
October 1984
$13.20 million underwritten
$825,000 fee
$12 per share
$.39 earnings per share last year

Harris Graphics Corporation*
Manufactures printing and publishing
  equipment
October 1984
$42.00 million underwritten
$2.94 million fee
$14 per share
$1.95 earnings per share last year

Laser Industries Limited
Manufactures opthalmic surgical laser
  systems
September 1985
$13.20 million underwritten
$900,000 fee
$11 per share
$.26 earnings per share last year

LSI Lighting Systems Inc.*
Manufactures high quality, energy efficient
  outdoor lighting fixtures
March 1985
$10.00 million underwritten
$720,000 fee
$12 per share
$.83 earnings per share last year

MacGregor Sporting Goods, Inc.
Manufactures team sports equipment and
  athletic apparel
April 1985
$12.50 million underwritten
$840,000 fee
$12 per share
$.37 earnings per share last year

MTV Networks Inc.*
Operates two channels of cable t.v.
  programming — MTV and Nickelodeon
August 1984
$76.88 million underwritten
$5.381 million fee
$15 per share
$1.25 pro forma earnings per share last year

Newmark & Lewis Inc.
Retails home entertainment and consumer
  electronics in metropolitan NY
June 1985
$19.20 million underwritten
$1.344 million fee
$16 per share
$1.01 earnings per share last year

Sylvan Learning Corporation
Franchises reading and math learning
  centers for children
July 1985
$7.65 million underwritten
$535,500 fee
$9 per share
$(.06) loss per share last year

Waxman Industries Inc.
Distributes products for the do-it-yourself
  home repair market
April 1985
$27.40 million underwritten
$500,000 fee
$10 per share
$.40 earnings per share last year

Westworld Community Healthcare, Inc.*
Operates primary healthcare facilities in rural
  areas
June 1984
$11.88 million underwritten
$837,500 fee
$10 per share
$.15 earnings per share last year

JAMES J. DUANE & CO., INC.
70 Pine Street
New York, NY 10270
212-248-6960

James J. Duane, Jr., Chm. & Pres.

**Edac Technologies Corp. and Cade
  Industries, Inc.**
Provides engineering services for the
  automotive industry
September 1985
$5.50 million underwritten
$550,000 fee
$5.50 per unit
$.51 earnings per share last year

Imreg, Inc.*
Products to treat immune system diseases
January 1984
$10.0 million underwritten
$900,000 fee
$10 per share
$.09 earnings per share last year

Penn-Med Technology, Inc.*
Manufactures dental equipment
March 1984
$1.60 million underwritten
$160,000 fee
$8 per unit
$(.55) loss per share last year

Power Recovery Systems, Inc.*
Disposes of waste and converts it to
  electrical and steam energy
November 1984
$4.50 million underwritten
$450,000 fee
$5 per share
$(.68) loss per share from 5/3/83 (inception)
  to 7/31/84

EASTLAKE SECURITIES, INC.
8767 Fifth Avenue
New York, NY 10153

Brooks Satellite Inc.*
Franchises stores selling satellite-delivered
  audio/video gear
April 1985
$4.38 million underwritten
$437,500 fee
$3 per unit
$(.56) loss per share for the nine months
  ended 1/1/84 (inception) to 9/30/84

A.G. EDWARDS & SONS, INC.
One North Jefferson Avenue
St. Louis, MO 63103
314-289-3000

Charles F. Fay, Mgr. & Corp. V.P.
Robert P. Barnidge, Corp. Fin.
Richard E. McDonnell, Corp. Fin.

Audio/Video Affiliates, Inc.
Sells home entertainment and consumer
electrical products through retail stores
July 1984
$15.95 million underwritten
$1.233 million fee
$11 per share
$.68 earnings per share last year

Engineered Support Systems, Inc.*
A military ground support equipment
contractor
August 1985
$9.75 million underwritten
$780,000 fee
$10 per share
$.42 earnings per share last year

Jumping-Jacks Shoes, Inc.
Manufactures Jumping-Jacks and little
Capezio children's shoes
October 1984
$5.43 million underwritten
$387,500 fee
$7 per share
$.94 earnings per share last year

Toys Plus, Inc.
Operates a chain of 20 specialty retail
toy stores
September 1985
$8.03 million underwritten
$588,000 fee
$13.38 per share
$.40 earnings per share last year

Top Brass Enterprises, Inc.
Sells consumer durables
January 1984
$12.7 million underwritten
$939,800 fee
$10 per share
$.60 earnings per share last year

ENGLER & BUDD CO.
930 Midwest Plaza Building
801 Nicollett Mall
Minneapolis, MN 55402
612-333-1161

Richard Heise, Exec. V.P./Corp. Fin.

Pizza Transit Authority, Inc.*
Franchises a chain of pizza stores featuring
home delivery
March 1985
$1.79 million underwritten
$178,750 fee
$2.75 per share
$.09 earnings per share last year

EPPLER, GUERIN & TURNER, INC.
2001 Bryan Street
Dallas, TX 75201
214-880-9000

Thomas F. O'Toole, Exec. V.P. & Mgr./
Corp. Fin.

National FSI, Inc.*
Provides systems for administering employee
benefit plans
August 1985
$12.25 million underwritten
$900,000 fee
$12 per share
$.84 earnings per share last year

Old Spaghetti Warehouse, Inc.*
Operates full-service, family-style Italian
restaurants
September 1985
$4.76 million underwritten
$380,800 fee
$7.00 per share
$.56 earnings per share last year

Plains Resources Inc.
Engaged in oil and gas exploration and
production
June 1985
$7.00 million underwritten
$546,000 fee
$10 per share
$.14 earnings per share last year

EQUITY SECURITIES TRADING COMPANY, INC.
2216 IDS Center
Minneapolis, MN 55402
612-338-8901

Nathan Newman, Pres., Secy. & Treas.

Heavy Duty Air, Inc.*
Manufactures air filters and items for heavy
duty replacement parts businesses
April 1984
$0.70 million underwritten
$70,000 fee
$2 per share
$(.18) loss per share for the year
ended 12/31/84

EUROPARTNERS SECURITIES CORPORATION
One World Trade Center
New York, NY 10048
212-466-6100

Kevin Clowe, Assist. V.P./Corp. Fin.
Francois Puton, Assist. V.P./Corp. Fin.

International Film Productions, Inc.*
Produces television programs and
feature films
November 1984
$1.10 million underwritten
$110,000 fee
$5 per unit
$(.51) loss per share last year

FAHENSTOCK & CO.
110 Wall Street
New York, NY 10005
212-668-8000

Sherburn M. Becker, Ptnr.
Michael Donald Grant, Ptnr.
Robert H. Warren, Ptnr.

Microsemi Corporation*
Manufactures discrete diodes
and assemblies
March 1984
$4.4 million underwritten
$352,000 fee
$5.50 per share
$.22 earnings per share last year

FERRIS & COMPANY, INCORPORATED
1720 Eye Street N.W.
Washington, D.C. 20006
202-429-3500

Dudley M. Patteson, V.P./Corp. Fin.

Hooper Holmes, Inc.*
Provides health care and information
  services to insurance industry
July 1984
$3.00 million underwritten
$240,000 fee
$10 per share
$1.27 earnings per share last year

QuesTech, Incorporated*
Provides technological services related to
  defense, aeronautics and energy
May 1984
$2.34 million underwritten
$163,620 fee
$8 per share
$.68 earnings per share last year

Ross Industries, Inc.*
Manufactures machines for use in the food
  processing industry
December 1984
$3.94 million underwritten
$334,680 fee
$9 per share
$.98 earnings per share last year

FINANCIAL FIRST SECURITIES, INC.
514 Fort Worth Club Bldg.
Fort Worth, TX 76102
817-877-1395

G. Rick Holder, Officer

Bar/Code, Inc.*
Manufactures devices that read bar codes
April 1985
$4.00 million underwritten
$375,000 fee
$1 per share
$(.22) loss per share last year

FIRST AFFILIATED SECURITIES
6970 Miramar Road
San Diego, CA 92121
619-578-9030

Jack A. Alexander, Prin.
Kenneth W. Eisberry, Prin.
William Patton, Sr. V.P./Corp. Fin.

Applied Genetics International*
Genetic evaluation and breeding of cattle
November 1984
$1.25 million underwritten
$250,000 fee
$2 per share
$.09 earnings per share for the six months
  ended 6/30/84

El Pollo Asado, Inc.*
Franchises char-broiled chicken fast food
  restaurants
October 1984
$2.00 million underwritten
$160,000 fee
$3 per share
$(.25) loss per share for the sixteen weeks
  ended 7/22/84

Haber, Inc.*
Develops technologies for metal separations
  and purifications
November 1984
$3.50 million underwritten
$350,000 fee
$20 per unit
$(.30) loss per share last year

Intermark Gaming International, Inc.*
Makes microprocessor-controlled, talking
  poker machines
May 1985
$3.08 million underwritten
$307,500 fee
$3 per share
$(.27) loss per share last year

Pyramid Magnetics, Incorporated*
Manufactures disk drive components
February 1984
$4.00 million underwritten
$400,000 fee
$5 per share
$.04 earnings per share last year

FIRST ALBANY CORPORATION
41 State Street
Albany, NY 12207
518-447-8500

George C. McNamee, Pres.

The Present Co., Inc.*
Retails diamonds, jewelry and hardgoods at
  discount prices
August 1985
$6.08 million underwritten
$445,500 fee
$9 per share
$.59 earnings per share last year

FIRST EQUITY CORPORATION OF FLORIDA
100 North Biscayne Boulevard
Miami, FL 33132
305-379-0731

Alan S. Pareira, Chm. & Pres.

American Land Cruisers, Inc.*
Operates rental fleet of recreational vehicles
  from offices in FL and CA
May 1984
$3.38 million underwritten
$303,750 fee
$6 per unit
$.18 earnings per share last year

FIRST FLORIDA SECURITIES, INC.
2401 East Atlantic Blvd.
Pompano Beach, FL 33062
305-943-8300

Nick P. Christos, Resident Officer

R2 Corporation*
Manufactures advanced disposable electrode
  systems
April 1985
$3.00 million underwritten
$300,000 fee
$2 per unit
$(1.08) loss per share last year

FIRST HERITAGE CORPORATION
Div. Office-First Florida Division
Southfield, MI 48086
313-353-4740

Jacob Feldman, Chm.
Nicholas Rucarean, Pres.
Richard L. Coskey, Exec. V.P. & Treas.

Inter-Active Services, Inc.*
Offers security management to homeowners
    and commercial buildings
February 1985
$1.20 million underwritten
$120,000 fee
$3 per share
$(.04) loss per share for 10/27/83 (inception)
    to 6/30/84

FIRST JERSEY SECURITIES
50 Broadway
New York, NY 10004
212-269-5500

Robert Brennan, Pres.

Cosmopolitan Care Corporation*
Provides temporary home health care
    personnel
May 1984
$4.80 million underwritten
$432,000 fee
$3 per unit
$.14 earnings per share last year

Fireplace Manufacturers, Inc.*
Factory-built wood-burning fireplace systems
April 1984
$2.5 million underwritten
$425,000 fee
$1 per unit
$.16 earnings per share last year

General Aero Products Corp.*
Manufactures electro-mechanical and
    electro-optical equipment
November 1984
$3.20 million underwritten
$528,000 fee
$1 per unit
$.06 earnings per share last year

Novo Corporation
Holding company providing information
    services
March 1984
$5.363 million underwritten
$858,000 fee
$3.25 per unit
$.20 earnings per share last year

Empire-Orr, Inc.*
Sells imported handbags, briefcases and
    leather goods
February 1985
$7.00 million underwritten
$980,000 fee
$2 per unit
$.04 earnings per share last year

Reprotech, Inc.*
Produces cattle embryos at clients' farms
July 1984
$4.50 million underwritten
$742,500 fee
$2 per share
$(.02) loss per share last year

Thermodynetics, Incorporated*
Manufactures metal tubing for energy
    transfer and heating
May 1984
$4.13 million underwritten
$701,250 fee
$1.50 per unit
$.01 earnings per share last year

Wright Air Lines, Inc.*
Regional air carrier serving Midwest and
    Mid-Atlantic states
February 1984
$7.00 million underwritten
$1.05 million fee
$1 per share
$.19 earnings per share last year

FIRST OF MICHIGAN CORPORATION
100 Renaissance Center
Detroit, MI 48243
313-259-2600

Joseph Mengden, Exec. V.P./Corp. Fin.
Frederick J. Schroeder, Jr., Sr. V.P./Corp. Fin.

Durakon Industries, Inc.*
Produces pickup truckbed liners
August 1984
$10.5 million underwritten
$760,000 fee
$10.50 per share
$.36 earnings per share last year

Inacomp Computer Centers, Inc.*
Retail outlets for microcomputer systems
January 1984
$12.65 million underwritten
$885,500 fee
$11.50 per share
$.30 earnings per share last year

Vortec Corporation*
Rents and sells home health care items and
    industrial products
June 1985
$4.95 million underwritten
$383,620 fee
$9 per share
$.66 earnings per share last year

FIRST UNITED SECURITIES GROUP OF CALIFORNIA
610 Newport Ctr. Dr., #1425
Newport Beach, CA 92660
714-752-9722

Linda A. Kochan, Pres.
Michael H. Stoltzner, Exec. V.P.
Catherine F. Siemer, Secy. & Treas.

Kinetic Design Systems, Ltd.*
Produces computer-generated animated
    video imagery
July 1985
$3.00 million underwritten
$300,000 fee
$3 per unit
$(.58) loss per share last year

FIRST WILSHIRE SECURITIES MANAGEMENT INC.
One Wilshire Blvd.
Los Angeles, CA 90017
213-464-3030

Bruce Jaell, Pres.
Joseph DeLillo, Exec. V.P.

Fanon/Courier U.S.A., Inc.*
Designs and markets telecommunications
    equipment
March 1984
$4.00 million underwritten
$400,000 fee
$8 per share
$.16 earnings per share last year

FITZGERALD, DE ARMAN & ROBERTS, INC.
6400 S. Lewis, P.O. Box 3094
Tulsa, OK 74101
918-743-1381

W. Fred Carlisle, Corp. Fin.

Identix Incorporated*
Produces terminals that electronically
  identify fingerprints
September 1985
$5.00 million underwritten
$500,000 fee
$4 per share
$(.59) loss per share last year

Video Image, Inc.*
Markets video instructional video products
  for home and education
January 1985
$1.58 million underwritten
$157,500 fee
$1.75 per unit
$(.01) loss per share from 5/2/84 (inception)
  to 9/14/84

FREDERICK & COMPANY, INC.
920 E. Mason Street
Milwaukee, WI 53202
414-271-1500

Paul A. Frederick, Pres. & Treas.
Joan C. Levine, V.P. & Secy.
Lon P. Frederick, V.P.

Circuit Systems, Inc.*
Manufactures double-sided and multi-layer
  printed circuit boards
September 1985
$3.00 million underwritten
$300,000 fee
$5 per share
$(.22) loss per share last year

FREEHLING & CO.
120 South LaSalle Street
Chicago, IL 60603
312-346-2680

Norman Freehling, Pres.

Kinetic Design Systems, Ltd.*
Produces computer-generated animated
  video imagery
July 1985
$3.00 million underwritten
$300,000 fee
$3 per unit
$(.58) loss per share last year

FURMAN SELZ MAGER DIETZ & BIRNEY INCORPORATED
230 Park Avenue
New York, NY 10169
212-309-8200

James M. Birney, Exec. V.P./Corp. Fin.
E. Camilla Dietz, Exec. V.P./Corp. Fin.

Brentwood Instruments Inc.*
Sells medical products to physicians' offices
  and nonhospitals
June 1985
$4.90 million underwritten
$399,000 fee
$7 per share
$.49 earnings per share last year

The Langer Biomechanics Group*
Products to assist feet ailments
January 1984
$5.9 million underwritten
$472,000 fee
$7.375 per share
$.05 earnings per share last year

Prism Entertainment Corporation*
Acquires home video rights to film, concert
  and other programs
August 1985
$4.72 million underwritten
$378,000 fee
$6.75 per share
$.58 earnings per share last year

Urgent Care Centers of America, Inc.*
Manages a chain of minor medical
  treatment centers
February 1984
$13.00 million underwritten
$1.04 million fee
$5 per share
$(.25) loss per share 9/13/82 (inception)
  to 2/28/83

GAINES, BERLAND, INC.
14 E. 60th Street, #511
New York, NY 10022
212-319-2050

Alan D. Gaines, Pres.

Praxis Pharmaceuticals Incorporated*
A fully integrated pharmaceutical concern
January 1985
$4.00 million underwritten
$4.002 million fee
$1.50 per unit
$.00 earnings per share last year

GALLANT SECURITIES INC.
717 Fifth Avenue
New York, NY 10022
212-593-2250

Alvin Gallant, Pres.

Sahlen & Associates, Inc.*
Investigative services to businesses
July 1984
$2.00 million underwritten
$200,000 fee
$2 per share
$.06 earnings per share last year

J.W. GANT & ASSOCIATES
7600 East Orchard Road #160
Englewood, CO 80111
303-850-7799

James A. Scott, Corp. Fin.

Edgewood Films, Inc.*
Produces feature-length motion pictures and
  television properties
February 1984
$2.20 million underwritten
$220,000 fee
$1 per share
$.00 earnings per share last year

GILFORD SECURITIES INCORPORATED
509 Madison Avenue #1512
New York, NY 10022
212-888-6400

Lucinda Morrissey, V.P./Corp. Fin.

CompuSave Corporation*
Computer video catalog system
May 1984
$5.00 million underwritten
$500,000 fee
$5 per share
$.02 earnings per share 5/10/83 (inception)
  to 2/29/84

Computerized Buying Network, Inc.*
Buying service database
April 1984
$2.50 million underwritten
$250,000 fee
$2.50 per unit
$(.31) loss per share last year

GridComm, Inc.*
Markets data transmission products using
   composite shift keying
July 1985
$3.00 million underwritten
$300,000 fee
$6 per share
$(.37) loss per share last year

**Magic Years Child Care & Learning
   Centers, Inc.***
Operates child day-care centers in
   Pennsylvania
August 1984
$1.20 million underwritten
$120,000 fee
$3 per unit
$(.02) loss per share last year

The Sporting Life, Inc.*
Sells traditional women's apparel and
   accessories by mail
May 1985
$2.50 million underwritten
$250,000 fee
$5 per share
$.12 earnings per share last year

**Sports Information Data Base,
   Incorporated***
Maintains information database for media
March 1984
$4.00 million underwritten
$400,000 fee
$5 per share
$(.52) loss per share 4/22/82 (inception)
   to 3/31/83

GOLDMAN, SACHS & CO.
85 Broad Street
New York, NY 10004
212-902-1000

Donald R. Gant, Ptnr./Inv. Bkg.
J. Fred Weintz, Jr., Ptnr./Inv. Bkg.
H. Frederick Krimendahl, II, Ptnr./Inv. Bkg.

Chili's Inc.*
Operates Chili's hamburger grill and bar
   restaurants
January 1984
$15.00 million underwritten
$1.05 million fee
$15 per share
$.55 earnings per share last year

DEST Corporation
Makes document readers to put paper-based
   data into computers
June 1985
$11.74 million underwritten
$880,200 fee
$6 per share
$.46 earnings per share last year

Pacificare Health Systems, Inc.*
Operates health maintenance organizations
May 1985
$24.30 million underwritten
$1.7 million fee
$18 per share
$.53 earnings per share for the six months
   ended 3/31/85

Zycad Corporation
High-performance computers for IC
   fabrication
June 1984
$30.00 million underwritten
$2.1 million fee
$15 per share
$.09 earnings per share last year

GREENTREE SECURITIES CORP.
23123 State Road #7
Boca Raton, FL 33433
305-483-2800

Bernice Lerner, Pres.

Jem Records, Inc.*
Manufactures phonographic records
   and tapes
August 1984
$2.10 million underwritten
$210,000 fee
$3.50 per share
$.18 earnings per share last year

GRUNTAL & CO., INCORPORATED
14 Wall Street
New York, NY 10005
212-267-8800

Michael Koblitz, Mgr.

Direct Action Marketing, Inc.*
Mail order promotions September 1984
$12.75 million underwritten
$960,000 fee
$8.50 per share
$1.13 earnings per share last year

HAMBRECHT & QUIST
  INCORPORATED
235 Montgomery Street
San Francisco, CA 94104
415-576-3300

Thomas S. Volpe, Pres.
Tim Howard, Mng. Dir./Corp. Fin.

Boole & Babbage, Inc.*
Designs management software for IBM
February 1984
$6.16 million underwritten
$446,600 fee
$10 per share
$.50 earnings per share last year

Certified Collateral Corporation*
Provides computerized auto claim service to
   insurance companies
July 1985
$9.63 million underwritten
$700,000 fee
$13.75 per share
$(.04) loss per share last year

Circadian, Inc.*
Manufactures ECG systems and diagnostic
   products for physicians
June 1985
$7.80 million underwritten
$546,000 fee
$6 per share
$.14 earnings per share last year

Telco Systems, Inc.
Voice frequency and fiber optic systems
February 1984
$11.00 million underwritten
$770,000 fee
$11 per share
$(.30) loss per share last year

VM Software Inc.*
Markets system software for use with the
   VM operating system
May 1985
$24.72 million underwritten
$1.73 million fee
$16 per share
$.52 earnings per share last year

Westwood One, Inc.
Radio programs broadcast worldwide
April 1984
$14.50 million underwritten
$1.02 million fee
$14.50 per share
$.56 earnings per share last year

Xidex Magnetics Corporation*
Supplies premium quality, high density, flexible magnetic disks
March 1984
$12.75 million underwritten
$897,600 fee
$12.50 per share
$(.03) loss per share last year

Zeta Laboratories, Inc.
Manufactures microwave components for defense and aerospace
April 1985
$5.22 million underwritten
$392,450 fee
$6.25 per share
$.35 earnings per share last year

HANIFEN, IMHOFF INC.
1125 17th Street #1700
Denver, CO 80202
303-296-2300

John Crum, Corp. Fin.
Frederic Birner, Corp. Fin.

Aspen Ribbons, Inc.*
Manufactures disposable inked cartridge and spool ribbons for computers
April 1984
$3.50 million underwritten
$350,000 fee
$2.50 per unit
$.10 earnings per share last year

Catalyst Energy Development Corporation*
Operates electric and thermal energy power plants
December 1984
$4.20 million underwritten
$336,000 fee
$6 per share
$.03 earnings per share last year
and
May 1985
$16.00 million underwritten
$1.12 million fee
$10 per share
$.06 earnings per share last year

Inertia Dynamics Corp.*
Manufactures grass and weed trimmers
February 1984
$2.55 million underwritten
$2.12 million fee
$8.50 per share
$.93 earnings per share last year

A.L. HAVENS SECURITIES, INC.
39 Broadway
New York, NY 10006
212-422-8882

Anthony L. Havens, Mgr./Corp. Fin.
Michael K. Hsu, Corp. Fin.

Infrasonics, Inc.*
Manufactures breath frequency ventilators and other medical items.
October 1984
$2.20 million underwritten
$220,000 fee
$1 per unit
$(.06) loss per share last year

Scott Science and Technology, Incorporated*
Aerospace technical service and precision parts
March 1984
$4.00 million underwritten
$400,000 fee
$1 per share
$.11 earnings per share last year

Wags Stores, Inc.*
Operates off-price retail stores in the metropolitan NY area
July 1984
$1.50 million underwritten
$150,000 fee
$1 per share
$.02 earnings per share last year

YVES HENTIC & COMPANY, INCORPORATED
30 Montgomery Street
Jersey City, NJ 07302
201-451-3300

Yves Hentic, Pres.

H.E. Ventures, Inc.*
Plans to fund development of videodisk instructional courseware
August 1985
$1.60 million underwritten
$160,000 fee
$2 per share
$(.02) loss per share for last year

HERZFELD & STERN SECURITIES CORP.
30 Broad Street
New York, NY 10004
212-480-1800

Paul A. Cohen, Co-Chm.
William Lendman, Pres.

Inmed Corporation*
Manufactures medical and surgical supplies and gauze products
October 1984
$4.20 million underwritten
$336,000 fee
$8 per share
$.85 earnings per share last year

HICKEY KOBER, INCORPORATED
122 East 42nd Street #2109
New York, NY 10168
212-692-9460

Paul K. Hickey, Pres. & Treas.

Fertil-A-Chron, Inc.*
Manufactures indicator for user to determine her fertility cycles
February 1985
$3.00 million underwritten
$300,000 fee
$1 per share
$(.03) loss per share last year

Nationwide Legal Services, Inc.*
Legal service membership plans
September 1984
$2.81 million underwritten
$281,250 fee
$3.75 per unit
$(.09) loss per share 12/27/82 to 11/30/83

J.J.B. HILLIARD, W.L. LYONS, INC.
545 South Third Street
Louisville, KY 40202
502-588-8400

E. Halsey Sandford, Corp. Fin.
Gerald R. Martin, Corp. Fin.

The Fresher Cooker, Inc.*
Franchises quick service restaurants featuring fresh light foods
May 1984
$3.68 million underwritten
$294,000 fee
$7 per share
$(.54) loss per share last year

HOPPER SOLIDAY & CO., INC.

1401 Walnut Street
Philadelphia, PA 19102
215-972-5400

David Fields, Mgr./Corp. Fin.
Robert S. Woodcock, V.P., Mgr./Synd.

EnergyNorth, Inc.
Distributes natural gas in New Hampshire
January 1984
$1.384 million underwritten
$115,500 fee
$10.25 per share
$1.12 earnings per share last year

HOUCHIN, ADAMSON & COMPANY, INC.

(Formerly Adams, James, Foor & Co., Inc.)
111 West 5th Street
Tulsa, OK 74103
918-584-6080

Peter Adamson, III, Pres. & Treas.
Larry C. Houchin, Exec. V.P.
C. Boyd Simmons, Sr. V.P.

Churchill Records & Video, Ltd.*
Produces "master recordings"
March 1984
$1.60 million underwritten
$160,000 fee
$4 per share
$(1.80) loss per share last year

Infoview, Inc.*
Develops video-tex system applications
  licenses
October 1984
$2.00 million underwritten
$200,000 fee
$1 per unit
$(.34) loss per share for 12/16/83 (inception)
  to 5/31/84

Total Assets Protection, Inc.*
Integrated computer protection services
May 1984
$4.0 million underwritten
$360,000 fee
$5 per share
$(.57) loss per share last year

HOWARD, WEIL, LABOUISSE, FRIEDRICHS INC.

1100 Poydras Street
Energy Centre, #900
New Orleans, LA 70163
504-588-2711

Alvin Pike Howard, II, 1st V.P./Corp. Fin.
Richard Foster Duncan, V.P./Corp. Fin.
Stanley E. Ellington, Jr., V.P./Corp. Fin.

TCBY Enterprises, Inc.
Franchises and owns soft-serve frozen
  yogurt stores
August 1985
$8.72 million underwritten
$544,500 fee
$19.38 per share
$.30 earnings per share last year

E.F. HUTTON & COMPANY INC.

One Battery Park Plaza
New York, NY 10004
212-742-5000

Peter M. Detwiler, Vice Chm./Corp. Fin.
C. Clarke Ambrose, Mgn. Dir./Corp. Fin.
W. James Lopp, II, Mgn. Dir./Corp. Fin.

Audio/Video Affiliates, Inc.
Sells home entertainment and consumer
  electrical products through retail stores
July 1984
$15.95 million underwritten
$1.233 million fee
$11 per share
$.68 earnings per share last year

Boole & Babbage, Inc.*
Markets IBM and compatible mainframe
  software
February 1984
$6.16 million underwritten
$446,600 fee
$10 per share
$.50 earnings per share last year

Develcon Electronics Ltd.
Data communications equipment
January 1984
$12.75 million underwritten
$860,000 fee
$19.125 per share
$.88 earnings per share last year

Geodynamics Corporation*
Provides software in support of U.S.
  intelligence and military
July 1985
$13.00 million underwritten
$960,000 fee
$13 per share
$.61 earnings per share last year

NICO, Inc.*
America's largest interior contracting firm
February 1984
$9.90 million underwritten
$729,000 fee
$11 per share
$1.27 earnings per share last year

Safeguard Health Enterprises, Incorporated
Operates the largest capitated dental care
  plan in California
July 1984
$21.25 million underwritten
$1.36 million fee
$12 per share
$.26 earnings per share last year

Top Brass Enterprises, Inc.
Sells consumer durables through
  chain stores
January 1984
$12.7 million underwritten
$939,800 fee
$10 per share
$.60 earnings per share last year

Triboro Communications, Inc.*
Markets computer-controlled communications
  system for business and institutional
  clients in New York
May 1984
$10.50 million underwritten
$800,000 fee
$5 per unit
$(1.02) loss per share last year

INTERSTATE SECURITIES CORPORATION

2700 NCNB Plaza
Charlotte, NC 28280
704-379-9000

J. Robert Philpott, Jr., Sr. V.P. &
  Mgr./Corp. Fin.
James H. Glen, Jr., Corp. Fin.
William F. Hubler, Corp. Fin.

The Flight Int'l. Group, Inc.*
Provides aviation service to U.S.
  Defense Dept.
January 1984
$4.25 million underwritten
$340,000 fee
$8.50 per share
$.39 earnings per share last year

Restaurant Management Services, Inc.
Operates franchised restaurants in Georgia
  and Florida
November 1984
$7.06 million underwritten
$493,920 fee
$10.50 per share
$.70 earnings per share last year

JANNEY MONTGOMERY SCOTT INC.

Five Penn Center Plaza
Philadelphia, PA 19103
215-665-6000

William Rulon Miller, V.P./Corp. Fin.
Jeff Price, V.P./Corp. Fin.

Bay Pacific Health Corporation*
A federally qualified, individual practice
  association HMO
November 1984
$4.95 million underwritten
$346,500 fee
$5.50 per share
$.02 pro forma earnings per share last year

Nu Horizons Electronics Corp.*
Active and passive electronic components
March 1984
$4.46 million underwritten
$391,000 fee
$7.75 per unit
$.03 earnings per share 10/22/82 (inception)
  to 2/28/83

Rocky Mount Undergarment Co., Inc.
Manufactures fashion and basic underwear
July 1985
$5.86 million underwritten
$490,000 fee
$8.38 per share
$.64 earnings per share last year

JEFFERIES & COMPANY, INC.

445 South Figueroa #3000
Los Angeles, CA 90071
213-624-3333

Boyd L. Jefferies, Chm.
Ronald A. Alghini, Pres.
James L. Owens, Exec. V.P. & Treas.
Reuben F. Richards, V.P./Corp. Fin.

Robert Bruce Industries Inc.*
Manufactures men's sweaters distributed
  under brand names in the U.S.
November 1984
$6.00 million underwritten
$464,000 fee
$7.50 per share
$1.50 earnings per share last year

JEROLD SECURITIES & CO., INC.

111 Broadway
New York, NY 10006
212-964-6300

Jerome Zeiff, Chm.
Harold Federbush, Pres.

Edudata Corporation*
Educational services for personal computers
July 1984
$2.50 million underwritten
$250,000 fee
$5 per share
$(.08) loss per share for the nine months
  ended 4/30/84

JESUP & LAMONT SECURITIES CO., INC.

360 Madison Avenue
New York, NY 10017
212-907-0100

James M. Rawdon, Chm., Treas. & CEO
Charles W. Cox, Sr., V.P./Corp. Fin.

Otisville BioTech, Inc.*
Develops biological products to treat
  diseases
February 1984
$3.60 million underwritten
$360,000 fee
$6 per unit
$(.36) loss per share from 2/23/83 (inception)
  to 12/31/83

JOHNSON, LANE, SPACE, SMITH & CO., INC.

101 East Bay Street
Savannah, GA 31401
912-236-7101

David T. Johnson, Pres.
B.H. Rutledge Moore, Exec. V.P.

TCBY Enterprises, Inc.
Franchises and owns soft-serve frozen
  yogurt stores
August 1985
$8.72 million underwritten
$544,500 fee
$19.38 per share
$.30 earnings per share last year

JOHNSTON, LEMON & CO.

1101 Vermont Avenue, N.W.
Washington, D.C. 20005
202-842-5500

John P. Crowder, Mgr./Corp. Fin.

**Gray and Company Public
  Communications Int'l.***
Provides public communications services to
  clients in U.S. and abroad
February 1984
$3.75 million underwritten
$280,000 fee
$7.50 per share
$.20 earnings per share last year

KIDDER, PEABODY & CO. INCORPORATED
10 Hanover Square
New York, NY 10005
212-510-3000

Henry S. Keller, V.P./Corp. Fin.

Automated Systems, Inc.*
Fabricates sophisticated printed circuit
  boards
November 1984
$12.30 million underwritten
$864,000 fee
$10.25 per share
$.48 earnings per share last year

Avant-Garde Computing, Inc.
Develops software-based systems to monitor
  large data communication networks
March 1984
$7.75 million underwritten
$425,000 fee
$15.50 per share
$.24 earnings per share last year

Bercor, Inc.*
A wholesale distributor of toys, appliances
  and electronics
July 1985
$19.58 million underwritten
$1.35 million fee
$14.50 per share
$.80 earnings per share last year

Computer Depot, Inc.*
Sells personal computers and products
July 1984
$9.00 million underwritten
$800,000 fee
$9 per share
$.22 earnings per share last year

Guest Supply, Inc.
Distributes customized toiletries to the U.S.
  lodging industry
June 1985
$13.28 million underwritten
$900,000 fee
$14.75 per share
$.49 earnings per share last year

Harris Graphics Corporation*
Manufactures printing and publishing
  equipment
October 1984
$42.00 million underwritten
$2.94 million fee
$14 per share
$1.95 earnings per share for the year
  ended 6/30/84

Integrated Device Technology, Inc.
Manufactures VLSI circuits with proprietary
  technology
February 1984
$16.13 million underwritten
$1.125 million fee
$10.75 per share
$(.64) loss per share last year

P. Leiner Nutritional Products
Vitamins and nutritional supplements
September 1984
$1.00 million underwritten
$750,000 fee
$10.25 per share
$.75 earnings per share last year

MMI Medical, Inc.*
Diagnostic imaging services utilizing mobile
  sophisticated equipment
July 1984
$5.60 million underwritten
$476,000 fee
$8 per share
$.61 earnings per share last year

Ribi ImmunoChem Research, Inc.
Researches and develops biological
  response modifiers
August 1985
$12.00 million underwritten
$810,000 fee
$8 per share
$(.04) loss per share last year

Scheduled Skyways, Inc.*
Regional airline serving southern and
  southwestern United States
April 1984
$2.60 million underwritten
$240,000 fee
$6.50 per share
$1.10 earnings per share last year

Silvar Lisco*
Markets integrated CAE software
May 1984
$10.00 million underwritten
$750,000 fee
$5 per share
$.06 earnings per share last year

Total Assets Protection, Inc.*
Offers assets protect program and services
  to preclude unauthorized access
May 1984
$4.00 million underwritten
$360,000 fee
$5 per share
$.10 earnings per share for the eleven
  months ended 11/30/83

Wilton Enterprises, Inc.*
Acquired the baking and cake decorating
  divisions of Pillsbury Co.
January 1984
$13.00 million underwritten
$910,000 fee
$10 per share
$.50 earnings per share last year

K.A. KNAPP & CO., INC.
171 Monroe Avenue, N.W.
Grand Rapids, MI 49503
616-459-3306

Kirk A. Knapp, Pres.
Thomas R. Malleis, Secy.
Michael J. Raterink, CFO

Circuit Systems, Inc.*
Manufactures double-sided and multi-layer
  printed circuit boards
September 1985
$3.00 million underwritten
$300,000 fee
$5 per share
$(.22) loss per share last year

Kinetic Design Systems, Ltd.*
Produces computer-generated animated
  video imagery
July 1985
$3.00 million underwritten
$300,000 fee
$3 per unit
$(.58) loss per share last year

LADENBURG, THALMANN & CO. INC.
540 Madison Avenue
New York, NY 10022
212-940-0100

Howard L. Blum, Pres. & Co-CEO
Ronald B. Koenig, Co-CEO
Stephen Weisglass, Director

Beeba's Creations, Inc.
Imports and distributes women's sportswear
September 1985
$9.07 million underwritten
$726,000 fee
$8.25 per share
$.48 earnings per share last year

Enseco Incorporated*
Provides hazardous and non-hazardous
waste monitoring services
June 1985
$5.20 million underwritten
$416,000 fee
$6.50 per share
$.10 earnings per 4/28/84 (inception)
to 12/31,84

Flakey Jake's, Inc.
Restaurants specializing in high quality
hamburgers
January 1984
$4.13 million underwritten
$330,000 fee
$4.125 per share
$(.04) loss per share from 3/3/83 (inception)
to 9/11/83

The Fresher Cooker, Inc.*
Franchises quick-service restaurants
May 1984
$3.675 million underwritten
$294,000 fee
$7 per share
$(.54) loss per share last year

HMO America Inc.
Operates health maintenance organizations
in metropolitan Chicago
June 1985
$7.35 million underwritten
$588,000 fee
$12.25 per share
$.47 earnings per share last year

LSI Lighting Systems Inc.*
Manufactures high quality, energy efficient
outdoor lighting fixtures
March 1985
$10.00 million underwritten
$720,000 fee
$12.50 per share
$.83 earnings per share last year

**S.P.I.-Suspension and Parts Industries
Limited***
Manufactures suspension system
components for military vehicles
July 1985
$5.63 million underwritten
$472,500 fee
$6.25 per share
$.47 earnings per share last year

Surgical Care Affiliates, Inc.*
Operates outpatient surgical care centers
January 1984
$14.00 million underwritten
$980,000 fee
$14 per share
$(.27) loss per share for the nine months
ended 9/30/83

R.F. LAFFERTY & CO., INC.
50 Broad Street
New York, NY 10004
212-269-6636

Henry Hackel, Pres.

Patient Medical Systems Corporation*
Sells enteral feeding equipment and
nutrients to home care patients
March 1984
$.75 million underwritten
$75,000 fee
$2 per unit
$.04 earnings per share 8/15/83 (inception)
to 6/30/84
and
September 1984
$1.65 million underwritten
$66,000 fee
$2 per unit
$.02 earnings per share for the three months
ended 6/30/84

LAIDLAW ADAMS & PECK INC.
40 Rector Street
New York, NY 10006
212-306-6100

James N. Cooke, III, Mgn. Dir./Corp. Fin.

American Restaurants Corporation*
Exclusive franchisee of Wendy's restaurants
for Southern CA
February 1984
$3.50 million underwritten
$350,000 fee
$5 per share
$.12 earnings per share last year

Diplomat Electronics Corporation*
Large U.S. electronic component distributor
March 1984
$6.00 million underwritten
$600,000 fee
$6 per share
$(2.07) loss per share last year

IEC Electronics Corp.*
A contract manufacturer of computer and
electronic products for OEMs
February 1985
$4.25 million underwritten
$425,000 fee
$5 per share
$.84 earnings per share for the year
ended 9/30/84

**Occupational Medical Corporation of
America, Inc.***
Operates occupational medical facilities in
CA, OR and WA
April 1985
$4.75 million underwritten
$475,000 fee
$5 per share
$.20 earnings per share last year

V Band Systems, Inc.*
Manufactures high density electronic key
telephones
January 1984
$5.50 million underwritten
$550,000 fee
$5 per share
$.18 earnings per share last year

**LEGG MASON WOOD WALKER
INCORPORATED**
Seven East Redwood Street
Baltimore, MD 21203
301-539-3400

Walter Frey, V.P./Inv. Bkg.

Phoenix Medical Technology, Inc.*
Manufactures disposable medical products
June 1984
$3.60 million underwritten
$324,000 fee
$6 per share
$.38 earnings per share last year

**LEHMAN BROTHERS KUHN LOEB
INCORPORATED**
(now Shearson Lehman Brothers Inc.)
Two World Trade Center
New York, NY 10048
212-321-6000

Francois de St. Phalle, Corp. Fin.
James A. Stern, Corp. Fin.

DNA Plant Technology Corp.*
Develops improved varieties of crop,
industrial and consumer products
January 1984
$12.65 million underwritten
$968,000 fee
$5.75 per share
$(.04) loss per share last year

LOWELL H. LISTROM & COMPANY INC.

1221 Baltimore Avenue, #500
Kansas City, MO 64105
816-421-1555

Lowell H. Listrom, Pres.
Marco R. Listrom, Exec. V.P.

ElDorado Motor Corporation*
Manufactures recreational and commercial
  vehicles
January 1984
$2.75 million underwritten
$230,000 fee
$5 per share
$.70 earnings per share last year

MAIN STREET SECURITIES, INC.

50 South Main Street, #400
Salt Lake City, UT 84144
801-531-7447

Mark Christiansen, Pres.
Walter Heyman, Mgr./Corp. Fin.

Microsize, Inc.*
Markets a microfiche camera and operates a
  service bureau
June 1984
$1.60 million underwritten
$160,000 fee
$1 per share
$(.04) loss per share last year

MCDONALD & COMPANY SECURITIES, INC.

2100 Central National Bank Building
Cleveland, OH 44114
216-443-2300

Frank B. Carr, Mgr./Corp. Fin.

Invacare Corporation
Manufactures line of medical equipment for
  home health care market
May 1984
$20.90 million underwritten
$1.463 million fee
$11 per share
$.69 earnings per share last year

LESCO Inc.
Golf course and lawn care products
August 1984
$6.60 million underwritten
$510,000 fee
$11 per share
$.85 earnings per share last year

MERRILL LYNCH CAPITAL MARKETS

(division of Merrill Lynch, Pierce, Fenner &
  Smith Incorporated)
One Liberty Plaza
New York, NY 10080
212-637-7455

Jerome P. Kenney, Sr. V.P. & Dir./Inv. Bkg.

Ceradyne, Inc.
Manufactures advanced technical ceramic
  products
September 1985
$11.88 million underwritten
$780,000 fee
$11.88 per share
$.31 earnings per share last year

Consolidated Stores Corporation
Operates a retail close-out merchandise
  store chain
June 1985
$33.35 million underwritten
$2.3 million fee
$14.50 per share
$.51 earnings per share last year

Optical Specialties, Inc.*
Manufactures automated microprocessor
  controlled water inspection stations
December 1984
$8.40 million underwritten
$696,000 fee
$7 per share
$.50 earnings per share last year

Personal Diagnostics, Incorporated*
Medical devices for in vitro diagnostic field
February 1984
$5.25 million underwritten
$392,000 fee
$7.50 per share
$(.66) loss per share last year

MONTGOMERY SECURITIES

600 Montgomery Street
San Francisco, CA 94111
415-627-2000

Alan Stein, Dir./Corp. Fin.

Integrated Device Technology, Inc.
Manufactures VLSI circuits with proprietary
  technology
February 1984
$16.13 million underwritten
$1.125 million fee
$10.75 per share
$(.64) loss per share last year

Sierra Spring Water Company*
A leading producer of bottle water products
May 1984
$6.00 million underwritten
$465,000 fee
$6 per share
$.29 earnings per share last year

MOORE & SCHLEY CAPITAL CORPORATION

45 Broadway
New York, NY 10006
212-483-1800

John J. Cranley, Jr., Chm.
Robert J. Figliozzi, Pres.

Institute of Clinical Pharmacology, PLC*
Test pharmaceuticals for European,
  American and Japanese companies
November 1984
$7.75 million underwritten
$660,000 fee
$7.75 per share
$.31 earnings per share last year

MORGAN, KEEGAN & CO., INC.

One Commerce Square
Memphis, TN 38103
901-524-4100

Richard A. McStay, Corp. Fin.
John W. Slater, Jr., Corp. Fin.
James R. Welsh, Corp. Fin.

Opto Mechanik, Inc.*
Manufactures sighting systems for tanks
  and howitzers
June 1985
$3.60 million underwritten
$288,000 fee
$6 per share
$.67 earnings per share last year

Reliability Incorporated
Manufactures integrated circuit testing
  equipment
May 1984
$4.94 million underwritten
$390,000 fee
$9.88 per share
$.29 earnings per share last year

MORGAN STANLEY & CO. INCORPORATED
1251 Avenue of the Americas
New York, NY 10020
212-974-4000

Allen Zern, Mgr./Corp. Fin.

Mentor Graphics Corporation
Computer-aided engineering CAE systems
January 1984
$49.95 million underwritten
$3.51 million fee
$18.50 per share
$(.30) loss per share for the nine months
    ended 9/30/83

Seaman Furniture Company, Inc.
Retails specialty furniture to middle income
    consumers
July 1985
$50.60 million underwritten
$3.54 million fee
$22 per share
$1.40 earnings per share last year

3Com Corporation
Manufactures high performance local area
    networks
March 1984
$12.78 million underwritten
$894,600 fee
$6 per share
$.00 earnings per share last year

MOSELEY, HALLGARTEN, ESTABROOK & WEEDEN INC.
60 State Street
Boston, MA 02109
617-367-2400

Frederick S. Moseley, III, Chm.
Jonathan A. Bulkley, Pres., CEO & Dir.

Guest Supply, Inc.
Distributes customized toiletries to the U.S.
    lodging industry
June 1985
$13.28 million underwritten
$900,000 fee
$14.75 per share
$.49 earnings per share last year

Rocky Mount Undergarment Co., Inc.
Manufactures fashion and basic underwear
May 1984
$4.0 million underwritten
$376,000 fee
$5 per share
$.64 earnings per share last year
and
July 1985
$5.86 million underwritten
$490,000 fee
$8.38 per share
$.70 earnings per share last year

S.A.Y. Industries, Inc.*
Manufactures plastic containers for motor oil
    and automotive chemicals
January 1984
$8.00 million underwritten
$624,000 fee
$10 per share
$.22 earnings per share last year

MOSTEL & TAYLOR SECURITIES, INC.
919 Third Avenue
New York, NY 10022
212-308-3700

Michael S. Taylor, Pres.
Michael A. Bresner, V.P. & Treas.

Medinet Inc.*
Developed an electronic display workstation
    for health care facilities
October 1984
$2.50 million underwritten
$250,000 fee
$2.50 per unit
$(.07) pro forma loss per share for the six
    months ended 6/30/84

The American Museum of Historical Documents*
Retails letters, documents and signatures of
    historic people
March 1985
$1.50 million underwritten
$150,000 fee
$3 per share
$.03 earnings per share last year

MULLER AND COMPANY, INC.
111 Broadway
New York, NY 10006
212-766-1700

Jerome Feldman, Mgr. Dir./Corp. Fin.

A.T.& E. Corporation*
Developing a voice mail system
February 1985
$9.00 million underwritten
$900,000 fee
$9 per share
$(.04) loss per share last year

Boro Recycling, Inc.*
Collects used carbonated beverage
    containers for recycling
September 1984
$3.85 million underwritten
$385,000 fee
$10 per unit
$(.35) loss per share last year

Cellufone Corporation*
Sells and rents telecommunications
    equipment through retail centers
February 1984
$8.00 million underwritten
$800,000 fee
$5 per unit
$.35 earnings per share 1/16/84 (inception)
    to 9/30/84

Enzon, Inc.*
Developing process to modify enzymes for
    treating diseases
February 1984
$4.08 million underwritten
$408,000 fee
$1.50 per unit
$(.01) loss per share last year

Great Western Systems, Inc.*
Operates used auto public auctions for its
    own and others' accounts
August 1984
$2.52 million underwritten
$252,000 fee
$6 per unit
$.03 earnings per share last year

International Film Productions, Inc.*
Produces television programs and
    feature films
November 1984
$1.10 million underwritten
$1.1 million fee
$5 per unit
$(.51) loss per share last year

Medication Services Inc.*
Develops unit dose drug distribution support systems
April 1984
$4.90 million underwritten
$490,000 fee
$7 per unit
$(.14) loss per share last year

Mercury Entertainment Corp.*
Produces and distributes prospective motion pictures
September 1984
$3.30 million underwritten
$330,000 fee
$6 per unit
$.00 earnings per share last year

Microcomputer Memories, Inc.*
Developing 3.5-inch Winchester hard disk drive for computer systems
January 1984
$5.72 million underwritten
`572,000 fee
$8 per unit
$.08 earnings per share from 3/3/82 (inception) to 7/31/83

Moleculon Biotech, Inc.*
Manufactures controlled release pharmaceutical and biomedical products
March 1984
$4.80 million underwritten
$480,000 fee
$8 per unit
$(.01) loss per share last year

Nutri-Foods Int'l., Inc.*
Manufactures frozen desserts-Ice Juicee, Italian Ice and Guido's Ices
April 1984
$4.00 million underwritten
$400,000 fee
$4 per share
$.19 earnings per share for the ten months ended 1/31/84

Pharmacontrol Corp.*
Will manufacture licensed or internally generated drugs
June 1985
$5.73 million underwritten
$572,750 fee
$7.25 per unit
$(.82) loss per share last year

Praxis Pharmaceuticals Incorporated*
A fully integrated pharmaceutical concern
January 1985
$4.00 million underwritten
$4,002,000 fee
$1.50 per unit
$(.00) loss per share last year

UCI Medical Affiliates, Inc.
Management for freestanding medical centers
September 1984
$5.5 million underwritten
$550,000 fee
$10 per unit
$.10 earnings per share last year

W.H. NEWBOLD'S SON & CO., INC.
1500 Walnut Street
Philadelphia, PA 19102
215-893-8000

Paul D. Keleher, Corp. Fin.
Paul H. Yeomans, Jr., Corp. Fin.

LESCO Inc.
Golf course and lawn care products
August 1984
$6.60 million underwritten
$510,000 fee
$11 per share
$.85 earnings per share last year

OBERWEIS SECURITIES, INC.
841 North Lake Street
Aurora, IL 60506
312-897-7100

Olin Neill Emmons, Corp. Fin.
Stirling Nellis, Corp. Fin.

General Metal & Abrasives Company*
Reclaims and recycles previously used steel abrasive materials
December 1984
$2.16 million underwritten
$216,000 fee
$6 per share
$.55 earnings per share last year

THE OHIO COMPANY
155 East Broad Street
Columbus, OH 43215
614-464-6811

Richard M. Blake, Exec. V.P./Corp. Fin.

ICEE-USA*
Produces and markets a semi-frozen carbonated beverage
January 1985
$5.60 million underwritten
$480,000 fee
$7 per share
$.45 earnings per share last year

NuVision, Inc.*
Markets prescription eyewear through franchised offices
January 1985
$6.82 million underwritten
$545,900 fee
$13.25 per share
$1.34 earnings per share for the nine months ended 9/30/84

Simmons Airlines, Inc.*
Provides regional air service to 20 cities in the Midwest
January 1984
$6.00 million underwritten
$495,000 fee
$10 per share
$1.30 earnings per share last year

OPPENHEIMER & COMPANY INC.
One New York Plaza
New York, NY 10004
212-825-4000

Jerome H. Grossman, Exec. V.P./Corp. Fin.

Crazy Eddie, Inc.
Operates consumer electronics stores in NY, NJ and CT
September 1984
$16.00 million underwritten
$1.2 million fee
$8 per share
$.75 earnings per share last year

National Pizza Company
Operates Pizza Hut restaurants under franchise agreements
August 1984
$9.07 million underwritten
$692,375 fee
$9.50 per share
$.79 earnings per share last year

ORIANS INVESTMENT COMPANY
529 S.W. 3rd Avenue
Portland, OR 97204
503-224-7885

Robert J. Orians, Pres.
Ernest Birchenough, V.P., Secy. & Treas.

Timberline Systems, Inc.*
Accounting and information management software
February 1984
$1.85 million underwritten
$185,000 fee
$4.625 per share
$.21 earnings per share for the nine months ended 9/30/83

PAGEL INC.
625 Marquette Avenue
Minneapolis, MN 55402
612-370-2900

Jack W. Pagel, Pres.
Joseph R. McCarty, Mgr./Corp. Fin./Synd.

Angiomedics Incorporated*
Manufactures intravascular and intracardiac
  catheters and related items
August 1984
$2.55 million underwritten
$255,000 fee
$4.25 per share
$.40 earnings per share for the nine months
  ended 6/30/84

Technology 80 Inc.*
Manufactures a computer system detecting
  defective data exchange
May 1985
$2.98 million underwritten
$297,500 fee
$3.50 per share
$(.22) loss per share last year

XTAL Corporation*
Develops components and installs computer
  systems for CAD/CAM application
May 1984
$2.28 million underwritten
$227,500 fee
$3.25 per share
$(.52) loss per share from 7/7/83 (inception)
  to 2/29/84

PAINE WEBBER INCORPORATED
1285 Avenue of the Americas
New York, NY 10019
212-713-2000

Donald B. Marron, Chm. & CEO

American Medcenters, Inc.*
Develops and manages health maintenance
  organizations
January 1985
$11.20 million underwritten
$840,000 fee
$8 per share
$.32 earnings per share last year

King World Productions, Inc.
Distributes or syndicates television programs
  to stations throughout U.S.
December 1984
$12.50 million underwritten
$937,500 fee
$10 per share
$.73 earnings per share last year

Lewis Galoob Toys, Inc.
Markets toy products throughout the world
September 1984
$12.50 million underwritten
$906,250 fee
$10 per share
$.93 earnings per share last year

Northern Data Systems, Inc.*
Markets turnkey computer systems
August 1984
$6.00 million underwritten
$480,000 fee
$7.50 per share
$.40 earnings per share last year

PARKER/HUNTER INCORPORATED
600 Grant Street, #4000
Pittsburgh, PA 15219
412-562-8000

David W. Hunter, Chm.
J. Mabon Childs, Pres.
Robert W. Kampmeinert, Pres. &
  CEO/Corp. Fin.

Duquesne Systems*
Designs software for IBM and compatible
  mainframe computers
January 1984
$8.63 million underwritten
$675,000 fee
$11.50 per share
$.49 earnings per share last year

PATTEN SECURITIES CORP.
26 Columbia Turnpike, #125
Florham Park, NJ 07932
201-966-6030

John Lewis Patten, Pres. & CEO
James T. Patten, Secy. & Treas.

Emery DataGraphic, Inc.*
Applies computer graphic developments to
  the mapping segment
April 1985
$2.00 million underwritten
$200,000 fee
$2 per unit
$(.15) loss per share last year

La Delite, Ltd.*
Manufactures premium ice cream and
  ice cream products
August 1985
$3.00 million underwritten
$300,000 fee
$15 per unit
$(.02) loss per share last year

Phoenix Financial Corporation*
Leases equipment to retailers of durable
  medical equipment
September 1985
$1.50 million underwritten
$150,000 fee
$1.50 per unit
$.10 earnings per share last year

PAULSON INVESTMENT
   COMPANY, INC.
811 S.W. Front Avenue
Portland, OR 97204
800-547-6710

Chester L.F. Paulson, Pres.

Advanced Logic Systems, Inc.*
Hardware and software products that
  enhance microcomputer capabilities
June 1984
$3.23 million underwritten
$322,500 fee
$1.50 per share
$(.79) loss per share last year

Financial News Network Inc.*
Distributes business programs to cable tv
  via satellite
January 1984
$9.50 million underwritten
$760,000 fee
$1000 per debenture
$(1.04) loss per share last year

Hosposable Products, Inc.*
Manufactures disposable bed pads
February 1985
$2.00 million underwritten
$200,000 fee
$5 per unit
$.69 earnings per share for the nine months
  ended 9/30/83

Timberline Systems, Inc.*
Accounting and information management
  software
February 1984
$1.85 million underwritten
$185,000 fee
$4.62 per share
$.21 earnings per share for the nine months
  ended 9/30/83

PENDRICK REEVES ASSOCIATES, INC.
2425 Post Road
Southport, CT 06490
203-259-5558

Brian M. Greenman, Pres.
Bruce Radler, V.P. & Treas.

Imtec, Inc.*
Microprocessor-based bar code printer
   accessories
June 1984
$0.68 million underwritten
$67,500 fee
$3 per share
$(.72) loss per share last year

PIPER, JAFFRAY & HOPWOOD INCORPORATED
222 S. 9th Street, Box 28
Minneapolis, MN 55440
612-342-6000

David. P. Crosby, Mgn. Dir./Corp. Fin.

Carver Corporation*
Manufactures high-fidelity audio system
   components
May 1985
$7.70 million underwritten
$581,000 fee
$11 per share
$.84 earnings per share last year

C.O.M.B. Co.*
Markets a broad range of close-out
   consumer merchandise
March 1984
$20.00 million underwritten
$1.35 million fee
$8 per share
$.32 earnings per share last year

GV Medical, Inc.*
Designs laser catheter system used to clear
   arteries
September 1985
$6.13 million underwritten
$455,000 fee
$8.75 per share
$(.88) loss per share last year

Horizon Air Industries, Inc.
A passenger airline serving the western
   continental U.S.
June 1985
$11.00 million underwritten
$852,500 fee
$10 per unit
$.69 earnings per share last year

Lieberman Enterprises Incorporated
Distributes pre-recorded music and provides
   merchandising services
November 1984
$18.00 million underwritten
$1.25 million fee
$10 per share
$2.52 earnings per share last year

United Healthcare Corporation*
Manages individual practice association
   model health maintenance organizations
October 1984
$5.74 million underwritten
$433,500 fee
$4.50 per share
$.03 earnings per share last year

United Tote, Inc.*
Manufactures wagering systems
August 1984
$7.2 million underwritten
$558,000 fee
$12.00 per share
$.87 earnings per share last year

Zycad Corporation
Develops computers to increase CAD/CAM
   productivity for IC fabrication
June 1984
$30.00 million underwritten
$2.1 million fee
$15 per share
$.09 earnings per share last year

E.J. PITTOCK & CO., INCORPORATED
7951 E. Maplewood, #230
Englewood, CO 80111
303-740-7272

George S. Yochmowitz, Exec. V.P./Corp. Fin.

Emery DataGraphic, Inc.*
Applies computer graphic developments to
   the mapping segment
April 1985
$2.00 million underwritten
$200,000 fee
$2 per unit
$(.15) loss per share last year

MegaCom, Inc.*
Developed the MegaCom LPE-1 computer
   system
June 1985
$3.00 million underwritten
$300,000 fee
$1 per share
$(.08) loss per share last year

PRESCOTT, BALL & TURBEN, INC.
1331 Euclid Avenue
Cleveland, OH 44115
216-574-7300

Page W.T. Stodder, Sr. V.P./Corp. Fin.
R. Gatzert, V.P./Corp. Fin.

Component Technology Corp.*
Manufactures critical tolerance and plastic
   subassemblies for OEMs
April 1985
$9.60 million underwritten
$648,000 fee
$12 per share
$.81 earnings per share last year

Consolidated Stores Corporation
Operates a retail close-out merchandise
   store chain
June 1985
$33.35 million underwritten
$2.3 million fee
$14.50 per share
$.51 earnings per share last year

Vector Automation, Inc.*
Interactive computer graphics systems
January 1984
$3.6 million underwritten
$324,000 fee
$6 per unit
$.09 earnings per share last year

PROVIDENCE SECURITIES, INC.
(division of Rooney, Pace Inc.)
Two Charles Street
Providence, RI 02904
401-861-4200

Tom dePetrillo, Pres.

CME-SAT, Inc.*
Produces educational television programs for
   health professionals
October 1984
$2.00 million underwritten
$200,000 fee
$5 per unit
$(.57) loss per share last year

Metalbanc Corporation*
Purchases and sells precious metals and
   alloy precious metals
March 1985
$1.10 million underwritten
$110,000 fee
$1 per unit
$.00 earnings per share last year

PRUDENTIAL-BACHE SECURITIES, INC.
100 Gold Street
New York, NY 10038
212-791-1000

Peter Bernard, Corp. Fin.

Barrister Information Systems Corporation
Markets integrated information systems for
  law offices
July 1985
$6.26 million underwritten
$437,850 fee
$9 per share
$.90 earnings per share last year

Bush Industries, Inc.*
Manufactures furniture for use with
  electronic equipment
April 1985
$10.40 million underwritten
$760,000 fee
$13 per share
$1.13 earnings per share last year

Cardis Corporation
Distributes supplies, tools and accessories to
  auto aftermarket
June 1985
$22.91 million underwritten
$625,000 fee
$916.23 per unit
$.22 earnings per share last year

The Fur Vault Inc.*
Retails and distributes luxury fur apparel
August 1984
$13.2 million underwritten
$924,000 fee
$11 per share
$1.21 pro forma earnings per share last year

Jumping-Jacks Shoes, Inc.
Manufactures Jumping-Jacks and little
  Capezio children's shoes
October 1984
$5.43 million underwritten
$387,500 fee
$7 per share
$.94 earnings per share last year

Keystone Camera Products Corporation
Manufactures popular price, easy to use
  cartridge and 35mm cameras
March 1985
$7.75 million underwritten
$580,000 fee
$7.75 per unit
$.70 earnings per share last year

Pancho's Mexican Buffet, Inc.
Operates cafeteria-style Mexican food
  restaurants
February 1985
$7.50 million underwritten
$550,000 fee
$7.50 per share
$.13 earnings per share last year

PDA Engineering*
Develops software for mechanical computer-
  aided engineering (CAE)
January 1985
$7.25 million underwritten
$520,000 fee
$7.25 per share
$.25 earnings per share last year

Personal Diagnostics, Incorporated*
Devices for the in vitro diagnostic field
February 1984
$5.25 million underwritten
$392,000 fee
$7.50 per share
$(.66) loss per share last year

Sbarro, Inc.*
Operates a national chain of italian
  restaurants
May 1985
$11.93 million underwritten
$862,500 fee
$10.38 per share
$.67 earnings per share last year

Western Health Plans*
Operates a health maintenanace
  organization in San Diego area
December 1984
$7.00 million underwritten
$496,000 fee
$8 per share
$1.20 pro forma earnings per share last year

QUINN & CO., INC.
301 Central Avenue NW
Post Office Box 528
Albuquerque, NM 87103
505-842-1000

J. David Stanford, Chm., Pres. & CEO
John F. Mohar, Sr. V.P.

Additive Technology Corporation*
Developed a "Wire ink" process
April 1984
$1.5 million underwritten
$127,500 fee
$5 per share
$(.44) loss per share last year

RAUSCHER PIERCE REFSNES, INC.
2500 Plaza of the Americas N.
Dallas, TX 75201
214-748-0111

Barry B. Conrad, V.P./Corp. Fin.

Dow B. Hickam, Inc.*
Manufactures low-volume, high-margin
  pharmaceutical products
April 1984
$5.20 million underwritten
$416,000 fee
$8 per share
$.54 earnings per share last year

Interphase Corp.*
Manufactures intelligent peripheral device
  controllers
January 1984
$4.80 million underwritten
$384,000 fee
$8 per share
$.35 earnings per share last year

Lancer Corporation*
Manufactures fountain soft drink dispensing
  systems
June 1985
$6.89 million underwritten
$525,625 fee
$9.50 per share
$.75 earnings per share last year

Pawnee Industries, Inc.*
Manufactures custom extrusion
  thermoplastic sheet materials
July 1985
$5.14 million underwritten
$397,300 fee
$7.50 per share
$.39 earnings per share last year

Technology Development Corporation*
Supplies interface hardware for automatic
  test equipment
August 1985
$7.65 million underwritten
$578,000 fee
$9 per share
$.16 earnings per share last year

RAYMOND, JAMES & ASSOCIATES, INC.
1400 66th Street, N.
St. Petersburg, FL 33710
813-381-3800

Francis Godbold, Exec. V.P./Corp. Fin.

Crown Rotational Molded Products, Inc.*
Manufactures plastic holding tanks for
  insecticide and herbicide
April 1985
$2.55 million underwritten
$255,000 fee
$6 per share
$.47 pro forma earnings per share for the
  year ended 9/30/84

Healthways Systems, Inc.*
Operates a health maintenance organization
  (HMO) in New Jersey
March 1985
$7.75 million underwritten
$740,000 fee
$7.75 per share
$.01 earnings per share last year

Iverson Technology Corporation*
A value added computer systems integrator
July 1985
$5.60 million underwritten
$532,000 fee
$8 per share
$.35 earnings per share last year

Stereo Village, Inc.*
Retails home entertainment and consumer
  electronics
May 1984
$1.86 million underwritten
$130,200 fee
$6 per share
$.39 pro forma earnings per share last year
and
June 1985
$11.67 million underwritten
$755,480 fee
$10.50 per share
$.76 earnings per share last year

ROBERTSON, COLMAN & STEPHENS
One Embarcadero Ctr., #3100
San Francisco, CA 94111
415-781-9700

Christopher H. Covington, Dir./Corp. Fin.
Sanford R. Robertson, Ptnr./Corp. Fin.

Compression Labs, Incorporated
Manufactures video compression equipment
  for two-way color teleconferencing
April 1984
$12.76 million underwritten
$893,340 fee
$9 per share
$(.21) loss per share last year

DEST Corporation
Makes document readers to put paper-based
  data into computers
June 1985
$11.74 million underwritten
$880,200 fee
$6 per share
$.46 earnings per share last year

Mentor Graphics Corporation
Manufactures computer aided engineering
  CCAE systems
January 1984
$49.95 million underwritten
$3.51 million fee
$18.50 per share
$(.30) loss per share for the nine months
  ended 9/30/83

Safeguard Health Enterprises, Inc.
Dental care plan
July 1984
$21.25 million underwritten
$1.36 million fee
$12.50 per share
$.32 earnings per share last year

Software Publishing Corporation
Markets packaged software for business
  professionals
November 1984
$11.21 million underwritten
$800,000 fee
$7 per share
$.69 earnings per share last year

Telco Systems, Inc.
Manufactures voice frequency and fiber
  optic transmission systems
February 1984
$11.00 million underwritten
$770,000 fee
$11 per share
$(.30) loss per share last year

3Com Corporation
Manufactures high performance local area
  networks
March 1984
$12.78 million underwritten
$894,600 fee
$6 per share
$.00 earnings per share last year

ROBINSON-HUMPHREY COMPANY, INC. (AMERICAN EXPRESS INC.)
3333 Peachtree Road NE
Atlanta, GA 30326
404-266-6271

Edward S. Croft, III, Mgr./Corp. Fin.

D'Lites of America, Inc.*
Franchises fast service restaurants featuring
  "lite" foods
September 1984
$14.25 million underwritten
$1.035 million fee
$9.50 per share
$.15 earnings per share last year

Stockholder Systems, Inc.*
Designs financial applications software
February 1984
$8.55 million underwritten
$646,000 fee
$9 per share
$.33 earnings per share last year

RONEY & CO.
One Griswold Street
Detroit, MI 48226
313-963-6700

Urban McDonald, Corp. Fin.

Simmons Airlines, Inc.*
Provides regional air service to 20 cities in
  the Midwest
January 1984
$6.00 million underwritten
$495,000 fee
$10 per share
$1.30 earnings per share last year

ROONEY, PACE INC.
11 Broadway, 16th Floor
New York, NY 10004
212-908-7700

Howard Sterling, Mng. Dir./Corp. Fin.
Faith Griffith, Dir./Corp. Fin.
Gary Griffith, Corp. Fin.

FCS Industries, Inc.*
Markets system for diagnosis and treatment
of allergies
March 1984
$3.70 million underwritten
$370,000 fee
$2 per share
$(.09) loss per share last year

**I.I.S. Intelligent Information Systems
Limited.***
Designs computer peripheral equipment for
use with compatible computer
November 1984
$4.16 million underwritten
$396,000 fee
$4.62 per share
$.33 earnings per share for the six months
ended 6/30/84

**Insituform Group Limited—
Channel Islands***
Owns the licensing rights to a pipeline
rehabilitation system
April 1985
$3.95 million underwritten
$376,000 fee
$4.20 per unit
$.36 earnings per share last year

International Record Carrier Inc.*
Provides international telecommunications
service
January 1984
$3.50 million underwritten
$350,000 fee
$5 per share
$.01 earnings per share last year

Perceptronics, Inc.*
Develops systems for training, simulation
and command support
June 1985
$2.80 million underwritten
$240,000 fee
$7 per share
$(.70) loss per share last year

**Rada Electronic Industries Limited—
Israel***
Supplies military equipment to Israeli
Ministry of Defense
April 1985
$5.00 million underwritten
$500,000 fee
$2.50 per unit
$.13 earnings per share for the nine months
ended 12/31/84

A.J. Ross Logistics, Inc.*
Provides storage and transportation for
structural steel
July 1985
$2.80 million underwritten
$280,000 fee
$2 per unit
$.06 earnings per share last year

Saratoga Standardbreds, Incorporated*
Horse management, breeding, boarding
and sales
September 1984
$3.00 million underwritten
$300,000 fee
$2.50 per share
$.03 earnings per share last year

Thermwood Corporation*
Manufactures industrial robots for spray
painting and material applications
April 1984
$4.65 million underwritten
$465,000 fee
$7.50 per unit
$(1.10) loss per share last year

Trio-Tech International*
Markets environmental test equipment for
ceramic pack of semiconductors
December 1984
$4.55 million underwritten
$364,000 fee
$6.50 per share
$1.10 earnings per share last year

Voicemail International, Inc.*
Manufactures computerized voice systems
for phone messages
May 1984
$4.50 million underwritten
$450,000 fee
$5 per unit
$(1.58) loss per share last year

ROSENKRANTZ EHRENKRANTZ
LYON & ROSS
Six East 43rd Street
New York, NY 10017
212-986-6700

Lester Rosenkrantz, Pres.

Sonex Research, Inc.*
Develops technology to control fuel
combustion in engines
April 1985
$2.50 million underwritten
$250,000 fee
$5 per unit
$(.68) loss per share last year

ROTAN MOSLE INC.
1500 South Tower
Pennzoil Place
Houston, TX 77002
713-236-3000

R. John Stanton, Jr., Pres./Corp. Fin.

Scott Cable Communications, Inc.
Owns and operates cable television systems
September 1985
$6.60 million underwritten
$528,000 fee
$8.25 per share
$.98 earnings per share last year

ROTHSCHILD INC.
One Rockefeller Plaza
New York, NY 10020
212-757-6000

Wilbur L. Ross, Jr., Mgn, Dir./Corp. Fin.

The Fur Vault Inc.*
Retails and distributes luxury fur apparel
August 1984
$13.2 million underwritten
$924,000 fee
$11 per share
$1.21 pro forma earnings per share last year

L.F. ROTHSCHILD, UNTERBERG, TOWBIN
55 Water Street
New York, NY 10041
212-425-3300

Thomas I. Unterberg, Chm.
A. Robert Towbin, Vice Chm.
Thomas A. Trantum, Corp. Fin.

Amistar Corporation
Equipment for inserting electronic
  components into printed circuit boards
May 1984
$7.5 million underwritten
$520,000 fee
$7.50 per share
$.60 earnings per share last year

Autodesk, Inc.*
Develops CAD and drafting software for
  desktop computers
June 1985
$15.40 million underwritten
$1.12 million fee
$11 per share
$.30 earnings per share last year

Centrafarm Group nv—Holland
Markets generic and branded
  pharmaceuticals
January 1985
$6.75 million underwritten
$475,000 fee
$6.75 per share
$.35 earnings per share for the nine months
  ended 9/30/84

DH Technology, Inc.*
Manufactures high performance dot matrix
  print heads
May 1984
$9.11 million underwritten
$675,000 fee
$6.75 per share
$.61 earnings per share last year

Invacare Corporation
Manufactures a line of medical equipment
  for the home health care market
May 1984
$20.90 million underwritten
$1.463 million fee
$11 per share
$.69 earnings per share last year

Nichols Institute*
Manufactures biomedical products
May 1985
$8.25 million underwritten
$618,750 fee
$6 per share
$.30 earnings per share for the year
  ended 11/30/84

PDA Engineering*
Develops software for mechanical computer-
  aided engineering (CAE)
January 1985
$7.25 million underwritten
$520,000 fee
$7.25 per share
$.25 earnings per share last year

Software Publishing Corporation
Markets packaged software for business
  professionals
November 1984
$11.21 million underwritten
$800,000 fee
$7 per share
$.69 earnings per share last year

Stereo Village, Inc.*
Retails home entertainment and consumer
  electronics
June 1985
$11.67 million underwritten
$755,480 fee
$10.50 per share
$.76 earnings per share last year

Thermedics Inc.
Markets a family of biomedical-grade plastics
May 1985
$4.69 million underwritten
$281,250 fee
$12.50 per share
$(.09) loss per share last year

Wyse Technology
Manufactures video display terminal
  workstations
October 1984
$12.67 million underwritten
$905,000 fee
$7 per share
$.30 earnings per share last year

Zeta Laboratories, Inc.
Manufactures microwave components for
  defense and aerospace
April 1985
$5.22 million underwritten
$392,450 fee
$6.25 per share
$.35 earnings per share last year

SALOMON BROTHERS INC.
One New York Plaza
New York, NY 10004
212-747-7000

Richard V. Schmeelk, Mgr./Corp. Fin.

Harris Graphics Corporation*
Manufactures printing and publishing
  equipment
October 1984
$42.00 million underwritten
$2.94 million fee
$14 per share
$1.95 earnings per share for the year
  ending 6/30/84

MTV Networks Inc.*
Operates two channels of cable television
  programming—MTV and Nickelodeon
August 1984
$76.88 million underwritten
$5.381 million fee
$15 per share
$(1.25) pro forma loss per share last year

Safeguard Health Enterprises, Inc.
Operates the largest capitated dental care
  plan in CA
July 1984
$21.25 million underwritten
$1.36 million fee
$12.50 per share
$.32 earnings per share last year

Telco Systems, Inc.
Voice and fiber optics transmission systems
February 1984
$11.0 million underwritten
$770,000 fee
$11 per share
$(.30) loss per share last year

SAN DIEGO SECURITIES INCORPORATED
1200 3rd Avenue, #910
San Diego, CA 92101
714-233-4721

Peter Korn, Corp. Fin.

Vortec Corporation*
Rents and sells home health care items and
  industrial products
June 1985
$4.95 million underwritten
$383,625 fee
$9 per share
$.66 earnings per share last year

SCHNEIDER, BERNET & HICKMAN, INC.
2400 InterFirst Two
Dallas, TX 75270
214-761-5100

John R. Muse, Sr. V.P./Corp. Fin.
Peter Gerard, Sr. V.P./Corp. Fin.

Advanced Tobacco Products, Inc.*
Developed smokeless tobacco product
May 1984
$8.13 million underwritten
$690,625 fee
$6.50 per unit
$(.04) loss per share last year

Clear Channel Communications, Inc.*
Operates FM and AM radio stations
April 1984
$7.5 million underwritten
$562,500 fee
$10 per share
$1.01 earnings per share last year

J. HENRY SCHRODER CORP.
One State Street
New York, NY 10004
212-269-6500

Jeffrey J. Collinson, Chm.

DNA Plant Technology Corp.*
Develops improved varieties of crop,
  industrial and consumer products
January 1984
$12.65 million underwritten
$968,000 fee
$5.75 per unit
$(.04) loss per share last year

SCOTT & STRINGFELLOW, INC.
Mutual Building
Richmond, VA 23219
804-643-1811

Jeffrey D. Levine, Corp. Fin.

Ross Industries, Inc.*
Manufactures machines for use in the food
  processing industry
December 1984
$3.94 million underwritten
$334,688 fee
$8.75 per share
$.98 earnings per share last year

SEIDLER AMDEC SECURITIES INC.
515 South Figueroa Street
Los Angeles, CA 90071
213-624-4232

Bruce P. Emmeluth, Sr. V.P./Corp. Fin.
James E. Moore, V.P./Corp. Fin.
Robert Campbell, Corp. Fin.

Comarco, Inc.
Provides technical and engineering support
  to the U.S. military
April 1985
$10.00 million underwritten
$500,000 fee
$17.25 per unit
$.86 earnings per share last year

SHEARSON/AMERICAN EXPRESS INC.
Two World Trade Center
New York, NY 10048
212-577-2845

Albert C. Bellas, Sr. Exec. V.P./Inv. Bkg.
Leonard A. Miller, Exec. V.P./Inv. Bkg.

MTV Networks Inc.*
Operates two channels of cable television
  programming—MTV and Nickelodeon.
August 1984
$76.88 million underwritten
$5.38 million fee
$15 per share
$(1.25) pro forma loss per share last year

Star Technologies, Inc.
Manufactures high performance scientific
  computer systems
December 1984
$19.80 million underwritten
$1.69 million fee
$9 per share
$(.77) loss per share last year

Thor Industries, Inc.
Produces travel trailers and motor homes
  through subsidiaries
January 1984
$8.80 million underwritten
$616,000 fee
$11 per share
$1.26 earnings per share last year

J.E. SHEEHAN & COMPANY, INC.
711 Fifth Avenue
New York, NY 10022
212-888-9020

Joseph E. Sheehan, Pres.
Dominique Bodvin, V.P.

Telecalc, Inc.*
Designs computer-based information
  systems for phone management
August 1985
$2.55 million underwritten
$255,000 fee
$6 per share
$(.32) loss per share last year

SHERWOOD SECURITIES CORP.
30 Montgomery Street
Jersey City, NJ 07302
201-332-8881

Raymond Meselsohn, Pres./Corp. Fin.
Lynn McCarthy, Sr. V.P./Corp. Fin.

Charvoz-Carsen Corporation
Distributes photographic, audio, scientific
  and engineering equipment
March 1984
$3.92 million underwritten
$352,687 fee
$7.13 per share
$1.06 earnings per share last year

Healthcare Affiliates, Inc.*
Provides services to computer supported
  medical imaging centers
June 1984
$3.50 million underwritten
$350,000 fee
$7 per unit
$(.25) loss per share 8/6/82 (inception)
  to 7/31/83

Zytrex Corporation*
Developing a proprietary CMOS process to
  manufacture logic and memory circuits
June 1984
$5.60 million underwritten
$499,500 fee
$9.25 per unit
$.34 loss per share last year

SHOENBERG, HIEBER INC.
Reade Street Plaza
66 Reade Street
New York, NY 10007
212-962-3800

Alfred Schoenberg, Chm., V.P. & Treas.
William G. Hieber, Jr., Pres.
Marilyn S. Wells, Secy.

Corporate Data Sciences, Inc.*
Manufactures a computer graphics and text
processing terminal
March 1984
$6.25 million underwritten
$625,000 fee
$6.25 per unit
$(.16) loss per share last year

Marcom Telecommunications, Inc.*
Sells electronic and private branch exchange
phone systems
May 1985
$2.03 million underwritten
$203,125 fee
$3.12 per unit
$.26 earnings per share last year

I.M. SIMON & CO., INC.
7730 Forsyth Boulevard
St. Louis, MO 63105
314-862-8800

James W. Byrne, Mgr. Syn.

Toys Plus, Inc.*
Operates chain of toy stores in S.W.
United States
April 1984
$2.88 million underwritten
$287,500 fee
$5.75 per share
$.19 earnings per share last year

SMITH BARNEY, HARRIS UPHAM
& CO. INCORPORATED
1345 Avenue of the Americas
New York, NY 10105
212-399-6000

J. Perry Ruddick, Exec. V.P. & Dir./Corp. Fin.

Clear Channel Communications, Inc.*
Operates four FM and three AM radio
stations in TX and OK
April 1984
$7.50 million underwritten
$562,500 fee
$10 per share
$1.01 earnings per share last year

Nanometrics Incorporated*
Manufactures automated microscope
measurement systems
November 1984
$8.53 million underwritten
$638,000 fee
$7.75 per share
$.32 earnings per share for the year
ended 12/31/83

Open Air Markets, Inc.
Operates supermarkets and convenience
stores
September 1985
$14.30 million underwritten
$1.07 million fee
$11 per share
$.88 earnings per share last year

XL/Datacomp, Inc.
Sells and distributes mid-range IBM
computer systems and peripherals
March 1985
$20.02 million underwritten
$1.4 million fee
$15 per share
$.86 earnings per share last year

Xidex Magnetics Corporation*
Supplies premium quality, high density,
flexible magnetic disks
March 1984
$12.75 million underwritten
$897,600 fee
$12.50 per share
$(.03) loss per share last year

SPECTRUM SECURITIES, INC.
300 Main Street, 3rd Floor
Cincinnati, OH 45202
513-241-6443

Mercer Reynolds, Chm. & CEO
Alan Gribbins, Exec. V.P.
John H. White, Secy. & Treas.

Health Images, Inc.*
Operates magnetic resonance imaging
medical diagnostic clinics
July 1985
$5.53 million underwritten
$552,859 fee
$2 per share
$(.03) loss per share last year

STARR SECURITIES, INC.
19 Rector Street
New York, NY 10006
212-509-5445

Martin Vegh, Pres.
Robert Fagenson, Mgr./Corp. Fin.

Animed Inc. (formerly Cardio Pet, Inc.)*
Provides electrocardiograph services to
veterinarians
March 1984
$3.00 million underwritten
$300,000 fee
$5 per share
$.07 earnings per share last year

Business Computer Network, Inc.*
Applications software for microcomputers
July 1984
$4.8 million underwritten
$6 per unit
$(.14) loss per share for the three months
ended 2/29/84

Carolyn Bean Publishing, Ltd.*
Publishes and markets a line of
contemporary greeting cards
July 1985
$3.78 million underwritten
$510,300 fee
$6 per share
$(.22) loss per share last year

Qmax Technology Group, Inc.*
Manufactures liquid crystal and
microencapsulation products for heat
measurement
November 1985
$3.10 million underwritten
$310,000 fee
$5 per share
$(.28) loss per share last year

R.J. STEICHEN & CO., INC.
1414 First Bank Place, W.
Minneapolis, MN 55402
612-341-6200

John D. Steichen, Pres.
Jack E. Feltl, V.P.
Joan C. Niedfeldt, V.P.

Digigraphic Systems Corporation*
Develops computer-based information
systems, software and components
January 1984
$5.63 million underwritten
$562,500 fee
$2.25 per share
$(.32) loss per share 9/25/81 (inception)
to 9/30/82

VICOM, Incorporated
Private commercial telephone systems
June 1984
$1.25 million underwritten
$125,000 fee
$2.50 per share
$.33 earnings per share last year

STEINBERG & LYMAN
1250 Broadway
New York, NY 10001
212-714-1470

Wallace H. Steinberg, Chm. & CEO
Richard P. Lyman, Pres. & COO

Bucknell Industries Incorporated*
A commercial printer of catalogs, brochures
and advertising literature
May 1985
$2.50 million underwritten
$250,000 fee
$6.25 per share
$(.24) loss per share last year

Circle Fine Art Corporation*
Wholesales and retails fine art and
art objects
April 1985
$2.55 million underwritten
$255,000 fee
$3 per share
$.19 earnings per share last year

Computer Telephone Corp.*
Designs communications systems using
phones and microprocessors
May 1985
$3.60 million underwritten
$360,250 fee
$5.50 per share
$.15 earnings per share last year

Control Resource Industries, Inc.*
Develops air filtration and asbestos control
systems
August 1985
$3.25 million underwritten
$325,000 fee
$5 per share
$.19 earnings per share last year

Perle Systems Limited—Canada*
Manufactures data communications control
hardware and software
April 1985
$3.60 million underwritten
$360,000 fee
$6 per share
$.20 earnings per share for the six months
ended 11/30/84

STEPHENS INC.
Stephens Building
114 East Capitol Avenue
Little Rock, AR 72201
501-374-4361

Jon E.M. Jacoby, V.P./Corp. Fin.
Mike Smith, V.P./Synd.

Institute of Clinical Pharmacology, PLC*
Test pharmaceuticals for European,
American and Japanese companies
November 1984
$7.75 million underwritten
$660,000 fee
$7.75 per share
$.31 earnings per share last year

Scheduled Skyways, Inc.*
Regional airline serving southern and
southwestern United States
April 1984
$2.60 million underwritten
$240,000 fee
$6.50 per share
$1.10 earnings per share last year

United Tote, Inc.*
Manufactures wagering systems
August 1984
$7.2 million underwritten
$558,000 fee
$12 per share
$.87 earnings per share last year

STIRES AND COMPANY INC.
130 E. 40th Streett
New York, NY 10016
212-696-9400

Sidney Stires, Pres.
Thomas Cloney, Exec, V.P.
Patricia Sheeria, V.P. & Secy.

American Mobile Systems Incorporated*
Operates Specialized Mobile Radio Service
systems
January 1985
$3.15 million underwritten
$315,000 fee
$4.50 per unit
$(.82) loss per share last year

SUMMIT INVESTMENT
CORPORATION
500 International Center
900 2nd Avenue S.
Minneapolis, MN 55402
612-338-1400

G. James Spinner, Pres. & Treas.

Discus Corporation*
Operates Fuddrucker's hamburger
restaurants in MN and WI
August 1985
$3.04 million underwritten
$304,000 fee
$4 per share
$(.33) loss per share last year

Infinite Graphics Incorporated*
Custom computer graphics
September 1984
$3.68 million underwritten
$368,000 fee
$5.75 per share
$.04 earnings per share last year

SUTRO & CO. INCORPORATED
201 California Street
San Francisco, CA 94111
415-455-8500

Thomas E. Bertelsen, Jr., Exec. V.P. &
Dir./Corp. Fin.

Expeditors International of Washington*
International airfreight
September 1984
$6.75 million underwritten
$540,000 fee
$9 per share
$.33 earnings per share last year

ICEE-USA*
Produces and markets a semi-frozen
carbonated beverage
January 1985
$5.60 million underwritten
$480,000 fee
$7.00 per share
$0.45 earnings per share last year

McGrath Rent Corp.*
Rents and sells relocatable modular offices
November 1984
$4.50 million underwritten
$360,000 fee
$6 per share
$.28 earnings per share last year

SWARTWOOD, HESSE INC.
21 West Street
New York, NY 10006
212-742-8900

T. Marshall Swartwood, Pres.
Richard Moyer, Corp. Fin.

Barrier Science & Technology, Inc.*
Manufactures cleaning, sanitizing and
 maintenance chemical products
August 1984
$1.38 million underwritten
$137,500 fee
$5 per unit
$.05 earnings per share last year

Dimis, Inc.*
Markets DIMIS 3000, a proprietary computer
 software package
July 1985
$1.40 million underwritten
$140,000 fee
$4 per unit
$(1.13) loss per share last year

GBI International Industries, Inc.*
Developed a patented tooling attachment,
 the "Superfinisher"
May 1985
$1.69 million underwritten
$169,000 fee
$1.30 per unit
$(.11) loss per share last year

Preco, Inc.*
Develops precoated microscope slides and
 diagnostic test kits
January 1984
$2.25 million underwritten
$225,000 fee
$5 per unit
$(.15) loss per share 5/27/82 (inception)
 to 4/30/83

SWERGOLD, CHEFITZ &
SINSABAUGH, INC.
110 Wall Street
New York, NY 10005
212-612-1300

Henrietta DeVeer, Corp. Fin.

Elan Corporation, plc*
Researches and develops drug delivery
 systems
January 1984
$13.20 million underwritten
$924,000 fee
$12 per share
$.10 earnings per share last year

Laser Industries Limited
Manufactures opthalmic sugical laser
 systems
September 1985
$13.20 million underwritten
$900,000 fee
$11 per share
$.26 earnings per share last year

THOMSON MCKINNON
SECURITIES INC.
One New York Plaza
New York, NY 10011
212-482-7000

David B. Hiley, Exec. V.P./Inv. Bkg.

Excel Industries, Inc.*
Manufactures metal framed windows
 for trucks
April 1984
$7.20 million underwritten
$520,000 fee
$9 per share
$1.39 earnings per share last year

TRIPP & CO., INC.
40 Rector Street
New York, NY 10006
212-608-6081

Donald L. Carman, Pres.
David Thomas Fettes, Exec. V.P.

Medco Group Incorporated*
Markets hand-held instruments to surgeons,
 dentists and veterinarians
September 1984
$2.50 million underwritten
$250,000 fee
$100 per unit
$(.07) loss per share last year

TUCKER, ANTHONY & R.L. DAY, INC.
120 Broadway
New York, NY 10271
212-618-7400

Kenneth D. Mann, Jr., Dir./Inv. Bkg.
V. Lee Archer, Mgn. Dir./Corp. Fin.

Lo-Jack Corporation*
Developing a system to locate and recover
 stolen vehicles
August 1985
$4.16 million underwritten
$415,625 fee
$4.75 per share
$(.16) loss per share last year

Stuarts Department Stores, Inc.*
Operates self service discount department
 stores in MA and NH
June 1984
$7.50 million underwritten
$570,000 fee
$7.50 per share
$.31 earnings per share 10/8/83 (inception)
 to 1/28/84

UNDERWOOD, NEUHAUS & CO., INC.
724 Travis Street at Rusk Avenue
Houston, TX 77002
713-221-2200

Robert S. Moore, Sr. V.P./Corp. Fin.

Reliability Incorporated
Manufactures integrated circuit testing
 equipment
May 1984
$4.94 million underwritten
$390,000 fee
$9.88 per share
$.29 earnings per share last year

VAN KASPER & COMPANY
50 California Street #2350
San Francisco, CA 94111
415-391-5600

F. Van Kasper, Pres.
Bernard Goldsmith, V.P. & Dir./Corp. Fin.

American Emergicenter, Inc.*
Manages freestanding walk-in
 medical centers
January 1984
$1.80 million underwritten
$148,000 fee
$9 per unit
$(.48) loss per share last year

Collins Industries, Inc.*
Manufactures specialty vehicles-ambulances,
 limosines, hearses etc.
November 1984
$11.96 million underwritten
$810,000 fee
$997 per unit
$.31 earnings per share last year

Computer Synergy, Inc.*
Markets integrated computer systems for
 acute care hospitals
April 1984
$3.23 million underwritten
$296,700 fee
$5 per share
$.18 earnings per share last year

Sunworld International Airways, Inc.*
A passenger airline serving seven Western
   U.S. cities
June 1985
$7.75 million underwritten
$680,000 fee
$7.75 per share
$(.28) loss per share last year

D.H. WALLACH INC.
1700 Market Street
Philadelphia, PA 19103
215-864-7850

D.H. Wallach, V.P./Corp Fin.

Computerized Buying Network, Inc.*
Operates buying service through database
   that provides price quotes
April 1984
$2.50 million underwritten
$250,000 fee
$2 per unit
$(.31) loss per share last year

Hosposable Products, Inc.*
Manufactures disposable bed pads to guard
   linens from incontinent soil
February 1985
$2.00 million underwritten
$200,000 fee
$5 per unit
$.12 earnings per share last year

WEAVER JOHNSON AND CO. INC.
56 Beaver Street
New York, NY 10004
212-344-5404

Mark G. Ross, Chm.
Robert T. Samila, Pres.

Solar Age Industries, Inc.*
Manufactures solar space and hot water
   heating systems
August 1985
$1.24 million underwritten
$123,750 fee
$1.50 per unit
$.07 earnings per share last year

**WEBER, HALL, SALE &
   ASSOCIATES, INC.**
1800 LTV Tower Building
Dallas, TX 75201
214-954-9472

Garry A. Weber, Chm.
Wallace L. Hall, Pres.
Terry D. Rader, Exec. V.P. & CEO

Bar/Code, Inc.*
Manufactures devices that read bar codes
April 1985
$4.00 million underwritten
$375,000 fee
$1 per share
$(.22) loss per share for the year
   ended 8/31/84

Cable Advertising Systems, Inc.*
Provides T.V. spots to advertisers served by
   cable systems
October 1984
$3.00 million underwritten
$270,000 fee
$1 per share
$(.09) loss per share last year

International Film Productions, Inc.*
Produces television programs and
   feature films
November 1984
$1.10 million underwritten
$1.1 million fee
$5 per unit
$(.51) loss per share last year

Intertrans Corporation*
Provides international transportation services
February 1984
$6.00 million underwritten
$540,000 fee
$6 per share
$.40 earnings per share last year

Satellite Music Network, Inc.*
Satellite transmission of stereo radio
   programming
June 1984
$4.00 million underwritten
$320,000 fee
$4 per unit
$(.59) loss per share last year

Scientific Measurement Systems, Inc.*
Develops computerized tomographic systems
   for government and industry
March 1985
$4.00 million underwritten
$360,000 fee
$1 per share
$(.01) loss per share last year

Shoppers World Stores, Inc.*
Operates retail discount department stores
July 1984
$2.44 million underwritten
$180,000 fee
$3.25 per share
$.60 earnings per share last year

WEDBUSH, NOBLE, COOKE, INC.
615 South Flower Street
Los Angeles, CA 90017
213-620-1750

Donald Royce, Jr., Sr. V.P./Corp. Fin.

Cybertek Computer Products, Inc.*
Supplies proprietary applications software
   and data processing to life insurance
August 1984
$5.25 million underwritten
$448,000 fee
$7.50 per share
$.46 earnings per share last year

U.S. Medical Enterprises, Inc.*
Network of industrial medical centers
June 1984
$8.75 million underwritten
$765,625 fee
$8.75 per share
$.41 pro forma earnings per share last year

L.C. WEGARD & CO., INC.
Highway 130 and Levitt Parkway
Willingboro, NJ 08046
609-877-3100

Victor L. Wegard, Pres.

Haganah Ltd. — Israel*
Develops technologies re: Israeli
   weapons systems
August 1984
$2.50 million underwritten
$250,000 fee
$5 per unit
$.00 earnings per share last year

Pathfinder Computer Centers Corp.*
Operates a chain of four retail computer
   centers
November 1984
$1.00 million underwritten
$100,000 fee
$1 per unit
$(.28) loss per share last year

WERBEL-ROTH SECURITIES, INC.
5560 West Oakland Park Boulevard
Fort Lauderdale, FL 33313
305-486-1500

Howard H. Roth, Pres.

Occupational-Urgent Care Health Systems, Inc.*
Manages medical centers serving industrial and commercial clients
June 1984
$1.95 million underwritten
$195,000 fee
$3 per unit
$(.01) loss per share last year

Warner Computer Systems, Inc.*
Provides computer services to brokers, banks and insurance companies
February 1984
$1.70 million underwritten
$170,000 fee
$1 per share
$.01 earnings per share last year

WHALE SECURITIES CORP.
650 Fifth Avenue
New York, NY 10019
212-397-2250

William Walters, Chm.

Color Systems Technology, Inc.*
Electronically converts black-and-white film to color videotape
August 1985
$4.00 million underwritten
$400,000 fee
$5 per share
$(.39) loss per share last year

Great Western Systems, Inc.*
Operates used auto public auctions for its own and others' accounts
August 1984
$2.52 million underwritten
$252,000 fee
$6 per unit
$.03 earnings per share last year

Howtek, Inc.*
Develops black, white and color ink jet printers and copiers
December 1984
$6.25 million underwritten
$625,000 fee
$5 per share
$(.21) loss per share for 2/24/84 (inception) to 8/31/84

International Container Systems, Inc.*
Sells Port-A-Pet molded cases for soft drink bottles
June 1985
$3.00 million underwritten
$300,000 fee
$5 per share
$.27 earnings per share last year

Lasermed Corp.*
Develops medical laser instruments
February 1984
$2.50 million underwritten
$250,000 fee
$5 per share
$.59 earnings per share 1/1/83 (inception) to 9/30/83

WHEAT, FIRST SECURITIES, INC.
707 East Main Street
Richmond, VA 23219
804-649-2311

John L. McElroy, Jr., Exec. V.P./Corp. Fin.

Open Air Markets, Inc.
Operates supermarkets and convenience stores
September 1985
$14.30 million underwritten
$1.07 million fee
$11 per share
$.88 earnings per share last year

The Peanut Shack of America, Inc.*
Franchises specialty retail food stores in U.S. shopping malls
August 1985
$4.31 million underwritten
$344,702 fee
$8 per share
$.32 earnings per share last year

Wiland Services, Incorporated*
Provides data processing to direct mail marketers
August 1984
$5.31 million underwritten
$425,000 fee
$6.25 per share
$.27 earnings per share last year

T.R. WINSTON & COMPANY, INC.
100 Menlo Park
Edison, NJ 08837
201-549-6311

Richard C. Novack, Principal

Edudata Corporation*
Provides education in PC use, markets software and provides consulting
July 1984
$2.50 million underwritten
$250,000 fee
$5 per share
$(.08) loss per share for the nine months ended 4/30/84

DEAN WITTER REYNOLDS INC.
130 Liberty Street
New York, NY 10006
212-524-2222

Robert M. Gardiner, Chm. & CEO
Philip J. Purcell, Pres.

AlternaCare Corp.*
Operates day-surgical outpatient centers
July 1984
$8.78 million underwritten
$721,500 fee
$6.75 per share
$.06 earnings per share for the three months ended 3/31/84

Columbia Data Products, Inc.*
Manufactures 16-bit IBM compatible personal computers
January 1984
$12.10 million underwritten
$869,000 fee
$11 per share
$.10 earnings per share for the 39 weeks ended 10/3/83

HMO America Inc.
Operates health maintenance organizations in metropolitan Chicago
June 1985
$7.35 million underwritten
$588,000 fee
$12 per share
$.47 earnings per share last year

MMI Medical, Inc.*
Diagnostic imaging services utilizing mobile sophisticated equipment
July 1984
$5.60 million underwritten
$476,000 fee
$8 per share
$.61 earnings per share last year

River Oaks Industries, Inc.
Manufactures mobile homes
January 1984
$10.8 million underwritten
$810,000 fee
$6 per share
$.19 earnings per share last year

Sierra Health Services, Inc.*
Owns a health maintenance organization
  in Nevada
April 1985
$18.75 million underwritten
$1.395 million fee
$12 per share
$.20 earnings per share last year

Stockholder Systems, Inc.*
Markets financial applications software for
  IBM and compatible mainframes
February 1984
$8.55 million underwritten
$646,800 fee
$9 per share
$.33 earnings per share last year

F.N. WOLF & CO., INC.
110 Wall Street
New York, NY 10005
212-635-5666

Franklin N. Wolf, Pres.

Birdfinder Corp.*
Cable television programming services
February 1984
$3.6 million underwritten
$360,000 fee
$4 per unit
$(.09) loss per share last year

Dental Management Services, Inc.*
Establishes dental centers
January 1984
$3.0 million underwritten
$300,000 fee
$6 per unit
$(.30) loss per share last year

Inland Vacuum Industries, Inc.*
Manufactures specialized hydrocarbon fluids
August 1985
$3.00 million underwritten
$300,000 fee
$4 per share
$.34 earnings per share last year

Medco Research Inc.*
Manages drug clinical studies for
  pharmaceutical companies
November 1984
$2.50 million underwritten
$250,000 fee
$1.67 per unit
$(.18) loss per share last year

Ovex Fertility Corporation*
Provides diagnostic and therapeutic infertility
  services
July 1985
$2.59 million underwritten
$258,750 fee
$4 per share
$.24 earnings per share last year

WOODMERE SECURITIES, INC.
1215 Station Plaza
Hewlett, NY 11557
516-374-5050

Richard A. Kahn, Pres.
Malcolm W. Basner, Exec. V.P./Treas.

Infotech Management, Inc.*
Provides computer-assisted services to the
  real estate industry
March 1984
$1.60 million underwritten
$160,000 fee
$2 per unit
$.03 earnings per share last year

**WILLIAM K. WOODRUFF &
  COMPANY, INC.**
7557 Rambler Road, #112
Dallas, TX 75231
214-987-2990

William K. Woodruff, III, Pres.
Joel K. Wittenbraker, V.P.

Irvine Sensors Corporation*
Engaged in R&D of infrared detection
  devices
June 1984
$2.00 million underwritten
$185,000 fee
$2 per share
$(.46) loss per share last year

Scientific Communications, Inc.*
Manufactures electronic radar
  reconnaissance receiving equipment
October 1984
$6.38 million underwritten
$510,000 fee
$8.50 per share
$.91 earnings per share last year

HERBERT YOUNG SECURITIES, INC.
98 Cuttermill Road
Great Neck, NY 11021
516-487-8300

Herbert D. Levine, Pres.

DocuGraphix, Inc.*
Developing a turnkey CAD document
  management system
July 1985
$3.45 million underwritten
$345,000 fee
$5.75 per unit
$(.33) loss per share last year

MacroChem Corporation*
Develops pharmaceuticals, drug delivery
  systems and industrial chemicals
February 1985
$3.60 million underwritten
$360,000 fee
$3 per unit
$(.01) loss per share last year

YOUNG, SMITH & PEACOCK, INC.
Financial Center
3443 North Central Avenue
Phoenix, AZ 85012
602-264-9241

Barry W. Peacock, Co-Chm. & Treas.
H. Holden Smith, Co-Chm., Exec. V.P.
  & Secy.

Inertia Dynamics Corp.*
Manufactures grass and weed trimmers
February 1984
$2.55 million underwritten
$237,000 fee
$8.50 per share
$.93 earnings per share last year

INDEX OF OFFERINGS 1982

	Companies With Net Worth Of $5 Million or Less		Companies With Net Worth Of $10 Million or Less	
	Number of Issues	*Dollars Underwritten (millions)*	*Number of Issues*	*Dollars Underwritten (millions)*
January	6	$ 24.68	10	$ 56.14
February	6	16.71	7	31.01
March	7	35.02	7	35.02
April	9	46.96	11	66.62
May	10	34.28	15	68.85
June	8	39.04	11	52.54
July	9	40.10	9	40.10
August	6	56.21	7	60.21
September	8	51.30	8	51.30
October	10	80.49	14	160.89
November	10	50.64	15	157.77
December	24	143.28	40	352.18
	113	$ 618.71	154	$1,132.63

INDEX OF OFFERINGS 1983

	Companies With Net Worth Of $5 Million or Less		Companies With Net Worth Of $10 Million or Less	
	Number of Issues	*Dollars Underwritten (millions)*	*Number of Issues*	*Dollars Underwritten (millions)*
January	14	$ 105.70	19	$ 163.38
February	16	175.61	26	345.06
March	28	220.93	42	431.71
April	26	215.01	29	267.73
May	37	268.38	42	348.79
June	50	585.47	68	931.90
July	59	549.37	75	771.94
August	50	430.78	64	678.51
September	45	254.51	56	395.81
October	38	208.16	53	467.42
November	46	264.99	57	383.19
December	68	392.48	80	554.83
	477	$3,671.39	611	$5,740.27

INDEX OF OFFERINGS 1984

	Companies With Net Worth Of $5 Million or Less		Companies With Net Worth Of $10 Million or Less	
	Number of Issues	Dollars Underwritten (millions)	Number of Issues	Dollars Underwritten (millions)
January	34	$ 234.15	43	$ 353.21
February	22	119.44	24	146.57
March	23	111.38	27	141.19
April	18	75.87	19	88.63
May	20	101.38	23	134.72
June	14	58.73	16	96.36
July	18	72.35	20	109.55
August	19	165.60	22	187.57
September	12	65.72	16	109.97
October	12	41.66	16	79.52
November	18	85.85	24	149.50
December	14	54.22	16	86.52
	224	$1,186.35	266	$1,683.31

INDEX OF OFFERINGS 1985

	Companies With Net Worth Of $5 Million or Less		Companies With Net Worth Of $10 Million or Less	
	Number of Issues	Dollars Underwritten (millions)	Number of Issues	Dollars Underwritten (millions)
January	13	$ 65.21	15	$ 88.15
February	11	51.74	12	59.24
March	13	76.46	16	109.24
April	17	94.23	24	204.60
May	15	96.06	18	141.05
June	15	85.68	25	228.42
July	20	114.48	25	195.04
August	18	92.19	21	124.66
September	9	39.00	17	123.29
October	28	216.70	35	300.20
November	27	236.46	31	236.46
December	23	152.08	25	177.33
	209	$1,320.29	264	$1,987.68

Company Index for Venture Capital Firms

Name Index for Venture Capital Firms

Atchie, Barbara, 623
Atkinson, Frank R., 204
Atkinson, Jeffrey C., 391
Augustus, Albert A., 510
Ault, Bromwell, 494
Aust, Michael J., 509
Austin, S.W., 586
Avery, Thomas A., 379
Avery, C. Stevens, II, 296
Avis, Gregory M., 379
Ayers, Brad C., 262

B

Bab, Donald Stuart, 420, 465
Babcock, Warner K., 272
Bachrach, Hillel, 598
Baer, Arthur Bugs, 425
Bagley, Taffy D., 581
Bailey, Mark, 213
Baird, Richard L., 348
Baker, Eric E., 634
Baker, John C., 474
Baker, Nathaniel B., 542
Baker, Philip G., 413
Baker, G. Leonard, Jr., 246
Balderston, James C., 229
Baldini, Daniel, 367
Ball, Debra A., 387
Ball, James R., 587
Ballantine, Paul J., 370
Ballantyne, Thomas A., 369
Balletto, John G., 202
Balzuweit, Herbert F., 278
Bamber, Frederick B., 352
Bangser, Andrew C., 276, 365
Bank, Raymond L., 224, 345
Banks, Barton M., 524
Banks, Stephen J., 204, 529
Bannon, Richard, 507
Barak, Philip E., 471
Barash, Irvin, 493
Barber, Gregory P., 543
Barber, Sandra P., 302
Barnes, Stanton J., 595
Barnett, Howard G., Jr., 516
Barnette, Fred A., Jr., 399
Barnum, William M., 177
Barnum, George G., Jr., 400
Barrett, Michael J., 323
Barrett, Robert G., 354
Barron, Thomas A., 243, 477, 487
Barrows, Timothy A., 215, 371
Barry, Martha A., 513
Barry, Roger J., 189
Barry, Thomas R., 308
Barth, Eugene F., 209
Bartlett, Thomas, 567
Bartlett, James L., III, 174, 436
Bartol, John G., 163
Barton, Arthur C., 544
Barton, Thomas U., 555
Bass, Mary D., 551
Basse, Marvin V., 331
Batterson, Leonard A., 311
Baty, Gordon B., 386, 540

Batza, Michael J., Jr., 345
Bauer, Dr. Charles A., 200
Bauman, William W., 164
Baumgartner, Walter F., 241
Bawlf, Charles W., 616
Baxter, James G., 534
Bay, Gerald B., 287
Bay, William, 597
Bayless, Jon W., 242, 486, 573
Bays, David A., 164
Bêique, Jean, 636
Beach, Murray M., 382
Beane, Donald, 350
Beaubien, J. Luc, 351
Beauchamp, Marc, 636
Beaurline, Andrew, 322
Beberman, Richard, 467
Bechmann, Mary C., 198, 276
Bechtold, Merle, 180
Beckett, William P., 601
Beecroft, Adrian, 474
Beecroft, Tom L., 578
Behr, Philip H., 431, 523
Behrman, Grant, 470
Beidler, J. Roger, 531
Bekenstein, Joshua, 352
Bell, Michael, 575
Bellas, Robert C., Jr., 512
Belser, Jess L., 483
Ben-Cnaan, Jonathan, 474
Bencivenga, Ernest V., 423
Beninger, Brian, 626
Beninger, Michael, 626
Bennett, Frank B., 402
Bennett, Wallace L., 585
Benoît, Germain, 637
Bentsen, Lloyd M., III, 552, 580
Berdell, James R., 253
Berdon, Matthew A., 449
Berezin, Evelyn, 458
Berg, Stan, 372
Berglund, James H., 194
Bergman, Bart, 405
Bergman, James R., 417
Bergmann, Roy N., 186
Bergstrom, John C., 394
Berkaw, John D., 387
Berkman, Bernard G., 357
Berliner, Arthur S., 255
Berliner, David L., 176
Berliner, Martha L., 176
Berman, Schorr, 372
Berman, Thomas D., 197, 275
Bernard, Thomas J., 480
Berner, H.S., 355
Berner, Robert C., 355
Bernhard, Robert A., 462
Bernstein, Arthur H., 181
Bernstein, Myral, 321
Best, David P., 202
Beste, Frederick J., III, 532
Bettigole, Robert A., 483
Bezuch, Robert A., 531
Bianchi, Annette M., 179, 358
Bianco, Aniello A., 483
Binford, Thomas W., 332
Binur, Yuval, 167, 430

Birchenough, Ernest, 520
Bird, Steven P., 198, 450
Birnbaum, Stevan A., 228, 282
Bise, John R., 404
Blaak, J., 280
Black, Foye F., Jr., 260
Blackburn, John W., 227, 375
Blackman, A. Wade, Jr., 351
Blair, David J., 333
Blair, Francis I., 321
Blair, James C., 417
Blair, Paul R., 173
Blakeslee, Thomas R., 258
Blakley, Harold W., 626
Blanchard, F. Dan, 375, 569
Blankenship, Mark R., 515
Blecki, David J., 189
Block, Michael I., 542
Bloomer, R.D., 264
Blumberg, David J., 167, 430
Bochnowski, James J., 248
Bock, Lawrence A., 197, 275
Boddorf, James E., 495
Boden, W.J., 617
Bodman, Samuel W., 363
Boeckman, Michael L., 508, 509
Boeger, William A., III, 187
Boehm, Bruce J., 251
Bogle, H.W., 450
Boissiere, Lionel P., Jr., 212
Bolland, Anthony J., 357
Bollier, Peter J., 369
Bolt, William J., Jr., 409
Bond, Johnetta B., 296
Bond, Cornelius C., Jr., 224, 345
Bonsal, Frank A., Jr., 224, 345
Bookin, Marvin L., 401
Boole, Robert A., 351
Borovoy, Roger S., 242, 486, 573
Bosch, John E., 174
Bosky, Dmitry, 241
Bosso, Raymond, 418
Bottoms, W.R., 474
Bottoms, W.R., Ph.D., 231
Bourke, Richard L., 411
Boury, Nissan, 495
Bowes, William K., Jr., 251
Bowman, D. Kirkwood, 206
Bowman, Donald E., 291
Boyd, Michael M., 621
Boydstun, John E., 237
Boyle, James H., 629
Boyle, John, 213
Bradbury, T.R., 635
Bradin, Bernice E., 378
Bradt, L. Jack, 532
Brag, Anders K., 458
Brancato, C.M., 488
Branch, Harvey C., 342
Brandewie, Richard J., 302
Brandt, Leonard J., 401, 519
Branham, Minta D., 294
Breeze, Janice L., 427
Breiner, James M., 276
Breiner, Steven, 276
Brenner, Nathaniel, 175
Brentlinger, Paul S., 512

Industry Preferences Index for Venture Capital Firms

Consumer

Distribution

Electronic Components and Instrumentation

Energy/Natural Resources

Industrial Products and Equipment

Medical/Health Related